S0-CAR-483

The Illustrated Encyclopedia of the

PLANET EARTH

The Illustrated Encyclopedia of the
PLANET EARTH

Exeter Books

NEW YORK

Academic Advisors:
Doctor Ray Hall,
Lecturer in Goegraphy,
Queen Mary College,
University of London.

Doctor P.F. Rawson, B.Sc., Ph.D., F.G.S.,
Lecturer in Geology,
Queen Mary College,
University of London.

Editors:
Michael Bisacre
Richard Carlisle
Deborah Robertson
John Ruck

First published in the United States of America
by Exeter Books

Distributed by Bookthrift, Inc.
New York, New York 10018

Library of Congress Catalog Card Number: 79-51914
ISBN 0-89673-015-8

Introduction

The Illustrated Encyclopedia of the Planet Earth is a comprehensive source of reference on every aspect of the physical world, and the elements that comprise it. The book contains the essential facts and figures, maps, and information on the planet from the beginning of its existence to the exploration of the solar system beyond.

Part I examines in detail the structure of the earth and its surrounding atmosphere. Taking account of the most up-to-date theories, it presents a whole range of sciences and explains the methods and development of each. Geology, meteorology and oceanography are fully discussed, as well as the causes and effects of weather and the nature of climatic zones.

Within these chapters there are articles on the evolution of plant life, the ice ages and the movement of oceans. The history of the earth and man's use of its resources – metals, minerals, oil – are some of the major concerns. These lead on through an explanation of our current knowledge of star systems and planets to the exploration of them that is only just beginning.

Part II contains general maps of the world and The Gazetteer, separately indexed for easy reference. This is a collection of maps of the world's countries annotated with information on population, industry, climate and topography.

The combination of the two sections, skillfully illustrated with photographs and artwork which expand and reinforce the text, provides a thorough and searching look at the world in which we live.

Contents

Part I The Elements of the Earth

Part II Atlas of the Earth

Part I

The Elements of the Earth

Susan Griggs Agency

Chapter 1
The Earth

Volcanoes are responsible for forming large areas of the Earth's crust, and much of its atmosphere. They release carbon dioxide – a gas basic to life – and create water by the combination of hydrogen and oxygen in steam.

Earthquakes

Earthquakes are movements within the earth caused by natural or man-made stresses. Many are so slight that they can barely be detected but others can be violent and catastrophic. In 1960 the Agadir earthquake in Morocco killed 12,000 people and nearly 50,000 died as a result of the Peruvian earthquake of 1970.

There are some parts of the world, *seismic* regions, where earthquakes are common occurrences. These lie along relatively narrow and unstable sections of the earth's crust which are also often areas of volcanic activity.

At these points a constant build-up of stress is released by sections of rock shifting along fault planes—cracks in the earth. These movements, known as *tectonic* events, are usually felt over a wide area and can be prolonged. In the San Fernando earthquake in 1971 small aftershocks went on for more than three days after the main shock.

Sometimes old fault areas can be briefly reactivated, causing minor earthquakes in *aseismic* regions such as Britain where they do not normally occur. The stresses which cause major earthquakes, however, build up along the edges of the plates or layers which form the earth's outer crust.

When rocks yield under stress a series of shocks radiate in all directions. If they are strong enough to reach the earth's surface the ground trembles, and ripples may be produced so that cracks, or fissures, open and close.

At the beginning of an earthquake there will be minor shocks which may be barely felt, then several more violent tremors spaced from a few seconds to a few hours apart. These are followed by small aftershocks, which can continue for several days or even weeks, while the disturbed rocks in the region of origin readjust and settle down.

Earthquakes quite frequently accompany or anticipate volcanic eruptions. Although they may have disastrous effects in the immediate vicinity, these die out rapidly away from the eruption.

Apart from the immediate effects of collapsed buildings, the earthquake can create havoc by burying settlements under landslides, destroying coastal regions with tidal waves, and causing fires from damaged cables, gas mains and petrol storage tanks. It is these secondary effects that most often cause the appalling loss of life associated with an earthquake. In the San Francisco earthquake of 1906 fire caused 400 million dollars worth of damage, and destroyed 700,000 homes in the Tokyo earthquake of 1923. The destruction of sewage systems and water supplies also tends to lead to epidemics breaking out in the disaster area.

Many earthquakes occur in coastal regions or under the ocean floor, resulting in a sudden shift in the level of the sea bed. Huge waves or *tsunami* are created by the water displacement and their effect may be felt for hundreds of miles. In the open ocean these waves are hardly noticeable and make no impression on passing vessels. As the wave nears shore and reaches shallower water, however, it gets larger and larger and travels at great speed. The 'tidal' wave may surge far

Above: Movement of the San Andreas fault in 1906 produced an earthquake which destroyed large areas of San Francisco. Much of the damage was caused by fires that broke out as gas mains fractured. The seismograph tracing of the vibrations was recorded in Albany, New York, 4,830 km (3,000 miles) away.

Left: These two views of the Peruvian village of Yungay show how it looked before and after an earthquake in 1970. The shock dislodged snow and ice from Nevados Huascarán, highest peak in Peru. A massive avalanche careered along the Santa valley at 480 km (298 miles) per hour, devastating Yungay.

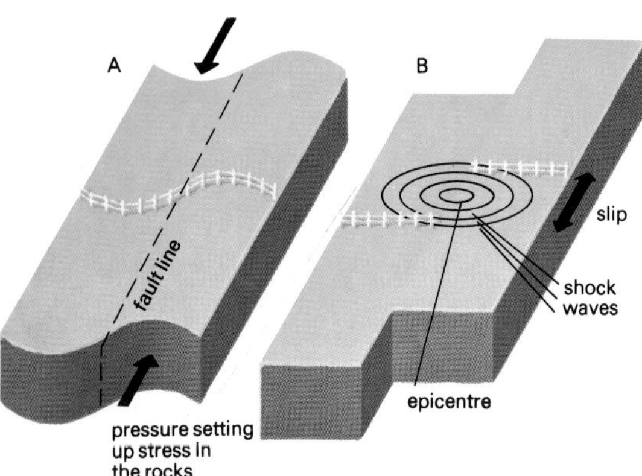

Left: The two sides of a fault have bonded since the last earthquake. As stress builds up around the bond, rocks bend to accommodate it in A. In B the bond fails and the rocks fracture. The stress is relieved and the rocks spring back causing vibrations from the spot, or focus, where the bond failed.

Right: Earth movements caused by earthquakes. A road in Hachinohe, Japan, has been partially destroyed by vertical subsidence. All the railway lines in Niigata, Japan (far right) were buckled by an earthquake in 1964. Undulatory features of this type are characteristic of earthquake damage and are often caused by soil liquefaction.

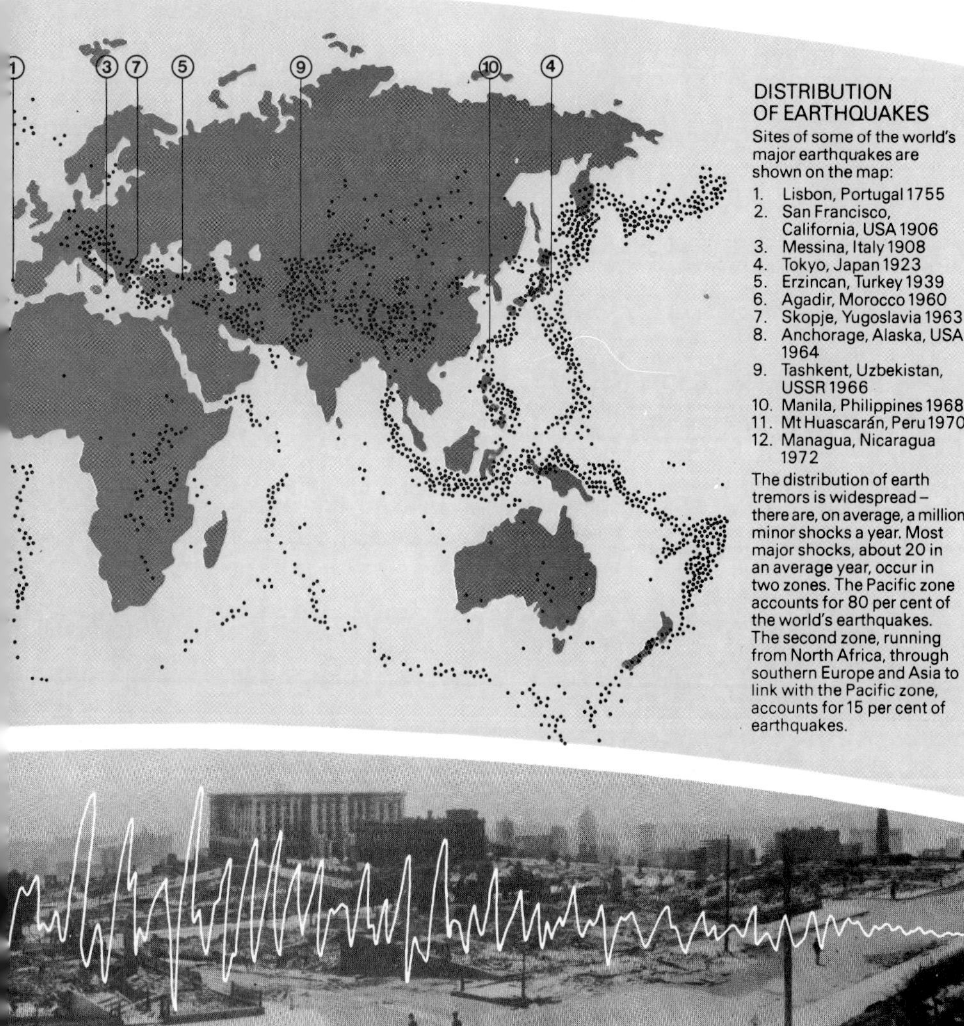

DISTRIBUTION OF EARTHQUAKES

Sites of some of the world's major earthquakes are shown on the map:

1. Lisbon, Portugal 1755
2. San Francisco, California, USA 1906
3. Messina, Italy 1908
4. Tokyo, Japan 1923
5. Erzincan, Turkey 1939
6. Agadir, Morocco 1960
7. Skopje, Yugoslavia 1963
8. Anchorage, Alaska, USA 1964
9. Tashkent, Uzbekistan, USSR 1966
10. Manila, Philippines 1968
11. Mt Huascarán, Peru 1970
12. Managua, Nicaragua 1972

The distribution of earth tremors is widespread – there are, on average, a million minor shocks a year. Most major shocks, about 20 in an average year, occur in two zones. The Pacific zone accounts for 80 per cent of the world's earthquakes. The second zone, running from North Africa, through southern Europe and Asia to link with the Pacific zone, accounts for 15 per cent of earthquakes.

of the continental shelf around land, however, the water piles up while continuing to move at a great speed. The result is a tidal wave or *tsunami* which sometimes surges far inland, especially along coasts with long narrow inlets. A tsunami can affect a region far removed from an earthquake. People have been drowned in Hawaii as a result of an earthquake in the Aleutian trench, over 3,000 km (1,900 miles) away in the North Pacific Ocean.

One of the most disastrous earthquakes in history, and one which first excited some scientific curiosity, was the Lisbon earthquake of 1 November 1755 in Portugal. This was felt over a wide area as witnessed by the account in *Gentleman's Magazine* of March 1756 by Mr Stoqueler, the Hamburg consul in Lisbon, who was about 30 km (19 miles) to the west-north-west of the city that day. 'The day broke with a serene sky, the wind continuing east; but at 9 o'clock the sun began to grow dim, and about half an hour after 9, we heard a rumbling like that of carriages, which increased so much as to resemble the noise of the loudest cannon; and immediately we felt the first shock, which was succeeded by a second, third and fourth.' In Lisbon itself, the first shock brought down many buildings while worshippers were at church—thousands were crushed. Many more were killed by the fires and tsunami which then swept parts of the city. The effects were felt, with diminishing intensity, as far away as Switzerland and Scotland where water levels in various lakes oscillated slightly. The resultant tsunami created noticeable waves in the North Sea and reached Martinique in the Caribbean.

While many in Europe found evidence

Left: Earthquakes under the sea or in coastal regions set up great waves, or tsunami, which can cause devastation far away from the earthquake site. Boats were flung inland at Kodiak by waves created by the Alaskan earthquake of 1964. A Pacific early warning system is now in operation.

Right: 'The Great Wave of Kanagawa', a Japanese print, shows a tsunami. Tsunamis are caused by rapid rise or fall of the sea floor during an earthquake. In open sea tsunami, often hundreds of miles long, may pass unnoticed. When they reach the continental shelf close to land, water piles up to heights of 12m (40ft).

Left: Another example of earth movement can be seen in this orange grove which was offset along the San Jacinto fault in California during the Imperial Valley earthquake of 1940. The photograph was taken 19 years later.

Right: The intensity of an earthquake diminishes from a zone of maximum effect, the *epicentre*, which is directly over its origin or *focus*, to areas where its effects can no longer be felt. The lines of equal intensity or *isoseismic* lines are arranged concentrically around the epicentre. The numerals show the intensity and the arrows show the movements of P and S waves and the two types of surface waves.

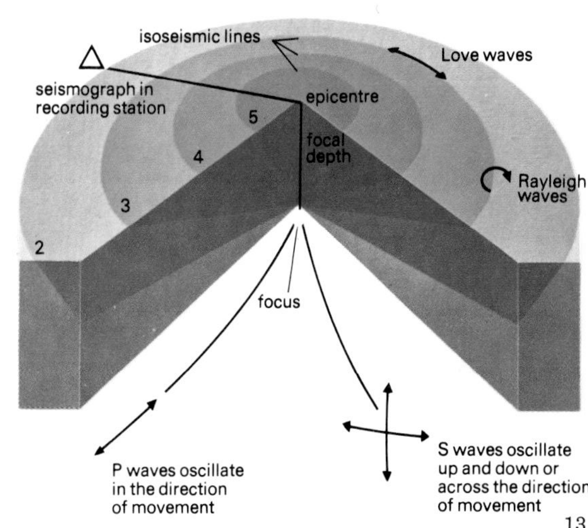

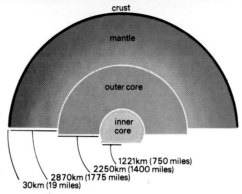

of God's or the Devil's work in these events, a small number of scientists pursued their own investigations. Thus Mr Stoqueler noted some of the local effects away from the city, such as springs drying up and new ones appearing, a swampy lake uplifted to form dry land, and the sea retreating so that 'you walk almost dry to places where before you could not wade'.

More importantly, as a result of collecting as many observations on the effect of the earthquake as possible, John Mitchell (1724-1793) suggested that an initial explosive shock could have given rise to waves spreading out through the rocks in all directions. This fundamental realization heralded an increasingly scientific approach to the study of earthquakes, or seismology.

Measurement of earthquakes

There are two main methods of measuring the strength of earthquakes—the Mercalli scale which relies on the comparison of eye-witness accounts of the effects of the earthquake and the Richter scale. In 1935 C. F. Richter, an American seismologist, devised a formula for calculating the strength of an earthquake from instrumental recordings of its magnitude. This is related to the total amount of energy stored in the rock under stress and released during an earthquake shock by the initial rock fractures at the point of origin, or *focus*.

The depth of the focus can be calculated. Shallow earthquakes have a focus above the boundary between the earth's crust and the deeper mantle. This boundary, known as the Moho after the Yugoslav seismologist Mohorovicic who discovered it, is 35 km (22 miles) deep. Intermediate

crust
mantle
outer core
inner core
1221km (750 miles)
2250km (1400 miles)
2870km (1775 miles)
30km (19 miles)

Above and below: The course of earthquake waves as they pass through the earth indicates its structure. The progress of the waves suggests a change in density and composition between the *crust* and the *mantle*. P and S waves that have travelled through the earth are registered on seismographs through an arc of 0°-103° from the epicentre. Both then disappear into the *shadow zone*. P waves alone, noticeably bent, reappear at 143°. This suggests a liquid outer core, since S waves cannot travel through liquids. Increased speed of P waves through the central part of the core suggests that the inner core is solid.

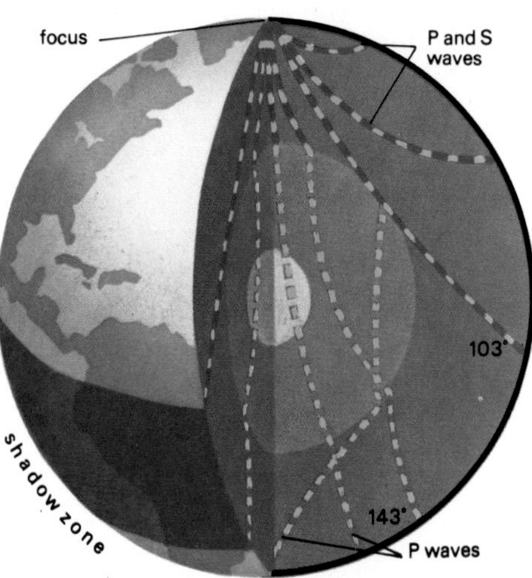

earthquakes have a focus between the Moho and a depth of 300 km (190 miles). Deep earthquakes have a focus below this, usually between 500 and 700 km (310 to 435 miles) from the surface.

A single earthquake produces three main types of shock wave, referred to as P, S and L waves. P or 'Primae' or 'Push and Pull' waves are analogous to sound waves in which each particle of rock vibrates longitudinally or parallel to the direction of the wave. S or 'Secundae' or 'Shear' waves are more like light waves in that each particle of rock has a shear motion, across the direction of movement of the wave. While P waves can pass through solids, liquids and gases, S waves pass through solids only. P waves also travel more quickly than S waves and therefore are picked up first by a distant seismograph.

A third, even slower set of waves are L or 'Long' waves which pass only through the earth's crust and are the last to be picked up by a seismograph. Conversely they are more easily detected than P and S waves at great distances from the source as they lose their energy more slowly. Surface waves set up by very large earthquakes have been recorded after they have travelled around the earth six times. There are two main types of L waves: Rayleigh waves and Love waves, which oscillate rather like P and S waves respectively.

A global network of seismological stations coupled with rapid exchange of information means that the focus, magnitude and *epicentre*, or the area of maximum effect, of an earthquake are quickly calculated. It also allows the study of the internal structure of the earth, using the

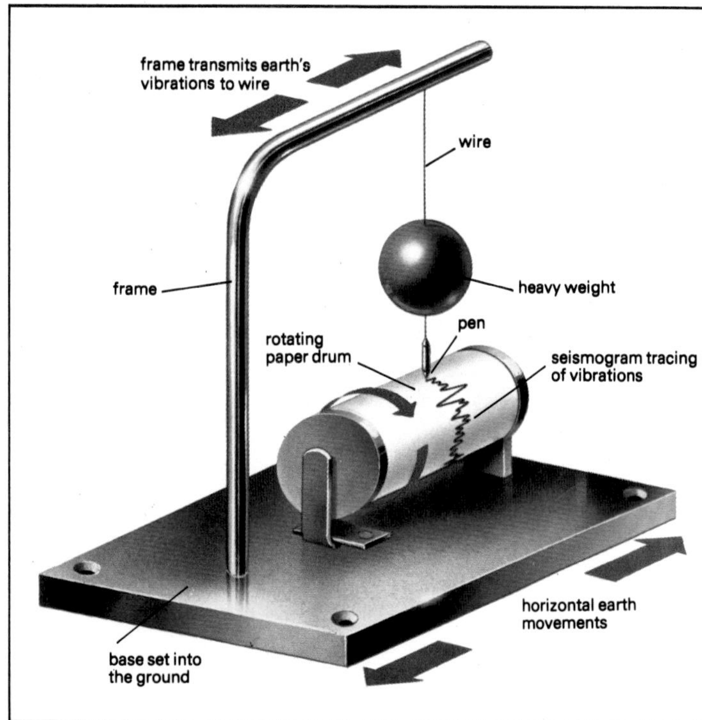

Above: A seismograph is a device for detecting and recording seismic waves. It consists of a spring suspended weight or pendulum and a clockwork-operated rotating drum. The frame of the device is set in bedrock. Seismic waves set up a horizontal motion which moves the frame backwards and forwards. The pen attached to the pendulum moves in the same way, marking the movements on the rotating drum. This produces a seismogram which indicates the duration and severity of the earth tremors. The record of an earthquake is a wavy line; when there is no movement the seismogram shows a straight line.

Right: The Mercalli scale uses observations of an earthquake's effect at a point on the earth's surface to assess its intensity. The scale is subjective and a reading can be exaggerated, for example, by the collapse of badly constructed buildings. However, it has given much useful information on the nature of earthquakes.

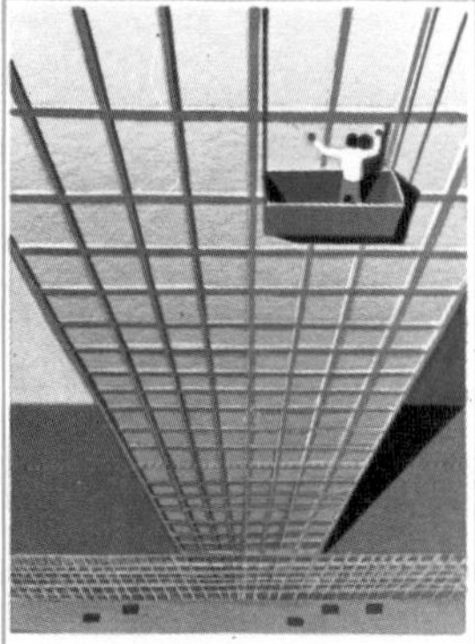

Point 2: Very slight. Felt by people on the upper floors of buildings and others favourably placed to sense tremors, such as those at rest.

Point 5: Quite strong. Small articles fall, liquids spill, sleepers wake, bells tinkle, doors swing open and closed. Noticed out of doors.

Point 7: Very strong. General alarm. Fall of loose plaster and tile. Some buildings crack. Noticed by people driving vehicles.

various shock waves to 'X-ray' the structure. The behaviour of the various types of wave can be used, for example, to study the nature and relative thickness of the earth's crust in different regions. A natural progression from this is the creation of small, man-made seismic shocks to study the structures within the crust when looking for oil.

Earthquake distribution

The overall pattern of distribution of earthquake epicentres follows closely the regions of the last two major periods of mountain building during the Tertiary (between ten and 70 million years ago) and Recent (the last 11,000 years) eras, the rift valleys of Central and East Africa and the submarine mid-oceanic ridges. The distribution of active and recently extinct volcanoes is very similar. The pattern fits well with the arrangement of crustal plates which cover the surface of the globe. Such a distribution indicates stresses build up at the places where the crustal material is being formed at the mid-oceanic ridges and where the plate edges are moving against one another or plunging back down into the mantle.

The distribution of earthquake focusses is even more instructive. The deeper focus earthquakes, over 200 km (120 miles) deep, are limited to the ocean trench and island arc systems, such as the Japanese islands. They appear to originate in the zones where one crustal plate is being forced beneath another. The pattern of focusses indicates that the inclination of these zones is about 45°. The zones were discovered by the American seismologist, Hugo Benioff, and are known as Benioff zones or subduction zones.

Man-made earthquakes

Significant man-made earthquakes are created by nuclear explosions, major constructions such as dams and reservoirs, and by liquid injection into undergound reservoirs. The energy released by a nuclear explosion can equal that of a moderately strong earthquake, although the pattern of shock waves is different and can be distinguished from that of natural earthquakes. In regions of structural instability sudden changes in water level of a reservoir may lead to earthquakes. The pumping of liquid waste into deep wells near Denver, Colorado, and of water under pressure in the Rangely oil-field, Colorado, have both triggered off earthquakes in previously quiet areas.

Earthquake prediction and control

It is unlikely that inhabitants of the major earthquake zones could ever be moved out permanently, especially in view of the fertility and wealth of some regions, but it may prove possible to protect people from major disasters. Attempts have been made to recognize physical changes prior to a major earthquake. This work is still in its infancy, but several lines are possibly worth pursuing.

In Japan and the Soviet Union slight changes in the inclination of the ground have been detected prior to an earthquake. Changes in the pattern of microearthquakes, which form the normal background seismic activity have sometimes been observed before a major shock. Possibly the most important observation is the local change in the earth's magnetic field which has sometimes been detected prior to an earthquake.

Another recent discovery suggests that there is a marked variation in the velocity of P waves recorded from microquakes during quite long periods prior to major earthquakes. According to this theory, observations suggest that San Francisco and central California will remain free from major earthquakes for at least the next 25 years.

The modification of earthquake patterns to avoid a major disaster may soon prove scientifically possible. Small earthquakes have been induced by injecting fluids into faulted areas. From this it has been inferred that strains built up along faults such as the San Andreas fault in California could be released in a relatively controlled manner by artificially triggering small earthquakes. This could prevent a major natural earthquake which would otherwise appear to be unavoidable along the Californian fault.

The reduction of loss of life is already being tackled in other ways. Specially designed modern buildings can withstand significant tremors. In the Tokyo earthquake of 1923, for example, the Imperial Hotel designed by Frank Lloyd Wright suffered little damage. Further research is being conducted on building resistance in Tashkent in the Soviet Union where there are empty apartment blocks with machines on their roofs to induce vibrations and thus test resistance of the buildings to stresses and strains. Populations are also slowly being educated to take sensible shelter indoors instead of running into the open streets where debris from collapsing buildings may cause them injury. By taking such precautions it may be possible to minimize the devastation and loss of life caused by earthquakes in the future.

Far left: The earthquake that hit Anchorage in Alaska in 1964 caused relatively little damage to timber buildings. The brick building on the left has suffered considerable damage; in the timber house even the windows are intact.

Left: These buildings in Niigata, Japan were built to withstand earthquakes. When strong tremors shook the city in 1964 the structures survived—there was not even a hair line crack in the walls. They toppled because certain soils lose their rigidity and 'liquefy' as a result of repeated seismic shocks. Few structures can survive this process—the ground simply slides away beneath them.

Above: The earthquake that struck Alaska in March 1964 was one of the most severe ever recorded and caused hundreds of millions of dollars-worth of damage. Landslides wrecked buildings, roads and railway lines. The houses shown here were smashed by a landslide with a front 2.4 km (1½ miles) long.

: 8. Destructive. chimneys and bell rs collapse, statues . Most buildings k and branches are from trees.

Point 10: Disastrous. Most buildings destroyed. Landslides and large cracks in the ground. Tsunami flood coastal regions.

Point 12: Catastrophic. Near total destruction. Major distortions and changes of ground level. Loose objects are hurled into the air.

Right: Chang Heng, a Chinese astronomer, first recorded distant earth tremors in 132AD. His seismoscope contained a pendulum which moved in a particular direction when an earthquake set up vibrations in the casing. This tipped one of the metal balls from the side of the seismoscope.

Volcanoes

A volcano behaves like a giant chimney, conducting material from shallow depths in the earth up to the surface. When a volcano erupts, hot liquid rock, called *lava,* gases and rock fragments are spewed on to the surface through its opening. This 'chimney' may take the form of a tall mountain *cone.* Volcanoes, however, may also appear as gently-sloping domes, or even as long, low-lying slits through which lava oozes out to produce a flat lava field.

A volcanic eruption starts deep down in the earth's *crust* or in the upper *mantle*—the thicker under-lying layer. Here rocks melt to form *magma,* essentially a mixture of volcanic gases dissolved in liquid lava. Underground pressure from the weight of the surrounding rocks forces the magma towards the surface.

As the magma wells up, sometimes into an underground reservoir, or *magma chamber,* under the volcano, the pressure drops and the gases start to bubble out of the liquid. The gases consist mainly of steam, most of which comes from water seeping through the rocks of the upper crust to meet the rising magma. They also contain carbon dioxide, nitrogen, sulphur dioxide and small quantities of such noxious gases as hydrogen sulphide and hydrogen chloride.

Eventually magma finds its way to the surface in a volcanic eruption, either through an existing vent or fissure from a previous eruption, or by forcing its way up through new cracks in the crust. On the flanks and around the base of an existing cone, secondary vents often produce small 'pimples' known as *parasitic cones.* Mount Etna on Sicily, for example, has 200 such satellite cones.

Gordon Gahan, Photo Researchers

Quiet eruptions

The thickness of the magma—whether it is thin and syrupy or tacky like toffee—depends on its temperature, pressure and chemical nature. This consistency determines how easily the volcanic gases will be able to escape into the atmosphere before or during an eruption.

In fluid, fairly flat magma—usually basaltic—that wells slowly up the central *vent* of a typical volcano, what little gas there is has plenty of time to separate peacefully from the magma. The gas-free lava collects in the funnel-shaped cup or *crater* at the summit of the volcano. When the crater is full, the lava spills over the edge and flows rapidly down the side of the cone in fiery rivers of *lava flows.*

When very liquid lava oozes out of a central vent or a big fissure it tends to spread out over a wide area, forming either huge plateaux or thin sheets of lava on the typically-gentle sloping dome of a *shield volcano.* Mauna Loa in Hawaii, the world's largest volcano with a base 100 km (62 miles) in diameter and rising 10,000 metres (32,820 feet) above the sea floor, is a perfect example of a shield volcano built up over the years.

When the lava first reaches the surface it is very hot and fluid at temperatures between 800°C and 1200°C. It quickly starts to cool and solidify into volcanic or *igneous* rock. As the molten lava cools, the different minerals it contains crystallize, just like ice crystals freezing in water.

Above: Volcanoes provide one of nature's most dramatic spectacles. Erratic bursts of lava create fountains of fire in this long-exposure photograph of a minor eruption on the slopes of Mount Etna. This type of activity creates a cinder cone, as fragments of solidified lava pile up around the vent.

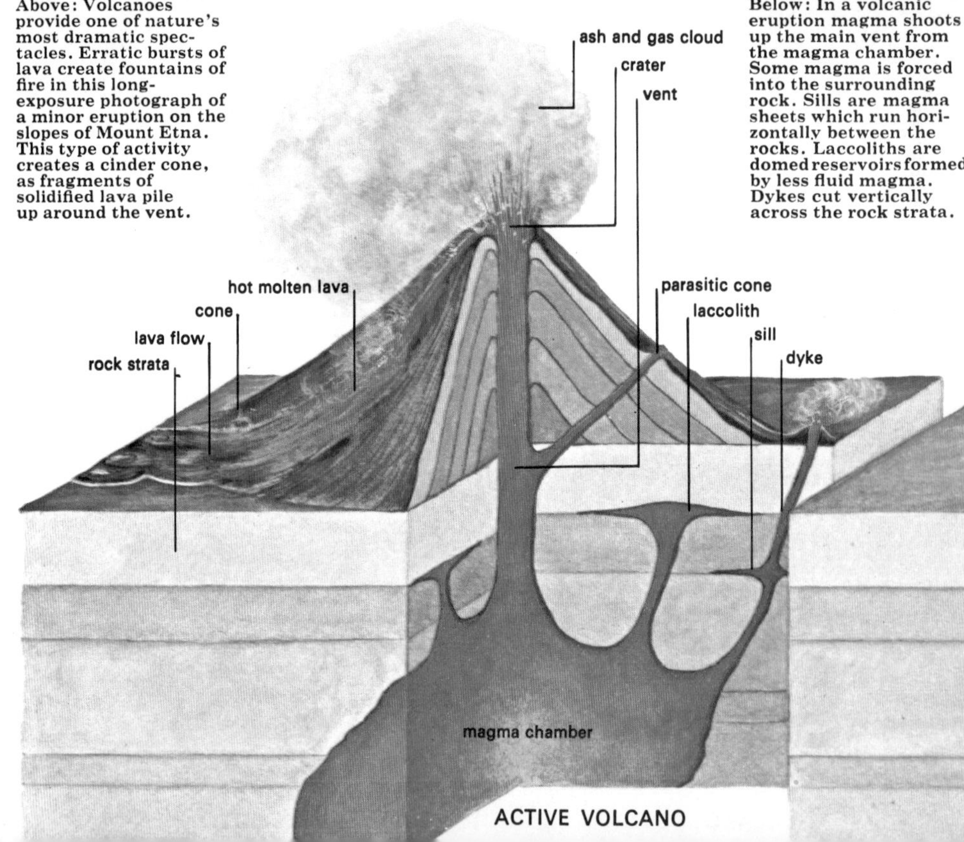

Below: In a volcanic eruption magma shoots up the main vent from the magma chamber. Some magma is forced into the surrounding rock. Sills are magma sheets which run horizontally between the rocks. Laccoliths are domed reservoirs formed by less fluid magma. Dykes cut vertically across the rock strata.

Left: Mt Fuji, the highest mountain in Japan, is a dormant volcano which last erupted in 1707. It has a perfect conical shape, with a summit crater. Volcanic cones of this type, also seen at Etna, Vesuvius and Stromboli, are strato volcanoes, formed by alternating layers of lava and ash.

Right: Cerro Negro in Nicaragua, a cinder cone built up over an older terrace of lava flows. Vast dark clouds of ash are disgorged when gases escape carrying minute particles of cooled lava powder. Eventually a rain of ash falls from the spreading cloud, burying settlements and countryside.

Aspect

Jacana/Explorer

Left: Fumaroles are small vents in the ground from which volcanic gases and steam escape.

Right: Cooler fumaroles are called solfataras. The steam they emit has a high sulphur content, and mineral deposits are formed as the water evaporates.

Jacana/Explorer

Popperfoto

Left: Bird's eye view of a volcanic crater, surrounded by liquid basalt flows.

Above right: Molten lava sweeps down from an Icelandic volcano. Lava flows can reach speeds of up to 100 km (62 miles) per hour, but usually they move more sluggishly.

Below: A composite cone is built of layers of lava and pyroclasts. If the main vent grows too high or becomes plugged by lava, a parasitic cone forms. The vents of a dormant or extinct volcano are plugged by lava. Pressure may build under a dormant volcano causing it to erupt after a long period of inactivity.

Below: The lava plug may remain as a hill after the rest of the cone has been eroded. Edinburgh's Castle Rock, for example, is the plug of one vent of the Arthur's Seat volcano, active 325 million years ago. Erosion also reveals the existence of sills and dykes when ash and rock has worn away.

Right: Pahoehoe is highly fluid lava, spread in sheets, which drags the cooling surface layer into folds.

Below right: 500 million year-old pillow lavas formed underwater now lie above sea level. Rapid cooling creates bulbous shapes inside a glassy skin.

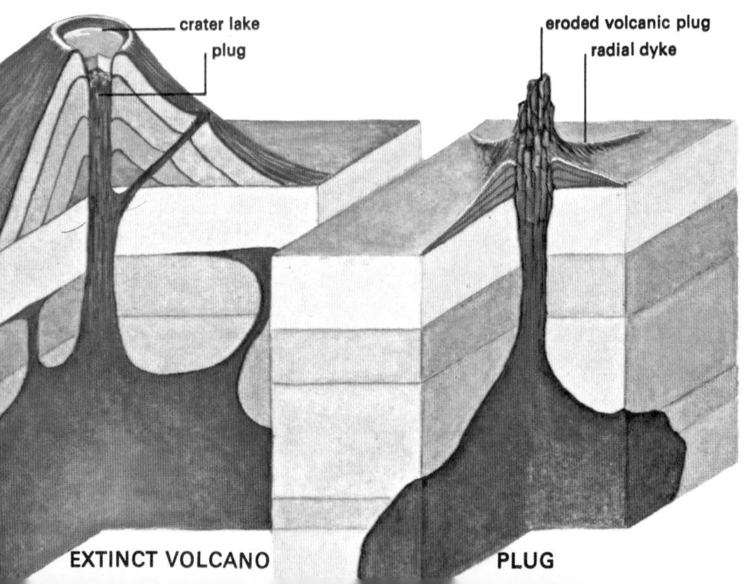

Mark Hurd Aerial Survey

Mats Wibe Lund

Heather Angel

Institute of Geological Sciences

TYPES OF ERUPTIONS

Icelandic: Quiet eruption of lava from fissures builds up horizontal lava flows.

Hawaiian: Fluid lava erupts quietly and builds up huge shield volcanoes.

Strombolian: Minor explosions throw out lava which cools into pyroclasts.

Vulcanian: Explosive escape of gas from viscous magma. Clouds of volcanic ash form.

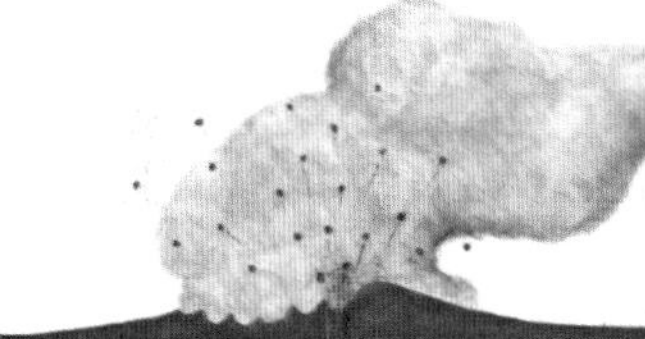

Vesuvian: Violent eruption produces huge quantities of ash. A vast cloud develops.

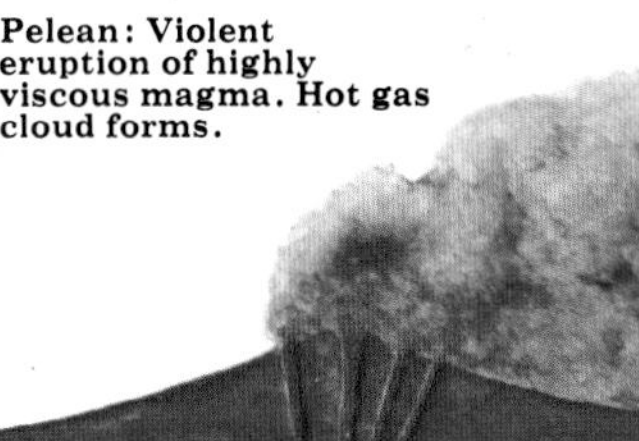

Pelean: Violent eruption of highly viscous magma. Hot gas cloud forms.

Plinean: Explosive outburst of gas sends ash several kilometres in to the air.

Thin sheets of lava cool quickly into fine grained rocks in which individual mineral crystals are invisible to the unaided eye. The more slowly the lava cools the larger the crystals grow before setting. Thicker blocks of lava take a long time to cool—they may still be too hot to touch several months after the eruption—and therefore form larger grained rocks. If the lava is chilled instantly, there is no time for this crystallization process to occur. Instead, it forms a volcanic glass called *obsidian*. This happens particularly in underwater eruptions, or where a stream of hot lava pours down into the sea.

Angry mountains

Where magma is of a slightly stickier consistency, the gas bubbles wind their way to the surface more slowly, growing as they climb and as more gas separates out of the rocky solution. These large bubbles burst when they reach the surface, splashing up a shower of lava spray that cascades over the sides of the vent in a spectacular natural fireworks display. The blobs of liquid lava clot quickly as they fly through the air, forming fragments of hard lava called *pyroclasts*. These missiles range in size from fine *dust* and *ash* to small pebble-sized particles called *lapilli* and large boulders or *bombs*. Bombs spin as they travel through the air, solidifying into characteristic shapes or spindle bombs. Breadcrust bombs on the other hand, have a zigzag pattern of cracks over the surface caused by the lava forming a solid skin which is broken by expansion and the escape of gas. Such bombs often shatter as they hit the ground.

A small pile of pyroclasts begins to form a *cinder cone* around the vent. The typical volcanic cone shape develops because most particles and all the larger, heavier fragments land near the vent, while smaller, lighter pieces are thrown further away. Consequently the volcanic mound grows more quickly nearer the vent, creating the classically rising slopes of a volcanic cone. Occasionally the globules of lava do not solidify in the air and form a *spatter cone* as they land.

In contrast to the fluid lavas, very tacky lavas barely flow at all but are squeezed out of the vent like toothpaste from a tube, forming steep-sided volcanic *domes* of hot lava in the crater. Sometimes a pocket of hotter, thinner lava forces its way through a crack in the dome creating a tall pinnacle of solid lava called a *spine* that towers over the vent. The spine of Mont Pelée on the island of Martinique in the Caribbean rose to the imposing height of 300m (984 ft) during its period of activity in 1902, before it cracked around the base and crumbled into the crater.

Thick lavas also tend to congeal in the vent and together with rubble from the crater form a plug that blocks the exit. Tremendous pressure builds up as gases are trapped under the plugged vent until the volcano literally 'blows its top' in a violent explosion.

Violent explosions, like the famous blast at Krakatoa in 1883, shoot vast quantities of rock, lava, gas and ash into the air. In the shock of the drop of pressure, the gases froth in the lava, but because of the thickness of the lava they are unable to burst free. If the lava drops back into the sea it sets very quickly, trapping the gas bubbles permanently into a petrified foam called *pumice*, which floats on water.

During a particularly violent eruption, the magma chamber may be completely emptied, leaving the central part of the cone unsupported. Often under such circumstances the crater and walls of the vent collapse into the hollow chamber, creating a large saucer-shaped depression known as a *caldera* across the summit of the volcano, which may be as much as several kilometres in diameter. An explosive eruption may cause the entire cone to fall into the magma chamber. After Krakatoa erupted, an underwater caldera 7 km (4.3 miles) in diameter was formed.

Life and death of a volcano

The sudden rise of a cinder cone called Parícutin on 20 February 1943—in the field of a surprised Mexican farmer—provided scientists with a rare opportunity to observe a volcano from its birth. In the first day of intense activity, it produced a huge glowing cloud of hot ash and a cone of pyroclasts 40 m (131 ft) high. After this astonishing effort, fissures opened around the base and lava seeped across the field. Eruptions continued with decreasing intensity until, when the volcano ceased eruption in 1952, the cone was 410 m (1,344 ft) high.

Library of Congress

The life-span of a volcano ranges from a few months to many thousands of years. Activity may vary greatly during that time. Of the 500 or so active volcanoes in the world today only a small number erupt each year. A few volcanoes, like Stromboli in the Lipari Islands off Italy, erupt continuously with successive bursts. The majority, however, erupt only irregularly and spend most of their time 'asleep'.

During these periods of inactivity, however, it is impossible to tell whether the volcano is really *extinct*—that is, stopped erupting for ever—or merely *dormant*, undergoing a temporary period of rest. Generally volcanoes are classified as extinct when no eruption has been noted in 'recorded history'.

Yet even then they may be potentially active, one day to wake up in a fresh eruption, with devastating results. Vesuvius, overlooking the Italian port of Naples, was thought to be extinct before its catastrophic eruption in 79AD which completely destroyed the Roman cities of Pompeii and Heraculaneum.

Causes of volcanic activity

Volcanoes are distributed in areas where conditions are suitable for the formation of magma. The concept of plate tectonics

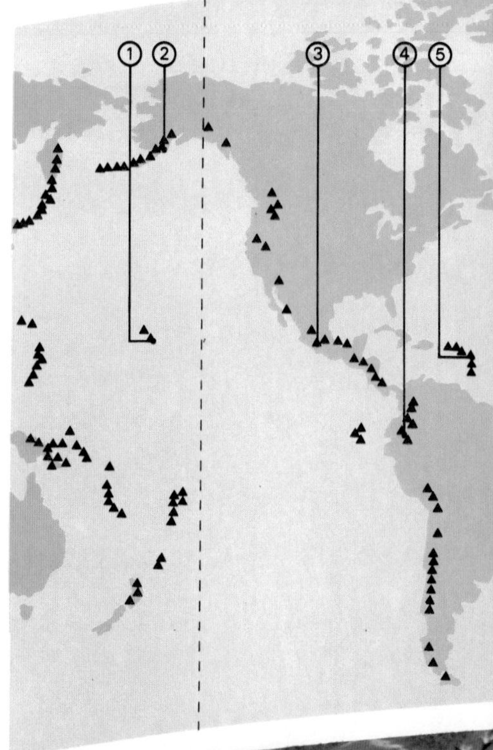

Above left: A nuée ardente, a glowing cloud of dust and gas, erupted from Mt Pelée in the island of Martinique at 7.50 am on 8 May 1902. The city of St Pierre, with its 30,000 inhabitants, was destroyed in seconds. The surge of gas that headed the cloud was hot enough to melt metal and glass.

Below: Krakatoa Island in the East Indies was formed by a group of volcanic cones built up from a prehistoric caldera. In 1883 a huge eruption destroyed most of the island and left a 300 m (1,000 ft) crater in the sea bed. The explosion, heard as far away as Australia, had worldwide effects. A tidal wave killed

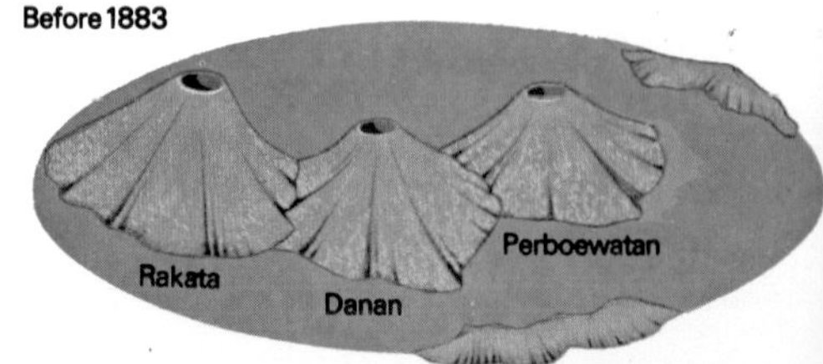

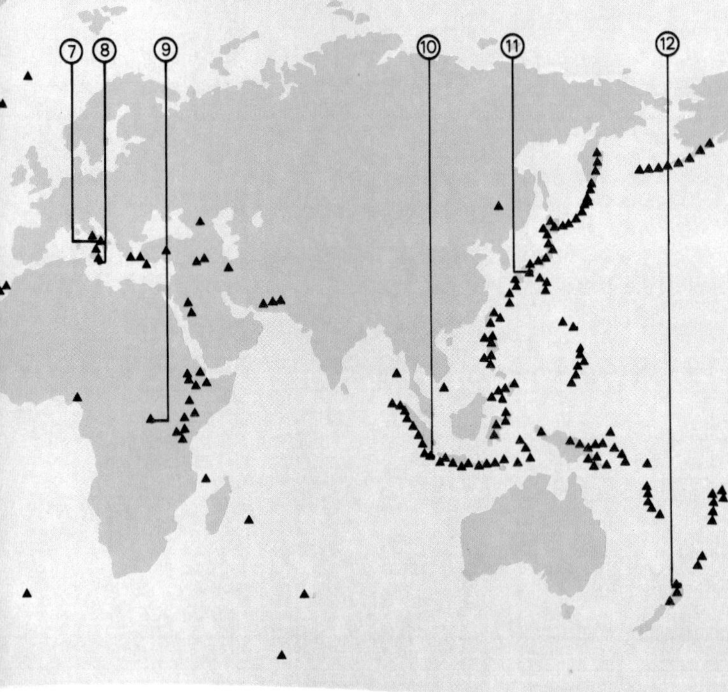

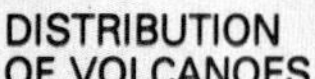

DISTRIBUTION OF VOLCANOES

Some of the world's major sites of volcanic activity are shown on the map:

1. Kilauea, Hawaii
2. Katmai, Alaska
3. Paricutin, Mexico
4. Cotopaxi, Ecuador
5. Pelée, Martinique
6. Surtsey, Iceland
7. Vesuvius, Italy
8. Etna, Italy
9. Nyamuragira, Zaire
10. Krakatoa, Indonesia
11. Sakurajima, Japan
12. White Island, New Zealand

Most active volcanoes are concentrated in a belt around the Pacific and one that extends through Indonesia and New Guinea. Indonesia has the greatest concentration of volcanoes with 29 actively emitting gases and 78 eruptions since records began.

Mats Wibe Lund

Left: The eruption of Eldfjell on the Icelandic island of Heimay in 1973 partly buried the town of Vestmannaeyjar in dust and ash. Volcanic areas may be quiet for many years—the only known volcano on Heimay last erupted 5,000 years ago—and then come suddenly and violently to life.

Above: The volcanic island of Surtsey appeared off Iceland on 15 November 1963. First eruptions were explosive as sea water entered the vent. When the cone was large enough to prevent this, lava flows were erupted. Surtsey was 2.3 sq km (1 sq mile) in area and 410 m (1344 ft) high by 1965.

Below: Anak Krakatoa, meaning the 'child of Krakatoa', has emerged on the site of the old island in the Sunda Strait between Sumatra and Java. Pressures from a lava pocket in the old volcano threw up a new submarine cone which reached the surface in 1928. A year later a geyser began to spout steam.

Pixfeatures

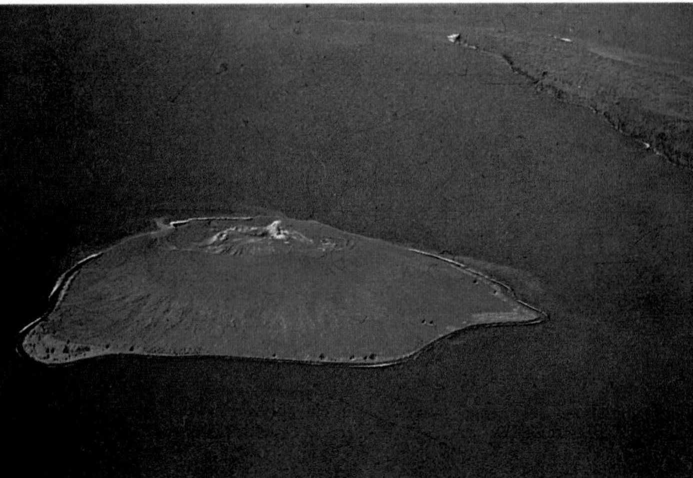

Ivan Polunin, Susan Griggs Agency

36,000 Indonesians and was recorded in the English Channel. For several years volcanic dust drifted around the earth in the upper atmosphere, causing brilliant red sunsets and reducing the earth's temperature by partly blocking the sun's rays. Recent volcanic activity has produced the tip of a new island.

ter 1883

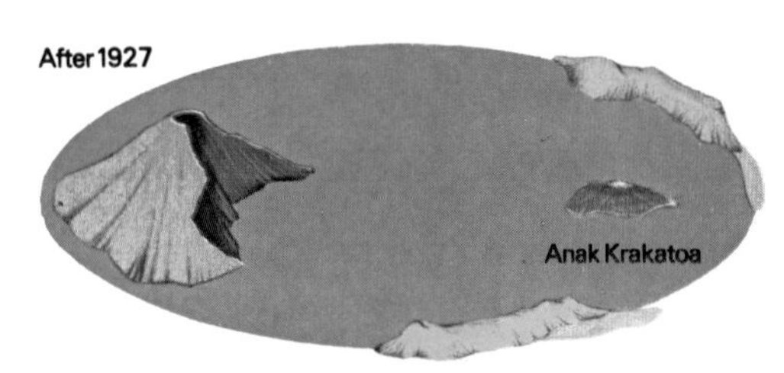

provides an explanation of the distribution of active volcanoes. The earth has a cool rigid crust which consists of a dozen or so plates which are free to move in relation to each other and to glide relatively freely over the earth's surface.

The mantle of the earth, the layer below the crust, is solid and its temperature is normally not high enough to start the melting which forms magma. Pressure here also prevents melting. Heat from the earth's interior does, however, cause the slow circulation of the mantle, or *mantle convection*.

A constructive plate margin, such as the mid-Atlantic ridge, is one where new crustal material is formed by rising magma. Lower pressure in these places allows the hot mantle to melt and produce magma. This rises and forms new oceanic crust and volcanoes at the plate margins. Iceland is an area that experiences this process.

At destructive plate margins, usually at oceanic boundaries such as the trenches around the Pacific Ocean, the edge of one plate is forced beneath that of another, or *subducted*. Oceanic crust is carried down into the mantle and starts to melt. It then rises and heats the overlying continental material and may cause further independent melting. These various kinds of magma reach the surface and produce the different types of volcano found around the perimeter of the Pacific and in the island arcs of Indonesia, West Indies and Japan.

Hawaii, lying in the centre of the Pacific plate, does not fit this pattern. The islands are thought to overlie a 'hot spot' or *plume* of rising mantle which provides the magma for eruptions.

Effects of volcanic activity

Volcanic activity is the main process by which material from the interior of the earth reaches the surface, and it must have contributed to the formation of the atmosphere and the oceans. Volcanic gases, for example, include carbon dioxide which is vital to life on earth. Fertile soils develop from the weathering of volcanic ash and lava, and are extensively cultivated even on the lower slopes of active volcanoes.

Crushed lavas make suitable roadstone. Pumice is used industrially and domestically as an abrasive, and, along with perlite, volcanic glass which expands when heated, for insulation in buildings. Volcanic pipes of an unusual rock, called kimberlite, are the source of diamonds, and sulphur is exploited in the volcanic areas of Japan and Sicily. Volcanic activity provides hot water for central heating in Iceland and steam-generated electricity in New Zealand, Italy and the United States.

The death and destruction inflicted by some volcanic eruptions makes the task of predicting eruptions one of real concern. The start of an eruption can be forecast fairly accurately by monitoring the temperature, pressure and composition of the gases within a volcano. Minor earth tremors, caused by movement of magma within a volcano, are recorded by seismometers positioned at selected sites, and portable machines can determine the exact location of an expected eruption. Observatories have been established on many volcanoes but it is still not possible to predict the intensity or duration of an eruption.

Continental Drift

A glance at a map of the Atlantic coasts of Europe, Africa and the Americas reveals a strikingly close match in their outline. With a little imagination, one could close the Atlantic and fit its western and eastern coastlines together, rather like matching up the pieces of a jig-saw puzzle. The startling conclusion this suggests is literally earth-shaking to scientists studying the history of planet earth. For the suggestion is that, sometime in the remote past, the distant continents were joined together, and have since drifted apart.

Early this century, an American geologist, Frank Taylor, became intrigued by the idea that the continents were once parts of a large land mass. In 1908 he put forward the imaginative theory that the continents may have been slowly drifting apart to reach their present-day arrangement. Meanwhile, working independently, the German meteorologist, astronomer and geophysicist, Alfred Wegener, was thinking along identical lines. His book, *Die Entstehung der Kontinente und Ozeane* — The Origin of Continents and Oceans — published in 1915, established him as a leading authority on the theory of continental drift.

For the next 40 years, however, the theory received little support. Critics pointed out that the reconstructions were based on flimsy evidence or were simply guess-work. Among the few who did believe in Wegener's idea was the South African geologist, Alexander du Toit. Working in South Africa and Brazil, he began to amass solid geological evidence in support of the theory.

Although some experts accepted du Toit's findings and those of other scientists, the majority discounted them on the basis that drift was impossible because there was no known mechanism which could cause whole continents to shift so dramatically. The breakthrough came, therefore, with the discovery of just such a mechanism — plate tectonics.

The concept of *plate tectonics,* which sees the continents as being carried along on the top of slowly moving crustal plates, reversed general attitudes to continental drift. By the mid-1960s the theory had

Right: One of the first to attempt a pre-drift fit was the American Antonio Snider. In 1858 he published a map showing how he thought the Americas were joined to Africa some 300 million years ago.

NASA

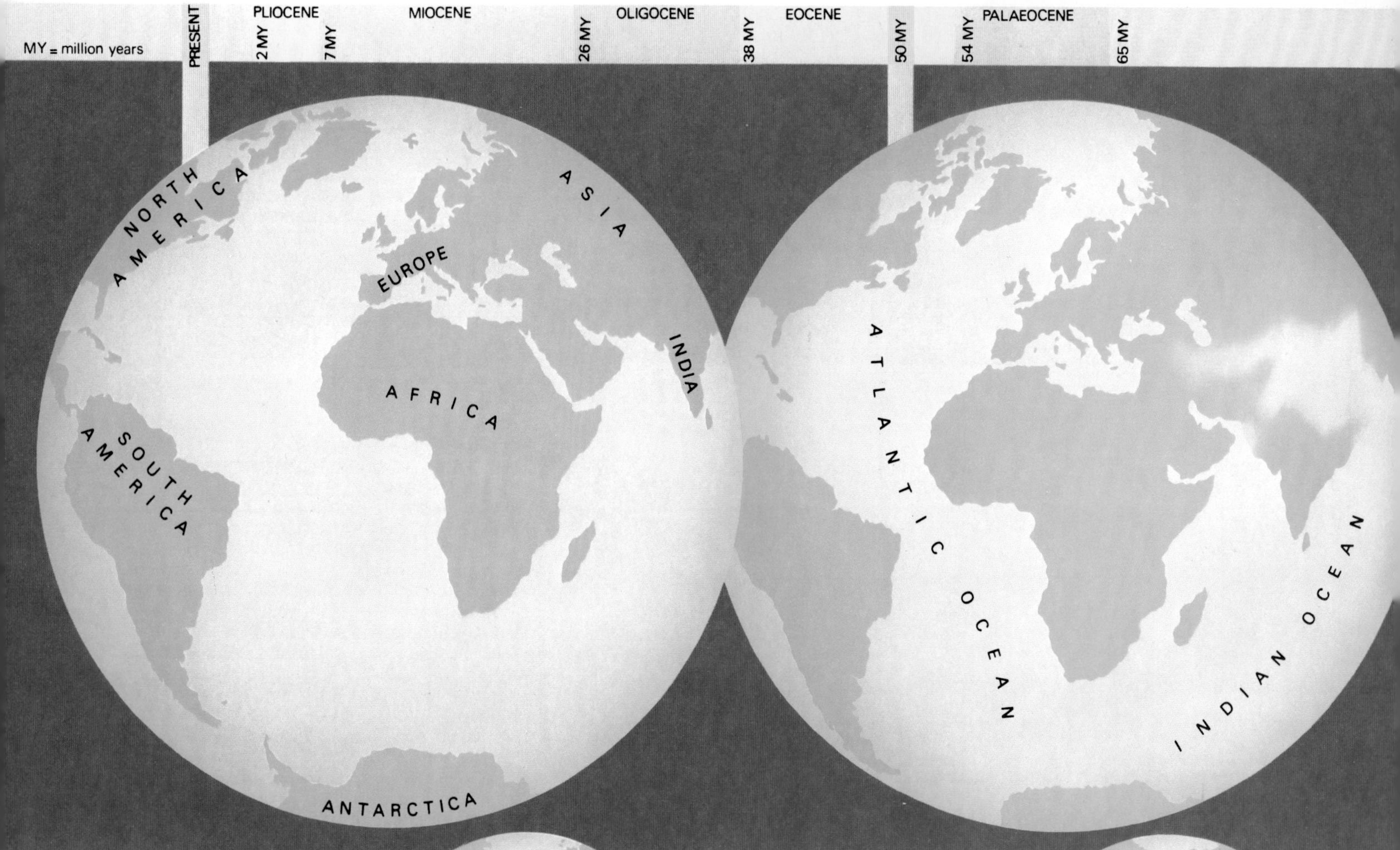

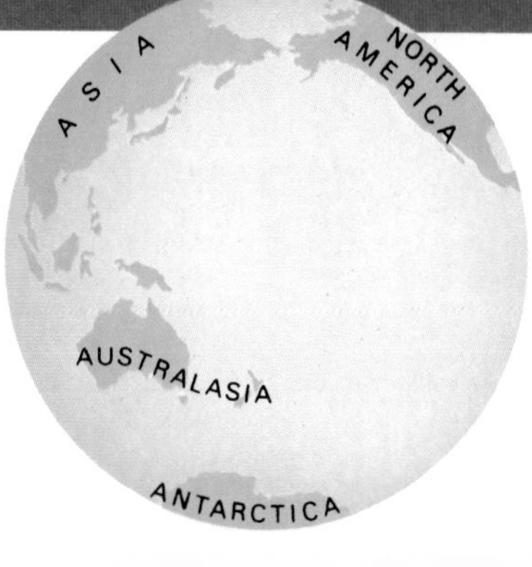

MY = million years

PRESENT | PLIOCENE 2 MY | 7 MY | MIOCENE | 26 MY | OLIGOCENE | 38 MY | EOCENE | 50 MY | 54 MY | PALAEOCENE | 65 MY

NORTH AMERICA · EUROPE · ASIA · AFRICA · INDIA · SOUTH AMERICA · ANTARCTICA · ASIA · NORTH AMERICA · AUSTRALASIA · ANTARCTICA

ATLANTIC OCEAN · INDIAN OCEAN · PACIFIC OCEAN

THE WORLD TODAY
The apparently static surface of the earth is in fact moving. It is noticeable at a glance how the two sides of the Atlantic Ocean easily match up. This fit first gave scientists the idea that the continents might have been joined and later drifted to their positions today.

50 m. YEARS AGO
The reconstruction of the earth's surface 50 million years ago is based on fossil, rock magnetism and other evidence. Australia lay next to Antarctica and India was drifting north to collide with Asia. Movement was slow—the Atlantic was growing by less than 10 cm (4 in) a year.

Below: South America (left) as seen from an orbiting NASA spacecraft. Cloud-ringed North America and the western bulge of Africa are also clearly shown. (right) Most of Africa and Antarctica's polar ice-cap are visible.

NASA

been accepted and the very evidence which had previously been ignored or explained away is now used to assist in continental reconstruction.

The search for evidence

No one piece of evidence is enough to assess whether continental drift has occurred. Several lines must be pursued. Firstly, a pre-drift reconstruction of the arrangement of the continents should provide a reasonable geometric or outline fit. Early workers have been rightly criticized for fitting the present-day coastlines together and making no allowance for the submerged part of the continent, that is the *continental shelf* which juts out under the ocean.

Subsequent reconstructions have taken this factor into consideration. Computers have been used recently to construct a 'best fit' between the continents. Following the assumption that the edge of the continent lies on the continental slope, which descends steeply from the edge of the continental shelf to the deep ocean floor, reconstructions have been made for various depth contours. For most parts of the world, the 'best fit' is at about the 1,000 m (550 fathoms) depth contour, and provides striking geometrical evidence that the continents were once joined together at the continental slope.

If the reconstructions are valid and drift has occurred, any two regions which formerly lay side by side, but are now far apart, should share common geological features. Ancient structural features such as the fold axes in mountain systems should match up. The detailed history of sedimentary rocks deposited in previously adjacent areas and the distribution of fossil animals and plants embedded in the rocks should likewise be almost identical.

This last line of evidence must be examined carefully. Geographically well-separated regions may have sedimentary and biological features in common just because they shared similar climates. The tropical rain forests of South America and Africa, for example, will both eventually produce the same type of coal bed deposits, but the plants enclosed within them may be very different.

Ancient climates also help in the work of reconstruction. Former climates leave their traces such as scratch marks where glaciers have dragged boulders over the land, and salt deposits which have developed in hot deserts. From such evidence a picture emerges of ancient climatic belts

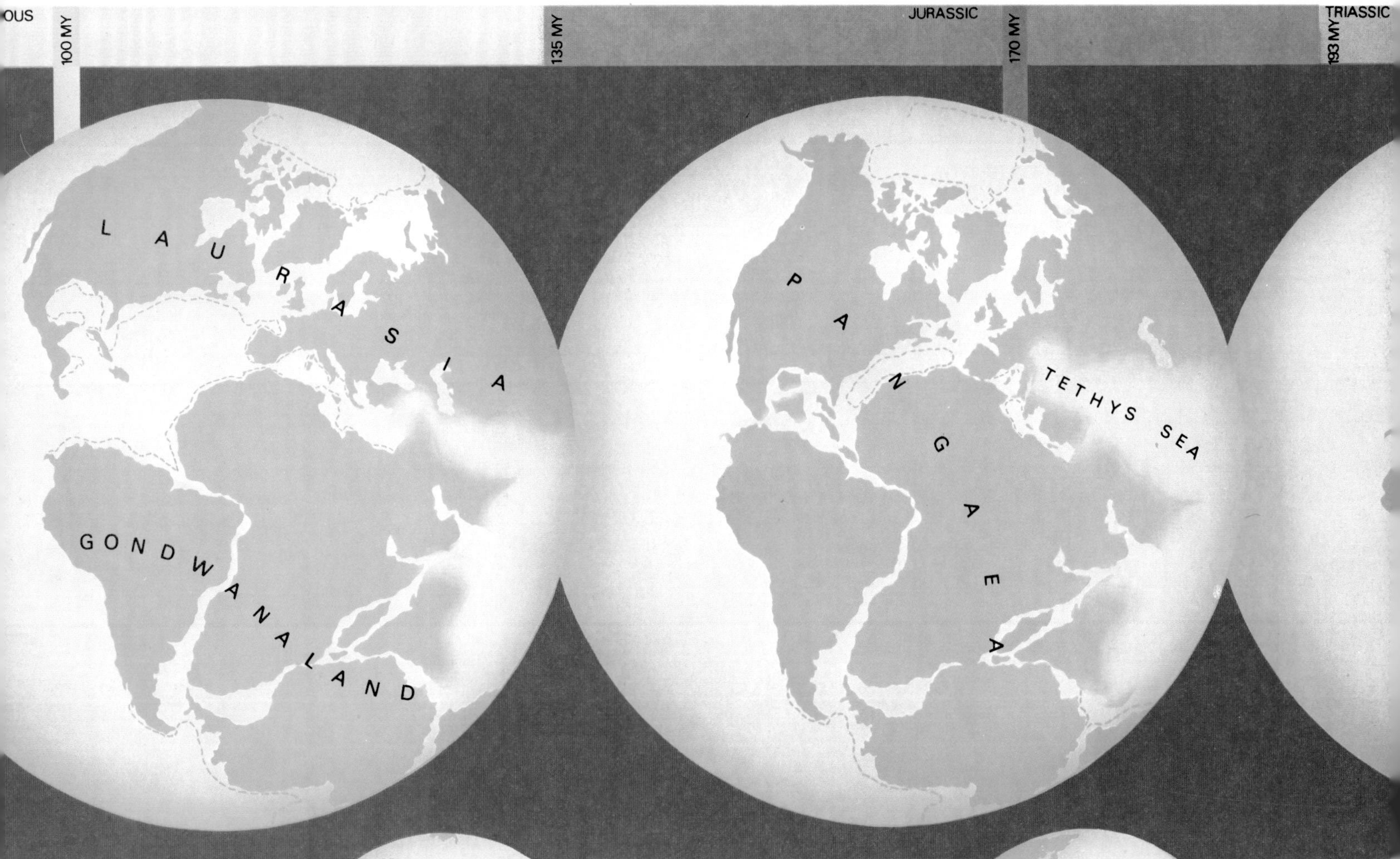

100 m. YEARS AGO India was nestled between Africa and the Antarctic. These three lands were joined to South America and Australasia to form *Gondwanaland*. North America and Eurasia made up the other great continent, *Laurasia*. The probable coastlines of the continents are marked by broken lines.

170 m. YEARS AGO The world was one giant land mass, named *Pangaea* and believed to be the result of even earlier drift. The *Tethys Sea*, dividing Eurasia from Africa, later formed the Mediterranean Sea. The reverse side of the globe shows *Panthalassa*, the Pacific Ocean's much larger ancestor.

which were in very different positions from those of today — hot deserts existed in modern polar regions and ice-caps invaded present equatorial zones. Presuming that the world's climatic pattern has always been basically similar to, though usually less extreme than, today's, the explanation must lie with the movement of the land masses which have drifted from one climatic zone to another. In a reconstruction, therefore, the original climatic belts, marked by rock and fossil clues, should line up and be roughly parallel to one another.

The most spectacular evidence for drift having taken place comes from palaeomagnetic work. *Palaeomagnetism* is the remnant of ancient magnetic traces preserved in rocks. Iron minerals crystallizing out from volcanic magma or molten rock generally become magnetized and line themselves up in the direction of the earth's magnetic field prevailing at that time. Even if, in the course of millions of years, magnetized iron mineral particles are eroded out of the parent rock and redeposited on the sea floor with other sediment, they will again orientate themselves exactly as a compass needle does in line with the earth's magnetic field.

In both cases, the magnetization is very stable and may be cemented within the rock to remain unaffected by subsequent changes in the earth's magnetic field. This means that the magnetism detected in a rock today can be used to fix the position of the earth's magnetic pole at the time when that rock was formed, though geological corrections may have to be made.

When there was no South Atlantic

The best examples of these various areas of evidence are found in South America and Africa. The fit of the Atlantic coastlines of these two continents shows an increasing gap north or south of a mid position. Much of that gap is filled in, however, if the continental shelf down to the 1,000 m (550 fathoms) depth contour is included in the fit. There are a few small areas of overlap, especially off the Niger River, but these are believed to date from after the break-up of the two continents.

There is ample data in support of the fit. Some was put forward by Wegener; much more was collected by du Toit and published in 1937. One aspect highlighted by both authorities was the distribution in Brazil and southwest Africa of glacial deposits from the Permo-Carboniferous age, some 300 million years ago.

These have since been intensively studied and tell a fascinating story. Southwest Africa was essentially an area of glacial erosion with material being moved from east to west towards the Atlantic. In contrast, the consolidated boulder clay, known as *tillite*, which covers Brazil was obviously deposited by extensive ice sheets moving in from the south east, from where the Atlantic now lies.

There are two conceivable sources for the tillite. Either this material was derived from the continental shelf — but this is unlikely considering the volume — or it came from southwest Africa.

Below: Continental drift explains the unexpected distribution of several fossils. Those of Cretaceous coral reefs and associated rudist bivalves (right) appear today in areas too cool for them to flourish. They could have grown further south, however, and been carried north by the drifting land.

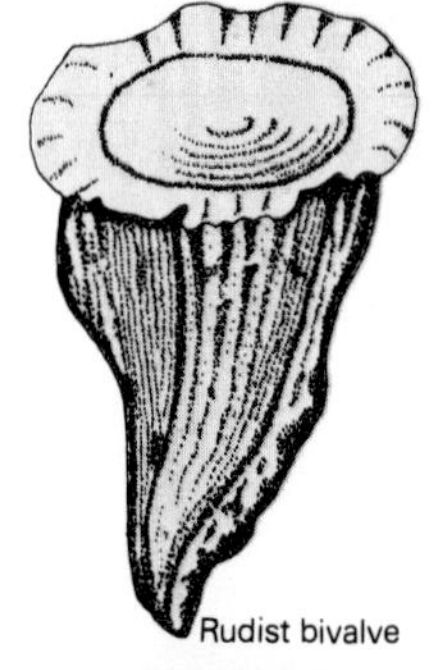

Gordon Roberton

Right: Characteristic of Permian plant beds is the *Glossopteris* fern with its blade-like leaves. It is found in all parts of Gondwanaland and gave an early lead to drift theory supporters. It could conceivably have been borne by wind over water and this casts some doubt on its value as conclusive evidence.

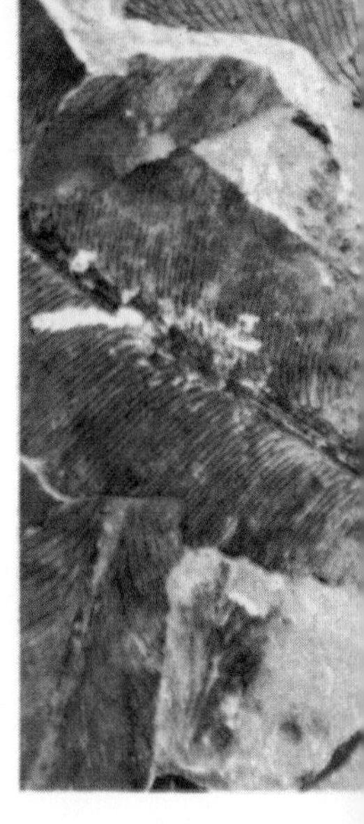

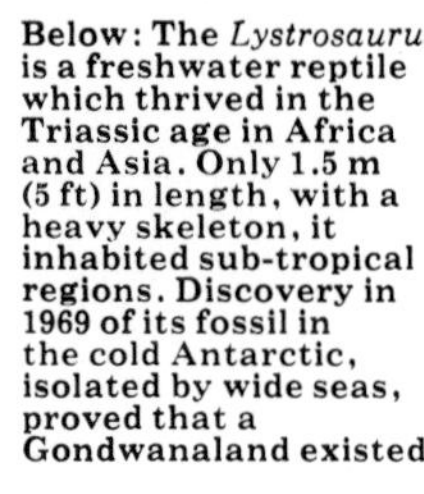

Below: The *Lystrosaurus* is a freshwater reptile which thrived in the Triassic age in Africa and Asia. Only 1.5 m (5 ft) in length, with a heavy skeleton, it inhabited sub-tropical regions. Discovery in 1969 of its fossil in the cold Antarctic, isolated by wide seas, proved that a Gondwanaland existed.

Coral

Lystrosaurus

CRETACEOUS | 135 MY | JURASSIC | 193 MY

NORTH AMERICA
EURASIA
ATLANTIC OCEAN
AFRICA
SOUTH AMERICA
ANTARCTICA
EQUATO

DISTRIBUTION OF EVIDENCE
Coral reefs
Lystrosaurus
Glossopteris
Mesosaurus
Carboniferous glaciation

Ancient coastline
Probable boundaries of Gondwanaland
Direction of ice flow
GONDWANALAND IN THE PERMIAN AGE

Above: Places where evidence from ancient wildlife and glacial activity has been found are pin-pointed on a map of the world today. Until quite recently, some scientists argued that giant land-bridges, across which ancient animals and plants might have spread, connected the continents—located then in their present positions. Such talk had to be discounted as these bridges could not have sunk without trace. When Gondwanaland, where most evidence has been found, is reconstructed (right) there is a perfect match both in outline and in locations of recorded fossil finds. The spread of Carboniferous glaciation is marked by arrows.

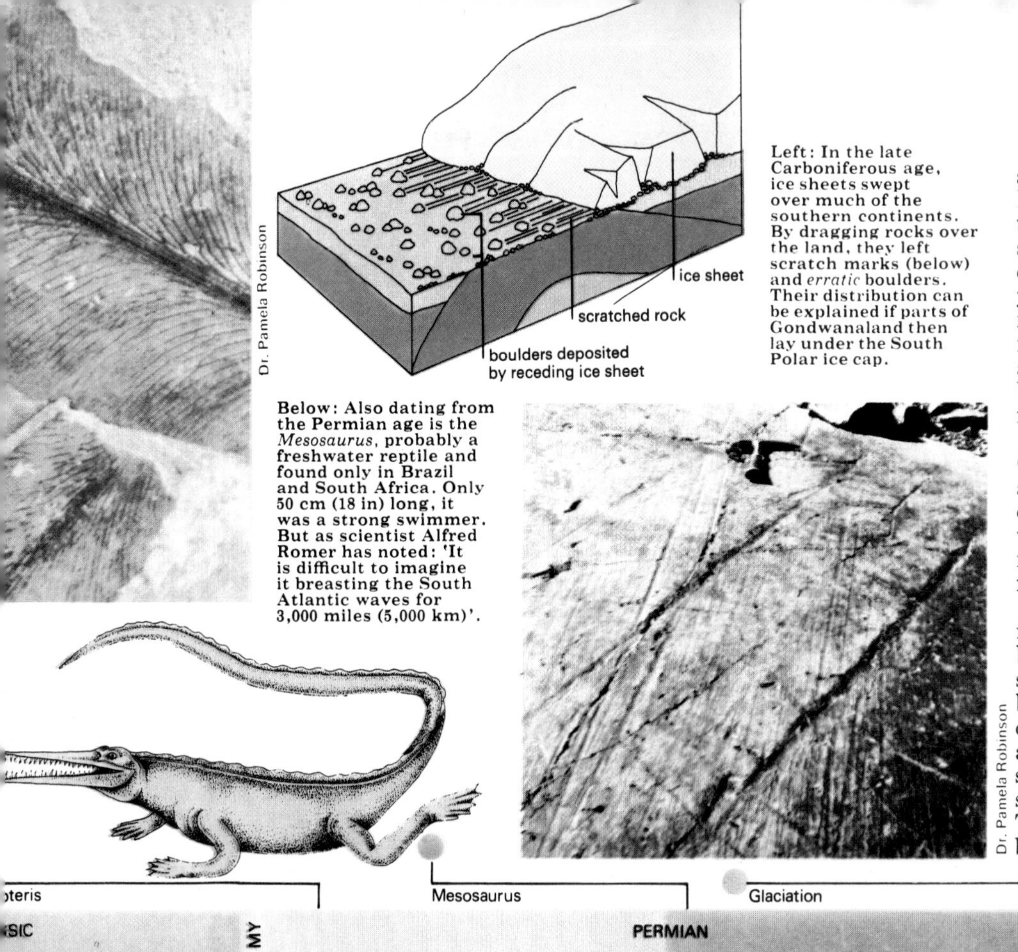

Left: In the late Carboniferous age, ice sheets swept over much of the southern continents. By dragging rocks over the land, they left scratch marks (below) and *erratic* boulders. Their distribution can be explained if parts of Gondwanaland then lay under the South Polar ice cap.

Below: Also dating from the Permian age is the *Mesosaurus*, probably a freshwater reptile and found only in Brazil and South Africa. Only 50 cm (18 in) long, it was a strong swimmer. But as scientist Alfred Romer has noted: 'It is difficult to imagine it breasting the South Atlantic waves for 3,000 miles (5,000 km)'.

pteris | Mesosaurus | Glaciation

SSIC | 225 MY | PERMIAN | 280 MY | CARBONIFEROUS

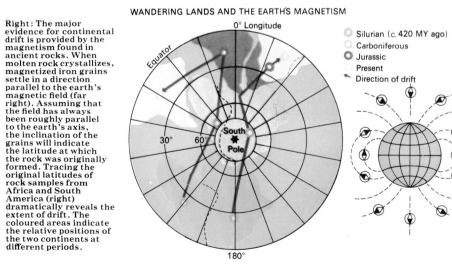

NORTH 30°

PACIFIC OCEAN

EQUATOR 0°

AUSTRALASIA

SOUTH 30°

Certain distinctive rock types enclosed within the Brazilian tillite can be matched with ones from southwest Africa. Moreover, palaeomagnetic observations confirm that the ice moving across southwest Africa was coming from the south polar region and that the pole at that time was lying to the southeast of South Africa.

Another outstanding piece of evidence has been established through the radio-active dating of rocks. Nearly all rocks contain minute amounts of radio-active elements which, in the course of time, decay to form other elements. As the various decay rates are known, it is possible to calculate the age of a rock by measuring the amount of the secondary element contained within it.

The Sahara shield was dated by this method and proved to be 2,000 million years old. Running alongside these ancient rocks is a group of younger rocks which are only 550 million years old. The dividing line between old and new is very clear and goes into the Atlantic near Accra, in Ghana. It reappears across the ocean at Sao Luis, in Brazil.

The sedimentary sequence on opposite sides of the Atlantic is remarkably similar, not only during Permo-Carboniferous times, but also from the Silurian age, some 400 million years ago, to the middle of the Cretaceous age, about 100 million years ago. Half-way through this 300 million year period, molten basalt rocks flooded parts of Brazil and South Africa and are overlain in both regions by red beds of desert origin which contain remains of similar vertebrate animals.

The sequence of sediments from the Cretaceous age along the coasts of Brazil and West Africa has recently attracted considerable attention. A series of fresh-water sedimentary basins have the same rock sequences and contain identical fish and microscopic crustacean remains.

The sequence is of interest for another reason. The non-marine conditions were brought to an end by a sudden influx of salt water. As the water evaporated it left behind deposits of salt. After this, marine conditions remained but the sediments, and eventually the animal life, developed separately and uniquely on the opposite sides of the present-day South Atlantic. This gradual division of formerly united basins of marine deposits during the middle of the Cretaceous age provides an accurate date for the beginning of the opening of the South Atlantic.

Laurasia and Gondwanaland

By the end of the nineteenth century, it had been suggested that in Carboniferous times the present-day continental masses could be grouped into two supercontinents. The more southerly one was called *Gondwanaland*, and the more northerly one called *Laurasia*. These two supercontinents were separated by the *Tethys Ocean*. South America and Africa form part of Gondwanaland, but some of the other fragments of this enormous land mass are more difficult to piece together — the positioning of India is particularly problematic. The geometrical fit of the northern continents to form Laurasia is better, although the geological evidence to support the fit is not as firm as the evidence for joining South America to Africa.

Wegener proposed that, originally, Gondwanaland and Laurasia had been joined together and he called this gigantic continent *Pangaea*, from the Greek 'all the earth'. It is now realized that Pangaea not only pre-dates the most recent phase of continental drift, but also represents the culmination of an earlier period of drift. Before that, there were others, and the present-day continents may be composed of fragments of several different earlier continental masses.

Today's map of the world is, then, a record of a moment in time, a static view of the ever-moving continents. Although there is still much detailed work to be done on continental drift, there is enough information available to stimulate a little informed speculation. The area of the Pacific basin, for example, is shrinking, which suggests that perhaps, in the next 50 to 100 million years, Asia will close with North America and the Philippines will lie in the shadow of the Andes.

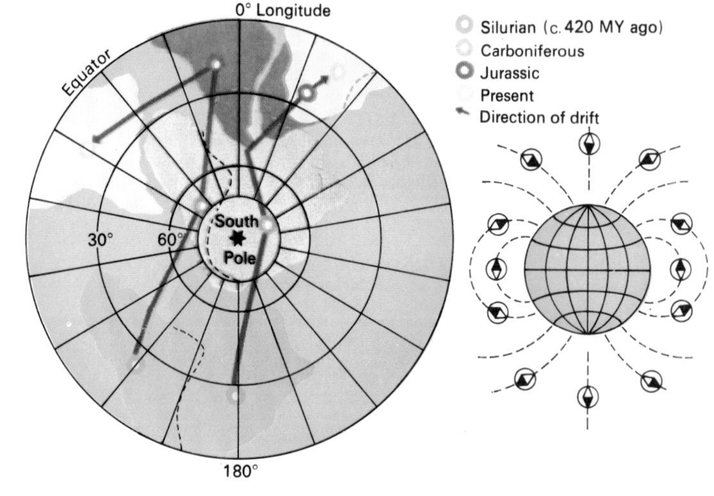

Right: The major evidence for continental drift is provided by the magnetism found in ancient rocks. When molten rock crystallizes, magnetized iron grains settle in a direction parallel to the earth's magnetic field (far right). Assuming that the field has always been roughly parallel to the earth's axis, the inclination of the grains will indicate the latitude at which the rock was originally formed. Tracing the original latitudes of rock samples from Africa and South America (right) dramatically reveals the extent of drift. The coloured areas indicate the relative positions of the two continents at different periods.

The Spreading Sea Floor

The theory of continental drift, as put forward by Alfred Wegener more than 60 years ago, suggested that the continents had once been joined as parts of a large land mass and then slowly drifted apart. The evidence for this imaginative idea was impressive but the theory gained little acceptance among scientists. This was primarily because it was hard to envisage a driving mechanism powerful enough to force apart and then to propel the apparently static continents over many thousands of kilometres.

It was not until the early 1960s that substantial evidence was collated to establish a theory explaining not only continental drift, but also the world-wide distribution of volcanic and earthquake activity. This evidence was not found in the continents themselves, however, but in the other two-thirds of the earth's surface—the oceans.

When scientists examined the ocean floor, they found its geology to be profoundly different from that of the continents. Along many coasts the sea is shallow, often less than 200 m (110 fathoms) deep, and relatively flat-bottomed. This is the *continental shelf* and is part of the continent. Further out to sea, the shelf gives way to the *continental slope* which drops steeply to the ocean bottom 5 or 6 km (some 3.5 miles) down. The slope is also made of continental rocks and on it and at its base there may be piles of debris that have slipped down from the shelf.

The layer of sediment covering the deep ocean floor is thin and nowhere more than 200 million years old. This is young in comparison to continental rocks which may be over 3,000 million years old. Below the sedimentary material is solid, dark, dense rock of volcanic origin, going down some 7 km (4 miles) to the surface of the mantle. This underlying rock forming the oceanic crust is known as *sime* because it is rich in silicon and magnesium. The land masses are known as *sial*—the rock is dominated by silicon and aluminium. The dense sima meets the lighter sial at the foot of the continental slopes and is believed to pass beneath them.

Mountains under the sea

Another important discovery was that the ocean floor is not flat. A great mountain chain or *oceanic ridge* with peaks 4,500 m (15,000 ft) high lies under the waves. One of the first sections to be investigated was the mid-Atlantic ridge. This stretches from Iceland to Tristan da Cunha in the South Atlantic, rounding the Cape of Good Hope then linking up with the rest of the submarine mountain system—80,000 km (50,000 miles) long. This ridge, like many of the others, has a central rift valley some 50 km (30 miles) wide and 2 km (1.2 miles) deep.

In contrast to ridges, which stretch upwards and sometimes break the surface to form volcanic islands, are *trenches*. These run along the edge of continents or close

Right: The cross-section of the earth's interior from the Pacific to Africa reveals great activity above and below the earth's crust. The Atlantic sea floor is expanding but the Pacific is shrinking. New oceanic crust is continually formed at the mid-ocean ridges, carried aside by the spreading *plates* and destroyed in the subduction zones. The South American plate consists of both continental and oceanic crust embedded in the *lithosphere*, a rigid shell of rock which 'floats' on the molten *asthenosphere*. It is drifting west and riding over the denser Pacific plate, which descends and remelts, creating volcanic and earthquake activity.

SOUTH AMERICAN PLATE MOVI
PACIFIC OCEAN
ANDES
SOUTH AMERICA
Peru-Chile trench subduction zone
active volcanoes
base of descending plate
partial melting of basaltic crust to feed volcanoes
Benioff zone–shallow earthquakes
lithosphere remelts
700 km discontinuity–deepest earthquakes
continental slope
continental s

Right: The cause of *plate tectonics* is unresolved. Four of the possible driving mechanisms are shown. The upwelling mantle may act as a wedge—pushing the plates apart as new material is added at the ridges (a). The raised ridges may provide a gradient down which plates slide under force of gravity. This may be coupled with sinking of cool, heavy ocean crust in subduction zones (b) due to the weight of very dense minerals formed as rocks pass under the overriding plate. Convection currents in the mantle may cause plate motion by (c) exercising a drag on the 'floating' plates. Alternatively, plate movements may be the outermost signs of powerful convection cycles (d), perhaps 700 km deep, of which the rigid *lithosphere* forms the cooled, brittle, upper boundary.

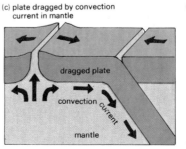

(a) plate pushed by addition of new material at spreading ridge

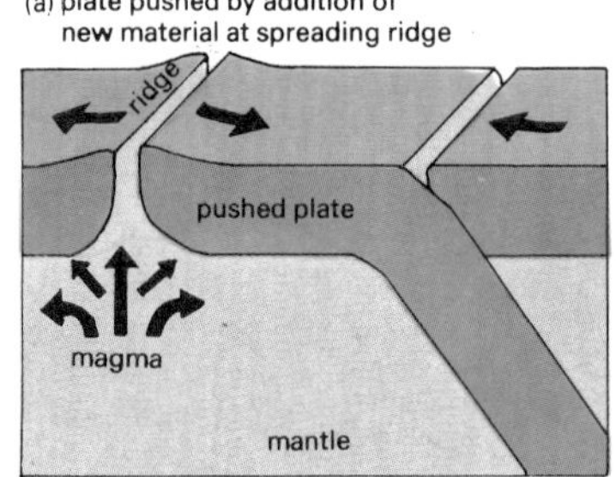

(b) plate pulled by weight of descending slab as it cools

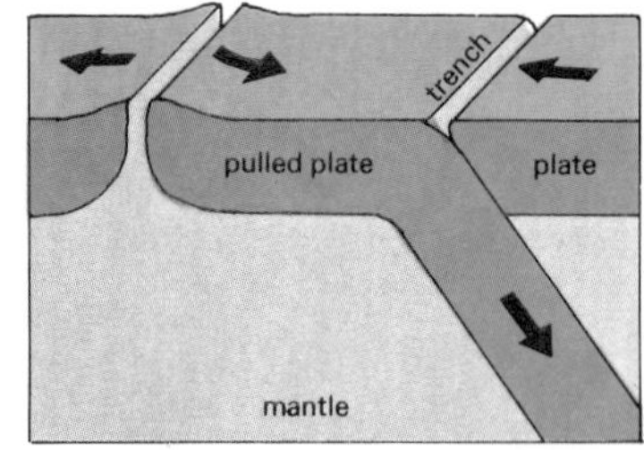

(c) plate dragged by convection current in mantle

dragged plate
convection current
mantle

(d) plate is cooled, upper boundary of mantle convection cycle

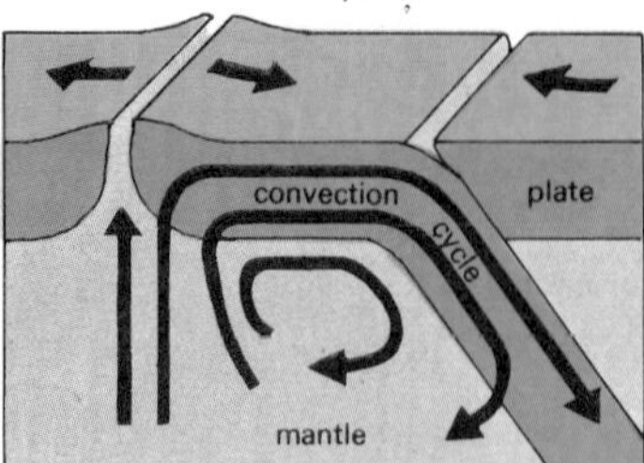

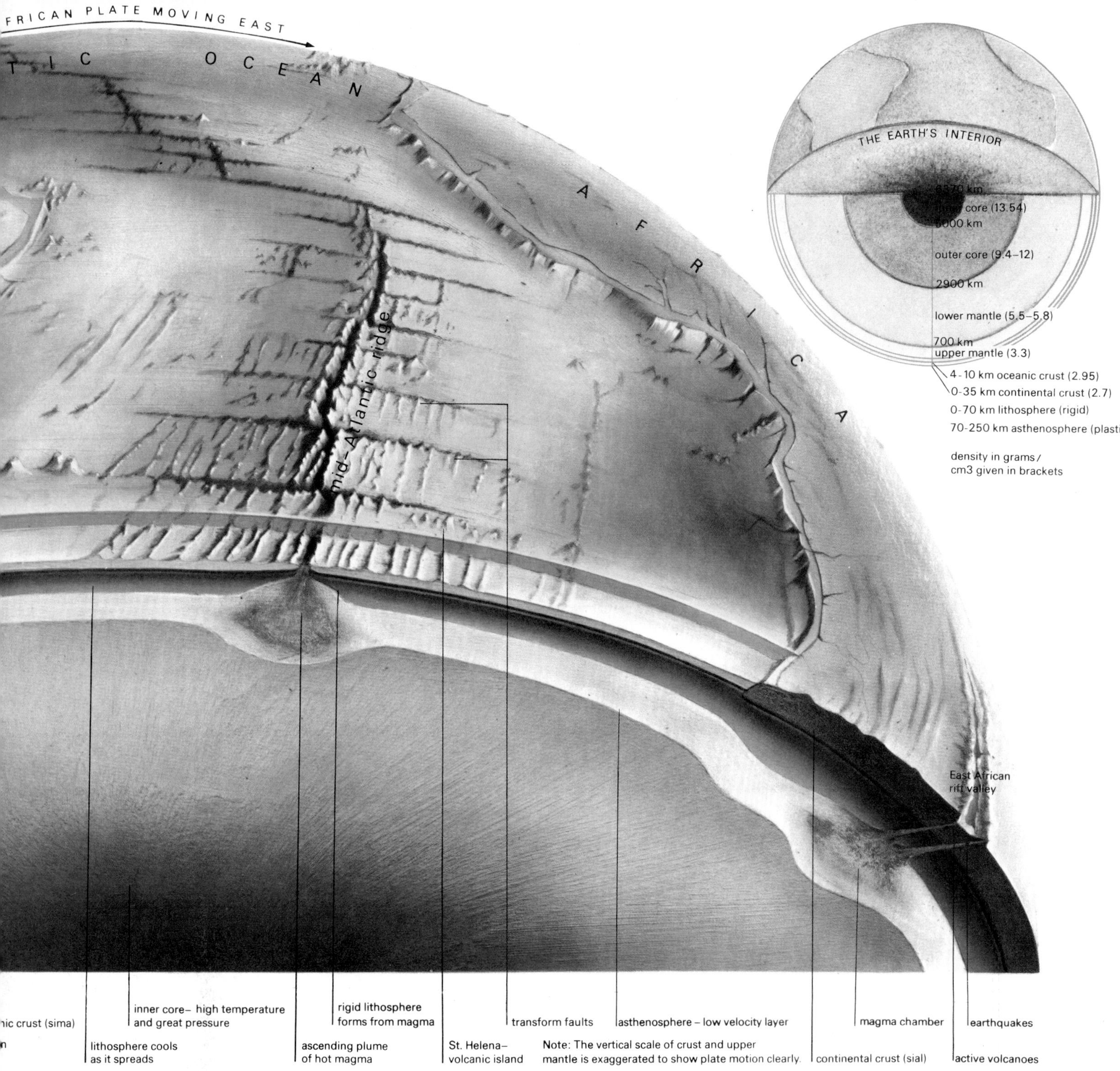

to chains of islands such as Japan and are the deepest parts of the earth's surface. The deepest point, 11 km (6.8 miles) down, is in the Marianas Trench in the Pacific.

There is another major difference between ridges and trenches. The *heat flow*, the rate at which heat is lost from the inner zones of the earth to the atmosphere, is extremely high at the ridges. But as one moves away from them, the heat flow decreases and becomes exceptionally low along the trenches. This, and the height of the ridges, is believed to be caused by the expansion of heated mantle material pushing up from below the crust.

One characteristic common to both ocean ridges and trenches is volcanic activity. The continental side of trenches are chains of volcanic islands or mountains, and mid-oceanic islands tracing the path of a ridge above sea level, are invariably made of igneous rocks. Moreover, these volcanic belts contain the epicentres of nearly all earthquakes.

All this data was pulled together by an American geologist, Harry Hess. In 1960 he put forward an idea that became known as *sea floor spreading*. Because all the sediments on the ocean floor are young, he argued, the ocean floor itself could not be very old. Either the earth must have expanded enormously—by about five times in the last 200 million years—or new oceanic crust must be both created and destroyed continuously.

Undersea 'conveyor belts'

Expansion at anything like that rate is considered highly unlikely. Hess therefore proposed that new oceanic crust was created at the ridges, carried sideways as though on a conveyor belt, and then taken down into the mantle along the deep sea trenches. He suggested that the conveyor belt could be driven by *convection currents*, movements caused by heat differences, in the mantle.

Hot materials, less dense than cold, tend to rise and create an upward plume of heat. Near the surface, the warm materials spread sideways and cool steadily, until an opposing current is met. Both then turn down to form a descending cold plume. This area of downward movement along the trenches is called a *subduction zone*.

The growth of the Atlantic Ocean, for example, can be pictured as follows. About 150 million years ago, a rising plume of heat generated vulcanism along the line that was to become the mid-Atlantic ridge. (Volcanic rocks of appropriate age are found in places along the present margin of the Atlantic). New oceanic crust was created steadily and the new ocean opened and widened. The continents, firmly embedded in the oceanic crust, were carried sideways away from the ridge and away from one another.

In the 1960s new evidence became available which supported Hess's idea. During the Second World War, instruments called *magnetometers* were developed to detect submarines by the magnetic disturbance they caused. Since the war, scientists have

NASA

John S. Shelton

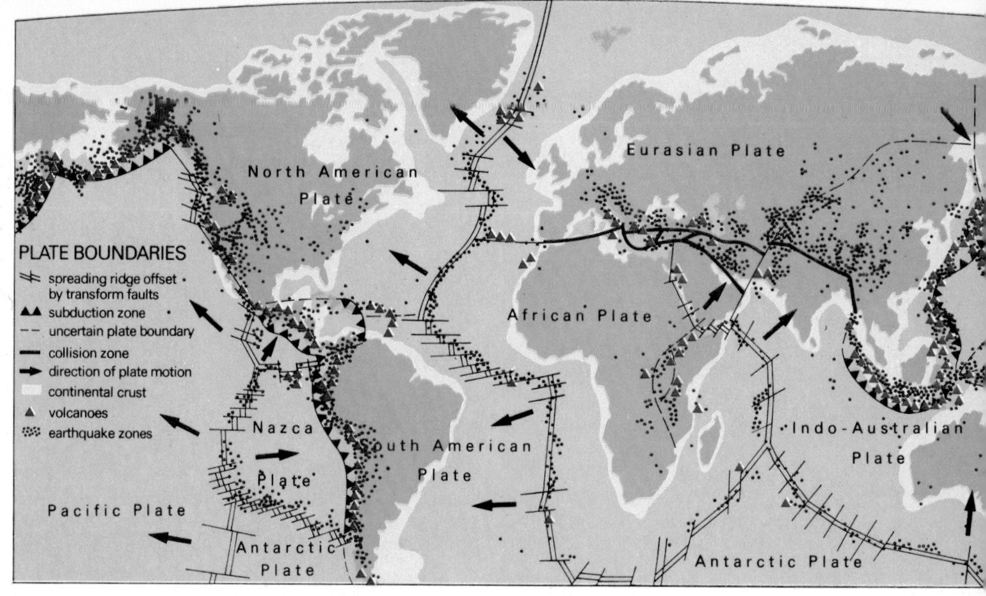

Top left: The Red Sea is a new ocean in the making. Africa (left) is being slowly forced apart from Arabia.

Left: California's San Andreas Fault is the earthquake-prone margin between two plates. A stream is being carried north (to the right) by the Pacific plate (top).

Above: The earth's outer shell consists of a mosaic of rigid plates, seven of which cover considerable areas. Plate boundaries are clearly indicated by interconnecting belts of major earthquake, volcanic and mountain-building activity, whose distribution is explained by plate tectonics. They occur along four types of plate margins. Plate material is created at *spreading ridges*. In *subduction zones* one plate is destroyed beneath another. Plates slide freely along *transform faults*, but push up high mountains along *collision zones*. Plate tectonics also confirms the theory of continental drift.

Top right: East Africa's Rift Valley, a volcanic area, may be the point of a future break-up in the African plate.

Right: Iceland is steadily growing larger. It is formed by the spreading mid-Atlantic ridge. The island has a jagged rift valley, and is an area of volcanic activity.

continued to use these instruments to measure variations in the strength of the earth's magnetic field. Over large areas of the ocean the magnetic intensity was found to vary in narrow bands parallel to the ridges.

Cambridge geophysicists Frederick Vine and Drummond Matthews showed that this pattern of *magnetic stripes* could be due to the rocks of the ocean floor. As lava solidifies, it is magnetized by the prevailing magnetic field. The pattern of bands could therefore be explained if the earth's present north magnetic pole had from time to time switched to the south. During such a *magnetic reversal* the volcanic rocks forming at the ocean ridges would have been magnetized in the reverse sense from those erupted today.

When Vine and Matthews put forward their idea, magnetic reversal was still just a theory. Soon after, however, examination of suitable volcanic rocks showed that a series of reversals had indeed occurred over the last 5 million years. So, using the 'stripes' it is now possible to estimate the age of sea-floor rocks and see how they become progressively older away from the ridges.

These successive ages of the sea floor have been double-checked by dating the sediments resting on the igneous rocks. Knowing how old an ocean is means that its growth rate can be calculated. The North Atlantic, for instance, is spreading at about 2 cm (0.75 in) a year, while the east Pacific ridge is producing 10 cm (4 in) of new crust annually. The rate of sea floor spreading is remarkable. It means that North America is moving west the length of a man's body in a lifetime.

Earthquakes at plate margins

Also in the 1960s, a world-wide network of sensitive seismographs was set up to detect minute earthquakes and to differentiate between them and nuclear explosions. From this it was possible to map the points where earthquakes begin. It was found that along the ocean ridges earthquakes are almost all less than 100 km (62 miles) deep.

MAGNETIC PATTERNS ON THE OCEAN FLOOR

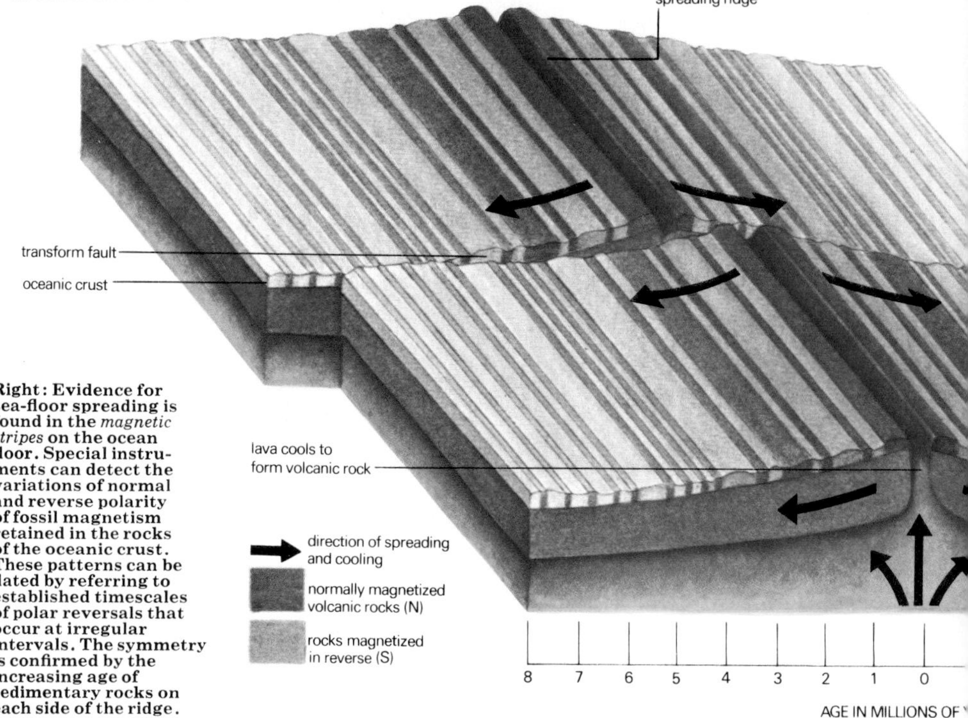

Right: Evidence for sea-floor spreading is found in the *magnetic stripes* on the ocean floor. Special instruments can detect the variations of normal and reverse polarity of fossil magnetism retained in the rocks of the oceanic crust. These patterns can be dated by referring to established timescales of polar reversals that occur at irregular intervals. The symmetry is confirmed by the increasing age of sedimentary rocks on each side of the ridge.

The deeper, stronger quakes are associated with the subduction zones. They all occur in a layer sloping at about 45°, the *Benioff zone*, and continuing down from the trenches to a depth of about 700 km (435 miles). There are a few shallow earthquakes situated at a maximum depth of 80 km (50 miles), probably caused by the rocks bending and cracking as they enter the subduction zone. Most of the quakes, however, happen much further down—between 300 and 700 km—and are probably the result of physical and chemical changes in the descending ocean crust.

In addition to ridges and trenches, another group of earthquakes is related to *transform faults*, great fractures that cut through the ocean ridges. These faults may extend for hundreds of kilometres across the ocean floor and, in some cases, go into the continents like the San Andreas fault in California. The fractures divide the ridge systems into segments. This raises some problems for the idea of sea floor spreading, for how can the conveyor belt operate differently in adjoining parts of the ocean floor?

An even greater problem is presented by continents such as Africa and Antarctica. These are almost surrounded by ocean ridge systems without the corresponding subduction zones. This means that crustal growth must take place by movement of the ridge system away from the continents. Attempts to answer difficulties such as these have caused sea floor spreading to be developed into the more comprehensive theory of plate tectonics.

The earth's crust is divided into stable areas bounded by ocean ridges, subduc-

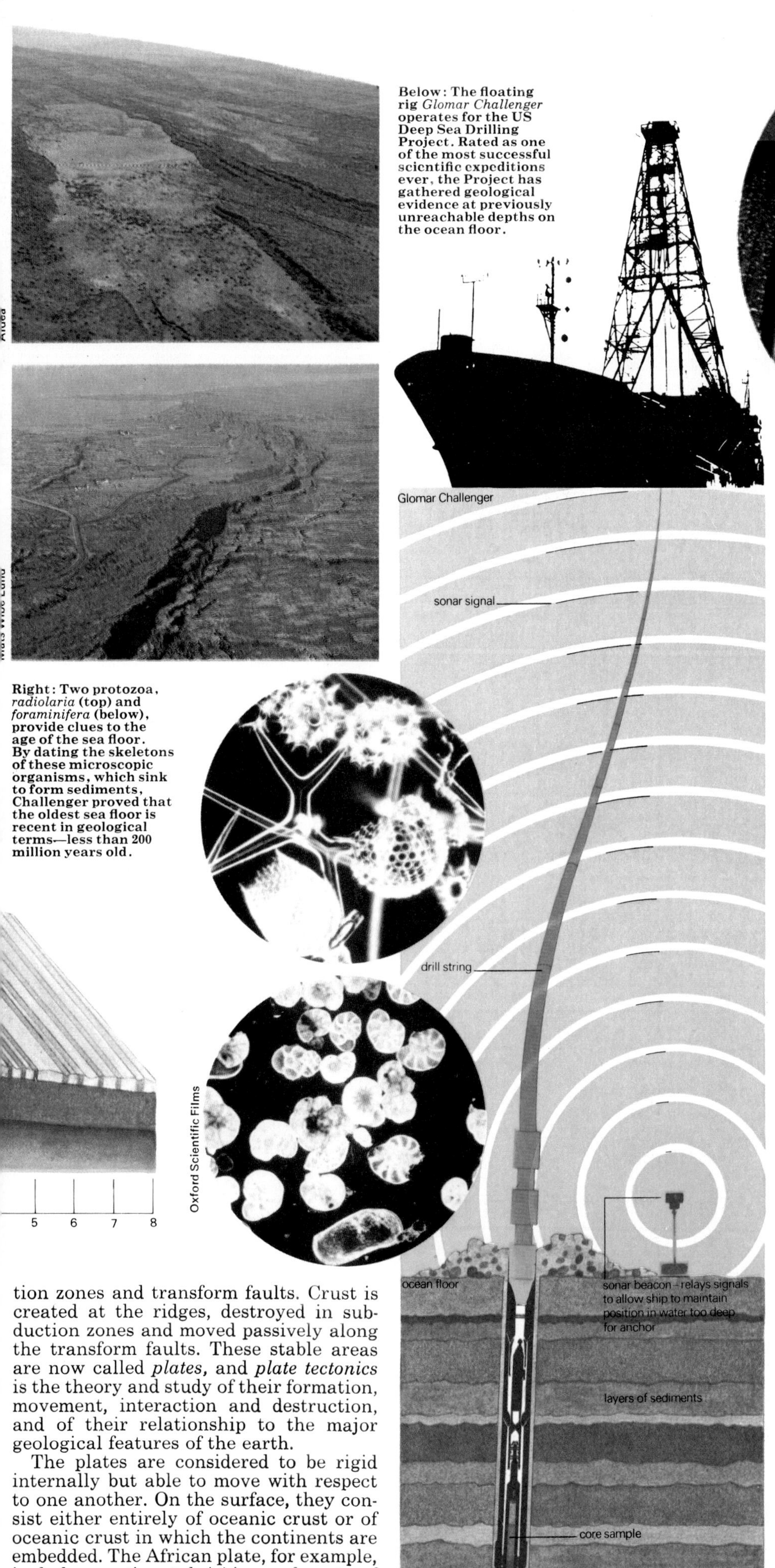

Below: The floating rig *Glomar Challenger* operates for the US Deep Sea Drilling Project. Rated as one of the most successful scientific expeditions ever, the Project has gathered geological evidence at previously unreachable depths on the ocean floor.

Left: Once on station, *Glomar Challenger* can drill without anchor. A sonar beacon is lowered and the ship uses four sideways thrusters to maintain position. From her 43 m tall derrick, the rig can lower as much as 6.7 km of pipe. Holes have been drilled more than 1.3 km deep into the ocean bottom.

Above: A scientist in a shipboard laboratory analyzes core samples. The fossil sequences and the stratas of sedimentary rocks tell the story of evolution and ancient climates in the oceans. The age and composition of the igneous rocks below the sediments confirm that oceanic crust is formed at spreading ridges.

Right: Two protozoa, *radiolaria* (top) and *foraminifera* (below), provide clues to the age of the sea floor. By dating the skeletons of these microscopic organisms, which sink to form sediments, Challenger proved that the oldest sea floor is recent in geological terms—less than 200 million years old.

tion zones and transform faults. Crust is created at the ridges, destroyed in subduction zones and moved passively along the transform faults. These stable areas are now called *plates,* and *plate tectonics* is the theory and study of their formation, movement, interaction and destruction, and of their relationship to the major geological features of the earth.

The plates are considered to be rigid internally but able to move with respect to one another. On the surface, they consist either entirely of oceanic crust or of oceanic crust in which the continents are embedded. The African plate, for example, includes continental Africa and parts of the Atlantic and Indian oceans.

These large, solid plates must be thicker than the depth of the oceanic crust. It is now believed that the plates are divisions of an outer, rigid shell of solidified rock, called the *lithosphere,* of which the crust forms the uppermost part. It is some 70 km (43 miles) thick under the oceans and perhaps 150 km (93 miles) thick under continents.

Floating continents in a sea of rock

Underlying the lithosphere is the *asthenosphere.* This is a world-wide 'plastic' layer through which seismic waves pass at low velocity and in which the rocks are partially molten or close to melting point. Its 'plasticity' bends to the shape of the lithosphere and allows the plates to glide relatively freely over the earth's surface. Continental drift is the result of plate movement.

The 'plastic' behaviour of the asthenosphere also explains the slow vertical adjustments which occur in the earth's crust. The continental crust is lighter than the rocks beneath it. Its average density is 2.7 grams/cm³ against 2.95 for the oceanic crust and 3.3 for the upper mantle. The lighter continents are in effect floating in a 'sea' of denser, but plastic, rock. The thickness of the continental crust is extremely variable.

This balancing act between 'floating' continents and underlying rock is termed *isostacy.* Isostatic adjustment is relatively rapid. About 10,000 years ago, for example, Scandinavia was covered by thick ice. The extra weight caused the crust in north-west Europe to sink, but now that the ice has melted, the land has risen some 200 m (650 feet) and is still rising.

Gradually the rates and directions of plate movement are being worked out, but its cause is still a mystery. Whatever its driving force, the theory of plate tectonics explains many aspects of earth history. Most changes occur at the plate boundaries, especially in the subduction zones where volcanoes and earthquakes are characteristic features. The moving plate theory is also important because it gives an idea of what will happen in the future. Knowing more about earthquakes, for instance, means that they can be predicted and, perhaps, controlled.

Mountain Building

There are two great chains of mountains on earth. One includes the South American Andes, the Rocky Mountains and other ranges encircling the Pacific; the other runs eastwards from the Alps of Southern Europe right across to the Himalayas and beyond. This system of 'linear' mountain belts appears to be unique to the planet earth.

Extending across the planet's surface for hundreds and even thousands of kilometres in continuous tracts, these mountains rise in places to peaks many kilometres above sea level. Their height means that most are snow covered. Frost-shattered fragments may break away to form jagged peaks surrounded by slopes covered in rock debris. Fast flowing streams cut gullies and gorges which are gradually widened and deepened, and may be cut still more savagely by glaciers flowing down from snow fields near the summit. Over millions of years such agents of erosion give mountains their characteristic features. Yet how did they originally form, and what forces were at work to create them?

Movements in the earth's crust

From the patterns revealed by volcanic and earthquake activity it has become clear that the earth's great mountain chains lie over unstable areas of the planet's crust. Indeed these mountains are not merely surface features, but are expressions of fundamental structures in the earth's crust. And it is this that has led scientists to regard mountain-building (known as *orogeny*) as part of an activity beginning beneath the earth's surface.

The earth can create mountains in a number of different ways, yet the great linear belts are an example of by far the most important mechanism, one which has been at work since early in the earth's history. These vast mountain chains of folded rock originate where the earth's crustal 'plates' converge, forcing layers of rock into great arcs which may rise far above sea level.

Investigation of the rocks of an 'orogenic' mountain belt like the Himalayas shows that over millions of years they have undoubtedly suffered severe distortion and displacement from their original position. The layers of sediment, deposited in the sea long ago and hardened to form sedimentary rocks, contain fossilized remains of marine animals. When these fossils are found in rock strata of mountain folds thousands of metres above sea level it is clear that astonishing forces have pushed the layers upwards. The flat and continuous layers originally formed have been shaped into huge folds, tilted into vertical layers, or broken and stacked in a series of slabs. Such was the force of compression when the Indian continental plate met the vast plate of Asia that the Himalayas were formed.

The effect of this convergence of plates does vary from place to place. For example, it is particularly where the leading edges of both plates consist of 'continental' crustal material—which is less dense than crust of 'oceanic' type—that the

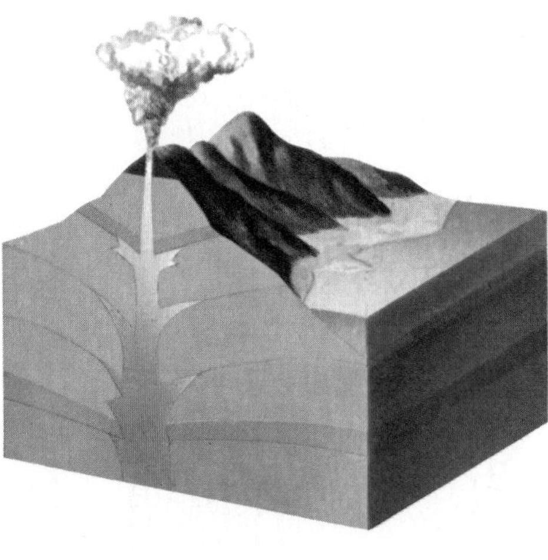

Left: Some of the world's most spectacular peaks are those formed by volcanic action. The classical shape of a volcanic cone is produced by the steady eruption of ash, pyroclasts and sticky lava from a central vent. Most volcanoes are located on the margins of the continental plates at mid-ocean ridges and deep sea trenches.

Right: The snow-capped peak of Mount Osorno reaches 2,660 metres into the South American skyline. A perfect example of a volcanic cone, Osorno is part of the Andes mountain range, formed when the Pacific plate was thrust under the South American plate.

Barnaby's

Left: Most mountain ranges are the product of continual pushing and compression of the earth's surface. Sideways pressure on layers of sedimentary rock can produce fold mountains of a simple, open shape, as in parts of the Jura range in France and Switzerland. In more complex belts like the Alps and Himalayas, distorted folds—overturned and recumbent—are more common.

Right: The Himalayan range contains the highest peaks in the world. They are formed by the compression and uplift of a land area between the colliding mass of Asia and the subcontinent of India.

R. Everts, ZEFA

Left: Under strong compression blocks of surface rocks may fracture rather than bend, producing a fault rather than a fold. Normal faulting produces a mountain with a steep fault face raised above a plain and a gentle dip slope on the other side.

Right: The Sierra Nevadas are a good example of 'tilt block' mountains, formed by the uplift of a tilted fault block. This view shows the steep eastern face—up to 3,000 metres high—rising above the floor of the Great Basin of eastern California and western Nevada. The Sierra slope coincides with a major fault area, which includes the San Andreas fault.

Barnaby's

Left: Some mountains are geological 'remnants' rather than 'constructions'. A mass of hard igneous rock such as granite intrudes into pre-existing rock, pushing up into the layers. Later, erosion of the softer surrounding rock leaves the igneous mass exposed as a dome or block-shaped mountain.

Right: Mighty Half Dome in the Yosemite Valley of California is a spectacular example of an intrusive mountain. Its tough granite face has resisted erosion better than the rock which once enclosed it. The sheer north-west face—now a mountaineer's delight—was carved by glaciation.

John Cleare

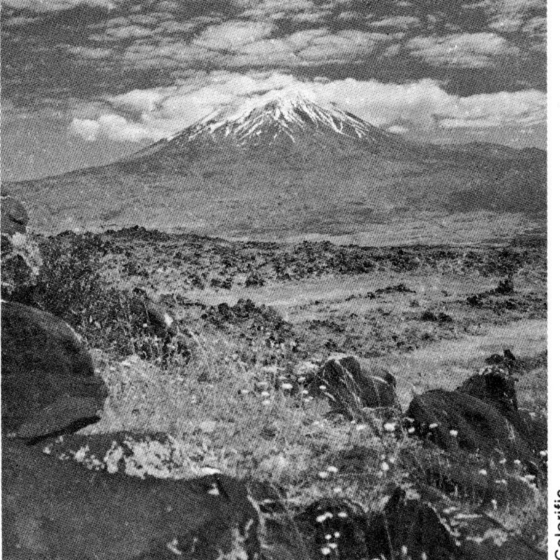

Left: Mount Ararat in eastern Turkey is a volcanic cone, 5,000 metres high. It lies in a 'collision zone' where volcanic and earthquake activity are caused by collision between the African and Eurasian plates. According to Biblical legend, Noah's Ark came to rest on Mount Ararat after the great flood.

Below: The sunlit slopes of Mount Ngauruhoe in New Zealand's Tongariro National Park. The mountain is a recently active volcano, the cone surmounted by an explosion crater which is still giving off gases. Mount Ngauruhoe lies on the fringe of the great 'linear' mountain belt that encircles the Pacific.

Below: The Elborz mountains near Teheran were formed by local tilting and faulting in an area of compression. They show a regular pattern of folding and deformation.

Below right: Diagram showing the features of a simple fold, created by horizontal pressure.

Right: Twisted layers of rock are clearly evident beneath the snow on a ridge along the western cwm of Everest, between Lhotze and Nuptse, at about 7,500 metres. These twisted strata indicate the kind of localized folding which produces minor anticline and syncline features in an area of compression.

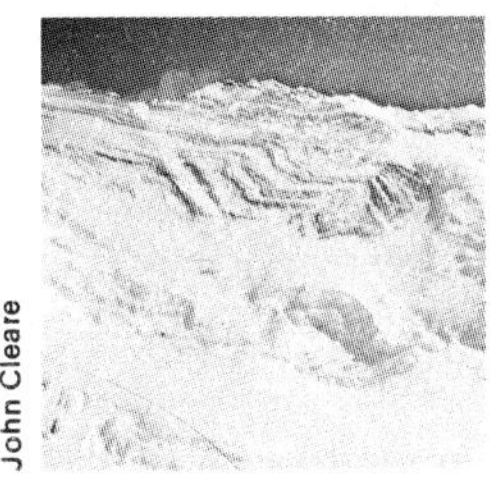

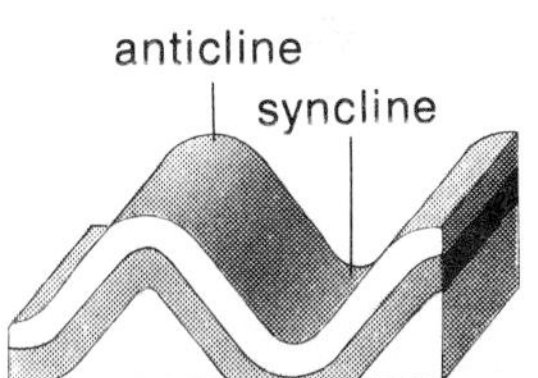

Above: The uplifted fault scarp of the tilt block of the Teton range forms a majestic panorama for visitors to the Grand Teton National Park in Wyoming, USA. Weathering processes have continually attacked the uplifted block, producing the present topography of sharp, angular peaks.

Left: A view of the Yosemite Valley from 3,000 metres up. Glacial action has smoothed a rounded valley in the granite rock, about 11 km long. The natural features of the area—sculptured granite cliffs and majestic waterfalls— are typical of heavy glaciation.

Right: The massive mountain dome overlooking Narssaq Harbour in Greenland. The slightly irregular shape is due to glaciation and frost action—exposure to extremes of temperature results in the fracturing of the rock which leaves jagged outlines and slopes which may be covered in a mass of rock debris.

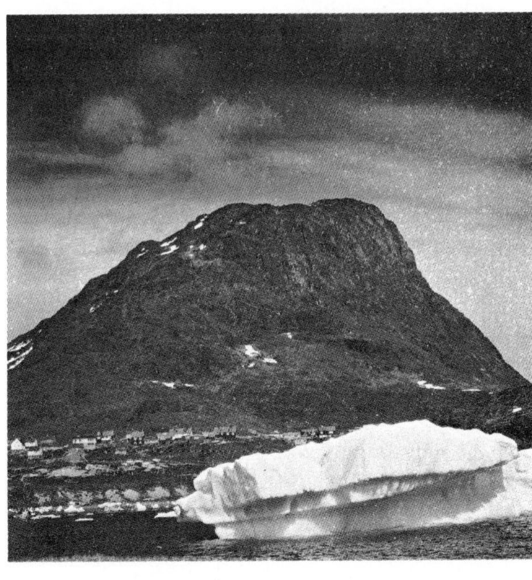

TYPES OF FOLDS

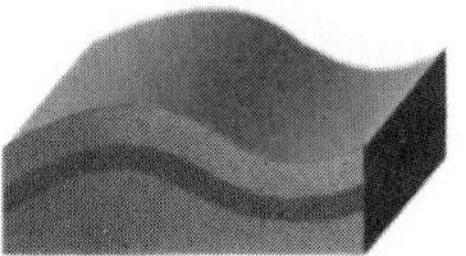

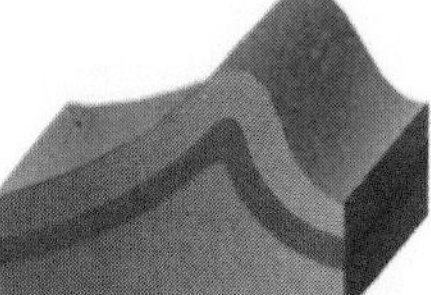

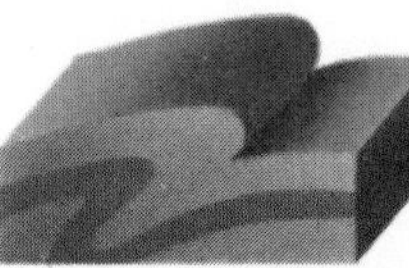

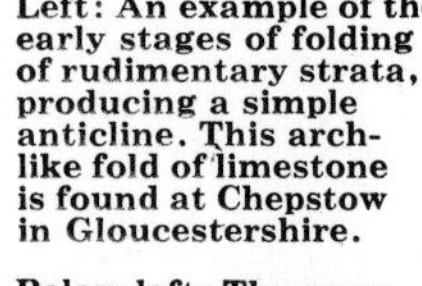

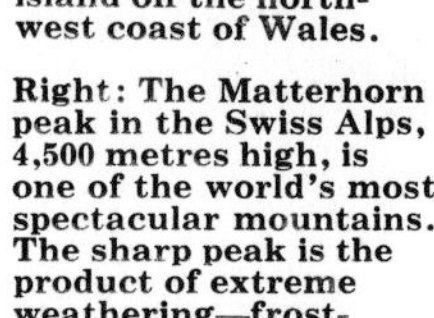

Left: An example of the early stages of folding of rudimentary strata, producing a simple anticline. This arch-like fold of limestone is found at Chepstow in Gloucestershire.

Below left: The more advanced stages of folding in which many minor anticlines and synclines occur within a larger complex anticline. This example is on Anglesey, an island off the north-west coast of Wales.

Right: The Matterhorn peak in the Swiss Alps, 4,500 metres high, is one of the world's most spectacular mountains. The sharp peak is the product of extreme weathering—frost-shattering caused by icy temperatures.

IGS

John Watney

forces of compression and uplift lead to formation of mountain belts. Where one of the plates consists of 'oceanic' crustal material, this may be overridden by the more buoyant continental plate, creating such features as oceanic trenches and volcanic island arcs. The Andes, the North American Cordilleras and the island arcs of Japan, the Philippines and Indonesia are products of the over-riding of the Pacific floor by the American and Asian continental plates.

The Geosyncline

Large parts of the world's orogenic mountain belts are carved from rocks which originated below the sea. Over periods of at least 100,000,000 years, marine sediments accumulated to thicknesses of ten or more kilometres on the sites of the belts. Most of these show features which indicate their accumulation in shallow seas and it is assumed that in the distant past, throughout the period of deposition, the sea-floor gradually subsided to make room for them. Such a well-defined region of long-continued subsidence of the earth's crust is called a *geosyncline*. For example, where the Appalachian Mountains (an 'orogenic' belt of mountains formed some 400 million years ago) now stand, a thick pile of sediment once lay beneath the sea. And this led two American geologists, Hall and Dana, to infer a connection between the development of a geosyncline and the subsequent operation of mountain-building forces.

The accumulation of great thicknesses of sedimentary and volcanic rocks in many such geosynclinal troughs has, however, been punctuated by phases of crustal instability and volcanic activity. In these periods portions of the trough filling were raised above sea level and subjected to erosion. The successive layers visible today as mountain belts may therefore have gaps which reflect erosion at several different periods. Lower layers, for example, may show folds developed before the accumulation of the most recent deposits.

In many belts, the continued deposition of sediment ended with the collision of two continental plates. As a consequence, the 'geosynclinal' sea was eliminated as the layers folded upward to form the mountain belt. This mountain-building stage at the plate margin is marked by severe distortion of the deposits. Other changes are associated with the great heat generated in the active zone. For example, where rocks undergo slow deformation, and especially where they are weakened by high temperatures, they yield like plastic to give gigantic folds. Where forces uplift as well as compress the layers, sedimentary rock strata may break away and cascade down to pile up at lower levels in flat-lying or *recumbent* folds.

On the other hand, where deformation is rapid and the rocks cold or strong, fracturing of the layers is common. As a result folds may be severed from their roots and piled up again, together with slabs wrenched from the underlying basement. By all these means, the orderly layers of sedimentary rocks and lavas laid down one by one on the geosynclinal floor may be disturbed, reversed or disrupted. In the Alps, for instance, the characteristic structures are recumbent folds or thrust-slices piled one above the

John Cleare

Above: A view of the last 900 metres of the south-west face of Everest. Man's greatest mountaineering challenge, the peak was first conquered by Sir Edmund Hilary in 1953.

Below: The mechanism that is thought to have formed the Appalachian Mountains is illustrated by these six stages. (1) Some 600 million years ago the North American and African continents were parted by a spreading rift. (2) The Atlantic ocean opens up and sediments are laid down on the continental margins, their weight causing subsidence of the sea bed and the formation of *geosynclines*. (3) The ocean begins to close and a trench is formed adjacent to the North American continent as the lithosphere is re-absorbed into the earth's hot mantle. This underthrusting compresses the North American geosyncline into folds, so creating the ancient Appalachians. An upthrust of magma and volcanic activity is triggered, so creating an intrusion of hard granite and surface volcanic mountains. (4) The Atlantic is now fully closed, so compressing the geosynclines of both continents and leaving only a vertical fault line. The two continents were joined in this way between 350 and 225 million years ago. (5) About 180 million years ago the Atlantic ocean began to open again along the old fault line, new oceanic crust material being formed as the continents drifted apart. (6) Today the rate of sea-floor spreading is some three centimetres per year, and new geosynclines are thought to be forming at the margins of the continents.

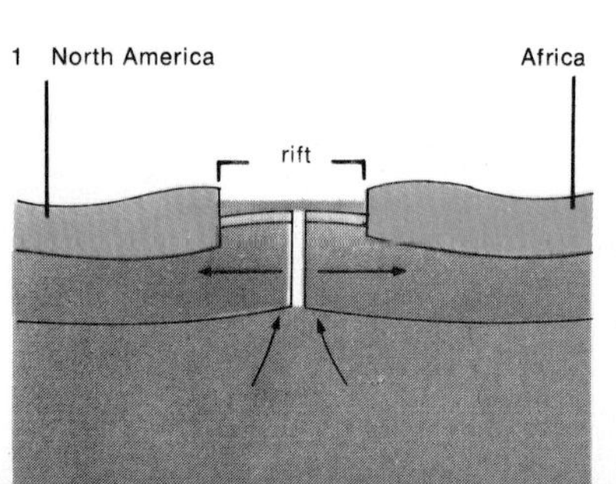

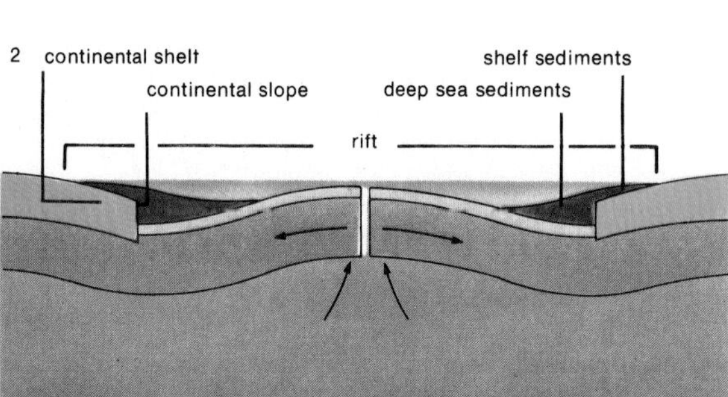

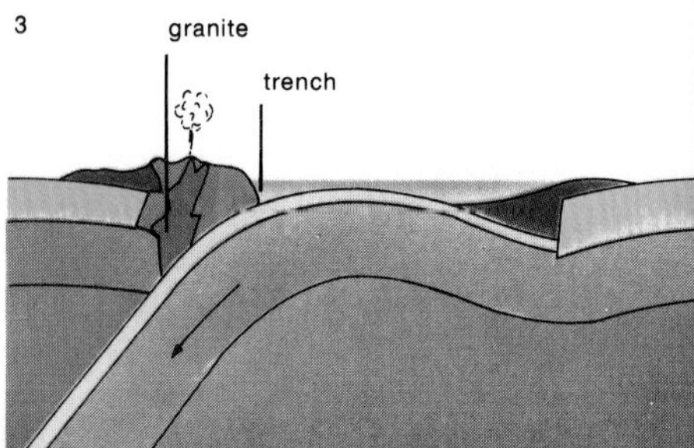

TYPES OF FAULTS

unfaulted blocks

normal

reverse

strike-slip

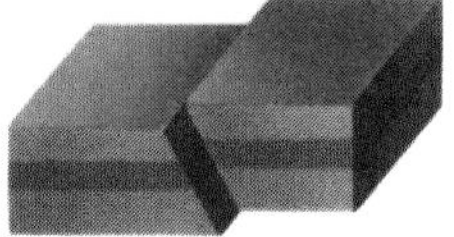

oblique-slip

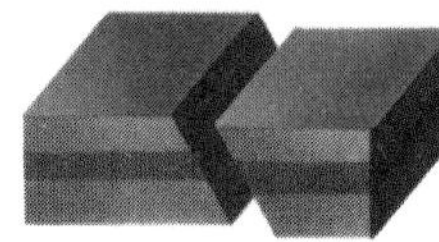

hinge

Left: The Grampian mountains in Scotland, an ancient, heavily-eroded mountain area. But crustal movements are still taking place—as erosion lessens a mountain's mass, it triggers movements to maintain a balance between the mountain's height and the depth of its 'roots' which lie in the molten mantle.

Picturepoint

Left: A faulted anticline of shales and sandstones near Saundersfoot in Pembrokeshire. The shale core has been eroded, leaving a cave.

Below: Close-up of a section of rock from Trevaunance Cove, in Cornwall, showing small faults in layers of grit and shale.

IGS

Right: A rift valley, or *graben*, is formed when the centre of an anticline slips down along fault lines.

Below right: A block mountain, or *horst*, is produced by a reverse movement—the middle block is forced up along fault lines. Erosion tends to round the rock surfaces.

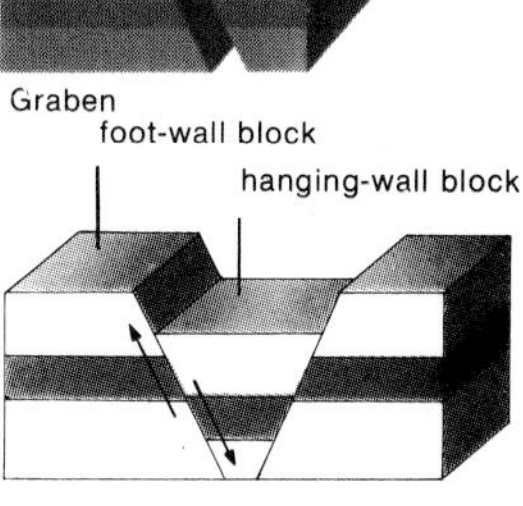

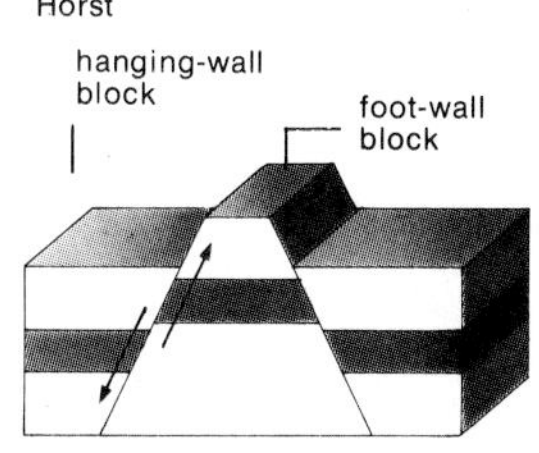

other.

Intense heat in the mountain-building belt results in two things: firstly, modifications, or the *metamorphism*, of the deformed rocks themselves; secondly, the rise of magma which is generated by partial melting of rocks at great depths. Chemical reactions during metamorphism lead to new minerals such as micas, garnet and hornblende. Different degrees of metamorphism also produce different rock types. For example, low intensities may produce slates, while higher intensities produce schists and gneisses whose parallel crystalline structure is related to the direction of the deforming forces.

The rise of granite is the dominant form of igneous activity during the mountain-building stage. The granite magma is derived largely from melting of rock near the base of the continental crust. Intrusive masses of up to several hundred kilometres in length occupy much of the interior of the Andes and the western Cordilleras of North America. Where one crustal plate over-rides another in a collision zone, magma may rise to the surface to build volcanic island arcs or volcanic mountain belts.

Mountain roots

The crumpling and disruption of rocks in a mountain-building belt do not only lead to a shortening of the belt, but also, in many instances, to a thickening of the crustal layer forming the belt. Like an iceberg in water, the mountain belt rises to a height above sea level which is balanced by a 'root' projecting deep into the denser material of the earth's mantle. This adjustment is the final stage in the mountain-building cycle, and is known as the *isostatic* stage.

Mountain massifs may be the product of forces other than the collision of crustal plates. Blocks of the earth's crust for example, may rise vertically along deep faults in response to abnormal temperatures at great depth. At first this kind of block-uplift tends to give level-topped plateaux. But the effects of erosion on the plateaux, and especially at the boundary faults, may transform them into spectacular landscapes. The Colorado Plateau in the US and the Drakensberg Mountains of South Africa, are both the result of such forces at work.

Volcanic mountains, on the other hand, are built up by the extrusion of lava and ash from volcanic vents or fissures. The symmetry of the volcano depends on the style of volcanic activity. For example, eruptions from a single centre give conical mountains; eruptions through cracks or fissures in the earth's surface result in irregular ridges or lines of cones. Yet volcanic activity is so commonly associated with deep fracturing that the resulting mountains may reflect several processes. In the African Rift Valley, for instance, central volcanic cones such as Mounts Kenya, Elgon and Kilimanjaro rise in a highland plateaux which is the result of the uplift of a block along deep fault lines.

Erosion over millions of years

The emergence of all new mountain massifs, whatever their origin, is accompanied by intense erosion. Millions of years pass before a new mountain range emerges and long before it has ceased to rise the rock is subject to heavy erosion. The Brahmaputra and Indus rivers, for example, which cross the Himalayas from sources in the Tibetan plateau, were able to deepen their valleys at the same time as the mountains rose, and so maintained their southward course to the sea. Continued denudation by the forces of erosion not only lowers the general level but also ultimately flattens out the topographical irregularities of the mountains. The end-product may be a *peneplain* of low relief and broad contours which exposes rocks and structures originally formed many kilometres below the surface.

The removal of rock-material as a result of erosion, however, also triggers off new crustal movements. This is because the isostatic balance is upset; the equilibrium is restored by a further rise of the eroded regions, which in turn stimulates further erosion. Many mountain terrains have been 'rejuvenated' more than once by this and other mechanisms. The Grampian Highlands of Scotland, for example, are the product of a mountain building belt 400 million years old which was rejuvenated comparatively recently. Successive cycles of erosion have revealed the roots of the old belt, made of deformed metamorphic rocks.

Indeed the forces which create and destroy mountains are at work all the time. Although uplift may occur at the rate of a metre or more in 100 years, erosion begins very rapidly, only slowing down as the elevation of the land diminishes. No highland area on the earth's surface can be regarded as 'stable'. All will change in some degree within a matter of a few hundred years. Within a hundred million years, the earth's surface will again be transformed.

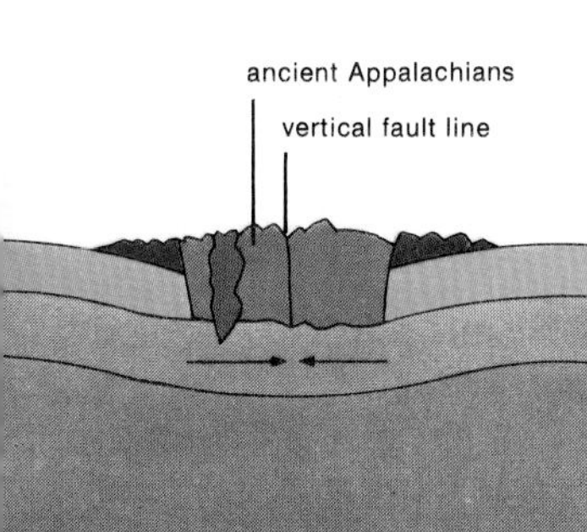

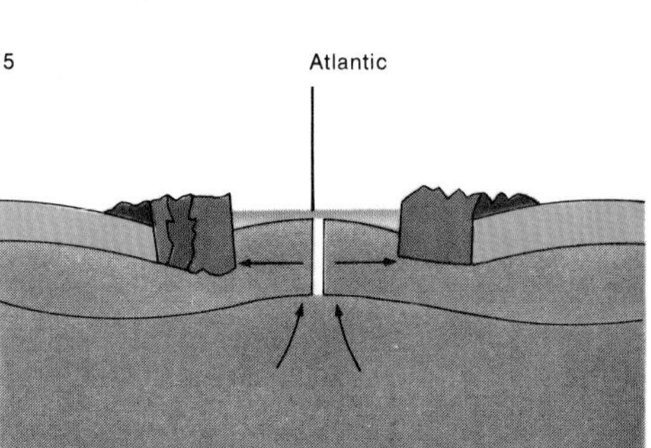

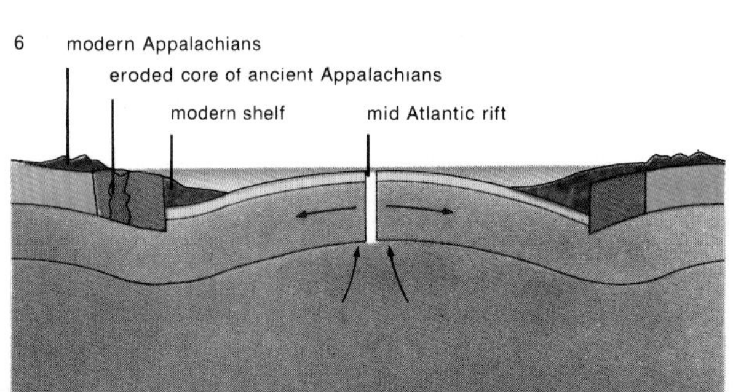

Minerals

Minerals are the building bricks of rocks. They are the basis of every rock except those of organic origin, like coal and chalk. A mineral is defined as any solid substance with a definite chemical composition occuring naturally in the earth, but which is not derived from plants or animals. By popular definition, anything that is mined is called a mineral, but the fossil fuels—coal, natural oil and gas—are excluded from the geological definition as they are formed from the remains of plant and animal life. One usual exception to the rule that a mineral must be solid is quicksilver, which is mercury in its native, liquid state.

Just as rocks are made up of combinations of minerals, the minerals themselves are composed of different fusions of chemical elements. Some minerals, however, such as gold or naturally-occurring copper and sulphur, contain only one element. The most common elements found in minerals, in descending order of occurrence, are oxygen, silicon, aluminium, iron, magnesium, calcium, potassium, and sodium. These are only eight of the 90 naturally-occurring elements, but they make up nearly 99 per cent by weight of the earth's crust. Oxygen and silicon alone account for nearly three quarters of the crust's constituents.

Secrets of atomic structure

The smallest particle of an element is a single atom. Examination of most minerals reveals that the atoms of the constituent elements have arranged themselves into a distinct and regular three-dimensional framework. These frameworks, known as *crystals* are geometric forms with their flat faces arranged symmetrically. Most minerals have this ordered atomic structure and are termed *crystalline.*

Under certain conditions that allow a crystalline mineral to grow without interference, it may form regular-shaped crystals. Silica, for example, may crystallize into perfect trigonal crystals of quartz. But if the growing crystals interfere with each other, then they may be distorted into mis-shapen grains of quartz which do not display regular crystal faces. Alternatively silica may develop into chalcedony, a *cryptocrystalline* mineral in which clusters of crystals are invisible except under the most powerful magnification. Finally, silica may take the form of opal, an *amorphous* or non-crystalline mineral, in which there is no regular arrangement of atoms. Each of these different manifestations of silica has a different atomic structure—directly affecting the crystal structure and thus the shape of each mineral.

How minerals are classified

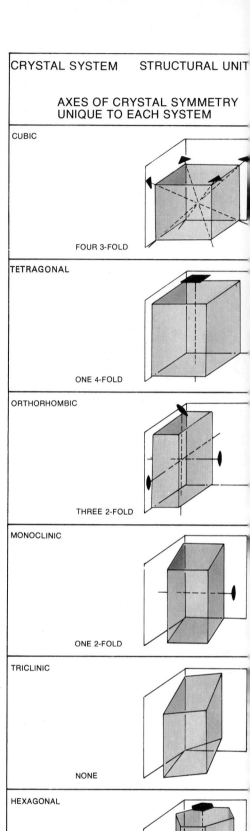

Crystalline structure is an important clue in distinguishing one mineral from another. There are seven basic shapes of structural unity, and this gives rise to seven categories or *crystal systems.* Each mineral crystallizes in a particular system and can be identified accordingly. For example, a diamond belongs to the cubic system, whereas a ruby has a hexagonal crystal system.

Minerals display a dazzling variety of

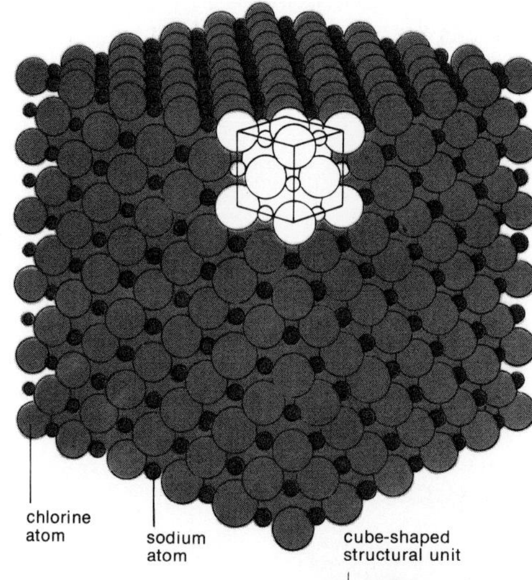

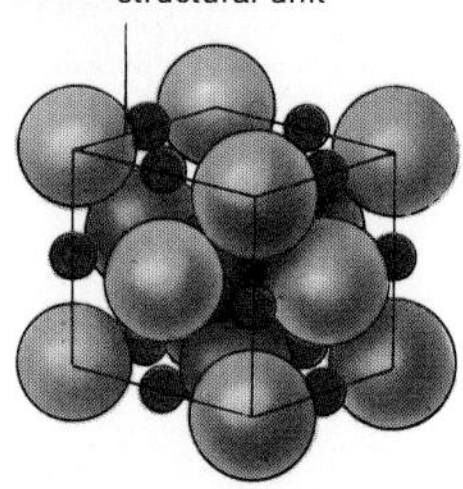

Above: Common table salt (sodium chloride) consists of finely ground crystals of a mineral called halite. When a crystal is magnified 100,000,000 times, its atomic structure is revealed. The large green circles represent chlorine atoms; the smaller red ones are sodium atoms. A 'detail' from the atomic structure model (right) outlines the molecular building block, or structural unit of the crystal. In this case it is the shape of a perfect cube.

Below: A scanning electron micrograph of a common salt crystal, magnified 800 times. Even in small quantities the cubic crystal structure is recognizable.

Alan Windle

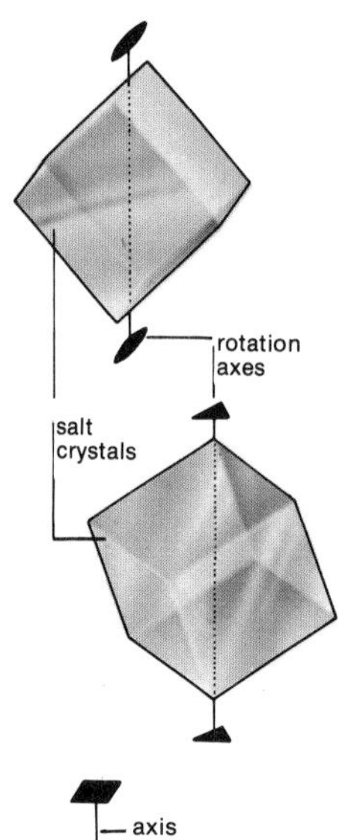

An important clue in identifying one mineral from another is symmetry—a property which allows a crystal to be spun on an axis and to appear identical twice or more before it has rotated one full turn. The number of axes of symmetry in a crystal are then counted. The cube of a common salt crystal, for example, reveals three axes of symmetry.

Top left: Rotated on an axis taken through the centres of diagonally opposite edges, the cube appears identical twice in a complete rotation of 360°. This is termed a two-fold axis of symmetry. There are six such axes on a cube.

Centre left: On an axis taken through the opposite corners, the cube looks the same three times in a complete rotation, and reveals four three-fold axes.

Left: In the same way there are three four-fold axes of symmetry emerging through the centres of the faces of a cube. Minerals can be categorized into seven distinct systems determined by their crystal symmetry.

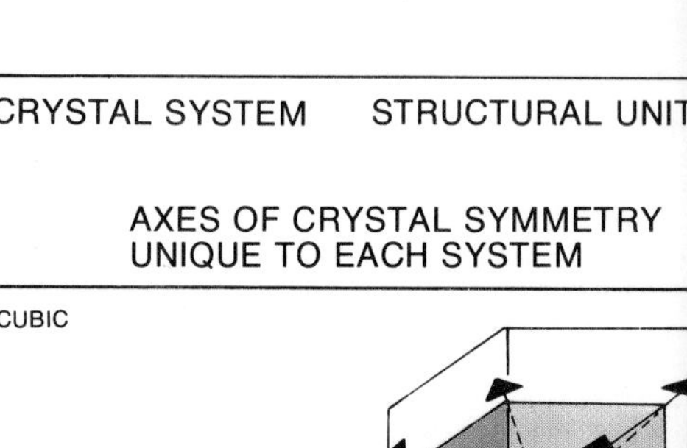

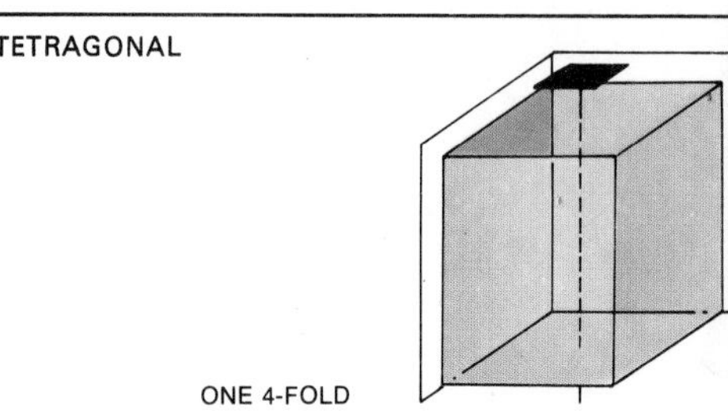

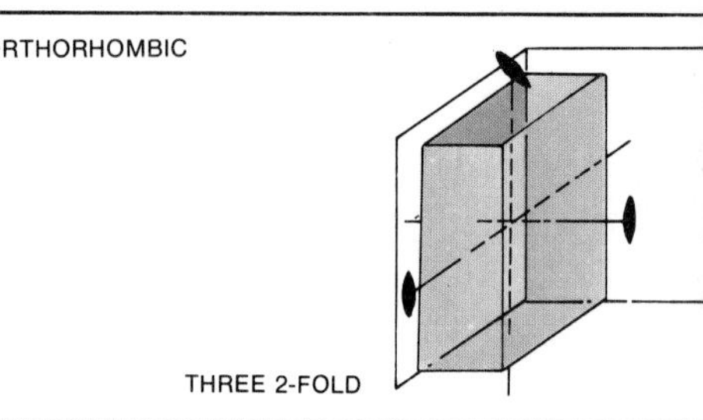

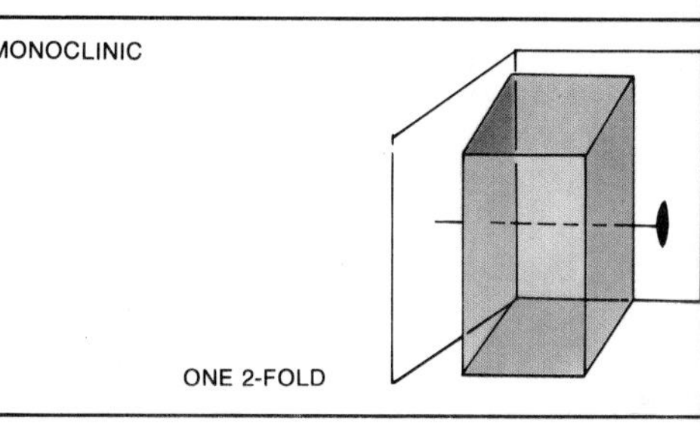

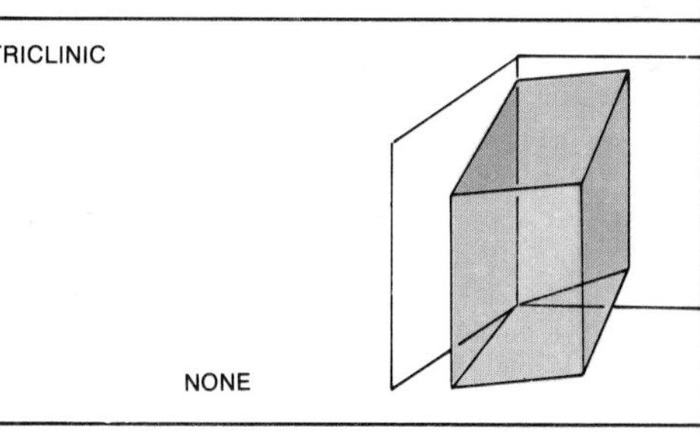

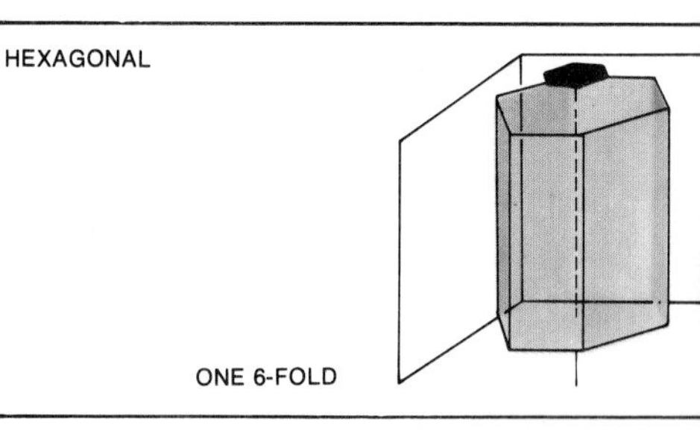

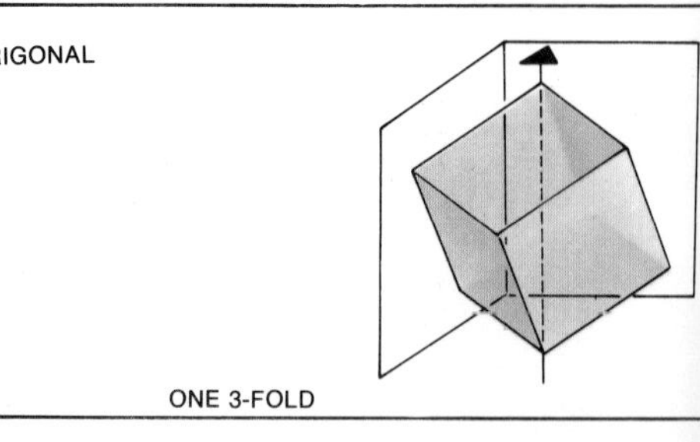

MPLES OF MINERALS CRYSTALLIZING IN EACH SYSTEM

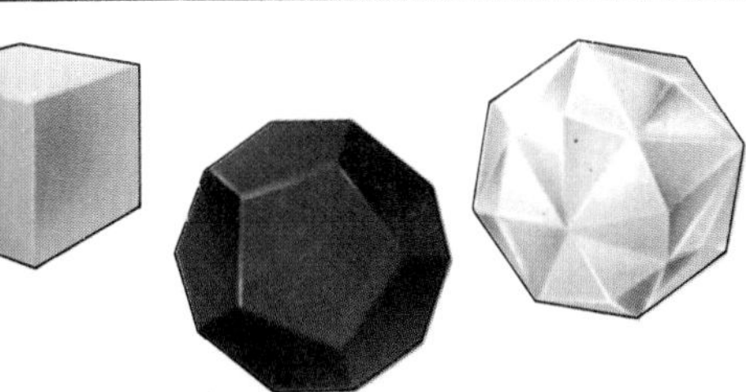

yrite

pyrite

diamond

1. A mineral belonging to the cubic system is pyrite which occurs with either 12 faces (left in photograph) or as a cube with six faces (right). Other examples of this system are diamond, galena and garnet.

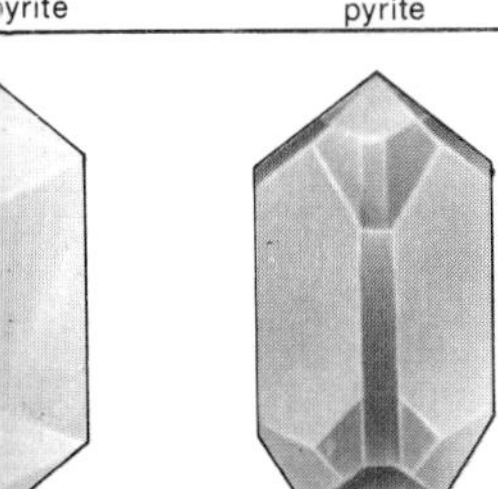

on

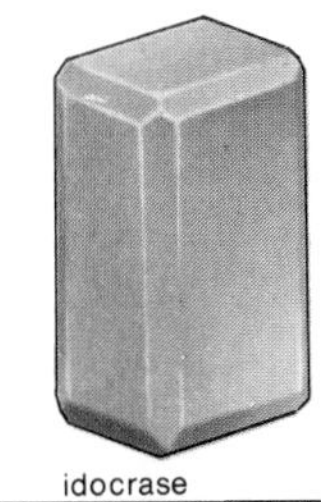

rutile

idocrase

2. Wulfenite is included in the tetragonal system and has fine orangish-yellow crystals. The mineral is found in zones of lead deposits. Its lustre varies but it leaves a distinctive white streak.

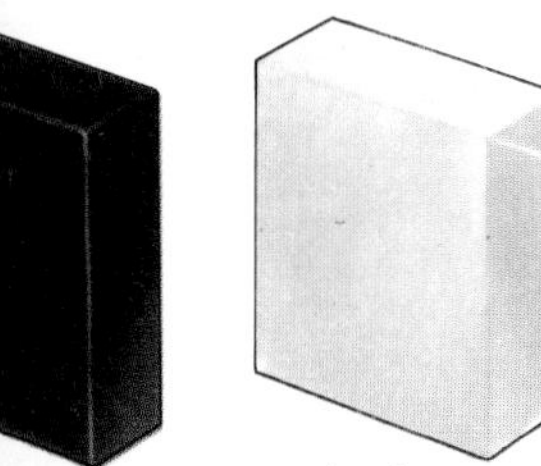

lite

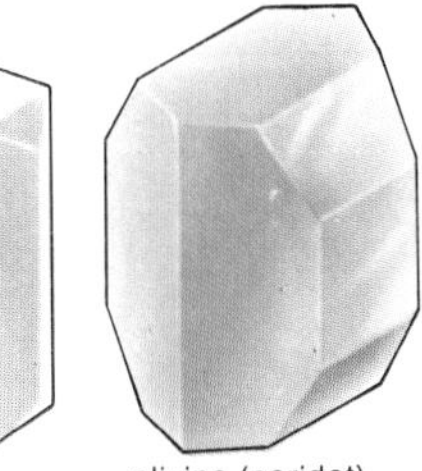

baryte

olivine (peridot)

3. Topaz crystallizes as orthorhombic crystals. This attractive gemstone is typically yellow but can also be colourless, skyblue, or even pink if subjected to heat. However, its streak is always colourless.

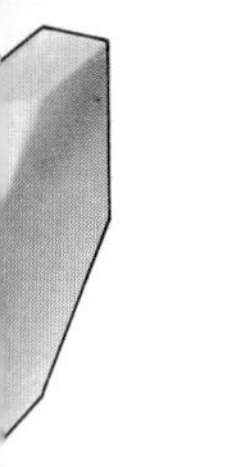

yroxene

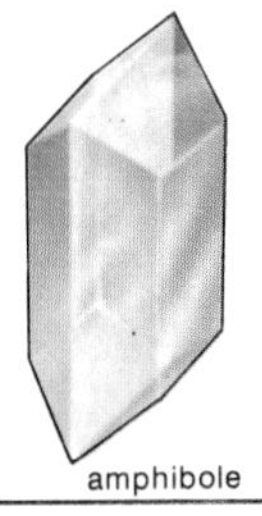

amphibole

orthoclase

4. Orthoclase occurs as white, pink, yellow or brown coloured monoclinic crystals. Most of the common rock-forming minerals are in the system. Orthoclase is important as a constituent of igneous rocks.

ise

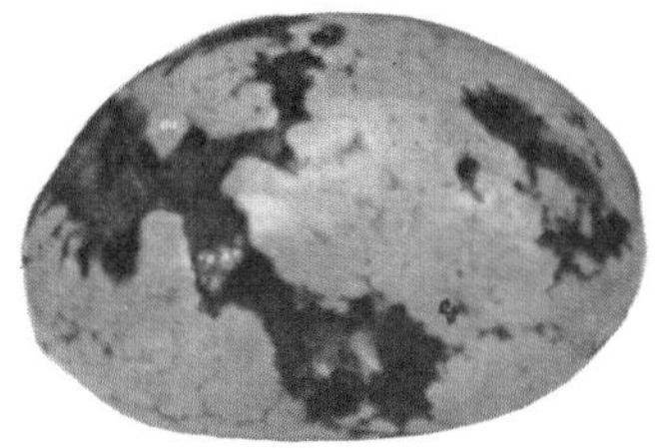

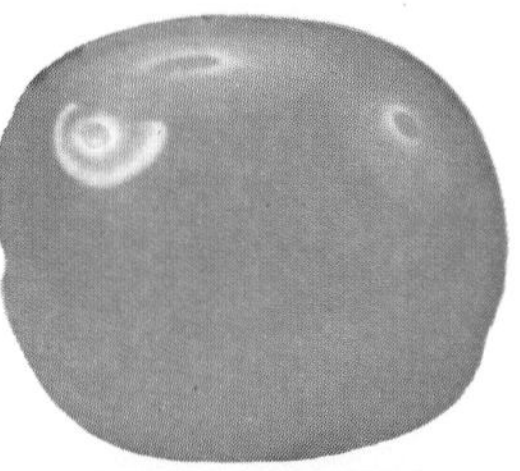

5. A fine example of a stone in the triclinic system is turquoise although it rarely forms perfect crystals. Normally it is found as an amorphous mineral. Two examples of polished turquoise are shown.

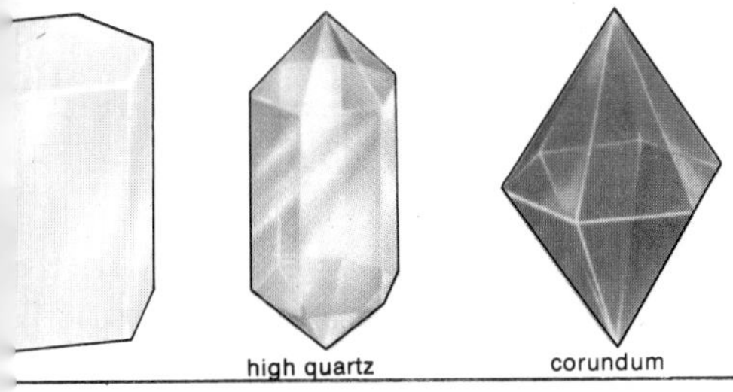

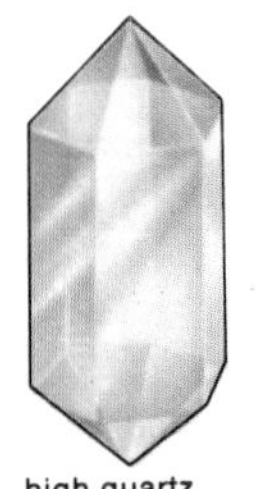

high quartz

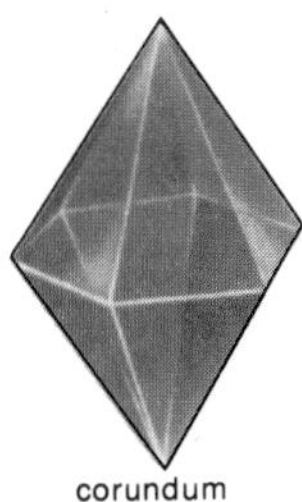

corundum

6. Beryl (below) forms emerald when shaded green by impurities of chromium. Ruby and sapphire are types of corundum which also crystallize as hexagonal minerals, as do certain types of quartz (above).

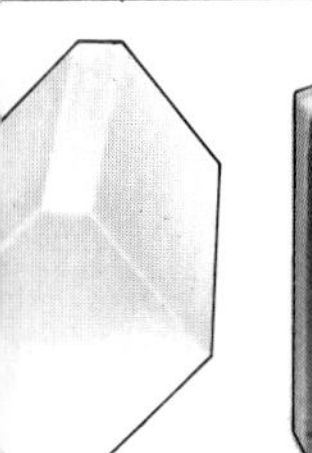

cite

tourmaline

7. Herkimer quartz (left) is a trigonal crystal of gem quality. Quartz crystals occur in two systems and some authorities consider the hexagonal and trigonal systems as one. Dolomite (right) also occurs in two systems.

The symmetry of the structural unit controls the symmetry of the crystal structure. Since the structure governs the crystal shape, the symmetry of the whole crystal is an exact indication of the shape of the structural unit. The cubic structural units of the mineral pyrite can build two crystal shapes. In both cases the symmetry requirements—four 3-fold axes—are satisfied.

Above and below left: Cube-shaped iron pyrite (iron sulphide).

Above and below right: An eight-sided pyrite crystal, galena (lead sulphide).

Paul Brierley

colour, which is determined both by their structure and by the presence of impurities. But colour is not always a reliable clue to identity. Many minerals are commonly white or colourless and others, such as quartz or calcite, may occur in a whole range of colours.

The most reliable colour indicator is obtained by scraping the mineral against unglazed porcelain. This leaves a finely powdered trail, the colour of which is the mineral's *streak*. In this way, for example, crystals of haematite, which have a red streak, can be distinguished from those of magnetite which leave a black streak—although the crystals appear as the same colour.

The way in which a specimen affects light is another important clue to its identity. Minerals reflect light in different ways; this characteristic, known as *lustre*, ranges from the dull quality of clay to the adamantine lustre of diamond.

Hardness and *specific gravity* are two other reliable diagnostic properties. Hardness is actually rated in terms of the resistance of a mineral to scratching, arranged in ascending order from talc, which is easily crushed by a finger-nail, to diamond, the hardest mineral known to man. The hardness of a mineral is measured in terms of Mohs' Scale—an arbitrary scale with very irregular intervals, devised in 1822 by Mohs, an Austrian mineralogist.

The specific gravity of a mineral is the ratio between its weight and the weight of an equal volume of water. Taking the specific gravity of water as 1.0, the great majority of minerals have a specific gravity ranging between 2.2 and 3.2. Only those minerals which are as light as graphite (1.9) or as heavy as gold (15.0 to 20.0 according to purity) can be distinguished by their specific gravity when held in the hand.

The world's great mineral deposits

The geological processes in which minerals are formed determines both the distribution and the type of mineral deposits. *Magmatic* minerals are those

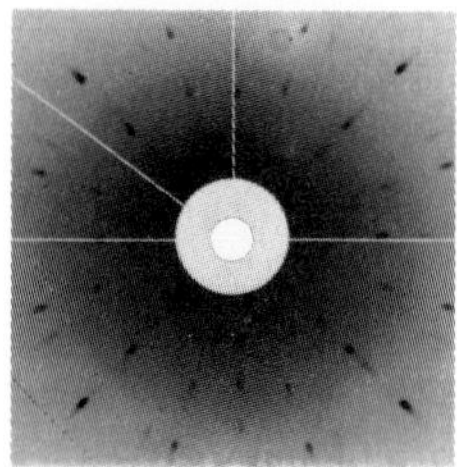

Above: The action of a crystal on X-rays is an important means of mineral identification. This X-ray diffraction photograph of common salt shows how the atoms deflect and reflect X-rays; the 4-fold rotation symmetry shown by the pattern of spots indicates that the atoms are packed in a cubic arrangement.

Paul Brierley

Left: A glowing piece of fluorite demonstrates the property of fluorescence. This refers to the way particular specimens of certain minerals emit visible light while bombarded with invisible radiation such as ultra-violet or X-rays. Fluorite, calcite and diamond all have this property.

George Gerster/John Hillelson

Right: The vast salt deposits in the Danakil region of Ethiopia. This is an area where hot springs bring up minerals in solution—solid deposits are left behind when the solution evaporates.

Below: The 'Big Hole' at Kimberley in South Africa—one of the world's richest diamond mines.

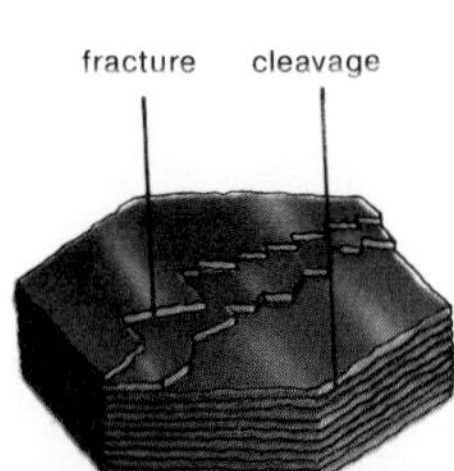

Left: The atoms of the mineral mica are strongly bonded in layers, but between the layers the bonds are very weak. The crystal will thus split smoothly between the layers—this is known as its cleavage tendency. Where the bonding is strong, across the horizontal layers, it fractures irregularly.

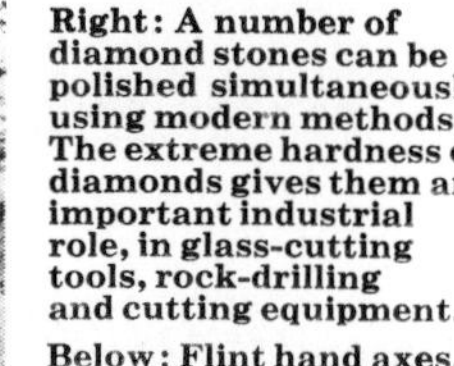

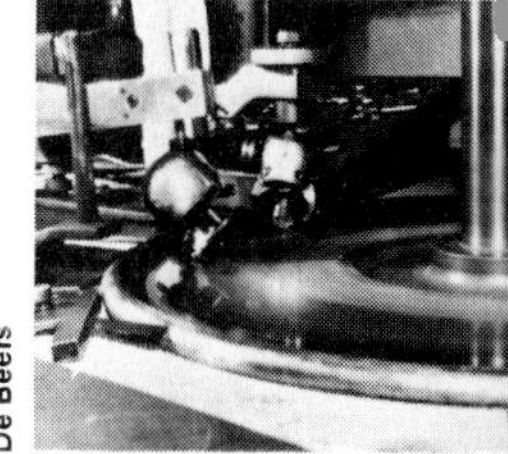

De Beers

Right: A number of diamond stones can be polished simultaneously using modern methods. The extreme hardness of diamonds gives them an important industrial role, in glass-cutting tools, rock-drilling and cutting equipment.

Below: Flint hand axes, some 250,000 years old, were one of man's first uses of minerals.

Paul Brierley

Left: A spectacular formation of magnetite, a common example of a magnetic mineral—one which is strongly attracted by an iron magnet. Magnetite also has the property of exerting and retaining its own magnetic field; in the form of 'lodestone' it was used by the ancients as a compass.

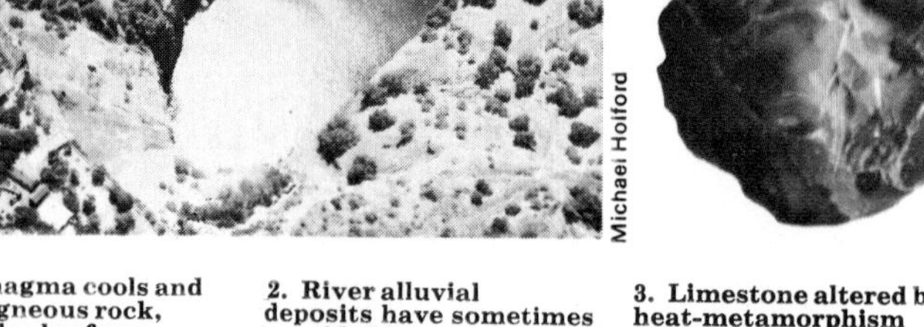

ZEFA

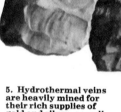

Michael Holford

which crystallize from molten magma as it cools to form igneous rock. The first minerals to crystallize in the cooling period—silicates with a high proportion of iron and magnesium—are free to grow without interference and form well-shaped crystals. For example, the important mineral chromite, used for toughening steel, was concentrated in enormous quantities in the huge Bushveld igneous complex of South Africa by this process.

As magma cools further, more minerals are formed until only a little 'residual liquid' is left between grains of rock. This liquid may be rich in volatile components and in elements that form valuable minerals, and may either be trapped in cavities known as *geodes*, *drusies* or *vugs* in which beautifully shaped crystals grow in towards the centre, or be violently squeezed out by pressure from solidifying minerals into cracks and fissures in surrounding rock. There it solidifies to form *hydrothermal veins* in which mis-shapen crystals of quartz grow, along with a wide variety of other minerals. These are commonly-mined deposits, as they often form at shallow depths.

Mineral deposits may also be of *sedimentary* or *metamorphic* origin. Deep down in the earth's crust, or near hot magma, metamorphic minerals are formed from pre-existing minerals in solid rock by intense heat and pressure. Most sedimentary rocks are the product of minerals weathered by wind, water and chemical action from igneous and metamorphic rocks and are consolidated in layers, such as shale and calcite-rich limestone. Other minerals, such as rock salts and gypsum, are *evaporites*, caused by evaporation in shallow seas or lakes.

1. As magma cools and forms igneous rock, minerals also form. Fine crystallized minerals, such as quartz, amethyst, galena and tourmaline, as well as feldspar and pyrite, occur in rock cavities called drusies, vugs and goedes. Diamonds from the Kimberley mine come from Kimberlite, an igneous rock.

2. River alluvial deposits have sometimes provided prospectors with easy pickings. Precious stones and metals may accumulate in places from the weathering and erosion of different types of rocks. Panning and dredging are used to sort out the potentially rich deposits from other sediments.

3. Limestone altered by heat-metamorphism and igneous gases is an important source of commercially valuable ores like copper, gold, 'fools gold' (pyrite), iron, lead and zinc.

4. Where heat has metamorphosed shale, minerals found include garnet, chiastolite, biotite and cordierite.

5. Hydrothermal veins are heavily mined for their rich supplies of gold and silver, as well as the silver- and lead-bearing galena, gems such as opals, emeralds and tourmaline, and sulphide minerals like pyrite and chalcopyrite. Secondary minerals like copper-bearing azurite and malachite occur.

HOW AND WHERE MINERALS OCCUR

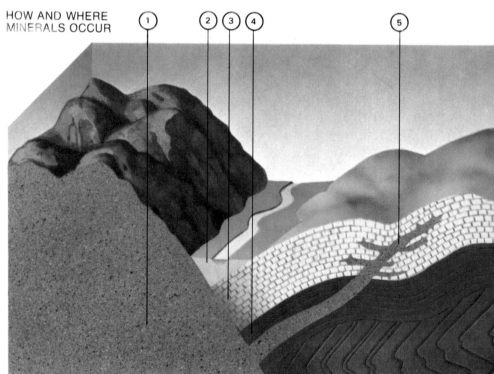

Institute of Geological Sciences

Robert Harding

Right: A variety of agate known as Mexican Lace, typical of the fantastic and colourful structures which make agate popular as an ornamental stone. Agate is in fact a variety of chalcedony, a mixture of quartz and opal.

Left: Panning gravel for diamonds in Borneo, a prospecting method still used today.

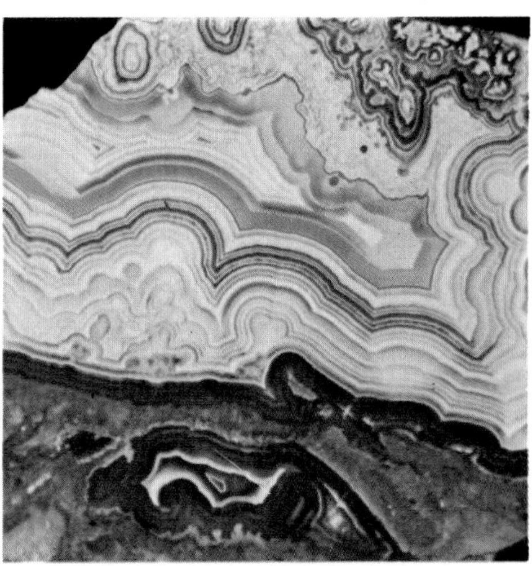

Jane Burton/Bruce Coleman

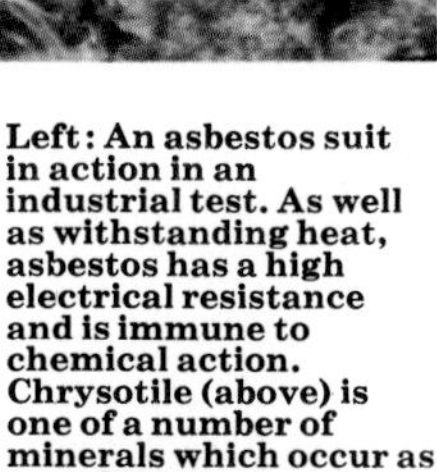

Left: An asbestos suit in action in an industrial test. As well as withstanding heat, asbestos has a high electrical resistance and is immune to chemical action. Chrysotile (above) is one of a number of minerals which occur as long fibrous crystals which can be spun to form asbestos.

Turner & Newall

Picturepoint

Above: A crystal of diamond, as it occurs in Kimberlite, the igneous rock which forms the famous South African 'diamond pipes'.

Left: The breath-taking Kohinoor diamond, originally found in India. It was cut in 1852 and is now part of the British crown jewels. This is one of the world's largest diamonds.

MOHS SCALE OF MINERAL HARDNESS

HARDNESS	MINERAL	TEST
1	talc	can be scratched by fingernail
2	gypsum	
3	calcite	
4	fluorite	can be scratched with steel point
5	apatite	
6	orthoclase	
7	quartz	will scratch glass easily
8	topaz	
9	corundum	
10	diamond	will scratch any other material

6. Beach sand and gravel retain deposits eroded from rocks and sorted by the continual action of waves. For example, chalcedony and calcite are eroded from limestone and sandstone, and pyrite and marcasite from shale. Some normally rare minerals like monazite may be concentrated here.

7. Ancient metamorphic rock, subject to great pressure and change, is the setting for garnet, asbestos, talc, serpentine, turquoise and some emeralds.

8. Sedimentary strata contain large deposits. Dolomite is an example of a constituent of many sedimentary rocks. Others are gypsum and halite.

Some rare minerals are very hard and have an unusually attractive colour and lustre. Those of greatest rarity, and therefore of greatest monetary value, are the precious gemstones, diamond, emerald, ruby and sapphire. Platinum, gold and silver, the precious metals, have also acquired great value because of their beauty, rarity and durability. These three metals together with copper and iron are the only metals to occur as *native*, or uncombined, elements in nature.

The precious minerals are both hard and, except for silver, chemically unreactive. When rocks bearing minerals of high specific gravity are exposed to weathering, the lighter material is gradually eroded away while the heavier, chemically stable minerals are concentrated in *placer* deposits.

Such deposits are called *residual* if they have remained at or near their original position, *eluvial* if they have been concentrated by rain-wash and gravity, and *alluvial* if they have been formed by streams. The famous deposits which sparked off the 1849 gold rush to California were alluvial placers. The discovery of diamond-bearing gravels caused a similar great rush to Lichtenburg in South West Africa in the 1920s.

Finding precious stones is still largely a matter of luck. Most occur in close association with particular types of rock, but suitable geological locations only rarely contain precious minerals and only exceptionally are these of gem quality. The most productive diamond mines are at Kimberley in South Africa, where the stones crystallized in an igneous rock called kimberlite. Other major producers are Angola and Zaire.

The weight of precious minerals is measured in *carats*, one carat weighing a mere 200 milligrams. Stones of gem quality are closely inspected for flaws and weaknesses, before being carefully cut and used in jewelry. The emerald, for example, owes its great value to the rarity of flawless crystals. This dark green variety of the mineral beryl occurs in highly metamorphosed shales called mica-schists. The finest emeralds come from near Bogota in Columbia, but other important deposits have been found in the Ural Mountains in the Soviet Union and in Austria, Norway and Australia.

The world's supply of fine rubies has come largely from the Mogok mines in Upper Burma, where they occur in metamorphosed limestone. The presence of minute quantities of chromium causes the red colour of ruby in the mineral corundum. Another, gem variety of the colourless corundum is the sapphire, tinted blue by iron and titanium impurities. Fine sapphires are found in gravels in Sri Lanka, Thailand and Kashmir.

Technological progress in exploiting minerals has determined the growth of civilization. The Stone Age began when the first crude but handy tools were fashioned from flint. From the Copper Age—when man first discovered a method of isolating metal from its natural mineral state—through the successive Bronze, Iron and Atomic Ages, man's activities and well-being have been affected by his increasingly sophisticated use of earth materials. The industrial and technological revolution which has reshaped society in every continent relies massively on a continued supply and large-scale exploitation of the earth's mineral wealth.

Metal Ores

The search for metals dates back almost to the beginning of civilization. Ores are minerals from which metal can be extracted, yet the first metal to be recognized by man was undoubtedly gold—which occurs naturally in a metal state and needs no extraction. Unaffected by weathering and other chemical processes, gold occurs in veins in rocks or as flakes and nuggets in river gravels. Gold was prized by the ancients for its unrivalled colour and lustre and for the ease with which it could be worked into objects of beauty and value. The Egyptians believed that gold had divine significance and established a state industry to exploit the metal over 4,000 years ago.

The Middle East also saw the beginnings of *metallurgy*, the extraction of metals from their ores. Archaeological excavations in Iran and Afghanistan have revealed that around 5,000 BC copper was being extracted from its easily-smelted ore, the beautiful emerald-green mineral malachite. The Greeks and Romans controlled extensive mining industries and their empires owed much of their pre-eminence to their wealth in metals.

In response to the needs of the technological revolution came a more scientific understanding of the formation of ores and their distribution patterns. Geologists now realize that nearly all the metals used in industry are very scarce. Copper forms 0.007 per cent of the earth's crust, tin 0.004 per cent, lead 0.0016 per cent, uranium 0.0004 per cent, silver 0.00001 per cent and gold a mere 0.0000005 per cent.

Usable ore deposits are therefore extremely rare features because they require a concentration of metals to as much as a million times their average distribution. There are two main processes by which ore deposits are formed. They may be concentrated within rocks formed by cooling magma or deposited by surface processes of erosion.

When magma cools slowly, insulated by the thickness of surrounding rocks, the minerals crystallize out in a particular order. Some minerals separate out early and sink to the bottom of the magma to form *magmatic segregations* such as the enormous quantities of chromite found in southern Africa. The remaining liquid then becomes more concentrated in other ore minerals and contains large amounts of dissolved gases and water vapour. At a late stage of the cooling process, the liquid may squeeze into cracks and fissures in the igneous rock to form *pegmatite* deposits.

The crystallizing minerals of pegmatite may grow very large. In the Black Hills of South Dakota, USA, for instance, one crystal of the lithium-aluminium mineral spodumene measuring over 15 metres in length and weighing over 90 tonnes was taken out of the pegmatite mine. Many of the rarer and more exotic minerals are found in pegmatites, including monazite, an ore of the radioactive metal thorium.

The solutions remaining in the late stages of separation are under great pressure and are chemically highly reactive. As they stream into the surrounding rocks they may react with them and deposit the metals they hold in solution as *pneumatolytic* mineral deposits. Deposits

Paul Brierley

Above: A polished example of malachite. This beautiful emerald-green mineral is often a result of secondary enrichment. Metallic copper was extracted from this easily-smelted ore as long ago as 5000BC.

IGS

RTZ

IGS

RTZ

Above: Bauxite (top) is the only important ore of aluminium. The rich specimen of copper ore (above) came from the Palabora mine in South Africa.

Above right: Dark red crystals of cinnabar, the ore of mercury. The white mass of crystalline calcite (right) is rich in gold flakes.

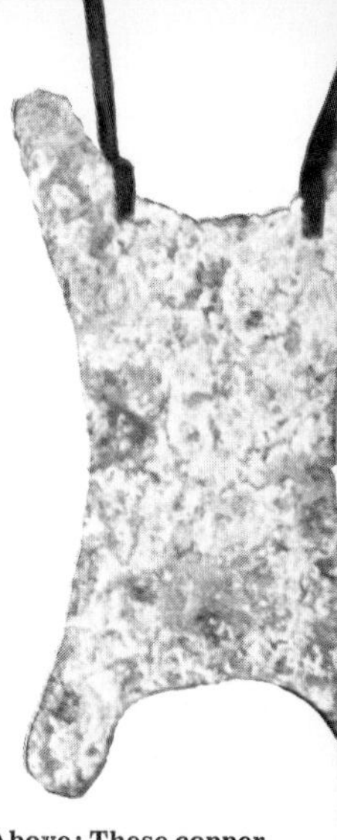

Above: These copper ingots, probably used as a trading currency, came from the oldest known shipwreck, dated 1000 BC, off the coast of Turkey.

Below: Geophysical techniques are used in the search for ores. The operator in this crew using a portable ground system carries a coil. This measures the responses to signals from an electromagnetic source.

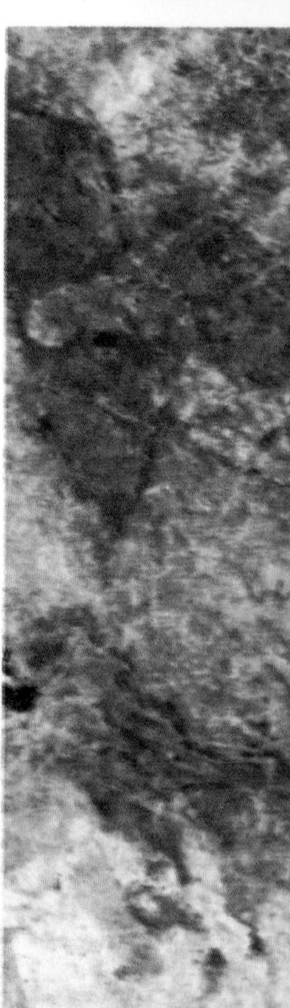

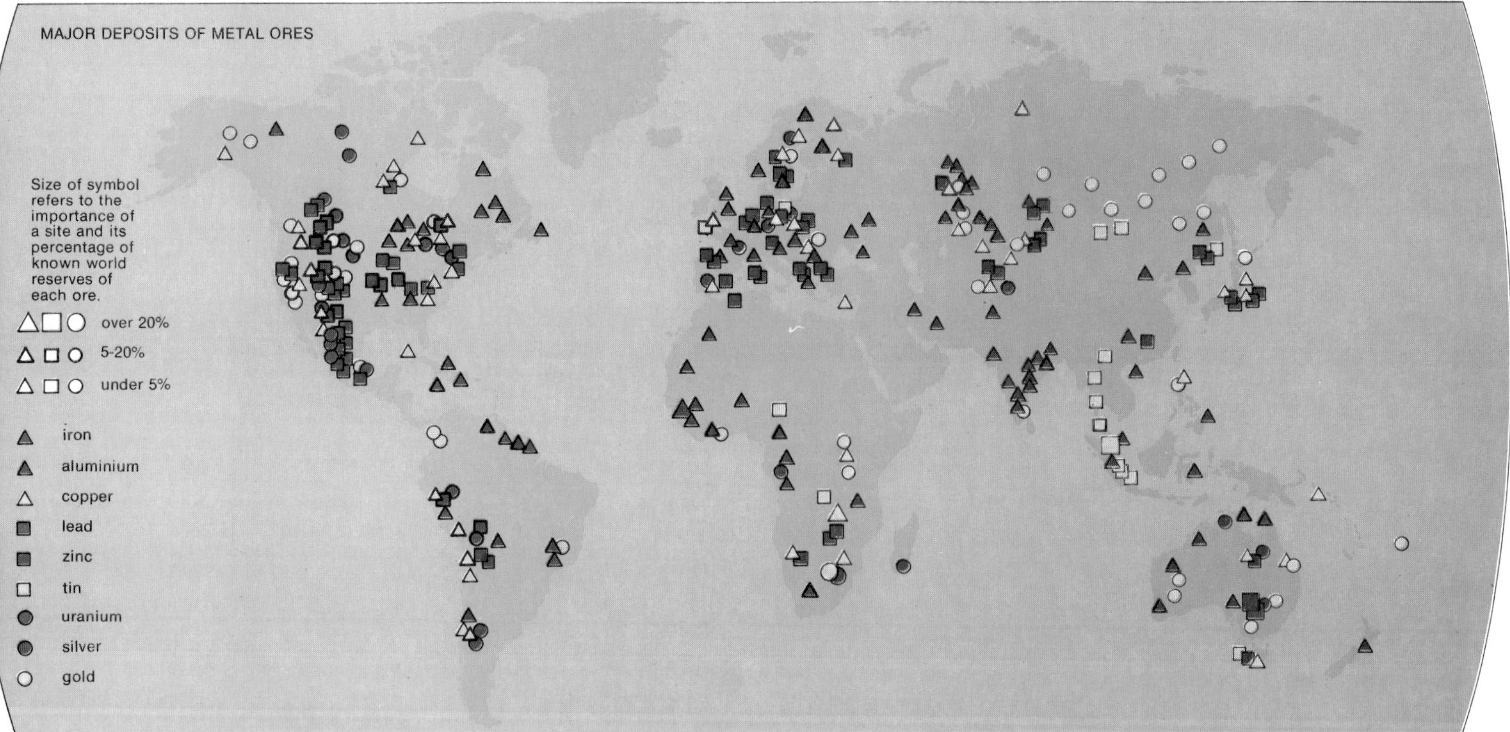

Above: The world map indicates the known distribution of major metal ore deposits. There are several thousand minerals but only about a hundred are of economic value. Distribution and production of the most important metal ores are detailed (right).

Below: This spectacular photograph of the southern half of Rhodesia was taken at a height of 500 miles from an orbiting NASA satellite. The picture emphasizes certain bands of the light spectrum and reveals many large-scale geological features unrecognizable on the ground. The long green strip is the Great Dyke, a major source of chromite ore.

RTZ

Iron is the fourth most plentiful element in the earth's crust and rich ores are widely spread. This is fortunate for the world uses over 800 million tonnes annually. USSR, USA, Australia and Brazil produce the most.
Aluminium is the most abundant metal in the earth's crust, but production is only 15 million tonnes, mostly from USA, USSR, Japan, Canada and Norway.
Copper production is some 6.6 million tonnes a year. Two-thirds comes from Chile, Zambia, Zaire and Peru whose economies largely depend on copper.
Tin is mined in large quantities in only a few areas in Asia, Africa and Bolivia. Low output—under 200,000 tonnes—makes tin an expensive metal.
Lead and **Zinc** usually occur together. Lead production is some 4 million tonnes annually, mostly from USA, USSR, Canada and Australia. The 6 million tonnes of zinc come mainly from the same four countries.
Gold is associated with South Africa which produces two-thirds of the world total of less than 1,500 tonnes. Other major sources are USSR and Canada.
Silver is also valuable but less rare. Leading producers are Mexico and Peru followed by USSR, Canada and USA. Annual supply is under 1,000 tonnes.
Uranium ore of a high-grade is of limited supply. Estimated consumption is 30,000 tonnes a year. Rich deposits occur in Canada, Australia and Africa.

of the tin ore cassiterite in Cornwall in southwest England, once a major source of the metal, are of this type.

The final stage of the formation of ore deposits of magmatic origin involves the watery hot, liquid residues called *hydrothermal* solutions. Under the right conditions, these solutions can move great distances and, being chemically and physically so different from the rocks in their path, they react with them to deposit their load of ore minerals. In cavities and fissures, *lodes* and *veins* are formed, while in the minute spaces between the grains of rocks, *impregnations* result.

Hydrothermal deposits are classified according to their temperature of formation. The Morro Velho gold mine in Brazil, still worked after two centuries of mining, is an example of the highest temperature deposits which formed nearest to the magma source. This is known because some of the minerals accompanying the gold only form at high temperatures.

Many of the world's great copper ore deposits are considered to have formed at a more moderate temperature. The enormous copper deposits found in the geologically-young mountain chains of the Andes, for example, are typically great masses of igneous rock peppered through with copper minerals. The world's largest copper mine is at Chuquicamata, some 3,000 metres up in the Andes. The richest mercury mine in the world is at Almaden in Spain. This is an example of the coolest hydrothermal deposits, usually formed at shallow depths.

The second major group of mineral deposits includes those formed by sedimentary processes. The action of rivers, seas and wind on rocks gradually wears them down and the heavier, ore minerals become concentrated together to produce deposits, such as the beach sand deposits along the eastern coastline of Australia, mined for titanium and zirionium.

Sedimentary deposits have also been formed by chemical or organic action. Many important iron ore deposits, such as the ironstones of the English Midlands and of Alsace-Lorraine in France, were formed by the action of acidic water on iron-bearing rocks.

More often, the chemical action of weathering produces new minerals. Under intense tropical weathering conditions, clays are broken down to leave their constituent aluminium minerals. The extensive layers of bauxite (aluminium oxide combined with water), like those

T. Spencer/Colorific

Left: Sinking a shaft at a diamond mine in Cape Province, South Africa. The deepest shafts extend over 3 km (2 miles) down into the earth at the Witwatersrand gold mines. Problems of water pumping, intense heat (rock temperatures increase 1°C for every 60 metres in depth) and high humidity have to be overcome before mining is possible.

Below: The gold mine at West Driefontein in South Africa is one of the world's largest. The tower on the right lies over the shaft. Winding gear hauls the skips of ore to the surface. The ore is then crushed at the plant in the centre and gold extracted. Waste is carried away by conveyor belt.

Consolidated Gold Fields

Above: The open-cast Toquepala copper mine in the Peruvian Andes. The open-cast method is suitable for mining large tonnages of low grade ore. First the barren rock or over-burden is removed and then each terrace or bench is mined back into the sides of the pit. After blasting, the ore is scooped up with mechanical shovels into waiting trucks. Ores with as little as 0.3% copper—once rejected as waste—can now be profitably mined.

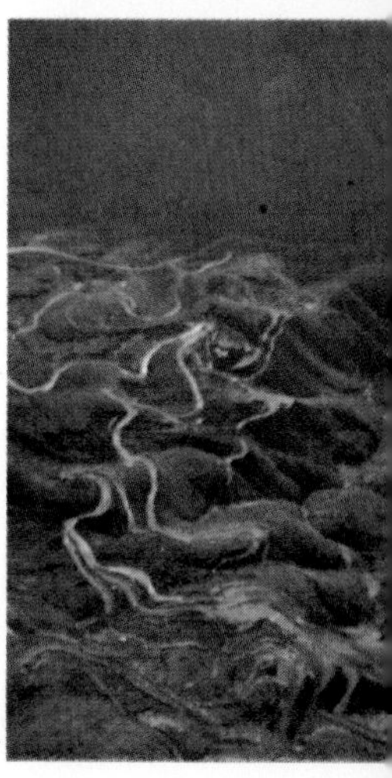
Aspect

Right: The residual deposits of gernierite on the Pacific island of New Caledonia form one of the world's most valuable reserves of nickel. It is mined by an open-cast method called strip-mining.

found in Jamaica which built up in this way, form residual deposits of virtually the only ore of aluminium.

Ore deposits, like other rocks, are also subject to chemical weathering at their surface outcrops. Water percolating through rocks often contains acid which attacks the ore and forms a metal-bearing solution. *Secondary enrichment* is the term applied to ore deposits carried downward in solution and later solidified in rich concentrations.

Exploration for the world's deposits

Many of the world's major ore fields have been discovered by chance. The great nickel deposits of Sudbury, Ontario, were found accidentally in the 1880s by workmen on the Canadian Pacific railway. Before the development of modern exploration techniques, minerals were located by prospecting. This involved searching directly for ore deposits on the surface, as in gold-panning, or indirectly by looking for the tell-tale signs of buried ore deposits. These signs include the *gossans* or 'iron hats' of rusty, spongy rock which sometimes cap sulphide ore deposits, or the staining of rocks by traces of the brightly coloured minerals of some metals.

Modern exploration involves searching an area in a much more elaborate way. Mining companies spend millions of pounds every year on exploration, with only very small chances of success. It has been estimated that perhaps one in a thousand prospects examined ever leads to a major ore discovery and an eventually productive mine.

Exploration usually follows a set sequence. First, a large area is selected because the right rock types and structure exist for a particular type of ore deposit. For example, rock fractures such as joints or faults may provide channels of easy access for metal-bearing hydrothermal solutions. At each stage in his exploration the geologist will build up knowledge of the type and distribution of rocks in the area by making geological maps. Here, he may be aided by aerial photographs. By careful interpretation, an enormous amount of information can be gained about the rocks and structure of the area which would otherwise take a great deal of time and work on the ground to obtain. A development of this technique on an even greater scale is the use of satellite photographs.

RTZ

Below: Molten gold poured from the furnace cascades into a set of moulds. After cooling, these ingots contain almost 99% pure gold but they are then even further refined to extract some of the valuable by-product metals. The gold in this picture was originally dispersed through many tonnes of rocks.

Gold generally occurs as the native metal, often mixed with silver and other precious minerals. Probably no metal has had more influence on the economics, politics and history of man than gold. Its principal use has been as a backing for currency but sizeable amounts go into jewellery.

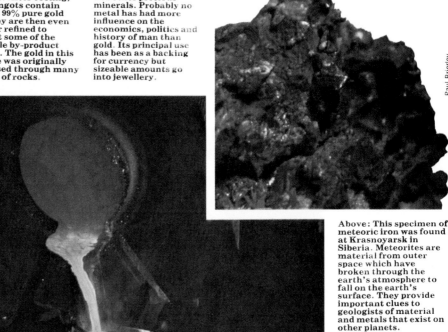

Paul Brierley

Above: This specimen of meteoric iron was found at Krasnoyarsk in Siberia. Meteorites are material from outer space which have broken through the earth's atmosphere to fall on the earth's surface. They provide important clues to geologists of material and metals that exist on other planets.

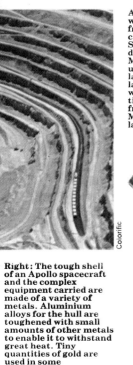

Colorific

Above: Most of the world's tin is mined from alluvial deposits of cassiterite (tin oxide) in South-East Asia. This dredger operating in Malaysia slowly works up and down a shallow lake. It is fitted with a large bucket-wheel which scoops up the tin-bearing gravels from the bottom. Malaysia is the world's largest tin producer.

Consolidated Gold Fields

Right: The tough shell of an Apollo spacecraft and the complex equipment carried are made of a variety of metals. Aluminium alloys for the hull are toughened with small amounts of other metals to enable it to withstand great heat. Tiny quantities of gold are used in some electronic components.

BASF

Right: Copper is an excellent conductor of electricity and some 60% of all copper extracted goes to the electrical industry. Several kilometres of copper wire were used in this modern telephone exchange system. Copper is also an essential ingredient of the alloys brass and bronze.

Direct geological observations are supplemented by the techniques of geochemistry and geophysics. Geochemistry utilizes the fact that traces of the metals in minerals can work their way to the surface, carried there by the water which circulates through the rocks. These metals then become dispersed in the soils carried into the sediment of streams and rivers or are even taken up by trees and plants. Geophysics depends on the fact that the physical properties of concentrations of ore minerals are measurably different from those of surrounding rocks. Instruments have been developed to detect the minutely different electrical, magnetic and gravitational response of ore bodies.

Both geochemistry and geophysics can only give a hint of what lies beneath the surface. Many features other than ore deposits can give rise to false indications and the real test of whether an ore deposit exists is to probe beneath the surface. The most widely used technique is *diamond drilling*. The cutting action of the rotating diamond-tipped drill bit produces a cylindrical *core* of rock. This is hauled up at intervals and examined.

Drilling can provide the first direct evidence of ore minerals. Using a grid pattern of drill holes over an area containing a deep-seated deposit, it is possible to get an estimate of a deposit's shape, size and grade of the ore even before the first tunnel is driven into the deposit.

Detailed exploration work provides enough information about the ore deposit for an entire modern mining operation to be planned and designed several years before mining actually starts. Advances in mining technology have meant that very low grade ores can be worked economically, provided the tonnages mined are sufficiently large. The bulk of the major, large-tonnage, new mines brought into production are enormous quarrying operations called *open cast*.

For ores deposited in veins or narrow layers, as well as for those lying too deep or at too steep an angle, underground mining methods have to be used. Shafts are sunk and horizontal tunnels driven at different levels into the ore deposit. The deposit is then explored from subsidiary tunnels. Alluvial deposits which are not amenable to either underground or open cast mining are extracted by dredging. For example, large dredgers scoop up tin-bearing gravels in lakes in Malaysia.

Coal

Coal is a unique deposit. No other rock (for coal is as much a rock in the geological sense as sandstone, limestone or granite) has played such an important role in the development of major industrial countries. Without coal, many modern technologies would be impossible, or prohibitively expensive. For example, coal is not only a fuel, but also—in the form of coke—an essential ingredient of steel. In addition, through making coke, many useful chemical by-products are generated.

The formation of coal

Coal is formed from the compacted and deeply buried remains of trees and plants which grew in forests millions of years ago. It is usually found in layers, or seams, each covering a large area, often hundreds of square kilometres, and ranging from one or two centimetres to several metres thick.

The oldest coal occurs in rocks of the Upper Devonian period, some 360 million years old, and is found subsequently in rocks of all ages up to the Tertiary period, which began 70 million years ago. However, most coals of economic importance were formed in the latter part of the Carboniferous period (the name means coal-bearing) some 265-290 million years ago. In this period conditions were just right for the prolific growth of forests, whose later burial led to the formation of the coalfields of North America, Europe and USSR. The climate was tropical and the trees grew in extensive swamps similar to the present-day jungles in such places as the Amazon basin and the Irrawaddy Delta of Burma.

Under these conditions, growth is very rapid. Dead trees and plant debris falling into the swamps quickly become waterlogged, and accumulate on the bottom. The stagnant swamp waters contain little oxygen, inhibiting the action of bacteria which would normally cause the vegetation to decay. Instead, the leaves and other soft parts gradually turn into a dark, jelly-like *humus*. This impregnates the harder, more woody plant debris until the end result is a layer of peat. (In present day swamps, peat layers 10 m (30 ft) thick have been found.) This is the first stage in the development of true coal. During peat formation, the weight of the upper layers compacts the lower layers, squeezing out some of the water. Chemical reactions accompany this compaction and result in the gradual enrichment of the peat with carbon. At the same time *methane*, or marsh-gas, is released.

To turn peat into coal, it must be buried and compacted still further beneath a thick pile of sediments. The consequent increase in pressure and slight rise in temperature results in progressive chemical changes. Water, methane, and other gases (known as *volatiles*) are further driven off and increasing carbon enrichment occurs until, ultimately, coal is formed. Such a decrease of volume takes place that a layer of peat more than 10-15 metres thick will produce only 1 metre of coal.

In Upper Carboniferous times, when coal formation was at its peak, the earth was in a general state of unrest. Fluctuating periods of earth movement caused

IGS

Above: Reconstruction of a typical coal-forming forest in the Carboniferous period reveals the luxuriant vegetation. Giant club-mosses, 'horsetails' and a dense undergrowth of smaller fern and creeper-like plants flourished in swampy terrain similar to the tropical jungles found in the Amazon basin.

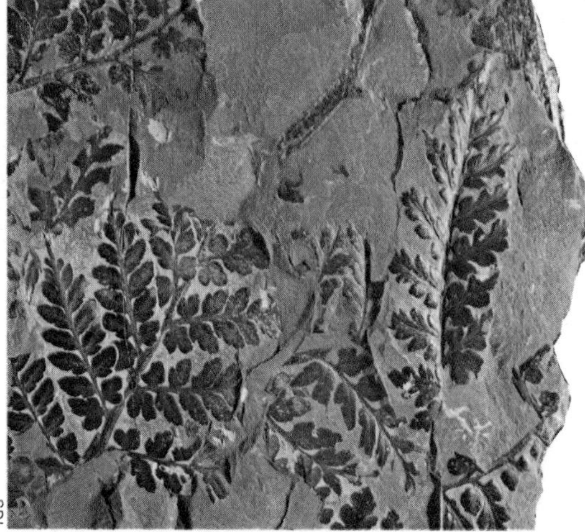

IGS

Below: The types of plants which grew in coal-forming forests are known because of fossilized remains commonly found in the rocks near coal seams. These well-preserved fossil ferns came from a coal measure in Yorkshire. Dead ferns and trees accumulated in the swamp to form peat and, later, coal.

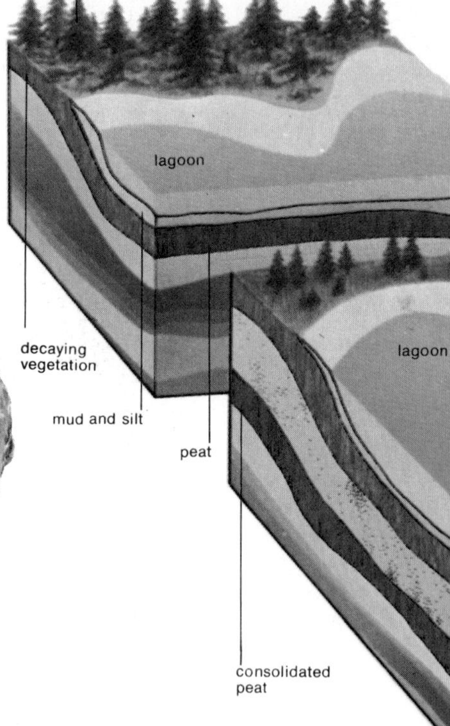

Picturepoint

Left: Peat forms also in temperate climates. In this hilly area of Scotland, with poor drainage, thick peat deposits have formed from fallen trees, heather and mosses. After digging and stacking to dry, the peat is used by local people as fuel but it gives off little heat and much smoke.

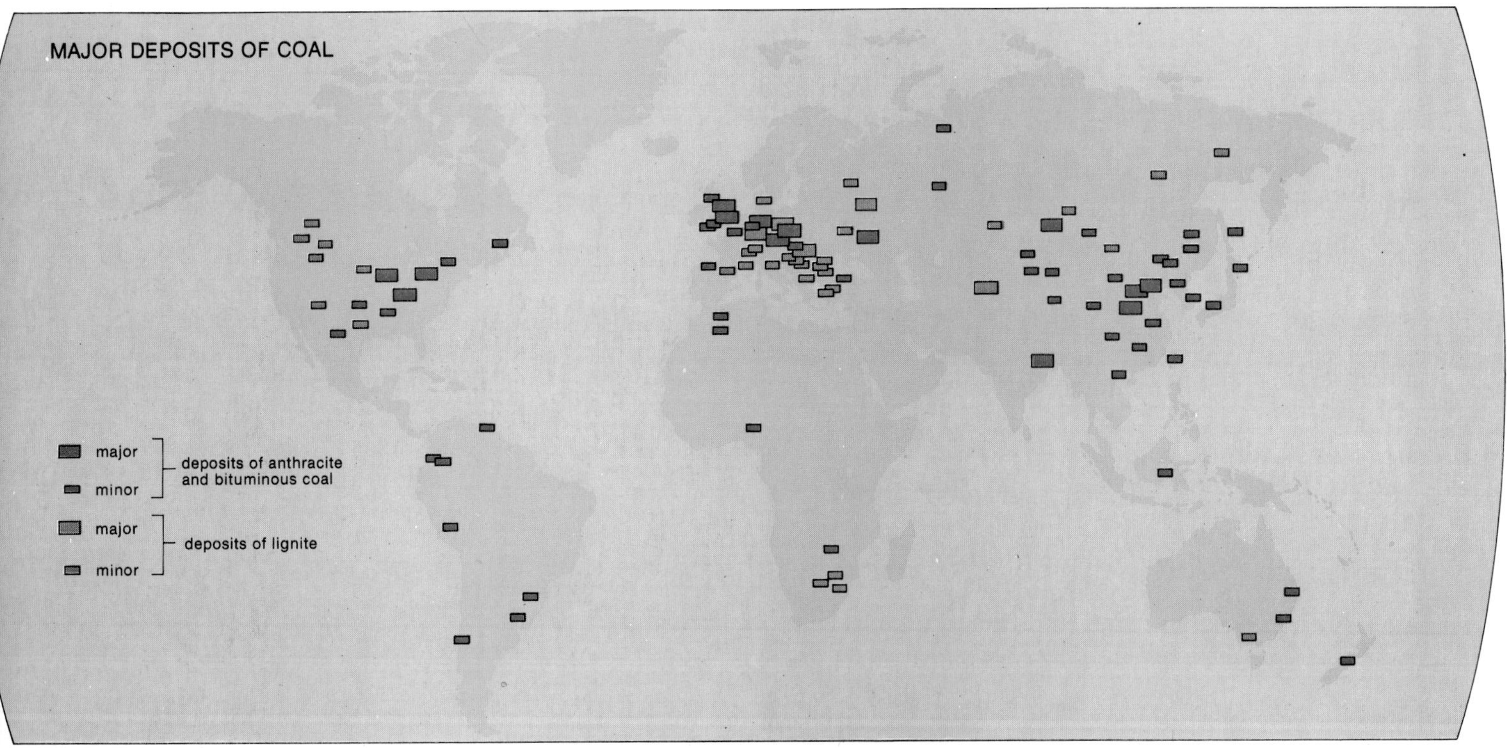

Below: Three stages in the formation of coal seams are shown. Dead vegetation falls into the swamp to form peat. After subsidence, water floods the forest and deposits a sedimentary layer of mud and silt which buries the peat to form coal eventually. As the water recedes, new forests grow and a new cycle begins.

Above: Coal deposits are widely distributed throughout the world and will offer a continuing supply of fuel to an energy-hungry world for many centuries. It is estimated that remaining resources are some 2.9 million million tonnes. Annual production is 3,000 million tonnes.

Right: The three main types of humic coal are classed by their degree of alteration. Lignite (right) is a soft coal, dark brown in colour, with a woody texture. Coals are broadly made up of carbon, hydrogen and oxygen. With high rank coals, carbon content increases. Lignite is typically 70% carbon.

BITUMINOUS

Left: Bituminous coal is the type most commonly used in the home. It is black and brittle with alternating bands of shiny vitrain and dull durain layers. Anthracite (below) is the highest rank coal produced by the greatest degree of alteration. It is very hard and has a 96% carbon content.

ANTHRACITE

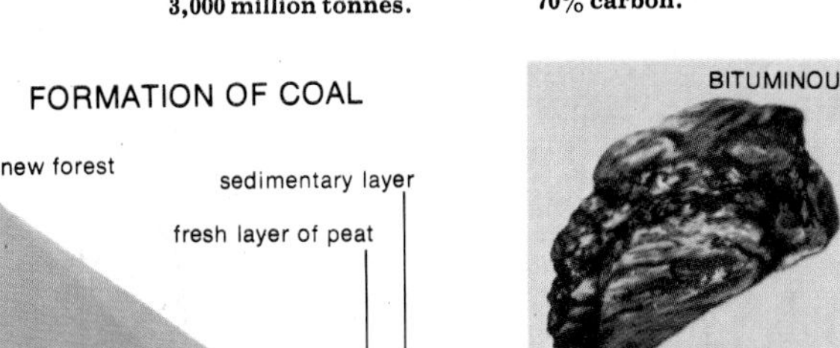

gradual subsidence of the coal-forming forests, with occasional periods of rapid subsidence in which the sea frequently flooded the forests and accumulating peat beds.

The forests occupied vast areas of swampland through which rivers and streams flowed. When they reached the sea, the rivers formed extensive deltas which were also colonized by forests. As rapid subsidence took place, the plants became submerged, and thick mud was deposited on top of the forests, burying and compacting the peat. When rapid subsidence ceased, the sea level remained much the same, but the waters became shallower as rivers carried down more sediments.

Eventually, so much sediment accumulated that sand-banks and mud flats appeared above water level. These were quickly colonized by plants and soon became new swampy forests. Peat formation started again, continuing until another rapid subsidence flooded the area, starting the whole cycle over again. Such a sequence of events is known as *cyclic sedimentation*.

Types of coal

Coals which have formed in seams by the process outlined above are known as *humic* coals and may be classed by the degree of alteration which the original peat has undergone. This is known as their *rank*. A whole range of coals can occur, but the main types are *lignite*, *bituminous coal*, and *anthracite*.

Lignite is a softish coal which is dark brown in colour. Nearest to peat in composition, it gives off a lot of smoke when burnt, without a great deal of heat. There are extensive deposits in central Europe and North America. Bituminous coal, on the other hand, is the type with which most people are familiar. It is black and brittle, with a tendency to fracture along one or two vertical planes, forming straight-sided blocks of coal.

Bituminous coals usually have horizontal bands of alternating shiny and dull layers. These represent different types of

J. Pfaff/Zefa

Left: Open-cast mining for low quality brown coal up to a depth of 50 metres near Cologne in Germany. This method is applied to shallow seams and vast excavating machines are used to mine a deep pit.

Right: For deeper deposits, underground mining is required. Miners working at the coal face are hampered by dirty and dangerous conditions. Modern mining techniques involve increasing use of mechanization.

Daily Telegraph Colour Library

Below: A plan of a typical coal mine shows the tremendous amount of careful planning and costly machinery needed to extract coal from deep coal seams.

original plant debris. The hard shiny, almost glassy, layers are known as *vitrain*. Microscopic examination shows that they consist of highly compressed bark and woody material. The dull layers are called *durain* and are formed mainly of the smaller and more resistant plant debris, such as spore-cases. Neither durain nor vitrain soil the fingers when touched. It is the presence of *fusain* that makes coal dirty to handle. Fusain is a soft and friable substance resembling charcoal, and was most probably formed from dead branches and trunks exposed to the air.

Anthracite is the highest rank of coal. Durain and vitrain bands are both present, but rarely fusain, and so anthracite is clean to handle. It burns with a very hot flame with hardly any smoke.

By contrast with the humic coals, the *sapropelic* coals are a group which do not appear to have formed from extensive tropical forest peat. There are two main types: *cannel coal* (the name is probably a corruption of 'candle' since it burns with a bright, smokey flame) is unbanded and breaks like glass. It is thought to have originated from the accumulation of fine floating plant material, such as spores. The remains of algae often form some of the constituents. *Boghead* coals, on the other hand, are dark brown or black, and resemble tough leather. They consist mainly of the remains of algae, which probably lived in large, well-oxygenated lakes.

The process of repeated seam formation leads to a great thickness of coal-bearing sediments being built up. These are given the general term *coal measures* and may reach a thickness of at least 1500 m, containing 20-30 main coal seams between one and three metres thick and many additional, much thinner ones. Their original horizontal layers, however, have often been disturbed by folding, tilting and faulting as a result of earth movements during the hundreds of millions of years in which they formed. Where coal-measures outcrop at the surface, an exposed coalfield is found but, over many

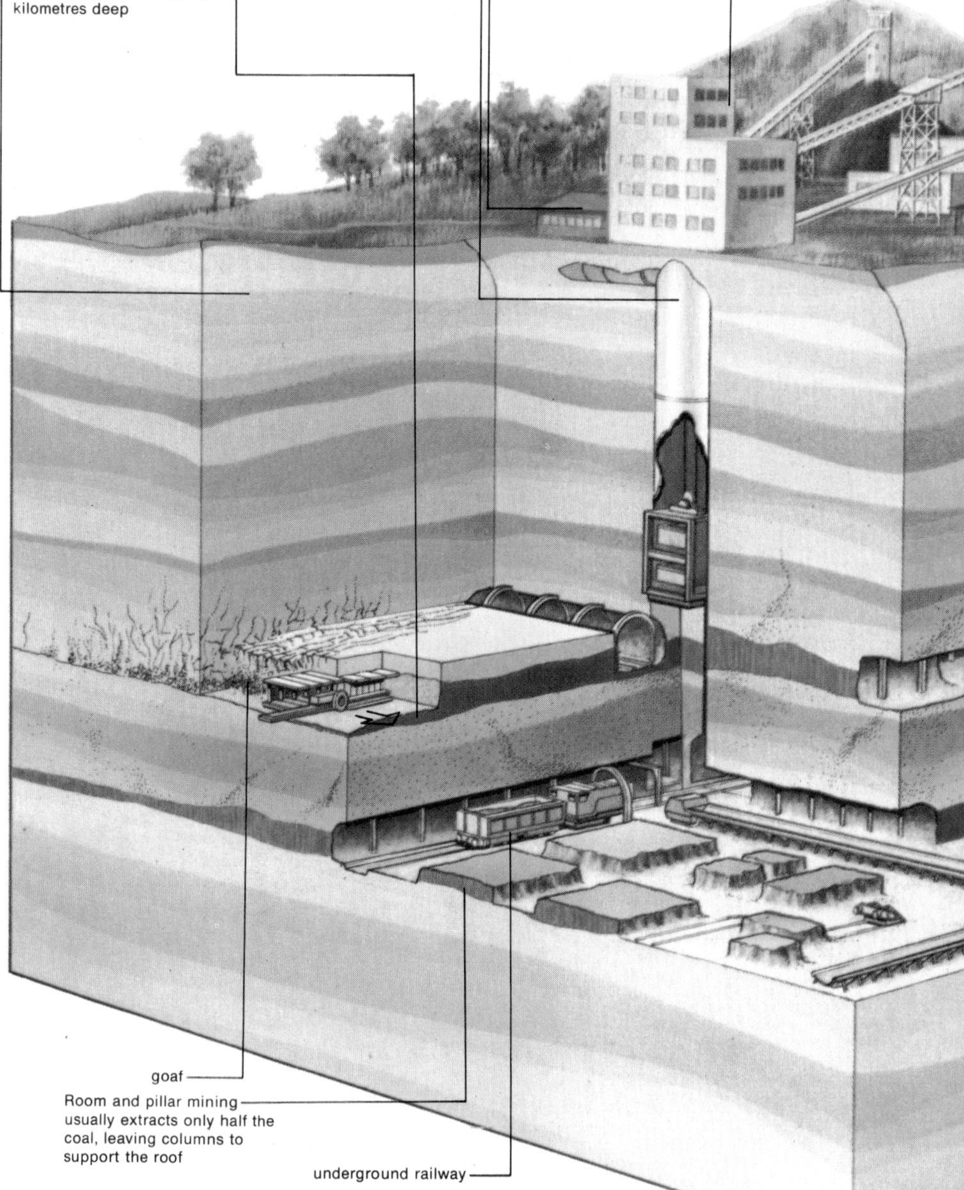
A cutaway section through the unmined coal shows the machinery used in longwall mining at work. The arrow shows the direction of mining into the coal face
Fan-house, with powerful fan to extract the foul air
The top of the upcast shaft is housed in a sealed building, to ensure that the fan operates efficiently in removing used air from the whole underground area
Intermediate rock strata. The diagram is not to scale — these strata may be several kilometres deep
Upcast shaft is used to bring coal, loaded in buckets called skips, to the surface
goaf
Room and pillar mining usually extracts only half the coal, leaving columns to support the roof
underground railway

Photri

Left: American coal mining is carried out on a large scale. Here an automatic loader is picking up the coal cut from the seam face and loading it on to a transporter. This is driven through the underground tunnels to a central conveyor belt.

S. Dumpleton

Below left: Two types of drilling bit are commonly used in coal exploration. An open-hole bit simply bores a hole through the rock. A coring bit is hollow with numerous industrial diamonds set in the rim. It retains a core of rock which is analysed for traces of coal seams. Often the borehole drilling rig is small enough to be mounted on a truck and moved from site to site.

Daily Telegraph Colour Library

Right: The Industrial Revolution began in Britain when the steam engine, fuelled by coal, replaced the water-driven wheel. This quiet valley town in Wales, now centred around the winding gear of a coal mine, grew rapidly in the 19th century as its rich seams were exploited.

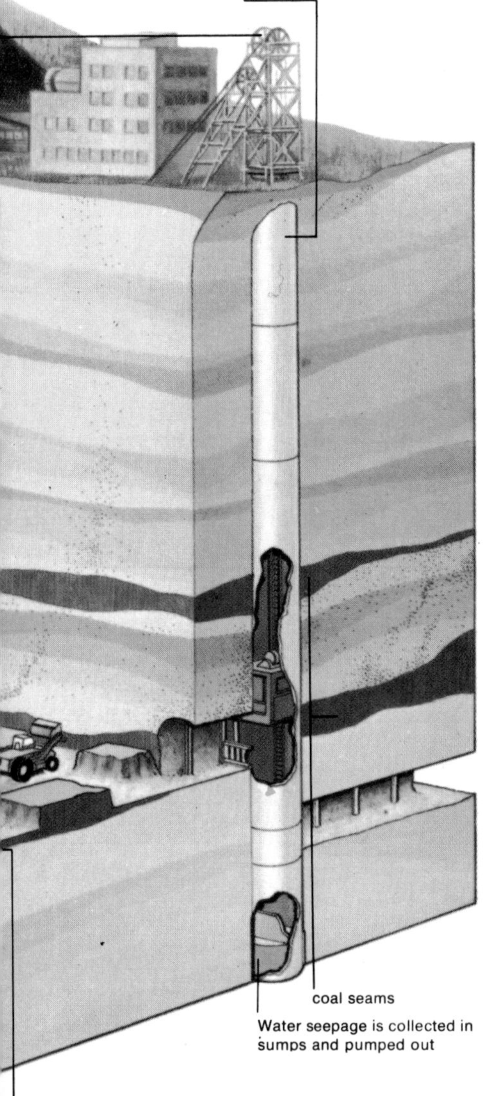
The headgear of the downcast shaft is made of an open lattice of steel girders, so that fresh air can enter to ventilate the mine
Downcast shaft is fitted with a cage, used to convey man and equipment into and out of the mine
coal seams
Water seepage is collected in sumps and pumped out
conveyor belts

areas, erosion has removed all trace of the coal. In other regions, younger rocks cover the coal measures completely, resulting in a concealed coal field at depth.

The search for coal

In completely unknown country, a thorough geological survey normally reveals coal deposits of some importance. The geologist will often employ aerial photography to help him with surface mapping but to prove the existence of a concealed coalfield boreholes have to be sunk.

The cores which are taken from the boreholes are analysed to determine their physical and chemical properties. These will indicate whether it would be economic to mine. Open-hole boreholes can also provide useful information, using a remarkable new technique called *electrical logging*. This involves lowering various instruments on a cable down the hole. These send back electrical impulses which vary according to the nature of the strata and the type of probe used. The results are recorded on graph-charts which build up an accurate picture of the borehole.

A comparatively new technique in coal field exploration is *seismic* surveying, although it has been used for many years in the search for oil. This kind of survey is carried out by drilling a line of shallow holes three metres deep. A small quantity of explosive is loaded into each hole, and then fired in succession. This produces a series of miniature earthquakes whose shock waves pass down into the ground. The different layers of rock reflect the waves back up again with different intensities, and these are picked up on the surface by special microphones, called *geophones*. The resulting picture built up shows different types of strata and, more importantly, the *structures*—for example, the folding or faulting of the layers.

Mining methods

Coal is extracted by either open-cast workings at the surface, or by deep mines underground. The average depth of open-cast mines in Britain is 33 metres (110 ft), although a working depth of 213 metres (700 ft) is planned at a Scottish site. To reach the coal seams, all the overlying soil and rocks, or overburden, must first be removed by large draglines and excavators. Later the overburden is replaced.

The main method of mining, however, is by fully mechanized *longwall* extraction. Two parallel tunnels or roadways, usually about 200 m apart, are driven into the coal seam. These are connected at right angles by a third tunnel, the height of the seam, which forms the coal face. Successive strips of coal are cut from the face, advancing it forward. Simultaneously the two roadways at each end are lengthened, to keep pace with the coal face.

The coal is cut by an electrically operated machine, mounted on a special armoured steel conveyor running along the length of the face. It pulls itself along the conveyor track by a chain and sprocket arrangement, cutting a strip of coal from the face, which falls onto the conveyor to be taken to one end of the face. There, it is loaded onto a belt conveyor which transports it to the mine shafts, where it is lifted to the surface.

Longwall *retreat* mining differs from advance mining in that the two parallel roadways are initially driven right to the furthest extent of the coal panel. The coal face is formed at the far end and retreats back towards the mine shafts. By 'blocking out' the panel in this way, any geological hazard like a fault can be assessed before the face starts production.

The world's remaining coal resources are estimated at 2,900,000,000,000 tonnes, of which only some 12 per cent can be economically worked by present day mining methods. Techniques such as *in-seam gasification* (which obtains energy by igniting the coal in its seam), however, may enable some of the energy of the remaining 88 per cent to be tapped. But in the meantime, much research is being carried out into methods of using coal more wisely and efficiently. The world is using coal many hundreds of thousands of times faster than it took to form—and the supply is not inexhaustible.

Petroleum

Petroleum, defined broadly to include crude oil, inflammable natural gas and the semi-solid black substance known as asphalt or bitumen, has been exploited on a small scale for centuries. Bitumen, for example, was used more than 5,000 years ago in waterproofing ships and as a mortar for bricks. But these early uses relied on natural escapes or *seepages* of oil and gas to the earth's surface and on hand-dug shafts near such places. Oil had also been recovered from the surface of some rivers, again provided by seepages, and small amounts had been found to contaminate wells drilled for water.

In Pennsylvania, on 27 August 1859, a retired railway guard named Edwin L. Drake sank a steam-powered drill into the ground, to produce petroleum commercially for the first time. Drake struck oil at a depth of only 21 metres (69 feet). Today, however, advanced technology enables oil and gas to be produced from depths well in excess of 6,000 m (20,000 ft), and the deepest well drilled to date in search of oil is 9,583 m (31,441 ft). Oil and gas fields have been developed in more than 60 countries, as well as offshore in many parts of the world, with wells in some cases more than 275 km (170 miles) from land and in depths of water of over 140 m (450 ft).

The Origin of Petroleum

The origin of crude oil and natural gas is still a subject of investigation and debate. However, most geologists now believe that oil and gas formed from changes in the remains of a variety of animals and plant life. This organic matter is thought to have been deposited with inorganic minerals as sediments on the bottom of ancient seas and lakes, most commonly in shallow, calm tropical seas. The organic matter generally constituted only a small amount of the total sediment, which was buried deeper by successive deposits of sediment and turned into rock.

The organic remains, imprisoned in the mud and sand, then underwent considerable change. They were partially modified by the action of bacteria and, after biochemical changes ceased, the total organic complex was slowly acted upon by heat. As the sedimentary strata were buried progressively deeper in the earth's crust, they entered zones of greater pressure and higher temperature. This heating, never strong, caused changes in which *hydrocarbons*—compounds of carbon and hydrogen—and other petroleum components were formed directly or developed by further alteration of previously released compounds.

Many of these changes may have taken place over several millions of years and at temperatures not more than about 180°C. In the process, an entire range of products—including crude oil and natural gas—were released. In the early stages in particular, the products will have been influenced by the nature of the parental matter. For example, coaly type organic matter is prone to give methane gas, and not the decidedly heavier hydrocarbons characteristic of crude oils. Like coal, which is also derived from organic material, oil and natural gas are known as *fossil fuels*.

Picturepoint

Above: Excess petroleum gas is burnt off at a field in Abu Dhabi. Much of the natural gas which occurs with oil is burnt off at the point of production, because of the cost and difficulty of transporting it to areas of consumption great distances away.

Drake Museum

Right: Edwin Drake drilled the first ever well in a specific search for oil at Titusville, Pennsylvania in 1859. The Pennsylvania Oil Company, founded in the same year, was the ancestor of the international oil companies of today. Drake was lucky—he picked a spot where oil lay just 21 metres below the surface.

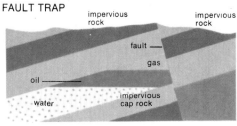

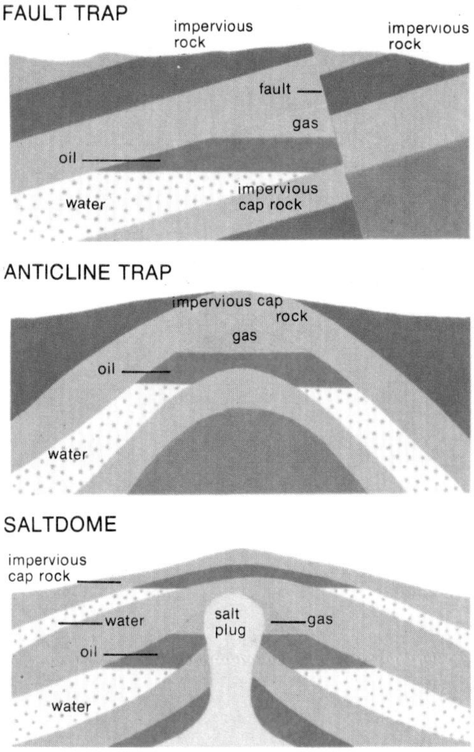

FAULT TRAP

impervious rock
impervious rock
fault
gas
oil
water
impervious cap rock

ANTICLINE TRAP

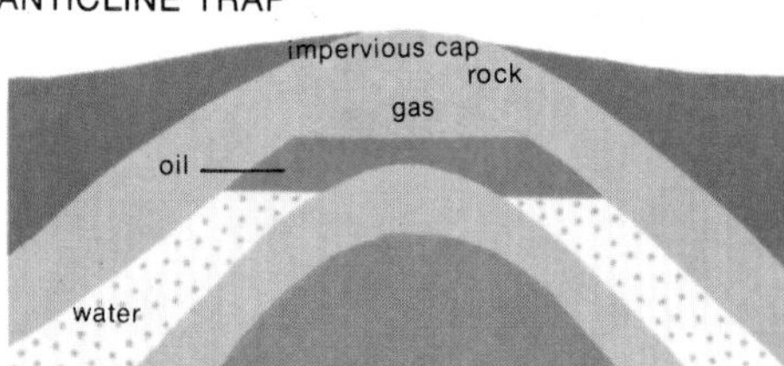

SALTDOME

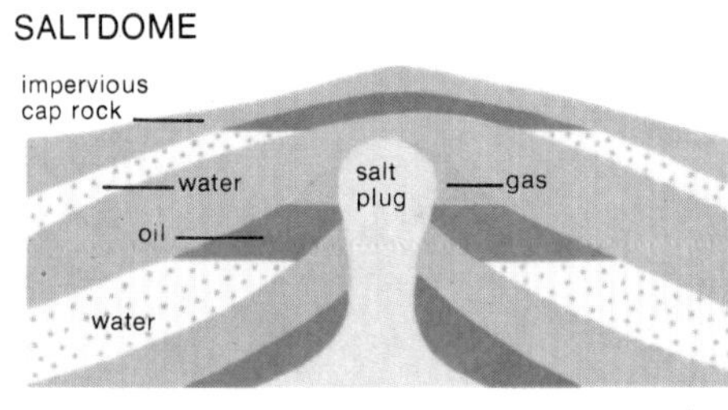

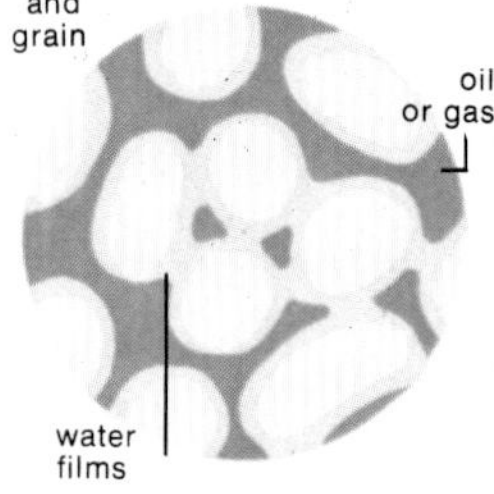

Above: Oil and gas are trapped between the pores of reservoir rock—the mineral grains are usually surrounded by a thin film of water.

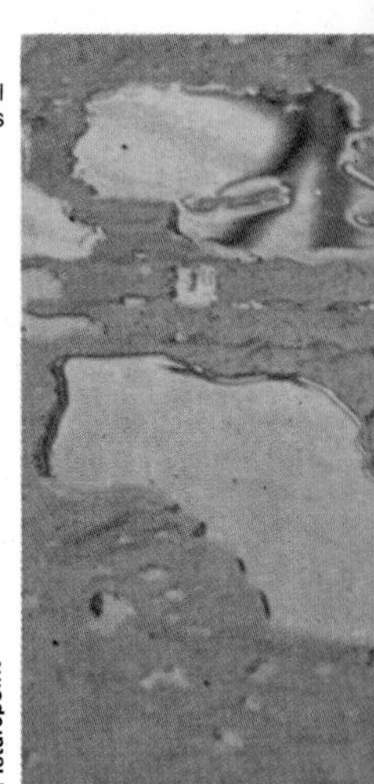

Picturepoint

Above right: Pools of iridescent colour created by natural seepage from a Venezuelan oil field. If petroleum leaks from underground, via a fault or crack, it floats on top of surface water.

Left: Three examples of the natural traps in which oil may be found. Oil is formed from microscopic marine organisms which died and sank to the bottom of water, becoming trapped beneath mud. Oil then rises until it reaches impervious rock.

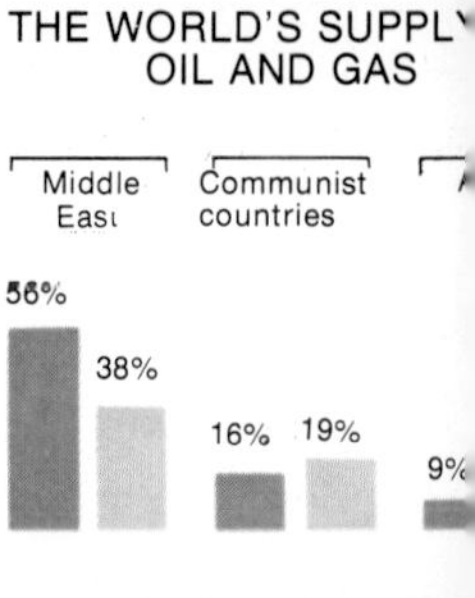

THE WORLD'S SUPPL OIL AND GAS

Middle East
Communist countries
56%
38%
16%
19%
9%

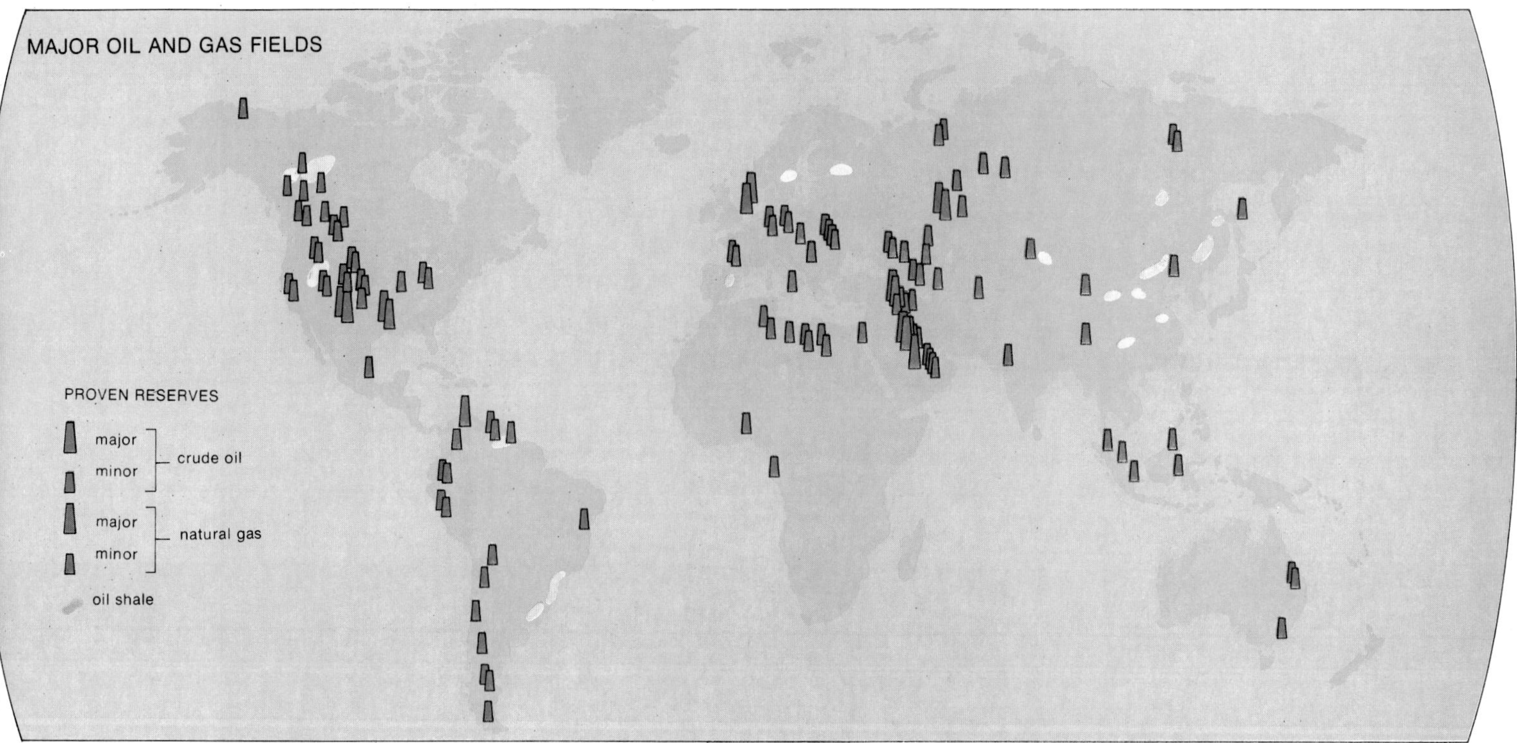

Where petroleum is found

Organic matter is generally deposited in greatest abundance in fine-grained rocks such as clays. Because only a small proportion of it is split off to give hydrocarbons, its concentration in these, the *source rocks*, is very low. Quite early it was recognized that, in order for oil or gas to accumulate to form a *field* or pool, the hydrocarbons must have moved away from their point of origin and that certain rocks with significantly different physical characteristics to those of the source rocks must be present. This movement, or *migration*, is caused by the pressure from the weight of overlying sediments.

Water trapped in the source rock is squeezed out and carries the petroleum with it into porous *reservoir rocks*, where the openings between the mineral grains allow fluid to percolate towards the surface. As the fluid slowly migrates through the porous rocks, the less dense petroleum separates from the salt water, which then accumulates below the crude oil and natural gas or occupies parts, sometimes as much as 20 per cent, of the pores in which the oil and gas occur.

Crude oils range widely in their physical and chemical properties. The colours range from green and brown to black with rare examples of straw-coloured oils. When they reach the surface, some oils are more fluid than water, yet others may be as viscous as treacle. The principal elements in their composition are carbon and hydrogen, with appreciable amounts of sulphur, oxygen and nitrogen, and yet smaller amounts of metallic elements, among which nickel and vanadium are outstanding. Natural gas is largely composed of methane in most cases, but small amounts of ethane and propane are commonly present. In addition some gases contain significant amounts of nitrogen, carbon dioxide, hydrogen sulphide and, more rarely, helium.

The most common reservoir rocks are sandstones and various types of limestones. Especially in the latter, some storage space is provided by openings other than inter-grain or inter-crystal openings, some of which may be decidedly larger than the pores between the sand grains. These are openings inside fossils, or between irregular fossil fragments; spaces are also formed by the solution or replacement of minerals, and by open fractures. Fractures are especially important in the finer-pored rocks, not so much because of the 'storage space', but because they make the rock mass much more permeable.

Accumulations occur when the petroleum is trapped in the reservoir rock by an overlying layer of suitably shaped impervious rock. This is known as the *cap rock*. Shales, clays, salt, gypsum and anhydrite are the principal cap rocks. Any pores in these rocks are much smaller than those in reservoir rocks, and are occupied by water. There is little if any penetration of the oil or gas into the cap rock. Natural gas may collect above salt water without the presence of oil. Free gas may also occur in a *gas cap* overlying crude oil containing dissolved gas. This in turn rests on the main body of salt water. On the other hand, some accumulations of petroleum have no associated gas cap, but do have dissolved gas in the oil.

Various types of geological formation

proven' oil reserves in 1974
gas reserves in million cubic metres
oil production in 1974

th erica: 20%
Latin America: 5% 9%
Western Europe: 4% 1%
Far East: 3% 4%

World Total
100% = 720,358 million barrels oil res.
100% = 20,943 million barrels oil prod.
proven world gas reserves 64,977
est. ultimate world reserves 339,600
2,000,000 million barrels est. ultimate world reserves

Shell

Right: An exploratory drilling rig. Mud is pumped down the drill shaft to lubricate the drill bit. Drilling mud disappearing below ground is a sign of porous rock and this in turn means there is possibly oil present. The cutting bit of the drill is rotated by turning the whole length of the pipe.

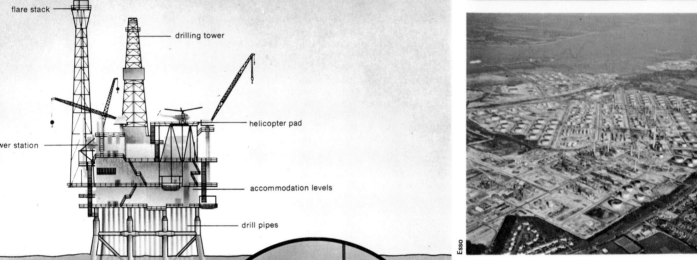

Right: The North Sea is among the most active fields for offshore oil exploitation. Worldwide, offshore fields offer a large potential of untapped oil and gas—they contribute only 17% of total world production but make up 21% of known world reserves. In the North Sea, oil reserves in the British sector alone may exceed 8,400 million barrels. Oil first came ashore in 1975 by tanker from the Argyll field. Since then, most oil has been pumped ashore via pipelines.

Below: The Forties rig—an anchored production rig standing on legs on the sea floor—is joined to the Scottish mainland by pipeline. The derrick, set high up on the rig platform above the waves, moves laterally so that the drill can be lowered to several positions down any one of the fixed drill pipes. These protect the drill which is driven through the *anticlinal cap rock* trapping the oil.

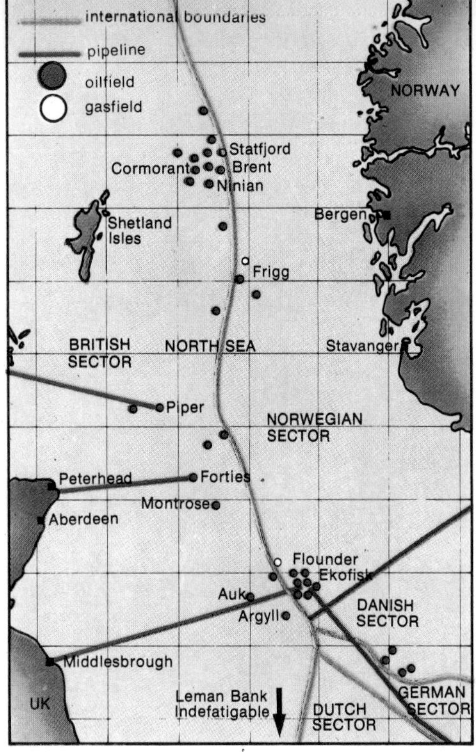

Right: A giant torch lights up a North Sea oil rig as excess gas is burnt off during production tests. Natural gas occurs both alone and with oil; its principal component is methane, an important raw material for the chemical industry.

Below right: The massive Esso refinery at Fawley on Southampton Water, is one of the largest in the world. Crude oil is refined into a vast number of primary products. Besides its use as a major fuel for all forms of air, sea and land transport, oil is also the raw material for a multitude of chemicals and synthetics. These are used in the manufacture of a range of products from agricultural feeds and fertilizers to perfume and plastics. Current research may lead to petroleum by-products providing a massive source of protein for a hungry world.

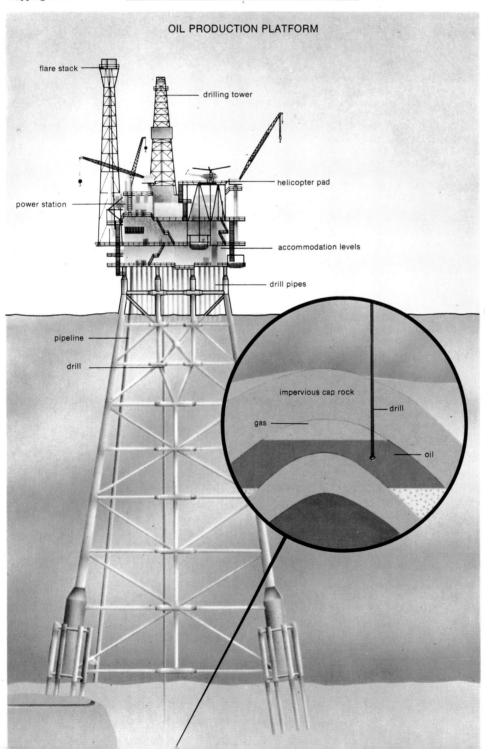

Shell

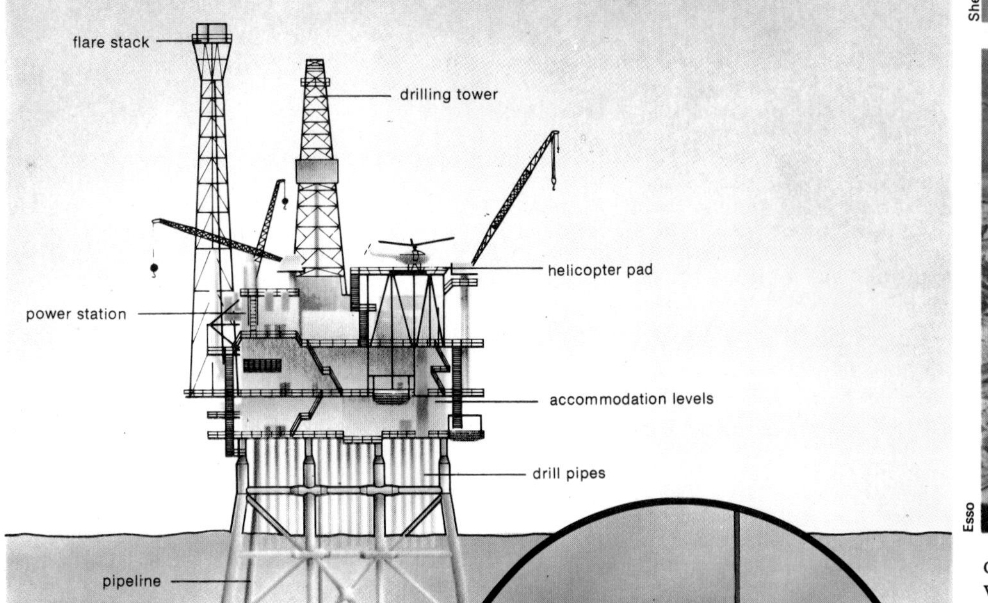

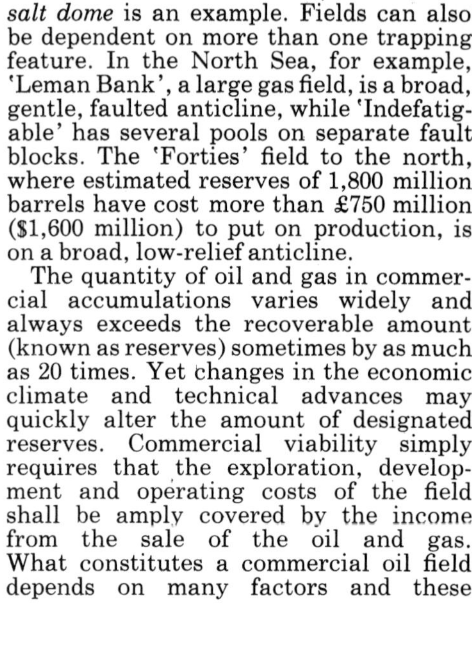
Esso

can produce traps. Some arise from the way the layers of sediment were at first deposited. Others are *structural traps*, formed by the folding or faulting of the earth as in *anticlinal* or *fault* traps, or by intrusions of different rocks, of which the *salt dome* is an example. Fields can also be dependent on more than one trapping feature. In the North Sea, for example, 'Leman Bank', a large gas field, is a broad, gentle, faulted anticline, while 'Indefatigable' has several pools on separate fault blocks. The 'Forties' field to the north, where estimated reserves of 1,800 million barrels have cost more than £750 million ($1,600 million) to put on production, is on a broad, low-relief anticline.

The quantity of oil and gas in commercial accumulations varies widely and always exceeds the recoverable amount (known as reserves) sometimes by as much as 20 times. Yet changes in the economic climate and technical advances may quickly alter the amount of designated reserves. Commercial viability simply requires that the exploration, development and operating costs of the field shall be amply covered by the income from the sale of the oil and gas. What constitutes a commercial oil field depends on many factors and these

Esso

Above: The giant oil tanker *Esso Scotia*, launched at Bremen in 1969, capable of carrying almost half a million tons of crude oil.

Below: Sheik Rashid of Dubai, one of the Arab rulers who have amassed great wealth from oil. Major producers like the Arabs have great economic influence.

Marc Riboud/Magnum

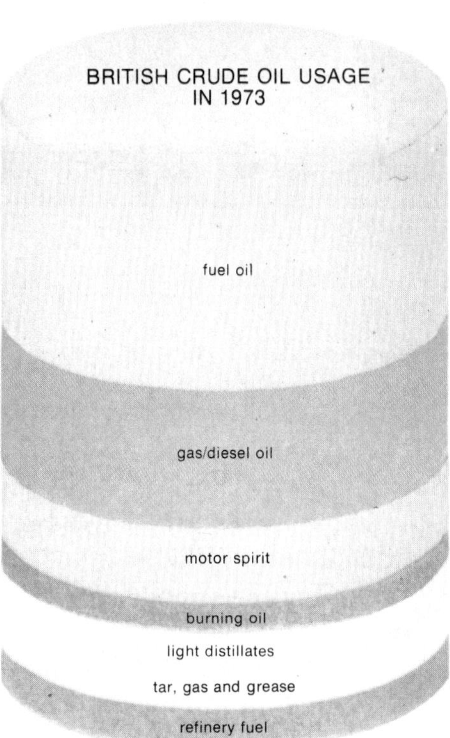

include the quality of the oil, the current price of oil and the depth of the reservoir.

Among the highest known reserves are the 66,500 million barrels of oil at the Ghawar field in Saudi Arabia and 65 million million cubic feet of gas under Slochteren in Holland. (One barrel of oil is about 0.16 cubic metres and contains 35 gallons. Gas reserves are in volumes calculated at atmospheric pressure and temperature.) Field areas vary from over 2,800 sq km (1,100 sq miles) to as little as 2.5 sq km (1 sq mile) for some pools. Individual well producing rates range from more than 20,000 barrels a day to less than 100 at the peak, and gas wells may flow at rates of tens of millions of cubic feet per day. There are, however, inevitable declines as the fields and wells are depleted.

There is no means of recognizing with certainty whether masses of oil or gas exist at depth before wells have been drilled. However, geologists can make reasonable predictions on the basis of rock forms which could constitute traps. In some areas, the surface rocks give clues to the different rock layers at depth. Surface mapping, often aided by the examination of aerial photographs, will often dictate accurately the positions of anticlines and faults at depth.

Where surface rocks are not a guide to the position of underground geological structures, or at underwater sites, geophysical techniques must be used to indicate the sites of structures at depth. One method uses readings of the intensity of the earth's gravitational pull. This may show where denser, and hence commonly older, rocks are nearer the surface than elsewhere. This indicates to geologists that violent earth movements have occurred in the past and could imply the existence of an anticline or point to a fault, both of which are capable of providing traps.

Seismic surveys are carried out as an alternative technique, or to confirm other indications. Pulses of energy, generated by explosives or other means, travel down from the earth's surface and, after reflection or refraction at boundaries between the rock layers, return to the surface and are detected by seismometers. Measurement of the travel times and the recognition of what are apparently the same boundaries from a series of observations allow the shapes of sub-surface boundaries to be plotted. In this way trapping forms can be recognized. Aeromagnetic surveys throw light on the broader features of sedimentary basins in which oil and gas accumulations are formed.

Drilling is an expensive operation, particularly in marine areas. Success is not assured even after extensive geological and geophysical surveys, because for various reasons traps can lack hydrocarbons, or contain quantities of hydrocarbons which are too small to justify commercial development.

The cuttings and other rock samples from a test drilling are carefully examined. These reveal the nature of the rocks penetrated and their fluid contents, and checks are kept on the returning mud for evidence of oil or gas. In addition, instruments are lowered into the hole from time to time to make electrical, radioactivity and other measurements. From these results, geologists can assess the type of rock, its porosity and the content of gas, oil or salt water. When hydrocarbons are recognized or thought to be present in exploratory wells, further special tests are made to check whether oil or gas can be produced at adequate rates. All of this is done before finally deciding to complete the well for production or to abandon it. Additional wells are normally needed to estimate the approximate size of the accumulation before embarking on full development, which includes the costly installation of pipe lines, storage and other major facilities.

To bring oil or gas to the surface, oil producers largely rely on the great pressure to which the petroleum at the bottom of a well is subjected. This pressure is reduced by opening surface valves or by other means, permitting fluids as a whole in the reservoir rock to expand, with gas coming out of solution in the oil, and the fluid itself being forced into and up the well.

Wells commonly produce oil unaided, for a time at least, but later many have to be helped in some manner, such as by pumping, in order to bring oil to the surface. Oil reaching the surface, as well as being accompanied by gas, is sometimes also associated with salt water, especially as the wells grow older. Gas, oil and water have to be separated before the saleable products are dispatched from the fields.

As the reserves of known accumulations of liquid hydrocarbons are used up, other sources become increasingly important. One such source—still so expensive that full exploitation lies in the future—are rocks impregnated with extremely viscous petroleum which will not flow into wells. These are referred to as *tar sands*, and include an enormous accumulation, known as the Athabasca Tar Sands of northern Canada. Special means, amongst which are excavation and washing, have to be employed in order to utilize these deposits. Such operations are commercially viable only rarely at present.

Another potential source may be the oil obtainable from *oil shales*. These are rocks rich in solid organic matter called kerogen, but not in free oil. However, by heating these shales at temperatures of several hundred degrees centigrade, the organic matter breaks down to yield considerable amounts of oil. This oil differs in various ways from crude oil, but may be refined by similar procedures although environmental problems arise from the disposal of large amounts of baked rock produced as waste. However, very extensive oil shale deposits exist, and they are potential sources of large volumes of oil, at a price.

Geological Time

Right: The Durdle Door in Dorset, England, forms a natural arch in the sea. Modern geologists recognize that it has taken millions of years for the natural processes of weathering and erosion to shape the rocks into such natural forms as this. However, many scholars in the past believed that supernatural forces were at work. Bishop Ussher (below) was a respected biblical scholar. His assertion that the earth was created 6,000 years ago caused great controversy for about 250 years. Some non-Christian cultures in Asia had a more realistic idea of the age of the earth, believed by Hindus to be 2,000 million years.

Heather Angel

The most accurate estimates available today indicate that the earth is about 4,500,000,000 years old. This figure presents a dramatic contrast with some estimates in the past. In 1644 John Lightfoot of Cambridge produced the unequivocal assertion that the moment of all creation was 9.00 am on September 17, 3928BC. Ten years later this was amended to 4004BC by Archbishop James Ussher of Ireland (1581-1656), who drew his date from a literal interpretation of the Book of Genesis. As late as 1900, his view of the creation was printed in the Authorized Version of the Bible by Cambridge University Press. This belief in a literal six-day creation and a 6,000 year-old earth was unquestioned by many Christians, until geologists began to produce conclusive evidence against it.

Leonardo da Vinci (1452-1515), the brilliant Italian artist and scientist, was perhaps one of the first to have an inkling of the modern concept of geological time. He recognized marine shells, found in the rocks of high inland mountains, as fossils—the remains of once-living organisms buried in the rocks by natural processes. He was convinced that the sea had covered the area at some time in a distant past. He rejected the interpretation of scholars who saw fossils as the Devil's work, put there to confuse mankind, or as evidence of the Biblical Flood, dated by theologians to 2348BC. Da Vinci sketched the rocks, showing their layered arrangement and the way in which they were buckled into folds.

Even so, it was not until 150 years later that Nicolas Steno (1638-87), a Dane living in Italy, rediscovered fossils and layering in rocks. Interpreting these features in the conventional manner, he attributed them to the Biblical Flood. But he did see that the layers stretched for great distances and that the upper beds of rock must have been deposited on the lower. This simple observation was to become the *Law of Superposition* and the basis of a geological time scale: more recent sedimentary rocks will always lie on top of the older rocks, unless later disturbed.

Steno's law of superposition was taken further by William Smith (1769-1839), a British engineer employed in canal construction. During his travels he collected fossils and noted that each form was restricted to certain beds. He found that the layers were always in the same order and contained the same sequence of fossils wherever they occurred.

After a quarter of a century of diligent observation, in 1815 Smith was able to publish a remarkable map of England and Wales. This showed the areas where each of his groups of beds came to the surface and their succession from oldest to youngest. Smith was unaware of the idea of organic evolution, which was put forward 44 years later by Charles Darwin, but he recognized that fossils were evidence of a constant process of change over a long period of time. By means of fossils, he proved that rocks in different places can be *correlated*, or shown to be of the same age, and that successions of rocks can be arranged in a relative time sequence.

Mary Evans

Hutton's 'Theory of the Earth'

The greatest step towards modern geological ideas, however, is justly attributed to a Scottish physician, James Hutton (1726-97). In 1788 he proposed a *Theory of the Earth* in which the formation of rock strata was only part of a process with 'no vestige of a beginning—no prospect of an end'. His great contribution lies in the recognition of the cyclical nature of geological change, with the implicit assumption that the earth must have had a very long history.

From his observations, Hutton reasoned that rocks were slowly weathered and eroded by the action of water and air and the debris transported to the sea to form new sedimentary beds. These beds in turn sank lower into the earth under the weight of successive deposition. In the depths they became crumpled and heating and compression produced new minerals and new structures. Along with this metamorphism, molten rock was forced into the strata which, upon solidification, gave rise to granites and related igneous rocks. Uplift of all this to make new land initiated a new cycle. According to Hutton the 'elements' that batter the land have always done so. 'The present,' he asserted 'is the key to the past.'

Hutton also described evidence of the relative age differences between rocks. On the island of Arran in Scotland, for example, he found sedimentary rocks folded by earth movements and metamorphosed, and then intersected from below by numerous thin granite veins. Here was evidence that not only did certain rocks

W. J. French

W. J. French

W. J. French

Top: At Loch Assynt in Scotland, the mountain structure has two unconformities. Quartzite on the surface rests on sandstone, deposited on older, folded gneiss.

Centre: Further evidence of relative age is found in conglomerates, which are formed of pebbles and boulders eroded from some pre-existing rocks.

Above: On this Yorkshire beach, marine erosion originally carved a cliff and shore platform out of chalk and clay. On the platform a beach deposit of chalk cobbles has been formed. Wind-blown sand coated this beach, and later deposits of glacial clay blanket the chalk, sand and old beach. Present marine erosion exposes the sequence.

Ronan

Right: Hutton, known as the 'Father of Geology' for his pioneering work.

Mary Evans

Below right: The law of superposition is assumed to apply unless it can be shown that the beds have been inverted as a result of earth movements. In the event of folding, the strata can become overturned so that some beds are upside-down and older beds rest on top of younger beds. Geologists are then faced with the problem of deciding the strata's original 'way-up'. Unfolded beds, occurring above an unconformity with folded beds, will be younger than the altered beds. Similarly, an igneous vein will be younger than the folded or metamorphosed rock into which it is intruded.

James Hutton based his unconformity principle on findings at Siccar Point (above) and Arran (right) in Scotland. The print, from an early geology book by Charles Lyell, and photograph both show strata of slightly inclined red sandstone resting on vertical schist. Here was proof to Hutton of a long interval of time. Hutton's work was not widely known until championed after his death by a student, John Playfair. Taken by Hutton to Siccar Point, Playfair later wrote: 'The mind seemed to grow giddy looking so far into the abyss of time, and while we listened . . . we became sensible how much farther reason may sometimes go than imagination can venture to follow.'

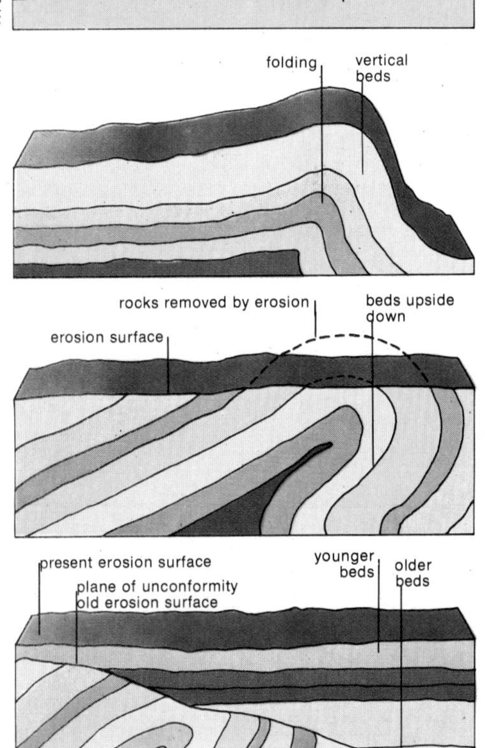

W. J. French

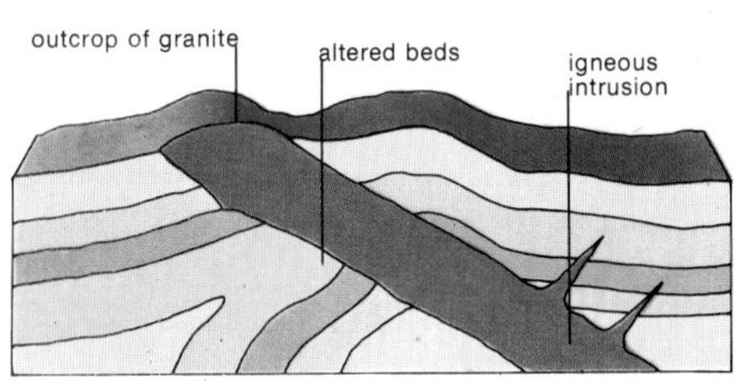

originate below the earth's surface, but also, as Hutton recorded, the granite must be younger than the pieces of sedimentary rock it engulfed.

Also on Arran, Hutton found the junction, termed an *unconformity*, between layered rocks of two different ages. An unconformity marks an interval in which deposition temporarily ceased and rocks already formed were eroded. On Arran, the older strata formed in some ancient sea had been buried deep in the crust, folded and recrystallized before being injected with quartz veins. Uplift and erosion eventually brought them to the surface where they formed the floor, upon which pebbly and sandy layers were deposited.

Hutton found additional evidence of relative age in the pebbly layers themselves, for the pebbles must have been made from some pre-existing rocks. The total series of events leading to the formation of a plane of unconformity obviously may occupy a very long period of time.

Layers of rock cannot themselves be considered as time planes. Nor for that matter can planes of unconformity. As the sea migrates over a land mass it may deposit similar material at each stage of its advance. These materials will not be of precisely the same age for they become younger as the sea spreads progressively over the land surface. Such deposits are termed *diachronous*, and are of only limited use in age correlation.

With these principles established, geologists began the task of building a chart of the relative ages of different rocks and areas of the earth. The law of superposition clearly had to be adjusted, however, where earth movement had occurred. For rocks may be folded and the strata then become inclined or vertical, or even over-turned. In such cases, the older rocks will rest upon the younger. It is then necessary to find ways of determining the original sequence of strata before the relative ages become clear.

Fortunately for the geologist, there are several types of evidence which point to the *way-up* in which rocks formed. Formation of sediments is a complex process involving deposition of fragments, chemical precipitation and the accumulation of organic debris. There are usually intermittent pauses in accumulation or even periods of erosion. One clue here is the ripple marks left by wind, wave or current action on the top of sediment. Traces of animals having bored or burrowed into the sediment while still in its soft state or even after it has been consolidated, may indicate what was then the surface. Any of these aspects of sediment formation can lead to preservation of evidence of 'way-up'.

The geologic column

Using the law of superposition, the fossils found in the rocks and the evidence of 'way-up', the sequence of layered rocks may be described and world-wide correlations made. Placing the rocks in order according to their relative ages makes it possible to construct a scale or *geologic column*. Until recently it was conventional to recognize at the base a series of rocks without fossils, the *Archeozoic*, and a younger series with scanty evidence of life known as the *Proterozoic*.

Resting on these old rocks are the *Phanerozoic* rocks containing many fos-

Zefa

W. J. French

C. R. Roberts

Left: Geologists use a variety of clues to determine 'way-up'. (1) In cross bedding, thin layers are deposited obliquely to the main bedding surfaces. These layers are usually abruptly truncated at the top by succeeding beds. This feature is found in Zion National Park, USA (above left) (2) Graded bedding may be a clue, where coarser deposits collect at the bottom. (3) Wash-outs occur where channels have been cut into older sediments, and then filled with sandy layers, leaving a record of the original 'way-up'. (4) Falling boulders form depressions in the upper surface of beds and (5) sand will fill surface cracks in drying clay.

Above left: Horizontal strata are usually no problem to the geologist interested in their relative ages. Using the law of superposition, he can assume that the younger rocks are at the top. The layers shown of light limestone and dark shales represent a few million years, only a relatively short span in earth's history.

1 CROSS BEDDING

erosion surfaces

truncated bedding plane

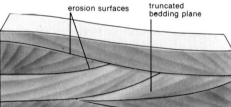

2 GRADED BEDDING

silt and mud towards top

pebbles and sand at base

3 WASH-OUT

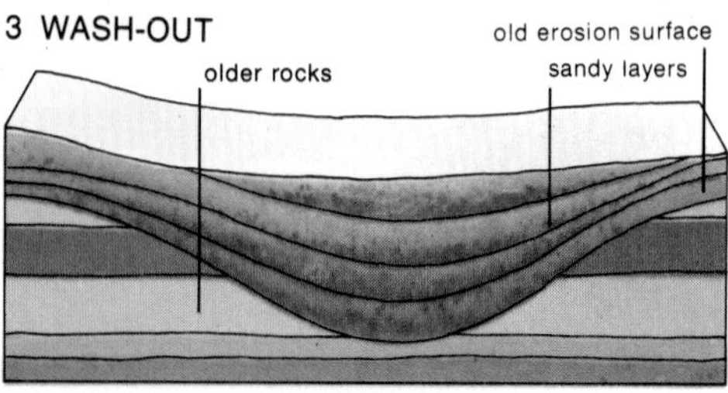

4 SURFACE DEPRESSION

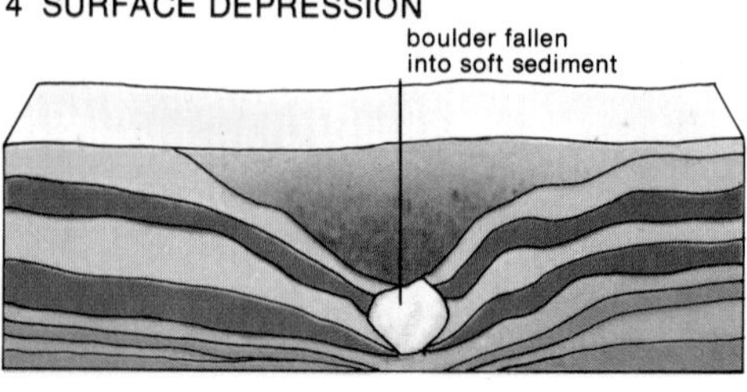

5 DESSICATION CRACKS

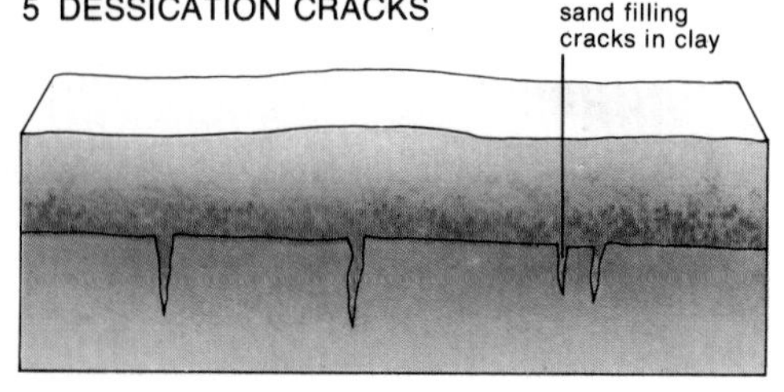

sils. So much detailed evidence is available from these beds that they have been divided into numerous rock *systems*, each formed in a specific geological *period*. The oldest belong to the *Cambrian* system, all older rocks are therefore collectively termed the *Pre-Cambrian*.

Most of the Phanerozoic systems and periods were worked out during the nineteenth century. The recognition of the systems took place in different regions and some of the names, such as Devonian, Permian and Jurassic, reflect these localities. Even today geologists continue to argue over the precise boundaries between the systems and the detailed correlations of rocks from one area to another. In the early days, definition was usually based on some strongly marked break in the rock sequence, such as an unconformity. However, where in one area there is an unconformity, in another area of the same age there may be successive strata undisturbed. Boundaries are therefore today based on detailed fossil lists and correlations.

Towards an appreciation of time

The work of Hutton and others allowed later geologists to grasp one concept of time—that of *sequence*, or the order of geological events. The other use of time is as a measure of *duration*—the length of time an event continues. At first there were few facts, but the evidence indicated that it had taken a very long time for the earth processes of erosion, deposition and uplift to occur.

Serious efforts to calculate the length of geologic time began in the late nineteenth century. The data gathered for the fossil record from the Phanerozoic led to attempts to estimate the age of the rocks from the number of evolutionary stages shown by the fossils. In 1867, Sir Charles Lyell (1797-1875), a friend of evolutionist Charles Darwin, decided by this means that the *Tertiary* period was 80 times as long as the *Quaternary*. Guessing one million years for the Quaternary gave 80 million years for the Tertiary and put the age of the Phanerozoic as a whole at 240 million years. Later studies of fossil horses again indicated that the Tertiary was about 80 times as long as the Quaternary. These figures, based on so many dubious assumptions, have little value, but the recognition of the origin, development and extinction of so many fossil forms testifies to the immensity of geologic time in relation to historic time.

Hutton's dictum that 'the present is the key to the past' leads to other ways of estimating age. Some geologists thought that if they found the rate at which sediment accumulates today and the total thickness of sediment formed throughout Phanerozoic time, they would have a simple method of assessing age. Obtaining these figures, however, is fraught with difficulty. Rates of sedimentation vary tremendously from place to place and the maximum thickness of sediment in each period is difficult to assess.

Another calculation giving an indication of the magnitude of time was first made by an Irish geologist John Joly (1852-1933). He calculated the minimum age of the oceans to be 90 million years by measuring the total amount of salt in the seas and its rate of accumulation.

Kelvin and the age of the earth

One of the great physicists of the nine-

C. R. Roberts

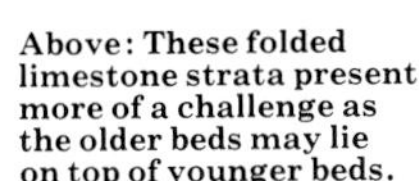

Jacana

Above: These folded limestone strata present more of a challenge as the older beds may lie on top of younger beds.

Left: Trace fossils are valuable as a means of determining 'way-up'. Animal bores or burrows and trails indicate the position of the surface of sediment when the animals were active.

Below left: The Petrified National Forest Park, USA, has a vivid example of strata to be found on a large scale in their original sequence of deposition. Here the beds of shales, marls and sandstones have been eroded over millions of years to reveal a wide range of bright colours, earning the area the name of Painted Desert.

Above: When strata occur vertically, as here in New Zealand, it is not immediately evident which rocks are older. Once 'way-up' has been discovered, age correlations can be made with rock systems throughout the world. These stratified rocks are of Jurassic age, a period of widespread deposition.

Bruce Coleman

teenth century, Lord Kelvin (1824-1907), sparked off a controversy by making three calculations, each indicating that the age of the earth was probably less than 100 million years and most likely about 30 million. Kelvin obtained his maximum age from studies of the rate of the earth's rotation and of the amount of heat given out by the sun.

For his more exact calculation, Kelvin assumed that if the earth began as a molten globe, the length of time required to cool to the present temperature could be obtained. Making the most reasonable assumption for the temperature at which crust would begin to form, the age of the earth was calculated to be about 30 million years. These results caused confusion and argument for a few years until another physical discovery proved them wrong.

Kelvin himself pointed out that the supposed cooling history of the earth depended on there being no other source for the generation of heat. The discovery in 1895 of radioactivity gave such a mechanism and quickly led to an explanation for the long period without notable change in the temperature of the crust. The decay of radioactive atoms involves the emission of radiation; the absorption of this radiation by the rocks liberates heat.

The discovery of this process of radioactive decay now also provides the method for measuring the age of rock beds by direct, rather than relative, means. Its discovery eventually resolved the long and bitter argument over geological history. The earth was shown to be not millions, but thousands of millions, of years old.

GEOLOGICAL TIME SCALE
showing the Geologic Column with explanations of the names used
(dates indicate numbers of million years ago)

	ERA	PERIOD of time / SYSTEM of rocks	EPOCH of time / SERIES of rocks	
PHANEROZOIC obvious life	CAINOZOIC recent life	QUARTERNARY an addition to the old tripartite 18th Century classification	RECENT	
			PLEISTOCENE most recent	2
		TERTIARY third from the 18th Century classification	PLIOCENE very recent	7
			MIOCENE moderately recent	26
			OLIGOCENE slightly recent	38
			EOCENE dawn of recent	54
			PALAEOCENE early dawn of the recent	65
	MESOZOIC middle life	CRETACEOUS chalk		135
		JURASSIC Jura mountains in Europe		193
		TRIASSIC from the three-fold division of the period made at a locality in Germany		225
	PALAEOZOIC ancient life	PERMIAN from Permia province in Russia		280
		CARBONIFEROUS coal abundance	UPPER Pennsylvanian in USA	
			LOWER Mississippian in USA	345
		DEVONIAN Devonshire, England		395
		SILURIAN Silures, ancient British tribe		435
		ORDOVICIAN Ordovices, ancient British tribe		500
		CAMBRIAN Roman name for Wales		570
	PRE-CAMBRIAN	PROTEROZOIC		
		ARCHEAN		

The Age of the Earth

The longstanding argument about the age of the earth was finally resolved by a breakthrough in a field of science quite separate from geology. In 1895, Henri Becquerel, a French physicist, realized that a mysterious form of energy was given out by certain substances independently of any external action. What Becquerel had discovered was the energy released by the spontaneous disintegration of the atoms of certain substances, the *radioactive elements*, into atoms of a different, stable element.

The process by which an unstable element spontaneously breaks up to form a second element is called *radioactive decay*. From the moment they exist, all radioactive elements are subject to decay from one form, or *isotope*, to isotopes of other, stable elements. The isotopes of an element differ in the number of particles in their atomic nucleii. They are therefore labelled according to this number. For example, uranium has two important radioactive isotopes—U^{235} and U^{238}. These *parent* atoms change slowly to the *daughter* lead (Pb) isotopes Pb^{207} and Pb^{206} respectively.

Just ten years after Becquerel's discovery of radioactivity, the pioneer English nuclear physicist Ernest Rutherford suggested that radioactive minerals such as uranium could be used to date rocks. Although the spontaneous decay of an individual atom is unpredictable, the overall rate of decay of the large number of atoms of uranium, as in all radioactive material, is constant and can be measured. Knowledge of this constant and of the ratios of parent to daughter isotopes provides geologists with a 'clock'.

The half-life

The intervals of time involved are enormous. It is more meaningful to express the rate of decay as the *half-life*, the time required for half the atoms in a specimen to have changed to the daughter isotope. Uranium-235, for example, has a half-life of 713 million years. This means that if there were 1,600 atoms of U^{235} in a specimen at the start, after one half-life there will be 800 atoms of U^{235} and 800 of Pb^{207}. After the next half-life of 713 million years, 400 atoms of U^{235} will remain and 1,200 atoms of Pb^{207} will have formed. The process of disintegration is effectively infinite, for as the radioactive material declines in abundance, its decline becomes progressively slower. The proportion of lead formed from decay indicates the length of time since decay began, and thus the age of the mineral.

Early results from this method were unreliable. Difficulties existed in measuring the proportions of the minute amounts of the isotopes. The development in the 1950s of the *mass spectrometer*, a machine capable of isolating different isotopes, meant a vast improvement in precision. Today, the isotopic decays that are valuable in determining geologic age include not only uranium to lead, but also thorium to lead, rubidium to strontium, potassium to argon, and carbon to nitrogen.

RADIOCARBON DECAY

0 years – death of plant

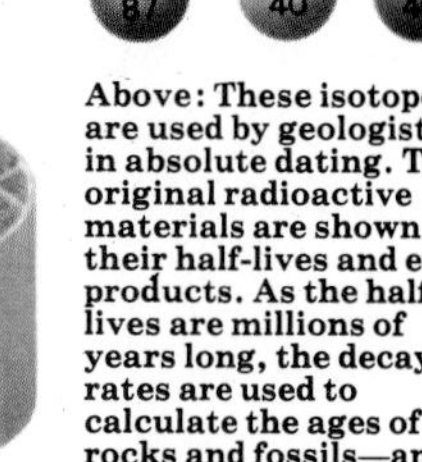

5,570 years – 50% remains

11,140 years – 25% remains

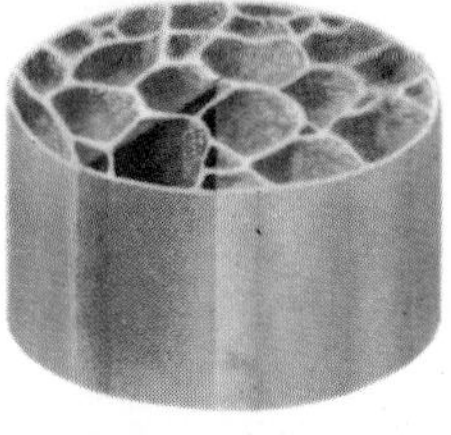

16,710 years – 12.5% remains

22,280 years 6.25% remains

55,700 years – 0.1% remains

Above: The rate at which radioactive carbon isotopes (C^{14}) decay to nitrogen isotopes (N^{14}) is shown here. All living plants and animals absorb radiocarbon from the atmosphere. This decay rate is known and the approximate time of death can be calculated by measuring the amount of C^{14} remaining in a specimen.

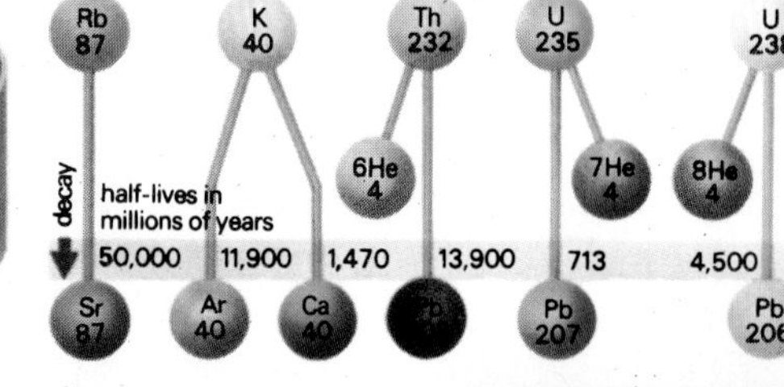
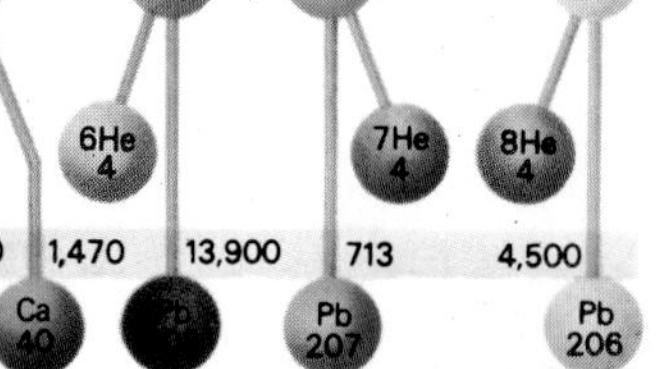

Above: These isotopes are used by geologists in absolute dating. The original radioactive materials are shown with their half-lives and end-products. As the half-lives are millions of years long, the decay rates are used to calculate the ages of rocks and fossils—and the earth's age, estimated to be 4,500 million years.

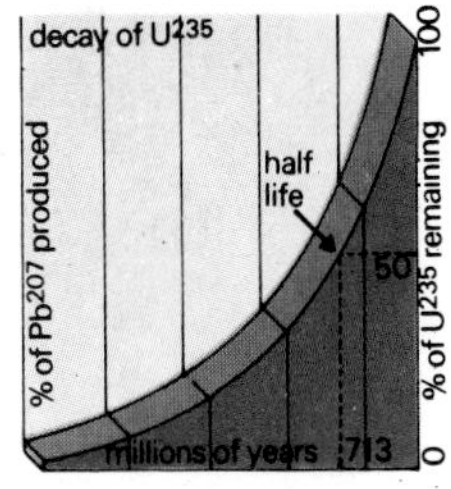

Above: Half-life decay follows the same curve, which can be plotted on a graph, for all radioactive materials. The curve remains constant although the rates vary considerably. Half the radioactive material decays quite early in the specimen's existence. The remainder decays by half again for each half-life period.

Right: The yearly growth of trees in spring is marked by a series of annual tree-rings in the wood. When counted these reveal the tree's age.

Below: The bristlecone pine, the world's oldest living thing, survives in the cold, dry White Mountains of California. Pines nearly 5,000 years old have been found.

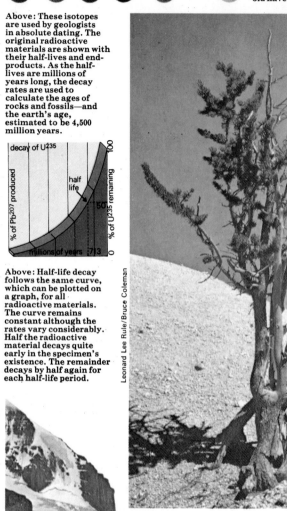

Leonard Lee Rule/Bruce Coleman

Robert Harding

Above right: The enormous Columbia ice fields in Jasper National Park in western Canada, an area where long sequences of glacial deposits allow a count going back thousands of years. Seasons of melting and freezing are clearly marked in the graded layers or varves (right) deposited in lake floors formed by melting ice.

Chaumeton/Jacana

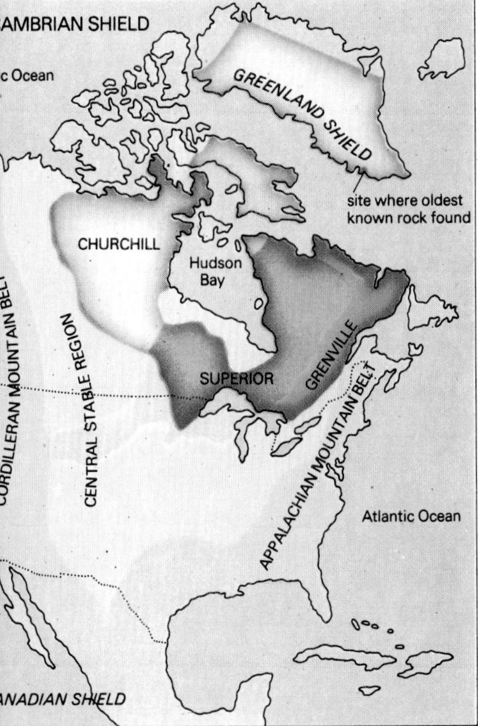

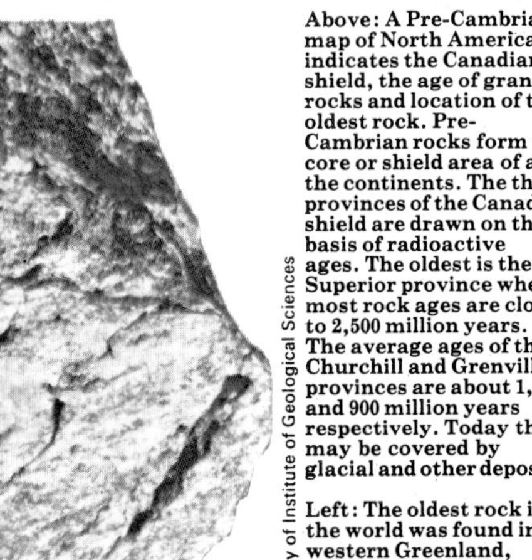

Above: A Pre-Cambrian map of North America indicates the Canadian shield, the age of granite rocks and location of the oldest rock. Pre-Cambrian rocks form the core or shield area of all the continents. The three provinces of the Canadian shield are drawn on the basis of radioactive ages. The oldest is the Superior province where most rock ages are close to 2,500 million years. The average ages of the Churchill and Grenville provinces are about 1,700 and 900 million years respectively. Today they may be covered by glacial and other deposits.

Left: The oldest rock in the world was found in western Greenland, where this amitsoq gneiss crystallized some 3,800 million years ago.

Courtesy of Institute of Geological Sciences

Two isotopes of uranium, U^{235} and U^{238}, occur in minerals. The rate of decay of U^{235} to Pb^{207} (with a half-life of 713 million years) is much greater than that for U^{238}, which slowly decays to Pb^{206} with a half-life of 4,500 million years. Since the two are found together in minerals, this permits geologists to make a third measurement of age by comparing the ratio of Pb^{207} and Pb^{206}.

The element thorium also produces lead—changing from its single natural isotope Th^{232} to Pb^{208} with a half-life of 13,900 million years. As with uranium decay, the disintegration of thorium releases helium gas. The best of these methods is U^{238} decay, for Pb^{206} makes up 95 per cent of the lead developed by radioactive decay or *radiogenically* and hence can be determined with the best precision.

Even in carefully controlled experiments, the ages determined by the three decay processes may be different. One correction often required, though usually small, arises from the presence of 'common lead' not produced by the decay being measured. Unless allowed for in the calculation, this will inflate the value of Pb^{206} and Pb^{207} and the age of the sample.

The ratio of the abundances of uranium isotopes can be used to estimate roughly the age of the earth. The result given is 5,400 million years. From the ratios of lead isotopes in certain minerals, the composition of lead existing at the origin of the earth can be calculated and this leads to another estimate of the earth's age. Early calculations gave around 4,000 million years but higher figures have been obtained more recently.

Certain meteorites, rock masses which have fallen to earth from space, contain a mineral known as troilite which is virtually uranium-free. Any lead they contain is considered to represent the original mix or ratio in the planetary system, a ratio frozen through time since their creation. Using this primaeval lead isotope ratio and applying it to terrestrial rocks gives an age for the earth of 4,500 million years. Intensive analysis of meteorites also revealed none older than 4,500 million years.

The ages of moon rocks given by uranium-lead and other methods range from 3,100 to 4,500 million years. Some lunar rocks have given slightly greater ages, but probably these result from special processes operating on the moon. In contrast, the oldest rock on earth found so far is about 3,800 million years old. The fact that maximum ages for the earth, moon and meteorites give the same date—4,500 million years—suggests to scientists that a major event occurred at that time throughout the solar system.

Finding the ages of rocks

The lead isotope methods have not proved very useful for dating crustal rocks. The elements are relatively rare, only a few minerals being suitable for analysis. These include zircon, monazite, sphene, uranite and pitchblende, the first substance to be analysed by Rutherford in 1904. Other techniques have been more widely used. The value of the rubidium-strontium method is that it can be applied to several common rock-forming minerals. The rubidium isotope Rb^{87} decays to strontium isotope Sr^{87} with a half-life of about 50,000 million years, giving useful age data for the oldest rocks including the oldest meteorites and moon rocks.

Paul Brierley

Above: This meteorite contains the virtually uranium-free mineral troilite. It offers scientists the chance to measure what is considered to be the 'primaeval' or original ratio of lead isotope Pb^{207} to Pb^{206}. Using this ratio gives a maximum age of 4,500 million years, the age of earth, for all meteorites.

Below: Information gathered from the face of the moon is immensely valuable in dating the rocks on earth. Moon rocks, which are as old as 4,500 million years, have escaped the weathering, erosion and transformation processes which occur on earth, where rocks older than 3,800 million years have probably all been lost.

Photri

This method is not so useful for younger rocks, but has provided valuable information on the source of igneous rocks, allowing a distinction to be made between igneous materials derived from the mantle and those from the crust. Extension of this idea has indicated to geologists the possibility that the crust has accumulated at a more or less consistent rate throughout geological time.

There are several factors that can cause dates derived from radioactive dating methods to be incorrect. On one hand, for example, the unnoticed presence of a 'common' or original isotope has exaggerated the findings. On the other, the escape of daughter elements may reset the 'clock' to zero or reduce the ages given. Argon is the gas given off in small amounts by decay of potassium isotope K^{40}, which has a half-life of 11,900 million years. The meaningfulness of results from this method is limited because the gaseous argon isotope Ar^{40} can be lost in some later, perhaps mild, heating of the rock. However, using carefully chosen materials, this method has yielded good results, and is applicable to a wide range of rocks and minerals containing sufficient potassium.

The long half-lives of all these radioactive elements restrict their use in dating to the distant past. This is exactly the period of the earth's history, however, about which relative dating methods can reveal little because of the lack of fossils. Pre-Cambrian rocks in which fossil evidence is rare form the cores of the continents, the so-called *shield areas.* Thousands of age determinations have been made, revealing provinces which are distinct in space and time. The Canadian shield, for example, contains three such provinces—Superior, Churchill and Grenville. Each is essentially the product of a cycle of sedimentation, volcanism, folding, metamorphism and igneous intrusion, and each took several hundred million years to complete. Provinces of comparable ages have been located on other continents, and geological maps drawn up which reveal the ancient history of the land masses.

In general, the most reliable radioactive dates are obtained from igneous and metamorphic rocks, in which the mineral crystallization provides a relatively sharp starting point in time.

Dating the recent past

For younger dates, much use has been made of the *radiocarbon* method, which measures the decay of carbon to nitrogen. All living plants and animals absorb the carbon isotope C^{14} in the form of carbon dioxide in their food cycles. The amount in organic bodies is the same as the small fixed proportion in the atmosphere, and remains constant through the life of the plant or animal. But when an organism dies, the intake of carbon ceases and the C^{14} slowly decays to nitrogen isotope N^{14}, starting a radioactive decay clock which can be applied to wood, peat, shells and certain limestones and bone materials.

The results can be subject to serious error. Contamination from other forms of carbon can upset the clock, and great care has to be exercised. One assumption which is basic to this method is that the concentration of C^{14} in the atmosphere, and thus in plants and animals, has remained constant through geological time. This assumption is now being questioned and corrections to some early radiocarbon dates have been made using age correlations with tree-ring dating.

Long-living trees like the bristlecone pine, found in California, Utah and Nevada in the United States, provide in their annual growth rings a precise method of dating for the last 8,000 years or so. Dates obtained by radiocarbon methods have been revised or *calibrated* both by tree-ring dating and by the yearly cycle of deposits left by melting ice. These deposits, called *varves*, mark the seasonal melting and freezing of ice as recorded in the debris deposited in lakes left behind by retreating ice sheets. The glaciers of the last ice age, in Scandinavia, for example, have created a time sequence of varves stretching back some 11,000 years.

One major contribution of radioactive methods has been to date the eras and periods included in the Geologic Column. This time-scale was constructed in the 19th century by correlating rock strata and fossil evidence, without any real idea of the dates of major earth events. Disputes as to the age of the earth are now substantially resolved and agreement exists that the earth's crust was created about 4,500 million years ago.

Man appears as no more than an afterthought, with an abruptly short record of existence. It has been calculated that if one thinks of the entire history of the earth as having occurred in one year, the first known living things would have appeared about 240 days before the end of the year. Early man would have appeared some 5 hours before the end of the very last day, and modern man some five minutes before midnight.

A RECORD OF LIFE ON EARTH

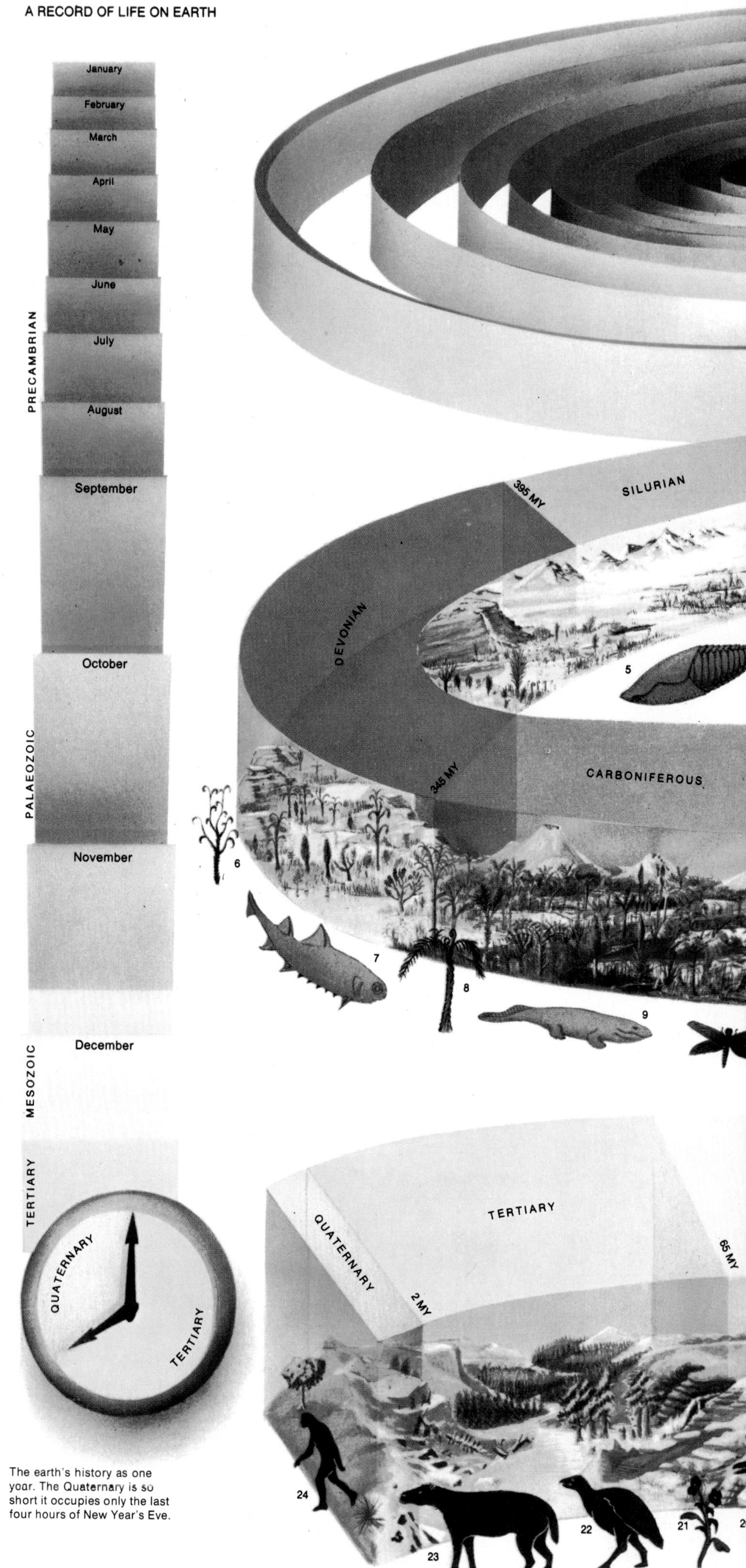

The earth's history as one year. The Quaternary is so short it occupies only the last four hours of New Year's Eve.

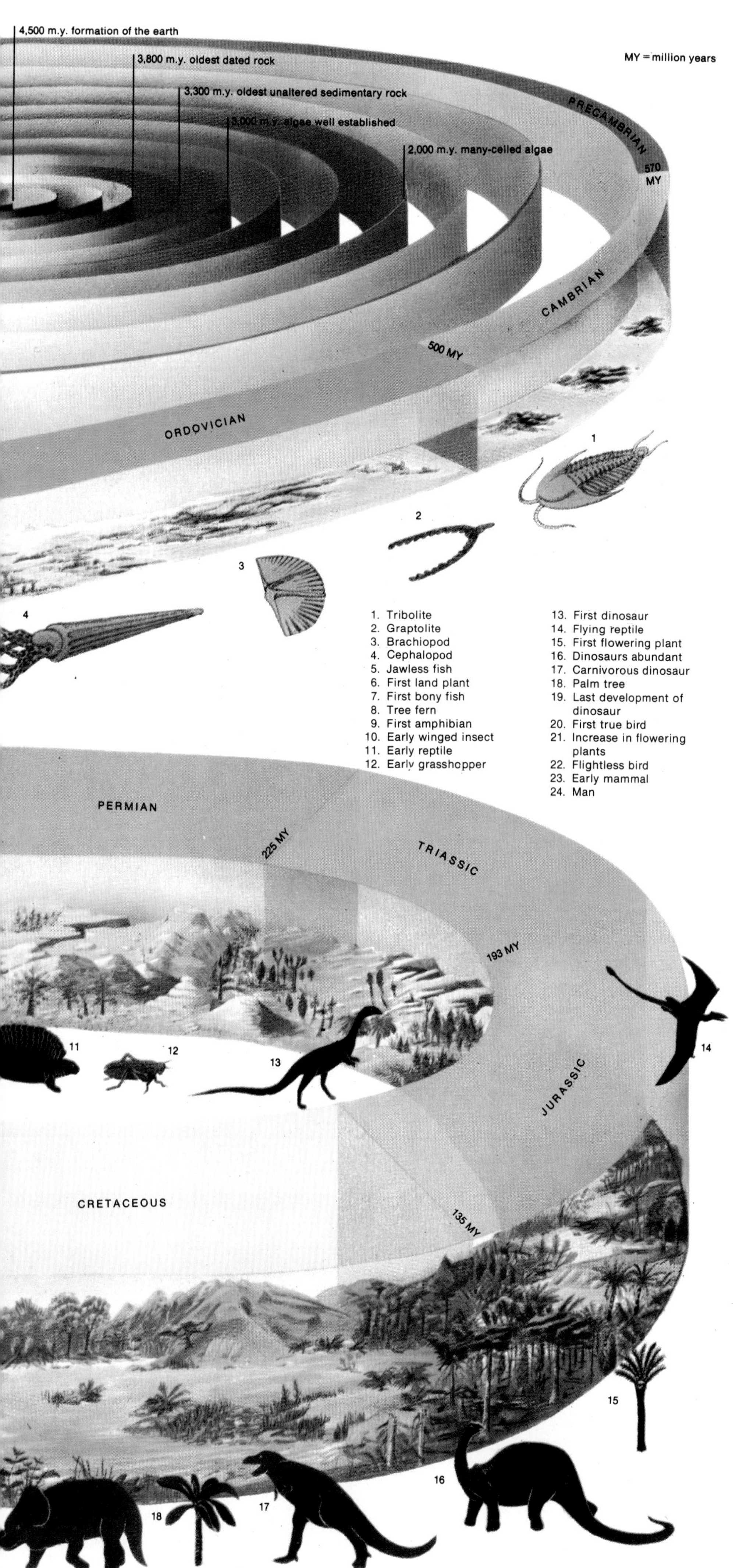

PRE-CAMBRIAN
The greatest part of geological time is represented by the Pre-Cambrian. The crust, land masses and seas formed and great volcanic activity occurred. Pre-Cambrian rocks form shield areas of all the continents. Traces of life are generally rare.

CAMBRIAN
The transition to the Cambrian is notable for the sudden appearance of abundant fossils. This marks the beginning of the Palaeozoic (ancient life) era. In the widespread shallow seas, early marine life proliferated. Tribolites were particularly common.

ORDOVICIAN
Much of the earth enjoyed a mild climate and seas still covered most of the surface. There was continuing sedimentation and important mountain-building occurred. Reef-building algae were notable and corals, sponges and molluscs such as cephalopods abundant.

SILURIAN
A dramatic development in earth's history came with the evolution of jawless fish, the first vertebrates (animals with backbones), which first appeared in the Ordovician. The late Silurian saw another important step — the growth of the first land plants.

DEVONIAN
Mountain-building movements reached a peak early in the Devonian but this was notably a period of explosive evolution. Land was colonized by the earliest seed plants. Fish grew in variety and size and the first land creatures — amphibians — evolved.

CARBONIFEROUS
Mountain building, folding and erosion continued. Richly forested swamps and deltas in North America and Europe were submerged and formed large coal measures. Extensive glaciation gripped the southern continents. Insects thrived. The first reptiles appeared.

PERMIAN
Desert conditions prevailed over much of Panagaea, the giant land mass made from all the drifting continents. The reptiles spread widely and modern insects evolved. Several marine creatures became extinct but new land flora, including conifers, developed.

TRIASSIC
As the Mesozoic era opened, Pangaea began breaking up. On land conifers became the dominant plants. This was a period of great diversity among the reptiles and the first dinosaurs and giant marine reptiles appeared. Small primitive mammals also evolved.

JURASSIC
Considerable volcanic activity was associated with the opening of the Atlantic Ocean. On land the dinosaurs reigned supreme and the air was first conquered by flying reptiles and later by primitive birds. There are traces of the earliest flowering plants.

CRETACEOUS
During the maximum extension of the seas of the world, great deposits of chalk formed in Britain. Dinosaurs remained dominant until they and many large reptiles became extinct at the end of the period. First true birds and early mammals became numerous.

TERTIARY
The opening of the Cainozoic (recent life) era heralded an explosive growth of mammals. Many large species evolved but some died out. Flowering plants increased rapidly and as climates later cooled grasslands appeared. Considerable uplift of land occurred.

QUATERNARY
This, the latest geological period, continues up to and including the present day. It is marked by climatic changes in which four major ice ages alternated with warmer intervals. Mammals increased and adapted and man evolved to dominate the earth.

Ancient Environments

Creating an image of the Earth's surface as it looked in the past requires information from all the many branches of geology. Occasionally, there is sufficient information to create a relatively clear picture and sometimes the evidence can be closely compared with present-day occurrences, all of which make it easier to envisage the environment of the past. Tlere are, however, some ancient environments which seem to bear no relation to the present, such as the Pre-Cambrian ironstone-forming lakes and the Cretaceous chalk-forming seas.

Some evidence can be read directly from the rocks. Volcanic bombs, for example, indicate the existence of an explosive volcano. Other evidence has to be read indirectly. Tracing the source of a particle in a sedimentary rock could give information on the nature of mountains and hills adjacent to the area of deposition. Indeed it is vital that the many lines of evidence should tell a consistent story and fit in to the overall picture.

Strictly, any image of an ancient environment can never be proved conclusively as the evidence can never be complete. In sediments the record provided by fossils is inevitably biased by the decay of soft-bodied organisms, such as marine worms, though they sometimes leave trace fossils as evidence of their activities. In addition, there may be a distortion or obliteration of the sedimentary record by later events such as earth movements, metamorphic or igneous activity, and erosion.

Despite these limitations, geologists have been able to make considerable advances in reconstructing ancient environments. As in any story of detection, the investigator relies on recognizable evidence which he must carefully select from a wealth of potential clues. Hutton's long-established geological axiom that 'the present is the key to the past' plays an important role, provided it is used cautiously.

On present-day coastal mud and sand flats, for example, it is possible to see features such as ripple marks, scour depressions and sun cracks forming. It is logical to assume that a similar environment and origin existed in the past if these features are found in old mudstones and sandstones. But if tree trunks, branches and twigs are found in the beds instead of marine shells then the deposits are more likely to be associated with an inland river system than a coastal flat.

Evidence from sea and land

Among the great variety of sediments some are more easily determined as marine beds than others. For instance, a collection of unworn, in-place fossil shells and algae resembling modern marine organisms in their morphology and ecology is usually taken as adequate evidence that the containing rock is marine. Certainly, a limestone body carrying a very rich fauna and flora of limey or *calcareous* corals, polyzoans and algae would be taken to be of marine origin. At present, extensive reef growth is

Left: Ripple marks are the undulations produced by the movement of water over sediments. They are not confined to marine conditions, and the information they give is substantial. Their size and shape indicate the speed of water across tidal flats or beaches. The orientation of the crests can often help in determining the approximate alignment of the nearby coastline or beach. This sample is a cast, formed when a layer of sediment was deposited on a lower bed in which traces of ripple marks and raindrops were sharp enough to leave imprints.

Below: Ripples forming on a present-day sandy beach exposed at low tide.

Right: The abundance of these relatively thin-shelled molluscs from Lincolnshire indicates marine conditions there in the Jurassic period. The ironstone rock, coloured brown in parts from weathering, is formed of *chamosite* and *siderite* minerals, which are normally widely precipitated in marine environments. The climate is not indicated directly, but the presence of the minerals commonly suggests fairly warm currents.

Below: Fossil coral from Derbyshire. The presence of dense patches of coral in these very poorly bedded Carboniferous layers suggests clear, shallow seas—conditions required for coral reefs.

Dr. John S. Shelton

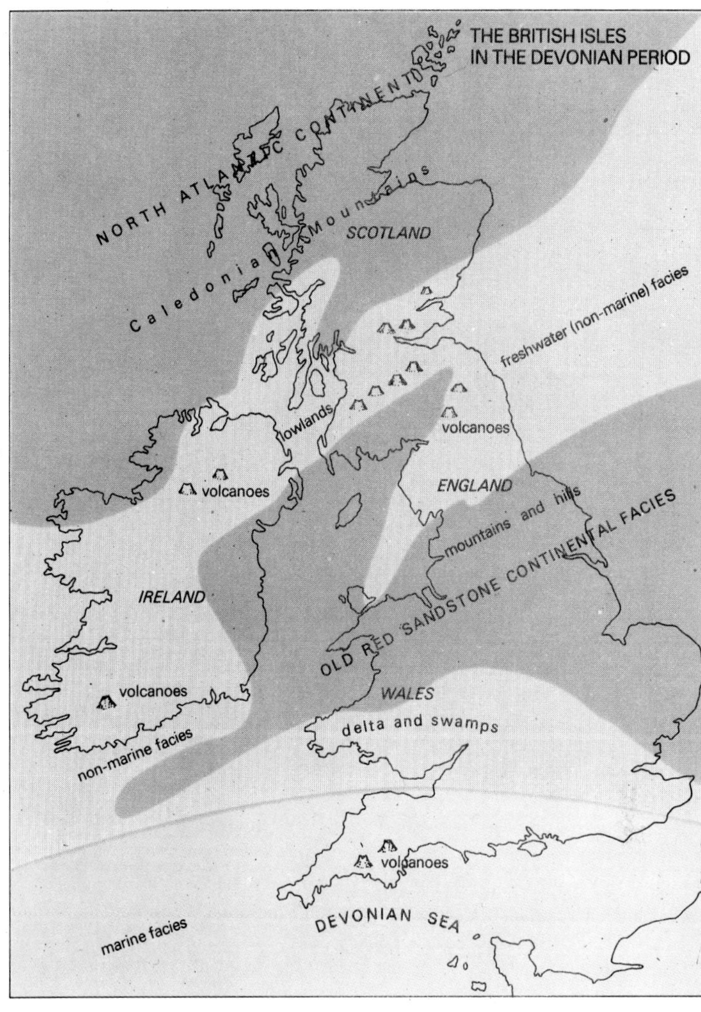

Right: This map of the British Isles shows the environment in the Devonian period, about 375 million years ago. Freshwater deltas and swamps surrounded the hilly sandstone area covering much of the present-day Midlands. Northern Scotland was part of another large land mass.

Left: Mudcracks are formed by compression and drying, and usually indicate exposure of a lake or stream floor to the air.

Below: This freshwater plant debris has been carried by silt and sand-laden water from its position of growth. The distance was not far as the leaves are relatively unworn. This is evidence of terrestrial conditions.

Jacana

only possible in particular ecological circumstances which include relatively clear and shallow sea waters and warm currents. These requirements appear to have remained comparatively stable throughout large periods of geological time. Reef-building calcareous algae are known from late Pre-Cambrian times onwards, but reef corals have become important since Ordovician times. The suggestion is that those northern regions must have been located in much warmer latitudes with coral reefs. Continental drift explains how this occurred.

A different style of marine deposition, on a muddy sea floor, is indicated by a shale or clay carrying a marine fauna. Unfortunately, these kinds of rock rarely give evidence of how near they were to land, nor the depth of the water.

In general, fossil preservation on land is poor. Ancient non-marine or *terrestrial* deposits, such as were laid down in deserts, lakes, rivers and deltas, are more likely to be deficient in fossils than the bulk of marine deposits. This is because processes of weathering and biodegradation actually have a much more persistent effect on land than in seas and oceans. Major exceptions to this scarcity of fossils are found in plant-rich beds and certain fish and bone beds. A prime example is the extensive development of coal seams in Carboniferous and Tertiary deltas throughout the world. These seams represent the mass accumulation of land plant debris in marshy environments.

A lack of fossils alone is not sufficient evidence to suggest a non-marine origin. This is particularly true of deposits from Pre-Cambrian times when few organisms with hard skeletal parts had evolved. Plants only began to adapt from a marine environment and colonize land areas in the Devonian period. For these and earlier periods, other techniques may have to be employed alone.

A characteristic property of clay minerals is the inclusion of certain elements such as boron in their crystal structures. Measuring the distribution of these *trace elements* provides a promising new technique which has shown, for example, that the proportion of very small amounts of boron is relatively high in some marine clay-rich deposits and relatively low in freshwater ones.

Ancient climates

Other techniques include analysis of soil varieties. Soils can be surprisingly well-preserved considering that they consist of an easily-eroded mixture of clay, carbonate and iron minerals. When they do survive, it is commonly as a consequence of land subsidence followed by gentle inundation either by river flood water or, in some instances, by sea water. The old soils found beneath many coal seams typify this style of preservation.

A more rapid form of preservation is burial under volcanic lava. For example, the upper surface of Carboniferous basalt lava flows in the Midland Valley of Scotland and Tertiary flows in Antrim in Northern Ireland were frequently exposed long enough for bauxitic and lateritic soils to develop prior to very rapid burial by the next flood of lava.

Laterites and bauxites in ancient successions provide fascinating information about the climate of the times. It is likely that they formed under wet sub-tropical conditions, as they do today. Other soils from the same area but of different age can be equally informative. In the Devonian rocks of northern Europe, including those in the Midland Valley of Scotland, there are certain varieties, known as *cornstones*, which are mostly carbonate-rich soils similar to those forming on the Russian steppes at present. These cornstones prove that a semi-arid, hot environment prevailed in Scotland over 50 million years before sub-tropical conditions.

The colour of some rock beds can also suggest an ancient environment. A red colour, caused by the iron oxide haematite, often pervades thicknesses of many metres of strata, including lava flows of comparable age, and may extend over vast regions. The creation of these rocks required oxidizing conditions over millions of years and could only be sustained on land areas subject to persistent semi-arid, and occasionally arid, climatic conditions. This deduction is supported by other evidence.

The lines of geological reasoning used to capture an image of ancient cold polar environments are basically no different from those adopted for deducing hotter climatic conditions. The distribution of animals and plants has to be assessed. Water temperature can be indicated in what are assumed to be the marine parts of sedimentary successions by oxygen isotope analysis of calcareous shells.

Areas once covered in great thicknesses of ice are revealed by such clues as boulder clay deposits and scratch marks on rock surfaces. Strong evidence for the

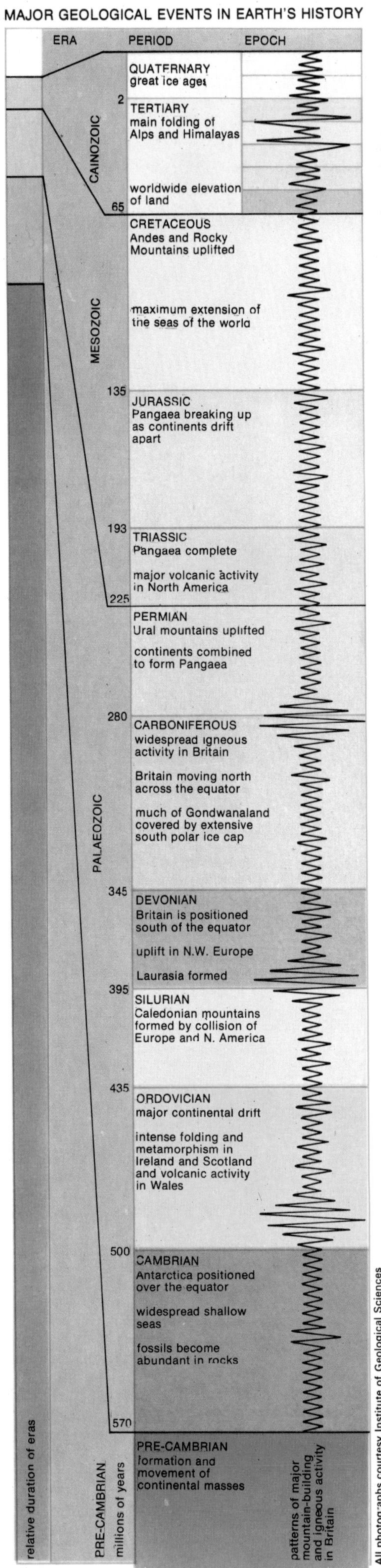

THE EDEN VALLEY THROUGH TIME

From Pre-Cambrian times until late in the Mesozoic era, what is now the British Isles lay near the heart of Pangaea, the super-continent composed of all the land masses. After the break-up of Pangaea, north-west Europe and Britain drifted over the changing earth's surface to reach their present position. These artist's reconstructions based on geological finds show the changes to one place—the Eden Valley in England's Lake District.

ORDOVICIAN PERIOD
Above: About 450 million years ago, the Eden Valley was the site of an open sea. The marine conditions are evident in the mud and sandstones deposited in the deeper parts of the sea. The growth of originally submarine volcanoes spread a considerable amount of debris into the adjacent seas. As the seas became shallower, the volcanoes eventually burst above the water level. The development of layers of volcanic ash and bombs, covering large areas at one time, is useful for correlation purposes. Many volcanoes were arranged in narrow zones. Much of the grand scenery of today's Lake District is a relic of this great period of volcanic activity. A long series of explosions poured out lavas and ashes to a thickness of many thousands of metres. Later, a shallow sea spread over the area, depositing in-shore sediments. The sea was probably warm at the time because there are rich deposits of organisms, such as crustaceans, molluscs and sea-urchins.

All photographs courtesy Institute of Geological Sciences

PERMIAN PERIOD
Left: 50 million years after the swampy Carboniferous, the Eden Valley was a hot desert. The contrast is illustrated clearly in the artist's reconstruction. Geologists have discovered several sources of evidence of the arid or semi-arid terrestrial conditions. For example, the process of oxidizing, when minerals react with oxygen, occurs on dry land. The record of this process is found in the weathered rocks in the background, whose red and brown colours indicate oxidizing conditions. The boulders, pebbles and sand produced by weathering occupy the middle and foreground. The sand dunes have wind-rippled surfaces and their shape indicates that prevailing wind probably blew from left to right at the time. Fossils generally are not well-preserved in terrestrial conditions, but the rocks from this period have a notable lack of fossils, suggesting that life in the Permian was minimal.

PLEISTOCENE TIMES
Below: One million years ago, the British Isles were in the grip of a great ice age. The painting shows how a record of glaciation was left behind. Glacial deposits and erratic boulders (transported by moving ice) are strewn over the denuded landscape. Boulders frozen into the underside of the ice left scratches on the rock surface, indicating the direction of ice-sheet movement.

CARBONIFEROUS PERIOD
Left: The Eden Valley of 300 million years ago was a tropical or subtropical swamp. The overall lack of red colours in the soil (instead greys, blacks and browns predominate) is evidence of wet conditions. Lush vegetation thrived in low-lying alluvial areas along valley bottoms and, closer to sea, between delta distributaries. In these complex, fertile soils, freshwater plants grew. As the plants died, they fell onto the forest floors or into the swamps, to accumulate as peat. At times of rapid subsidence, submergence of this area by fresh or salt water buried the plants beneath mud and sand. The beds of peat were compacted to form seams of coal, from which geologists have been able to identify the original plants. Giant club-mosses, tree-ferns and horse-tail plants thrived in the moist, mild, humid climate. The *Lepidodendron* and *Sigillaria* trees grew to a height of 30 metres. While the Eden Valley enjoyed an equatorial climate, much of the southern continents that then made up Gondwanaland lay around the South Pole and were covered in extensive ice-sheets.

THE PRESENT DAY
Right: The Eden Valley as it appears today. Clearly the interpreting and reconstruction of ancient environments is a slow process requiring the sorting and detailed examination of a variety of evidence.

theory of continental drift has been collected by proving that during the Permo-Carboniferous age, ice sheets covered parts of the modern warm temperature zones in South America, South Africa, India and Australia.

Creating a picture of the past

Putting together the jig-saw of evidence to build a picture of an ancient environment begins with the fine details of rocks. Once these are pieced together, the groups of related, interbedded rocks on a larger scale are examined until, finally, the extent of their distribution over very large regions can be considered.

For this broad environmental picture it is important to ensure that the rocks are of the same age. The age-equivalence, or *correlation*, of rocks is most reliable with beds laid down under uniform marine conditions. The Cretaceous Chalk series in Britain is a good example of this, although there is not a great deal of evidence to indicate that the depths of seas were uniform. However, towards Scotland the Chalk series becomes more sandy, probably indicating the nearness of land. This change is known as a facies change. The term *facies* encompasses all the physical, chemical and biological properties shown by a single bed or group of beds.

The correlation of different marine facies can be troublesome if certain of the rocks lack fossils. But the greatest problems arise when correlating marine and terrestrial facies. It is possible to radiogenically date volcanic ash which, by chance, may fall on both the land and in the sea. This would establish a reference level, yet such ash falls are rare.

Facies changes in rocks are usually deduced by tracing the rocks of comparable age from one area to another. The succession of rocks in Britain from the Devonian age illuminates quite well the lessons learnt from the long-established principles of correlation. Because of the presence of such fossils as cephalopods, trilobites and brachiopods, the Devonian succession of south-west England appears to be predominantly marine in origin.

The mixed successions represent sand and mud laid down in shallow, turbid seas with occasional shallows of clearer water where reefs grew. Submarine volcanoes were also active. As the marine facies is traced northwards towards Wales, marine fossils become scarce and the rocks become thickly bedded, and sometimes red-coloured sandstones and siltstones occur, with many features typical of coastal deposition.

In the Welsh borderland, and indeed as far north as the Orkney Islands of Scotland, rocks believed to be of the same age are called the Old Red Sandstone facies. There is no doubt of their land origin as they are extensively red-coloured, contain land plant beds, calcareous soils, river and lake deposits, and are associated with volcanic larvas and ashes, and weathered by terrestrial conditions. The overall picture is of a northern land mass, semi-arid and volcanic in nature. It was sparsely vegetated except near spasmodic water-courses, which contained a few fish. This land mass abutted a rather shallow, turbid sea supporting relatively little life except in clearer water where reef faunas could proliferate.

The Fossil Record

The term *fossil* originally referred to any object dug from the ground, but its use is now limited to the remains of once-living animals and plants. Although the study of the fossil record often seems of distant relevance to the practicalities of modern life, it does in fact have great importance. One outstanding example is the use of fossil evidence by geologists in their search for sources of fuel. Most importantly, however, its study provides us with a fascinating glimpse of the colourful assortment of life on earth during its long history. 'Glimpse' is, unfortunately, the most appropriate word, for the fossil record is far from complete and much of the existing record remains poorly explored by *palaeontologists*, the scientists who study fossils.

The fossil record depends on how much has survived the ravages of time. Only the hard parts, such as the bones and shells of animals, the tree trunks or leaf cuticle of plants, are normally preserved in the rocks. Consequently, information about the function of the hard and soft parts has to be deduced from the skeletal remains.

Completely soft-bodied animals usually leave little or no direct evidence of their former existence. However, certain 'freak' sediments, such as the Burgess Shale (Cambrian) of British Columbia, preserve such creatures and give a fleeting impression of the real diversity of life hundreds of millions of years ago. In addition, many animals burrowed into sediment, or briefly rested on it, or bored into a hard sea floor. The traces of these activities are preserved surprisingly often as *trace fossils*.

Even fossil excreta are found and can sometimes be attributed to a particular kind of animal living long ago. Evidence of damage during life, or of disease, are also often visible. Palaeontologists have found such examples as ammonites that have patched up tears in their shell and dinosaurs that suffered rheumatoid arthritis.

The fossil record is biased towards the marine realm because the seas and oceans have always been the main area of deposition of sediment. Because land areas are essentially regions of weathering and erosion, even those animals with backbones, the *vertebrates*, may have been poorly preserved on land. The remains of many vertebrates—amphibians, reptiles, mammals and many birds—are rare except at certain limited geological levels or *horizons* where non-marine deposits have been preserved.

Fossils can provide an immense amount of information. Historically, it is their role in the correlation of rock strata that was first appreciated, but they are also used in the interpretation of past environments, in studying the rates, processes and paths of evolution, and in testing alternative models of plate movement and continental drift. The correlation of rocks by the fossils they contain—a key principle in *stratigraphy*, the study of rock strata—reflects the evolution of life through time. The stratigrapher collects

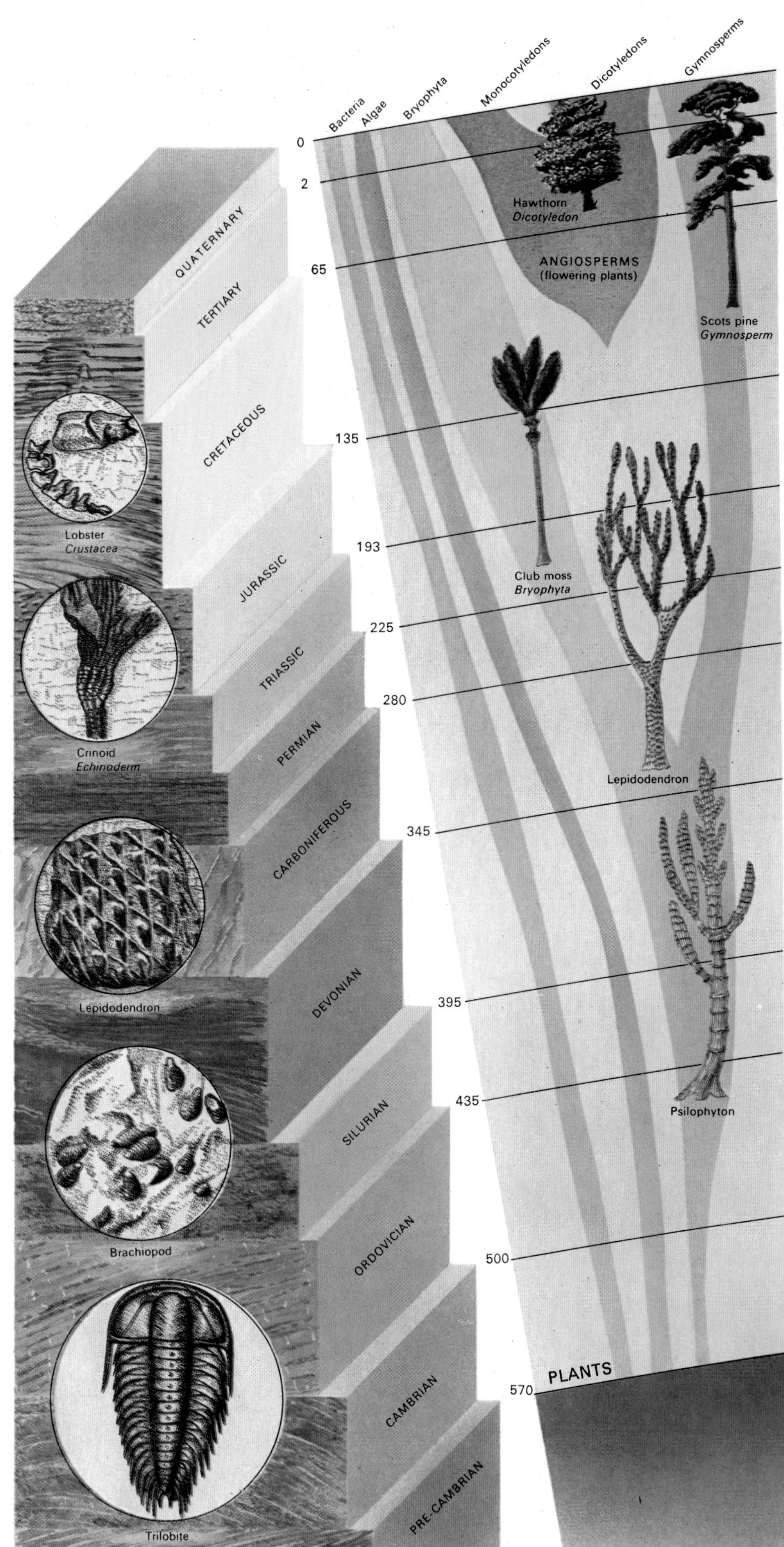

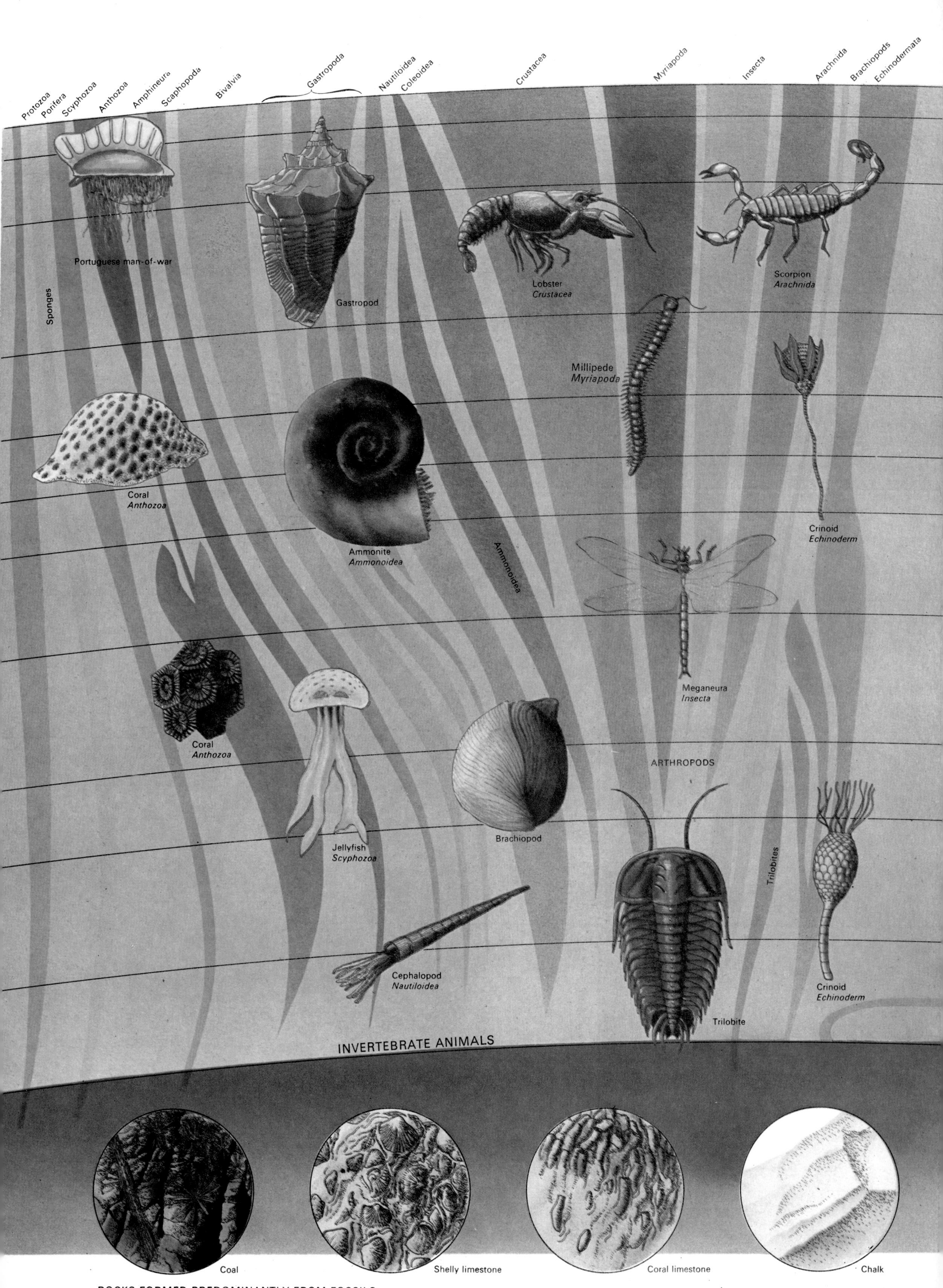

Protozoa
Porifera
Scyphozoa
Anthozoa
Amphineura
Scaphopoda
Bivalvia
Gastropoda
Nautiloidea
Coleoidea
Crustacea
Myriapoda
Insecta
Arachnida
Brachiopods
Echinodermata
Portuguese man-of-war
Sponges
Gastropod
Lobster
Crustacea
Scorpion
Arachnida
Millipede
Myriapoda
Coral
Anthozoa
Ammonite
Ammonoidea
Ammonoidea
Crinoid
Echinoderm
Meganeura
Insecta
Coral
Anthozoa
ARTHROPODS
Jellyfish
Scyphozoa
Brachiopod
Trilobites
Cephalopod
Nautiloidea
Crinoid
Echinoderm
Trilobite
INVERTEBRATE ANIMALS
Coal
Shelly limestone
Coral limestone
Chalk

ROCKS FORMED PREDOMINANTLY FROM FOSSILS

Hemichordata
Urochordata
Cephalochordata
Cyclostomes
Elasmobranchs
Cephalochordata
Teleosts
Crossopterygii
Lung fishes
Urodeles
Apoda
Anura
Chelonia
Crocodilia
Ophidia
Aves
Acorn worms
Herring
Teleost
Newts
Legless lizards
Turtles
Snakes
Lizards
Birds
Archaeopteryx
Aves
Rays
Sharks
Bony fishes
Turtle
Chelonia
Acorn worm
Coelacanth
Crossopterygii
Ornithopods
Theropods
Sauropoda
Icthyosauria
Holosteans
Chondrosteans
Lungfish
Dipterus
Protosuchus
Crocodilia
Shark
Elasmobranch
Rachitomes
Ichthyosaur
Icthyosauria
Acanthodires
Sea squirt
Urochordata
Ichthyostega
REPTILES
Lepospondyls
Agnatha
Ostracoderms
Cheirolepis
Chondrostean
Dipterus
Pterosaur
Ceratopsian
Sauropod
Pteraspidomorph
Ostracoderm
Carnosaur
Amphioxus
Cephalochordata
Acanthodes
Acanthodire
Ichthyosaur
Plesiosaur
CHORDATES
Pliosaur
VERTEBRATE ANIMALS
Dominant reptiles of the age of Dinosaurs
Nautiloid dies
Sediment settles
Earth Movements
Erosion exposes fossil
THE STORY OF A FOSSIL

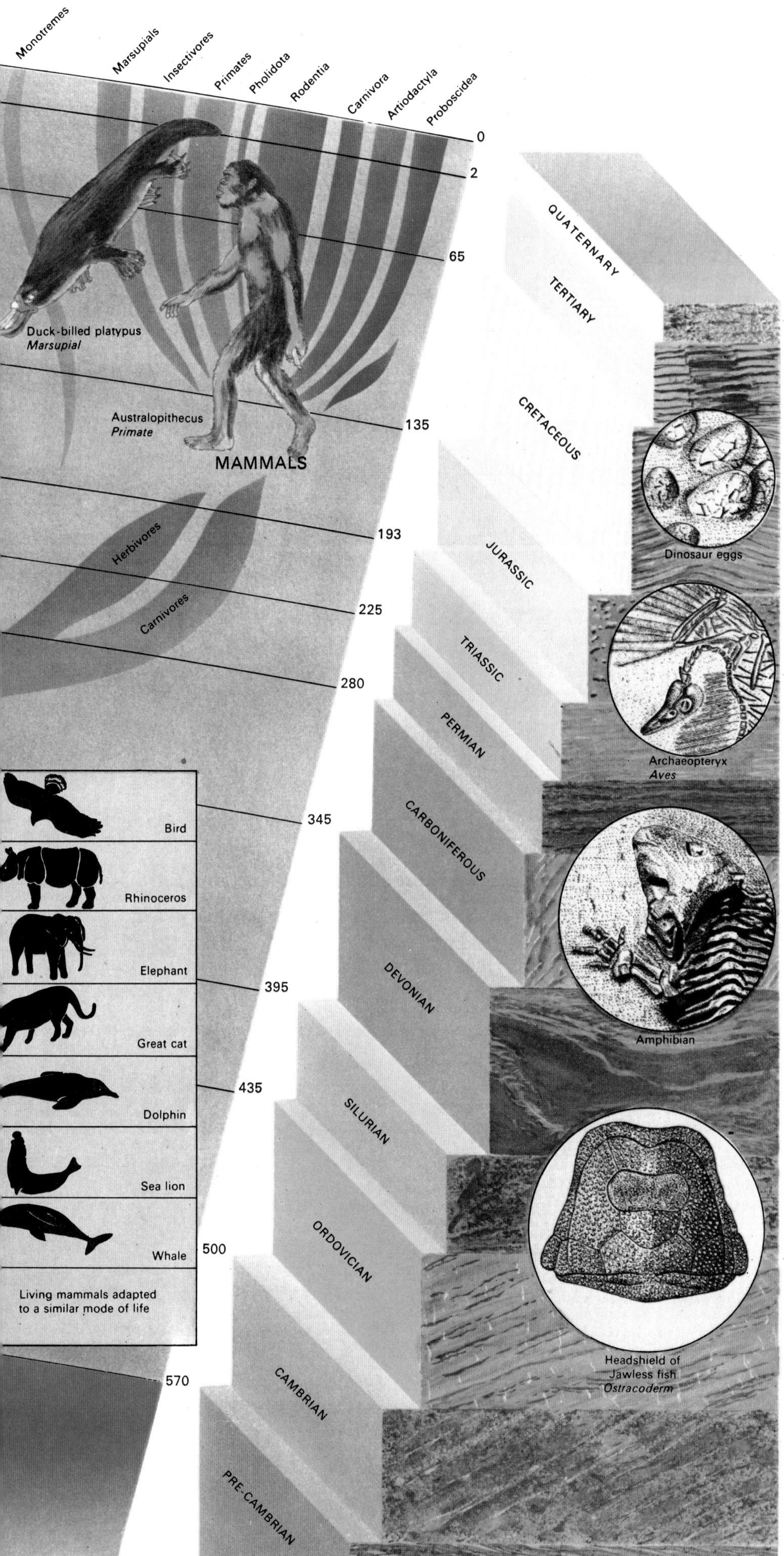

fossils layer by layer to establish the time-sequence of the various forms, and then recognizes that any rock succession containing the same sequence of species spans the same period of geological time —no matter how different the rock types themselves may be. In this way the relative geological time scale was built up.

The *palaeoecologist* studies the relationship of a fossil animal or plant to the environment in which it lived. Study of whole *fossil assemblages*, the complete entity or number of fossils in an area, can indicate differing depths of sea water, while research into the geographical distribution of fossil organisms, the study of *palaeobiogeography*, sheds light on ancient climates or geography.

Fossils and evolution

The present is simply a brief cross-section of geological time. Biologists build up much of their understanding of the processes and result of evolution by studies in such fields as the comparative morphology, embryology, genetics and biochemistry of living forms. But present-day life represents only the culmination of over 3,500 million years of evolution, the direct evidence of which is locked into our fossil record. Charles Darwin (1809-82), in his celebrated work *The Origin of Species*, was fully aware of the potential importance of fossils in testing his evolutionary theories, but he stressed the many imperfections of the record. Since Darwin's day our knowledge has vastly expanded and a more rigorous approach has demonstrated definite patterns in evolutionary processes, though these are certainly not to be regarded as 'laws' of evolution.

The most spectacular pattern is that of *explosive evolution*. On several occasions through geological time there have been relatively sudden bursts in the evolution of major groups of animals and plants. One instance is the rapid diversification or *radiation* of fish during the Devonian period nearly 400 million years ago. Such bursts interrupted the more usual, slow or *progressive evolution* within individual groups, and often seem to be associated either with periods of major extinctions or with significant environmental changes such as the flooding of extensive areas of continental margins to form shallow shelf seas.

Explosive evolution often affected unrelated groups of animals or plants at the same time. The sudden diversification of a group to exploit an environmental change is called an *adaptive radiation* because it usually results in a great variety of new forms evolving. Some of these prove to be successfully adapted to live in the new environment, but others quickly become extinct.

For periods of more normal, progressive evolution, *rates of evolution* can be worked out. Although absolute rates have rarely been calculated, there has long been tacit recognition among palaeontologists that some fossil groups evolved faster than others. The most rapidly changing groups have always been used as *zone fossils*, those fossil species which are used to characterize a particular horizon and are restricted to it in time.

Rates of evolution can apparently vary considerably within any division of the animal kingdom, or *phylum*. Some bivalve species, for example, apparently lasted at least six times as long as contemporaneous

Bruce Coleman

Ardea

Above: These extinct ammonites date from the Jurassic. Some species lived for less than half a million years before evolving into another species and their sequence gives an accurate relative time scale for Jurassic and Cretaceous rocks.

Left: Trilobites are extinct marine arthropods which superficially resemble woodlice. They are zone fossils, used in the age correlation of rocks, for the Cambrian and Ordovician periods.

Below: These shellfish are brachiopods. Living examples are quite rare but they are significant as zone fossils from the Ordovician period to the Permian.

Institute of Geological Sciences

ammonites during the Cretaceous, yet both belong to the phylum *Mollusca*. However, some authorities point out that the rate of evolution of some groups may appear faster simply because they have more characters which can vary and are therefore more readily divided into chronological 'species'. This reflects the problem that affects every palaeontologist. He is dealing not with a single slice of time but with a continuum, and therefore has to distinguish both contemporaneous and chronological species.

Evolutionary convergence is known from both the fossil and modern records. It is the tendency of completely unrelated groups to give rise to similar looking forms, usually reflecting a similar mode of life. Thus the fossil plesiosaur developed into a form very much like a fish although it was a reptile. Repeated or *iterative evolution* is a similar tendency which occurs in related organisms. Many different ammonites, for example, give rise to tightly coiled shells at the end of their evolutionary lineages.

Extinction of fossil species

While many fossil species became 'extinct' simply by evolving into another species, there were periods when whole groups disappeared. Such wholesale extinctions are quite common in the geological record and, as explained earlier, their occurrences have been linked with bursts of explosive evolution. Indeed, the boundaries between our major divisions of Phanerozoic time—the Palaeozoic, Mesozoic and Cainozoic eras—and to a lesser extent the boundaries between the geological periods were based essentially on the recognition of major periods of extinction followed by bursts of evolution.

Some of the extinctions were spectacular. Some were so impressive, as for example the disappearance of the giant reptiles about 65 million years ago at the end of the Cretaceous period, that external catastrophies, such as changes in the sun's radiation or collision with a huge meteorite, have been invoked. However, more thorough study has demonstrated that most extinctions and evolutionary radiations actually occurred over a period of time, though accelerated in relation to more normal periods of evolution and extinction. The changes probably reflect major but progressive changes in the environment, such as extensive marine retreats or advances, or significant changes in the world's climate.

The progress of life through time

Despite its major imperfections, the fossil record, when properly interpreted, provides an immense amount of information on the progression of life through geological time. The record starts very early in the earth's history. Indeed, so-called *chemofossils*, minute agglomerations of organic acids possibly of living origin, are known from rocks almost 4,000 million years old, and algae were well established by 3,000 million years ago. Much more advanced, though soft-bodied, animals are known from a variety of late Pre-Cambrian rocks and trace fossils of this age are common. All are *invertebrates*, animals without a backbone, but some are difficult to assign to their correct phylum.

Invertebrate fossils are common from the beginning of the Cambrian period (some 570 million years ago) onward. This resulted from the development of hard shells, initially often chitinous but soon mainly calcareous, by most invertebrate phyla at that time. With one exception—the *Archaeocyatha*, a group of extinct marine forms—all the phyla which had appeared by the end of the Cambrian still flourish today, though many of the early forms look very different from their modern descendants.

The phylum *Arthropoda* probably originated in the Pre-Cambrian and is represented at first by marine creatures called *trilobites*. These became extinct during the Permian period of 280 to 225 million years ago, but the phylum is by then represented by many other forms including abundant crustaceans—a group represented today by such creatures as crabs, lobsters and shrimps. 'Modern' crabs originated some 100 million years later during the Jurassic. To the palaeontologist some of the most important crustacean arthropods are the microscopic *ostracods* which originated late in the Cambrian and are of importance as zone fossils in the correlation of rock strata of Silurian and later age. An equally important group for this purpose are the *foraminifera*, a division of the single-celled phylum *Protozoa*. The phylum must have had a long Pre-Cambrian history, and foraminifera appeared early in the Cambrian.

The phylum, *Coelenterata*, which includes present-day corals, sea-anemones and jelly-fish, is represented in the Pre-Cambrian by the traces of jelly-fish and in many later systems by the skeletons of fossil corals. The latter often formed reefs in ancient tropical areas. The phylum *Mollusca* has reached its peak today, but its fossil record is varied and impressive. The *cephalopod* molluscs, forms with chambered shells, appeared at the end of the Cambrian and radiated rapidly at the beginning of the Ordovician 500 million years ago. They gave rise during the Devonian, 100 million years later, to the *ammonoid* cephalopods, whose shells are so common in some Mesozoic sediments.

Another cephalopod group, the *belemnites*, appeared in the Carboniferous and are ancestral to the modern squid and cuttlefish. Other molluscan groups include the *bivalves*, which are rare until the Silurian, 400 million years ago, but then become increasingly common to achieve enormous diversity today, where they include the common cockles, mussels and scallops. The *gastropod* molluscs, common today as snails, slugs and whelks, have coiled shells and a geological history similar to that of the bivalves.

The phylum *Brachiopoda* is another shellfish group. In contrast to the Mollusca they are relatively insignificant now, although their geological record, especially from Ordovician to Permian times, was much more important. The phylum *Echinodermata* also originated in the Cambrian or earlier, and its two major fossil groups are the *Crinoidea* (sea lilies) and the *Echinoidea* (sea urchins). The former were most important in the distant Palaeozoic where their skeletal remains are sometimes important rock builders, while the latter diversified during the Mesozoic to reach a peak in the Cretaceous.

The *graptolites* appeared in the Ordovician and became extinct 200 million years later in the Carboniferous. They are colonial organisms that were once classified with the Coelenterata but are now placed among the most primitive members of the phylum *Chordata*, which includes the vertebrates. The first true vertebrates, the fish, evolved in the Ordovician. Land was first colonized in the Devonian, when amphibians as well as the first land plants appeared, to be followed by reptiles in the early Carboniferous.

The conquest of land left only one realm to be fully occupied—the air. Flying insects were well established by the Carboniferous, and the first flying reptiles are of Triassic age (over 200 million years ago). Some 50 million years later, true birds appeared in the late Jurassic, by which time many forms of life were taking on a modern appearance while the land was roamed by the dinosaurs, now long extinct. Man appeared only about 2.5 million years ago, at about the beginning of the Pleistocene epoch.

In fossilised wood (as here, in the Petrified Forest National Park, East Arizona) the wood fibres have been replaced, through the action of hot, silica bearing waters, by opal or chalcedony.

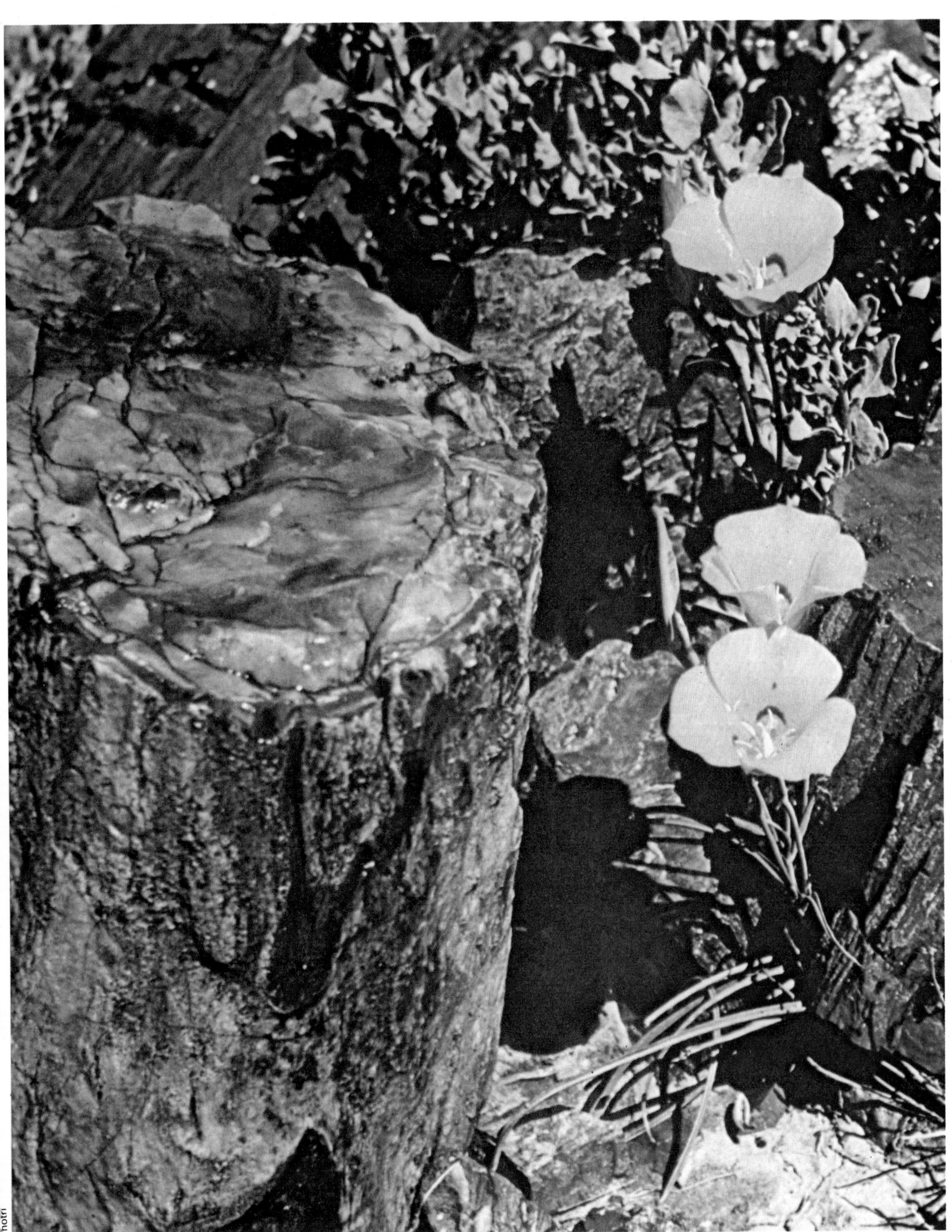

Photri

The Evolution of Plants

Throughout much of geological time, plants have been preserved as fossils in sedimentary rocks. Today this fossil record provides evidence of some of the major steps in the evolution and astonishing diversification of the plant kingdom. But the usefulness of this record goes far beyond the palaeobotanist's interest in the ancient history of plant life. Buried in this fossil record, there are clues to the origin of life itself.

Indeed, research into the Pre-Cambrian fossil record has been encouraged by the advances in space exploration. For, in anticipation of finding some primitive form of life on other planets, earth scientists are examining the oldest and most primitive remains of life on earth.

The first evidence of life

At present the oldest known remains of cellular organisms are found in the Fig Tree chert (black, glassy rocks made of silica) in Swaziland, which is some 3,100 million years old. The simple morphological structures are presumed to be bacteria because of their size and shape. From the same rocks scientists have also extracted many different kinds of complex organic substances which are the essential biochemical constituents of living matter. These include, for example, certain familiar amino acids and carbohydrates.

The search has been extended to other slightly younger rocks. This has shown that as the age decreases so cellular structure and chemical complexity increase. For instance, 2,800 million year old rocks in the Bulawayan Group from Rhodesia contain fossils of multi-cellular organisms, thought to be the remains of colonial algae which form reef-like calcareous banks called *stromatolites*. These are easily preserved as fossils because of the hard calcareous dome-shaped mats which the algal cells secrete.

Very similar organisms still survive today and grow in profusion in the quiet intertidal zones of western Australia. These *procaryotes* (lacking a true nucleus) are among the simplest known organisms. Their occurrence 2,800 million years ago marks the beginning of plant life as we know it, and the start of the development of greater complexity by living things.

The next major stage in the increasing sophistication of the fossil plant record is found in Canada. Certain blue-green algae have been identified in the 1,900 million year old Gun Flint chert. These still have simple procaryotic organization, but they are more complex than the algae which produced the stromatolites because their cells are ordered into filamentous chains. Once again, the specimens that have been found in these old rocks are very similar to types of blue-green algae that grow in ponds and lakes today.

More and more of these very old fossils are being discovered every year, particularly in Australia, where suitably preserved sediments a little younger than 1,000 million years old are quite common. The best known are from Bitter Springs where large numbers of multi-cellular photosynthetic organisms have been discovered. These fossils are among the oldest records of *eucaryotes*, organisms with highly organized cytoplasm, the earliest of which gave rise through evolution to all other types of plants. These more sophisticated organisms become widespread in younger fossil-bearing deposits and, though they often occur alongside the simpler procaryotes, they begin to dominate the vegetation from about that time.

Until about 400 million years ago, single-celled, colonial and filamentous algae formed the basis of plant life on this planet. Much of today's land surface was covered with water.

An environmental change enabling plants to adapt to new forms came over 400 million years ago. During the Silurian period, the seas retreated from earlier continental coastal regions. Palaeobotanists believe that multi-cellular algae began to colonize the new intertidal areas and to have differentiated into forms of plants that could best survive away from the seas. The new land environments had many advantages: they offered a stable base, a source of food in the newly developing soil and a warm humid atmosphere, with some concentration of oxygen for more efficient respiration.

Dr Michael Boulter

Left: About 400 million years ago, plants first made the transfer from sea to land. The oldest known vascular plant (with fluid-conducting cells) is *Cooksonia* (shown beside tall fern) which grew up to 10 cm high at the edge of the water. The fossil (above) shows the simple branching of the stem and the spore capsules. Many other very simple fern-like plants also colonized the land and some grew to over 1 m high. Intertidal zones continued to support the dome-shaped mats of secretions from various blue-green algae, which form the easily fossilized stromatolites. These vary from a few centimetres to several metres across. (Below) Section of a stromatolite dome. Stromatolites date back to 2,800 M.Y. ago.

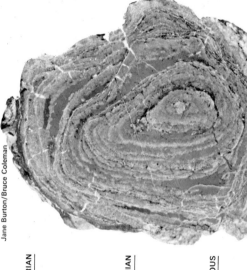

Jane Burton/Bruce Coleman

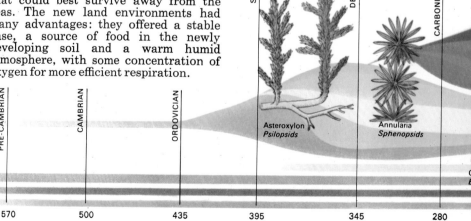

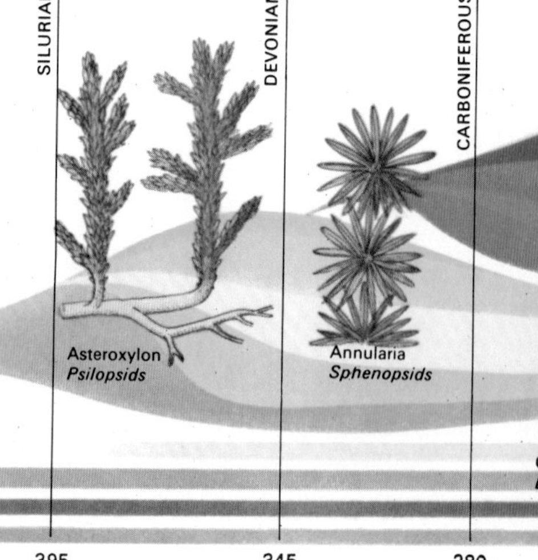

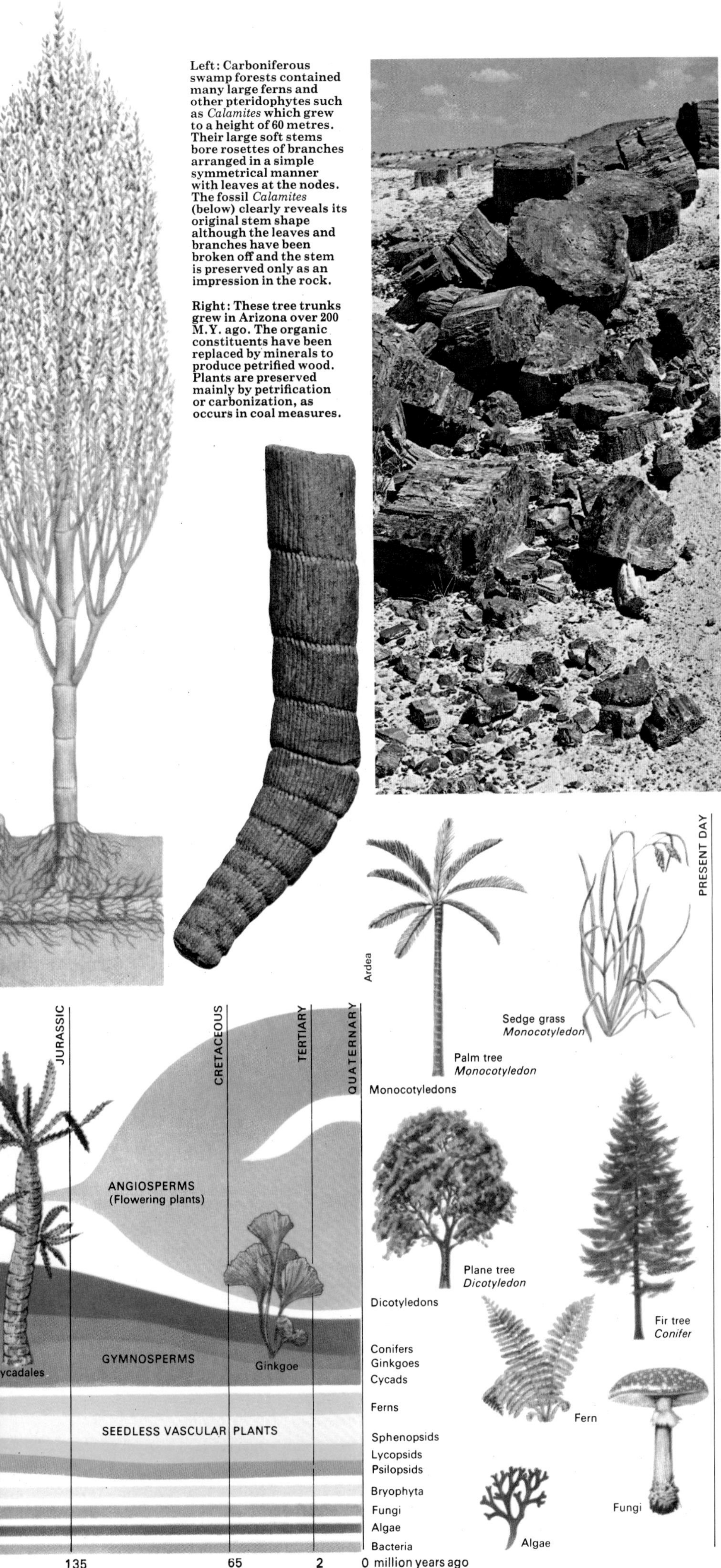

Left: Carboniferous swamp forests contained many large ferns and other pteridophytes such as *Calamites* which grew to a height of 60 metres. Their large soft stems bore rosettes of branches arranged in a simple symmetrical manner with leaves at the nodes. The fossil *Calamites* (below) clearly reveals its original stem shape although the leaves and branches have been broken off and the stem is preserved only as an impression in the rock.

Right: These tree trunks grew in Arizona over 200 M.Y. ago. The organic constituents have been replaced by minerals to produce petrified wood. Plants are preserved mainly by petrification or carbonization, as occurs in coal measures.

At the end of the Silurian, there began a rapid burst of evolution within the plant kingdom. Within just 25 million years—a very short length of geological time—land plants evolved complex vascular systems to transport food all over the plant body, leaves which specialized in photosynthesis, roots and stems for support, and, most dramatically of all, *sporangia* (in which spores were produced) and even seeds for reproduction. Moreover, the biochemical, physiological and genetical processes needed to support such complex organisms developed too.

Plants of the past

These events occurred during the Devonian—a period when much land surface was exposed—and now recognized as being one of the two intervals of greatest expansion in plant evolution. Consequently, at the end of the Devonian, 345 million years ago, not only were there diverse types of marine and freshwater algae, but also a huge variety of spore-bearing plants such as ferns, tree-ferns, horse-tails, club-mosses and many now unfamiliar little plants with simple stems and small sporangia.

All these plants are now extinct, though modern ferns, club-mosses and horse-tails do survive as rare representatives of the ancient lineages. Particularly unfamiliar to us would be the Devonian tree-ferns which are thought to have grown up to 25 metres (88 feet) in height with woody trunks, fern-like leaves and simple seeds which were fertilized by wind-blown pollen.

A similarly unfamiliar, completely extinct group of plants was particularly common during the Carboniferous period that followed. These were the *pteridosperms*, with fern-like leaves, underground stems and very simple large seeds hanging loosely from the leaves. They relied on the wind blowing large pollen grains over the mouth of the seed for pollination to take place. Because this was a very inefficient process which encouraged inbreeding, they quickly became extinct. For a time, however, they achieved some success and are commonly found as fossils in the Carboniferous coal measure deposits.

The equatorial swamps of North America and Europe, then joined as a single land mass, also supported forests of very large *pteridophytes*. These plants reproduced by spores, like modern ferns, and were formed of very soft parts with a high water content. The best known of these is *Lepidodendron* which grew up to 35 metres (115 feet) in height and had a stem over 1 metre (39 in) in diameter. Just as common were giant horse-tails such as *Calamites* and ferns similar to, but larger than, those of modern times. These very warm, wet and humid swamps were environments in which plant life flourished, and where the rate of growth has been shown to have been considerable.

The relatively sudden and major changes in world environment that took place at the end of the Carboniferous period marks the end of this botanical paradise. Climatic and other changes forced an end to the profusion of the luxurious forest swamps, and large numbers of once abundant plants became extinct very quickly. The environmental changes enabled those plants with the more sophisticated seed reproduction systems, the *gymnosperms* (which include the conifers and their relatives), to win over those with the simpler sporangia. Their woody nature also proved to be most suitable for the drier environments that were to follow.

The periods of the Mesozoic era saw a great diversification of these plants. Gymnosperms with short hard trunks and crowns of hard waxy leaves up to four metres (13 feet) long were commonplace. For 150 million years, until some 100 million years ago, the plant kingdom diversified more than it had done before. Trees with naked seeds relying on wind for pollination, ferns, and relatively few smaller pteridophytes formed the basis of the floras of the world. As in the Carboniferous, plants were able to consolidate on this type of structure once they had become established within a reasonably stable environment.

World vegetation during the Mesozoic was based on four separate floras, whose origins can be traced back to Carboniferous times. The Euramerican flora occupied most of Europe and North America, the *Glossopteris* flora most of what was Gondwanaland in the south, the Angaran flora most of northern Asia, whilst the Cathaysian flora occupied what is now central Asia, China and S.E. Asia.

The Glossopteris flora was the most distinctive. Alone, it has representatives of another quite extinct group of plants, which had veined spear-shaped leaves and complex seeds. Moreover, plants from this flora have been recognized for many years from South America, southern Africa, India, Australasia and Antarctica. They provided one of the major proofs that these land masses formed a single continent 280 million years ago.

Many recent studies of these Mesozoic floras have involved not only examination of the fossilized leaves, stems and seeds, but also of their pollen grains. Since these are well preserved (they are formed of *sporopollenin* which is one of the most stable and resistant chemical substances known) they are easily observed with a microscope. And since they are more readily obtained in narrow bore-hole samples than large fossils, the recognition of pollen is particularly important in the exploration for oil and other minerals. Most of the oil deposits in the North Sea, for example, are of Mesozoic age, and have been discovered with the help of fossil pollen studies to identify the age of the sediments.

The success of flowering plants

The Cretaceous period some 100 million years ago saw the second really large explosion of evolutionary activity in the plant kingdom. The environmental circumstances that were responsible for this event are more controversial than those for the Devonian expansion as many more factors were operating to cause the changes. But the effect of this second revolution was that the dominating gymposperms of the Mesozoic were replaced by the much more successful *angiosperms*, or flowering plants, with their widely varied morphology and specialized seeds enclosed in a protective carpel.

One current explanation for this dramatic evolutionary growth is that during the relative stability of the Mesozoic plants had been able to build up a large reserve of genetic facility, needing only the opportunity to use it. Whether this opportunity was afforded by the sudden expansion of insects during the Cretaceous (most angiosperms are pollinated by insects) or whether the particular climate and environmental circumstances of the Cretaceous were suddenly favourable is not fully understood.

Dr Michael Boulter

Left: This fossil moss grew in Derbyshire in the English midlands, then enjoying a warm climate, about 8 M.Y. ago. Its perfect preservation shows many botanical features though no living moss is quite the same. It is one of the few fossils that record the warm climate of the time and like them it is extinct.

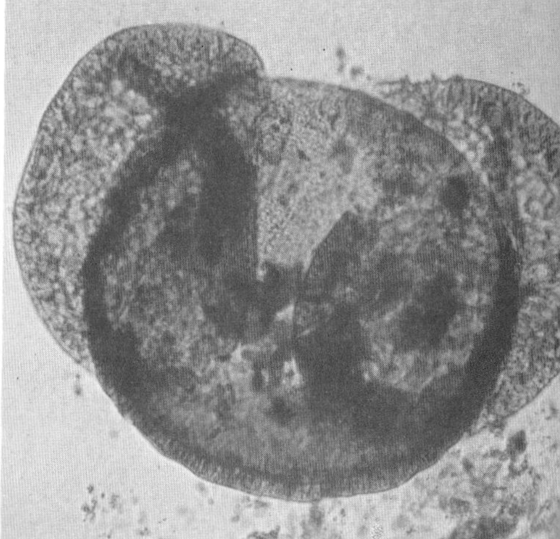

Dr Michael Boulter

Below: A fossil pollen grain from an extinct species of silver fir. The grain is only 0.1 mm long but its delicate features are revealed under a microscope to aid in identifying the plant. *Palynology*, the study of pollen grains, is widely used in oil exploration to determine the age of sediments found in boreholes.

The effect of this evolutionary explosion of plant life was far reaching. The first groups of flowering plants succeeded so well that they caused the greater number of Mesozoic gymnosperms to become extinct quite quickly. The disappearance of others has been more gradual, and even today there is one surviving species of the *Ginkgoales*, a few species of *Cycads* in isolated parts of the world and many conifers, though the last are restricted to extreme environments such as deserts and cool temperate regions. These are the only survivors. Today most areas of the world are more or less dominated by angiosperms.

The continuing debate on the evolutionary origin of the angiosperms remains the one most substantial unanswered question in palaeobotany. One difficulty is that there are very few fossil remains of early angiosperm plants, possibly because they first appeared on mountain tops where erosion has destroyed all evidence. Another is that so many advanced gymnosperm groups, such as the members of the Glossopteris flora, have leaves and other organs that are very similar to what the earliest angiosperms may have resembled. Also, many of the parts of simple angiosperms are likely to have been very soft and so unlikely to survive as fossils. But fossil pollen grains may hold important clues since they are distinctive and easily preserved. Current research suggests that discoveries of very primitive angiosperm pollen from Cretaceous rocks from south-east Asia and Africa may represent some of the first appearances of the flowering plants.

Once they had developed, angiosperms became established very quickly. The fossil record of 90 million years ago shows few traces. Yet at the end of the Cretaceous 25 million years later they form the dominant group of plants in most fossil floras. So rapid was the rate of change that, by the beginning of the Tertiary 65 million years ago, the characters of primitive angiosperms were giving way to the relatively advanced features recognizable in modern plants.

The last 60 million years

The last 60 million years of history of the plant kingdom have been dominated by climatic fluctuations in most parts of the world. These have helped create a wider range of ecological niches and thus an increase in the potential for plant evolution to produce more species. The climax occurred just two million years ago with the beginning of the extensive ice ages, when ice at the poles produced a maximum range of climate from north to south.

The climate of the whole planet had been fluctuating from the beginning of the Tertiary. Successive waves of cooling were directed from the poles towards the equator. These changes in temperature had themselves caused a pattern of plant migration away from the poles for most of the temperate plants living in what are now polar regions, 50 and 60 million years ago. At the same time, substantial climatic changes were being caused by the effects of sea floor spreading and continental drift.

Scientists are in the process of trying to piece together the fossil evidence to explain the details of these effects of plant migration. Not only were subsequent generations of the same species of plants migrating as the climate changed, but new forms were also evolving and others were becoming extinct. One difficulty is that we know little enough of modern plants, particularly those that grow in the unexplored tropical parts of the world, to make adequate comparisons with the fossils that we might luckily find. From the huge variety of environmental and genetical factors influencing their development, it seems as though the last 50 million years in the history of plants are the hardest to understand.

The Venus fly-trap (*dionaea*) has evolved something appraoching a primitive nervous system. The touch of an insect on two trigger hairs is enough to snap shut the trap formed by the hinged leaves.

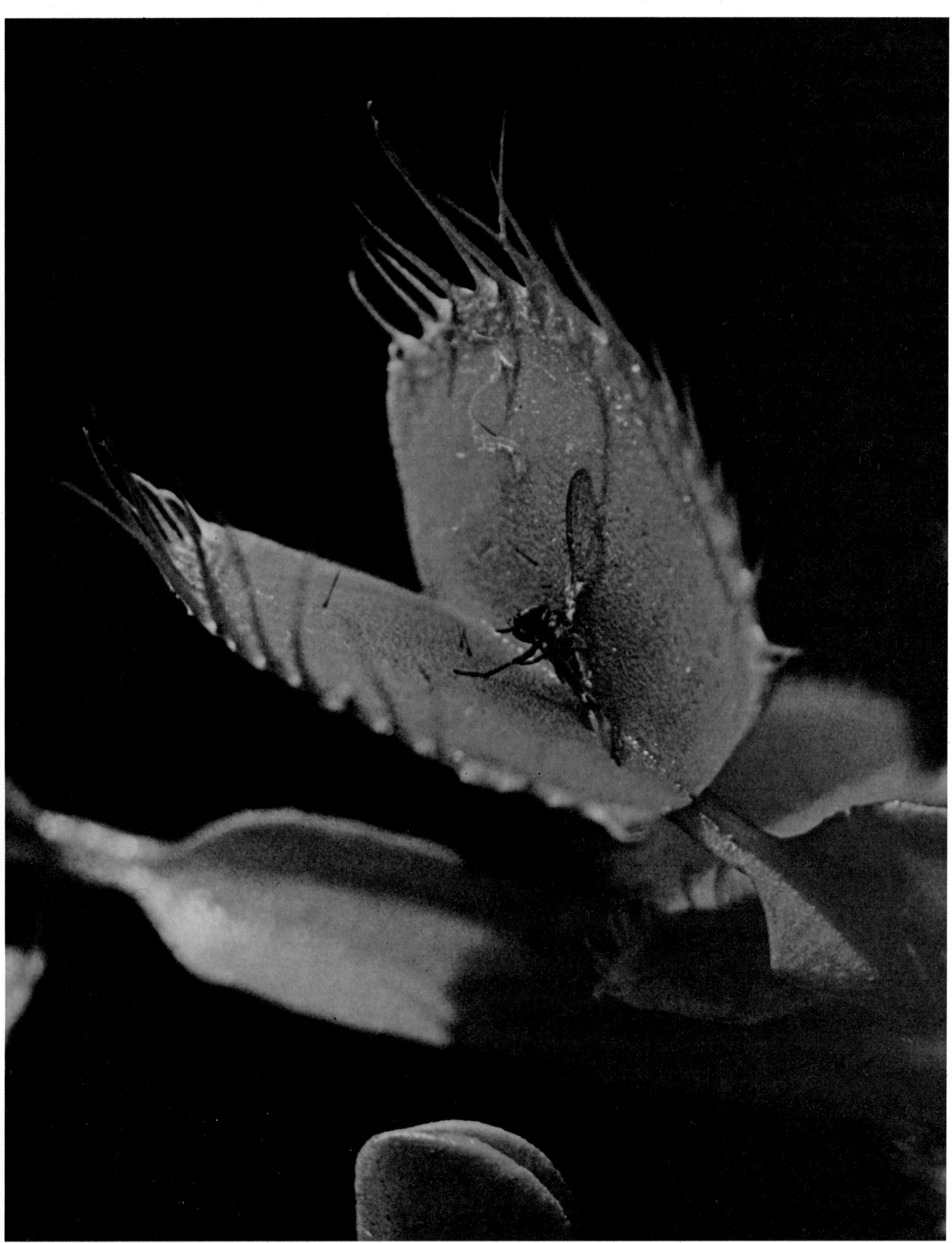

Barnaby's Picture Library

Life in Ancient Waters

In tracing the evolution of life on earth, the story of the first vertebrate animals is of vital importance. In fact the first vertebrates were fish and during the Devonian period—which is often known as the 'Age of Fish'—there is evidence of the origins of both modern fish and many other fish-like animals which have long since become extinct. Moreover, from fish evolved the first amphibious creatures which could live on land. And from them, ultimately, evolved all the reptiles, birds and mammals that now inhabit this planet.

Jawless fish

The earliest evidence of vertebrate animals is found in sandstones of middle Ordovician age, about 465 million years old. It consists of small plates of bone-like material, and the animal that possessed these plates was a fish-like vertebrate belonging to a group that includes the modern eel-shaped lamprey. This group is distinguished from other vertebrates by its lack of true jaws or teeth. It is called *agnatha*, meaning 'without jaws'.

Unlike the modern lamprey, the Palaeozoic agnathans were covered with bony plates and scales and are consequently called *ostracoderms*, 'shell-skinned'.

Most ostracoderms lived in lakes, rivers and lagoons during the late Silurian and the Devonian periods, 400-350 million years ago. It is probable that they were rather idle, spending much of their time resting on the bottom, only occasionally darting from place to place feeding on organic debris which accumulated on the bottom sediments. The end of the Devonian witnessed the extinction of ostracoderms, but the agnathan lineage continued with the lamprey.

The advantages of jaws

The appearance of upper and lower jaws with associated teeth was a major step forward in vertebrate evolution. It transformed the rather weak, circular mouth of ostracoderms into a long, powerful organ potentially capable of grabbing active prey. However, in order to realize this potential there had to be improvements in mobility to aid the pursuit of likely victims. Not surprisingly, therefore, the development of jaws is accompanied by the development of true paired fins—the *pectoral* or breast fins, one on each side behind the head, and *pelvic* fins, on either side of the lower surface of the body. These helped control the movement of the fish through the water.

One of the early groups to exploit the advantages of jaws was the *placoderm* fish, sometimes called the 'armoured fish'. The head was encased in a bony shield and this *articulated* or moved by means of a ball and socket neck-joint, with another bony shield covering the foremost part of the trunk. The neck-joint was an interesting innovation. It allowed the front part of the skull to be raised at the same time as the lower jaw was lowered. Effectively, therefore, this considerably increased the size of the mouth opening.

Despite the great variety of placoderm

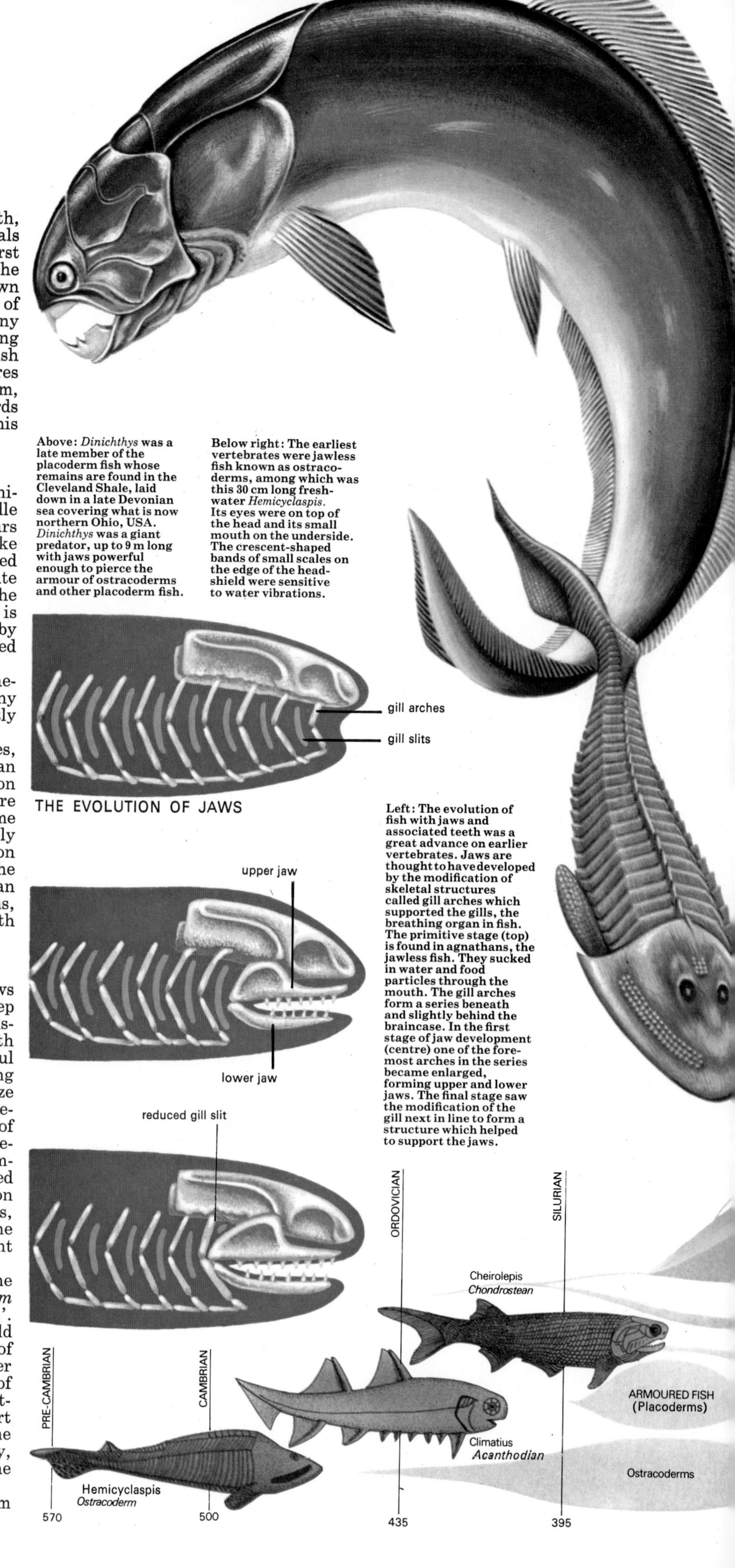

Above: *Dinichthys* was a late member of the placoderm fish whose remains are found in the Cleveland Shale, laid down in a late Devonian sea covering what is now northern Ohio, USA. *Dinichthys* was a giant predator, up to 9 m long with jaws powerful enough to pierce the armour of ostracoderms and other placoderm fish.

Below right: The earliest vertebrates were jawless fish known as ostracoderms, among which was this 30 cm long freshwater *Hemicyclaspis*. Its eyes were on top of the head and its small mouth on the underside. The crescent-shaped bands of small scales on the edge of the head-shield were sensitive to water vibrations.

Left: The evolution of fish with jaws and associated teeth was a great advance on earlier vertebrates. Jaws are thought to have developed by the modification of skeletal structures called gill arches which supported the gills, the breathing organ in fish. The primitive stage (top) is found in agnathans, the jawless fish. They sucked in water and food particles through the mouth. The gill arches form a series beneath and slightly behind the braincase. In the first stage of jaw development (centre) one of the foremost arches in the series became enlarged, forming upper and lower jaws. The final stage saw the modification of the gill next in line to form a structure which helped to support the jaws.

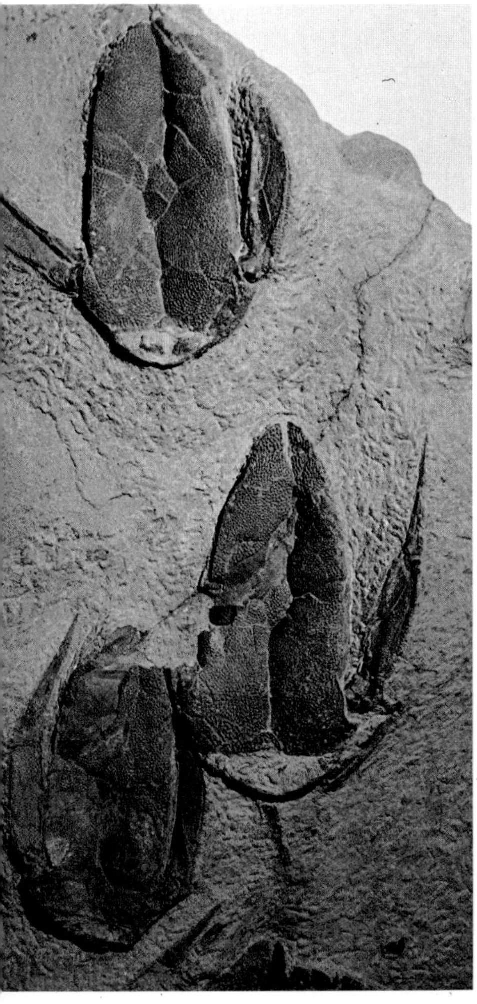

P. Morris/Ardea

fish, particularly in late Devonian times, all had become extinct by the end of that period. This fact is difficult to explain but two factors may have been important. The solid head shields may have imposed restrictions on breathing, and hence on activity; also the bony shearing blades were not replaceable once they had been worn down. Perhaps these limitations became too great at a time when fish with more efficient breathing mechanisms and methods of tooth replacement were making their appearance.

Cartilaginous fish

The cartilaginous fish are today represented by the sharks, rays and the deep-sea ratfishes. This group is characterized by an internal skeleton made of cartilage and a body covering of tiny denticles or scales. Throughout their history, cartilaginous fish have been a predominantly marine group. Unfortunately, the fossil record is rather poor since, with a few exceptions, only the isolated denticles, teeth and fin spines are preserved.

From their appearance in the middle Devonian the cartilaginous fish were a group which became adapted to an active swimming, predatory existence. There is no restrictive bony shield covering the head and the teeth are hard-wearing, being composed of dentine with a tough coat of enamel, and replaceable.

Sharks of truly modern form appeared by the late Jurassic, some 150 million years ago. This period also marks the appearance of modern rays which, in all probability, evolved from a shark-like ancestor. The rays became adapted to life on the sea floor. They became flattened with enormously expanded pectoral fins.

Bony fish

The dominant group of modern fish are the *bony fish*, such as salmon, cod, herring, perch and angel fish. They are numerous as fossils, particularly in deposits of late Mesozoic and Cainozoic age. As the group name suggests, the skeleton, both internally and externally, is composed of strongly calcified bone. An important internal structure that was developed in early bony fish is the paired lung. In one group of bony fish, the fleshy-finned fish, the lung retained its original form and function—that of gaseous exchange—but in the ray-finned fish the lung became modified to form a swim-bladder and took on the function of a buoyancy tank. This was an important energy saving development. It provided the fish with neutral buoyancy and eliminated the need for constant swimming in order to stay at one level.

The ray-finned group of bony-fish were numerous and have shown great variation throughout their geological history. The first ray-fins were found in freshwater Devonian deposits but by the end of that period a few had taken up life in the sea and this has remained their principal environment. In the late Mesozoic and the Cainozoic several kinds of ray-fin fish re-invaded freshwater and formed most of the freshwater fish fauna of today.

The earliest, most primitive of the ray-fins were members of a group called the *chondrosteans*. This was essentially a Palaeozoic group although a few members, such as the sturgeon, survive today.

Above: *Bothriolepis* was a late Devonian freshwater placoderm with bony pectoral fins. These may have been used as props when the animal was at rest. Remains of this fish are world-wide, lending support to the argument that in Devonian times the present continents were joined together.

Below: The chart shows, in simplified form, the evolution of fish and amphibians. The width of the lineage strands represents the relative abundance and diversity of the groups through geological time. It can be seen that the Devonian was an important period of evolution and that the bony fish are the dominant modern group.

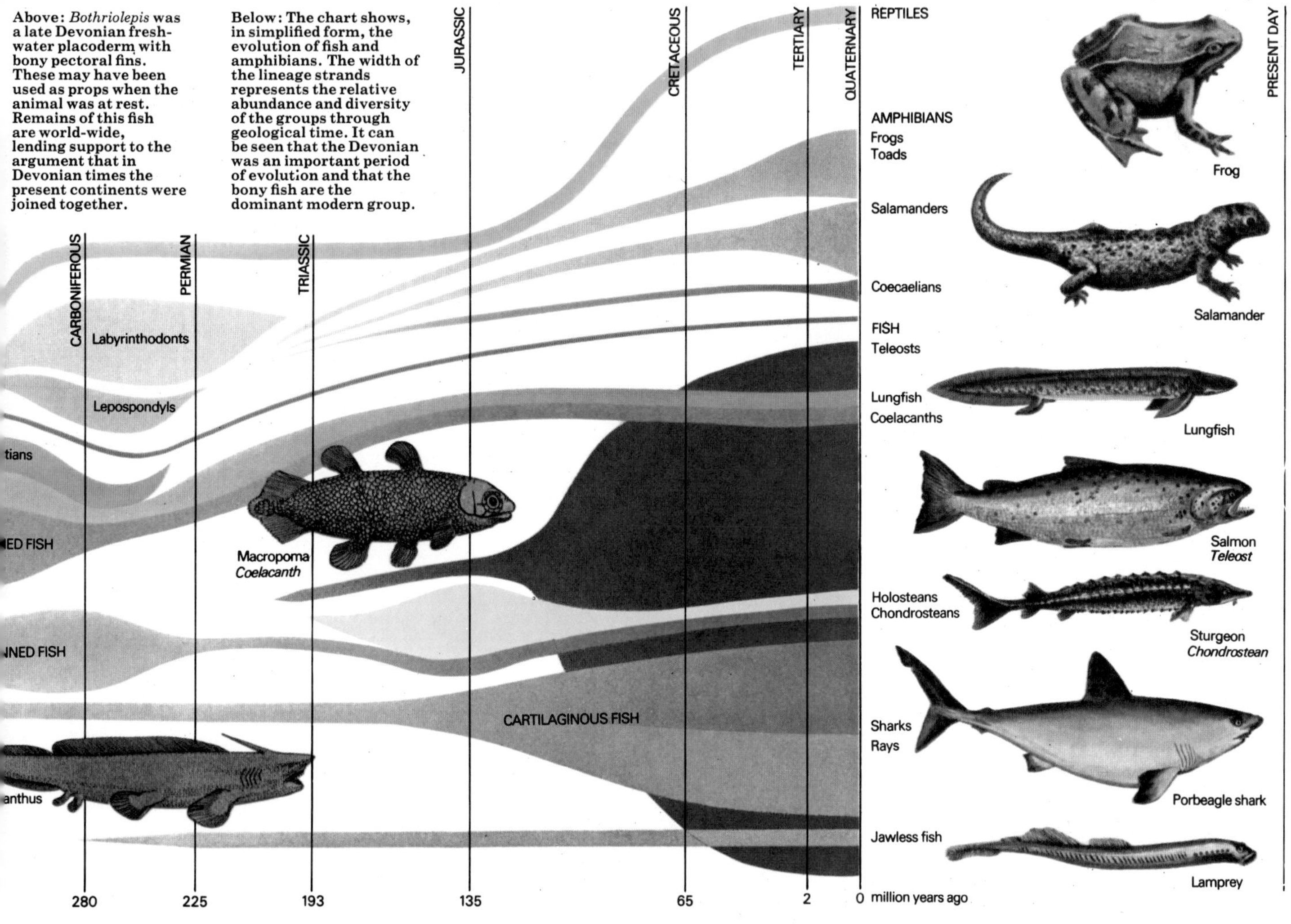

CARBONIFEROUS
PERMIAN
TRIASSIC
JURASSIC
CRETACEOUS
TERTIARY
QUATERNARY
PRESENT DAY
REPTILES
AMPHIBIANS
Frogs
Toads
Salamanders
Coecaelians
FISH
Teleosts
Lungfish
Coelacanths
Holosteans
Chondrosteans
Sharks
Rays
Jawless fish
Labyrinthodonts
Lepospondyls
tians
ED FISH
NED FISH
CARTILAGINOUS FISH
anthus
Macropoma
Coelacanth
Frog
Salamander
Lungfish
Salmon
Teleost
Sturgeon
Chondrostean
Porbeagle shark
Lamprey
280 225 193 135 65 2 0 million years ago

Another more advanced level of ray-fin evolution is represented by the *holosteans*. This was essentially a Mesozoic group, and only two types have survived.

At the top of the ray-fin evolutionary ladder stand the *teleosts*. This group first appeared in the Triassic but became particularly important in the late Mesozoic and the Cainozoic when they show a great variety of body forms. The evolution of ray-fin fish is marked by repeated improvements in feeding methods and mobility.

Ray-finned differ from another group of bony fish, the fleshy-fin fish, in the structure of the paired fins. In fleshy-fin fish, the skeleton and muscles, which support and move the paired fins, extend outside the body and give the fin a fleshy lobe at the base.

Of the three groups of fleshy-fin fish, lungfish are a very specialized group. They possess solidly constructed skulls and large grinding plates which are adapted for crushing molluscs and plant material. Lungfish are so-called because the primitive lung has been retained and can be used for obtaining oxygen in unfavourable climatic conditions. Structurally, the lungfishes have remained relatively unchanged since their appearance in middle Devonian times.

Another structually conservative group of fleshy-fin fish are the *coelacanths*. The Palaeozoic coelacanths inhabited freshwater but they migrated to the sea in the Mesozoic. They were thought to have been extinct for 65 million years until one was caught in 1938 off the coast of Africa.

In contrast to the lungfish and coelacanths, the *rhipidistians*, the third fleshy-fin group, were short-lived. They were, however, a very important group since it is likely that the first animals to exist on land, the amphibians, arose from rhipidistian stock. During the Devonian, most lived in freshwater where they must have been voracious carnivores.

Many of the rhipidistian features foreshadowed those in early amphibians. Not only was the backbone composed of strong vertebrae, but also the skeleton of the pectoral and pelvic fins was comparable with that of the fore and hind limbs of amphibians. Perhaps more importantly, the arrangement of limb muscles allowed for multi-directional movement of limbs. Rhipidistians also possessed internal nostrils which opened through the roof of the mouth. This totally unfish like feature is precisely that found in amphibians and is an adaptation to air breathing. Such air breathing might have been very impor-

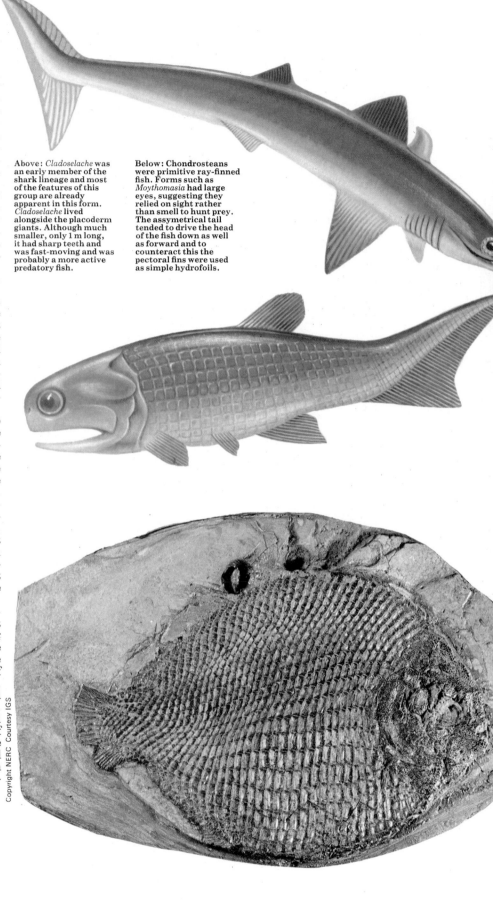

Above: *Cladoselache* was an early member of the shark lineage and most of the features of this group are already apparent in this form. *Cladoselache* lived alongside the placoderm giants. Although much smaller, only 1 m long, it had sharp teeth and was fast-moving and was probably a more active predatory fish.

Below: Chondrosteans were primitive ray-finned fish. Forms such as *Moythomasia* had large eyes, suggesting they relied on sight rather than smell to hunt prey. The assymetrical tail tended to drive the head of the fish down as well as forward and to counteract this the pectoral fins were used as simple hydrofoils.

Below: Life in certain late Devonian pools may have been rather harsh with times of drought and stagnant water. Early lungfish, such as *Dipterus* (left), probably gulped air and may even have had the ability to 'hibernate' in the mud during droughts. Rhipidistians such as *Eusthenopteron* (centre) were capable of walking out on land to seek new pools. *Ichthyostega* (right) was better at walking with much stouter limbs with fingers and toes. This early amphibian shows some terrestrial adaptations but it probably spent most of its time in the water since there was very little animal food on land in the Devonian.

tant as geological evidence suggests that at least some of the Devonian freshwaters were periodically subject to low oxygen levels.

From water to land

About 350 million years ago, some rhipidistian fish probably left the water for brief periods. The reasons for these temporary excursions on to land are not clear but the late Professor A. S. Romer, an eminent American palaeontologist, suggested that it may have been to escape from oxygen-depleted pools which were drying up to more favourable bodies of water. Whatever the reason, it is from a land-venturing rhipidistian that the first amphibians are descended.

On land the early amphibians made an attempt to raise the body off the ground on to four legs. Fossil remains reveal that both the shoulder and pelvic girdles were large, and that the pelvic girdle was rigidly anchored to the backbone. These primitive land-venturers needed to travel more efficiently in their new environment and there was modification of the rhipidistian paired fins to form the first kind of fore and hind limbs with fingers and toes.

The first amphibian, *Ichthyostega*, lived in late Devonian times. Ichthyostega was structurally intermediate between rhipidistians and later amphibians and belongs to a large group of fossil amphibians called the *labyrinthodonts*.

Labyrinthodonts reached the peak of their radiation about 300 million years ago in the late Palaeozoic, but 100 million years later by the end of the Triassic period they had become extinct.

Another Palaeozoic group of amphibians were the *lepospondyls*. Most were small aquatic forms. Some became eel-like while others had highly flattened heads that were extended on each side.

The amphibians living today are the frogs and toads (anurans), the salamanders (urodeles) and the coecaelians. The frogs are known as fossils from the Triassic, 200 million years ago, and the salamanders from the Jurassic, about 50 million years later. However, when they appear in the fossil record they are already very similar to their modern-day counterparts and their ancestry from older Palaeozoic amphibians is obscure.

But this was only the beginning, for from the early amphibians many new forms of life were to evolve, animals that severed completely any connections with the sea. These animals were the reptiles, birds, mammals and, ultimately, man.

Above: In teleost fish the tail is fully symmetrical and this produces a horizontal thrust. This example, *Acanthonemus*, was found in Eocene marine deposits in Italy. The fish fauna of this area, rich in teleosts, is very similar to that found in lagoons and shallow seas of the Indo-Pacific region today.

Left: Holostean fish were the dominant ray-fins of the Mesozoic era. *Dapedium* was a Jurassic form with a deep body about 60 cm long and a small mouth with a profusion of sharp peg-like teeth. The teeth indicate that this fish may have lived around coral reefs feeding on hard-shelled invertebrates.

Left: Coelacanths had been known as fossils for a long time but were thought to have become extinct in the late Cretaceous, 65 million years ago. However, in 1938 a local fisherman hauled up a rather unfamiliar fish off the coast of East London, South Africa. Tremendous excitement was aroused in the scientific community when it was realized that the fish was a coelacanth, named *Latimeria*. Since then about 80 more specimens of this 'living fossil' have been recovered from the deep waters around the Comoro Islands. The coelacanth is very important for it is the nearest living relative of the amphibians.

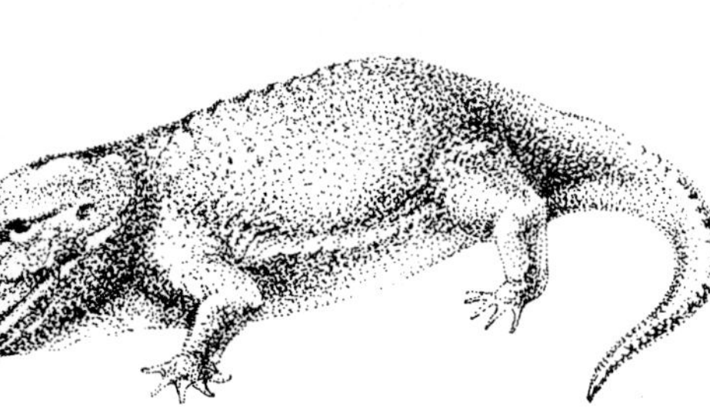

Left: *Eryops* was a Permian amphibian which reached a large size of about 1.5 m. No doubt its powerful jaws made it an aggressive carnivore. It appears capable of spending much of its time on land but it probably returned to the water to feed. Its prey were fish and other amphibians.

Fossil Reptiles and Mammals

Right: The strange 'sail' of the mammal-like reptile *Dimetrodon* may have been a device to keep its body temperature constant. If it was cold, it would have basked broadside to the sun, with a network of blood-vessels circulating the heat to its body. When it was warm enough, it would have faced the sun or retired to the shade.

The key to successful life on land seems to have lain in the development of the reptilian egg. Apparently simple, it gave the reptiles a distinct advantage over their ancestors, the amphibians. The egg contains a complex set of adaptations to allow the unborn or *embryonic* reptile to develop with its own enclosed supply of food and water, while at the same time allowing it access to the life-giving air around it. The evolution of this egg made it possible for reptiles to dispense with the vulnerable, aquatic *larval* stage—characteristic of amphibian reproduction.

The reptilian egg probably evolved over 300 million years ago, in the Carboniferous period. But reptiles were not immediately able to evolve into a complete range of land animals. The first reptiles were small and lizard-like, for the only other land animals available as food were small invertebrates—insects, spiders and snails. As larger reptiles evolved, each in turn was potential food for yet larger *carnivores* or flesh-eating animals.

Even more complex problems had to be overcome before *herbivorous* or plant-eating reptiles could evolve. This is not only because the digestion of plant material takes a long time—and therefore requires a bulky body—but also because, like most animals, reptiles cannot digest that material unaided. They first had to develop a special bacterial flora which, living within the digestive passage or *alimentary canal*, could carry out the preliminary stages of digestion. When herbivorous reptiles did evolve, they in turn provided yet more food for larger carnivores, forming new links in the increasingly complex community of plant and animal land life.

The earliest major group of successful reptiles are called *mammal-like reptiles*, for it was from them that the mammals eventually evolved. The mammal-like reptiles seem to have originated in a continent made up of what is now North America and Europe. Their remains are common in early Permian deposits, about 270 million years old, laid down in a great river delta which lay in what is now northern Texas. These animals, both herbivores and carnivores, were still slow and clumsy, but more active mammal-like reptiles evolved later in the Permian.

The first mammals evolved from advanced mammal-like reptiles about 200 million years ago. But their eventual success was still far in the future, for alongside them there also evolved the first of those reptiles which were to dominate the world for the next 135 million years—the dinosaurs.

The massive dinosaurs

Some dinosaurs were surprisingly small; one called *Compsognathus* was only the size of a chicken. But most were large and some were enormous. As always, the largest were the herbivores, especially the great four-footed, long-necked types known as *Sauropods*. It was long thought that these animals could only support the weight of their massive bodies if they spent most of their time in lakes or

Below: *Cynognathus* lived about 220 million years ago. It was about the size of a pig and was probably close to the line of ancestry of the mammals. Whether it had a covering of hair is not certain, but it was doubtless an active predator, with teeth capable of biting, stabbing and chewing like those of living mammals.

Above: The egg of both a reptile and a bird looks deceptively simple. But it contains a complex system of blood-vessels and membranes which allow the embryo to obtain the nourishment from the yolk, to get rid of its waste products and to breathe air. The air passes through pores in the shell, which protects the embryo from damage.

Right: The chart shows, in simplified form, the evolution of reptiles, mammals and birds. The width of the strands represents the relative abundance and diversity of groups through geological time. Most notable is the sudden extinction of all the dinosaurs at the end of the Cretaceous and the evolutionary explosion of mammals.

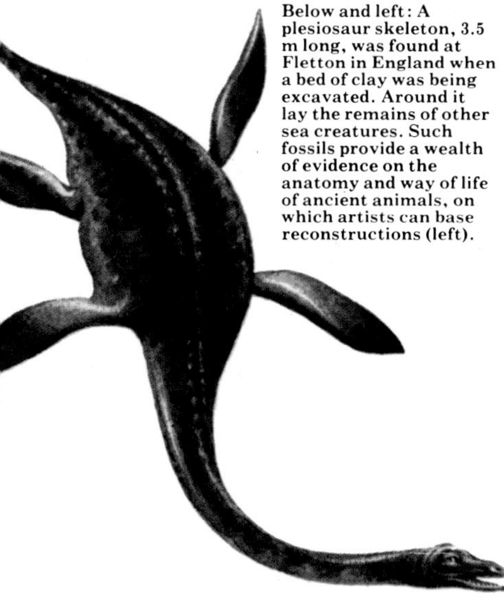

Below and left: A plesiosaur skeleton, 3.5 m long, was found at Fletton in England when a bed of clay was being excavated. Around it lay the remains of other sea creatures. Such fossils provide a wealth of evidence on the anatomy and way of life of ancient animals, on which artists can base reconstructions (left).

swamps. But many scientists now believe that they were dry-land animals, using their long necks to reach high vegetation.

Some herbivores, such as *Stegosaurus* or the Certopians, were protected from their enemies by bony plates, frills or spikes. Some such protection was certainly necessary. For some of the carnivorous dinosaurs were fearsome animals, with great heads bearing dagger-like teeth, armed also with sharp, ripping claws on their limbs.

The dinosaurs inhabited the world at a time when the great supercontinent of Pangaea was breaking up. Separated continents drifted apart and some became partly covered by shallow seas. Though scientists are still uncertain, it is even possible that this process was the cause of the extinction of the dinosaurs.

The spectacular extinction of dinosaurs occurred at the end of the Cretaceous period, 65 million years ago. At that time continental drift was slowing down and the shallow seas were withdrawing from the continents. This would have led to the climate becoming colder and more variable, perhaps causing serious physiological problems for the dinosaurs, which were adapted to a more genial and uniform climate. Whatever may have been the reason, they all died out and their only surviving relatives today are the lumbering, aquatic crocodiles.

While the dinosaurs were dominant on land, the surrounding seas were dominated by other reptiles. Some, the *ichthyosaurs*, swam by powerful strokes of their tails which bore a large fin. They would have found it difficult to move on land and there is evidence that they gave birth to live young in the water, as whales do today.

Other marine reptiles, the *plesiosaurs*, swam like turtles, by strokes of their enlarged, paddle-like limbs. They were probably able to haul themselves ashore to lay their eggs. Some of the plesiosaurs had long, thin necks, flexible enough to allow them to catch agile, darting fish. Others, with great powerful heads and jaws, had turned to prey on their own reptilian relatives.

The main flying animals in Jurassic and Cretaceous skies were the *pterosaurs*, related to the dinosaurs. They were like bats in many ways, with a leathery flight membrane supported on their fourth finger and with tiny hind limbs which must have made it impossible for them to walk on land. There is even evidence that, more like a mammal than a reptile, pterosaurs had an insulatory covering of hair so that their body temperature and

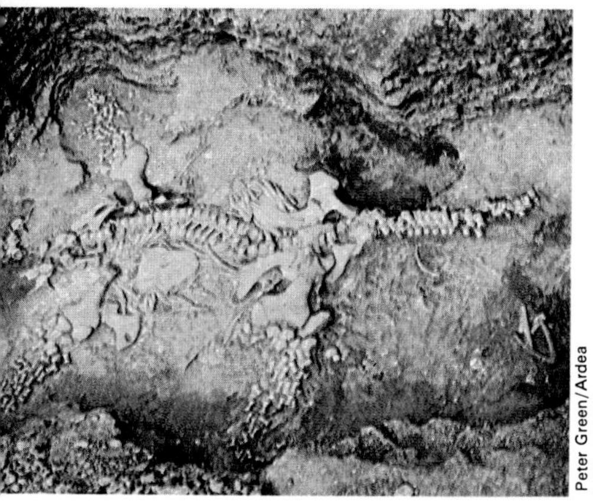

Peter Green/Ardea

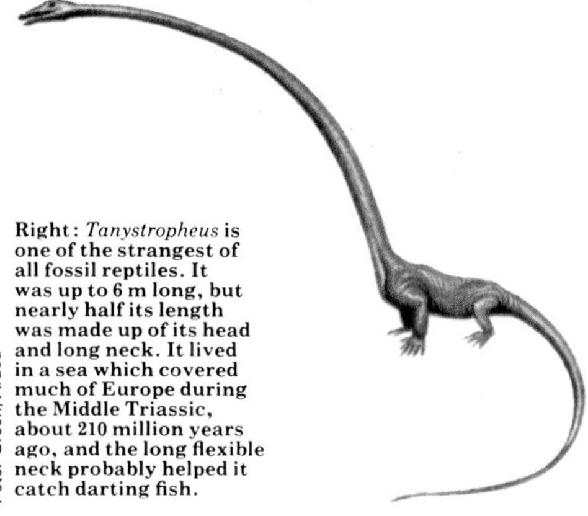

Right: *Tanystropheus* is one of the strangest of all fossil reptiles. It was up to 6 m long, but nearly half its length was made up of its head and long neck. It lived in a sea which covered much of Europe during the Middle Triassic, about 210 million years ago, and the long flexible neck probably helped it catch darting fish.

Left: *Coelophysis* was one of the first of the small carnivorous dinosaurs. Only about 2.5 m long, it probably ran on its hind limbs and grasped its prey with its forelimbs. Within this fossil can be seen traces of its food which seems to include the remains of some young individuals of its own species.

Above left: The world inhabited by dinosaurs about 70 million years ago was very different from today's. Eastern N. America and Europe were still connected to one another but seaways across North America and Asia separated this land area from another which included Asia and western N. America. Fossil dinosaur finds are marked.

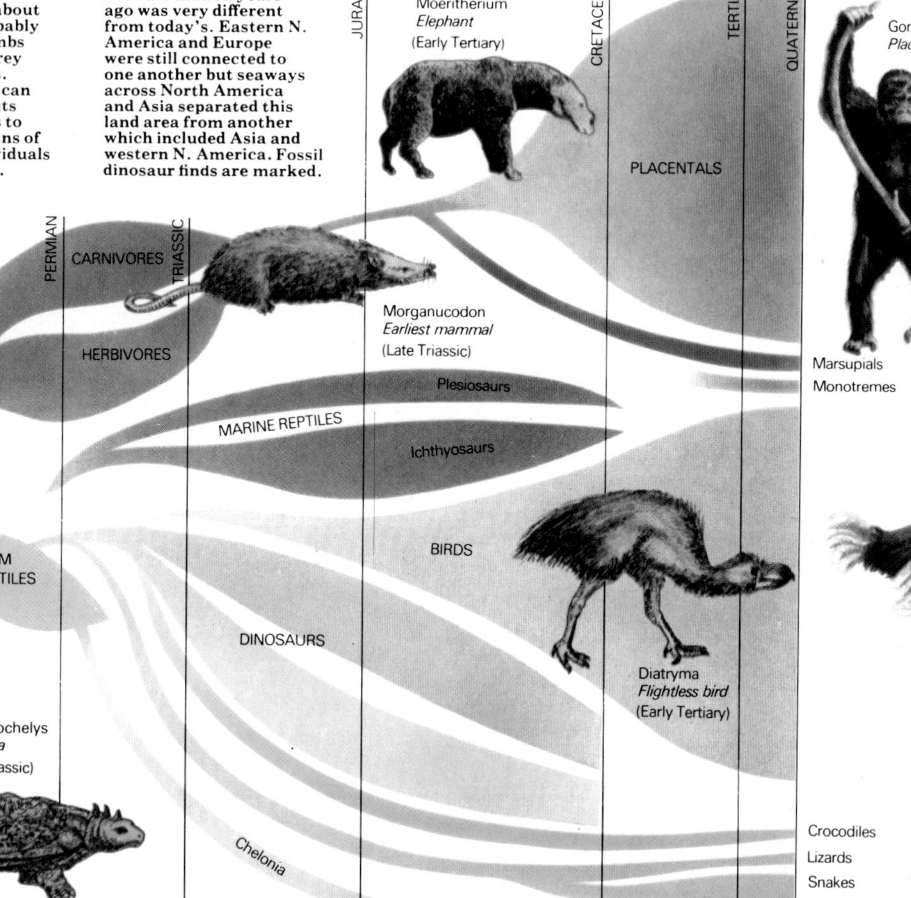

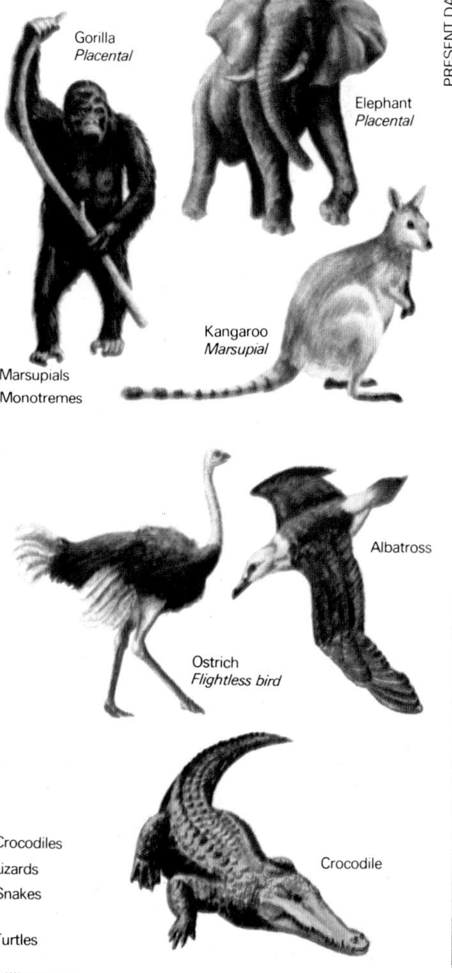

activity did not vary if the daily or seasonal temperature increased or decreased.

Prehistoric birds

The bones are usually all that remains of a fossil animal. Occasionally, however, impressions of softer structures are preserved. In at least one case, this has given us vital clues about the course of evolution. In late Jurassic rocks from southern Germany, a few specimens that might well have been thought to be merely skeletons of small dinosaurs have been preserved in very fine-grained sediments. However, around the skeletons these showed the clear impressions of feathers, proving that these animals, called *Archaeopteryx*, were really almost perfect intermediates between a reptile and a bird.

Archaeopteryx is the oldest known bird. There is a great gap in time, over 75 million years, between the Jurassic *Archaeopteryx* and the next birds in the fossil record. But specimens from late Cretaceous deposits show a high degree of specialization and by the early Tertiary, 60 million years ago, many modern kinds of bird were represented.

Like ostriches and emus today, some fossil birds lost the power of flight and became large, fast-running birds. The powerful beaks and claws of such extinct creatures as *Diatryma* or *Phororhachos*, with a head the size of that of a horse, must have deterred even the most savage predatory mammal.

Mammals themselves evolved in the late Triassic from advanced, active mammal-like reptiles rather like *Cynognathus*. Mammals, including birds, are 'warm-blooded', able to maintain a constant body temperature. This adaptation was an advance over 'cold-blooded' reptiles, whose body temperature is determined by the outside temperature. Though a number of different types of little mammals evolved during the next 135 million years, the real burst of adaptive radiation of mammals only became possible after the dinosaurs became extinct at the end of the Cretaceous period.

Early in their evolutionary history, the mammals divided into two stocks. The young of the *placental* mammals are born at an advanced stage of development, whereas those of the *marsupials* are born more prematurely but continue their development in the mother's pouch. The marsupials may have evolved in the great southern land mass, Gondwanaland, made up of South America, Antarctica and Australia. The marsupials also colonized North America and Europe, but soon became extinct there due to competition from the placental mammals. These evolved in Asia, but soon spread all over the northern hemisphere.

At the beginning of the Tertiary, 65 million years ago, Africa was still isolated from the northern continents by the Mediterranean Sea which then extended

Below: The great sauropod dinosaurs such as this *Barosaurus* were the largest land animals ever to exist. They were up to 30 m long. To provide enough energy for their gigantic bodies, these herbivores must have spent much of their time eating. The size of the head seems remarkably small in comparison with that of the body.

LATE JURASSIC

Below: This reconstruction of what life was like in both Asia and western North America about 70 million years ago gives some idea of the diversity of dinosaur life. The largest known carnivorous land animal is the *Tyrannosaurus*. It is shown attacking a hadrosaur, the head of which bears a strange bony crest, of uncertain function. Though these animals had no defence—except perhaps speed—the ceratopian *Triceratops* had bony rhino-like horns on its head, and *Anklyosaurus* had protective plates and spikes of bone on its body and tail. Overhead swoops *Pteranodon*. These flying reptiles, which had a wingspan of up to 13 m, are known as pterosaurs and were closely related to the dinosaurs. The diversity of giant reptiles, just before their final extinction, indicates that they were not gradually dwindling in numbers or importance. Instead, they seem to have reached a peak of dominance, making their sudden and complete disappearance from land, sea and air 65 million years ago very puzzling.

LATE CRETACEOUS

Left: The reconstruction of the earliest known bird, *Archaeopteryx*, shows that it still had a long, reptile-like tail, clawed fingers and teeth. A perfect intermediate between reptiles and birds, it is one of the best proofs of evolutionary theory. The skeleton of *Archaeopteryx* is compared (below left) with a modern bird's.

Below: This fine fossil *Archaeopteryx* was found in Upper Jurassic limestone in Germany. It shows not only the skeletal structure, but also the clear impression of the feathers attached to its wings and tail. The size of the tail suggests that it was as yet only capable of gliding flight and not of true powered flight.

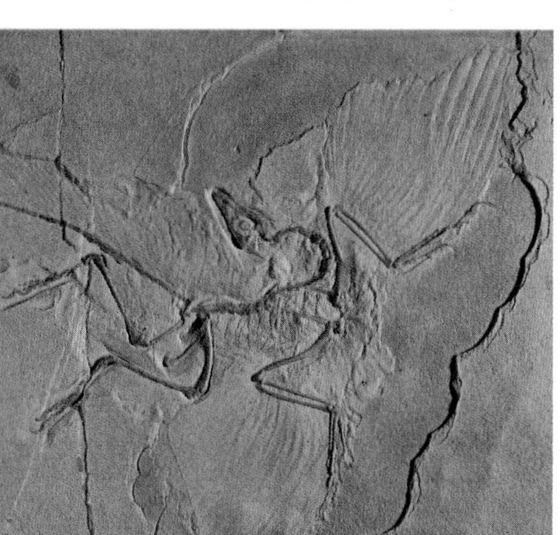

Ardea

eastwards into Arabia. A few types of placental mammal did, however, reach Africa. There some of them became the ancestors of the elephants which, when dry land later connected Africa to Eurasia, eventually spread over most of the rest of the world. Only the Indian and African elephants survive today.

Evolution of superior mammals

In the great connected landmass of Eurasia, Africa and North America, placental mammals continued to evolve and compete throughout the Cainozoic era. As a result of this evolutionary competition, even more efficient types had evolved by the Miocene epoch, about 25 million years ago. These included the ancestors of not only the great cats, wolves and other carnivores, but also such browsing and grazing herbivores as cattle and deer.

The superiority of these new types of placental mammals became dramatically apparent at the end of the Pliocene epoch. At that time, about two million years ago, a continuous land bridge connected North and South America for the first time. For the previous 60 million years South America had been almost totally isolated from the rest of the world. Apart from monkeys and rodents, which had later found their way across the surrounding ocean barriers, its only mammals had been marsupials and some early, primitive types of herbivorous placental. A variety of strange mammals had evolved such as the giant ground-sloth *Megatherium* and the giant armadillo-like *Glyptodon*.

But these once-isolated stocks were no match for the new placental mammals which poured across the Panama isthmus from the north. A great wave of extinction of the South American mammals took place. All the less advanced herbivorous placentals died out and the opossums are almost the only marsupials that survived there.

As a result, another island-continent—Australia—became the last refuge of the marsupials. There they evolved undisturbed into a great diversity of animals, including types similar in appearance and habits to many of the placentals, and also such unique types as the kangaroos.

Man and climate have also had a great effect on the mammals of the rest of the world, together or separately causing the extinction of many. During the last two million years, a series of ice ages brought vast sheets of ice and snow southwards over enormous areas of Eurasia and North America. Some mammals were able to adapt to these conditions. Both elephants and rhinoceroses, for example, evolved types with thick, warm coats of hair. But many others became extinct, either when the ice ages arrived or later, when the ice was receding and the climate changed once more. Also, at this time man was becoming an increasingly numerous and skilled hunter.

Below: *Baluchitherium*, about 7 m tall, is the largest known land mammal. It lived in Asia about 25 million years ago and it became extinct soon after elephants spread there from Africa. It seems likely that the long trunk and great grinding teeth of elephants provided a more economic way of reaching high foliage.

Below: Yet another way of feeding on the leaves of trees is shown by *Megatherium*, the 6 m long ground sloth that lived in South America until a few thousand years ago when it became extinct. *Megatherium* probably reared up on its haunches and used its clawed forelimbs to pull the branches down to its mouth.

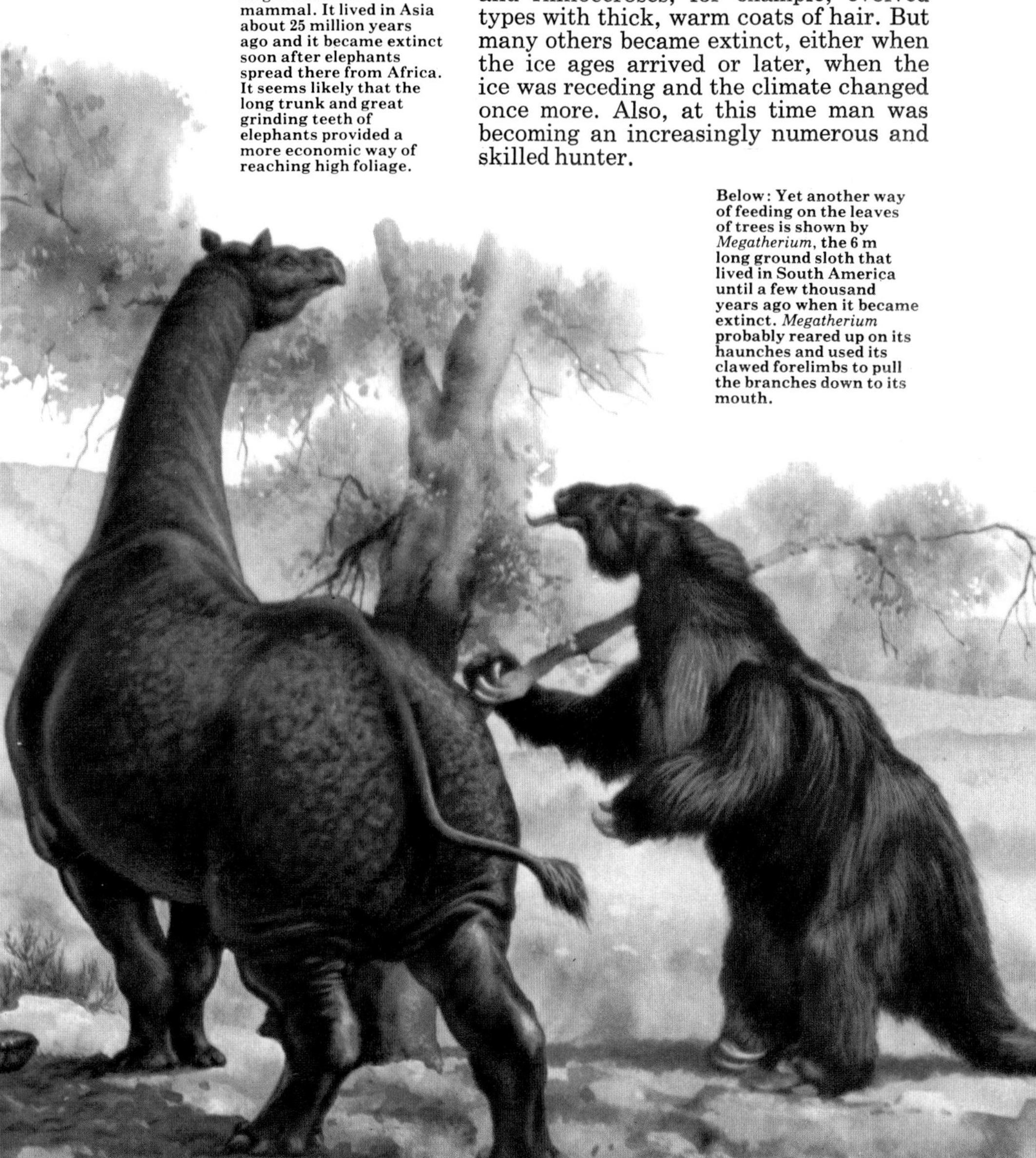

EARLY TERTIARY

LATE TERTIARY

Cave painting at Altimira, northern Spain. Inside the cave, 270 metres long, have been found remains from the upper Solutrian and middle Magdalanian periods (between approximately 30,000 and 10,000 B.C.).

The Emergence of Man

Man belongs to a major group of mammals known as the *primates*. Two sub-groups are recognized. These are the *anthropoids* (man-like forms including the monkeys, apes and man himself) and *prosimians* (early monkeys or pre-monkeys, including the tree-shrews, lemurs, lorises and bush-babies and tarsiers) and they jointly form man's living relatives. The primates also include a range of extinct ancestral forms known only as fossils.

The earliest prototype primates, resembling modern tree-shrews, were long-snouted, insect-eating tree dwellers which flourished over 65 million years ago. They differed little from other groups of ancestral mammals.

The prosimian descendants of these primates flourished until 45 million years ago. They were also small, tree dwelling forms, leading retiring and often largely nocturnal lives. The characteristic large eyes, grasping hands and stereoscopic vision—needed for well-judged movement through the trees and found in such forms as the fossil primate *Adapis*—suggest that they lived in a similar manner to prosimians of today.

Many of the prosimians have now been replaced by the 'higher' primates. However, some survive in isolated parts of the world—the only surviving lemurs, for example, live on the island of Madagascar, where they were free from competition with other more advanced primates until the arrival of man there 10,000 years ago.

Fossil monkeys and apes

The living monkeys are distributed in two major groups, inhabiting respectively the Old World of Asia and Africa and the New World of the Americas but sharing a common ancestry. This common stock dates from a period before the separation of South America and Eurasia by continental drift. From the period of separation the two monkey groups evolved along independent but parallel lines.

The way of life, and death, of monkeys, and the fact that the forest floor provides poor conditions for preserving bones, result in a scanty fossil record of monkeys. However there is sufficient material to show that two major groups of Old World monkeys—the Cercopithecine and Colobine monkeys—were already well differentiated at least 20 million years ago.

More than 30 million years ago small, unspecialized ancestors of the modern great apes (chimpanzee, gorilla and orang) are known as fossils. The best preserved find dating from this time is a skull of *Aegyptopithecus* from the Fayum area of Egypt.

The fossil evidence becomes much more abundant by about 20 million years ago. It shows that ancestral gorilla-like forms (*Dryopithecus* (*Proconsul*) *major*) were already markedly different in appearance from ancestral chimpanzee-like forms (*Dryopithecus* (*Proconsul*) *africanus*). Over 400 specimens of these two forms have been collected from Kenya. Other fossil Dryopithecines, or 'oak apes', are known from various localities in Europe and Asia.

Norman Myers/Bruce Coleman

NHPA

NHPA

Above left: The lemurs are a surviving prosimian group which found refuge from competition with higher primates on the island of Madagascar. The slow loris (above) is another prosimian. The chimpanzee (left) and gorilla (below left) found in equatorial Africa are man's closest living relatives.

Below: The cast of the skull of *Dryopithecus* (*Proconsul*) *major* (top), an 18 M.Y. old fossil ape from east Uganda. It represents a creature resembling, and ancestral to, the modern gorilla. The smaller cast (bottom) is of the skull of *Dryopithecus* (*Proconsul*) *africanus*, a chimpanzee-like form found in Kenya by Dr. Mary Leakey and dating from about the same time.

Ardea

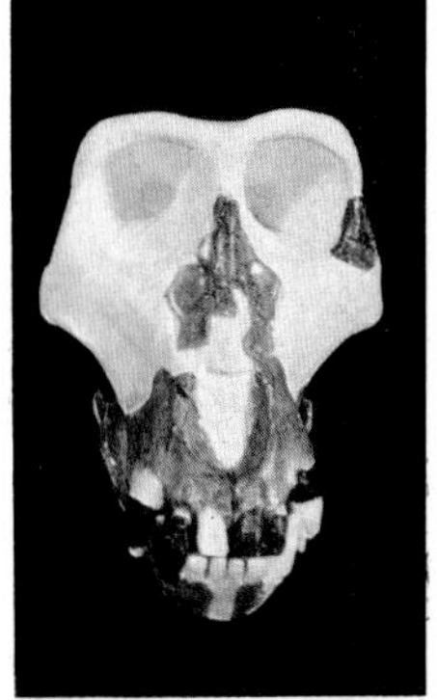

Gordon Roberton/A. C. Cooper

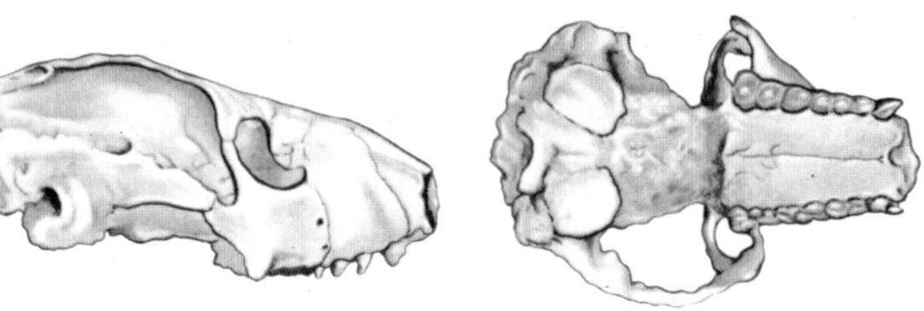

Left: The skull of the fossil *Adapis*, a four-footed, squirrel-like animal. Abundant in Eurasia from 55 to 45 M.Y. ago, it probably moved by clinging and leaping between nearly vertical branches—similar to the way modern bushbabies move. *Adapis* resembled the stock from which the later primates developed.

The earliest hominids

It has been claimed that signs of the earliest hominids can be detected in some of the specimens from this collection of 20 million year old unspecialized ape-like ancestors. The *hominid* family is the one which includes all forms of true fossil men and also modern man. However, this is a speculation and a 20 million year old origin for the hominids is not generally accepted.

Instead, it is a creature called *Ramapithecus* which is generally thought to represent the first recognizable hominid. Originally discovered in the Siwalik Hills in northern India, *Ramapithecus* also includes a fossil hominid known as *Kenyapithecus wickeri* which was found in Kenya. The oldest fossil specimens of this group are dated to about 14 million years ago.

There is a major gap in the trail of fossil evidence from between 14 million years ago and about 5 million years ago. Only two separate molar teeth (one about 10 million years old and the other about 6.5 million years old), both from Kenya, provide slender evidence of the forms that one day may be found to close this gap.

In 1925 Professor Raymond Dart, an Australian anatomist, discovered in Taung in southern Africa the fossil skull of a child aged about 7 years. This was the first discovery of what was to become an important and large group of fossils, the *Australopithecines* or southern apes. Numerous fossils have since been recovered from deposits infilling three former caves in the area between Pretoria and Johannesburg in South Africa. The three infilled caves all lie virtually in line and about a mile apart in a broad valley cut in limestone. Investigation has been carried out by combining careful excavation with diligent detective work by the noted palaeontologist Dr. Robert Broom and numerous later workers.

Detection and reconstruction of former conditions were necessary because quarry workers extracting limestone had been active at all the sites before the palaeontologists arrived on the scene. Large numbers of good fossil hominid specimens had been torn from their matrix of cave fill and thrown onto the quarry dumps still in rough hewn blocks. Over the years this material has been carefully sorted and many fossils have been retrieved from the dumps to add to the excavated specimens. Other specimens have been found at another cave in the northern Transvaal.

The fossils consist mainly of two different species of Australopithecine. One is the sturdy form *Australopithecus robustus* and the other a more lightly built creature *Australopithecus africanus*, which includes the original Taung infant. A few other specimens from the caves represent the genus *Homo*, the same genus as modern man.

Unfortunately, it has not been possible to accurately date the South African cave deposits with the use of radioactive 'clocks'. The fossil mammals that they contain allow a broad assignment of age to a period between 3 and 1 million years ago. Statistical analysis of 111 Australopithecine specimens from one site does, however, reveal something about their life expectancy—27 per cent of the individuals died before reaching the age of 10 years; a total of 88% had died before reaching the age of 25 years, and only one was more than 35 at the time of death.

Ian Berry/John Hillelson

Left: The late Dr. Louis Leakey working at Olduvai gorge in Tanzania. His discovery of fossils of the 'near man' known as *Australopithecus* made a significant contribution to understanding man's evolution.

Dr. Georg Gerster/John Hillelson

Below left: The Olduvai Gorge, a dry valley for most of the year, is about 100 m deep and numerous fossil hominids have been discovered in its well-stratified deposits. This has enabled most of the finds to be accurately dated.

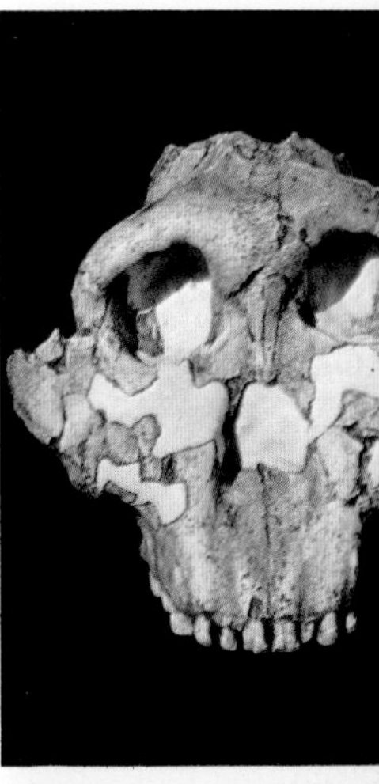

Above right: The skull of *Australopithecus (Zinjanthropus) boisei*, a robust fossil of a 'near man' who was contemporary with some of the early 'true men' about 1.75 M.Y. ago. Found in 1959 in Olduvai Gorge, it is known as 'nutcracker' because of the large molar teeth.

Dr. W. Bishop

Right: A more lightly-built hominid, *Australopithecus africanus*. This fossil, thought to be a female and nicknamed 'Mrs Ples', was excavated from the infill of a former cave near Johannesburg in South Africa. This was one of first fossils of *Australopithecus* to be found.

The East African Rift Valley

In 1959 two British anthropologists, Dr Louis Leakey and his wife Mary, announced the discovery of the first important Australopithecine find from East Africa. This was the skull of *Australopithecus boisei*, or 'Zinj', from Olduvai Gorge in Tanzania. It is interesting that this discovery was made just 100 years after Darwin published *The Origin of Species*. Although in 1859 there was almost no evidence of fossil man, and none from Africa, Darwin suggested that Africa was the place where such evidence would be found. He argued that this was because man's closest living relatives, the chimpanzee and the gorilla, are found there.

Following the Leakeys' breakthrough, the focus in fossil 'head hunting' switched to East Africa. The discovery of 'Zinj' (East African Man or 'Nutcracker' as he was nicknamed because of his large molar teeth) was the first of more than 400 hominid fossils recovered from Tanzania, Kenya and Ethiopia. They are all from the flanks of or within the great East African Rift Valley. This wealth of fossil remains has been of outstanding value in providing evidence of man's evolution.

A further 50 hominid fossils have been found from Olduvai Gorge. Since 1969, 125 fossils have come to light from the east of Lake Turkana (formerly Lake Rudolf) in Kenya, and 180 have been found since 1967 in the Omo Valley in southern Ethiopia. Rich finds have been made recently in northern Ethiopia.

The Rift Valley situation not only favours the preservation of bone and tooth, but its well exposed, layered sequences of fossil-bearing rocks are also highly suitable for accurate dating by

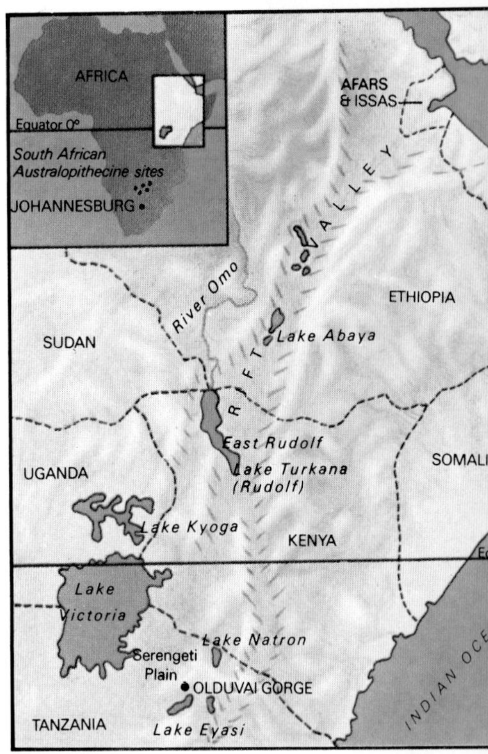

Below: The map of Africa shows the main areas yielding fossils of early man. The earliest finds of *Australopithecus* came from South Africa, but the wealth of fossils—different forms of Australopithecines, and the earliest men *Homo habilis* and '1470' man—has come from the Rift Valley area of East Africa.

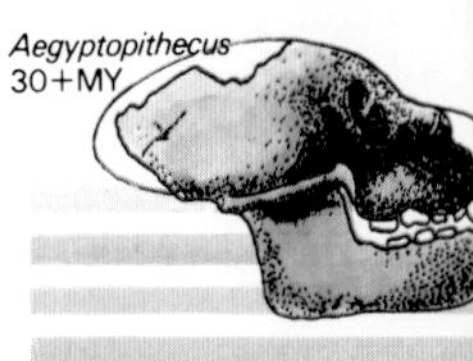

Right: Our present knowledge of man's emergence is shown in this generalized chart. Important skull finds reveal the evolution of the hominid family, but the story remains incomplete. One notable discovery was that the Australopithecines and the early *Homo*, known as '1470 man', were contemporaries.

Left: Deposits east of Lake Turkana (formerly Rudolf) have proved to be a rich source of remains of fossil man and of his early stone tool kits. Richard Leakey and his team made their dramatic discovery of '1470 man' to the east of the lake in 1972.

Right: The skull of '1470' man. It is thought to represent the genus *Homo*, and the fossil has been given an age of almost 3 million years.

Below right: A skull of modern *Homo sapiens* gazes towards those of some of his fossil ancestors. These are grouped in order of increasing antiquity, with Cro-Magnon man, who had many features in common with modern man, at the top. Both Neanderthal man and Java man had heavy brow ridges. The bottom cast is believed to be an Australopithecine skull.

Below: Stone tools are useful indicators of man's former presence. These tools illustrate the range of types fashioned by early man. (1) Two very early tools of Oldowan type (named after Olduvai Gorge) showing a core and a primitive chopper, up to 2 M.Y. old. (2) Two very early bifaces. These were later to develop into neatly shaped hand axes. (3) The tools of Acheulian culture (named after St. Acheul in France) include hand axes and cleavers made from quartz, flint and a variety of lavas. (4) Various evolved types of tool including points, spearheads, arrowheads and polished stone axe.

Douglas Botting

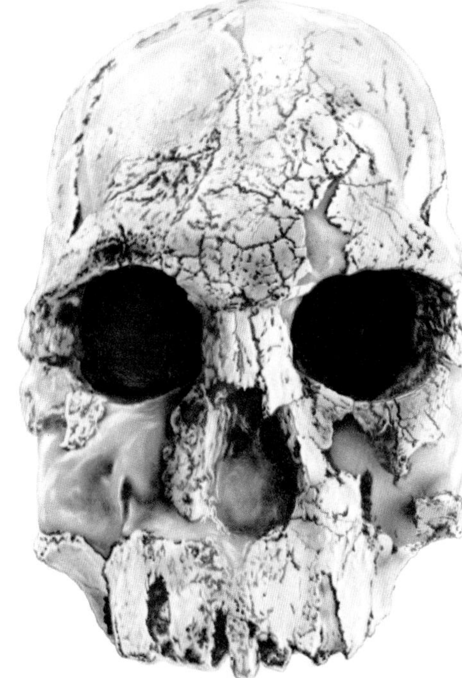

radioactive methods. For example, decay of potassium-40 to produce the gas argon-40 is used to date rift valley lavas and other strata rich in potassium that occur interbedded with fossil-bearing sediments.

The dates may then be compared with the ages obtained by using the fossils themselves as in classical geology. The result is that the Rift contains an exceptional sequence of rocks and fossils dated more firmly than has previously been possible. This makes it quite unique for the study of the nature and rate of evolutionary change in fossil man over the last 3 or 4 million years.

The fossil evidence shows that Australopithecines, both *robustus* and *africanus* forms as in South Africa, were living virtually side-by-side throughout the Rift area. Contemporary with these 'near men' are remains of 'true men' that have been assigned to the genus *Homo*.

Evidence of man

The first *Homo* specimen was from Olduvai Gorge and dates from about 1.75 million years ago—almost the same level that yielded 'Zinj'. This was *Homo habilis* (or handy man) who was named because the fossil hand bones revealed his capability of using the precision grip thought necessary in order to be a successful tool maker.

Other evidence of the *Homo* line has now been found by Richard Leakey, the son of the late Dr. Louis Leakey, in the form of various fossils from east of Lake Turkana. These include the specimen numbered '1470'. This fossil startled the scientific world by having a brain capacity of 800 cc (the Australopithicenes range around 500 cc) and by dating back to almost

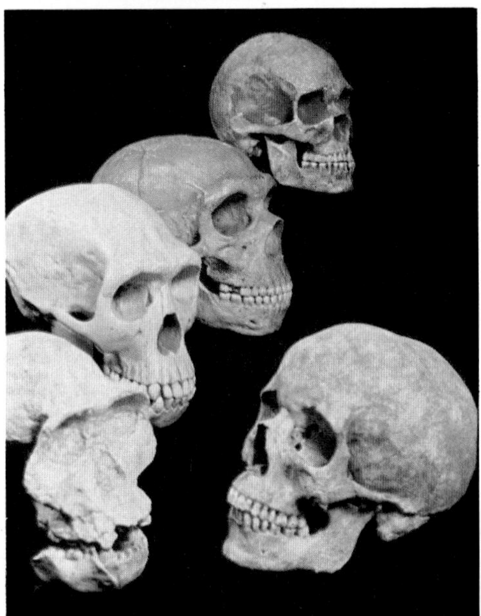

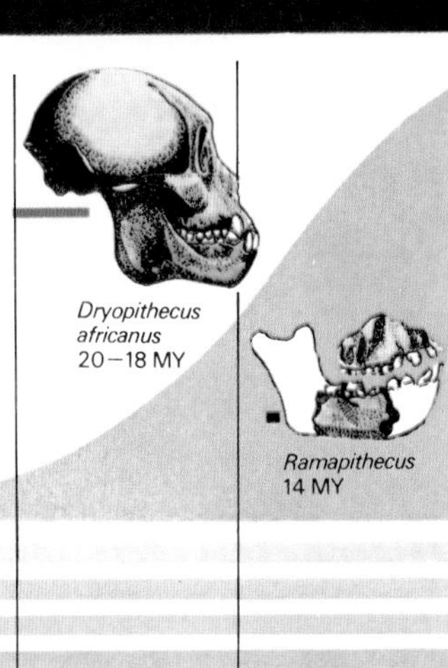

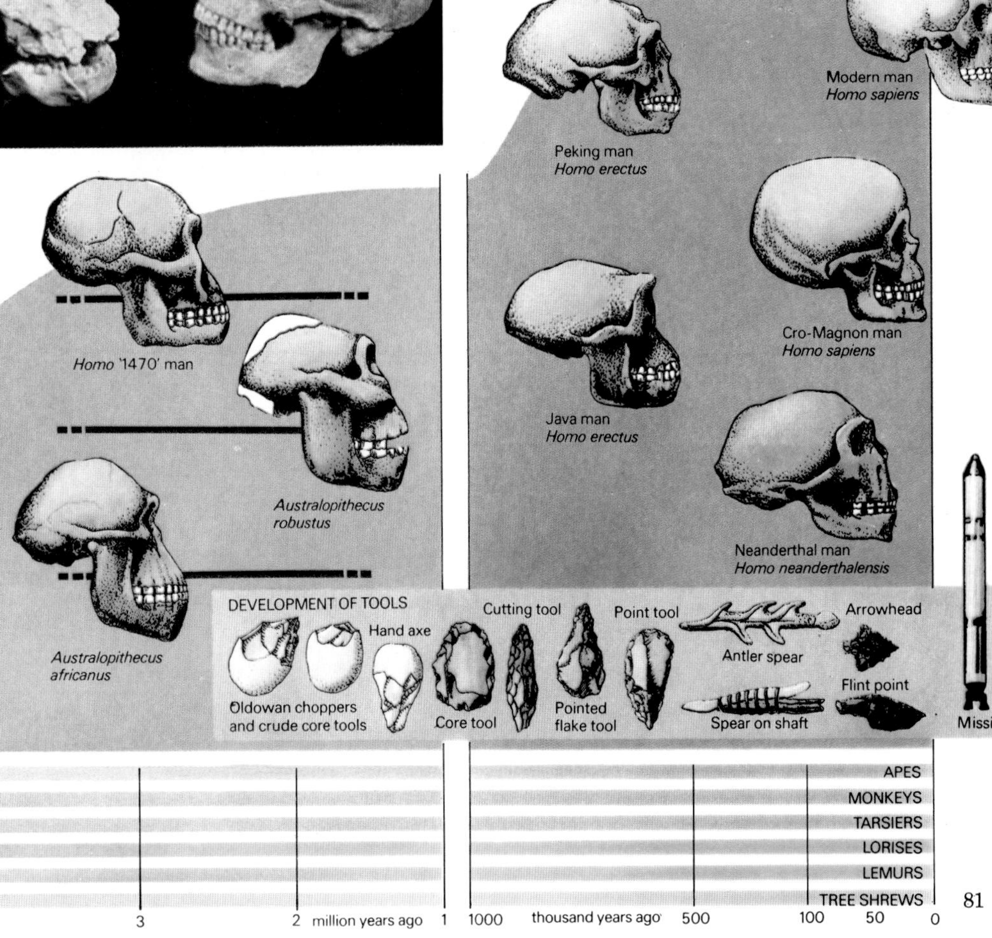

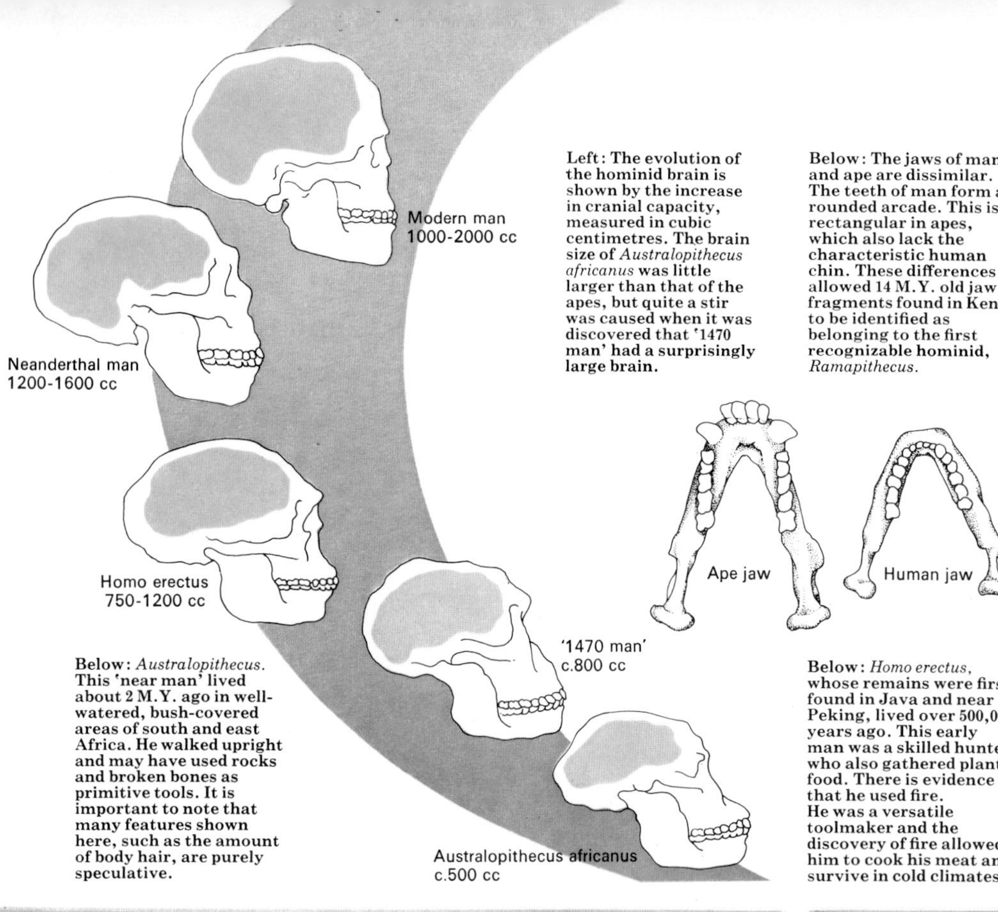

Left: The evolution of the hominid brain is shown by the increase in cranial capacity, measured in cubic centimetres. The brain size of *Australopithecus africanus* was little larger than that of the apes, but quite a stir was caused when it was discovered that '1470 man' had a surprisingly large brain.

Below: The jaws of man and ape are dissimilar. The teeth of man form a rounded arcade. This is rectangular in apes, which also lack the characteristic human chin. These differences allowed 14 M.Y. old jaw fragments found in Kenya to be identified as belonging to the first recognizable hominid, *Ramapithecus*.

Below: *Australopithecus*. This 'near man' lived about 2 M.Y. ago in well-watered, bush-covered areas of south and east Africa. He walked upright and may have used rocks and broken bones as primitive tools. It is important to note that many features shown here, such as the amount of body hair, are purely speculative.

Below: *Homo erectus*, whose remains were first found in Java and near Peking, lived over 500,000 years ago. This early man was a skilled hunter who also gathered plant food. There is evidence that he used fire. He was a versatile toolmaker and the discovery of fire allowed him to cook his meat and survive in cold climates.

3 million years ago. Still older material probably representing *Homo* has now been found in the extreme northern part of the Rift, the Afar region of Ethiopia.

Thus there is evidence of at least three, and possibly more, different types of 'near men' and early man living as contemporaries in the Rift Valley area from about 3.5 million years ago to 1.5 million years ago.

Having seen the origins of the genus *Homo* traced back to such an early date, it remains only to note that three other species are known spanning the last million years. These are *Homo erectus*, *Homo neanderthalensis* and *Homo sapiens*.

Evidence of *Homo erectus* came first from south-east Asia when the original find of this heavy-browed man with a shallow vault to the top of his skull was made in Java at the end of the last century. Other similar finds have since been made from the same area, from caves near Peking in China and from other parts of the world, including East Africa. Although, the finds from the river terrace gravels in Java and from the Peking cave have proved impossible to date with accuracy, and the African finds are not yet dated, *Homo erectus* is generally thought of as belonging in the range between 1,000,000 and 500,000 years ago.

AUSTRALOPITHECUS about 2 million years ago

HOMO ERECTUS about 1 million years ago

The fossils of *Homo neanderthalensis* (Neanderthal man, named from the Neander River in Germany) are much more recent and a great deal of evidence has been found in Europe from deposits broadly equivalent in age to part of the last Ice Age (100,000 to 50,000 years ago). This is shown by the fossil remains of cold climate animals such as the woolly rhinoceros, mammoth and reindeer from the rock-shelters where Neanderthal man has been found. The Neanderthals also lived in places such as Africa.

By this time man had learned the use of fire and his brain capacity was in some cases as large as that of modern man. Despite his rather heavy-browed and massive skull form, Neanderthal man was close to *Homo sapiens* (modern 'thinking' man) in both time and evolutionary development. Indeed he is sometimes classified as a sub-species (*Homo sapiens neanderthalensis*).

The features of the group characterized by the fossils of Cro-Magnon man (*Homo sapiens*) are very similar to those of ourselves and are of no great antiquity. And from this point on, it is early man's tool-making abilities rather than his fossils which provide evidence of his development.

THE PILTDOWN HOAX
Left: Sir Arthur Keith measures the infamous Piltdown skull. Charles Dawson (standing centre right) 'found' the pieces of this skull near an English village in 1912. When the skull was reconstructed (below left) it had a cranium of modern human type with a fully ape-like jaw. It seemed to be the missing evolutionary link. But in the early fifties, modern testing methods were applied to the skull. It was proved a definite fake—the skull was recent and the jaw was that of an ape with the teeth filed down. Dawson had long since died and it was never discovered who was responsible for the elaborate hoax. But palaeontologists are not likely to be fooled again. For one thing, modern detection techniques and dating methods have improved considerably. In addition, scientists are now much more aware of how evolution operates. It is accepted that no such 'missing link' as Dawson's Piltdown man, which possessed some specialized features of both modern ape and man, ever existed.

Below: *Neanderthal man.* The rather brutish-looking Neanderthal man first appeared over 100,000 years ago. Fossils have been found in many parts of Europe, Asia and Africa. He survived the last Pleistocene ice age by living in caves, building fires and wearing skin clothes. There is even evidence that he buried his dead.

Below: *Cro-Magnon man.* The last fossil man was also the first true *Homo sapiens.* The 30,000 year old remains from many sites in Europe show these early stone-age people, with advanced tools and weapons, were skilled hunter-gatherers who were becoming more settled. Their fine cave paintings reveal a developed culture.

NEANDERTHAL MAN about 100,000 years ago

CRO-MAGNON MAN about 30,000 years ago

Paul Hagdorn/Zefa (UK) Ltd.

Chapter 2
The Land

Cedar Brakes Canyon, Utah. In arid regions crossed by rivers whose water sources are elsewhere, deep valleys are cut into the rocks. These channels are also shaped by weathering of the valley sides and by mass movement of the resulting debris.

Landforms

Every day, physical and chemical processes are at work, changing the apparently solid face of the earth. *Geomorphology* is the study of these processes and of the landforms shaped by them. *Weathering*, which is the breakdown or decay of rocks, is perhaps the most fundamental of all geomorphic processes, for without it landforms created by structural movements of the earth's crust, such as rift valleys and mountains, would undergo very little subsequent alteration.

Mechanical weathering or physical disintegration is distinguished from *chemical weathering*, in which rock decomposition is achieved by such agents as acid contained in water. In turn, a distinction is generally drawn between weathering and *erosion*, which is the process of destruction by those agents—wind, moving ice and running water—which carry away the debris at the same time. Indeed, the development of erosional landforms by wind-blasting, glacial abrasion or stream action depends on the production of coarse particles by weather-

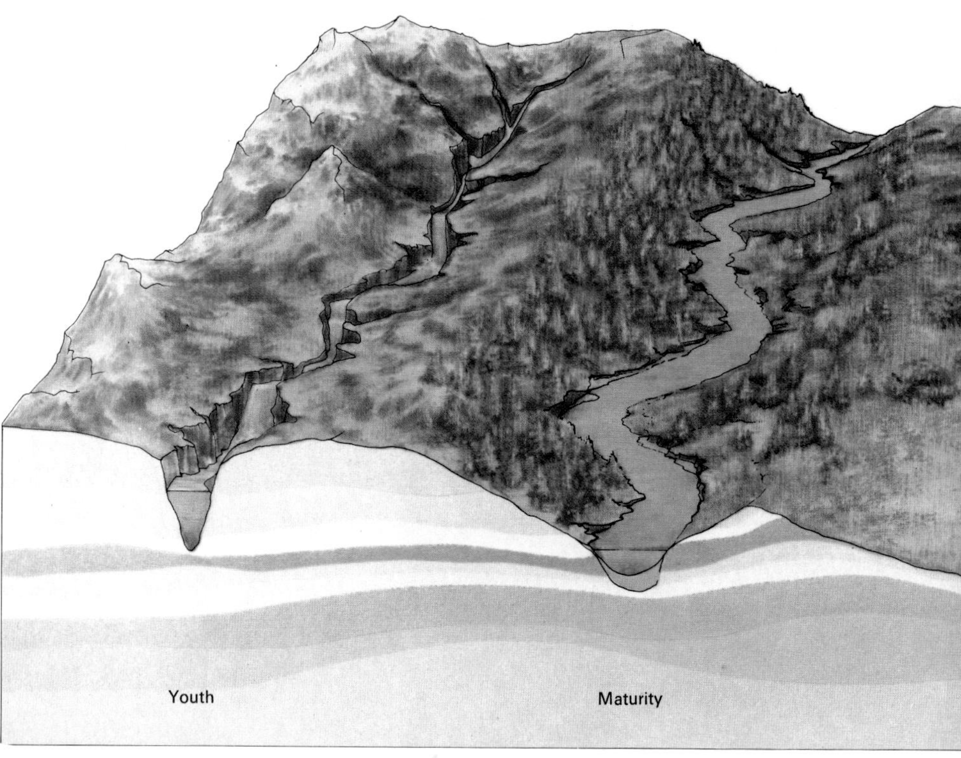

Left: A spectacular example of the effect of underground water. Limestone, like all porous rock, stores water but, being composed of calcium carbonate, it is soluble. This cave in France was opened up by the solvent action of underground water. Water seeped down the joints, dissolving the calcium carbonate. As it dripped from the cave roof, partial evaporation caused it to deposit some of the calcium carbonate. This grew downwards as a *stalactite*. Water landing on the floor formed a similar deposit, producing a *stalagmite*.

Below: A river in the Northern Territory of Australia has reached its 'old age' stage. The river, in the last stage of development, is close to *base level* (usually sea-level), the point at which it cannot cut its bed down any deeper. The curves of a river always tend to become exaggerated because of the effect of centrifugal force. This causes the current to swing against the outer bank of a curve and wear it away, a process called *lateral erosion*. In the middle distance is a meander soon to be cut off by lateral erosion.

Right: This section across the Weald of southern England shows clearly a landscape in old age. The contrast with the 'ideal type' as advanced by Davis is striking. Instead of a flat peneplain, the Weald is an irregular landscape of hills and vales from the English Channel to the River Thames. It was originally uplifted as a large anticline, but rivers flowing off the dome cut through the chalk to expose the underlying layers, leaving the resistant ridges forming the North and South Downs.

CYCLE OF EROSION

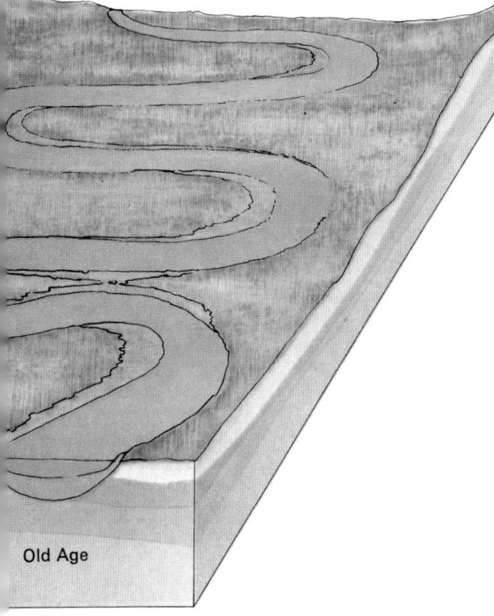

Left: A theoretical 'cycle of erosion' was advanced by the American geomorphologist W. M. Davis. His theory was based on an 'ideal case' of a block of sea-floor being uplifted to form land. The first or *youthful* stage is characterized by fast-flowing rivers which cut steep valleys into the land. In the *mature* stage, the original surface has been eroded away by the enlargement of the valleys, now broader and more open, and the curves of the rivers are more developed. By the *old age* stage, the valleys have broad, flat floors, only a little above sea-level, over which the sluggish rivers meander. This final stage Davis termed a *peneplain*, the lowest level of reduction.

Right: Ingleton Falls in Yorkshire, a river in its youthful stage causing vigorous downwards erosion. Most erosion happens when a river is in flood—at that time it has sufficient velocity to carry large rock fragments which wear away the river bed. The boulders seen here will be rolled downstream next time the river is in flood.

EALD OF SOUTHERN ENGLAND

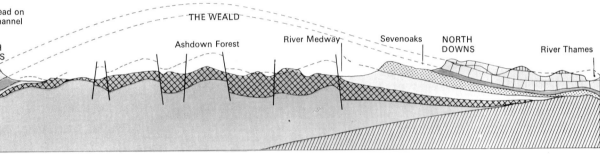

Head on
Channel
THE WEALD
Ashdown Forest
River Medway
Sevenoaks
NORTH DOWNS
River Thames
Eocene rocks
Chalk
Upper Greensand and Gault
Lower Greensand
Weald Clay
Hastings sands
Jurassic rocks
Palaeozoic rocks

ing to provide the weapons of erosion and landform sculpture.

Some of the first explanations of landforms were derived from a blend of geology and theology. As late as the nineteenth century, thinking was shaped by an effort to link the age of the earth with the Creation, and landforms with such supernatural catastrophes as the Biblical flood. After 1900, however, English-speaking geomorphologists were encouraged to explain the land surface in terms of 'youth', 'maturity' and 'old age' after the pioneering work of W. M. Davis. An American, whom many call 'the father of geomorphology', he postulated an ideal *Cycle of Erosion* to account for landforms which proceeded with a gradual flattening of relief by weathering and erosion, until the levelling was nearly complete and a *peneplain* (meaning 'almost a plain') was achieved at the 'old age' stage.

The scope of geomorphology

Currently, there is no neat framework into which landforms can be realistically placed. But there is little doubt about the scientific ingredients of a modern geomorphological explanation. These are drawn from a study of geomorphological *processes*, a study which in turn depends on a working knowledge of a wide range of sciences. These include geology as the indispensable, basic science concerned with the properties of the raw materials of landforms.

But to understand the geomorphological processes which sculpture rocks, transport debris and which modify geological structures, information is essential from other sciences, including *climatology*, *hydrology* (the study of water), *pedology* (the science of soils) and *ecology* (the study of organisms in relation to their environment). Furthermore, an appreciation of the physical motions of water, wind and ice and the nature of their role as transportation agents may be deepened by an understanding of physics.

Chemistry and biology are also important, since much of rock weathering, particularly in tropical areas, is a biochemical process. Chemical reactions are involved that are difficult to simulate in the laboratory but which depend on the vital biological contribution of carbon dioxide to the soil from plant and animal respiration. Carbon dioxide concentration in soil is commonly between 10 and 100 times greater than the 0.03 per cent found in the atmosphere. The intensified carbonic acid dissolved in soil water accounts, for example, for the impressive *solutional* weathering associated with limestones.

Biophysical processes are also at work, shaping the landforms around us. The rate of reworking of soils by animals has been known since the late nineteenth century to be impressive. In 1880, the English naturalist Charles Darwin calculated that earthworms annually bring to the ground surface about 25 tonnes of soil per hectare (10 tons per acre). Equally noteworthy is the varying effectiveness of a given vegetation cover in protecting soil from erosion. Even the social sciences are involved here since many of man's activities, such as agriculture and engineering, have an important, and often underestimated, influence on the nature and rate of some contemporary processes.

At the outset, however, the influence of geology on landforms is fundamental. The disposition of rocks at the earth's surface is determined by earth movements and expressed in structures like folds or faults. Moreover, the characteristic properties of rocks are important in relation to their resistance to erosion.

Controversy exists about the influence of climate on landforms, but some of the processes which lead to rock breakdown and the subsequent movement of the fragments or *detritus* are most distinctive in a given climatic zone. Particularly instructive in this context are studies of the processes operating in arid and semi-arid areas, such as the waterless deserts of Africa and the inhospitable 'badlands' of North America. The scant vegetation cover in these areas leaves the actual shapes of landforms starkly obvious. Such areas also show clearly the physical breakdown of rocks and the implications of a sparse vegetation cover when an occasional downpour of rain beats upon unprotected earth.

Below: Elegant, sculpted sand dunes—the result of wind deposition. Sand grains are carried along quite near the ground and deposited when the wind velocity slackens. The smooth windward slope coupled with a steep lee-face is the commonest shape of sand dune. Eddies moving sand grains along the surface cause the ripple pattern.

Right: The major factors which control the erosion and weathering of rocks are closely interrelated and occur over time. The nature of the rocks themselves is of basic importance. In particular, some types of rock are more susceptible to chemical weathering than others, even where conditions of topography and climate are the same.

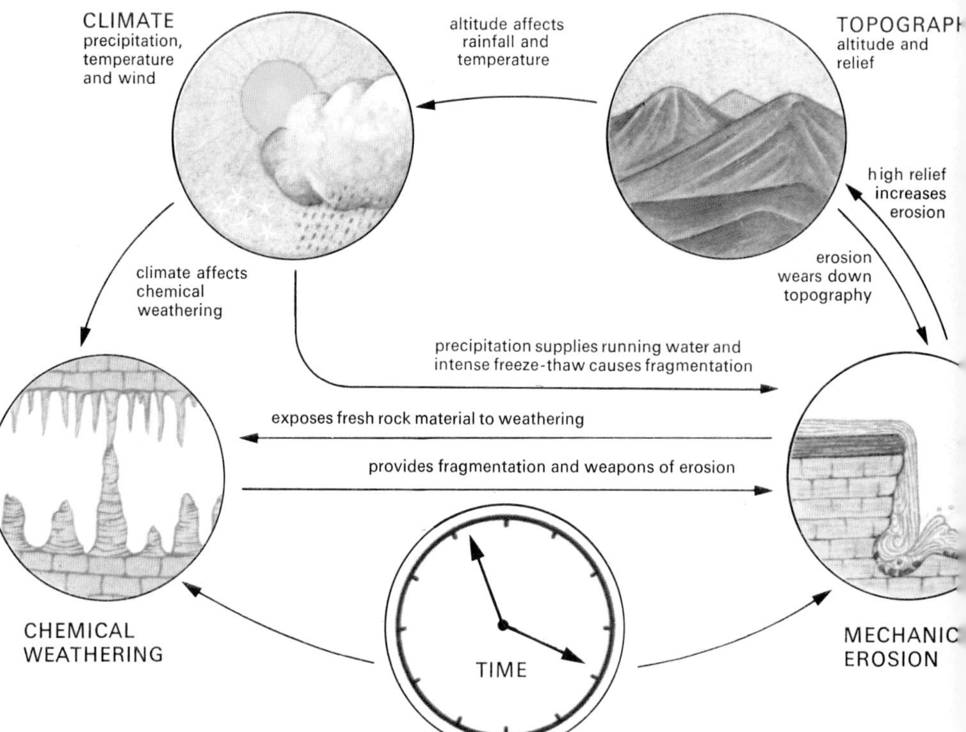

CLIMATE
precipitation, temperature and wind
altitude affects rainfall and temperature
TOPOGRAPH
altitude and relief
high relief increases erosion
erosion wears down topography
climate affects chemical weathering
precipitation supplies running water and intense freeze-thaw causes fragmentation
exposes fresh rock material to weathering
provides fragmentation and weapons of erosion
CHEMICAL WEATHERING
TIME
MECHANIC EROSION

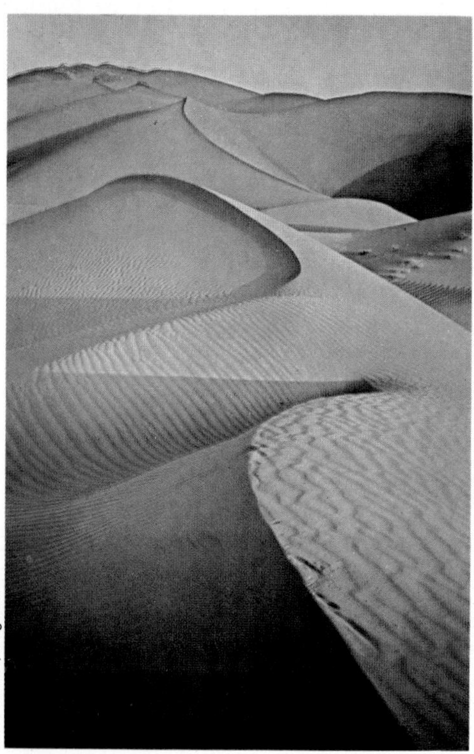
Marc Riboud/Magnum

Water at work

Water, flowing down to the oceans over the land surface, is the dominant agent of erosion. In upland areas with moist climates, fast-moving rivers may flow with sufficient volume to shift enormous, abrasive loads of sand, pebbles and even boulders. Erosion by stream action tends to broaden and deepen a valley floor, particularly if undercutting leads to landsliding. There is, however, a theoretical *base level*, or lowest point, below which most *fluvial*, or river, processes cease to be effective.

In the lowland reaches of a river, opposite valley slopes may be wide apart, separated by a broad plain made up of stream-deposited sediments, termed *alluvium*. Rivers usually wind across alluvial plains in sweeping loops or *meanders*, but there are interesting exceptions. In Arctic environments, for example, innumerable interlinking channel branches meet and diverge to form a *braided* channel pattern. The characteristics of river mouths or *estuaries* also vary greatly, in part depending on the amount of silt that may be deposited in tidal reaches of rivers. One finding from this area of research is that such deposition or *siltation* has increased notably within historic times.

Not only river waters come under close scrutiny. Geomorphology also includes the study of lakes, swamps and underground water. Only a portion of the *precipitation* (rain, snow, hail, fog and dew) that falls on to a soil runs off as a surface stream. For instance, only about 25% of the 1500 mm (about 60 in) of annual precipitation in the Congo basin enters the river, due to the intense *evapotran-*

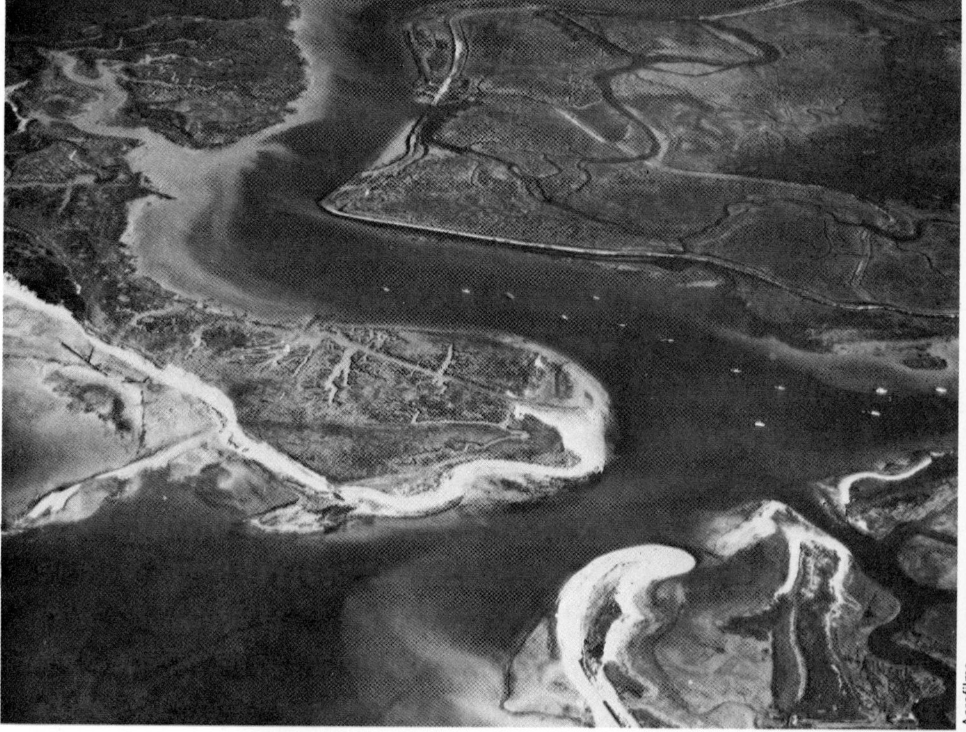
Aerofilms

Above: River estuary on the Isle of Wight. An estuary occurs at the mouth of a river where fresh water and sea water mix. Sediment is both brought down by the river and carried in by the tides, hence an estuary tends to become silted up. The light-coloured areas seen here in the rivers are the sediment below water level.

Right: The steep chalk cliffs of Flamborough Head in Yorkshire are the result of wave erosion cutting away at the base. As the cliffs are worn back a shallow platform is left behind, indicated by the zone of breaking waves. All the inlets and caves are eroded along the main joints in the rock—the usual pattern of marine erosion.

J. Allan Cash

Above: Rocks in Saudi Arabia show how *exfoliation* (the splitting of successive layers from the rock surface) can create dramatic shapes.

Below: A natural arch in Utah (USA). Wind erosion has cut along vertical joint planes, leaving columns of rock isolated, and has carved an arch in the process.

R. Everts/ZEFA

Right: Two glaciers flow like rivers of ice into the sea at Spitzbergen in the Arctic. They have carved steep-sided, U-shaped valleys, with floors well below sea-level. Stresses within the moving glaciers cause cracks and crevasses in the surface. The tops of the mountains show the sharply fretted shapes created by frost.

ZEFA

Spectrum

spiration (the total loss of moisture in the form of water vapour) typical of tropical areas. Much of such *effective* precipitation infiltrates the soil.

Usually, water percolates vertically through soil, then down through the pores and joints of the underlying rock, where it increases the store of underground water. This water slowly continues to attack the deep rock, termed *deep-weathering*, an action which, in tropical areas, may extend down to 100 m (over 300 ft) below the land surface. Such effects on landforms are most thoroughly investigated in limestone terrains.

Regions of ice and snow

In the higher latitudes and at higher altitudes, an important concept may be the *snowline*, often defined as the lower limit of perennial snow. Snow becomes consolidated beneath accumulations which are at least 30 m thick and it recrystallizes into granular snow or *firn* and finally into ice. The observation, measurement and understanding of the physical mechanisms by which ice begins to flow downvalley as a *glacier* are an exceptional challenge to all the skills of the glaciologist. Although glacier-flow velocities range from a few millimetres to a few metres each year, large volumes of soil, frost-shattered debris and deep-weathered materials are pushed forward by the glacier's advance.

The land surfaces of glaciated uplands are thus areas of gaunt, bare-rock outcrops. By contrast, after the ice has retreated, lowland areas of glacial deposition are often paved smooth by a thick layer of *ground moraine*, composed of the debris dragged along at the base or *sole* of the glacier.

A significant portion of the debris moved by ice is initially loosened and transported by *periglaciation*. This term refers to a set of processes associated with the repetitive fluctuation between intense freezing and thawing characteristic of zones marginal to ice-caps, or, indeed, of any bare ground where the annual temperature is at or below freezing point. The ground of such areas is usually permanently frozen, a condition termed *permafrost*. However, the top metre or so often melts in summer and periglaciation includes the rapid downslope debris movements termed *solifluction* that then occur in this thawed or 'active' layer above the permafrost.

A compelling fascination about landforms is to enquire how long they have been there or perhaps how they may have changed with the passage of time. However, it is no longer thought realistic to confine consideration of the stages in the evolution of a land surface within an over-idealized framework. One reason is the number of quite extraordinary and rapid oscillations in ice volumes and in areas covered by ice that occurred in the high latitudes during the Ice Age of the Pleistocene epoch. Moreover, there were repeated oscillations of climate from rainy periods or *pluvials* to dry phases or *inter-pluvials* in lower latitudes.

Geomorphology includes the study of the narrow zone where land meets sea. Somewhere within that zone, geomorphology hands over to oceanography, but along the coast itself the influence of geological control and the nature and role of processes of rock breakdown, transport and deposition are as obvious as anywhere inland.

The Grand Canyon in northwest Arizona is one of the most magnificent sections of the great gorge of the Colorado river. The Canyon is 217 miles (349km) long and between 4 and 18 miles (6-29km) wide.

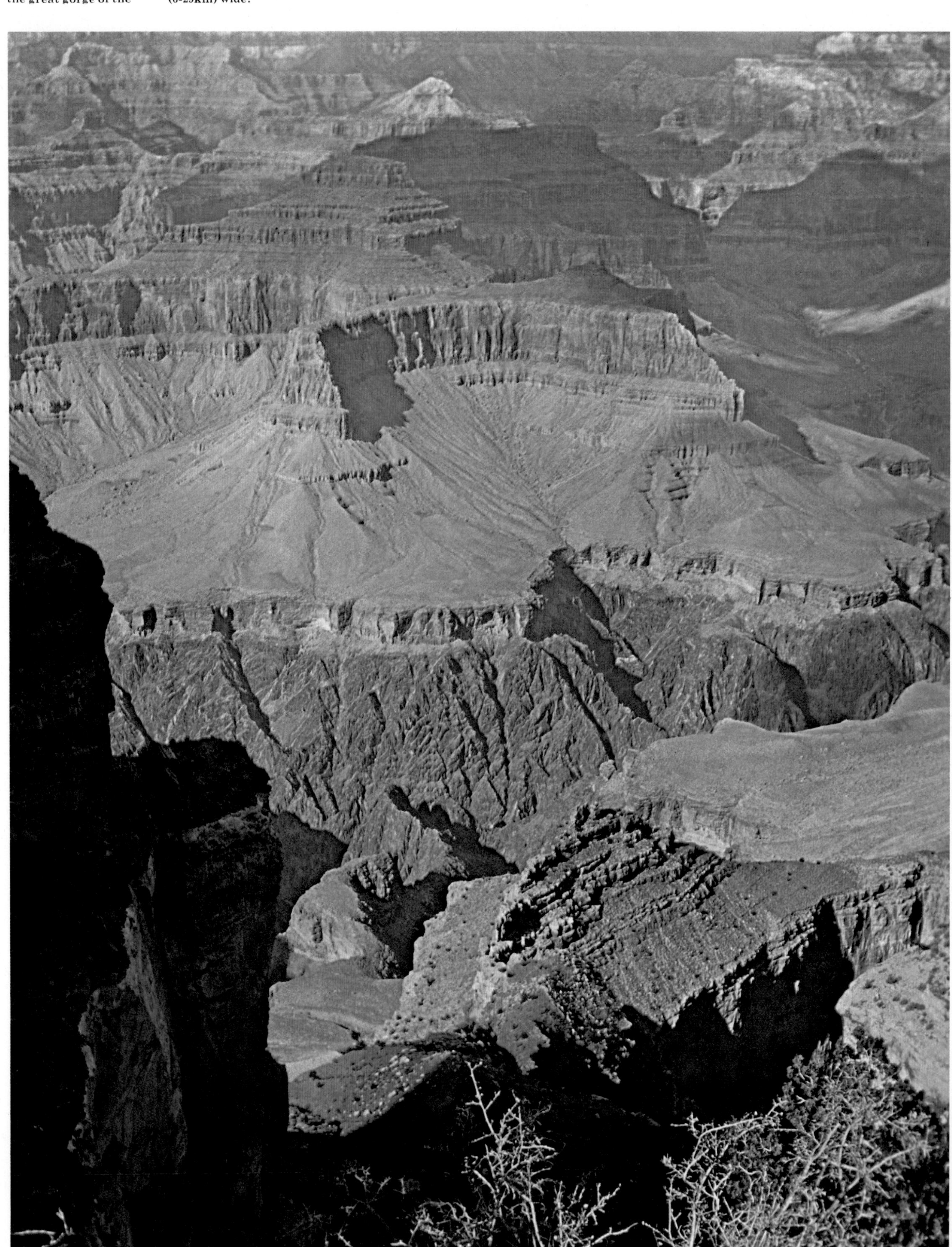

Rocks and Landscapes

The hills, valleys, plains and bays that form the landscape we see around us are sculptured by the processes of weathering, and then shaped by the erosion and deposition of rivers, glaciers, wind and sea. Nevertheless, these relief features depend on geology, for both the nature or *lithology* of the rocks and their structures are fundamental to visible landforms.

Igneous and metamorphic rocks, because of their interlocking crystalline texture, are usually resistant to erosion and tend to stand up as high ground. This resistance, however, also depends upon the chemical stability of the minerals making up the rocks.

Some minerals resist chemical weathering better than others. For example, quartz and white mica, which form a large part of granite, are relatively stable. But feldspar, the most common mineral in most igneous and metamorphic rocks, is less stable and tends to break down to form clay. Silicates of iron and magnesium, abundant in *basic* (low silica content) igneous rocks like basalt and dolerite, decompose still more readily under weathering.

Granite therefore usually forms high ground, as in Dartmoor in south-western England and the Cheviot Hills between England and Scotland. Basalt, dolerite and gabbro, on the other hand, may or may not form high ground, depending upon how active chemical weathering is. This in turn depends mainly upon the climate.

Young volcanoes usually form steep hills of lava and volcanic ash, but are eroded comparatively quickly. Volcanic *necks* (the pipes of old volcanoes, from which the surrounding deposits of lava and ash have been eroded away) often form sharp hills. A familiar example is Edinburgh's Castle Rock, the remains of the Arthur's Seat volcano which was active 325 million years ago.

Metamorphic rocks are sometimes more resistant than igneous rocks, as they have been intensely compressed. And sedimentary rocks vary still more in their resistance to erosion. Clay rocks are chemically stable, but are physically very unstable. They tend to 'flow' downhill and collapse along slip planes and so will stand at only a very low angle. This means that any hillside slopes formed of clay or shale will necessarily be gentle and the side view or transverse *profile* of a valley eroded in such rocks will appear wide and low-angled.

Sandstones and limestones do not have this tendency to flow and usually stand at a high angle with consequently steeper slopes. When alternated with clays, the sandstones or limestones often stand out as steep, bare edges, separated by gentler, grassy slopes on the clays. However, this arrangement is obviously dependent upon the extent of rock consolidation. In the case of sandstones this is determined by the degree of cementation; in limestones it depends on the degree of crystallization. Unconsolidated sand, for example, will stand in steeper faces than clay, but not as steep as a well-cemented sandstone.

Chalk country is characterized by

Picturepoint

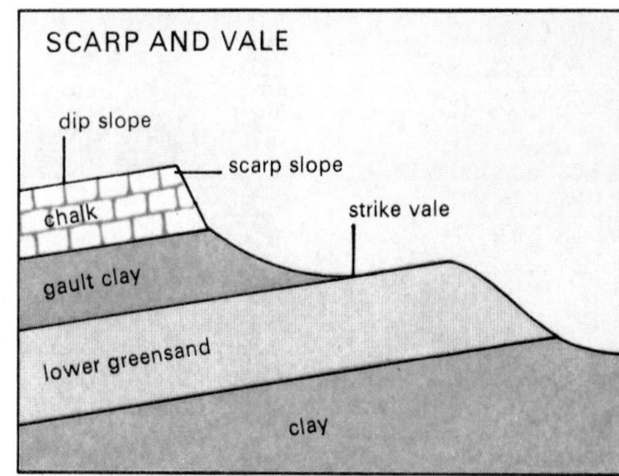

Above: The scarp at the Devil's Dyke in Sussex.

Left: The section shows that the hills, formed of chalk, are dipping to the left, with a steep scarp slope facing north. Beneath the chalk is the Gault Clay which has been eroded to form a strike vale. The Lower Greensand forms a ridge further north.

Below: A section taken through a rift valley bounded by successive fault scarps. The faults have thrown the strata down on both sides, so that a low strip of land runs along the centre, often the site of a river. Most rift valleys have one dominating pair of faults, but some, like this one, are formed by a number of small faults.

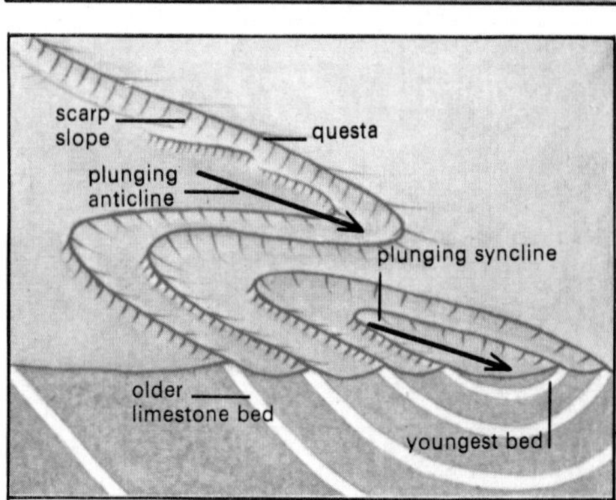

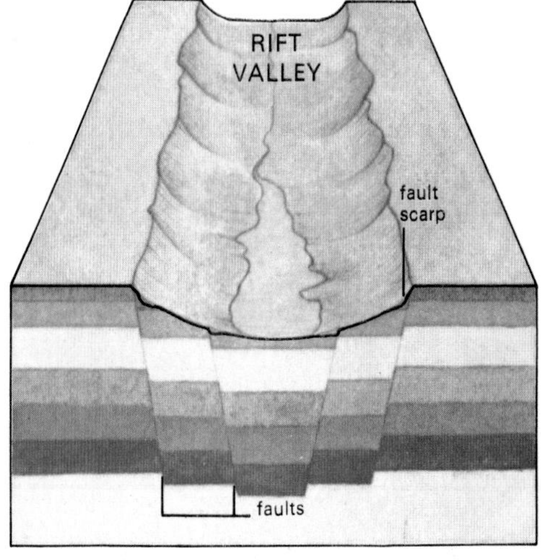

Right: The view from the summit of St Victor in south-west France, an area of much folding. The anticline (upfold) and syncline (downfold) share an axis of folding (as shown above) which is plunging to the right. Resistant limestones, interbedded with less resistant strata, form ridges or cuestas. These curve round the plunging folds and are bare of covering vegetation. On the anticline the oldest beds come to the surface in the centre and are surrounded on three sides by the steep scarp slopes of the limestones. As the limestones are dipping away from the crest of the anticline, their dip-slopes stretch away from the outcrop of the oldest beds. On the syncline the youngest beds appear in the centre.

Dr. Middlemiss

gently rounded hills with no steep slopes. The Salisbury Plain and the Chilterns of England, for example, are wide areas of grassy downs and smooth, rolling hills where the occasional chalk pit unveils the underlying rock. Chalk is an example of a poorly-crystallized limestone which is liable to flow downhill, especially under the influence of alternate freezing and thawing of the water it contains. On the other hand, a thoroughly crystalline limestone, as in the Pennines or the Niagara Limestone over which the Niagara Falls plunge, will easily stand in resistant, vertical faces.

The steepness of the slopes of a valley-side depends upon the relationship between the rate of erosion by the river running through the valley and the rate of movement downhill of rock material weathered from the sides of the valley. Anything which gives the river an advantage over the downhill movement will produce a steeper profile. Downhill movement may be inhibited by resistant rocks, or the energy of the river may be increased by recent uplift of the area. Conversely, the nature of clay gives the advantage to downhill movement and a gentler profile will result.

The influence of rock structure

The famous six-sided columns of basalt at the Giants' Causeway in Northern Ireland show how the shape of a landscape is influenced by the structure of the rocks, and not just by their nature. Structure is primarily important in opening the rocks to attack from rain, ice and streams along joints and faults. *Joints* are fractures in the rock along which there has been little or none of the movement associated with faults. But both these features act as planes of weakness where weathering and erosion can work effectively. The pattern of a river system is often found to be guided by joints and faults and this confirms that running water finds it easiest to erode the rocks along such planes.

When a fault has recently taken place—'recently' in a geological sense can, of course, extend to two or three million years—the fault plane is visible as a steep slope or *fault scarp*. A *rift valley*, for example, is a strip of country let down between two fault scarps, like the East African Rift Valley and the Rhine valley between Basel and Bingen. The opposite is a *block mountain*, a block of land pushed up between two fault scarps.

Eventually a primary fault scarp will become eroded away. More resistant rocks may, however, have been thrown by the fault against less resistant rocks. In that case the more resistant rocks, whether they are on the upthrown or the downthrown side of the fault, will be less affected by erosion and will stand up parallel to the outcrop of the fault as a *fault-line scarp*. The edge of the Ochil Hills near Stirling in Scotland and the northern front of the Harz Mountains in Germany are good examples.

Where inclined or *dipping* rock beds are being eroded, the more resistant strata will stand up as ridges, or *cuestas*, while the less resistant ones are eroded to form strips of lowland or *strike vales* between the ridges. In the scarp and vale landscape of the Weald in southern England, the Chalk and the Lower Greensand form cuestas separated by the vale of the Gault Clay. Another very good example can be seen further north in Shropshire, where limestones form the cuestas of Wenlock Edge and View Edge, with the strike vale of Hope Dale on shales between them.

A different, but equally distinctive, landscape is found in regions subjected to folding. In the simplest case, the *anticlines* of the folds form hills and the *synclines* appear as valleys. Such simple correspondence is rare, but good examples are found in the Jura Mountains of eastern France and Switzerland. Here resistant limestones have preserved the anticlines from erosion.

It is much more usual for anticlines to have been breached by erosion. When this happens, the more resistant beds form cuestas which slope in opposite directions on the two sides of the fold, with the scarp slopes facing towards each other in an anticline and facing away from each other in a syncline. For example, the scarp slopes of the South Downs and the North Downs, both formed by chalk, face each other across the Weald. In fact, it is common to find that anticlines have been hollowed out to form valleys while synclines stand up to form hills, so that the topography is opposite to the structure. Although this is known as *inverted relief*, it is in fact the more usual case in an area where the rocks have been folded.

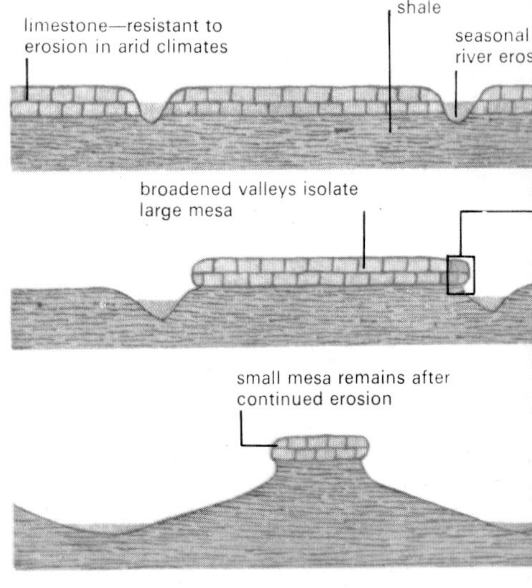

Above: How a mesa is formed: where resistant rocks are horizontal and lie over less resistant beds, weathering and erosion tend to work down the main joints until the soft rock is exposed. This is then easily eroded, leaving a remnant of the resistant bed as an isolated table which becomes steadily reduced in size.

Below: Monument Valley in Utah (USA) is famous for its sculptured mesas. In this arid region, wind has probably done most of the erosion. The steep angle of slopes on the resistant sandstones contrasts sharply with the more gentle slopes formed by the debris eroded from the less resistant shales.

Picturepoint

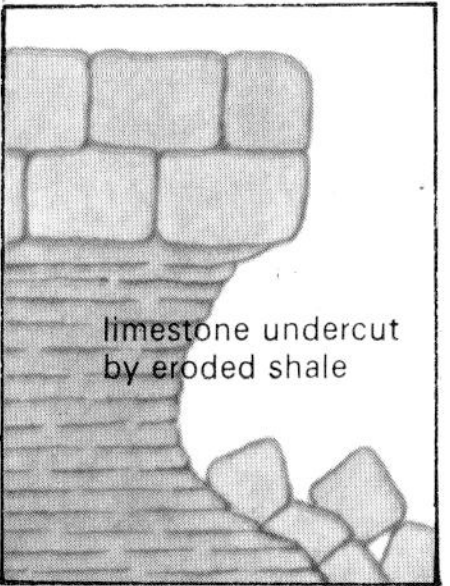

Below: The spectacular Giants' Causeway in Antrim, Northern Ireland. The regular six-sided columns of basalt were formed long ago by rapidly cooling volcanic lava flowing into the sea. Today, these joints act as planes of weakness where weathering and erosion by water, sea and ice are constantly wearing away the columns.

Spectrum

ROCKS AND THEIR ORIGINS

There are three kinds of rocks. **Igneous** rocks have cooled and solidified from molten rock material or *magma* produced by heating deep in the earth. The magma is squeezed upwards through the earth's crust and may be forced in among the pre-existing rocks where it solidifies as *intrusive* igneous rock. Granite is a well-known example. Alternatively, magma may reach the surface at a volcano and flow out as *lava* to solidify as *extrusive* igneous rock, of which basalt is a common example.

During cooling the constituent minerals crystallize out from the molten mass, in approximately the reverse order of their melting points (the temperature at which minerals become molten). Consequently, an igneous rock is composed of interlocking crystals.

Sedimentary rocks are composed of fragments derived from weathering of pre-existing rocks. The fragments are commonly transported by wind, water or ice and deposited, usually in water and especially on the sea-floor, where the sediments become compacted to form rocks. There are again three main types of sedimentary rocks. First, there are those in which the fragments are recognizable pebbles of pre-existing rocks (*conglomerates*) or grains of identifiable minerals (*sandstones*). These rocks become consolidated when mineral matter becomes deposited between the particles to act as a cement. The second type is *clay*, in which the particles are extremely minute crystals of clay minerals formed from the chemical breakdown of other minerals during weathering.

Chemical deposits form the third main type of sedimentary rock. These are composed of material dissolved out of pre-existing rocks during weathering. The most important of this type is limestone, often formed of calcium carbonate from the shells and skeletal remains of dead animals accumulated on the sea-floor. Recrystallization takes place and the calcium carbonate consolidates to form limestone.

Metamorphic rocks were originally either igneous or sedimentary rocks which were thoroughly altered or *metamorphosed* by heat and pressure within the crust of the earth without being completely melted. In its original form marble, for example, was limestone.

IGS

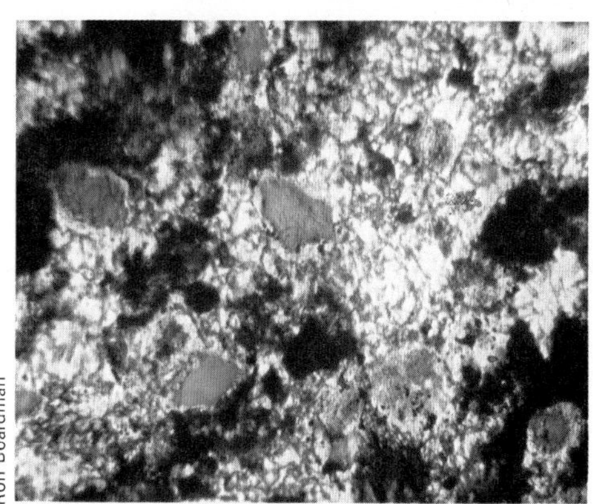

Ron Boardman

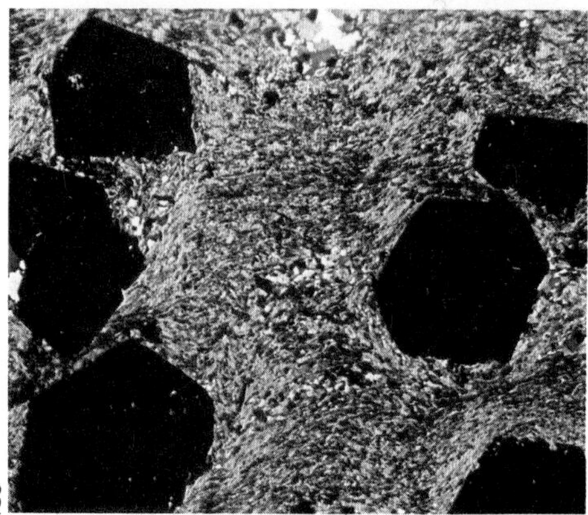

IGS

Above: Examples of the three main types of rock photographed under a microscope between crossed-polarizing lenses. This process gives distinctive colours to minerals. The igneous *gabbro* (top) is made up of intimately interlocking crystals of feldspar (black and white stripes) and silicates of iron and magnesium. The sedimentary *sandstone* (centre) is composed of grains of quartz (bright blue) cemented together by chert (fine-grained silica). The *schist* (bottom) is mainly composed of mica, but the large black crystals of garnet grew in the rock during its metamorphism.

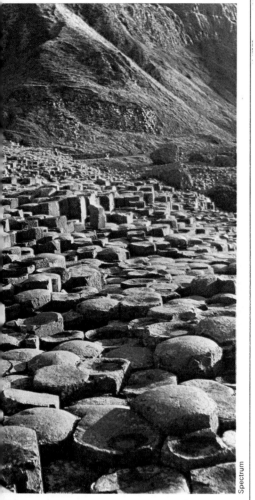

Right: The spectacular Niagara Falls interrupt the flow of water from Lake Erie to Lake Ontario. At the Falls, the massive, resistant and almost horizontal Niagara Limestone caps less resistant shale. The shale is being rapidly eroded into a deep plunge pool (left) beneath the falls and, as this is enlarged, the undercut limestone collapses along its main joints. Large limestone blocks can be seen in the foreground of the photograph. These will eventually become broken up by weathering and carried away by the river. In this way, the limestone edge is being cut back and the falls are retreating upstream towards Lake Erie by about 1m each year.

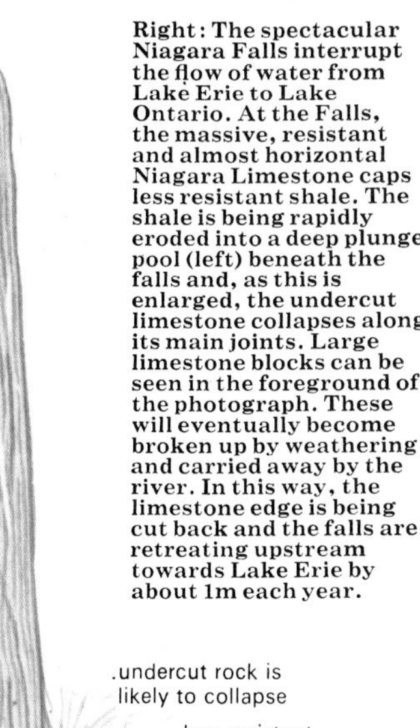

Canadian High Commission

Climate and Landforms

In 1883, Albrecht Penck, a German, became the first geomorphologist to consider the possible relationship between distinctive climates and landform development. Later, in 1910, he suggested that five separate landform groupings could be recognized in the world from their correspondence to climatic regions. The five regions were *humid* (moist) and *sub-humid* areas, where precipitation exceeds evaporation; *arid* (dry) and *semi-arid* areas, where evaporation exceeds precipitation; and *glacial* areas, where the land surface is shaped by a mass of moving ice.

At the same time W. M. Davis, an American whom many call the 'father of geomorphology', put forward his theory of the *geographical cycle of erosion*. He suggested that, depending on the rock structure, landforms develop in stages through a 'normal' cycle of erosion in which running water is the dominant process. 'Landscape', he said, 'is a function of structure, process and stage.'

Davis's cycle, which really described the evolution of steep slopes (young landscapes) to a level surface or *peneplain* (old landscapes), was based upon humid, temperate conditions which he considered as 'normal'. In these 'normal' areas, slope angles vary, but are usually *convex* (bulging) on their upper parts and *concave* (hollowed) on their lower parts and have a relatively uniform covering of rock debris. Landforms which developed in extremely cold or hot areas, he considered climatic accidents or interruptions to the 'normal' development. Later, however, he too recognized special cycles for arid and glacial areas.

Differences of opinion

The ideas of Penck and Davis were the beginnings of *climatic geomorphology*, the study of climatic influence on landforms. Although their notions are now thought to be gross over-simplifications, both men were very influential at the time. After Penck, other Germans such as Carl Troll and Julius Budel, and the Frenchmen Jean Tricart and André Cailleux, have developed the concepts of climatic control of landforms, whereas in the US and Britain the idea has diminished in popularity. Most English-speaking geomorphologists either assume climate to be of secondary inportance or neglect it altogether. Instead, emphasis has been placed more on the processes of weathering and erosion themselves.

This difference may be attributed to the emphasis given by the German scientists to detailed landform description rather than explanation. Or it may have been due to the language barrier, which enabled British and American workers to criticize and reappraise Davis's theories of landform evolution whilst overlooking the ideas of climatic influences developed by Penck.

There are some processes, such as the action of ice, which are limited to certain climatic areas. Glaciated areas at high latitudes, and elsewhere in mountainous regions, produce unique landforms, such as deposited *moraines* and U-shaped

D. H. Teuffen/ZEFA

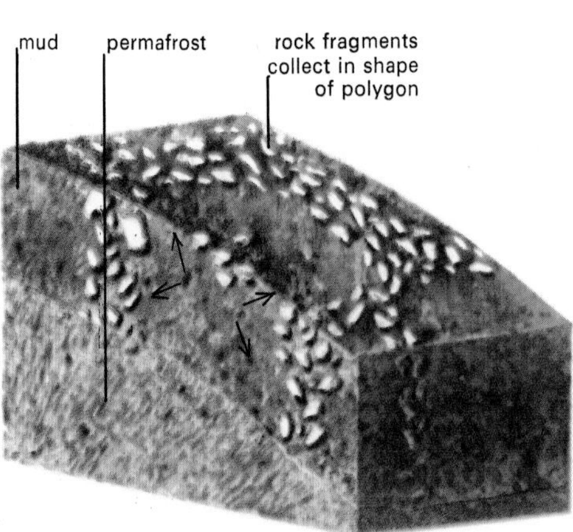

STONE POLYGONS AND STRIPES

Above: A typical U-shaped valley created by glacial erosion in the Swiss Alps. Glaciers and frost shattering shape landforms unique to very cold, wet climates; but similar features exist in more temperate areas which were once glaciated. England's Duddon Valley (above centre) derives its primary shape from Ice Age glaciation, but the rounded hilltops and slopes are typical of humid, temperate areas.

Left and below: Some distinctive ground patterns only occur in periglacial regions. Repeated freezing and thawing force coarser rock fragments through the mud to collect in curious shapes, which depend on the angle of slope as shown below.

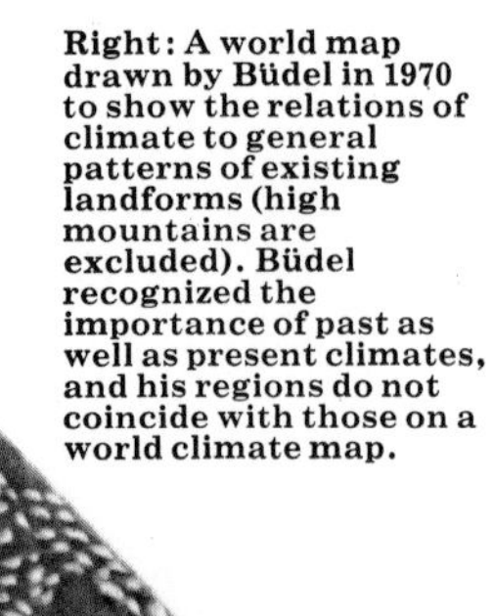

Right: A world map drawn by Büdel in 1970 to show the relations of climate to general patterns of existing landforms (high mountains are excluded). Büdel recognized the importance of past as well as present climates, and his regions do not coincide with those on a world climate map.

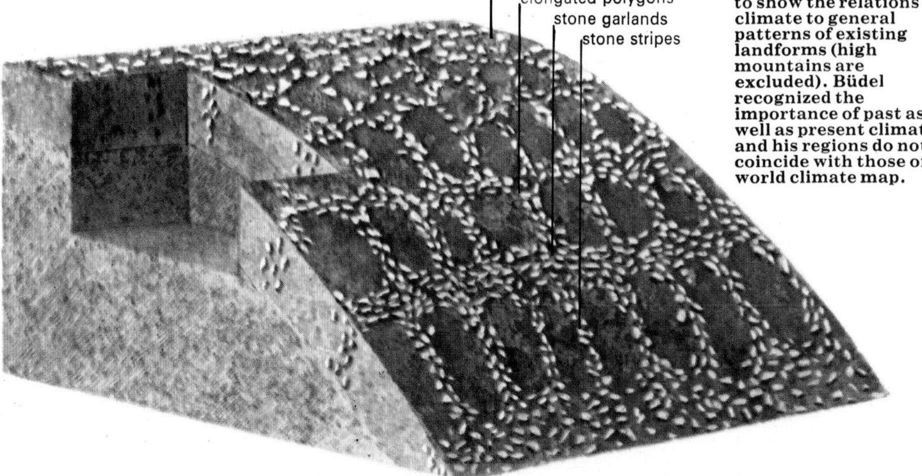

Patrick Thurston

G. D. Plage/Bruce Coleman

Mary Evans Picture Library

Above: In extremely arid areas like the Namib desert, climate affects landforms largely by inhibiting the growth of vegetation. There is little or nothing to bind the unconsolidated surface materials and strong winds can then sweep the loose particles into giant sand dunes.

Left and right: Cleopatra's Needle, an Egyptian obelisk of granite, was presented to the British people in 1878. It now stands on the Thames Embankment (right). However, after only a century of exposure to the humid, temperate atmosphere of London, it has weathered more extensively than after 3,500 years of exposure in Egypt's arid environment.

Angelo Hornak

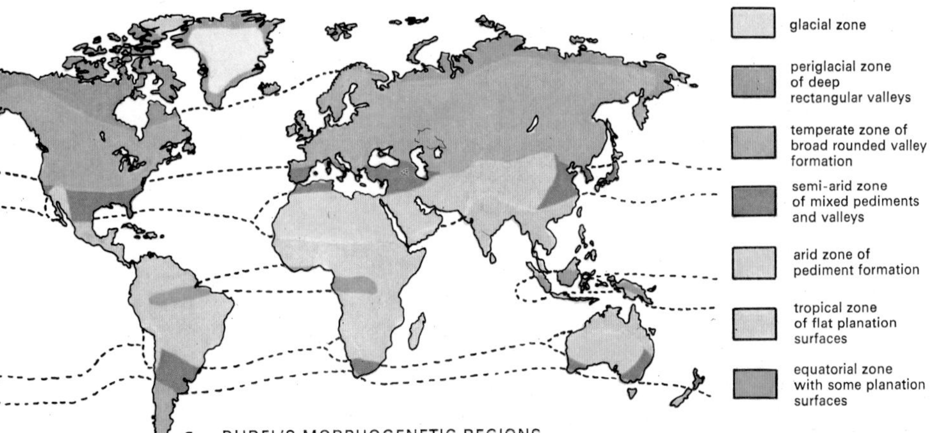

valleys. On the margins of glacial areas, in *periglacial* regions, where mean annual temperatures are still low but the temperature range is greater, other distinctive forms are found.

Here *mechanical weathering* or physical disintegration is more important than *chemical weathering*, in which rock decomposition is achieved by agents such as water, carbon dioxide or organic acids. In cold, moist periglacial conditions, the lack of vegetation and the low temperatures retard chemical reactions, but abundant moisture and frequent freezing and thawing of ice and snow in rock joints and below ground is highly conducive to mechanical disintegration.

Mechanical weathering by frost-shattering is most important in high mountain or *alpine* areas and in the vast, treeless plains known as *tundra* in North America and Siberia. As a result, the debris produced there is typically angular in shape. Because water increases its volume by nine per cent on freezing, its presence in rock joints and pores can easily shatter rocks. Low temperatures alone are not sufficient but prolonged temperature fluctuations around 0°C will cause severe breakage if water is available. In addition, the daily freezing and thawing of the 'active layer' above the permanently frozen subsoil or *permafrost* may create a mobile surface of mud and rock fragments. In such climates wind action is strong but water removal is sporadic and weak as most water is frozen.

The topography created as a result is unique. Steep rocky cliffs tower over layers of frost-shattered debris known as *scree* or *talus*. On gentler slopes, slow downhill flow or *solifluction* of saturated

George Hall/Susan Griggs

Left: Climate rarely acts alone in shaping landforms. Ayer's Rock in Australia is a giant dome of sandstone and conglomerates. Earth movements tipped the strata into a vertical position and erosion removed less resistant rocks to form an almost level erosion plain or *pediplain*. Present-day erosion processes have rounded the surface, but the rock structure is mainly responsible for this feature.

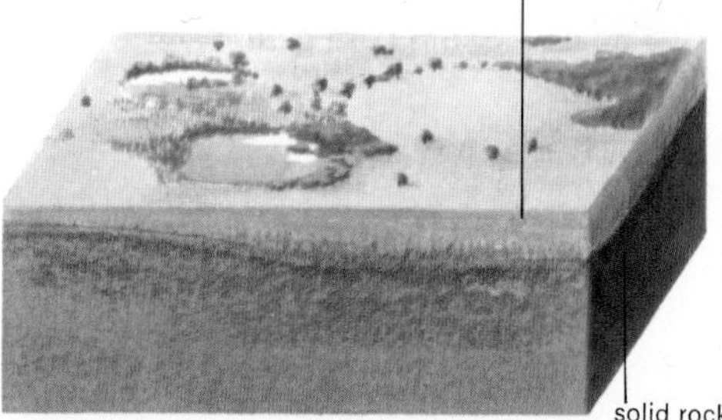

Above right: How an inselberg is formed: (1) With high temperatures and seasonal abundance of surface and ground water, chemical weathering may penetrate to great depths. (2) An irregular weathering 'floor' in the rocks often forms due to local differences in rock resistance and jointing. Subsurface domes are produced. (3) When erosion removes the weathered surface rock, the domes are exposed. Subsequent disintegration of the outcrops produces *inselbergs* 'island mounds' typical of arid and tropical areas.

Right: Isolated inselbergs found in Iran.

Colorific!

Left: A reef of coral fringing the Society Is. in the Pacific. Coral reefs are an indisputable example of landform determined by climate—they grow only in seas where temperature never falls below 18°C.

Below: The gaunt topography of dry regions is shown in this view of Dead Horse Point, Utah.

rock fragments and mud often occurs, giving rise to huge valley-side lobes, and mass movements such as *rockfalls* and *landslides* are common in the unconsolidated surface materials. On level ground occur plateaux of frost-shattered boulders, known as *blockfields*, and poorly-drained plains covered with curious ice-formed patterns and hollows. Braided river channels interweave through wide, rock-choked alluvial valleys.

By contrast, landforms in arid and semi-arid areas are quite different. These dry landscapes take many forms, from the deeply-dissected plateau blocks of the south-western USA to the flat, eroded plains of Africa and Australia; from stony deserts to sandy dunes. Two essential features are apparent in arid and semi-arid landscapes. Firstly, the existence of broad, gently-sloping surfaces known as *pediments* descending from steep slopes distinguishes dry climate landscapes from all others. Secondly, the angularity and sharpness of the landform profiles are impressive: the slightest change in rock type is at once reflected by a sharp break in slope.

A wide 24-hour temperature range, small but critical water supply, strong winds, lack of vegetation and the occurence of flash floods are the factors controlling landform development in arid climates. One of the major causes of rock decay is mechanical weathering by *insolation* (expansion and contraction of rock minerals by rapid heating and cooling); other causes are *salt crystal growth* and very active chemical weathering induced by high temperatures acting with small amounts of rainfall and dew.

ZEFA

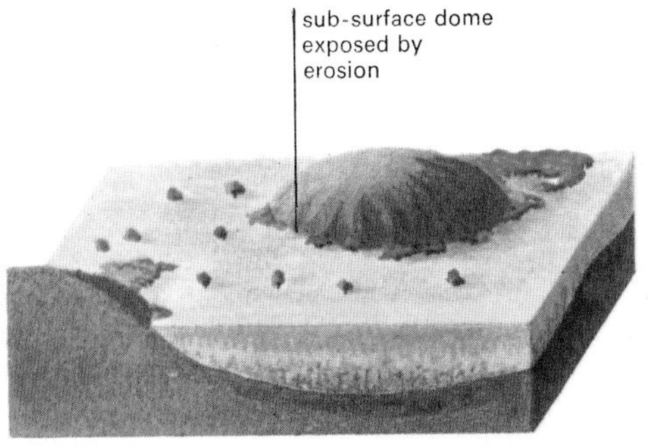

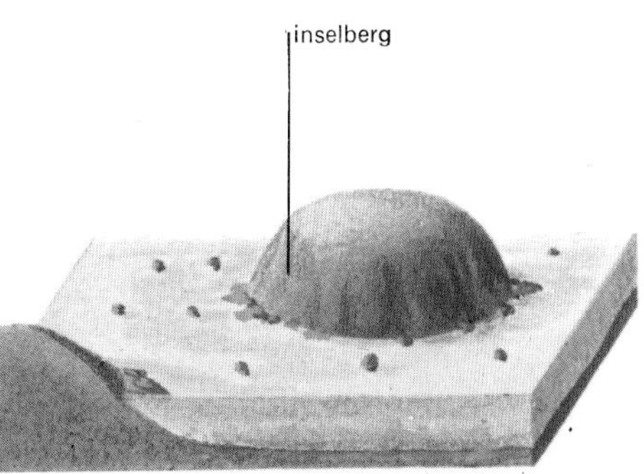

C. Weaver/Ardea

TEMPERATE
CAPE

harder rock
eroded down

Below: A typical humid, temperate landscape has modified plateau remnants, broad valleys, meandering rivers and rounded hills.

TROPICAL
CAPE

Below: By contrast, the humid tropical landscape shows a more extensive plateau cut by steep valleys over broad plains. Harder rock masses form dominant sugarloaf hills.

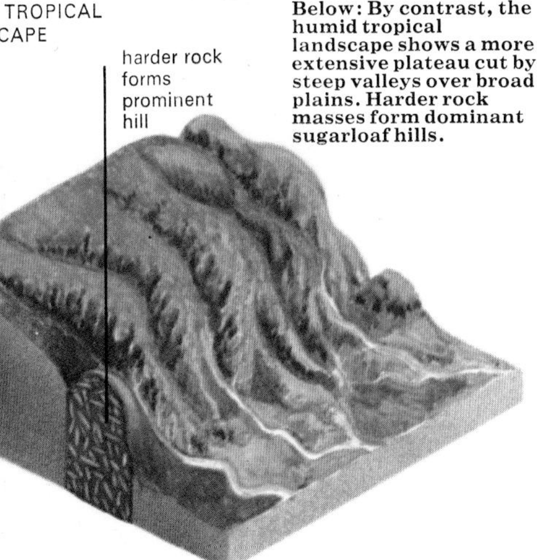

In the drier parts, combined mechanical and chemical weathering affects only rock cracks. Intervening grains are loosened to produce mostly granular sands. With sparse vegetation and strong winds these are soon removed or used to carve wind-blasted stones. Residual hills known as *mesas* or *buttes* are often left isolated due to the protection of more resistant cap rock.

In semi-arid climates, increased water leads to a more extensive penetration of rock joints and the production of rounded boulders from joint blocks. Active erosion by *sheet wash*, a broad flood of rainwater, in wet periods easily removes the surrounding weathered mantle, leaving only isolated hills called *inselbergs* or piles of rocky boulders, *castle koppies*, rising above a flat surface.

In humid, tropical climates chemical weathering is extremely intense. Soluble products of weathering such as calcium bicarbonate are removed by rainwater into the river system. On slopes, however, rock decomposition is generally faster than the transport of slope material. Consequently, deep soils are formed of the abundant clays produced by chemical weathering aided by intense biochemical activity. It is the balance between the products of weathering and the effects of heavy tropical rain which controls slope evolution in this zone. Rounded hillslopes, sugarloaf-shaped hills, and silty rivers are the typical landforms of tropical regions.

The highly variable landforms of temperate areas show forms intermediate between those of arid and humid, cold and tropical areas. As has been observed, a rolling landscape of hills and broad valleys is determined by the typically 'convexo-concave' shaped hillslopes. Both mechanical and chemical weathering processes occur but the relative importance of each depends upon local conditions such as rock type, exposure, temperature and the amount of water present. Neither process acts as intensely as in polar or tropical climates.

Transportation of debris in river systems is most effective in this area because the amount of sediment supplied is roughly equal to the ability of the stream to transport it. As a result, the channel is not overloaded with coarse debris as in periglacial areas, nor is it laden with fine silt and dissolved material as in tropical areas.

Mapping the effects of climate

In 1948, Julius Büdel devised a world map showing the distribution of nine *morphogenetic regions*, in which distinctive individual landforms and physical landscapes are found, and in which the same geomorphic processes are supposed to predominate. The variations between these regions, however, do not arise because processes are operating there which do not occur elsewhere. Rather, the landforms are shaped by the way in which 'universal' geomorphic processes operate in different climates.

Several geomorphologists have tried to map the distribution of such large-scale regions. For example, one French scientist, Louis Peltier, even used measurements of temperature and precipitation to define his morphogenetic regions. None of these classifications, however, accurately shows the world distribution of landforms as it presently exists. There are a number of reasons why this is so.

The detailed form of most landscapes reflects past as well as present climatic effects. In *polygenetic* landscapes, several types of climatic conditions have left their imprint. This is especially so in middle-latitude, temperate areas which have experienced many fluctuating cycles of glacial and periglacial conditions. Many parts of Britain, for instance, have glacial valleys. Similarly many of the blockfields of present periglacial regions, and dry river channels or *wadis* in deserts, are due to former climates when conditions were very different.

Many so-called distinctive climatic landforms occur in widely differing climatic zones. Inselbergs, for example, occur in both arid and humid areas. Similar forms often develop in different rock types from a different set of processes and in different climates. Moreover, when landforms over small areas are considered, no clear relationship with climate emerges.

Today, geomorphologists do not agree on the relative importance of climate in landform development. It is possible that the influence of climate is felt most directly through the effect of vegetation. Certainly vegetation greatly affects the nature of the processes operating. It also seems that many landforms are influenced more by infrequent climatic events than they are by average or typical events. This is the case with rivers where the shape of the channel is generally adjusted to the maximum flow rather than the average, and in deserts where the most important landform modifications are brought about by the occasional flash flood.

Desert Landscapes

Approximately one-third of the earth's land surface has a scarcity of water. Some of these arid (dry) and semi-arid regions, like the Sahara and Kalahari of Africa, the Thar in India and Pakistan, and the great Australian desert, are vast, hot deserts, created mainly by the global pattern of climate. Other arid zones, such as the Great Basin and Mohave deserts of the United States and the Gobi desert in Mongolia, are sheltered from rain by mountain ranges or vast continental expanses.

Dry regions may be broadly described as deserts or semi-deserts, but not all of them are hot. Patagonia in South America and the Siberian steppes, for example, are seasonally very cold. But in all deserts the amount of moisture that can be lost through evaporation exceeds the amount of water received as precipitation.

As a result of this deficiency of water, vegetation is either totally lacking or very sparse, and consists of remarkable drought-resistant species of plants such as the American cacti. Despite the wide range of rock types and topographies found in arid areas, certain very distinctive landforms are produced. These are the result of the predominance of bare ground, and the effects of infrequent, and often violent, rainfall and high *insolation* (radiation received from the sun).

Wind and sand

Deserts are often thought of as vast expanses of drifting sands. Yet, no more than 30 per cent of the Arabian desert, for example, is sandy terrain, and only 11 per cent of the Sahara and two per cent of North America's arid lands are sand deserts. These wastes are dominated by seas of sand (known as *ergs* in the Sahara) which are swept by the wind into ripples, dunes and sand ridges, some of which are 450 m (1,500 ft) high. The distance between adjacent crests, the *wavelength* of these features, tends to grow when the dominant wind speed increases.

Wind is a major agent of removal and transportation in deserts. The process by which unconsolidated sand and dust is caught up and swept away by wind is termed *deflation*. Eventually, such material is deposited to form ripples, dunes, sand ridges and sheets of loess.

Ripples form transversely to the wind direction. Some are *aerodynamic ripples*, created by regular patterns of turbulence in the moving air. Others are *ballistic ripples*, formed by the bouncing motion or *saltation* of most wind-blown sands. When a saltating grain lands, it ejects several other grains into the airstream. In their turn, these grains land downwind

Photri

Left: The effect of weathering is clearly visible in deserts. This rock in Death Valley, California, was attacked at its base by chemical and mechanical weathering and the wind has removed the debris to reveal its shape.

Right: A satellite photograph of the Namib Desert, SW Africa. This view, covering about 40,000 sq km, shows a series of enormous dunes (lower left) which were swept into parallel lines by off-shore winds. North of the Kuiseb River, an eroded landscape of Pre-Cambrian rocks is partially veneered by sand. The large sand-bar in the middle part of the Atlantic coast forms Walvis Bay, the largest settlement in this thinly-populated but diamond-rich desert.

Below: The Bad Lands of South Dakota give their name to badly gullied, semi-arid areas. Once natural vegetation is removed by man, short but violent flash floods erode weak and unprotected sediments into an intricate pattern of gullies. More resistant beds form ledges and benches.

Picturepoint

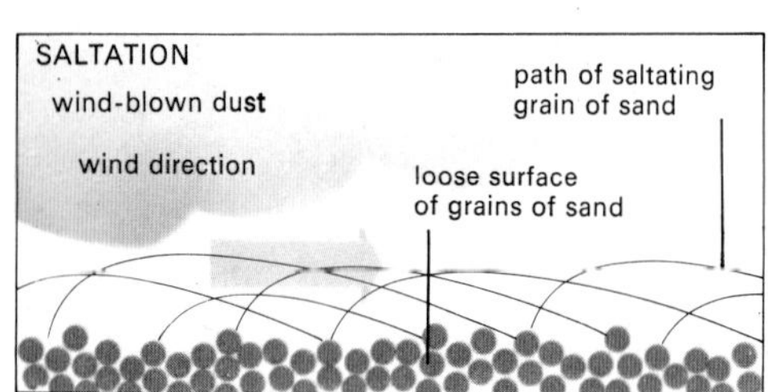

Left: This illustration shows the bouncing movement or *saltation* of wind-blown grains over a sandy surface.

Right: The alignment of long, narrow sharp-crested dunes, known in the Sahara as *seifs*, is the result of the combined effect of winds blowing in different directions.

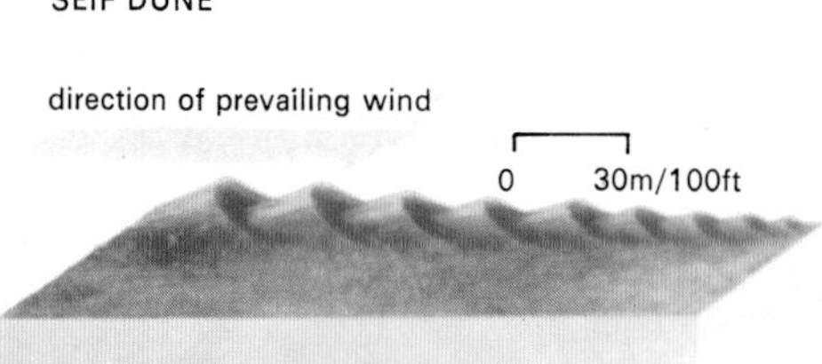

Photri

Pierre Jaunet/Aspect

Above right: An approaching sandstorm in the Sahara. The finer particles in sand deserts are swept up and kept in suspension by air turbulence. If the winds are strong enough, sand as well as dust is blown along and threatens unwary travellers with burial.

Dr. C. Vita-Finzi

Right: These hillocks in the Sarazac area of northern Chad are called *yardangs*. Ancient lake beds were weakened by salt weathering and then carved by sand-laden winds into streamlined, undercut hillocks. The ridges are roughly parallel and lie in the direction of the dominant wind.

George Rodger/Magnum

Right: Tall sharp-crested sand dunes tower over the palm trees at an oasis in the Sahara. Plant roots bind the sand and help prevent it being carried away by the wind. However, dunes may gradually encroach on an oasis and bury it.

Below: How a *barchan* is formed. These crescent-shaped dunes generally develop over hard, poorly-sanded desert surfaces. Having accumulated, the sand moves forward as grains blown up the windward side fall over the lee side to form a slip face. The sides of the mound, being lower, move faster.

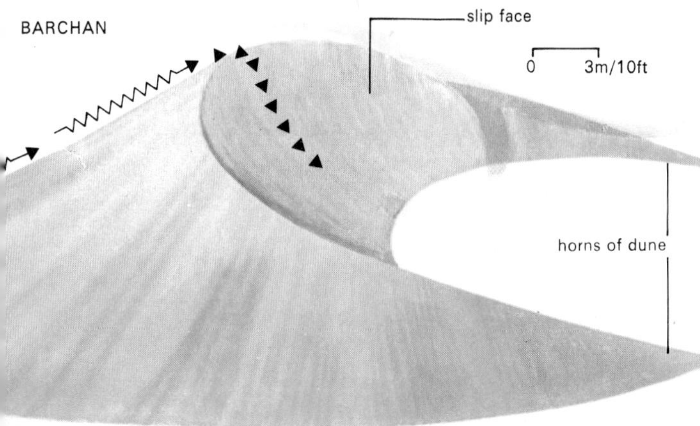

at a distance equivalent to one bounce, dislodge more grains, and so perpetuate a regular spacing between the ripples created in the sand.

Dunes come in a wide range of shapes, sizes and patterns. The classic crescent-shaped *barchan* is only found on hard desert surfaces which have little sand covering. A barchan has a gentle wind-ward face and a steep leeward or slip face. Sand is swept over the crest and slides and slumps until it reaches its angle of rest (typically 34°). As a result of this transfer of sand, the dune slowly advances. The margins of the original mound, being lower, move more quickly and so develop into the characteristic horns.

Sand ridges and dunes occur also in long, narrow lines. These linear types may be parallel, diagonal or transverse to the dominant winds, and their alignments can sometimes be traced over tens, or even hundreds, of kilometres. The alignment of some of the long and narrow sharp-crested dunes known as *siefs* results from the combined effect of all the local winds which are capable of moving sand. Others arise from the interaction between a dominant wind and a cross wind. Even more complex wind patterns are thought to account for intersecting linear dunes and for sand mountains called *rhourds*.

Large sand grains are said to 'creep' when rolled by the wind or nudged along by saltating particles. Those which are fine enough to be held aloft in suspension by the wind may be carried far afield. The 'blood rains' occasionally experienced in Italy and other parts of Europe, for example, are coloured by red Saharan sand blown across the Mediterranean Sea. Extensive sheets of such fine dust, or silt, laid down by the wind are called *loess*. They resist further wind displacement because the particles tend to stick together to form a protective *silt crust*. But once the surface is broken up—perhaps by animal hooves, ploughs or traffic—deflation readily follows. This has created disastrous results in areas such as the North American prairies. In the 1930s, for example, the 'dust bowl' of the Midwest was created by the ploughing up of prairie lands—devastating dust storms resulted which removed vast amounts of soil.

Despite both the spectacular nature of dust storms, however, and the likelihood that the breakage of colliding sand grains is constantly producing additional particles, the volume of dust generated by deserts appears to be inadequate to account for any of the world's major loess deposits. The loess of the Huang Ho valley in China, for example, is usually traced to the Gobi Desert. However, it is more likely that it consists of silt produced by the grinding action of mountain glaciers from the Pleistocene epoch.

Where deflation removes sand and dust, basin-like depressions are left behind. However, it seems unlikely that this process alone could account for some of

Right: Unlike the barchan sand dune, this *parabolic dune* travels with its points trailing behind. Also known as a 'blow out', this type of 'hollow' dune may be the result of upsetting the delicate balance between vegetation and sand, exposing loose, finely-grained sand which is easily carried forward by the wind.

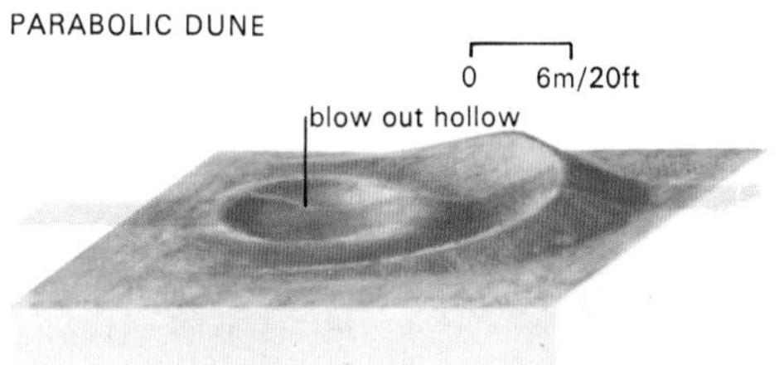

the giant hollows, such as the Qattara Depression of Egypt, which are found on arid plains. The Qattara Depression is over 160 km (100 miles) wide, and the soft shale floor lies over 300 m (100 ft) below the level of the surrounding limestone plateau.

Wind is very ineffective in eroding solid rock. Unless armed with abrasive particles, it lacks 'teeth' and even when suitably equipped for erosion its action is confined to within a few metres above the ground. The only landforms definitely shaped by wind erosion are streamlined, undercut hillocks called *yardangs*, carved from soft deposits such as lake clays. Some major channels cut into the rock in the Sahara are thought to be of similar origin, but they could well have been scoured out by glaciation of the area some 450 million years ago.

Rocky deserts

Most of the world's arid landscapes, both lowlying and mountainous, have rocky surfaces. Rock breakdown is performed by a variety of agents. At high altitudes, and in the cold, continental deserts, frost weathering produces coarse, angular debris. Elsewhere, salts—brought to the surface by high evaporation—enlarge cracks and pores in the rocks when they crystallize, or when the crystals themselves expand on combining with water and on being heated by the sun.

The extent to which temperature fluctuations cause rock breakdown remains controversial. Some geologists attribute mysterious 'shots' heard in the desert to the collapse of stressed rocks, and others explain them as pistol shots. On the other hand, it is clear that plant roots, lichens, and the cycles of wetting and drying created by dew formation, are all effective agents of breakdown.

Fluctuations in temperature, as well as chemical changes, promote the distinctive onion-like peeling called *exfoliation* of granitic and other rocks. Similarly, hollows or *tafoni* worn in rock faces by weathering promote their own expansion by harbouring moisture. Eventually, a striking honeycomb effect is produced.

On some desert floors, the stones fit closely together as though deliberately laid down in a mosaic. These gravelly *desert pavements* are produced by the removal of fine debris by wind and water and the upward migration of stones through mixed ground deposits, following repeated cycles of wetting and drying or of freezing and thawing. Local names for this feature include *gibber plain* in Australia and *hammada* in North Africa. The stones are commonly coated with dark 'desert varnish' composed of iron and manganese oxides. Desert varnish also occurs on rock faces, and iron oxide coatings account for the characteristic redness of many desert sands. In this sense the colourfulness of arid landscapes is only 'skin deep'.

In semi-arid areas, the landscape features may be capped by pale crusts of calcium carbonate or of gypsum. These minerals are either derived from waters drawn to the surface by capillary flow and brought in by rare floods, or have formed beneath the surface and been subsequently exposed by the erosion of the overlying material. These crusts are often very resistant to erosion and tend to fossilize the topographies on which they have developed.

Bruce Coleman

Above: This steep-sided ravine in Tunisia is a *wadi*. The violent floods that occasionally sweep down rocky desert wadis carry a heavy load and can achieve a great deal of erosion during their brief lives. In addition, the flood waters carry away rock material loosened by weathering, leaving behind the more resistant rock strata. The sharp, angular landscape is typical of many arid areas.

Below: Death Valley in California exhibits a variety of arid landforms. In some places, great dunes have formed from drifting sand. This view of another part of the valley from Zabriskie Point shows the dramatic effect of desert floods. Deep gullies have been eroded and the valley floor is choked by the heavy load of sediments washed down by the flood-waters from distant mountains. The exposed sediments reveal the lines of flow and their colour and composition are in marked contrast to those of the local rocks.

Photri

band of resistant rock

accumulated debris

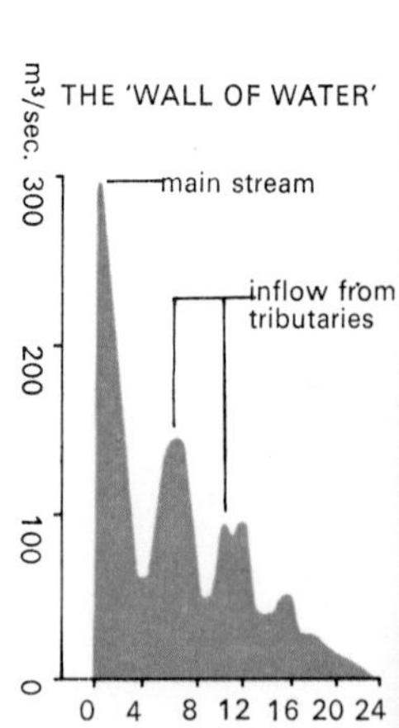

Below: The landscape of arid and semi-arid regions is distinctive. Steep cliffs rise above shattered rock debris and flat areas of alluvium. When the infrequent downpours follow the same course, they cut deep, wide channels, leaving wadis and residual mesas and buttes. Dry conditions help to maintain the steep sides. Where the wadis open onto a plain, the streams dump their loads and build up alluvial fans. A series of such fans is termed a *bahada*. If the flow is sufficient to sweep away all the products of weathering, a broad, gently-sloping *pediment* of bedrock is formed. The water itself often flows into saline lakes and evaporates, creating a salt pan.

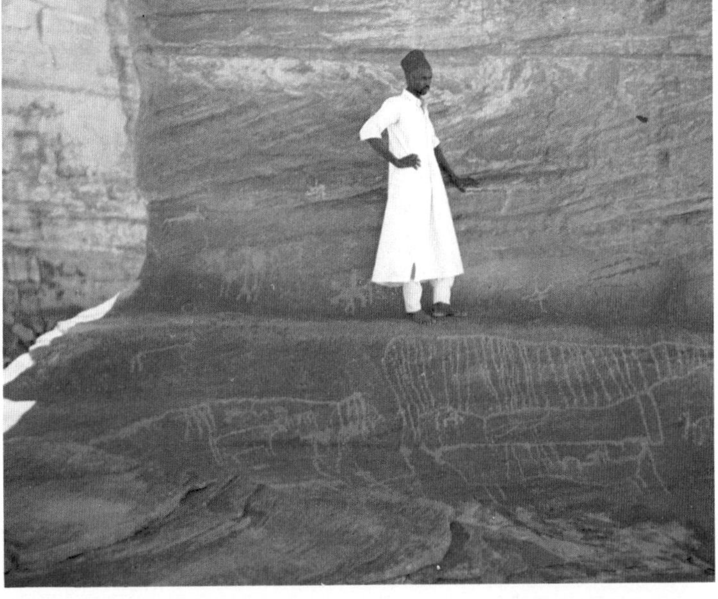

Dr. C. Vita-Finzi

Above: Prehistoric rock drawings in the Tibesti Mountains of the Sahara. The surfaces of long-exposed rocks and pebbles sometimes gain a coating of iron and manganese oxides and other minerals. The red, brown or black crusts protect the underlying rock. Prehistoric inhabitants of the Sahara scratched out drawings of familiar animals on this 'desert varnish'. The fact that these animals once lived in what is now a barren desert is often cited as evidence of former wet climates in the Sahara.

butte
wadi
run-off channel
gently sloping pediment —sheet wash carries fine debris to the basin
alluvial fan
salt lake
salt pan
note: vertical scale is exaggerated
alluvial fans unite to form a bahada

The spectacular effect of water

When water does flow through desert regions, the effects are dramatic. The great drainage networks characteristic of many arid landscapes have often been explained as relics of wetter climates in the past. But anyone who has witnessed the violence of a desert flood will have little difficulty in accepting that such features are still forming today, albeit in a random fashion.

Dry desert gullies which contain running water only after heavy rainfall are called *wadis* or *arroyos*. The walls of these ravines are typically steep and irregular, and they undermine residual mesas and buttes. Regions which are scored with numerous ravines and gullies carved into alluvium and other weak rocks are called *bad lands*, named after the inhospitable Bad Lands of South Dakota, USA.

In arid regions crossed by rivers which gain their waters elsewhere and manage to maintain a regular flow, very deep valleys or *canyons* are cut into the rocks. The most dramatic of all is the Grand Canyon in the western United States. Carved by the Colorado River on its way from the Rocky Mountains to the Gulf of California, the Grand Canyon extends more than 350 km (217 miles), reaches a depth of over 2,000 m (6,550 ft) and varies from 6.5 km (4 miles) to 21 km (13 miles) wide.

The growth of drainage channels, however, does not depend on water erosion alone. The channels are also shaped by weathering of the valley sides and by mass movement of the resulting debris. This sediment is ultimately carried out of the wadis and gullies to be dumped at the mouths in alluvial fans which, when joined together, produce aprons of alluvium termed *bahadas*. In the absence of fans and bahadas, weathering may act with the spreading floodwaters to produce very gently sloping, broad, rock-cut surfaces termed *pediments*.

Many arid-zone drainage systems fail to reach the sea and are termed *endoreic*. They either fall prey to evaporation and infiltration, or are confined within closed basins. In endoreic systems, the salts carried by run-off gradually accumulate on the floors of temporary lakes to form a salt pan, known as *playa* or *salina* in North America.

Salt pans may be bordered by swamps, as in the Lop Nor basin in China. Saline lakes which increase in size or perhaps only come into being during wet periods sometimes occupy the floor of such desert basins.

Left: Violent downpours on bare desert terrain lead to rapid run-off and flash floods. This graph of the volume of water rushing through a wadi, which was totally dry only a few minutes earlier, plots the sudden flood—described by desert travellers as a 'wall of water'—and the gradual decline after the peak has passed.

Right: A salt pan in the cold, arid region of the Bolivian altiplano, an elevated plateau in the Andes of South America. This salt pan, known locally as *salar*, was deposited when rare flood waters evaporated leaving an accumulation of salts, which are often economically valuable, at the base of an extinct volcano.

Dr. C. Vita-Finzi

Slopes and Landslides

Slopes occur in almost all landscapes and, apart from providing variety in the scenery, more significantly they give the geomorphologist clues to the evolution of that landscape. In addition, it is important to understand the processes whereby slopes are formed and changed, since most of man's activities take place on the surface. Soil erosion, damage to property, roads and railways, and even loss of life, may all be avoided to some extent if these processes are understood.

Previously the study of slopes involved the use of simple, descriptive words, such as steep and gentle, feral (uncultivated) and non-feral. Recent research, however, has become more mathematical and slopes are now the subject of careful measurement. One method of gauging the rate of downward movement on a slope, for instance, is to follow the change in position of stakes hammered into the ground. Deeper movements are measured by the use of buried nails or wooden pins, although these can be difficult to retrieve. These two methods are among the easiest and least expensive.

Quantification has revealed the fascinating complexity of slopes. Research topics include, for example, investigation of the angle of inclination at which different soils and rocks tend to remain stable without slipping. One discovery

Dr. Lauri Wright

Above: This island in Fiji in the Pacific presents a panorama of rugged relief composed entirely of slopes. This type of landscape occurs in areas of infrequent but high intensity rainfall. Various processes—such as surface wash, rain splash and chemical weathering—are at work, stripping the slopes of their soil covering.

Robert Harding

Above: In many areas of the world, man has now interrupted the natural slope-forming processes. The most obvious example is terracing, as here in Peru. But deforestation and ploughing have also helped to speed up some processes and initiated others. In extreme cases an accelerated rate of erosion creates severe problems for land use and water supply.

Spectrum

Left: Middle Tongue in the Yorkshire Dales. Smooth, long slopes characterize many of the world's temperate areas, like the British Isles, where the consistent rainfall is of low intensity. Slope processes are usually slow-acting, and solutional weathering and soil creep are important though barely perceptible. Many slopes in these areas originated under a different climate from that occurring today.

Dr. Lauri Wright

Right: Many landslides require a trigger action, such as an earthquake, before movement occurs. This relatively small slide in Buller Gorge, New Zealand, is one of many initiated by the 1968 Murchison earthquake.

pressure of buildings on ground

FORCES ACTING ON A HILL SLOPE

soaking and drying out of soil by precipitation and evaporation loosens grains

movement by animals and humans disturbs the soil

surface wash carries soil and stones down stream

channel flow widens and deepens streams bearing away more debris

soil movement hindered by vegetation cover

fluctuations in upper level of saturated rock

ground water infiltration

sub-surface seepage of water

soil movement

river erodes the base of slopes

expansion and contraction of soil due to freezing and thawing

Above: A landslide occurs when some force upsets the delicate balance between the stress on a slope and the resistance of the soil or rock.

Right: A scree slope looms over the dark waters of Loch Aire in Scotland. Screes are a frequent result of the destruction of slopes by frost action. The loosened material falls downslope under the pull of gravity and accumulates at the base. The angle of rest is closely related to the size and shape of the fragments. The slope is often so steep that a slight disturbance—perhaps by sheep, whose tracks can be seen across the face of this slope—may send the whole mass sliding downwards.

Heather Angel

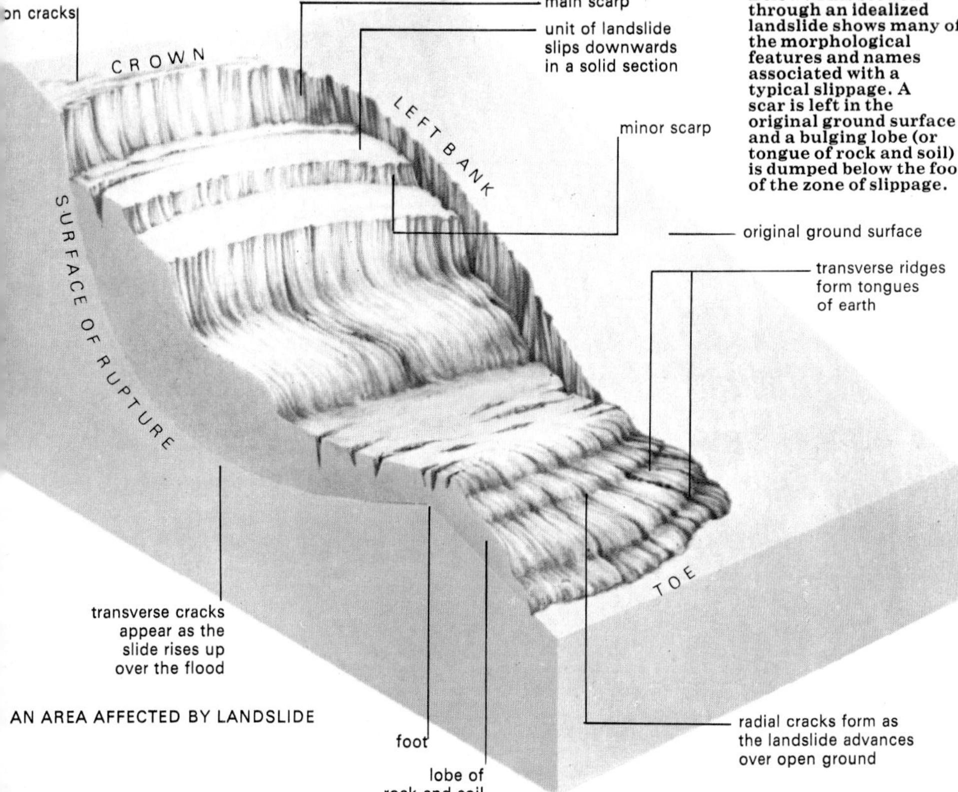

Below: This section through an idealized landslide shows many of the morphological features and names associated with a typical slippage. A scar is left in the original ground surface and a bulging lobe (or tongue of rock and soil) is dumped below the foot of the zone of slippage.

is that most slope angles fall into two or three groups, 25°-29° slopes predominating in sandstones and shales, for example, while 8°-12° slopes are typical of clays.

Landslides

It has long been known that slopes do change, but attention has previously been focused on the more spectacular events. Among recent ones, these include the landslide which fell into the Vaiont reservoir in Italy in 1963, washing a great wave of water over the dam and causing a flood which killed 3,000 people, and the 1970 Huascaran disaster in Peru of which more than 20,000 people were victims.

Events of this magnitude have occurred from time to time throughout history and evidence of catastrophic landslides goes back into the distant geological past. However, the processes responsible for such devastations are also those which create movements on a much smaller scale, and which affect all slopes to a greater or lesser degree. It is the study of these processes with which much modern research is concerned.

The downward movement of material under the influence of gravity is termed *mass movement* or *mass wasting*. Such movement generally occurs when the force of the weight of rock and soil (and of the water it contains) along with the pull of gravity exceeds the forces of resistance within the rock and soil mass itself. In essence, movement occurs when the balance between *stress* and *resistance* is shifted sufficiently in favour of stress. This effect can be achieved either by an increase in stress or by a reduction in resistance.

Increase in stress can be brought about in a number of ways. Under natural conditions, undercutting by a river or the sea at the base of a slope leaves the slope unsupported, thereby placing greater stress on those parts of the slope lying immediately above. An increased load on the slope, possibly through the addition of rainwater or the deposition of a *moraine* by a glacier would have the same effect. The tilting of an area by geological forces could also be responsible.

Similar effects are often produced by man. The cutting of a road into a hillside effectively undermines the slope, while the dumping of spoil from mines at the top of valley sides increases the load on the slope. These changes in applied stress, as in the construction of a road, are often clearly visible. However, decreases in the internal strength of rock and soil masses caused by weathering can go largely unobserved.

For example, underground caves may be opened up in limestone when the calcium and magnesium are dissolved by water. No indication of this would appear on the surface, but if enlargement of the caves continued there would come a point when the ground above, being insufficiently supported, would collapse. Nearly all minerals can, in fact, be taken into solution. Although this would happen at a much slower rate than with calcium and might not form caves, the rocks would become progressively weaker and progressively less able to withstand the stress.

Slope failure, nevertheless, does not occur immediately whenever stress exceeds resistance. If it did, slopes would be showing continual adjustment and this does not happen. In reality, many slopes are inherently unstable and slippage may occur at any time, given the appropriate stimulus.

Among the factors contributing to mass movement are the angle of rest of the soil and waste material, and the looseness or lack of consolidation of the soil or rock. But water is certainly one of the chief agents. Most sudden mass movement is, in fact, associated with heavy or prolonged rain or snow melt. Water acts in several ways. It can, for example, provide an additional weight on the slope. More importantly, it can enter the pore spaces within the rock and soil and weaken the bonds between mineral grains. Rarely, if ever, does the passage of water through the rock and soil cause movement by lubrication; in many cases water actually increases the friction between particles and so acts against movement.

Melting snow plays its part, too. It produces its own moisture and a surface on which it can slide, creating avalanches which carry boulders and rock fragments along in their path. The spring thaw is the time for avalanches, which may be caused by an exceptional rise in temperature (and thus an uneven but rapid thaw), or triggered off by the smallest vibration. Avalanches usually flow at great speeds.

Types of mass movement

Many attempts have been made to classify the different types of mass movement and their causes, and a number of names have been coined. Among the more common are rock fall, soil creep, mud flows, earth flows, rain splash action and surface wash. The term landslide is noticeably missing from this list. This is because it is often used in a general sense to cover any sudden movement on a slope.

Rock fall, a rapid mass movement in which rocks slide down along a plane of weakness, is intermittent and typically produces uneven, irregular slopes. Rock fall activity can produce a *scree* or *talus*, accumulations of rock fragments which pile up at the bottom of slopes. The fragments are dislodged by the action of frost and weathering from the face of a slope. Screes are unstable, and material continues to slide downwards, while new material is constantly added from above. Normally, a scree will lie at a fairly steep angle of rest, but heavy rain or melting snow can upset this situation. The entire scree may be cemented by ice and, when the ice thaws, it may slip downhill, burying the slopes below under rocks and stones.

In contrast to rock fall, *soil creep* is gradual, operating more or less continually, and only detectable by careful measurement. It is caused by the expansion and contraction of soil particles due to wetting and drying, freezing and thawing, or even heating and cooling. Downslope movement occurs because expansion tends to be at 90° to the angle of the slope, while contraction tends to be vertical and unrelated to the slope angle. Following a zig-zag path, the soil slowly moves downhill, often no faster than a centimetre (0.39 in) a decade. If this increases to between 5 and 10 cm a year, as can happen on steep slopes subject to repeated frost action and a marked spring snowmelt, the surface may crack to produce a series of steps known as *terracettes*. Similar features can also be produced by the tramping and burrowing

Dr. Lauri Wright

Below left: Not all slopes are affected by water. Sand on this dune in the Namib Desert was built up by wind to an unstable angle before collapsing.

Below: How 'piping' develops. This type of slope-forming process, particularly important in regions where periods of drought alternate with heavy rainfall, affects only a small area. Below the surface, a cemented layer of soil, often consisting of clay, or an abrupt change from soil to the weathered rock, prevents the seepage of soil water down into the ground. The existence of a pipe is revealed only when the overlying soil collapses.

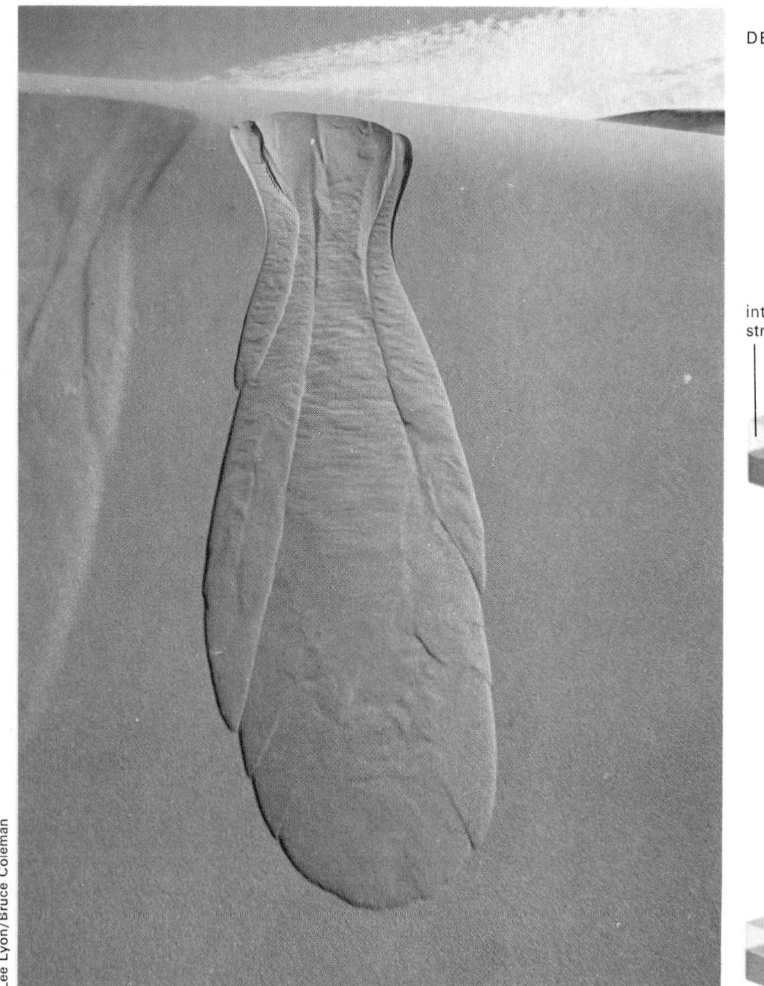

Lee Lyon/Bruce Coleman

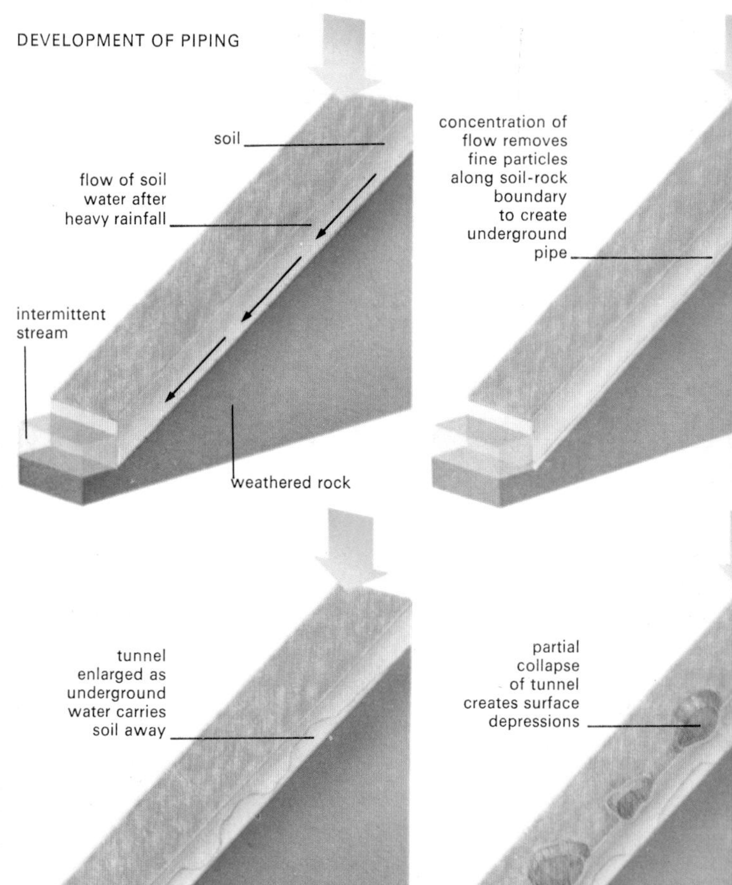
DEVELOPMENT OF PIPING
soil
flow of soil water after heavy rainfall
intermittent stream
weathered rock
concentration of flow removes fine particles along soil-rock boundary to create underground pipe
tunnel enlarged as underground water carries soil away
partial collapse of tunnel creates surface depressions

Left: The sudden collapse of a slope can have serious human and economic consequences, causing deaths and destroying property, farmland and lines of communication. No casualties resulted from this small slump in New Zealand, triggered by an earthquake, but the new house was made uninhabitable.

Below: The main types of mass movements, from an almost vertical rock-fall to a flat mudflow. Slopes are far from simple features, for both their form and the processes at work are constantly changing. In practice, larger slopes will often be subjected to a variety of mass movements at the same time.

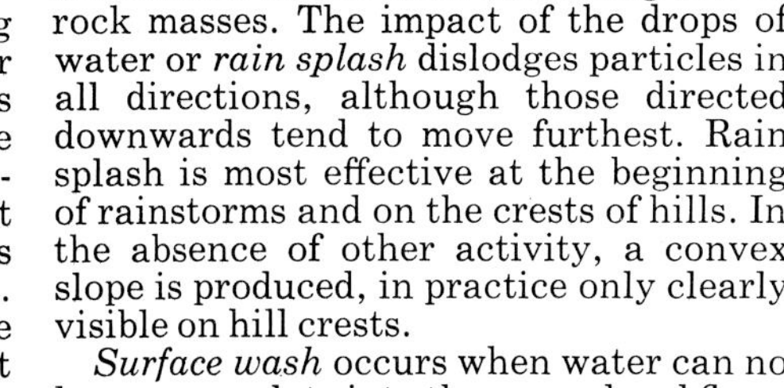

MASS MOVEMENTS

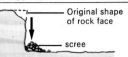

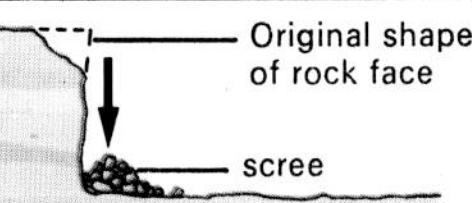

Original shape of rock face
scree
ROCK FALL
rapid collapse of rock from top of coastal cliff or steep mountain side creates scree at foot of slope.

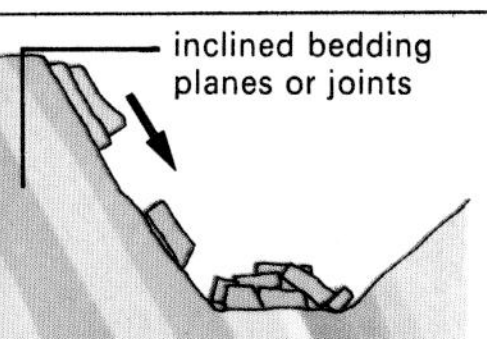

inclined bedding planes or joints
ROCK SLIDE
occurs when beds or joints of cliff are steeply inclined. Depending on the height and angle of slope, large chunks may break away. Occurs in high mountains and on coasts.

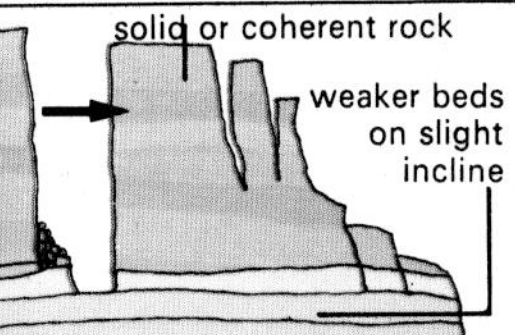

solid or coherent rock
weaker beds on slight incline
BLOCK GLIDE
large blocks of solid or coherent rocks glide on a very gently inclined floor or more sensitive beds. Movement is mainly sideways and is often considerable.

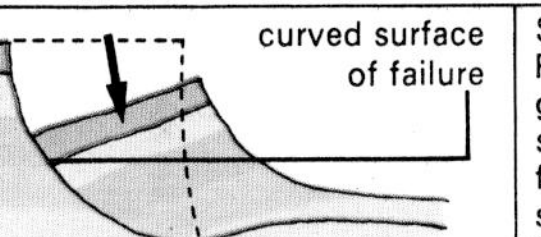

curved surface of failure
SINGLE ROTATIONAL SLIP
ground rotates by both slipping down and forward on a curved surface of failure. Often occurs in silts, clays and shales.

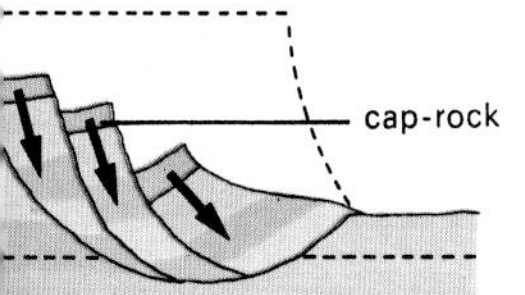

cap-rock
MULTIPLE ROTATIONAL SLIPS
several blocks all rotate backwards on a shared, curved surface of failure. Slippage of this kind occurs in clays with a caprock and very sensitive clays.

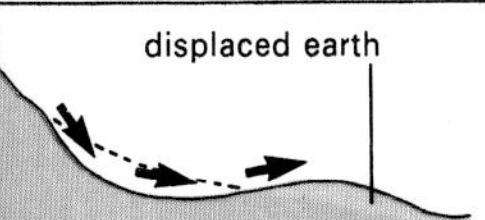

displaced earth
EARTH FLOW
occurs in saturated shale or clay which is disturbed by vibration. Movement is usually small.

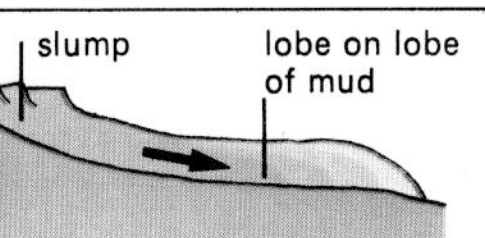

slump
lobe on lobe of mud
MUDFLOW
often occurs in arid regions where fine deposits slump or slide when saturated with water. Usually long and shallow.

of animals along a hillside.

Earth flows are movements involving finely grained material, such as clay or shale. These materials can sometimes become so saturated with water that the slightest vibration causes the whole hillside to flow downwards. One of the most disastrous examples of an earth flow was the Aberfan landslide in October 1966. Undermined by heavy rains, a man-made hill of pit waste collapsed, engulfing part of the village and killing 144 people, including 116 children.

Similar to earth flows, but occurring in dry, sloping valleys of arid and semi-arid areas, are *mud flows*. Quantities of sand and dust accumulate in these valleys and after a heavy rainfall are mixed with the rainwater to form a thick mud. This then flows downwards, sweeping away everything in its path.

Lahars are a type of mud flow which occurs on the slopes of volcanoes, and are thought to cause greater loss of life than volcanic explosions or flows of hot lava. Fine ash, sand and dust accumulate on volcanic cones and are transformed into liquid mud by the addition of water. This water can come from volcanic steam or melting snow or ice, but most frequently its origin is seasonal rainfall. Probably the most famous lahar occurred in 79 AD, when a river of hot mud flowed over the Roman town of Herculaneum.

Slopes bare of vegetation

In semi-arid regions, slopes are largely unprotected by vegetation cover. When not affected by rock fall, they are often subjected to the action of rainwater, which removes individual particles from the surface rather than disturbing soil or rock masses. The impact of the drops of water or *rain splash* dislodges particles in all directions, although those directed downwards tend to move furthest. Rain splash is most effective at the beginning of rainstorms and on the crests of hills. In the absence of other activity, a convex slope is produced, in practice only clearly visible on hill crests.

Surface wash occurs when water can no longer percolate into the ground and flows over the surface. In areas of heavy but occasional rainfall this is not uncommon and, acting under the same forces as river water, the process tends to produce smooth, slightly concave slopes. Contrary to what its name implies, surface wash does not occur in the form of a flowing sheet of water. Rather, myriads of tiny streams or *rills* are created. These fill up as their sides collapse between rainstorms, so that with further rain new rills are formed in a slightly different position. The overall effect is as if sheet erosion were taking place.

The clearing of natural vegetation on slopes in order to plant crops can be counter-productive, as once vegetation cover is removed, the soil can be eroded. Only strict measures to limit the area cleared at any one time and to direct the flow of water into concrete culverts can prevent severe erosion, particularly in regions with high rainfall. Alternatively, erosion can be allowed to continue, and the eroded debris collected and spread out behind long walls at a lower level. This creates flatter fields, which are easier to farm than the steep slopes and are less susceptible to erosion.

Right: An avalanche on the flanks of Mt Nuptse in the Himalayas. On steep slopes, snow may start to slide when its own weight or a sudden thaw makes it unstable. Once under way, an avalanche tends to pick up speed and may sweep up thousands of tonnes of soil, rock and vegetation before finally reaching a halt.

Below: Movements include not only such spectacular events as avalanches, but also slow, barely perceptible processes such as soil creep. One of the common indications of creep is a series of terracettes, often formed (like these in New Zealand) by the tramping of animals across the face of a hillside.

Dr. Lauri Wright

Chris Bonnington/Bruce Coleman

Rivers at Work

Until the late seventeenth century, the continuous flow of water from the earth to rivers was thought to be magical. Then two Frenchmen, Pierre Perrault and Edmé Mariotte, measured the flow of the River Seine, which runs from the hills of Burgundy through Paris to the English Channel. They concluded that there was more than enough rain and other precipitation falling on the *catchment area*, the entire region drained by a river, to account for the flow of the river. The first step had been taken into *hydrology*, the science dealing with the many properties of water.

Recent research into the total world stock of water has revealed some unexpected facts. In 1960, R. L. Nace, an American hydrologist, calculated the amount of water in storage and in transit in the various parts of the *hydrological cycle*, the continuous process in which water evaporates from the seas, is precipitated on to the land, and eventually runs back to the seas. It may not be surprising that the oceans contain 97 per cent of all the water in the world, but what is surprising is that the amount stored in the atmosphere is no more than one-thousandth of one per cent. Yet it is this small percentage that provides water to sustain vegetation and ultimately to flow in the rivers of the world.

The quantity of water to be found both in and on the continents is only three per cent of all the earth's stock. Of this, over 77 per cent is locked up in the ice caps and glaciers and another 22.5 per cent lies under the ground. This leaves a mere one half of one per cent of the waters in and on land to flow in the world's rivers, streams and lakes.

Nevertheless, running water is the most widespread and effective agent of landscape sculpture, continually carving deep valleys and broad plains and altering the surface features of the earth. In general, work starts with the rainfall and other forms of precipitation which provide, directly or indirectly, all the waters guided into natural channels to form streams and rivers. The source of a stream may be the immediate run-off from rainfall, or sub-surface water from a spring, or the release of water held temporarily in lakes or ice.

The anatomy of a river

On their course to the sea, rivers develop a distinctive slope or *gradient*. The side-view of the entire gradient, known as its *long profile*, reveals a generally concave shape, steeper towards the source of a river and flatter towards the mouth. Throughout a river's course, material is constantly being eroded from some sections and deposited in others. Where the river beds are very irregular and full of holes, it is likely that erosion is taking place; where the beds are floored with alluvial material, deposition is taking place. Erosion occurs where the stream has an excess of energy. When its energy is decreased, by a fall in gradient or by an obstacle, such as the still waters of a lake, the stream is no longer competent to transport its debris and must start to deposit it.

A river is often described as passing

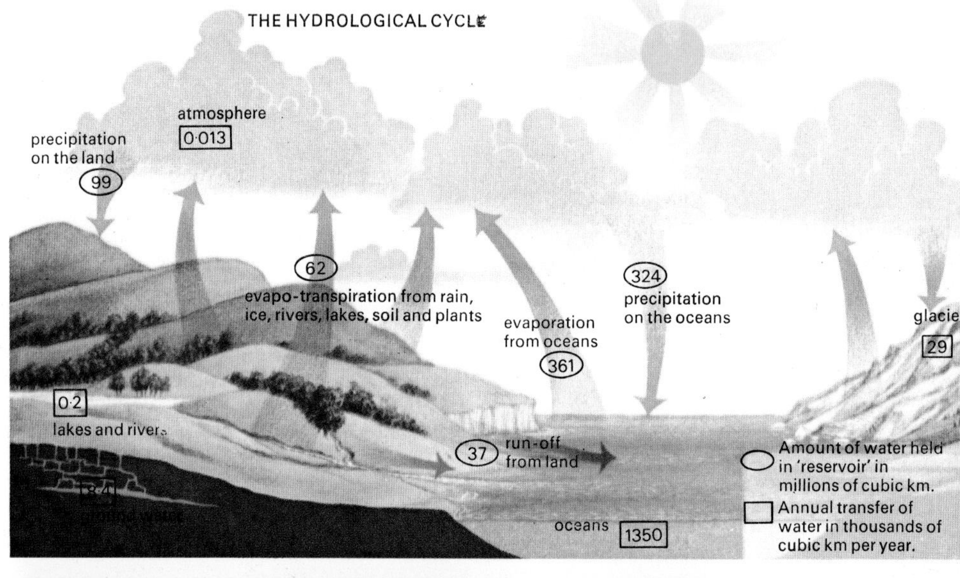

Above: The natural cycle of water from land to ocean, up to the atmosphere and back to land again is known as the *Hydrological cycle*. The sun's heat provides the energy by which water is evaporated from the surface of land and sea and transpired from vegetation. Precipitation falls as rain or snow; some is absorbed by the soil and plants, some is held as ice or seeps into the ground. What is left runs off the surface to enter the complex network of lakes, streams and rivers.

Colorific!

Left: Rushing water, large boulders and pot holes (worn into the bed rock by the constant rocking of boulders) are typical of a youthful mountain stream.

Spectrum

Right: An aerial view of the Rakaia river near Windwhistle gorge in New Zealand. It shows several features of a mature river adjusting to changes in base level. In the foreground, several raised terraces have been created as the river has cut down into the land surface uplifted by earth movements. The present river is developing a new flood-plain with deposition on inside bends, erosion on the outer-side. In the distance, interlacing of distributaries, known as *braiding*, is in evidence where the river leaves its gorge.

Below: In a straight channel, frictional drag is greatest along the bed and banks, so the river current is fastest towards mid-channel and close to the surface. Straight uniform channels are unstable and meanders soon develop.

Below right: In curved or meandering channels, erosion develops at the outside of bends where the velocity is highest, and deposition occurs on the innerside of bends where the current is slackest.

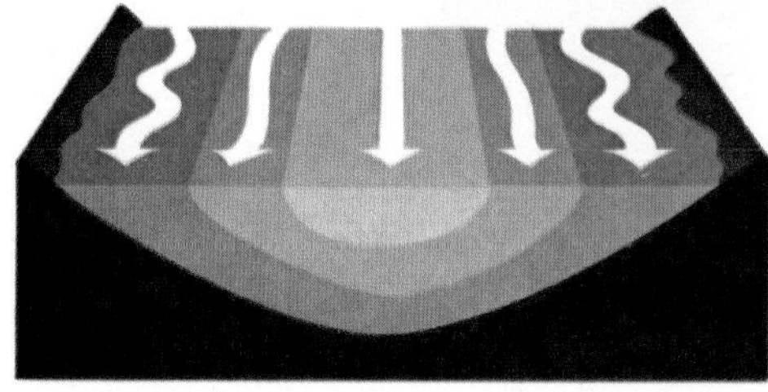

Jaroslav Poncar/Bruce Coleman

G. R. Roberts

Above: The colourful Agua Azul (meaning blue water) cascades down a series of steps on its way through the Mexican jungle. A resistant band of rock acts as a temporary base level for a stream until it is cut through by waterfalls, cascades and rapids.

Left: A stream is likely to encounter rocks of varying resistance in its course. The variations predispose the stream to change its direction and so to develop a winding course, creating a series of interlocking spurs.

Below: An incised 'goose-neck' meander cut by the river Saar flowing through Bavaria in south-west Germany.

Bavaria

through successive stages of development, from youth to maturity and on to old age. Because of the erosive energy of youthful streams, the upper course of a river is characterized by steep-sided, V-shaped valleys and gorges, through which the water rushes and tumbles over many rapids and waterfalls. Running water by itself has very little erosive power. River erosion is the cumulative effect of a great variety of processes including *corrosion*, the solvent and chemical activities of river water on the materials with which it comes into contact, and *hydraulic action*, which loosens and removes bed and bank material.

Once armed with loosened debris, running water becomes very destructive. *Corrasion* (not to be confused with corrosion) is the process by which the river bed is worn away by the boulders, pebbles, sand and silt being carried along in the stream. *Attrition* is a mechanism in river erosion whereby the transported materials or *load* are themselves broken down into smaller pieces by the continuous battering they receive as they move downstream.

A river's load can be transported in four different ways; by *traction* where the load is rolled along the stream bed; by *saltation* where the particles are moved in a series of short jumps; by being held up in *suspension*; and in *solution*, dissolved in the water. As the velocity of the river slackens, the larger boulders and pebbles come to rest, leaving only the material in suspension and solution to continue its journey downstream.

In any inspection of a natural river, the nature of the bed and land adjacent may indicate erosion or deposition although the river itself may appear to be incapable of either. But if the same river is looked at in flood, the large and apparently immovable boulders are being bounced along the bed, and material is being deposited in the lower reaches. In this way an estimated 8,000 million tonnes of eroded rock waste are transported from all parts of the world to the sea every year. This represents an annual loss corresponding to 77 tonnes per sq km (200 tons per sq mile).

Erosion cuts into steeper sections of the river profile and deposition occurs on the gentler sections. Consequently, there is a tendency to reduce the differences in gradient and so form a smooth profile which irons out any irregularities such as small lakes, waterfalls and rapids, often produced when a river course crosses resistant rock bands. The deepening of the river valleys by erosive processes is limited by sea level, which acts as the lowest point or *base level* for erosion. All rivers attempts to smooth out their long profiles from source to mouth. When a river attains this condition it is said to be at a state of equilibrium or *grade* and the profile is known as a *graded profile*.

Rivers in maturity

When rivers reach middle age or maturity, sideways or *lateral erosion* becomes more important. Broad valleys with gentle slopes are produced and the rivers tend to meander. A *meander* (named after the classical River Meander of Troy) is the name given when a river follows the natural gradient of the land and forms semi-circular bends with geometrically perfect curves.

William MacQuitty

Aerofilms

Left: This dry river valley in the Gilgit region of Kashmir contains a steeply sided alluvial cone. The cone was formed by the stream as it deposited its load when it left the mountain tract of its course.

Above: The valley of Glendaruel in Scotland. As a river develops its meanders, it deposits material on the inner sides of bends. The area of deposits is enlarged as the meanders move downstream. Eventually, this migration leads to the formation of a flood-plain which widens as the meanders swing freely from one valley side to the other, smoothing out headlands or bluffs as they go.

It was once thought that chance irregularities in a river's curve were the cause of meanders, but if this were so there would be odd meanders here and there, whereas meanders always conform to a pattern. Laboratory experiments have shown that even those rivers developing on a uniform slope of uniform sediment are always found to modify their channels by erosion and deposition so that a series of symmetrical bends develops.

Braiding is another feature of a mature river valley. This occurs when a river which is laden with debris emerges from a ravine onto a bordering plain. The velocity of the river is suddenly checked by the abrupt change of gradient and much of its sediment load is dropped. The large volume of debris thus deposited obstructs the flow of the river which divides into *distributaries* which continually separate and unite.

Meandering rivers develop their flood plains by depositing silt and alluvium as they migrate seawards. Further deposits known as *overbank deposits* are left on the flood plain by flood waters each time the river overflows its banks. The flow of the water which floods onto the banks is not controlled by the main current since it is outside the river channel. As the flood slows down, it drops the coarsest part of its load, gradually building up a low embankment or *levee* on either side of the river. As the levee develops so too does the river bed. Silt, carried down by flood waters too small to overtop the levees, is deposited on the river bed as the flood subsides. If, however, the flood waters do breach the levees the consequences can be disastrous.

J. Allan Cash

Above: An ox-bow lake and sloughs (areas of dead water) formed on a flood plain by a meandering river in Alberta, Canada.

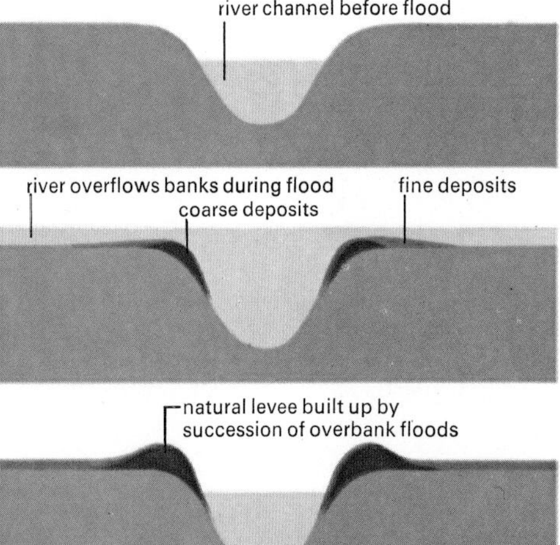

Left: Natural levees, often many metres high, are built up from the sediment deposited by a succession of overbank river floods.

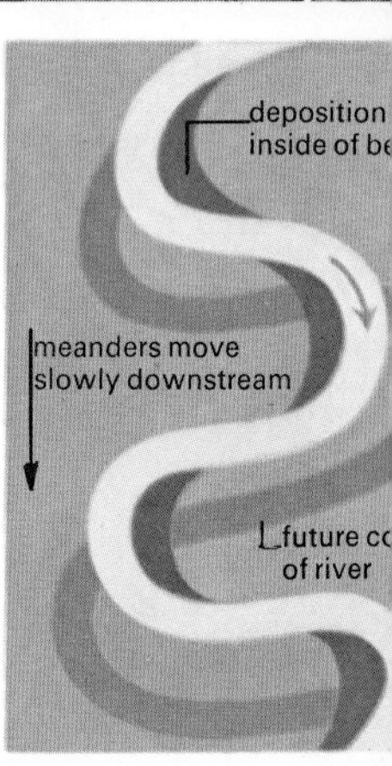

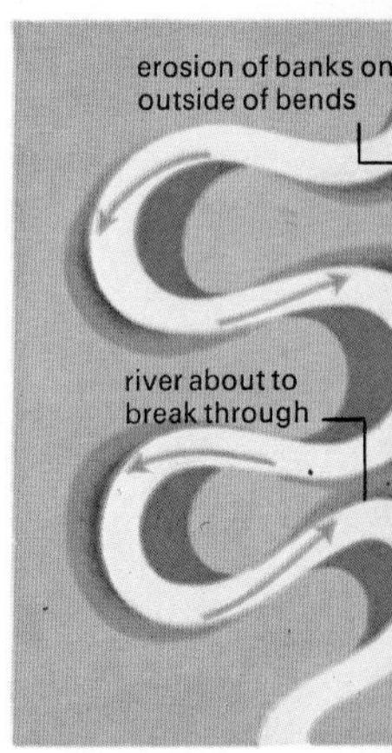

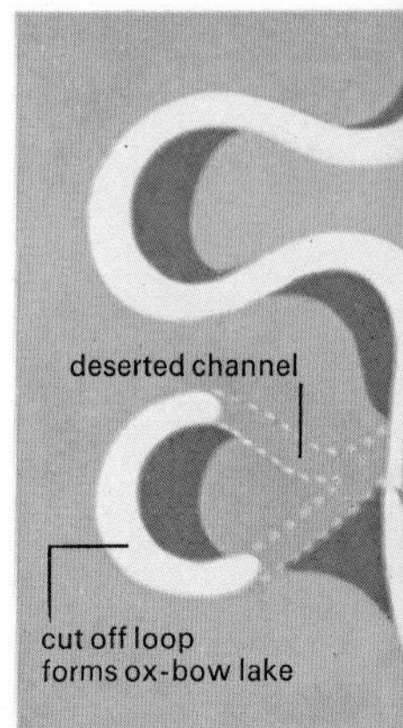

Right: How an ox-bow lake is formed. As a river develops its winding course, each bend is enlarged and the meanders migrate downstream in a serpentine fashion. Meanders continue to swell in broad loops with gradually narrowing necks. In times of flood, the neck is gradually cut off and a deserted channel or ox-bow lake is formed.

Robert Harding

Above: Braided channels in the Matanuska River in Alaska. Braiding occurs when a river emerges from its energetic mountain stage laden with debris on to a bordering plain and is slowed down. In the above example, the complex interlacing network of channels are separated by shoals of sand and islands of shingle.

Michael Freeman/Bruce Coleman

Right: The junction of the Amazon and Negro rivers in South America. The Negro is stained black with sediment and the Amazon is muddy. Their silt loads are so heavy that the waters do not mix until several kilometres downstream. This is known as *encontro das aguas* or meeting of the waters.

Aerofilms

Left: The fan-shaped Maggia Delta protruding into Lake Lugano in Switzerland provides an ideal setting for the town of Lugano. The main distributary of the river has been channelled into a canal to combat flooding.

Below: A section taken through the sediments of a fan-shaped or *arcuate* delta. The foreset beds are built up outwards into the sea or lake by successive loads of sediment tipped in that direction. The marked cross-bedding of layers of silt is notable. Finer sediments are deposited further out to sea to form the bottom-set beds. The veneer of top-set beds form the seaward continuation of the river's floodplain.

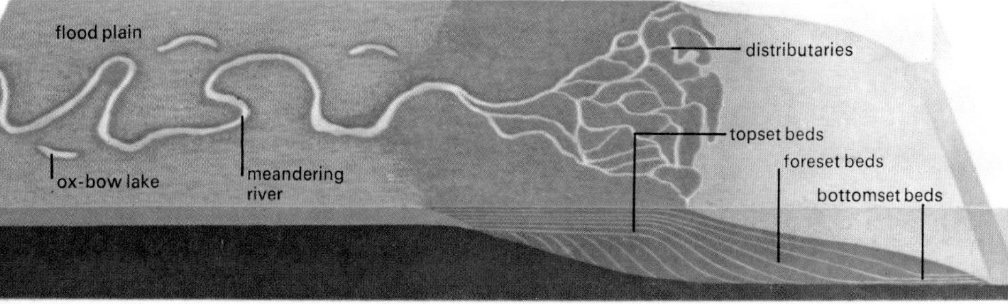

The effect of base level change

Rivers are rarely allowed to achieve a state of equilibrium or grade. More often they are interrupted by changes of base level, caused either by a change in the sea level or by earth movements which have uplifted or lowered the earth's surface. If a region is depressed by earth movements, its surface is brought nearer to base level, and because the work to be done by erosion is diminished, the stages of the cycle then in progress are passed through more quickly.

On the other hand, if a river that has already established a flood plain is rejuvenated—that is, the base level is lowered—the river will cut through the alluvium onto the rocks below in an attempt to re-grade its course. The margins of the original valley floor are then left as *terraces* above the level of the rejuvenated river. Subsequent rejuvenation would result in a second pair of terraces left on the valley sides. A *knick-point* results where the regraded profile meets the old profile. It is characterized by cascades and waterfalls and may often be difficult to distinguish from a break in the long profile caused by resistant rock bands.

If at the time of rejuvenation a stream was freely meandering on a floor of alluvium underlain by more resistant formations, the deepening channel would soon be etched into the underlying rocks with a winding form inherited from the original meanders. In England the 'hair pin' gorge of the River Wear, Durham, is a familiar example of such an *incised* meander.

Activity in old age

In old age, the wide, heavily-laden river glides sluggishly over a very broad, almost level plain. Its main work is deposition. Most of the sediment load of a river is carried out to sea or to a lake where the velocity is checked and, provided that deposition is at a greater rate than removal by currents, much of the load is deposited as an alluvial tract called a *delta*.

There are three basic types of delta formation. If the river water is denser than the sea or lake because of its load of sediment, it flows along the bottom and forms an *elongated* delta. If the river water has the same density as the sea or lake, it spreads out in the shape of a fan and an *arcuate* delta, like that of the River Nile, is formed. Finally, if the river water is less dense, it makes a few confined channels for itself and a *bird's foot* delta, like that of the Mississippi, is formed. Deltas can grow with great rapidity. For example, the delta below Astrakhan in the Soviet Union, where the Volga meets the Caspian Sea, was at one time growing at the rate of 1.6 km (1 mile) every five or six years.

Deposition does not only occur in the lower parts of a river course. Many youthful mountain rivers descend steeply to neighbouring lowlands where they drop their suspended load to form *alluvial fans* (so called because of their shape) or, in special cases, steep sided *alluvial cones*. Where closely spaced streams discharge from a mountain region their deposits may eventually unite to form a continuous plain or *piedmont alluvial plain*. For example, the Indo-Gangetic Plain in India extends from the delta of the Indus to that of the Ganges-Brahmaputra.

River Systems

On their journey to the sea, individual streams and rivers merge together to form a characteristic network or design, which is referred to as the *pattern of drainage* of a river system. In most areas, this pattern is one of considerable complexity, and in fact drainage patterns vary greatly from one kind of terrain to another: they are influenced by the slopes over which the rivers flow, the differences in rock hardness and structure that the streams meet during their course, and the recent history of earth movements in the drainage area.

Patterns and texture of drainage

In areas of uniform layers of sedimentary rocks, such as clays, drainage patterns emerge which resemble the branching of a tree. The *dendritic* patterns (from the Greek word 'dendron', meaning a tree) resemble the branching of trees. In scarplands and other areas of gently dipping rocks where branches of smaller streams tend to join the larger streams or rivers at right angles, a lattice-shaped or *trellised* pattern is more likely. *Radial* or *concentric* drainage patterns, in which the channels radiate in all directions from a central area, develop on the slopes of volcanoes or conical-shaped hills.

The relative spacing between the streams of a river's network is aptly described as *drainage texture.* Fine-textured drainage indicates a closer network of stream channels than coarse-textured drainage. Drainage texture is influenced by many factors, including climate: for example, areas which receive all their rain in short, sharp thunderstorms often develop a fine-textured network. Texture is also affected by rock structure: drainage lines are more numerous over highly impermeable surfaces such as clays which do not allow water to soak into them than over permeable rock like chalk or limestone.

The Bad Lands topography in parts of the western United States illustrates one set of conditions which leads to the development of fine texture—impermeable clays, sparse vegetation and rain falling in violent thunderstorms. Coarse drainage texture is well displayed on the sand and gravel outwash plains in front of glaciers.

In 1945, a useful method of measuring drainage texture was suggested by R. E. Horton, an American hydrologist. He developed several numerical measures so that objective comparisons could be made between the texture of different drainage networks. For example, he defined *drainage density* as the value of the sum total of the stream lengths in the system divided by the total area drained by the system under investigation. In this way the texture of several drainage systems may be compared.

Horton also devised a system of listing streams in an order of rank. A stream with no branches or *tributaries* joining it was called a *first-order* stream. Where such streams join they form a *second-order* stream. It is possible for a second-order stream to receive another first-order tributary without being promoted to the next (third) order, but where two second-order streams join up then a *third-order* stream begins, and so on. The complexity

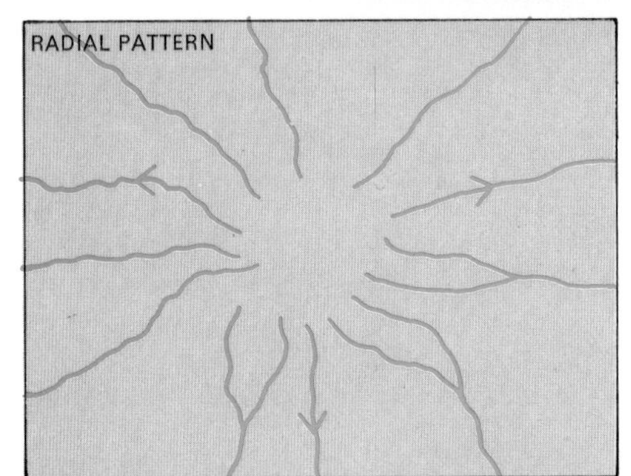

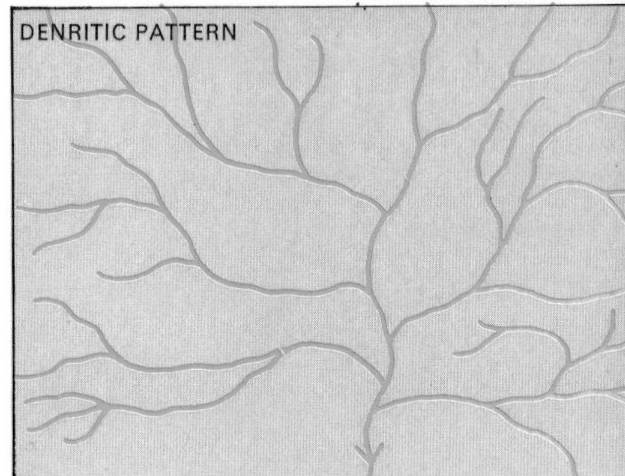

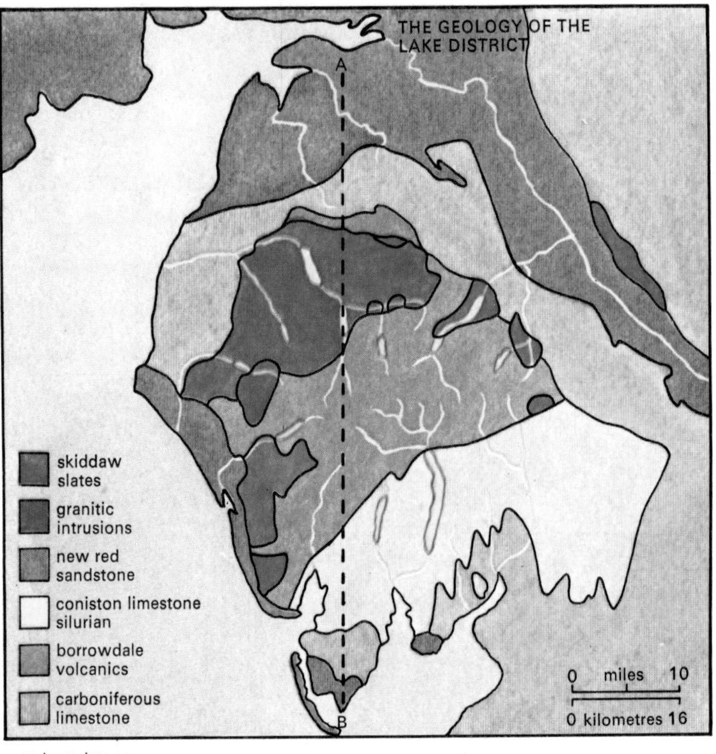

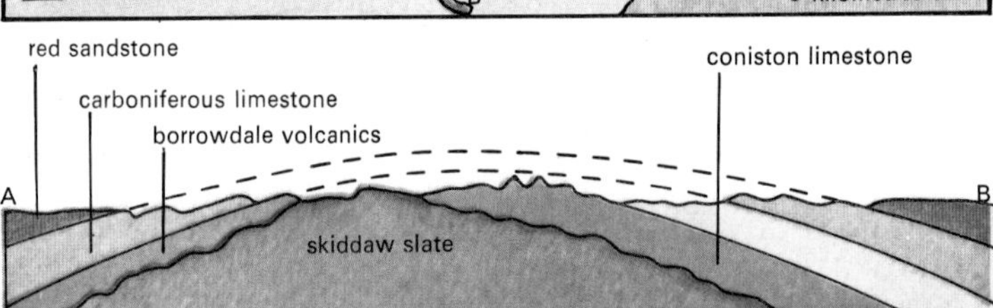

Left: Map and geological section of the English Lake District, showing a radial pattern of superimposed drainage. The area consists of folded early Palaeozoic rocks enclosed by a frame of limestone and sandstone, which were themselves once covered by later layers. In the Tertiary period the region was uplifted into a dome and the first streams were consequents that flowed radially down the slopes of the rising dome. These cut their valleys deeply into the underlying rocks. Today there is little evidence left of the younger rocks, but the drainage pattern of the vanished cover still substantially remains—it has been *superimposed* on the older rocks. Note how the rivers radiate from a central area.

Right: A spectacular aerial view of the Colorado river system as it cuts through the Kaibab plateau near the Arizona-Utah border. It shows the typical coarse-textured drainage of a mature river flowing through an arid area. The junction of the Colorado tributary is indicated by a circle. The dark mass of water is Lake Powell on the Colorado, upstream from the Grand Canyon. The lone peak to the east of the picture, south of the Colorado, is the Navajo mountain.

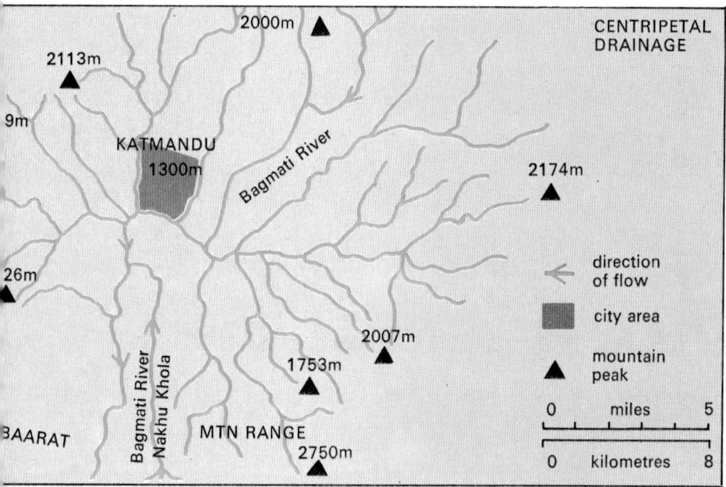

Left: Aerial view of the Colorado delta, often known as the 'burning tree' delta. The tributary streams join at various angles and resemble the twigs of a tree. This example shows how numerous branching systems, if allowed to develop freely in uniform layers of material, will take on a dendritic pattern.

Above: The Katmandu valley in Nepal has a remarkable example of *centripetal drainage*, in which streams flow towards a central depression. Along the single line of exit the Bagmati flows southwards towards the Ganges, while just a few miles east the Nakhu Khola flows in the opposite direction.

Right: Aerial view of the dry river beds near Lake Turkana in Kenya. These form a pinnate-type of drainage pattern. This is a special form of dendritic drainage in which the tributaries join the main river at acute angles, an effect produced by the unusually steep slopes on which the tributaries have developed.

Anthony Howarth/Susan Griggs

SED PATTERN

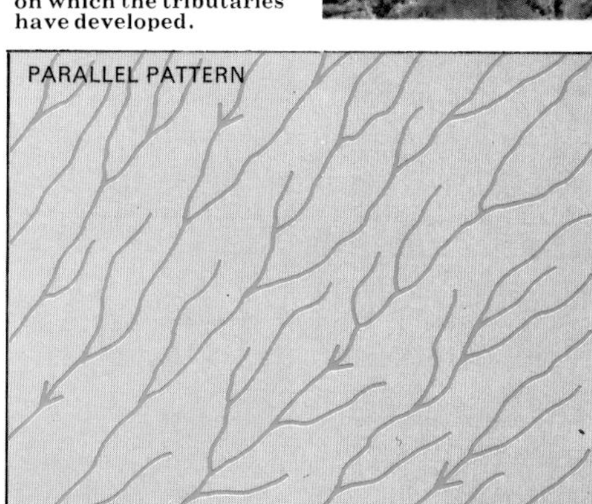

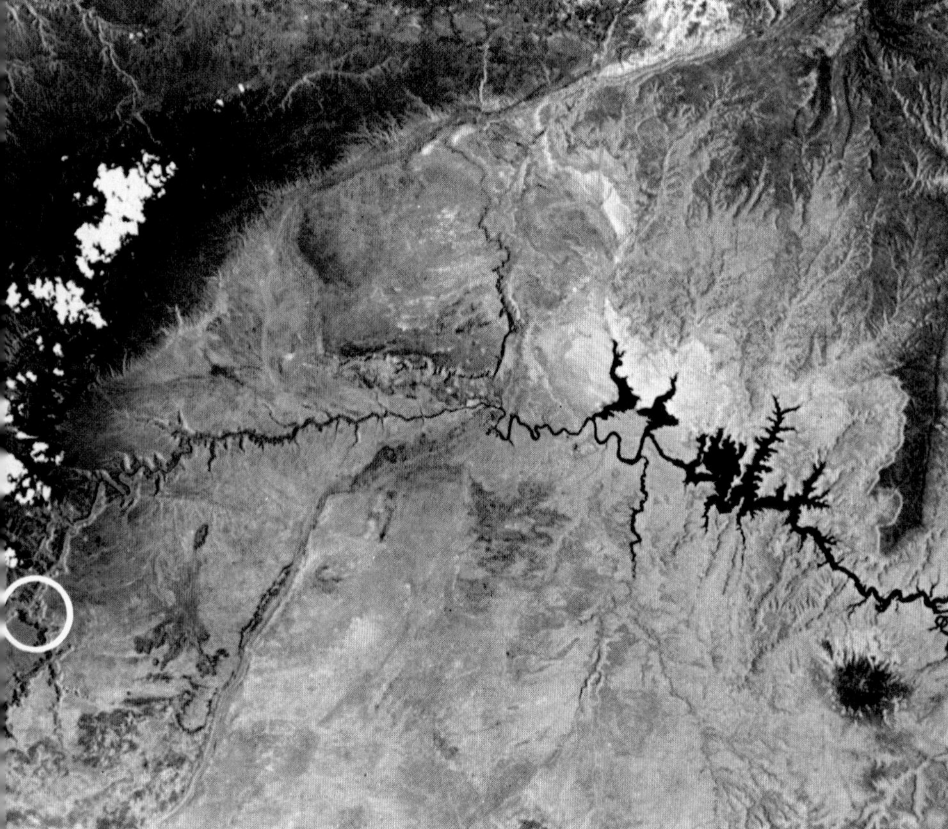

Photri

of different drainage systems can be measured by determining which have the highest order streams.

The origins of river systems

Names given to drainage systems often relate to the effect of structure and topography on their development.

A newly formed land surface is immediately exposed to weathering and erosion. In regions of sufficient rainfall, streams are created by the run-off of rain. Thus the streams and rivers whose original downhill course was determined by the initial slopes of the land are termed *consequent streams*, because their flow is a consequence of the pre-determined slopes. The final pattern of drainage to emerge then depends on the nature and structure of the rocks over which the consequent stream flows. If the rocks are uniformly resistant, a dendritic pattern will form. The branching drainage system developing from consequent streams is known as *insequent* or *lateral consequent*.

However, it is more common that an area consists of alternating strata of hard and soft rocks. As the consequent stream cuts its way down to the sea, it behaves in a different way as it passes over differing rock beds. Narrow valleys will be carved through the more resistant rocks, which will stand up as ridges, and the stream will wear away the clays and softer rocks to produce broad valleys.

In this situation, the tributaries feeding the main consequent stream are much more likely to take advantage of the weaker bands and to make rapid upstream or *headward erosion* along these. These tributaries are then known as *subsequent streams*. A typical trellised drainage pattern then develops, with the consequent rivers flowing parallel to the gentle dip slope of the rock and the subsequent tributaries flowing at right angles to this.

The valley of a subsequent stream steadily widens between the ridges formed by the bands of more resistant rock on either side. As the valley is broadened, the gentler slope will become steeper or gentler to approximate the angle of dip of

FORMATION OF INVERTED RELIEF

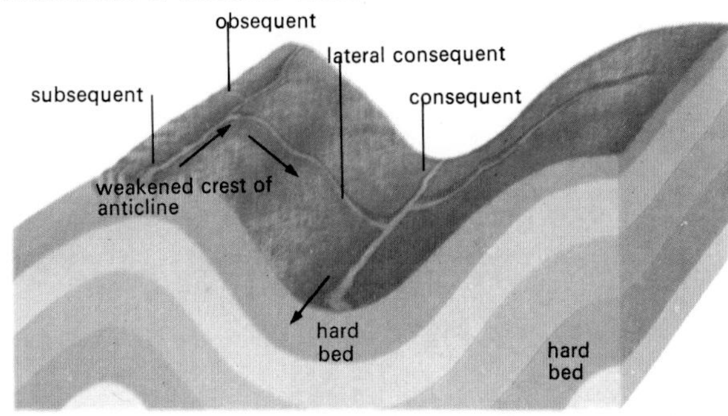

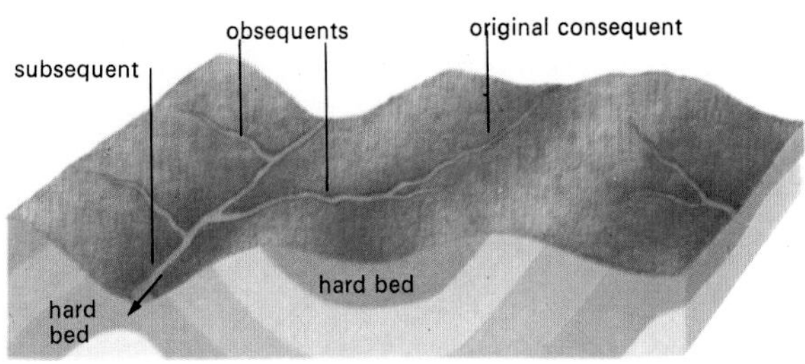

Left: The main stages in the development of inverted relief. On the original land surface (top), a consequent stream follows the hollow of the syncline. It is fed by a lateral consequent stream, and subsequent and obsequent streams are eroding the weakened peak of the anticline. At a later stage (bottom left), the pattern has been reversed and the relief is inverted. The subsequent stream has cut deeper than the consequent, which now acts as just one of several obsequent streams flowing into the lower stream valley.

Right: How a river system is superimposed over a landscape. In the initial stage (top), a river has established its course over horizontal beds of rock laid down unconformably over folded beds of varying resistance. After a period of down-cutting (bottom), the river has encountered the underlying rock but has maintained its original pattern. Where it has reached the buried anticline of resistant rock, it has eroded a narrow gorge.

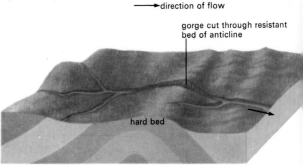

FORMATION OF SUPERIMPOSED DRAINAGE

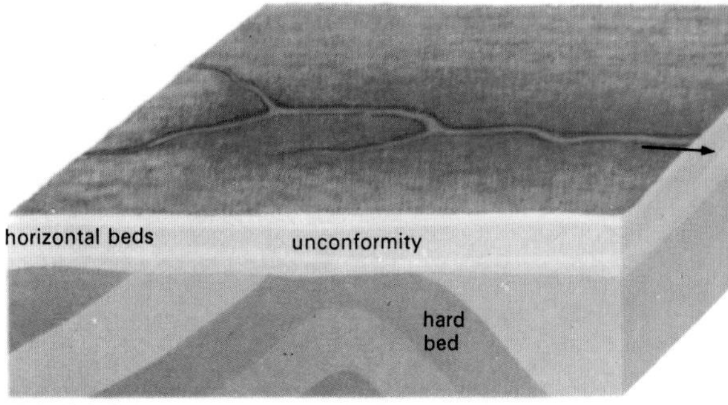

the underlying hard rock. Gradually, run-off from these slopes will form new streams, called *secondary consequents* or *dip streams*, as they flow down the dip slopes to meet the subsequent.

These new streams are sometimes called *resequent streams* since they appear to be consequent in direction, but they are of a later generation, forming only when the original incline down which the consequents flow is broken up into dip slopes. Shorter streams will also flow in the opposite direction down the steeper escarpment slope of resistant rock to join the subsequent stream, and are known as anti-dip or *obsequent* streams.

Inverted relief

The original surface of the land on which some drainage systems develop takes the form of a series of synclines (dips) and anticlines (rises). If, for some reason, the erosive powers of rivers wear away the anticlines at a greater rate than the synclines, then the synclines eventually form the mountains and the anticlines will form the valleys. This phenomenon, where the topography is 'opposite' to the structure, is known as *inverted relief*, although it is in fact the more usual case in areas of folded rocks. For example, Snowdon, the highest mountain in Wales, has developed from a synclinal structure.

During the first stage in the development of inverted relief, the main consequent stream follows the natural hollow of the syncline. However, the peak of the anticline is often so weakened or even cracked by folding that the hard bed capping the structure is easily breached near the crest of the anticline. Subsequent streams will easily develop here, whilst obsequent streams will begin to flow down the inward-facing scarps. If the arrangement of the hard and soft beds on the anticline is suitable, erosion of the anticline by the subsequent streams may be much faster than erosion by the consequent streams in the synclinal valley. The relief now becomes inverted.

After erosion has continued for a period of time, the subsequent streams may cut

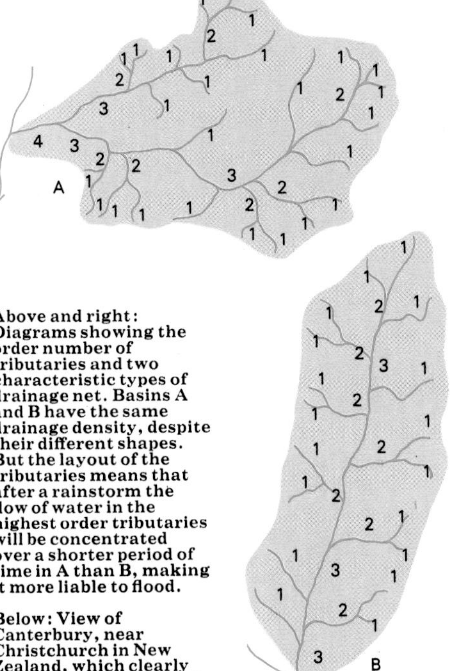

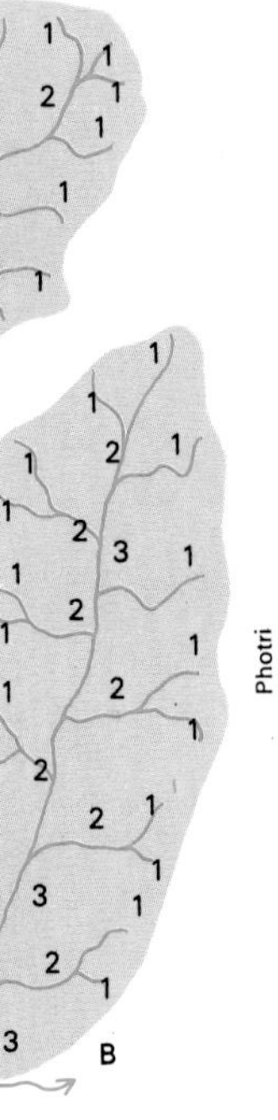

Above and right: Diagrams showing the order number of tributaries and two characteristic types of drainage net. Basins A and B have the same drainage density, despite their different shapes. But the layout of the tributaries means that after a rainstorm the flow of water in the highest order tributaries will be concentrated over a shorter period of time in A than B, making it more liable to flood.

Below: View of Canterbury, near Christchurch in New Zealand, which clearly shows relative orders of streams.

Photri

Above: NASA satellite picture of the Amazon tributaries in western Brazil. The smaller river Tarauaca flows into the Jurua, which meanders across the flat Amazon basin. An example of how drainage systems simplify in time, myriads of streams have been gradually superseded by a few main drainage lines.

Below right: The Brecon Beacons in south Wales. The streams on the right, which drain into the sea at Newport, are cutting into the watershed by headward erosion, thus lengthening their valley upstream. They will eventually capture the streams on the left, which drain to a different river and meet the sea at Cardiff.

G. R. Roberts

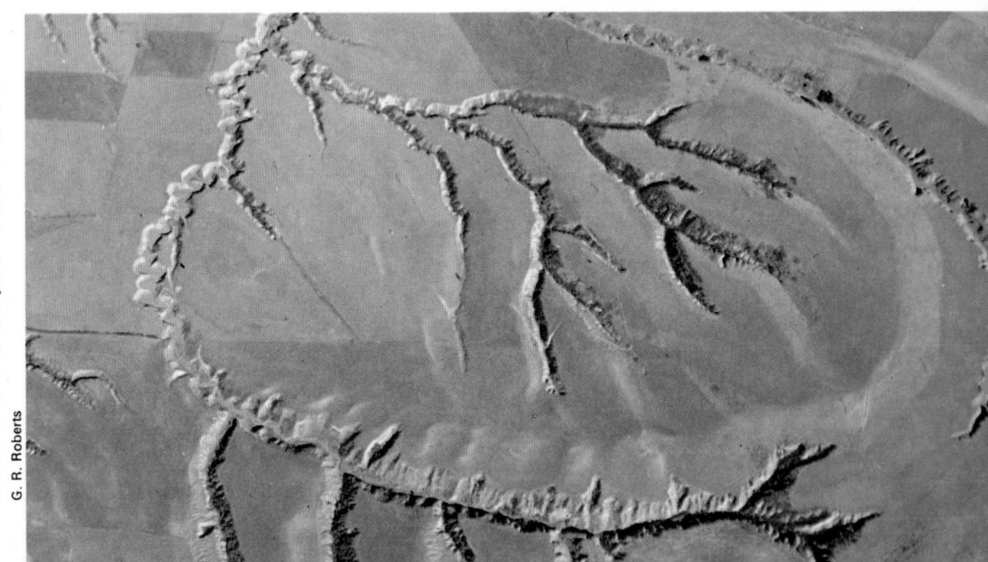

Below: How a river is captured. In the first stage, the streams have formed a trellised drainage pattern over gently dipping hard and soft beds. The detail shows a powerful subsequent stream making headward erosion through soft rock about to capture its neighbouring consequent stream.

Right: The River Thames flowing through the Pool of London below Tower Bridge. Before the last Ice Age and the subsequent reflooding of the North Sea, Britain was joined to the Continent and the Thames was a tributary of the Rhine. Once the English Channel formed, the Thames gained its own outlet to the sea.

RIVER CAPTURE

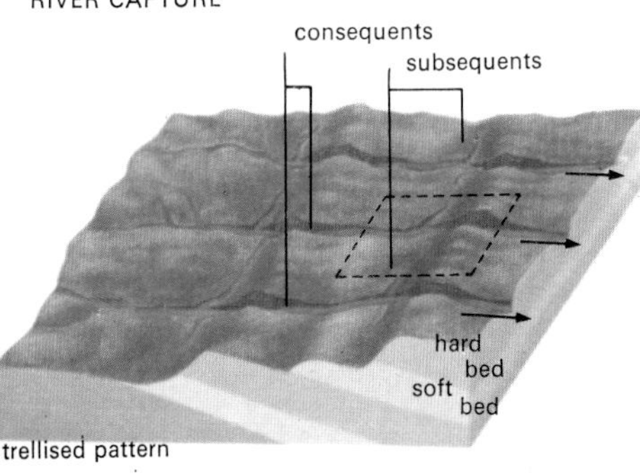

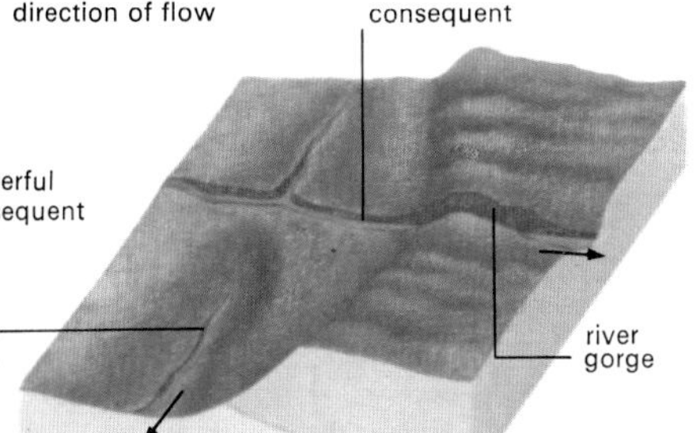

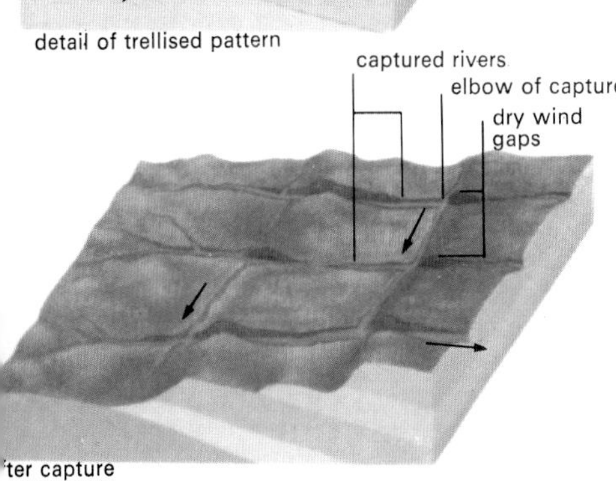

Above: Capture is complete. The powerful subsequent has pirated the headwaters of its neighbouring consequent and has continued its headward erosion to capture the next stream. The sharp bend where the two streams meet is known as the elbow of capture. Below the elbow, the course of the captured stream soon diminishes and a wind gap develops where the stream used to flow.

Right: The junction at which the Ouse has captured the river Nidd in Yorkshire. The Ouse, a major consequent aided by active subsequents, has acquired a large drainage area at the expense of other rivers.

Picturepoint

Aerofilms

down as far as a lower hard bed of rock. Its downward path is then checked, but the original consequents may erode relatively easily through the remains of the upper hard bed and underlying soft beds. Ultimately a pattern very like the original develops, but as the streams are not direct descendants of the original consequents, they are more properly described as secondary consequents.

Watersheds

The ridge of high land separating two neighbouring streams or river systems is known as a divide or *watershed*. As early as 1877, the American geologist G. K. Gilbert discovered that, in the later stages of the fluvial cycle, watersheds between streams of similar size are uniformly spaced and stream gradients are roughly equal on opposite sides of the watersheds.

However, Gilbert found that this was not true in the earlier stages of the cycle. A stream flowing down the steeper slope on one side of an unequally inclined ridge erodes its valley more rapidly than one flowing down the other, more gentle slope. As a result the watershed gradually recedes or migrates towards the side with the gentler slope. The dividing ridge quickly takes on a characteristic ruggedness, varying in height. This concept came to be known as the *Law of Unequal Slopes*. Sometimes the crest is lowered until it develops into a depression or *col* in the divide which often becomes useful as a pass for roads built across mountain ranges.

River capture

A strange phenomenon which has come to light in the study of drainage systems is that of *river capture*. This interesting example of natural piracy takes place when a major consequent river acquires a vigorous subsequent tributary which is etching its way by headward erosion back along a very weak outcrop of rock, wearing back its watershed as its goes. Eventually the subsequent stream may break through the divide and intercept an adjacent river system whose upper tributaries or *headwaters* are captured and

Aerofilms

G. R. Roberts

Above: An incised meander in the Macdonnell Ranges, Australia, about 125 km from Alice Springs. A deeply cut meander like this indicates that the river course is *antecedent* to (older than) the earth movement that uplifted the area. The river cut deeper as it was raised to a greater height.

Right: Ethiopia, the river Yonder and the Lali-Bela. The ridge of rock between the two streams is a clear example of a watershed.

Below: The Shenandoah is a famous example of a subsequent river valley. In a folded landscape, a subsequent river usually carves out a broad deep valley because it flows over weak rocks, becoming a powerful stream. The Shenandoah is one of the Appalachian rivers in the eastern United States. These have been interpreted as distinctive examples of superimposed drainage. Powerful subsequent streams cut their way through the Cretaceous rock cover onto the Palaeozoic rocks beneath, dissecting the Appalachians into long mountain ridges.

Georg Gerster/John Hillelson

Picturepoint

diverted along the course of the subsequent stream. The *beheaded* stream is left as a *misfit* since the reduced volume of water is no longer appropriate to the valley through which it flows. If river capture is predominant in a region, a pattern commonly occurs in which tributaries join the main river in backward looping or 'boathook' bends, providing a *barbed* drainage system.

Most river capture is largely explained by differences in rock resistance. However, in areas of permeable rocks there is the possibility of underground diversion preceding and aiding surface capture. Active erosion at the head of a lower but vigorous stream may cause it to approach close to a higher level valley and gradually sap more and more of the upper stream's ground water supply. Tower Creek in Yellowstone National Park, USA, is an interesting example of the underground diversion of drainage.

A river's course can also be diverted or deranged by the imposition of a barrier in its path. Although *stream derangement* has several of the features attributable to river capture, including barbed tributaries, it is the result of an entirely different mechanism. Glaciation is the chief cause of stream derangement. An example of this is to be found in North America where the present course of the Upper Missouri River is largely the result of the advancement during the Pleistocene Ice Age of the ice-sheets across the preglacial course of the Missouri. At that time it had its outlet to the north in the Hudson Bay in Canada. The glacial advance caused the Upper Missouri to abandon this route and establish a new course, roughly following the glacial boundary, to the Mississippi flowing south to the Gulf of Mexico.

Superimposed drainage

Some river systems have managed to maintain their original patterns despite obstacles erected during the geologic history of the area. Much of Britain, for instance, was originally covered by chalk and Jurassic rocks, lying unconformably above more ancient Palaeozoic rocks. As the land emerged from the sea during the late Cretaceous period, rivers were formed consequent to this surface.

As the valleys deepened, stripping away much of the younger cover, the rivers cut into the older, more resistant rocks, many with structural features which resulted in barriers across the river courses. In highland Britain, although the chalk cover has disappeared, the rivers remain carved into spectacular valleys through older rock while maintaining a close approximation to their original courses. This type of drainage pattern, in which a river system has been let down over an older landscape, is referred to as *superimposed* or *epigenetic* drainage.

If a stream continues through its erosive cycle whilst mountain uplift and folding are in progress it is said to be an *antecedent stream*, for the river is older than the earth movements. The resulting features of this antecedent drainage pattern will depend on the rate of the earth's uplift compared with the rate of the river's downcutting. Antecedence has been used to explain the nature of some of the rivers flowing across the Himalayas, notably the Arun and Tista, which flow against the structure of the mountains through impassable gorges.

The Rhine, on its way through western Europe from its source in the Swiss Alps to the North Sea, links up with a number of other rivers – among them, the Sieg, the Wupper, the Ruhr and the Lippe.

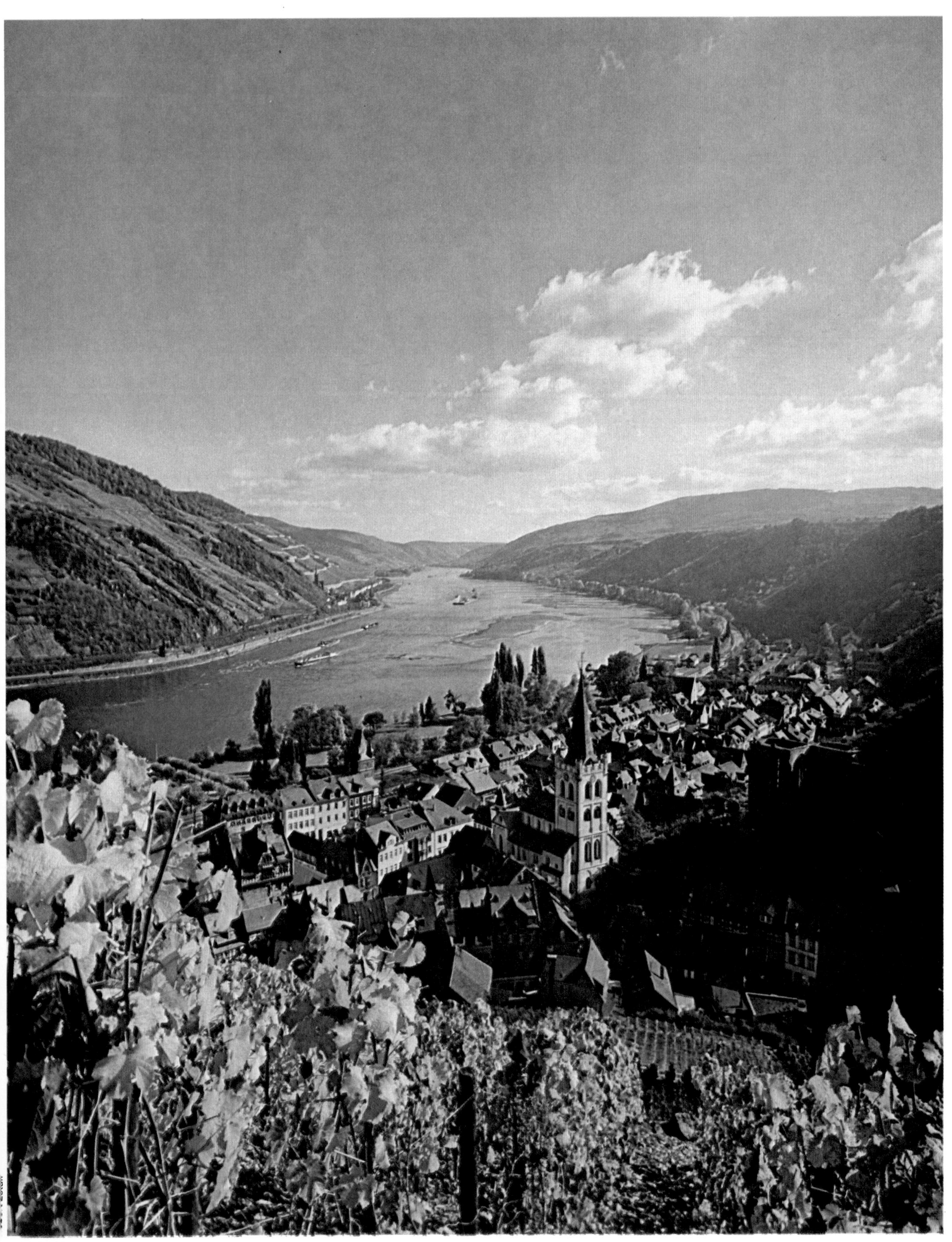

Lakes

Lakes are a familiar sight in most landscapes, but they are notoriously difficult features to define except in the most general terms. Broadly speaking, *lakes* are bodies of water enclosed by land, occupying hollows on the earth's surface. They form when the floor of a hollow is relatively impermeable, preventing the water from seeping into the ground, or when the floor lies below the *water table*—the highest level at which the pores of underlying rock are saturated with water.

Despite this basic common feature, lakes have a huge variety of different characteristics. They may be very large or very small, deep or shallow, natural or man-made, freshwater or salty, and even permanent or seasonal. They vary in size from the small ponds known by different names in different parts of the world—for example, *tarns* in England, *lochans* in Scotland, *étangs* in France, and *billabongs* in Australia—to the large features frequently referred to as *inland seas* and in some cases given the name 'sea'. In fact, the Caspian Sea in central Asia is the largest lake in the world, with a total area of 371,800 km^2 (143,550 sq miles).

Larger lakes often exhibit characteristics very similar to those of seas or oceans, though usually on a smaller scale. For example, winds blowing over large lakes can generate waves of sufficient size to result in erosion processes similar to those at the sea coast. Another similarity between seas and lakes is the creation of

Above: A lake is a perfect example of a complete 'system', in which the inputs and outputs of material and energy are readily identified. Once the hollow has been formed, water can be supplied by inflowing rivers, underground water, melting ice and precipitation. Sediment and decaying organic material accumulate on the floor. Lake water is lost to evaporation and to outflowing rivers, which may drain the lake completely by eroding through the lake wall.

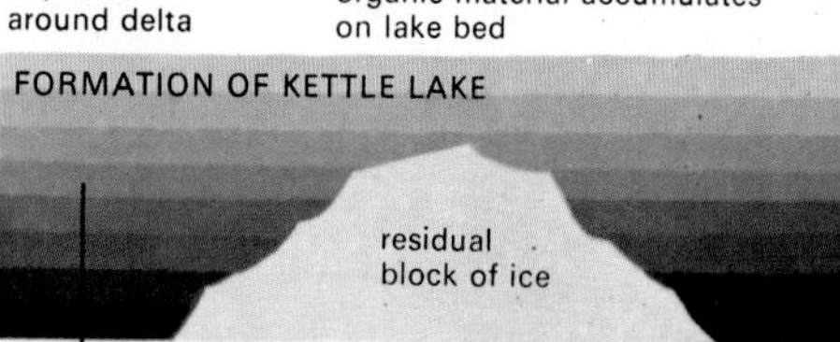

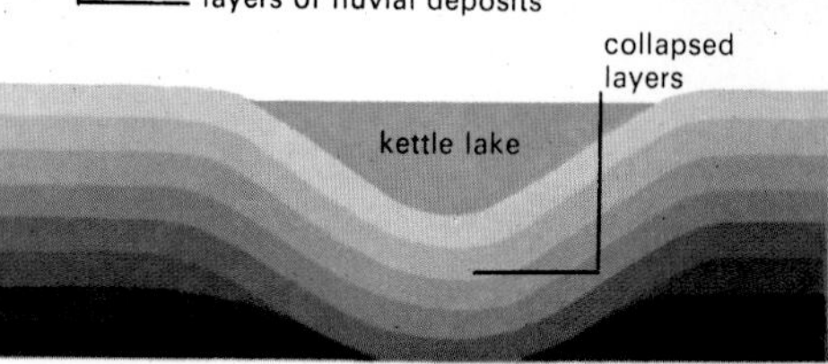

Right: Rivers issuing from glaciers may deposit sand and gravel around and on top of residual blocks of ice. When the block melts, the sediments will collapse, forming a surface depression. If this fills with water it is called a *kettle lake*.

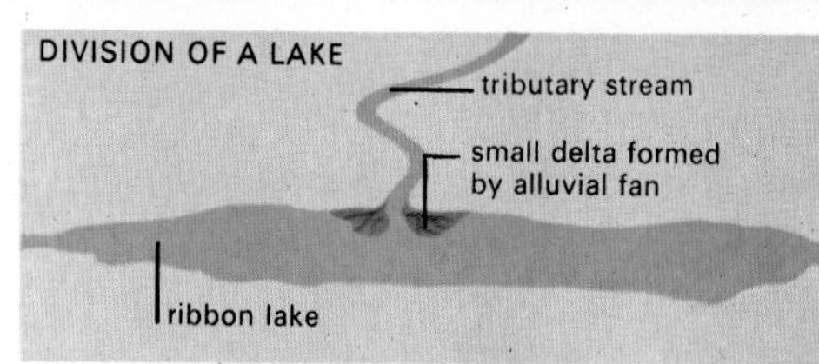

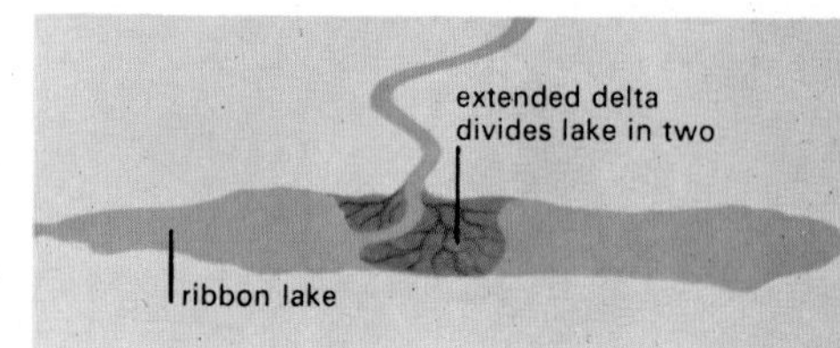

Below right: Ribbon lakes often receive fast-flowing tributary streams which deposit alluvial fans on the valley floor. In time the fans may spread out and divide the lake in two, as happened at Interlaken in Switzerland.

Photri

Left: An aerial view of the Dead Sea between Israel and Jordan. The Dead Sea formed in the basin of the Great Rift Valley—its floor lies over 800 metres below the surface of the Mediterranean to the west. Its high concentration of salt brought in by rivers results from rapid evaporation of the water.

Right: Crater Lake in Oregon (USA) occupies a giant caldera formed by the collapse of a volcanic crater about 8,000 years ago. The lake is 9 km in diameter, 600 m deep and the steep inner walls stand a further 600 m high. Wizard Island in the centre of the lake is the exposed summit of a volcanic cone pushed up by later activity.

Natural Science Photos

Aerofilms

Above: Loch Einich in Scotland is a ribbon lake, lying on the floor of a glacial trough with typically steep, smoothly curving sides. Lakes are very common in glaciated areas as glacial erosion and deposition leave behind an irregular surface, with an abundance of hollows in which water can collect.

Left: Loch Ness, home of Nessie, a prehistoric 'monster' supposed to have survived the extinction of the dinosaurs 65 M.Y. ago. Towards the end of the last Ice Age about 12,000 years ago, Loch Ness was joined to the sea. Subsequent uplift of the land resulted from the melting of ice which had depressed the surface of Scotland by its weight. Any 'monsters' in the loch would have been trapped as Loch Ness was cut off from the sea.

Below: 'Bottomless lakes' carved out of gypsum in New Mexico (USA). Certain rocks—such as gypsum, rock salt and especially limestone—dissolve under the action of acidic water. Hollows are created that may become lakes if they lie below the water table or if the underground outlet of running water becomes clogged with inwashed clay. Lakes also form above collapsed caverns.

H. Steenmans/ZEFA

Jerome Wyckoff

deltas where rivers flow into them, and lakes even have a type of tidal movement known as a *seiche*. Although seiches usually involve rises and falls in lake level of only a few centimetres they occur on a much shorter time-cycle than oceanic tides and may produce over 20 high 'tides' per day.

Although the water in lakes is usually described as fresh, under certain circumstances lake water can have a higher salt concentration than sea water. Thus in semi-arid parts of the world, rather than being drained by an outflowing river, lakes frequently lose water by large-scale evaporation from their surfaces, leading to the build-up of salts in lake water. The Great Salt Lake in Utah, USA, and the Dead Sea between Israel and Jordan, for example, both have salt concentrations six to seven times that of sea-water.

Creation of lakes

The most convenient way to classify lakes is to explain how the hollows containing them first originated, although it is common for a single lake to be due to more than one cause. However, apart from those produced artificially, all these hollows can be said to be manifestations of the unstable land surface and climate of the earth.

Firstly, a significant number of lakes are formed as a result of crustal or *tectonic* movement, volcanic activity, or changes in relative sea-level. Tectonic activity involves subsidence of the earth's crust, a mechanism that was responsible for the creation of Lough Neagh in Northern Ireland and Lake Victoria in East Africa, or down-faulting of a block of land, as occurred in an area of central Asia to produce the deepest lake in the world, Lake Baykal, 1,940 metres (6,365 ft) deep. The best known down-faulted blocks occur in the rift valleys that extend in a linear belt from Jordan to East Africa.

Craters are frequently created by volcanic eruptions and under suitable circumstances these hollows may be filled with water after volcanic activity has ceased. One of the best known and largest examples of this type is the characteristically circular Crater Lake in Oregon, USA, with a diameter of 9 km (6 miles). On a smaller scale the numerous *Maaren* of the Eifel district of Germany are crater lakes between 500 metres and 1 km (1,600 to 3,200 feet) in diameter. Occasionally a lava flow or accumulation of other volcanic material may block a valley and so form a lake. One example of this is Lake Kivu in East Africa, which originally drained northwards to the Nile but, following the eruption of the Birunga volcanic field, has since overflowed southwards to Lake Tanganyika.

If relative sea-level falls, either by a rise in land-level or fall in sea-level, or both, numerous lakes will be left in hollows on the former sea floor. This happened on several occasions during the Ice Ages, for at various times sea-level fell due to the abstraction of ocean water to form ice, and land-level rose as ice sheets that had depressed the land surface by their weight melted.

Hollows scooped out of the land

A second group of processes responsible for lake formation involves erosion of various kinds. Moving bodies of ice are probably the most important of these erosion agents, leaving a variety of

IN-FILLING OF A LAKE

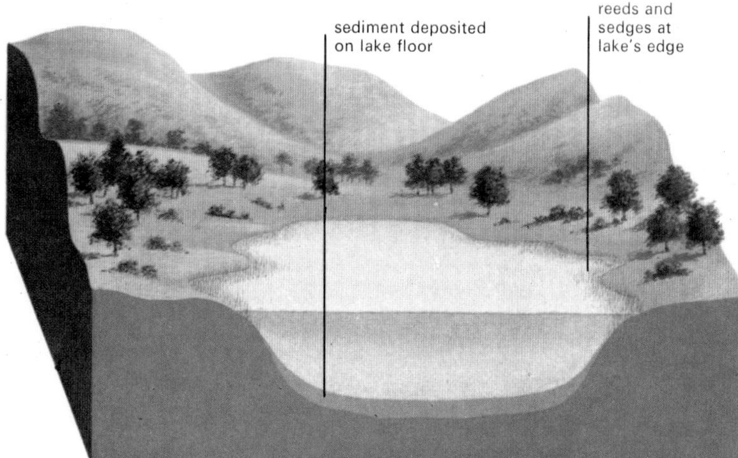

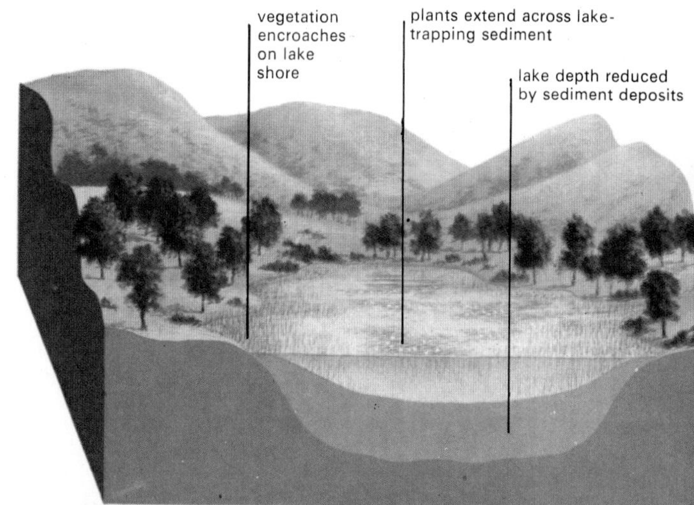

Michael Freeman/Bruce Coleman

Left: An ox-bow lake in the forests of the Amazon Basin. The lake was left behind when the River Jutat cut through the narrow neck of a looping meander and changed its course. Ox-bow lakes soon disappear unless fed by a fresh supply of water. Already the trees and other vegetation have quickly colonized the ends of the loop, disguising the original course of the meander.

Right: Lakes Maurepas (below the river) and Pontchertrain were created partly by levee deposits from the Mississippi river and partly by the coastal deposits from the Gulf of Mexico (top right corner).

Below: The Parallel Roads of Glen Roy in Scotland gained their name from a legend that they were the hunting tracks used by giants. In fact they mark the former shorelines of an old lake, formed about 10,000 years ago by glaciers that blocked the mouth of the valley and trapped the waters of melting ice. The highest level of the lake has thus been recorded at 350 m.

attractive lakes in formerly glaciated areas. They form, for example, in deep, rounded hollows, known as *cirques* or *corries*, that have a rock lip or in deepened basins in troughs scoured out by glaciers. These are termed *ribbon lakes*, of which the Finger Lakes of New York State and the lakes of the Italian Alps—Maggiore, Como and Garda—are good examples.

In lowland areas, glacial erosion has often produced a very irregular topography that becomes a landscape of lakes and rocky outcrops. Topography of this type is found in parts of the Canadian Shield, north-west Scotland, as well as in Finland.

Another type of erosion that produces lakes is solution, by which rock material is dissolved in acidic water. In limestone areas this process may form steep-sided hollows known as *swallow holes* up to 30 metres (100 ft) deep which can fill up with water if they either lie below the water table or become clogged with inwashed clay. Lough Derg on the River Shannon in Ireland is thought to be due to the expansion and deepening of the limestone bed of the river by surface solution.

Deflation, the erosive action of the wind in desert regions, can also produce hollows of substantial size. If the hollows are eroded down to a level below that of the water table, they become shallow salt lakes or swamps. Many oases in the Sahara originated in this way.

There are rare examples of lakes that

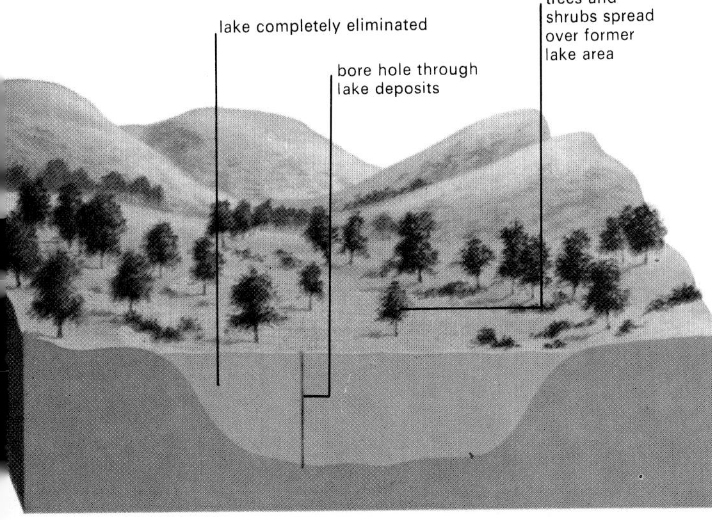

Left: How a lake is filled by sedimentation and vegetation growth. In the initial stage the lake is clear of vegetation, but rivers flowing through carry sediment loads that are largely trapped by the calmer waters of the lake. Coarser deposits form deltas and beaches around the shores and finer deposits collect on the floor, gradually filling up the basin. When the depth is reduced to 1-2 m, plants may extend across the lake, greatly accelerating silting by trapping sediment. Eventually the lake becomes a swamp, a marsh and then firm ground on which trees and shrubs grow. Bores taken through old lake deposits reveal evidence of past environments.

Heather Angel

Right: A salt lake on Santiago Island in the Galapagos Group, East Pacific. Salts left behind in the dry season are used commercially.

Below: Lake Tekapo in New Zealand is silting up. Where rivers flow into lakes, their velocities are checked and the sediment being transported is deposited in the form of deltas, as here where the muddy waters enter the lake.

Bottom: The Hoover Dam was built across the Colorado River in 1935, creating the 190 km long Lake Mead. The variation in lake level—shown by the light zone above the lake surface—is partly due to climatic factors and partly to human control of the water allowed to escape. The Colorado River deposits 700,000 tonnes of sediment in Lake Mead every year and if left to itself the lake will become completely infilled by 2250 AD.

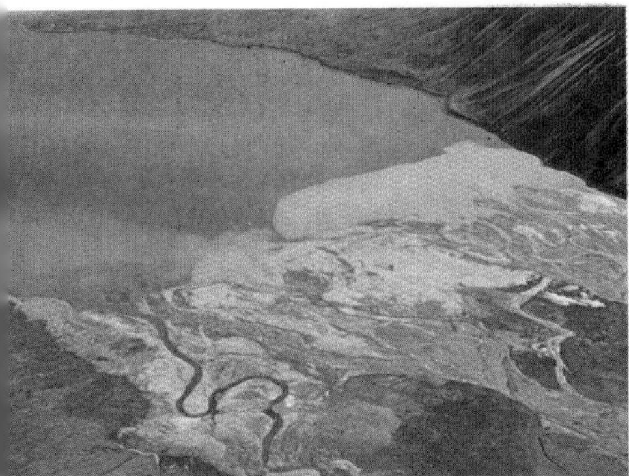

G. R. Roberts

Photri

have developed in the impact craters of large meteorites. The largest positively assigned to this origin is Lake Bosumtwi which occupies the Ashanti Crater in Ghana and is about 10 km (6 miles) wide.

Barrier lakes

A third group of processes which form lakes involves various types of deposition. Glacial deposits are often laid down in irregular sheets, in which the numerous hollows may fill up with water. Two other lake types associated with glacial deposits are those formed behind a barrier of terminal moraine and *kettle lakes*, formed in hollows produced by the melting of blocks of ice.

River deposits also form lakes. Common examples occur where river deposits seal up both ends of abandoned meander loops, thus forming *ox-bow lakes*, while the building of natural levees on both sides of river channels can prevent flood waters from flowing back into the river channel, creating flood plain lakes. In coastal locations this action produces delta *lagoons*, though these are often partly sealed by marine deposits.

Vegetation growth and animal activity can create barriers for lakes, but man is by far the most effective dam constructor. The growing demands for water have led to the large-scale impounding (blocking off) of rivers or enlargement of previously existing lakes. In the United States alone over 40,000 km² (15,000 sq miles) is now covered with artificially impounded water, an area larger than Belgium.

Elimination of lakes

One feature common to all lakes is their transient existence. Not only can their level change from time to time but eventually all lakes tend to be eliminated altogether. Lakes have been observed to drain temporarily after earth tremors, while the tilting of blocks of the earth's crust may lead to a more permanent elimination. Where lakes owe their existence to the position of the water table above the floor of a basin, it is clear that a fall in the water table will result in a drop in the level of the lake and in some cases to its complete disappearance.

Climatic change can produce changes in lake levels. For example, during the Ice Ages, evaporation rates were much lower in many presently semi-arid areas and a number of so-called *pluvial lakes* existed. The largest of these was Lake Bonneville in Utah which covered an area of 50,000 km² (20,000 sq miles) and was over 300 metres (1,000 ft) deep in places. The Great Salt Lake is a present day remnant of it. Similarly, most desert lakes or *playas* are particularly transient features. They may form during an occasional heavy shower but due to rapid evaporation they quickly disappear.

Just as lakes can be formed by a fall in relative sea-level, they can be destroyed by a relative rise of sea-level. This must have happened many times at the end of the Ice Ages as ice masses melted and returned water to the oceans. The best known example is probably the Baltic Sea which at one time towards the end of the last Ice Age was a fresh water body known as Ancylus Lake. As sea-level rose its threshold was overtopped and it became an arm of the sea.

Lakes may also disappear if the dams impounding them are broken through or removed. Ice-dammed lakes, for example, are drained if the water is able to escape under the ice or if the ice melts.

Lakes are of great importance to man. They not only provide natural reservoirs of water, but also help to regulate the flow of rivers, thus preventing excessive flooding and intermittent flow. However, outlet rivers supplied by the overflow from the lake tend to erode down through the barrier holding back the lake waters and may eventually drain the lake.

Another slow process by which lakes eventually disappear is sedimentation or *silting up*. If none of the previously described processes leads to elimination of a lake, then gradual sedimentation on the lake floor and vegetation growth will eventually fill it in, although this may take thousands of years.

One interesting aspect of lakes that have been filled by sediment and vegetation is that they can yield considerable information regarding the geomorphological, vegetational and climatic histories of surrounding areas. Radiocarbon dating of the bottom deposits gives a date for the creation of the lake and in glaciated areas gives a clear indication of when the area was deglaciated. Analysis of the pollen present throughout the core allows scientists to work out the vegetational history of the area and together with the study of beetles and other insects present is valuable in deciphering the climatic changes since the lake was created.

Limestone Terrain

Of all the major rock types, limestones produce one of the most distinctive types of terrain. A variety of features associated with limestone outcrops are recognizable throughout the world; some of these have been known for centuries by local names and as a result words from many different languages make up the current vocabulary describing limestone features. Many such words are either Slovene or Serbo-Croat, borrowed from the limestone terrain in Yugoslavia, an area composed of rugged mountains, the Dinaric Alps, and the low plateau of Istra. This region is known as the *Karst*, a term which is now commonly used by geologists to mean limestone terrain.

Natural waters, whether in the soil or in a stream, are actively erosive or *aggressive* when they first come into contact with the limestone of karst areas. All limestones, including both marble and chalk, are largely composed of calcite (calcium carbonate), one of the most common and readily dissolved minerals. As water percolates through the soil it picks up a considerable amount of carbon dioxide from the high percentage found in soil air. Calcium carbonate reacts with carbon dioxide and water to form the very soluble salt, calcium bicarbonate, which may be carried away in solution.

Limestones are mainly dissolved in two ways. Firstly, water percolating through the soil cover gradually lowers the overall land surface. In humid, mid-latitude areas, the rate at which the ground-surface is lowered may be as much as 50 to 100 mm (2-4 in) in a thousand years. Secondly, water which has converged into surface streams over non-limestone rocks concentrates solutional activity at the point where the river passes on to a limestone outcrop.

The other important feature of limestones is the fact that they are well-jointed. *Joints* are fractures in which little or no movement parallel to the walls of the fracture has taken place. Vertical joints originated due to contraction following the drying out of the limestone when it was first deposited. If the joints are horizontal, they mark changes in the character of the sediment or pauses during its deposition, and are termed *bedding joints* or *bedding planes*.

Joints allow water to find a path through the limestone. Some features of karst areas are due essentially to jointing and are very similar to comparable landforms in other well-jointed rocks which are non-soluble. For example,

Sonia Halliday

Above: The most striking feature of any limestone country is the general lack of any surface water. This dry, steep-sided gorge in Cappadocia, Turkey, was carved into massive, horizontally-jointed limestone. The cracks and bedding planes provided passages for water which dissolved the rock, creating large cavities. Debris at the foot of the cliffs suggests the gorge may be a collapsed cavern; alternatively it may be the steep-sided valley of a now vanished river.

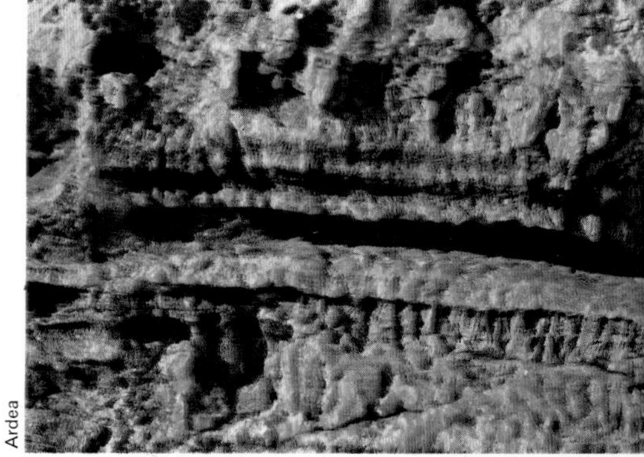

Ardea

Right: Calcite and aragonite may be deposited in layers of colourful crystals along the joints in limestone.

Below: This section reveals several underground features of well-jointed limestone. A surface stream running off impermeable rock disappears down a swallow hole and opens up a series of vertical shafts, chambers and narrow passages along the joints, before it reappears. Frequently, dripping water will form stalactites, stalagmites and pillars of limestone.

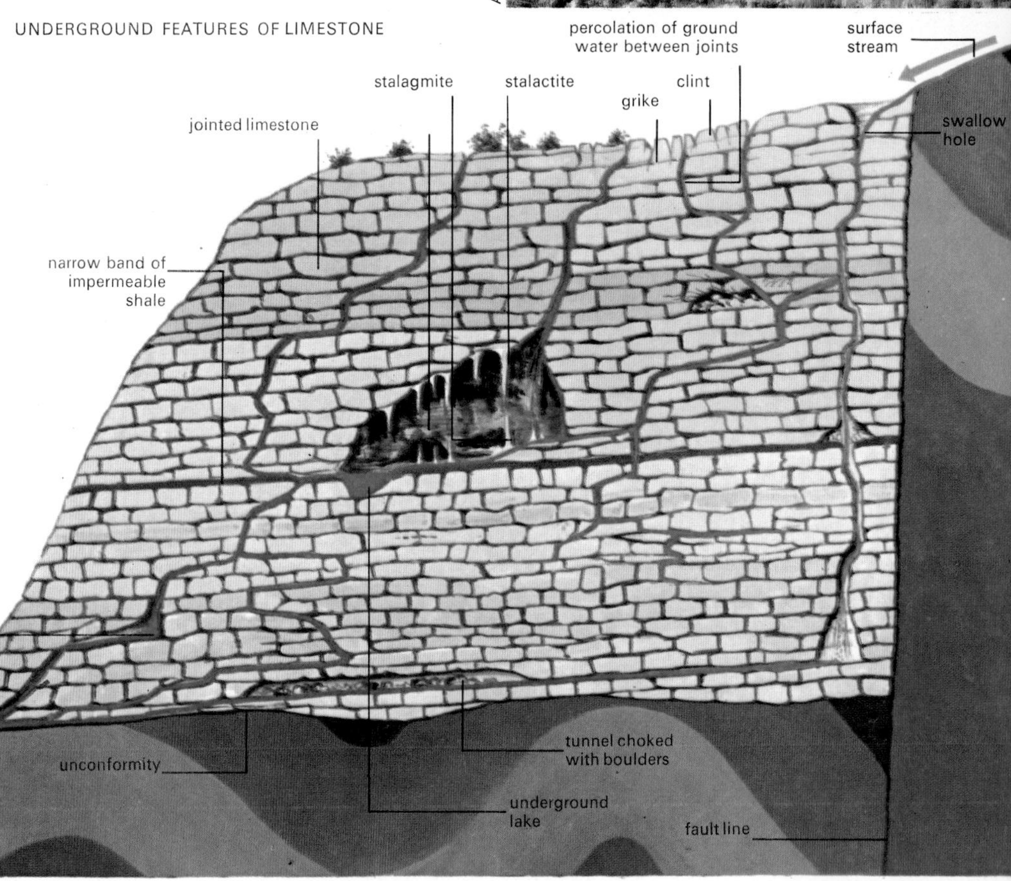

SURFACE FEATURES OF LIMESTONE

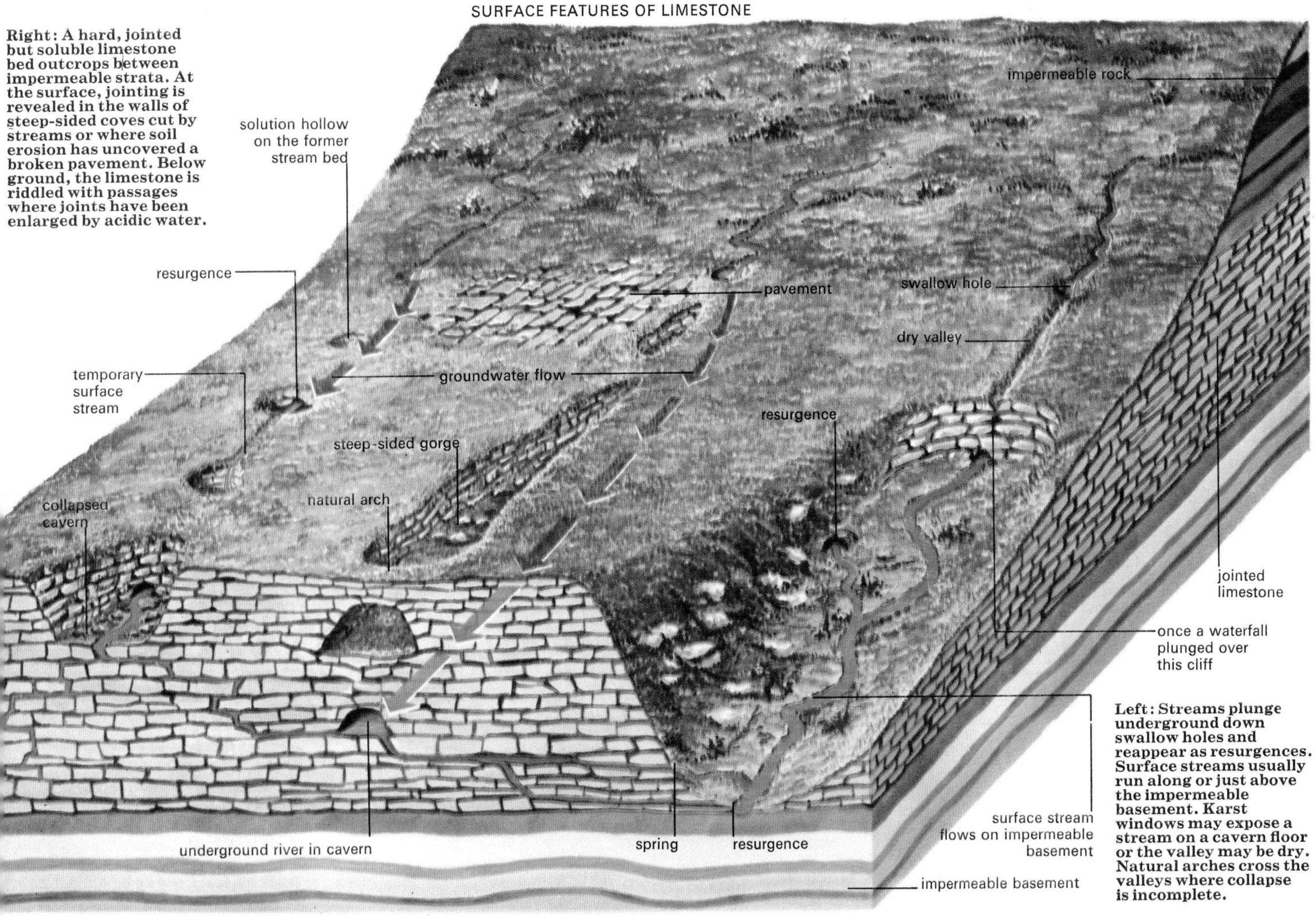

Right: A hard, jointed but soluble limestone bed outcrops between impermeable strata. At the surface, jointing is revealed in the walls of steep-sided coves cut by streams or where soil erosion has uncovered a broken pavement. Below ground, the limestone is riddled with passages where joints have been enlarged by acidic water.

solution hollow on the former stream bed
impermeable rock
resurgence
pavement
swallow hole
dry valley
temporary surface stream
groundwater flow
resurgence
steep-sided gorge
collapsed cavern
natural arch
jointed limestone
once a waterfall plunged over this cliff
surface stream flows on impermeable basement
underground river in cavern
spring
resurgence
impermeable basement

Left: Streams plunge underground down swallow holes and reappear as resurgences. Surface streams usually run along or just above the impermeable basement. Karst windows may expose a stream on a cavern floor or the valley may be dry. Natural arches cross the valleys where collapse is incomplete.

J. L. Mason/Ardea

Above: At Hutton Roof Crag in North Yorkshire, a well-drained upland limestone pavement (or lapiés surface), bare of soil, has been eroded. As shown in the detail (above left) solution has worked along the roughly rectangular pattern of joints to hollow out the deep grooves called grykes between the masses of limestone clints. The largest clints are about 1 m across and the grykes may be over 0.5 m deep.

Institute of Geological Sciences

Left: A dry valley in Somerset, England. Theories vary as to the origin of such features. Some authorities view them as the product of cavern collapse; others as relics of a colder climate, when streams eroded the frozen, and thus impermeable, rock.

gorges cut into the rock are often flanked by sharp sides and steep cliffs that follow the outline of the jointing pattern. If a limestone is less well-jointed, like the porous chalk outcrops, smoother outlines develop in the landscape. Chalk is a soft, white type of fine-grained limestone. Because of its purity—chalk is composed almost entirely of calcium carbonate—it is highly soluble and easily eroded, giving rise to the gently rolling scenery found in the hills of eastern and southern England and the hills of Picardy and Artois in France.

It is the combination of these properties of limestone, being both soluble and well-jointed, that explains the distinctiveness of karst areas. For example, a surface stream may disappear at the junction of major joints, creating the limestone feature known as a *sink* or *swallow hole*. In England, a well-known example of a swallow hole is Gaping Ghyll, a deep opening in the Carboniferous Limestone in the Yorkshire Pennines. If a disappearing stream continues to erode its bed upstream from a swallow hole, the valley ends abruptly in a horseshoe-shaped cliff above the opening. This is termed a *blind valley*. The valley of the River Reka in Yugoslavia ends in this way.

Underground cave systems

Once underground, the stream continues to eat along the joints, enlarging caverns in the limestone. In horizontally-bedded strata, caves are made up of a series of vertical drops or *pitches* linked by horizontal *passages*. In mountain karsts, the total depth of caves is considerable. Near Lyon in eastern France, for example, the Gouffre Jean Bernard is estimated to be 1,200 m (4,000 ft) deep.

Just below the surface, beneath a soil cover, solution slowly etches out the joint pattern. Due to deforestation and the consequent soil erosion in many areas in the Middle Ages, roughly rectangular blocks known as *limestone pavements* or as a *lapiés surface* are now revealed as a feature of well-jointed limestones. In north-west Yorkshire, the pavement is called a *clint* and the solution-enlarged joint is termed a *gryke*. The German word *karren* is widely used to describe grykes and solutional gutters on bare limestone outcrops.

Where major joints intersect, solutional activity may tend to concentrate and develop a funnel-shaped surface cavity, now widely described by the Slovene word *doline*. Dolines may be as much as 100 m (330 ft) in diameter. If the base intersects an underground drainage system, the doline sides may collapse to form a circle of sheer cliffs, termed a *shaft doline*. Such a doline, broadened to afford a view of the underground river emerging from one cave then disappearing into another, is called a *karst window*.

However, shaft dolines and karst windows are not common. Cave systems often have no noticeable effect on landforms developed above them on the surface, although some authorities suggest that a number of valleys in karst areas have formed by caverns collapsing.

Dry valleys

Drainage patterns, however, are markedly affected by cave systems; in many cases entire valleys are now streamless because all precipitation finds its way into underground fissures, voids or caves before it can concentrate as a surface stream. Such *dry valleys* can therefore be attributed to a lowering of the groundwater levels, as solution progressively enlarged joints which were once very narrow.

Dry valleys are also partly explained by climatic changes during the Quaternary and post-glacial periods of the last two million years. For instance, during the Quaternary period, the Karst in Yugoslavia was under the strong meteorological influences of the sub-Polar front and the ice cap of the Alps. Cyclones from the sea brought great quantities of moisture to the Karst mountains, much of it falling as snow, and the enormous floods of summer melts exceeded the capacity of the cave systems to lead all the water underground. This abundant surface flow over the permeable limestone cut out valleys, which today are dry.

Dry valleys and a lack of surface drainage are characteristic of most chalk country. One explanation suggested for the formation of streamless valleys in the highly porous English chalk areas is that they were cut when the ground was permanently frozen, which meant that the limestone was temporarily impermeable.

Climate is an important factor when present-day comparisons are made between the main karst areas of the world. Because solutional processes are governed by the amount of effective precipitation that falls, and by temperature, limestone terrains are not the same in different climatic zones. For example, in arctic or alpine areas, the main agent is the large volume of snowmelt which runs over bare rock surfaces in late spring and summer. Karren are therefore distinctive characteristics of such regions.

S. Schmidt/Bavaria

Left: The Karst region of Yugoslavia slopes down from the Dinaric Alps to the Dalmatian coast on the Adriatic Sea. This barren, rocky land is the most distinctive and closely studied of all limestone areas and many of the names given to local features are now used to describe limestone terrains found elsewhere.

Barnaby's

Right: A polje, a large steep-sided depression, in the Montenegro hills. Poljes appear to be almost exclusively Yugoslavian features. They are of considerable agricultural importance in this bare, barren area as their alluvial floors often provide the only cultivable land available. Thus settlements often develop on the perimeter.

Below: A section through a typical Yugoslavian karst area. The landscape is dominated by the large polje, bounded by limestone hills. The origin of poljes is problematic: they may be due to erosion, or to earth movements such as faulting. Poljes often flood in winter to form large temporary lakes.

THE YUGOSLAVIAN KARST REGION

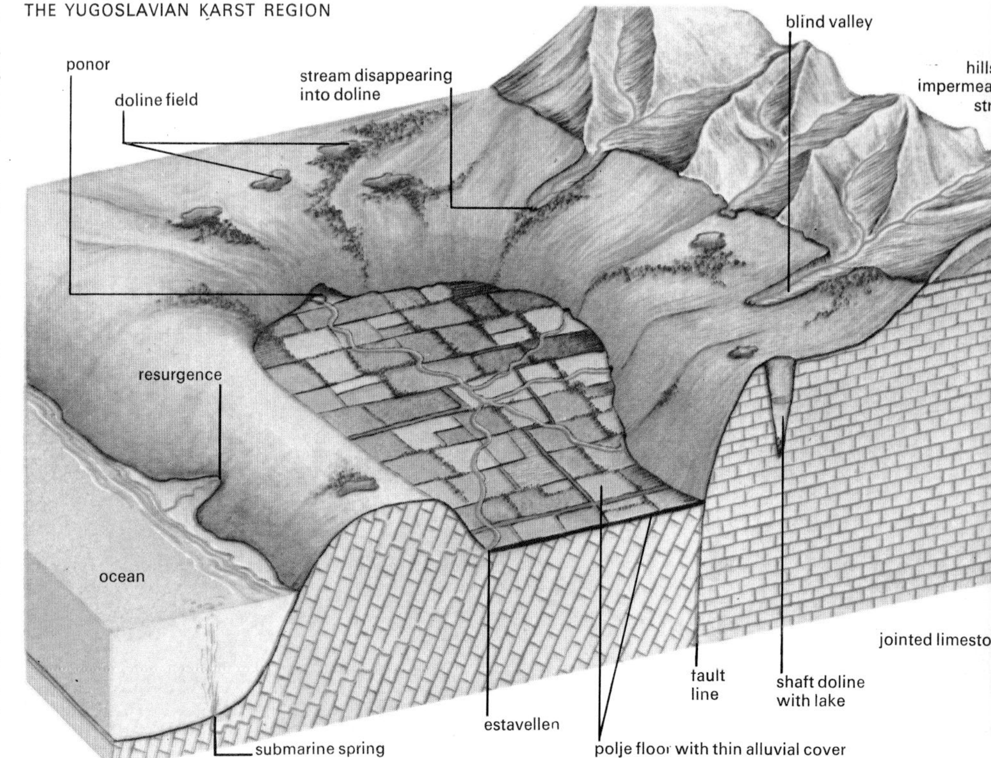

Below: Cockpit country in central Jamaica is the classic area for cone karst—a landscape of limestone peaks which looks rather like an egg box. Cockpit karst is restricted to limestones with widely spaced joints in tropical regions, other examples being found in Cuba, Vietnam, New Guinea and Indonesia.

Right: Tower karst in Kwangsi province, China. These precipitous peaks were probably formed when dolines and other holes coalesced to produce wide plains with hums (isolated hills). The tower karst landscape has been the inspiration for the spectacular background scenery of many Chinese drawings and paintings.

A. L. Waltham

William MacQuitty

Terence Spencer/Colorific!

Above: White Horse Hill above Uffington in Berkshire. The large figure of a horse, thought to date from the Iron Age, was sculpted on the scarp slope by removing the turf to show the white chalk subsoil. Chalk is highly porous and its gentle topography is characteristically streamless.

Below: A steep gorge cut by the fast-flowing River Cunningham in Somerset Island in the Canadian Arctic. The underlying permafrost renders the limestone impermeable and prevents the surface stream from percolating into the rock. Usually rivers on a limestone surface are only found in areas of permafrost.

D. I. Smith

In contrast, warmer karst areas are dominated by large depressions known as *poljes*, from the Serbo-Croat word for field. A polje, however, is a very unusual type of field. It is the very flat floor of a large, isolated karst depression, cut across the bedrock and bounded by steep slopes on all sides. Poljes, which are often several kilometres long, experience seasonal flooding. Winter run-off from the surrounding hills is too great to be drained off by the existing cave systems. So a large temporary lake forms. Swallow holes at the edge of poljes are called *ponors*. Some underground systems act as springs in winter when water is plentiful and as swallow holes in summer. These seasonally fluctuating features are termed *estavellen*.

Poljes have not developed in cooler environments, although the *turloughs* of County Clare in western Ireland are very similar. The slopes of the perimeter of high land around the turloughs are gently inclined, whereas in humid, tropical regions the contrast between polje floor and the surrounding hills is more accentuated. The major reason for this is the increased acidity of water in warm, moist areas, caused by the swift decay of dead vegetation on the ground. Highly acidic water subjects the limestones to rapid erosion.

In karst country in the humid tropics where the hills have become isolated in a flat plain, the distinctive *tower karst* country is developed. The junction of the polje floor with the karst tower is very abrupt and there is often solutional undercutting of the tower. Rock falls at such points have been recorded in recent years in Malaya. Another distinctive feature of tropical karst is the enlargement of adjacent dolines until any flat land between them is eliminated. The higher land is reduced to a series of isolated peaks or *cone karst*. The classic example of cone karst is the Cockpit country of Jamaica.

Much of the calcium carbonate dissolved from limestones remains in solution until the drainage waters reach the ocean. But in certain circumstances, deposition of calcium carbonate may occur in sufficient quantities to create new landforms. Deposition seems to happen more in warmer climates and at points where water is slow-moving or running as a thin film over rock. Precipitated calcium carbonate is called *travertine* and occasionally forms *waterfall screens*, which look like petrified waterfalls. Within the tropical belt the best-known limestone terrain, the coral atolls, are formed by the abstraction of calcium carbonate from sea water by coral polyps.

There is always an impermeable basement to any limestone block which will halt the downward percolation of ground water. Within the limestone strata, thin impermeable layers like shale, volcanic ash or marl act as the floor of an extensive cave passage system and of the outlet of a spring or resurgent stream—until the layers are eventually breached. In a *covered karst*, a non-soluble or impermeable stratum remains above an underlying limestone mass. If the cover is relatively thin and the limestone strata beneath undergoes extensive solution, they may collapse, creating dolines in the cover rock itself.

Glacial Erosion

About ten per cent of the earth's land surface is covered in ice. As recently as 70,000 to 10,000 years ago, during the last major advance of the Pleistocene Ice Age, almost 30 per cent of the earth was blanketed by ice and snow, profoundly affecting the landscape of many areas. Today, the erosional effects of ice are reshaping such spectacular scenery as the mountains and valleys of the European Alps.

The ice which feeds the world's vast ice sheets and glaciers primarily forms through prolonged accumulation of snow. However, fresh snow is light and easily disturbed and, before it is converted into heavier, more tightly compacted ice, various processes have to take place. The change is mostly due to the compression of snow by the weight of successive additions from direct snowfalls and from avalanches down surrounding slopes.

In some areas summer temperatures and the increasing pressure of successive layers of snowfall cause some of the ice particles to melt. The *meltwater* produced then trickles down through the snow and refreezes, so that the compressed snow is further compacted. In this state, the snow is a porous mass of small, rounded granules known as *firn* or *névé*. The continued pressure of overlying snow concentrates the trapped air into gas bubbles under very high pressure, and the particles become even more closely locked together. When the ice finally forms a solid state composed of interlocking ice crystals, it is termed *glacier ice*.

Types of glacier

Broadly speaking, there are two types of glacier: valley glaciers and continental glaciers. By far the most extensive are *continental glaciers*, vast areas of ice spreading out under their own weight. The larger spreads, such as those covering Antarctica and Greenland, are usually called *ice sheets*, while smaller areas of ice, such as those in Iceland and Norway, are known as *ice caps*.

The largest European ice cap is in Iceland, covers about 19,500 km² (7,500 sq miles) and is about 230 m (750 feet) thick. This is relatively unimpressive, however, when compared with the Antarctic ice sheet which extends over 13,000,000 km² (5,000,000 sq miles), and the Greenland ice sheet, which covers an area 10 times the size of England and Wales—and in places is 3,000 m (10,000 ft) thick.

Much of Greenland is permanently covered in ice and, except for the south-west of the island (where the ice terminates before reaching the sea), the ice sheet spills through the coastal mountains and descends in the form of outlet glaciers.

Valley glaciers are slow-moving rivers of ice which flow downwards from higher to lower land along the easiest route, namely valleys. They can be divided into three sections, starting with the source or *zone of accumulation* where accumulated snow is transformed into glacier ice.

Moving out of the basin, the mass of ice

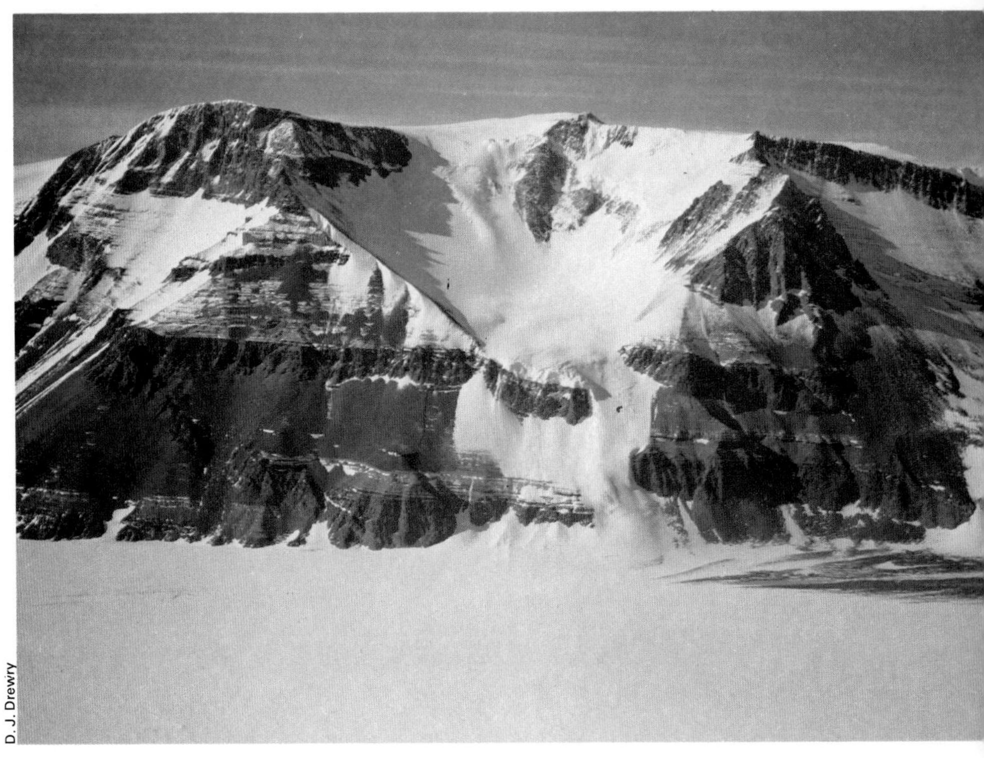

D. J. Drewry

Above: Small glaciers on mountain sides may erode a bowl-shaped *cirque*. This ice-filled cirque in Antarctica lies above the 200 km-long Beardmore Glacier, one of the world's largest.

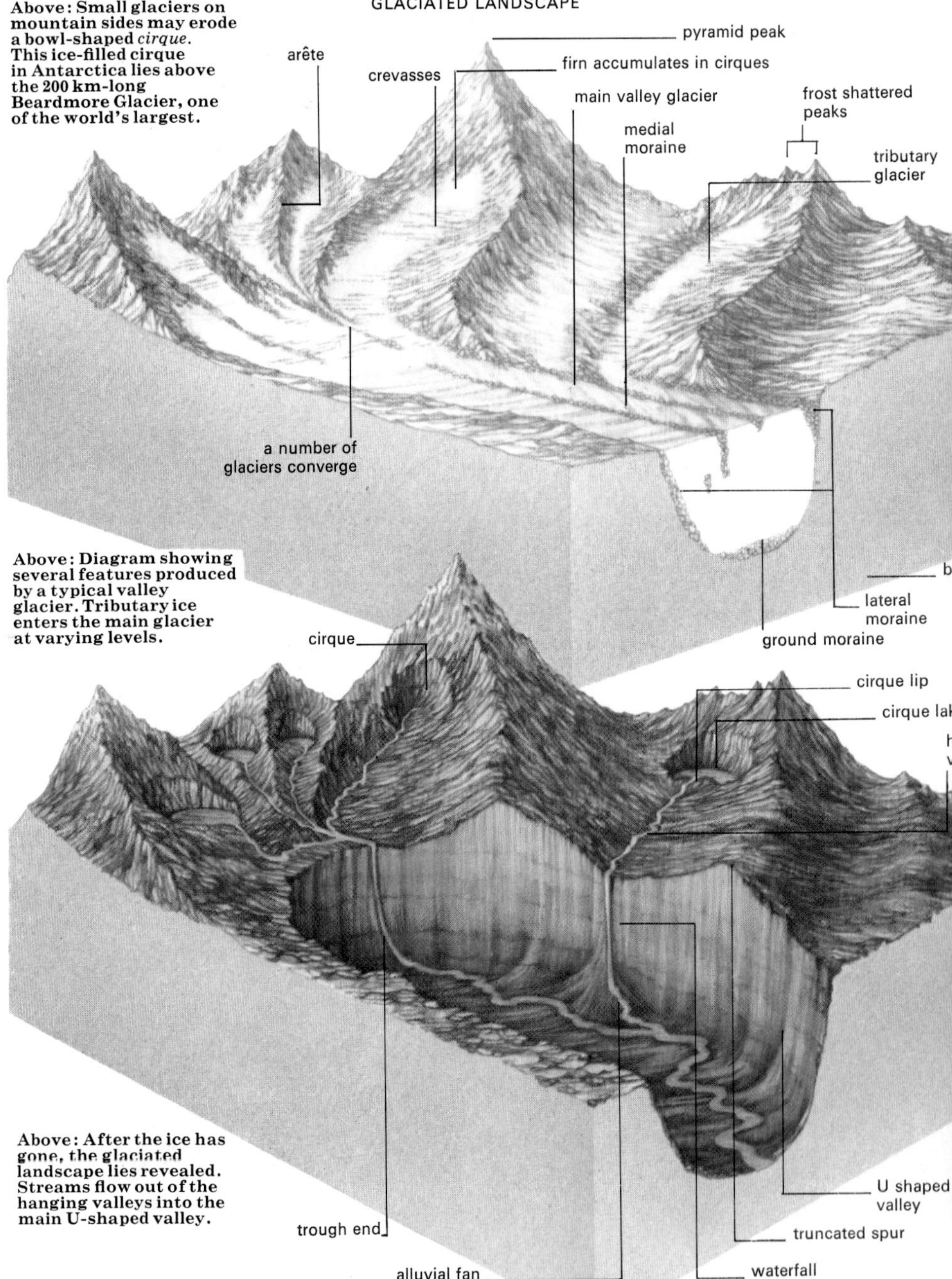

Above: Diagram showing several features produced by a typical valley glacier. Tributary ice enters the main glacier at varying levels.

Above: After the ice has gone, the glaciated landscape lies revealed. Streams flow out of the hanging valleys into the main U-shaped valley.

G. R. Roberts

enters its zone of transit. As it flows downwards, its surface begins to split and crack, probably due to movement within the ice mass itself, to form openings or *crevasses*.

Crevasses also occur along the margins of the glacier, due to the difference in the rate of movement of ice in the middle of the glacier and along the valley wall. Other features of this stage are steep ridges called *seracs*, and *ice falls*, masses of ridges and crevasses, caused by a change in gradient of the glacier bed. The Khumbu ice fall in Nepal, for example, is badly crevassed, proving an obstacle to climbers using the southern approach to Mt. Everest.

During its downward journey, the glacier acts on, and wears away, the underlying rock. In addition, rock fragments detached from the valley walls by the action of frost, fall on to the glacier and are carried along by it. Debris transported and deposited by glaciers is termed *moraine*.

Finally, the ice mass moves beyond the *snow line* (the lower limit of permanent snow) into an area of decline or *zone of ablation*. Here the glacier is subject to the effects of evaporation and melting which contributes to this decline.

Above: A glaciated valley in the Southern Alps of New Zealand. Glaciers flowing through mountainous country carve out deep, straight, U-shaped valleys by concentrating erosion at the bed and sides. After the glaciers have melted, these valleys provide some of the most impressive scenery of alpine areas. Peaks above the smoothed valley are fretted with spires and jagged pinnacles formed by the action of frost and ice.

Below: Mt Blanc, the highest peak in the European Alps, lies in a sea of moving ice spread over 100 km². Various parts of glaciers move at different rates and this view shows how the centre of a glacier flows faster than the sides.

R. Everts/ZEFA

Left: Geiranger Fjord in Norway was scooped out by very thick glaciers flowing swiftly out of the former Scandinavian ice sheet. These powerful outlet glaciers were able to erode very deep, steep-sided valleys, even below sea level. When the ice retreated and sea level rose, the great trenches were flooded to form fjords.

Below: Sutherland Falls in the Southern Alps (NZ) where much of the landscape was once covered by ice and valley glaciers. Less powerful tributary glaciers often left a valley perched above the deeper trunk channel. Such *hanging valleys* may have lakes in the overdeepened basins, from which waterfalls tumble.

C. M. Dixon

Brian Brake/John Hillelson

The processes of glacial erosion

Glacial erosion forms the first part of a continuous chain of glacial activity, which ends with transportation of debris to its place of deposition. Various factors contribute to the degree and rate of erosion: the strength, hardness and pattern of joints and fractures in the underlying rock, the thickness and speed of the glacier, and the concentration and characteristics of the rock fragments within the base or *sole* of the ice.

Three key processes are involved in glacial erosion. *Abrasion* refers to the scraping or scratching action on the glacier bed of rock fragments held in the lowest levels of ice. *Crushing* involves the grinding or breaking-down of bedrock by the weight and pressure of ice and debris, while *plucking* is the direct incorporation of crushed or abraded material into the glacier base. The processes of crushing and plucking are sometimes collectively known as *quarrying*. A fourth, less crucial process involves erosion by meltwater beneath the ice, concentrated into channels or cavities. Such fluvial erosion may constitute an important method of entirely removing loose material from a glacier basin.

Abrasion at bed level is principally controlled by the pressure of overlying ice. As the ice thickness increases, so the pressures at the base of the glacier also increase, resulting in accelerating rates of abrasion. It appears, however, that beyond a certain ice load rates of abrasion begin to decline and may be eliminated altogether.

Crushing of bedrock to produce rock fragments and boulders is also dependent upon the weight of the load of ice. Here too, however, it is thought that as ice thickness increases so the degree of crushing will reach a peak and then decline.

The action of plucking requires that ice comes into direct contact with loosened materials. These materials are then incorporated into the mass of ice in two ways: fragments may be picked up and encased in the viscous flow of the ice; or a mixture of water and rock debris may amalgamate by being frozen on to the glacier sole.

The type and extent of these processes depends particularly on temperatures at the glacier bed. The temperatures at the sole of *wet-based* or temperate glaciers and ice caps are at the *pressure melting point* (the lower melting point of ice when under great pressure) due to the sheer weight of overlying ice and warmer mean annual temperatures at their surface. A thin layer of water may consequently exist on the bed, causing the ice mass to move faster. For example, most valley glaciers in the Alps, in Scandinavia, in parts of the Rocky Mountains and in Iceland are wet-based. The whole range of erosional processes—abrasion, quarrying and melt-water beneath the ice—are vigorous in these glaciers.

Dry-based or cold ice masses, on the other hand, are characterized by temperatures at their base below the pressure melting point. In other words, they are frozen to the rock and no water can exist at the bed. Such conditions occur over large areas of the Antarctic and Greenland ice sheets and in some valley glaciers in high latitudes. Naturally the action of meltwater is completely suppressed here, and although plucking of materials appears to be somewhat enhanced under cold conditions, in general erosion is less effective.

Landforms produced by erosion

A great variety of distinctive landforms are created by glacial erosion. On a small scale, scratches known as *striations* are produced mainly by abrasion. Rock

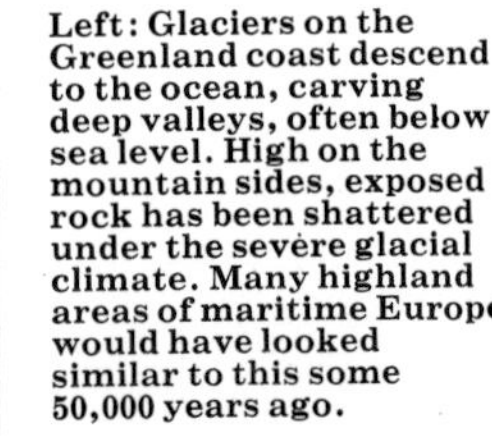

Norman Myers/Bruce Coleman

Left: Glaciers on the Greenland coast descend to the ocean, carving deep valleys, often below sea level. High on the mountain sides, exposed rock has been shattered under the severe glacial climate. Many highland areas of maritime Europe would have looked similar to this some 50,000 years ago.

Right: An aerial view of ice-scraped plains in Jameson Land, north-east Greenland. Vast lowland areas of Canada and Eurasia were once covered by enormous ice sheets thousands of metres thick and similar to those still present in Antarctica and Greenland. Erosion by such ice has scoured the rock surface, producing a gnarled, hummocky and now barren terrain.

D. J. Drewry

Right: Vestfjella in Antarctica are present-day *nunataks*. This is the Eskimo name given to isolated protruberances of land which look like islands in a sea of ice. They occur when ice sheets develop, drowning the former landscape, leaving only the highest mountain tops above the surface of the ice sheet. There they may be etched and fretted by the frost.

Below: The head of a glacier may be a deepened cirque in which accumulated snow is converted to ice. A deep vertical crack or *bergschrund* develops in the ice where the moving ice-mass pulls away from the cirque wall. The detail shows how frost-shattered rock falls into the bergschrund and is carried away by the ice.

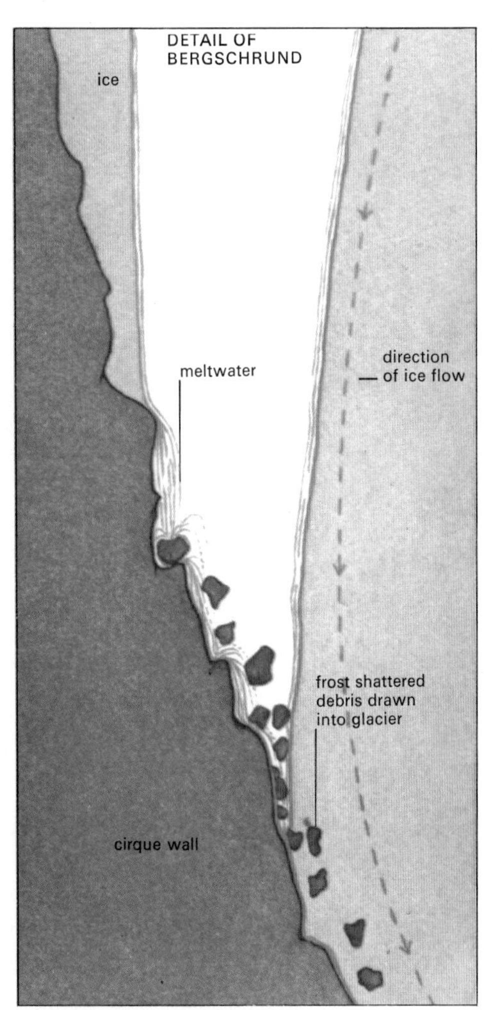

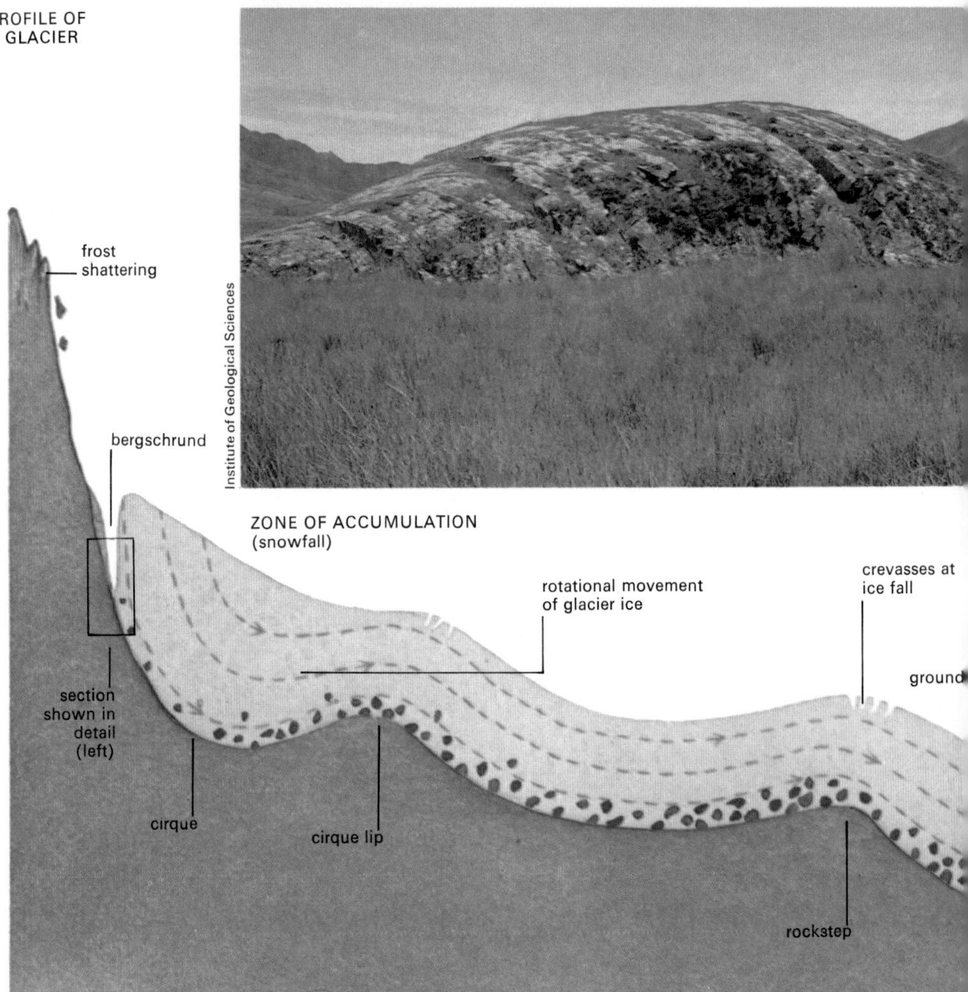

Institute of Geological Sciences

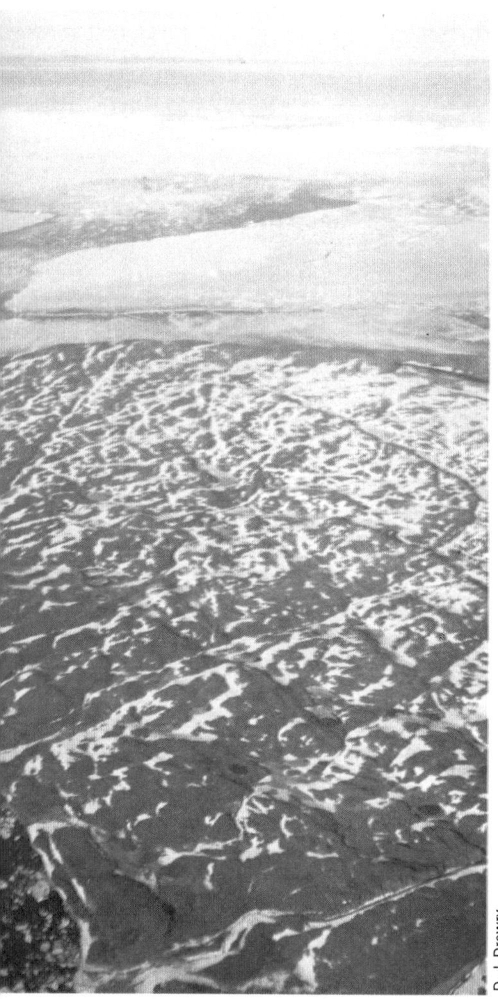

D. J. Drewry

fragments, held tightly in the glacier base, are dragged across the bedrock cutting linear scratches of varying depth (from a few millimetres to a metre or more) and up to 100 m (330 ft) long. *Gouges*, crescent-shaped cracks, and *chattermarks*, close series of gouges, also originate from boulders coming into contact with the bed and causing it to fracture.

On a larger scale, ice may mould hummocks, mounds and small hills of hard rock into asymmetric, streamlined landforms. Such features, termed *roches mountonnées* or *whalebacks*, are found widely in glaciated regions such as Scotland, north Wales and Scandinavia.

In mountainous regions, such as the Alps and Rockies, hollows or *cirques* (known as *cwms* in Wales and *corries* in Scotland) are found above and at the heads of many glaciated valleys. These deep bowl-shaped rock depressions, with a steep backwall and a flatter floor, frequently contain a small lake or tarn once the ice has melted. Many cirques have diameters up to 1-2 km (0.6-1.2 miles), with cliffs up to 1,000 m (3,300 ft) in height.

Glacial valleys are distinguished by their generally straight, deeply hollowed appearance and constitute one of the most spectacular elements of glacially sculptured highlands. In cross-section their shape is broadly that of a 'U' contrasting strongly with the 'V' shape of valleys produced by fluvial erosion. Nevertheless most glacial troughs have evolved due to the modification of former river valleys occupied by temperate glaciers during glacial episodes.

Tributary glacial valleys are frequently left as *hanging valleys* above a main glacial trough since glaciers, unlike rivers, do not combine to erode to a common base level. Each individual glacier acts as a semi-independent force, and the main, usually thicker glacier erodes its valley more deeply than the tributaries.

Fjords are valleys reaching to sea-level in mountainous coastal localities, created either by glacial erosion below sea level, or by the submergence of glacial troughs as the sea level rises. They usually have excessively deepened basins and precipitous sides, the result of vigorous erosion due to considerable ice thickness and high ice velocity. The Skelton Inlet in Antarctica (at present still ice-covered) has a maximum water depth of 1,933 m (6,350 ft) and a full vertical elevation range of 4,500 m (14,750 ft). Other equally impressive fjords occur in western Norway, Greenland and Scotland (where they are known as sea-lochs), and on the north-west coast of North America, in Chile and in South Island, New Zealand.

Some elements of mountainous glacial landscape are the combined result of a variety of erosional processes. *Arêtes*, for instance, are the knife-edged, serrated ridges that separate glacial valleys or cirques. Pointed pyramidal peaks or *horns*, such as the Matterhorn and Weisshorn in the Alps, form as a result of erosional retreat of a series of cirques around a central mountain massif.

In contrast to highland regions, the topography produced by glacial erosion in lowland areas is less marked and exhibits quite different characteristics, which are related to ice sheet activity rather than that of valley glaciers. Frequent among landforms here are ice-scoured plains made up of numbers of rounded rock-knobs and hollows, often termed *knock and lochan topography* in southern Scotland. In some locations ice has imprinted a dominant grain or lineation on the scoured terrain, which mirrors the overall direction of ice flow and is called *fluting*. Large tracts of the Scandinavian and the Canadian shields display this kind of landscape. On a greater scale, extensive basins may be formed by glacial erosion, especially near the margins of former ice sheets. A key element governing the glacial processes which produce these types of landform is the condition of the bedrock, and the relief of undulating lowland regions, exposed when the ice melts, may closely reflect varying degrees of abrasion and quarrying of weak and resistant strata.

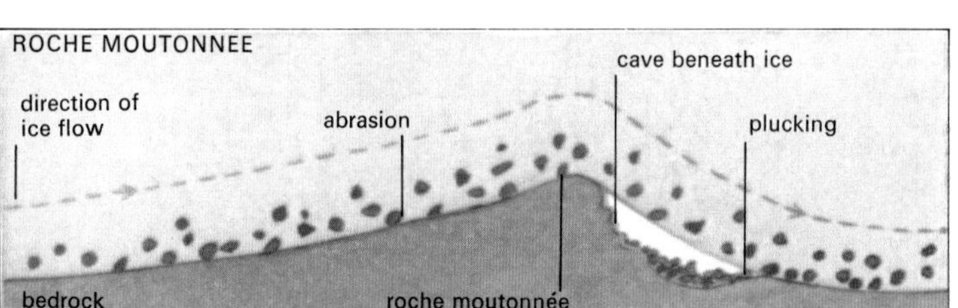

Right: Formation of a roche moutonnée. The ice sheets covering upland areas in the last Ice Age shaped the underlying hard rocks into streamlined features reflecting the movement of the ice. Rock is scraped away on the up-glacier side, while loosened material on the down-glacier flank is plucked away.

Left: A roche moutonnée in Caernarvonshire, Wales.

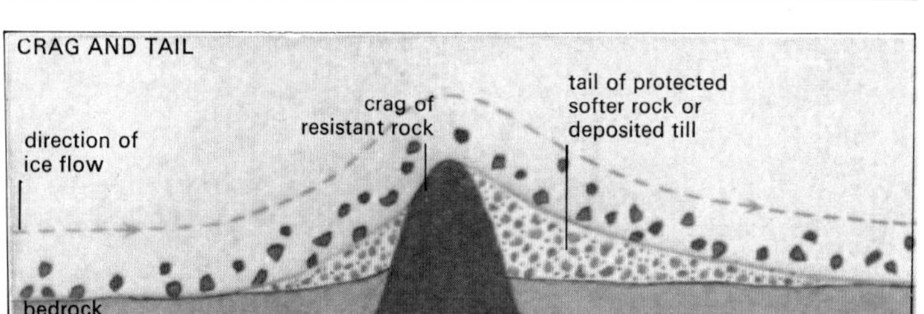

Right: A *crag and tail* is produced where a mass of resistant rock lies in the path of an oncoming glacier or ice-sheet. The 'crag' protects the softer rocks in its lee from erosion and the movement of the glacier over the top leaves a gently sloping 'tail'.

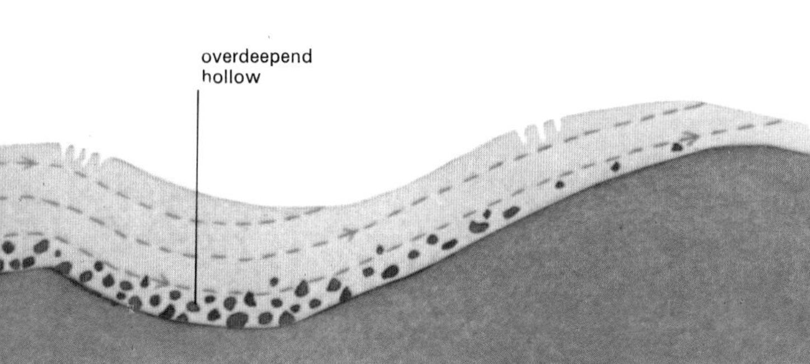

Left: The long profile of a glacier reveals the usually low gradient of the ice as it flows from high relief to lower ground. Unlike water, ice can flow uphill under the right circumstances and carve out *overdeepened* hollows. The early stages of the glacier, where ice forms faster than it melts, is known as the *zone of accumulation*. The *zone of ablation* begins when the glacier loses more ice to evaporation and melting than it gains.

Right: The entrance to an ice cave in Norway. In such caves or tunnels in the ice, scientists can view the bed of a glacier and study how moving ice erodes the underlying rocks. Stones held in the glacier base are scraped over bare rock surfaces.

Ardea

Glacial Deposits

During the last two million years, over 30 million square kilometres (11,500,000 sq miles) of northern Europe, North America and Asia were periodically covered by great ice sheets. The melting of the ice left large expanses of these continents covered by a veneer of glacial sediments, varying from a few centimetres to more than 400 metres (1,300 ft) thick.

On land, glacial sediments are now of great economic importance. They constitute some of the world's most fertile agricultural land and are a major source of sand and gravel for building aggregate (material added to cement to make concrete). On the deep-sea floor, glacial debris produced by the melting of icebergs, covering vast areas, has lain relatively undisturbed since deposition and thus provides crucial clues to the recent glacial history of the earth.

Glacial deposition forms the final part of a train of glacial processes beginning with the incorporation of soil and rock into a glacier as it erodes the land. These materials are then transported and often modified by moving ice and water before their final deposition in a range of environments, often producing distinctive landforms.

Glacial sediments are classified into two main groups: 'till' and sorted deposits. *Till* is a random mixture of rock particles, including at times both tiny clay particles and massive boulders (hence the alternative name, *boulder clay*); it is deposited directly by the glacier. Stratified or *sorted deposits*, on the other hand, require the action of water or wind to sort their particles according to size and weight. Once deposited, sediment is also altered by chemical processes, which adds to the distinction between younger and older material.

Till and moraine

Deposits of till produced by the ice are generally described as *moraine*, a term which is also applied to all debris transported by a glacier.

Till can be transported by ice in various ways. If it is carried at or near a glacier's surface, elongated lines of sediment may form, either at the sides of a glacier in the ablation or melting zone (*lateral moraine*), or where laterals from tributary glaciers coalesce in the centre of a main glacier (*medial moraine*). If sediments are carried at the bed of a glacier, they may form closely stacked layers with occasional lumps of other materials. The thickness of these basal layers is about one per cent of the glacier's depth and the concentration of debris decreases upwards from the base. As it is carried along, till is often modified as pebbles are broken, scratched, smoothed and frequently changed in shape. Only a very small percentage of material survives such destructive processes for more than about 30 km (20 miles)—and then only in a ground-up form. Granite and metamorphic rocks, for instance, may be reduced to fine sand over long distances, while shales persist only as clay-sized particles. However, very large boulders may be transported many kilometres by ice and, when deposited, stand out as *erratics*, rocks or rock fragments foreign to their new geological setting.

SECTION THROUGH VALLEY GLACIER

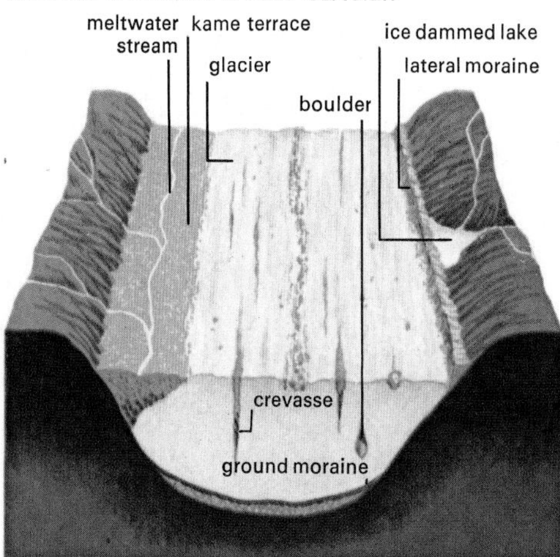

Above: Far from being rivers of pure ice, glaciers are typically 'dirty'. Vast amounts of material are picked up and carried as moraine in the sides, base and body of glaciers. Debris is also supplied by meltwater streams, which may flow alongside a glacier, adding to the deposits of lateral moraine.

Below: When the ice has melted, a variety of glacial deposits decorate the landscape. *Kame terraces*, laid down by streams which flowed along the margins of valley glaciers, and other lateral moraines are subject to stream erosion. Former ice-crevasse fillings and erratics are strewn over the valley floor.

DEPOSITS LEFT AFTER ICE HAS MELTED

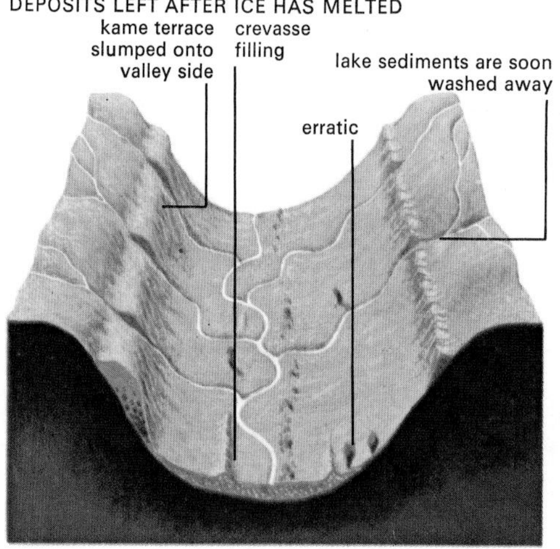

Till carried at the base of a glacier is often deposited in horizontal sheets. Sediments close to the glacier sole are continuously transported by the force of the moving ice until this force becomes insufficient to carry the debris with it. The immobile till is then described as *lodged*. Basal till is also deposited by *melting-out*, which occurs when the lower layers of a glacier melt, leaving their sediment on the bed.

Till can also originate from sediments carried on the surface of a glacier. As the surface melts, a thick deposit is produced on top of the glacier, heavily charged with meltwater; this is known as *flow-till*.

Landforms produced by till

By far the most predominant form taken by till, after the ice masses have disappeared, is that of a shapeless sheet of boulder clay, such as those found in eastern England, northern Germany or parts of the eastern USA. Such sheets are usually the product of lodgement and sometimes carry a superficial layer of flow or melt-out till. Within spreads of the till, however, a variety of other forms occur, related to special conditions on the glacier bed during deposition.

Aerofilms

Above: Small glaciers have withdrawn from the precipitous flanks of the Breithorn-Monte Rosa massif in the Swiss Alps, leaving behind long moraine ridges of rock debris. These impressive lateral moraines, lying parallel to the sides of the former glacier, are being rapidly lost to landslides and mountain torrents.

Below: A trail of loose rock fragments stretches along the centre of this glacier in Greenland. Such linear ridges are called *medial moraines* and originate from the union of lateral moraines when two adjacent glaciers come together. They are best developed in the lower reaches of melting glaciers.

D. J. Drewry

D. H. Teuffen/ZEFA

Left: High up on the right bank of the Glacier du Collon in the Swiss Alps, a close-up shows lateral moraine, formed by material incorporated into the glacier from rock-falls on the valley side. Here the glacier (on the left) has shrunk back, revealing the moraine, subsequently gullied by rain waters.

Below: Tottering pillars of earth in the Val d' Hérens, Switzerland. The constituents of a thick layer of *till* (a mixture of clay, rock fragments and boulders carried and then deposited by ice sheets and glaciers) have been exposed to view by heavy rainfall. The larger boulders have protected the earth spires from rain erosion.

Picturepoint

Bavaria

Left: The *sandar* plains of southern Iceland consist of large amounts of sediment and debris carried away by streams and rivers of melting snow and ice from glaciers and ice caps. These pro-glacial rivers have built up spectacular spreads of sand and gravel stretching over many tens of square kilometres.

Below: A floating tongue of ice near Scoresby Sund, Greenland. In severely glaciated areas such as Greenland and Antarctica glaciers may reach the sea and start to float. Icebergs break off from the edges and drift out into open sea, often for great distances. When they melt, debris and moraine carried in and on the ice is deposited on the sea floor.

D. J. Drewry

Drumlins are streamlined mounds of till, commonly appearing in clusters. They may have rock cores and often occur behind moraines formed at the front of an ice sheet. The drumlins which extend over much of Northern Ireland, are one of the largest groups in the world. They vary considerably in size, ranging from a few metres in length and height, to over 1.5 km (1 mile) long and 60 m (200 feet) high. It seems probable that drumlins originated as masses of debris lodged beneath the glacier and subsequently streamlined by moving ice. Other moulded till forms such as *flutes* (ridges parallel to the former direction of ice flow) are produced by similar processes.

Both basal and surface till are often continuously deposited at the front of a glacier or ice sheet. While the ice front remains fairly stationary, materials falling down the front or carried along by meltwater build up a ridge of debris or *terminal moraine* along the margin of an ice sheet or at the end or *snout* of a glacier. Only terminal moraines from the last or furthest glacial advance usually remain, but those left after the retreat of powerfully erosive glaciers can be most spectacular. The largest terminal moraine in Britain is the Cromer Ridge near the coast of Norfolk, which is 8 km (5 miles) wide, 24 m (15 miles) long, and over 90 m (300 ft) high.

Sorted sediments

Sorted deposits, often with well-developed layering or *bedding*, have very different characteristics from till. They accumulate either close to an ice mass (where they are termed *ice-contact* deposits) or at a greater distance beyond the ice front

Right: Erratic boulders at Cwm Idwal in Snowdonia, N. Wales. A glacier will pick up and transport large rocks like these for long distances. They are later deposited well away from their original location as erratics, often in a different geological setting.

Below right: The hills in the foreground of this view of Bantry Bay on Ireland's S-W coast are called *drumlins*. Moraine or till, forming these stable mounds, were carried beneath an ice sheet before being deposited in their present positions. Their streamlined shape aided the passage of overlying ice. Large groups of drumlins are aptly described as 'basket of eggs' topography.

Below: These banded deposits found in Finland are *varves*, laid down in a lake near the margin of an ice-sheet by meltwater. Each varve (about 3 cm deep) marks a year's deposits and consists of two layers: a coarse, light band from summer and a fine, dark band from winter. The analysis of varves gives valuable information on glacial chronology.

Courtesy Institute of Geological Sciences

E. A. Francis

J. Allan Cash

(*pro-glacial* deposits).

Some of the most important groups of sorted sediments are those deposited by glacial meltwater. Where these are of the ice-contact variety, a distinctive morphology and sediment texture may be produced. *Eskers* are long, narrow ridges which snake sinuously up and down over gently undulating terrain, often reaching several hundred kilometres in length and hundreds of metres in height. In some cases they are made up of mounds joined by low ridges, in others of complex networks of criss-crossing ridges. The sediments forming eskers are sorted pebbles and cobbles, often with little sand or silt. Crude stratification is present with cross-bedding and structures such as ripples and dunes.

Eskers are primarily formed by streams tunnelling beneath, within or on a glacier, carrying sediment which sinks to ground level when the ice melts. Observations have indicated that some eskers may also be produced from sediments carried by melt-water streams flowing into pro-glacial lakes. Some of the best developed eskers are to be found in the lake country of Finland and other examples occur in central Ireland and parts of northern Canada.

Other ice-contact deposits include *kame terraces* which are laid down mainly by streams flowing in a trough between valley glaciers and their valley walls. As the ice retreats, deposits are left on hillsides, which sometimes slump down into the valley.

Meltwater deposits

Pro-glacial sediments, washed out of an ice mass by meltwater, are deposited beyond the ice front and form fan-shaped spreads of sediment called *outwash*. Where confined in a narrow valley, outwash deposits are called *valley trains*. The condition of meltwater and debris issuing from a glacier determines the nature of the sediments in these trains. Close to the glacier, they may be coarse but decrease in size down the valley.

Where sedimentation is not confined by a valley, outwash fans may coalesce to produce broad alluvial expanses or *outwash plains*. Much of the south coast of Iceland is made up of outwash material, called *sandar*. In New Zealand, the Canterbury Plains on the east-central side of South Island constitute an outwash plain of over 10,000 km^2 (4,000 sq miles) left by sediment-laden meltwaters from glaciers in the Southern Alps.

D. J. Drewry

DEPOSITS LEFT BY A MELTING ICE SHEET

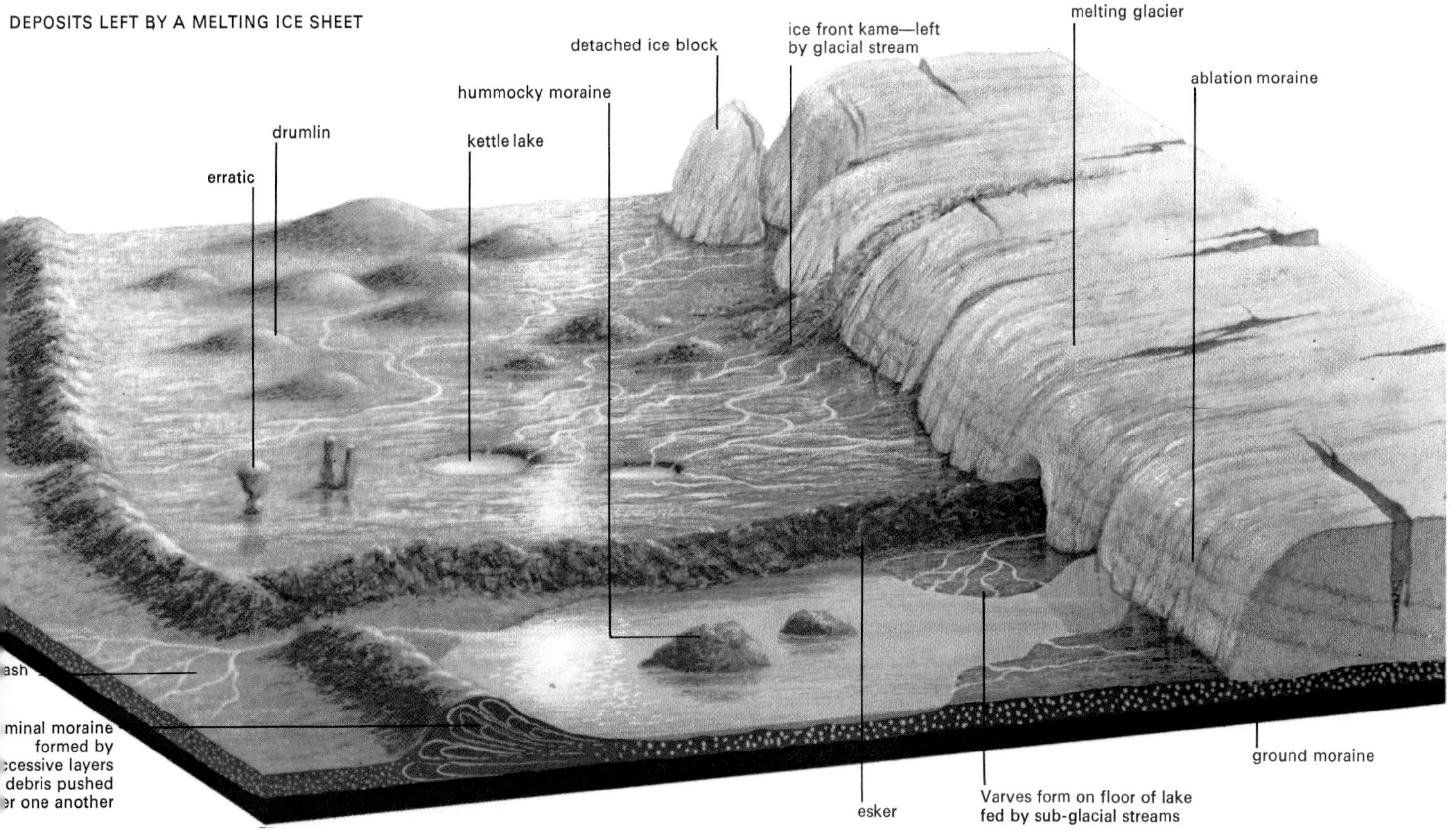

Above: Several of the depositional features left behind by a retreating ice sheet or glacier. The ridge of terminal moraine marks the furthest advance of the ice front and has formed a natural dam for a lake fed by meltwater. A blanket of ground moraine covers the whole glaciated area. On the lake floor, annual deposits of varves are also being laid down. The shapes of the winding esker and streamlined drumlins reveal the direction of the former ice-flow. Kettle lakes form in hollows left by large, detached melting blocks of ice. Beyond the ice front, streams spread out over a broad outwash plain.

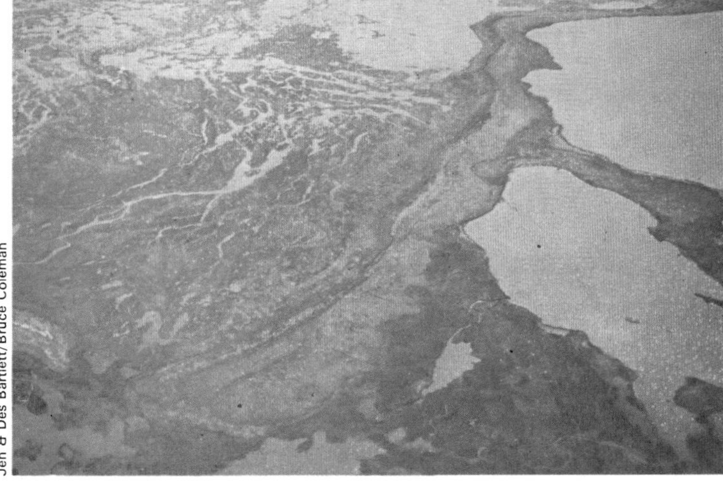

Right: An aerial view of an *esker* lying between lakes in the Canadian tundra near Hudson Bay. Eskers are long, sinuous ridges of sediment formed by water flowing in tunnels near the bed of a glacier. When the ice disappears they are left as long piles of sorted debris, snaking across barren ice-scoured terrain.

Below: A glacier will often deposit a girdle of rock and debris at its front or *snout*. Such curved ridges are called *terminal moraines* and their size depends on how long the glacier snout remains stationary. The terminal moraine of the Roslin Glacier in East Greenland, shown here, is large and marks the furthest advance of the ice in recent years.

Jen & Des Bartlett/Bruce Coleman

Where glacial meltwaters are blocked by rock-bars, moraines or other obstructions, pro-glacial lakes may form and sediments in these are termed *glacio-lacustrine* (that is, deposited in glacial lakes). As streams enter the lakes, their speed is checked and part of their load is deposited, creating deltas.

Glacial chronology

Within lakes, finer materials also settle, forming *varves*, distinctive banded deposits. Each varve consists of two layers, one coarse and light in colour, the other darker and finer. During the summer thaw, the flow of water is able to carry and deposit the coarser material, while in winter, when water movement diminishes due to freezing, the finer particles settle; thus each varve represents one year's deposit. Exceptionally well-preserved varves found in southern Sweden were investigated late in the nineteenth century by Baron de Geer. His pioneering and painstaking work of counting varve 'couplets' gave some of the earliest accurate dates to the fluctuations and overall retreat of ice in Europe.

During the Pleistocene Ice Age, strong winds were generated by the climatic conditions. Fine materials (silt and clay constituents) were picked up and carried over many hundreds of kilometres, eventually to be deposited as *loess*. This is a porous, crumbly silt deposit, usually without bedding, coloured yellow, orange or brown due to staining by iron minerals. Loess occurs in sheets many metres thick, particularly in central North America, eastern and central Europe, and China, and it is highly fertile. The loess zone of Europe is one of its most important agricultural areas.

Glacial deposits at sea

The most extensive area of glacial deposition is to be found, not on land, but on the sea-floor. Glaciers descending from coastal mountains may reach the sea and float out if the water is sufficiently deep. The edges of continental ice sheets may also terminate as a thick shelf of ice over the sea. In both cases chunks of ice may regularly break off at the edges to form *icebergs*. These are then carried by currents and wind into the open sea where they eventually melt away.

Any sediments carried by these icebergs will then be deposited as a mantle on the sea-floor. These glacial sediments contrast strongly with normal marine deposits because of the greater size of particles, their lack of fossils and the often distinctive scratches, cracks, grooves and polish on individual grains. Extensive accumulations of such deposits in the Southern Ocean today completely girdle the ice-covered Antarctic continent and date back 25 million years. In the Northern Hemisphere they cover the floor of many sea areas, testifying to the presence, in the not-too-distant past, of ice sheets on adjacent land.

Frozen Landscapes

In many of the cold regions of the world, the land is free from glaciers and ice sheets but temperatures are low enough to result in distinctive processes and landscape features. In 1909 the term *periglacial* (literally meaning 'around the ice') was introduced into geomorphology to describe the climate and associated features found on the margins of past and present ice sheets. The term periglaciation is now used to include all cold climate phenomena except those directly related to ice itself or glacial meltwater.

At present about 20 per cent of the world's land area is periglaciated. In the southern hemisphere, periglaciation occurs in those parts of the Antarctic not covered in ice, on the tops of the South American Andes and mountains in New Zealand, Australia and New Guinea. But the main periglaciated areas are in the northern hemisphere, where they are associated with the freezing peaks of many mountain ranges, Arctic Canada and Greenland, and the cold tundra of high latitudes. Tundra areas are barren, treeless plains where the average temperature of the warmest month never reaches above 10°C. They stretch across Alaska, northern Canada and parts of northern Europe and Asia, including vast tracts of Siberia. Something like 50 per cent of the total area of the USSR may be underlain by permanently frozen ground.

Left: Aerial view of the thawing Canadian tundra. Snow geese are migrating over a scene typical of much of northern Canada and USSR in spring. Much of the snow and ground has melted but the water is unable to drain through the underlying permafrost. In some places, lakes and swamps have formed; in others, the saturated soil forms a very muddy, active surface layer.

Jen & Des Bartlett/Bruce Coleman

Below: A drilling rig on the oil-rich North Slope of Alaska. The tundra surface presents an unstable foundation on which to build as it melts in summer. Beds of gravel have been spread over the ground where roads and buildings are laid out in an attempt to insulate the surface from seasonal warming.

Robert Harding

Frozen ground

There are two main types of frozen ground: seasonally frozen and permanently frozen ground, known as *permafrost*. Seasonally frozen ground is the zone near the surface where annual freezing and thawing takes place. It varies in thickness from a few millimetres to some four metres (up to 13 ft).

Below seasonally frozen ground and towards the poles lies the permafrost, which can be hundreds of metres thick. One exceptional figure of 1,500 m (almost one mile) was recorded in Siberia but there have been few other records of permafrost extending deeper than 500 m (1,650 ft). The maximum depth will vary with different rock types, but is largely determined by the heat-flow from the

Below: Permafrost is the perpetually frozen layer of the earth's crust, found where ground temperatures remain below freezing for a period of years. A section taken through Siberia (right) shows the relative thickness of permafrost and the active layer (the surface layer above the permafrost subject to annual freeze and thaw). The active layer is thinnest above the continuous permafrost and thickest above the discontinuous permafrost. Further south only the surface layer freezes.

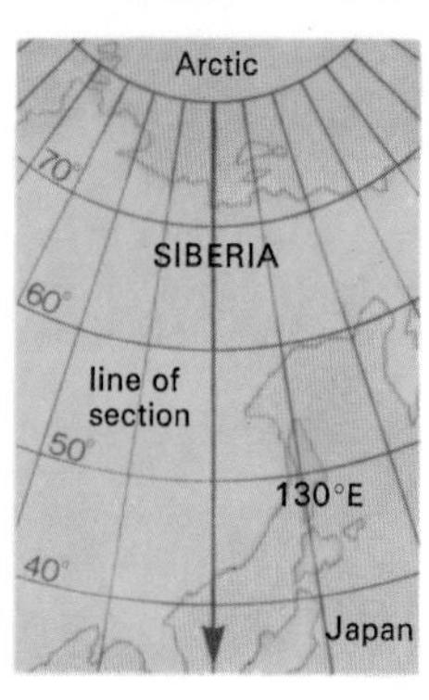

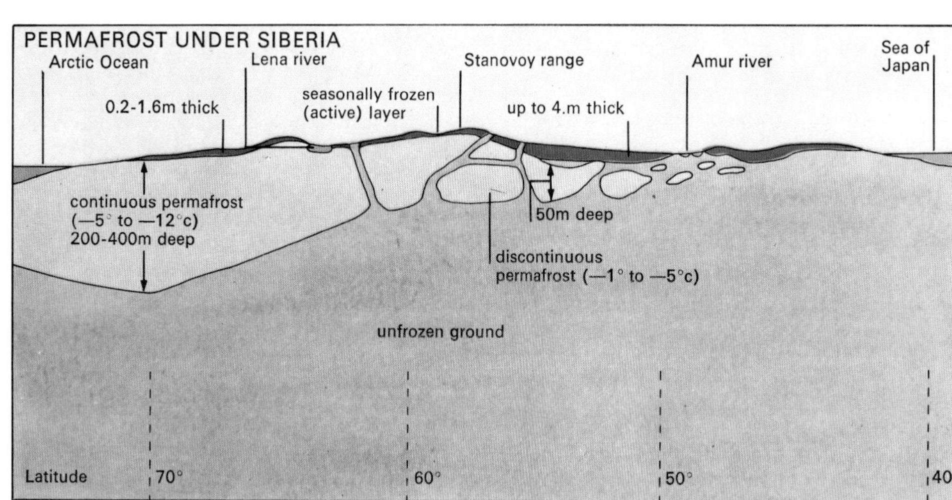

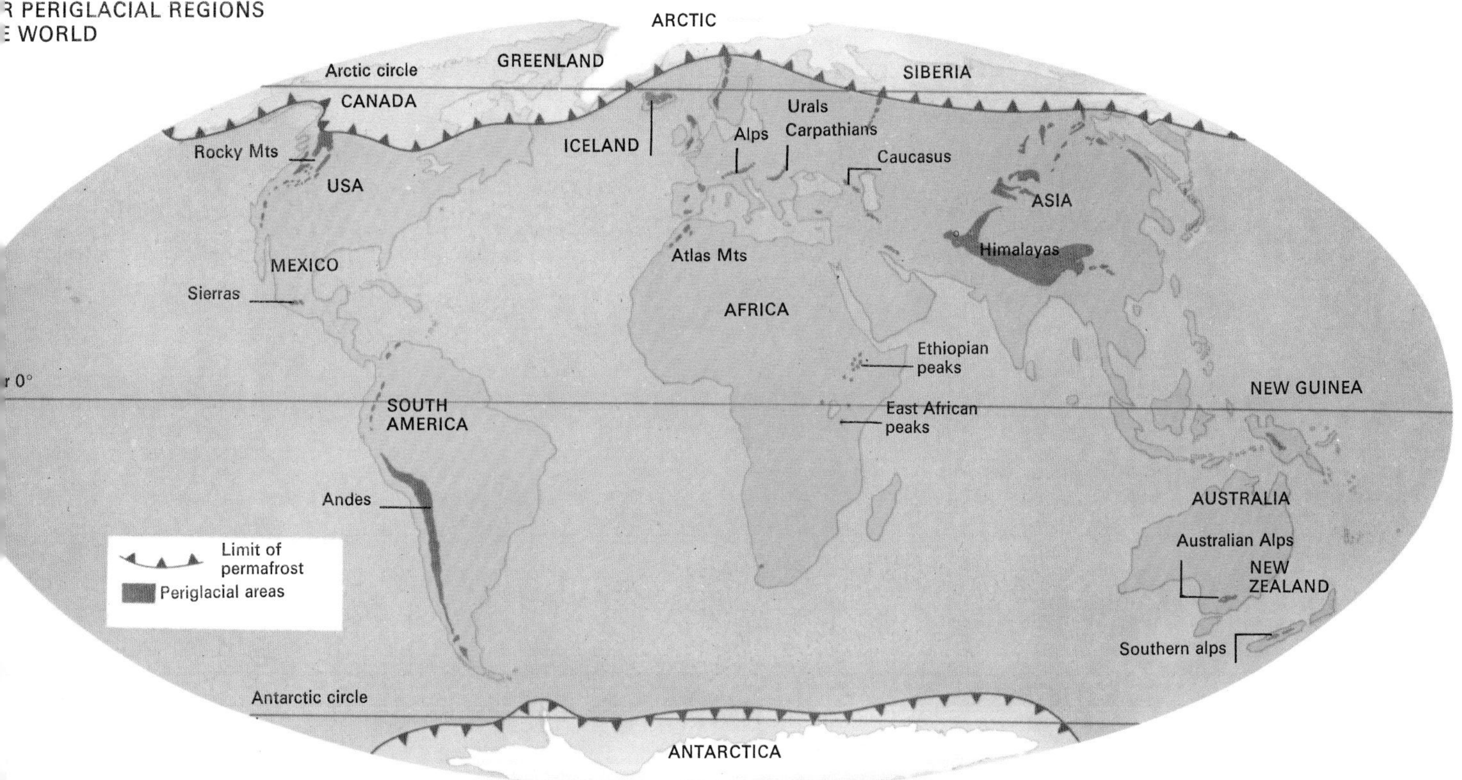

Above: Most of the world's periglacial regions are found in the high latitudes above the line marking the limit of continuous and discontinuous permafrost. Periglacial processes also occur in lower latitudes on high, cold mountains (even in the tropics) and in places where the ground freezes sporadically.

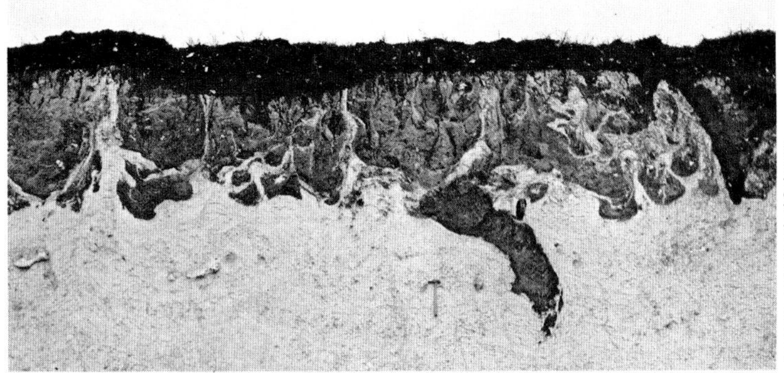

Right: This quarry face of an involuted till layer overlying chalk displays the severe disruption which periglacial action can cause in freezing ground.

Institute of Geological Sciences

Left: Frost shattered boulders near the summit of Glyder Fawr (1000 m) in Snowdonia, Wales. Rock shattering is an important periglacial process which occurs in cold areas throughout the world. Water penetrates lines of weakness such as joints, then freezes and expands, thus widening the crevices in the rock.

Picturepoint

Above: This ice-wedge cast in a gravel pit in East Anglia is a relic of former periglaciation. When a cooling surface contracts, cracks form which fill with water in spring. During winter freezing, an expanding ice wedge further opens the crack. Later, in a warmer climate, stones and debris fall into the crack as the ice melts.

Dr. Rendel Williams

earth's warm interior.

In summer, when the seasonally frozen layer melts it becomes very fluid. The water in this layer—known as the *active layer* if it is underlain by permafrost—is unable to drain through the frozen ground and creates a very muddy surface layer which may gradually begin to flow downhill. This slow, viscous flow is known as *solifluction* and often takes place in the form of huge soil tongues called *solifluction lobes* which are distinctive features of many hillsides in tundra areas.

In winter, when this active layer refreezes, two other related processes may come into play. These are known as *frost heave* and *frost thrust*. The surface of the ground freezes first and the frost gradually penetrates downwards towards the deeper permafrost. For a time the intervening layer remains unfrozen. But it becomes subjected to considerable pressure as when water freezes it increases in volume by about nine per cent. Thus as the ground gradually freezes, it expands by thrusting horizontally and heaving vertically between the solid permafrost and rigid surface layer. The tremendous pressure is most easily released by upward heaving of the surface, producing contortions known as *involutions* in the soil layers. The rigid surface becomes considerably disrupted and objects such as stones, trees, fence posts and even telegraph poles have been seen to be completely heaved out of the ground.

On a smaller scale, surface displacement occurs when thin spikes of ice grow in the active layer as it freezes in winter. These spikes of *needle ice* consist of ice crystals which usually range from one to three centimetres (up to one inch) long, but can significantly alter the landscape; they can lift soil particles and stones above the surface and, if this occurs on a slope, when the crystals melt the material will fall and roll downhill.

A further example of the powerful action of freezing and thawing is *frost shattering*, one of the most intense forms of rock fragmentation on earth. When water freezes in cracks, joints or other

Right: How a closed system or Mackenzie type of pingo may be formed. (1) A broad, shallow lake overlies frost-free ground. (2) The climate may get colder, or the lake may drain or be filled with sediment or vegetation. The lake water and sediments then freeze and the area of permafrost spreads, trapping the saturated unfrozen ground. (3) Eventual freezing and expanding of entrapped ground water exerts sufficient upward force to create a dome on the surface. (4) Any unfrozen water is expelled upwards from the saturated ground beginning to freeze and becomes concentrated below the pingo. It too eventually freezes as permafrost completely envelopes the area.

FORMATION OF A MACKENZIE DELTA TYPE PINGO

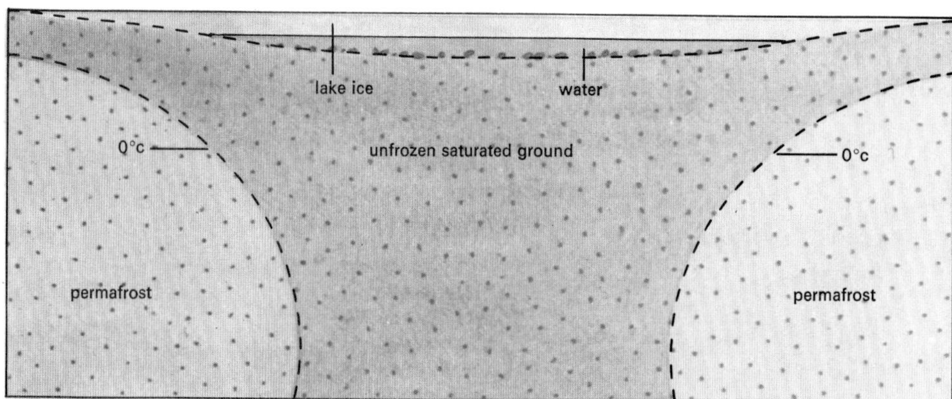

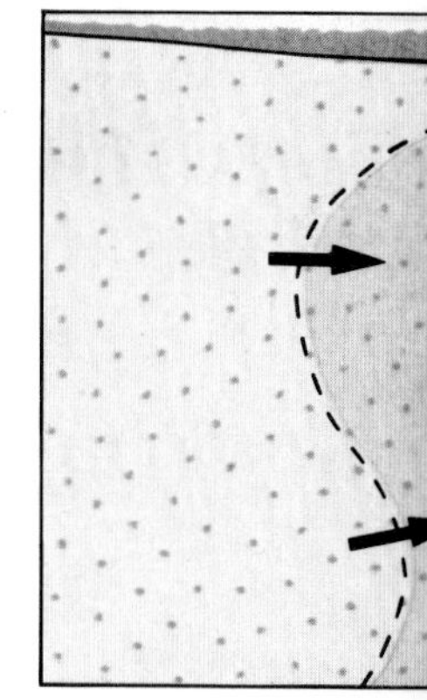

lines of weakness in rock, its nine per cent increase in volume exerts considerable pressures. The expanding ice acts like a wedge driven into the rock, and this *ice* or *frost wedging* results in splitting and shattering of the rock.

Frost shattering varies greatly with rock type. Sedimentary and other relatively soft, porous rocks have a great water-holding capacity and are usually well-bedded. Consequently, such rocks are generally more susceptible to frost wedging than igneous or metamorphic rocks. However the cleaveage planes in metamorphic rocks such as slate and schist provide lines of weakness where frost shattering may occur, producing flat, angular slabs of rock.

A variety of features resulting from the melting of ground ice in permafrost areas resemble those found in limestone karst areas. These include such features as caverns, disappearing streams and troughs, known collectively as *thermokarst*. However, rather than being the work of chemical processes, thermokarst is created when the permafrost is disrupted by large-scale climatic changes or by local environmental disturbance.

For example, in the early 1920s forest was cleared from land near Fairbanks, Alaska (USA), to prepare the area for agricultural purposes. The area had been underlain by vertical wedges of ice and, when the vegetation was removed, the ice wedges began to thaw, causing the soil to collapse into them. An extensive pattern of depressions and thermokarst mounds developed, varying from 3 to 15 m (10-50 ft) in diameter and up to 2.5 m (8 ft) high, creating an undulating topography quite unsuitable for its intended agricultural use.

Perhaps the most spectacular features of periglaciated areas are *pingos*, an Eskimo word describing scattered, isolated hills. The term was introduced into geomorphology in 1938 to describe the conspicuous domes with radially cracked summits that are particularly common in the continuous permafrost zone. They can be over 50 m (165 ft) high and up to 600 m (2,000 ft) in diameter.

There are two types of pingo: closed and open system types. The closed system has been best examined in the Mackenzie River delta area of Canada where 98 per cent of the 1,380 pingos mapped occur in fairly level, poorly-drained sites such as former lake basins.

The open type of pingo is best developed in East Greenland and most common on slopes rather than on level areas. It appears to be associated with artesian springs which provide a continual supply of ground water under presure. As this water approaches the surface it freezes, and the expanding ice exerts considerable upward pressure on the ground above.

Patterned ground

One of the most striking and controversial features of a periglacial landscape is the unusual geometric patterning found in the soil. The most common shapes are circles, polygons (many-sided forms) and stripes so perfectly arranged as to appear deliberately laid out; yet these patterns occur naturally in the cold terrain. The circles are stony areas measuring from a half to three metres (18 in to 10 ft) across, often with vegetation growing around their margins. In some the stones are smaller in the centre of the circle than towards the edge.

The polygons are usually larger, sometimes reaching over 10 m (33 ft) in diameter. They are delineated by vegetated furrows or lines of stones enclosing areas of finer debris. Polygons are best developed on fairly level areas. Where the ground steepens, stripes form—these are thought to be the downslope extension of polygons; an intermediate form is the extended polygon or net.

Patterned ground has been the subject of considerable debate in geomorphology; its origin remains unclear, although some polygons seem to result from ice wedging.

Wind, water and snow

Violent winds sweep over the cold, exposed periglacial terrain, leaving a trail of wind-scoured features and transported sediments. In fact, wind action is one of the most important processes at work, capable of sand-blasting the rocks to produce sharp-edged, polished stones, termed *ventifacts* or *dreikanter*. The thick deposits known as *loess* are fine-grained sediments swept up and carried sometimes great distances by the wind from bare areas of glacial and outwash deposits.

River flow in the periglacial zone is characteristically irregular. Water will cease to flow altogether during prolonged periods of sub-zero temperatures, but during the spring thaw powerful torrents rush over the river beds causing considerable erosion and movement of debris. Similarly, coastlines in periglaciated areas are usually frozen up during winter, but in summer intense shattering of coastal rocks may take place as each tidal

Dr. D. Drewry

Below: Perhaps the most striking, and puzzling, features of periglacial areas are the patterns found in the ground. These stone circles on Devon Is. in Arctic Canada are well sorted, with a border of stones surrounding the finer material in the centre. The diameter of the near circle (shown by the red gloves) is about 1 m.

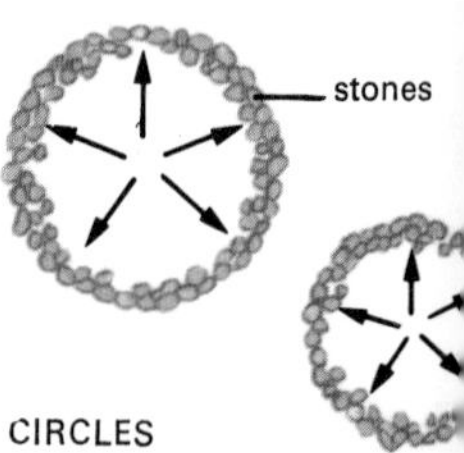

Dr. C. Embleton

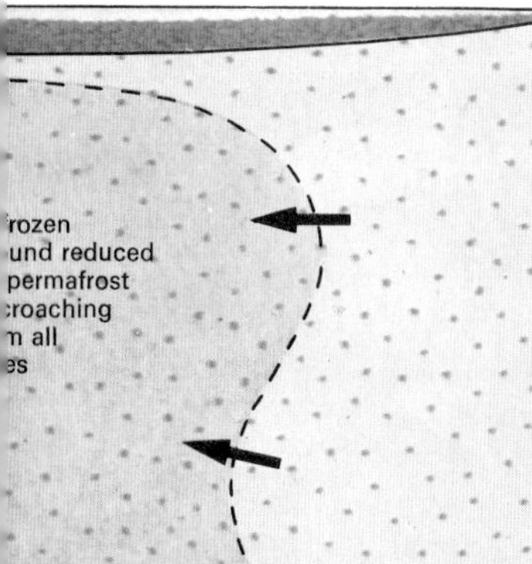

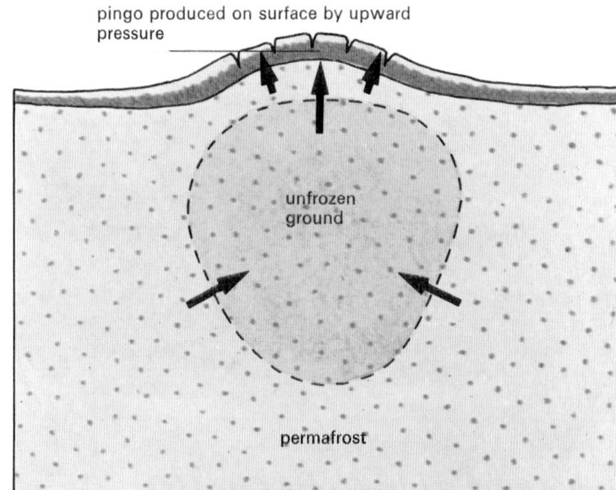

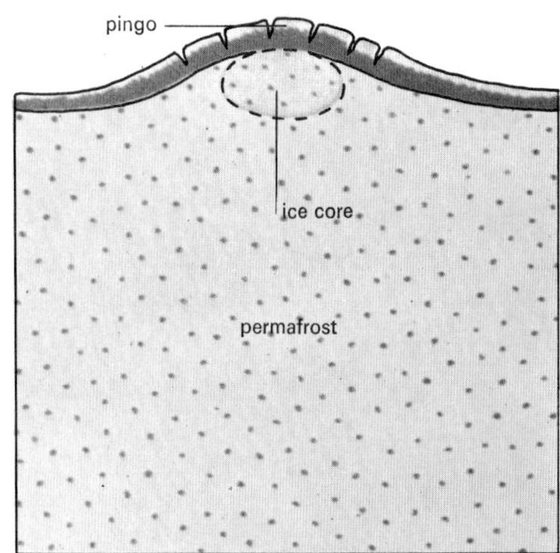

Left: Isolated mounds, known by the Eskimo name *pingos*, in the Mackenzie delta area of Arctic Canada. These surface 'blisters' form on the sites of former floodplain lakes and overlie areas where the pressure of freezing and expanding ice has heaved up the ground. Summer meltwater may collect as lakes in the cracks and hollows on the summits of the domes.

Above right: Blocks of frost-shattered dolomite near Platteville in Wisconsin, USA. Toppled by former periglacial conditions, these rocks slid downhill to their present resting place.

Dr. C. Embleton

Right: These rounded tongues of earth, known as solifluction lobes, on Baffin Is, Canada, are water-logged surface deposits which flow slowly downhill when activated by summer thawing. The rounded stones suggest that the lobe material is reworked glacial till.

Prof. C. A. M. King

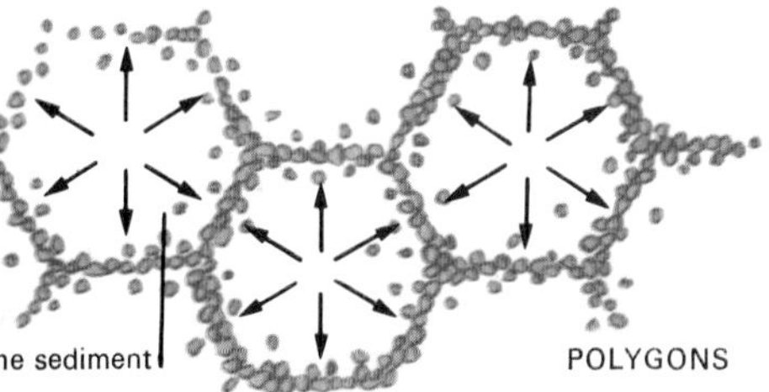

Herta Grondal/ZEFA

Above left and left: Scientists are still debating how such remarkably perfect geometric shapes can form in patterned soil. One possible reason is that fine material has a greater water-holding capacity than stones. Areas of fine water-saturated sediments or mud expand on freezing, thrusting embedded stones outwards and upwards, but draw back more effectively during thawing because of their greater cohesion. Continued freezing and thawing may produce patches of fine material separated by narrow bands of stones, which appear as circles or polygons on level ground as shown in the diagram (above left) and as stripes on slopes. The polygons on Spitzbergen (left) are well sorted, with stone bands bordering patches of fine debris. Small plants and flowers typical of tundra areas are growing in the fine soil.

rise fills cracks with sea-water which freezes when exposed to air at low tide.

Erosion also occurs in areas apparently protected by a blanket of snow. Beneath patches of snow continual thawing by day and freezing by night leads to bed-rock weathering, with the loosened particles being washed out by meltwater. Snow-patch erosion or *nivation* thus tends to create large, distinctive hillside hollows that may eventually become cirques.

Man in periglacial areas

Man faces considerable problems as he penetrates further into periglacial areas in order to exploit their mineral reserves. The difficulties stem largely from the presence of permafrost and its susceptibility to melting when disturbed by human activities. When the ground is frozen it has great bearing strength but when thawed it turns into mud with no strength at all. Consequently it is impossible to build centrally-heated dwellings directly onto the permafrost. A common solution is to raise the buildings off the ground by using stilts or piles so that air can circulate between the heated building and the permafrost. However, the piles are open to attack by frost heaving and must be lubricated and placed sufficiently deep to prevent this happening. Where roads and airport runways are constructed, the ground is insulated by spreading a gravel blanket about one metre (3 ft) thick over the ground.

The provision of services, particularly water and sewers, to polar settlements creates many problems. In summer there are few difficulties, but in winter water is in short supply and chunks of ice must be melted down. A number of the larger settlements have piped-in water supplies but the problem is in preventing freezing.

Sewage is often hauled by bucket or wagon and dumped on the river ice to be carried away with the spring break-up. Some settlements have heated sewage-disposal systems but it is not possible to put the pipes underground since the heat would disrupt the permafrost. This is also true of the pipelines constructed in such cold, remote areas as Alaska to carry the relatively warm oil from polar oil fields to more temperate latitudes. Buried pipes can be fairly effectively insulated. An alternative is to construct the pipelines above ground on piles, but this is expensive and may inhibit the migration of such animals as caribou to their traditional breeding grounds.

The Ice Age

There have been several ice ages in the earth's history, periods when for one reason or another ice caps and glaciers became much more extensive than usual and large areas of the earth's surface were dominated by glacial and periglacial processes. The evidence of these ice ages is there to be seen in the rocks and, although the further one goes back in time the fainter the evidence becomes, we can be certain that there was an ice age in the late Pre-Cambrian period some 700 million years ago; another in the Carboniferous, about 300 million years ago; and a third, known as the *Pleistocene Ice Age*, which began only two million years ago and is probably still going on.

A variety of theories have been put forward about the causes of the latest Ice Age—some suggest extra-terrestrial explanations such as variations in the heat radiated by the sun. A recent theory suggests that the positions of the drifting continents relative to the pole may account for the earlier ice ages as well as for climatic changes which affected both hemispheres. Ice caps form more easily on land than on oceans, and during the Carboniferous ice age extensive ice sheets swept over much of Gondwanaland, the massive continent then located over the South Pole.

Some scientists have stressed the increase in cold, high elevations on which glaciers could develop during the mountain-building activity in the late Tertiary period. Others argue that intensive volcanic activity may have ejected great clouds of dust and ash into the upper atmosphere which shielded the earth's surface from the sun's rays. However, critics of both theories have pointed out there have been periods of mountain-building and great volcanic activity in the past which were not followed by ice ages. The conflict of opinion and lack of real evidence means that what actually caused the ice ages remains at present a matter of pure speculation.

The Pleistocene Ice Age

The events of the Pleistocene had a profound effect on the landscape and its soils, on the distribution of land and sea and thus on the migration and settlement patterns of our ancestors. For example, London is built on a series of river terraces formed during the Pleistocene as a result of climatic and sea-level changes. Without them the Thames valley would be an arm of the sea and the Romans would never have chosen the site of London as a crossing place.

All the great harbours of the world, such as New York, Vancouver, Sydney and Wellington owe their existence to the melting of the Pleistocene ice caps which raised the sea to its present level. Long before man was settling the land and developing his farming methods, the Ice Age was moulding it and controlling the ways in which he might use it.

But it would be wrong to think of the Ice Age as one long freeze-up. In fact it consisted of a series of alternate cold and warm periods, probably seven cold with six warmer ones separating them. During the cold periods the climate was a good deal colder everywhere than at present,

Courtesy Director, Institute of Geological Sciences

Above: An artist's reconstruction of a glacial landscape during the Pleistocene Ice Age shows the edge of a great ice-sheet, with cold, barren terrain in its immediate vicinity. Vegetation in the poor soil consisted of mosses and small arctic-alpine plants. Among the animals to withstand the intense cold were hairy mammoths.

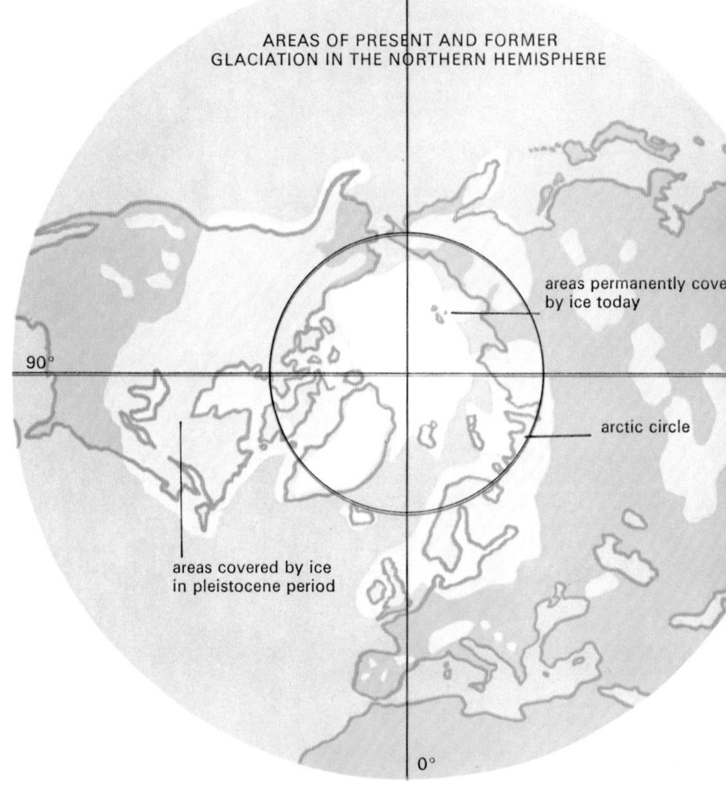

Right: The areas of permanent present-day ice are shown with the maximum extent of Pleistocene ice sheets in the northern hemisphere. (The ice may have reached its furthest limit in different areas during different glacial periods.) Most of the increased volume was due to the growth of large ice sheets over N.W. Europe and N. America.

Below: About three times more of the earth's surface was covered by ice in the Pleistocene than at present. The impact was less dramatic in the southern hemisphere where there are fewer high latitude land masses on which ice sheets could grow. But the Antarctic ice sheet (below) grew thicker, there were ice caps in New Zealand and thick ice on the Andes.

Bavaria

/armer → sent	British standard stages	Probable equivalents elsewhere
	Holocene Flandarian 10,000 yrs ago	Post-glacial
	Devensian	Weichsel Würm Wisconsin
	Ipswichian	Eem Sangamon
	Wolstonian	Saale Illinoian Riss
	Hoxnian	Holstein Yarmouth
	Anglian	Elster Kansan Mindel
	Cromerian	Aftonian
PLEISTOCENE	Beestonian	North European Alpine North American
	Pastonian	LIMITS OF THE ICE ADVANCE
	Baventian	
	Antian	
	Thurnian	
	Ludhamian	
	Waltonian 2 million yrs ago	

Devensian
Wolstonian
Anglian

Left: The record of climatic change in Britain during the last 2 million years. The Pleistocene was not a period of continuous glaciation. There were lengthy periods, the *interglacials*, when the climate became as warm or warmer than today's. (Shorter cold and warm episodes termed *stadials* and *interstadials* also occurred.) The stages have different names in other parts of the world, where the ice may have advanced at different times. Attempts have been made to roughly equate them, but correlation becomes more uncertain further back in time. The map shows the limits of ice advances in England and Wales during the Pleistocene.

Above: The severity of past climates in parts of Britain which escaped glaciation during the last ice advance is demonstrated by fossil periglacial features. These fossil polygons (on level ground) and stripes (on slopes) occur in East Anglia. Fossil pingos are found in Wales and elsewhere in Europe.

Professor K. St. Joseph

Georg Gerster/John Hillelson

ight: The entrance to art of the South Pole tation in the frozen ntarctic wastes. About 9 per cent of ice on arth today is in the ntarctic ice-sheet. onsiderable research s being carried out on he glaciology of the olar ice sheet, as well as he biology, geology and eomorphology of areas ot covered by ice.

elow right: There is lear evidence of ice ges prior to the leistocene. Outcrops of *illite* (consolidated ill) on top of Table ountain near Cape own are relics of the arboniferous ice sheet which covered parts of ondwanaland.

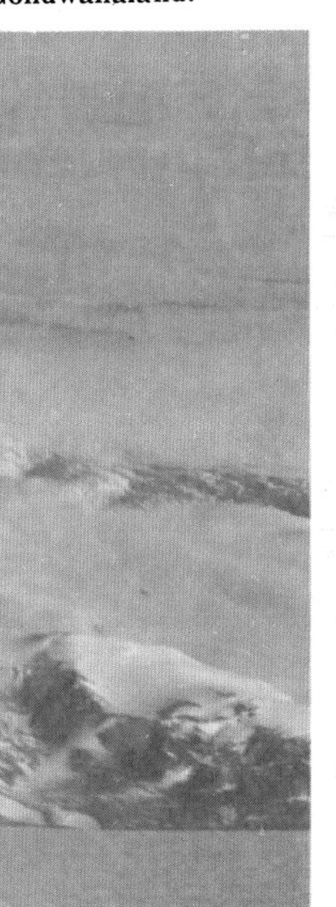

Spectrum

but only during the last three was it actually glacial in northern latitudes. (In Britain, these are known as the Anglian, Wolstonian and Devensian stages.)

At such times the polar ice extended far beyond its present limits, in Europe reaching as far south as southern England, the Netherlands and south Germany. In North America, the ice reached a line running roughly from Seattle in the west to Long Island in the east, and passing well south of the Great Lakes. During the last major advance, 15,000 to 20,000 years ago, ice covered about 30 per cent of the earth.

However, the ice advanced only during the coldest of the cold periods. In the intervening ones, known as *interglacial periods*, the climate was as warm as, or even warmer than, the present day. For example, during the last interglacial in Britain (the Ipswichian), elephants, rhinoceros and hippopotami wandered as far north as Yorkshire, where their bones are sometimes found in caves or in river and raised beach deposits. So although in Britain the Pleistocene is thought of as an Ice Age, glacial conditions existed for only a very small part of that time. In more southerly countries they never existed at all—for what fell as snow in northern Europe, came down as rain further south. In Africa there is evidence of alternate wet and dry phases, known as *pluvials* and *interpluvials*, which may correspond with the glacial and interglacial periods in Europe.

Each time the ice advanced, animals and plants were forced to migrate southwards. Later, as the ice retreated, they were able to move north again and recolonize the land. Consequently their remains, preserved as fossils by natural burial, can be used to record the climatic changes which the area has undergone. These fossils include vertebrates, such as elephants and rhinoceros for the warm periods, and reindeer and mammoths for the cold. The distribution of invertebrates such as molluscs can be equally revealing. In a warm period molluscs of southern type migrate northwards, whereas in a cold period they move south again and their place is taken by more boreal (northern) species.

Trees too are good indicators of climate, and the course of an interglacial can often be plotted by tracing the changes in tree cover from arctic tundra to fully developed temperate forest and back again. The evidence is gained by studying the proportions of different kinds of pollen that are preserved, layer by layer, in the sediments of ponds or lakes. This has proved to be a most effective way of building up chronological sequences based on climatic change.

The periodic expansion of ice sheets during the Pleistocene inundated about 30 million square kilometres (over 11 million square miles) of northern Europe, North America and Asia, covering large areas with a veneer of glacial sediments. The most characteristic of these is the till, or boulder clay, deposited by the ice itself. Much can be learnt by studying these deposits. For example, an exposure of till on the Yorkshire coast of eastern England might yield erratics (far-travelled stones) of Shap granite, Permian Breccia, Carboniferous Limestone, Magnesian Limestone and even a battered Liassic ammonite. This would tell geologists that the ice which deposited the till came from

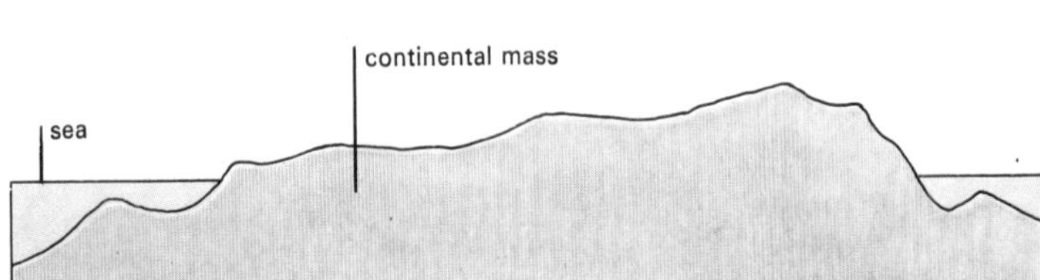

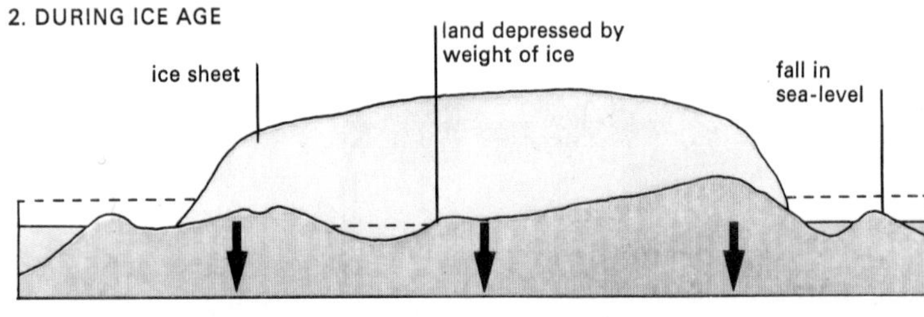

Above: Eustatic (sea-level) and isostatic (land level) changes. Before a glacial period, land and sea-level are stable (1). When thick ice builds up on land, its weight depresses the crust. The seas also fall, as water is lost to form ice (2). When the climate warms, the ice melts and returns to the seas. But the land also rises as its burden is removed (3). Shorelines will be formed along the boundaries where the land meets the sea. If the land subsequently rises more than the sea, old beaches will be raised above the present shoreline (4). Canada and Scandinavia are still rising, although the ice melted several thousand years ago.

Below: Drowned drumlins in Strangford Lough, Northern Ireland. The drumlins, moulded by an Ice Age glacier, were flooded by a rise in sea-level when the ice melted. However, relative sea-level was once even higher, as shown by the raised beaches and cliffs in shadow on the right sides of the drumlins.

Aerofilms

Explorer

the Lake District in north-west England by way of the Vale of Eden, over the Pennines (ice can go uphill, unlike water) to Teesside, and so down the North Yorkshire coast. Such an assemblage is the 'trade-mark' of that particular till; it serves to identify it wherever it is seen, or to distinguish it from other tills which may contain different assemblages.

Almost as extensive as till are the sheets of outwash sand and gravel which spread out from the margin of an ice cap or glacier. The bulk of our present resources of sand and gravel, so vital to the building and heavy construction industries, originated from this water-sorted debris during the Pleistocene. In dry weather a third kind of deposit may become important. Strong winds, blowing over the outwash plains, pick up the silt (sand is too heavy, and clay is usually bonded by moisture) and carry it in the form of dust storms, perhaps for many miles, before re-depositing it as an even spread of loess, blanketing the landscape. Many of the superficial deposits known as *brickearth* on British geological maps are actually thin beds of loess. Much thicker deposits extend from France right across Europe into the USSR—in fact all along the line of the Pleistocene glacial limit.

Changes in sea level

The impact of the Pleistocene Ice Age on the earth as a whole was not restricted to the deposits of glaciation and a changing pattern of plant and animal life in the immediate vicinity of fluctuating ice sheets. As the ice was retreating and advancing, so world sea-level was rising and falling. During a glacial period immense quantities of water are locked up in the form of ice. With less water left to fill the oceans, sea-level falls equally all over the world, leaving raised beaches and river terraces to mark its former height. In the warmer periods most of the ice melts again and sea-level rises, flooding the former land surface and its vegetation, which may later be identifiable as a buried forest.

These world-wide changes in sea-level, brought about by an actual rise or fall of the oceans, are termed *eustatic movements*. During the coldest part of the last glacial period (the Devensian in Britain) sea-level was at least 100 m (330 ft) lower than now, so the English Channel and much of the southern North Sea were dry land and other land bridges existed wherever there are now shallow epicontinental seas. On the other hand, if all the existing ice in the world (most of which is held in

Below: The fossil remains of small land animals are particularly useful in learning about past climatic changes. Snails have become accepted as helpful indicators of Pleistocene temperature fluctuations. This is the shell of an interglacial species, *Vallonia enniensis*, found in Ipswichian deposits in Britain.

Right: Mammal remains are often found in interglacial deposits. This excavation of a skull of a woolly rhinoceros was carried out about the turn of the century at Barrington in eastern England, with great care to retrieve the skull intact. Other cold climate mammals were mammoth bison, reindeer, musk oxen and wolves.

B. W. Sparks

3. AFTER ICE MELTS

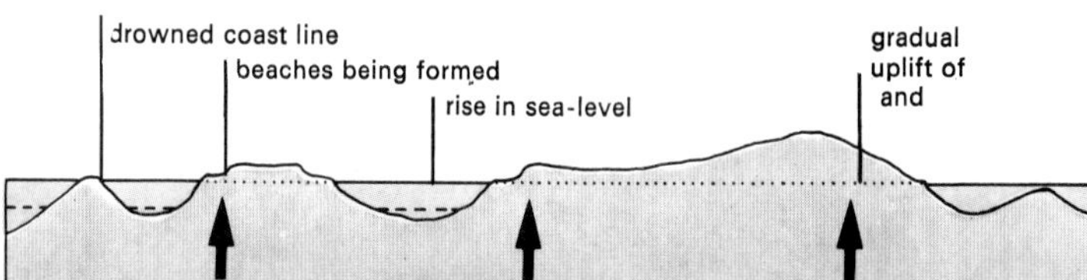

4. FINAL UPLIFT

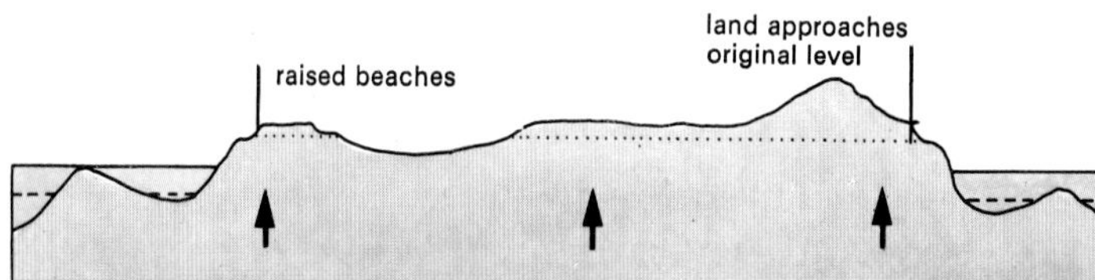

Left: A string of icebergs 'calving' off from the Antarctic ice cap. Pleistocene glaciers in northern latitudes could spread over land, but Antarctic ice spilled into the deep water around the continent and icebergs drifted north to warmer latitudes where they melted. Only about 10% of an iceberg appears above water.

Below: The Dog Stone near Oban, west Scotland, is a raised, undercut sea-stack, eroded by the sea and left high above the present coastline by isostatic uplift of the land. Its name comes from a local tradition that the stack was used by a giant to tie up his dog, which wore a groove at the base by trying to get free.

Right: Blocks of ice dug or drilled from the Antarctic and Greenland ice-sheets reveal strata in the ice. Each layer represents a year's snow-fall, and their age can be found by counting the number above a certain point. By measuring the amounts of oxygen isotope O18 in the ice, past temperatures can also be identified.

Dr Murray Gray

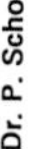

Dr. P. Schoeck/ZEFA

Sedgwick Museum

the two great continental ice sheets, Antarctica and Greenland) were to melt at once, the sea would rise a further 50 m (115 ft)—with catastrophic effect.

While the level of the sea was rising and falling during the Pleistocene, the land in the glaciated areas was rising and falling as well. This is because the continents behave, in the long term, as though they are 'floating' on the denser rock beneath. Extra weight such as thick ice depresses land masses and removal of it allows them to recover their original level. This adjustment, which happens only gradually, is the *isostatic effect*.

In a glaciated area there will thus be the interaction of two processes, one raising and lowering the land, and the other raising and lowering the surface of the sea. Where the shoreline eventually lies depends on many factors, but broadly speaking in the glacial centres isostasy is more effective than eustasy. In Scandinavia and northern Scotland, for instance, there is a series of raised beaches representing former shorelines, now elevated well above present sea-level. However, away from the glacial centres, for example in southern England and France, the eustatic effect is more important, and these areas are characterized by submerged coastlines, drowned valleys and buried forests.

Increasing awareness of the history of the recent past provokes fascinating questions about the future. Will the polar ice caps melt, drowning major population centres? Or are we still in an ice age, and will another cold period eventually lead to the depopulation of the densely settled areas of the northern hemisphere?

The correct answer is that nobody knows. All that is certain is that the time elapsed since the end of the last glacial period (about 10,000 years) is less than the duration of most of the interglacials, so there is no real reason to assume that the Ice Age is over and done with.

Perhaps post-glacial time (the Holocene or Flandrian stage) is just another interglacial period. What is more, perhaps the mid-point of that interglacial is already past, for there was undoubtedly a time, around 4000BC, when the climate was slightly warmer than it is now. One consoling thought is that climatic change takes place very slowly. It has taken 10,000 years—about 400 generations—for the climate in southern England to change from arctic to temperate; so we need not really worry that another glaciation is imminent.

Photri

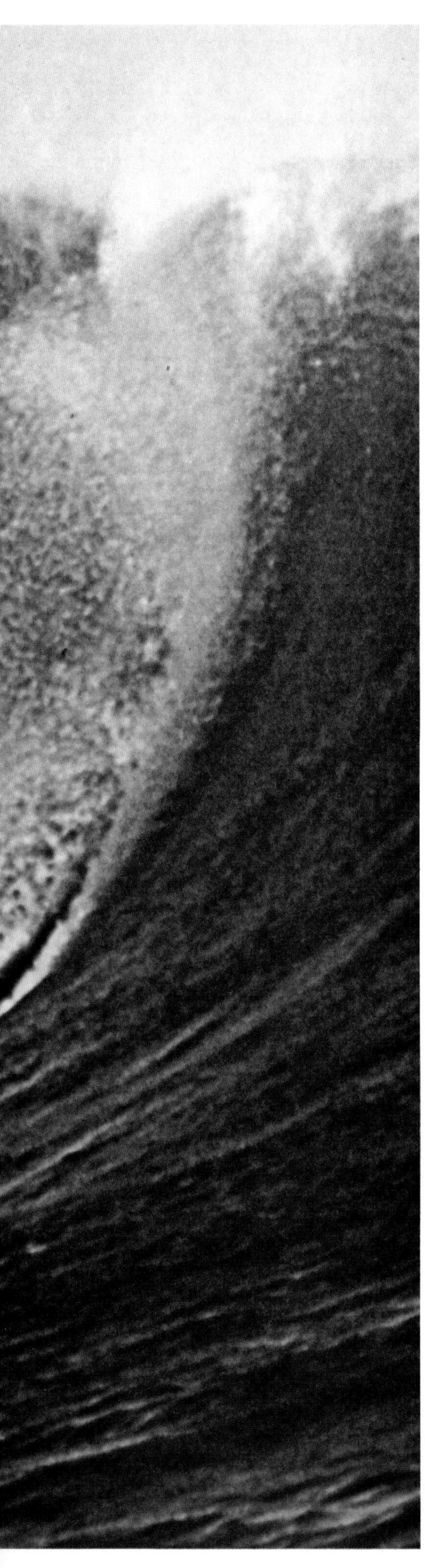

Chapter 3
The Oceans

The Polynesians are believed to have used small wooden boards to surf among the Pacific Islands from New Zealand to Tahiti. They passed on the skill to the Hawaiians, who gave it to the rest of the world.

Caves hollowed on both sides of a headland sometimes meet and form an arch. When the action of the sea causes the top of the arch to collapse, the seaward support of the arch which is left standing is called a *stack*.

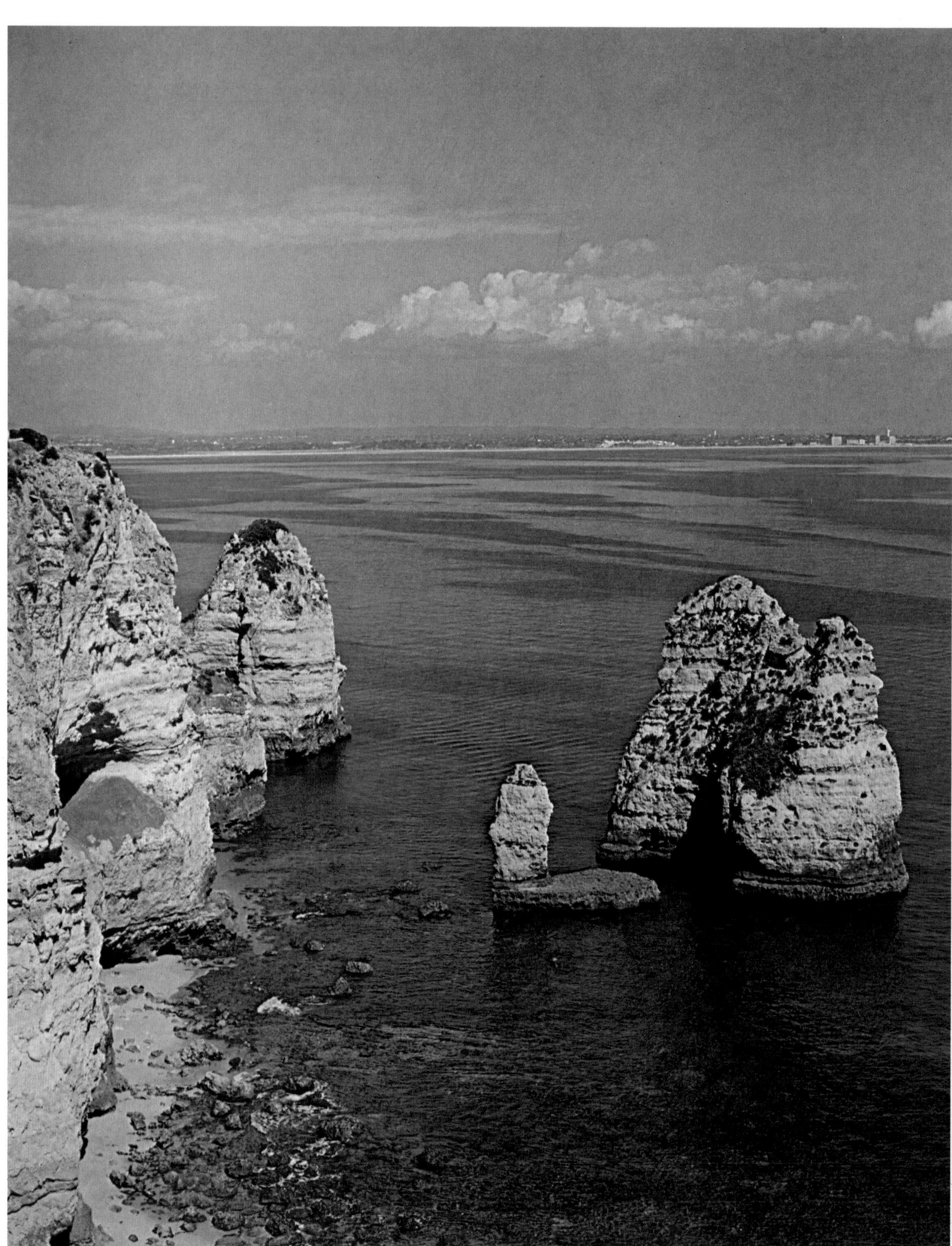

The Sea at Work

The seas make a constant assault on our coasts. Yet the pounding action of the waves is not only destructive, for while cliffs and other coastal landforms are being eroded, the resulting rock debris (often quickly reduced to fine material like sand) may be deposited by that same wave action elsewhere.

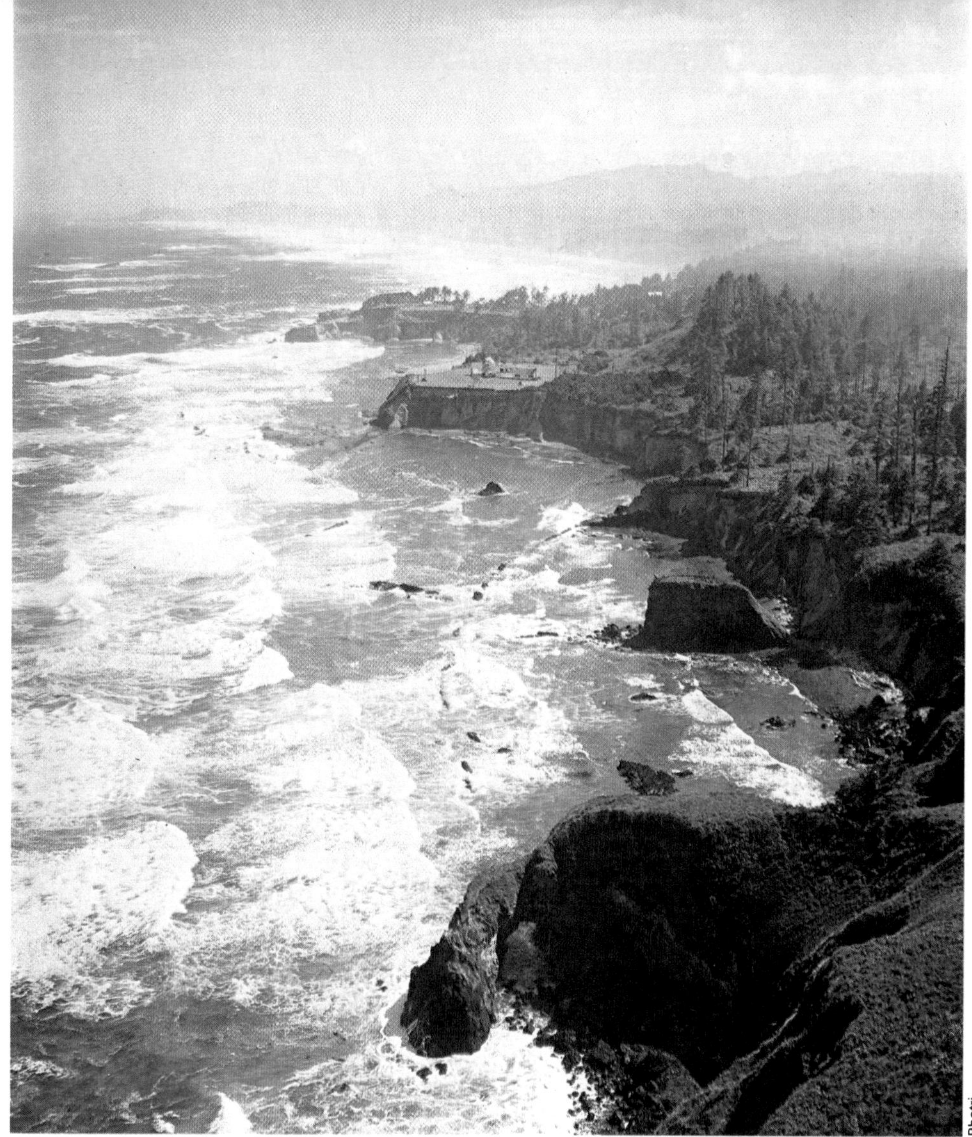

Photri

Above: Waves breaking on the rocky shore of Oregon's Pacific coast. The cliffs are fairly low (about 10 m high) but their vertical faces indicate active erosion by waves. Weaknesses in the rock have been exploited to create an attractively varied coastline of capes and bays. Outcrops of more resistant rock have produced an intertidal island (centre right of the photograph) and a curving arch (bottom). Rock debris and driftwood are deposited at the cliff-base by the gentle swell waves.

The power of waves

Most coastal changes occur under storm conditions, when the destructive powers of waves are at their greatest. The energy of a wave depends on its *length* (the distance from crest to crest), its *height* (the distance from trough to crest) and its swiftness or *celerity* (measured by the period of time between waves). Variation in any one of these characteristics will change the ability of a wave breaking on a coast to erode and move material.

However, the most important factor in the power of a wave is its height. Because this depends in part on wind speeds, the highest waves most commonly occur in storms, when gales whip the sea into a furious assault on the coast. The crash of storm waves on a cliff traps pockets of air in the rock cavities and compresses them. Then as waves fall back, the air expands explosively, throwing spray, pebbles and shattered rock high into the air. Further erosion is the result of the *corrasive* action of the debris hurled by waves against the coasts. The material itself is worn into smaller particles by the constant grinding or *attrition*.

The immense amount of damage that can be caused by storm waves was dramatically illustrated in January 1953 along the coasts of the North Sea. Under strong northerly winds and the high tide, a surge of water was forced into the southern part of the North Sea. The effect was devastating. In many places along the eastern coast of England, the beach was completely washed away by the sea, and once this protection was lost, the cliffs were exposed to rapid erosion. In some areas of Lincolnshire, low cliffs were cut back by more than 10 m (33 ft).

The sea can also change a shoreline considerably without actually eroding the cliffs or beach. On tropical coasts, for example, huge waves are generated by violent hurricanes. In 1960 Hurricane Donna in two days shifted an estimated 5,000,000 m^3 (176,500,000 cubic ft) of sand from one part of the Florida coast to another. Under normal conditions it would take about 100 years to transport that amount. Although very little erosion—that is, breakdown of material—had occurred, at the end of the storm, each resort had an entirely new beach similar in all respects to the pre-storm beach.

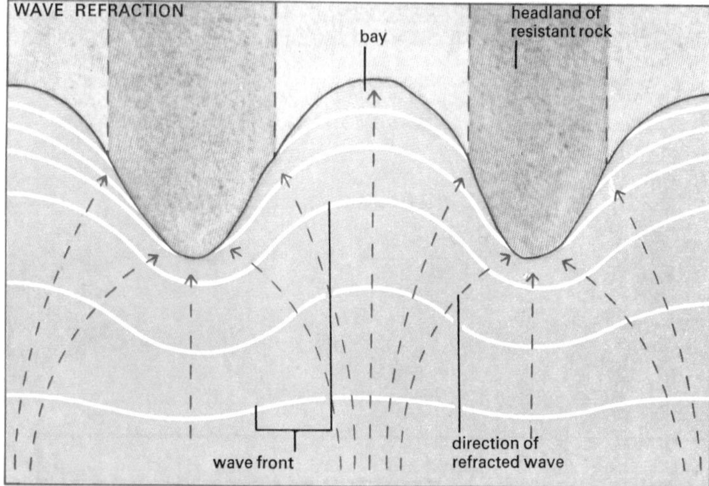

Right: Waves tend to reach the shore at right angles. As they approach the coast, the waves 'feel' the sea bottom. The increased friction slows the waves as they bear down on the protruding headlands. Initially, the brunt of the sea's attack is borne by the headlands and the less disturbed conditions in the bay offer safer anchorage for shipping. However, since the sea-floor is uneven, waves will advance more quickly into the bays where the water is deepest and a wave front becomes curved as the water shallows. The bending, or *wave refraction*, increases until, at the moment of wave break, the front is almost parallel to the coastline.

Cliffs

Perhaps the clearest example of the erosive action of the sea is the way a cliff is undercut by wave action, and then eventually recedes as the unstable slope above collapses. Cliffs are undoubtedly the most striking landform to be seen along a coast, and although their height is entirely determined by the relief of the land, the sea can have dramatic effects. In England, for example, some parts of the Isle of Sheppey are retreating by more

Dr. John S. Shelton

Right: Aerial photograph of Sakonnet Point on Rhode Is. (USA) showing waves being refracted as they near the coast. In the lee of the offshore rocks the waves produce an interference pattern.

than three metres (10 feet) every year. On another part of the eastern coast of England, the cliffs are being eroded even further—as much as 10 metres (33 feet) a year.

Yet the sea can attack the cliffs only within a very restricted vertical range, in effect up to a level reached by the highest waves. Concentrated at the base of the cliff, the sea's erosive force obviously varies with the strength of the waves. In sheltered locations, for example, cliffs are eroded much more slowly than those on exposed coasts. However, the other major factor affecting the rate of erosion is the geology of the area. Cliffs composed of soft rocks, such as clays or glacial sands, can be attacked and the rock debris washed away very quickly.

Cliffs of harder rock such as granite offer much greater resistance to the pounding force of the sea, even along exposed shores such as Land's End at the tip of southwest England and the stormy Cape Horn of South America. Where harder rocks alternate with softer ones, the sea often carves out *bays* and *coves* in the less resistant rocks, leaving the harder ridges jutting into the sea as *headlands*. Straight shorelines are characteristic only of faulted coasts and those formed of rocks of generally uniform resistance to erosion. Along the English Channel, for example, the famous White Cliffs of Dover and the Seven Sisters coast near Eastbourne are composed of chalk of very even texture.

Marine erosion at the cliff-base occasionally creates unusual landforms. Most hard rocks have fault joints and other lines of weakness which are exploited by the sea, sometimes cutting *inlets* and *caves* deep into the cliffs. The explosive pressure of trapped air and surging water inside a cave may be sufficient to erode upwards through the roof to form an opening known as a *blowhole* from which clouds of spray may shoot upwards. Quite often, caves hollowed on both sides of a headland join up to form a natural arch. In time, when the top of the arch collapses, the remnant of the headland stands as a detached pillar, known as a *stack*. All tall, offshore rock pinnacles are called stacks, irrespective of how they were formed. Many well-known examples occur around the coasts of Britain, such as the chalk pinnacles known as the Needles off the Isle of Wight, and the Old Man of Hoy, a 137 m (450 ft) high pillar of Old Red Sandstone, in the Orkney Islands of Scotland.

Beaches

A beach is a deceptively transient feature, a sloping accumulation of loose material —which may consist of boulders, *shingle* (coarse gravel), pebbles, sand, mud and shells—along the sea-shore. Movement of material both up and down and along the beach ensures that it is constantly changing. Beaches may be removed overnight by a violent storm, as occurred in 1953 along the Lincolnshire coast—but they usually build up again during long periods of calm weather. Often, a thin layer of material is moved nearly continuously, being deposited at one end of the beach, washed by *longshore drift* along the length of it, and carried out the other end.

The continuous interplay of waves and this loose material contributes to the

Dr. John S. Shelton

Left and right: The changing appearance of beaches from one season to another is familiar to people who live near sandy sea-shores. Usually a beach loses sand during storms when the waves are highest and most destructive, and regains it during calmer periods. These two photographs of the same part of Boomer Beach near La Jolla, California, show a dramatic gain and loss of sand. In summer (right) gentle swell waves carry material up to the shore, building up a soft sandy beach. In winter (left) storm waves wash away the easily-moved, fine material such as sand, carrying it out to sea, and expose the coarse fragments at the base of this beach.

Picturepoint

Right: Waves thump against the protective sea-wall at Portmellon in Cornwall. In winter the south-western corner of England often suffers storm waves swept across the Atlantic Ocean. Such waves possess a large amount of energy and can bring major changes to shorelines in a very short time. It has been estimated that Atlantic storm waves pound exposed coasts with an average force of 10,000 kg per square metre (2,000 lb/sq ft).

Far right: Tidal mud-flats at Dawlish on Devon's south coast. In sheltered coastal areas such as this where waves are feeble, deposition dominates over erosion. Fine silt and sand are laid down by the sea and rivers add their alluvium. Salt-tolerant vegetation tends to colonize the flat ground and this helps to trap more silt. In tropical areas, mud-flats support mangrove swamps.

Below: This former island in the Scottish sea-loch Eriboll is joined to the mainland by a *tombolo*, a linking deposit of sand and shingle.

Picturepoint

Dr. John S. Shelton

Picturepoint

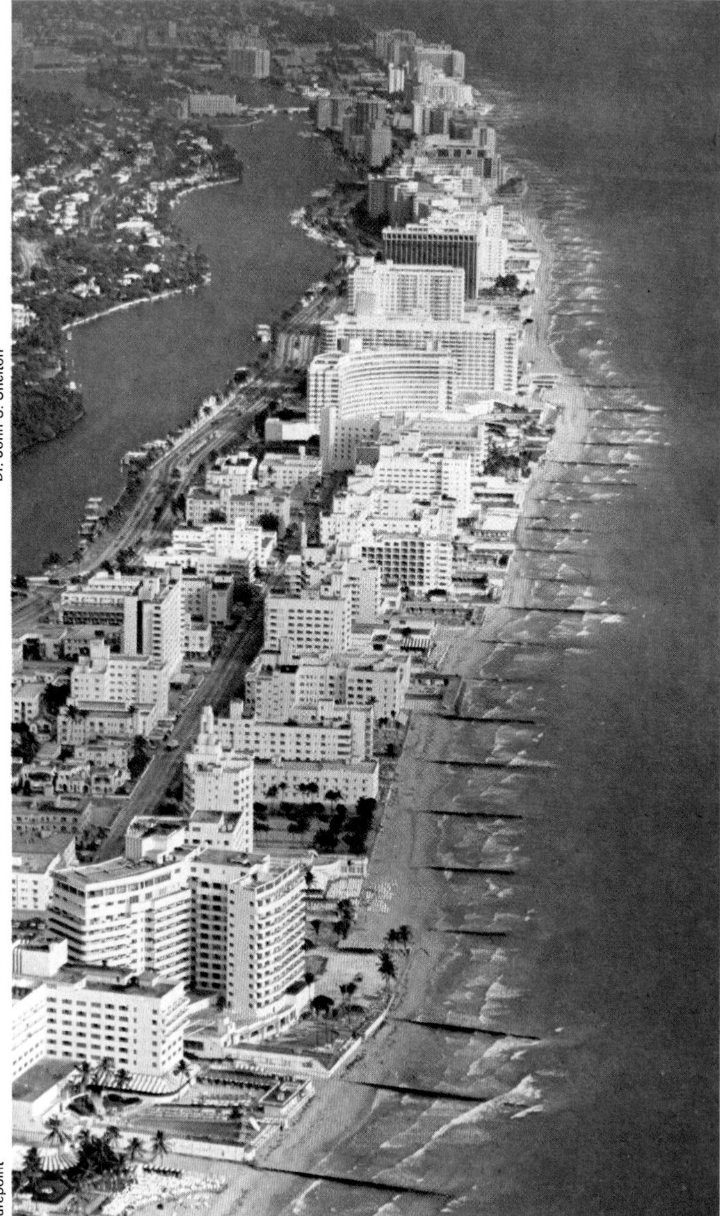

Carl Purcell/Colorific!

CAPE COD, MASSACHUSETTS

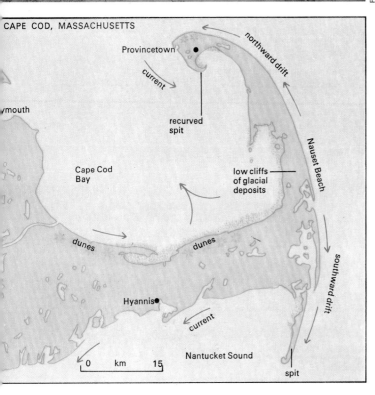

Provincetown
northward drift
current
recurved spit
ymouth
Cape Cod Bay
low cliffs of glacial deposits
Nauset Beach
dunes
dunes
southward drift
Hyannis
current
Nantucket Sound
0 km 15
spit

Above: Miami Beach, the tourist and convention centre in south-eastern Florida (USA), is built on an offshore sand-bar. Separated from the mainland by shallow Biscayne Bay, the island was a mangrove swamp until developed and joined to Miami proper by causeways in 1912. The growth of coastal deposits such as bars and spits depends on sizeable longshore drift of material along an irregular coastline. Here the drift is from the south, as shown by the sand trapped on the near-side of the groynes, low walls or jetties built to protect the beach from further erosion.

Left and right: At Cape Cod on the coast of Massachusetts, the easily-eroded glacial debris is gradually drifting both north and south along Nauset Beach. Long bands of shingle and sand, known as *spits*, are extending the length of the beach. Spits are formed by *longshore drift*, which occurs when waves arrive obliquely at a beach (right). Material carried both up and along the beach by the swash is pulled straight down the slope by the backwash.

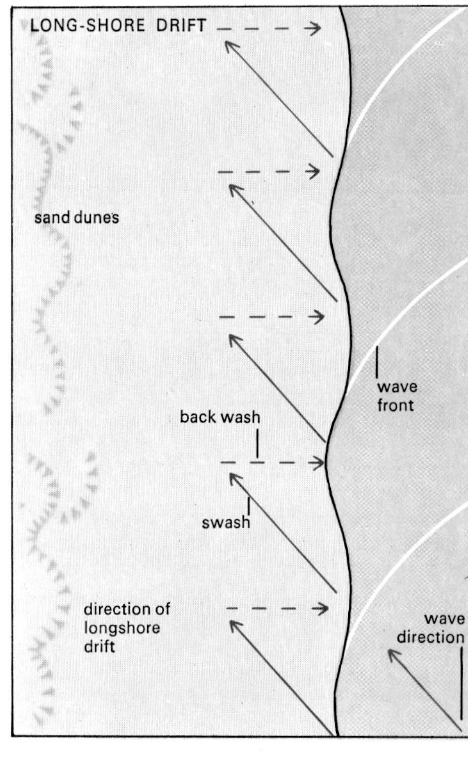

great variety of beaches. Sand and shingle may be washed up from the sea-floor and a small amount of debris is provided by cliff erosion, but most of the material comes from sediment carried to the sea by rivers and then transported along by the waves and currents. The river Nile, for example, is responsible for nearly all the beach sediments in the south-east corner of the Mediterranean Sea. The remains of shells, corals and other organisms may be a further source of beach material.

It is often possible to trace the varied origins of material. For example, at Cap Griz Nez, near the French Channel port of Calais, the beach consists of huge boulders more than a metre (39 in) across, which have fallen from thick limestone bands in the cliff face. Flint cobbles the size of a fist are found on Chesil Beach in Dorset, having been eroded from the chalk on the Channel floor, then washed up by the waves.

Coarse sand is common in the beaches of Cornwall, having been eroded from the granite rocks inland, while extremely fine sands from the Old and New Red Sandstone areas provide a popular holiday beach at Weston super Mare on the Bristol Channel coast.

On all beaches, eroded material is gradually broken down into smaller pieces by the constant pounding of the sea. The surge or *swash* of waves pushes pebbles and sand up the beach, while the *backwash* (the return of seawater down a beach after a wave has broken) or underwater currents drag the material down the slope. Generally, the coarser the material, the steeper the beach slope will be. The steep profile of the shingle beach at Chesil Beach, for example, is partly due to the large size of the flints, whereas the beach at Weston-super-Mare slopes gently because of its fine sand. Where a mixture of sediment sizes occurs, as at many beaches of East Anglia, the coarser material tends to gather at the highest part, and there is usually a marked change in slope between this and the finer sediments towards the low water level.

The shape of a beach is also affected by

Aerofilms

Above: The *cuspate foreland* at Dungeness on the English Channel is one of the best examples of this very unusual feature. Its origins are unclear but shingle has been added to the foreland in a sharply defined series of beach ridges. Many fine ridges were destroyed by the construction of the Nuclear Power Station.

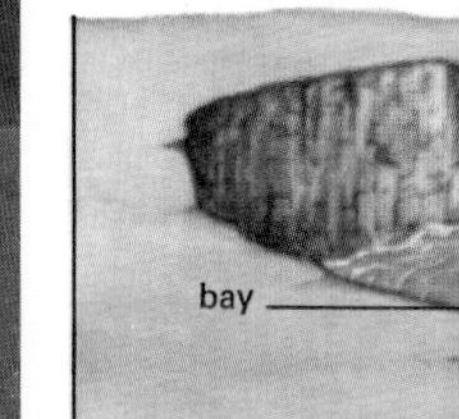

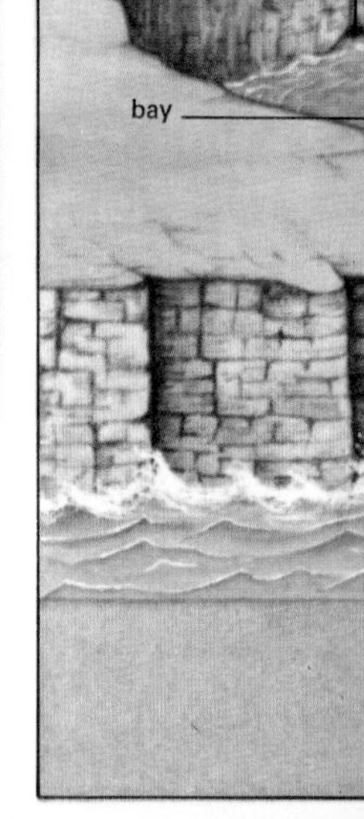

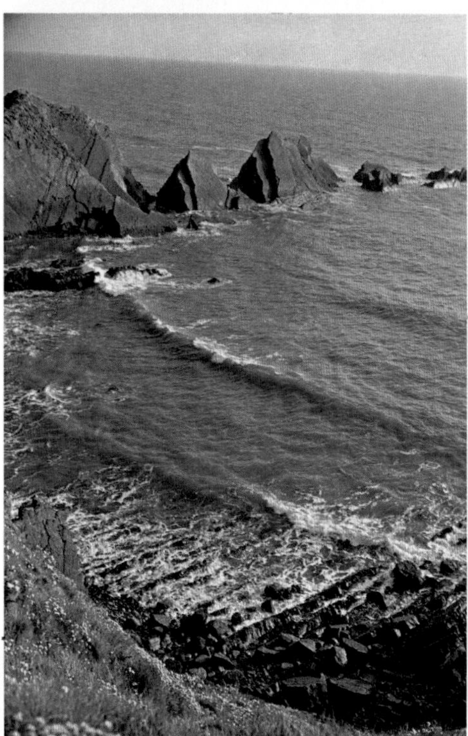
Bruce Coleman

Above: Seastacks and a rocky shore platform project out to sea at a cove near Hartland Quay on the north coast of Devon. The gently inclined *platform* was built and extended as the cliffs were eroded back. Debris from the cliff face has fallen onto the platform, to be swept away by the waves. On coasts like this—battered by strong storm waves—mechanical erosion by the sea picks out the weaknesses in the rock strata. Harder rocks resist destruction and many cliffed coasts end in a series of offshore rocks or *sea stacks* on which lighthouses are often built. Well-known examples include the Needles off the Isle of Wight.

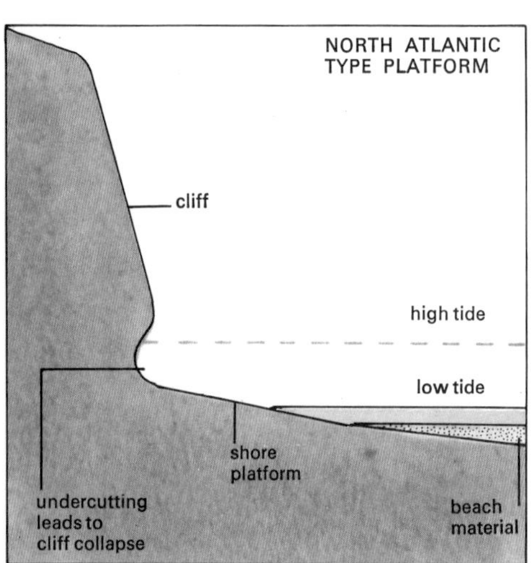

Above and right: There are two basic types of shore platform. The North Atlantic type (above) has an inclined surface stretching from the cliff-base to beyond the low-water mark. It is typical of storm wave coasts, where erosion by the sea leads to undercutting of the cliff. The abrasive and quarrying action of the waves is usually concentrated into joints and cracks in the rock, producing an irregular surface, as seen at Hartland Quay. The SW Pacific type (right) is characterized by a near-horizontal platform that ends abruptly at a low tide cliff. Here chemical weathering is important. The sea merely removes loosened material.

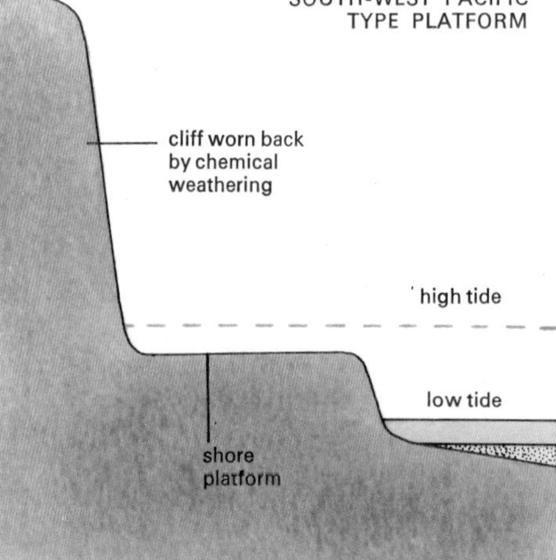

J. Rufus/Robert Harding

Above: These inspiring arches on the coast of the Algarve, Portugal, are known locally as the 'bridges of piety'. Natural arches are an attractive feature of many cliffed coasts. They are most likely to form where horizontally bedded rocks are cut by major vertical joints. Limestones and basalt are particularly suitable.

Right: A fountain of spray shoots out of a *blowhole* on Española or Hood Is. in the Galapagos. Blowholes occur where a chimney extends from the cliff top down to a sea cave. As waves enter the cave, usually at high tide, air is forced up the chimney, carrying water with it, usually with a great roaring noise.

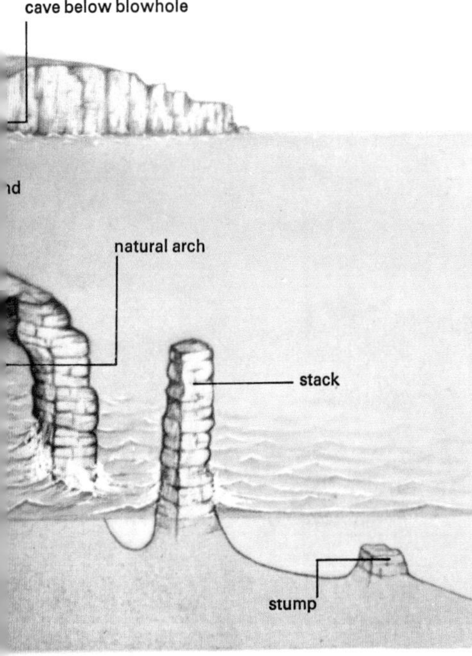

Above: Some of the most striking features along a cliffed coast are those sculpted by the ceaseless battering of the sea. Caves occur quite commonly at weak points in the rock face; for once the sea has cut a hole in the rock, it enlarges it by compression and erosion. Collapse of the cave roof may produce a blowhole. If two caves develop on opposite sides of a headland, the waves may erode through their back walls to carve a natural arch. The sea will continue to erode the arch. When the roof of the arch gives way and debris is carried away by the waves, a large pillar or stack is left offshore. Further erosion may leave a stump, only revealed at low tide.

variations in the movement of waves. Once the direction of prevailing waves or the swash and backwash change, the beach is modified, either by erosion or deposition. If the beach is battered by high waves, as often occurs in winter, the loose material raked from the beach is carried back to the sea, producing a more gentle slope (often separated from the beach beyond the level of wave attack by a small sand or shingle cliff). By contrast, when these steep waves are replaced by more gentle *swell waves* (those which are not driven by winds) material tends to be built up and the beach slope is increased. This produces the generally steeper, larger beaches of summer.

Waves tend to approach the shore at right angles. This is true even of a cape and bay coastline, for as the waves approach the shore, they first encounter the shallower water opposite the headlands, and are slowed down. Opposite the bays, however, the water usually remains deep, so that the waves advance more rapidly. As they too begin to 'feel bottom' they slow and a swinging effect, known as *wave refraction*, occurs by which the line of advance of the waves becomes generally parallel to the shore so that they break head-on.

In many places, however, waves are not fully refracted, and approach at an angle to the coast. This results in *longshore drift*: the movement of shingle and sand along a coastline. Where longshore drift is strong, an abrupt change in the direction of the coast or the entry of a river can produce a *spit*, a narrow ridge of sand, gravel and pebbles piled up by the waves.

Orford Ness on the Suffolk coast is a shingle spit which first sealed off the estuary of the River Alde and then extended southwards for several kilometres across the mouth of the River Butley. The town of Orford lies inland between the two rivers, but 750 years ago it was a port facing the open sea. The curiously shaped triangular beach known as a *cuspate foreland*, and found for example at Dungeness in Kent and at Cape Kennedy (Canaveral) in Florida, is the result of material adjusting to a particular pattern of wave or current action.

Man has attempted to arrest the drift of material along some beaches by constructing barriers or *groynes*. While they may prove a temporary success, groynes all too frequently upset the natural relationship between beach supply, wave action and sediment transport, so that at the end of the protected zone serious erosion occurs. As an alternative to this a number of attempts have been made to artificially replenish beaches by dumping material of an appropriate size. For example, Portobello beach near Edinburgh—robbed of its sand by a long history of erosion—has received this treatment with some success and the technique has been quite widely adopted in California and Florida.

Shore platforms

Along rocky coasts, a level rock shelf or *shore platform* extends seawards from the cliff-base. Shore platforms show almost as much variety as beaches but two basic forms can be recognized. The first, typical of storm wave coasts where mechanical erosion is dominant, consists of an inclined surface stretching to low tide and below. The second consists of a near-horizontal platform that ends abruptly at what is called a *low tide cliff*. This form is typical of tropical and warm temperate areas, such as the New South Wales and Victoria coasts of Australia, where chemical weathering is important.

The surface form of the platform owes much to the waves and the underlying geology, but it also depends on the processes by which a platform is eroded. Alternating hard and soft sands in shore platforms are eroded at differing rates so that miniature scarps and vales are produced. Biological activity is often a notable feature of shore platforms and in warm seas becomes very important. A continuous sea-weed cover tends to protect the platform surface, but a variety of intertidal organisms cause erosion. Some creatures such as piddocks survive by drilling a hole into the platform surface, enlarging it as they grow. Others, like the sea urchin, excavate a shallow hollow or cave. On limestone rocks a number of animals, as for example the limpet, create a variety of hollows by exuding acids which eat into the rock. In these limestone areas, chemical solution is often an important weathering process. But, inevitably, it is slow and its effects may be overtaken by other, more powerful, erosive processes such as the pounding of storm waves.

Heather Angel

Below: Robin Hood's Bay in Yorkshire, created by the rapid erosion of cliffs of soft rock. In many such cases, the sea actually erodes very little material, but it encourages mass movement processes to operate on the cliff and then removes material that slumps onto the beach—as in happening in the foreground.

Alphabet & Image

The Ocean Floor

Like the back of the moon, the floor of the ocean was almost entirely unknown until a few years ago. In the days of the great circum-global expedition of HMS *Challenger* in 1872-1876 the depth of the ocean was still being determined by line sounding. This was achieved by laboriously unwinding a line with a weight attached to the end until it touched the ocean bottom. As the ocean is commonly 5,000 m (3 miles) deep, this was very time consuming and required careful judgement.

During and after the First World War, echo sounding was introduced. At first it consisted of letting off a single sound pulse into the ocean and 'listening' for its echo from the bottom. Knowing the speed of sound in water and the time taken for the echo to return to the surface, the depth of water could then be determined.

Under the stimulus of the Second World War continuously recording deep-sea echo sounders were developed which synchronized the repeated firing of a sound pulse with a recording device, such as an electrically-activated 'pen' scanning a moving paper roll. These echo sounders produced a continuous profile of the ocean floor along the line of the ship's course.

Because of this invention we now have a comprehensive and detailed idea of the morphology of the floors of seas and oceans—comprehensive because it can be obtained automatically whenever a ship is under way; detailed because it can provide precision within 2 m (6 ft) or so in depths of 5,000 m (3 miles) of water. For maximum accuracy it is necessary to actually measure the temperature of the ocean water from top to bottom, because this, together with salinity (saltiness) and pressure, affects the precise speed of transmission of sound.

Other methods similar to echo sounding include *continuous seismic profiling*, which can also be obtained from a moving vessel. However, this method uses a more powerful and lower frequency sound source than echo sounding. This will not only reflect back off the immediate ocean floor, but also in part penetrate through it, to be reflected back by underlying sediment layers and rock surfaces. In this way more information is gained about the structure of the rocks beneath the sea bed.

The *sidescan sonar* is a further advance, as it can look obliquely sideways from a ship, instead of vertically downwards, and therefore cover a broad band across the ocean floor. It is particularly good at picking out the pattern of rock layers which outcrop on the sea floor.

Ocean floor provinces

From all this wealth of information we can conclude that the ocean floor has just as varied a 'landscape' as the surfaces of the continents. The floor is made up of a series of major 'provinces', each with its own special characteristics. Working outwards from the coast, the first is known as the *continental shelf*, followed by the *continental slope* and the *continental rise*, and then out on to the *abyssal plains* and *hills*. However, at destructive plate margins, where the oceanic crust is subducted below the continental crust at the foot of the continental slope, deep *ocean trenches* are

Above: This idealized panorama of the ocean floor illustrates the major sea-floor features to be expected in any ocean basin. In order to show these features clearly, the vertical scale is greatly exaggerated and the features have been grouped closer together than they are actually found. The depths are shown as if they were illuminated, although in reality there is little light below 200 m and it is completely dark below 1,000 m in the oceans.

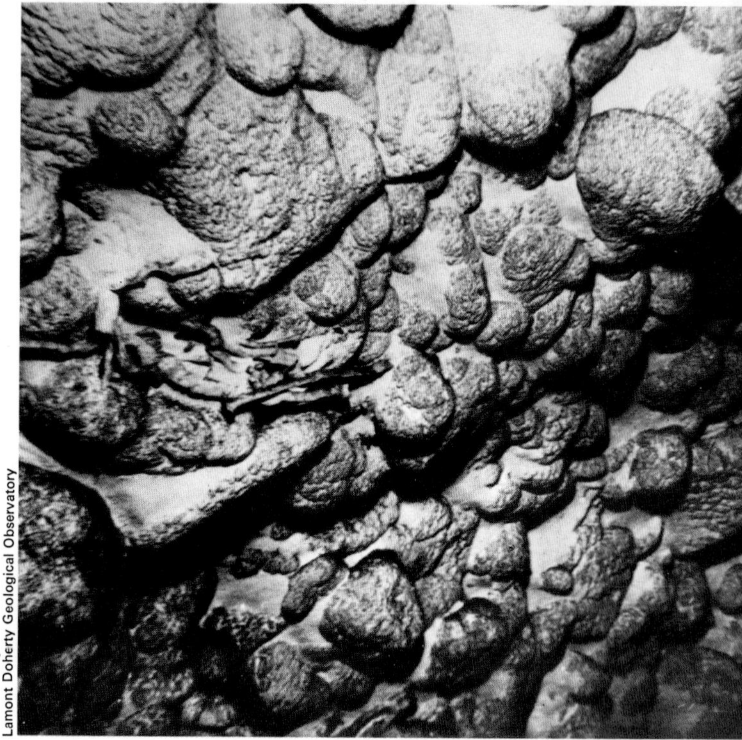

Right: Recent pillow lavas on the mid-Atlantic ridge. Where molten lava erupts underwater, the leading edges of the flow cool very quickly and solidify into these pillow-like masses. Sediment is often trapped between the pillows and this helps to date the period of eruption. Unfortunately, chemical reactions between the fresh lava and seawater often make the usual radioactive methods of age determination unreliable, but the oldest known sediments brought up from beneath the ocean floor are 165 million years old.

Lamont Doherty Geological Observatory

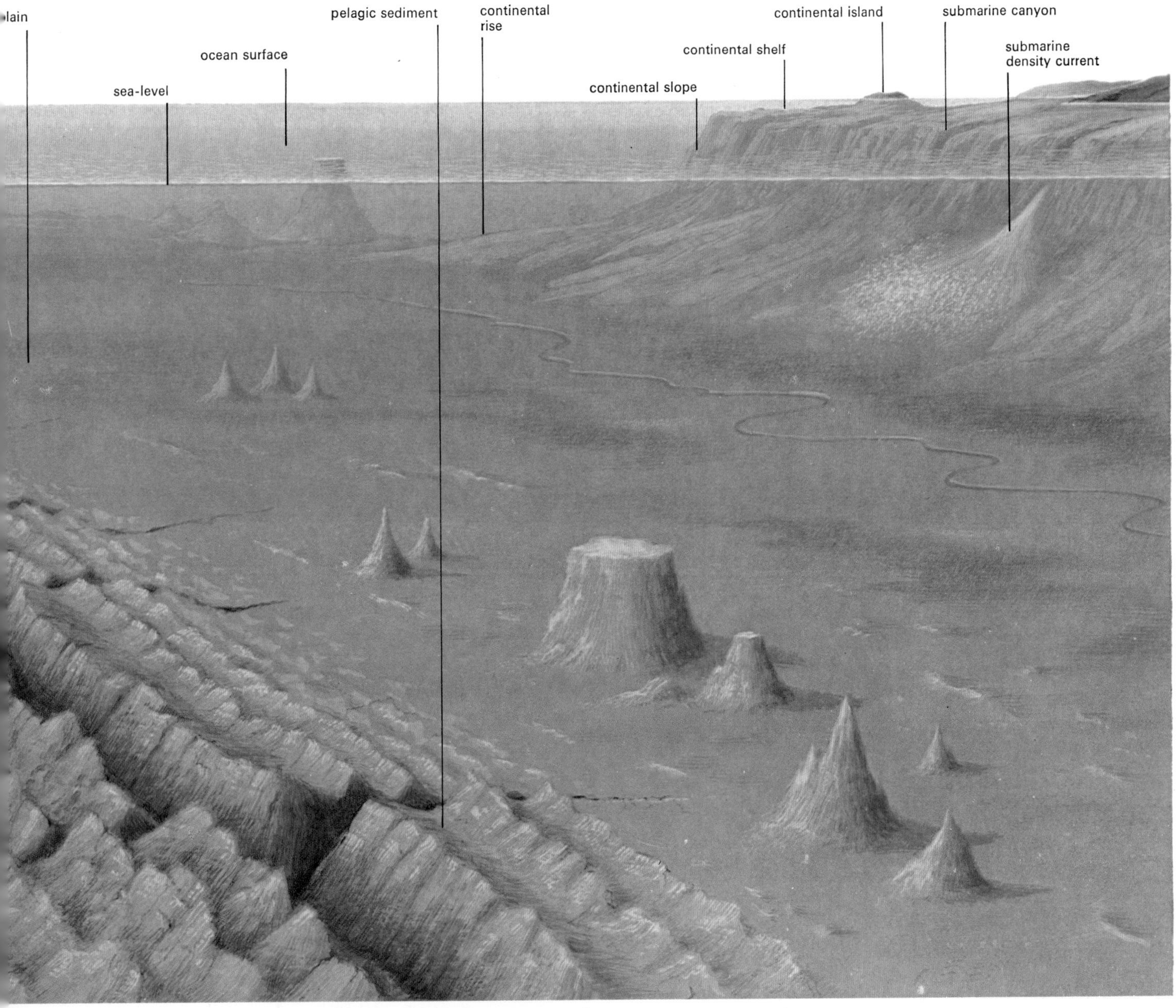

lain
pelagic sediment
continental rise
continental island
submarine canyon
ocean surface
continental shelf
submarine density current
sea-level
continental slope

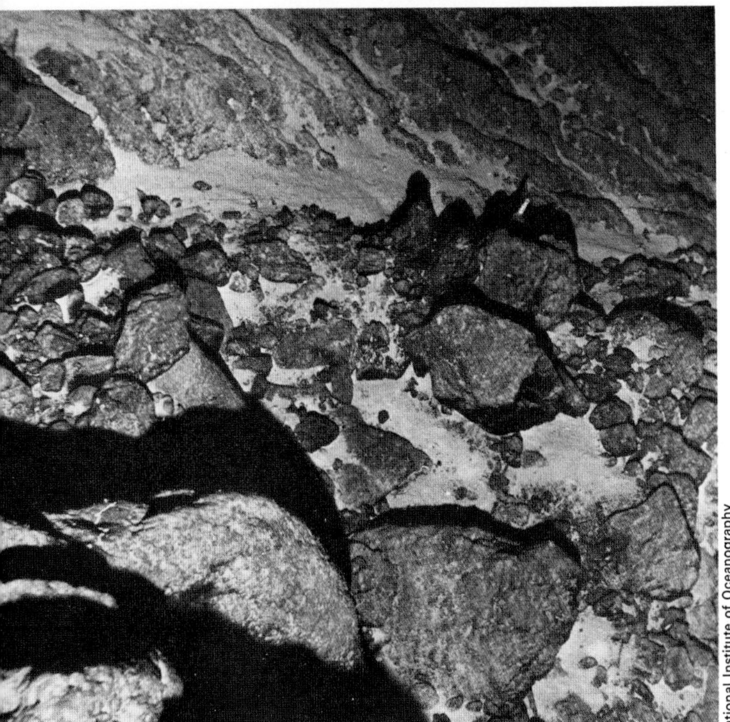
National Institute of Oceanography

Left: In the ocean, as well as on land, rocks are often broken by large fractures or faults and form cliffs or escarpments. In this photograph, taken at a depth of 3,390 m (1,850 fathoms), boulders up to a metre across and other smaller angular blocks of rock can be seen at the bottom of a bare rock slope, on Palmer Ridge in the NE Atlantic. Samples of rock can often be obtained by dredging the sea floor.

Below: This picture shows ripples (about 20 cm from crest to crest) produced by currents passing over calcareous sands (rich in calcium carbonate) between outcrops of basaltic rock on top of a seamount, on the Carlsberg Ridge in the Indian Ocean. The photograph was taken 2,500 m down. Despite the conditions of darkness and great pressure, animals still thrive. A sea lily (or crinoid) is visible, its branched arms open to catch small organisms on which it feeds.

National Institute of Oceanography

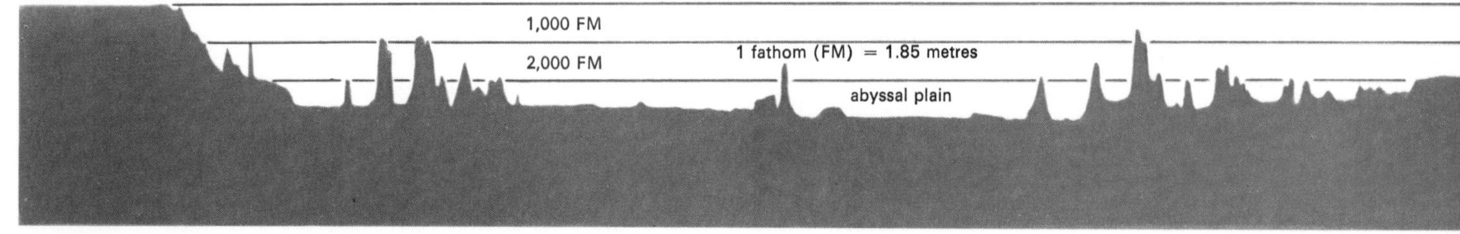

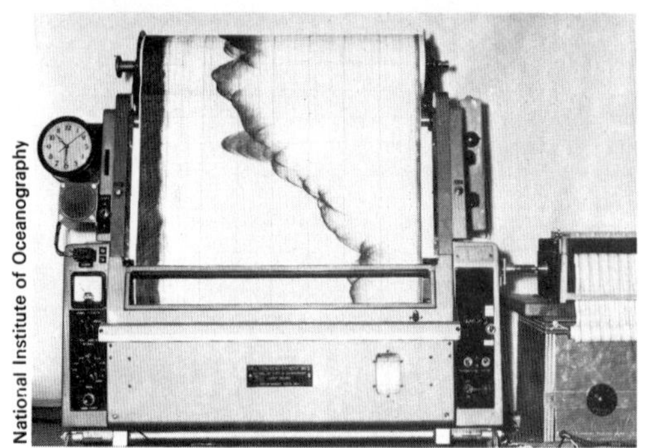

National Institute of Oceanography

Above: A cross-section of the bottom of the N Atlantic. The topographical profile shown is of the sea floor from Martha's Vineyard, Massachusetts (USA) to Gibraltar, 5,600 km away. An accurate picture of the undersea 'landscape' is given by modern devices such as this echo-sounding machine (left), which is producing a trace of the sea-floor off the Canary Islands in the Atlantic as the sounding ship moves over it. Each line records the echoes from one sound pulse.

National Institute of Oceanography

developed instead of a continental rise. The final major province of the ocean floor comprises the flanks and crest of the *mid-oceanic ridges* or *rises*.

The *continental shelves* are the submerged edges of the continents. The water over them is usually no more than about 200 m (660 ft) deep. Because of its shallowness the sea bottom here is strongly affected by tidal and other currents which disturb and transport the sandy, clayey and shelly sediments produced by coastal erosion and by the growth of plants and animals in these shallow ocean waters. The width of the continental shelves varies in different parts of the oceans, from 2 km (1.25 miles) or less off the coast of Chile, to 320 km (200 miles) off Land's End in England, to over 1,200 km (750 miles) off the Arctic coast of Siberia.

At the seaward limit of the shelf there is usually an abrupt change in slope, and the sea bottom then descends steeply towards the deep ocean floor. This steep slope is known as the *continental slope*. It often declines at a rate of between 1 in 40 and 1 in 6 (the latter comparable with the steeper hillsides on land) from a depth of about 200 m (660 ft) to around 3,000 m (about 2 miles) deep. In parts of the ocean it is covered by a mantle, sometimes unstable, of clay and silty clay. Elsewhere it consists of the more or less cut-off edges of the layers of sediment making up the continental shelves. It is the continental slope, not the coastline, that marks the true boundary of each continent.

Many continental slopes are incised with vast steep-sided *submarine canyons* that cut back into the continental shelves —often nearly to the coast itself. Sometimes they occur directly off the mouths of major rivers: one, for example, has been discovered directly in front of the mouth of the River Congo in Africa. The canyons cut deep into the sea-floor, usually emerging somewhere near the foot of the continental slope, where there is often a fan-shaped sedimentary deposit on the deep-sea floor. These troughs are the result of submarine erosion by sediment en route more or less directly from the near-shore to the deep-sea floor.

At the base of the continental slope there is generally a more gently inclining province (sloping at a rate of 1 in 100 to 1 in 700) known as the *continental rise*, which takes the sea-floor down gradually to truly oceanic depths of 4,000 to over 5,000 m (16,500 ft). The rise is made up of sediments brought down by dense, heavy flows of sediment-laden water called *submarine density currents*, sometimes along submarine canyons from the adjacent continent, thereby building up the ocean floor above its normal level. The rise represents the coarser deposits of slowing density currents. Beyond it are the extensive *abyssal plains*.

The almost flat, featureless abyssal plains have been called 'the smoothest surfaces on earth'. Their actual inclinations are between 1 in 1,000 and 1 in 10,000. Beneath them is the irregular igneous basaltic crust. Over them are deposited the finer suspended debris which ultimately settle out from the larger density currents.

Mainly in the Pacific Ocean, beyond the influence of density currents, the ocean floor is composed of a series of gently moulded *abyssal hills*. The undulations reflect the original unevenness of the igneous basement. On these abyssal hills rain the slowly accumulating remains of planktonic (floating) plants and animals, which lived in the surface waters, but whose skeletons fall to the depths to form a fairly uniform blanket of sediment. In the narrower Atlantic Ocean, however, the abyssal plains stretch right out to the flanks of the *mid-oceanic ridge*.

The mid-oceanic ridge consists of a crestal region adjacent to the centre line along which new igneous crustal material (basalt) is being injected, and a flank region in which the crust very gradually subsides as it cools and is pushed away from the centre line. A slow-spreading ridge often has a characteristic median rift valley, as in the Atlantic, with peaks rising thousands of metres on either side of a fissure on average 50 km (30 miles) wide. Some points along the crest may actually project above sea-level as an island, such as Iceland, or as a sub-aerial volcano, such as Tristan da Cunha in the South Atlantic. Faster-spreading ridges, as in the south-east Pacific, generally lack such a central rift valley and have a lower profile.

The mid-oceanic ridges or rises are the site of formation of new ocean floor. Old ocean floor is consumed by underthrust-

Above and below: Echo sounders beam sound waves to the bottom and measure the time taken for the echo to be reflected back to the ship. A major advance came with seismic surveying, which uses more powerful low-frequency equipment to penetrate the sea floor and record underlying sediment layers and rock. By towing the array of devices, interference from ship-board noises can be avoided. These seismic reflection profiles (above) across the Bay of Biscay show that great thicknesses of sediment have accumulated under abyssal plain conditions. Multilayered profiles are often an indication that numerous episodes of deposition have occurred, by deep-sea density currents.

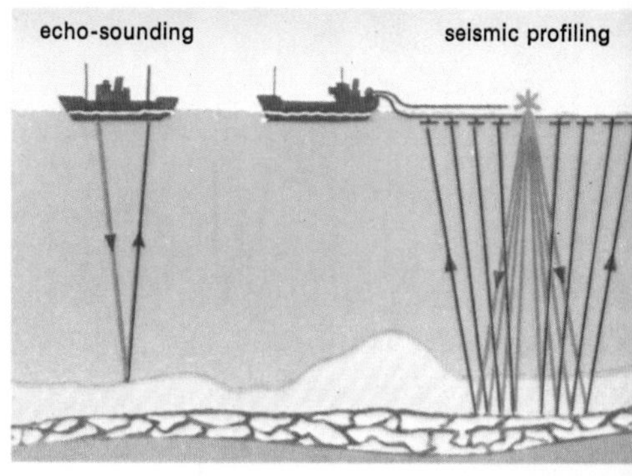

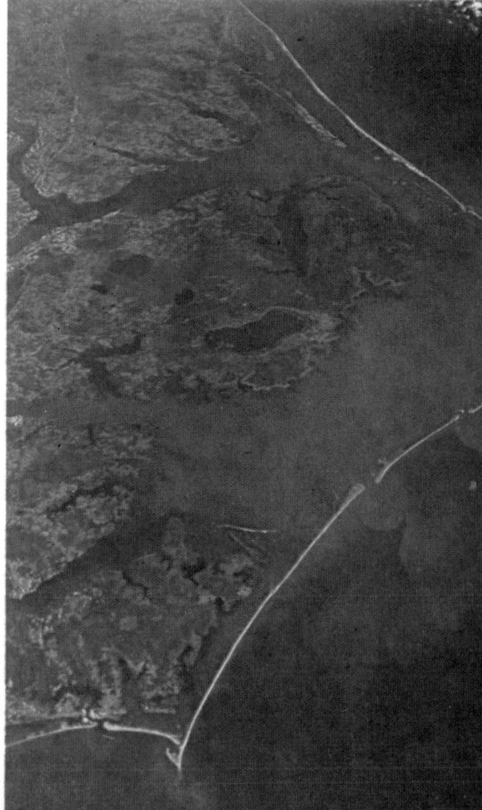

Photri

ntic Atlantic Seamount Azores Josephine Seamount Gettysburg Seamount Gibraltar

Seaphot

Above: A diver inspects the wreck of the sunken *Cooma* in the shallow waters of the continental shelf of Australia.

National Institute of Oceanography

Right: The radiating feeding tracks on this abyssal plain (more than 5,500 m deep) indicates an animal buried in the soft calcareous *Globigerina* ooze. A sea lily can also be seen.

Left: This NASA shot of the Atlantic coast off Cape Hatteras shows the extent of the continental shelf off the NE United States beneath the ocean waters. The line of puffy clouds marks the junction between the colder water covering the shelf and the warmer Gulf Stream waters further out. The shelf is an average 120 m deep.

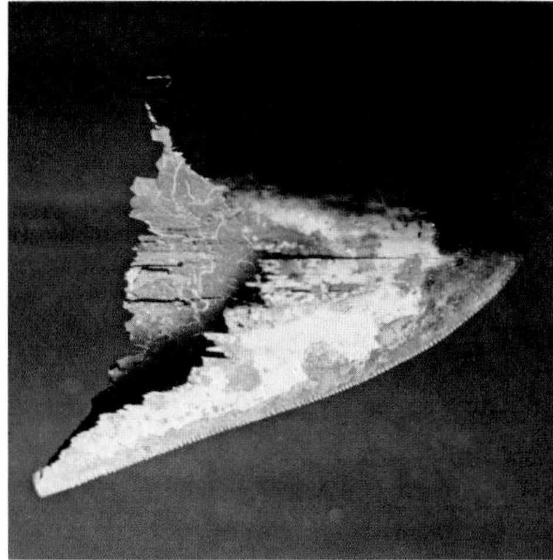

Alphabet & Image

Right: The very slow rates of sediment accumulation on the deep-sea floor may leave very resistant remains, such as whales' earbones and sharks' teeth, at or near the surface of sediment for very long periods. This now-extinct shark's tooth was dredged in the Pacific from a depth of over 4,000 m by HMS *Challenger* in 1874.

ing, either beneath continents, or beneath other pieces of oceanic crust. At the point where the ocean floor is deflected downwards by crustal activity an *ocean trench* is formed. It is in these trenches that the greatest depths on the deep ocean floor are found. A depth of 11,033 m (36,198 ft) was recorded by echo sounding from the Marianas Trench off the Philippines.

Composition of the ocean floor

New ocean floor, freshly created at the mid-ocean ridges, is made of basaltic igneous rock. This may be either extruded onto the ocean floor as pillow lavas, or intruded as horizontal sills or vertical dykes into pre-existing sediments or igneous rocks. These rocks form the crest of the mid-ocean ridges. They also form the foundations of individual volcanoes or chains of volcanoes, and of their submerged counterparts, the volcanic *seamounts*. Seamounts are isolated peaks rising from the ocean floor, and are especially numerous in the Pacific Ocean. Here, in the Tonga Trench between Samoa and New Zealand, is the highest known seamount, its summit being some 8,690 m (28,500 ft) above the sea bed.

The original surface of the volcanic mid-oceanic ridge crest is very rugged. In time the depressions get filled in with *pelagic sediment* (mostly the skeletal remains of planktonic organisms) which is often re-deposited by slumping off the steep slopes of the surrounding volcanic rocks. The deposit in these so-called sediment 'ponds' is likely at first to be calcareous, because of the calcium carbonate content of the remains of the microscopic algae called *coccolithophores*, and the microscopic animals called *foraminifers*. In time the whole of the original surface will be blanketed by these deposits, known as *calcareous ooze*, and this is generally the case on the upper flanks of mid-ocean ridges.

At greater depths the ocean floor passes below the level (4,000 to 5,000 m) at which calcium carbonate dissolves. Here the sediment consists only of insoluble clay or the remains of siliceous (silica rich) organisms such as *diatoms* and *radiolarians*. Therefore drilling through those parts of the ocean floor covered by the oldest sedmiments will often reveal a sequence of non-calcareous, then calcareous sediments, then volcanic basalt rock.

From the shallowest water to the greatest depths, the ocean floor is almost universally colonized by animals of one kind or another. In soft sediment they live by burrowing into the sediment, on hard rock attached to the surface. Where currents run near the bottom it may be patterned by ripple marks, and near areas influenced by the past and present polar ice caps are found sand, silt and blocks of erratic rock, carried and eventually dropped by drifting icebergs. In fact the ocean floor is a veritable repository of the entire history of our planet.

Coasts and Islands

G. R. Roberts

Coasts are the zone where the forces of the sea conflict with all other processes of land sculpture, and no two coastlines are ever exactly alike. Indeed the variety of coasts poses enormous difficulties for scientists trying to draw together the coasts of the world into even the broadest groupings.

The character of a coastline is, of course, strongly influenced by wave action, and a few areas can be identified by distinctive wave characteristics. The mountainous storm waves battering Cape Horn on the tip of South America are legendary. However, comparable if less extreme conditions apply to many coasts where storms are a common feature, at least in winter, such as the coasts of northwest Europe.

In contrast, the high latitude coasts of the Arctic and Antarctic are areas of relatively feeble wave action since a protecting fringe of ice blunts the energy of the winter storm waves. In most inter-tropical areas the frenzied, episodic activity of storm waves is replaced by the regular beat of trade-wind generated swell waves. Yet in a few tropical areas, notably north Australia, south China and Vietnam, Bangladesh and the Caribbean, short-lived tropical hurricanes do produce enormously destructive waves.

Above: The series of raised beaches on this New Zealand coast show clearly the effects of tectonic activity such as faulting. Above the present grey strip of shoreline lies an old beach, raised some 2.5 m by an 1855 earthquake. Above that are four other distinctive raised beaches. The greatest uplift occurred about 3,100 years ago, when the land was lifted some 8 m by faulting.

G. R. Roberts

Right: Looking out to sea over Sydney Harbour—a fine example of a coastline of drowned river valleys. In this case, the existing lowlands and valleys were submerged by a rise in sea-level when Pleistocene Ice Age glaciers elsewhere melted.

The influence of plate tectonics

A recent attempt at a comprehensive classification of the world's coasts, however, is based not on wave action but on the theory of plate tectonics. This sees the earth's crust as composed of enormous plates moving laterally away from 'zones of spreading' towards 'zones of convergence'. Three broad categories of coasts can be recognized.

The first, termed *collision coasts*, occur where a continental margin is located along a zone of convergence between two plates. These important areas of volcanic and earthquake activity are characterized by fairly straight, clifted coastlines and include much of the west coast of the Americas. *Island arc collision coasts*, such as those of Japan, the Indonesian islands and the Caribbean, are found where plates are colliding some distance from the edge of a continent.

The second group, termed *trailing edge coasts*, has much lower levels of tectonic activity and is generally less mountainous. These occur where a coast firmly imbedded in a crustal plate faces a spreading zone. However, a distinction is drawn between an *Afro*-trailing edge coast (where the coast on the opposite side of the same continent is also trailing, as in Africa and most of Australia) and an *Amero*-trailing edge coast, illustrated by the east coast of North and South America, where the opposite continental coast is a collision coast.

The distinction is important. Since the whole continent of Africa is associated with low tectonic activity, there are low yields of sediment to rivers and thus to the coast. On the other hand, the mountainous areas in the Americas produced by the collision between two plates, although located close to one of the continental margins, supply large quantities of sediment to rivers draining to both west and east coasts. Both the Amazon and the Mississippi, for example, carry much more sediment than the Congo or the Niger. As a result the coastal plains of the eastern Americas are much more extensive.

The east coasts of Asia and Australia illustrate the third group of coasts classified by the ideas of plate tectonics. These *marginal sea coasts* display a diversity of relief, but they are tectonically relatively stable like the Afro-trailing edge coasts and could perhaps be considered as part of that group.

The wide acceptance in the late 1960s of the concepts of plate tectonics gave new significance to the long-standing grouping drawn up in 1892 by Edward Suess, an Austrian geologist. Suess had distinguished between *Pacific type coasts*, where geological structures are aligned parallel to the coast, and *Atlantic type coasts*, where the structures are at right angles to the coast. It is now clear that Pacific type coasts, like those of California and Yugoslavia, correspond closely with collision coasts. Similarly, Atlantic type coasts as illustrated by those of south-west Ireland and Brittany are associated with trailing edge coasts.

More local level geological conditions often determine the precise form and orientation of a coastline. Faulting and

Below: The remains of a submerged forest exposed at low water on a beach in Sussex, England. During past glaciations, sea-level was lower and woods and marshes extended far beyond the present shoreline. As sea-level rose they were drowned and gradually eroded. This forest probably flourished several thousand years ago.

Below right: A coastal mangrove forest in Trinidad. Mangroves are often associated with areas of restricted wave action in the humid tropics—fine-grained sediments produced by intense chemical weathering on land accumulate to provide a base for the many stilt roots of the mangrove shrubs and trees

Heather Angel

Right: A broad but revealing grouping of the world's coasts can be made in terms of plate tectonics. Rocky *collision coasts* are formed where two crustal plates converge and the crust bordering the continent is folded and raised, as along most of the west coast of the Americas and much of the Mediterranean. Very steep collision coasts are mainly found around the Pacific ring of trenches and active mountain building. The Atlantic is largely bordered by tectonically quieter, but varied, *trailing edge* coasts. *Amero-trailing edge* coasts are characterized by more extensive coastal plains than found along *Afro-trailing edges*. *Marginal sea coasts*, such as the east coast of Australia, are also fairly stable, low-lying areas. *Neo-trailing edge coasts* are found where a new zone of spreading is separating a land mass, as is happening in the Red Sea.

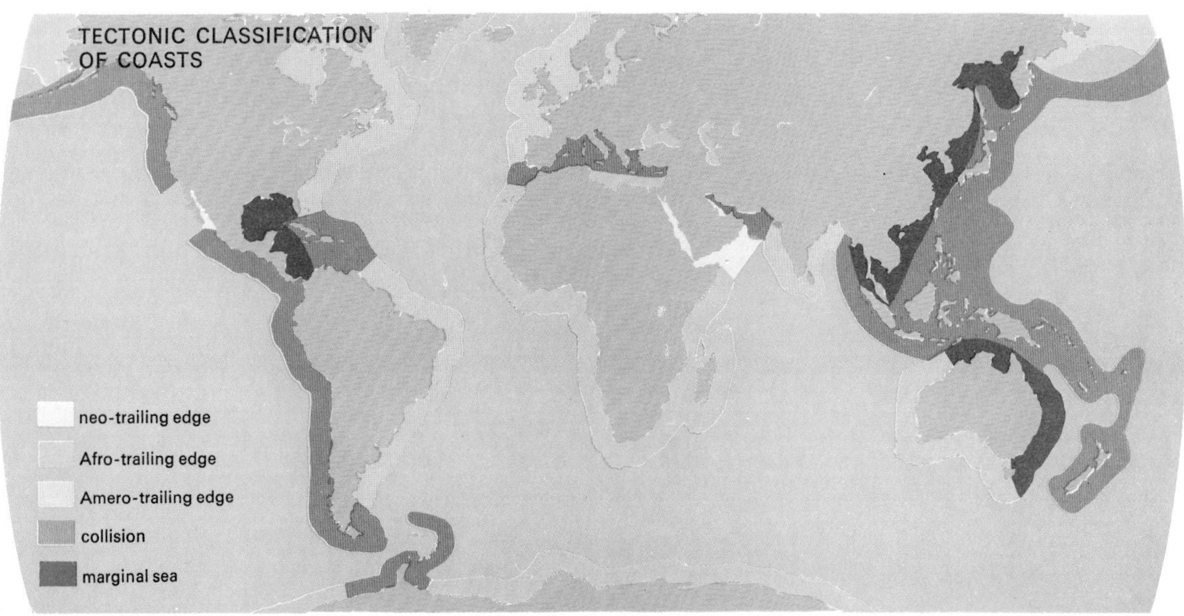

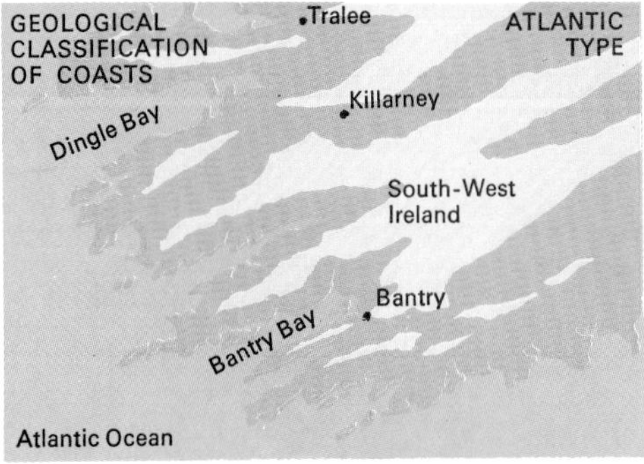

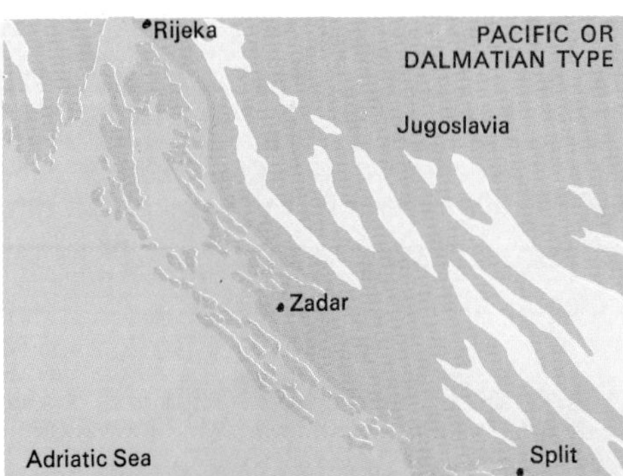

Left and right: In 1892 Suess recognized two strongly contrasting types of coast based on geological structure. The SW coast of Ireland (left) is an example of an *Atlantic* type in which fractures and folds lie at right angles to the shoreline. Along *Pacific* type coasts (below left) geological structures are aligned parallel to the coast. When partially drowned, as on the Dalmatian coast of the Adriatic Sea (right), such coasts are called *Dalmatian*. Suess's classification can be largely replaced by that based on plate tectonics. The Dalmatian coast is a collision type, created by the convergence of the African and Eurasian plates, whereas SW Ireland is a trailing edge coast.

Ardea

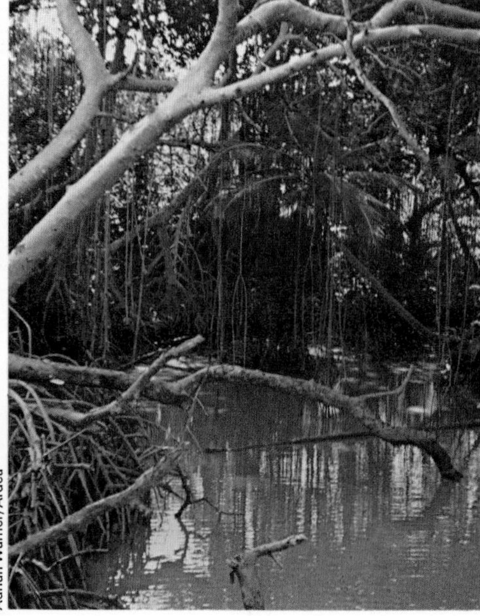

folding may produce local cliffs and bays and the character of a rock also helps determine whether a coast is basically cliff-dominated or lowland-dominated.

Much of the variety in coasts is derived from the influence of the processes of land sculpture. The most obvious examples of this are the steep-sided fjord coasts of Norway and Fjordland, New Zealand, which owe their distinctiveness to glacial erosion. The rather subdued coastline of low cliffs and extensive beaches so typical of East Anglia in England is associated with areas of glacial deposition.

Delta coasts, on the other hand, bear the hallmark of river activity. *Deltas* are tracts of alluvium formed at a river mouth, where water movement is slowed as it enters the sea, thereby allowing deposition of the suspended load carried by rivers. If the river supplies more material than can be removed by the sea the delta will grow, as is currently occurring at the Mississippi delta.

Although many other coasts are low-lying and dominated by river deposition, different conditions result in a broad *coastal plain* rather than a delta. Coastal plains are especially associated with humid, tropical areas such as Sumatra and Borneo where the large numbers of streams carry heavy sediment loads. Since the swell waves characteristic of these coasts dissipate most of their energy crossing the wide, shallow near-shore zone, they have little energy left when they finally reach the shore. Under these circumstances fine sediments accumulate and very often swamp vegetation and mangroves colonize them.

Changes in sea level

Many coasts are dominated by cliffs, beaches and shore platforms which originated hundreds, and even millions, of years ago. Once this time span is considered the fact that sea-level has changed so much becomes of vital significance. In recent earth history the main cause of relative sea-level change has been the varying amount of water held as ice during Pleistocene and recent times.

Local changes in the level of the land may be due either to direct tectonic activity or to isostatic change (vertical adjustment of sections of the crust). The first is best illustrated by the sudden uplift that sometimes accompanies an earthquake. For example, the shores of Port Nicholson in New Zealand were raised almost 2 m (6.5 ft) by faulting in 1855. Although less spectacular, tectonic warping is no less effective. Much of the present subsidence in coastal Essex and Holland is the result of this type of movement. One result of isostatic changes in the level of the land is evident in the northern Baltic region which has risen some 200 m (660 ft) since its ice cap melted 10,000 years ago—and the area is still being uplifted.

As a consequence of the changing sea-

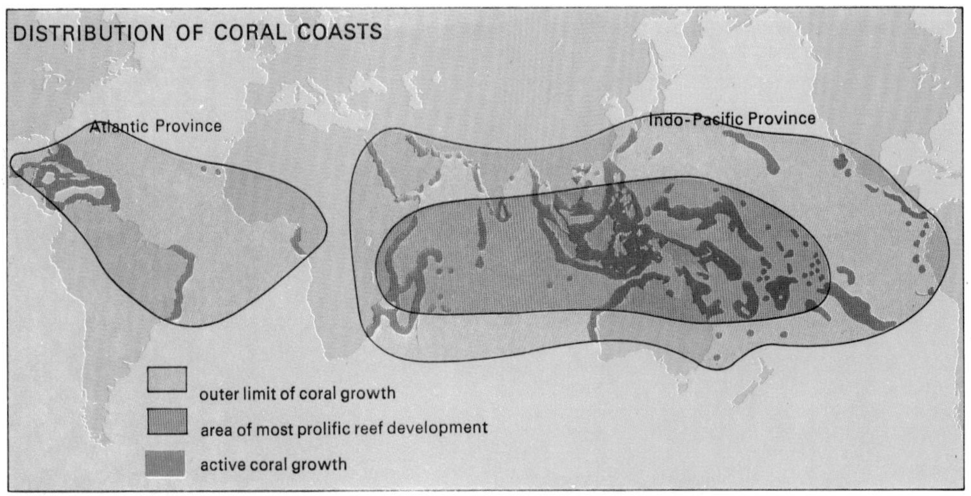

Above: The map shows the distribution of coral growth coasts, largely concentrated in the tropical parts of the Indian and western Pacific Oceans, although they also occur in the Caribbean. The most important factors influencing coral growth are the temperature and salinity of the water and the amount of sunlight the coral receives.

Left: A coral atoll off Queensland, Australia, showing the fringing reef and the coral sand beach around vegetated areas of coral.

Below: The three diagrams show how a coral atoll forms. First stage is the growth of a fringing coral reef round the island. As the island begins to sink, the coral grows upwards to form a barrier reef. Finally the island sinks beneath the surface, leaving only a coral atoll and the enclosed area of water known as a lagoon.

Below: On the coast of Namibia (S.W. Africa) near Walvis Bay, sand dunes dominate the coast. A combination of strong winds, gentle coastal slopes and a large tidal range are the best conditions for such coastlines, particularly if they occur in the dry tropics.

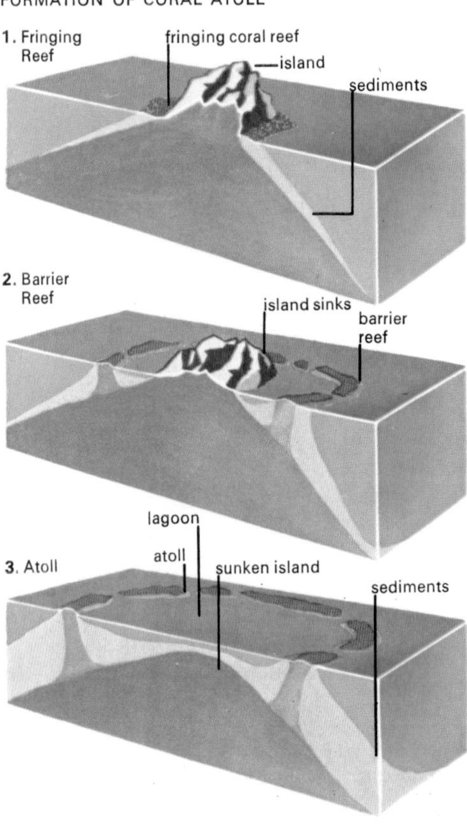

level, features associated with coasts are sometimes found high above or well below present sea-level, and some features associated with land areas are now drowned. Raised beaches, stranded shore platforms and old cliff lines high above present sea-level are to be found in many areas, especially in those which have recently been deglaciated such as Scotland, Scandinavia and Arctic Canada. On the other hand, drowned cliffs and platforms are also quite common. Submerged forests, drowned glacial moraines, estuaries, long, narrow inlets called *rias* (such as those in south Devon and Cornwall) and drowned river systems, such as those traceable on the floor of the North Sea, all bear witness to a rise in sea-level.

Islands

Discounting Australia, which is usually regarded as a continental land mass, the world's largest island (a piece of land surrounded by water) is Greenland, with an area of about 2.2 million km (840,000 sq miles). Islands fall into two broad groups: continental and oceanic.

Continental islands, such as the British Isles, are considered part of a continental mainland which has been cut off, perhaps by a change in sea-level. Island arcs such as the Caribbean islands and Indonesia are the result of tectonic activity within the crust relating to plate movements. Although often composed of rock material similar to that of the continental shelf or mainland, many of the individual islands are dominated by volcanic activity.

Oceanic islands are also intimately related to plate tectonics, but rise out of the deep sea. These include the islands associated with mid-oceanic ridges such as Iceland, Madeira, the Azores and Tristan da Cunha. These are invariably composed of volcanic material and are frequently noted for their volcanic eruptions. A number of oceanic islands such as Hawaii appear to be associated more with local hot spots in the crust than plate activity, but these too are entirely volcanic in origin.

Coral reefs

A fascinating variety of islands and coasts are formed by coral growth. Corals are actually small marine organisms called *polyps* which have skeletons of calcium carbonate. Millions of these skeletons bind together to form coralline *reefs*.

Reef-forming corals are very selective about where they live. They grow best in clear, salt-water tropical seas where the water temperatures are normally 25-29°C. Vigorous growth is restricted to the top 20 m (65 ft) of water. The tropical parts of the Indian and western Pacific oceans are the main areas of coral islands and coastline through they do occur in the Caribbean and a few other localities. The most widespread form is the *fringing reef*, an offshore coral platform.

All the other forms of coral structures are in some way connected with slow subsidence, indicated by the fact that the thickness of the coral usually greatly exceeds 20 m (65 ft). A barrier reef is one such large-scale feature and is classically illustrated by the Great Barrier Reef of Australia. Continued subsidence of oceanic islands can lead to a situation where coral eventually occupies all the surface area and encloses a lagoon to produce a *coral atoll*, illustrated by many of the islands of the western Pacific.

Ocean Exploration

The voyage of the Greek explorer Pytheas beyond the Mediterranean Sea and along the Atlantic coast of Europe, around 325BC, is often considered as the start of ocean exploration. Perhaps its chief significance, indeed, lies in the fact that the voyage seems to have been deliberately undertaken and a written record of it was preserved. Others such as the Phoenicians had certainly been at least some of the way before.

The next milestones in ocean exploration are commonly taken to be the Spanish and Portuguese explorations of the Atlantic and Indian Oceans in the fifteenth century, culminating in the circumnavigation of the globe by Ferdinand Magellan's expedition in the early sixteenth century. But here again, others had explored these oceans before. The Vikings in the North Atlantic and the Polynesians in the Pacific had made remarkable journeys in small and often open boats in the first millenium AD. The record of these explorations is, however, contained only in the Nordic Sagas and oral traditions of the Polynesians. The Spanish and Portuguese on the other hand provided tangible and written testimony of their exploits to their royal sponsors, which we can still read today.

The centuries which followed saw a continuing and systematic exploration of the world's oceans by European navigators. The rewards were trade, wealth and colonies. By the eighteenth century, in the light of the developing interest in science, exploration was being deliberately sponsored to push back human knowledge of the limits of the oceans. In this spirit the English sea-captain James Cook made three major voyages mapping out the Southern Ocean which surrounds Antarctica and later, in the early nineteenth century, Sir James Clark Ross followed him southwards to explore the ice-rimmed margins of the 'last continent'. Previously Ross had been engaged in seeking a Northwest Passage from the Atlantic to the Pacific via the frozen seas of the Arctic region.

Perhaps the middle of the nineteenth century should be regarded as the end of the heroic age of ocean exploration. Certainly with the voyage of HMS *Challenger* around the world in 1872-1876, the systematic study of the world's oceans, in all their aspects, had begun in earnest.

The oceans of the world

We now know there are five major oceans—the Atlantic, the Pacific, the Indian, and the Arctic, with the southern extremities of the first three, around Antarctica, being gathered up as a fifth: the so-called Southern or Antarctic Ocean. Together with the adjacent seas, these make up 71 per cent of the surface of planet earth. They contain over 97 per cent of the water which occurs at the earth's surface.

The Pacific Ocean is the largest, measuring 15,500 km (9,600 miles) from Bering Strait in the north to Antarctica

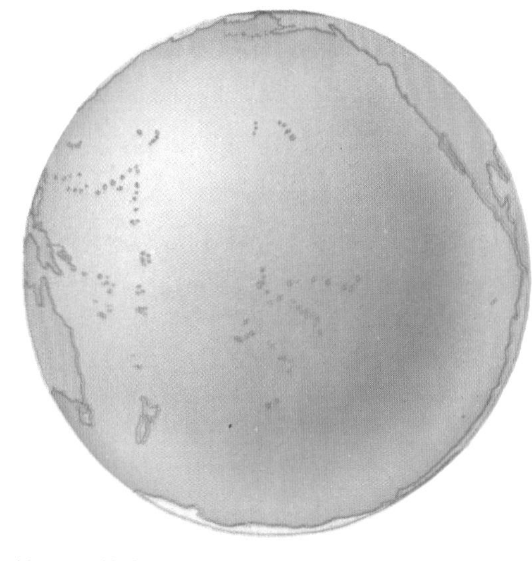

Above and below left: Planet earth or planet water? Looking down from a position directly over Tahiti in the Pacific, the earth appears to be almost totally covered in ocean. In contrast, this world map from about 1480, possibly known to Columbus, reflects man's long-standing ignorance of the vast oceans (and much of the continents) before the great voyages of discovery.

Below: It is not known when man first tried to explore the sea depths. The earliest record of a diving bell is by the Greek philosopher Aristotle (4th century BC). This 13th-century French painting shows Aristotle's pupil Alexander the Great in a glass barrel, in which he was reputed to have been lowered to the sea-floor. The king claimed he saw a great monster which took 3 days to pass.

M. Pucciarelli

Bildarchiv Preussischer Kulturbesitz

Michael Holford

Left: HMS *Challenger* under sail in the cold Antarctic Ocean. This 3-masted British Navy corvette, her guns replaced with scientific gear, sailed from the Thames in December, 1872, covering 110,844 km in a three and a half year around-the-world expedition. *Challenger's* auxiliary steam engine enabled her to hold steady over the sea-floor during bottom soundings. The team of six scientists, led by Sir Wyville Thomson, also collected water and bottom samples, plants and animals, and observed sea temperatures and currents. The voyage was a turning point in the science of oceanography.

Right: The chemical laboratory aboard HMS *Challenger*.

Michael Holford

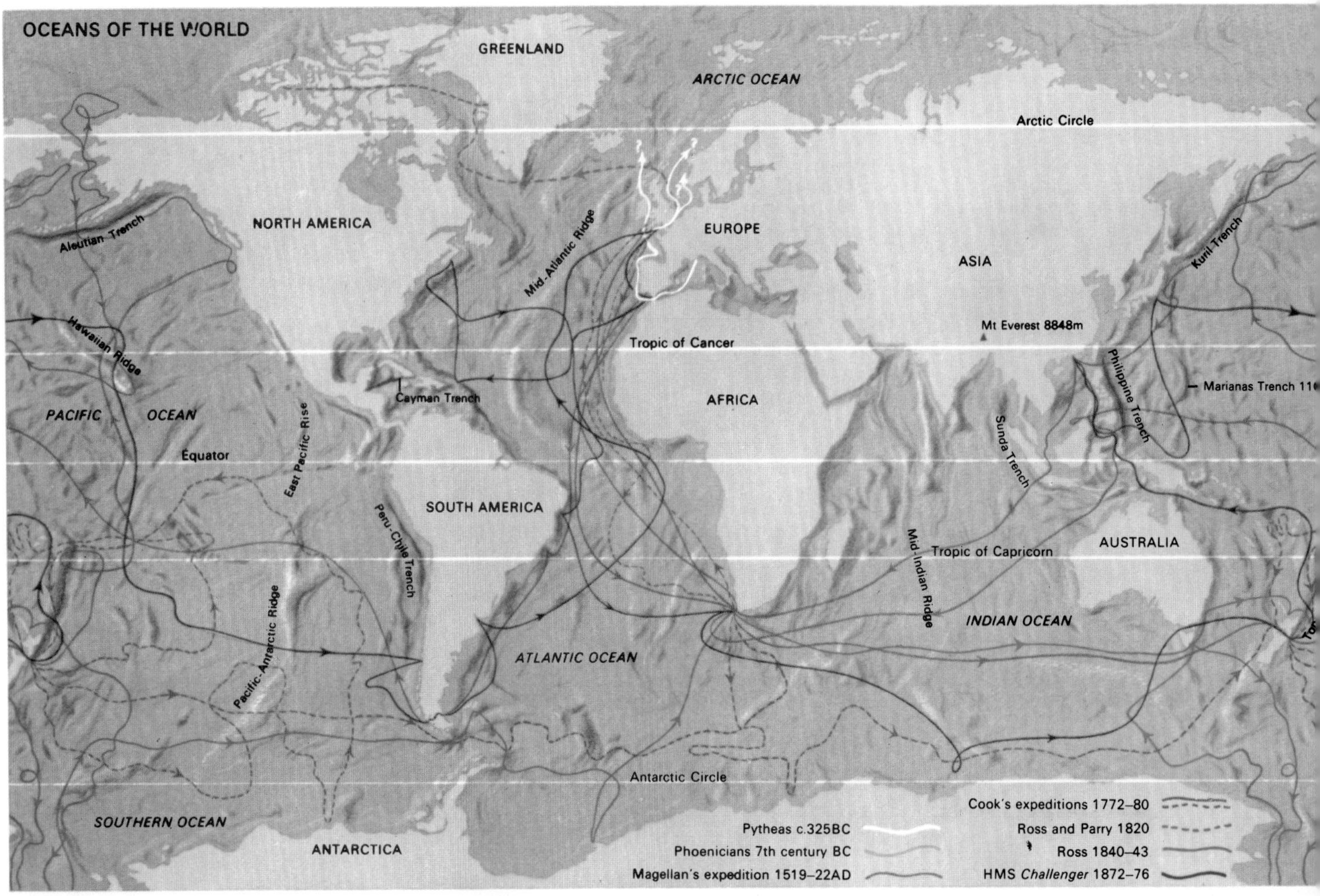

Above: If the world's oceans are drained of water, the varied 'landscape' of the sea-floor is revealed. The deepest trench is 25% further below sea-level than the highest land mountain is above it. The routes of some of the major sea voyages show man's increasing awareness of his watery planet.

Right: This corer is a hollow steel tube that is dropped into the sea-floor sediments. When withdrawn, it retrieves undisturbed samples of clay, ooze, volcanic ash and other bottom deposits.

Below: This probe is used to measure deep-sea temperatures and salinity (saltiness).

Seaphot

National Institute of Oceanography

in the south, and 17,550 km (10,905 miles) at its widest between Panama and Thailand. Altogether, the Pacific covers some 180 million km² (69.5 million sq miles). The other oceans are much smaller: the Atlantic covering 106 million km² (40 million sq miles) and the Indian Ocean 75 million km² (29 million sq miles). By comparison the North Sea covers a mere 600,000 km² (230,000 sq miles).

These figures begin to bring home to us the immensity of the unknown task that the early ocean explorers undertook when they started their endeavour. It also illustrates the uniqueness of planet earth in our solar system, where all the other planets lack water almost completely.

Below the surface

Knowing the extent of the ocean is, however, only half the story. The other major dimension of the oceans is their depth. The environment of deep water is quite alien and mysterious to man, but exploration of it has developed intensively in recent years.

The surface waters of the oceans are illuminated and heated by the sun's rays. They are therefore, at least in lower latitudes, both well-lit and warm. Gradually the sun's rays are absorbed as they penetrate the ocean water, and below about 100 m (330 ft) the water becomes increasingly cold and dark.

Moreover, at the surface the ocean water has only the pressure of the atmosphere above it, and the movement of the atmosphere to stir it. Pressure increases rapidly with depth owing to the weight of the overlying water. Water movement, especially wave motion, is largely reduced below a few tens of

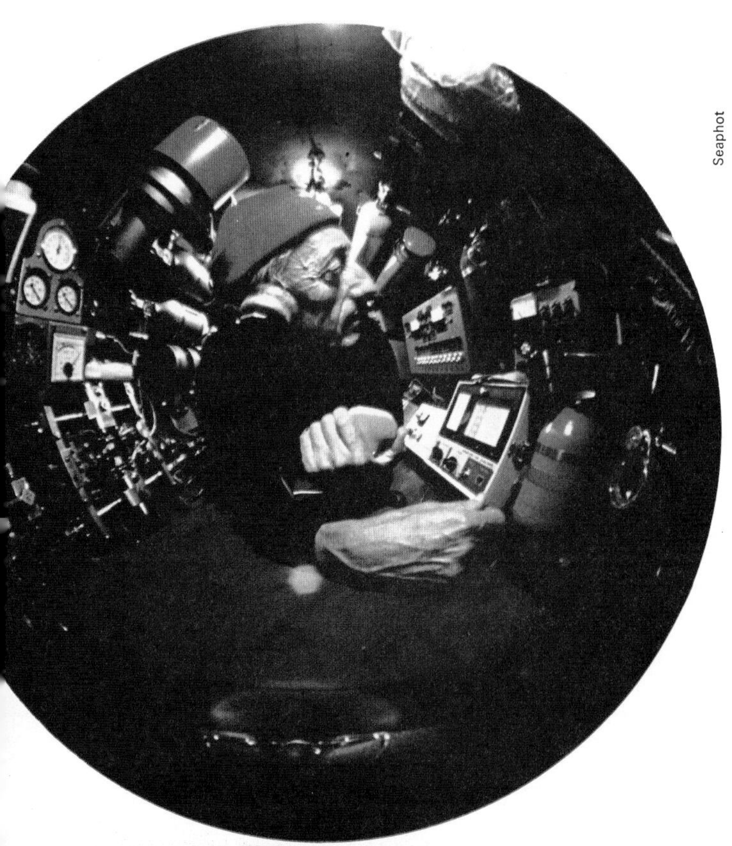

Seaphot

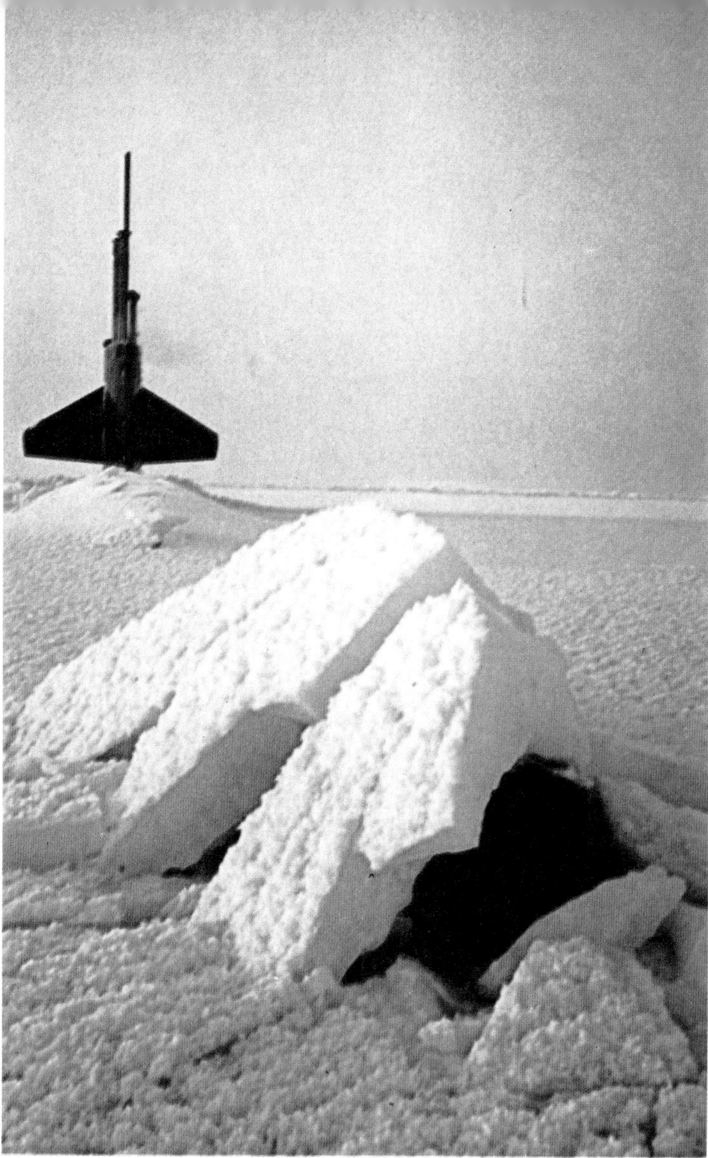

Photri

Above: Jacques-Yves Cousteau in one of his submersible *Sea Fleas*. This Frenchman has perhaps done more than any other living man to excite the public imagination about life under the sea. He also perfected the aqualung, fed with compressed air, which has freed divers to explore the shallower sea depths.

Below: This unmanned, underwater, self-propelled television camera has been nick-named 'Snoopy' by its operators at the US Naval Undersea Center. By sending its pictures back to the surface vessel, Snoopy can be used over wide areas. Linked flash-units are needed at depths which lack natural light.

Right: The American nuclear submarine USS *Whale* surfaces at the North Pole in 1959. In the previous year, its sister submarine USS *Nautilus* made its epic voyage—the first crossing, underwater and under the ice, of the frozen Arctic Ocean by way of the North Pole. A new dimension was added to ocean exploration.

Seaphot

metres from the surface. To live at depth in the oceans, animals must be adapted to the pressure, the cold and the dark. Plants cannot live there at all. Because of their dependence on light energy for photosynthesis they are restricted to the top 100 m (330 ft) of the oceans' waters.

Most of the investigation into conditions in the ocean depths has been carried out remotely—by suspending instruments from lines operated overboard from surface ships. The number of devices available for this kind of exploration is enormous, but they generally fall into a smaller number of categories. There are thermometers, water-bottles and current meters for measuring the physical and chemical characteristics of the water; dredges, corers, heat probes and cameras for studying bottom sediments and bottom life; weighted lines for measuring the depth of the bottom.

Bottom depths were routinely measured by weighted line before the First World War. As small sampling or *coring tubes* were usually attached to the end of every sounding line, this had the incidental advantage that a small sample of the sea-bed was brought back on most occasions. Modern coring devices are very much larger, and heavily weighted. They are allowed to fall freely for the last few metres to the sea-floor by the action of a trigger mechanism and penetrations of up to 30 m (100 ft) can be made into soft sediment in this way. Steel chain-link dredges are used to break off sedimentary and igneous rocks and bring them back to the surface—a crude but effective way of bringing samples back to the surface from 3 to 5 km (2 or 3 miles) down. Cameras in pressure-sealed containers with linked

Below: This chart illustrates the limits encountered as man explores the 'inner space' of the oceans. As greater depths are reached, natural light disappears, temperatures fall and pressure increases enormously. The average depth around the world of the various ocean floor provinces is indicated.

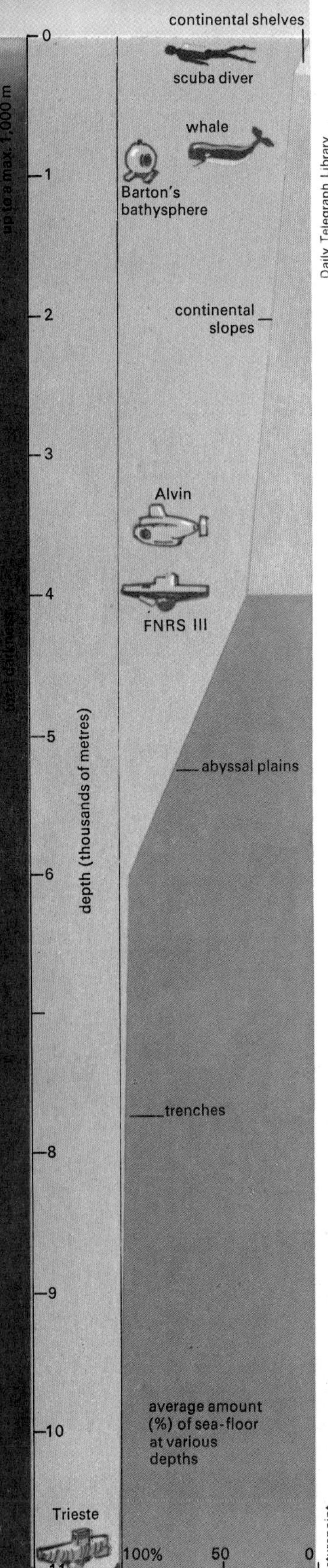

Above: A bell and decompression chamber (left). Decompression presents a hindrance to divers, but is necessary to avoid decompression sickness ('the bends') caused by returning too rapidly to the surface from the ocean depths.

Left: A 'deep sea spacesuit', specially designed to withstand pressures at 300m. The suit is made of magnesium alloy. The diver breathes air at normal atmospheric pressure from a 20-hour supply of oxygen strapped to his back. There are four portholes for the diver to view the undersea world, and tools can be manipulated by lever-controlled fingers which protrude from the bulbous gloves.

Below: One of the most ambitious series of undersea experiments involves a carefully designed habitat in which 'aquanauts' can live for weeks at a time in shallow depths. This US-built *Sealab III* is a non-propelled craft from which divers can undertake salvage and construction work and scientists perform oceanographic and biological studies.

flash-units (there is no natural light in the deep sea) are used to take photographs either continuously or automatically by triggering with a weight suspended below the camera.

The temperature of the deeps is taken by special thermometers, called *reversing thermometers*, which break their mercury thread at the desired depth so that they can be read when returned to the surface. Water samples are often taken at the same time using *reversing water-bottles* such as the Nansen bottle. These are clamped in series on to the hydrographic (water measuring) wire carried on most research ships, lowered to the required depth and then triggered in rapid sequence by sending a mechanical messenger down the wire. Some instruments such as the *bathythermograph* are self-recording and continuously plot temperature (as measured by thermal sensors) against depth (as measured by pressure sensors) during lowering and raising.

Most meters used for measuring the strength and direction of ocean currents are also self-recording. They can be suspended in series at different depths beneath a stationary ship or, alternatively, fixed to a buoy and anchor system for weeks or occasionally months on end.

These routine and often tedious explorations of the oceans may not appear very glamorous, but they have probably contributed the most to our understanding of how the oceans work physically, chemically and biologically. We now have records made in this way that span more than a century of investigation, during which this last frontier of our planet has been well and truly probed.

The inconvenience of having to manipu

Photri

John Hillelson Agency

Left: The *bathysphere* developed by Otis Barton. This iron diving bell, only 145 cm in diameter, was taken down to a depth of over 900 m off the coast of Bermuda by Barton and his fellow American, Dr William Beebe, in 1934. It was to be fifteen years before any other men would beat their record dive.

Above: The deepest descent ever achieved by man was made in this bathyscaphe (Greek for 'deep boat'). In 1960, the *Trieste*, manned by Piccard and Walsh, reached the ocean bed 10,917 m down in the Marianas Trench. The pressure was over one tonne per cm^2 (7.5 tons per sq inch) and the temperature a cold 3°C.

Right: The two-man submersible *Alvin* is built to survive pressure down to about 2,000 m. The *Alvin* has recently explored the Cayman Trough on the Caribbean floor for the Woods Hole Institution, but hit the headlines in 1966 by recovering the nuclear bomb lost by the US Air Force off the coast of Spain.

late instruments in deep water rather like a puppeteer has led many oceanographers to dream of actually venturing into the deep ocean to see conditions at first hand. Contingencies of war or prospect of financial rewards have gradually led to the development of submersibles that can operate in deep water. The problems faced are enormous, and the principal one is pressure. This increases rapidly with depth and any underwater vessel—which must (in order to support human beings) contain air at more or less atmospheric pressure—is liable to collapse or leak under the very great water pressures applied to it.

Over the continental shelves, water depths are only moderate, and in recent years, free-swimming divers using *SCUBA* (Self-Contained Underwater Breathing Apparatus) equipment have been able to dive routinely to 100 m (330 ft). By gradual pressurization and depressurization, and use of unusual combinations of gases for respiration, the extreme depth limit of this system has been trebled. This has been particularly useful in off-shore oil and gas field development, and in the exploration of submerged wrecks and cities, as for instance around the Mediterranean. This approach to diving has proved far more effective and flexible than the use of diving bells or heavy helmeted suits, although it is still not without its considerable dangers.

In these same fairly shallow depths, conventional submarines, with their reinforced cigar-shaped steel hulls and buoyancy-modifying devices (enabling them to dive or surface at will) can operate easily. Most if not all of these vessels are, however, designed for military activities and are not suitable for making underwater explorations. Nevertheless, some of the earliest successful measurements of gravity at sea were made in submarines. Also, in 1958 the first successful crossing of the Arctic Ocean was made underwater —and under the ice—by the United States nuclear submarine *Nautilus*. It actually surfaced between the ice floes near the North Pole itself. In many ways this was the last great geographical voyage of ocean exploration and was a remarkable combination of technological and navigational skill, with a blend of traditional audacity and good fortune.

Voyage to the greatest depths

Descending to very great depths, like rising to very great heights, has always been an especial dream and ambition for some human beings. Sometimes both ambitions have been held by the same man. Professor Auguste Piccard, a Swiss physicist, broke both the existing altitude record in a balloon (in 1931) and then the diving record (in 1953). Like Piccard, most divers attempting to descend deep into the ocean have agreed on the necessity for a spherical container to provide the main pressure vessel, as this shape is strongest under compression. The technical problems which arise thereafter concern the use of strong and flawless materials, the problem of creating portholes in such a vessel so that observations can be made through them, and the balancing of the thickness and thus the strength of the shell against its volume and buoyancy.

Several attempts were made earlier in this century to develop the technology of deep diving. In 1934, the Americans Dr William Beebe and Otis Barton descended 923 m (3,028 ft) in their US-manufactured bathysphere. In August 1953, the French *FNRS 3* reached 2,112 m (6,930 ft) in the Mediterranean, only to have this record broken a month later by Auguste Piccard and his son Jacques, who descended 3,150 m (10,334 ft) to the Mediterranean sea-floor in the Italian-built bathyscaphe *Trieste*. The *FNRS 3* achieved 4,050 m (13,287 ft) in 1954 off the coast of West Africa, but the *Trieste*, purchased by the US Navy and piloted by Jacques Piccard and Lieutenant Donald Walsh, went on to establish an all-time record on January 23, 1960. They descended to 10,917 m (35,820 ft or 6.78 miles) in the Challenger Deep of the Marianas Trench, the deepest part of the deepest trench in the world.

Since that time emphasis has been placed on gaining greater flexibility and potential for observing and collecting from submersibles, rather than achieving record depths. Recent studies on the igneous rocks outcropping on the mid-Atlantic Ridge have been completed using submersibles at depths of around 2,000 m (6,560 ft).

In the Pacific, *Sealab III* has been used to maintain men at a depth of 200 m (650 ft) for a period of two months, making continuous observations of the sea-floor during that time. Scripps Institution of Oceanography in California operates a strange-looking vessel called *Flip* which can be up-ended to provide a very stable working laboratory extending to 100 m (330 ft) below the surface. We may expect continuing development of many other bizarre submersibles directed to economic exploitation or exploration of the sea-floor in the years to come.

The Movement of Oceans

The waters of the oceans are always in motion. As the earth rotates within the gravitational fields of the sun and moon, a pull is exerted by these extra-terrestrial bodies. Their attractive force has little effect on solid objects on the earth, but ocean water, being fluid, is free to move towards both the points of strongest and weakest gravitational pull. The movement of these two bulges around the earth produces the ocean tides, the daily rise and fall of the sea. Because the earth rotates in relation to the moon every 24 hours and 50 minutes, high tides in most places occur every 12 hours 25 minutes or so (known as *semi-diurnal*). Sometimes, however, the *diurnal* (24 hour 50 minutes) frequency is dominant, as in the Gulf of Mexico.

The sun is much further away than the moon, but its greater mass also causes tides, though these are a little less than half the height of lunar tides. Every 28 days, when its gravitational pull directly reinforces that of the moon, the tides are both higher and lower. This is the time of the *spring tides*, when the *tidal range* (the difference in water height at low and high tide) is at its greatest. *Neap tides*, on the other hand, occur when the gravitational pulls of the sun and moon oppose each, producing the lowest tidal range.

Although it is possible to regard the tide as a progressive tidal wave that moves around the world, always keeping opposite the moon as the earth rotates, this is not a truly accurate picture. In reality, each ocean basin or sea acts like an independent container of water with a *natural period of oscillation*, the time it takes a disturbance in the water to travel from one end to the other. A simple analogy is the way that bath water can be made to oscillate, or 'slosh' back and

HOW TIDES ARE FORMED

high tide
water drawn away from moon
earth
low tide
water drawn towards moon
high tide
moon

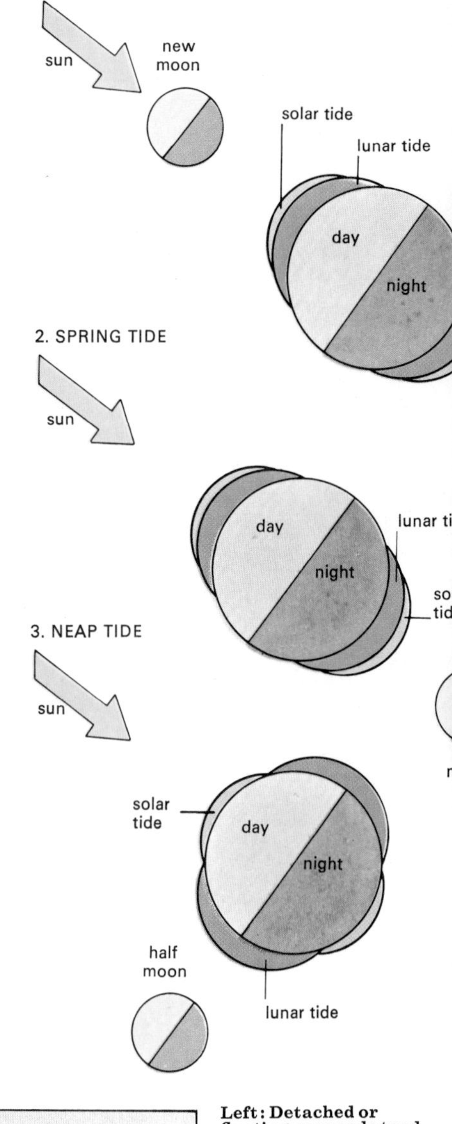

Above: Ocean water is drawn towards the side of the earth directly opposite the moon by the moon's gravitational attraction. It also rises on the diametrically opposite side of the earth because of the greater distance from the moon's pull. Thus as the earth rotates, high and low tides are produced twice a day.

Above right: A similar but weaker effect is produced by the sun. When the sun's and moon's effects act in the same direction (at full and new moon) they reinforce one another to give the higher (and lower) than normal *spring tides*. At *neap tides*, the tidal range is minimized as the lunar and solar tides oppose each other.

Heather Angel

Left: Detached or floating seaweeds tend to be left behind on the beach at the limit reached by the waves at high tide. As each successive high tide in the monthly cycle becomes lower (on going from spring to neap tides), the line of seaweeds marking the previous high tide is preserved, as here at La Roque, Jersey.

Right: When a rising tide is constricted as it floods into the narrowing mouth of an estuary, it may pile up to form a wall of water which is steepened by friction at its base and a strong opposing river current. The wave, known as a *tidal bore*, then passes up-river until it dies out. The bore on the River Severn, shown here, is sometimes 1 m high.

Spectrum

Left: Low tide along the Normandy coast of France shows the rocky islet of Mont-Saint-Michel surrounded by a vast sandy tract. The mount is connected to the mainland by a 1.6 km-long causeway. The incoming tide can travel at dangerous speeds, faster than a running horse.

Keystone

Right: During the early hours of February 1, 1953, the winds and low barometric pressure raised the high tide level 2 to 3 m above its normal height as the water crowded into the southern North Sea. This *storm surge* caused very extensive flooding, damage and loss of life in the Netherlands and eastern England. These houses on low-lying Canvey Island were amongst the casualties.

ZEFA

Barnaby's

Above: The light swells which characterize this wide expanse of ocean were generated by distant winds. However, local winds, under a sky with high cumulus clouds, are affecting the swell waves, causing their crests to be broken or *capped* by 'white horses' of broken water.

Left: A ship crashes through the storm waves in the wind-swept North Sea. Most waves in the open sea are less than 3.5 m high, but may reach 12 to 15 m high. The highest wave so far recorded was 34 m, measured in 1933 by an officer on an American tanker. Even higher, and more destructive, than wind waves are *tsunamis*, the great waves produced by volcanic eruptions or earthquakes.

Arnold Madgwick/National Institute of Oceanography

forth, with a characteristic frequency when disturbed; the amplitude of that oscillation can be increased with an added push in the same direction, or reduced if you work against it. In the same way the water in individual ocean regions or basins reacts differently to the frequency of the gravitational tidal pull, depending on whether or not it coincides with the natural frequency of oscillation or *harmonic* of the region or basin. Both the amplitude of the tidal range and the relative timing of high tide are affected.

Like the Baltic and Mediterranean, some enclosed seas are, because of their harmonics, almost tideless. Other seas connected to the oceans, as the North Sea joins the Atlantic, may have much larger tidal ranges, often of 5 m (16 ft) or more. Exceptionally, as in the well-known case of the Bay of Fundy in eastern Canada, the tidal range exceeds 10 m (33 ft).

Tideless seas are particularly prone to modern pollution problems because of the lack of tidal currents, and the consequent failure of the waves regularly to re-work a wide zone of the beach. Seas and estuaries with strong tides, however, benefit from the scouring and cleansing action of the tides.

Tides may also provide a new source of energy. The first steps have already been taken to harness their power: in a barrage thrown across the Rance estuary in France, turbines driven by the now-controlled tidal flow of water are used to generate electricity. This is a technique which is being seriously considered for application to the Severn estuary in the United Kingdom.

Waves

Most waves are generated by the frictional drag of the winds blowing over the surface of the oceans. Once generated, wind waves can cover a great distance or *fetch* across the ocean. All waves are noted for their destructive power, exerted both on ships at sea, and on coastlines around the world. The most destructive waves, however, are the surface waves known as *tsunamis* (sometimes wrongly called 'tidal' waves), created by submarine earthquakes or volcanic eruptions. These fast-moving (800 km per hour/500 mph) waves are of greater wavelength (often up to 160 km/100 miles) than wind waves, and may cross entire oceans in hours, causing severe damage along the coasts they hit.

The passage of a wind wave or tsunami across the ocean does not normally involve any actual transport of water. As with the serpentine waves that can be generated along a length of rope, the particles of water involved in the passage of a wave only move in a closed ellipse or circle. Lateral movement of water by waves only occurs in coastal zones where the water drags against the sea bottom. In the open sea, particularly when waves have been originally generated some distance away and have become regular in form to produce *swell waves*, the only effect on a ship is a regular vertical movement as it rises and falls with the wave surface.

In the zone of wave generation, however, strong and gusting winds will cause oversteepening and breaking of the wave crests, and trains of waves moving in differing directions may be created. The chaos of vertical and horizontal accelerations and breaking water inherent in *storm waves* can be extremely dangerous to

Right: The individual particles of water involved in the passage of waves move in elliptical orbits, which decrease in size from the surface downwards. In the open ocean, the orbit is circular but near shore, as the bottom comes nearer to the surface, it becomes flattened. Friction with the bottom causes flattening of the orbits and the front of the wave steepens and falls over or *breaks*. At this instant the energy of the rising and falling ocean wave is translated into lateral movement, and it is this which thrusts the water up the beach, erodes cliffs and may be strong enough to knock someone over in the surf.

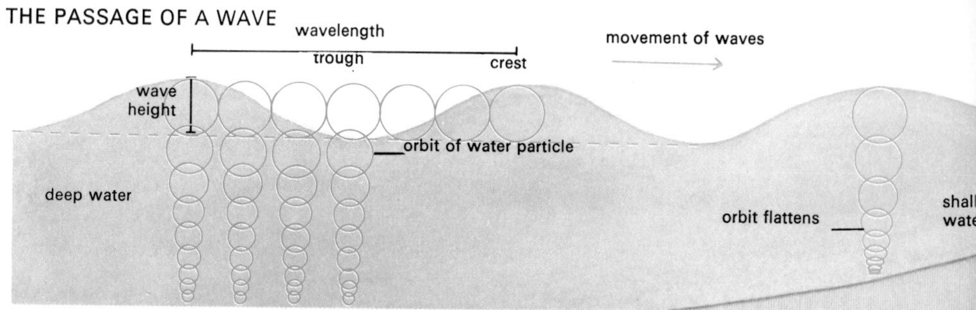

Above: Large spilling breakers on the Pacific coast of Oregon in the United States. A *spilling breaker* is a foaming mass of water that surges forward. In contrast, a *plunging breaker* has a steeper wave front in which an unstable hollow may form just as the crest curls over and plunges forward, often with great violence.

Above right: 'Catching a wave' in California the expert surfer uses the forward movement of a plunging breaker for his exhilarating ride in towards the beach. The energy he is taking advantage of may have been generated by storms hundreds or even thousands of kilometres out in the Pacific Ocean.

ships and boats. Amplitudes can reach 10 or 20 m (33 or 66 ft), with relatively short wave lengths. Lying head-on to the wind is the only expedient in these conditions, so that the largest oncoming waves can be met prow-first.

Another hazard caused by waves results from the piling-up of water on the shore as wave after wave breaks on it and runs up the beach. Much of this water escapes back to the ocean under the next incoming wave as *undertow*. This in itself may be hazardous. But in the higher velocity of the incoming water and the friction of the bottom on the returning underflow of water often means that not all the water can return in that way. Fast-flowing surface currents develop which run out from the shore beyond the zone of breaking waves. These are called *rip* currents and can be a major hazard for sea bathers.

Currents

In addition to the movement of waves and tides, ocean waters also move as currents. In the open sea, *surface currents* are everywhere under the influence of the wind and the earth's rotation. The trade-wind and westerly-wind belts in particular, with their consistent year-round winds, drive the surface waters of the ocean along with them.

This drive provides the initial impetus to a clockwise movement of waters in the northern hemisphere and a counter-clockwise movement in the southern hemisphere. This movement is reinforced by the earth's rotation which causes any water not moving parallel to the equator to turn towards the right in the northern hemisphere, and to the left in the southern. The *Coriolis force* which causes this results from the more rapid rotation of the earth's surface near the equator compared with the poles.

Other types of current also affect the general circulation of the ocean waters. *Tidal currents* are produced from the inevitable lateral movements of water required to compensate for the vertical, up-and-down movement of the water surface during the tidal cycle. *Density currents* of several kinds are formed when denser ocean water flows under less dense ocean water, and gravitates towards the deeper parts of the oceans. *Cold* dense water, which is produced in particular around the Antarctic continent (where the mean annual temperature of the surface water is only 1°C/30°F), flows down to the ocean floor and towards the equator (where mean annual water temperature is 27°C/80°F) to cover much of the floors of the Pacific, Atlantic and Indian Oceans.

The *salinity*, or amount of salt in the water, also affects the density of seawater. Average salinity varies between 33 and 37 parts of salt per thousand parts of water, and this variation also produces density currents. Dense saline water, produced in enclosed seas such as the Mediterranean Sea by high evaporation

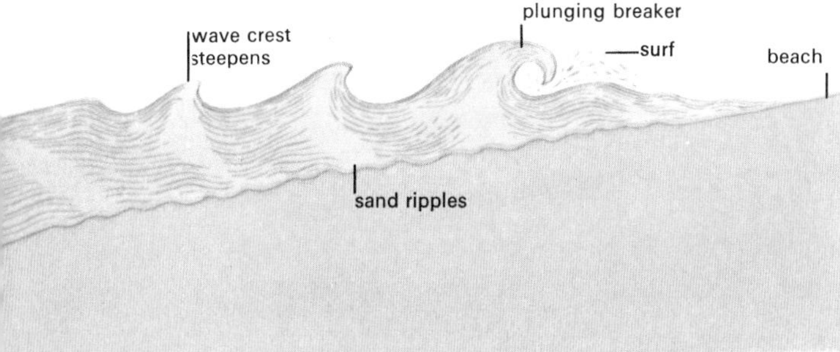

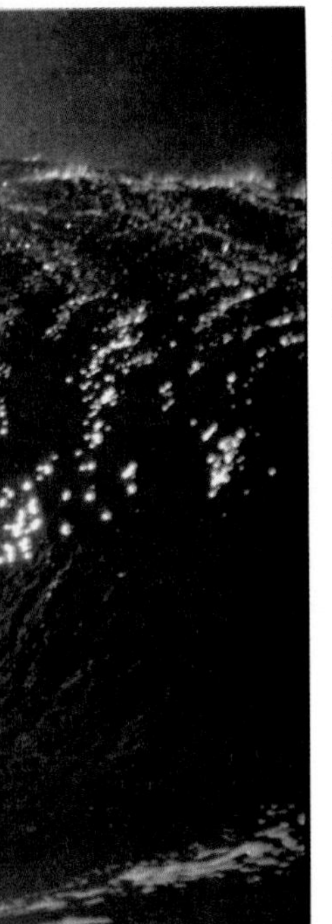

Below and right: The great circulations of ocean waters, the currents, have a considerable influence on climate. Here the climate and vegetation of eastern Canada and south-west Devon are shown in sharp contrast although both places are on about the same latitude. The cold Labrador Current passes close to the shore of Newfoundland, where Terra Nova National Park supports a cold, barren coniferous forest. Yet a lush vegetation of trees, shrubs, flowers and semi-tropical plants is found in the Shapiter Gardens, Salcombe, Devon, where the climate is favoured by the warm waters of the Gulf Stream brought by the North Atlantic Drift.

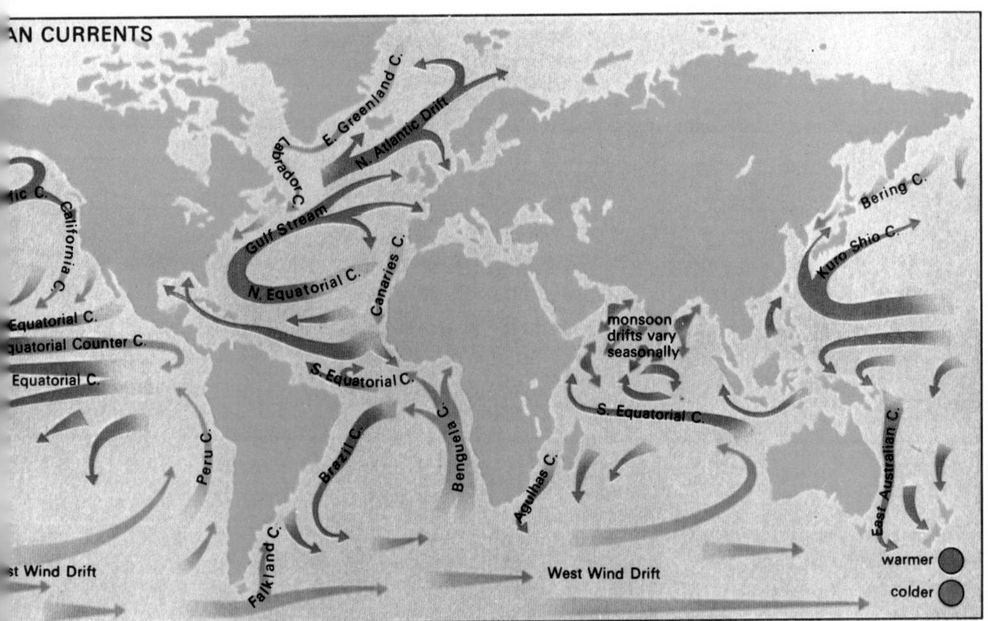

Above: The surface ocean currents swirl clockwise in the N. Hemisphere, anti-clockwise in the South.

Left: Dead anchovies on the beach at Chimbote, Peru. Colder currents often support highly productive fisheries, but a shift in the nutrient-rich waters can have disastrous results, as these dead fish show.

Right: This diagram of the N-S Atlantic Ocean circulation of water shows how the cold dense water from the Antarctic displaces other waters from the ocean bottom.

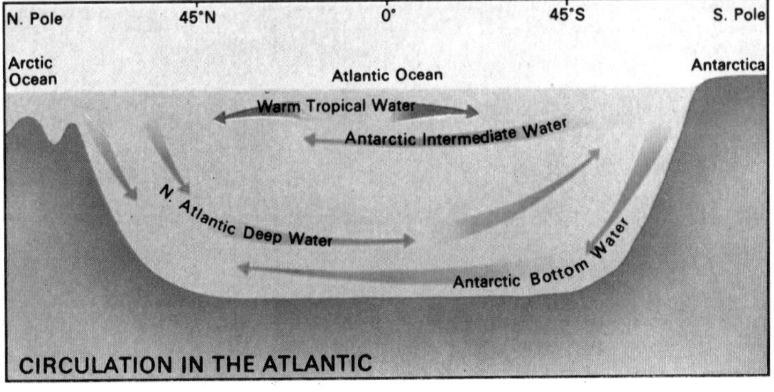

rates, flows out and under adjacent less dense waters, in this case the Atlantic. Dense *turbid* water, on the other hand, is injected by large rivers in flood, or created by slumping of unstable muds and silts on the continental slope. This water will flow out across the ocean floor to form the deposits of continental rises and abyssal plains as the current is slowed.

Surface currents have always been much exploited by mariners. Across the Atlantic, for example, a course set within the *North Atlantic Drift* en route to Europe gives the benefit of all its intrinsic eastward velocity. This same North Atlantic Drift transports warm water from the *Gulf Stream*, issuing from the Gulf of Mexico, to the relatively high latitude shores of north-western Europe, and is responsible for the comparatively mild and equable climates enjoyed there.

In the trade-wind belts on the eastern sides of the oceans, where the surface currents flowing towards the equator are pushed seawards by the offshore-blowing winds, deep nutrient-rich water wells up to replace the surface water. This gives rise, in the Peru Current off South America, for example, to some of the richest ocean fishing in the world. In contrast, the central ocean *gyres* (the relatively quiet centres of the circulating surface current systems) are deprived of nutrients, which sink through the water to deeper levels and are not replaced. Here, therefore, fertility and fishing are poor.

The year to year and decade to decade fluctuations of the major ocean current systems are of major importance to man. Not only do they strongly influence variations in the climate of the adjacent continents, but they also lead to considerable variations in fish yields. Observation of the behaviour of these currents, their annual mass transport of heat, and fluctuations in their speed, temperature and salinity are therefore most important in commercial and economic terms.

Bottom currents are important in a biological sense. In returning surface water to the ocean floor they simultaneously displace nutrient-rich bottom waters back to the surface to continue the cycle of ocean fertility. They also introduce oxygen to the deep-sea floor, enabling numerous animals to live there, even at the greatest depths. And they are responsible, more than was suspected until recent years, for the transport of fine-grained sediments even in the deepest water. Movement is a byword in the oceans; they are never still.

Ardea, London

Chapter 4
Weather and Climate

The formation of glaciers depends on low temperatures, heavy snowfalls and mountain slopes gradual enough to permit the accumulation of snow fields. Layer upon layer of snow becomes compacted into glacier ice.

The Atmosphere

Seen from outer space, the earth's atmosphere appears no more than a thin skin of air, which is prevented from escaping into space by the force of the planet's gravity. Nevertheless, the atmosphere is vital to our natural environment. It not only provides the air essential for life on earth, it also protects that life from the harmful effects of the sun's rays and from bombardment by meteors and other bodies travelling through space.

The atmosphere, moreover, is the source of our weather. In fact, *weather* is defined as the conditions of the atmosphere in terms of wind, rain, temperature, and so forth at a particular time. *Meteorology*, the scientific study of weather, is concerned primarily with the changes taking place in the atmosphere.

The atmosphere

The atmosphere is a mixture of gases. Over the last 300 years, scientists have discovered over ten constituent gases, some of them permanent and occurring in large quantities, others transient and miniscule in amount. By volume, nearly 80 per cent of the atmosphere is nitrogen, just over 20 per cent oxygen and nearly one per cent carbon dioxide. Inert (chemically inactive) gases such as argon, helium and neon are also found in very small quantities.

Among the principal variable gases are sulphur dioxide, ammonia, carbon monoxide and ozone (a gas related to oxygen). Some of these constituents are significant air impurities or *pollutants*, having harmful effects even when present in very low concentrations. Notable amounts of solid particles, such as smoke, salt, dust and volcanic ash, may also be found locally in the atmosphere and may substantially decrease the amount of sunshine received. For example, as a result of smoke controls imposed in Britain by several Clean Air Acts, there has been a 50 per cent increase in the amount of winter sunshine in Central London.

The most vital variable constituent, however, is water vapour. It occurs in very small amounts—varying from one to four per cent—but nowhere in the world, even above the hottest desert, is the lower atmosphere completely dry. Variations in the amount of water vapour affect the behaviour of the atmosphere and therefore influence our weather.

This mixture of gases is compressible, and the weight of overlying air results in the density of air being greater nearer the ground than at high levels. Air pressure thus falls with an increase in altitude, but at a variable rate—falling far more rapidly near the ground than at higher levels. As a result, roughly 80 per cent of atmospheric gases and nearly all of its water vapour lie below a height of 12 km (7.5 miles).

Like density and pressure, temperature also varies with height. Until the late nineteenth century, temperature was believed to fall steadily with increasing altitude to 'the top of the atmosphere'. However, findings from manned and unmanned balloon flights and, more recently, from rocket probes have revealed four well-defined thermal (heat) layers in

NASA

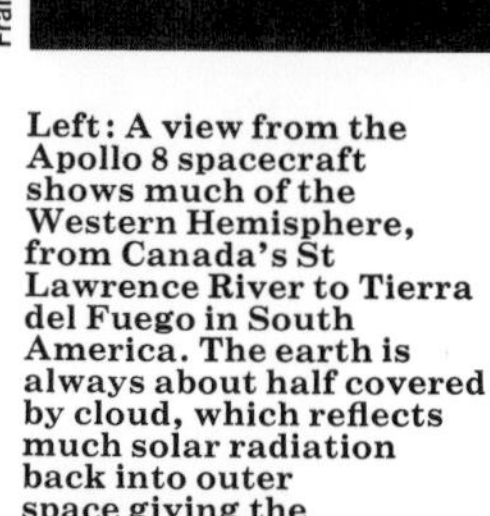

Frank Lane

Left: A view from the Apollo 8 spacecraft shows much of the Western Hemisphere, from Canada's St Lawrence River to Tierra del Fuego in South America. The earth is always about half covered by cloud, which reflects much solar radiation back into outer space giving the earth its 'brightness'.

Above: A meteor, or 'shooting star', photographed just before burning up 40 km above earth. Large bodies of matter frequently enter the atmosphere from space. They heat up because of friction in the air and eventually burn out. The head of this meteor was 10 km in diameter and its tail was over 3 km wide.

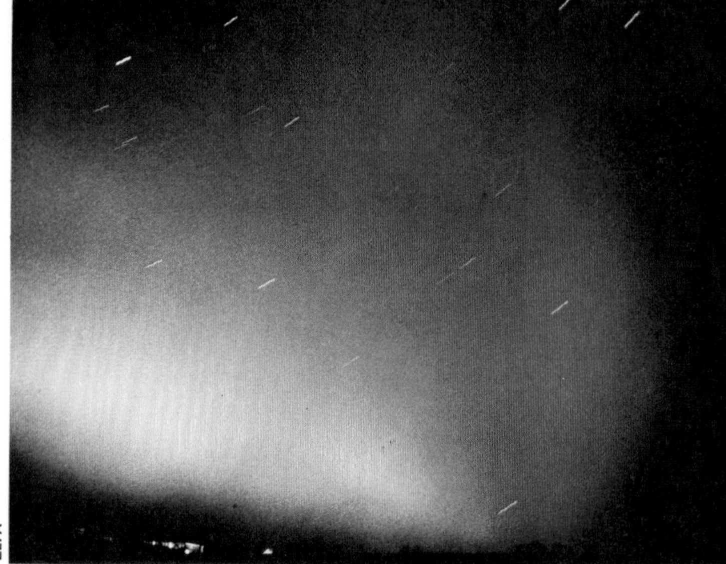

ZEFA

Right and below: The earth's atmosphere is very shallow compared to the diameter of the planet, and the colours within it are due to the scattering of light by gases and pollution. Manned spaceflights have brought back spectacular pictures of the atmosphere viewed 'from the side' (below), while *auroras* (right) can be seen from the earth's surface. They occur in many shapes and colours, being due primarily to irregular bursts of radiation from the upper atmosphere, usually between 80 and 100 kms up at high latitudes. In the northern hemisphere the phenomenon is known as the *aurora borealis* or 'northern lights'; in the southern hemisphere as *aurora australis*. They are thought to be due to the influence of the earth's magnetism on particles received from the sun during sun-spot activity.

Photri

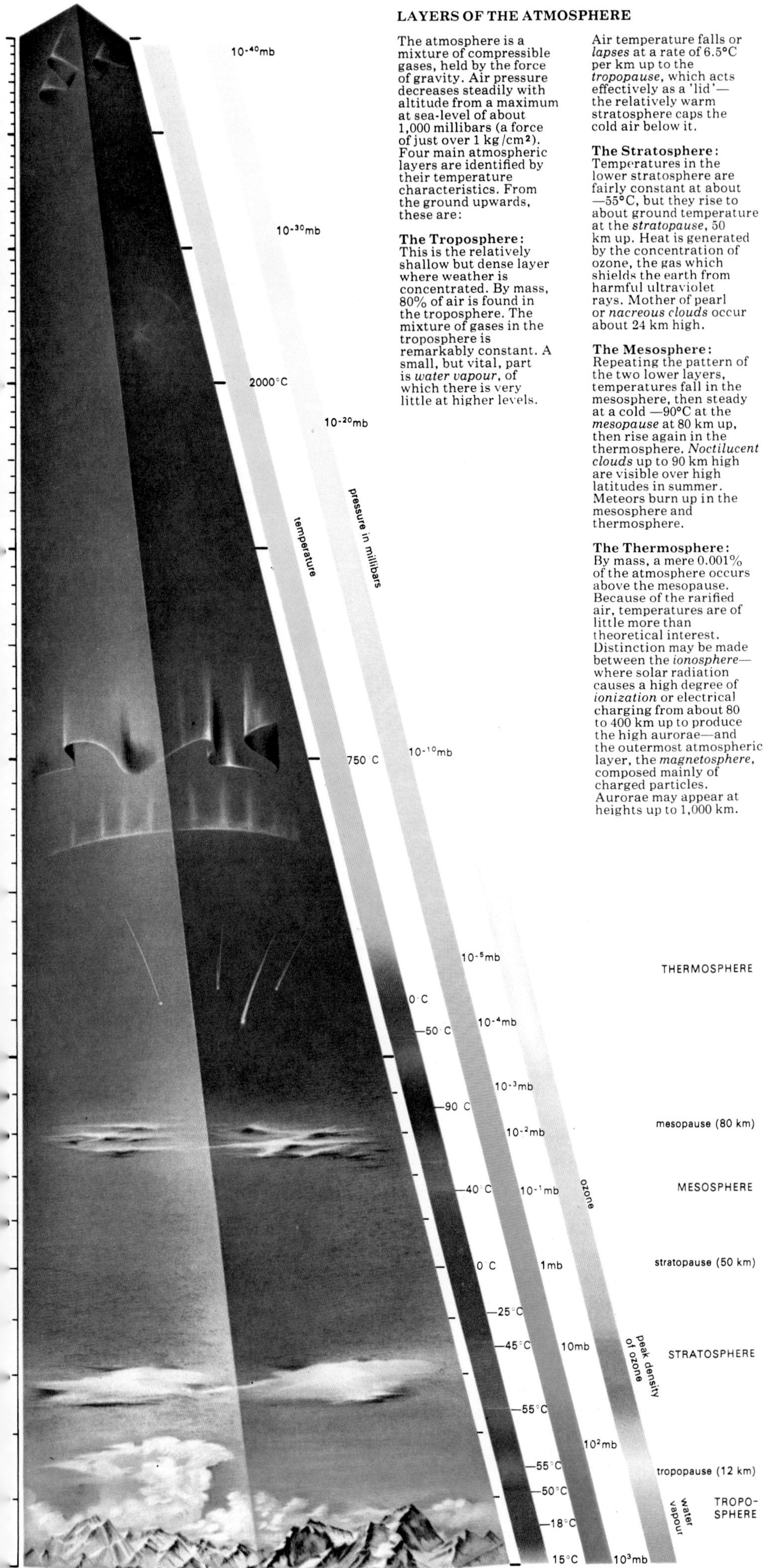

LAYERS OF THE ATMOSPHERE

The atmosphere is a mixture of compressible gases, held by the force of gravity. Air pressure decreases steadily with altitude from a maximum at sea-level of about 1,000 millibars (a force of just over 1 kg/cm²). Four main atmospheric layers are identified by their temperature characteristics. From the ground upwards, these are:

The Troposphere: This is the relatively shallow but dense layer where weather is concentrated. By mass, 80% of air is found in the troposphere. The mixture of gases in the troposphere is remarkably constant. A small, but vital, part is *water vapour*, of which there is very little at higher levels. Air temperature falls or *lapses* at a rate of 6.5°C per km up to the *tropopause*, which acts effectively as a 'lid'—the relatively warm stratosphere caps the cold air below it.

The Stratosphere: Temperatures in the lower stratosphere are fairly constant at about —55°C, but they rise to about ground temperature at the *stratopause*, 50 km up. Heat is generated by the concentration of ozone, the gas which shields the earth from harmful ultraviolet rays. Mother of pearl or *nacreous clouds* occur about 24 km high.

The Mesosphere: Repeating the pattern of the two lower layers, temperatures fall in the mesosphere, then steady at a cold —90°C at the *mesopause* at 80 km up, then rise again in the thermosphere. *Noctilucent clouds* up to 90 km high are visible over high latitudes in summer. Meteors burn up in the mesosphere and thermosphere.

The Thermosphere: By mass, a mere 0.001% of the atmosphere occurs above the mesopause. Because of the rarified air, temperatures are of little more than theoretical interest. Distinction may be made between the *ionosphere*—where solar radiation causes a high degree of *ionization* or electrical charging from about 80 to 400 km up to produce the high aurorae—and the outermost atmospheric layer, the *magnetosphere*, composed mainly of charged particles. Aurorae may appear at heights up to 1,000 km.

the atmosphere. These layers are known as the troposphere, stratosphere, mesosphere and thermosphere.

In the lowest layer, the *troposphere*, the average rate of temperature decrease, known as the *lapse rate*, is about 0.6°C for every 100 m ascent (1°F per 300 ft) over the average depth of 12 km of the troposphere. As this is the same height below which most of the atmosphere is found, this is where all our weather occurs.

An abrupt change in the lapse rate is marked by the *tropopause*, the boundary between the troposphere and the thermal layer above it, the *stratosphere*. Here the temperature is nearly constant in its lowest 10 km (6.2 miles) and then, instead of falling, temperatures actually rise until the *stratopause* is reached at about 59 km (31 miles) high. The pattern of steadily falling, then constant, then rising temperatures is repeated in the highest layers, the *mesosphere* and the *thermosphere*, which are separated by the *mesopause* at a height of about 80 km (50 miles). The thermosphere decreases in density until the atmosphere ceases to exist.

Solar radiation

The constant turmoil of the earth's thin gaseous envelope gives us our wind weather. But the atmosphere moves only because of a perpetual fuel supply—the sun. Energy is received from the sun in the form of electro-magnetic waves, and is commonly known as *solar radiation*. These waves transfer energy which becomes available to sustain the planet when intercepted by the earth. Yet, unless protected from the full power of the sun's rays, the earth would be a highly inhospitable place. Much of the solar radiation is in fact prevented from reaching the earth's surface by a series of natural 'filters'.

The amount of solar radiation received at the outer limit of the atmosphere is called the *solar constant*, for it varies only rarely if at all. But the average intensity of radiation reaching the earth's surface does vary, both with the time of day and the day of the year—largely as a result of the varying inclination of the earth's axis during its orbit of the sun—and with latitude. In polar regions (the high latitudes), the sun's rays strike the earth at a lower angle than at the equator (low latitude) because of the earth's curvature. They therefore pass through a greater thickness of atmosphere and are distributed over a wider surface area.

If there were no atmosphere, equatorial areas would receive an annual average of 35 megajoules (units of energy) per square metre per day (written as 35 MJ/m²/day), with little variability throughout the year. But the atmosphere lets through less than half of the solar radiation initially received. Actual equatorial values range from 20 to 24 MJ/m²/day throughout the year, whereas polar values range from zero to 18 MJ/m²/day.

These figures reveal how the differences in path-length through the air at different latitudes and seasons affect the amount of solar radiation filtered by the atmosphere. In absorption, air molecules actually take up part of the radiant energy and convert it into internal energy. This energy increase is felt as a temperature change.

The sun has a surface temperature of over 5,700°C (10,000°F). The wavelength of radiation emitted by a hot body depends on its temperature. The wavelengths of solar radiation vary, but most are short. Harmful ultraviolet radiation (of short wavelength) is strongly absorbed by the ozone in the stratosphere, producing the maximum temperature at a height of 50 km (31 miles). Solar radiation of longer wavelengths is absorbed only weakly or not at all by the atmosphere. Most of the lower stratosphere and the troposphere is transparent to solar radiation.

As well as being absorbed, solar radiation is scattered in all directions as it passes through the atmosphere. The result is to send half of the radiation hitting the air molecules back to space. The sky is generally its familiar blue colour because very small particles scatter a larger proportion of blue and violet light waves than the longer-wave yellow and red light. Larger particles, such as those found in haze, scatter all wavelengths more equally, giving us a whiter sky, particularly near the horizon.

Radiation is also subject to reflection from clouds and the earth's surface. The fraction reflected is called the *albedo* and it varies with the nature of the reflecting surface. White clouds and fresh snow, for example, may reflect back as much as 80 to 90 per cent of the sun's rays, while trees and wet earth may reflect as little as ten per cent. For the earth and atmosphere as a whole, the so-called *planetary albedo* is about 35 per cent.

The remnants of solar radiation that do reach the earth's surface are absorbed and converted into ground temperatures. If the surface is dry soil or rock, then the temperature increase is large; on the other hand, if the surface is water, the radiation can penetrate and be absorbed through a depth of several metres, so that the same amount of heat is spread through a larger mass, resulting in a much smaller temperature increase. Some of the heat is also used to evaporate water. This is known as *latent heat* and it is released to the atmosphere during condensation.

Once heated by radiation, the earth's surface in turn heats the air above it. Air, like all other substances, may be heated in three ways: by *conduction* (direct contact), *convection* (up and down movement of air) and *radiation* (absorption of heat-waves). Air itself is a poor conductor of heat. If conduction alone provided transfer of heat upwards from the earth's surface, the air would be very hot along the ground on a summer's day and quite cool a few metres up. Within the air, heat conduction is insignificant compared with convection, which accomplishes transfer of heat through movement of air itself.

As the average surface temperature of the earth is about 15 °C, most of the energy radiated out by the earth is of longer wavelength than the sun's and is readily absorbed by water vapour and carbon dioxide. Consequently, the air layers near the ground absorb a large part of terrestrial radiation. It is this heating from below that creates the warmth of the lower atmosphere and the decrease of temperature in the troposphere.

Heat balances

Just as the earth radiates heat, so does the atmosphere. With an average temperature of —18 °C, its radiation is also in longer wavelengths than the sun's. However, atmospheric radiation passes both upwards to space and downwards to the

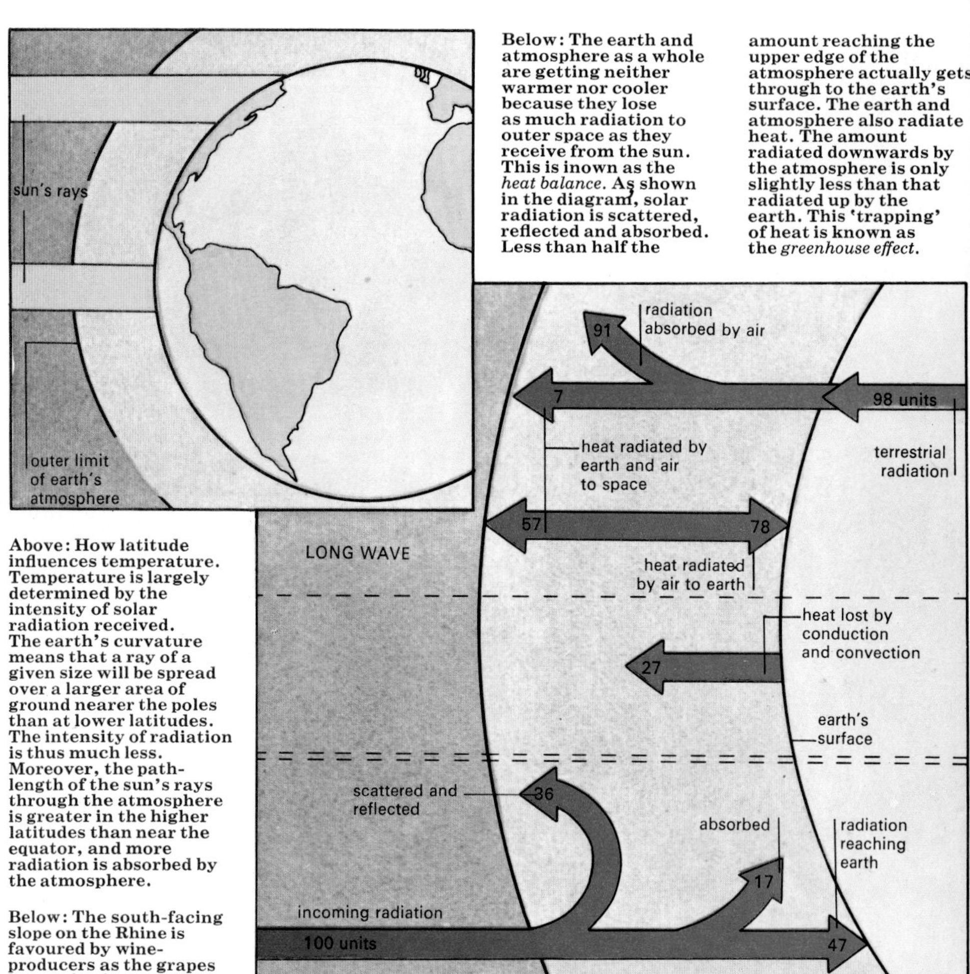

Below: The earth and atmosphere as a whole are getting neither warmer nor cooler because they lose as much radiation to outer space as they receive from the sun. This is inown as the *heat balance*. As shown in the diagram, solar radiation is scattered, reflected and absorbed. Less than half the amount reaching the upper edge of the atmosphere actually gets through to the earth's surface. The earth and atmosphere also radiate heat. The amount radiated downwards by the atmosphere is only slightly less than that radiated up by the earth. This 'trapping' of heat is known as the *greenhouse effect*.

Above: How latitude influences temperature. Temperature is largely determined by the intensity of solar radiation received. The earth's curvature means that a ray of a given size will be spread over a larger area of ground nearer the poles than at lower latitudes. The intensity of radiation is thus much less. Moreover, the path-length of the sun's rays through the atmosphere is greater in the higher latitudes than near the equator, and more radiation is absorbed by the atmosphere.

Below: The south-facing slope on the Rhine is favoured by wine-producers as the grapes here enjoy intenser radiation than those on the opposite bank.

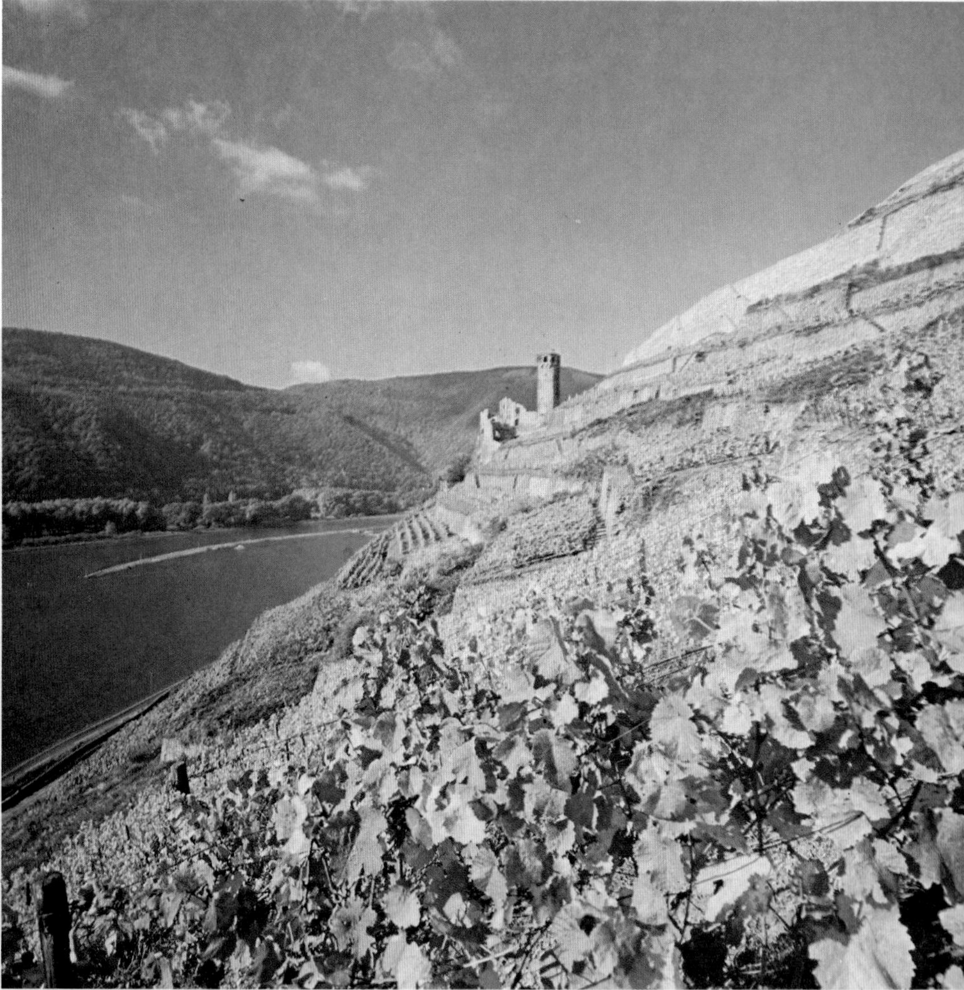

Robert Estall

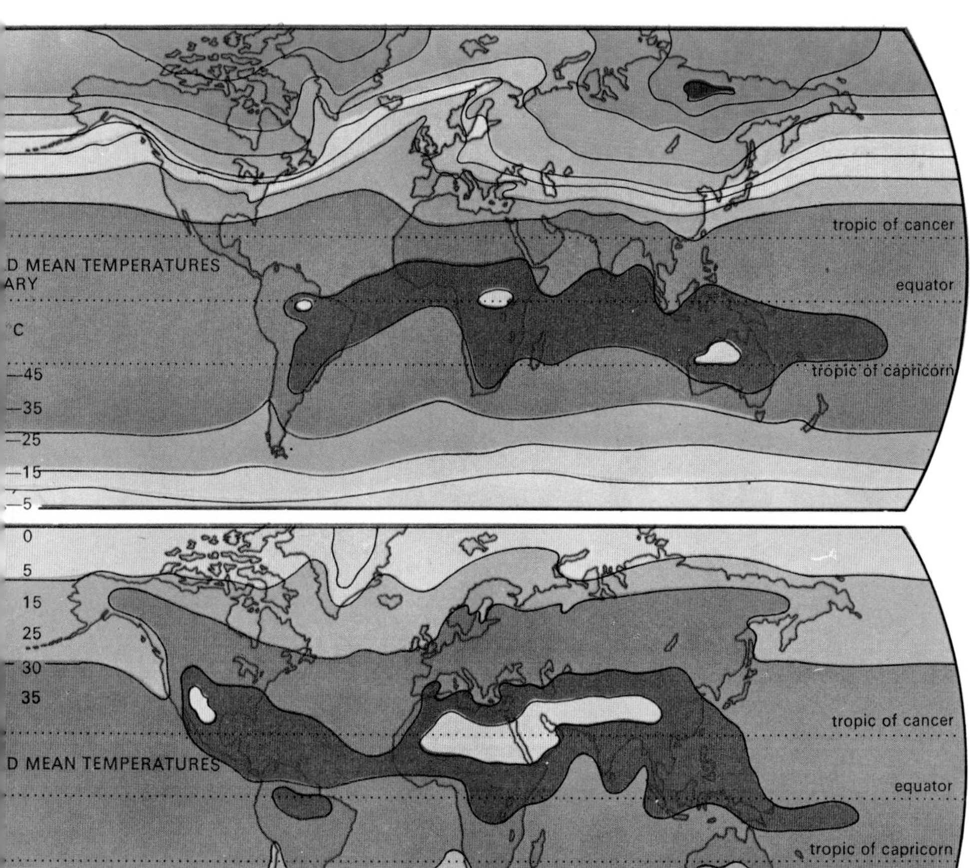

Left and below left: World distribution of surface air temperatures in January and July. Temperatures are shown by *isotherms*, lines drawn through places sharing the same mean sea-level temperature. Their distribution reveals the close relationship between latitude and temperature, which falls gradually from equatorial to polar regions. There is a marked latitudinal shift of isotherms between January and July due to seasonal changes in the sun's relative position. Isotherms are also affected by prevailing winds, ocean currents, and distribution of land and sea. The hottest and coldest places are both on land.

Emil Schulthess/Transworld

Above: The cold Siberian winter is illustrated by the fantastic ice formations on this house in Yakutsk. Some 600 km to the north of Yakutsk is Verkhoyansk, known as the 'Siberian cold pole'. The greatest annual temperature range ever recorded—from —50.6°C in January to 13.3°C in July— was observed here.

Kessell/Time/Life

Left: These Russian children in a nursery group at Bratsk in Siberia are enjoying the warm summer weather. June temperatures here average 15°C. In winter, however, temperatures plunge well below freezing point and thus limit the length of the growing season and the types of plants found.

Below: The hottest place on earth. The highest annual average temperature—34.4°C—was recorded at Dalul in the Danakil desert in Ethiopia. The town lies in a basin 116 m below sea level, but water does not collect. It evaporates in the intense, unrelenting heat, leaving salt formations in the basin.

summer winter
−70°C −60°C −50°C −40°C −30°C −20°C −10°C 0°C 10°C 20°C 30°C
60° 45° 30° 0 30° 45° 60°
degrees latitude

Left: This diagram shows the distribution of average upper-air temperatures when it is summer in the Northern Hemisphere. (The effects of oceans and continents have been eliminated). The highest mean temperatures are found at low latitudes near the equator, as this is where net radiation is greatest. There is a gradual temperature gradient between equatorial and polar areas, where temperatures are much lower. Mean temperatures also fall with height in the tropopause, which varies in height from 15 to 20 km over the equator to about 10 km over the poles. Higher up in the stratosphere, temperatures are not as variable as those in the troposphere.

Georg Gerster/John Hillelson Agency

Left: Klukhorsky Pass in the Caucasus range (USSR). Changes in vegetation illustrate the general rule that temperature decreases with height. The rate of decrease or *lapse rate* is on average 6°C per 1,000 m, although this varies. The peak shown here, near the Turkish border, is over 3,600 m above sea level.

Above: A mirage photographed in the western Sahara. In very hot areas the air may shimmer because of intense convection near the ground. *Mirages* are optical illusions created by light waves bending in the layer of convection. What looks like water is usually an image of part of the sky.

Below: The plume of smoke from this factory chimney at Larne Lough, Northern Ireland, is prevented from rising by *temperature inversion*, an increase of air temperature with height in contrast to the normal decrease. This phenomenon occurs mostly at night, when the ground cools the air immediately above it.

earth's surface. But because the amount of radiation from a body depends on its temperature, more radiation goes upwards to space from the earth and the lower, warmer layers of the atmosphere than is returned to the surface from the atmosphere, which on average is cooler.

The net effect of these vertical transfers is that heat is lost to space from the earth-atmosphere system. If the amount of heat lost to space did not equal the amount of heat entering the system as short-wave solar radiation, there would be a cumulative imbalance—resulting in the planet becoming either warmer or cooler. We now know from many years of records that the temperature of the earth and atmosphere is effectively constant. This equality of input and output is known as the *heat balance*.

Another heat balance exists which prevents the tropics from becoming intolerably hot and the polar areas intolerably cold. Between 38° N and S and the equator, more solar radiation is received than terrestrial radiation is lost. The opposite is true polewards of 38°. The balance is restored by the movement of air and latent heat (in water vapour) so that heat is transferred polewards and upwards in the atmosphere before being radiated back to space. This transfer of heat is the basic driving force of both the atmosphere and the ocean movements.

Temperature

If latitude were the only factor controlling the amount of radiation received, we would expect a world temperature map to show the lines of equal temperature, the *isotherms*, as lying parallel to each other, in the same way as parallels of latitude. But this does not happen.

Such an orderly arrangement is broken up by the irregular distribution of land and sea. The seas both heat up and cool down much more slowly than the land. As a result, sea air remains generally mild throughout the year, and it moderates the climate of any land areas over which it is blown. In contrast, continental air is hot in summer, and cold in winter. For example, under the influence of the North Atlantic Drift, Glasgow has an average temperature of 3°C in January and 15°C in July. Although Moscow lies at the same latitude—56°N—the city has a continental type of climate. January there is a cold 9°C below freezing, whereas July temperatures average 18°C.

Closely related factors include altitude and exposure or *aspect*. On a local scale, poleward-facing slopes—those facing north in the northern hemisphere, and south in the southern hemisphere—generally receive less radiation than slopes facing towards the equator, and temperatures are normally lower.

The highest surface temperatures on earth occur in the sub-tropic deserts well away from cooling oceanic influences. Here the skies are clear (resulting in a long duration of radiation input), the sand is dry (thus radiation is used to heat sand rather than evaporate water), and the angle of the sun is high (giving high intensity of radiation). All these factors frequently combine to produce temperatures of over 30°C. The record high temperature is probably 59.4°C observed at Insala in Algeria in 1973.

The lowest surface temperatures are found in Antarctica, where high latitudes, high albedo and continentality are complemented by high altitude. The lowest ever recorded at the earth's surface was in 1960 at Vostok, Antarctica, where a reading of —87°C was taken. Within these two extremes, variations according to the season and time of day interact with surface conditions to produce a wealth of different temperatures throughout the world.

Air Pressure and Winds

The air in the lower part of the earth's atmosphere is in perpetual motion. A wind is simply the movement of air over the surface of the earth which results from a difference in air pressure between two points. In building up an understanding of how winds work, scientists have progressed from simple models of air moving in ideal conditions to a realistic picture of the processes actually operating in the atmosphere.

Winds vary significantly in strength and direction and with height. They may be as short-lived as a gust, or as persistent as the dominant wind patterns which generate the movement of ocean currents. Their importance to meteorology lies in the fact that winds are the prime regulators of weather and climate. They are essential in maintaining the balance of temperature in the atmosphere, carrying heat from the equator to the poles. Moreover, they bear water vapour from the seas to the land, thus controlling the world distribution of rainfall.

Air pressure

The air enveloping the earth constantly exerts a downward force on the surface. Man is rarely conscious of this weight, as it presses on him from all directions and his body is fully adjusted to it. Air pressure is measured by a barometer, usually in millibars (mb)—for example, 1,000 mb is the pressure exerted by a column of air which supports a column of mercury at a height of 750 mm (29.5 in). At sea level—where the whole weight of the overlying atmosphere is felt—pressure reaches an average of 1013.2 mb, enough to register 760 mm (29.9 in) on a barometer.

Air pressure decreases with height in just the same way as air density. For example, at a height of about 5.5 km (3.5 miles) above ground, pressure is only about 500 mb, half that at the surface. This change in pressure from one point to another is known as a *pressure gradient.* Although the vertical pressure gradient is dramatically steep, air is prevented from escaping from the high pressure at ground level towards outer space by the force of gravity. The equilibrium of these two forces is known as *hydrostatic balance.*

It is the horizontal pressure gradients, the differences in pressure between two places at the same level, which give rise to winds. Here the great variations in temperature at the earth's surface play a vital part. Heated air expands, becomes lighter and rises, while cool air becomes relatively denser and sinks. Since the earth's surface is heated unevenly by the sun, winds are created by air moving from cool, high pressure areas to warm, low pressure areas.

If no other forces came into play, the winds would soon iron out all the horizontal pressure gradients and the atmosphere would come to rest. However, winds themselves also help to maintain pressure gradients. They can blow air of different densities over an area, contributing to pressure change there. More importantly, the variations in speed of a wind result in air being 'piled up' in some areas, thus helping to create a new pressure gradient.

Set into motion by a pressure gradient, air would normally rush in a direct line from areas of high to areas of low pressure. However, as the air flows over the earth's surface, it is constantly deflected from its original path by the pull of the earth's rotation beneath it. In the Northern Hemisphere air is deflected to the right, and in the Southern Hemisphere to the left. The deflecting force caused by the earth's rotation is known as the *geostrophic* or *Coriolis force.* The Coriolis force varies with latitude, from a negligible pull near the equator to a maximum at the poles.

In time, the two forces acting in opposite directions on the moving air—the pressure gradient and Coriolis force—achieve a balance, known as *geostrophic equilibrium.* The air is then deflected at right angles to its original down-gradient flow and the winds are termed *geostrophic winds.* Now, instead of flowing down the pressure gradients from high to low pressure, the deflected air moves along the gradients, parallel to the *isobars,* the lines on a pressure map joining points of equal pressure.

Left: The distribution of pressures and winds on an idealized rotating earth of uniform surface. Winds are created by air moving from high to low pressure areas. Warm air rises at the equator to form part of the *Hadley Cell* and cold air sinks at about 30° latitude to form the sub-tropic surface high pressures. The surface winds created are known as *Trade Winds.* Deflected by the earth's rotation, they blow remarkably consistently from NE and SE, depending on the hemisphere. Winds in the mid latitudes form part of another vertical cell but are far more variable in speed and direction. Generally they blow from the west. High pressures over the cold poles cause winds to blow towards the equator.

Below: Buys Ballot's Law, formulated in 1857. If one stands with one's back to the wind in the Northern Hemisphere, low pressure is on one's left and high on the right. The reverse is true in the Southern Hemisphere. The diagram also shows how *isobars* join up places of equal air pressure. The closer the isobars are, the stronger the wind is.

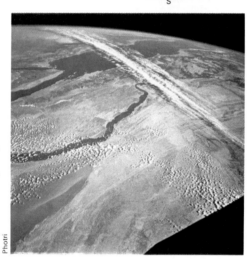

Photri

Left: A *jet stream* picked out by clouds high over the Red Sea. Jet streams are parts of the general wind flow which reach high speeds (over 110 km/h) high in the atmosphere. They occur in the sub-tropics, but most frequently in the mid latitudes and are usually hundreds of km long, tens of km wide and 1-2 km deep.

Below: Five off-shore racing yachts take advantage of a brisk 17 knot (31.5 km/h) wind off Miami, Florida. These fresh breezes may last for no more than a few hours and blow over relatively short distances. In the days of great sailing ships, mariners sought the more reliable prevailing winds.

Eric North

When there is a rapid change in pressure over a short distance, a steep pressure gradient is said to exist, and strong winds result. On a pressure map, this is shown by the isobars being close together. Where the pressure change is spread over a longer distance, the gradient is gentle, the winds are light and the isobars are spaced further apart. A reduction in wind speed in turn means a reduction in the effect of the Coriolis force.

Following the curved lines of the isobars has an additional influence on air flow. When air moves along a curved path, it is subject to *centripetal forces*, forces which exert a pull towards the centre, and is again caused to change direction, as the geostrophic equilibrium has been upset. Winds influenced in this way are known as *gradient winds*.

The earth, of course, is not a rotating globe with a perfectly uniform surface. Friction produced by obstacles such as buildings dissipates the energy and momentum of the wind, and results in another force, so that the wind ceases to blow along the isobars but tends to blow across them.

The degree to which this happens depends on the degree of friction. Over the sea, where friction is minimal, the wind direction will be only about five degrees different from the isobar direction, and its speed about two-thirds that of winds higher up. Over the land, however, the difference in direction may be as much as 15 degrees, and the wind velocity only half that of higher winds.

Friction has a notable effect on winds only in the lowest few hundred metres of the atmosphere. Higher up, winds may exist where none exist below. This is due to uneven pressure distribution at higher levels, even though it may be relatively uniform below. Although pressure falls with height, it falls at different rates at different points. In cold, dense air the fall is more rapid than in warm, light air. This leads to horizontal pressure gradients at different levels in the atmosphere, which in turn produce winds, known as *thermal winds*. The strongest thermal winds are known as *jet streams*. These are high-altitude westerly air movements of strong winds concentrated in a narrow belt.

World wind patterns

When the world-wide pressure variations and their associated winds are considered certain wind patterns emerge. In every part of the world some winds are more common than others; these are termed *prevailing winds*. A knowledge of the prevailing winds was essential in the days of sailing ships. For example, ships en route from Europe to North America made use of the steady and reliable easterly *Trade Winds* which blow across the Atlantic from the coast of north-west Africa to Central America. The return journey then took a more northerly path, using the Westerlies.

The Trades are the most widespread and persistent winds in the tropics. The name comes from the nautical expression 'to blow trade', meaning 'to blow along a regular track', and has nothing to do with commerce. These remarkably consistent winds blow from the east towards the equator, beginning in the high pressure belt of the sub-tropics and moving towards the equatorial low pressure belt.

The Trades form part of a massive vertical circulation of air in the tropical troposphere known as the *Hadley Cell*. The other parts of the cell are the rising air near the warm equator, the poleward flow of this air at the level of the tropopause about 15 km (9 miles) high, and 'sinking' of now-cool air over the sub-tropics. However, recent observations have modified this simple picture. It now seems possible that there may be smaller circulations within the Hadley Cell itself.

Outside the tropics, the prevailing winds are the Westerlies. Unlike the Trade winds, the Westerlies vary in force and direction, particularly in the Northern Hemisphere where there is a greater distribution of land. The southern Westerlies, being relatively unobstructed by land, blow with great strength and regularity, creating some of the roughest seas and fiercest gales in the world. For this reason, the area across which they blow—40° to 50° south—is known as the *Roaring Forties*, a term sometimes applied to the winds themselves.

In the broadest terms, the Westerlies blow because of high pressures over the sub-tropics and low pressures over the higher latitudes. But these winds also take on a wave-like character, particularly above a height of three kilometres

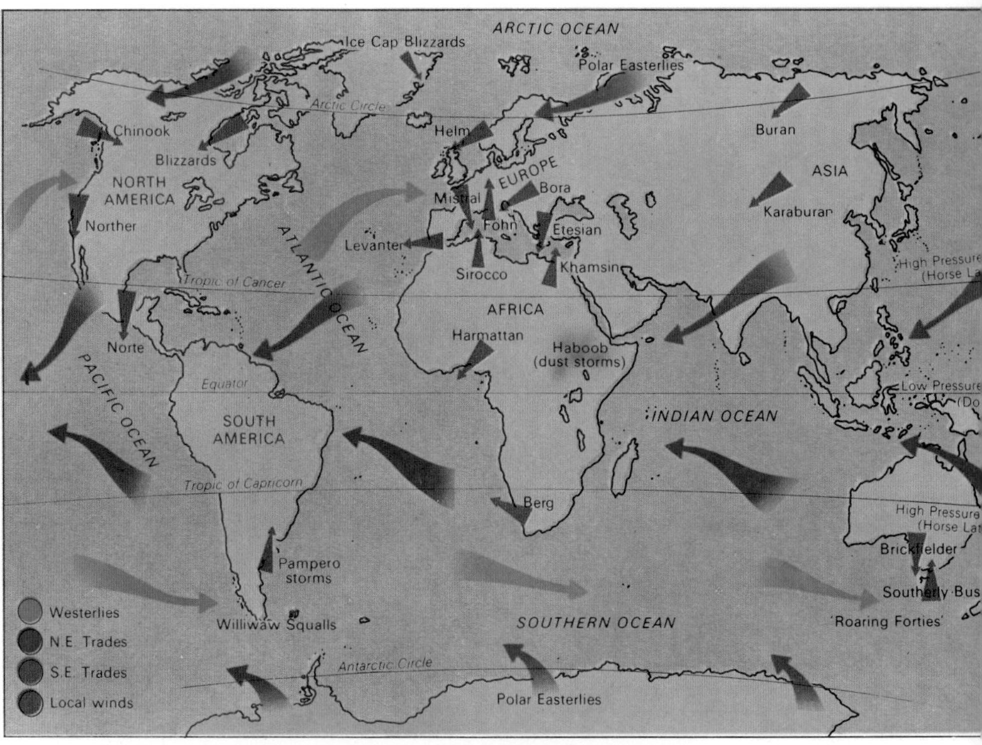

U.S. Dept. of Interior/Alphabet & Image

Above: The major wind systems of the world. This view gives a more realistic map of world winds than the schematic diagram of the globe, as the effects of land and sea and local conditions have been taken into consideration. This tree (left) in Yosemite Park, California, has bent to the persistent power of the prevailing westerlies.

Below: One of the world's major local winds is the *Föhn*, shown here by a wall of cloud coming down the Maloja valley in the Swiss Alps. The Föhn is a hot wind formed by air sinking and warming as it flows down the leeward side of the Alps. When it occurs, the local temperature may rise as much as 15°C in 24 hours melting ice and snow.

G. Seider/ZEFA

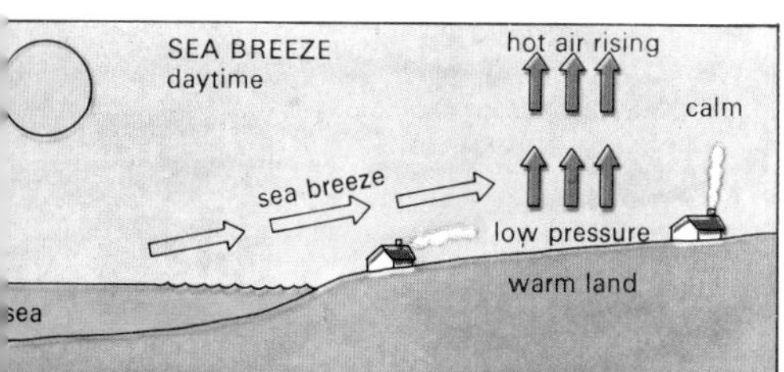

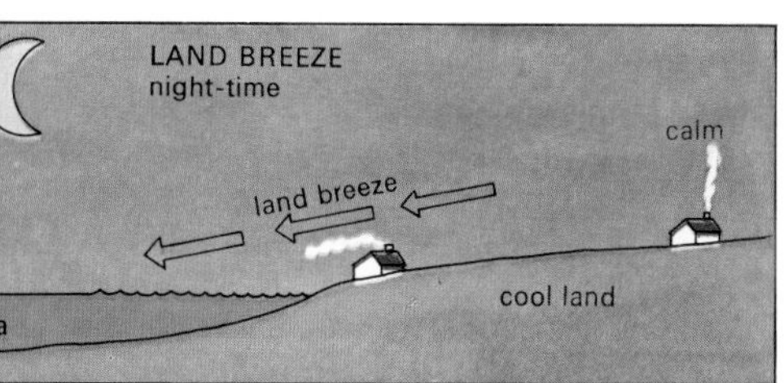

Above and below: Local winds may result from the uneven distribution of temperature over land and sea. During the day, the land heats more rapidly than the sea, creating low pressure at ground level. Air moves in from the sea to replace the rising air and a *sea breeze* develops. Sea breezes usually extend 30-50 km inland, but are only 0.5-1 km deep. At night, the land cools more rapidly than the sea. This cools the overlying air which becomes relatively dense and flow from land to sea occurs, giving a *land breeze*. Not as strong as sea breezes, they are usually shallower and extend 10-20 km seawards.

Radio Times Hulton Picture Library

Above: 'Off she goes'. When winds reach cliffs, the air is forced to rise—providing a strong 'lift' for kites and other buoyant objects.

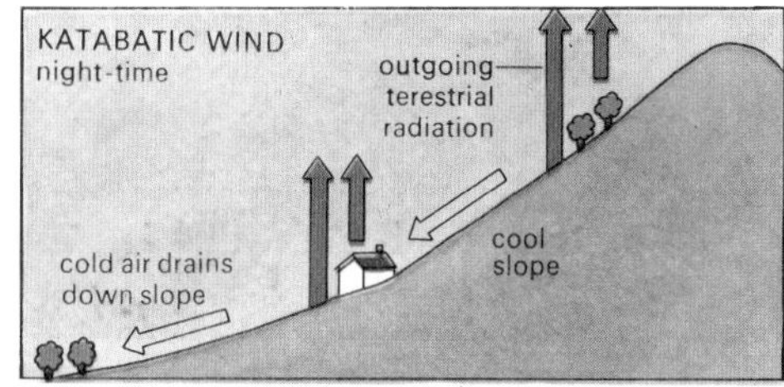

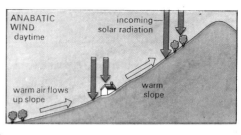

Above and below: Anabatic and katabatic winds are localized flows created by the same basic mechanism as land and sea breezes. *Anabatic winds* blow up hillsides in daytime. Air in contact with the warm slopes becomes warmer than air at the same level above the valley. The warm air rises and flows up the slope, with air from the valley moving in to take its place. *Katabatic winds*, on the other hand, are downhill flows of cold air. At night, air above the cooling slope becomes denser than air above the valley at the same level. Katabatic winds blowing off the Greenland glaciers can last several days and reach speeds of over 100 km/h.

Below: Trees in Nigeria blown by the *Harmattan* wind. In the Sahara, the air is very dry and the Harmattan, which blows out of the desert towards the W African coast, is likewise dry. Although often unpleasantly dust-laden inland, it brings welcome relief from the prevailing humidity and is known locally as 'the doctor'.

J. Samways

Below: A dust-storm in Australia. In semi-arid areas, winds sweep up dense clouds of dust, sometimes in a 'wall' of dust up to 3,000 m high.

Bruce Coleman

(1.8 miles). These massive waves are known as *Rossby waves* after the scientist who first suggested their existence. Within the meandering westerly flow, winds at heights of 8 to 10 km (5 to 6 miles) frequently have speeds over 60 knots (110 km per hour). This is the threshold speed for the jet streams, the fastest-moving part of the overall flow.

Local winds

At a local level, several different types of small-scale winds may have a notable effect on the weather. *Gusts*, sudden blasts of wind, are really short-lived (a few seconds) turbulences in the larger circulation of air. They bring a temporary increase in wind speeds followed by a lull.

Along coastal areas, small-scale winds are typified by *land* and *sea* breezes. Sea breezes develop as a result of the unequal heating of land and sea during the day. After sunrise the land heats up more rapidly than the adjacent water and in turn the air over the land becomes warmer than the air over the sea. Consequently the 'land' air at the surface expands and raises the pressure of the air immediately above it. This leads to a flow of air (at a height of perhaps one kilometre) from land to sea and thus a fall in pressure over the land. Consequently air flows in from the sea at the surface as a sea breeze. The circulation is completed by air rising over the land and sinking over the sea.

Initially the sea breeze blows at right angles to the coastlines. But as the day progresses, the wind is deflected by the Coriolis force, and by late afternoon, sea breezes will blow virtually parallel to the coast.

At night, the land cools more rapidly than the sea. The cooler air over the land then blows towards the lower pressure area above the sea, giving a land breeze. Both land and sea breezes tend to last for less than 12 hours and blow over distances of only a few tens of kilometres.

Other localized winds are associated with hill slopes. During the day, if the slope becomes heated by the sun, the air in contact with it becomes warmer than the air at the same level above the lower ground in the valley. The warm air is less dense and tends to rise. This uphill flow is known as an *anabatic wind*. Air from the valley moves in to take its place.

At night, however, the reverse effect occurs. Air in contact with the cooling slope becomes denser than the air at the same level above the valley. This cold air tends to flow down the slope, producing a *katabatic wind*.

In certain areas of the world, special local conditions give rise to regional winds which affect much larger areas. Several regional winds are found around the Mediterranean. For example, the *sirocco* is a hot dusty wind which blows out of the Sahara, covering parts of the North African coast in dust before bringing high humidity to the shores of southern Europe. The same wind is known as *khamsin* in Egypt and *leveche* in Spain. The *mistral* and *bora* are cold northerly winds which bring unseasonally low temperatures to southern Europe and may damage valuable crops.

In several mountainous areas, a warm, dry wind blows down the lee side of a range of hills. In the European Alps, this wind is known as the *Föhn*. Its mechanism is not yet fully understood, but the warmth and dryness of the Föhn are known to result from compression as the air sinks down the lee of the mountains. Its warmth often causes rapid melting of snow. Similar winds occur elsewhere, but are given different names, such as *chinook* in the Rocky Mountains, *zonda* in Argentina, and *puelche* in the Andes.

Weather Systems

To most of us weather simply means sunshine or rain, high or low temperatures, windy or calm days. Yet any combination of these features will usually occur in a particular type of weather system. These systems are usually described in terms of the variations in air pressure and the winds which blow within them. Thus a roughly circular area of low pressure is known as a *cyclone* or, more commonly, a *depression*. The winds blow around a depression in an anticlockwise direction in the Northern Hemisphere, but clockwise in the Southern Hemisphere. A similar area of high pressure in which the winds blow clockwise in the Northern Hemisphere is known as an *anticyclone*.

Analysis of maps of the weather tells us that systems exist in many different sizes. The largest are 12 to 15 km (7-9 miles) deep (the average depth of the troposphere). The small, fast-moving ones are 1-3 km deep and vary enormously in their horizontal dimensions. Small weather systems tend to have high wind speeds, large ones low wind speeds.

Tornadoes and thunderstorms

Tornadoes are, considering their size, probably the most destructive of weather types. Also known as 'twisters' in the United States, *tornadoes* are tubes of very rapidly spinning air which create havoc wherever they touch the ground. The tube is usually a few hundred metres across and wind speeds may reach over 320 km/h (200 mph).

Tornadoes are usually short-lived, but often leave a trail of destruction in their path. At any one time and place several tornadoes (up to eight have been observed) may exist and they tend to move at between 10 and 30 km/h (6-20 mph) across the countryside. Frequently the bottom of the tube leaves the ground, thus sparing the inhabitants of devastation; yet the rushing noise of the wind in the funnel may be clearly heard. Over the sea, they appear as *waterspouts*, a swirling funnel of water.

The cause of tornadoes is not clear. However, they are frequently associated with thunderstorms and, when viewed from above by airplane or satellite, seem

Robert Harding

Photri

Above: A whirlwind is a rapidly rotating column of air, only a few metres across, made visible by the dust picked up in the air. Whirlwinds are the result of a high temperature gradient close to the ground. In this unstable situation, the hot air spontaneously rises and spins to form the whirlwind.

Right: A tornado over Oklahoma in the USA. Larger than whirlwinds, tornadoes often grow down from thunderclouds; low pressure in the dark funnel causes condensation thus making the vortex visible. Tornadoes are also known as 'twisters' and although short-lived they can be enormously destructive, with wind speeds of over 320 km/hr. (The red streak in this picture may be a photographic fault.)

Frank Lane

Below: This house exploded outwards when a tornado passed close by. The reason is simply the large pressure gradient while air pressure inside the house remains steady. In a tornado and its path the air pressure drops sharply, producing a strong suction effect.

Camera Press

Georg Gerster/John Hillelson

Left: A picture from the Apollo 7 spacecraft of Hurricane Gladys sweeping over the Gulf of Mexico off the coast of Cuba. This unique view of the storm shows its vast horizontal extent as well as the highest mass of clouds punching into the stratosphere some 12 km above the earth's surface.

Below: A cross-section of a hurricane, showing the vast extent of the storm on the ground—it will often cover an area 400 km across. The diagram also shows the vertical currents of air spiralling upwards in the clouds and sinking in the calm eye. Rainfall is very heavy, with as much as 50cm (20 in) falling within 24 hours.

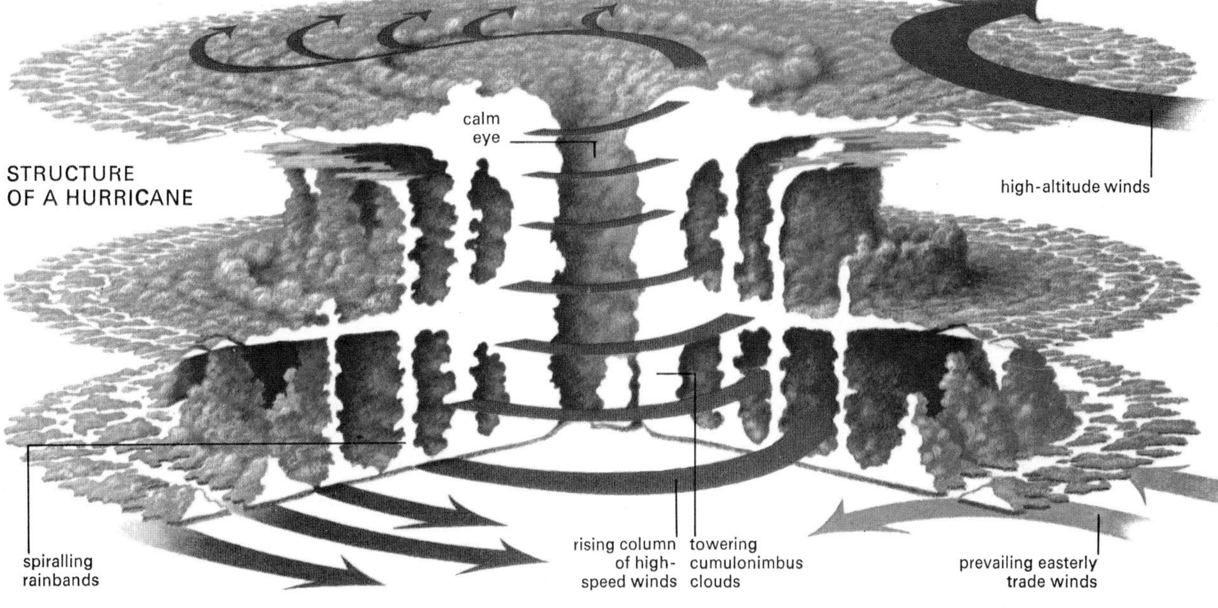

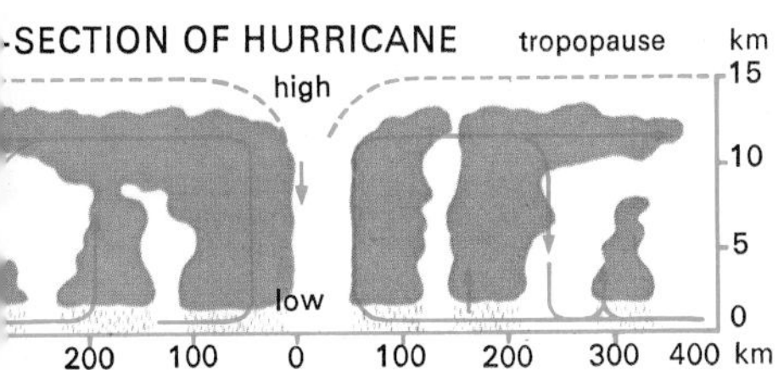

Left: The high winds (over 160 km/hr) of hurricane *Inez* ravaging the Miami region of Florida in 1966. Leaving a trail of destruction behind it, the hurricane lasted more than a week, covering as much as 500 km every day. It followed a track out of the Gulf of Mexico towards the Atlantic coast of the US and across Florida.

Above: The swirl of clouds rotating about the calm eye of a hurricane extends right through the troposphere. The cumulonimbus clouds are arranged in bands around the eye. When the storm begins to die (usually over colder water or over land) the eye fills with clouds and the storm dissipates.

Keystone

Below left: Large clouds characteristic of a thunderstorm. Formed by rapidly rising moist air, thunder-clouds may be up to 10 km deep.

Below: The drama of a thunderstorm lies in the thunderous noise and flashes of lightning. The huge electrical discharges that cause this are the result of the top of the clouds becoming positively charged, while the lower levels become negative. The very high voltage discharge does not only occur within the clouds, but may also reach the earth. The rapid expansion of air in the path of the discharge generates the sound waves we hear as thunder.

Picturepoint

to occur most frequently in the rear right-hand side of such storms. But it is very difficult to explain how the winds reach such high speeds and how the spin is concentrated into such a narrow tube. Common in both Australia and the United States, the best recorded tornadoes occur in the central states of the latter country where their frequency has earned the area the name of 'tornado alley'.

Unlike tornadoes, thunderstorms can occur virtually anywhere on the globe outside the polar areas and it is estimated that at any one time some 2,000 exist throughout the world. Characterized by thunder and lightning, *thunderstorms* are simply very large clouds—usually 8-12 km (5-7 miles) deep and possibly a similar size across—in which intensely powerful up-currents of air occur.

Heavy rain, hail and high winds are usually associated with thunderstorms. For example, during a storm over Hampstead in London in August 1975, a record 170 mm (nearly 7 ins) of rain fell within 150 minutes. Rainfall of this intensity, however, is far more frequent in the tropics where as much as 600 mm (24 in) may fall in one day.

Thunderstorm clouds may exist singly or in clusters. They travel up to 30 km/ph (20 mph), but the heaviest rains fall from stationary ones. Often the storms move over an observer on the ground in a different direction to that of the surface wind. This occurs because the storm moves with the winds at higher levels (perhaps four or five kilometres high) rather than the surface wind.

Thunderstorms occur in *unstable air*, that is, air likely to move upwards or downwards with the slightest provocation. One circumstance in which air is highly unstable is when warm, moist air lies beneath cold air.

During the summer in Britain, for example, the sum often heats the air near the ground to such an extent that it rises. If the air is moist and rises to great heights it eventually causes a thunder cloud and is known as a *heat thunderstorm*. Storms may also be caused by air becoming cooler at high levels (5 to 10 km up) or by 'undercutting' near the ground, where a mass of cold air forces warm air to rise. Collections of thunderstorms may last for 10 to 12 hours and die out only when all the instability has been 'de-fused'.

Hurricanes

In the tropics, thunderstorms frequently form part of a *hurricane*. This weather system, otherwise known as a *tropical cyclone*, is much larger, usually about 200 to 400 km (125 to 250 miles) across, and has a very definite cyclonic spin (in the Northern Hemisphere it will be anti-clockwise). It usually starts from a cluster of large thunder clouds which merge over a period of a day or two to form an almost circular low pressure system, with a solid mass of cloud from near ground up to the tropopause. At the centre of the storm is the calm *eye* where the sky is clear and there are no winds. Here, air is sinking, thus preventing the development of clouds. Around the eye, however, the air is rising into the thunder clouds.

A hurricane is likely to bring very heavy rainfall (tens of centimetres) and wind speeds of over 100 km/h (60 mph) are frequently recorded. In a single day, the storms may move as much as 200 km (120 miles) but their speeds are erratic. Because of their winds and their enormous size, hurricanes can wreak havoc over vast areas.

Anticyclones and depressions

In the middle and high latitudes of the world most of our weather is associated with distinct pressure systems known as cyclones (or depressions) and *anticyclones*. They were recognized as distinct pressure and wind (and therefore weather) systems in the nineteenth century but we still do not completely understand how they work.

Cyclones may cover enormous areas, sometimes up to 4,000 km (2,500 miles) in diameter. In the early 1920s, two Scandinavian meteorologists suggested that cyclones tend to occur in lines or 'families', with the youngest at the western end of the line and the oldest at the eastern end of the line. One family, for instance, could stretch right across the North Atlantic.

This discovery of families of cyclones was closely linked to the discovery of the *polar front*, the boundary found in the mid latitudes separating the cold 'polar' and warm 'tropical' air. Research showed that cyclones formed on the polar front and, because of their spin, deformed it into waves. Thus, the younger the cyclone, the less the deformation and the smaller the wave. As the cyclone matured the wave on the polar front became more pronounced, usually having its 'crest' sharpened and coincident with the lowest surface pressure in the depression.

At this stage the part of the polar front within the individual depression can be divided into a 'cold' front and a 'warm' front. From the point of view of a ground observer, the *cold front* indicates the part of the front where cold air replaces warm, and the *warm front* where warm air replaces cold. The cold front travels faster than the warm front and so, by the cyclone's maturity at the eastern end of the family, the fronts meet. This is known as an *occlusion*. Soon after the occlusion process, the cyclone dies out because it has completed its task of moving warm, tropical air from low levels at low latitudes to higher levels at high latitudes.

This outline of the life history of cyclones accounts for many sequences of weather experienced in the mid-latitudes. For example, in the British Isles, at the approach of a warm front (the leading part of a cyclone moving towards the east), clouds become thicker and lower because the advancing warm air rises over the colder air ahead of the front. Rain may fall for several hours before the warm front passes. Behind the front, the *warm sector* is usually cloudy and may produce drizzle or light rain. The western boundary of the warm sector is the cold front where the cold air undercuts the warm. This frequently leads to shower clouds and can be the cause of thunderstorms. Rainfall is often heavier than at the warm front but does not usually last as long. Finally, behind the cold front the weather is usually clear, cooler and bright.

An anticyclone is a region of high pressure, generally characterized by light winds and clear skies. Usually of rather larger size than cyclones, anticyclones have opposite characteristics: air spins clockwise (in the Northern Hemisphere) rather than anticlockwise and generally sinks, so preventing the formation of clouds. At night, the same clear skies that give us our sunny days allow a great deal of terrestrial radiation to be lost. The result is that the ground and the nearby air cools, and in winter this may lead to frost or, in a moist air, to mist or fog. The very light winds of anticyclones help the formation of both of these. For if winds were stronger, as in cyclones, the air would be thoroughly mixed and the

Above: Typical weather brought by an anticyclone (left) and a depression (right). In an *anticyclone*, high pressure and sinking air tend to give calm, cloudless conditions and produce valley fog. The passage of a *depression* (cyclone) brings unstable conditions associated with low pressure. Warm air behind the *warm front* is pushed up by the moving wedge of denser cold air behind the *cold front*, producing clouds and rainfall. The warm front gives steady rainfall, but the cold front brings the heaviest showers. As the cold front clears (right) blue skies appear as the rain continues to fall from the dark clouds moving away from an observer on the ground.

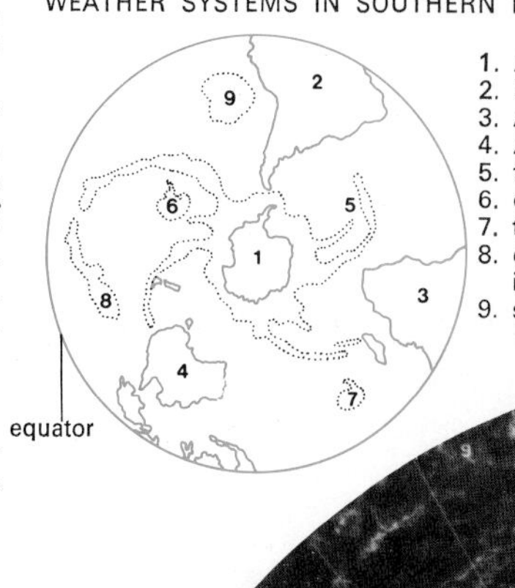

Below: This view of the entire hemisphere from over the South Pole is in fact a 'mosaic' of numerous photographs taken by a satellite on one day in October 1968. Cloud patterns are clearly complex but several major weather systems are shown (left). Four main arms of cloud pick out fronts stretching from Antarctica into middle latitudes. Also visible are cyclones, around which winds blow clockwise in the Southern Hemisphere. Broad troughs of low pressure are created at both the polar front and inter-tropical zone of convergence where different air masses meet. Australia and much of southern Africa are enjoying clear skies.

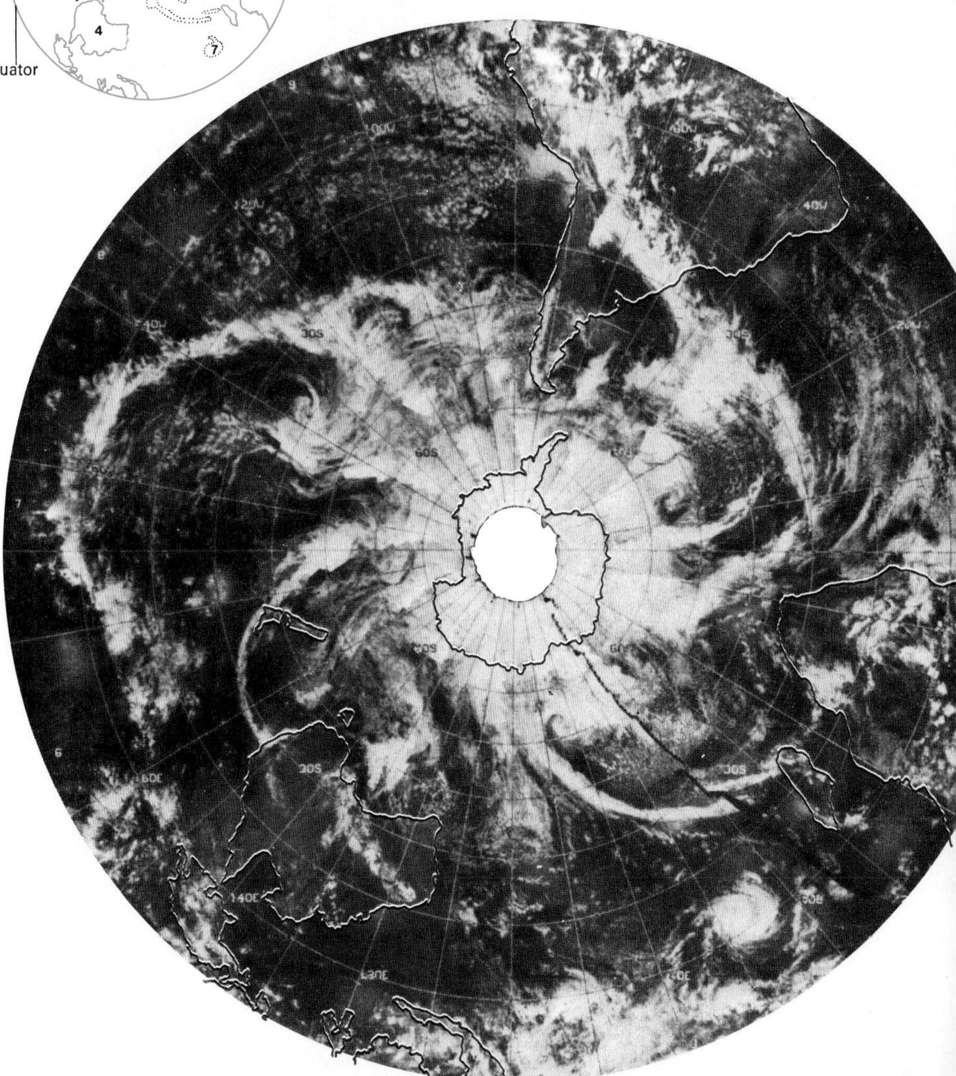

Environment Science Service Administration/Alphabet & Image

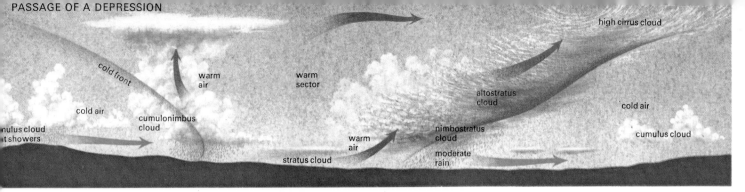

PASSAGE OF A DEPRESSION

high cirrus cloud
cold front
warm air
warm sector
altostratus cloud
cold air
cold air
cumulonimbus cloud
nulus cloud
t showers
nimbostratus cloud
cumulus cloud
warm air
moderate rain
stratus cloud

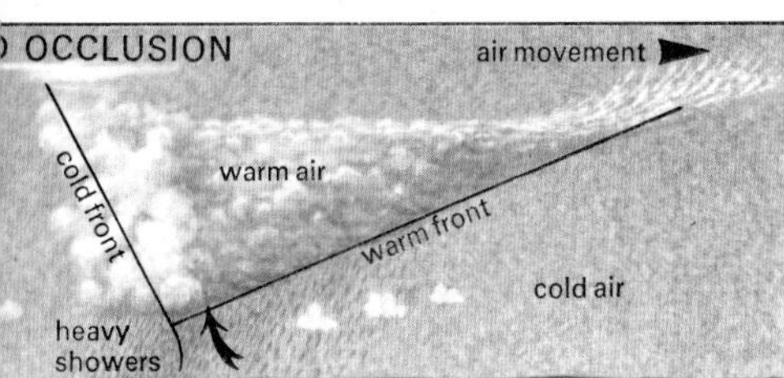

Above and below: An *occlusion* is formed in a depression when the generally faster-moving cold front catches up with the warm front and lifts the warm sector off the ground. The cold air behind the depression now meets the cold air against which the warm front was formed. If the overtaking air is colder than the advance cold air, this is termed a *cold occlusion* (above). Resulting weather is similar to that at a cold front with heavy showers. If it is not as cold as the air ahead of the warm front, then the cold front rises over the warm front to give a *warm occlusion* (below). The weather here is similar to that at a warm front.

M OCCLUSION
air movement
cold front
warm air
warm front
colder air
moderate rain

Below: The dry months preceding the south-west monsoon in India cause severe depletion of water resources, and if the monsoon rains are delayed drought and famine can easily occur. This has been happening more often in recent years, following a southerly shift of the main wind belts and thus of the monsoons.

Right: During the winter months from November to April, the pressure of the air over central Asia is much higher than that of the air over the southern seas. This is because the land mass gets much colder than the seas, and it results in the dry, offshore winds of the north-east monsoon.

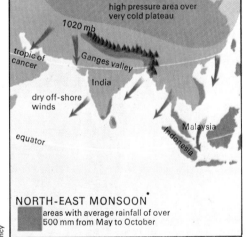

Marilyn Silverstone/John Hillelson Agency

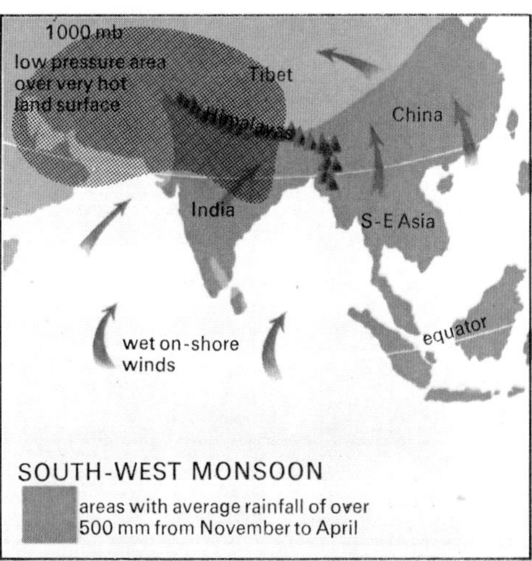

Above: During the summer the upper westerly winds blowing over Asia shift their path north of the Tibetan plateau. This allows the monsoon winds and rains to surge northward towards the large area of low pressure created by the heating of the land to the north-west of the Indian sub-continent.

Right: The monsoon rains hit India between June and September. The rains are eagerly awaited after the months of hot, dry weather, and below-average monsoon rains can bring famine conditions in southern India due to crop failure. Too much rain, however, can cause disastrous flooding.

high pressure area over very cold plateau
1020 mb
tropic of cancer
Ganges valley
India
dry off-shore winds
equator
Malaysia
Indonesia
NORTH-EAST MONSOON
areas with average rainfall of over 500 mm from May to October

Below: World distribution of tropical storms. The regions affected and tracks taken are shown. They originate over all the tropical oceans except the S Atlantic. *Hurricanes* form in the E Atlantic and move westward, and tend to turn north near Florida although some go straight on and devastate Texas. *Cyclones* in the Indian Ocean also often result in extensive damage and deaths. Tropical cyclones originating in the seas off China, Japan and the Philippines are known as *typhoons*, and off N. Australia as *willy-willies*. All these varieties of cyclones bring torrential rains and high winds.

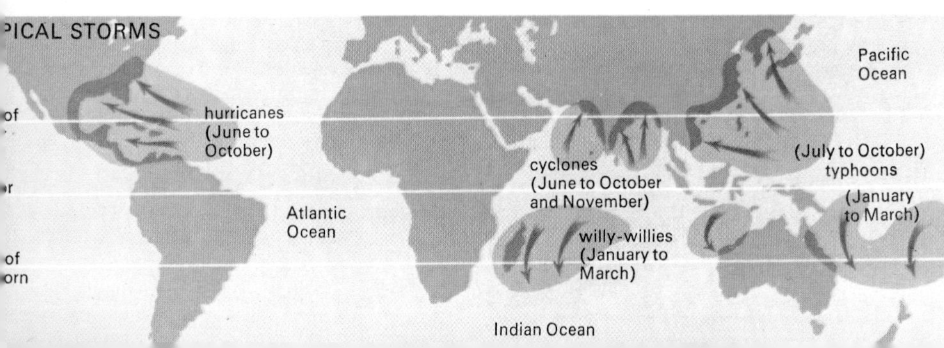

Raghubir Singh/John Hillelson Agency

near-surface cooling would be spread over a much deeper layer of air.

Anticyclones are caused in two basic ways: by temperature and by sinking air. Cold air, such as occurs over Siberia and Canada in winter, is dense and thus causes a high pressure at ground level. Such anticyclones are, however, usually shallow, only about 3 km deep. By contrast air which sinks around latitudes 20-30° causes deep, warm anticyclones, such as those frequently found over the Azores. They are larger, more permanent features of the atmosphere than the cold, shallow anticyclones.

Monsoons

The monsoon is perhaps the most significant of all rain-bearing winds. The name describes seasonal winds, and was first applied to the winds over the Arabian Sea, which blow for six months from the north-east and for six months from the south-west. However, it now includes similar winds in other parts of the world, particularly on the southern and eastern sides of Asia, where such winds are strongest and the rains they bring most dramatic.

No complete explanation of monsoon winds is yet possible. But part of the story lies with the seasonal differences in temperature that arise between central Asia and the seas to the south and east. Whatever the full explanation, however, the unfortunate reality is that the monsoon's intensity and duration are never uniform. A season of heavy rainfall bringing disastrous floods may be followed by years of low rainfall when crops fail and famine results.

Clouds and Precipitation

Both heat and water are essential for life on earth. The sun provides us with a steady source of warmth and the world's natural supply of fresh water is provided by precipitation from the clouds in the atmosphere. Rainfall is the most common form of precipitation, but the term includes all the water, both liquid and solid, which falls from the clouds (sleet, snow and hail) and dew and hoar frost.

Clouds

Clouds appear in an almost endless variety of shapes, sizes and heights. Yet there are some common features which form the basis of a fairly simple classification first suggested by Luke Howard, a London chemist, in 1803 and later modified by the World Meteorological Organization. The WMO recognizes ten main types of cloud on the basis of height and according to whether they form layers (*stratus*), heaps or piles (*cumulus*) or hair-like filaments (*cirrus*). The high-level clouds, *cirrus*, *cirrostratus* and *cirrocumulus* occur from six to 18 km (4-11 miles) high. Medium-level clouds (2-6 km or 1-4 miles) are *altocumulus* or *altostratus*, and low clouds up to 2 km high include *stratocumulus*, *stratus*, *nimbostratus*, *cumulus*, and *cumulonimbus*. The WMO groups cumulus and cumulonimbus as a fourth type of cloud —those with considerable vertical development—as their tops often go far beyond the 2,000 m (6,500 ft) level. The world *nimbus* is combined with stratus or cumulus if there is precipitation falling from these clouds.

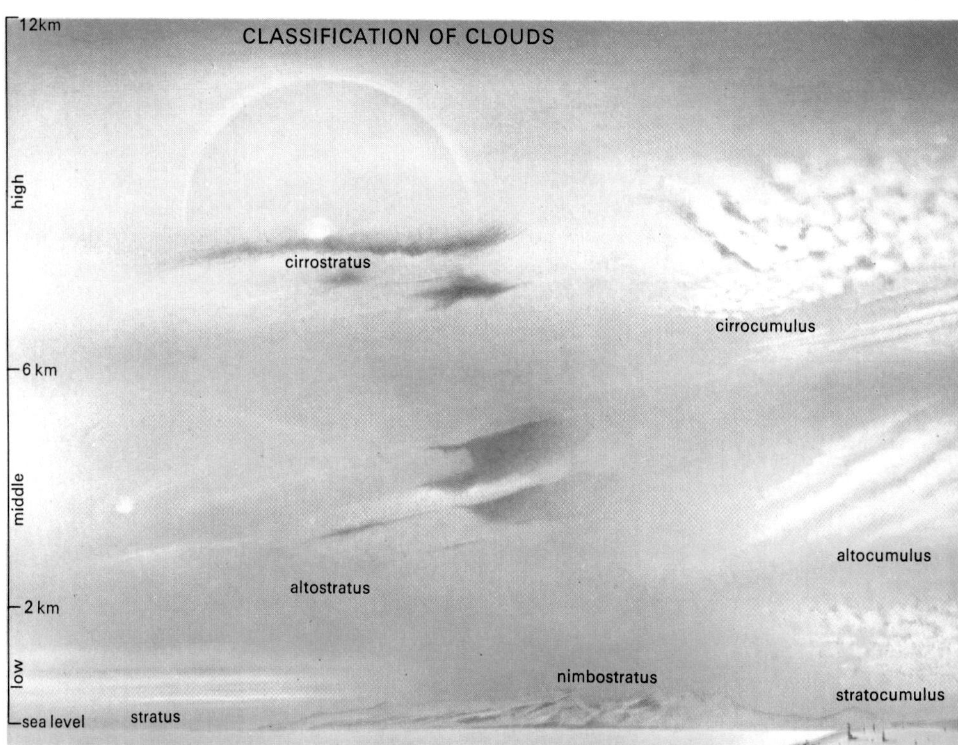

Above, left and below: The basic cloud types, identifiable by shape and height. The highest clouds are cirrus (left) which stretch out into long streaks 6-12,000 m above the earth's surface. They are formed entirely of ice crystals. An irregular arrangement of these wisps of cloud often indicates fair weather; if bad weather is approaching, the cirrus will appear in bands or lines. Clouds lying between 6,000 and 2,000 m are known as altocumulus and altostratus. This picture (below) shows the latter, covering an area of hundreds of square kilometres in a grey sheet which shrouds the sun. Altocumulus clouds are more patchy.

Right: At a lower level are these thick cumulus clouds. They are the result of convection currents rising from the ground, and may reach the highest levels. As the air cools it is less able to hold its water as vapour. The water condenses at the dew-point. The level at which this happens is visible as the *cloud base*.

Clouds are made up of liquid water or ice, or a combination of the two. The lower in the atmosphere they occur, the more likely they are to be water clouds. By contrast, the delicate and feathery cirrus clouds, confined to high levels, are always made of ice.

Both the ice and water come from the condensation of the water vapour which is largely derived by evaporation from the earth's oceans, lakes and rivers. Water vapour is present, to varying degrees, everywhere in the atmosphere: the amount contained in a given volume of air is termed its *absolute humidity*. The higher the temperature, the more water vapour the air can contain. However, there is a limit; when the air contains the maximum water vapour possible for a given temperature, the air is said to be *saturated* or to have a *relative humidity* of 100%. This critical temperature, at which the air becomes saturated at a constant pressure, is known as the *dew point*.

Condensation is the process by which water vapour changes into liquid or solid form, and it occurs when air containing water vapour is cooled and becomes saturated. The cooling itself results from the air being lifted—for example, as it passes over a range of hills—and expanding due to the lower pressure. In expanding, the air uses some of its heat and when the temperature of the air drops low enough, the excess water vapour condenses into droplets and forms clouds. If, on the other hand, air sinks into higher pressures, it is compressed and warms and is thus able to hold more water as vapour.

Not until the late nineteenth century was it appreciated that clouds formed because of cooling by expansion in lift-

Right: These diagrams illustrate the formation of clouds by three different processes. The first shows air being forced to rise over the barrier of a mountain. Cloud forms when the dew-point level is reached and water condenses—the height at which this actually occurs will depend on the air's humidity. These are known as *orographic* clouds and they often bring rain to the windward side of mountain ranges. On the leeward side, the cloud base is higher as the air is less humid. The descending air produces a drier *rain shadow* area.

The second diagram shows the formation of a *convection* cloud when warm currents of air rise from a hot land surface. Again, cloud forms when the air reaches its condensation level. Violent summer thunderstorms result from convection clouds forming under unstable conditions.

The third diagram shows the meeting of two air masses, one warm and one cold. As a result, air rises along the front between the two and cloud forms as the rising air cools and condenses. Such *frontal* clouds may be 10,000 m thick and extend over thousands of square kilometres.

Below: A *banner cloud* streaming off a peak in the Himalayas. Air has been lifted to its condensation level to form a cloud. Because of the high wind speeds at the top of mountains, the cloud is blown downstream like a banner.

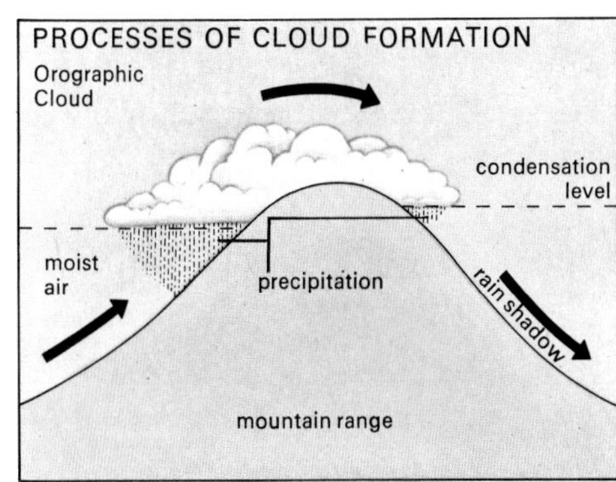

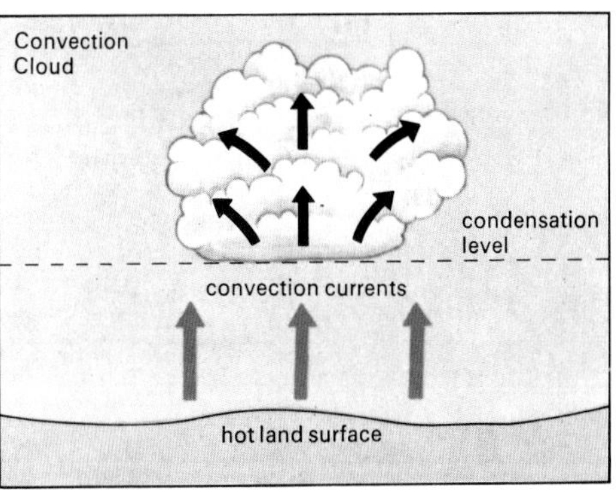

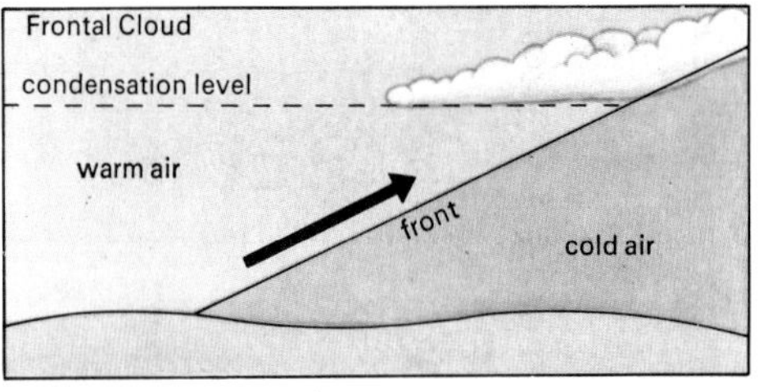

ing rather than—as was previously believed—by air being cooled by contact with cold mountain tops. The height at which cooling by lifting is sufficient to cause condensation is called the *condensation level* and this can vary considerably.

Water vapour condenses on to particles of material known as *condensation nuclei*. Their exact beginnings and operation are not fully understood, but it is known that these nuclei include dust and smoke particles, salt from sea-spray and pollen. Small ice-crystals have similar origins. Vapour is deposited on the ice-nuclei to form ice crystals. The form of the ice crystal depends on the temperature of the cloud. Cloud droplets may remain liquid at temperatures well below 0°C, sometimes as low as —15°C. The cloud is then said to be *supercooled*.

Cloud shapes

The shapes and types of cloud are closely related to the nature of the upward movement of air which created them. Sheet-like clouds are usually caused by slowly rising air (about 5-10 cm/sec or about 0.2 mph) over an area of thousands of square kilometres. Such movement is common at the warm front of depressions.

Cumulus clouds, on the other hand, are formed by warm air rising off the land at a rate a hundred or more times faster in a process called *convection*. American scientists have in fact measured vertical motion of cumulus clouds in thunderstorms at speeds up to 100 km/hr (60 mph). These clouds are large and deep, sometimes developing into the 6,000 m (20,000 ft) tall cumulonimbus, the anvil-shaped mass that is the hallmark of a typical thunderstorm.

The typical 'bumps' on a cumulus cloud are caused by the rise of *thermals*, distinct volumes of air which rise through the lower atmosphere rather like a hot-air balloon. As they ascend under their own buoyancy, they turn themselves inside out, thus mixing their warm air with the surrounding cold air. When the thermals are cool enough to allow the water vapour within them to condense, they become visible as cloud.

The height to which any current of air will rise, however fast it is moving, is governed largely by whether the air through which it moves is 'stable' or 'unstable'. If the drop in the temperature of the surrounding air is more than the rate at which the rising air cools—1°C per 100 m (330 ft)—then the current will

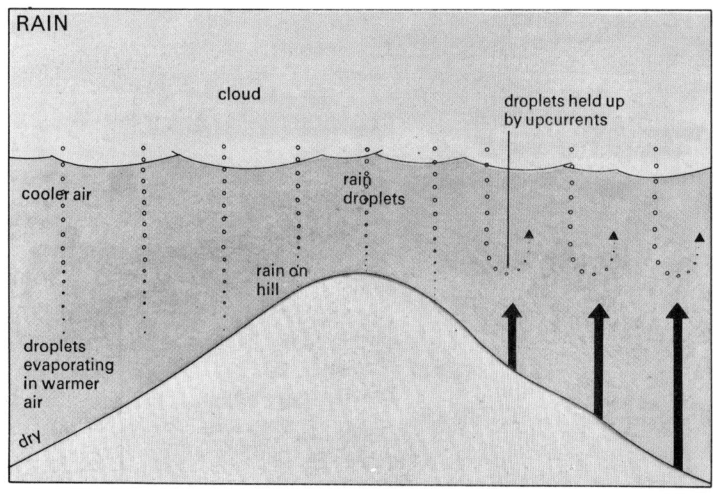

Above: Precipitation falls as rain, snow, sleet or hail. It rains when water droplets start to fall from clouds, which were formed when droplets condensed from water vapour on to particles or *condensation nuclei*. Once large enough, the raindrops will fall, but may not reach the ground. They may evaporate in the warmer air below, or strong upcurrents of air may hold them aloft. The diagram shows how it may rain on the hills, while surrounding lowlands are dry.

Near right: Below cumulonimbus clouds, strong upcurrents may lift the raindrops repeatedly so high that they freeze into *hail-stones*. A fresh layer of ice is collected each time the hailstone is uplifted until it becomes too heavy, and falls to the ground as hail.

Far right: Ice crystals form in clouds where the temperature is well below 0°C. When large enough they fall as snowflakes. If ground temperatures are above freezing, the snow melts partially to form *sleet* or melts fully to give rain.

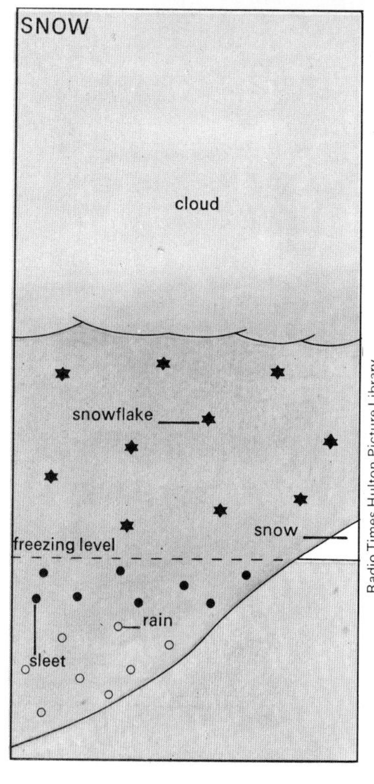

Radio Times Hulton Picture Library

Above: The fantastic shapes in this specially compiled photograph are delicate *snow crystals*. The variations in their patterns are apparently infinite, but all have a basically hexagonal form. When water vapour condenses in a cloud at temperatures below —4° to —15°C, it forms minute 'spicules' of ice which unite to produce these ice crystals. In turn, the crystals agglomerate into snowflakes.

Right: In this town in central Norway, the postman uses a motorized sledge to deliver the mail through the heavy winter snows.

continue to rise and conditions are said to be *unstable*. If the drop in the temperature is less than 1°C per 100 m, the thermals will soon reach the temperature of the air around. Ceasing to be buoyant, they will stop rising. Thus clouds rise higher when conditions are unstable.

Why it rains or snows

The amount of water suspended in the air in a cloud is enormous. A small cumulus cloud may hold up to 1,000 tonnes of water, a large one possibly a hundred times that weight. However, the tiny drops do not float in the air (water is many times denser than air) but rise or fall through the cloud extremely slowly. The problem is that in liquid form the water droplets in a cloud are very small—about ten micrometres across (ten millionths of a metre)—and are not heavy enough to penetrate the rising air which created them. Even if they could overcome this updraught, as well as the general motion of the cloud, the droplets would evaporate in the drier air beneath the cloud after travelling only a few tens of metres. This was once a great puzzle of meteorology: how exactly does precipitation from the clouds reach the ground?

There are two explanations. One is called *coalescence* and the other, named after the Swedish expert who first described it (and who, by his discovery, provided the first plausible method of commercial 'rainmaking') is known as the *Bergeron process*.

If drops are of different sizes they tend to unite or *coalesce* on impact and form a larger one. This in turn will pick up small droplets as it falls through the cloud. An average raindrop, in fact, represents the accumulation of up to a million droplets. If it reaches a diameter of a millimetre (0.04 in) it stands a chance of surviving the trip to earth, but if it reaches five millimetres it may break up due to air resistance, and start the process again.

When ice-crystals hit each other in clouds where the temperature is well below zero, they tend to cement together or *agglomerate* because of the thin film of supercooled water on their surfaces. Ice crystals can also grow by *accretion*, by collecting water droplets as they fall. All three types of coalescence have been shown by laboratory experiments to be capable of producing precipitation within the lifespan of a cloud.

Bergeron's theory, put forward in 1935

ZEFA

Left: The complexity of atmospheric movements is shown by the co-existence of differing cloud types at various heights over any one place. In this picture, the low-level cumulus cloud is overlain by an alto-cumulus. Rain is falling from the cumulus over a limited area out to sea.

Right: The seasonal distribution of rainfall tends to follow the pattern of mean annual precipitation. Thus areas of high rainfall—with the significant exception of the tropical storm areas— tend to receive a year-round supply of precipitation.

Below: Hailstones on the ground. The largest is shown by the ruler to be about 1.5 cm across.

Bruce Coleman

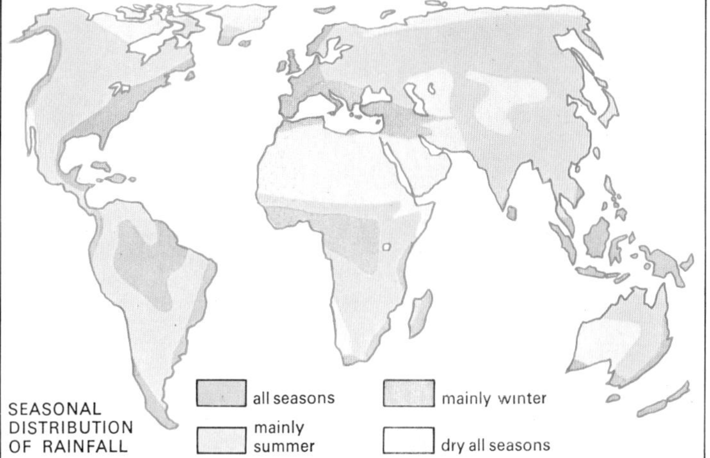

Below: The world mean annual distribution of precipitation. As the map shows, the wettest regions are the tropical, monsoonal and mid-latitude areas where depressions (cyclones) are active and frequent. Local factors include air temperature—as this governs humidity—and the height of land over which moist air is blown. Continental interiors are dry because of their remoteness from the oceans. Very hot, dry deserts such as the Sahara are often associated with sub-tropical anti-cyclones, where air is sinking and prohibits rainfall. In some deserts, no rainfall has ever been recorded. Rainfall is slight in colder, higher latitudes and leeward of mountain ranges.

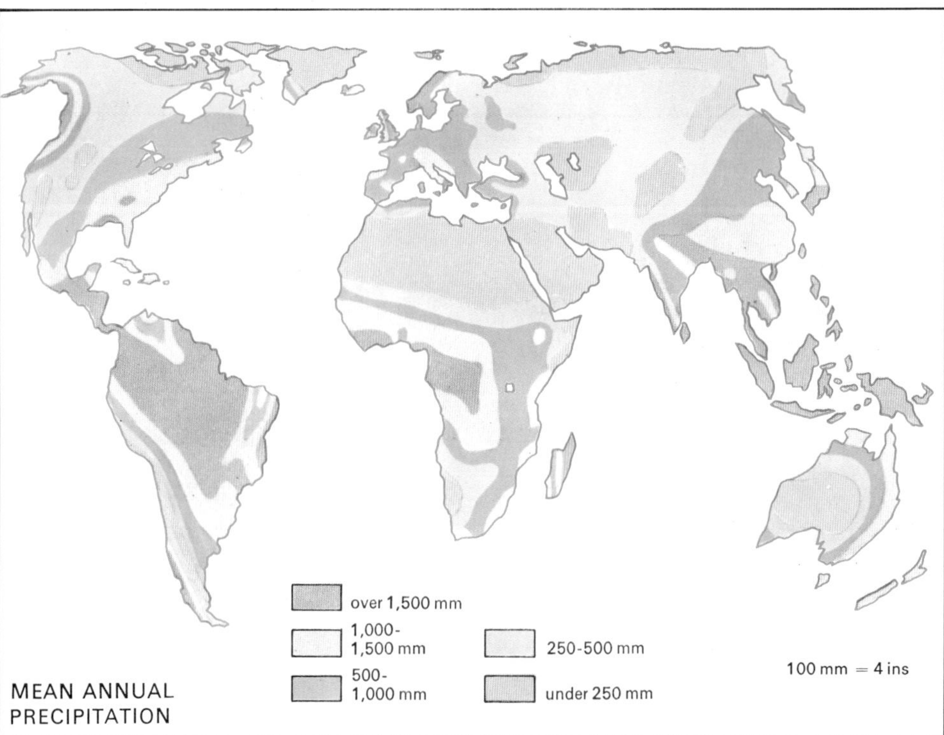

Left: A rainbow brings colour to a grey sky over Lüneburg Heath in West Germany. Rainbows appear as a multi-coloured arc when a shower of rain is falling in front of the observer and the sun is behind him (as shown here by the shadows). The drops of rain refract and internally reflect the sun's rays, breaking up the white light into the colours of the spectrum. The larger the raindrops, the more vivid are the colours.

Right: Heavy flooding in this Vietnamese street resulted from the torrential downpours which accompany the summer monsoons. Saigon receives an average of over 2,000 mm of rain each year, mostly in the summer.

David Hurn/Magnum

Keystone

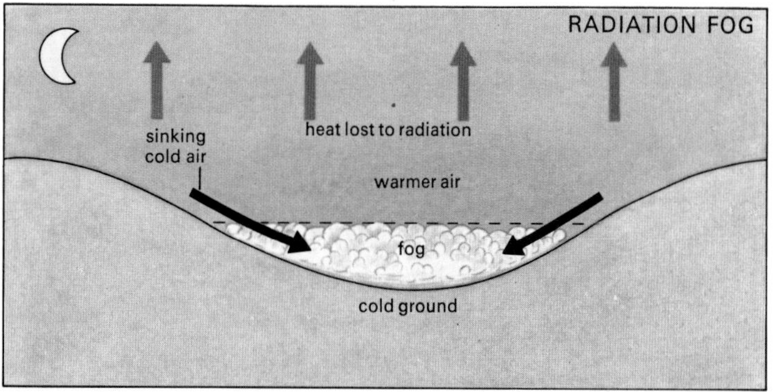

Left: This diagram illustrates the formation of *radiation* fog. Clear skies at night allow a great deal of the ground's surface heat to radiate into the atmosphere. As long as there are no strong winds, the cool ground in turn cools the overlying air up to a height of 20-30 m. Fog will form when this cooling effect takes moist air below its condensation temperature. As cool air tends to sink and flow into valleys, this is where fogs tend to accumulate, greatly reducing visibility.

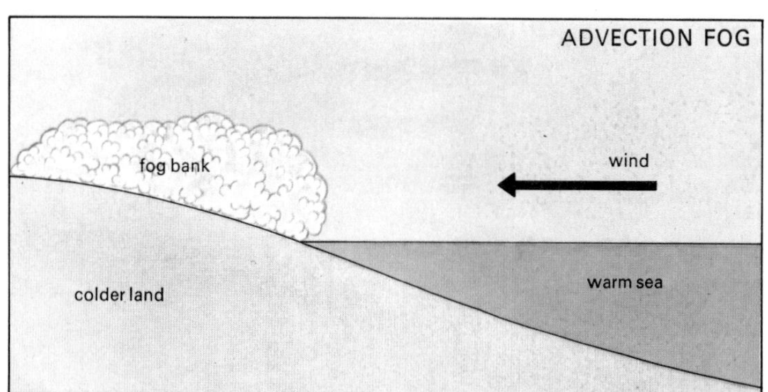

Right: Moist warm air blown across a cold surface may thus be cooled to below its condensation point. The fog caused is known as an *advection* (meaning horizontal flow) fog and occurs over both land and sea. Around the coasts of Britain, for example, these fogs develop when warm sea air blows over the colder land.

Below: Radiation fog—associated here with industrial air pollution—shrouds St Mary's Cathedral in Armidale, NSW, Australia.

David Moore

G. R. Roberts

Left: Hoar frost in a forest—formed instead of dew by deposit of ice crystals on objects when the dew point is below the freezing point.

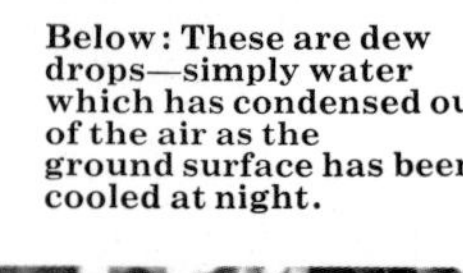

Below: These are dew drops—simply water which has condensed out of the air as the ground surface has been cooled at night.

Bruce Coleman

and later confirmed by the German meteorologist Findeisen, depends on the existence of both ice crystals and supercooled water at the top of a cloud, where the temperature is below —10°C. In such a situation, the liquid water evaporates and its vapour is deposited on the ice crystals. Once the crystals are large enough, they fall to the ground, giving either snow or rain depending on whether the snow melts during its descent.

Radar studies have shown that most rain clouds in the temperate latitudes do have snowflakes in their upper layers. However, Bergeron's explanation clearly cannot apply to clouds where the temperature never reaches freezing point or anywhere near it. Most tropical rain, therefore, starts from coalescence. In the mid-latitudes it is not easy to distinguish which process is in operation, but the fuzzy outline of glaciated upper parts of cumulus clouds is a sure sign that the Bergeron process is working.

Drizzle and hail

Drizzle is a very light rain which results from the coalescence process in low-level, shallow stratus cloud. The small droplets survive the short journey because of the high humidity of the air below the cloud. Technically, drizzle is said to occur where the raindrops are less than 0.5 mm (0.2 in) in diameter. Drizzle will travel to earth at 3 km/h (2 mph) or less, whereas the large drops of a thunderstorm may reach over 30 km/h.

While rain and snow may fall from both stratus and cumulus clouds—snow obviously being more likely in winter when the air is colder—hail falls mostly from cumulonimbus clouds. *Hail*, not snow, is actually frozen rain. Snowflakes form when water vapour condenses at a point below freezing; if the snow partially melts before it lands it is known as *sleet*.

World patterns of rainfall

As the upward movement of air is essential for the formation of clouds and for precipitation, both are more common in those weather systems where the air is rising. This occurs in both tropical and mid-latitude cyclones and thus on a world scale, the wettest areas tend to be those where such cyclones are most frequent. Perhaps the wettest place on earth is Cherrapunji in Assam, India, where 26,461 mm (1,042 in) of rain once fell in a single year—9,299 mm (366 in) in one month alone—from the tropical monsoon. By contrast London normally receives about 600 mm (24 in) each year. Deserts occur in regions where sinking air in anticyclones prevents the formation of cloud and thus of precipitation.

As well as the amount of rain, the seasonal distribution or *rainfall regime* is very important to man, as a regular supply of water is essential for cultivation, industry and domestic supply. In the tropics the diurnal (within-a-day) variation is frequently stronger and more regular than the seasonal distribution because the afternoon sun may trigger off cumulonimbus clouds. In the middle latitudes, the more frequent visits of cyclones to areas such as the British Isles bring slightly higher levels of rainfall in the winter than in the summer months. Nevertheless, many such places have more than 150 rainy days per year.

A lightning flash is a very powerful discharge of static electricity. Friction caused by air currents in a thunder cloud builds up until a massive discharge takes place between the cloud and the ground, or an object on it.

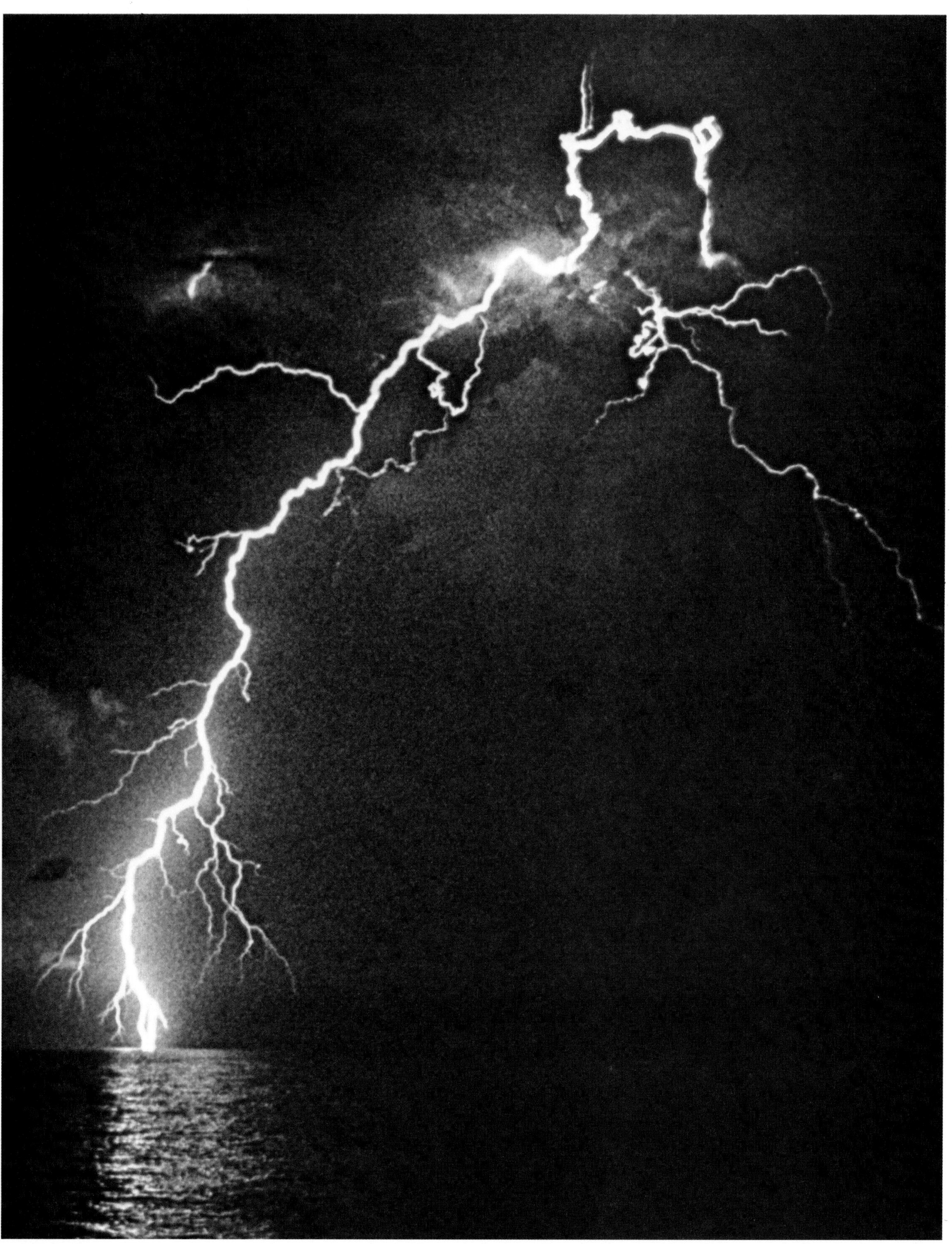

Weather Forecasting

The daily weather forecast on radio, television and in the newspapers probably provides the main point of contact between the public and the science of meteorology. The brief presentation of the forecast and the very simple symbols used may give the impression that forecasting is easy, requiring little scientific and technological knowledge. Such an impression is often encouraged by the apparent success of many traditional weather sayings or 'old saws' drawn from a mixture of experience and superstition.

Some 'old saws' have stood the test of time because they are based on experience of the typical behaviour of weather in certain areas. One of the best-known in Britain is the old adage: 'Red sky at night, shepherd's delight; red sky in the morning, shepherd's warning'. This saying simply recognizes the fact that the prevailing winds over the British Isles are westerlies. Redness in the sky at sunset or sunrise is caused by the presence of dust particles in the air. There is most dust when the air is dry and calm, so if the sky is red at sunset (in the west), dry air is moving towards the observer, bringing fair weather. On the other hand, if the dry, calm air appears in the east (red sky in the morning), there is a good chance that the spell of fine weather has passed, with the likelihood of wetter conditions not far behind moving in from the west.

Although weather lore sometimes represents a useful shorthand of observed conditions, modern scientific forecasting requires the collection of millions of observations, their analysis and translation into understandable meteorological patterns and projections of future weather events based on this analysis.

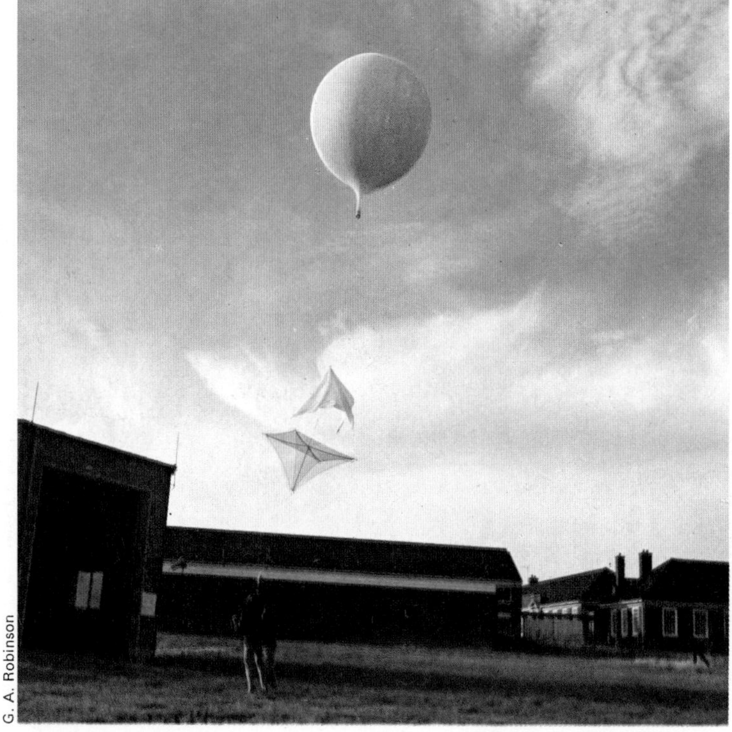

G. A. Robinson

Plessey

Above: Launching a *radio-sonde*. Carried up by a balloon, this device measures air pressure, temperature and humidity in the lower atmosphere. A radio signals back their values to a ground station. Its reflector is tracked by radar so that wind speed and direction can be deduced. The parachute aids recovery of the instruments.

Right: Air pressure is measured by a barometer. The diagram shows how the height of the column in a *mercury barometer* varies with pressure. The greater the 'weight' of air, the higher the mercury rises up the glass tube. The force exerted by atmospheric pressure of 1,000 mb supports 750 mm (29.5 in) of mercury.

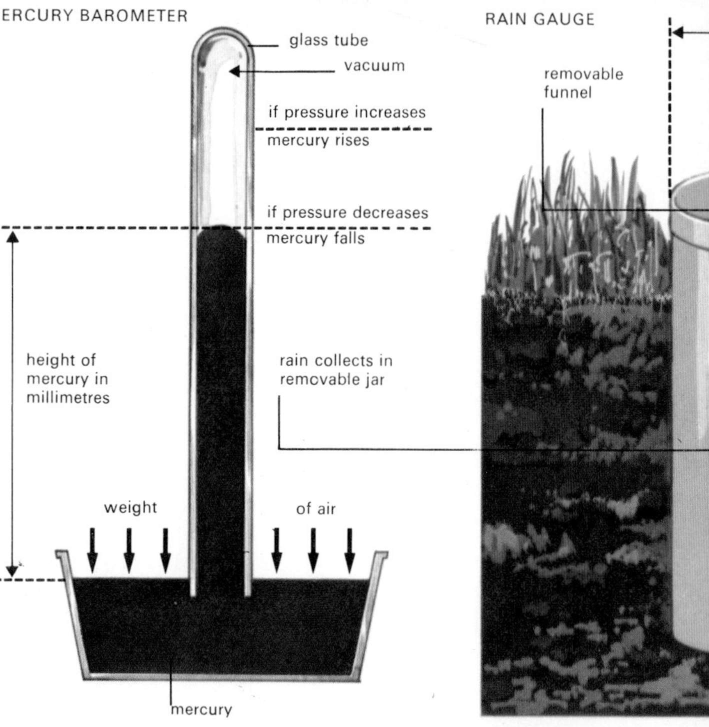

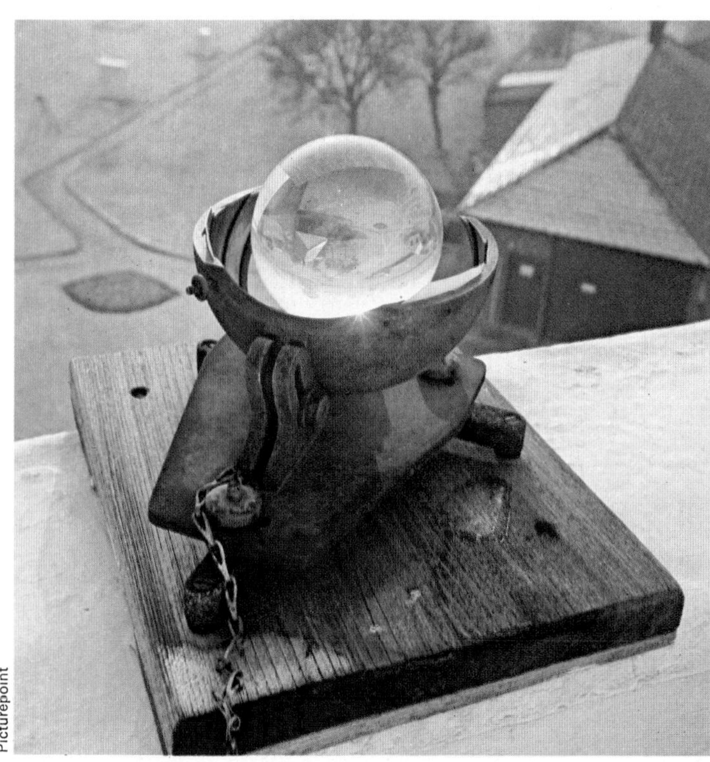

Picturepoint

Left: The sunshine recorder at Kew Observatory, London. The sun's rays are focused through the glass ball so that they burn a trace on a piece of card. As the sun moves across the sky, the trace is also moved. The length of the burn records the duration of bright sunshine.

Right: The Beaufort Scale is a system of estimating and reporting wind speeds invented in the early 19th century by Admiral Beaufort of the British Navy. It was originally based on the effects of various wind speeds on the canvas sails that a fully-rigged frigate of the period would carry. It has since been modified so that the 'effects' are shown on land as well as at sea.

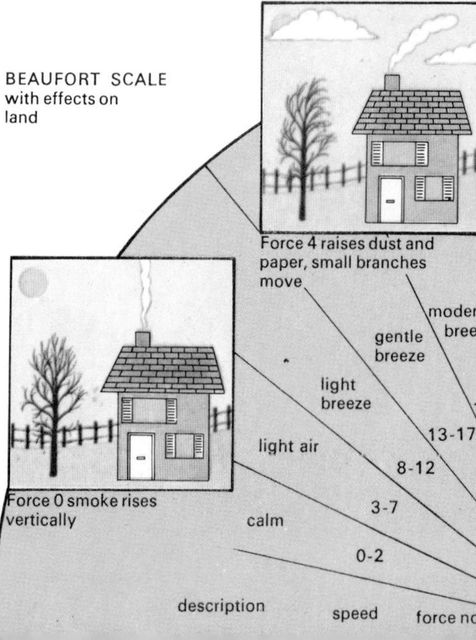

Collecting the information

Serious attempts at weather forecasting became possible only after the perfection of the electric telegraph in 1844 by the American inventor Samuel Morse. Reliable forecasts require the rapid collection of weather conditions reports from widely distributed observing stations. A vast global system served by a fast and efficient communications network now exists to speed information around the world.

At a meteorological station on the ground or on board a weather ship, observations are taken regularly of temperatures, dew point, humidity, atmospheric pressure and recent changes in pressure, wind speed and direction, precipitation, visibility and the type of cloud and height of visible cloud layers. At an airport observations may be reported as often as every half hour but it is more usual to report every 1 or 3 hours. Lesser stations report every six hours and some only once per day. All the information gathered by these stations is communicated in an internationally agreed code to a collecting centre.

To gain a comprehensive picture of weather conditions, meteorologists also need information from the higher levels in the atmosphere. Observations here are restricted to pressure, temperature, humidity, wind speed and direction. These elements are measured by a *radio-sonde*. This device, attached to a free balloon, carries instruments to measure pressure, temperature and humidity and a radio to signal back to a ground station their values continuously as it rises through the atmosphere. A 'target' attached to the balloon allows the whole package to be tracked by radar to reveal the course and speed of its drift. Twice a day from several hundred points around the globe, radio-sondes are released at the same time, thus providing a network of observations of the pressures, temperatures, humidities and winds throughout the depth of the troposphere and the lower stratosphere.

In the 1940s, ten years after radio-sondes were first used, radar was added to the meteorologists' observational armoury. During the Second World War, it had been noticed that aircraft could escape detection by flying into rain-cloud—the radar beam was intercepted by the precipitation in the cloud. In the postwar years, meteorologists put this discovery to good use and developed special radars to detect areas of precipitation. Radars are now used at many forecasting stations in the US and UK.

Satellites are a more recent observational tool. The first weather satellite was launched on 1 April 1960 by the US and has been followed by about thirty more. Satellite meteorology has proved invaluable in opening up those remote and often inhospitable areas of the globe, including much of the tropics and the Southern Hemisphere, which lack adequate coverage by observing stations on the ground. Some satellites orbit around the earth tracking approximately north-west to south-east; others are so high—about 35,000 km (22,000 miles) above the earth—that they provide 'snapshots' of whole hemisphere.

Most of the satellites provide both photographs of clouds and also information on radiation in different wavelengths.

Above left: An automatic weather station (AWS). Since 1960 these stations have been developed to give surface observations from previously poorly-observed areas on land and at sea. This AWS is recording temperature and humidity in the Stevenson screen (the white box at right). Wind speed is measured by the rotating cup of the *anenometer* and solar radiation by the device at top. These stations must be sufficiently sturdy and reliable to be left for weeks without attention. Measurements are either stored on magnetic tape or transmitted directly to a manned station at pre-set times. The information is then added to the total supply of meteorological observations.

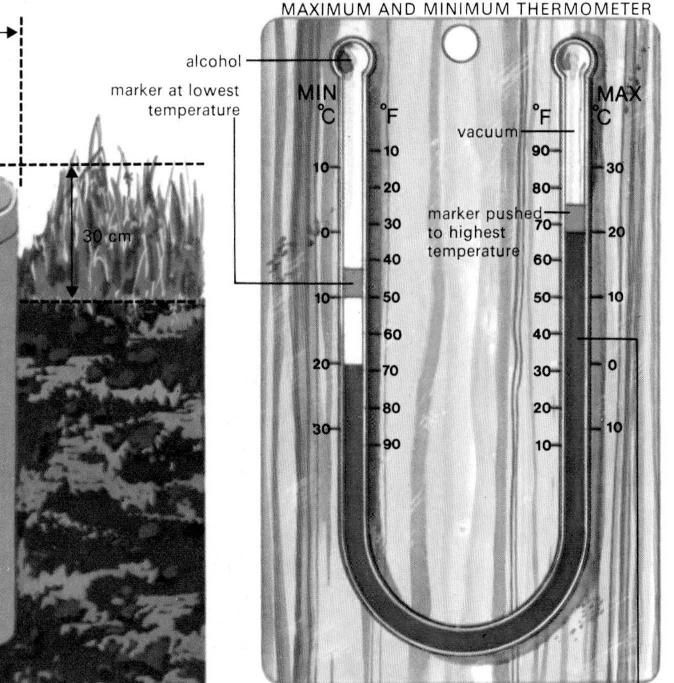

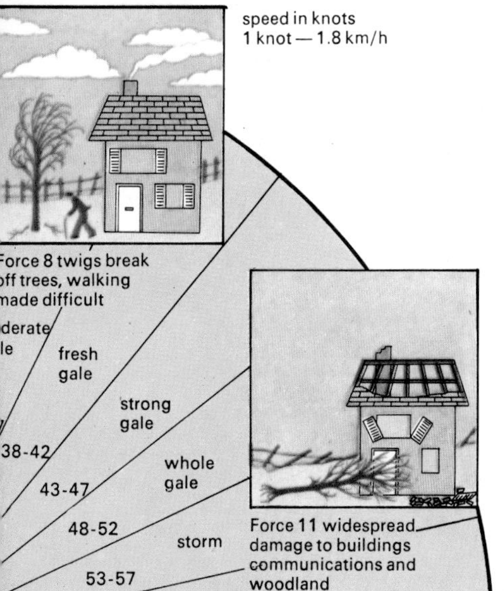

Above left: Rainfall is collected in a rain gauge and measured each day. Snow and hail are melted to give the water equivalent. Over 7000 such gauges in the UK are read daily for the Meteorological Office by volunteers, many of them at schools.

Above: The lowest and highest temperatures reached in a day are recorded by the metal markers in a maximum-minimum thermometer.

Right: A barograph is a self-recording *aneroid barometer*. Changes in pressure are picked up by sensitive vacuum chambers and transferred by a moving pen to a slowly rotating chart. This chart is recording atmospheric pressure over the course of a week.

G. A. Robinson

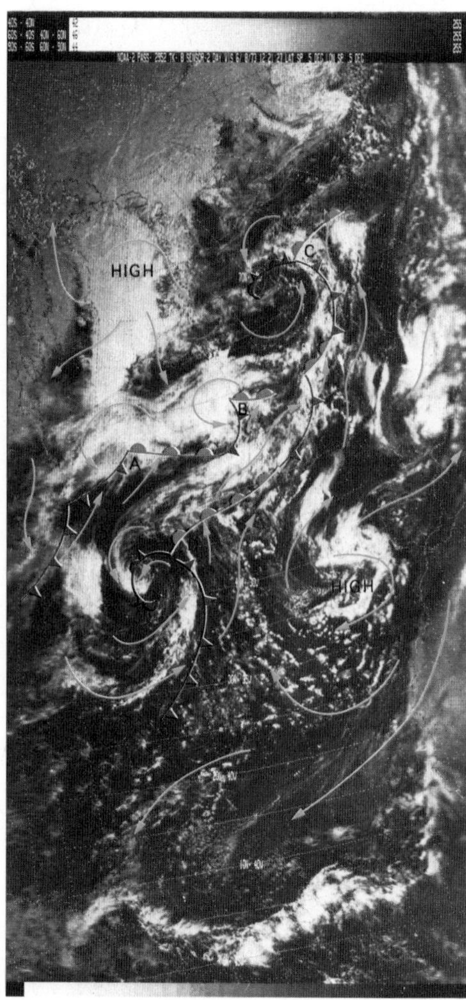

N.O.A.A.

Left: A satellite photograph of weather conditions over the NE Atlantic at noon on June 8, 1973. Clouds show up brightly, allowing areas of high and low pressure approaching Europe to be mapped out. There are two open-wave cyclones with cold and warm fronts at A and B. Two occluding cyclones, where the cold front has caught up with the warm front, appear at C and D. Both areas of high pressure are cloudy and a cluster of cumulus clouds are visible in the sub-tropics to the south.

Right: Information monitored by weather satellites can be radioed to aircraft in flight. Here the co-pilot is examining a visual report of the weather he is about to fly in.

Camera Press

METEOROLOGICAL OFFICE WEATHER MAP

CLOUD amount in oktas (eighths)
clear sky
1 or less
2
3
4
5
6
7
8
sky obscured
figure beside each station circle shows temperature in °C
cold front
warm front
occluded front

WIND direction shown by arrow
calm
1-2 knots
3-7 knots
8-12 knots
13-17 knots
for each additional 5 a half feather is adde
48-52 knots

WEATHER
mist
fog
drizzle
rain
snow
shower
hail
thunderstorr
sleet
snow showe
O.W.S. ocean weath station

HOW INFORMATION IS PLOTTED ON A STATION MODEL

high and medium cloud
temperature
visibility
present weather
dew point
wind direction
pressure
rise or fall in pressure
past weather
low cloud

temperature 10°C
visibility 15m. raining
dew point temperature 10°C
SW wind 23-27 knots (moderate breeze)
pressure 996 mb
pressure decreasing then steady
rain in past hour
stratus (low cloud)
complete low cloud cover
base of low cloud 100-200m. hig

Birmingham 18

Above: A synoptic weather map for much of W Europe at 1800 GMT on January 2, 1976. A well-developed depression is centred over Scotland, with central pressure at 972 mb. Fairly steep pressure gradients indicate strong winds—about 40 knots in Wales and the Hebrides. Cloud covers virtually all of the UK, but is clearing behind the cold front in W Ireland. It is raining and drizzling in all parts of the UK, with mist in SW Ireland. Temperatures range from 4°C ahead of the warm front, to 9-12°C in the warm sector, to 8-10°C in Ireland behind the cold front. High pressure over NW Spain has given clear skies, with mist and fog on the coast.

Of these two types of observation the cloud photographs were of most value at first, as they provided much fuller information on cloud distribution. In recent years, however, the prospect of calculating the vertical distribution of temperature from the radiation measurements has given the latter a renewed importance, especially as an alternative to using radio-sondes.

Cloud photographs from satellites provided spectacular confirmation of the theory of the 'life history' of cyclones suggested in the 1920s by the two Scandinavian scientists Bjerknes and Solberg. The photographs also revealed many cloud patterns previously unseen, particularly over the oceans where there had been no observations.

How forecasts are made

Before a weather forecast can be drawn up, some sense has to be made of the millions of observations collected at any one time. As many observations as possible are plotted on a weather map known as a *synoptic chart*. The term 'synoptic' simply means that the chart gives a synopsis or summary of the known state of the atmosphere at one particular time. The location of cyclones, fronts and anticyclones, together with any other distinguishable weather systems, are then easily located by drawing isobars between points of equal pressure. The isobars provide an immediate picture of the areas of high and low pressure. Indirectly they also reveal wind direction and speed because of the close relationship between pressure gradient and wind.

The distribution of both pressure and wind gives the forecaster his best estimate of how the air is moving. Such informa-

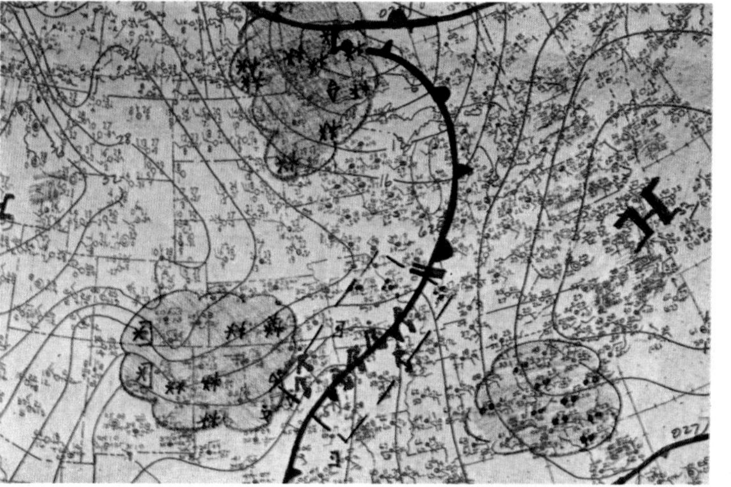

Photri

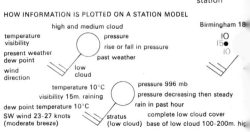

Left: A photograph of an actual synoptic chart of weather observed over much of the central US. It shows the bewildering amount of detail that mus be taken in and analysed by a forecaster, before he can predict future weather conditions. High pressure exists over the eastern seaboard and the Rockies to the west. Between the two lies an occluded front.

Right: A radar picture of rainfall over Wales on November 15, 1975. Radar can 'see' precipitation within clouds. Its receiver picks up echoes whose strength depends on the intensity of the rainfall. The results are displayed on a screen, with the most intense rainfall shown in yellow.

Left: An artist's conception of a Nimbus weather satellite. This family of US satellites, in use since 1964, is powered by solar energy received via the wing-like 'paddles'. A steady stream of weather pictures, over 1,000 daily, have been relayed by Automatic Picture Transmission (APT) aerials (right) on the ground.

Below: Daily forecasts are now made by computers using complicated models. This simulated global map of surface pressure (shown in isobars) and cloud cover (in white) for a typical January was calculated and drawn by a computer at the National Centre for Atmospheric Research in Colorado, US.

Photri

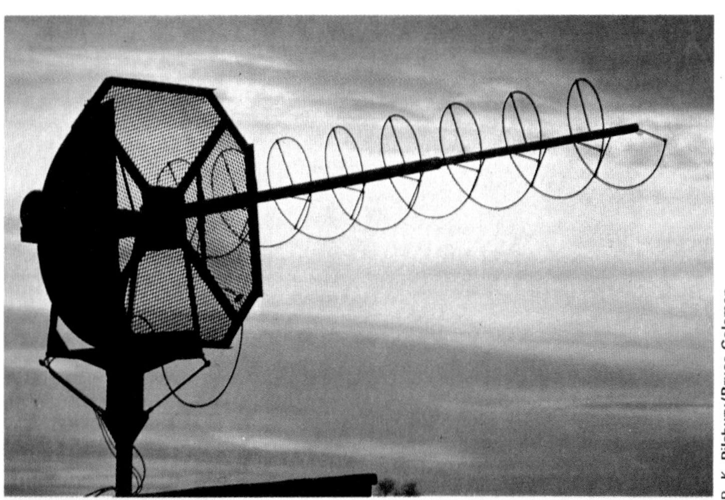

R. K. Pilsbury/Bruce Coleman

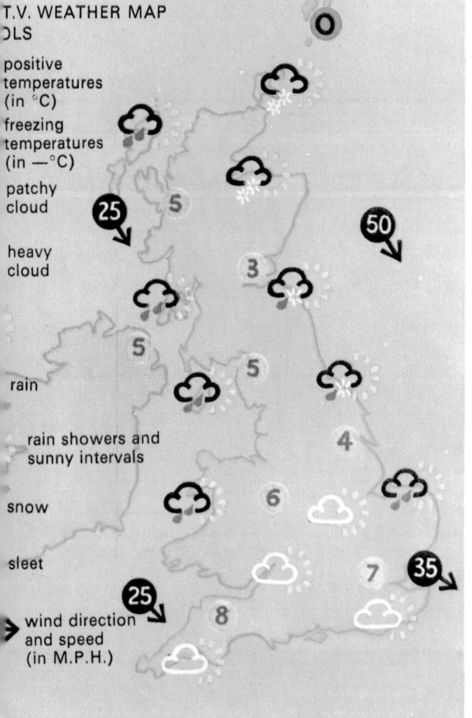

Left: Observations recorded at a weather station are plotted on a *station model*, using special symbols. The diagrams show where all the symbols are plotted around the station's circle. Both present and past weather are shown. The example given is that of Birmingham, taken from the large synoptic map.

Above: The forecast for noon next day (based on the synoptic chart) as would have been seen on BBC TV. The depression has moved away, to be followed by a ridge of high pressure, bringing a general 4°C drop in temperatures; sunny intervals in S and central England and snow or rain showers elsewhere; winds NW.

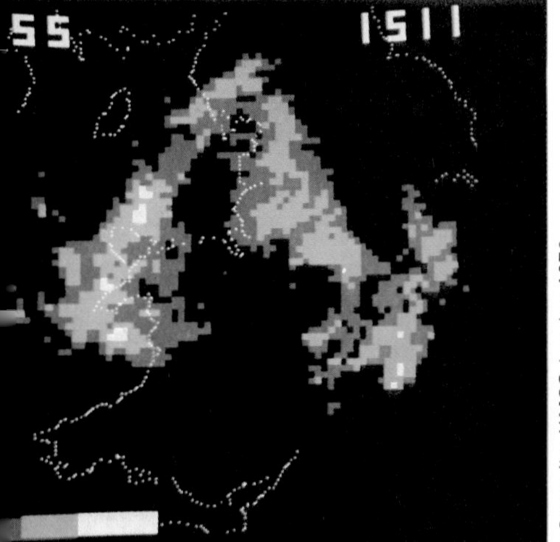

National Centre for Atmospheric Research

tion is critical as moving air is the ultimate cause of our weather. Upward moving air tends to cause cloud and precipitation; downward moving air tends to give us clear, sunny skies.

Once the meteorologist is satisfied that his chart is a fair representation of the observations, he is confronted by the forecast problem. His public wants to know whether it will be hot or cold, wet or dry tomorrow. The easiest way to provide such information is to forecast what the weather map will look like the next day and in essence this means forecasting how the air will be moving within that time. An accurate forecast assures a reliable prediction of the locations and intensities of the cyclones and anticyclones. Only then can the forecaster 'put in' on his chart the weather, such as cloud, rain, wind and sun, using a knowledge of how they are related to the structure of cyclones and anticyclones.

The traditional or synoptic method of forecasting is based on analysis of a series of weather charts. The forecaster uses all his knowledge and experience to produce a weather map for 24, 36 or 48 hours ahead which he interprets into a 'plain-word' forecast. For example, if the forecaster locates an active warm front (one along which rain is falling) over the west coast of Ireland in the circulation of a depression which is travelling from west to east and providing he thinks that the front will remain active, then he may feel fairly confident in forecasting rain 12 to 24 hours later for those parts of England and Wales over which the front will pass. Rain belts associated with warm fronts, cold fronts and other troughs of low pressure are usually between 20 and 200 km (12-125 miles) wide. Their normal speed of at least 30-40 km/h (18-25 mph) means that the period of rain associated with their passage rarely lasts for more than 4 or 5 hours. This is recognized by the old saying: 'Rain before seven, dry by eleven'.

Long-range forecasts

There are many factors which can change within 24 hours and it is virtually impossible to keep an eye on all of them. This explains why forecasts are not always correct. The longer the period for which the forecast is made, the more general and less reliable the forecast tends to be. Most forecasts are for a day ahead, and these maybe updated every six or twelve hours, but some forecasts are for an entire month ahead. In India attempts have been made to forecast a whole season, that is, to predict when the monsoon will arrive.

Whereas short-range forecasts (for a few days) can be quite detailed in their coverage of places and times, monthly forecasts have to rely on records of past weather behaviour for that time of year and are restricted to statements of whether it will be drier, wetter, warmer or cooler than normal over large areas. Despite their generality, such forecasts are useful to planners in industry and agriculture. For example, gas and electricity suppliers need both short- and long-range forecasts of such elements as temperature as these may influence the demands made for energy.

Since 1960 short-range forecasts have increasingly been made by computers. The millions of mathematical calculations and equations needed to forecast the distribution of pressure and wind and how they may change are done by a computer in a matter of minutes. The machine even draws the maps of the predicted pressure and wind distributions. The general procedure clearly parallels that used in the synoptic method. The forecaster then 'puts in' the actual weather that he thinks will result from his predicted systems.

In recent years, computers have begun to do this job also. In the British Meteorological Office at Bracknell a very complicated mathematical model can now predict weather (particularly precipitation) from systems as small as 100 km (60 miles) across. At the other extreme scientists in the US have simulated the whole general circulation of the atmosphere for the month of January. Whilst this is not forecasting, it does show the depth of understanding of the atmosphere now achieved by meteorologists.

Tropical Climates

It is often assumed that *climate* simply represents the 'average weather' of a particular place, especially in terms of mean temperature and rainfall figures. In fact, these figures only partly describe the climate of a locality, for the climate of any area is the synthesis of all the weather conditions experienced there over a period of time. Thus it incorporates both the weather systems which produce the temperature and rainfall figures and the large variability within a climate which averages may hide.

The climate of a given place is determined by three main factors: latitude, continentality and altitude. Latitude determines the amount of solar radiation to be received, and a locality's latitude also determines its position within the general circulation of the atmosphere. The geographical position in terms of how near or far it is from the moderating influences of the sea determines whether the climate will be essentially maritime or continental; its height above sea-level will modify its rainfall and temperature.

Because most living things require warmth and moisture to varying degrees to survive, their distributions over the earth are strongly influenced by climate. If the earth's climates are classified into major groupings, certain patterns emerge and these boundaries often coincide with the major boundaries in the distributions of natural vegetation and soils. The classifications vary according to the rainfall and temperature criteria adopted, and the transition zones are often difficult to incorporate. However, natural vegetation is a better indicator of the effects of climates than any instrument, and is thus a good index of prevailing climatic conditions.

Bruce Coleman

Above: A typically lush equatorial rain forest in Guyana. The plants shown here are well adapted to the conditions of high temperatures, high humidities and heavy convectional rainfalls (often falling in short, intense downpours lasting only 3 hours). The evergreen leaves can withstand the intense radiation and high midday temperatures which would kill the leaves of most deciduous trees. Despite often infertile soils, rain forests are the densest on earth. In the East Indies, the dense foliage of tall (60-90 m high) trees form a canopy over a thick undergrowth inhabited by species adapted to the heat and lack of light.

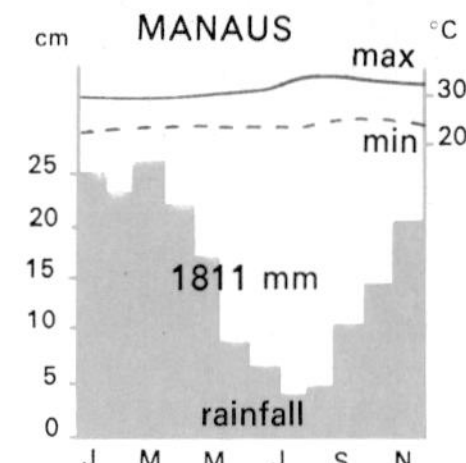

Left: The station graph for Manaus in the equatorial Amazon basin. Mean monthly equatorial temperatures are consistently 25-27°C. Typically, the high rainfall totals also vary little (Singapore averages no less than 170 mm each month) but Manaus shows greater local variation and even has a fairly dry season.

Climates in the tropics

The regions of the world with tropical climates fall largely between 23½° N and S (the Tropics of Cancer and Capricorn), but are by no means restricted within these latitudes. Tropical climates have been defined quantitatively as those regions where the average temperature for any month does not fall below 18°C (64.4°F), that is, they all lack a cold season. Nevertheless, within these regions there are striking variations, most notably in the amount of rainfall received. An analysis of the dominant factor in tropical climatology—the Hadley Cell—helps to explain these variations.

The Hadley Cell is the name given to the continual overturning of the atmosphere which is vital in transporting heat and energy polewards to maintain the earth's heat balance. Air flows towards the equator in the Trade Winds belt, rises near the equator in the Intertropical Convergence Zone (ITCZ), flows towards the poles in the upper troposphere, and then sinks beneath the westerly subtropical jet stream in the subtropical anticyclones.

From the sub-tropical anticyclones, characterized by deep and extensive sinking air and dry sunny conditions, the Trade Winds blow westwards and equatorwards in both hemispheres (north-east winds in the Northern Hemisphere and south-east in the Southern Hemisphere). These winds are known for their constancy of direction and speed. Nevertheless, while the steady fair-weather conditions are typical of the central and eastern oceanic areas, their constancy declines the further they move from this source area. By the time they have traversed vast expanses of tropical ocean, they frequently have small disturbances embedded within them, especially in the vicinity of the ITCZ, in the form of easterly waves and occasionally hurricanes.

The air within the Trades, however, is generally stable (in contrast to the unstable air associated with convection). Cloud development is limited by the trade-wind inversion (a layer where temperatures increase with height) which occurs at a height of about 500 m (1600 ft) near the centre of the subtropical highs and rises equatorwards and westwards. Above the inversion the air is extremely dry. Because the clouds are not deep enough to produce rain, all the moisture that evaporates from the warm ocean waters is transported equatorwards to the ITCZ where deep clouds form, rainfall totals are large and much latent heat is liberated.

The Intertropical Convergence Zone is a low pressure area between the Trade Wind systems of both hemispheres. Here the Trades converge, causing the air to rise vertically upwards to produce deep cumulus and cumulonimbus clouds with heavy showery rain and thunderstorms. Vast amounts of latent heat are liberated and this adds to the air's instability. Wind conditions in this area are complex: some areas (known as the *doldrums*) have light, indeterminate winds, while in others light easterlies are common.

Within the tropics temperatures are uniformly high. The most important factor which differentiates tropical climates is rainfall—its amount, its seasonal occurrence and its balance with the amounts of evaporation occurring. On this basis five broad climatic types can be distinguished.

Equatorial climates

The main areas of equatorial climates occur in the Amazon Basin, the Congo Basin, the oceanic margins of tropical West Africa, and South East Asia. This irregular belt some 10 to 20 degrees latitude wide around the equatorial girdle of the earth is only interrupted by areas

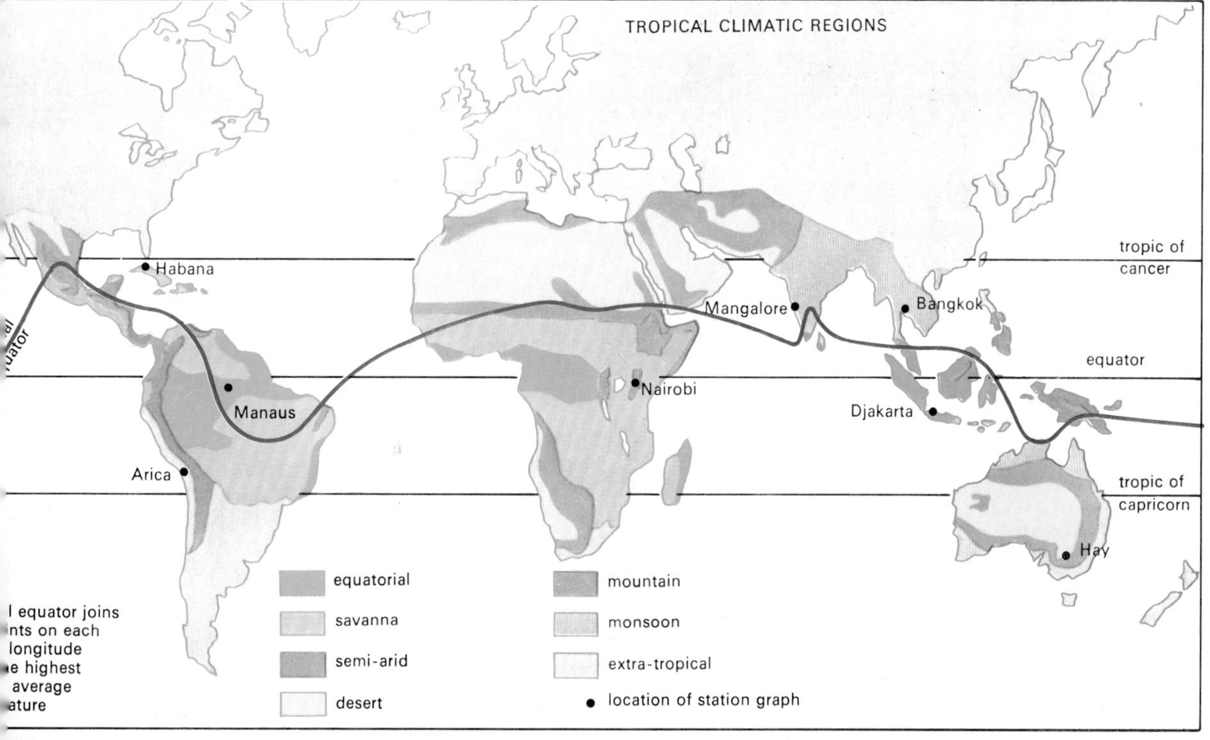

Left: The tropical climates of the world. Climatic regions are drawn where climatic conditions are fairly uniform over a wide area. This classification is based on the widely accepted scheme devised by W. Köppen, one of the founders of modern climatology. Köppen was impressed by the close correlation between vegetation types and the amounts of mean monthly temperature and precipitation amounts. Within the tropics, temperatures are uniformly high. The most important difference is that of rainfall—its amount, its seasonal occurrence and the balance between precipitation and evaporation rates. 'Wet' climates are those where precipitation exceeds the rate of evaporation. 'Dry' tropical climates —the deserts and semi-arid areas—are distinguished by greater evaporation rates.

Below: In the Assam province of India, these elephants are being employed to clear the jungle to make way for a railway line. The teak forest is typical of such monsoonal areas, and the sale of the lumber provides income.

Robert Harding

Left: Rice terraces and coconut palms on the island of Bali, Indonesia. Rice is a most important part of the diet in Asian countries: it provides a higher yield per sq km and feeds more people than any other cereal. The rice crop needs large amounts of water during its growing period and, in order to trap the rainfall, horizontal terraces like these are constructed on every available space. In this part of Bali, rainfall totals are high (over 2,500 mm), but the rain comes in short, heavy downpours, to be lost without terraces. Cultivation can continue during dry periods.

Below: The station graph for Djakarta, the capital of Indonesia.

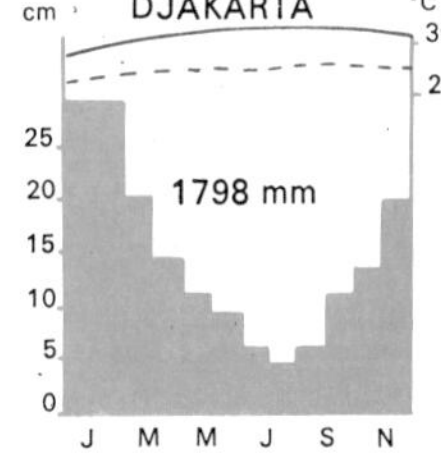

Robert Harding

of highland and areas affected by oceanic influences.

The climate is characterized by high temperatures—around 25-27°C (77-81°F) —and large precipitation totals uniformly distributed throughout the year. This, together with the high humidity and intense sunlight, gives rise to a lush, rich and dense tropical rainforest vegetation.

The sun is almost always vertically overhead at midday. Consequently solar radiation figures are high and the length of day varies little during the year. The cloud cover prevents excessive temperatures, but the uniformity and monotony of the never-ending succession of hot months without relief, together with the slight air movement and high humidities, produces oppressive, sultry and energy-sapping conditions for humans. These are, however, superb growing conditions for the dense rainforest. The main relief comes at night (the tropical equivalent of winter), for although afternoon temperatures may reach 29-34°C (85-93°F), typical night-time values are between 20 and 24°C (68-75°F).

The equatorial region contains some areas of notably heavy precipitation, primarily because of rainfall from the ITCZ. Average figures are 1,800-2,500 mm

(70-100 ins), but these may be increased by local topographic effects. For example, near the foot of Cameroon Mountain in equatorial Africa some 12,000 mm (400 ins) are recorded annually. Most of the rains come in the form of torrential downpours, and in general this region has between 75 and 150 days with thunderstorms each year.

Savanna climates

The regions experiencing these climates lie in zones immediately polewards of the equatorial areas and experience smaller annual rainfall totals, which tend to come from a shorter wet season followed by a long dry season. The savanna lands include the Sudan/Sahel region of Africa south of the Sahara, much of central, eastern and south-eastern Africa, and areas north and south of the Amazon Basin.

Here the vegetation is dominated by deciduous forest and tree-studded grasslands. Savanna climates represent a transition zone between the influence of the ITCZ and the subtropical high pressure regions. They experience unstable convective airmasses at the time of high-sun and sinking anticyclonic air at other times of the year. Temperatures remain high and similar to those experienced in the hot, wet equatorial regions, but the annual range of temperature is greater (usually some 3 to 8°C). The hottest months occur at the end of the dry season, the cooler months during the wet season (when there is a lot of cloud).

The typical annual rainfall for this region is 1,000-1,600 mm (40-60 ins), but is highly seasonal. During the dry months desert-type weather prevails, for the drought is usually intense, but as the ITCZ migrates with the overhead sun so the convective disturbances migrate with it and produce the rainy season. Rainfall is much less reliable than in the hot, wet climates.

Tropical Semi-Arid climates

The tropical semi-arid climates represent a transition zone between the very dry desert regions and the bordering, moister savanna lands. The dominant feature of the climates is that there is a lack of sufficient effective rainfall (that is, rainfall sufficient to overcome evaporative losses) to sustain dense vegetation. Such areas are found north and south of the Sahara desert, in south-west Africa, in a belt through the Middle East towards India, and around the periphery of the Australian Desert.

The seasonal distribution of rainfall is usually better defined than in the neighbouring deserts, but its variability from year to year is a critical factor in determining agricultural land-use.

Desert climates

The main tropical deserts coincide with the heart of the dry, subsiding air found in the subtropical anticyclones. All the major examples—the Sahara desert, the Kalahari of South Africa, the Sonoran and Baja Californian of north-west Mexico, the Atacama-Peruvian desert of South America and the Australian desert—lie adjacent to the west coasts of their respective continents. The stable, sinking anticyclonic air is often further stabilized by cool offshore currents.

Desert rainfall is notoriously small in total: at Lima in Peru, for instance, the

Right: Monsoon clouds over Bangkok, the capital of Thailand. Bangkok is 30 km from the sea and experiences a typical monsoon climate. It receives an annual total of 1,390 mm of rain, with a marked wet season between May and October. It is much drier, but only slightly cooler, during the winter months.

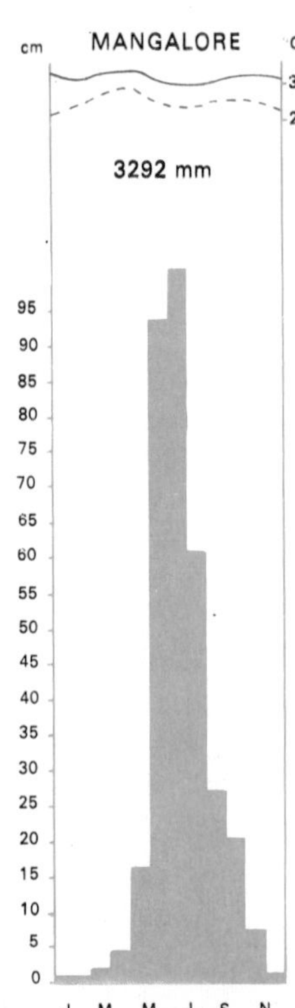

Explorer

Left: Mangalore is on the west coast of India—the windward side when the wet south-westerly monsoon winds blow across the sub-continent. Thus rainfall totals are high, with June, July and August as by far the wettest months.

Right: The station graph for Bangkok, a monsoon station.

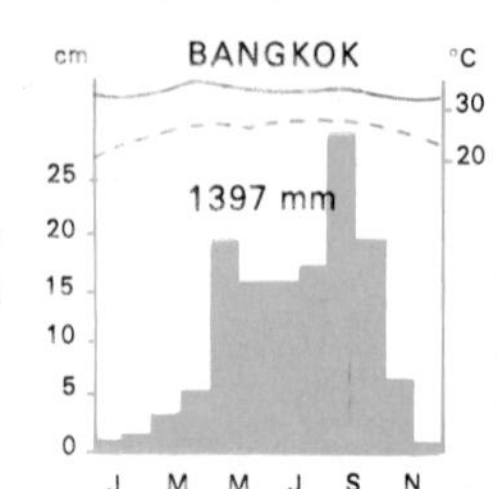

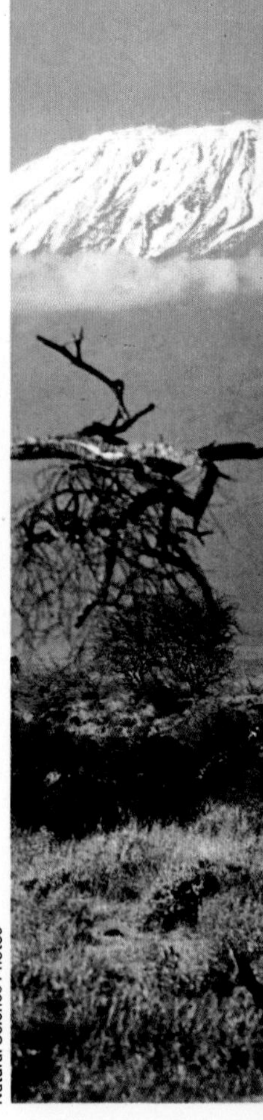

Natural Science Photos

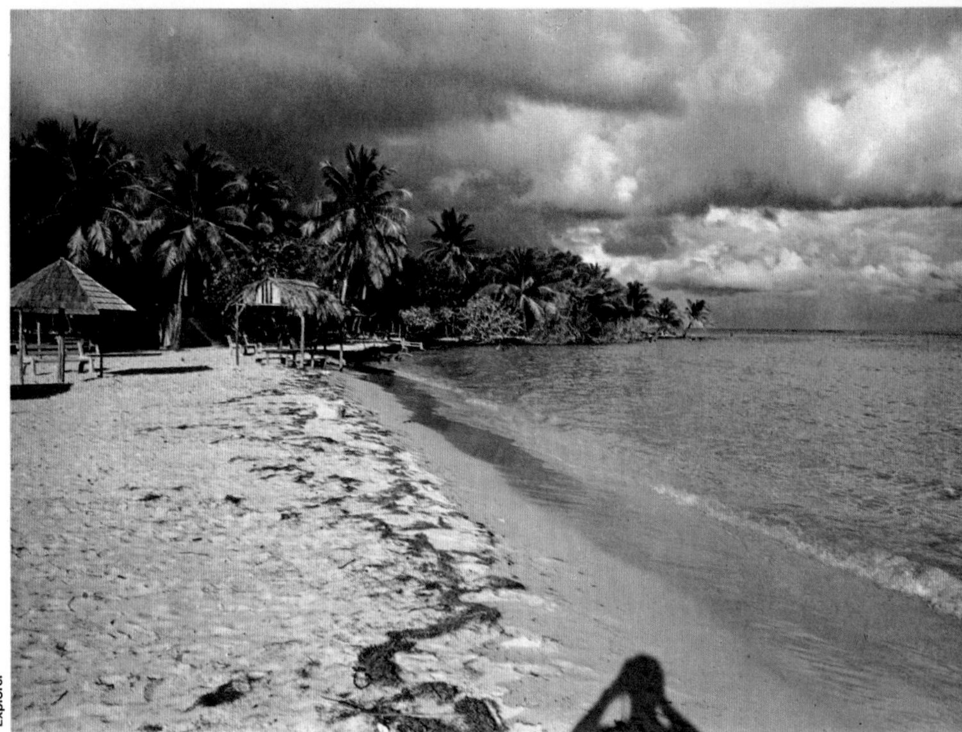

© Explorer

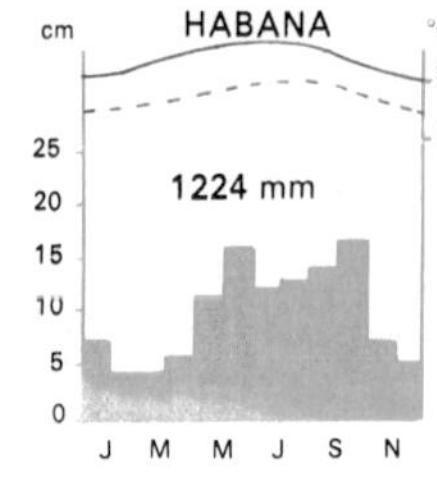

Above: A beach on the island of Guadeloupe in the West Indies. The east coast margins of tropical areas, such as the Caribbean and the north-east Queensland coast of Australia, are sometimes classified as a separate climatic region. They are normally sunny regions, directly facing the Trade Winds, in which disturbances, such as easterly waves and the occasional tropical cyclone, occur. For most of the year, Guadeloupe has temperatures of about 26°C; sea temperatures are warm and onshore breezes maintain pleasant conditions, ideal for its tourist industry. The station graph for Habana, Cuba, shows the rainy summer months.

Right: Tall saguaro cacti, brittlebush and flowering golden poppies in the desert. The cactus family (native to America) is specially adapted to the dry heat. The stem contains fleshy tissue to retain moisture and the long roots tap water from the soil. The poppies burst into flower soon after any sudden rainstorms.

Right: The semi-arid country of the Murray River basin in NSW, Australia. Tropical semi-arid climates lack sufficient effective rainfall to sustain more than a short cover of grasses and drought-resistant shrubs like the saltbush, shown here. Nearby Hay (graph below) receives only 350 mm of rain in a year.

G. R. Roberts

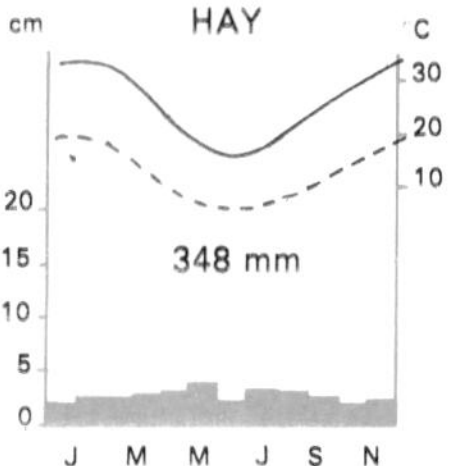

Left: Mt Kilimanjaro (5,895 m high) towers over the savanna lands of East Africa. Low rainfall totals (500-750 mm) over the grasslands contrast with the 1,800 mm of orographic precipitation (much of it snow) on the mountain. Nairobi's graph (below) reflects its altitude (1,650 m) more than the regional climate.

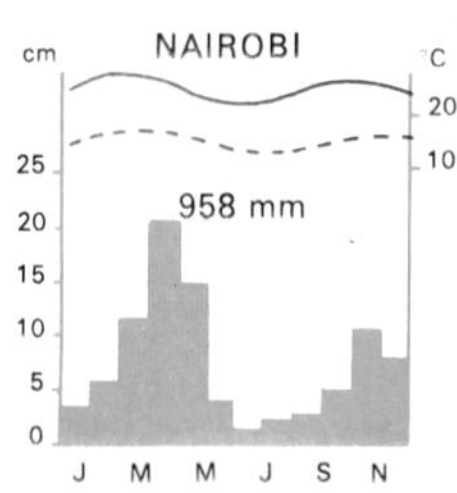

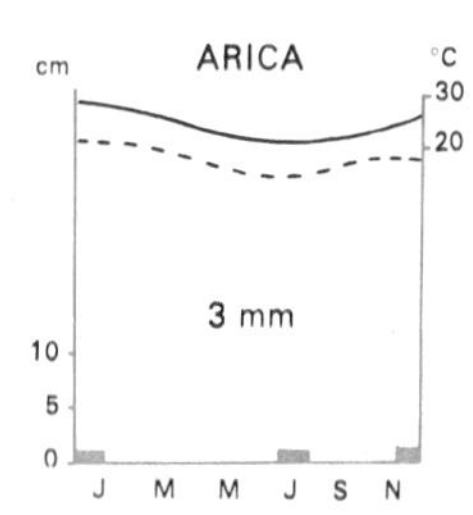

Below: Atacama desert in northern Chile is one of the world's driest places. The station graph for Arica, on the coast of Chile, shows a negligible amount of rainfall. The air is very dry, the sky normally cloudless, and the unbroken arid landscape with its salty soil means that few plants can survive.

Bruce Coleman

Bruce Coleman

annual average is 51 mm (2 ins), at Yuma, Arizona, it is 59 mm (2.3 ins), and at Calama in northern Chile it is said that no rain has ever been recorded. Totals are low, but the rain is also highly erratic: when it does come it will fall as a sudden torrential downpour.

Annual temperature ranges (some 11-17°C or 20-30°F) are larger than in any other tropical climate, due to the seasonal variation of solar radiation under conditions of clear sky. Daily ranges are often larger. One station in Libya has recorded a minimum temperature of —1°C (31°F) and a maximum of 37°C (99°F) on the same day. During the high-sun period scorching, dessicating heat prevails; at Insala, south of Algiers, 59.4°C (139°F) has been recorded, the highest air temperature in the shade ever registered. The temperature decreases towards the period of low sun and in this season the nights feel distinctly chilly.

Vegetation is very sparse because the little rain that does fall soon evaporates under the scorching conditions. Hence the only vegetation which can survive is either peculiarly adapted to these extreme conditions such as the agave and American cactus, or, like the blooming desert flower, can take advantage of the sudden downpours, or, like the date palm, have access to groundwater, particularly near oases.

Monsoon climates

The monsoon climates are known for their great reversals. They are found in much of South East Asia and with less intensity in northern Australia, but the tropical monsoon climate is most dramatically illustrated on the Indian subcontinent. Here, the winter period is dry with north-easterly surface winds and westerly upper winds; the summer is wet with south-westerly surface winds and easterly upper winds. The Indian monsoon is still not completely understood—it is as if the atmosphere undergoes a huge somersault.

The winter season is dominated by the stable, continental north-easterly flow. Cloud development is restricted and the only rainfall comes from occasional disturbances in the north. During the spring the weather becomes hot, dry and squally in response to the greater insolation. Temperatures rise quickly from 23°C (73°F) in March to 33°C (91°F) in May in Delhi; this is the hot, dry and dusty season of India. Overall rainfall is minimal.

From early June, a surface flow of unstable, maritime air pulsates northwards, the 'burst of the monsoon' replacing the continental air. This south-west monsoon generally consists of two branches. One comes from the Arabian Sea to meet the west coast of India at right angles, giving rise to heavy orographic rain. Another comes from the Bay of Bengal, converging with the other air stream in the Monsoon trough over the Ganges valley, producing heavy rainfall.

India's summer rain is variable in amount and distribution. 2,080 mm (82 ins) falls on Bombay, 1,250 mm (49 ins) at Madras, 2,900 mm (113 ins) at Chittagong and an astonishing 10,800 mm (426 ins) at Cherrapunji in the Khasi Hills of north-east India. These amounts vary from year to year causing drought one year and flooding the next, important factors in the Indian economy.

Temperate and Cold Climates

The climate of any area incorporates all the weather elements (especially temperature and precipitation) experienced there over a period of time. Once one moves out of the tropical regions into the temperate and cold climates of middle and higher latitudes, average temperatures fall and rainfall patterns become noticeably different. The climate of an extra-tropical area is largely determined by how often, and how intensely, cyclones and anticyclones occur. Cyclones tend to bring cloud and rain, whereas anticyclones frequently bring clear, sunny days and foggy (sometimes frosty) nights.

These weather systems themselves are basically caused by variations in airflow in the massive air waves, known as the *Rossby waves*, within the prevailing Westerlies. If the number and location of Rossby waves change, then so do the frequency and intensity of cyclones and anticyclones in any given area. Seasonal climatic changes are due to the massive latitudinal shift in the Rossby waves .

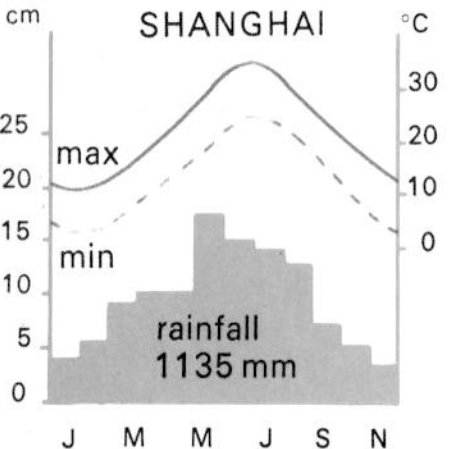

Below: Taiwan has a humid sub-tropical climate. Winters are warmer than on the Chinese mainland, but both areas share a seasonal pattern of rainfall. Rainfall in other humid sub-tropical areas is more uniformly distributed. The station graph for Shanghai in China (left) plots rainfall and temperature.

ZEFA

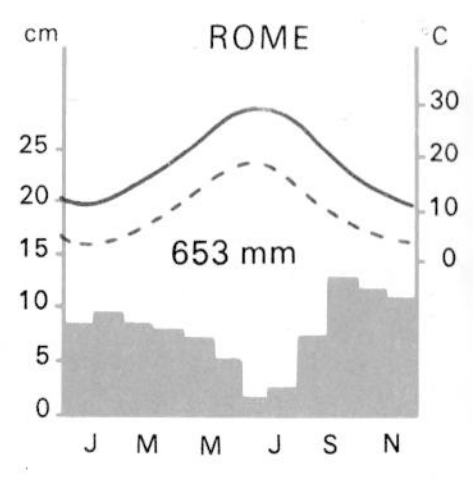

Above: The station graph for Rome, which enjoys hot, dry summers but mild, rainy winters.

Left: The Adriatic coast of Yugoslavia has a typical Mediterranean climate. Natural vegetation consists mainly of scrub and trees able to survive the dry summers. These areas are famous for the wines produced from cultivated vineyards.

Right: The temperate and cold climates of the world. The divisions are based on the classification originally devised by W. Koppen, who drew correlations between maps of natural vegetation and mean monthly temperature and precipitation. The most notable features of the extra-tropical regions are that they become progressively colder towards the poles and that west coasts are the wettest areas due to the prevailing westerlies in middle latitudes.

Photri

Superimposed on this basic mechanism are the effects of land and sea distribution and mountains. In general terms, areas which are great distances from the oceans experience air which has been 'dried out' somewhat in its passage from the ocean. Consequently these so-called *continental regions* tend to be drier than areas nearer the oceans. Moreover, because they are unaffected by the ocean's moderating effect on temperature ranges (both daily and seasonal), they experience greater extremes of heat and cold.

An increase in altitude also exerts a profound influence on climate. Mountains have the effect of lowering mean temperatures (because temperature falls with height in the atmosphere) and increasing precipitation and windiness. Thus mountainous areas, both inside and outside the tropics, are considered as a distinct climatic type. With the aid of the classification of climates originally devised by the German climatologist W. Köppen, it is possible to recognize nine other climatic types in extra-tropical latitudes.

Mediterranean climates

Although first recognized in the coastal lowlands around the Mediterranean Sea, this particular climate prevails on the west coasts of all continents in the lower middle (warm temperate) latitudes. A

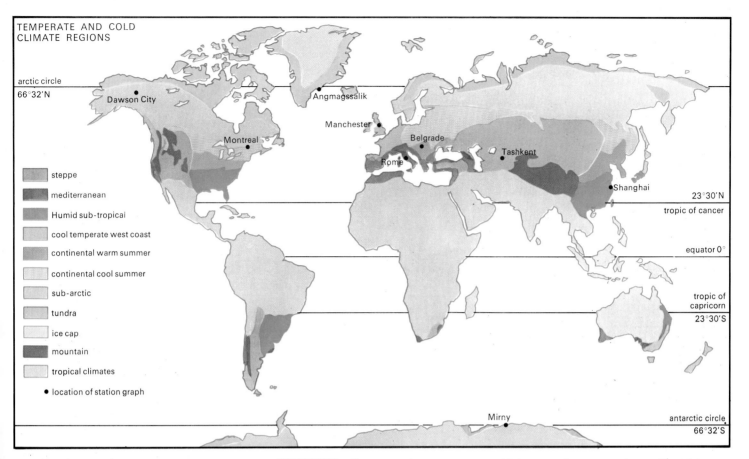

TEMPERATE AND COLD CLIMATE REGIONS

arctic circle 66°32′N

Dawson City

Angmagssalik

Manchester

Montreal

Belgrade

Rome

Tashkent

Shanghai

23°30′N tropic of cancer

equator 0°

tropic of capricorn 23°30′S

Mirny

antarctic circle 66°32′S

- steppe
- mediterranean
- Humid sub-tropical
- cool temperate west coast
- continental warm summer
- continental cool summer
- sub-arctic
- tundra
- ice cap
- mountain
- tropical climates
- • location of station graph

Picturepoint

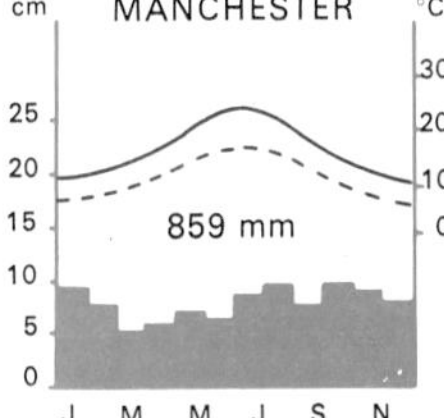

Left: The records for Manchester are typical of the cool temperate west coast type of climate experienced in the British Isles.

Far left: Early autumn in the English Lake District. A mixed deciduous and coniferous woodland flourishes in the reliable rainfall and equable temperatures.

Mediterranean type of climate is found in central California, central Chile, the Cape Province of South Africa and the coasts of western and southern Australia around Perth and Adelaide. The chief features of the climate are a hot, dry summer and a mild, rainier winter. Monthly average temperatures in summer do not often exceed 27°C (80°F), although higher temperatures have been recorded. With clear skies and low relative humidity, intense daytime heating is followed by rapid night-time cooling. The winter months are cooler, the coolest usually having a mean temperature below 10°C (50°F). Frosts are rarely severe.

Annual precipitation amounts in the Mediterranean climates are not great, generally totalling 350-900 mm (14-35 ins). Little or no rain falls in the summer, and this, combined with the high temperatures, results in extremely low soil moisture content. Consequently, the natural vegetation consists mainly of scrub and trees which can resist the lack of water in the summer.

Humid sub-tropical climates

The humid sub-tropics lie along approximately the same latitudes as the Mediterranean climates, but on the eastern side of the continents. Widely known as the east coast warm temperate climates, the main areas are the south-eastern United States; the Pampas of Argentina, Uruguay and southern Brazil; Natal in South Africa; south-eastern Australia; Taiwan; southern Japan; and eastern China.

These regions have similar temperatures to those in Mediterranean climates, but annual precipitation is greater due to the influence of unstable tropical air in summer. The mean monthly temperature of the warmest month is a pleasant 27°C (80°F), but the humidity is also high and summer conditions can be oppressively sultry. Both diurnal (within a day) and day-to-day variations of temperature in summer are small.

In all humid sub-tropical climates (except that of eastern China) temperatures in the coldest month average between 5° and 12°C (41-53°F), giving mild winters with few frosts. In China, however, cold winds blow out of the massive winter high-pressure system over central Asia, and temperatures drop steeply. Averages fall below 5°C (41°F) and frosts are frequent. The January average at Shanghai is as low as 3.9°C (39°F), whereas Charleston in South Carolina enjoys an average 10°C (50°F) for the same month.

Eastern China also has distinctly seasonal rainfall, with a clear summer maximum brought by the south-westerly monsoon winds blowing over the South China Sea. Because of this and the much colder winters, the area is usually considered as a special type of humid sub-tropical climate, known as the temperate monsoon or China type.

Elsewhere in the humid sub-tropics, annual precipitation may vary from 750 to 1,500 mm (30-60 ins), the lower values occurring in places such as Bahia Blanca, Argentina, near the semi-arid climatic regions. Most areas have a fairly uniform distribution of rainfall throughout the year. In summer, most of the precipitation falls from thunderstorms. Winter precipitation falls mainly along cyclonic fronts, and is far lighter but more continuous.

George Rodger/John Hillelson

Cool temperate west coast climates

As the name suggests, this type of climate is found on the west coasts of continents, in the middle latitudes, where on-shore westerly winds bring maritime conditions. Western Europe including the British Isles shares this type of climate with the west coasts of Canada and southern Chile and North and South Islands of New Zealand.

Mean annual temperatures are mostly in the range of 7° to 13°C (45-55°F), and the mean monthly temperature of the warmest month is usually 15-20°C (59-68°F). The moderating marine influence is seen in low diurnal ranges as well as low annual ranges of temperature. However the effect decreases inland. For example, at Brest on the Atlantic coast of France, the annual range is about 11°C (20°F), but increases to about 17°C (30°F) at Strasbourg on France's eastern border.

In winter, temperatures are abnormally high compared with areas at similar latitudes well away from the warming oceanic influence, often being 5-15°C (9-17°F) warmer. This means that mean monthly temperatures in winter are above freezing throughout the climatic region. At times, however, outbreaks of very cold polar air, such as occurred for several weeks over the British Isles in the winter of 1962-63, are responsible for periods of freezing and often snowy weather.

Annual precipitation amounts vary from about 545 mm (21 ins) in lowland areas such as Cambridge, England, to over 2,500 mm (98 ins) in some regions of high relief near the coast. There is usually a slight winter maximum but a characteristic feature of this climatic type is the reliability of the precipitation and thc large number of days on which it falls. Many stations have more than 150 rainy days per year.

Bruce Coleman

MONTREAL
cm
°C
1036 mm
25
20
15
10
5
0
J M M J S N

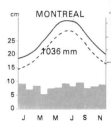

Left: The rich display of colour in the forests of Vermont heralds the approach of the winter cold. New England and the provinces of Canada around the Great Lakes experience a continental climate with cool summers.

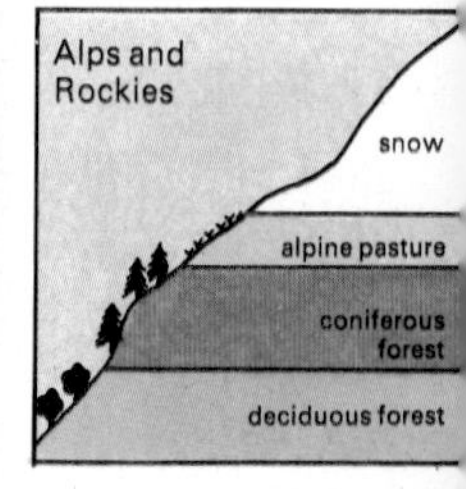

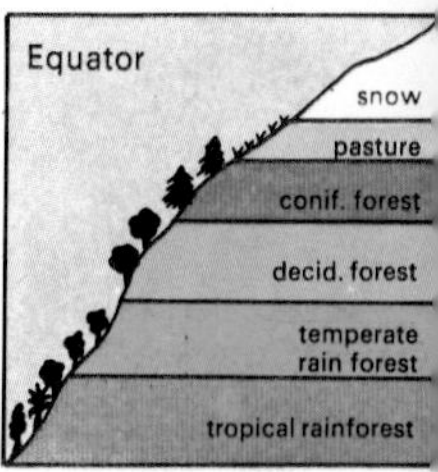

Right: The Jungfrau in the Swiss Alps. Mountain areas are generally cooler, wetter and windier than neighbouring low-lying areas. The diagrams (above) show the zones of vegetation on slopes at different latitudes.

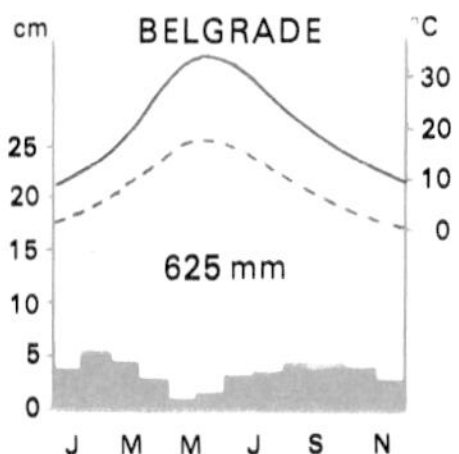

Left: A shepherd drives his flock to fresh pastures across the parched grasslands of Romania. Much of SE Europe including Belgrade (above) has a continental type of climate with warm summers (mean temperatures over 22°C).

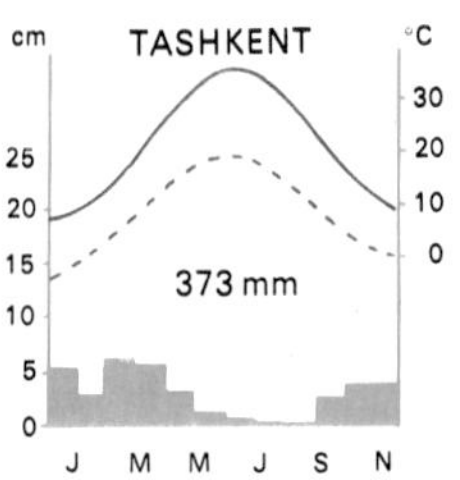

Right: The golden wheat fields of Nebraska are evidence of the productive potential of the world's semi-arid steppe lands. However, cereal crops are often at the mercy of rain failure. Tashkent (above) is in the Russian steppe.

Photri

Bruce Coleman

Warm summer continental climates

The Southern Hemisphere lacks any sizeable land masses in its middle latitudes. Consequently, both types of temperate continental climates (warm-summer and cool-summer types) are found only in the Northern Hemisphere.

The continental type with warm summers lies in three areas between 35° to 45° north. These are northern and eastern central US; south-eastern Europe; and Manchuria, north-eastern China and Korea. In the summer months, mean temperatures are near or above 22°C (72°F) whereas winter monthly means are typically below freezing. This illustrates the great annual range of temperature. Yet the diurnal ranges are small in summer, so summer nights in places such as New York City are often uncomfortably warm and humid.

Typical annual precipitation totals in this climate vary from about 580 mm (23 ins) in Bucharest, Romania, to 1090 mm (43 ins) in New York, with amounts typically decreasing towards the northern latitudes and towards continental interiors. Spring or summer is the season of maximum rainfall with convective showers accounting for most of the warm-season precipitation. Some of the winter snowfalls occur in severe blizzards.

Cool summer continental climates

In central Canada; the north-eastern US sea-board; eastern Europe; central and south-eastern Soviet Union; and northern Japan, a continental climate with cooler summers and a shorter growing season results from their location in higher latitudes. Mean summer monthly temperatures are typically less than 22°C (72°F), but extremes may exceed 35°C (95°F) in a 'heat wave' of tropical continental air. The coolness of these climatic regions is shown by the length of the frost-free season, less than 150 days long.

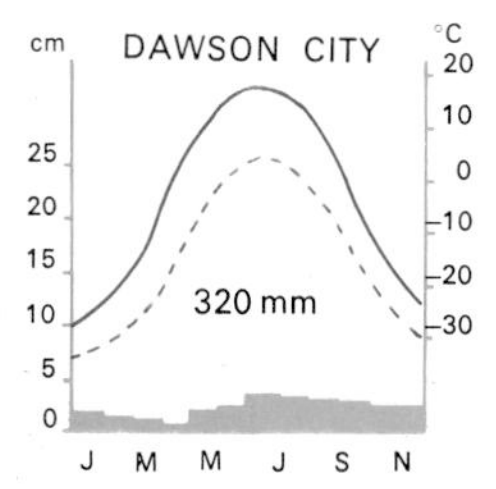

Above: Dawson in the Yukon Terr. of Canada has a notable annual temperature range, typical of sub-arctic climates. As here in Alaska (left), the cold northern winter means that coniferous forests are the dominant type of vegetation. The frost-free season is short and snow may lie for most of the year.

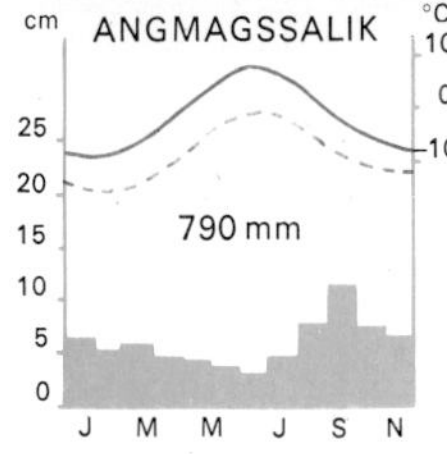

Right: Bird Island, South Georgia, in the S Atlantic has a tundra climate—named after the vegetation of bog, shrubs and moss found there. However, nearly all tundra regions lie in northern latitudes between the northern tree limit and the polar wastes. Angmagssalik in E Greenland (above) is a tundra station.

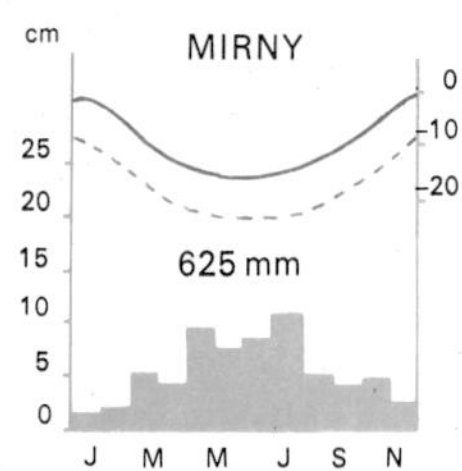

Below: Anvers Island in the Frozen Antarctic. Even in summer, mean temperatures remain below 0°C. Because it is so cold, the little snow that actually falls builds up to great thicknesses. The climate prohibits all plant growth. The station graph is for Mirny, a Soviet research station on the coast.

Annual ranges of temperature may be larger than in warm-summer continental types. For example, Winnipeg in Canada has a range of 38°C (68°F). Annual precipitation is usually less than in the warm-summer types, ranging from 350 to 700 mm (13.5-27 ins), but again most precipitation falls in the summer. In winter, however, the proportion of snow is greater and it lies on the ground for longer periods.

Steppe climates

These mid-latitude arid and semi-arid climates occur well away from the oceans in large areas of central North America and Asia, and in much of Argentina including the cold Patagonian desert. Temperatures show a marked annual range from about 24°C (75°F) in summer to about 0°C (32°F) in winter. Diurnal ranges are also large because of intense daytime heating and night-time cooling. Annual precipitation is often a meagre 150-200 mm (6-8 ins), and the high summer temperatures mean that evaporation far exceeds precipitation in that season.

Sub-Arctic climates

Often known as 'taiga' from the Russian word for the coniferous forest found in these areas, the sub-arctic climatic region covers vast areas of Canada and Siberia. Mean monthly summer temperatures are fairly warm—about 15-20°C (59-68°F)—but the winter monthly means fall to as low as —20° or —40°C (—4° to —40°F).

Because of the high latitude, summer days are short. The frost-free season is similarly short and the summer ends abruptly, usually with a hard freeze. Winter usually consists of eight months with mean temperatures below freezing. Annual precipitation is generally less than 500 mm (20 ins) with a definite summer maximum. Winter snow therefore accounts for a smaller part of the annual total.

Tundra climates

Like 'taiga', 'tundra' is a vegetation term which has also been applied to the associated climate. Tundra is a composite of bog, muskeg and low bush vegetation. The climate is cold: mean annual temperatures are usually below 0°C (32°F), with temperatures about 5°C (41°F) in summer and —25°C (—13°F) in winter. Most weather stations record only two to six months with average temperatures above freezing.

Annual precipitation is less than 350 mm (14 ins) and it comes mostly from cyclones in the warmer half of the year. Snow contributes a greater proportion of the precipitation in the tundra than in the taiga.

Ice caps

The coldest places on earth are the polar areas—mean monthly temperatures are all below freezing. Vegetation is entirely absent and snow and ice or barren rock cover such areas. The lowest mean annual temperatures recorded are those on the polar ice caps of Greenland and Antarctica: summer temperatures generally reach no higher than —5°C (23°F), whereas in winter, monthly means may fall to less than —65°C (—85°F). Despite, or rather because of, the cold, annual amounts of snowfall are small—ranging from 50 to 500 mm (2-20 ins). In such low temperatures, the cold air is unable to hold much water for precipitation.

Glaciers form in areas above the permanent snow line, where accumulated winter snow does not melt completely in summer.

The permanent snow line varies between sea level at the Poles, and 17 to 18 thousand feet in the Andean region of Argentina.

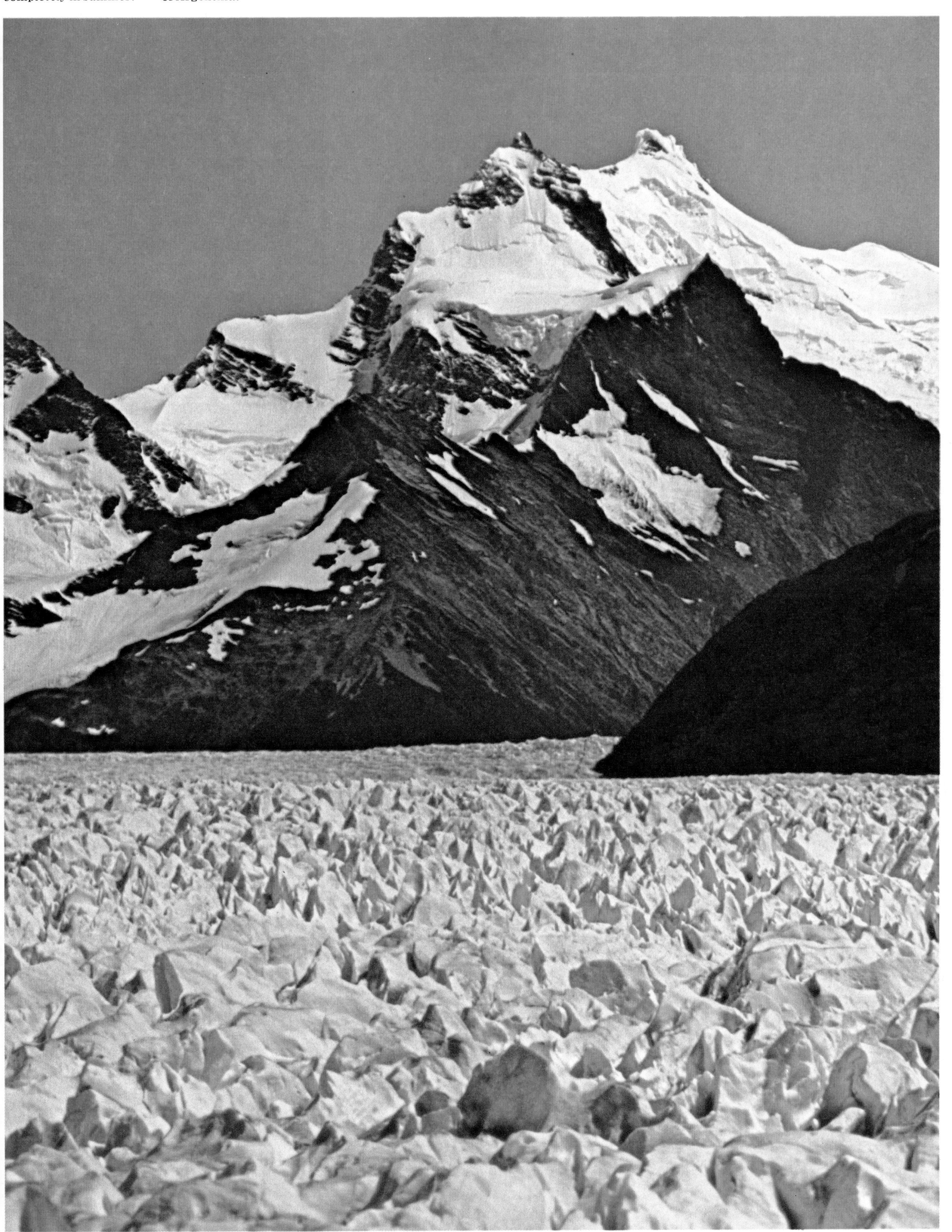

Climatic Changes

Despite enormous technological advances in recent decades, man is still very much at the mercy of the elements. There have been several major climatic fluctuations since the end of the last (Pleistocene) Ice Age about 10,000 years ago and, as recently as the early 1970s, unusually large-scale droughts brought poor harvests and widespread suffering to many parts of the world. In trying to predict future climatic conditions, so critical for world agriculture and food supplies, scientists attach great importance to a knowledge of the causes and the magnitude of past climatic changes.

After the break-up of the main Scandinavian ice sheet over north-west Europe, about 10,000 years ago, the climate warmed rapidly. Evidence from fossil pollen grains, found preserved in peat bogs and lake sediments, show that forests spread over Europe during the dry climatic periods known as the *Pre-Boreal* and *Boreal* periods, when winters were cold, but summers warm.

Then, about 7,000 years ago, conditions became the warmest since the end of the Ice Age. Average summer temperatures in Europe were about 2° to 3°C warmer and winter temperatures about 1°C warmer than today. This was the beginning of the *Atlantic Climatic Optimum*, so called because conditions were favourable for the development of plants and animals. Over most of Europe the snow-line, the lowest limit of continuous snow-cover, was about 300 m (1,000 ft) higher than now. Cave drawings from that period in the Sahara show that human settlement and migration took place in areas which are now desert, suggesting that at the end of the last Ice Age summer monsoon rains spread further north, making the Sahara moister than today.

Towards the end of this climatic optimum, about 5,000 years ago, an increase in pine pollen in north-west Europe (showing that pine forests replaced the earlier oak forests) indicates a return to drier, cooler conditions in the *Sub-Boreal* period. The decline was gradual at first, with some rapid, short-term fluctuations, but by 900 BC—at the beginning of the *Sub-Atlantic* climatic phase—the decline had become rapid, with a marked increase in precipitation.

The levels of many European lakes rose abruptly, swamping lakeside settlements. Many ancient routes were affected by the widespread growth of peat bogs, and the advance of Alpine glaciers blocked mountain passes for several centuries. It is possible that the poleward shift of the main climatic zones which had taken place during the Atlantic Climatic Optimum had reversed, allowing the sub-polar storms once again to sweep across northern Europe.

Man's interference with the natural vegetation by burning and clearing forests means that pollen records are not a reliable indicator of climates for later periods. Fortunately, other evidence, for instance from archaeological sources and historical documents, is more abundant. There is also good evidence—for the whole post-glacial period—based on modern geophysical techniques using deep-sea cores and ice sheet borings.

Picturepoint

Above: The river Thames in 1677. In the 17th century, at the height of the *Little Ice Age*, the Thames froze over 20 times, allowing Frost Fairs to be held on the ice. The old London Bridge aided freezing by impeding the tidal flow and passage of ice down river. The severe cold of the period was carefully recorded in the diary of Londoner Robert Hooke. This page (below) is for March 1, 1673.

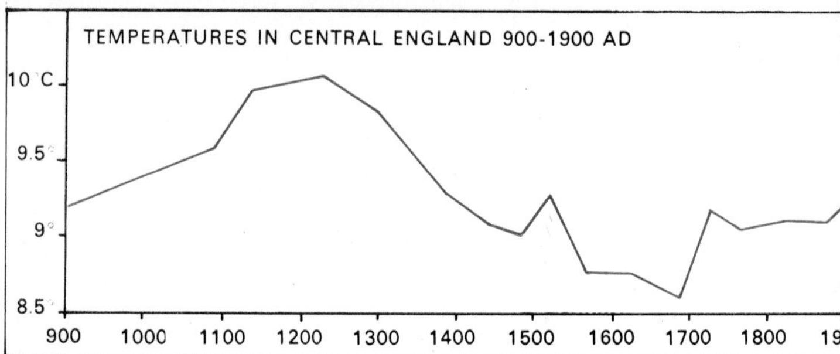

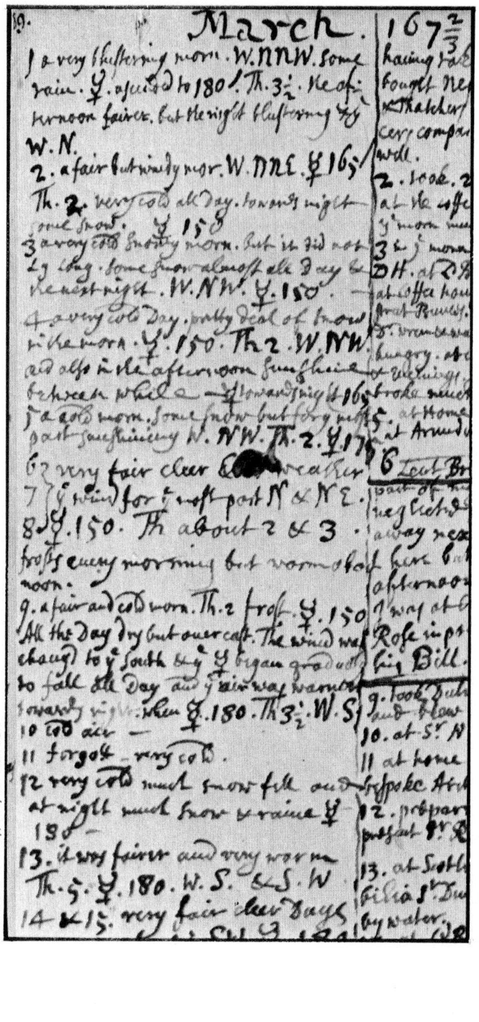

Guildhall Library/City of London

The next few centuries saw a gradual warming and drying, leading to a *Secondary Climatic Optimum* between about 400 and 1200 AD. This remarkably warm, dry, storm-free period in much of the North Atlantic area saw the great Viking voyages and the settlement of Iceland and Greenland, whose coasts were almost completely free of Arctic pack-ice in the tenth century AD. These northern lands must have been considerably more hospitable than today as areas once cultivated by Norse settlers are now covered by ice. In England, historical records of vine growing confirm this very mild climate, implying summer temperatures at least 1°C to 2°C warmer than today.

During the thirteenth and fourteenth centuries, these genial conditions came to an end. Old ships' logs and weather journals mention the reappearance of Arctic pack-ice which, together with increasing storminess of the North Atlantic, began to affect the traditional sea routes between Iceland and Greenland.

The extreme climatic fluctuations of the thirteenth and fourteenth centuries are evident in many different areas of the Northern Hemisphere. In the south-west US, climatic evidence from the growth rings of old trees indicates that the thirteenth century was extraordinarily dry. India too experienced its most disastrous recorded drought and famine due to failure of the summer monsoons.

Left: Temperatures in central England from 900 to 1900 AD. Estimates for early periods are rather subjective, but careful scrutiny can be made of other evidence, such as historical accounts and harvest records. The great climatic changes of the 13th and 14th centuries brought harsh droughts to SW US, and lead to the abandonment of these cliff dwellings in Mesa Verde, Colorado (below right).

Editions Flammarion

Explorer

Above left: The glacier at Agentière, France, about 1850-60. Advances and retreats of Alpine glaciers provide chilling evidence of climatic fluctuations. Their greatest advances since the end of the Pleistocene Ice Age occurred during the Little Ice Age. This engraving made just before the glacier began to retreat, shows the ice front very close to the village.

Left: By 1960, when this photograph of the same glacier was taken from a similar position to that of the engraving, the glacier had retreated far up the valley, leaving masses of larch-covered moraine. The warming trend of the early 20th century is reflected in the recession of many other Alpine valley glaciers, which have not yet reacted to the recent downturn in temperatures.

In Europe, years with severe winters, when rivers like the Danube, Thames and Rhine froze over, and cold rainy summers causing crop failure and famine in England, often alternated with years of severe drought. Records of grape harvest dates and grain prices have been used as evidence of the prevailing climate in this period, but must be interpreted with care, as factors other than climate are often involved.

The Little Ice Age

Fortunately in north-west Europe there exists a very long series of instrumental records of weather conditions, dating back to the middle of the seventeenth century. These records cover much of the period known as the *Little Ice Age*, between about 1550 and 1880, when temperatures declined to their lowest since the Ice Age. Apart from instrumental records, well-documented advances of Alpine glaciers like the Rhône, which reached its furthest extent in 1602, also indicate the magnitude of the cooling.

Ice advances in other parts of the world, especially North America, occurred at approximately similar times and indicate a pattern for at least the Northern Hemisphere, if not for the whole world. Ships' logs record that polar ice reached its most extensive limit ever seen, extending halfway between Greenland and Norway. In Norway and Iceland crops failed and upland farms were abandoned—some farms were actually overridden by the advancing ice. Many large rivers froze over, including the Thames.

Jerome Wyckoff

Changes in the last hundred years

Although early instruments were slightly unreliable, and the degree of their exposure uncertain, it appears that January mean temperatures in central lowland England in the 1780s were around 2°C lower than in the twentieth century. As instruments became more refined and their exposures standardized, a great wealth of climatological data from many parts of the world became available for the nineteenth and twentieth centuries, allowing recent changes to be studied in great detail.

The most important trends over the last hundred years have been a steady increase in global temperatures by about 0.5°C, accompanied by an increasingly vigorous general atmospheric circulation, until the 1940s. Since then temperatures have declined by 0.2-0.3°C. The early part of the twentieth century, from which most climatic 'normals' are calculated, is therefore highly abnormal when compared with the remainder of the post-glacial (Flandrian) period.

Associated with these global temperature trends have been notable—and recently disastrous—changes in the global distribution of rainfall. In the early twentieth century, the mid-latitude zones of prevailing westerly winds experienced a general increase in rainfall, and, in the zones equatorward of the sub-tropical anticyclones, the monsoon rains penetrated further into desert areas like the southern Sahara. However, since the early 1960s, this rainfall distribution has changed because of a slight equator-ward displacement of the climatic zones.

Rainfall in equatorial areas has increased dramatically since the poleward extent of the monsoon rains has become more restricted. An increase of as much as 130-140 per cent in East Africa has caused abrupt rises in lake levels. Lake Victoria, for example, has risen 1.5-2 m (5-6.5 ft) since 1961, threatening lakeshore settlements. On the other hand, because of the reduction of monsoon rains, latitudes 10-20° north and south of the equator have suffered several successive years of drought. As these are areas of marginal agriculture, where even in good years it is only just possible to raise crops and cattle because of the low rainfall, the droughts have caused disastrous starvation and loss of life.

Causes of climatic changes

What causes these changes and can they be predicted? Explanations of climatic change abound, but no single theory has been shown to account for all known fluctuations, and several different processes are likely to interact.

As the sun is the major source of the energy which drives the general circulation of the atmosphere, and hence controls climate, it is reasonable to look to the sun for an explanation of long-term climatic changes. Variations in the *solar constant*, that is the amount of solar radiation reaching the outer edges of the earth's atmosphere (which affects temperatures on the earth's surface), may have taken place in the past because of alterations in the sun's behaviour. It has been known for many years that solar activity varies in a regular fashion, but the climatic influence of these well-known 11-year *sunspot cycles* continues to be the subject of much controversy, and the precise effects are still uncertain.

Even without sunspot cycles, variations in the earth's elliptical orbit around the sun, combined with the tilt of the earth's axis, control the amount of solar radiation available in different climatic zones at different times of year. These so-called *Milankovitch radiation curves* (after the Yugoslav who first calculated them) show considerable solar radiation variations over thousands of years. Although many previous attempts to match radiation curves with climatic curves have proved rather unsatisfactory, recent calculations have shown that the fluctuations are probably of the correct order of magnitude to cause large climatic changes.

However, the nature of the earth's surface and the composition of the atmosphere may have similar climatic effects. In the course of earth history, the shifting positions of the continents and the main periods of mountain building have undoubtedly influenced the distribution of sources and sinks of heat energy, and the circulation of the atmosphere. But equally obviously, they occur on too long a time-scale to explain recent changes. Operating on a much shorter time-scale are changes in the composition and transparency of the atmosphere. Fine volcanic ash, injected high into the atmosphere,

Right: In semi-arid areas, notably in the SW US, where rainfall is the main control on tree growth, the study and correlation of tree rings can provide information on annual rainfall variations over hundreds of years.

J. R. Pilcher

Below right: By careful adjustment of early instrumental records, temperatures for central lowland England can be extended back to 1659. The curves illustrated here show the marked decline of temperatures around 1700 in the Little Ice Age, and the warming trend of the early 20th century, followed by the slight cooling since about 1950.

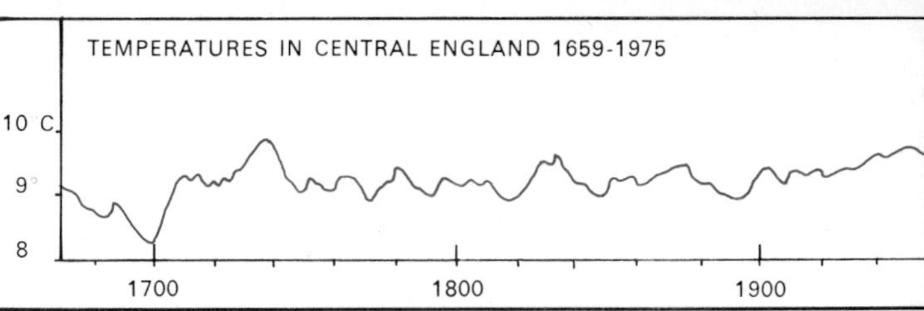

Below: A victim of the drought in Senegal in 1973. The equatorward shift of the main climatic zones in recent years has lead to several successive failures of summer monsoon rains in the Sahel region on the southern edge of the Sahara. This has caused widespread drought and starvation. If this trend continues large numbers of people will be forced to alter their ways of life.

John Hillelson Agency

may cause a noticeable reduction in the amount of solar radiation reaching the earth's surface. For example, radiation measurements at Montpellier, France, averaged 10 per cent below normal for three years after the enormous 1883 Krakatoa eruption. Periods of worldwide volcanic activity may therefore cause a reduction of radiation for many years, and the Little Ice Age seems to have coincided with a period of high volcanic activity between 1750 and 1900.

Is man an agent of climatic change?

In recent years, man's influence on the atmosphere has become a major potential cause of global climatic change, although there is still some debate over the magnitude of the possible effects. The trend towards warmer weather of the early twentieth century coincided with an increase in atmospheric carbon dioxide concentrations from 290 ppm (parts per million) before 1900, to 328 ppm in 1973. It is suggested that this rise is due to increased burning of fossil fuels (coal, oil and gas) which, if continued at its present rate, will lead to a concentration of 370 ppm by the year 2000. However, such estimates of future trends are unreliable because economic factors will play an important role. A rise in carbon dioxide concentrations causes more of the earth's outgoing long-wave radiation to be trapped, increasing the 'greenhouse effect' and raising global temperatures.

Despite the continued rise in carbon dioxide emissions, however, global temperatures have now declined, possibly because of another effect of human activity. Dust in the atmosphere, like volcanic dust, intercepts incoming solar

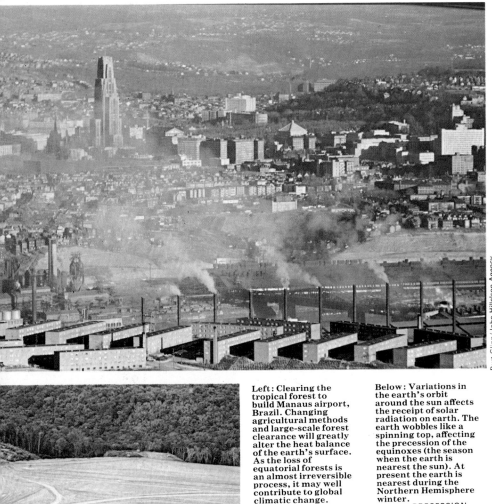

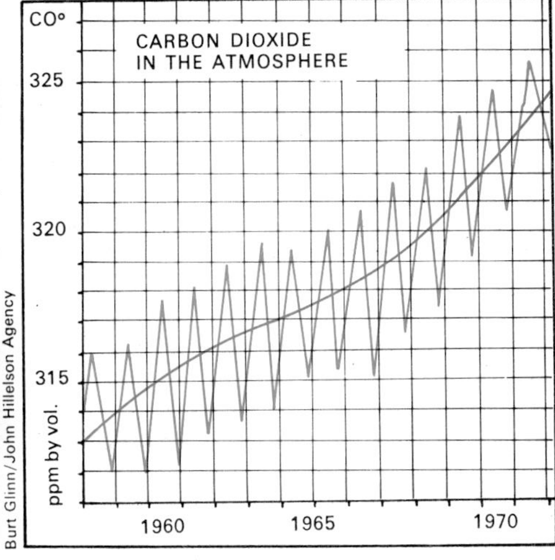

Burt Glinn/John Hillelson Agency

Left: Industrial air pollution in Los Angeles, California. The emission of large quantities of pollutants into the atmosphere significantly alters the ability of the atmosphere to transmit solar and terrestrial radiation. Emissions of dust and smoke particles block out some sunshine. But increases in carbon dioxide concentrations tend to increase surface temperatures. The record (below) of CO_2 concentration at Mauna Loa, Hawaii shows that, superimposed on a regular seasonal variation, there is a steady upward trend from 315 ppm in 1958 to about 325 ppm in 1971.

Left: Clearing the tropical forest to build Manaus airport, Brazil. Changing agricultural methods and large-scale forest clearance will greatly alter the heat balance of the earth's surface. As the loss of equatorial forests is an almost irreversible process, it may well contribute to global climatic change.

Bruno Barbey/John Hillelson Agency

Below: Variations in the earth's orbit around the sun affects the receipt of solar radiation on earth. The earth wobbles like a spinning top, affecting the precession of the equinoxes (the season when the earth is nearest the sun). At present the earth is nearest during the Northern Hemisphere winter.

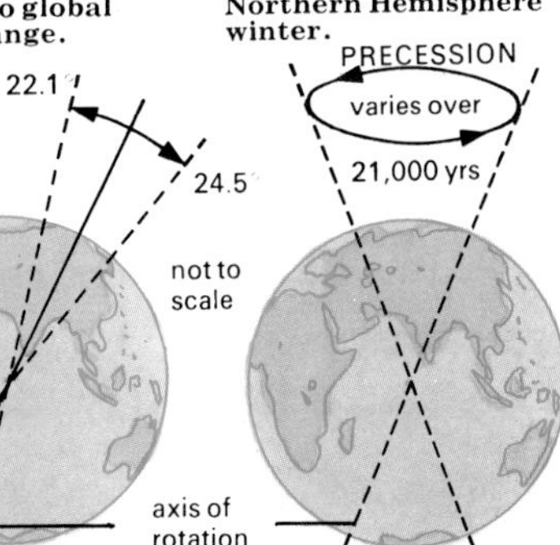

Above: The tilt of the earth's axis causes changes in the latitudes of the tropics and polar circles. When the tilt is large, differences between summer and winter are most extreme.

Below: The eccentricity of the elliptical orbit. When the orbit is most eccentric (when the sun is furthest from the centre of the ellipse) the amount of radiation reaching the earth varies the most.

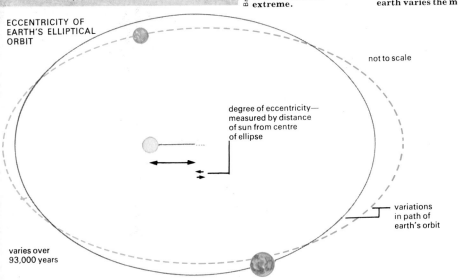

ECCENTRICITY OF
EARTH'S ELLIPTICAL
ORBIT
not to scale
degree of eccentricity—
measured by distance
of sun from centre
of ellipse
variations
in path of
earth's orbit
varies over
93,000 years

radiation. Measurements of this atmospheric turbidity at Davos in Switzerland have shown a doubling of concentrations in recent years, caused by industrial emissions and changing agricultural methods. However, the influence of dust in the atmosphere is complex. An increase in the amount of dust in the lower atmosphere may actually add to the 'greenhouse effect', causing surface temperatures to rise.

Recently, concern has been expressed that the emission of water vapour and chemicals from the exhausts of high flying supersonic aircraft such as the Anglo-French *Concorde* may seriously affect important layers of the atmosphere, like the ozone layer which intercepts harmful ultra-violet radiation. But too little is known at present to predict the consequences.

Predictions of the climate over the next few decades have been attempted by extrapolating present trends and cycles. For example, deep ice-cores bored in north-west Greenland have revealed regular variations in the oxygen isotope ratios (more heavy oxygen means warmer conditions). If these fluctuations continue, this would suggest a cooling in the next 10 to 20 years followed by a renewed warming until the beginning of the twenty-first century. However, such predictions are largely based on simplistic assumptions of the meteorological processes involved, and often produce conflicting results. In fact, the weight of opinion at present suggests that the global cooling trend, and the associated shifts in precipitation distribution, are likely to persist for some years to come.

The repercussions for world agriculture, for food supplies and human survival in marginal areas, are so enormous that it has been suggested that man should attempt to alter deliberately the global climate to prevent such consequences. Yet, until the workings of the atmosphere are known in much greater detail, such a course of action may lead to greater climatic disasters than those it is trying to prevent.

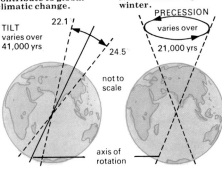

Zefa (UK) Ltd.

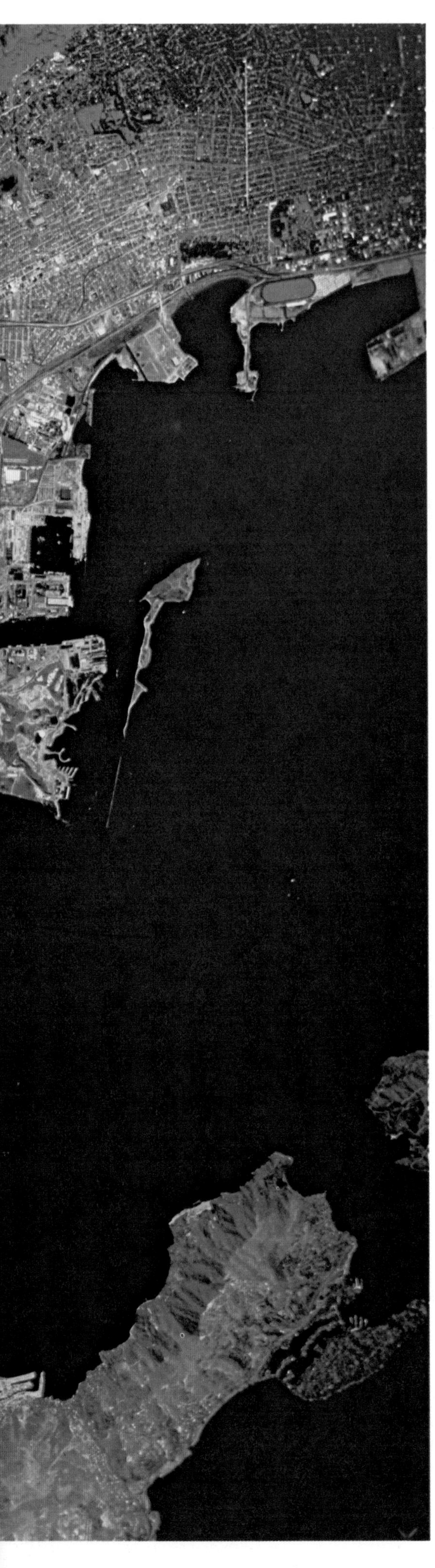

Chapter 5
Mapping the Earth

Large scale maps can be produced with a photographic base. This photograph of San Francisco is taken on infra red film, which will penetrate mist – the wavelength of infra red light being greater than the diameter of dust and air molecules.

Mapping the Globe

Many people, asked to describe an area, would give a purely verbal outline based on the relative positions of various landmarks. But any two maps of the same area based on such a description would probably be quite different. True map making depends on the setting up of some system of co-ordinates.

Everyone has seen street maps with square grids superimposed, so that a particular street can be found in, say, square B3. This system is called *Cartesian:* there is a starting point, called the *origin,* for the two scales, which are at right angles to each other.

Such a two dimensional system works well over small areas and on flat ground. If the Earth were flat, a simple Cartesian system would be quite satisfactory. Since the Earth is a globe, however, another system has to be used. Each place is located by its *latitude* and *longitude.* The zero value for latitude, corresponding to the origin, is the equator. Lines of latitude are then imaginary circles parallel to the equator and called *parallels.* These circles get smaller towards the poles, and are numbered according to their angle from the equator as seen from the Earth's centre. The equator is then 0° and the poles 90°N and 90°S.

The circles of longitude, on the other hand, are not parallels but are all *great circles*—that is, circles of the same diameter as the Earth. Each one passes through both poles, and is called a *meridian,* running from north to south. The zero point of the longitude system is internationally agreed to be at Greenwich, England. All other lines of longitude are described as either east or west of Greenwich.

The position of any place on Earth, therefore, is given by two co-ordinates. Each can be measured as accurately as required, using degrees, minutes (sixtieths of a degree) and seconds (sixtieths of a minute). A second of latitude is just under 31 m (102 ft); for greater accuracy than that, decimals of a second are used. The size of a second of longitude varies between the equator and the poles.

Latitude and longitude can be measured using a sextant to observe the positions of astronomical bodies. In theory a complete map of the world could be built up by measuring the latitude and longitude of each place individually, and this is indeed how explorers made maps of the territories they visited. A few places would be located accurately and the rest filled in by eye. But to make a detailed map in this way would be very time-consuming. Instead, the mapping of an area is based (on a nationwide basis, for example) on triangulation control.

Triangulation

The first stage in surveying a previously unmapped area is to establish a *ground control*—the relative positions of a few easily-visible points. To do this the process of *triangulation* is carried out. This hinges upon the proposition that, if the length of one side of a triangle and the three angles within the triangle are

Left, right and far right: Depiction of the Greek mathematician and geographer Claudius Ptolemy (left), who lived during the second century AD. His great work, *Geographia,* discusses the making of a world map based on a conical projection, estimates the latitude and longitude of some 8,000 places and has instructions for 26 regional maps. During the Dark Ages, classical advances, including the notion of a spherical Earth, were lost. Instead, the world was thought of as a flat disc. Mapping was based on Christian doctrine rather than on geographical fact, as the map (far right) shows. Dated around 1300 this has Jerusalem at the world's centre and includes many biblical references. With the Renaissance, great advances were made in cartography, Ptolemy's scholarship was discovered and his world map, together with its inaccuracies, was copied. By the sixteenth century terrestrial globes (such as the one seen right, dated 1541) were made, indicating a return to maps suited to practical needs.

Left: Mercator, the 16th century geographer. His 1569 map projection has become world famous.

Below: Mercator's cylindrical projection is one of the most commonly used. If a light is projected through a glass globe, it throws shadows of the parallels and meridians on to the surrounding cylinder. This projection distorts rapidly towards the poles. If the cylinder is placed horizontally (as in the small diagram), a *transverse* Mercator projection results, in which the line of zero distortion runs from north to south, not east to west.

Right: The *azimuthal* projection is often used to represent polar areas. With this, all parallels of latitude increasingly distort away from the centre.

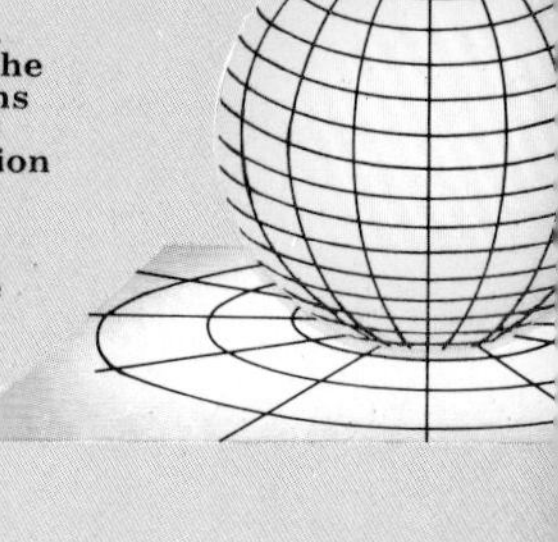

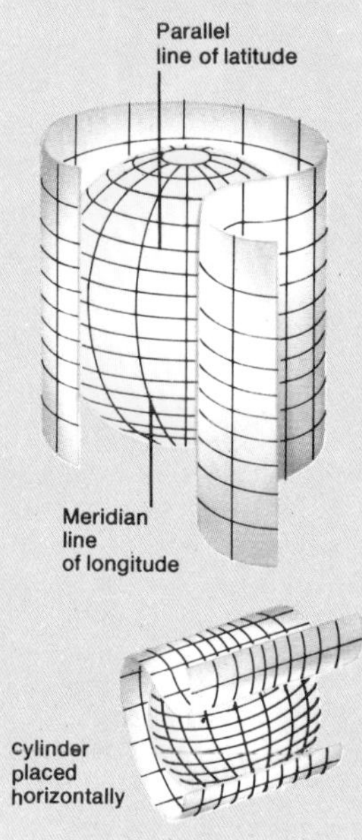

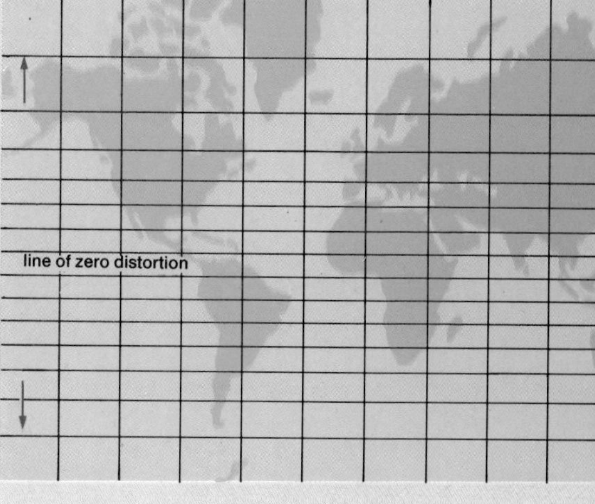

Michael Holford/National Maritime Museum

Woodmanstone Colour Slides

'HAL PROJECTION

point of zero distortion

TION

line of zero distortion

Below left: In the *conic* type of map projection all meridians (lines of longitude) are projected as straight lines and the parallels of latitude are arcs of concentric circles. The line of zero distortion is the circular arc where paper and globe meet. Mapping parts of the US was based upon local versions of this.

Below: Much topographic survey is now carried out by *photogrammetry*. This involves collecting aerial photographs of the area and correcting these by plotting the true relative positions of certain points on the ground by field survey. Overlaps in adjacent photographs must occur to provide the necessary stereoscopic image.

Aerofilms

known, it is possible to calculate the lengths of the other sides and whatever *closing error* has occurred in the measurement process. The closing error is the internal discrepancy within the measurements of the triangle as made from all three stations. Once this is done, the other sides can be used as the bases for new triangles and the whole process repeated. Sometimes the resulting chains of triangles will be chosen so that they are orientated roughly along parallels or along meridians.

Triangulation involves measuring a baseline, then taking observations of the angles between other points which can be seen from each end of this line. The 'altitude' of the other points is also observed from the baseline by measuring their position above or below the horizontal.

Generally speaking, a country is first covered by a primary triangulation in which the sides of the triangles average about 50 km in length. Once this has been established and the average closing error for any triangle is no more than about 3 cm, secondary triangulation is carried out within the primary triangles, followed by tertiary triangulation within each of the secondary triangles. Closing errors in the tertiary triangles are not so critical since they do not accumulate throughout the whole survey, but they are normally less than 30 cm in about 4 km.

Until the 1960s almost all triangulation measurements were made with optical instruments such as *theodolites*, which measure angles, and *tacheometers*, which measure the size of a staff of known height, thus giving its distance. Since then, triangulation has been increasingly carried out with electronic distance-measuring devices; these measure the lengths of the sides of the triangle directly and, in favourable conditions, provide an accuracy of a centimetre or less over two kilometres.

Filling in the details

Once the ground has been established by triangulation, most large and medium scale (say 1:50,000 scale or larger) mapping is now carried out by *photogrammetry*. The scale of a map gives its size in relation to the land it represents. Thus a distance on a 1:50,000 map is 50,000 times shorter than the real thing. Such a map has a scale of 2 cm to 1 km.

Photogrammetry involves taking overlapping air photographs, so that each point on the ground is seen from two positions. Once processed, the photographs can be used to give stereoscopic images, so that the height of the ground, as well as surface details, can be measured.

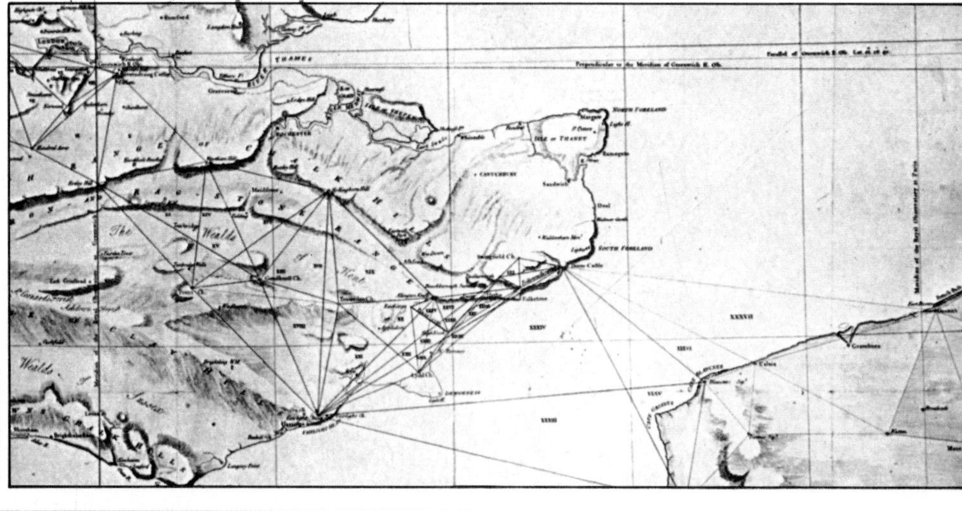

Ordnance Survey

Above right: The first triangulation, carried out by Sir William Roy from Hounslow to Paris (1784-1790). It established the relative position of Great Britain and Europe.

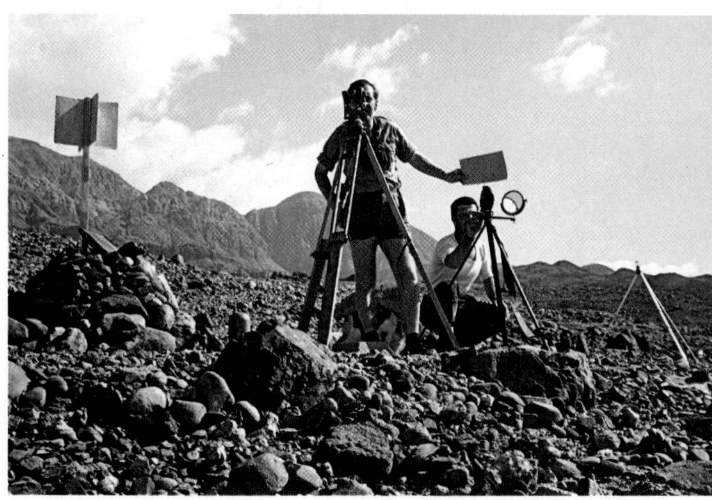

Fairey Surveys

Right: *Theodolites* used in a survey of Bahrain. Theodolites are used to measure angles between survey points in conspicuous locations such as hill tops. The angles are measured in both the horizontal and the vertical planes. If the distance between any two stations and the height of one is known, the distance between all others and the height of all survey points may be calculated through a triangulation network. Triangulations often span distances of over 50 km (30 miles).

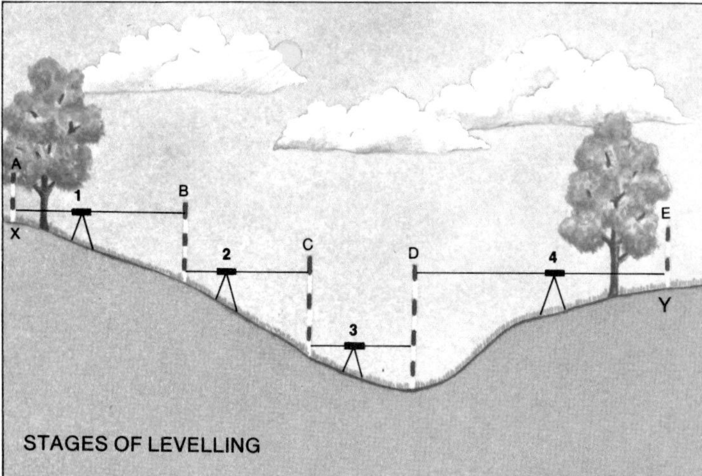

Left: A simple and accurate way of measuring height differences between two points (X and Y) is provided by levelling. In principle, the operator sets up his telescope to be horizontal at position 1. He then looks back to a calibrated staff A, reads off the height on the staff and repeats this with the staff at B, C and so on.

Below: Satellites are now used as survey beacons. A satellite observed simultaneously from three triangulation points on Earth appears against a different star background in each case. By knowing exact star positions, the locations of the Earth stations can be traced back.

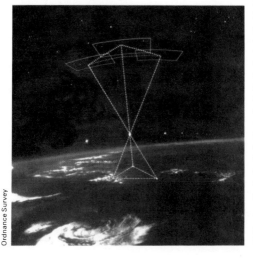

Ordnance Survey

An alternative method is to carry out a levelling survey on the ground. This gives accurate height values over short distances and uses a levelling telescope which can accurately be made horizontal. The procedure is to observe a calibrated staff (that is, a staff with heights marked off in bands) through the telescope, so that the height difference between the two stations can be measured directly. This process is repeated with the staff and telescope in different positions.

Representing position

Once the basic survey measurements of relative position have been made and checked, they need to be represented in a convenient form. Much the simplest way is to plot them on a globe, a model of the world, since this gets over the problems of transferring information collected on a near-spherical world to a flat sheet of paper. Globes, however, are inconvenient to use in many situations and numerous map *projections* have been devised to permit the convenient representation of all or part of the spherical world on flat paper.

The simplest form of map projection is to 'peel the skin' off a globe. This gives a series of *gores*, strips of paper joined at the equator and tapering to points at the poles. In effect, this produces a form of *interrupted* map projection but its very fragmentary nature makes it difficult to use: oceans and continents are frequently split into two or more parts.

Geographers have suggested that there are four vitally important properties of a map projection. These are that the resulting map should accurately reproduce correct areas, correct shape, correct angular relationships and correct distances between points. Unfortunately it is totally impossible to have all these properties in any projection for a flat sheet of paper and the map maker therefore has to select the projection according to which property is most important for the purpose of the map.

The representation of *conformality* is one in which all angles and shapes over small areas are correctly reproduced: because of these properties, such projections are normally used for topograhic maps (that is, the familiar straightforward maps of an area), navigation charts and military maps. A consequence of the correct angular representation is that parallels and meridians meet at right angles. Equal area projections, on the other hand, often give extremely distorted shapes to countries but represent the area of one correctly in regard to all the others shown. Because of this property, they are commonly used in mapping distributions, such as of population density, of agricultural produce and output. If an equal area projection were not used in these circumstances, the same values for two equally sized countries, one at the equator and one near the pole, would look very different indeed. It can be shown by simple algebra that no map projection can be both conformed and equal area, though there are many which are neither but are created as a compromise between these two extremes.

Map of Europe and the Atlantic from the 1513 edition of Ptolemy's *Geographia*. It shows how the distance from Europe to America had been underestimated since the second century, thus misleading Columbus and other explorers. The criss-cross lines mark compass points.

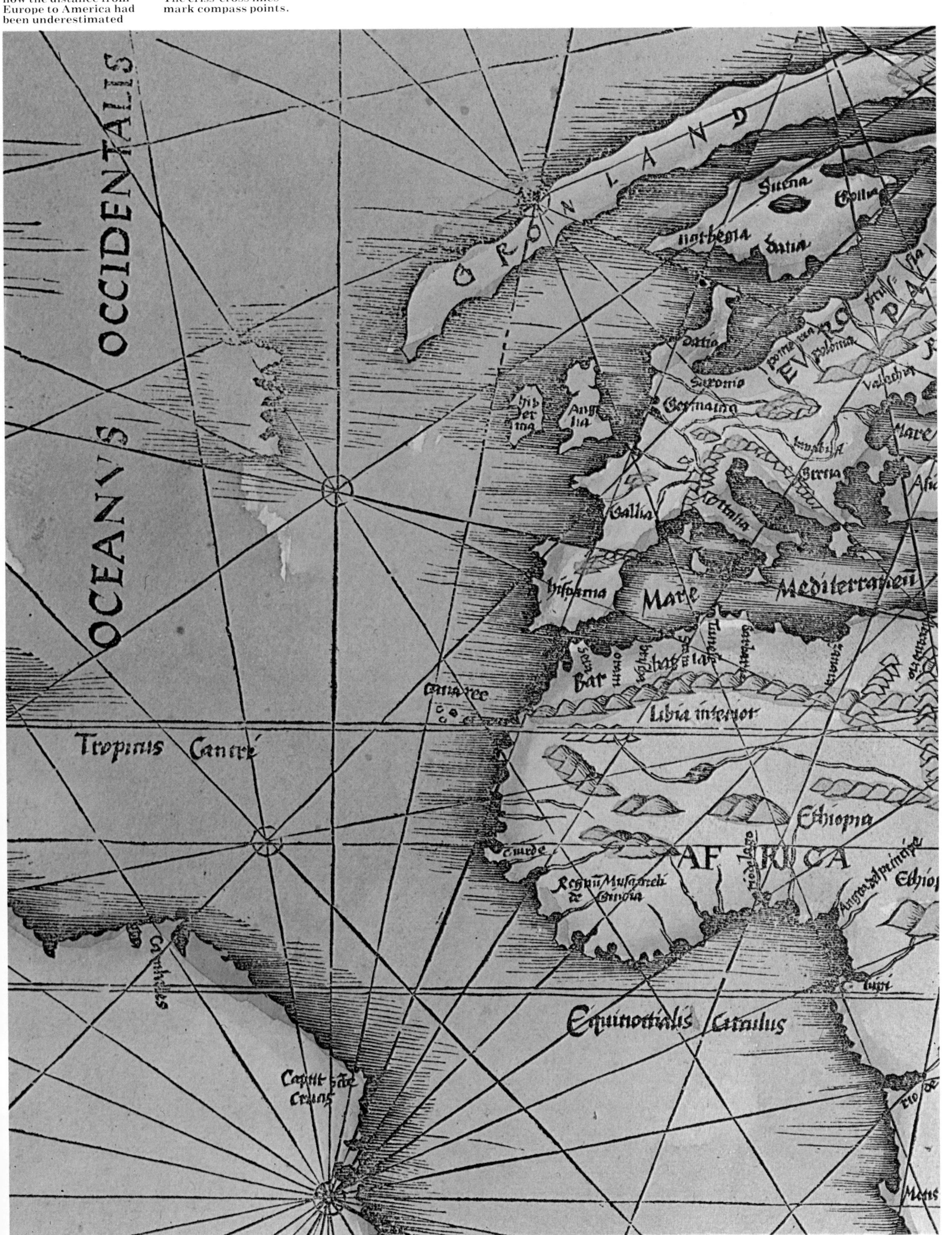

Making Maps

Maps have been made for at least 4,500 years. However, the manner in which they have been made has changed dramatically over the last few hundred years. The change has been from individually constructed manuscript maps to maps reproduced in quantity on a printing press though now, in certain respects, there is a return to the production of single maps suited to a particular purpose. All of these changes have been largely brought about by changes in technology.

Before a map is made, the map-maker or *cartographer* must make certain decisions which determine the form of the map, bearing in mind its purpose. There will of course be great differences between maps intended for trained map users, for tourists, for display purposes and so on, and the design must be appropriate to each. What the particular map needs to show determines to some extent the scale which is used. Small scale maps, which can cover a large area such as a whole country, usually show major details—rivers, cities, towns, roads—only. For greater local detail, large scale maps covering a smaller area are used.

Leonie Finlay

Collecting information

When the information for a map is constructed from original survey measurements the product is called a basic map. For this, the cartographer will plot the relative positions of the survey points and the detail of the landscape in between these will either be provided for him by a trained user of air photographs—a photogrammetrist—or will be sketched in using whatever other information is at hand.

When an overlapping pair of aerial photographs is mounted in a *stereoscope*, the photogrammetrist sees a three-dimensional view of the ground to be mapped. First the two photographs are tilted if necessary to correct for the tilt of the aircraft and so on when the photographs were taken. The operator can now recognize variations in height in the stereoscopic view. The machine he uses may have, for example, a small dot or bar in the optical system. This dot can be moved around by the operator. The procedure may then be to move the dot across the surface keeping it at the same apparent height as judged in the stereo view. The dot's movements then trace out a *contour*—a line of constant height. Quite often the dot controls are linked to a pen mechanism which draws a map directly. Such devices are called *stereoplotters*.

Up to 80 per cent of the survey information comes from air photographs. The remaining information must be collected by observers on the ground, who check and correct the material provided by the photogrammetrist and stereoplotter and who add details which might have been obscured in an aerial photograph. These details, necessary for large scale maps such as those produced by the British Ordnance Survey, include the accurate naming of features, the type of vegetation, buildings which are covered by trees or otherwise not visible in an aerial view, the ground measurements of buildings, house numbers, boundaries and divisions under roofed areas.

Leonie Finlay

Above and left: Stereoplotters, such as the high precision version shown here, are used to create corrected images of three-dimensional models of the terrain from aerial photographs. On this, the operator follows 'lines of interest' such as field boundaries. Imaginary lines, such as contours, may also be followed. Some stereoplotters can produce a map directly as a result of this process by being linked to a pen mechanism, or co-ordinatograph. This instrument, a detail of which is seen left, is tracing the lines of buildings, fields and paths followed by the operator onto a stable base plastic material.

Compilation

It is probably more common, however, for the cartographer to create a 'derived' map, that is, a new map from several existing ones, especially when he is mapping to a small scale. These, however, may be at different scales and on different projections, and only certain parts of the information on each may be required. The conversion of all the information to a common scale is normally carried out by photographic enlargement or reduction. Alternatively another simple, if tedious, process can be carried out by overlaying grids of appropriate sizes on the old and new maps—the location of the features on the old are transposed to the new using the grid lines as guides. If the grids are replaced by graticules, that is, lines of longitude and latitude as depicted on the

Ordnance Survey

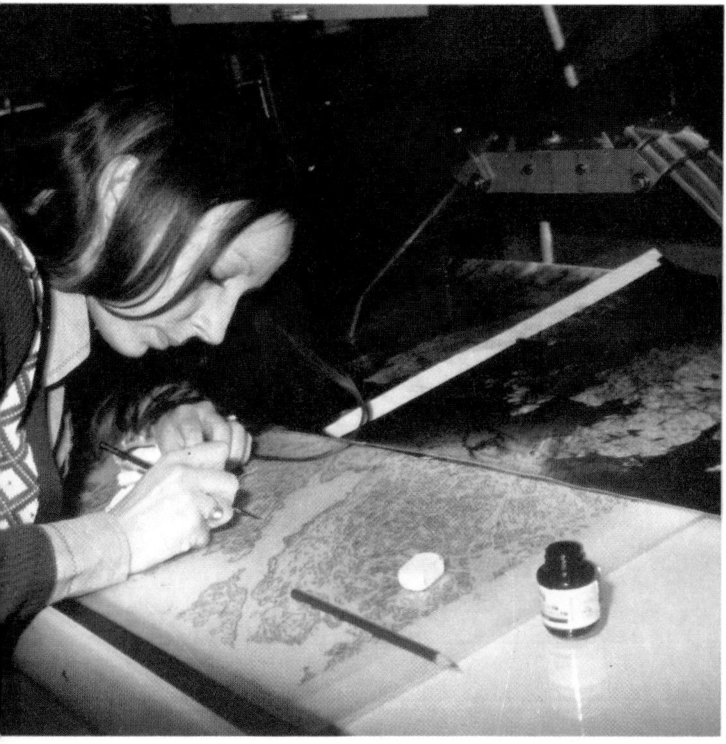

Ordnance Survey

Fairey Surveys Ltd.

Left: Altitude is often shown on British maps by the use of contours—imaginary lines joining all places of the same height. Where very steep slopes occur, however, the contour lines on the map are so close together that they coalesce. In such places they are often removed and a drawing of a steep rock face inserted by hand.

Right: A minimum of overlap must occur between the names and other details on a map. Most names are now set on a phototypesetter in the size and language required—in this case Arabic. The self-adhesive film can be stuck down in the appropriate place. When photographed, it will appear as part of the original map.

Below: This camera is designed to reproduce lines and other cartographic details of consistent width and clarity over an area of more than one metre square. The map or section of a map being photographed is held in a glass frame by a vacuum. It can be accurately reduced or enlarged in scale.

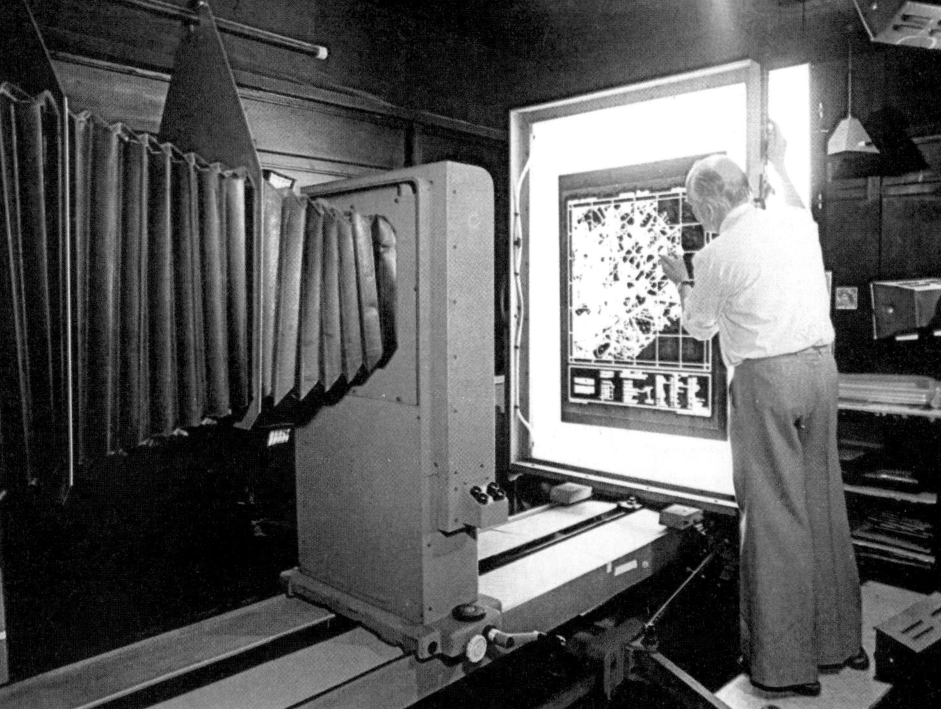

Leonie Finlay

Below: Map making is becoming increasingly automated. Here a girl is digitizing an Ordnance Surveyor's map; she is following the lines of the map and these are being stored by the computer as repeated pairs of co-ordinates. Labels are then added to indicate the meaning of each line. Once this is complete, the same data may be used to produce a wide variety of maps with different scales, symbols and projections. Alterations need simply to be digitized and the old parts deleted within the computer. Ordnance Survey cartographers were pioneers in this field; by the end of 1976 they had digitized about 4,000 maps.

old and the new maps, then conversion from one map projection to the other may be carried out in addition to the change of map scale; it is not simple to change map projection by photographic means.

Once the scale and projection of all the source maps have been brought to a single, common standard, the features which are required are traced off by the cartographer and then re-drawn. Only rarely can satisfactory maps be made by merely assembling pieces of existing maps and reproducing these without re-drawing. Because the original maps may have been drawn differently and at different scales, the photographic process produces lines of different thickness and symbols of different types representing the same feature within the composite map. In addition, the cartographer normally brings the mapped features into a conformity to suit his own process.

In a description of the map-making process, the amount of information carried in the margin of the map is easily overlooked. But these margins often contain valuable information such as the date of survey and of any revisions; the name of the publisher; information on latitude and longitude; the variation between true north and magnetic north; the type of projection used; and the key, the scale and the grid system.

Until the 1960s, the map image was normally created by drawing on paper or on film with a dense black ink. High quality maps of certain types were still made in some places by direct engraving and etching of a copper plate which was subsequently used for printing. Now the majority of high quality maps available are drawn using a *scriber*. With this, the cartographer in effect chisels lines in a coating on plastic material. This coating, often red or yellow, is transparent so that the cartographer can see the base map below, but is opaque when seen by the blue-sensitive emulsions on the films used for copying.

Dotted and pecked lines are achieved by scribing continuous lines and then filling in alternate sections with an opaque liquid; double lines, such as those used to show roads, are drawn with a special double headed scribing tool.

Scribing gives much higher and more consistent quality of linework than does the use of pen and ink and is much easier than engraving. The use of plastic-based materials avoids the problems of shrinkage which occur with paper when the temperature and humidity of the air change. Before the ready availability of easily-handled plastics, very high quality maps had to be drawn on glass.

Though lines are usually now scribed, a different approach is taken in depicting symbols and in shading or colouring areas. If a cartographer makes frequent use of a particular small symbol—say for a telephone box—he will draw it at perhaps twenty times its final size, then have it photographically reduced and reproduced many times on 'stripper film'. The mini-symbols on this may then be stuck down in the correct position on a positive copy of the map. Place names are commonly set in this way though the originals are produced by machine rather than via an enlarged drawing. The use of stripper film ensures that different type styles and

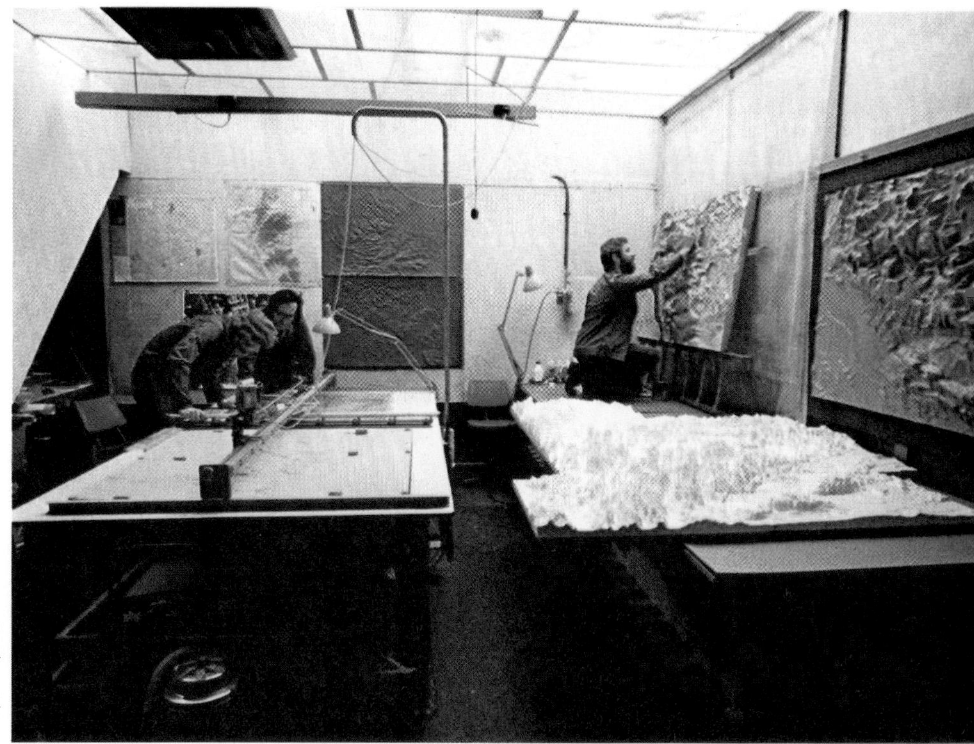

Fairey Surveys Ltd.

Above: 3-dimensional models of terrain are an easily understood form of mapping. They are usually cut by hand from expanded polystyrene but can be cut under computer control from a map stored in digital form. Normally, terrain models must use a greatly exaggerated vertical scale before the relief is noticeable.

Below: Air photograph and details from two maps of Hatfield, Hertfordshire, England. The larger scale map (1:10,000, that is, one unit on the map represents 10,000 units on the ground), top, shows details such as individual houses. The small scale (1:50,000) map, lower, is heavily generalized. Symbols rather than drawings of features are used and roads have exaggerated widths so they can be coloured, important to road classification. Colour is used more extensively in this map. The air photograph resembles the larger scale map in some respects, but is on a different scale and needs skilled interpretation.

Below right: Infra-red photograph of part of the Blackwater estuary, Essex, England. Since World War II, infra-red (or *false*) colour film has been used in mapping to distinguish areas of healthy (red) and diseased (blue) vegetation and to show up the depth of water (seen here as light and dark blue areas).

Aerofilms

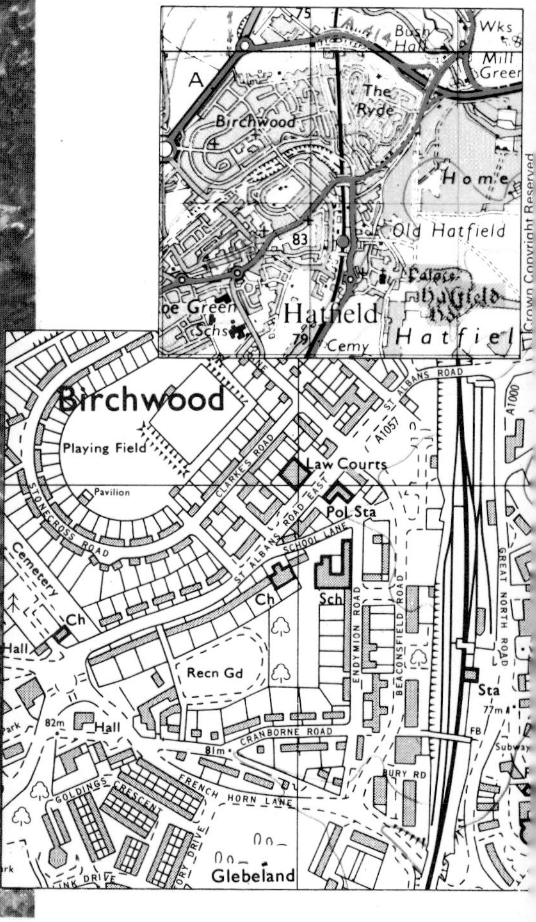

Crown Copyright Reserved

weights may be used, the names can be set at any angle and may easily be positioned so as not to overlap important crossroads and other features in the map.

If the map is to be produced in colour, each colour is prepared separately as a black and white overlay. The colour only appears when the final plate is printed using the chosen ink colour. Up to 10 colours are common, each one having its own plate.

Automated cartography

Since the late 1950s, attempts have been made to introduce computers into the map-making process. The reasons for this are the speed and flexibility of their operation and the basic repetitiveness of some parts of map-making. Many organizations now use computing, but a milestone was the production in Britain in 1971 of the Abingdon geology map by the Experimental Cartography Unit: this was the first map to be made by automated means and published as one of a conventional map series.

The essence of map-making by computer is similar to manual cartography. Compilation of the materials, however, is done inside the computer. The most common method of obtaining information is to digitize (convert into numbers) the location of roads and other features from existing maps. In this process lines are stored as repeated co-ordinate pairs, each pair giving a measure of so many millimetres to the east and so many to the north of the south-west corner of the map.

The greatest advantage of computer cartography is that it greatly simplifies selection of an area of interest, of features of interest within that area, of the projection on which the results are to be produced and the graphic symbols used to show them. A change of features of interest, for example, does not involve the cartographer in manual re-drawing: he specifies which ones he wants and the machine will draw them on film or paper, often to very high accuracy indeed.

Different machines use different means of drawing such as pens, beams of light and laser beams. The use of cathode ray tubes is becoming much more common—these appear like televisions and *ephemeral* maps may be drawn on them if no *hard copy* map is needed. Some of these can draw at speeds of more than 100 metres per second. In addition to this speed and flexibility, the basic cartographic information can often be used for other tasks. A suitably programmed computer, for example, will be able to draw sections through the topography along a given road or find the answers to such questions as 'how many buildings lie within this area?' Though a very important and far-reaching development, the use of computers in mapping still necessitates the cartographer's design skills to produce maps which can be used by the average person.

Photomapping

A number of maps, particularly in Sweden and the US and at large scales, are now produced with a photographic base rather than the normal line depiction of the topography. This is particularly useful in areas which do not already have accurate maps or in areas of rapid change, such as in cities.

Often these maps consist of mosaics of air photographs. Since each photograph is distorted because of the variations in the height and orientation of the survey aircraft and because of variation in ground height, they often have to be *rectified* before being pieced together. Such rectification can remove all of the distortions apart from those due to variations in ground altitude. To get rid of this, a special electronic or optical process termed *orthophotography* has been devised. It produces planimetrically correct photographs, that is, photographs which are as free of geometric distortion as the best maps.

Whatever the sophistication of the rectification carried out, the photographs have to be converted from their continuous tone nature (in which all shades of grey are present in the film) into a half-tone before they can be printed. This involves breaking up the original into dots of different sizes, the larger dots representing the darker areas: the coarse half-toning in newspaper pictures illustrates the end result. The infills for roads, lakes and so on are printed, often in different colours, on top of the half-tone image to enhance the appearance and to make the map easier to use. The more annotation, the more the photomap comes to resemble the conventional map, but it retains one important difference—all the features of the landscape are on it, not merely ones selected and interpreted by the cartographer. Some training is usually necessary before photomaps can be used successfully, since the user must be able to interpret air photographs as well as map-read.

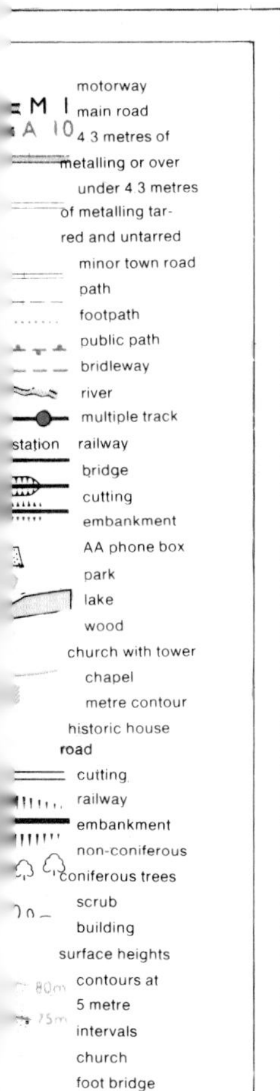

Ordnance Survey

Using Maps

Maps are a familiar feature of modern life: they are seen everywhere. On television the weather forecast is explained with the help of a map, in town centres the road systems and important local buildings, like the hospital and police station, are displayed on a map, and on railway stations maps show how to travel from one place to another. The appearance of maps varies enormously. Just how a particular map is designed depends on its intended use, and a map designed for one purpose may be quite useless for another: there is, for example, no need for a map of a railway system to be geographically accurate.

Maps are basically of two kinds: *topographic* and *thematic*. The first shows the form of the landscape and the man-made features upon it, while the second shows the distribution of particular phenomena such as the spread of Dutch Elm disease through England in 1976.

The most common use of topographic maps is for route finding by motorists at both very large (town plan) and very small (1:250,000 to 1:1,000,000) scales. In between these two extremes, a variety of other uses, such as for walking and cycling, predominate.

Even if motoring information is the most common use for many maps, other very different kinds of route finding needs exist. Military uses for maps include finding routes where all movements will be out of sight of an observer on a particular hilltop and planning routes for armoured vehicles that avoid valleys in which they might get bogged down. Both military and civilian aircraft have special requirements for route-finding maps. One type of screen display sometimes provided in modern aircraft is the *moving map:* a background map moves continuously to maintain the aircraft's current position at the centre of the screen.

On a more individual level, the Scandinavian sport of orienteering—running in races through forested terrain with the aid of a map and compass—is becoming widespread in Europe and new large scale maps are in continuous production to meet the needs for maps of terrain unfamiliar to all the contestants. Other leisure maps are also now widely available, often tailored to one particular user: in Britain, for example, a special series of maps is available to dinghy sailors.

In most countries, the planning departments of both central and local government are major map users. Central government is chiefly interested in strategic planning, and so most of their maps tend to be small scale, covering the whole of the country. A good example is the *Atlas of the Environment* produced by the Department of the Environment in Britain. This contains about 50 maps of England and Wales and the major conurbations: most are derived from the census of population carried out every ten years and show such features as 'percentage of homes lacking all standard amenities' (inside toilet, bath and hot water). Such maps very quickly show which areas of the country are more 'deprived' than

Cooper-Bridgeman Library

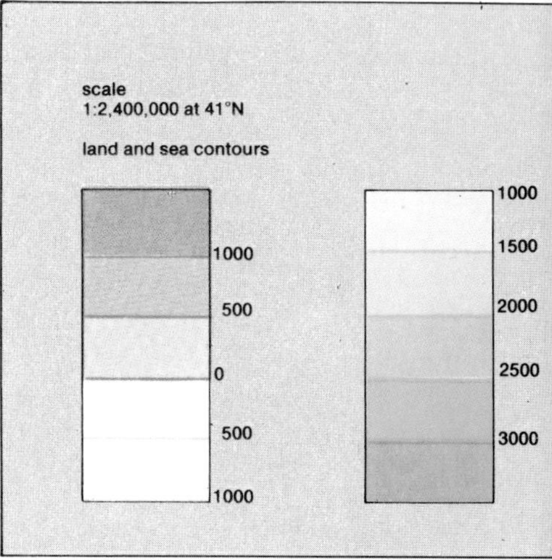

Left: This topographic map of Chelmsford in England was made by John Walker in 1591. Maps like this provide historians with information that would be extremely hard to obtain from any other source: for example, an accurate measure of the extent, and therefore an estimate of the town's population.

Right: Part of a contour map and key (above) of the east Atlantic. The map is based on many thousands of soundings each checked for consistency by an oceanographer. The position of each sounding is shown as a black dot. Maps of this type are important for navigation and studies of the sea bed.

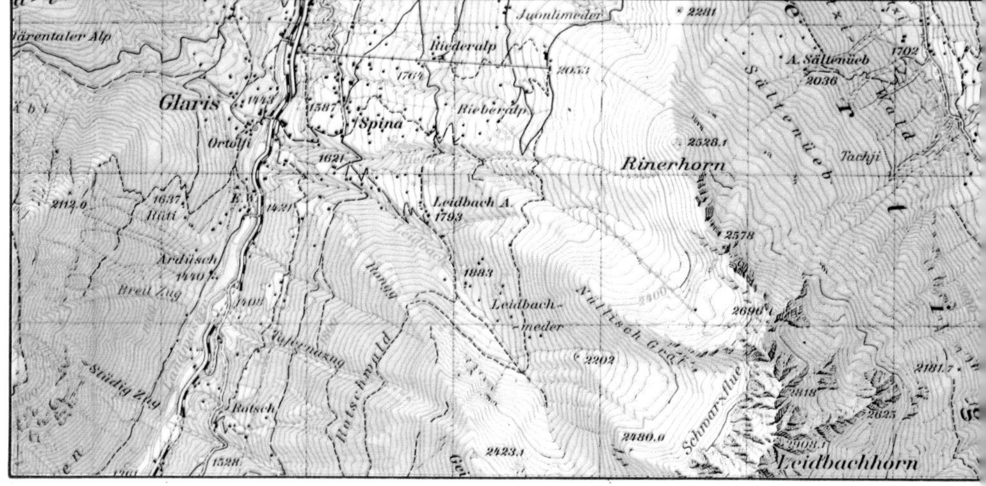

Above: On this Swiss topographic map, relief is shown by contours, by rock drawing and by shading of east and south-facing slopes. Although the scale is only 1:50,000 individual houses are shown. The map provides an enormous amount of detail of the topography of the area.

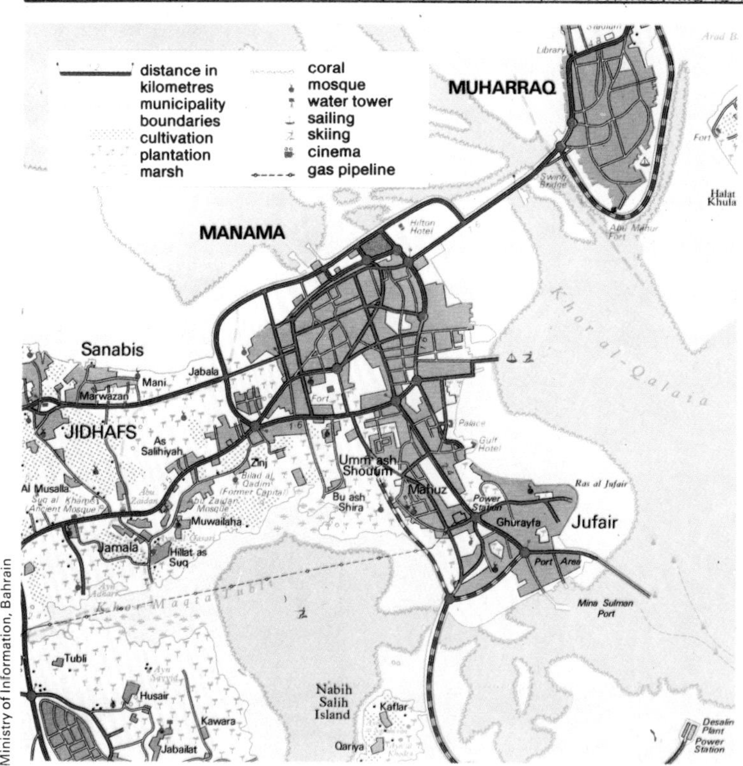

Ministry of Information, Bahrain

Left: The features shown on this map of the northern part of Bahrain have been selected to be of interest to visitors. The map is shown at about half the scale of the Swiss map (above) and the amount of detail is much less. The sizes of certain features on the map (such as the widths of some roads) have been exaggerated for clarity.

Right: A navigational chart showing the arc of visibility of the light on the Needles Rocks at the western tip of the Isle of Wight, England. The chart also shows depths (in fathoms), the type of sea bottom (such as shingle, weed or mud), the direction of magnetic north and the positions of anchorages, radio beacons, radar reflectors and wrecks.

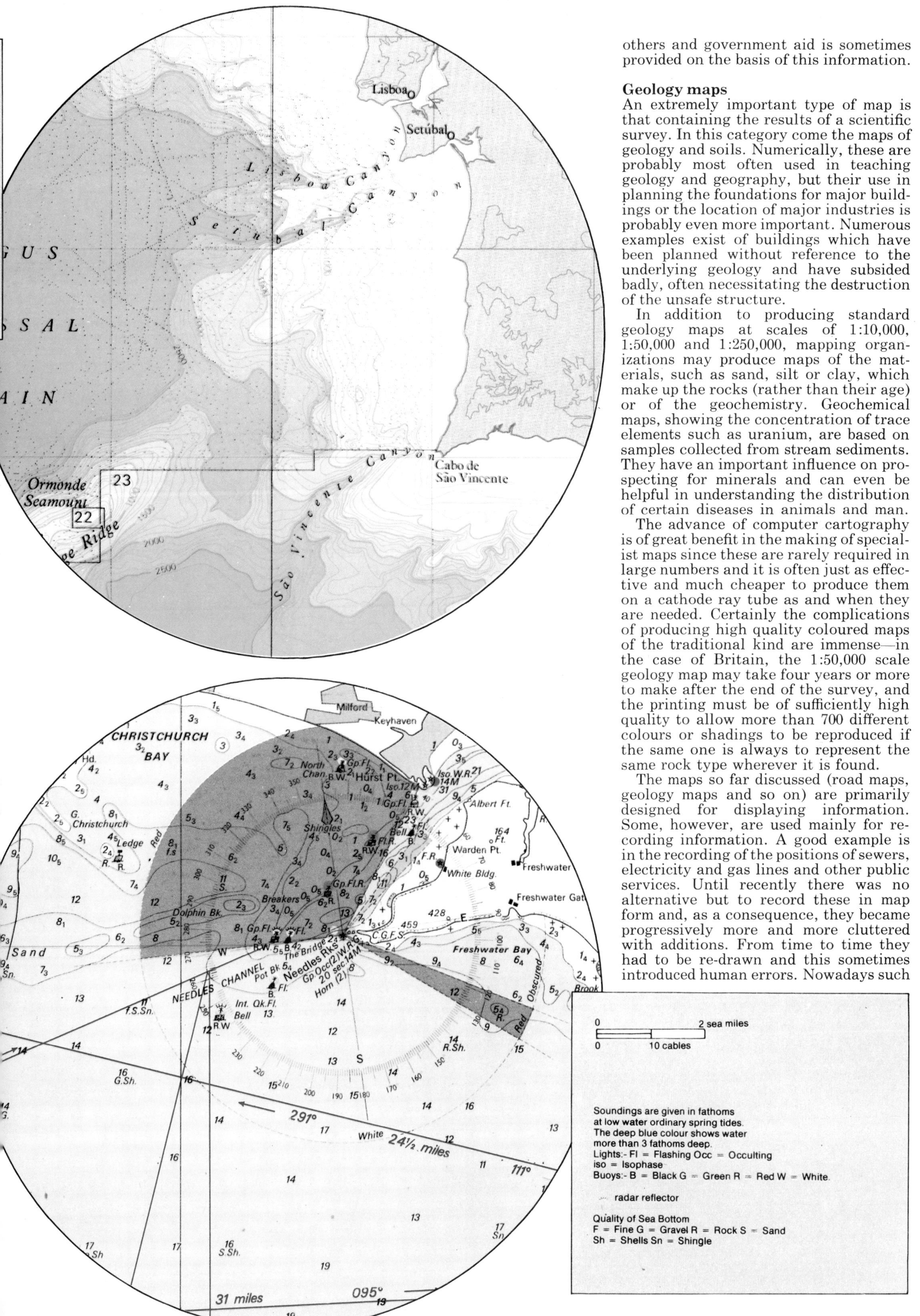

others and government aid is sometimes provided on the basis of this information.

Geology maps

An extremely important type of map is that containing the results of a scientific survey. In this category come the maps of geology and soils. Numerically, these are probably most often used in teaching geology and geography, but their use in planning the foundations for major buildings or the location of major industries is probably even more important. Numerous examples exist of buildings which have been planned without reference to the underlying geology and have subsided badly, often necessitating the destruction of the unsafe structure.

In addition to producing standard geology maps at scales of 1:10,000, 1:50,000 and 1:250,000, mapping organizations may produce maps of the materials, such as sand, silt or clay, which make up the rocks (rather than their age) or of the geochemistry. Geochemical maps, showing the concentration of trace elements such as uranium, are based on samples collected from stream sediments. They have an important influence on prospecting for minerals and can even be helpful in understanding the distribution of certain diseases in animals and man.

The advance of computer cartography is of great benefit in the making of specialist maps since these are rarely required in large numbers and it is often just as effective and much cheaper to produce them on a cathode ray tube as and when they are needed. Certainly the complications of producing high quality coloured maps of the traditional kind are immense—in the case of Britain, the 1:50,000 scale geology map may take four years or more to make after the end of the survey, and the printing must be of sufficiently high quality to allow more than 700 different colours or shadings to be reproduced if the same one is always to represent the same rock type wherever it is found.

The maps so far discussed (road maps, geology maps and so on) are primarily designed for displaying information. Some, however, are used mainly for recording information. A good example is in the recording of the positions of sewers, electricity and gas lines and other public services. Until recently there was no alternative but to record these in map form and, as a consequence, they became progressively more and more cluttered with additions. From time to time they had to be re-drawn and this sometimes introduced human errors. Nowadays such

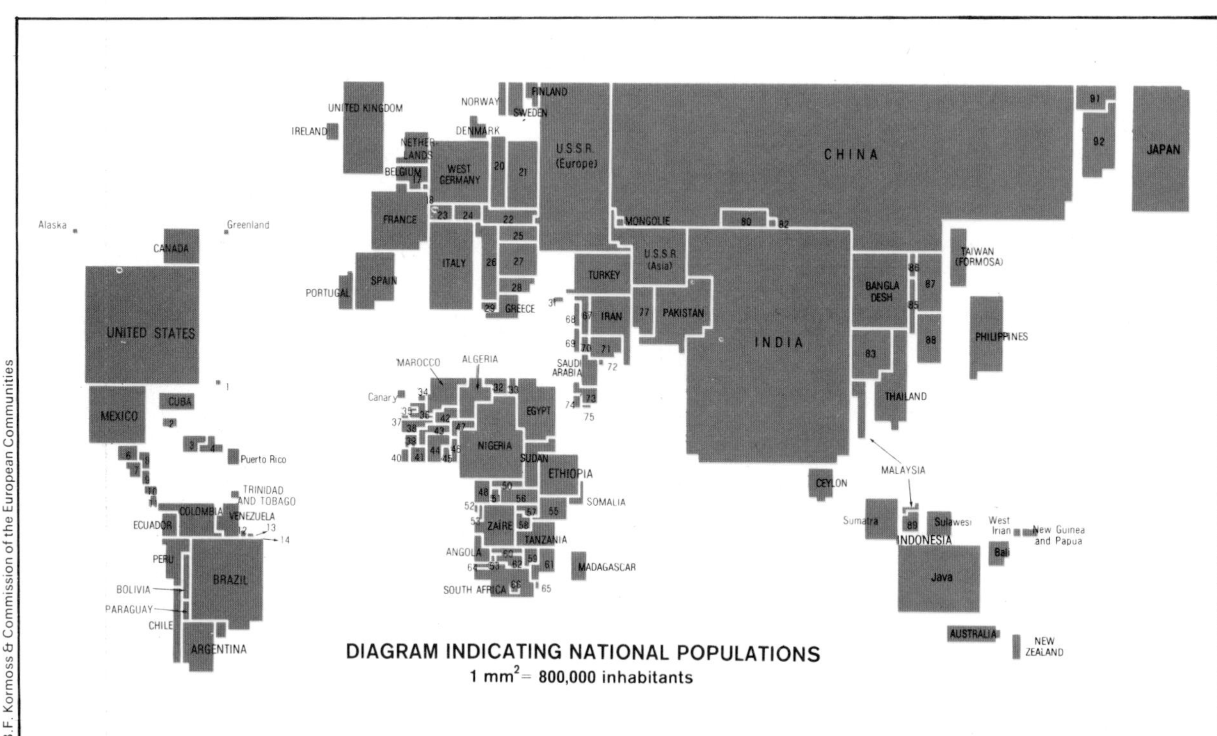

I.B.F. Kormoss & Commission of the European Communities

Left: A cartogram of world population. The area each country occupies on the map has been adjusted to correspond with its population. In a normal thematic map a large country like Australia or Canada would receive, from the point of view of population, more space than it really deserved.

Right: A map of the Mersey region of England showing the distribution of unemployment in the area at the time of the 1971 census. The map is based on information for 1 km square areas. Census information for the whole country was mapped in this way, providing a remarkably accurate picture of the distribution of population.

Below: Preparing a map for an Open University geography course. Land or property use is perhaps the most common type of information to be stored on maps. In Britain as many as 800 categories of land use may be recognized, so the preparation of such maps is a painstaking business. They are chiefly used by planning authorities.

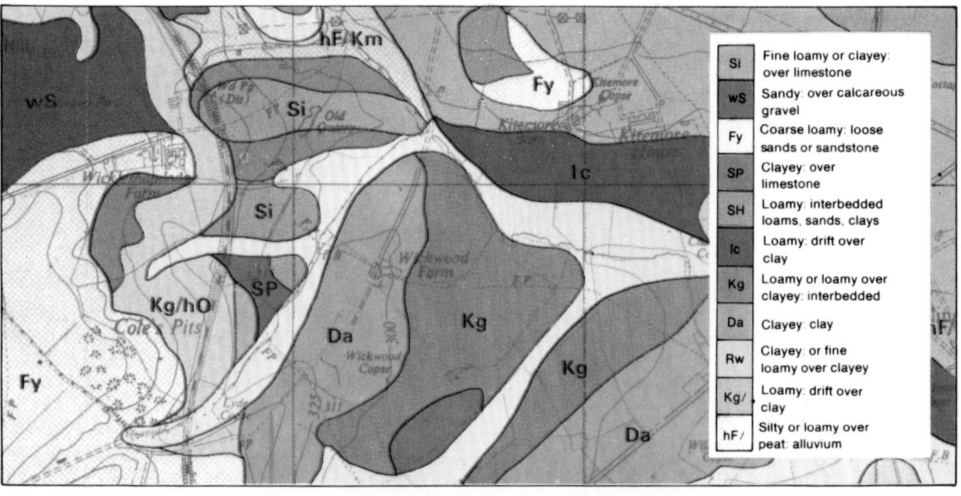

RNIB

Above: This soil map of the region around Faringdon in England was drawn by computer from information compiled in the field on numerous other maps, to a scale of 1:25,000. The usefulness of such a map depends largely on the existence of a separate memoir giving detailed information about each of the different soil series.

Left: A map maker engraves a mould from which a map for the blind will be formed. The map, made from a plastic sheet, is read by touch, like writing in braille.

Right: Computers can be used to produce block diagrams with perspective. This diagram shows variation in population, looking southwards towards London. The higher the peak, the greater the population density. The computer has been programmed to suppress contour lines which lie 'behind' any of the peaks. Other views of the same population chart can be prepared quite simply by specifying a different angle or altitude of viewing.

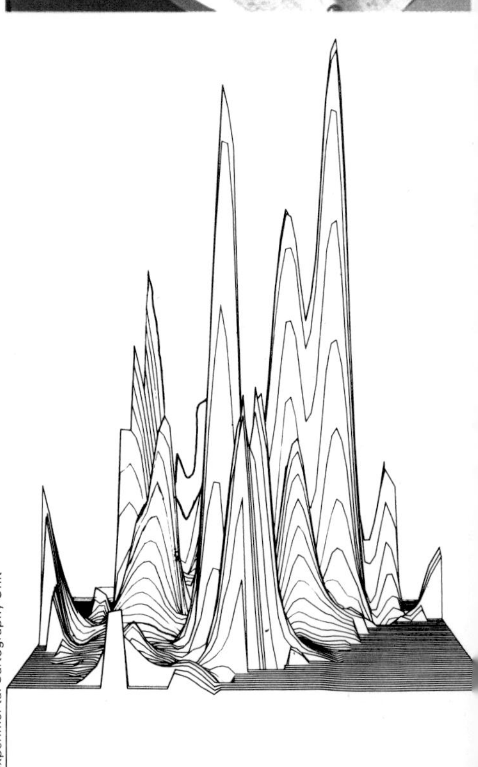

Experimental Cartography Unit

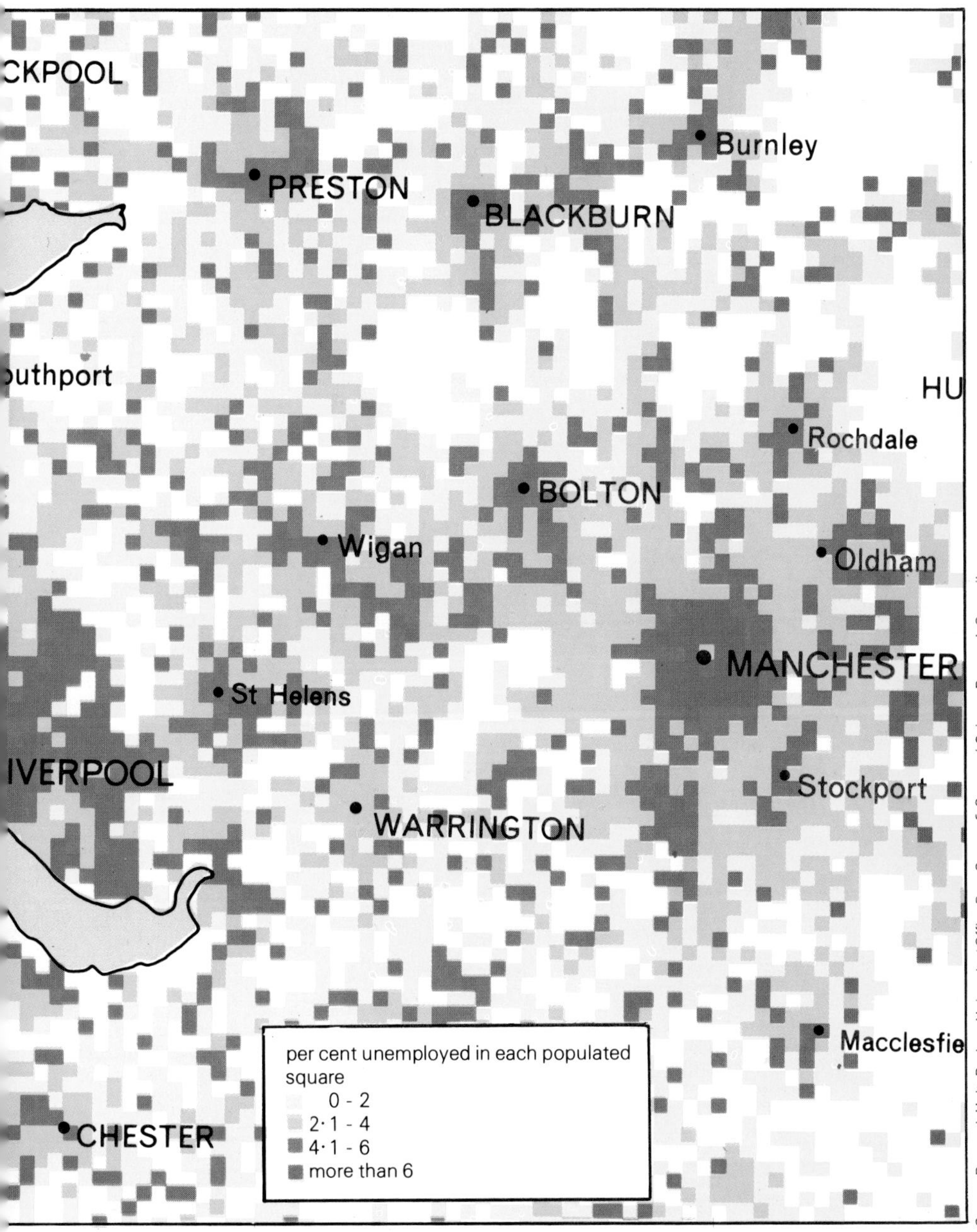

Census Research Unit, Durham University/ Office Pop. Census & Surveys/ Science Research Council

information is often digitized from maps and stored on magnetic tape; a computer can then draw out maps of selected portions of the network at a given scale or can be instructed to correct any mistakes which have been discovered.

Another important use of maps is to link the real world to some other store of information. Perhaps the best example of this is the soil map which normally contains coloured areas, each with a symbol indicating the soil type or, in technical terms, the *soil series*. The characteristics such as depth, colour, stoniness, acidity and so on, of any particular soil series may be found in an accompanying *memoir*. This combined use of map and memoir is necessary to interpret soils or plan their future use.

Using maps

Whatever the task the map reader must be familiar with the conventions and limitations of the map. Perhaps the most common conventions are those of having north at the top of a published map and using colours similar to those of the features in the real world, such as blue for sea and green for grass. The limitations of the map are quite another matter and most of these stem from the question of map scale. A simple example illustrates this: on a 1:10,000 scale map (one unit of length on the map represents 10,000 of the same units on the ground) a road represented as 2 mm wide would be 20 m wide in reality. On a 1:50,000 scale map, the same 2 mm would represent a road 100 m wide and on a 1:250,000 scale map, it would represent a width of no less than 500 m.

Such scale considerations ensure that the cartographer must adapt the way he shows the world to what is possible on a relatively small piece of paper. As a result, he will often show some features on small scale maps by caricatures—twisting alpine roads have many individual bends missed out but are still shown as being very sinuous to maintain the impression of their character. In topographic maps, this sort of generalization normally begins at scales of about 1:50,000 and smaller: at larger scales most features can be represented without significant distortion.

A second limitation of any map is in what it shows. The conventional line map, like the British Ordnance Survey maps, show only a selection of what might have been put on the map. Relatively little, for example, is shown of land use except for the location of wooded areas, and nothing is shown of underground features such as subways or sewers. Maps in different countries, even if they are drawn to the same scale, will show different things, as can be seen by comparing maps of adjacent areas on either side of an international boundary.

Sometimes, however, a map shows more than is apparent. A good example of this is seen in a geology map now published in Britain at 1:50,000 scale. This shows the age and, to some extent, the physical character of the rocks making up the landscape by different colours and by symbols. Underneath the colours, however, is an Ordnance Survey topographic map printed in grey. By comparing the Ordnance Survey contours and the position of the boundaries of the rocks on the geology map, the geologist can tell not only where the rocks appear on the ground but also whether they are tilted underground and, if so, where the boundary between any two strata is to be found at all depths. Thus the amount of information that can be derived from the whole map is more than can be obtained from all the parts considered separately.

Map reading

An essential ability in using maps is to be able to think spatially: to be able to establish a mental picture of the mapped area by translating the symbols on the map into real features. Until relatively recently it was thought that such spatial abilities were not acquired until the age of six or seven, but experiments have shown that children as young as three years can occasionally think in this way, though they are incapable of sophisticated work, such as working out whether one point can be seen from another, until they are eight or nine.

It is clear from everyday experience that some people can understand and read maps much better than others. To improve map design, geographers need to understand the mechanisms by which the map user finds and selects the information he is seeking on the map. Many studies have been carried out—some as long ago as the 1920s—but the majority of these were inconclusive and more recent studies have only served to illuminate the difficulty of carrying out perception tests on map users.

In standard tests maps with only slight differences are given to different users who are then assessed for speed and accuracy in carrying out tasks such as finding the most direct route from place A to place B. In theory, with a well-designed experiment and with careful use of statistics, it should be possible to determine just which difference has had the greatest effect on the usefulness of the map. Unfortunately, however, it is virtually impossible to change an item in a map design without changing many others: changing scale without altering the map size or the area displayed is, for example, quite impossible. Some findings of value have come out of these studies. For example, map users regularly underestimate the values represented by the circular symbols commonly used to indicate the sizes of towns on maps. The larger these are, the larger the town they represent, but the increase is usually underestimated: the problem is easily solved by making the symbols larger still. Perhaps the most important finding, however, is that individuals can vary hourly in their accuracy and speed of map reading.

Chapter 6

Beyond the Earth

Andromeda, the nearest major external galaxy to Earth's Milky Way system. It is perhaps twice as large as our own galaxy, 2 million light years in length and containing 100,000 million stars.

The Universe

With hardly an exception, the variations we see in the astronomical sky are the results of effects within our own solar system. The sequence of night and day is produced by the Earth's rotation, the phases of the Moon by its orbiting of the Earth and the march of the constellations across the sky by the Earth's orbit around the Sun. Otherwise the night sky seems remote and uncommunicative. However, the very fact that the sky is dark at all reveals fundamental information about the universe.

Imagine a universe consisting of luminous *galaxies*, systems of billions of stars bound together by their own gravity, like our own Milky Way, spread fairly uniformly throughout a space extending in all directions to infinity. Because the fact that galaxies appear increasingly dim to us the further away they are is compensated by the greater number that can be seen from such a distance, the sky in between the nearby stars should then be as bright as the galaxies themselves and not dark at all. Without artificially limiting the universe in extent or age the most plausible explanation of this paradox (called Olbers' Paradox) is that the universe is expanding, which means that all the galaxies in the universe are moving away from each other. Looked at from any one galaxy (ours, for example) the more distant a galaxy the faster it appears to be receding from us.

As two objects separate, the light from one seen from the other is reddened in its wavelength—that is it loses energy (known as the Doppler effect)—so the light from more and more distant galaxies makes less and less contribution to the brightness of the sky seen from the Earth.

The Doppler effect is useful to astronomers since the speed of recession of a galaxy can actually be measured by observing by just how much recognizable lines in its spectrum are *red shifted*, that is, by how much its wavelength has reddened. This red shift was discovered by the American astronomer Edwin Hubble in 1928 to be directly related to the observed faintness of a galaxy, proving that distant galaxies recede faster.

One theory about the universe's age emerges if we imagine the expansion of the universe reversed. Then the contraction would bring all the matter in the universe to a very high density after between 10,000 and 20,000 million years. This number can be thought of as the age of the universe—and not surprisingly exceeds geophysical estimates of the age of the Earth (4,500 million years)—if we suppose the universe to have started from such a high density state by expanding after a 'big bang'.

Once the expansion of the universe was established, people looked for alternatives to the rather awkward notion that matter once existed in a very dense state, and the idea of continuous creation was put forward in 1948. Since the universe is constantly expanding, the matter it contains would become more spread out with time so, according to this theory, matter must be continuously created to fill the space caused by the expansion.

Subsequent observations have made the idea of continuous creation difficult to

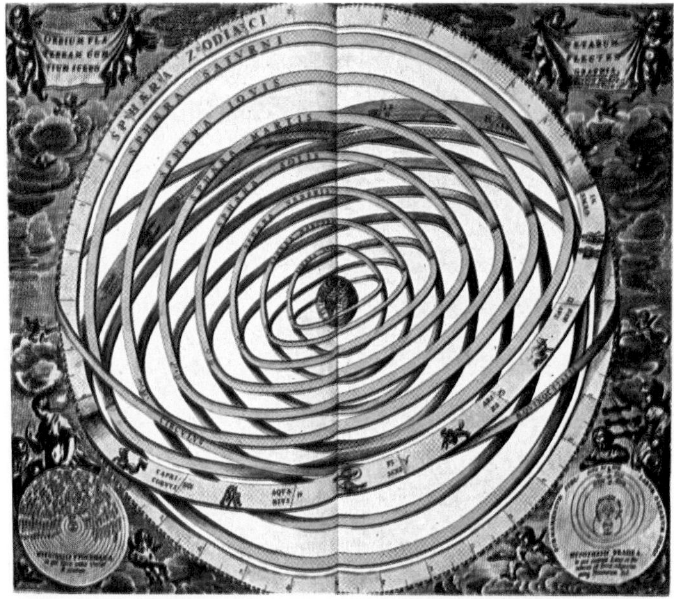
Ann Ronan Picture Library

Ann Ronan Picture Library

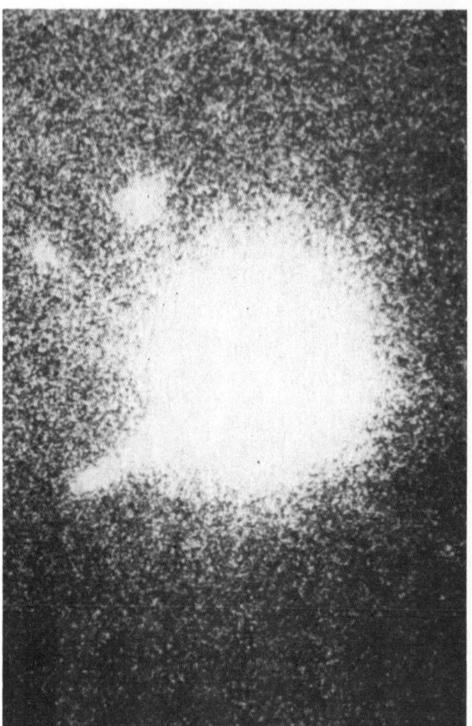
Royal Astronomical Society

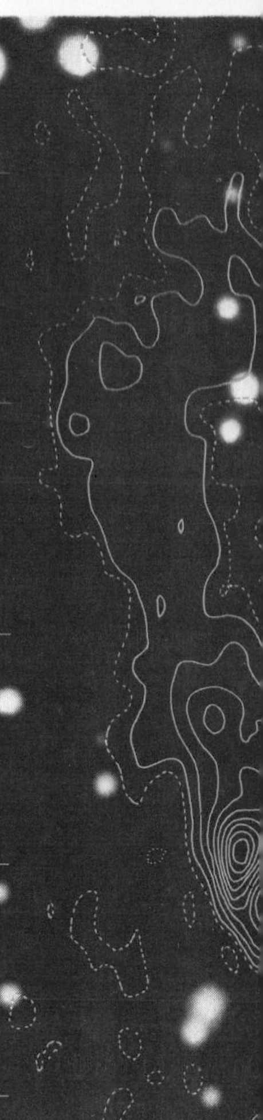

Top: Plate from an 18th century Dutch book, illustrating the ancient view of a *geocentric*, Earth-centred universe. Minute in comparison with the infinite universe that we now believe exists, it consists of the planets encircled by the stars of the zodiac.

Above: An early astronomical telescope, mounted at Slough, England, by Sir William Herschel in 1789. Large optical telescopes have contributed greatly to the 20th century advance of astronomy.

Left: The nearest quasar, referred to as 3C273, was discovered in 1963. Given a long exposure, this picture shows the 'jet' which extends from one side. Normally, quasars appear as mere points of light and can only be distinguished from stars in our own galaxy by analysis of their light, which appears bluish, although they are receding from us at high speed. The first quasars were picked up because they seemed to be ordinary stars emitting radio waves. Many quasars are sources of radio waves; others, however, are *radio quiet*.

Alphabet & Image

Left: Embedded in a cluster of galaxies, the galaxy NGC 1265 is also a radio source Here its radio emission is superimposed on its optical appearance. Most radio galaxies have two radio 'blobs'; NGC 1265 has emitted several blobs which stream from it, due possibly to its movements through thin intergalactic gas.

Above: Radio telescopes at Jodrell Bank, Cheshire, England. Radio telescopes do not give images as do optical telescopes, although they focus the radio waves just as an optical telescope's mirror does. They are useful in collecting information about matter which is invisible to an optical telescope.

Below: Each blurred spot here is a galaxy; the hard round dots, including the bright one with spikes, are stars in our own galaxy. Such clusters seem to contain a large amount of invisible matter, now being discovered as sources of X-rays. Over 100,000 million galaxies probably exist in the observable universe.

Leiden Observatory—Netherlands Foundation for Radio Astronomy

Anglo-Australian Observatory © 1977

accept and have tended to give more credence to the big bang theory. In 1965, a low level of background radiation was detected, coming from all directions of the sky equally. Its temperature, 2.7°K (degrees above the absolute zero of temperature) is best interpreted as the radiation remaining from the big bang. During the earliest moments of the universe this radiation was equivalent to an enormously high temperature, but the subsequent expansion of the universe has red shifted it so much that now it is at a very low temperature. On the continuous creation theory such radiation would have to come from individual sources at least as numerous as ordinary galaxies. No such distribution has been observed.

New cosmologies

Such an intriguing study as the origin of the universe is bound to attract many descriptions and explanations. These *cosmologies* attempt to explain the structure, history and future of the universe.

At present, important questions are whether the universe is infinite in extent, allowing one to travel for ever through new parts of space, or whether it is a finite system where the curvature of space itself brings the cosmic traveller back to his starting point. Also, will the universe continue expanding just as it is doing now? Two observable quantities would answer these questions.

First, if scientists could measure the average density of matter in the universe they would know whether its gravitational attraction could slow, halt and even reverse the expansion. There are observational problems which probably prevent us 'seeing' all the forms of matter in the universe, so we almost certainly underestimate the average density. To 'close' the universe, that is provide enough matter to eventually make the universe halt its expansion and contract again, requires roughly ten times the density currently detectable. Possibly the 'missing' mass is present, but in a form we can see only rarely, for example as black holes or as gas between the galaxies. The most recent evidence from observations is that the universe is infinite in extent and will expand for ever.

Secondly, can the rate at which the expansion rate is changing with distance, called the *deceleration factor*, be measured? This factor can be estimated from the way the red shift ceases to be directly related to the brightness of a galaxy at distances beyond about 1,500 million light years. Unfortunately, present astronomical telescopes and techniques are not quite sensitive enough to make reliable estimates of red-shift and brightness at this distance, so the deceleration factor is as yet unmeasured.

Evolution of the universe

Using one of the big bang cosmologies, the way in which the present contents of the universe have evolved can be examined. In the highly compact young universe the enormously high temperature and consequent highly energetic radiation prevented the existence of all but fundamental nuclear particles.

As the universe expanded the density of radiation decreased rather more rapidly than the density of matter, and so the existence of further particles became possible. First of all neutrons were formed and, when the universe was a

Above: A large 4 m (157 in) telescope at Cerro-Tololo in Chile. The mirror at the base of the skeleton tube reflects light to a focus near the top of the tube, where a photographic plate can be placed. The light can be reflected into a room to apparatus too large to be carried on the telescope.

Above right: Astronomers require mountaintop sites in order to be free from most of the pollution and vapour in the atmosphere. The Cerro-Tololo Inter-American Observatory, at an altitude of 2,160 m in the Chilean foothills of the Andes, was opened in 1967 and has remarkably steady air for much of the time.

Below: A sequence of galaxy types:
1. A giant *elliptical* galaxy, M87, also a radio source. Around it are faint blurred blobs which are globular clusters, each containing up to a million stars. Elliptical galaxies contain almost no visible gas or dust.
2. The *Sombrero Hat* galaxy, M104, a spiral galaxy with a large hub. A spiral galaxy has two parts—the hub (similar to an elliptical galaxy, with little gas) and the spiral arms, laden with gas and dust, from which new stars are created.
3. A *regular spiral* galaxy, possibly similar to our own.
4. A *peculiar spiral*, showing that galaxies can be deformed into strange shapes, often as a result of the gravitational pull of other galaxies.
5. This spiral exhibits widely spread arms and a comparatively small hub. Spiral galaxies are typically 100,000 light years across.
6. The tightly wound spiral arms of this galaxy could indicate rapid rotation; our own galaxy rotates once every 250 million years (called a galactic year).
7. The *whirlpool* galaxy has a small companion linked by a stream of material. Our own galaxy has two companions, the *Magellanic Clouds*.
8. A *barred spiral* galaxy, in which the hub is elongated, with the arms projecting from its ends.

few seconds old, a proportion of these decayed into protons and electrons. These three particles were the building blocks for all the chemical elements. By the time the universe was several hundreds of seconds old the simplest elements would have appeared, including hydrogen (one proton and one electron), deuterium or *heavy hydrogen* (one proton, one neutron and one electron) and helium (two protons, two neutrons and two electrons). Helium was probably formed by the pairing of deuterium nuclei, and it is estimated that about 35 per cent of the mass of the universe should have become helium by this process, a figure which compares quite well with the 25 per cent observed today. To form a large amount of helium from hydrogen requires the kind of temperatures and conditions that would have been present in the big bang; ordinary stars do not seem to be hot or bright enough to have produced all the helium detected now.

From the hydrogen and helium mixture within the universe condensations started to appear as fluctuations in gas density caused gas clouds to collapse under their own gravitational attraction. Eventually *protogalaxies*, containing individual *protostars*, were born.

Galaxies

Not only is the matter in the universe clumped into galaxies but about three quarters of all galaxies reside in clusters of galaxies containing from a few to thousands of members. On even larger distance scales, clusters may be members of superclusters stretching hundreds of millions of light years across space.

It is possible to estimate the mass of a

1

2

5

6

Anglo-Australian Observatory © 1977

Science Research Council

Anglo-Australian Observatory © 1977

Above left: Centaurus A, a nearby radio galaxy, surrounded by a mass of opaque dust that is hiding the light from the centre.

Left: A typical spiral galaxy, M83. The arms are regions of new star formation and thus are bluish; the centre, where the older stars are, appears redder.

Above: the British X-ray satellite Ariel 5, launched by the US in 1974. Carrying X-ray telescopes and detectors, it observes the X-rays coming from the sky, often from the centres of galaxies with disturbed, very energetic nuclei such as Seyfert galaxies, radio galaxies and quasars.

4

Kitt Peak National Observatory

Kitt Peak National Observatory

7

© Hale Observatories

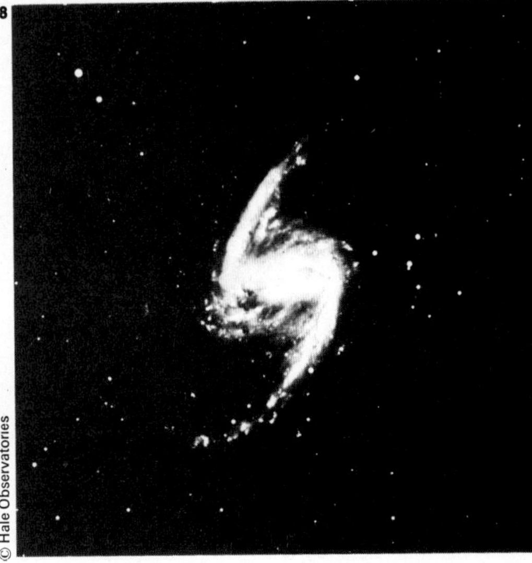

8

Anglo-Australian Observatory © 1975

cluster of galaxies, and the result of such a calculation shows that there is more mass present than can be accounted for by observation. A clue to this discrepancy was provided when it was discovered, by means of scientific satellites, that the clusters are diffuse X-ray sources. The X-rays could be generated by the individual galaxies ploughing through a very thin inter-galactic gas and heating it to tens of millions of degrees. The presence of such a gas would not only account for the missing mass of the galaxy cluster, but would certainly have a bearing on the mass required to 'close' the universe.

Advancing astronomy

By investigating wavelengths other than visible light, radio and X-ray astronomers have been obtaining new information about the matter present which does not show up visually. In particular, radio astronomy's discovery of radio galaxies opened up research in 'active' galaxies and debate as to their energy mechanisms. About one galaxy in a thousand is a radio galaxy and it is often the brightest elliptical member of a cluster of galaxies.

Further evidence that vast amounts of energy are released in the nuclei of galaxies came with the discovery of quasi-stellar objects (QSOs or *quasars*), radio sources which are identified with bright, blue star-like objects quite unlike the giant elliptical radio galaxies. Red-shift measurements implied that these quasars were at considerable distances and therefore must have an unusually high energy output. The optical *spectra* (range of optical wavelengths) emitted by quasars are much like the spectra of another class of active galaxies named after their discoverer Carl Seyfert. The bright star-like nucleus of the Seyfert galaxy is surrounded by the arms and even possibly the bar of a normal spiral galaxy. X-ray astronomers have found that Seyfert galaxies in which clear signs of violent motion are apparent are invariably X-ray sources. This implies that either very high temperatures (tens of millions of degrees) or very fast electrons are being produced within the nucleus. Since quasars have red shifts greater than about 0.1 (equivalent to 1,500 million light years) compared with red shifts of only about a tenth of this for Seyfert galaxies, it has been suggested that quasars are just bright Seyfert galaxies so distant that only the star-like nucleus remains visible, but this test awaits the more sensitive X-ray telescopes of the future.

A mechanism able to power an active galaxy must be unusual if we place quasars at cosmological rather than 'local' distances. In the X-ray sources of our own galaxy the X-rays are produced when hydrogen from the surface of a normal star is heated to very high temperatures as it falls on to the surface of a binary companion which is a neutron star or black hole. As much as one tenth of the equivalent in energy of the falling mass (given by Einstein's famous $E = mc^2$) can be released in the process compared with only a small fraction of this if the hydrogen were converted to helium by nuclear fusion, as occurs in the centres of stars or in a hydrogen bomb. This highly efficient process may be responsible for powering active galaxies if the nucleus contains a supermassive black hole (a hundred million times the mass of our sun) which is sucking in gas and stars.

The Galaxy

Most galaxies reside in clusters, and our own is no exception. We are in what is called the 'local group' of galaxies which comprises about two dozen members including the spectacular Andromeda Galaxy (known to astronomers by its catalogue number Messier 31). This spiral galaxy is not unlike our own in structure although it is somewhat larger: our own galaxy has about 150,000 million stars, while M31 has about twice that number. M31 and our galaxy are the largest galaxies in the local group, most of the other galaxies being dwarfs. The nearest members are the Large and Small Magellanic Clouds (LMC and SMC), irregular galaxies each about 170,000 *light years* away (a light year is the distance travelled by light during one year; it travels 300,000 km per second).

Although it might appear to be a simple matter to observe the structure of our own galaxy, the Milky Way, we are prevented from seeing all parts of it clearly. Often the astronomer is forced to observe many parts of it simultaneously,

Ann Ronan Picture Library

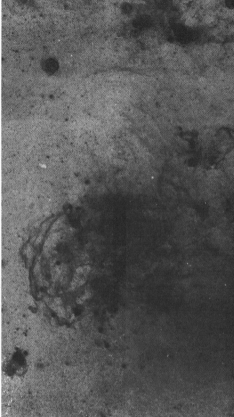

UK Schmidt Telescope Unit/Royal Observatory, Edinburgh

Lund Observatory, Sweden

Anglo Australian Observatory

UK Schmidt Telescope Unit/Royal Observatory, Edinburgh

Top: Sir William Herschel (1738-1822), pioneer of stellar astronomy, discoverer of the planet Uranus and of infra-red radiation. From observations, he concluded that the Milky Way actually forms a flat, lens-shaped disc.

Above: Panoramic chart of the Milky Way, made by plotting the 7,000 brightest stars in the sky and mapping in the distribution of nebulae from photographs. The stars and gas clouds shown here are mostly between 100 and 5,000 light years from us. Gas and star clouds concentrate towards the nucleus (centre), while to the left of the centre dust lanes obscure the stars. Our small companion galaxies, the Magellanic Clouds, can also be seen (below right).

Left: Globular clusters such as this surround the centre of our galaxy. Each contains between 100,000 and a million old, red stars and has no dust, gas or young stars. Globular clusters, approximately 13 billion years old, are among the oldest objects in the galaxy.

Left and below: Photographs of the Large Magellanic Cloud, one of the two small companion galaxies, about 170,000 light years distant, that orbit our Milky Way. The colour picture (below) shows the fuzzy appearance of the Cloud, which is composed of similar material to the spiral arms of our galaxy (stars, gaseous nebulae and dust clouds). The large glowing area to the left is the Tarantula Nebula. The black and white negative (left) was taken using a filter which only lets in light from hydrogen gas. The small rings visible are sites of past *supernova* explosions, in which a star releases its material into the area around it, to become incorporated in new stars. Such supernova remnants are a sign of young regions; if this were an old region, all the traces would have long since vanished.

Below right: Glowing hydrogen in our galaxy, seen here in the Lagoon Nebula. Areas such as this, composed mainly of hydrogen gas in a hot, ionized form, are called H II regions. Dark lanes and *globules* (circular or oval dark nebulae made of dusty gas, seen against the bright star or nebula background) can be seen; stars may form from these globules.

making the observations difficult to disentangle. Data from external galaxies can be used to assess the plausibility of theories based on observations within our own galaxy so it is perhaps fortunate that M31 is comparatively local—only two million light years away.

Structure of the galaxy

The flattened shape of our galaxy is apparent from the appearance of the Milky Way, suggesting we are embedded in a disc-like distribution of stars. Using a telescope the numbers of faint, and therefore presumably distant, stars in equal, small areas of the sky can be estimated. This 'star density' decreases dramatically with increasing angular distance above and below the Milky Way. Along the Milky Way a maximum density occurs roughly in the direction of the constellation Sagittarius and a minimum in the opposite direction, in Auriga. We conclude that the Sun is not in the middle of the disc of stars but that the hub or *galactic centre* is in Sagittarius.

As well as the galactic disc containing the spiral arms, which is roughly 100,000 light years across and between 3,000 and 5,000 light years thick, there is a central spherical region around the nucleus (the *galactic bulge*) about 30,000 light years across. The Sun is about 25,000 light years from the centre and the constellations of stars we see from the Earth are patterns of comparatively nearby stars.

Observations by Walter Baade in 1944 showed that the distribution of different types of stars and groups of stars is not uniform throughout the M31 galaxy. There are two distinct 'populations' of stars in spiral galaxies such as M31 and our own, and these two populations are revealed by the different colours of the spiral arms and the nuclear region. The spiral arms, rich in gas and dust, look bluish by virtue of the dominating presence of bright, massive *main sequence* stars (stars in the prime of their lives, when energy is produced by the fusion of hydrogen at their cores). Such stars belong to Population I. In contrast the nuclear region, which contains little gas or dust, consists mostly of comparatively low mass Population II stars, which appear reddish. All the massive stars have long since evolved into old age, and are no longer visible.

There are other differences between these two populations of stars which are highly relevant to the history and structure of the galaxy. By analyzing the light from a star using the techniques of spectroscopy, astronomers can identify spectral lines which are characteristic of certain elements, revealing the relative abundance of those elements in the outer layers of the star. Any consistent shifts in wavelength of these lines (red or blue shifts) compared with laboratory values can give us the relative recession or approach velocities of the Earth and the star. Population I stars in our galaxy have low space velocities but are rich in heavy elements (elements up to iron which are synthesized by nuclear fusion in the cores of stars). Population II stars have high velocities but contain very little of the heavy elements.

One other feature of resemblance between M31 and our galaxy is the presence of globular clusters distributed around each galaxy in a spherical halo which has the same radius and centre as the disc. Globular clusters are composed of extremely old stars.

These observations fit fairly well with how we think our galaxy has evolved from the original gas cloud. In a collapsing gas cloud successively smaller fragments formed. Collisions between particles caused each cloud to generate internal heat until it became almost impossible for the heat released during the collapse to escape from a fragment. This occurred when the fragments were about as massive as typical stars and so the galaxy of stars was born. The existence of the spiral arms is less easy to explain. Presumably as the collapse proceeded, processes (which are not well understood but which probably included rotation and possibly a magnetic field) came into play to produce a spiral rather than an elliptical

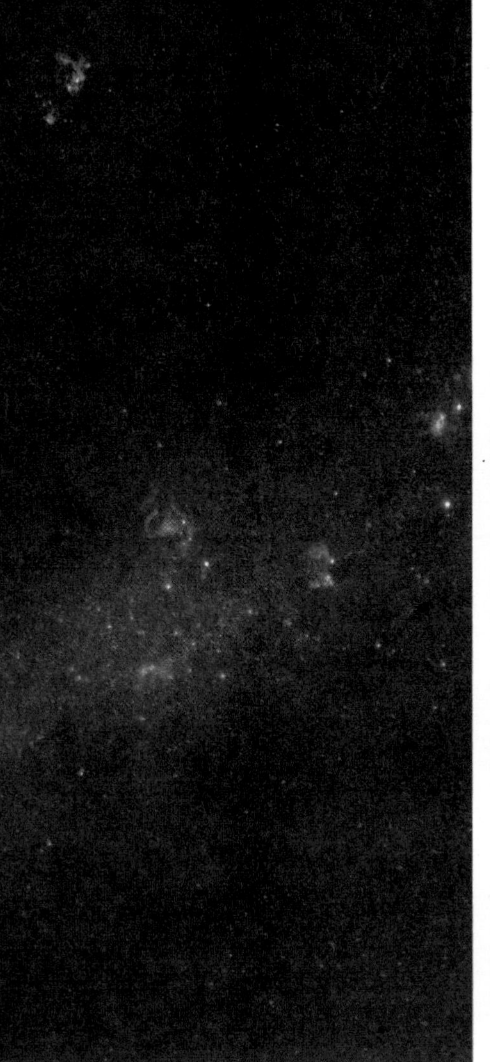

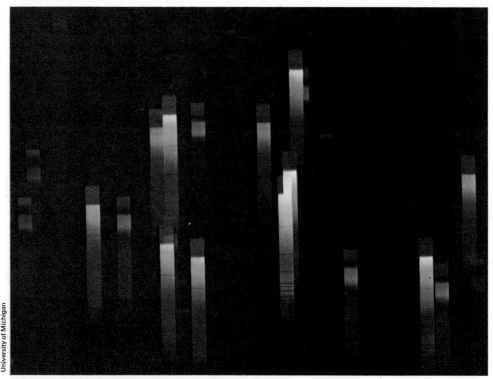

University of Michigan

UK Schmidt Telescope Unit/Royal Observatory, Edinburgh

Above: An *objective prism spectrum* is made by placing a prism in front of a telescope to split light into its component colours. The thin dark lines running across each spectrum show up elements present in the star as well as its temperature.

Left and below left: Important advances in the study of stars in our galaxy came with the Schmidt camera-telescope (below left), constructed in 1975. Using a spherical mirror with a correcting lens in front, the telescope can take a comparatively wide angle view of the sky. One of its uses is illustrated (left). Here the image of a galaxy is viewed on a television monitor. This image, retaining excellent definition, is magnified from a tiny portion (only a few square millimetres in size) of the original 350x350 mm Schmidt plate mounted on the left.

Courtesy Science Research Council

galaxy. Fragments left behind became the globular clusters we see in the galactic halo. The stars in the nuclear region were born at the same time.

The halo and central regions used up almost all their available material in one burst of star formation during the energetic phases of the birth of the galaxy. Violent activity at this time may have resulted in the high velocities of those old Population II stars which we can still see. But star formation continues to take place in the spiral arms of the galactic disc, where we can clearly see gas, dust and new stars—as in the Orion Nebula.

The hottest, most massive stars go through their life cycles quickly, forming heavy elements in their inferno-like cores. At the end of their lives they explode as *supernovae*, scattering their material throughout interstellar space and into the gas clouds from which subsequent generations of stars will form. In this way the more recent stars to form, Population I stars such as the Sun, have a higher metal content than the Population II stars.

The spiral arms

There are two important ways in which we can study the spiral structure of our galaxy. Observations can be made of the distribution of young stars, whose copious ultraviolet radiation excites light from clouds of hydrogen. This optical method is much hampered by the obscuring dust in the rest of the Milky Way. Apart from this, the radio emission from neutral hydrogen, at a wavelength of 21 cm, can be used to map the positions of clouds to greater distances. These clouds orbit the galactic centre at differing velocities, depending on their distance from it. Doppler shifts in the 21 cm wavelength separate these velocities and allow us to build up a picture of the position of clouds in different directions in the galaxy.

It is believed that this side of the galaxy probably has four nearly parallel spiral arms, the Sun lying between one arm passing through the constellation Perseus and the other through the Carina and Aquila constellations.

How do the spiral arms form? They so resemble the spirals produced when cream is stirred slowly into coffee that the answer seems inevitably to be a rotation process. The stars in the spiral arms orbit the galactic centre, just as the planets orbit the Sun, with those furthest out travelling the slowest. As seen from Earth, therefore, stars' individual velocities vary. The Sun's velocity can then be inferred from the velocities at which these stars seem to be receding from or approaching the Earth. The Sun is found to travel at roughly 220 km per second, which at our distance from the galactic centre implies a galactic or *cosmic year* of about 250 million years. In the lifetime of the galaxy, the Sun has orbited the galactic centre some 25 times, but the spiral arms have been 'wound-up' only a few times. This result is confirmed in other spiral galaxies where the velocities of gas clouds are measured by observing their optical emission.

It is possible that although individual stars in a galaxy are orbiting the centre at the measured velocities, the spiral structure is moving more slowly or is even stationary. But how the spiral structure started and what prevents it from decaying are poorly understood.

Galactic activity

The rotation rate of material at a certain distance from the galactic centre can be used to estimate the mass of the galaxy. Our galaxy has a mass of about 150,000 million times that of the Sun and so very roughly contains this number of individual stars. About five per cent of this mass is thought to be interstellar hydrogen gas.

In common with active galaxies, but on a much smaller scale, the nucleus of our galaxy shows signs of activity. The nucleus, containing a variable X-ray source, has been investigated by radio astronomers measuring its radio emission. They find that within the brightest of the discrete radio sources in the central region (Sagittarius A, probably at the true centre of the galaxy) there is an emitting region less than 1,000 million kilometres across. The high star densities expected in the nuclear region have led to the speculation that a supermassive black hole (equal to 100 million solar masses) is responsible for the X-ray and radio activity.

Star Systems

Stars are only visible as points of light seen through our own unsteady and obscuring atmosphere. Even with large telescopes these points of light are simply smeared out by atmospheric turbulence, obliterating details on even the closest stars. Yet today a great deal is known about the distances, masses, physical conditions and other features of the stars. How have these details been discovered?

Spectroscopy yields many clues to the true nature of the stars. By splitting light into its constituent colours with a prism or diffraction grating, the light of stars can be analyzed in detail. As well as the composition of the outer atmosphere of a star, information on its surface temperature, pressure, magnetic field, and overall motion can be gleaned. But some important details, such as distance, mass and luminosity (true brightness) cannot be found in this way.

How distant are the stars?

Some stars are sufficiently close that a slight shift in their position (known as their *parallax*) can be measured as the Earth moves in its annual orbit round the Sun. This works for stars within about 100 light years, and the distances of several thousand stars can be measured with a greater or lesser accuracy in this way. When a star's distance is known its luminosity can be found: normal stars range in brightness from about 0.0001 to 1,000 times that of the Sun.

Once the distances and brightnesses of a range of star types are known, it is possible to compare other stars with them. A star with a similar spectrum to Sirius, for example, can be expected to have a similar luminosity, 26 times that of the Sun. Its brightness as seen from Earth is also measurable, so astronomers can work out how distant the star must be to appear that bright.

Another method depends on finding clusters of stars. The Pleiades or 'Seven Sisters' is the most famous of these *open clusters*, but there are many others of different ages and sizes. When the motions of the stars in a cluster are measured against more distant stars they all appear to be moving towards or away from a common point—the *convergence point*. This convergence is an effect of perspective since even if the stars in the cluster are on parallel paths they will seem to converge, just as parallel railway lines converge on the horizon. By finding the convergence point (a painstaking task) and measuring the velocities of the stars from the Doppler shifts of their spectral lines and their slow movements across the sky, astronomers can estimate the distance of the cluster.

Most of the stars in a cluster lie on the *main sequence*, ranging from cool red to hot blue stars. The distances of remote clusters can be found by matching their main sequences with those of known clusters, to find their true brightnesses and hence distances.

Another method of obtaining the distances of stars, clusters and even nearby galaxies is by observing the variable stars known as *cepheids*. These vary in brightness regularly at a rate which has been found to be closely related to their luminosity. The pulsation rate of a cepheid therefore betrays its luminosity, enabling its distance to be found. Cepheids in open clusters, whose distances are known from the methods described above, provide the necessary calibration. Cepheids are among the brightest stars, and are visible out to 10 million light years, providing a link between our galaxy and others.

Stars with companions

Only about 15 per cent of all stars are single, like the Sun. The rest are members of multiple systems consisting of two (a *binary* star) or more stars. In fact binaries turn out to be some of the most useful of

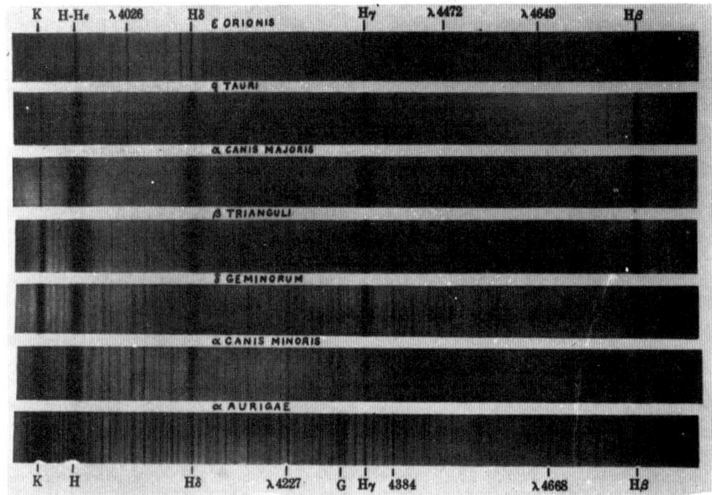

Royal Astronomical Society

Right: A series showing the spectral types of stars of different temperatures. At the top are the hot blue stars, showing a prominent series of lines due to hydrogen. The cooler stars lower down have more lines due to a wide range of molecules and elements. The lines are caused by gases in the stars' outer atmospheres.

Below: An 18th century map of the heavens, showing the signs of the zodiac. All the *constellations*, or star patterns, are back to front, matching the celestial globes of the period. Many of the constellation figures are very ancient and can be traced back before the Greeks to Babylonian times.

Below: Sir William Huggins (1824-1910), a pioneer of stellar spectroscopy. His observations were made with the eye alone, not with photographic plates. He found that many of the hazy nebulae in the sky have spectra of glowing gas, while others consisted of stars—these are now known to be galaxies.

Ann Ronan Picture Library

stars, since their movements reveal far more than we could ever discover from single stars.

In the solar system, it is true to say that the planets orbit the Sun. But in the case of a binary star the two components are usually of comparable mass, so they have similar gravitational attractions for each other. When the stars are equally massive they rotate about a point (called the *barycentre* or *centre of mass*) halfway between them. Where one star is more massive than the other the barycentre is closer to the more massive star.

If two close stars are observed for a long period and found to be orbiting each other, they are known as a *visual binary*. Our nearest star system, Alpha Centauri, is a visual binary 4.3 light years away. Its two stars, A and B, have a separation 23 times that of the Earth from the Sun (which would put B somewhere between Uranus and Neptune in our own solar system) and a period of rotation of about 80 years. There is actually a third component, Alpha Centauri C, which orbits A and B at a distance of at least 12,000 times the Earth-Sun distance. This makes Alpha Centauri C our nearest star, for which reason it is sometimes called *Proxima* Centauri.

Many double stars, however, are so close together that they appear as a single star. But the spectrum of this star may reveal two sets of lines, showing that there are really two stars there—a *spectroscopic binary*. Sometimes the two sets of lines may periodically separate slightly as the stars orbit each other, one approaching and one receding, so that the Doppler effect shifts the lines from each star to the blue or red respectively. Alternatively just one set of lines may be visible but may shift, implying that the star has a much fainter companion.

Knowing the period of the orbits and the stars' velocities it is possible to work out the true size of the system. From this, the combined mass of the stars involved can be calculated using Kepler's laws of planetary motion.

The only unknown factor is the inclination of the plane of the orbits: that is, whether we see them face on, edge on, or at some intermediate angle. Only rarely is this known for certain—in the case of visual binaries where the two stars can be seen moving, and in the case of *eclipsing binaries*.

Eclipsing binaries

Eclipsing binaries are pairs whose orbits are seen edge on, or nearly so. This means that each star will periodically pass in front of the other (an eclipse), causing the combined light to dim. The periodic nature of the dimming gives the orbital period of the stars, while the way in which the light dims and the duration of the eclipse make it possible to estimate the diameters of the stars involved. In eclipsing binaries, therefore, astronomers can determine fairly accurately the mass, luminosity and diameter of each of the stars involved as well as their other physical features and distance.

The classic example of an eclipsing binary is the star Algol in Perseus. Astronomers have found a paradox with Algol and other eclipsing binaries. These systems generally consist of a giant or supergiant star in orbit with a less massive subgiant. The subgiants in these systems, however, often appear to

Sproul Observatory

Above: The refracting telescope at Sproul Observatory, Pennsylvania, US, has a 61 cm lens set in a tube 11 m long. Such long-focus refracting telescopes are important in *astrometry*—the precise measurement of star positions, which leads to a knowledge of the distances and motions of stars.

Anglo-Australian Observatory

Above: At the centre of this image is a star as seen by the Anglo-Australian telescope. The telescope was then moved in a spiral to trail the star image. The Earth's atmospheric variations have smeared the trail, often to twice its original width. On this scale the Moon would be four times the height of this page.

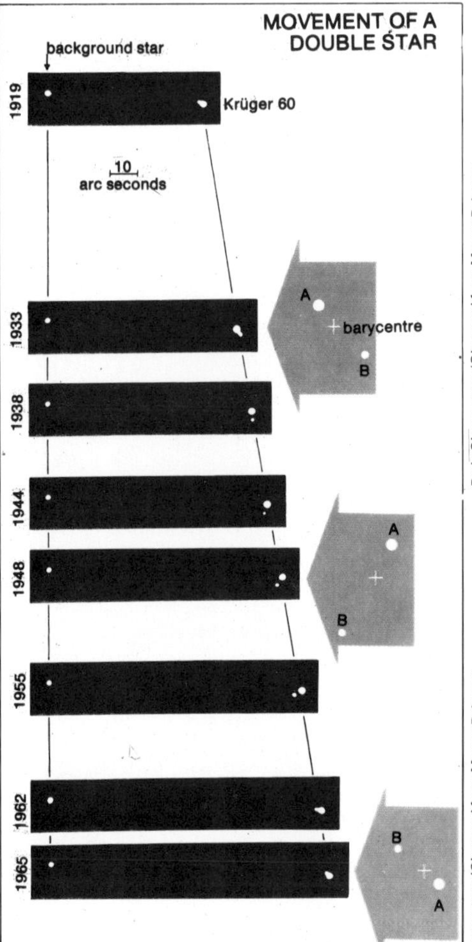

Below: Observations of the nearby binary star Kruger 60, made at Sproul, show the motion of the two stars about each other, along with their combined motion through the sky. Magnified views on the right show the positions of the stars on three dates, with the barycentre marked by a cross.

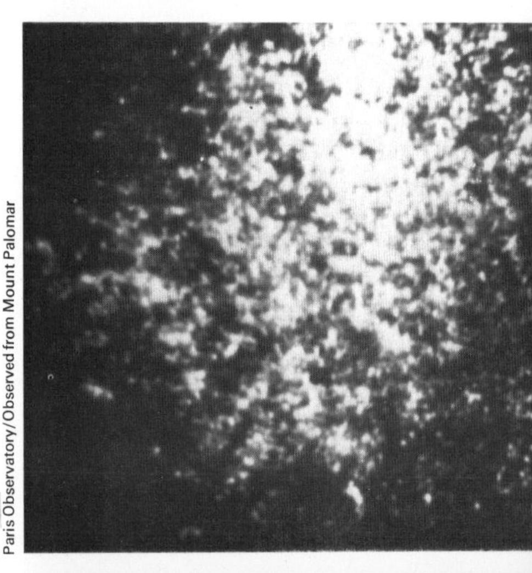

Paris Observatory/Observed from Mount Palomar

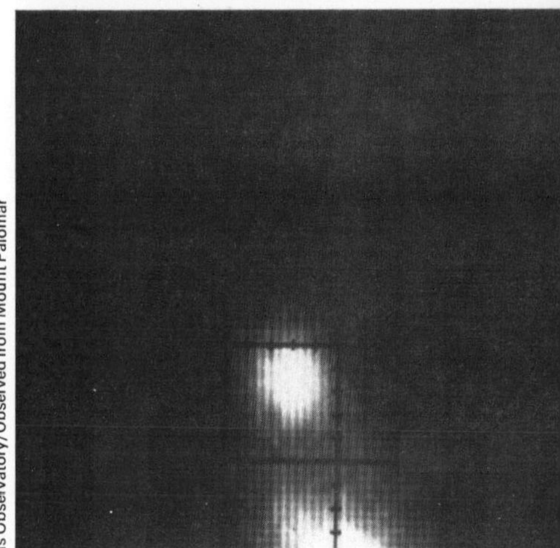

Paris Observatory/Observed from Mount Palomar

Below and bottom: To overcome the effects of atmospheric turbulence, the technique of *speckle interferometry* is used. Below is a double star photographed at 15 times the scale of the picture above. After computer processing, the speckle pattern is converted to a true image (bottom) on a scale five times larger.

Right: Many new objects in the sky are discovered by amateur astronomers. George Alcock of Peterborough, England, has discovered a record four novae and four comets using only binoculars and his knowledge of the sky.

Below: Sirius, the brightest star in the sky, has a white dwarf companion. The bright spiked object is Sirius and the row of dots are extra images to help measurements. The single dot is the white dwarf.

Bottom: Two ways of finding out about stars. Parallax gives distance of a nearby star; the light variations and Doppler shifts of an eclipsing binary give diameters and masses of the two stars.

Irving Lindenblad/US Naval Observatory

Leonie Finlay

PARALLAX

distant stars

nearby star

photograph taken at A

photograph taken at B

Earth's orbit

Sun

B (January)

ECLIPSING BINARY

A B C D E F G H

duration of eclipes and orbital speed give star diameters

B F G H C D E

spectrum at A

spectrum at B

doubling of lines at A (exaggerated here) shows orbital speed of 100 km/sec

Sproul Observatory

be stars of advanced age, no longer on the main sequence. Theories of stellar evolution demand that the more massive star should evolve first, so we would expect that in any pair of stars the more massive one would be the older. The solution to the 'Algol Paradox' gives clues as to the nature of many of the more exotic stars now being discovered: it involves the transfer of mass from one star to another.

Evolution of close binaries

The behaviour of two stars very close together is unlike anything we are used to within the solar system. The gravitational attraction of each star affects the other, sometimes leading to distortion of their shapes so that each star may be egg shaped, with the narrower end continually pointing towards the other star. Between the stars is a critical point where the gravitational attraction of each is equal: any body at this point could fall on to either star with equal ease.

The more massive star in a binary does evolve faster than the other, as theory predicts, eventually reaching the red giant stage when it starts to expand. When its material reaches the critical point, it can easily flow across to the companion star. Thus a funnel is formed through which gas flows from the outer layers of the more massive star to be *accreted* or accumulated on the less massive one which, in effect, 'eats' the other. The timescale on which all this happens —about a million years—is rapid compared with the lifetime of a star, and the process more than reverses the original ratio of masses. The less massive star, which began life as the more massive, now looks like an evolved star containing lots of helium (since we see only the core of the red giant) and the other star looks like a massive main sequence star. This process can happen in any close binary star, but it is only the case of the Algol-type binaries that the masses of the individual stars can be determined.

Runaway stars and X-ray sources

The evolution of the binary is not finished when it has reached the stage of one star appearing paradoxically evolved. This star may settle down to become a white dwarf or, if it is still massive, may evolve even further to end its life as a supernova producing a neutron star or even a black hole. Surprisingly enough, binaries often seem to be able to withstand the explosion of one of the components. In the cases where the system is disrupted, the less evolved companion star may be flung through space by its orbital velocity and by the force of the explosion, becoming a *runaway star*.

Even though the compact star remaining after a supernova is small compared with normal stars it still has appreciable mass, and the transfer of mass between the components of the binary can still occur. If the star which previously gained mass now itself evolves and expands during its evolution then mass will flow back again. Another possibility is that the more massive star will have such a high surface temperature that many particles on its surface will be moving fast enough to exceed the escape velocity and leave the surface. This stellar wind will blow across to the compact companion star and some of the mass will fall on to it, heating the gas to tens of millions of degrees and creating an X-ray 'flare'.

A solar eruption. The sun's *prominences* – arches and spikes of hydrogen gas – can be quiescent or eruptive. The latter are in violent motion and can extend more than 310,000 miles (500,000km) above the sun's surface.

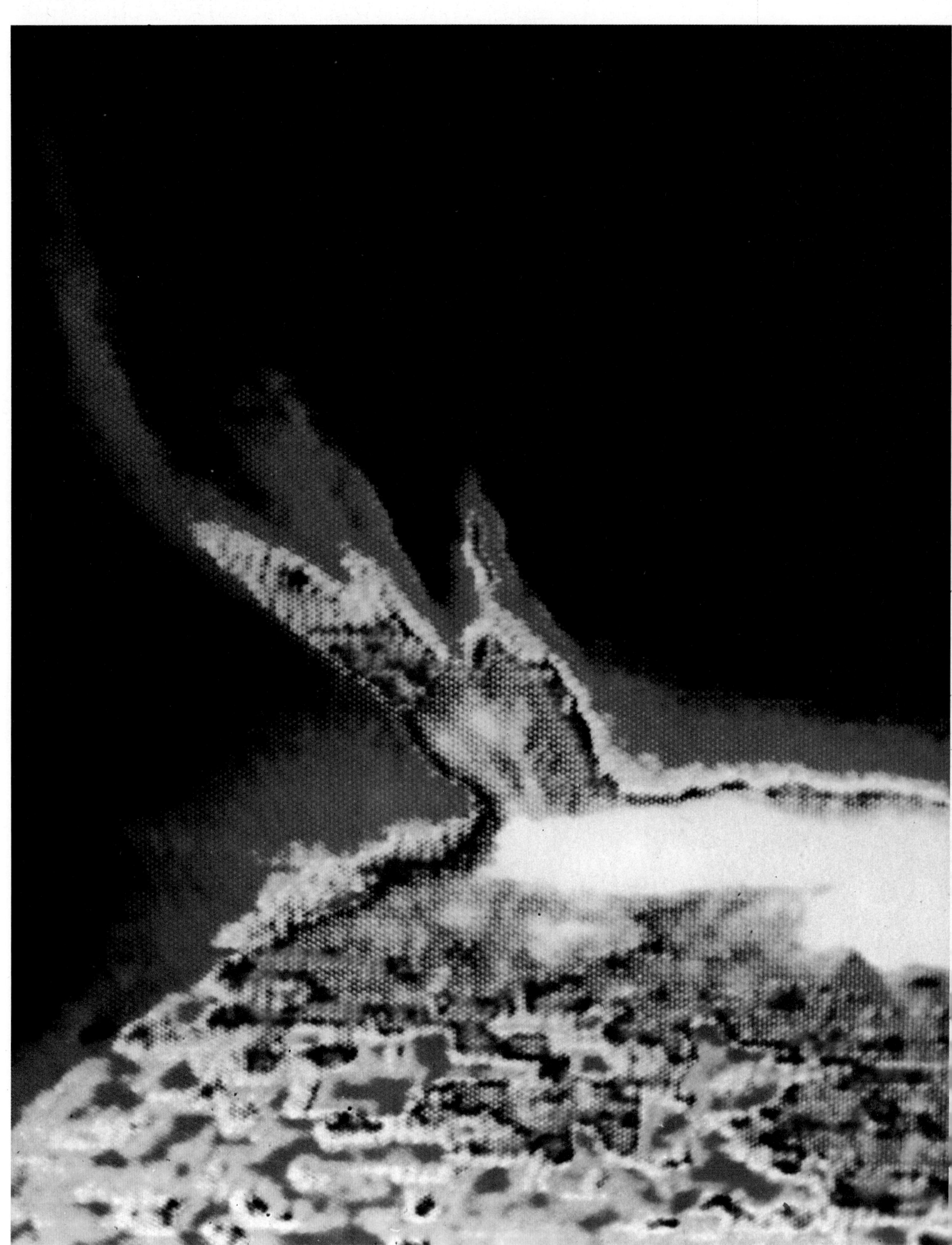

The Solar System

The Earth is one of a family of nine planets, at least 33 satellites, and thousands of chunks of assorted rocky debris. Together they make up the *solar system*, a collection of relatively small, cold bodies in orbit about an ordinary star—our Sun.

Physically the Sun is very different from the other members of the solar system. As a star, it has its own internal power source, arising from the nuclear fusion of hydrogen to helium, and so produces its own light and heat. This fundamental difference between the Sun and its planets is simply due to the Sun's huge mass, 1,000 times greater than the rest of the solar system put together. Any body held together by gravity becomes hot at the centre, because of compression by the overlying layers. The Earth's centre has a temperature of some thousands of degrees; the core of the massive planet Jupiter is at about 30,000°C.

Not unless a body is more than 50 times heavier than Jupiter does its central temperature reach the millions of degrees needed for nuclear reactions to begin. An astronomical body more massive than this limit—about one-twentieth of the Sun's mass—will shine in its own right as a star; anything less massive remains a relatively cold planet.

As a result of its huge mass, the Sun's gravity is responsible for controlling the motions of all the bodies in the solar system (except the planetary satellites). Its influence is felt well beyond the 5,900 million km distance of the most remote planet, Pluto. The planets travel around the Sun in oval paths—called *ellipses*—and all their orbits are in very nearly the same plane.

The make-up of the solar system also gives clues as to its origin. The innermost part, out to 250 million km from the Sun, contains the four 'terrestrial' planets—Mercury, Venus, Earth, and Mars. These are small, dense worlds, rich in rocks and metals. The region from 750 million km to 4,500 million km is the domain of the giant planets—Jupiter, Saturn, Uranus and Neptune. All have vast, extended atmospheres made up of lightweight gases, with perhaps some rock and metals in their innermost cores.

Separating the terrestrial planets from the giants is a zone containing thousands of small rocky bodies, the *asteroids*. The largest are hundreds of kilometres across, but many are no more than space boulders, detectable only when their sometimes elongated orbits bring them close to Earth. Other small bodies of the solar system include the planetary satellites (some of which are as large as the smaller planets), and the comets, whose icy coating evaporates in spectacular streaming tails as they approach the Sun from beyond the orbit of Jupiter. Finally, the whole system is cluttered with debris, from boulders down to dust.

Is the solar system unique?

Do other stars have planetary systems, or is our solar system unique? At the distance of even the nearest star—a 'mere' 40 million million km—any planets would

Camera Press

Michael Maunder

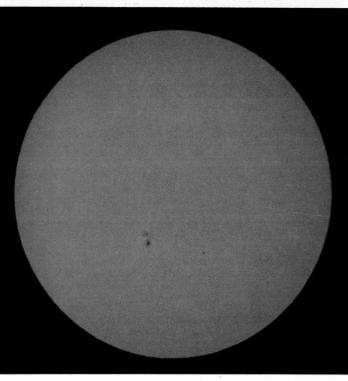

Arthur Davies

Top: The Sun's atmosphere, pictured in X-rays by the Skylab astronauts, shows intensely hot, patchy 'active regions'. At the top, a plume of gas erupts from one such region into space. The colours here are false, arising from laboratory reconstruction of the original film.

Above: During a total solar eclipse the Moon blocks the Sun's brilliant disc from view, revealing its pearly-white atmosphere —the *corona*. The very thin coronal gas is at temperatures of millions of degrees and its top layers stream off into space as the solar wind.

Right: The Sun's visible surface, measuring 1,400,000 km across, is a glowing layer of gas at a temperature of 6,000°C. Energy from the Sun's surface is discharged through this layer, called the 'photosphere'. Where this flow is blocked by the magnetic field which threads the surface, cooler regions are formed which appear as dark *sunspots*, although their temperature is 4,000°C.

Right: How the solar system probably formed. Part of a large dust and gas cloud began to contract under gravity and flattened into a disc because of rotation. Gradually the heavier dust particles settled towards the centre of the rotating disc leaving the gases farther out. Accretion among the dust particles built up larger and larger bodies. As the centre of the disc accumulated more material it grew hotter until the Sun was formed. The heat drove the remaining gases away from the centre, leaving the heavier material. Thus the solar system today has giant, gaseous outer and rocky inner planets (not to scale).

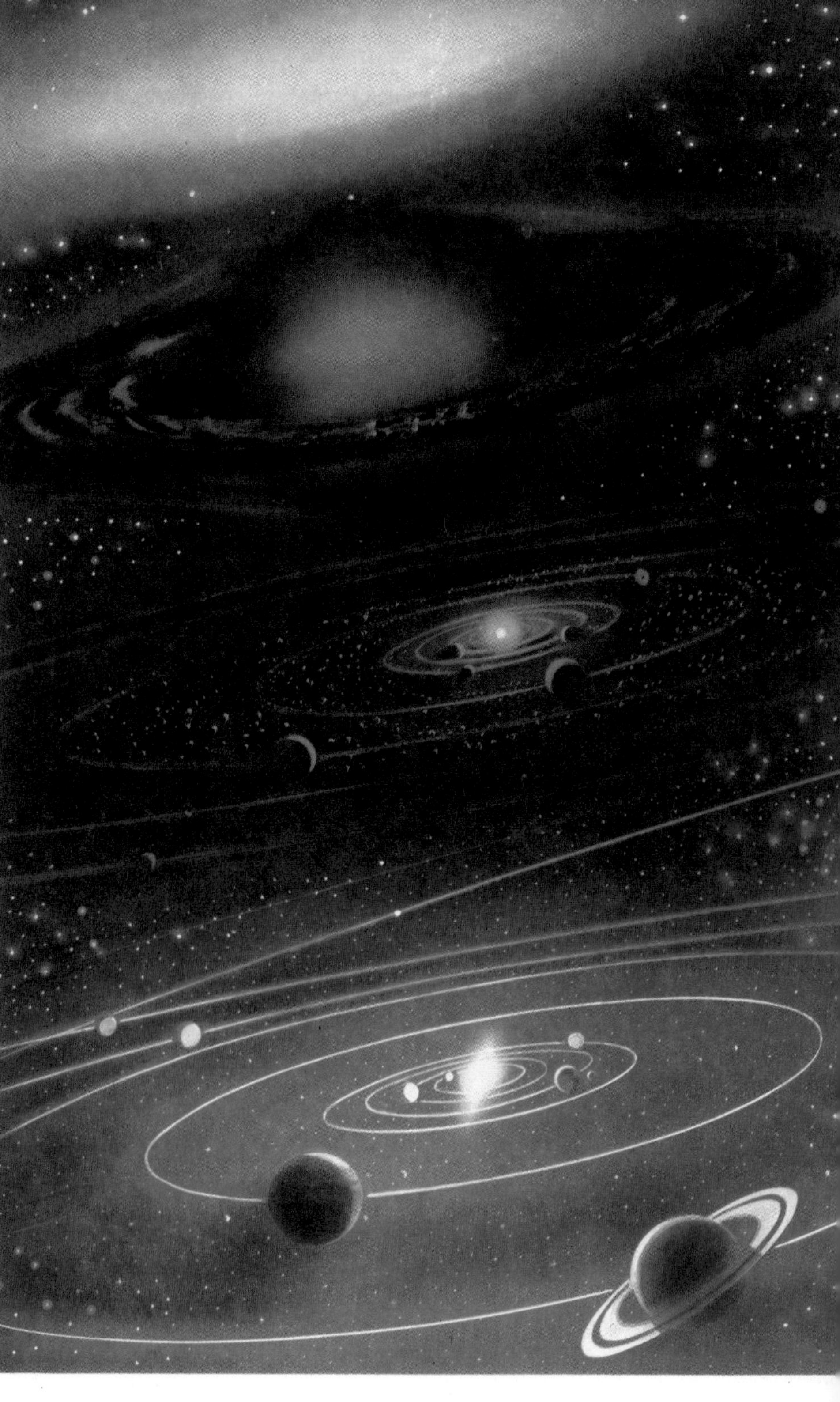

be completely invisible, even with the world's largest telescopes. Their faint reflected glow would be completely drowned by the glare of their star.

During the early twentieth century several theories of the origin of the solar system were advanced, all based on the assumption that planets are made up of material which has somehow condensed from the stars. Some proposed that a passing star raised huge tides on the Sun, dragging out a stream of gas which subsequently cooled to form planets. More speculative theories have the Sun as a member of a double star system whose companion exploded, releasing huge clouds of material into space. Some of this gas was later captured by the Sun, and subsequently formed the planets.

Recent research, however, supports the view that planets cannot be formed by way of such stellar catastrophes. Spectroscopic analysis of the planets, revealing their chemical make-up, indicates that they formed from cold material which has never been 'processed' inside a star. Other measurements strongly suggest that the planets were formed at the same time as the Sun, and not, as the catastrophe theories maintain, at a later stage. And now it seems certain that planets are not the rarities that these theories predict. Astronomers believe that several nearby stars, notably Barnard's star and Epsilon Eridani, are accompanied by one or more planets; these reveal their presence by causing minuscule 'wobbles' (revealed by years of painstaking observation) in the stars' paths through space.

Birth of the solar system

Planetary systems are now seen as a natural by-product of star formation, so that any average single star—like the Sun—is expected to have planets. This is a more realistic standpoint, for it removes our solar system from the 'rarity' class. It also strongly increases the possibility of there being Earthlike, lifebearing planets elsewhere in the universe.

Clouds of hydrogen gas are very common in space. Their densest and coolest parts are enriched with the products from nuclear reactions in previous generations of stars—elements heavier than hydrogen, complex molecules, and cosmic dust grains. Many clouds glow brightly as a result of the young, hot stars embedded within them. It is very tempting to view these gas clouds, with their abundance of raw materials, as prime sites for star and planet formation, and modern theories have concentrated on this possibility.

Formation of the planets

Some 4,600 million years ago, when the universe was already 10,000 million years old, the theories suggest that one such cloud of dust and gas began to collapse under its own gravity. The cloud shortly broke up into thousands of fragments, each of which continued to contract independently. One of these fragments—the 'solar nebula'—was ultimately to form our Sun and the solar system.

The motion of the gas cloud through space had made this fragment rotate slowly. But as it contracted, it spun faster and faster—like a spinning ice-skater who speeds up by clasping her arms to her body—and slowly assumed a flattened, disc-like shape. As the collapse continued, two very important things happened. The grains of dust, which had hitherto been mixed in with the gas, rapidly coalesced to form an extremely thin disc inside the gaseous one. And the temperature towards the centre began to rise steeply as the pressure increased.

Now the process of planetary creation could begin. The dust grains provided the necessary sites upon which the gas from the nebula could condense out, and all the matter gradually became concentrated towards the central region. But the temperature difference between the middle and the edge of the nebula meant that this was by no means a uniform process. In the cool outer parts, the grains became coated with the ices of frozen water, methane and ammonia. As the raw materials—hydrogen, oxygen, carbon and nitrogen—were very abundant in the nebula, these ices soon built up in enormous quantities.

But in the inner regions, where temperatures ranged from some 200°C to over 1000°C, condensation of ices was out of the question. Here, only non-volatile substances (those with very high evaporation temperatures, like metals and silicates) were able to stick to the grains.

The coated dust grains, packed closely

Ann Ronan Picture Library

NASA

Left: Huge arches and spikes of glowing hydrogen gas called 'prominences' hang in the Sun's atmosphere above sunspots. These drawings by a 19th century astronomer and priest, Father Secchi, show their fantastic shapes and strange behaviour, now believed due to the gas following loops of magnetic field.

Right: Phobos, one of the two tiny potato-shaped moons of the planet Mars, has a surface scarred by impacts. It seems that, like the asteroids, 21 km-wide Phobos is made of virtually unaltered material from the early solar nebula. Some astronomers believe that Phobos may even be an asteroid captured by Mars' gravitation.

Institute of Geological Sciences

Institute of Geological Sciences

Above and below: A chunk of the Canyon Diablo meteorite (above) which formed the Arizona crater (below) about [illegible]0,000 years ago. Most of the body (weighing about 250,000 tons) vaporized on impact, creating by explosion a crater 180 m deep and [illegible].2 km across. This is one of the Earth's best-preserved craters.

Above right: Section through a stone meteorite which ended its 4,600 million year journey through space in Leicestershire, England. This magnified section seen in polarized light, with round silicate droplets (*chondrules*) among finer grains, shows the *accretion* process through which the solar system formed.

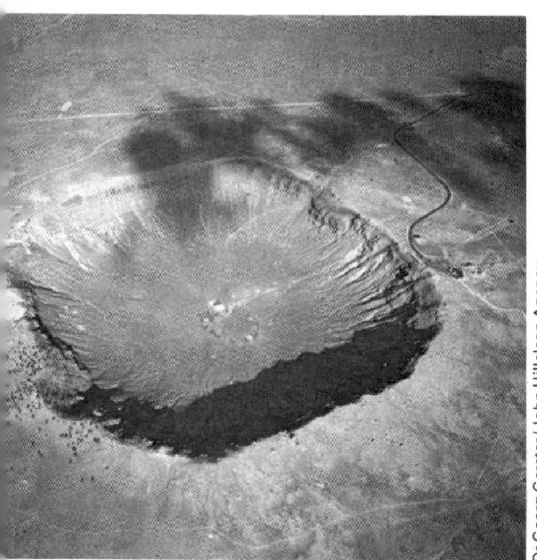

Dr Georg Gerster/John Hillelson Agency

together in the disc, jostled and collided with each other. Clumps soon formed, which in turn rapidly grew under gravity. Those in the cold outer reaches of the disc, where ices were abundant, grew much larger than the thinly-coated inner-most clumps. Because of their greater mass they could catch and hold on to even the lightest gases from the nebula, hydrogen and helium. The end result was the family of giant, gassy outer planets from Jupiter to Neptune. The small clumps in the inner part of the disc had insufficient gravity to capture and retain any quantity of these light gases; and they eventually became the compact, rocky terrestrial planets with their small atmospheres.

As the young planets gradually accreted from the dusty disc, the gaseous part of the nebula continued to contract and heat up. The contraction of the gaseous nebula proceeded until its central temperature reached the millions of degrees necessary for the onset of nuclear reactions. At this point, the nebula—our young Sun—became a star. Its tendency to collapse under its own gravity was now perfectly balanced by the outflow of energy from its interior. Over millions of years, the continuous stream of particles from the Sun—the solar wind—acted as a brake on its initially rapid rotation, and the Sun settled down to a stable existence.

The outlook was not quite as peaceful for the young planets. The early solar system was a dusty, debris-strewn place and there still remained many sizeable clumps of grains which had not become incorporated into planets. The newly-formed surfaces of the planets suffered enormous crater-producing collisions with these bodies. The terrestrial planets all bear the scars from this episode of bombardment. After a relatively short period, however, most of the smaller bodies had been 'mopped up'.

But even today, the solar system is by no means empty of dust and rocks. Much of the debris is concentrated in the asteroid belt and in the cloud of comets much further out in the solar system. But the process of accretion on to the planets still continues, albeit in a much less intense manner. Bodies called *meteoroids* rain down to the extent of some 16,000 tonnes per year on the Earth's surface alone. Some meteoroids derive from the slow break-up of asteroids and comets; others are unaltered clumps of original grains, representing the first materials to condense out of the solar nebula thousands of millions of years ago.

The Giant Planets

The outer regions of our solar system are still largely uncharted territory. They are the domain of the giant planets—Jupiter, Saturn, Uranus and Neptune—with strange, tiny Pluto and the swarm of frozen comets outermost of all. Of these planets, only Jupiter and Saturn were familiar to ancient man; the last three have all been discovered in the last 200 years, Pluto as recently as 1930. Although their motions have been mapped with considerable accuracy—to a precision sufficient to detect the tiny perturbations produced by the gravity of other planets—comparatively little is known of their structure and physical make-up.

But in the last decades of the twentieth century our knowledge of these distant worlds is destined to undergo a revolution. Already, Jupiter has been viewed by two spaceprobes which flew past in 1973 and 1974, sending back detailed information about the huge planet and its environment. One of these probes—Pioneer 11—reaches Saturn in mid-1978. The major breakthrough, however, may be made by two American spacecraft, Voyagers 1 and 2. The first will pass only 350,000 km (217,000 miles) from Jupiter in 1979, and 197,000 km (122,000 miles) from Saturn in 1980. Voyager 2 will not approach these planets as closely, for it is specially targeted to fly on to encounter and survey the giant worlds Uranus and Neptune.

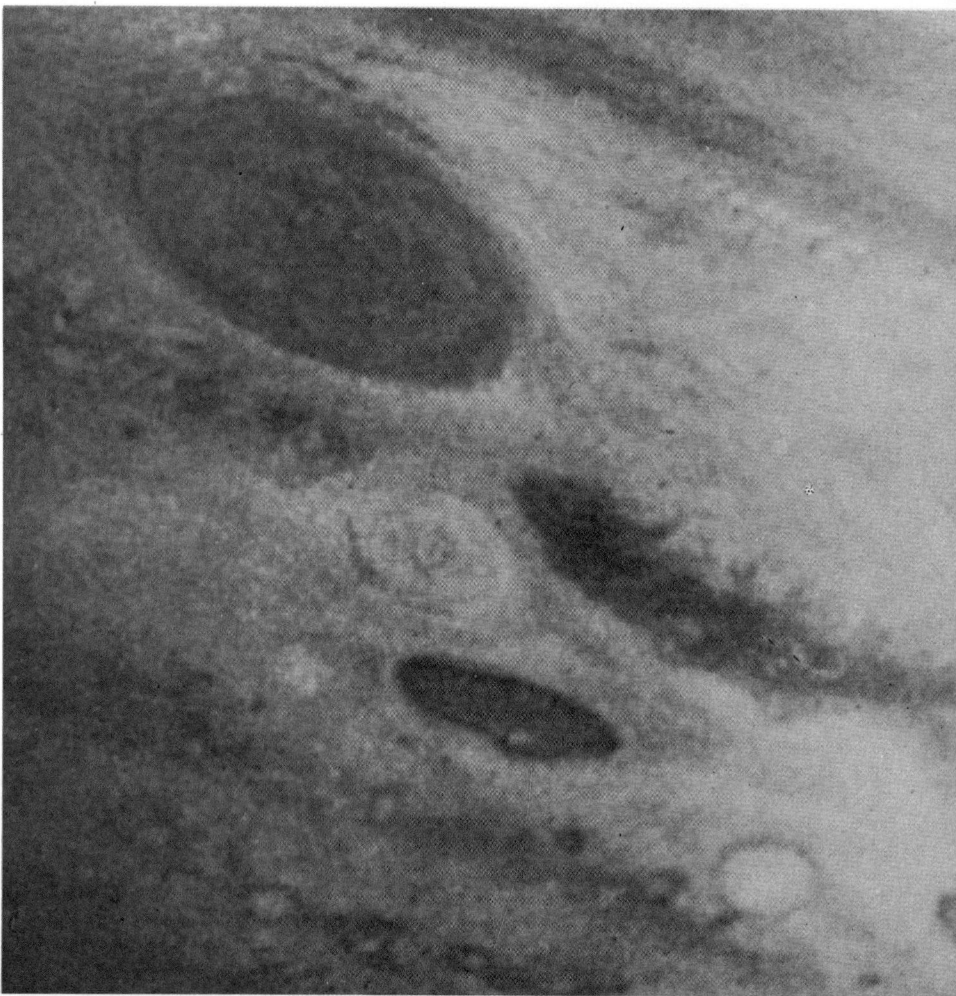

Photri

NASA

Above: Jupiter's Great Red Spot (upper left) is now thought to be a cyclonic disturbance like a hurricane—but on a vast scale. About 40,000 km (25,000 miles) long, it is nearly three times the size of the Earth.

Left: Jupiter's cloud belts are separated by whitish-yellow 'zones'. The light zones are areas of high, ascending gas and the dark belts are cooler areas where the gas decends again.

Right: Ganymede, the largest of Jupiter's satellites, is bigger than the planet Mercury. It is thought to be heavily cratered, with a rough surface composed of rocky or metallic material embedded in ice.

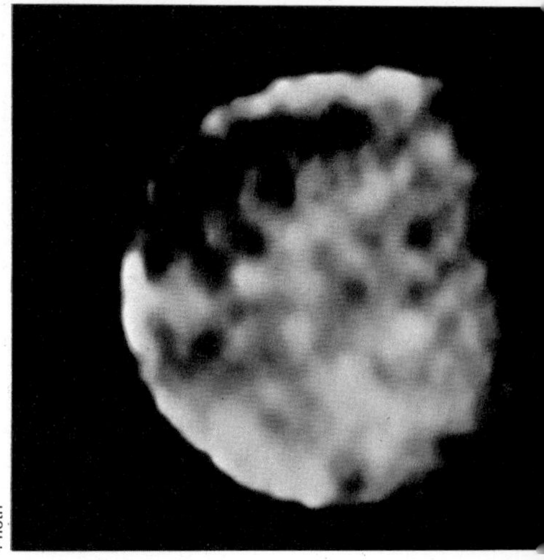

Photri

Jupiter

Jupiter, 143,000 km (89,000 miles) across, is by far the largest planet in the solar system, being more than twice as massive as all the other planets put together. It is accompanied on its 12-year journey round the Sun by a retinue of at least 13 satellites, four of which are similar in size to the smaller planets. Its gravity controls the orbits of a group of some thousand asteroids—the Trojans—and is powerful enough to cause permanent changes in the motions of many of the solar system's small members.

Telescopes and spaceprobes reveal Jupiter to be a world completely covered by bands of cloud and considerably flattened at the poles by its rotation. It is the most rapidly rotating planet—spinning once on its axis in only 9 hours 50 minutes—and the enormous rotational speed of 46,000 kph (29,000 mph) at the equator drags out the clouds into belts encircling the planet. These reddish-brown belts are permanent features of Jupiter's atmosphere, but can change in colour and intensity or suddenly break out in spots, loops and whorls.

However, one spot has persisted in Jupiter's atmosphere ever since it was discovered by Giovanni Domenico Cassini in 1665. Varying over the centuries from deep brick-red to anaemic pink in colour, the so-called 'Great Red Spot' slowly drifts around the planet.

The colour of the Great Red Spot, and indeed of Jupiter's cloud belts, is more difficult to explain. Jupiter's atmosphere is known to be largely made up of the hydrogen and hydrogen compounds it was so easily able to obtain from the primeval solar nebula—such as methane, ammonia and hydrogen sulphide. But all these gases are colourless; and although the high, whitish zones are probably made up of pure, frozen ammonia crystals, the belts are more likely to be orange ammonium sulphide or hydrosulphide.

What lies below Jupiter's clouds? There is certainly no Earthlike solid surface. Jupiter's average density works out as only a third more than that of water, less than a quarter of the Earth's, and so we would expect its make-up to be very different. The giant planet also differs from the terrestrial worlds in having its own, quite powerful, internal heat source. It radiates twice as much heat as it receives

Right: Saturn, the second largest planet in the solar system—an imaginary view from one of its satellites. Saturn's rings measure 275,000 km (172,000 miles) across, but must be only a few kilometres thick since they disappear from view when seen edge on. There are four concentric rings differing in brightness and transparency; they are thought to be composed of swarms of centimetre-sized particles. These are coated with ice, but it is uncertain whether rock or simply ice lies beneath. The rings may be the remains of a moon which trespassed too close to Saturn, or the components of a satellite which failed to coalesce.

David Hardy

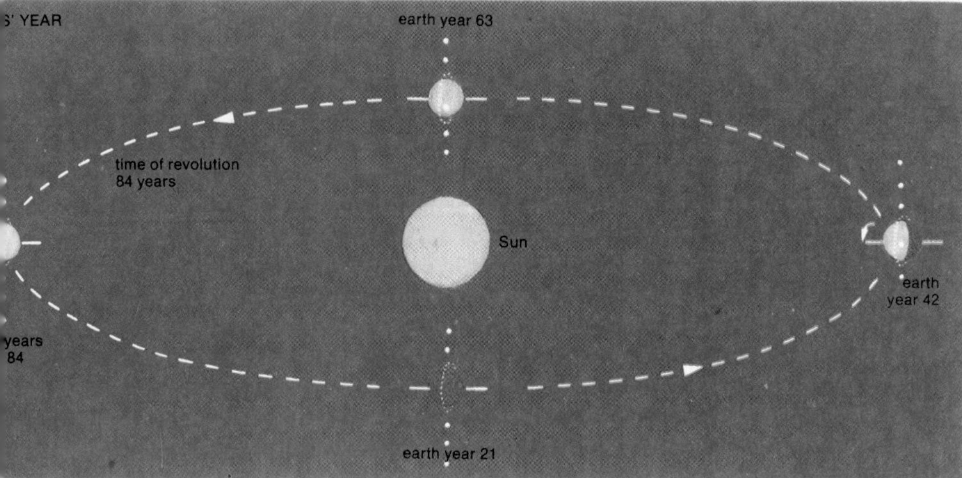

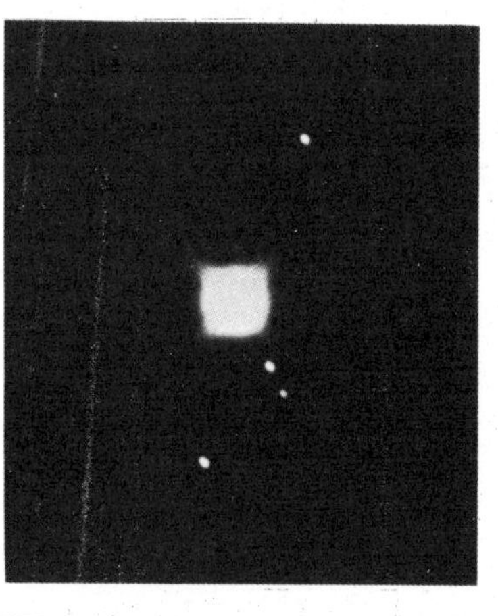
Above and right: Uranus is unusual in that it effectively travels round the Sun on its side, with its pole inclined at an angle of 98° to the vertical. This tilt, as yet unexplained, means that each of the planet's poles experiences 42 years perpetual darkness during the planet's 84 year journey around the Sun. Uranus has five known moons (seen right in long exposure photographs): Miranda, Ariel, Umbriel, Titania and Oberon. These have orbits parallel to the planet's tilted equator, that is, in a plane at right angles to the plane of Uranus' orbit. Astronomers are uncertain how the satellites have followed the planet's extreme axial tilt so exactly.

McDonald Observatory

from the distant Sun, thereby providing a power source for the huge convection currents in its atmosphere. The origin of this excess heat is still uncertain.

The Pioneer probes, perturbed by Jupiter's gravitational field, have yielded most information on its internal structure. It now seems that all of the planet's rocks and metals are confined to a tiny dense core, at a temperature of about 30,000°C. Above this core are thought to be two concentric thick layers of dense hydrogen, which make up most of the planet's mass. The inner layer, extending to a distance of 46,000 km (29,000 miles) from the centre, is under enormous pressure—millions of Earth atmospheres. In these conditions, hydrogen behaves as a metal. Overlying the metallic hydrogen is a less dense, 25,000 km (15,000 miles) thick layer of compressed molecular (ordinary) hydrogen, topped by 1,000 km (620 miles) of atmosphere.

Surrounding Jupiter's atmosphere lies the *magnetosphere*, a huge zone containing energetic particles from the solar wind trapped by Jupiter's magnetic field. This magnetic field has been known for some years, as it gives rise to strong radio emission from Jupiter. The Pioneers have shown Jupiter's field to be extremely complex and some twenty times stronger than the Earth's. Radio emission from Jupiter's magnetosphere is enhanced when one of its major satellites, Io, is at certain positions. It seems that, although most of the radio emission is caused by the trapped solar wind particles, some of it originates in high-speed electrons generated by the motion of Io.

Saturn and Uranus

Without its ring system, Saturn would look somewhat like a smaller version of Jupiter. As the second largest planet in the solar system, it is still a giant, measuring 120,000 km (75,000 miles) across its bulging equator. Like Jupiter, it spins very fast, completing a revolution in about ten hours, and its yellow disc is similarly striped with cloud belts. But Saturn's belts are much paler, and far less likely to break out in sudden activity. This may be a result of the intense cold at 1,400 million km (870 million miles) from the Sun—Saturn's cloud tops are at a temperature of —170°C (—274°F).

Saturn's composition and internal structure are probably very similar to Jupiter's, although it is even less substantial. With its average density of only 0.7 that of water—the lowest in the solar system—it would float, given an ocean large enough! Saturn may have a weak magnetic field, and, like its giant neighbour, it radiates more heat than it receives from the Sun.

Saturn is encircled by ten satellites as well as its famous rings. The largest satellite, Titan, is massive enough to have a methane atmosphere.

Writing in his journal of 13 March 1781, William Herschel reported that he had observed 'a curious either nebulous star, or perhaps a comet'. Four days later, he found 'that it is a comet, for it has changed its place'. In actual fact, Herschel had discovered a new planet.

At the vast distance of 2,900 million km (1,800 million miles) from the Sun, Uranus is only just visible to the naked eye, and appears small and unremarkable in a telescope. But with a diameter of 51,800 km (32,000 miles) it is the third largest planet in the solar system. In structure and composition, Uranus probably bears a great resemblance to Jupiter and Saturn, although its smaller size means that it must contain proportionally less hydrogen. Its atmosphere is largely made up of methane—one of the few substances to remain gaseous at —210°C (—346°F)—and faint cloud belts have been reported from time to time.

An important discovery concerning Uranus was made in March 1977. During that month, Uranus passed briefly in front of a distant star, which was unexpectedly seen to dim several times before and after the actual occultation. Astronomers have concluded that these dimmings occurred as the star passed

Michael Holford

Above: Traditionally, the appearance of a comet has been taken as a sign of impending disaster, as this scene from the Bayeux tapestry—in which a comet (probably Halley's Comet) is sighted over England—clearly shows.

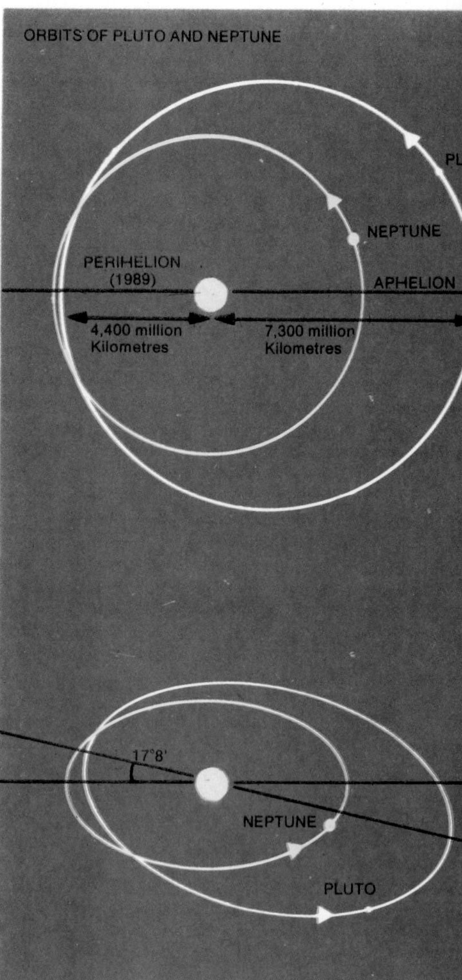

Right: Diagrams to show Pluto's unusual plane of orbit, inclined at 17°18′ to that of Neptune and to the solar system plane. Because of its highly elliptical orbit, Pluto sometimes comes nearer to the Sun than Neptune.

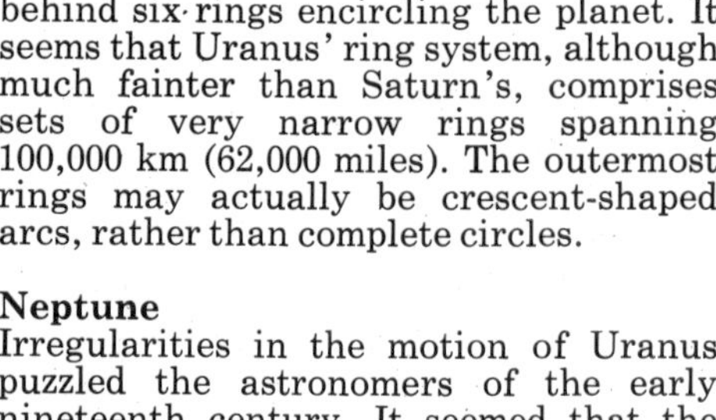

behind six rings encircling the planet. It seems that Uranus' ring system, although much fainter than Saturn's, comprises sets of very narrow rings spanning 100,000 km (62,000 miles). The outermost rings may actually be crescent-shaped arcs, rather than complete circles.

Neptune

Irregularities in the motion of Uranus puzzled the astronomers of the early nineteenth century. It seemed that the planet was being perturbed by an unknown body. Using Newton's Theory of Gravity, mathematicians set about calculating where the perturbing body must lie. An undergraduate at Cambridge, John Couch Adams, sent his predicted position to the Astronomer Royal, Sir George Airy, in 1845, but it was apparently disregarded and no search was started. Meanwhile Urbain Leverrier in France had arrived at the same results. He was luckier; a search was commenced at Berlin, and in September 1846 the planet Neptune was discovered at its predicted position. Today, as is only fair, both Adams and Leverrier share the credit for the planet's discovery.

Lying 4,500 million km (2,800 million miles) from the Sun, Neptune is virtually Uranus' twin. At 49,500 km (30,000 miles) across, it is slightly smaller, but rather more massive; its internal structure is likely to be identical to that of its neighbour, with perhaps more ice overlying the innermost, rocky core. Neptune is so distant that it is invisible without a telescope; and even with a large telescope no features can be made out on its tiny disc. But astronomers have found that its brightness changes, suggesting that it

Lowell Observatory

Below right: The planet Pluto was discovered in 1930, after a search for the cause of perturbations in the motions of Uranus and Neptune. The American Clyde Tombaugh noticed that an image (marked here with arrows) on these two photographic plates had moved over a period of a week. The planet was near its predicted position but smaller and fainter than expected. Recent measurements make Pluto's diameter only 3,000 km (1,875 miles)

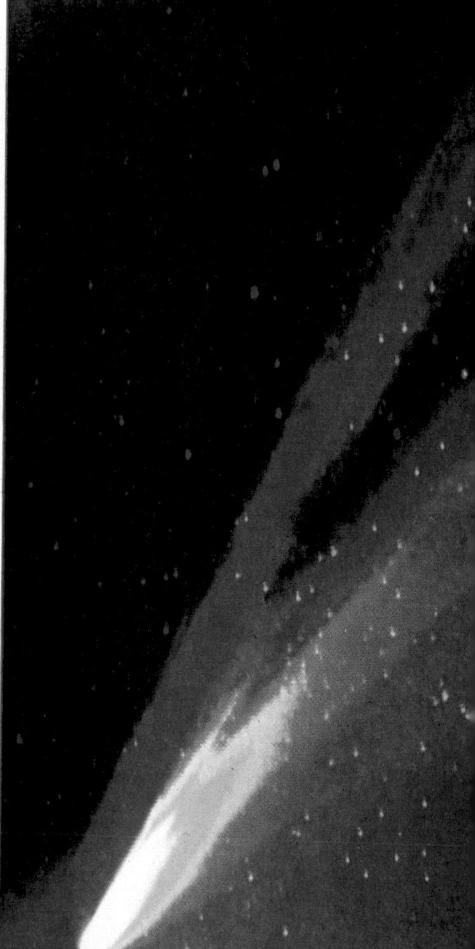

Below: The discovery of rings encircling Uranus was made in 1977 by astronomers in an airborne observatory over the Indian Ocean, hoping to record photoelectrically the occultation (obscuring) of a distant star by Uranus. 35 minutes before the occultation, the star's light dimmed for a few seconds. Five such dimmings occurred at intervals of several minutes. These dips in the star's intensity, together with similar dips recorded after the main occultation, were identified as probably being caused by a system of rings passing in front of the star.

Right: Uranus and its system of five, almost vertical, rings.

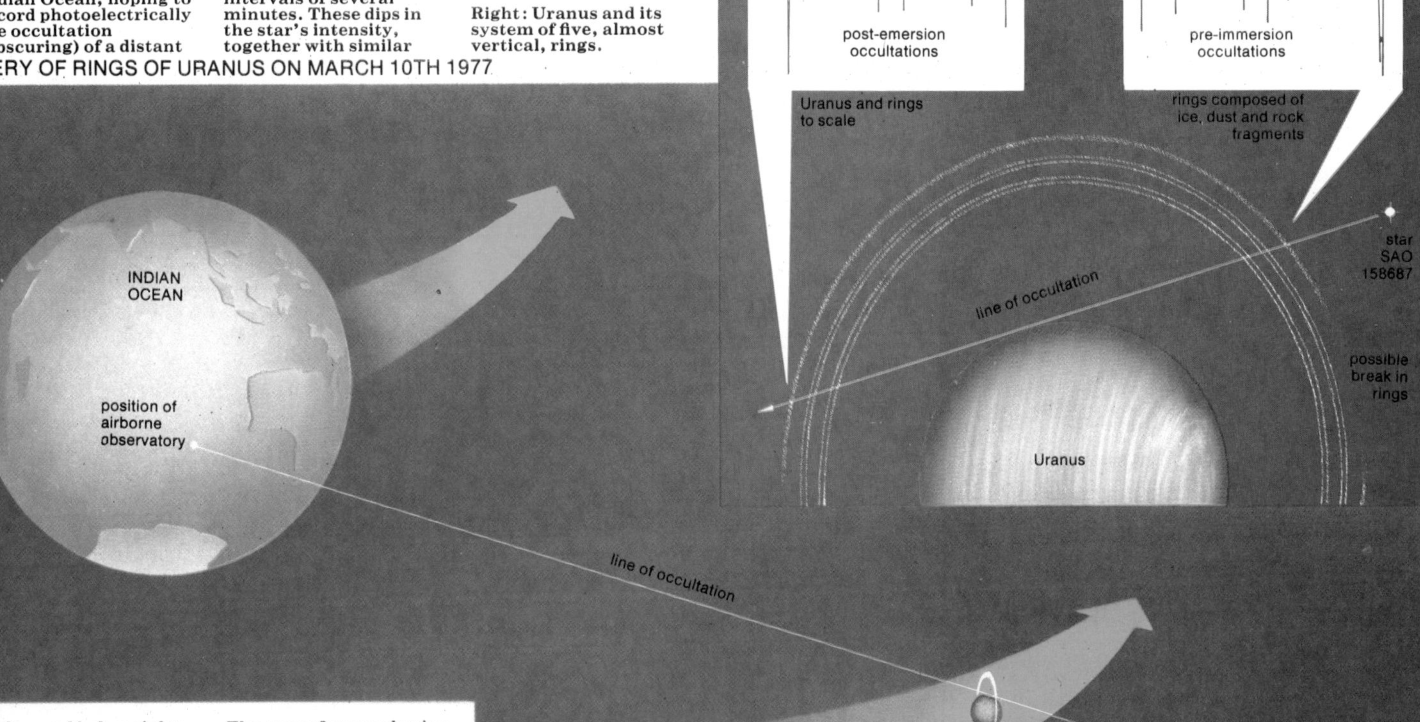

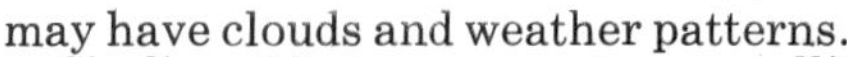

Below and below right: Comet West, with a computer-processed image (left) to enhance details. The blue tail is gas streaming away from the Sun and the red tail is composed of dust released from the comet's icy nucleus. The gases form a glowing trail millions of kilometres long. Cometary nuclei form a swarm far beyond Pluto's orbit, from where they may be perturbed by a passing star to plunge towards the centre of the solar system.

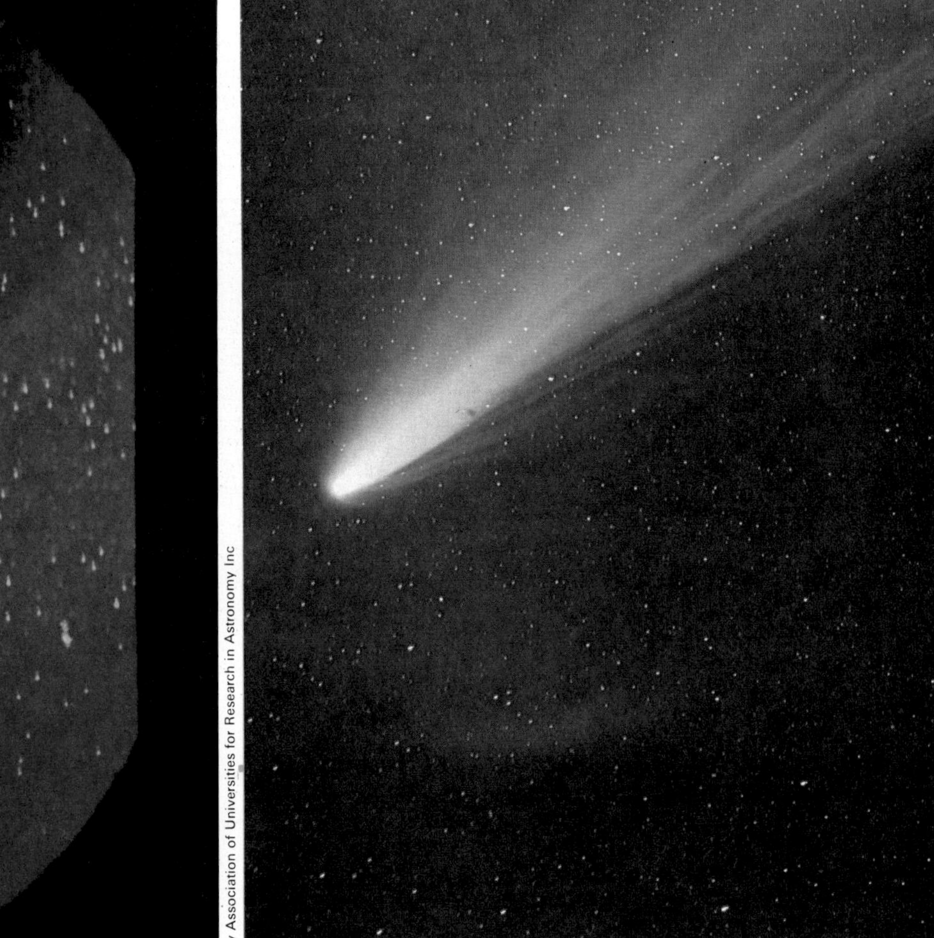

By Association of Universities for Research in Astronomy Inc

McLean Observatory, Sierra Nevada College

may have clouds and weather patterns.

Circling Neptune are two satellites, both rather strange. Triton, 6,000 km (3,700 miles) across, is the largest satellite in the solar system—almost as big as the planet Mars—and travels around Neptune in an east-to-west (*retrograde*) orbit, rather than the normal west-to-east orbit of the other planets' major satellites. Nereid, discovered in 1949, has the most elongated orbit of any satellite. These anomalies may be related in some way to the peculiar orbit of Pluto.

Pluto

Tiny Pluto sits at the edge of the solar system almost like an afterthought. It is unrelated to the family of giant planets and seems to have little in common with smaller planets, like Earth. It is even beginning to look as if Pluto is not the planet astronomers began to search for when they detected perturbations in the motions of Uranus and Neptune.

At Pluto's average distance from the Sun of 6,000 million km (3,700 million miles), the bitter cold of —230°C (—382°F) means that almost all the gases are frozen. Pluto seems to be a low-density body, covered in frozen methane—similar to some of the giant planets' satellites.

But Pluto is not strictly the outpost of the solar system, for between 1979-1999, its eccentric orbit will carry it within the orbit of Neptune. This behaviour has suggested to some astronomers that Pluto is not a true planet at all, but an escaped satellite of Neptune. An interaction between Pluto and Triton could have sent Triton into a retrograde orbit around Neptune and Pluto hurtling out of the system, to orbit the Sun alone.

Mercury, Mars and the Moon

The inner planets of the solar system have seen the most far-reaching effects of the space age. Each has been visited by spaceprobes several times and craft have landed on the Moon and Mars. In nearly every case, there have been unexpected new discoveries which have greatly extended our knowledge and understanding of the solar system. At the same time, these discoveries have generated a host of questions which, as yet, remain unanswered.

The inner or 'terrestrial' planets—Mercury, Venus, Earth and Mars—seem at first sight to form a close-knit group. To this group, we can add our Moon. Although not strictly a planet, it is certainly of planetary dimensions, being 30 per cent smaller than Mercury. All these bodies are small, rocky, dense worlds circling close to the Sun. But it appears that the inner planets, as a group, show far more diversity among themselves than do the giant planets.

The Moon

Since time immemorial, Earth's only natural satellite—the Moon—has fascinated mankind. At a distance of only 385,000 km (238,855 miles) it is close enough for its most prominent surface markings to be clearly seen—prompting the popular idea of a 'Man in the Moon'.

The early users of telescopes during the seventeenth century believed that they had discovered the Moon to be another world like the Earth. They saw the smooth, dark markings as vast tracts of water and named them accordingly. Such names as 'Ocean of Storms' and 'Marsh of Dreams' are used even today. The lunar mountain ranges were christened after counterparts on Earth so the Moon, too, has its Alps and Apennines.

NASA

Above: Apollo 17 picture of the full Moon, its surface clearly showing the effects of severe bombardment in the past. The right hand side in this view is invisible from Earth. The dark plains (maria) are concentrated almost entirely on the side facing Earth.

Below: This crater, some 80 km (50 miles) across, lies on the rugged far side of the Moon. More recent craters are smaller and less eroded by the effects of particle bombardment.

Below and right: The six Apollo missions left a variety of scientific equipment on the lunar surface. Below, tracks left by a transporter lead back to the Apollo lunar module. At right, seismic traces obtained from lunar instruments are compared with those observed by seismometers on Earth. The lunar trace was due to an impact some 100 km away, which set the Moon vibrating almost like a bell. The tiny vibrations took almost an hour to die away, indicating deep layers of rock fragments.

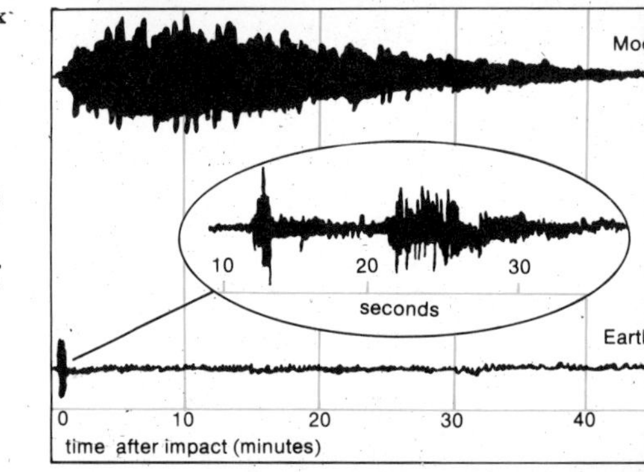

Photri

NASA

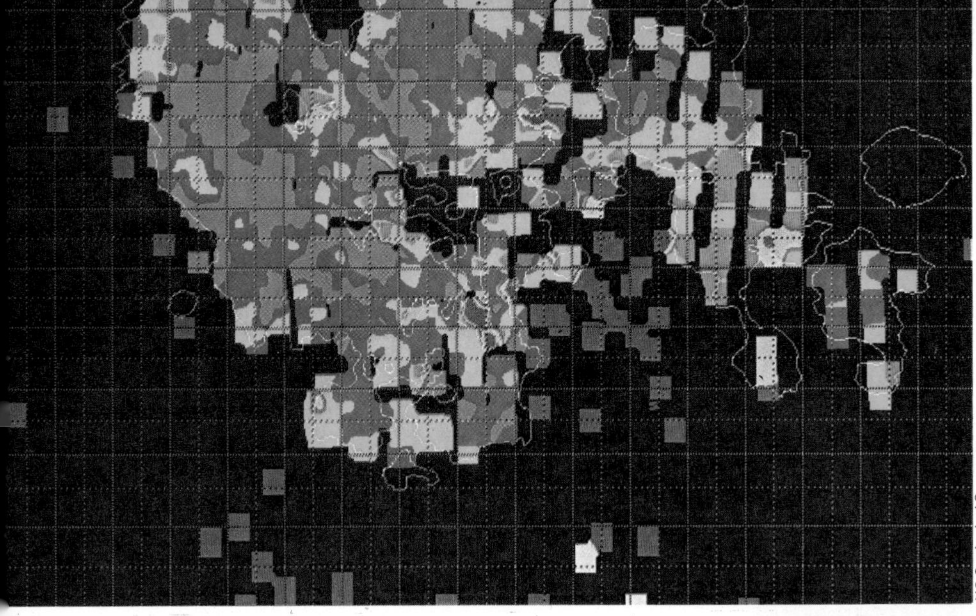

US Geological Survey

Over the centuries, it slowly became apparent that the Moon could not be another Earth. The most fatal objection is its size—only 3,500 km (2,160 miles) in diameter—which means that it is too small to be capable of holding down an atmosphere. So not only is the airless Moon unable to support life; it is also exposed to all the extremes of space. As the fortnight long lunar 'day' gives way to two weeks of 'night', the surface is alternately baked to 120°C and frozen to minus 180°C. It is incessantly bombarded by radiation and streams of charged particles from the solar wind, which scour and blacken the surface. Thousands of craters, ranging in size from tiny pits to colossal walled plains hundreds of kilometres across, testify to violent onslaughts by chunks of space debris, which continue on a reduced scale even today.

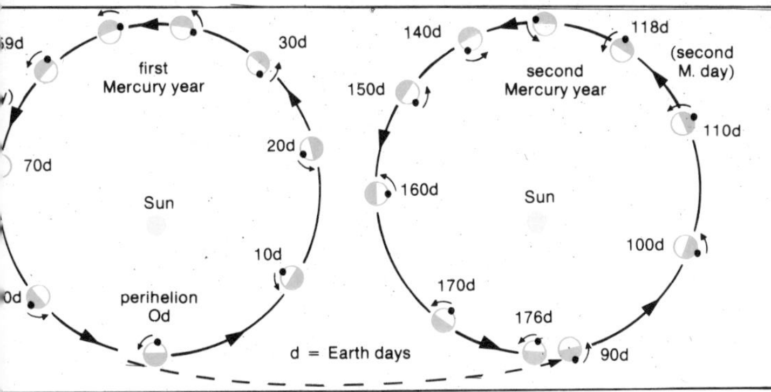

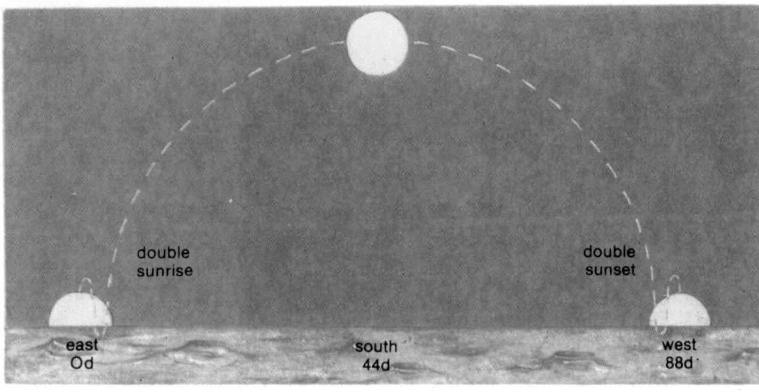

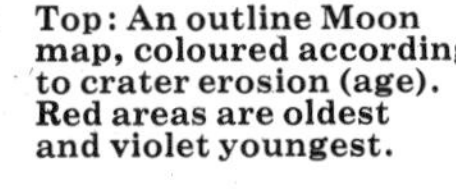

Top: An outline Moon map, coloured according to crater erosion (age). Red areas are oldest and violet youngest.

Left: At first glance, Mercury's surface looks similar to the Moon's. But there are no dark 'seas', and long scarps cross the surface.

Above and above right: The combination of Mercury's 88-day year and 59-day rotation period lead to odd effects. A point on the surface turns only slightly faster than the planet orbits the Sun. It is in the same position relative to the stars after 59 days but only faces the Sun again after 176 days—two Mercury years. At perihelion Mercury moves faster in its orbit than it turns so the Sun will briefly reverse its motion through the sky. At some places this could result in two sunrises and two sunsets per 88-day Mercury year.

Below: Craters on Mars are more eroded and dust filled than the Moon's. Atmospheric haze veils the horizon.

NASA

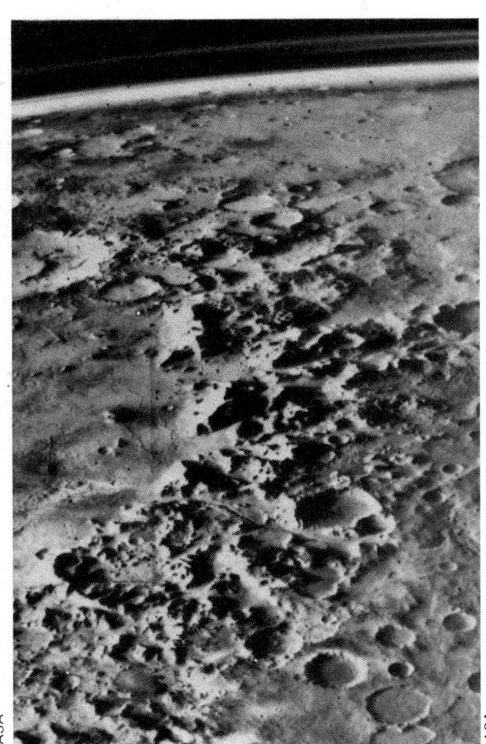

NASA

The Moon keeps one hemisphere permanently turned towards us, because its rotation has been enormously slowed by the powerful pull of Earth's gravity. Before the days of spaceprobes, speculations abounded that the 'other side' of the Moon might be less hostile. But orbiting craft showed it to be even more rugged, lacking the extensive dark plains of the near side.

These orbiters were just five out of the dozens of spacecraft despatched towards the Moon in the 1960s, which culminated in the brilliantly successful Apollo series of manned lunar landings. Although sometimes dismissed as merely a political device, the Apollo missions changed the Moon from an astronomical object into a body which could be studied in the laboratory.

Results taken from the rock samples and recording instruments have enabled scientists to build up a fairly detailed picture of the Moon's history. Right from the beginning, its story differs strikingly from that of the Earth. From the Moon's lighter, less volatile rocks it seems that it formed much closer to the Sun, and was subsequently 'captured' by Earth's gravity. For the next thousand million years, it was bombarded violently by space debris, which excavated vast craters and shattered the crust to a depth of 25 kilometres. As the meteorite onslaught abated, the largest craters (the lunar 'seas') were filled by outwellings of magma from the Moon's interior, which later cooled and solidified. Apart from a few later impacts which created the craters Copernicus, Tycho and Aristarchus—young formations still outlined by bright 'rays' of ejected material—the Moon's surface effectively died some 3000 million years ago. It is too small a world to have the internal heat necessary for maintaining an active and changing crust.

Yet, from time to time, strange glows are seen in a few lunar craters. Some astronomers claim that these are emissions of gas akin to small volcanic eruptions on Earth; others believe them to be electrical discharges in lunar dust clouds. It is clear that our exploration of the Moon has not yet ended.

Mercury

Mercury, the innermost planet, orbits the Sun in just 88 days, at a distance of only 58 million km (36 million miles). Never straying far from the Sun in our skies, it is a very difficult object to glimpse. Until the 1960s, Mercury was virtually an unknown world. Although dusky markings had been suspected on its surface, these were at the limit of observation. With a diameter of only 4,900 km (3,032 miles), Mercury appears to us as the Moon would if moved some 300 times further away.

The new tool of planetary radar—bouncing radio waves of a planet's surface and timing the echo—added much to the knowledge of Mercury and Venus. In particular, Mercury was found to have a 'day' of 59 Earth days, instead of keeping the same face forever turned towards the Sun. But the biggest breakthrough happened in 1974 and 1975, when the spaceprobe Mariner 10 made three close approaches to the planet.

Mariner 10 revealed Mercury to be a remarkable cross between the Earth and the Moon. Its surface is astonishingly lunar, with the same mixture of craters, mountains and lava plains. It is, if anything, even more hostile. Lacking any appreciable atmosphere, and lying so close to the Sun, its surface temperature ranges from over 400°C during the day (hot enough to melt lead and tin) to minus 170°C at night.

The similarity between Mercury and the Moon stops as soon as its structure is analyzed. Whereas the Moon is of a shattered, lightweight construction, Mercury more closely resembles the Earth in having a dense, iron core and a magnetic field. But Mercury's core is proportionally far larger, taking up 80 per cent of the interior. It appears to have modified some of Mercury's surface features for, as the core gradually cooled and contracted, the whole planet shrank, wrinkling the crust into shallow cliffs some hundreds of kilometres long, which are quite unlike any other features in the solar system.

Mercury's magnetic field—although only 1 per cent of the Earth's in strength—is problematical. The Earth's field arises from a dynamo action in its fast-rotating iron core; but Mercury spins too slowly to produce a field in this way. Some astronomers believe that it could have arisen from heavy bombardment by charged particles of the solar wind.

NASA

Above: Sunrise over Noctis Labyrinthus (Labyrinth of the Night) on Mars reveals mist in the canyons. This view, about 100 km (60 miles) across, provides evidence for water on Mars. The mist is probably water ice clouds, while the canyons seem to have been formed by large volumes of running water in Mars' distant past. Meteoroid impacts may have melted vast frozen reservoirs beneath the surface, releasing flash floods which carved the winding channels.

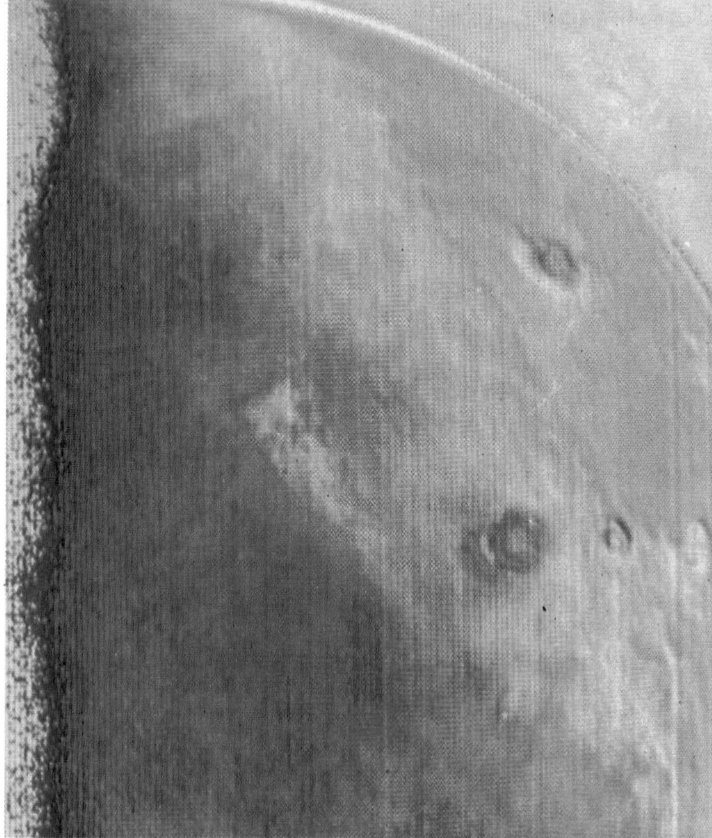

NASA

Right: Slight colour differences in Mars' normally reddish hue are exaggerated in this computer-processed view of one hemisphere of Mars. The technique picks out the huge Martian volcanoes as darker circles. Olympus Mons, the largest of these, rises some 27 km (17 miles) above the surrounding plains, making it by far the largest volcano yet discovered in the solar system.

Below: Sand dunes and boulders feature in this early morning view seen by the Viking I Lander craft. The boom carrying the meteorology instruments extends diagonally across the picture. Measurements show that the weather on Mars is remarkably similar from day to day.

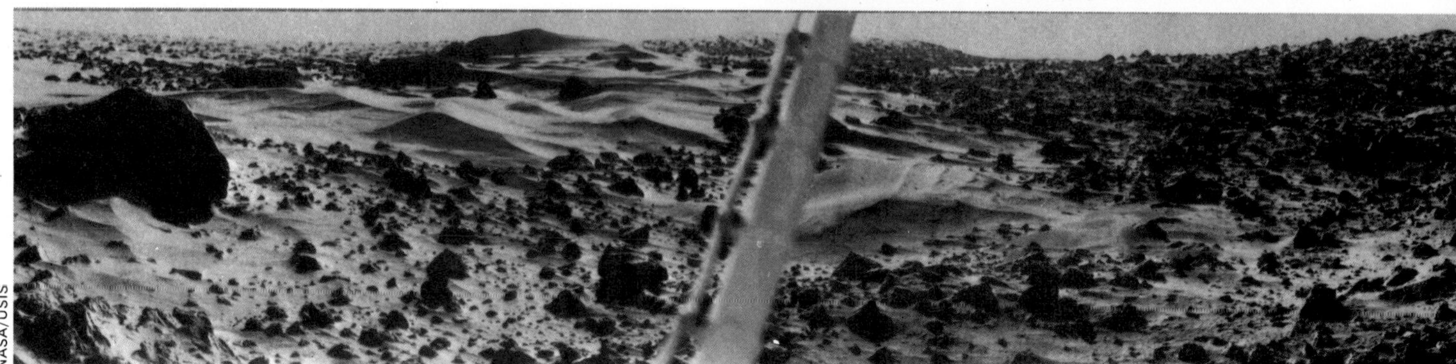

NASA/USIS

NASA

Above: This view of the Martian surface, taken on 25 September 1977, shows late winter frost beneath boulders. From the rate of melting, scientists deduce that the frost is six parts water to one part carbon dioxide. The light pink colour of the Martian sky results from scattering of red light by particles.

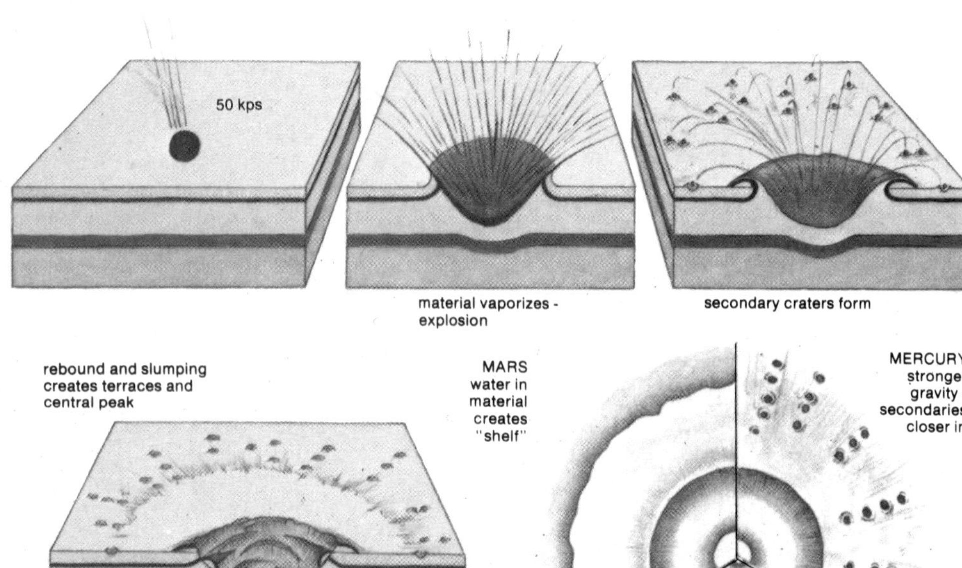

Stages in the formation of an impact crater. The impact vaporizes the surface material instantaneously, producing an explosion. Dynamic rebound fills in the interior in the case of larger craters. Comparison of craters on all three bodies reveals differences due to surface gravity and permafrost layers.

Mars

The blood-red planet Mars has been associated with carnage and war since Babylonian times. With the invention of the telescope, large dark markings could be seen on the red globe, and the slow motion of these markings revealed that Mars' rotation period—its 'day'—is 24 hr 37 min, remarkably similar to the Earth's. The rotation axis of Mars is tilted to its orbit at almost exactly the same angle as Earth's, with the consequence that Mars goes through similar seasons in the course of its 687-day 'year'.

Naturally, there was considerable speculation that Mars might harbour life and attention focused on the dark markings, which changed in colour and intensity with the Martian seasons in a way strikingly similar to vegetation. The case seemed strengthened in 1877, when Giovanni Schiaparelli announced that thin, straight dark lines—'channels', or *canali* in Italian—connected the dark markings. The sensational mistranslation as 'the canals of Mars' implied they were artificial constructions by intelligent Martians.

Better observations have revealed, however, that the straight canals were merely an optical illusion: an eye straining at the limit of visibility tends to connect up individual faint features into straight lines. In the last few years, spaceprobes have proved that the canals do not exist, and that the large dark areas are merely regions where wind has blown off the normal bright dust covering of Mars' surface. Seasonal changes in wind direction and strength cause the brightness and colour changes.

From the Mariner probes it seems that like the Moon, Mars has two hemispheres of very different appearance and age. The early probes had photographed only the 'highland' southern hemisphere, which has remained unaltered since the planet's formation and is very heavily cratered—the largest crater, Hellas, is a dust-filled bowl some 2,000 km across. The northern hemisphere consists of vast lava plains which have flooded the older surface like the lunar maria ('seas'), but Mars' atmosphere has oxidized both hemispheres to the same red tint. Most surprising, the northern hemisphere has several vast volcanoes, each larger than any which exist on Earth.

Mariner 9's other remarkable discovery was the presence of various types of dried-up river beds, clear evidence for running water at some time in Mars' history. The temperature is now too low for liquid water to exist on the surface of Mars—rising above freezing point for only a few hours at noon, even in the Martian summer, and remaining below freezing all day in winter. The tiny amount of water vapour in the atmosphere would form a layer only a hundredth of a millimetre thick if it could be condensed out. But the polar caps consist of water ice perhaps hundreds of metres thick in places and the entire surface of Mars is probably permeated with frozen water (*permafrost*).

The two Viking landing craft which touched down on Mars in 1976 carried clever experiments to test for primitive life, assuming it was either lying dormant awaiting an improvement in the climate, or has adapted to the present severe conditions. The experiments all gave initially positive results, but not in the way expected for biological activity. Most planetary scientists now think that chemical reactions with the unusual soil were responsible, and that Mars does not bear even the simplest forms of life.

Below: Midsummer view of part of Mars' north polar cap, showing layering as the carbon dioxide cap melts to reveal water ice and rock beneath. The cliff face at the top of the picture is about 500 m (1640 feet) high; the view is some 60 km (37 miles) across. The rippled areas are probably sand dunes.

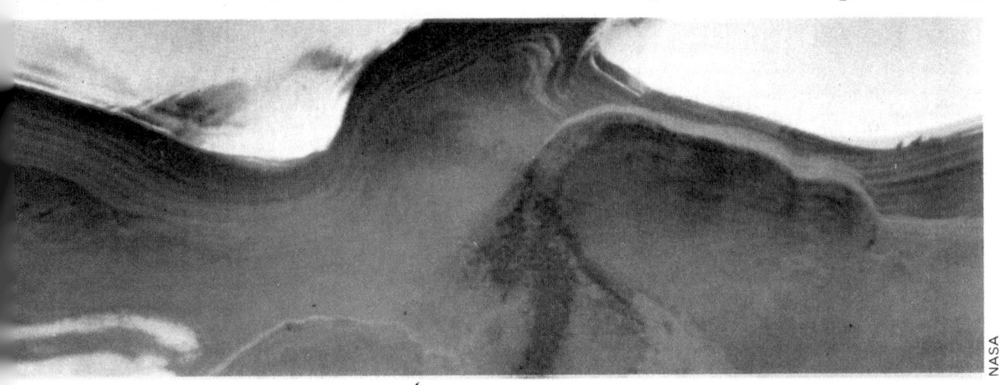

NASA

Venus and the Earth

Venus and the Earth are twin planets in the inner solar system. They are almost identical in size, mass and density, with Venus slightly the smaller of the two. Venus is actually Earth's closest planetary neighbour—it can approach within 41 million km (25 million miles)—and it is hardly surprising that astronomers once imagined these companion worlds to be alike in almost every detail.

In 1962 the spaceprobe Mariner 2 first showed up flaws in our rosy picture of Venus. Since then, it has been revealed to be horrifyingly unlike Earth and extremely hostile. To explain why these two well-matched planets have developed along such strikingly different paths is a puzzle which scientists have only recently solved.

Venus, seen shining like a lantern after sunset as the 'Evening Star', or heralding dawn as the 'Morning Star', is the brightest and most beautiful of the planets to the naked eye. But it has always been the planet of mystery. Even in the largest telescopes, Venus reveals nothing but impenetrable layers of unbroken cloud, encouraging early speculations that a moist, tropical paradise might lie beneath.

A suggestion that Venus was markedly different from Earth came from radar astronomers in 1962. By bouncing radio waves (which penetrate thick cloud) off the planet, they were able to measure the length of Venus's 'day' for the first time. Astonishingly, Venus takes 243 Earth-days to make just one turn; and even more surprisingly, it was found to spin in the opposite direction to all the other planets (apart from tipped-up Uranus). Some radio astronomers had found hints that the surface of Venus was rough, cratered and searingly hot. But these results were very unexpected, and difficult to confirm. It was not until probes reached Venus that a more definite picture emerged.

The early American probes—Mariners 2 and 5—flew past the planet at a distance of only a few thousand kilometres, and confirmed the earlier high temperature measurements. But the Russian Venera craft, which descended through the atmosphere to land on the surface, provided the most startling results. The first three capsules were completely crushed by the enormous pressure of Venus's atmosphere even before they reached the surface. Not until 1970 was a craft—the enormously reinforced Venera 7—able to land safely. Since then, three more Russian craft have successfully landed, and Venus's bleak landscape has now

NASA

Above right: The blue planet—Earth's unique water covering has prevented us from sharing the same fate as arid, scorching Venus. Unlike Venus, Earth's surface is often visible through its clearer atmosphere.

NASA

Below: Venus in false colour; dark and light areas reveal circulating currents in the dense atmosphere. Well-defined belts towards the poles show more uniform flow patterns and give an impression of the rapid (four day) rotation.

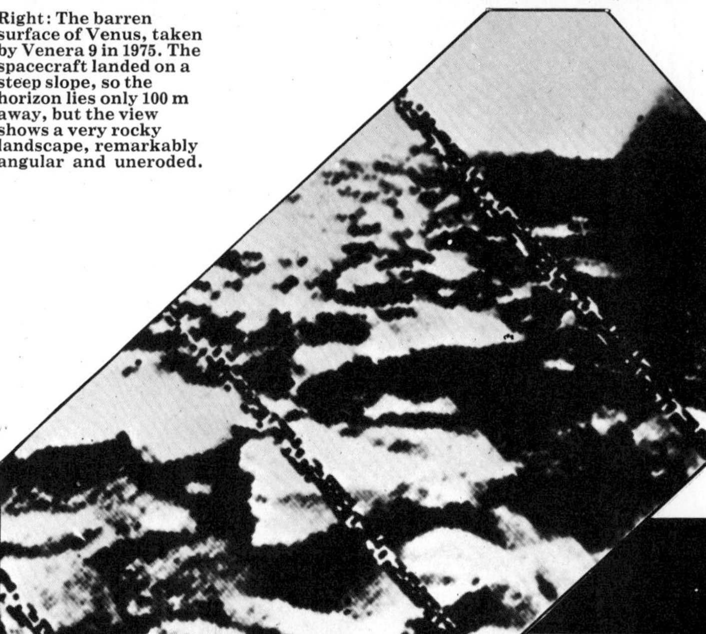

Novosti

Right: The barren surface of Venus, taken by Venera 9 in 1975. The spacecraft landed on a steep slope, so the horizon lies only 100 m away, but the view shows a very rocky landscape, remarkably angular and uneroded.

Above: The first observation of the transit of Venus across the Sun was made by Crabtree and Horrocks in Lancashire on 6 December 1639, from calculations made by Horrocks, a curate. The transits of Mercury and Venus were widely observed in the 18th and 19th centuries as a means of determining the scale of the solar system. This mural depicting Crabtree is by the Pre-Raphaelite artist Ford Madox Brown.

Right: Earth's nearest neighbours, the Moon and Venus, in the morning sky. Venus is the brightest object in our skies after the Sun and Moon and is sometimes visible in broad daylight. Its brilliance arises from its dense cloud cover, which reflects some nine-tenths of the sunlight which falls on it.

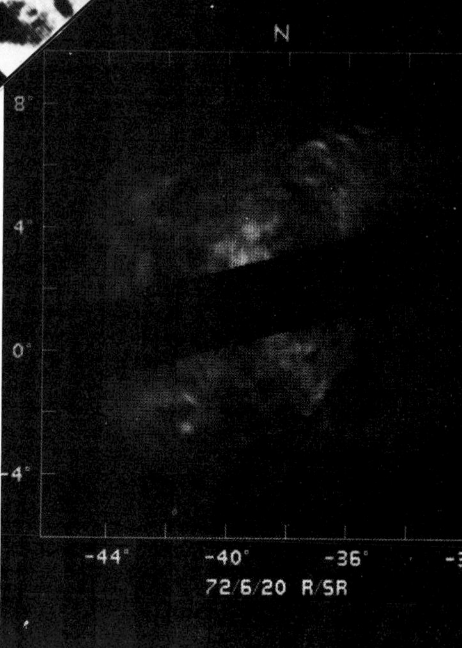

Jet Propulsion Laboratory

Below: Radar 'photograph' of Venus shows ill-defined surface features. The bright markings are peaks of high reflectivity, indicating high mountain areas and crater rims.

Manchester City Council

Photri

Above: Details which our planet reveals from space, shown in this satellite view of south Saudi Arabia. Sand dunes show the presence of winds, and to the left the river valley cutting through a mountainous area shows water erosion. From this, both the atmosphere and the presence of liquid on Earth could be deduced.

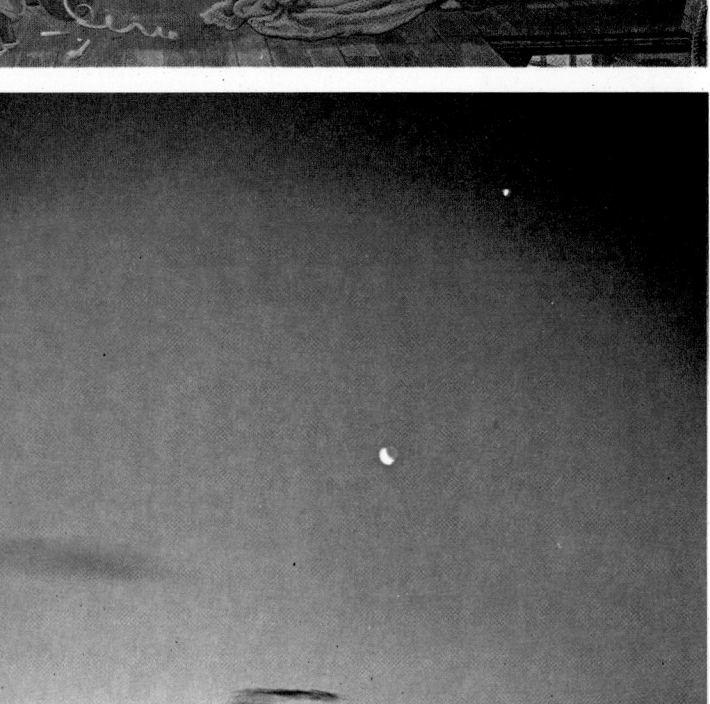

James Shepherd

Below: Satellites and space probes have made possible this view of our *magnetosphere*—the pattern made by lines of force from Earth's magnetic field. It acts as a huge cocoon, trapping charged particles and protecting Earth from electrical bombardment by deflecting the incessant flow of particles and radiation from the Sun.

European Space Agency

been recorded by camera.

As revealed by spaceprobes, Venus is the complete antithesis of the fertile, tropical rain forest once expected. It is enveloped in a thick, choking atmosphere composed of 97% carbon dioxide, with scarcely any water vapour. Although the planet spins very slowly, the atmosphere itself rotates every four days, giving rise to tremendous winds in its upper layers which can reach 350 kph (220 mph). The dense, grey clouds in Venus's atmosphere are quite unlike the low-lying clouds of Earth. They float some 80 km (50 miles) above the surface, and more closely resemble choking industrial smogs. It seems likely that they are composed of sulphuric acid droplets, with other strong acids mixed in. If rain can fall on Venus, then it must be the most corrosive natural liquid in the solar system.

At the surface, the atmospheric pressure is some 90 times greater than on Earth, which is why early spaceprobes were crushed. Venus's dense atmosphere also ensures that the temperature is the same over the whole of the planet's surface. At a constant 475°C (887°F) it is hotter even than the sunward side of Mercury. The Venera 9 and 10 photographs reveal Venus as a dry, dusty desert, littered with boulders of all sizes, their angular shapes only slightly worn.

What lies beneath the surface can only be speculation. Because of the similarity in density between Venus and Earth, it is very likely that they resemble each other in structure. The young-looking boulders on Venus point to it being a geologically active world; and there is every reason to suppose it has a liquid iron core like Earth. But we would not expect Venus to have a magnetic field, as it spins far too slowly for a dynamo action to occur.

Why have two basically similar planets developed so differently? It seems that in the early days of the solar system, Earth's slightly greater distance from the Sun allowed liquid water to condense, dissolving the atmospheric carbon dioxide, which subsequently became locked up forever in calcareous or carboniferous rocks. But on Venus, the surface temperature was slightly too high to allow water to stay liquid. The initial carbon dioxide remained in the atmosphere, trapping more and more heat by a process known as the 'greenhouse effect'. This led to the searing temperatures of today. Had the Earth been a few million kilometres nearer the Sun, it might have suffered the same fate as Venus.

Earth

The third planet from the Sun is of course the most familiar. Our Earth, the largest terrestrial planet, has been intensively studied by geologists, geophysicists and geochemists; its history has probed by palaeontologists, its life-forms by biologists and its atmosphere by meteorologists. These, and many other disciplines have enabled scientists to understand much of the Earth's structure and evolution, but the detailed study of other planets in recent years has added a new dimension to the study of the Earth. *Comparative planetology* enables us to distinguish between features which are common to all terrestrial planets, and hence are an inevitable consequence of the formation of 'rocky' planets; and those which are unique to Earth, resulting from its different mass and distance from the Sun.

Robin Scagell

Alphabet & Image

Above: Both Venus and Mars have atmospheres rich in carbon dioxide, which is comparatively lacking in Earth's air. On Earth, life processes removed carbon atoms from the air; these now remain locked within calcareous rocks such as this limestone reef in Dorset, England.

Left: The volcanic island of Surtsey, off Iceland. An erupting volcano marks the site where molten rock from the Earth's interior gushes to the surface. Most volcanoes are strung along the boundaries of Earth's crustal plates and, like earthquakes, act as safety valves for the release of the enormous quantity of energy produced by the plates grinding together.

Below: The spinning Earth; demonstrated by these trailed images of stars carried around the South Pole of the sky by the Earth's rotation.

Approached from a distance, Earth would appear as the 'blue planet'. Its bright azure hue is a result of the oceans which cover seven-tenths of its surface, and which are frozen at the poles to form the glaring white polar caps. Although Mars has icy polar caps and water frozen into the soil, Earth is the only planet with liquid water. The continental areas of the Earth are coloured reddish-brown and green. The former—the colour of the deserts—is due to oxidized iron compounds, like the red deserts of Mars, but the green of the chlorophyll in plant leaves is unique to our planet: Earth is the only known planet with life-forms. Earth's atmosphere too is unusual. Unlike the predominantly carbon dioxide atmospheres of Venus and Mars (and the airless Moon and Mercury), our atmosphere is composed almost entirely of *nitrogen* (78%) and *oxygen* (21%), with carbon dioxide present to the extent of only three parts in ten thousand. (For comparison, Mars' atmosphere is 96% carbon dioxide, with only 2.5% nitrogen and 0.1% oxygen.) These three most obvious differences between Earth and the other terrestrial planets are in fact closely related, as will become evident when we consider the Earth's history.

Anglo-Australian Observatory

In some ways the broad geology of Earth is similar to that of the Moon and Mars, the other best-studied terrestrial bodies. Like them it has 'highland' regions (the *continents*) raised some 4,500 m (15,000 ft) above the 'lowland' areas (the *ocean floors*). (This interesting comparison is not entirely accurate—the ocean floors, for example, are less than 200 million years old, compared to the 3,500 million year age of the lunar *maria*.) The continental regions of the Earth, however, show no obvious sign of the craters which abound on the surfaces of all the other terrestrial worlds. This lack is readily explained by the water erosion and intense geological activity to which the Earth's surface is subjected. Crumpling of the crust to form mountain ranges destroys fold structures; the material of mountains is quickly eroded away and areas temporarily submerged beneath the sea are covered with washed-down sediments which hide the original surface. Only a small fraction of the Earth's surface is older than 1,500 million years, and on these ancient 'shields' there is ample evidence of old craters, eroded almost to oblivion.

The continental regions of the Earth differ from the lunar and Martian highlands in being split up and scattered over the globe, rather than forming a continuous highland hemisphere. A visitor to the Earth 200 million years ago would however have found just one 'supercontinent' near the South Pole, containing all the Earth's land surface. This land mass of *Pangaea* began to break up some 180 million years ago into our present-day continents, which are still moving over the surface of the Earth.

The confirmation of *continental drift* has been the most exciting development of the earth sciences in recent years, and has radically changed previous geological ideas. According to the present theory, the surface of the Earth is composed of at least 15 separate rigid *plates*, seven of them very large. These plates slide about on a lower layer of 'slushy' rock, the *asthenosphere*, and some of them carry the continents 'piggy-back'. Continental drift thus becomes just one aspect of the movement of crustal plates, and the general theory is now dubbed *plate tectonics*. As two plates move apart, fresh rock appears between them, at the mid-ocean ridges; and where two plates clash, one dives under the other and melts. The material of the plates is thus constantly being renewed, and so the rocks of the ocean floor are comparatively young. The lighter continents always stay on top, however, and thus preserve far older rocks.

Earth is the only planet where plate tectonics is definitely known to operate. The process driving the plates is still not completely understood, although it is probably related to convection currents in the mantle underlying the crust and asthenosphere. The Moon, Mercury and Mars seem to have too little mass for this activity to occur; it is not yet known whether Venus's crust is composed of moving plates. In view of its similar mass to the Eearth. Venus may hold important clues to the mechanism of plate tectonics.

The northern hemisphere of Venus, seen through an infra red radiometer aboard the Pioneer Venus Spacecraft. (December 1978).

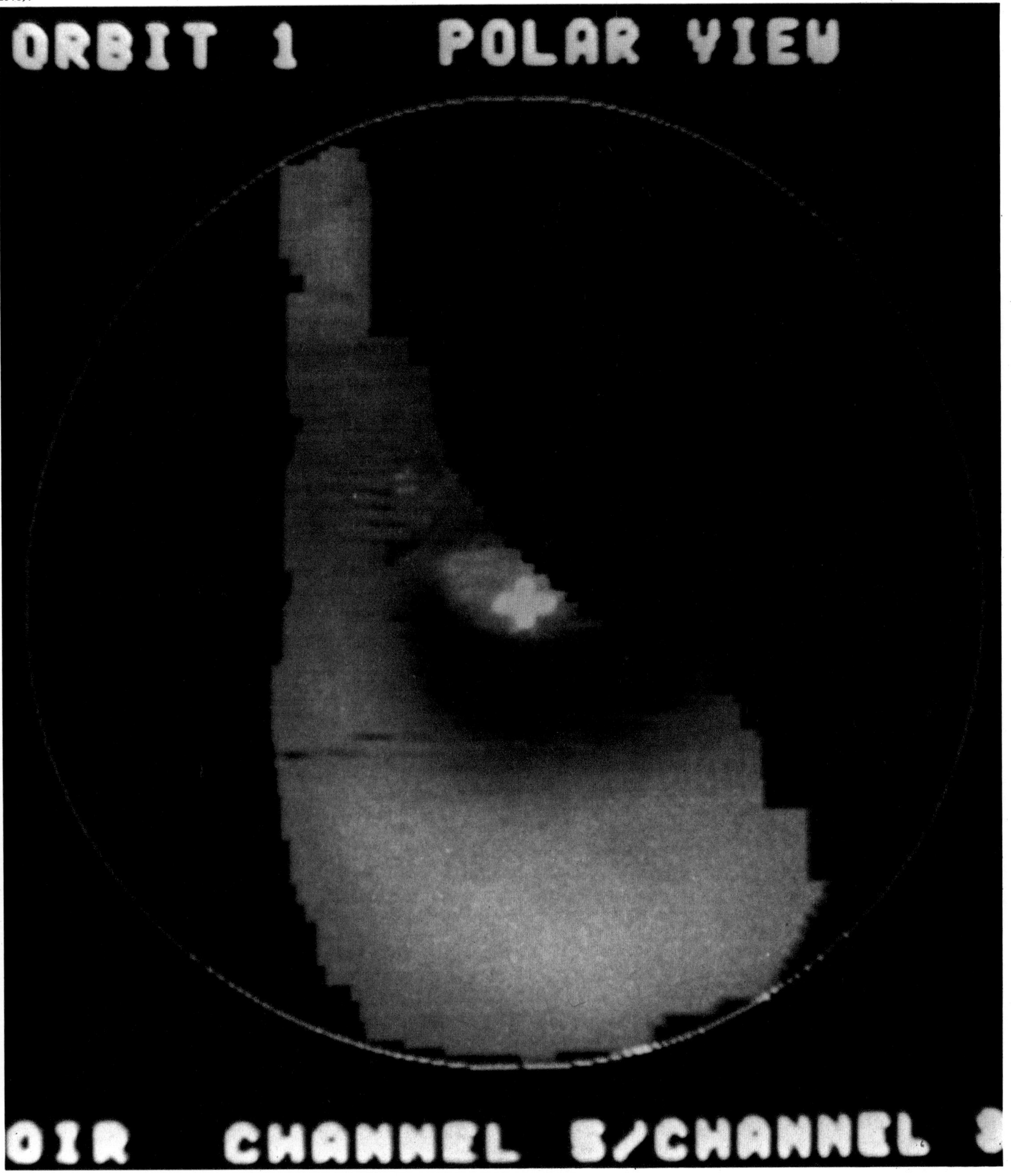

Part II

Atlas of the Earth

The World in Hemispheres
Physical and Astronomical Geography

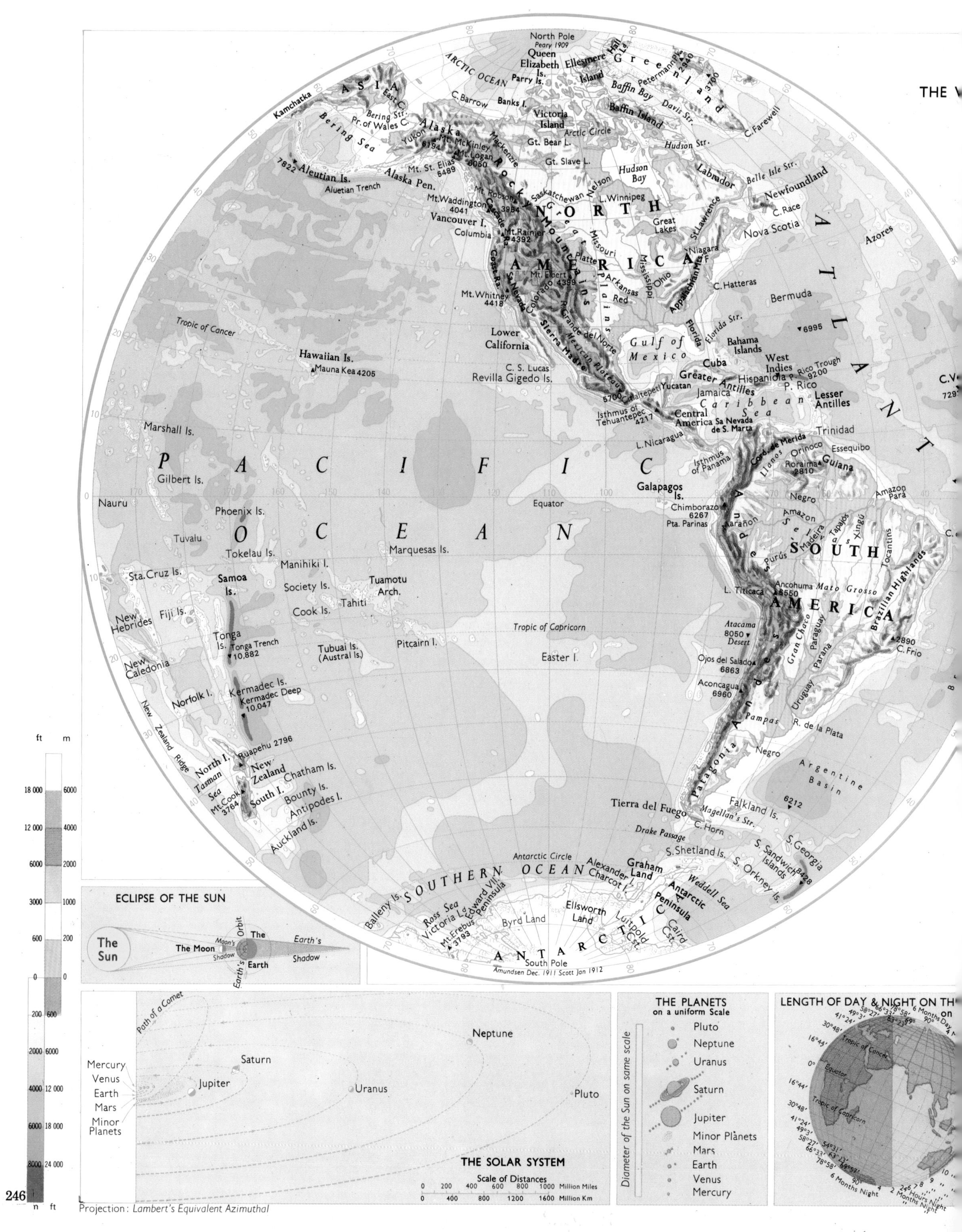

Projection: *Lambert's Equivalent Azimuthal*

ICAL

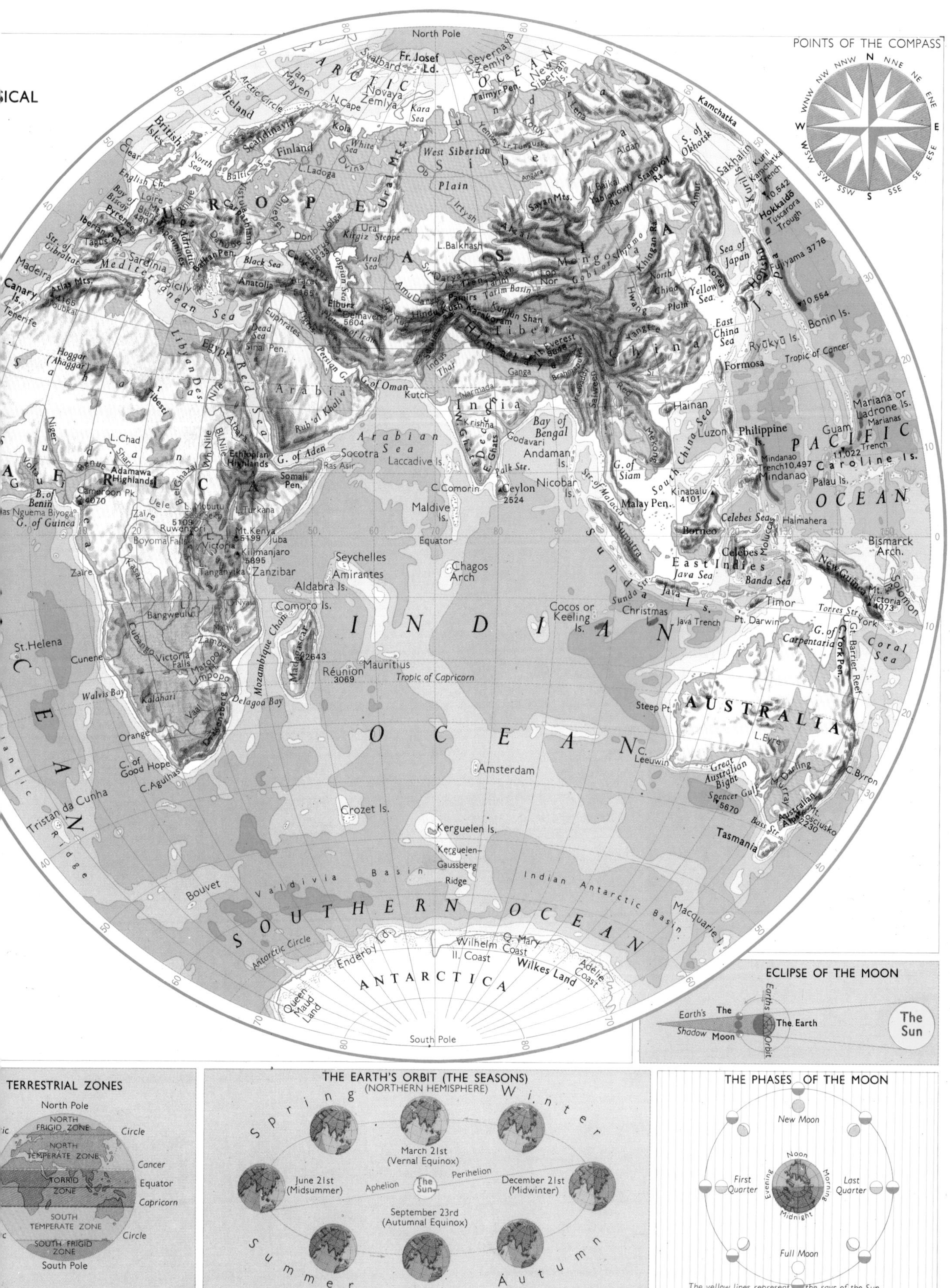

POINTS OF THE COMPASS
N
NNE
NE
ENE
E
ESE
SE
SSE
S
SSW
SW
WSW
W
WNW
NW
NNW
North Pole
Fr. Josef Ld.
Svalbard
Severnaya Zemlya
New Siberian Is.
ARCTIC OCEAN
Jan Mayen
Iceland
Arctic Circle
Novaya Zemlya
N.Cape
Kara Sea
Taimyr Pen.
Kamchatka
British Isles
Scandinavia
Kola
White Sea
Finland
North Sea
Baltic
L.Ladoga
Ural Mts.
West Siberian Plain
Siberia
Yenisei
Lena
Aldan
S. of Okhotsk
Sakhalin
Kurile Is.
Kamchatka Trench
10,542
Hokkaido
Tuscarora Trough
English Ch.
Bay of Biscay
Loire
Pyrenees
Iberian Pen.
Tagus
Str. of Gibraltar
Madeira
Canary Is.
Tenerife
Atlas Mts.
Alps
Adriatic
Apennines
Carpathians
Danube
Dnieper
Don
Volga
Balkan Pen.
Sardinia
Sicily
Mediterranean Sea
Black Sea
Caucasus
Elbrus
Caspian Sea
Anatolia
Ararat
5165
EUROPE
ASIA
Ural
Kirgiz Steppe
Aral Sea
L.Balkhash
Irtysh
Ob
Sayan Mts.
L.Baikal
Yablonovy Ra.
Stanovoy Ra.
Amur
Altai
Mongolia
Gobi or Shamo
Khingan Ra.
Sea of Japan
Korea
Honshu
Japan
Fujiyama 3776
10,554
Bonin Is.
Syr Darya
Tien Shan
Tarim Basin
Lop Nor
Amu Darya
Pamirs
Hindu Kush
Karakoram
Kunlun Shan
Tibet
Himalaya
Mt. Everest
8848
Elburz
Demavend
5604
Plateau of Iran
Euphrates
Tigris
Persian G.
G. of Oman
Indus
Thar
Ganga
Brahmaputra
North China Plain
Hwang
Yangtze
Yellow Sea
East China Sea
China
Ryūkyū Is.
Tropic of Cancer
Formosa
Dead Sea
Sinai Pen.
Egypt
Libyan Des.
Nile
Red Sea
Arabia
Rub 'al Khali
Kutch
Narmada
India
Deccan
W. Ghats
E. Ghats
Krishna
Godavari
Bay of Bengal
Salween
Mekong
Red
Hainan
South China Sea
Luzon
Philippine Is.
Mariana or Ladrone Is.
Marianas Trench
11,022
Guam
PACIFIC OCEAN
Mindanao Trench 10,497
Mindanao
Caroline Is.
Palau Is.
Hoggar (Ahaggar)
Sahara
Tibesti
Niger
L.Chad
Shari
Benue
Adamawa Highlands
AFRICA
Atbara
Bl. Nile
Wh. Nile
Bahr el Ghazal
Ethiopian Highlands
G. of Aden
Socotra
Arabian Sea
Laccadive Is.
Ras Asir
Somali Pen.
Palk Str.
Andaman Is.
Nicobar Is.
G. of Siam
Str. of Malacca
Malay Pen.
Kinabalu 4101
Ceylon
2524
C.Comorin
Maldive Is.
B. of Benin
Cameroon Pk.
4070
G. of Guinea
Uele
L. Mobutu Sese Seko
L. Turkana
Zaire
Ruwenzori
5109
Mt. Kenya 5199
Juba
Boyoma Falls
L. Victoria
Kilimanjaro 5895
Zanzibar
Tanganyika
Kasai
Equator
Seychelles
Amirantes
Chagos Arch.
Aldabra Is.
Comoro Is.
Sumatra
Sunda Is.
Borneo
Celebes Sea
Halmahera
Celebes
Moluccas
East Indies
Java Sea
Banda Sea
Bismarck Arch.
New Guinea
Mt. Victoria 4073
Solomon Is.
Sunda Str.
Java
Christmas
Java Trench
Timor
Pt. Darwin
Torres Str.
C. York
G. of Carpentaria
Coral Sea
Gt. Barrier Reef
York Pen.
Cocos or Keeling Is.
INDIAN OCEAN
St.Helena
Cunene
Bangweulu
Malawi
Cubango
Victoria Falls
Zambezi
Matopo
Limpopo
Kalahari
Walvis Bay
Mozambique Chan.
Madagascar
2643
Réunion
3069
Mauritius
Tropic of Capricorn
Delagoa Bay
Vaal
Drakensberg
Orange
C. of Good Hope
C.Agulhas
Steep Pt.
AUSTRALIA
L.Eyre
C. Leeuwin
Great Australian Bight
Spencer Gulf
Darling
Murray
C.Byron
Australian Alps
Mt. Kosciusko 2230
Bass Str.
Tasmania
Amsterdam
Crozet Is.
Kerguelen Is.
Kerguelen-Gaussberg Ridge
Tristan da Cunha
Atlantic Ridge
ATLANTIC OCEAN
Bouvet
Valdivia Basin
Indian Antarctic Basin
Macquarie I.
SOUTHERN OCEAN
Antarctic Circle
Enderby Ld.
Q. Mary Coast
Wilhelm II. Coast
Wilkes Land
Adélie Coast
ANTARCTICA
Queen Maud Land
South Pole
ECLIPSE OF THE MOON
Earth's Shadow
The Moon
Earth's Orbit
The Earth
The Sun
TERRESTRIAL ZONES
North Pole
NORTH FRIGID ZONE
NORTH TEMPERATE ZONE
TORRID ZONE
SOUTH TEMPERATE ZONE
SOUTH FRIGID ZONE
South Pole
Circle
Cancer
Equator
Capricorn
Circle
THE EARTH'S ORBIT (THE SEASONS)
(NORTHERN HEMISPHERE)
Spring
Winter
Summer
Autumn
March 21st (Vernal Equinox)
June 21st (Midsummer)
December 21st (Midwinter)
September 23rd (Autumnal Equinox)
Aphelion
Perihelion
The Sun
THE PHASES OF THE MOON
New Moon
First Quarter
Last Quarter
Full Moon
Noon
Evening
Morning
Midnight
The yellow lines represent the rays of the Sun

North America: Physical

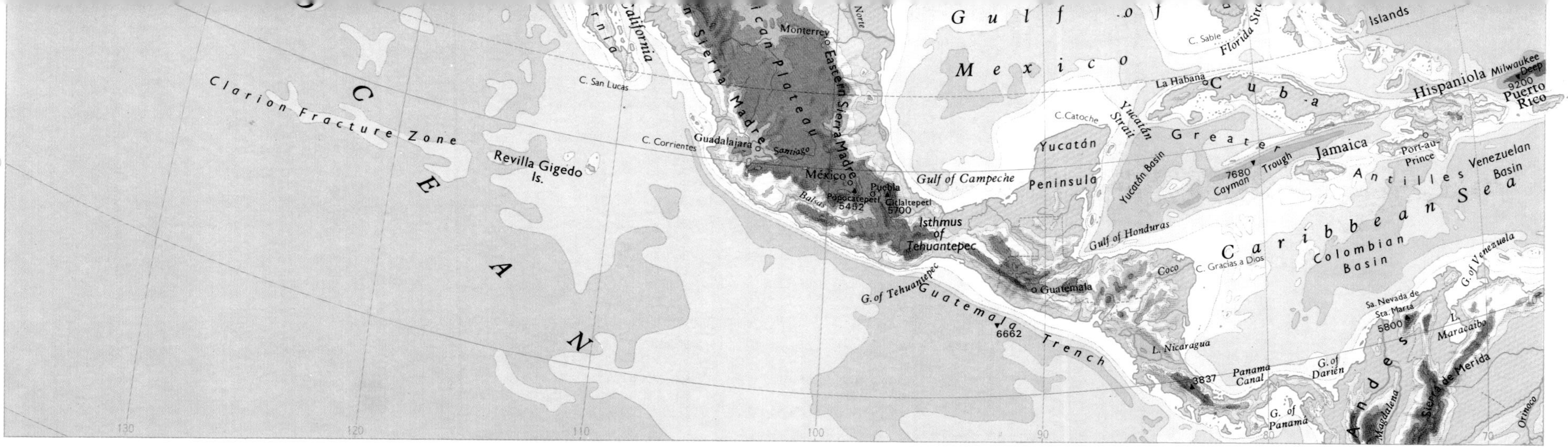

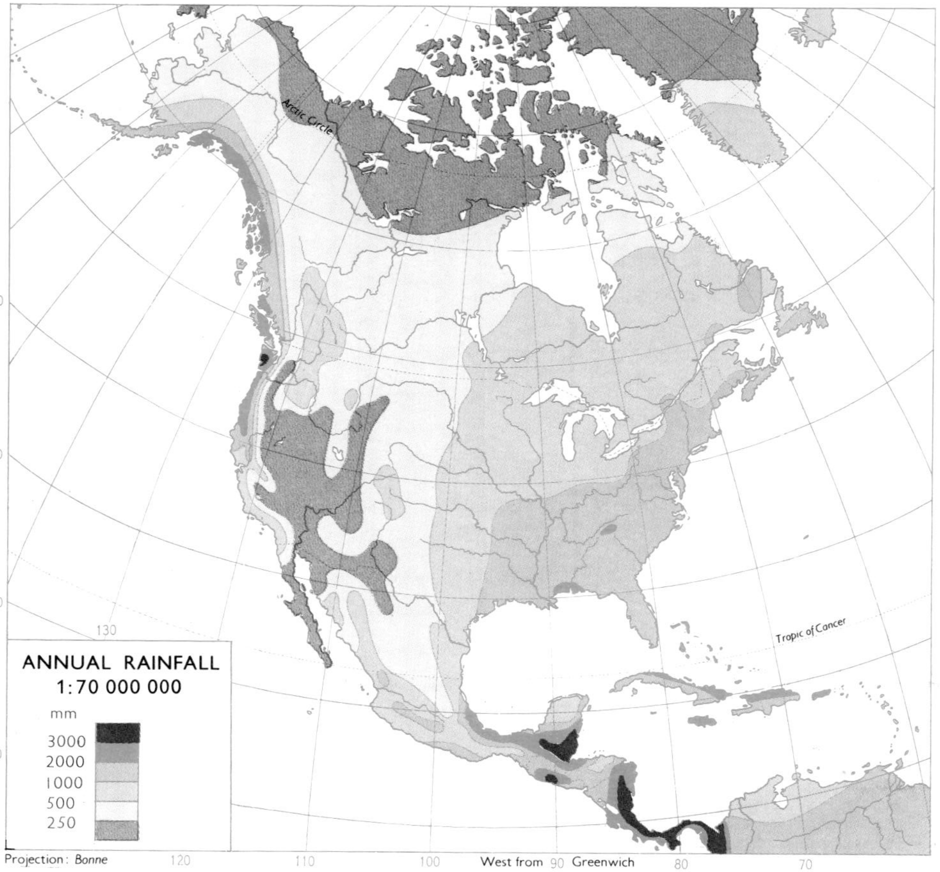

1:30 000 000

200 0 200 400 600 800 1000 km

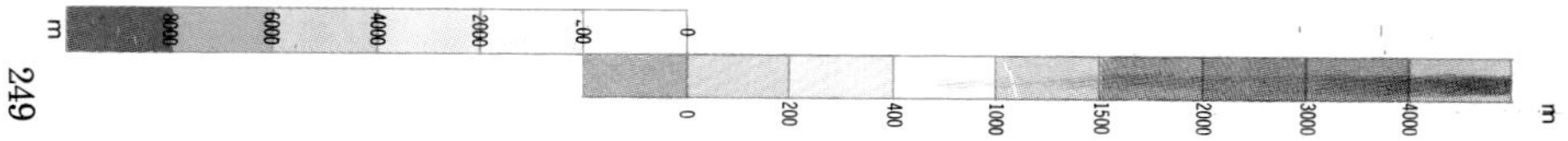

ANNUAL RAINFALL

1:70 000 000

mm
3000
2000
1000
500
250

Projection: Bonne

West from 90 Greenwich

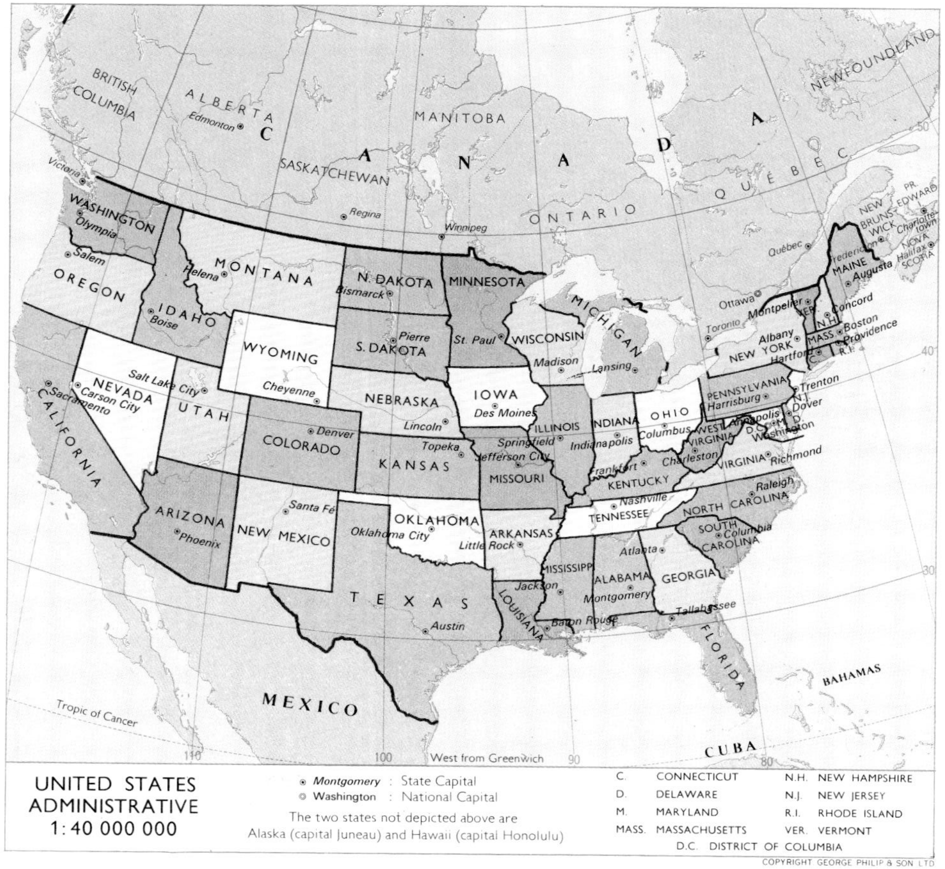

UNITED STATES ADMINISTRATIVE

1:40 000 000

⊛ Montgomery : State Capital

◎ Washington : National Capital

The two states not depicted above are Alaska (capital Juneau) and Hawaii (capital Honolulu)

C.	CONNECTICUT	N.H.	NEW HAMPSHIRE
D.	DELAWARE	N.J.	NEW JERSEY
M.	MARYLAND	R.I.	RHODE ISLAND
MASS.	MASSACHUSETTS	VER.	VERMONT
	D.C. DISTRICT OF COLUMBIA		

North America: Natural Vegetation

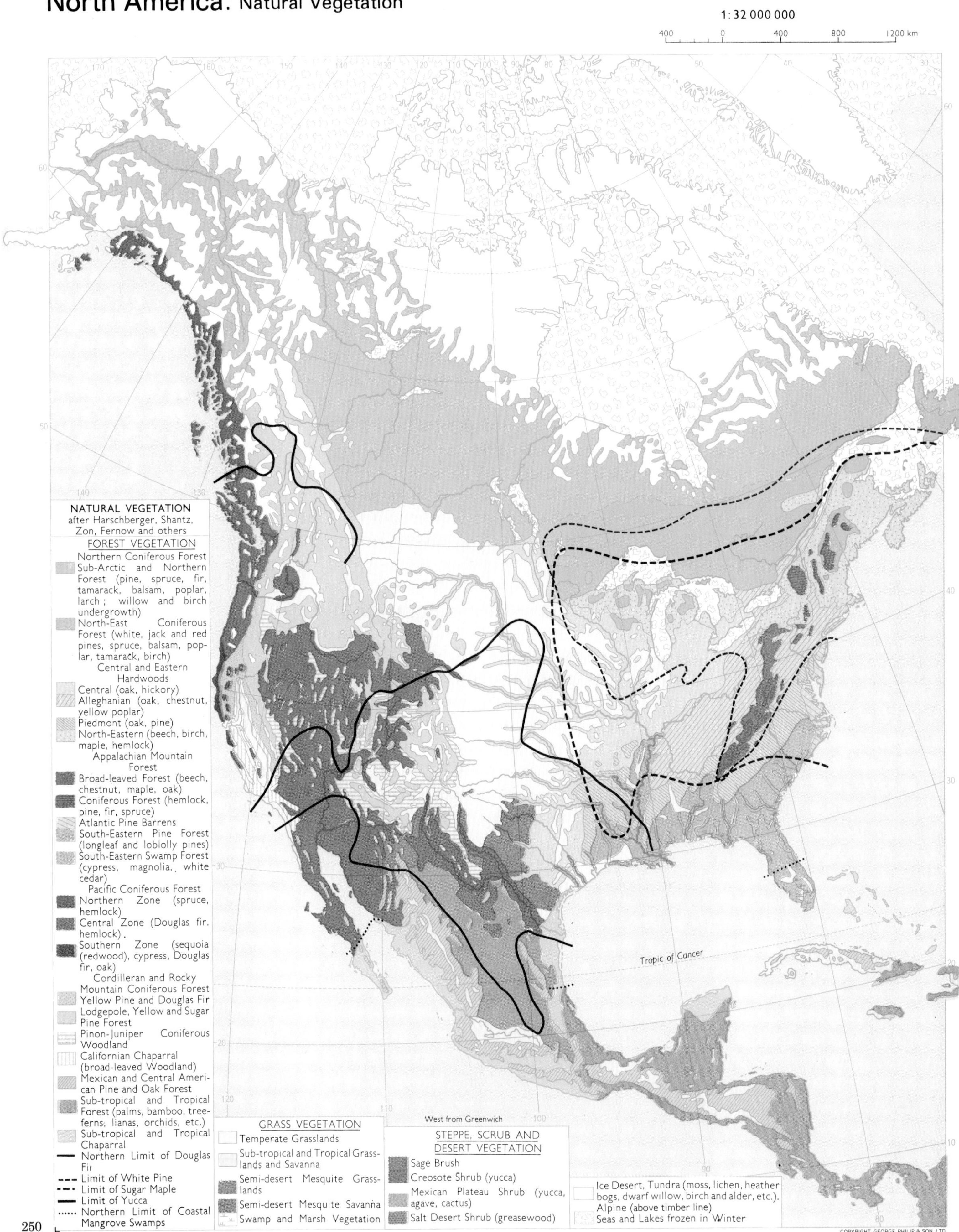
1: 32 000 000
400 0 400 800 1200 km
NATURAL VEGETATION
after Harschberger, Shantz, Zon, Fernow and others
FOREST VEGETATION
Northern Coniferous Forest
Sub-Arctic and Northern Forest (pine, spruce, fir, tamarack, balsam, poplar, larch; willow and birch undergrowth)
North-East Coniferous Forest (white, jack and red pines, spruce, balsam, poplar, tamarack, birch)
Central and Eastern Hardwoods
Central (oak, hickory)
Alleghanian (oak, chestnut, yellow poplar)
Piedmont (oak, pine)
North-Eastern (beech, birch, maple, hemlock)
Appalachian Mountain Forest
Broad-leaved Forest (beech, chestnut, maple, oak)
Coniferous Forest (hemlock, pine, fir, spruce)
Atlantic Pine Barrens
South-Eastern Pine Forest (longleaf and loblolly pines)
South-Eastern Swamp Forest (cypress, magnolia, white cedar)
Pacific Coniferous Forest
Northern Zone (spruce, hemlock)
Central Zone (Douglas fir, hemlock).
Southern Zone (sequoia (redwood), cypress, Douglas fir, oak)
Cordilleran and Rocky Mountain Coniferous Forest
Yellow Pine and Douglas Fir
Lodgepole, Yellow and Sugar Pine Forest
Pinon-Juniper Coniferous Woodland
Californian Chaparral (broad-leaved Woodland)
Mexican and Central American Pine and Oak Forest
Sub-tropical and Tropical Forest (palms, bamboo, tree-ferns, lianas, orchids, etc.)
Sub-tropical and Tropical Chaparral
Northern Limit of Douglas Fir
Limit of White Pine
Limit of Sugar Maple
Limit of Yucca
Northern Limit of Coastal Mangrove Swamps
GRASS VEGETATION
Temperate Grasslands
Sub-tropical and Tropical Grasslands and Savanna
Semi-desert Mesquite Grasslands
Semi-desert Mesquite Savanna
Swamp and Marsh Vegetation
STEPPE, SCRUB AND DESERT VEGETATION
Sage Brush
Creosote Shrub (yucca)
Mexican Plateau Shrub (yucca, agave, cactus)
Salt Desert Shrub (greasewood)
Ice Desert, Tundra (moss, lichen, heather bogs, dwarf willow, birch and alder, etc.).
Alpine (above timber line)
Seas and Lakes frozen in Winter
Tropic of Cancer
West from Greenwich
Projection: Polyconic
COPYRIGHT GEORGE PHILIP & SON. LTD.

South America: Physical

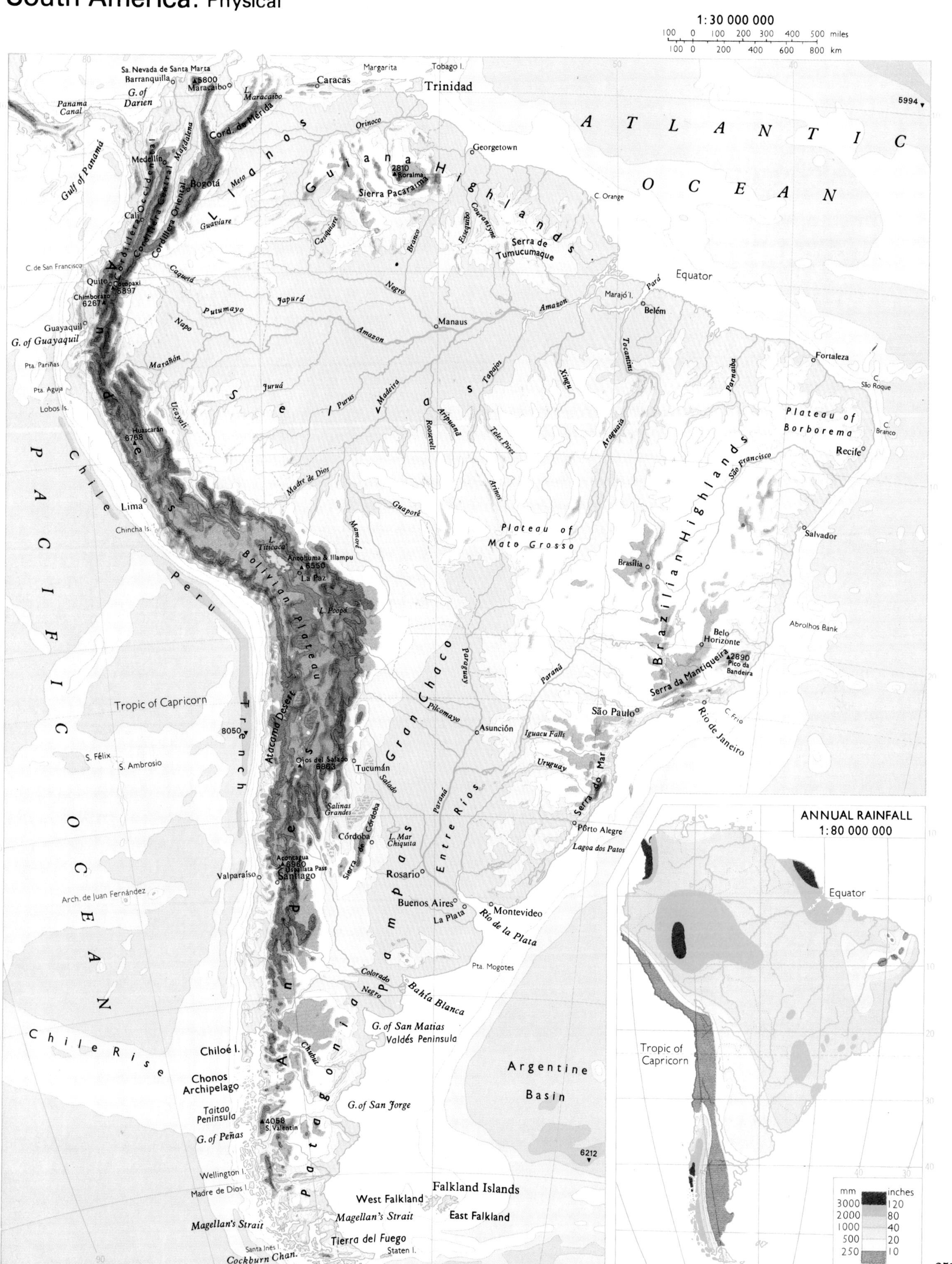

Europe: Physical

ANNUAL RAINFALL
1:40 000 000
mm inches
1500 60
1000 40
750 30
500 20
250 10
Arctic Circle
Iceland
Reykjavik
Hekla 1491
Öræfajökull 2119
NORWEGIAN SEA
Faroe Is.
Rockall
Hebrides
St. Kilda
Shetland Is.
Orkney Is.
British Isles
Ben Nevis 1343
Edinburgh
NORTH SEA
Ireland
Belfast
Irish Sea
Dublin
Great Britain
St. George's Channel
Snowdon 1085
Cardiff
Thames
London
Amsterdam
Netherlands
Lands End
Scilly Is.
English Channel
Channel Is.
Str. of Dover
Brussel
Ardennes
Eifel
Meuse
Paris
Seine
Brittany
Vosges
Loire
Saône
C. Clear
ATLANTIC OCEAN
Flores
Terceira
Pico
Azores
São Miguel
Bay of Biscay
4861
Gironde
C. Finisterre
Massif Central
Mt. Dore 1886
Mt. Blanc 4807
Jura
Cevennes
Rhône
Garonne
Cantabrian Mts.
Old Castile
Iberian
Douro
Maladetta 3404
Pyrenees
Ebro
G. of Lion
Madrid
Lisboa
C. da Roca
Tagus
Peninsula
New Castile
Guadiana
Sierra Morena
Corsica
Sardinia
C. St. Vincent
6293
Madeira
Guadalquivir
Andalusia
Mulhacen 3478
Sa. Nevada
Balearic Is.
Str. of Gibraltar
C. Trafalgar
Gibraltar
MEDIT
Er Rif
Casablanca
Alger
Maritime Atlas
Plateau of the Shotts
Great Atlas
Saharan Atlas
Toubkal 4165
Palma
Tenerife
Canary Is.
Gran Canaria
Fuerteventura
Sahara
Tropic of Cancer
Projection: Bonne.
West from Greenwich
East from Greenwich
ft m
12,000 4000
6000 2000
3000 1000
1200 400
600 200
0 0
200 600
2000 6000
4000 12,000
m ft

1:17 500 000
100 0 100 200 300 400 500 miles
100 0 200 400 600 800 km
Nordkapp
Nordkinn
Lofoten
L. Inari
Kebnekaise 2123
Torne älv
Lappland
Kola Peninsula
Kanin Peninsula
Tundra
Pechora
Narodnaya 1894
Telpos Iz. 1617
Ural Mountains
West Siberian Plain
Ob
Irtysh
Tobol
White Sea
Mezen
Scandinavia
Ume älv
Indalsälven
Gulf of Bothnia
Onega
N. Dvina
L. Onega
Finland
Lake Ladoga
Svir
Åland Is.
Helsinki
Oslo
Stockholm
Mälaren
Vänern
Vättern
Gotland
Gulf of Finland
Neva
Leningrad
Rybinsk Res.
L. Chudskoye
Valdai Hills
Volga
Moskva
Gorkiy
Oka
Kama
Volga Heights
Obshchi Syrt
Ural
Kirgiz Steppe
BALTIC SEA
København
Dvina
North European Plain
Central Russian Uplands
Neman
Vistula
Oder
Warszawa
Pripet
Pripet Marshes
Kiyevo
Dnieper
Ukraine
Sudetes
Moravian Hts.
Tatra 2655
Carpathians
Wien
Budapest
Bakony Forest
Plain of Hungary
Drava
Mureş
Tisza
Sava
Transylvanian Alps
Bucureşti
Wallachia
Danube
Beograd
Dinaric Alps
Dalmatia
Morava
Sofiya
Balkans
Rhodope
Balkan Peninsula
Prut
Dniester
Bug
Odessa
Don
Tsimlyansk Res.
Volga
Ust Urt Plateau
Karagiye Depression -132
Caspian Sea -28
Kara Bogaz
Sea of Azov
Kuban
Terek
Crimea
Mouths of the Danube
Strait of Kerch
Elbrus 5633
Caucasus
Transcaucasia
Kura
Baku
Araks
Black Sea
2211
Pontine Mts.
Ararat 5165
L. Van
L. Urmia
Elburz Mts.
Tehrān
İstanbul
Bosporus
Sea of Marmara
Ankara
Kizil
Anatolia
L. Tuz
Erciyas 3770
Taurus Mts.
Kurdistan
Gran Sasso 2914
Adriatic Sea
Str. of Otranto
Pindus
Dardanelles
Aegean Sea
Athinai
Ionian Is.
Ionian Sea
Messina
Calabria
C. Spartivento
Morea
5121
C. Matapan
Malta
Rhodes
Crete
Cyprus
Halab
Euphrates
Tigris
Mesopotamia
Baghdād
Levant
Bayrūt
Syrian Desert
Tel Aviv-Yafo
Dead Sea -396
Persian Gulf
MEDITERRANEAN SEA
Gulf of Sidra
Nile Delta
COPYRIGHT, GEORGE PHILIP & SON, LTD

Africa: Physical

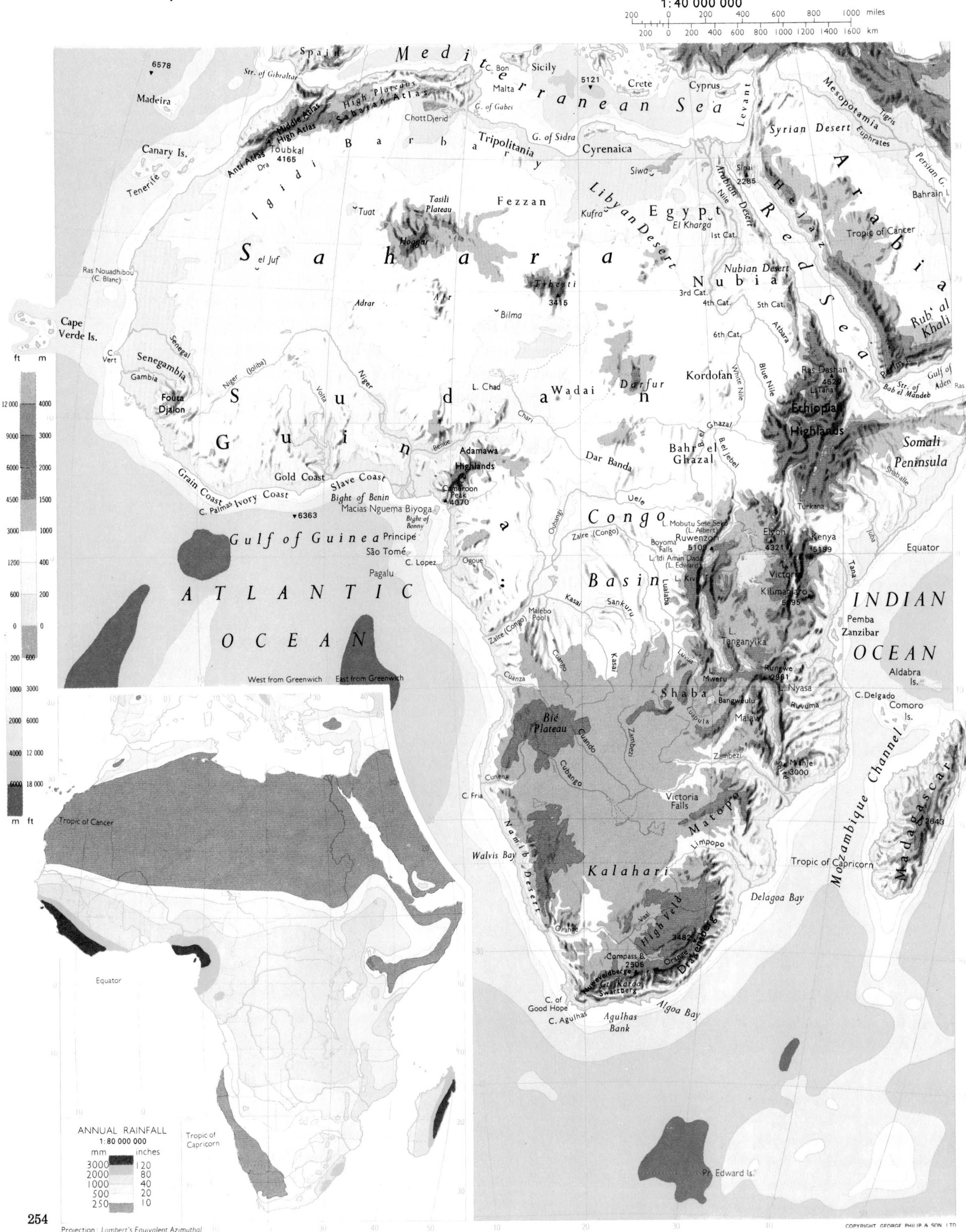

Asia: Physical

The Gazetteer

The Gazetteer is a collection of maps of the countries of the world, arranged regionally. As well as providing topographical information each map contains details of population, industry, climate and language. The countries are listed below.

United States 1

Kilometres 0 300 600

0 150 300 Miles

● Towns over 1 million
◉ Towns over 500,000
• Towns under 500,000

N

m f
4000 13125
2000 6560
1000 3280
500 1640
200 656
0 0
200 656
2000 6560
m f

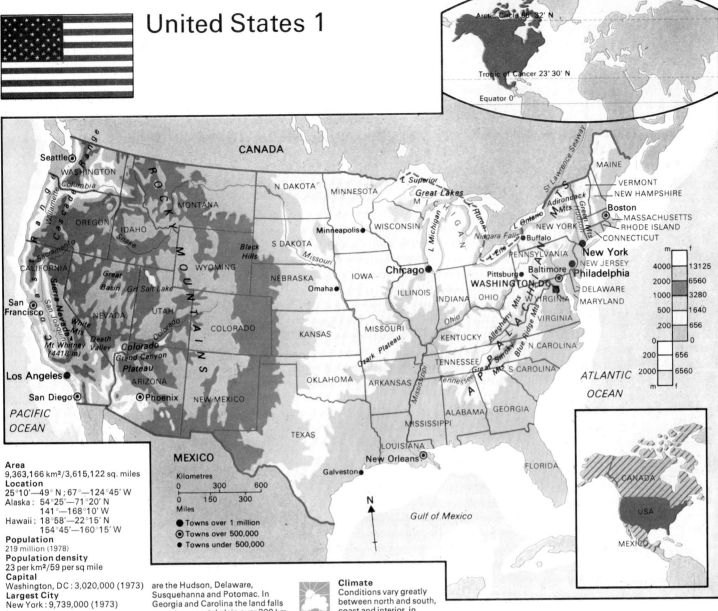

Area
9,363,166 km²/3,615,122 sq. miles
Location
25°10′—49° N; 67°—124°45′ W
Alaska: 54°25′—71°20′ N
141°—168°10′ W
Hawaii: 18°58′—22°15′ N
154°45′—160°15′ W
Population
219 million (1978)
Population density
23 per km²/59 per sq mile
Capital
Washington, DC: 3,020,000 (1973)
Largest City
New York: 9,739,000 (1973)
Language
English
Major Imports
machinery, transport equipment, petroleum, foods, textiles, electrical goods
Major exports
machinery, vehicles and aircraft, chemical manufactures, wheat and other foods
Currency
dollar (1 dollar = 100 cents)
Gross National Product
1,397,300 million dollars (1974)
Status
federal republic

The US consists of 50 states and the District of Columbia (the site of the federal capital). The above facts relate to the whole territory.

Physical features
The US, the world's fourth largest nation both in area and in population, can be roughly divided into three regions: a hilly east, a flat centre and a mountainous west. The principal feature of the eastern sector is the Appalachian system, a mountain chain extending southwestwards from Canada to Alabama. This chain includes the White, Green and Adirondack mountains in the north and, further south, the Allegheny, Blue Ridge and Great Smoky ranges. Although some peaks rise to almost 2,000 m, most are under 900 m. The main rivers penetrating the Appalachian block are the Hudson, Delaware, Susquehanna and Potomac. In Georgia and Carolina the land falls away to a coastal plain over 300 km wide. The Atlantic coast is rocky in the north but consists of marshes, dunes, lagoons and sandbars south of Maine. The central plains are broken by a few upland blocks, such as the Black Hills of South Dakota and the Ozark Plateau but the main feature is the Mississippi-Missouri river system (6,212 km), the third longest in the world. Every minute the Mississippi deposits a further 200 tonnes of silt in the delta which is slowly expanding into the Gulf. The Ohio is the major eastern tributary of the Mississippi. To the north lie the Great Lakes. In the west, the Rockies, running from Alaska to Mexico, climb to over 4,000 m. These rugged mountains contain some of North America's most spectacular scenery with snowy peaks, waterfalls, gorges, geysers, lakes and forests. West of the Rockies lies a region of tablelands, basins, canyons and deserts. It includes the Colorado Plateau (mostly over 2,000 m high,) the Grand Canyon, the arid Great Basin of Nevada, the Great Salt Lake and California's Death Valley (85 m below sea level). This region is bordered by the high Sierra Nevada and Cascade ranges whose highest point is Mt Whitney (4,418 m). Between these and the Coast Ranges lie a series of sheltered valleys including the Willamette, Sacramento and San Joaquin valleys which are important agriculturally. The chief rivers in the west are the Snake, Columbia, Sacramento and Colorado.

Climate
Conditions vary greatly between north and south, coast and interior, in a country the size of the US. Summers are generally hot and, in coastal areas, humid. July averages 24°C in New York, 28°C in New Orleans, 32°C in Phoenix but only 17°C in San Francisco (because of cool currents and sea breezes). Winters are mild on the west coast but colder east of the Rockies: January averages 12°C in San Francisco,—7°C in Omaha, —1°C in New York but 15°C in Florida. In the east, annual rainfall is over 100 cm and occurs throughout the year; the central plains receive under 50 cm, mostly in summer. On the west coast, winters are wettest but the amounts range from 180 cm in the north to less than 20 cm in the desert south.

Flora and fauna
A third of the country is forested. Conifers (spruce, pine, fir, hemlock, redwood) cover the western mountains; mixed forest (pine, hemlock, fir, spruce, birch, maple, beech) predominates in the east but gives way to deciduous (oak, beech, hickory) in the southeast. Pine, cypress, palm and mangrove grow on the Gulf coast and in southern Florida. Grasslands characterize the centre while desert scrub and cactus occur in southern California and Arizona. Wildlife includes the Rocky Mountain goat and marmot in the west; buffalo and prairie dog on the plains; bear, deer, racoon and beaver in the north-east; and alligators in Florida.

Transport
Life in the US is car-dominated with almost one car for every two Americans. The 6,000,000 km road network (the world's longest) is densest along the eastern seaboard, the Mississippi and Ohio valleys and the Pacific coast. Although the US has a quarter of the world's railway track, rail transport is in decline: in the mid 1970s, 90% of passenger travel was by car, and only 1% by train; transcontinental passenger services have been discontinued. But railways are still important for goods transport and carry about 40% of the country's freight. Chicago is a major terminus and ranks as the world's largest railway centre. Other freight movements are by road, pipeline (oil, gas, acids) and water. The principal inland waterways are the Mississippi-Missouri-Ohio system extending to Omaha, Minneapolis and Pittsburg; the Great Lakes-St Lawrence Seaway which brings ocean-going vessels as far inland as Duluth; and the New York State Barge canal which links New York to Buffalo and the Great Lakes. Chicago is the main inland port with New York the leading seaport followed by New Orleans. Other ports are Galveston, Baltimore, Boston, Los Angeles, San Francisco and Seattle. Railways have also lost traffic to buses and planes; there is a comprehensive network of internal air routes, with some 4,000 public airports served by 50 airlines.

Energy
The US, using 33% of the world's energy, ranks as the largest energy-consuming nation; it also leads in energy production, accounting for 27% of the world total. Petroleum (25% imported) and natural gas provide about 65% of the nation's energy needs. The main oil and gas producing states are Texas, Louisiana, California, Oklahoma, New Mexico, Wyoming and Kansas. The pipeline network, totalling 282,000 km, is densest between the southern fields and the industrial Great Lakes region; oil from the Gulf Coast fields is transported to the northeast by tanker. Coal is also a major source of power and 70% of output comes from the Appalachian fields, especially in West Virginia, Kentucky and Pennsylvania. Appalachian coal (providing 25% of world output) is one of the main reasons why 75% of American industry is concentrated in the northeast. The Indiana-Illinois field is the other chief coal-producing area and lignite occurs in the Rockies. Over 80% of the country's electricity is generated in thermal stations by oil, gas or coal but other sources of electricity are water and nuclear power. Major hydro schemes are located on the rivers Columbia (producing 25% of all US hydro-power), Tennessee, Colorado and Sacramento and at Niagara Falls. The US produces over 50% of the world's nuclear power, using uranium from the Rockies.

United States 2
(Eastern)

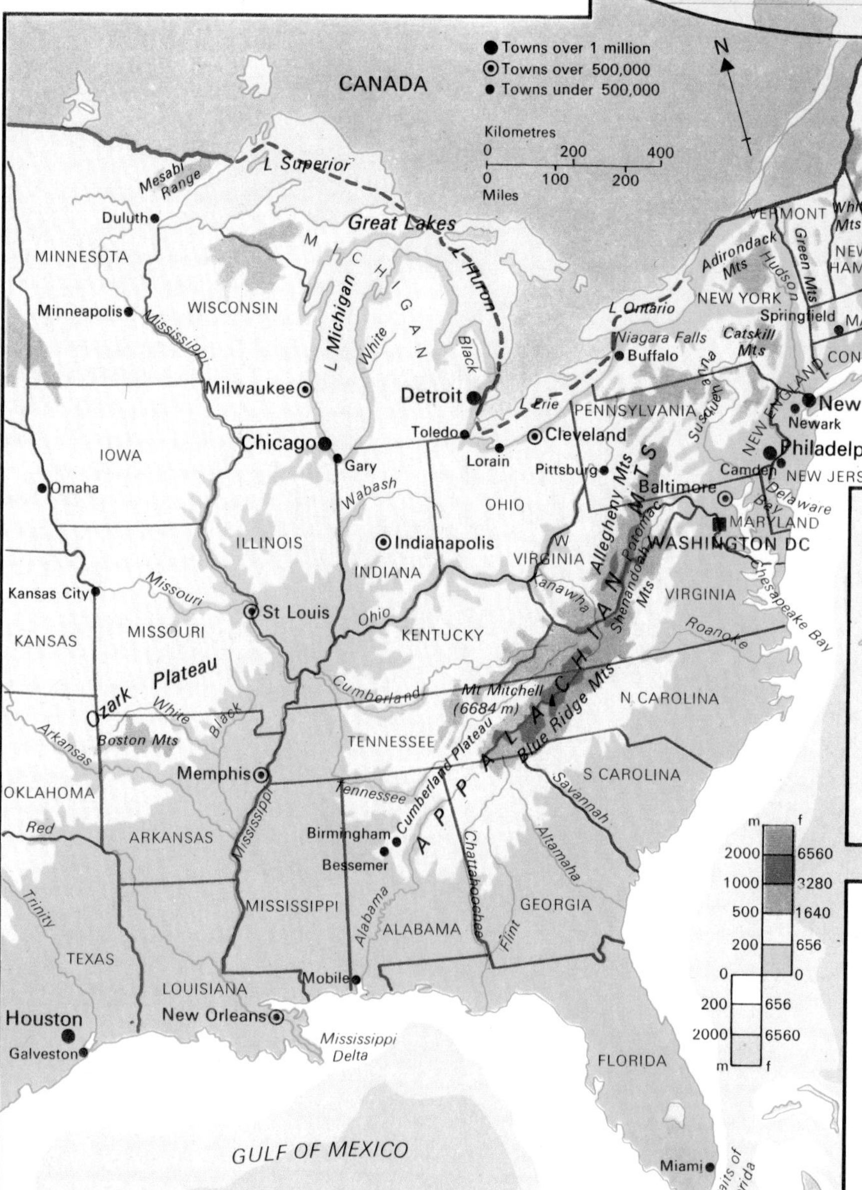

Mining

Although the US leads the world in mineral production, imports are vital, especially of tin, nickel, asbestos, bauxite, industrial diamonds, platinum, manganese and tungsten. Most of America's minerals are located in the west except for iron ore, sulphur and phosphates. Over 80% of iron ore comes from the Lake Superior fields of Minnesota (Mesabi range), Michigan and Wisconsin; some iron ore is mined in the Adirondacks and Alabama. The US is the world's largest producer of phosphates and sulphur; both occur on the Gulf Coast, sulphur in Louisiana and Texas, phosphates in Florida and Tennessee. The western Ozark mountains are important for lead and zinc.

Iron and steel

The US makes a quarter of the world's steel and 78% of national output comes from the Pennsylvania—Great Lakes region. Factors behind the industry's growth are Lake Superior iron ore, coal from the Appalachians, limestone near Lake Huron and a navigable waterway (the Great Lakes) linking these reserves. Ore is also imported from Canada, Venezuela and Liberia. Major iron and steel centres include Philadelphia, Baltimore, Pittsburg, Cleveland, Lorain, Toledo, Detroit, Gary, Chicago, Milwaukee and Duluth. Outside the northeast, the main steel-making region is at Birmingham and Bessemer (Alabama). Local ore, coal and limestone are used and steel goods are shipped via the Black Warrior river and the Gulf port of Mobile.

Other industry

Around 75% of US manufacturing is concentrated in the area between Minneapolis, St Louis, Baltimore and Boston. In addition to iron and steel, the northeast is also the centre of the engineering, electrical, chemical and textile industries. About ten million motor vehicles (25% of the world total) are made each year in the Detroit district.
Other engineering products coming principally from the northeast are agricultural machinery (Chicago), ships (Philadelphia, Camden, Baltimore), machine tools (New England) and industrial machinery. Pittsburg, Boston and Springfield are major centres of electrical and electronic equipment. Chemical plants are mostly located in northeastern seaports, steel towns, along the Kanawha (W Virginia) and Tennessee valleys and the Gulf coast. The textile industry has spread from its original New England base; in particular, cotton textiles have moved south to the Carolinas and Georgia. Food processing is widespread and is mainly centred on producing areas.

Forest industries

The US produces a large share of the world's timber products, providing 20% of its lumber, 35% of pulp, 11% of newsprint and 44% of all other paper. The eastern forests are important, especially in New York, South Carolina, Mississippi and Minnesota, which together account for 85% of paper output, 78% of pulp and 33% of its lumber.

Farming: the centre

The central plains contain some of the world's richest and most extensive farmlands. Dairying predominates in the north; Wisconsin alone produces 15% of America's milk and 50% of its cheese and butter. South of the dairy belt lies the corn belt, stretching across Iowa, Illinois, Indiana and Ohio. Corn (maize) covers 30% of arable land in this area; other crops are wheat, oats, hay and soybeans. The corn belt is also a major meat-producing zone and 85% of corn is used as stockfeed for cattle and pigs. Southwards lies a mixed farming region, followed by the cotton belt in the lower Mississippi basin. The name 'cotton belt' now belongs to history as cotton production has moved west, mainly to Texas. Traditional sources such as Mississippi, Arkansas, Louisiana and Alabama provide only 45% of the national total. In place of cotton, the South is growing soybeans, peanuts, vegetables and fodder. Rice and sugarcane grow on the Gulf coast.

Farming: the east

The urbanized east coast, particularly from Boston to Washington, offers a big market for fresh fruit and vegetables; consequently, truck farming (market gardening) is highly developed in the northeast. This region, especially New England, is also important for dairying and poultry. In Virginia, the Carolinas and Georgia, tobacco is a major cash crop. Other crops are: peanuts and soybeans on the coastal plain, maize and cotton inland and, further south, fruit. Florida is noted for citrus.

Fishing

Fishing is important and supplies a highly developed processing industry. The catch from the Atlantic and Gulf is very varied and includes lobsters and cod off New England, oysters and crabs off Delaware and in Chesapeake Bay, shellfish and menhaden (herring-like fish used for fertiliizer and oil) from the Gulf. Boston is the main fishing port.

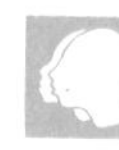

Peoples

The first European settlers were Spaniards, moving up from Mexico, followed by English colonists who came to Virginia and Massachusetts. Since then, over 50 million people have migrated to the US. Some of the non-European groups are concentrated in certain areas: most Mexican immigrants live in Texas and California, Japanese in San Francisco, Chinese in San Francisco and New York, and Puerto Ricans in New York.
During the first centuries of settlement, frequent wars between white colonists and native Indians threatened the Indian population with extinction. Protection measures have, however, contributed to an increase in numbers (800,000: 1970). Many live on reservations in the mid- and far west. Black Americans (22.6 million: 1970) are the descendants of slaves brought in to work the southern plantations. In 1900, 90% lived in the south but, with the decline in southern agriculture, 40% have since moved north.

Urban growth

Initially, the US was a rural country: in 1790, only 5% lived in towns and there were no centres with more than 50,000 inhabitants. Today, 75% of Americans are urbanized and 35 metropolitan areas have populations of over one million. A recent trend is suburban growth coupled with inner-city decline: for every one person moving into a city, five move to the suburbs. As the middle classes escape to the less crowded, less polluted and less expensive suburbs, city centres are left to the rich and the poor; the latter are often black migrants from the south in search of employment.

Cities

One American in two lives in the industrial northeast. New York started as a trading post in 1624 on Manhattan Island and is now the world's second largest city. Manhattan is still the heart of New York and the country's financial and commercial centre although the port, factory and residential districts have spread far beyond the island. About 10% of US industrial output comes from New York while the port handles 20% of the country's trade. Chicago (3.2 m) leads the world in steel production and has important food-processing industries based on produce from the hinterland. Other major urban centres in the east are Philadelphia (1.8 m), Detroit (1.4 m), Washington DC, Boston (618,000), St Louis (558,000), Pittsburg (479,000), Baltimore (878,000), Newark (368,000) and Buffalo (450,000).

United States 3
(Western)

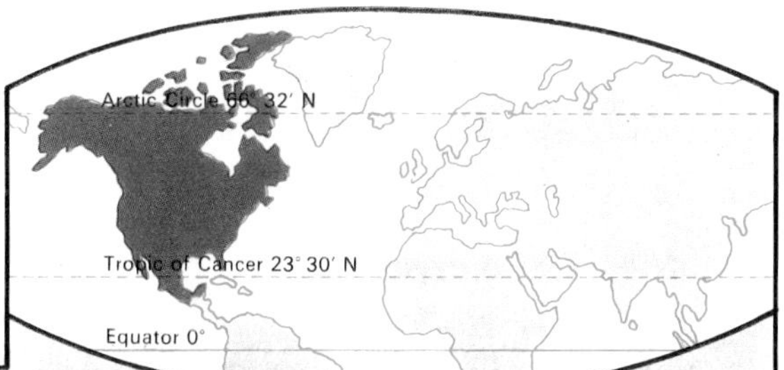

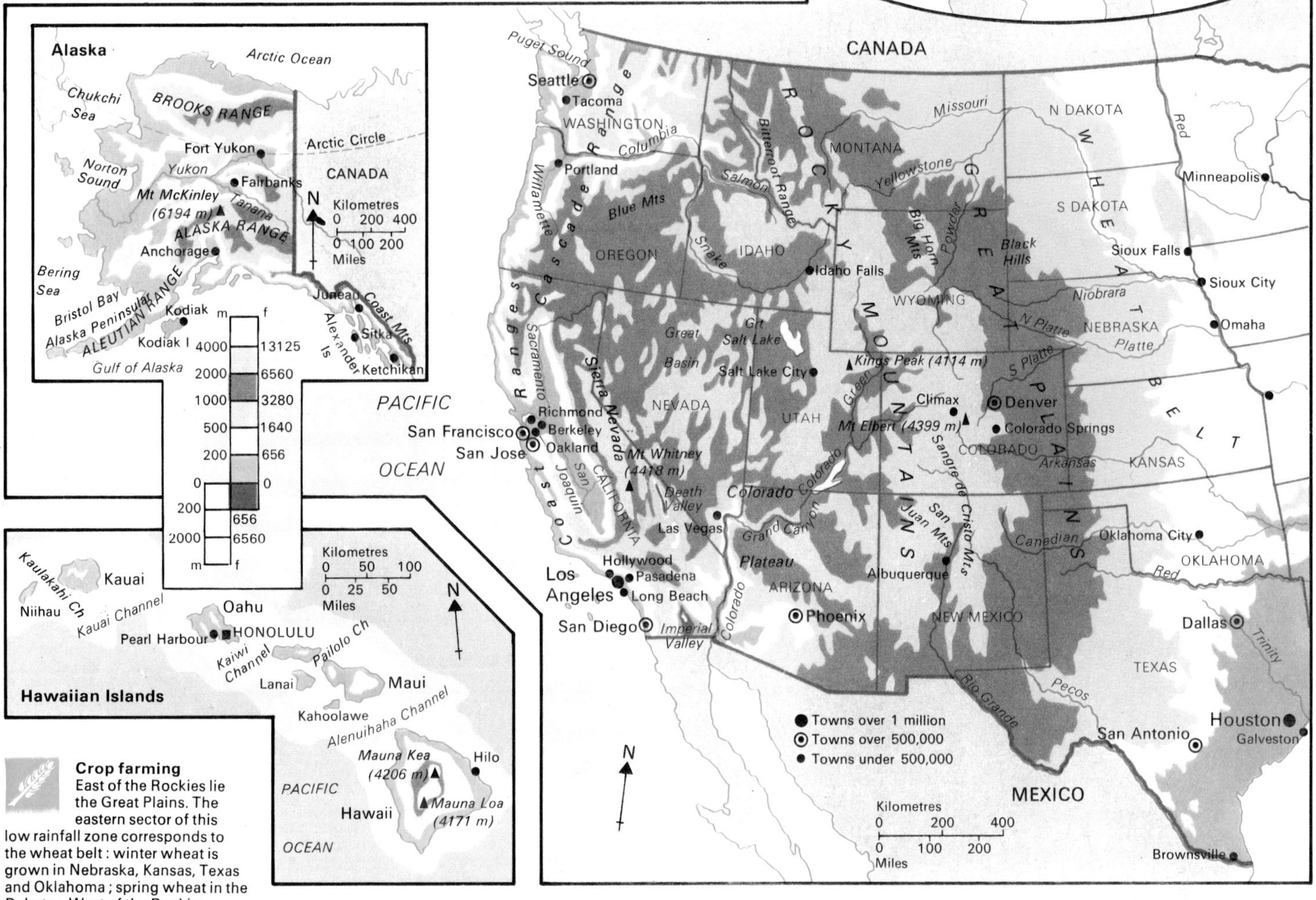

Crop farming
East of the Rockies lie the Great Plains. The eastern sector of this low rainfall zone corresponds to the wheat belt: winter wheat is grown in Nebraska, Kansas, Texas and Oklahoma; spring wheat in the Dakotas. West of the Rockies, cultivation is limited to areas where water is available: alfalfa, sugarbeet and wheat are grown in the Columbia and Snake valleys and near Great Salt Lake; cotton, fruit and vegetables along the Salt and Rio Grande rivers and in Imperial Valley. The main cash crop of the Pacific Coast is fruit: apples and pears in the northwest and grapes, citrus, peaches, apricots, plums and nuts from the California central valley and Los Angeles region. Cotton, sugar beet, rice and alfalfa are also grown in the central valley.

Livestock
The Great Plains and some arid zones of the western plateau are used for grazing cattle. Except in the south (Arizona and Texas) the cattle winter in sheltered valleys and feed on alfalfa and other fodder grown under irrigation. Animals are mostly fattened on the plains of the Midwest or in lowland California. Sheep are kept for wool. Dairying is important along the Pacific coast and well developed in the Willamette valley and near Seattle.

Fishing
Fishing is an important west coast activity, providing 25% of the total US catch. Tuna and halibut are caught in the Pacific, salmon in Puget Sound, the Columbia and Sacramento. Fishing ports, all with canning and freezing plants, include San Diego, San Francisco and Seattle.

Mining & industry
The US is the world's largest producer of copper, uranium and molybdenum. Copper comes mainly from Arizona, Montana and Utah; uranium occurs in Wyoming and New Mexico; Climax (Colorado) is the world's chief source of molybdenum. Northwest Montana has important lead-zinc deposits. In the 19th century, thousands of adventurers went west in search of gold and silver. Gold is still produced in South Dakota, Utah, Nevada and California; silver in Idaho and Utah. Industry in the Great Plains and Rockies is basically concerned with primary products (flour milling, meat packing, metal refining and timber processing). The port of Houston is important for oil refining, metallurgy, engineering, food processing, chemicals and textiles. Dallas has oil refining, engineering and leatherwork. A wide range of manufacturing exists on the Pacific coast (Seattle, Portland, the San Francisco Bay towns, Los Angeles and San Diego). The leading sector, engineering, specializes in aircraft and missile construction; other branches are motor vehicles, ships, machinery and electrical equipment. Food processing is next in importance and includes dried fruit, wine, canned fish and fruit juices. The other major industry is timber. Tourism, chemicals and textiles (wool in the northwest and cotton in California) are well established.

Forestry
The coniferous forests that cover 75% of Washington and 50% of Oregon and California are a valuable resource. In Washington and Oregon, the timber industries employ 50% of the industrial workforce and, although the eastern US leads in pulp and paper manufacture, over half the country's softwood lumber comes from the west. Seattle, Tacoma, and Portland are timber centres.

Cities
While the Great Plains and western mountains are thinly populated, parts of the Pacific coast, especially in California, are highly urbanized. About 90% of Californians live in urban areas and 40% of these in the Los Angeles district where the main industries are aerospace, tourism and fruit processing. The Los Angeles conurbation (8.3 m) covers 600 km² and over 100 municipalities including Long Beach, Pasadena and Hollywood. The San Francisco conurbation (3 m) includes bay towns such as Richmond, Berkeley and Oakland. San Francisco's industrial growth has been stimulated by its port activity and by the rich agriculture of the central valley. Other major cities in California are San Jose and San Diego. Outside California, the two leading west coast cities are Seattle (515,000) in Washington and Portland (386,000) in Oregon.

Alaska: the land
Alaska (1,518,776 km²), situated partly within the Arctic circle, is a desolate, mountainous territory. The Alaska and Aleutian ranges, which terminate in the Aleutian islands, are part of the Pacific mountain system, while the northern Brooks range is a continuation of the Rockies; Mt McKinley (6,194 m) is North America's highest peak. A region of low hills, drained by Alaska's longest river, the Yukon, lies between the southern and northern highlands. Beyond the Brooks massif a flat coastal plain extends to the Arctic Ocean. Winters are cold (−40°C), summers are cool (6°C).

Alaska: the economy
Fishing, forestry and mining are the chief activities. Alaska ranks as the world's leading supplier of salmon, caught offshore and in the Yukon. Juneau, Ketchikan, Sitka and Kodiak have big canneries. Other species taken are halibut, herring, crab and shrimp. In the southeast, coniferous forests provide large volumes of lumber and pulp; there are pulp mills at Ketchikan, Sitka and Juneau. Mineral production includes petroleum, natural gas, gold and coal. There is a little arable and dairy farming in the Anchorage region. Anchorage, Fairbanks, Ketchikan and Juneau account for 60% of the total population (377,000).

Hawaii: the land
Hawaii, the only non-mainland US state, consists of 312 islands lying about 4,000 km southwest of San Francisco. The islands rise from a submerged mountain ridge and form a 3,000 km-long chain across the north Pacific. At the eastern end, the 8 main islands (Hawaii, Maui, Oahu, Kauai, Molokai, Lanai, Niihau and uninhabited Kahoolawe) make up all but 7 km² of the state's total area of 16,705 km². Hawaii is the largest (10,458 km²) and has the groups highest mountain, Mauna Kea (4,206 m), and an active volcano, Mauna Loa. The other islands are just volcanic stacks, coral reefs and shoals. The climate is warm (23°C) with heavy winter rainfall.

Hawaii: the economy
The activity generated by the US naval base at Pearl Harbor (Oahu) is the state's chief source of income. Next in importance is tourism with 3 million visitors a year. Farming is highly commercialized: the two main crops, sugar cane and pineapples, occupy 90% of cultivated land. Skipjack tuna accounts for half of the fish catch. Food-processing industries are important with sugar, canned pineapple and juice, canned tuna, tropical fruits and flowers sent to the US mainland. About 75% of the 847,000 inhabitants live on Oahu which has the state capital, Honolulu (338,000).

The Arctic and Greenland

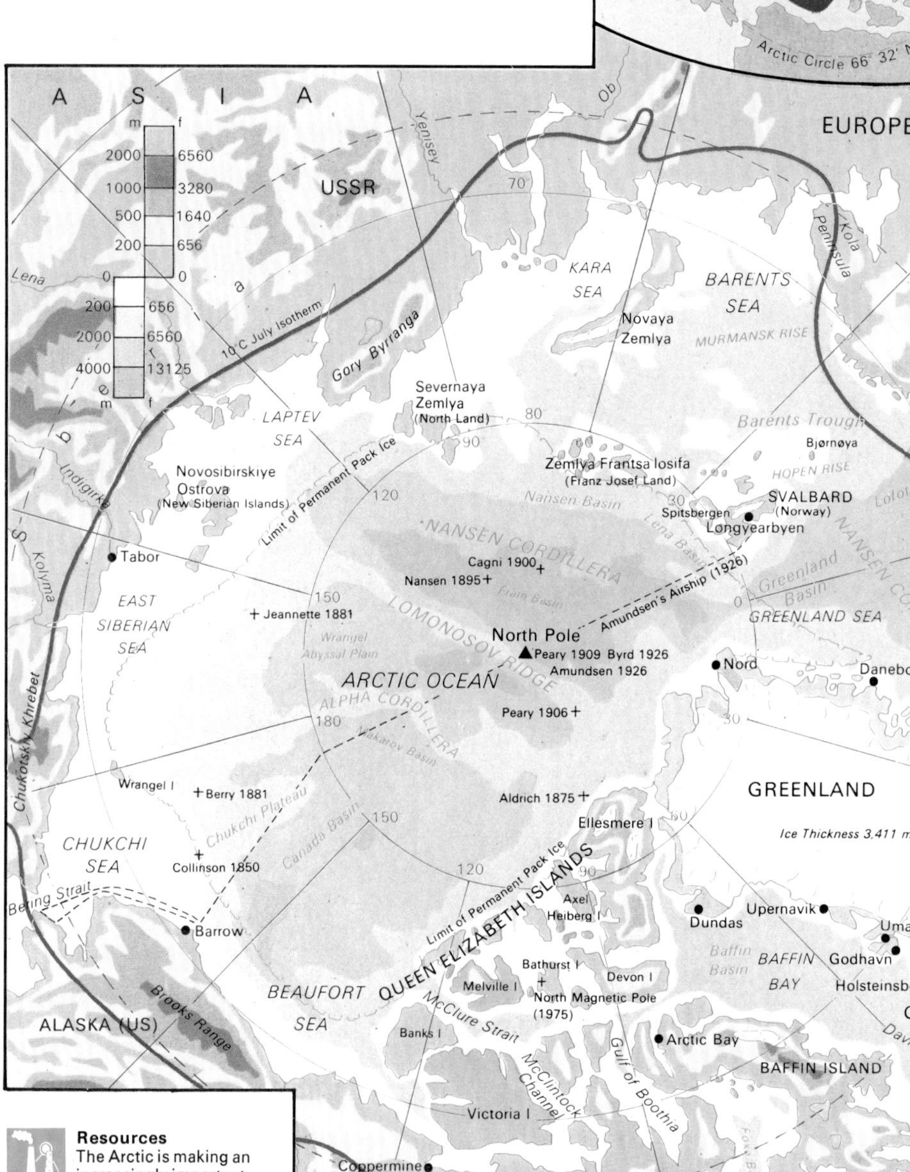

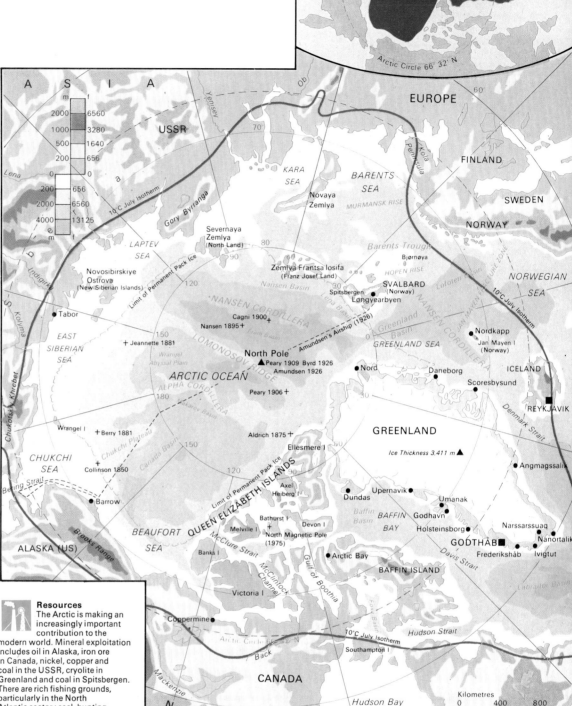

The Arctic

The Arctic, the vast northern polar region, consists of an immense central ocean fringed by innumerable islands and the shores of Asia, Europe and North America. Its southern limit lies along an astronomically determined line, the Arctic Circle (66°32′ N); above this latitude the sun never rises in midwinter nor sets in midsummer. For geographical purposes, however, the polar boundary is often defined by the 10°C July isotherm: an imaginary line passing through all places with an average July temperature of 10°C. This line roughly coincides with the northern limit of trees and brings within the Arctic the whole of Greenland, most of Iceland and a broad belt, up to 500 km wide, along the north coast of the American and Eurasian continents.

Physical features

The Arctic's dominant feature is its great ocean, 3,000 m deep and covering 14,200,000 km². Much of the surface of this huge ocean is permanently frozen, but in summer some melting occurs along the southern margins and navigation is possible. The Arctic lands bordering the ocean are partly mountainous and in some places are liable to earthquakes; Jan Mayen island has the world's most northerly volcano. With the exception of Greenland and neighbouring islands, most land is free of ice and snow in summer. Several major rivers drain into the ocean, including the Mackenzie (Canada), Lena, Yenisey and Ob (USSR).

Climate

Over most of the Arctic, mean temperatures for the warmest and coldest months are about —1°C and —35°C. On the continental land masses, temperatures are more extreme, rising to 9°C in summer but falling to —46°C in winter. Winters are generally milder on the islands: Spitsbergen averages —20°C in February. Much of the Arctic is basically desert as precipitation (in the form of snow blizzards) seldom exceeds 20 cm.

Vegetation

Between the tree line and the shores of the Arctic Ocean lies the *tundra*—a forlorn monotonous plain, littered with swamps and lakes, which early explorers called 'the barrens'. During the short summer, when temperatures remain above freezing, the tundra bursts into life: mosses, lichens, grasses, low shrubs and small flowering plants form a dense, colourful carpet. The vegetation draws its moisture from the thawed surface of the permanently frozen subsoil (permafrost), a feature of all Arctic lands.

Wildlife

The Arctic Ocean, with its rocky shores, freezing waters and pack-ice, is the home of polar bears, walruses, seals and whales. Many land animals, such as caribou, wolves, wolverines and grizzly bears, migrate in winter; others, including the musk-ox, lemming and Arctic fox, are permanent tundra residents.

Resources

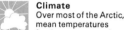

The Arctic is making an increasingly important contribution to the modern world. Mineral exploitation includes oil in Alaska, iron ore in Canada, nickel, copper and coal in the USSR, cryolite in Greenland and coal in Spitsbergen. There are rich fishing grounds, particularly in the North Atlantic sector; seal-hunting and whaling also take place. Large herds of reindeer are kept for their meat and skins on the Eurasian mainland and in Canada, the breeding of musk oxen is being developed as the animals produce a very valuable fine wool.

Peoples

The Arctic has a total population of about half a million; the majority are Americans, Canadians, Danes and Russians who have moved into the area to develop its economic, scientific and strategic potential. The indigenous peoples are: Eskimos in North America, Greenlanders (mixed Eskimos and Europeans), Lapps in the Kola peninsula and north Scandinavia, Samoyeds, Yakuts, Tungus and other tribes in Siberia. Although these groups are spread over a vast area, their cultures are similar and their traditional activities of hunting and fishing provide them with food, clothes and oil (for heat and light).

Greenland

Area
2,175,600 km²/840,000 sq miles
Location
59°45′—83°40′ N
12°—73° W
Population
48,000 (1975)
Population density
1 person per 45 km²/17 sq miles
Capital and largest town
Godthåb: 8,600 (1971)
Languages
Greenlandic, Danish
Major imports
fuels, foods, machinery, vehicles
Major exports
fish, cryolite, skins
Currency
Danish kroner
Gross National Product
80 million US dollars (1970)
Status
island territory of Denmark

The land

Most of Greenland, the world's largest island, lies within the Arctic Circle. The low-lying interior is covered by a giant ice-sheet (1,833,900 km²) some 2,000 m thick. The surrounding coastal zone, seasonally free of ice and snow, features mountain ranges rising to 3,700 m and deep fjords. The island's polar climate is harshest in the north: July and February in Upernavik are 5°C and —23°C, in Ivigtut, 10°C and —8°C; temperatures on the ice-cap are always below freezing. Rainfall decreases from 110 cm in the south to 20cm in the north.

The economy

Greenlanders, of mixed Eskimo and Danish origin, mostly live on the southwest coast where they work in fishing (cod, halibut, shrimp) and associated industries; Godthåb, Frederikshåb and Holsteinsborg are the principal centres. Other activities include sheep-farming in the south, seal-hunting in the north and some mining (marble, coal, lead, zinc and cryolite). Deposits near Ivigtut are the world's only commercial source of cryolite, used in making ceramic glazes and aluminium. There are important meteorological and radio stations on the island.

Canada

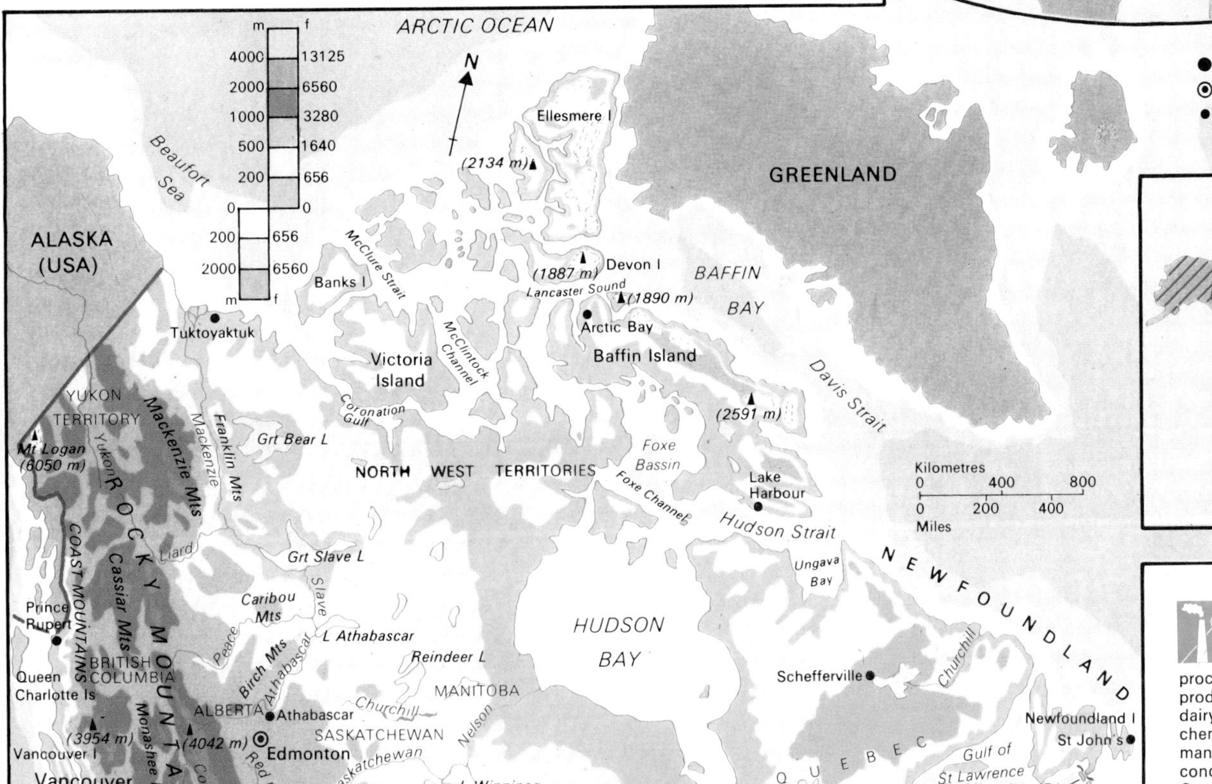

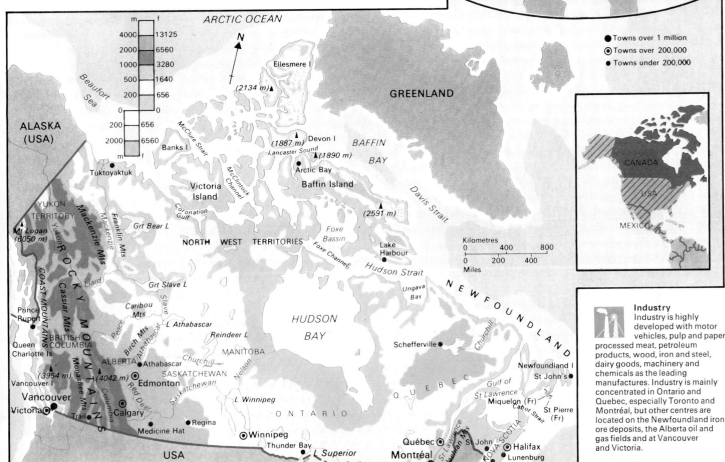

Area
9,976,185 km²/3,851,809 sq miles
Location
41°40′—83°10′ N
52°40′—141° W
Population
22,830,000 (1975)
Population density
2 per km²/6 per sq mile
Capital
Ottawa: 613,000 (1972)
Largest city
Montréal: 2,761,000 (1972)
Languages
English, French
Major imports
vehicles, machinery, foods, metal manufactures, chemicals, textiles
Major exports
vehicles, machinery, ores and metals, wheat, other edible products, lumber, petroleum, newsprint, pulp
Currency
dollar (1 dollar = 100 cents)
Gross National Product
160,000 million US dollars (1975)
Status
independent federal state

Forestry

Canada's forests, which cover a third of the country, stretch from the Atlantic to the Pacific. About 80% are coniferous (spruce, fir, pine, cedar, hemlock) but some mixed forest occurs near the southeastern border. Forestry and allied industries are most important in British Columbia, Québec and Ontario. Forest products provide 12% of total exports and Canada ranks as the world's leading producer of newsprint and the second largest producer of wood.

Physical features

Canada is the world's second largest country. The Canadian shield underlies half the territory; this core of very old, hard rock spreads from the Arctic Ocean and the Mackenzie river, down to Lakes Superior and Huron and the St Lawrence and up into Newfoundland. Glacial action has left the area thin-soiled and badly drained with many lakes and swamps. Flat plains stretch between the shield's western rim and the Rockies. To the southeast lie peninsular Ontario and the St Lawrence valley—both fertile and densely populated regions. Uplands west of the river are an extension of the Appalachians. Western Canada consists of a central plateau flanked by the Rockies, which rise to over 3,000 m, and by the Coast Mts, which climb steeply from the sea and reach 6,050 m at Mt Logan. There are three main river systems: the Great Lakes/St Lawrence river to the Atlantic; the Saskatchewan/Nelson system draining into Hudson Bay and Canada's longest river, the Mackenzie (4,241 km), flowing into the Arctic Ocean.

Climate

Canada has a continental climate with mountain barriers limiting ocean influences. Winters are cold: January averages —31°C at Arctic Bay, —20°C at Winnipeg. Summers are cool in the north warm in the south (6°C at Arctic Bay in July, 19°C at Winnipeg). Most areas have 75-130 cm of rain; the Coast Mts have over 250 cm.

Agriculture

Although Canada is basically an industrial country, agriculture is still important and accounts for 12% of total exports. Farmland, covering less than 8% of the country, lies mostly south of 55°N and is concentrated on the west. Canada's main crop, spring wheat, is grown on the Prairies (southern Alberta, Saskatchewan and Manitoba) and 75% is exported. Other Prairie crops are oats, barley and oilseeds. British Columbia is noted for fruit, particularly apples. Southern Ontario and Québec specialize in maize, tobacco, fruit and dairying (73% of Canada's milk comes from this region). Meat animals are reared in Ontario, Quebec, the Prairies and northern British Columbia.

Fishing

Canada is the world's fourth largest fish exporter with 65% of the catch exported. About 85% of the catch comes from the Atlantic where the main species are cod (off Newfoundland), herring, halibut and lobster. Salmon is caught off the west coast. The Great Lakes yield eel, whitefish and pickerel. St John, Lunenburg, Yarmouth and Halifax in the east, and Vancouver and Prince Rupert in the west are fishing ports.

Mining

Canada has immense mineral wealth and leads the world in output of nickel, zinc and asbestos. It holds second place for uranium, sulphur and molybdenum, exports more iron ore than any other country and produces a large share of the world's gold, lead, potash, silver and copper. The chief mining regions are west Newfoundland (iron ore), south Québec (asbestos, copper, gold), southeast Ontario (copper, zinc, nickel, lead, uranium, gold and silver) and southeast British Columbia (zinc). Sudbury (Ontario) and Trail (British Columbia) are important mining centres. About 65% of minerals are exported, accounting for 25% of total exports.

Energy

Canada is self-sufficient in energy resources with petroleum its leading mineral. Alberta produces 85% of petroleum requirements, 40% of the coal and some natural gas. Further vast reserves of oil and natural gas occur in the Athabasca tar sands and there are valuable coal fields in British Columbia, Saskatchewan and Nova Scotia. Hydro-electric stations generate 75% of electricity with major plants located on the Churchill, St Lawrence, Niagara, Peace and Columbia rivers.

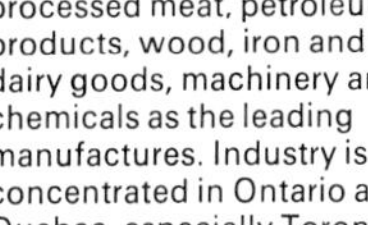

Industry

Industry is highly developed with motor vehicles, pulp and paper, processed meat, petroleum products, wood, iron and steel, dairy goods, machinery and chemicals as the leading manufactures. Industry is mainly concentrated in Ontario and Quebec, especially Toronto and Montréal, but other centres are located on the Newfoundland iron ore deposits, the Alberta oil and gas fields and at Vancouver and Victoria.

Transport

Transport plays a vital role in a country as large as Canada. Passenger traffic is mainly by road and air, while freight moves by road, rail and water. The 829,300 km road network includes the Trans-Canada Highway (7,776 km), the world's longest paved road. There are also two trans-continental railways. The St Lawrence Seaway/Great Lakes system is one of the world's main commercial waterways: the chief cargoes are wheat (downbound) and iron ore (upbound). Increased trade with Japan has made Vancouver the leading port with Montréal second; other major ports are Halifax, St John, Québec, Toronto, Hamilton and Thunder Bay.

Towns

About 75% of Canadians live in urban areas, mainly in the south. Ontario and Québec account for two-thirds of the population. In particular, peninsular Ontario and the St Lawrence valley are highly urbanized and include Montréal, Toronto (2,672,000), Ottawa, Hamilton and Québec. Other centres are Winnipeg, Edmonton and Calgary in the Prairies, and Vancouver (1,098,000) in the west.

St Pierre & Miquelon

The French Overseas Territory of St Pierre and Miquelon, lying 25 km off the south coast of Newfoundland, consists of 8 small rocky islands with a total area of 242 km² and 5,000 inhabitants. The chief economic activity is cod-fishing with salted, frozen, smoked and canned fish as the main exports.

Mexico

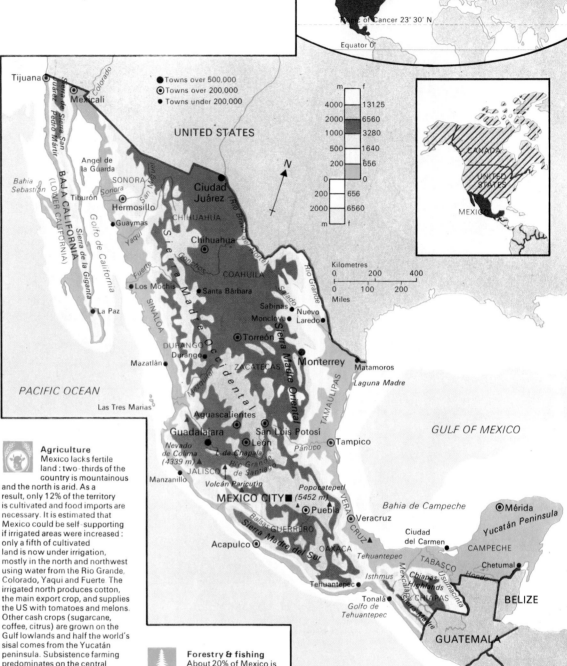

Area
1,972,547 km²/761,601 sq miles
Location
14°30'—32°40' N
86°50'—117°10' W
Population
60,145,000 (1975)
Population density
30 per km²/79 per sq mile
Capital and largest city
Mexico City: 8,600,000 (1975)
Language
Spanish
Major imports
machinery, vehicles, fertilizers, food, steel, paper
Major exports
cotton, coffee, oil, zinc, silver, shrimps, vegetables, machinery
Currency
peso (1 peso = 100 centavos)
Gross National Product
34,000 million US dollars (1971)
Status
federal republic

Physical features

Mountains cover most of Mexico. The chief feature is the wedge-shaped central plateau with its base along the US border and its apex south of Mexico City. The northern part of the plateau, averaging 1,200 m altitude, contains wide shallow basins and isolated upland blocks. It is an arid region with only two permanent rivers, the Rio Grande and its tributary, the Conchos. Southwards, the plateau becomes higher (2,500 m) and more mountainous—ending in a belt of snow-capped volcanoes including the still active Popocatepetl (5,452 m). The central plateau is bounded on the west and east by the steep and rugged Sierra Madre ranges, the western chain rising to over 3,000 m. Beyond the volcanic zone, the southern part of the country consists of a high, mountainous plateau crossed by deep river valleys. In the southeast are the Chiapas uplands. Lowland Mexico is limited to the narrow Pacific coast, the wide swampy plain bordering the Gulf, the Tehuantepec isthmus and the Yucatán peninsula. The Santiago, Pánuco and Balsas are major rivers.

Climate

Altitude has a major influence on Mexico's climate with temperatures of 27°C on the lowlands, 21°C on the central plateau and 15°C in the mountains. Rainfall, occurring mostly in summer, varies greatly from one region to another. The eastern lowlands and the south are the wettest parts (100 to 300 cm of rain a year), being in the path of the trade winds. The central plateau, sheltered by the Sierra, is dry (60 cm near Mexico City to under 10 cm in the north). The northern Pacific coast and lower California are also arid, but in the southwest, the Sierra and Chiapas highlands receive up to 200 cm.

Flora & fauna

Lowland vegetation consists of rainforest in wet areas, savanna and scrub in drier parts. In the mountains, mixed forest occurs up to 1,800 m with pine and fir on higher slopes. Grasslands cover the central plateau giving way northwards to scrub, cacti and desert. Wildlife includes jaguars, pumas, monkeys, iguanas, toucans and parrots.

Agriculture

Mexico lacks fertile land: two-thirds of the country is mountainous and the north is arid. As a result, only 12% of the territory is cultivated and food imports are necessary. It is estimated that Mexico could be self-supporting if irrigated areas were increased: only a fifth of cultivated land is now under irrigation, mostly in the north and northwest using water from the Rio Grande, Colorado, Yaqui and Fuerte. The irrigated north produces cotton, the main export crop, and supplies the US with tomatoes and melons. Other cash crops (sugarcane, coffee, citrus) are grown on the Gulf lowlands and half the world's sisal comes from the Yucatán peninsula. Subsistence farming predominates on the central plateau and in the south. Maize, grown on 50% of all arable land, is the basic food crop followed by wheat, beans and rice. Beef cattle are reared on large ranches in the semi-arid north. There is some small-scale dairying in the centre and south.

Mining

Mining, the main industry, plays a significant part in the economy. Mexico has considerable energy resources. Oilfields, mostly on the Gulf lowlands (Tamaulipas, Veracruz, Campeche, Tabasco, Chiapas), supply all the country's petroleum and natural gas. There are also big reserves of coal: Sabinas is the main producing area. Mexico leads the world in silver production with the principal mines (many worked for centuries) on the central plateau. These same mines yield lead, zinc and copper. Mexico is also a major world producer of sulphur, found in the Veracruz region. Other important minerals are iron ore (mined at Durango) and manganese. Large deposits of uranium and phosphates exist.

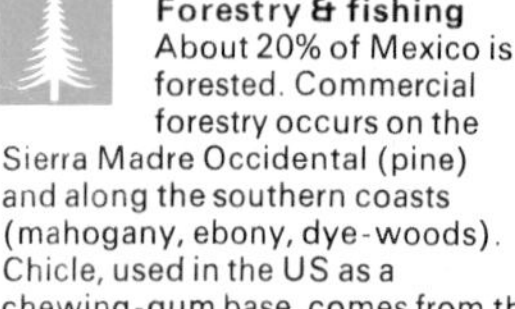

Forestry & fishing

About 20% of Mexico is forested. Commercial forestry occurs on the Sierra Madre Occidental (pine) and along the southern coasts (mahogany, ebony, dye-woods). Chicle, used in the US as a chewing-gum base, comes from the forests of the Yucatán peninsula. Fishing is important off the 9,660 km-long coast, particularly in the Pacific. The catch includes sardine, tuna and shrimp.

Industry

The past few decades have seen considerable industrial growth. The main sectors are textiles, steel and petrochemicals. The textile industry, based on cotton from the north, is located at Mexico City, Puebla, León, Guadalajara and Veracruz. Steel manufacture, using Durango ore and Sabinas coal, is centred on Monterrey and Monclova. Fruit, meat and fish canning and other food processing is widespread. The Mexico City area is the chief industrial region, accounting for over 50% of all manufactures. Monterrey is the hub of the second manufacturing zone.

Tourism

Tourism accounts for 40% of foreign earnings. Visitors, 80% from the US and Canada, are attracted by the beaches (Acapulco is world famous), mountain scenery and the remains of the Mayan and Aztec civilizations.

Transport

Transport systems have been improved to meet the growing demands of tourism and economic development. Hard-surfaced roads, totalling 85,000 km, carry 70% of the country's passenger traffic and 60% of its freight. The 25,000 km rail network is densest on the central plateau. In places mountains make road and rail traffic difficult but this is overcome by an extensive internal air service. There are 50 seaports of which the most important are Veracruz, Tampico and Manzanillo.

People & cities

About 70% of Mexicans are *mestizo* (of mixed white and American Indian descent), 20% are white and 10% Indian. Half the population lives in towns and 25% of these in Mexico City where densities exceed 5,000 per km². Mexico City, built on the site of Tenochtitlan (the ancient Aztec capital), is expanding rapidly and has doubled its population since 1960. Consequently, overcrowding and shanty-town growth are major problems. Its central position has stimulated its development as the chief commercial and manufacturing centre and as the focus of national transport systems. The capital's industry is powered by hydroelectricity from installations in the nearby mountains and by oil and gas piped from the Gulf fields. Other major cities are Guadalajara (2 m) and Monterrey (1.5 m).

Honduras

Nicaragua

Honduras and Nicaragua

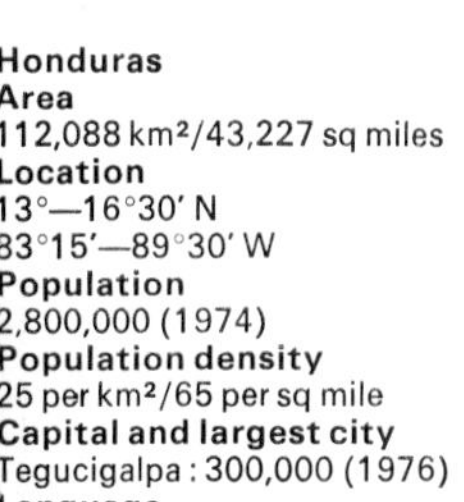

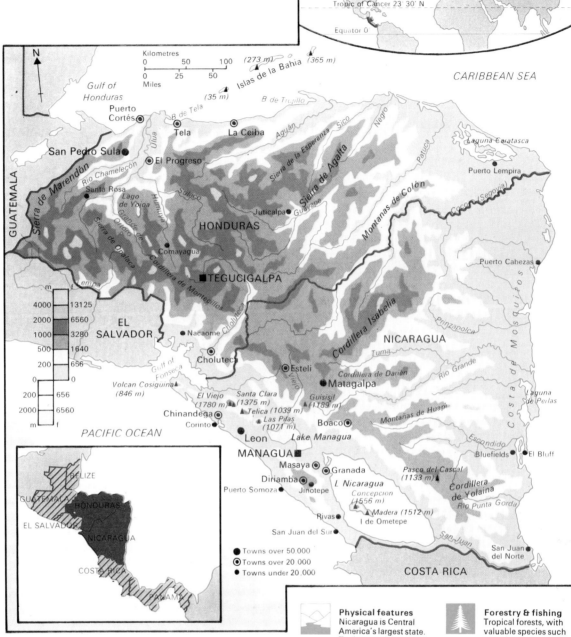

Honduras
Area
112,088 km²/43,227 sq miles
Location
13°—16°30′ N
83°15′—89°30′ W
Population
2,800,000 (1974)
Population density
25 per km²/65 per sq mile
Capital and largest city
Tegucigalpa: 300,000 (1976)
Language
Spanish
Major imports
machinery and transport equipment, fuels, chemicals, foods
Major exports
bananas, coffee, timber, lead and zinc, meat, sugar, tobacco
Currency
lempira (1 lempira = 100 centavos)
Gross National Product
970 million US dollars (1975)
Status
republic

Physical features
Honduras is a mountainous country. Ranges, lying east-west, cover most of the territory and are highest in the south where rugged peaks rise to 2,500 m. The mountains enclose numerous basins with fertile volcanic soils. Lowland areas are limited to the small Pacific coastal plain and the alluvial valleys formed by rivers draining into the Caribbean Sea.

Climate
The Caribbean coast is hot and humid with average temperatures of 27°C and 250 cm of rain. Inland, the tropical climate is modified by altitude: at 2,000 m temperatures average 15°C and, in central areas, rainfall seldom exceeds 100 cm. The country is exposed to hurricanes and was devastated by one in 1974.

Flora & fauna
Dense tropical rain-forest occurs along the Caribbean coast and the northern margin of the highlands; inland, savanna grasslands and pine forests predominate. The varied wildlife includes jaguars, pumas, wild pigs, deer, crocodiles, alligators and many exotic birds.

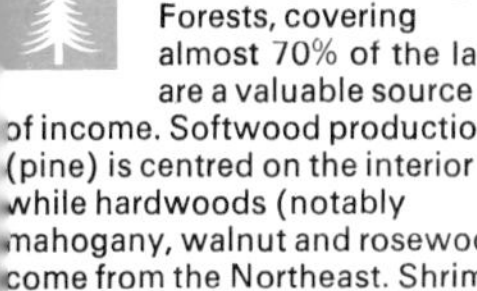

Forestry & fishing
Forests, covering almost 70% of the land, are a valuable source of income. Softwood production (pine) is centred on the interior while hardwoods (notably mahogany, walnut and rosewood) come from the Northeast. Shrimp and lobster fishing, mainly on the Caribbean, is being developed.

Agriculture
Honduras is the poorest Central American state and its backward economy depends largely on agriculture. Bananas, the chief export, are grown on plantations along the northern coast and Honduras ranks as a leading world producer. Coffee, from upland zones, is the second important cash crop. Some sugar, cotton and plantains are also exported. Food crops include maize, beans and rice. Livestock is important, particularly in the southern highlands. Less than a quarter of the country is under cultivation.

Mining & industry
The search for precious metals first drew the Spanish conquerors to the area in the 16th century and some gold and silver are still worked. Lead and zinc, however, are far more important and are exported. Deposits of copper, iron, asbestos and platinum are, so far, unexploited. Industry is small-scale and very limited: products include cement, sugar, cigarettes, beer, furniture, flour and clothing. San Pedro Sula is the most important manufacturing centre.

Transport
Communications are inadequate. Most of the roads, totalling 6,200 km, are unpaved and the 1,000 km rail network primarily serves the banana plantations in the north. As road and rail systems are so poor, internal air services (linking some 40 centres) are of vital importance. The main ports, Puerto Cortés, Tela, La Ceiba and Trujillo, are all on the Caribbean, but a new port is under construction on the Pacific.

Nicaragua
Area
148,000 km²/57,143 sq miles
Location
10°45′—15°10′ N
83°15′—87°40′ W
Population
2,200,000 (1975)
Population density
15 per km²/38 per sq mile
Capital and largest city
Managua: 282,000 (1974)
Language
Spanish
Major imports
manufactured goods, machinery, vehicles, chemicals, food
Major exports
coffee, cotton, meat, sugar, timber, bananas
Currency
córdoba (1 córdoba = 100 centavos)
Gross National Product
1,540 million US dollars (1975)
Status
republic

Climate
Temperatures vary from 26°C on the lowlands to 18°C in the mountains. Rainfall is heavy (over 350 cm) on the east coast.

Physical features
Nicaragua is Central America's largest state. To the east lies a wide, swampy plain dissected by river valleys. The central region consists of a mountain block, 1,500 to 2,000 m high, which extends southwards like a wedge with its base on the Honduran border. West of the highlands is a depression which contains Lakes Managua and Nicaragua as well as several active volcanoes. A chain of hills separates the depression from the forested Pacific coastlands.

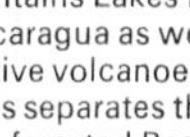

Agriculture
Although agriculture employs 65% of the workforce and provides 75% of exports, farmland occupies only 15% of the total area—mostly in the western half of the country. The principal cash crops are coffee (from the lower mountain slopes) and cotton, sugar and bananas from the Pacific coastlands. Some cocoa, tobacco and sesame seed are also exported. Maize, rice, sorghum, beans, oranges, pineapples and sweet potatoes are grown for domestic consumption. About 50% of agricultural land, mostly in the southern highlands, is pasture and beef is a leading export.

Forestry & fishing
Tropical forests, with valuable species such as mahogany, cedar and rosewood, cover 36% of the country. Production is centred on the Pacific plain and the eastern river valleys. Fishing is important off both coasts; shrimp and lobster are exported.

Mining & industry
Various minerals occur in northern Nicaragua but, so far, gold, silver and copper are the only ones mined. The manufacturing sector is expanding; products include soluble coffee, canned meat, cocoa powder, plywood, cigarettes, textiles, cement, flour, dairy foods and shoes.

Transport
Economic development is hampered by poor communications. Roads are mostly unpaved; the rail network, linking major towns in the west, totals only 350 km; air services are limited. Corinto, handling 60% of all trade, is the main seaport followed by Puerto Somoza, San Juan del Sur, Puerto Cabezas and El Bluff. The state airline, LANCIA, operates overseas and internal flights from Managua airport.

Guatemala, Belize and El Salvador

Above: **El Salvador**
Above left: **Guatemala**
Left: **Belize**

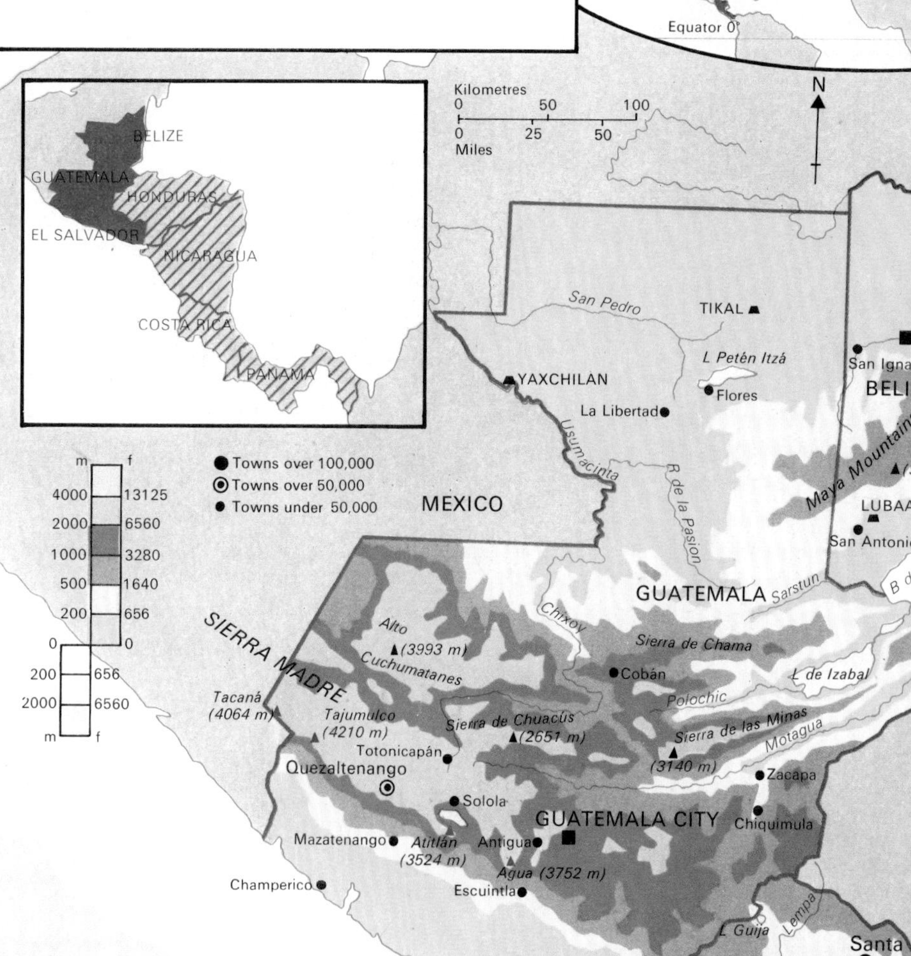

Guatemala
Area
108,889 km²/42,042 sq miles
Location
13°40′—17°50′ N
88°15′—92°15′ W
Population
5,540,000 (1973)
Population density
51 per km²/132 per sq mile
Capital and largest city
Guatemala City: 800,000 (1973)
Language
Spanish
Major imports
machinery, vehicles, chemicals, fuels, foods
Major exports
coffee, cotton, bananas, sugar, meat
Currency
quetzal (1 quetzal = 100 centavos)
Gross National Product
3,500 million US dollars (1975)
Status
republic

The land
The Sierra Madre range dominates southern Guatemala and includes a chain of volcanic peaks rising to over 3,500 m; dormant Tajumulco (4,210 m) is the country's highest point. In the south, the highlands fall sharply to the narrow Pacific plain but northwards they drop gently to a low limestone plateau covered with tropical forest. The main river, the Motagua, drains into the Caribbean. Temperatures decrease from 28°C on the lowlands to 20°C in the mountains; rain occurs in summer on the Pacific coast but all year round on the Caribbean side. The Pacific coast is most densely populated.

Farming & forestry
Agriculture is the basis of the economy. The leading export crops are coffee (grown on the fertile mountain soils), cotton and sugar (on the Pacific coastal plain) and bananas (in the Motagua valley). Guatemala is also a major world supplier of chicle (a chewing-gum base) and essential oils (citronella and lemon grass). Maize, beans and rice are cultivated for food. Livestock farming, mostly beef cattle, is important. As the northern forests are largely inaccessible, valuable hardwoods remain underexploited.

Mining & industry
Various minerals occur but production is limited to nickel, zinc and lead; oil deposits on the northern plateau are being developed. The manufacturing sector includes food-processing, textiles, chemicals and electrical goods, but expansion is checked by inadequate power supplies. Tourism is being encouraged: the main assets are the spectacular mountain scenery and vestiges of Mayan and pre-Mayan civilization.

Transport
The 13,000 km road network, densest in the south, is being improved and expanded. Railways, which total 1,000 km, link the Pacific and Caribbean coasts and connect Guatemala with neighbouring Mexico and El Salvador. Puerto Barrios and Champerico are the chief ports. There is an international airport.

El Salvador
Area
21,393 km²/8,236 sq miles
Location
13°10′—14°25′ N
87°40′—90°10′ W
Population
4,000,000 (1976)
Population density
187 per km²/486 per sq mile
Capital and largest city
San Salvador: 500,000 (1976)
Language
Spanish
Major imports
chemicals, machinery, transport equipment, fuels, food
Major exports
coffee, cotton, sugar, shrimps
Currency
colón (1 colón = 100 centavos)
Gross National Product
1,800 million US dollars (1975)
Status
republic

The land
El Salvador, the smallest and most densely populated of the Central American republics, is a highland country. Behind the Pacific coast, two parallel chains of volcanoes rise to over 1,500 m; Izalco still shows signs of activity. The ranges enclose a central plateau some 600 m high where most of the population dwell. Lowland areas comprise the narrow coastal plain and the valley of the Lempa, the main river. The coast is hot but temperatures decrease inland with altitude: San Salvador (670 m) averages 23°C. The wet season, with up to 170 cm of rain lasts from May to October.

Farming & forestry
El Salvador is primarily agricultural: about 30% of the land is used for crops and 30% for pasture. The main cash crop, coffee, provides 50% of all exports and is grown on the rich volcanic soils of the plateau and lower slopes. Cotton, another major export, is cultivated on the coastal plain. Sugar production is increasing. Rice and maize are the basic food crops. Forests cover a third of the country from which cedar and walnut lumber, mahogany and balsam are produced. El Salvador is the world's chief source of balsam—a medicinal gum.

Industry
El Salvador is the most industrialized state in Central America. Many industries are based on agriculture and include sugar refining, flour milling and cotton spinning; others, such as chemicals and engineering, rely on imported materials. Fishing is important and frozen shrimps are exported. Industrial development owes much to good transport systems and to the development of hydro-power resources. The main ports are Acajutla, La Libertad and La Union and there is a rail link to the Caribbean port of Puerto Barrios in Guatemala. Mountain scenery, Mayan remains and surf beaches are tourist attractions.

Belize
Area
22,966 km²/8,867 sq miles
Location
15°55′—18°30′ N
88°10′—89°10′ W
Population
130,000 (1973)
Population density
6 per km²/15 per sq mile
Capital
Belmopan: 4,000 (1974)
Largest city
Belize City: 39,000 (1970)
Language
English
Major imports
machinery, vehicles, foods
Major exports
sugar, citrus, timber, lobsters
Currency
dollar (1 dollar = 100 cents)
Gross National Product
76 million US dollars (1972)
Status
UK dependent territory

Transport

Although swamp, jungle and mountain hamper communications, there is a good all-weather road network. Belize City and Stann Creek are the main ports.

The land
Swamps, lakes and sluggish rivers characterize the low-lying north. In contrast, southern Belize is dominated by the Maya Mountains which rise steeply from the coastal plain to over 1,000 m. Offshore, a chain of coral cays forms a long barrier reef. The climate is hot (26°C) with rainfall increasing from 125 cm in the north to 460 cm in the south. Hurricanes occasionally ravage the coast.

The economy
Belize's weak economy is largely based on farming and forestry. Cultivated land, accounting for 25% of the total area, is concentrated along the coast and in forest clearings. The chief cash crops are sugar, citrus (mainly grapefruit) and bananas. Forests, covering 60% of the country, are a valuable resource: mahogany, rosewood and cedar are the principal species exported. Fishing is important and lobsters are supplied to the US. Industry, confined to processing primary products, is very limited.

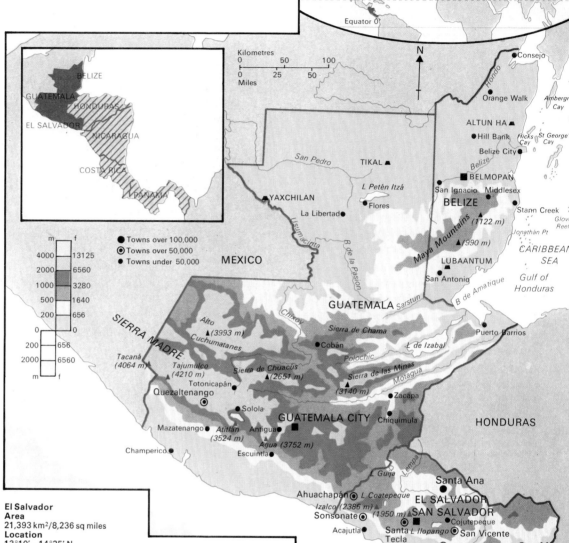

Costa Rica

Panama

Costa Rica and Panama

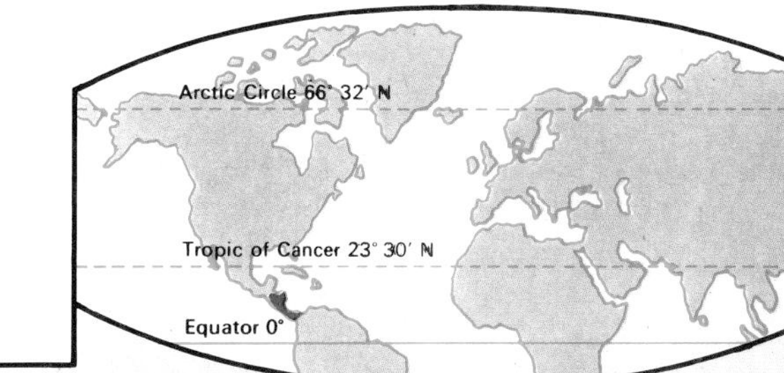

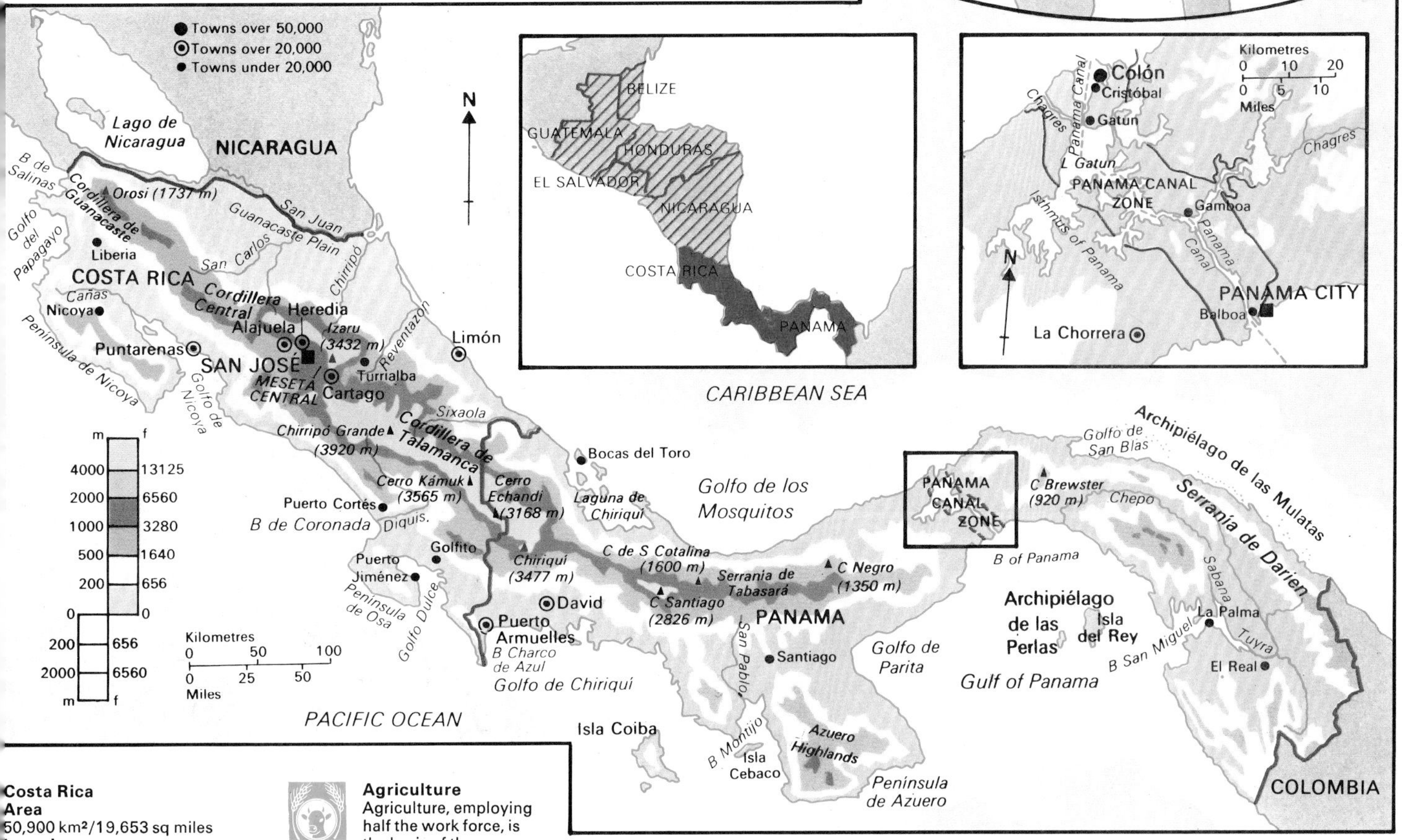

Costa Rica
Area
50,900 km²/19,653 sq miles
Location
8°—11°15′ N
82°35′—85°55′ W
Population
1,990,000 (1976)
Population density
39 per km²/101 per sq mile
Capital and largest city
San José: 228,000 (1976)
Language
Spanish
Major imports
manufactures, machinery, chemicals
Major exports
coffee, bananas, sugar, live animals and meat, cocoa
Currency
colón (1 colón = 100 centimos)
Gross National Product
1,870 million US dollars (1975)
Status
republic

Physical features

Mountains (1,000 to 3,600 m high) cover most of Costa Rica. The three principal blocks, lying northwest-southeast, are the Guanacaste, Central and Talamanca ranges. The Guanacaste and Central Mountains contain active volcanoes including Izaru (3,432 m). The Cordillera Central flanks the Meseta Central, a tableland 1,000 to 1,500m above sea level, which is the country's economic hub. Lowland Costa Rica consists of the narrow Pacific seaboard, the Caribbean coastland (a swampy forested area, widest in the north) and the Guanacaste plain (between the mountains and the Nicoya peninsula).

Climate

The lowlands have a hot, humid tropical climate, but more temperate conditions characterize the Meseta Central. Rainfall is heaviest on the Caribbean coast.

Agriculture

Agriculture, employing half the work force, is the basis of the economy. The Meseta Central, the chief farming region, provides most of the country's coffee, sugar and dairy produce plus a large share of food such as maize, beans and potatoes. Coffee accounts for 50% of all exports. Bananas, the second main cash crop, are grown on the coastal lowlands with the Caribbean zone also producing hemp and cocoa. Stock-raising is important on the Guanacaste plain. Forestry and fishing are both underdeveloped.

Mining & industry

Mineral output is limited to gold, limestone and salt (extracted from the sea). Bauxite and manganese also occur. Manufacturing is small-scale: products include textiles, foodstuffs, fertilizers, furniture, pharmaceuticals, cement and tyres. Most industry is located on the Meseta and at Limón and Puntarenas. The exploitation of hydro-power resources in the Cordillera Central is aiding industrial development.

Transport

The Meseta Central, home of 65% of the population, is the focal point of Costa Rica's transport systems. Roads connect San José to the principal towns: Alajuela, Heredia, Cartago, Turrialba—all on the Meseta. The capital is also linked by the Pan-American Highway to Nicaragua and Panama and by rail to the ports of Limón and Puntarenas. Golfito is the third major port. The state airline, LACSA, provides overseas and domestic services.

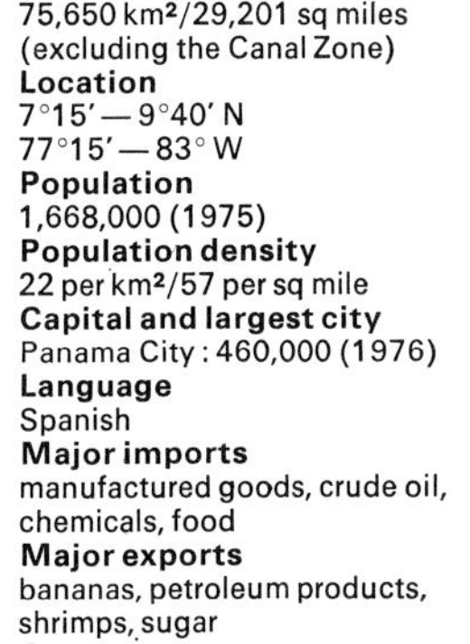

Panama
Area
75,650 km²/29,201 sq miles (excluding the Canal Zone)
Location
7°15′—9°40′ N
77°15′—83° W
Population
1,668,000 (1975)
Population density
22 per km²/57 per sq mile
Capital and largest city
Panama City: 460,000 (1976)
Language
Spanish
Major imports
manufactured goods, crude oil, chemicals, food
Major exports
bananas, petroleum products, shrimps, sugar
Currency
balboa (1 balboa = 100 centésimos)
Gross National Product
2,130 million US dollars (1975)
Status
republic

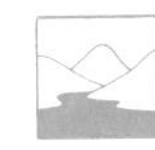

The land

Panama is a mountainous country with three dominant highland blocks. A central ridge, extending westwards from the canal, contains several volcanic cones near the Costa Rican border, including Chiriquí (3,477 m). In the southwest are the Azuero highlands, while east of the canal a range runs parallel to the coast into Colombia. Lowland areas comprise narrow coastal plains and fertile basins between the ranges. The lowlands are hot (27°C) and humid; mountain areas are cooler (17°C). Rainfall (May to November) is heaviest by the Caribbean (300 cm). Tropical forest predominates with savanna on the drier, Pacific coast.

Agriculture

Despite Panama s arable potential (rich soil and favourable climate) only 14% of the land is cultivated. Leading cash crops are bananas (grown round the Gulf of Panama and along the northeast), sugar (from the Perita Gulf lowlands), coffee (from the western uplands) and some cocoa, hemp and coconuts. Rice, maize and cassava are produced for food; cattle are raised on the Pacific savannas.

Forestry & fishing

Forests cover 60% of the country but are largely unexploited except for some production of mahogany. There is a well developed shrimp-fishing industry centred on Bocas del Toro, Chiriquí and the Gulf of Panama. Shrimps are a major export.

Mining & industry

There is little mining. Some limestone and salt are worked, but deposits of manganese, iron, copper and bauxite are so far undeveloped. Industries include oil-refining, food-processing, cement and clothing. In addition to farming, fishing and industry, receipts from the canal and services to the Canal Zone are vital sources of income.

People

About 35% of the people (of European, Indian and Negro descent) live in Panama City and Colón (94 000) both enclaves in the Canal Zone. The rural population is mostly based on the Pacific coast, west of the canal.

Transport

The 7,000 km road network includes a section of the Pan-American Highway which runs the length of the country. The principal railway connects Cristóbal port (near Colón) with Panama City; most cargo destined for the capital is unloaded at Cristóbal and brought overland by rail. The Panamanian merchant fleet is one of the world's largest; ships are mainly foreign owned but registered in Panama because of low fees and lenient regulations. All maritime traffic for Colón and Panama is handled by the canal ports of Cristóbal and Balboa.

The Panama Canal Zone

The US-controlled Canal Zone is a narrow strip of land flanking the Canal. Extending 8 km on each side of the waterway, the Zone has a total area of 1,673 km² and about 50,000 inhabitants (mostly employed by the Panama Canal Company or the Canal Zone Government). The canal itself, opened in 1914, is 82 km long and cuts northwest to southeast across the isthmus from Cristóbal on the Caribbean to Balboa on the Pacific. By eliminating the long haul round Cape Horn, the canal has transformed trade between, on the one hand, the east coast of the Americas, Europe and the West Indies and, on the other, the west coast of the Americas, Australia and Asia. Coal, oil, grain, ores and metals are the principal cargoes carried by the 15,000 vessels that pass through the canal each year. The average transit time is 15 hours, including a 7-hour wait.

Bahamas

Cuba

Caribbean Islands 1

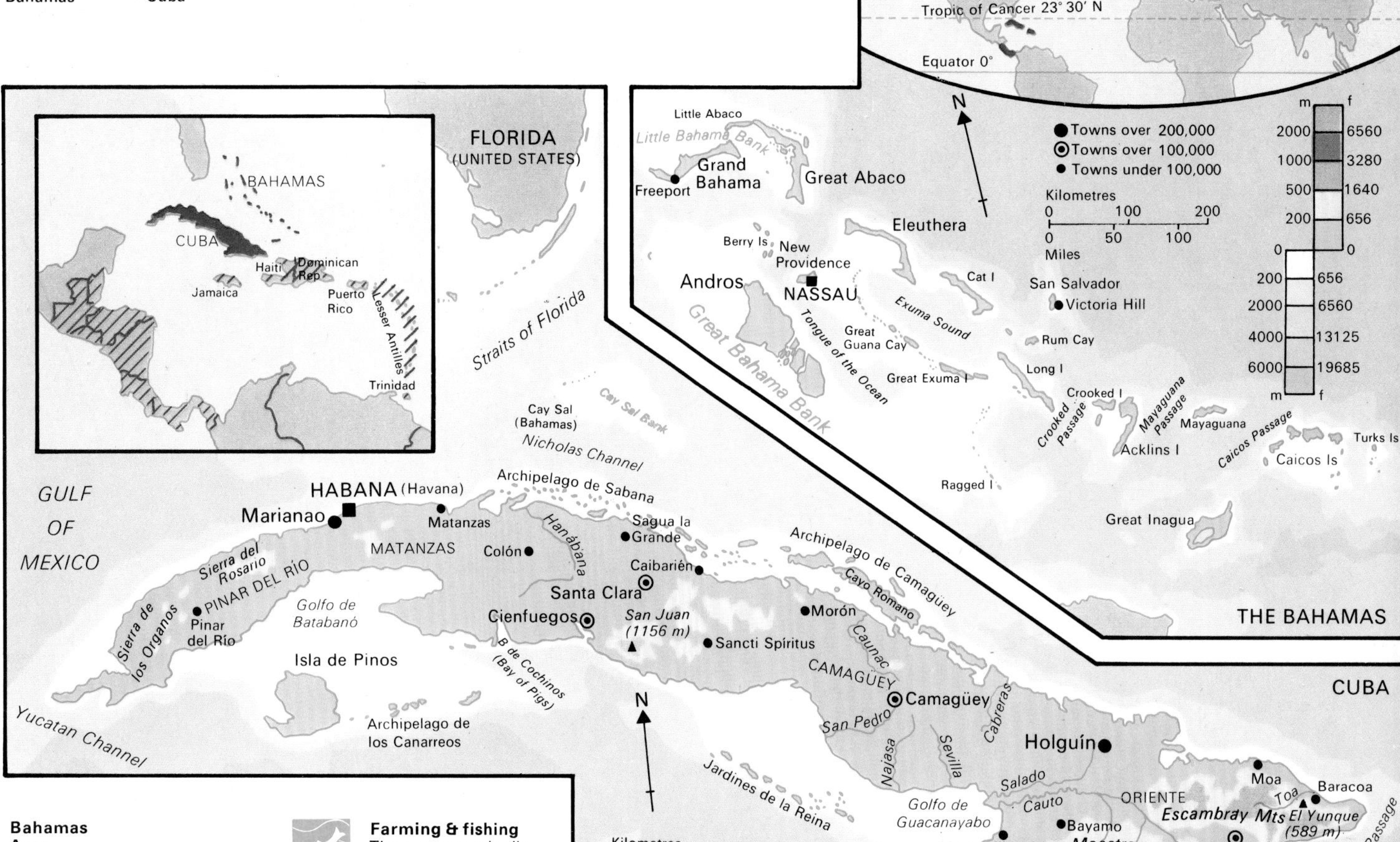

Bahamas
Area
11,396 km²/4,400 sq miles
Location
21°—27°17′ N
72°45′—81°10′ W
Population
218,000 (1973)
Population density
19 per km²/50 per sq mile
Capital and largest city
Nassau : 101,500 (1970)
Language
English
Major imports
crude oil, foods, machinery, vehicles
Major exports
petroleum, petrochemicals, cement, rum
Currency
dollar (1 dollar = 100 cents)
Gross National Product
400 million US dollars (1972)
Status
parliamentary state

Physical features
The Bahamas, extending 1,200 km southeastwards from Florida, consist of some 700 islands and over 2,000 cays and rocks ; only 30 islands are inhabited. The archipelago, formed of coralline limestone, represents the highest parts of two submarine banks : the Little Bahama Bank and the Great Bahama Bank. All the islands are flat with sandy beaches, saltmarsh and mangrove along the coast. Inland, bare rock and cacti characterize the dry, eastern islands, while forests of pine and mahogany occur in the wetter west. Andros is the largest island, but New Providence is the most important and most populous, with 60% of the total population.

Climate
The climate is sub-tropical : winters are modified by the Gulf Stream and are mild (21°C) but summers are hot (29°C). Rain ranges from 75 cm in the east to 120 cm in the west.

Farming & fishing
The porous coral soils are infertile and less than 2% of the land is cultivated. Some peas, beans, papayas, bananas and mangoes are grown by the Negro population but large food imports are necessary. A few plantations produce tomatoes, cucumbers, onions, pineapples and citrus for export. Fishing is more profitable : the catch is mostly consumed locally, but some crayfish is frozen and sent to Florida.

Industry
The huge oil-tanker terminal at Freeport with its refinery and petrochemical complex is the main source of income. Tourism is next in importance : the sunny beaches and warm seas make the Bahamas a luxury resort. There is little other industry except for some rum-distilling, cement manufacture, saw-milling, fruit-canning and fish-freezing. Salt, produced by evaporation, is exported.

Transport
The growth of tourism has resulted in good sea and air links with the outside world, especially North America. There are numerous inter-island boat and plane services. Roads on New Providence and Grand Bahama are hard-surfaced and fairly extensive, but are less developed on the other islands.

Turks & Caicos
The Turks and Caicos Islands, at the southeast end of the Bahamas, are a British Colony. The group, consisting of six inhabited islands and about 30 cays, has a total area of 430 km². The 6,000 islanders live by fishing : crayfish provide 90% of all exports. Salt and conch shells are also exported. Tourism is being developed.

Cuba
Area
110,922 km²/42,827 sq miles
Location
19°52′–23°5′ N
74°10′—85° W
Population
9,200,000 (1974)
Population density
83 per km²/215 per sq mile
Capital and largest city
Habana : 1,755,000 (1970)
Language
Spanish
Major imports
food, machinery, transport equipment, fuels, chemicals
Major exports
sugar, nickel, tobacco, fish, citrus
Currency
peso (1 peso = 100 centavos)
Gross National Product
4,500 million US dollars (1971)
Status
republic

Physical features
Cuba, the largest and most westerly of the Caribbean islands, is 1,200 km long but only 32-145 km wide. The coast is swampy, especially in the south, and is fringed with reefs, sandbanks and about 1,600 islands, including the large, forested Isla de Pinos (3,060 km²). Broad plains and low hills cover most of Cuba. The main highlands are the Sierra de los Organos and the Sierra del Rosario in the west, the Escambray Mountains in the centre and, in the east, the Sierra Maestra with Pico Turquino (2,005 m), Cuba's highest point. The rivers are mostly short, swift-flowing and seasonal.

Climate
The moderating effect of constant trade winds gives Cuba a mild climate ; Habana averages 22°C in winter, 28°C in summer. During the wet season (May-November), 130 cm of rain falls on the lowlands rising to 250 cm in the mountains.

Agriculture
Sugar, accounting for 80% of exports, is the basis of the economy ; it is grown throughout the island and Cuba ranks as the world's second largest sugar producer. Tobacco, cultivated in the west, is next in importance with coffee, from the eastern highland slopes, citrus and pineapples also exported. Rice is the staple food. Other major crops are pangola (for fodder), maize, potatoes, henequen and kenaf fibres (both used for sacking) and cotton. Dairy and beef cattle are kept on the central and eastern plains. Cuban agriculture is state controlled and 60% of farmland is state-owned.

Forestry & fishing
Less than 15% of the land is forested. Tropical hardwoods cover high slopes in the west while pine grows in the eastern mountains and on Isla de Pinos. To increase timber output and aid soil conservation, new forests are being planted—mostly of eucalyptus, pine and some cedar (for cigar cases). Fishing is organized into co-operatives and is expanding ; Manzanillo and Habana are major centres.

Mining
Cuba has considerable mineral wealth. There are extensive nickel deposits in the eastern mountains and production is centred on Moa where there is a nickel and cobalt smelter. Manganese and copper occur in large quantities in the Sierra Maestra and in the western province of Pinar del Río and chromite is mined near Holguín and Camagüey. Iron reserves in the mountains of Baracoa are among the world's richest. Energy minerals, however are lacking : Cuba has no coal and only a little oil. All mineral resources are nationalized.

Industry
Following the 1959 revolution, when Fidel Castro came to power, there has been steady industrial development. Aid from the Eastern Bloc, in the form of technical training and factory building, has played a major part in Cuba's industrialization programme. Processing agricultural products is the main industry and includes sugar-refining, textile manufacture, leather-working, fruit-canning and cigar production. The metallurgical and construction sectors are also important.

Transport
The main road is the 1,240 km-long Central Highway which runs from Pinar del Río via Habana to Santiago. About 60% of the railways serve the sugar estates. Habana is the main seaport with an international airport.

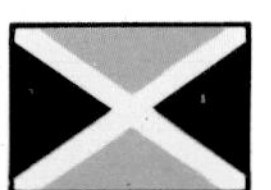

Caribbean Islands 2

Above: Dominican Republic
Top left: Jamaica
Left: Haiti

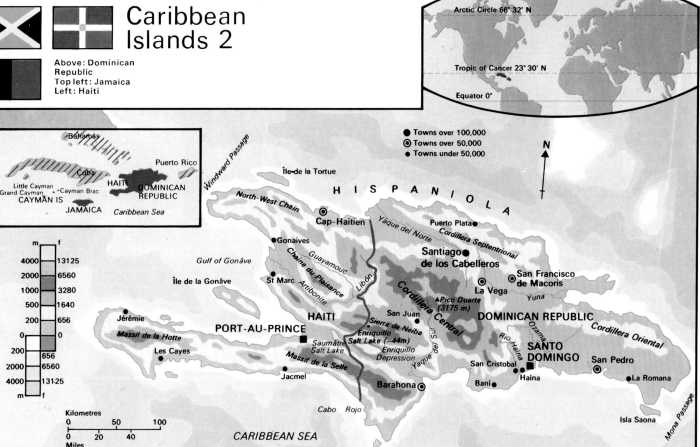

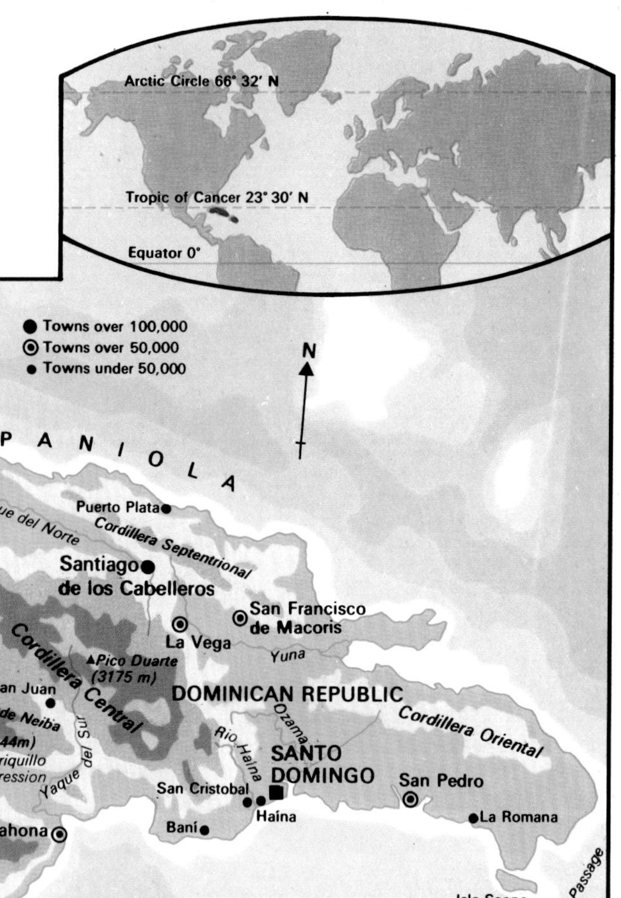

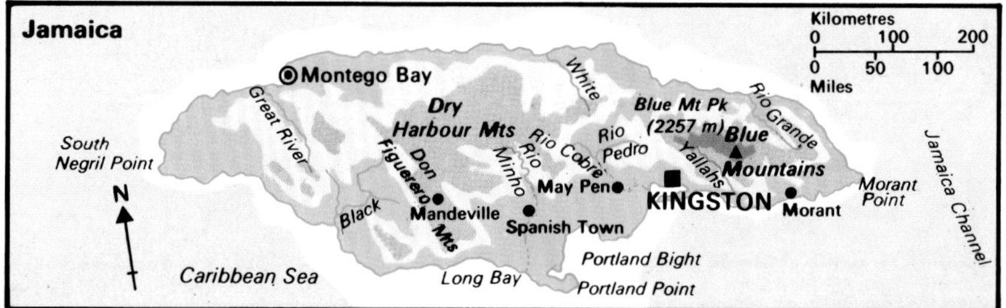

Jamaica
Area
11,424 km²/4,411 sq miles
Location
17°40'—18°30' N
76°10'—78°20' W
Population
2,025,000 (1974)
Population density
177 per km²/459 per sq mile
Capital and largest city
Kingston: 614,000 (1974)
Language
English
Major imports
consumer goods, foods, machinery vehicles, fuels, chemicals
Major exports
bauxite and alumina, bananas, sugar, rum
Currency
dollar (1 dollar = 100 cents)
Gross National Product
2,420 million US dollars (1974)
Status
parliamentary state

Physical features
Jamaica, the third largest Caribbean island, lies 150 km south of Cuba. In places the forested highland interior is almost impenetrable; it comprises rugged limestone plateaux in the centre and west and, in the east, the Blue Mountains reaching 2,257 m. The surrounding coastal plain is narrow in the north, but wider in the south and west. Rivers are swift flowing with steep, rocky courses.

Climate
Coastal areas are warm; tempeatures average 26°C but the upland interior is cooler. Rain, falling between August and November, ranges from 500 cm in the Blue Mountains to approximately 100 cm in the southwest.

Agriculture
A third of the land is farmed, producing a wide range of cash crops: sugarcane and citrus on the alluvial plains in the south and west; bananas along the wetter north coast; coffee in the Blue Mountains; pimento, ginger and cocoa in the interior; coconuts and tobacco. Sugar and bananas are most important. Rice, maize, vegetables and rootcrops are grown for food. Jamaica is increasing its dairy and beef cattle stocks.

Mining & industry
Jamaica has rich bauxite deposits in the Mandeville area and ranks as the world's second producer of bauxite and alumina. In recent years, a variety of industries have been established; products include textiles, shoes, cement and paints as well as traditional goods such as rum, molasses and cigars. After sugar, tourism is the chief source of income with Montego Bay as the leading resort.

Cayman Islands
The low lying, coral Cayman Islands, a self-governing British colony, are situated 300 km northwest of Jamaica and consist of Grand Cayman, Little Cayman and Cayman Brac with a total area of 260 km². Most of the 12,000 islanders live by fishing. Turtle products, shark hides and crayfish are the main exports. About 90% of the population is concentrated on Grand Cayman which has the capital, Georgetown.

Dominican Republic
Area
48,442 km²/18,703 sq miles
Location
17°40'—19° N
68°15'—71°55' W
Population
4,696,800 (1975)
Population density
97 per km²/251 per sq mile
Capital and largest city
Santo Domingo: 922,500 (1975)
Language
Spanish
Major imports
machinery, chemicals, foods, vehicles, fuels
Major exports
sugar, ferro-nickel, cocoa, coffee, tobacco, bauxite
Currency
peso (1 peso = 100 centavos)
Gross National Product
2,260 million US dollars (1973)
Status
republic

The land
The Dominican Republic extends over the eastern two-thirds of Hispaniola, the Caribbean's second largest island. Mountains cover the west and centre; the principal range is the Cordillera Central which rises to 3,175 m in Pico Duarte—the highest peak in the Caribbean. The central ranges are separated from coastal chains by the Yaque del Norte and Yuna rivers in the north and by the Enriquillo depression in the south; the Enriquillo salt lake (44 m below sea level) is the lowest point in the West Indies. The east is largely lowland. Temperatures average 26°C but are lower in the mountains; rainfall is heaviest in the north. Hispaniola lies in a hurricane belt.

Agriculture
Agriculture is the chief economic activity. Sugar, grown on plantations in the southeast, is the main cash crop and accounts for 50% of all exports. Other leading cash crops are coffee (from the coastal uplands), cocoa and tobacco (both cultivated on the northern plain) and bananas. Rice, maize and groundnuts are produced for domestic consumption. Stock-raising is concentrated in the north and east and dairying in the south.

Mining & industry
Mining makes a significant contribution to the economy: bauxite is exploited at Cabo Rojo, nickel at Bonao in the Cordillera Central, and rock salt in the Enriquillo lowland. Silver, copper and gypsum are also worked. Industrialization is progressing steadily: the principal sectors are food processing, cotton textiles, cement and fertilizer. Santo Domingo and the new port of Rio Haina are important manufacturing centres.

Haiti
Area
27,750 km²/10,714 sq miles
Location
18°—20° N
71°40'—74°30' W
Population
4,583,800 (1975)
Population density
165 per km²/428 per sq mile
Capital and largest city
Port-au-Prince: 458,700 (1975)
Language
French
Major imports
foods, textiles, machinery, fuels
Major exports
coffee, bauxite, sugar, sisal, essential oils, handicrafts
Currency
gourde (1 gourde = 100 centimes)
Gross National Product
727 million US dollars (1974)
Status
republic

The land
Haiti, occupying the western third of Hispaniola, is a mountainous country. The main ranges thrust westwards into two peninsulas enclosing the Gulf of Gonâve. The principal lowlands are the Artibonite valley and the plain between Port-au-Prince and the Saumâtre salt lake. The climate is tropical but modified inland by altitude; rainfall decreases from 300 cm in the north to 50 cm in the south.

The economy
Haiti is one of the poorest Caribbean states. Its weak economy is based on peasant agriculture which employs 85% of the work-force and provides 80% of exports. Coffee is the main cash crop followed by sisal and sugar. Maize, millet, yams and rice are grown for food. Various minerals occur, but only bauxite from the south peninsula is mined. Apart from food-processing and handicrafts, there is little industry. Tourism is important.

Caribbean Islands 3

top left: **Trinidad and Tobago**
above: **Grenada**
left: **Barbados**

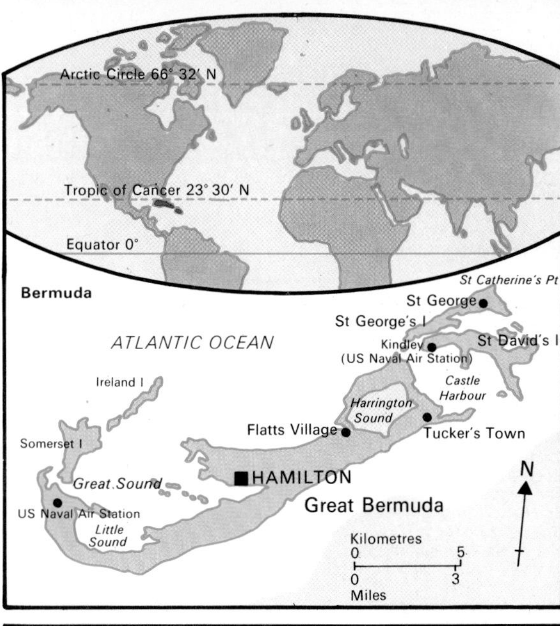

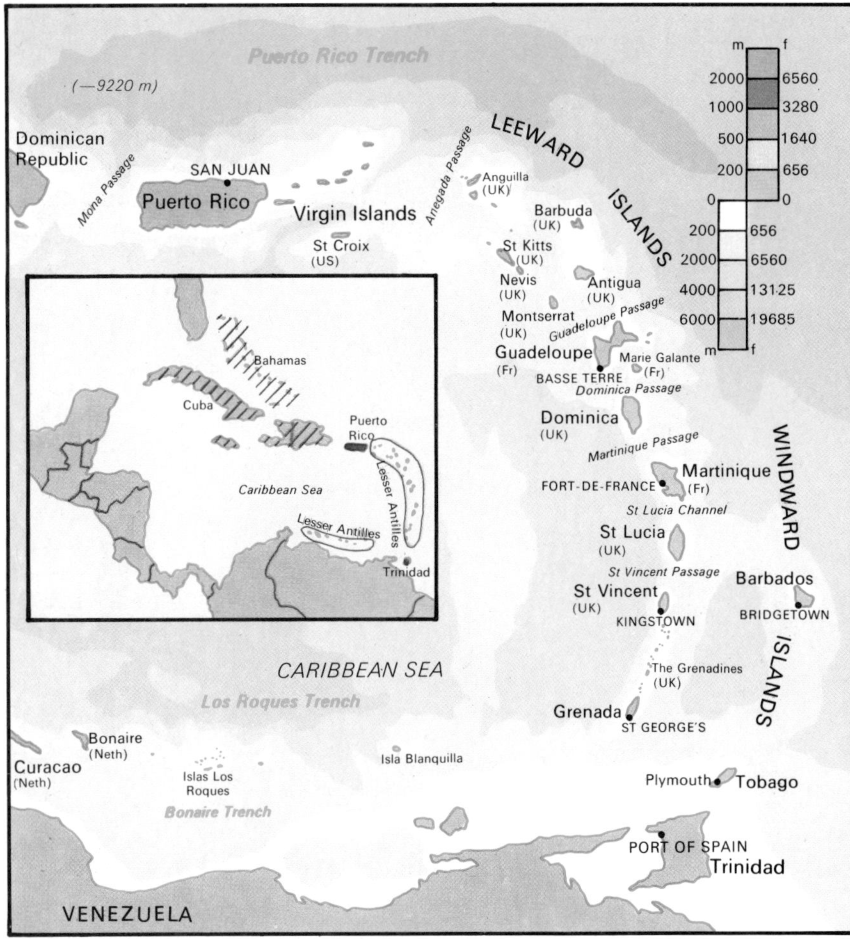

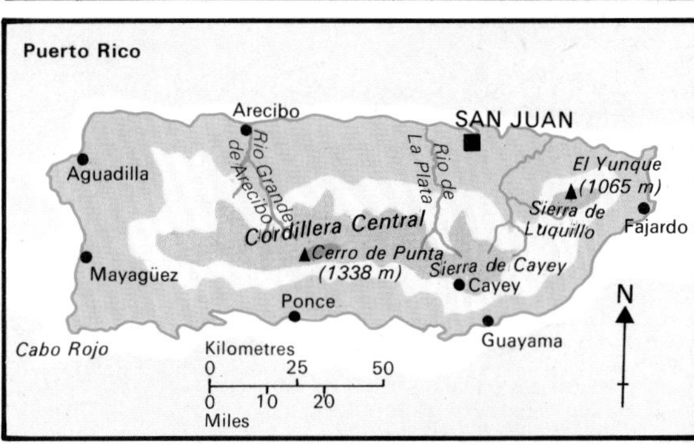

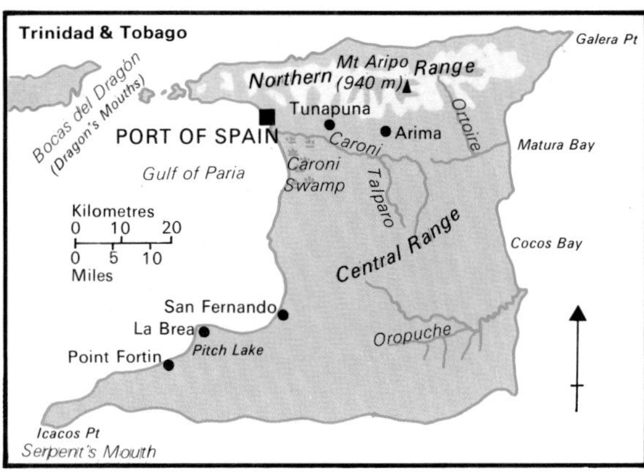

Bermuda
Area
53.3 km²/20.6 sq miles
Population
55,000 (1973)
Population density
1,031 per km²/2,669 per sq mile
Capital and largest city
Hamilton : 3,000 (1973)
Language
English
Major imports
foods, textiles, vehicles
Major exports
essences, perfume, flowers

The British colony of Bermuda consists of some 300 small coral islands situated in the western Atlantic 1,120 km southeast of New York. The largest island, Great Bermuda, is 20 km long and, like the rest of the group, it is low-lying (no point exceeds 75m) and fringed with reefs. The climate, modified by the warm Gulf Stream, is mild with temperatures ranging from 16°C in winter to 30°C in summer. Rain occurs throughout the year and averages 150 cm. As only 20 islands are inhabited, Bermuda has one of the world's densest populations. Many islanders are involved in tourism—the colony's major source of income. Agriculture is limited to 5% of the land : the main crops are vegetables, flowers, bananas and citrus. Small-scale industry includes pharmaceuticals, beauty preparations and essential oils. The larger islands have a good road network and are connected by bridges and causeways ; inter-island ferry services are good.

Puerto Rico
Area
8,891 km²/3,435 sq miles
Population
3,112,500 (1975)
Population density
350 per km²/906 per sq mile
Capital and largest city
San Juan : 485,000 (1972)
Languages
Spanish, English
Major imports
raw materials, foods, machinery
Major exports
sugar, tobacco, rum, petroleum and petroleum products

The Puerto Rican Commonwealth, politically linked with the US, lies about 2,400 km southeast of Florida and groups Puerto Rico (8,648 km²) with several smaller islands. The main island has a mountainous interior rising to 1,338 m surrounded by a narrow, alluvial coastal plain. The northeast trade winds keep average temperatures between 24°C and 27°C and bring heavy rains (500 cm) to north-facing slopes, but under 75cm to southern parts. In spite of industrialization, centred on the ports of San Juan, Ponce and Mayagüez, agriculture is still significant. About 50% of arable land is used for sugar ; tobacco, coffee and pineapples are also major export crops. Sugarcane processing is the leading industry ; other industries, such as textiles, electronics and petrochemicals, mostly use imported materials. The islands are popular with American tourists ; 90% of all trade is with the US.

Trinidad & Tobago
Area
5,128 km²/1,980 sq miles
Population
1,050,000 (1972)
Population density
204 per km²/529 per sq mile
Capital and largest city
Port of Spain : 65,000 (1972)
Language
English
Major imports
crude oil, machinery, food
Major exports
petroleum and petroleum products, chemicals, sugar, asphalt

The tropical islands of Trinidad and Tobago form an independent state. Trinidad (4,828 km²) lies 11 km off Venezuela and consists of three east-west highland zones covered with rain forest and separated by broad alluvial plains. Tobago (300 km²), situated 32 km northeast of Trinidad, has a mountainous north and a low-lying coral limestone plateau in the south. Temperatures are generally high (28°C) with rainfall decreasing from 250 cm in the northeast to 120 cm in the west. Only 3% of the population lives on Tobago. Trinidad has two major resources : oil and pitch. There are oil fields in the south and in the Gulf of Paria ; the pitch lake near La Brea is the world's largest asphalt deposit. Oil refining (including Venezuelan oil) and petrochemicals are the main industries, providing 80% of exports. About half the land is farmed and the chief cash crops are sugar, cocoa, coconuts and citrus.

Leeward Islands
The Leeward Islands, forming an arc on the Caribbean's northeast edge, comprise an inner chain of volcanic islands and an outer chain of coral reefs: Principal (and mountainous) islands are Guadeloupe (1,779 km²), the Virgin Islands (100 islands : total area of 497 km²), St Kitts (176 km²), Nevis (93 km²) and Montserrat (97 km²). The main low-lying outer islands are Anguilla (91 km²), Barbuda (161 km²) and Antigua (280 km²). The climate is humid and tropical, averaging 27°C with 130 cm of rain. Except in the Virgin Islands, agriculture is the basic economic activity. The main crops are sugar (St Kitts, Antigua), cotton (St Kitts, Nevis, Antigua, Barbuda), coconuts (Nevis, Montserrat), fruit and vegetables (Montserrat). Tourism is the chief source of income in the Virgin Islands and is also important in Antigua, St Kitts and Montserrat. Stock-rearing and fishing are significant in the Virgin Islands and Anguilla ; Anguilla also produces salt. Off South America, Aruba (193 km²) and Curaçao (444 km²) depend on refining Venezuelan oil ; nearby Bonaire (288 km²) is a major world supplier of aloes (from which is derived a laxative.)

Windward Islands
The Windward Islands, extending south from the Leewards to Trinidad, form the Caribbean's eastern perimeter. These islands are mountainous (of volcanic origin) and partly covered with dense rain forest. The chief islands in the group are Martinique (1,116 km²), Dominica (790 km²), St Lucia (616 km²), Grenada (344 km²) and, to the east, Barbados (430 km²). The climate is hot with average temperatures of 24°C in winter and 29°C in summer and heavy summer rainfall ranging from 120 cm to 300 cm ; hurricanes sometimes occur. On all the islands, agriculture is the basis of the economy with sugar and bananas as the main crops. Other cash crops are cocoa, coconuts, citrus and cotton. Yams, cassava and groundnuts are grown for food. Dominica is noted for limes, Grenada for nutmeg and other spices and Barbados for shrimps. St Vincent (389 km²) ranks as the world's leading producer of arrowroot. Industry, based on agriculture, is small-scale : the principal products are refined sugar, molasses, rum, fruit juice and essential oils. Throughout the Windward Islands tourism is increasing in importance.

Colombia

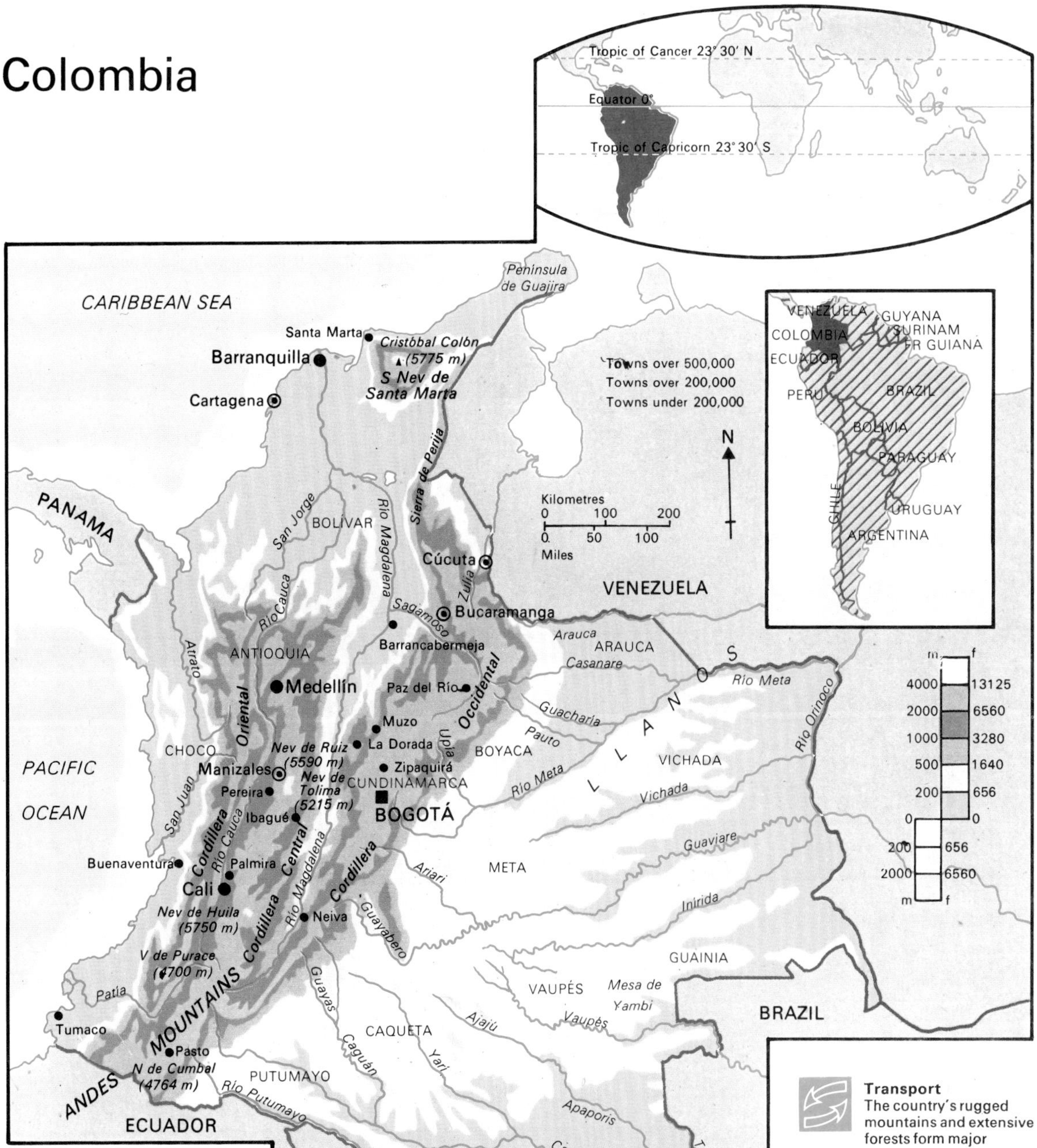

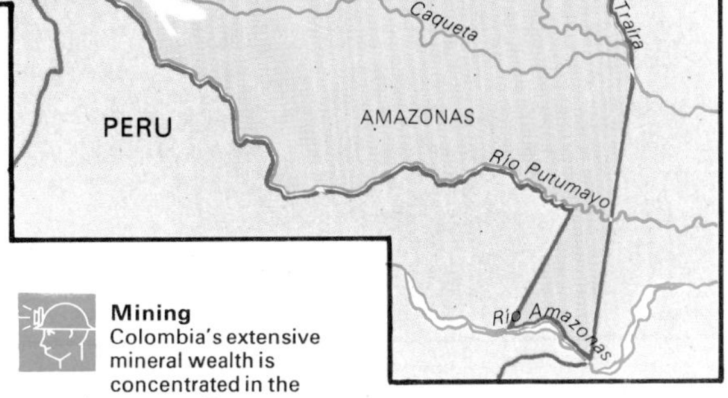

Area
1,138,911 km²/439,734 sq miles
Location
12°30′N—4°15′ S
66°50′—79° W
Population
23,210,000 (1973)
Population density
20 per km²/53 per sq mile
Capital and largest city
Bogotá : 2,850,000 (1973)
Language
Spanish
Major imports
chemicals, machinery, metals, vehicles, paper, rubber
Major exports
coffee, textiles, fuel oil, rice, cotton, bananas, beef, flowers, sugar, emeralds
Currency
peso (1 peso = 100 centavos)
Gross National Product
14,500 million US dollars (1975)
Status
republic

Physical features

Colombia, named after Christopher Columbus, is the only South American state with coastlines on both the Caribbean and the Pacific. The western part of the country is dominated by three parallel north-south ranges of the great Andes Mountains with altitudes of between 3,000 and 5,000 m ; the Cordillera Occidental, the Cordillera Central and the main range, the Cordillera Oriental. These ranges are separated by the deep valleys of Colombia's two main rivers : the Cauca and the Magdalena. A lowland belt, up to 100 km wide, lies between the western mountains and the Pacific. In the north, the isolated Sierra Nevada de Santa Marta rises from the marshy Carribean plain to 5,684 m in Pico Cristóbal Colón, the country's highest point. Beyond the Andean ranges, the eastern two-thirds of the territory consists of vast savanna plains (the *llanos*) drained by Orinoco and Amazon tributaries.

Climate

Colombia's contrasting climate zones reflect the country's varied relief. Lowland areas, comprising the river valleys, coastal plains and llanos, are hot with mean annual temperatures of 24° to 30°C. At altitudes between 900 and 1,800 m, conditions are healthier and range from 16° to 22°C. A cooler zone from 1,800 to 3,000 m averages below 15°C. Bogotá at 2,650 m averages 14°C. The high mountain regions have freezing temperatures and snow-storms. Rainfall varies greatly, but is heaviest west of the Cordillera Occidental ; some parts receive over 1,000 cm a year.

People

The Colombian people are the product of three ethnic types : native Indian, Spanish conqueror and Negro slave. Over the centuries, these groups have intermarried and today, *mestizos* (mixed Indian and white) constitute 60% of the population and *mulattoes* (Negro and white) a further 14%. Most Colombians live in the mountainous west ; steady migration from rural areas is causing overcrowding in cities and shanty towns are a major social problem.

Flora & fauna

The vegetation shows great diversity. Lowland plant cover includes mangrove swamps bordering the Pacific, equatorial jungle in the Amazonian region and grass savanna on the plains. More temperate areas feature forest, grasslands and scrub while meadows and alpine flowers characterize the treeless high mountain zones. Wildlife is equally varied, ranging from bears and jaguars to condors and hummingbirds.

Agriculture

Although less than 5% of the country is cultivated, agriculture employs almost half the work-force and plays a major part in the economy. The range of relief and climate permits cultivation of many different crops : rice, bananas, sugar, cotton and cocoa in the tropical lowlands ; coffee, maize, tobacco and beans in the temperate zone ; potatoes, wheat, barley, deciduous fruits and fodder at higher, cooler altitudes. Coffee, providing 50% of all exports, is the dominant cash crop : Colombia ranks as the world's second largest coffee producer after Brazil. Stock-rearing is important on the vast llanos and the Caribbean lowlands ; dairying occurs near major towns. Forest products include rubber and fibres but are not developed.

Mining

Colombia's extensive mineral wealth is concentrated in the mountainous west. Resources currently exploited include gold and silver in Antioquia department, platinum near the headwaters of the Atrato and the world's largest deposit of emeralds at Muzo. Salt is extracted from the great Zipaquirá mine and from pans along the Caribbean coast. Coal comes from Cundinamarca and Boyaca, the Guajira peninsula and the southern Cauca valley ; iron ore also from the departments of Cundinamarca and Boyaca. Petroleum is found near Cúcuta, Barrancabermeja and in the Putumayo region. Copper, lead mercury and manganese also occur and further exploration is taking place. Principal mineral exports are emeralds and gold ; the large volumes of crude oil formerly shipped abroad have largely been replaced by refined petroleum and petroleum products. Colombia is South America's largest producer of gold and coal.

Industry

Industry's contribution to the Colombian economy is becoming increasingly significant. Food-processing is the leading sector and includes rice-milling, sugar-refining, cheese and butter production, coffee-processing, fruit and vegetable canning, oil extraction and chocolate manufacture. The textile industry is next in importance. Other major manufactures are steel, refined petroleum and associated products, paper, cement, chemicals, pharmaceuticals, metal goods and wood products. Over 60% of the country's electricity is generated by hydro-power and further installations are planned : the role of natural gas is expanding. Except for the iron and steel complex at Paz del Río, manufacturing is centred on Bogotá, Medellín and Cali.

Transport

The country's rugged mountains and extensive forests form major obstacles to communications and many areas remain isolated. Consequently, air transport is important. In 1919, Colombia made aviation history by establishing the world's first commercial airline ; today, domestic flights link over 400 centres. The 48,000 km road network includes the Caribbean Trunk Highway connecting the ports of Cartagena, Barranquilla and Santa Marta with the Venezuelan system and a section of the Simón Bolívar highway running from Venezuela to Ecuador. The railways are being modernized. On the Magdalena, the main waterway, steamers reach La Dorada, 960 km upstream. Barranquilla and Buenaventura are the chief ports.

Cities

Colombia's four main cities are widely dispersed. Bogotá, the capital, is located in the Cordillera Oriental. To the northwest, Medellín (1,100,000) lies in the Cordillera Central in a region noted for its coffee and orchids ; it is the country's industrial capital and South America's largest textile producer. The third largest city, Cali (920,000), is situated in the fertile Cauca valley and is a commercial and agricultural centre ; sugar and paper production are important. Near the mouth of the Magdalena lies Barranquilla (650,000)—the country's chief port.

Venezuela

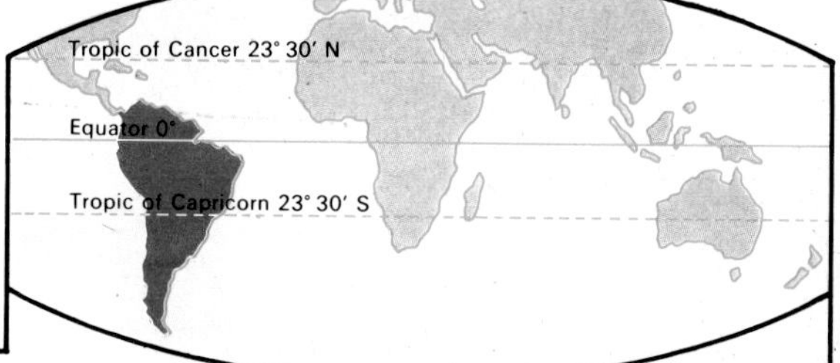

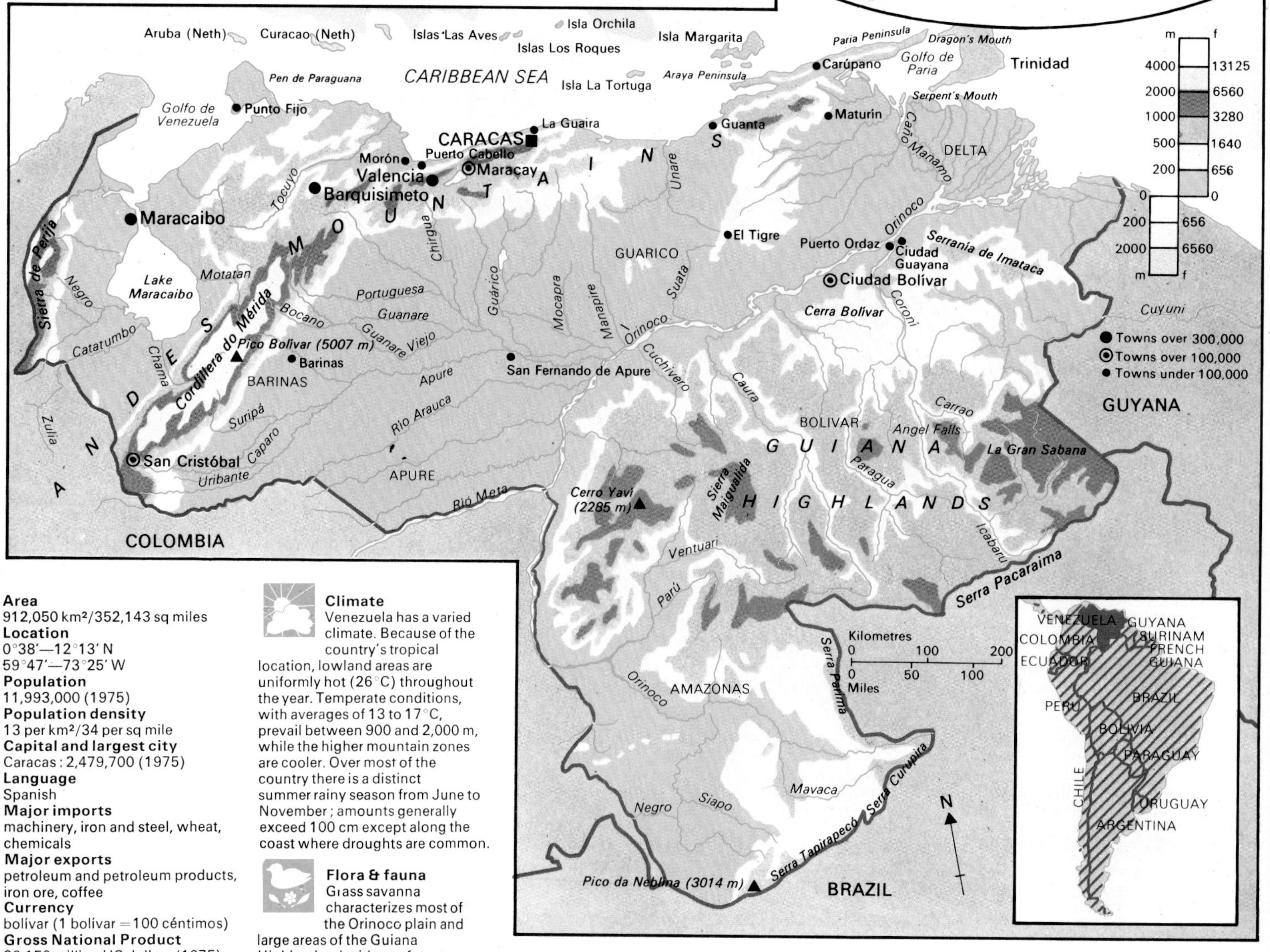

Area
912,050 km²/352,143 sq miles
Location
0°38′—12°13′ N
59°47′—73°25′ W
Population
11,993,000 (1975)
Population density
13 per km²/34 per sq mile
Capital and largest city
Caracas: 2,479,700 (1975)
Language
Spanish
Major imports
machinery, iron and steel, wheat, chemicals
Major exports
petroleum and petroleum products, iron ore, coffee
Currency
bolívar (1 bolívar = 100 céntimos)
Gross National Product
26,150 million US dollars (1975)
Status
federal republic

Physical features

Venezuela divides into four regions: the Andes, the Maracaibo basin, the Orinoco lowland and the Guiana Highlands. The Andes enter the country from the west and divide into two ranges which enclose Lake Maracaibo (12,950 km²): to the west, the Sierra de Perija and to the east the magnificent Cordillera do Mérida with snowy peaks over 4,500 m; Pico Bolívar reaches 5,007 m. This latter range extends along the coast to the Paria peninsula near Trinidad. In the 16th century, Lake Maracaibo's swampy shore, fringed with huts on stilts, gave Venezuela its name: Little Venice. The Orinoco basin (300,000 km²) is a vast alluvial plain subject to flooding. The Orinoco, 3,000 km long, rises in the Guiana Highlands and hugs the edge of the massif before entering the sea via a huge delta. The Highlands are an ancient plateau with summits of over 2 000 m. They occupy half the country and are largely unexplored. The Highlands contain precipitous cliffs with many spectacular waterfalls; Angel Falls, the world's highest, has a drop of 980 m.

Climate

Venezuela has a varied climate. Because of the country's tropical location, lowland areas are uniformly hot (26°C) throughout the year. Temperate conditions, with averages of 13 to 17°C, prevail between 900 and 2,000 m, while the higher mountain zones are cooler. Over most of the country there is a distinct summer rainy season from June to November; amounts generally exceed 100 cm except along the coast where droughts are common.

Flora & fauna

Grass savanna characterizes most of the Orinoco plain and large areas of the Guiana Highlands; deciduous forest covers other parts of the plateau. Vegetation in the Andes ranges from thorn scrub in the drier regions to dense tropical jungle on the wet slopes. A variety of wildlife inhabits the humid Andean rain forest including mountain lions, anacondas and humming birds. Alligators, turtles and iguanas frequent the Orinoco and its tributaries.

Agriculture

About 30% of the workforce is engaged in agriculture although only 3% of the land is cultivated (mostly in the north, one of the main agricultural areas being the intermontane basin centred on Valencia). Subsistence farming predominates but some coffee, cocoa and sugar are exported. High quality coffee is mostly grown on the slopes of the Andes between 1,000 and 2,000 m; cocoa, sugar-cane, cotton and bananas are also produced in the Andean zone, but at lower altitudes where conditions are warmer and wetter; coconuts grow along the coast. Rice is the chief lowland food crop, while wheat, maize, barley, beans and potatoes are cultivated in the cooler uplands. Dairying is important in the Valencia and Caracas basins. South of the Andes, the Orinoco plain specializes in beef-cattle.

Forestry & fishing

Venezuela's forests, covering half the country, contain over 600 species of timber trees; exploitation is, however, limited because of inaccessibility. Fishing, both inland and coastal is also underdeveloped, but some sardines and tuna are canned for export.

Petroleum

Venezuela's important oil resources have made it one of South America's richest states. Since production began in 1917, the growth of the petroleum industry, now nationalized, has been phenomenal. With a current output of over 2 million barrels a day, Venezuela ranks as the world's third largest oil producer and its leading exporter. About 75% of production comes from the shore and shallow waters of Lake Maracaibo; there are also oil-fields in the Maturin basin and the Barinas region. Almost half the oil is refined in Venezuela. Natural gas is piped to Caracas and other centres where it is used as fuel and as a raw material in the petrochemical industry. The channel linking Lake Maracaibo to the Gulf of Venezuela has been deepened for tankers to enter Maracaibo port.

Mining

In addition to its valuable oil resources, Venezuela has vast iron-ore deposits and ranks as the world's tenth largest producer; production is centred on the Caroní valley in the Guiana Highlands. The Highlands are also rich in other minerals: gold, diamonds and manganese are exploited, but reserves of nickel, bauxite and chromium are underdeveloped because of poor communications. North of the Orinoco, mining activity includes asbestos near Puerto Cabello, coal and lignite in the Andean foothills, salt on the Araya peninsula and limestone. Copper phosphate, sulphur, vanadium, zinc and lead also occur.

Industry

Industrialization is making steady progress. Originally, manufacturing was concentrated in the Caracas area, but other centres have developed including Ciudad Guayana (steel), Ciudad Bolívar (metallurgy), Morón (petro-chemicals) and Maracaibo (paper, food-processing, engineering). So far, natural gas is the main energy source but a giant hydro-scheme on the Caroní is being built to supply electricity to Venezuela and neighbouring states.

Transport

The 50,000 km road network is densest in the north and northwest and includes a section of the Pan American Highway from Caracas to Colombia. Except in the Highlands, where lines link iron ore mines to Ciudad Guayana, railways are unimportant and cover less than 500 km. Inland shipping is significant: sea-going vessels dock at ports on Lake Maracaibo and sail up the Orinoco as far as Ciudad Guayana. The main seaports are La Guaira, Puerto Cabello, Puerto Ordaz, Guanta and Maracaibo. Internal air services are important, especially in remote areas.

Cities

The population, concentrated in the Andean zone and northern coastal belt, is mainly urban: 75% of Venezuelans now live in towns and cities and by 1980 the figure is expected to exceed 80%. Caracas, situated in a steep-sided rift valley, is a modern city based on oil wealth; it is served by the port of La Guaira. Next in importance is the port and oil city of Maracaibo (655,000). Other major centres are Valencia (367,000), Barquisimeto (331,000), Maracay (255,000) and San Cristóbal.

Guyana

Surinam

Guyana, Surinam and French Guiana

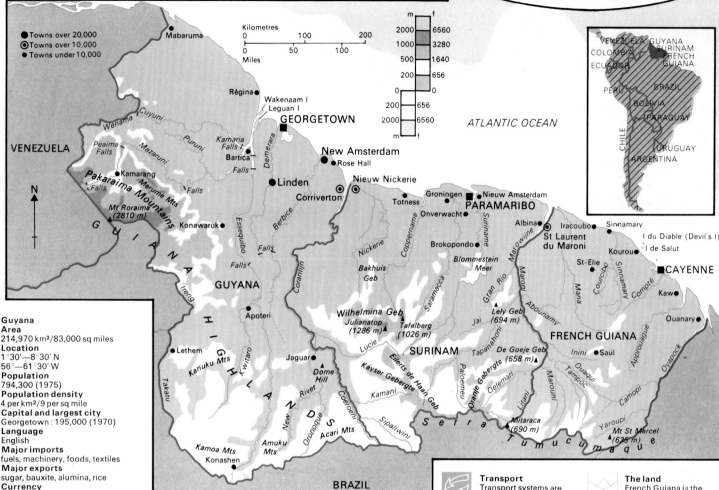

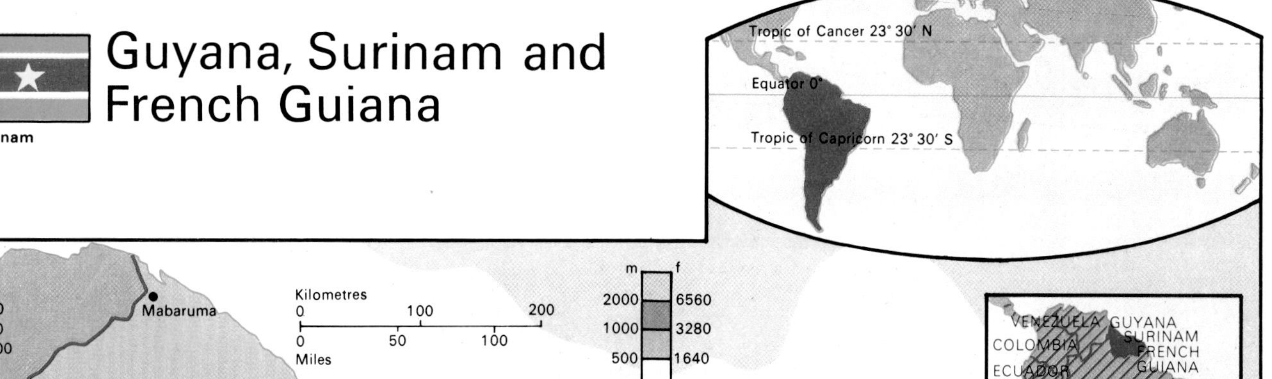

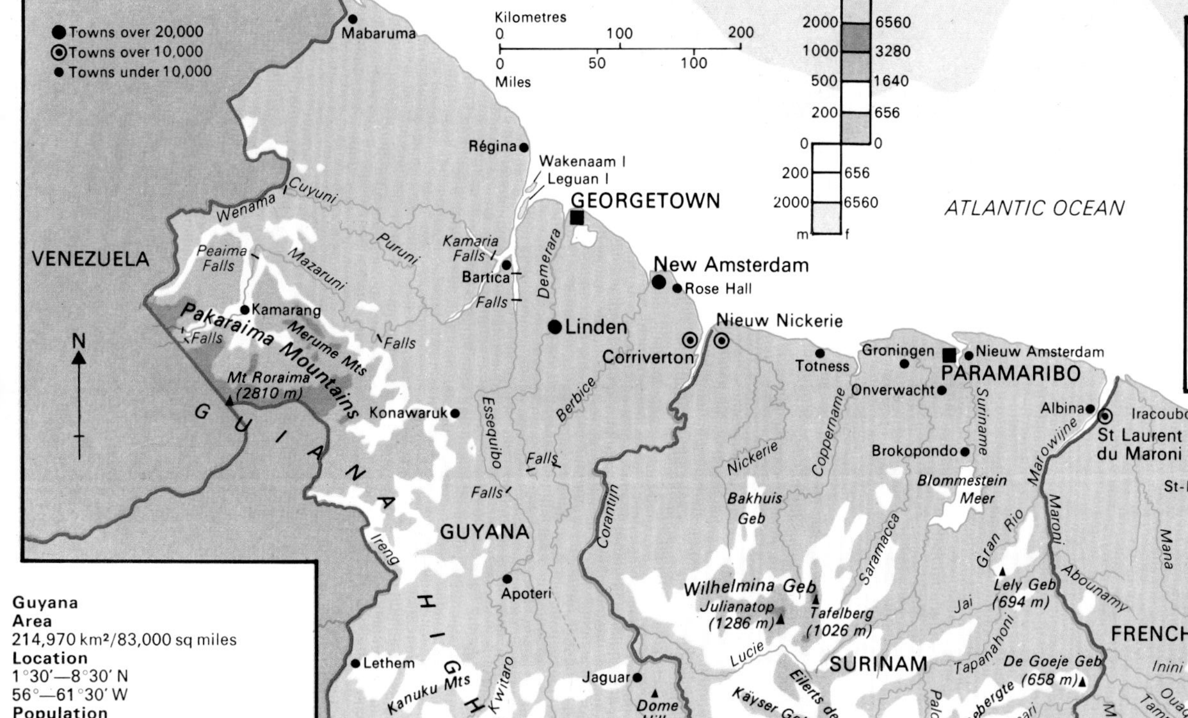

Guyana
Area
214,970 km²/83,000 sq miles
Location
1°30′—8°30′ N
56°—61°30′ W
Population
794,300 (1975)
Population density
4 per km²/9 per sq mile
Capital and largest city
Georgetown : 195,000 (1970)
Language
English
Major imports
fuels, machinery, foods, textiles
Major exports
sugar, bauxite, alumina, rice
Currency
dollar (1 dollar = 100 cents)
Gross National Product
440 million US dollars (1974)
Status
co-operative republic

The land
The coast, fringed with mangrove, sandbars and lagoons, is backed by a narrow plain lying below sea level. Some 20 km inland, the land rises to an area of dense tropical rain forest which gives way to mountains in the south-west and to a savanna-covered plateau in the south. The coast is hot and wet: Georgetown averages 28°C and has 230 cm of rain; in the interior, temperatures rainfall and humidity decrease with altitude.

The economy
Farming is the basic activity. Cultivated land is located in the coastal belt where sugarcane and rice are the main crops followed by citrus and coconuts. Output of groundnuts, palm oil, cotton and vegetables is increasing. Fishing and forestry are being expanded, but at present forests, covering 87% of the country, are underexploited. Guyana has considerable mineral resources: bauxite is a major export and significant amounts of gold, diamonds and manganese are also produced. Industrial development plans include a hydro-electric plant and an aluminium smelter in the Upper Mazaruni district of the Pakaraima Mountains.

Transport
Along the coast (the most populous and developed region) the road network is fairly dense and 75% paved. In the interior, however, where dense forest hampers communications, tracks are unsurfaced and less extensive, and access is primarily by river. The main waterways are the Berbice, Demerara, Essequibo, Cuyuni and Mazaruni. Georgetown and New Amsterdam are the chief seaports. Near the capital there is an international airport.

Surinam
Area
163,265 km²/63,037 sq miles
Location
1°50′—6° N
54°—58°10′ W
Population
405,000 (1974)
Population density
2 per km²/6 per sq mile
Capital and largest city
Paramaribo : 151,500 (1971)
Language
Dutch
Major imports
manufactures, fuels, foodstuffs
Major exports
alumina, bauxite, aluminium, rice, forest products
Currency
gulden (1 gulden = 100 cents)
Gross National Product
462 million US dollars (1974)
Status
republic

The land
Coastal Surinam features mangrove swamps and sandy stretches of savanna. The thickly-forested interior climbs to a plateau over 1,000 m high. The country's main rivers, the Corantijn, Coppername, Saramacca, Suriname and Marowijne, drain northwards from the highlands. Inland, the hot, wet tropical climate is modified by altitude.

The economy
Bauxite is the mainstay of the economy and, together with alumina and aluminium, accounts for 90% of all exports. Alluvial gold is extracted from the rivers Marowijne and Tapanahoni, but other mineral resources are unexploited. Surinam's next most valuable assets are its forests which cover 85% of the country: products include lumber, plywood and balata (a type of latex). Although 75% of the workforce is in agriculture, output is inadequate and food imports are necessary. About 80% of farmland, concentrated in the coastal zone, is used for rice, the staple food. The area under rice is being doubled by reclamation and irrigation schemes. The other main crops are sugar, citrus, bananas and coconuts. Shrimp fishing is being developed. Other industries process timber, farm produce and fish.

Transport
Transport systems are poor: the road network is minimal and there is only one short railway. Inland, passengers and freight travel mostly by water using some 1,500 km of navigable rivers and canals; remote districts are also linked by air. Paramaribo is the chief seaport.

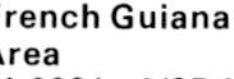

French Guiana
Area
91,000 km²/35,135 sq miles
Location
2°—5°45′ N
52°—54°30′ W
Population
55,100 (1975)
Population density
0.6 per km²/1.6 per sq mile
Capital and largest city
Cayenne : 30,000 (1975)
Language
French
Major imports
food, manufactures, petroleum products, cement, iron and steel
Major exports
timber, shrimps
Currency
franc (1 franc = 100 centimes)
Gross National Product
40 million US dollars (1970)
Status
French overseas department

Transport
Roads, totalling 500 km link the main centres which are all on the coast. Small craft, travelling along the coast and up the rivers, provide the chief means of transport. There are no railways. Cayenne is the major seaport.

The land
French Guiana is the smallest country in South America. The land is highest in the south and descends gradually to the swampy seaboard. Many streams, draining northwards through deep valleys, dissect the country; the two main rivers (the Maroni and Oyapock) flow along its borders. Except for mangrove and savanna in the coastal zone, dense rain forest blankets the territory. Its near-equitorial location gives French Guiana a hot, wet climate (27°C; 300 cm).

The economy
French Guiana is economically backward and relies heavily on French assistance. The forests, covering 90% of the total area and containing many valuable hardwoods, are the country's greatest resource, but apart from a very limited output of timber they are virtually unexploited. Mineral reserves, notably of gold, bauxite and tantalite, are similarly underdeveloped. Cultivation is confined to about 33 km² but the area could be greatly increased by draining the swampy coastlands. Subsistence farming predominates with cassava, bananas, maize, rice and sweet potatoes as the chief food crops. Sugarcane is the only significant cash crop. Some cattle, pigs and sheep are kept. Although the coastal waters are rich in fish there is little fishing except for shrimps and this is controlled by American companies for the US market.

Brazil

Area
8,511,965 km²/3,286,473 sq miles
Location
5°15′N—33°45′ S
34°50′—74° W
Population
110,124,000 (1976)
Population density
13 per km²/34 per sq mile
Capital
Brasília: 950,000 (1976)
Largest city
São Paulo: 7,415,000 (1976)
Language
Portuguese
Major imports
crude oil, metal products, chemicals, machinery, transport equipment, wheat
Major exports
soya, sugar, coffee, iron ore, electrical apparatus, cocoa, cotton
Currency
cruzeiro (1 cruzeiro = 100 cents)
Gross National Product
77,200 million US dollars (1973)
Status
federated republic

Physical features

Brazil, the world's fifth largest country, occupies almost half South America and has frontiers with ten states. It is a country of low-altitude plateaux and only 40% of the territory exceeds 200 m. The two upland regions are the vast central plateau and, north of the Amazon, the Guiana Highlands which contain the country's highest peak, Pico de Neblina (3,014 m). Both regions have similar features: rounded hills, low mountains, extensive tablelands and, in the south, great lava sheets. The two upland areas are separated by the Amazon basin (3,984,500 km²) covering almost half of Brazil. The Amazon, flowing 6,500 km to the Atlantic, is the world's second longest river after the Nile and the greatest by volume. This tremendous waterway is wide (320 km at its mouth) and deep: ocean-going vessels can sail 3,700 km upstream. As, from the foot of the Andes eastwards, the river falls only one centimetre per kilometre, widespread floods occur. Brazil's other lowland zones are the narrow coastal strip running from the northeast to Rio de Janeiro and, in the south and southwest, the Paraguay, Paraná and Uruguay river basins. The country's other main river is the São Francisco (2,900 km long) which rises in the Brazilian Highlands.

Climate

Around 93% of Brazil lies between the Equator and the Tropic of Capricorn and mean temperatures range from 18 °C in the sub-tropical south to 27 °C in the equatorial north. Rainfall, mostly between January and June, varies widely from region to region. The northeast is the driest area with long droughts and an annual total of under 70 cm; Amazonia, with over 200 cm of rain, is the wettest zone.

Flora & fauna

Brazil has several distinct vegetation zones. The Amazonian forest is the world's largest tropical rain forest with more species of flora than any other equatorial forest. South of the Amazon, the interior is covered with woodland savanna while the dry northeast features thorn scrub and cacti. Semideciduous forest occurs along the coast below Salvador and in the Paraná region. Pine forest and prairie characterize the extreme south. Apart from jaguars and tapirs, Brazil lacks large mammals but is rich in fish, reptiles, birds and insects.

Forestry & fishing

The Amazonian forest accounts for 75% of Brazil's timber resources but exploitation is limited by inaccessibility. Hardwood production (largely for export) is centred along the coast. Softwoods, from the southern forests, are mostly for domestic use. The fishing industry, spread along the 7,400 km coastline, is expanding: balsa rafts are used in the north, but in the south there are motorized fleets. Shrimp and lobster are exported.

Energy

The São Francisco and Paraná rivers form Brazil's chief energy resource. There are 30 hydro-plants under construction, including the world's largest power station at Itaipu.

Agriculture

Despite industrial expansion, agriculture remains vital to the economy: it provides 95% of domestic food needs, 60% of exports and employs almost half the workforce. The staple foods are rice, manioc, maize and beans: maize and beans are particularly important in the south and south-east; irrigated rice is grown in the extreme south but upland dry rice is grown elsewhere; manioc predominates in the northeast. Soya, cultivated in the south, is the main cash crop followed by sugar mostly grown in the southeast. Coffee is next in importance and Brazil ranks as the world's leading producer: 75% of output comes from the states of São Paulo and Paraná. Other major export crops are cocoa and bananas (from the hot wet coast between Salvador and Vitória), cotton (from Paraná, São Paulo and the northeast) and citrus and tobacco. Stock-raising is widespread and Brazil has the world's fourth largest beef herd; cattle are bred in the interior and brought to the seaboard for fattening. Dairying is developing.

Mining

Brazil's immense mineral wealth is underexploited. Mining activity is based on the state of Minas Gerais which has one of the world's largest reserves of iron ore as well as major deposits of nickel, bauxite, mica, beryl, quartz crystal, dolomite, gold, zirconium, niobium ore and diamonds. Elsewhere, lead, zinc, manganese, copper, tungsten, barite, chrome and asbestos are produced and many other minerals occur. Domestic output of coal and oil has to be supplemented by large imports. Mineral exports (13% of all exports) consist of iron ore, manganese, diamonds and niobium ore.

Industry

Brazil is Latin America's most industrialized state. The main industries, concentrated in the São Paulo region, are food-processing, textiles, iron and steel, vehicle manufacture, shipbuilding, chemicals, cement and electrical goods. Tourism is expanding: attractions include Rio de Janeiro and its beaches, Brásília and Amazonia.

Transport

Communications are handicapped by Brazil's enormous size and physical geography. Roads, totalling 1,400,000 km, carry 70% of all traffic. The network is expanding and recent projects include roads linking Brásília to all regions and the Trans-Amazonian Highway from the Atlantic to Peru. Railways, mostly in the southeast, play a minor role but are being modernized. As the forest is sparsely populated, there is relatively little traffic on the Amazon—the world's greatest inland waterway; Manaus is the main river port. Rio de Janeiro and Santos are the chief seaports followed by Paranagua, Recife, Salvador, Vitória and Rio Grande. Internal air services are being developed; Rio and São Paulo have the main international airports.

Cities

One South American in two lives in Brazil, giving it the world's seventh largest population. Most Brazilians inhabit the coastal zone, especially the southeast, and the interior is sparsely settled with an average of under one person per km². The population, growing by 3 million a year, is 60% urban. The largest city and chief industrial centre is São Paulo: Rio de Janeiro (5 million), the former capital, remains the cultural centre. Brásília, 900 km from the coast, was inaugurated in 1960 and is famous for its daring architecture. Other major cities are Belo Horizonte (1,600,000) Recife (1,290,000) and Salvador (1,270,000).

Ecuador

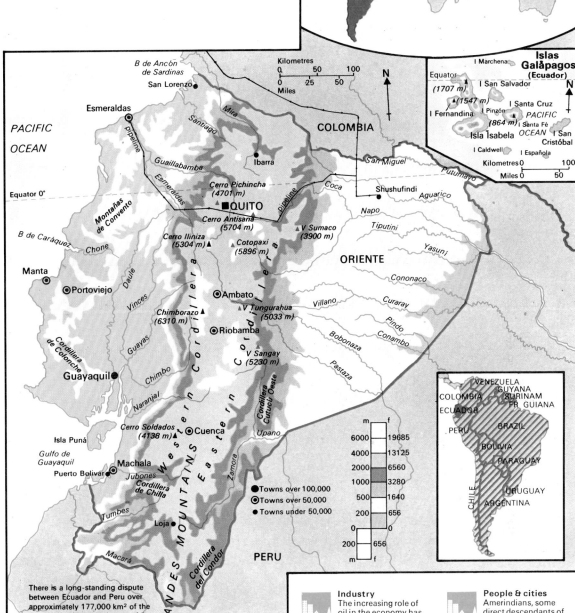

Area
455,452 km²/175,850 sq miles
Location
1°20′ N—5° S
75°15′—81° W
Population
7,100,000 (1975)
Population density
15 per km²/38 per sq mile
Capital
Quito: 575,000 (1972)
Largest city
Guayaquil: 947,000 (1972)
Language
Spanish
Major imports
raw materials, vehicles, building equipment
Major exports
petroleum, bananas, cocoa, sugar, fish, balsa, straw hats
Currency
sucre (1 sucre = 100 centavos)
Gross National Product
4,200 million US dollars (1975)
Status
republic

There is a long-standing dispute between Ecuador and Peru over approximately 177,000 km² of the Amazon basin currently part of Peru.

Towns over 100,000
Towns over 50,000
Towns under 50,000

Physical features

The name Ecuador (Spanish for 'equator') is derived from the country's position astride the equator; just 25 km north of Quito stands the Equatorial Monument with its inscription 0°00′00″. The territory divides into three major regions: the Pacific plain, the central mountains and the eastern lowlands. The Pacific coastline, a hilly area broken by swampy river valleys, is most extensive in the south where the Guayas river flows across a wide plain and enters the Gulf of Guayaquil via a great delta. Central Ecuador is dominated by the Andes with two parallel north-south ranges containing over 30 volcanoes, among them Chimborazo (6,310 m) and the still active Cotopaxi (5,896 m). These two ranges are separated by a structurally complex trough which includes a series of inter-mountain basins. East of the mountains, the land falls away into the lowlands of the Amazonian basin. This eastern region, the *Oriente*, occupies a third of the country and remains largely unexplored.

Climate

Ecuador has a varied climate. The coastal zone, averaging 24°C, is humid in the north with two rainy seasons but arid in the extreme south. Temperatures decrease with altitude in the Andes and drop below freezing above the perpetual snowline. Quito, almost on the equator but situated at 2,860 m, averages 13°C and is known as the 'city of eternal spring'. In the mountains there is only one wet season (November-May) with about 145 cm of rain. Conditions in the Oriente are very warm and wet with temperatures of 27°C, 300 cm of rain and 90% humidity.

Vegetation

On the Pacific coast, the rain forests and mangrove swamps of the north give way southwards to thorn scrub, short-grass savanna and, near the Peruvian border, cacti and drought-resistant plants. In the mountain zone, forest predominates up to 3,500 m and is then replaced by grasses and shrubs up to the snowline. Dense tropical rain forest smothers the Oriente.

Agriculture

There are two agricultural zones: the tropical Pacific plain and the temperate Andean highlands. The three staple export crops (bananas, cocoa, coffee) dominate land use in the coastal region; bananas and cocoa are cultivated on lowland plantations while coffee comes from the coastal uplands and Andean foothills. Ecuador ranks as the world's leading banana exporter and second largest producer (after Brazil). Other crops grown in this fertile zone are sugarcane, cotton, pineapples, citrus and rice. In the mountains, the cooler climate favours stock-raising and the production of barley, wheat, maize, potatoes and vegetables; on the higher slopes (up to 3,600 m), Indians grow subsistence crops of potatoes.

Fishing

The Pacific waters are rich in fish and Ecuador's fishing industry, centred on Guayaquil and Manta, is expanding. The main species caught are tuna, sardine and shrimp.

Forestry

Ecuador's vast forests, covering 75% of the country, are under-exploited; this is especially true of the valuable, but inaccessible, hardwood resources of the Oriente. The coastal forests are important for Carludovica palm fibre (used in the manufacture of Panama hats) and lightweight balsawood; Ecuador is the world's chief producer of balsa. Castor-oil seeds, kapok, palm nuts (for making buttons) and quinine (from the cinchona tree) are among other forest products.

Mining

Oil is transforming the Ecuadorian economy. The newly-developed fields are located in the Oriente and production is piped across the Andes to the tanker port of Esmeraldas. Four refineries, with a total daily capacity of 100,000 barrels, are in operation and a gas liquefaction plant has been built on the Shushufindi field. Small-scale mining activities include copper and gold, both in the Andes.

Industry

The increasing role of oil in the economy has stimulated industrial development and manufacturing is expanding rapidly; the most important sectors are cement and steel, pharmaceuticals and petrochemicals. Long-established industries include textiles, food-processing, ceramics and the weaving of Panama hats. The main manufacturing centres are Quito, Guayaquil and Cuenca. Vast hydro-power potential in the Andes is mostly unexploited. Tourism, based on the country's scenic beauty and cultural heritage, is being developed.

Transport

Transport systems are greatly handicapped by forest and mountain. The road network basically comprises the Pan American Highway (running through the inter-Andean trough) with branch roads to the coast. River transport is important and the lower reaches of the Guayas, Mira and Esmeraldas are navigable for 200 km. The main seaport, Guayaquil, handles 75% of foreign trade (excluding petroleum); other leading ports are Manta, Esmeraldas, San Lorenzo and Puerto Bolívar. All major towns are linked by air; Guayaquil and Quito have international airports.

People & cities

Amerindians, some direct descendants of the Incas, form nearly 60% of the population and mestizos (mixed Indian/white) about 35%; whites, Negroes and mulattoes make up the remainder. The population is most sparse (less than 2%) in the Oriente and densest in the Andean basins. Quito, the world's second highest capital and a former Inca city, retains much of its Spanish colonial atmosphere. The largest city and chief port, Guayaquil, at the head of the Guayas delta, is the country's industrial and commercial capital.

Galápagos Islands

These islands, 1,000 km west of Ecuador, consist of 15 large and numerous small islands totalling 7,964 km². Volcanic in origin, many of the islands are arid lava cones, but the higher ones attract rain and are densely forested. Only five are inhabited and the 4,000 islanders live by farming and fishing (lobster and tuna). The archipelago is named after its giant tortoises; these and other animals (including various species of finches) helped Darwin develop his theory of evolution when he visited the islands in 1835. The Galápagos Islands are now a wildlife reserve.

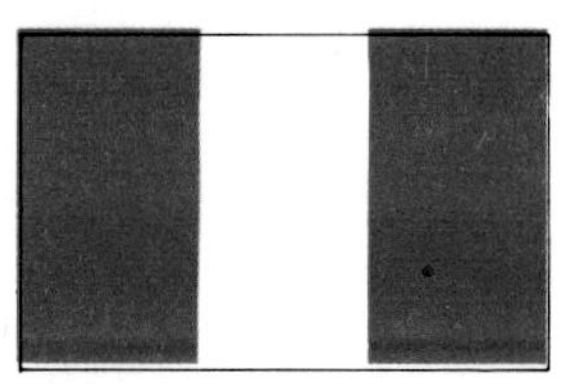

Peru

Area
1,285,220 km²/496,224 sq miles
Location
0°05′—18°20′ S
68°40′—81°20′ W
Population
15,900,000 (1975)
Population density
12 per km²/32 per sq mile
Capital and largest city
Lima: 3,274,000 (1975)
Language
Spanish, Quechua, Aymará
Major imports
machinery, foodstuffs, metal goods, transport equipment, chemicals
Major exports
copper, fish and fish products, silver, sugar, cotton, lead, iron, coffee
Currency
sol (1 sol = 100 centavos)
Gross National Product
7,940 million US dollars (1975)
Status
republic

Physical features

Peru, South America's third largest state contains three major relief regions: the coastal zone, Andes and Amazonian lowlands. A narrow strip of desert, broken by the valleys of short, fast flowing rivers, faces the Pacific. This coastal belt is widest in the north where it forms a dune-covered plain but almost non-existent further south where the mountains drop steeply to the sea in a series of plateaus and ledges. Inland, the massive bulk of the snow-capped Andes climbs to over 5,500 m; the country's highest peak, Huascarán, reaches 6,768 m. Many of the southern peaks are volcanic cones, including the beautifully symmetrical El Misti (5,822 m). Also in the south, on the Bolivian border, the Andean ranges enclose a high plateau containing Lake Titicaca, South America's largest lake (6,900 km²). Beyond the Andes, the land descends into the Amazon basin. Deep gorges, carved by some of the Amazon's main headwaters, dissect the eastern Andean slopes.

Climate

Coastal Peru is cool, cloudy and arid. Onshore winds are cooled by the cold Humboldt current and low, rainless cloud is then formed by condensation: Lima averages 18°C in temperature with 5 cm of rainfall. Andean temperatures vary with altitude: the annual mean at Arequipa is 14°C, 11°C at Cuzco and 5°C at Cerro de Pasco. Most rain falls between October and May and is heaviest in the eastern range. The Amazon basin is warm (26°C) and wet (up to 250 cm).

Fishing

Peru has developed the vast fish resources of the Pacific Ocean to become the world's foremost fishing nation. The catch, accounting for 15% of the world total, includes anchovy, tuna, bonito, mackerel, hake, shrimp and sardines. Anchovies are mostly processed into fishmeal (a protein-rish animal feed) and exported; Peru now supplies 45% of the world's fishmeal. Canned and frozen tuna and bonito are also major exports. In addition, guano is collected from the coastal rocks and is used as fertilizer.

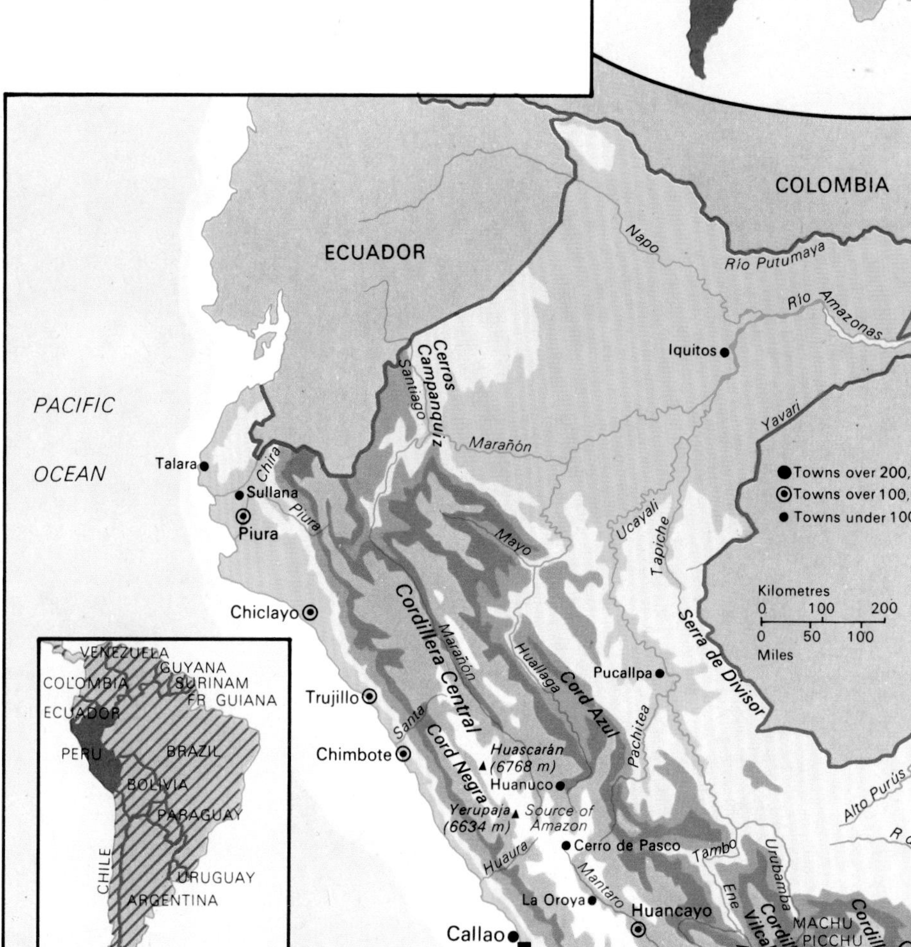

Vegetation

The arid coast is barren except for cacti and desert grasses. In the Andes, the dry western slopes feature drought resistant plants but grassland and forest cover the wetter east. Thick tropical jungle characterizes the Amazon basin.

Forestry

Peru's forest resources are mostly inaccessible but some exploitation occurs in the eastern Andes. Products include mahogany, cedar, rubber, balata, milk caspi (a chewing gum base), quinine and coca (source of cocaine). The main outlet for these products is by river from the Amazon port of Iquitos.

Agriculture

Although 50% of the population depend on agriculture, only 3% of the land is cultivated and Peru is a major food importer. The most productive region is the irrigated coastal belt which is used for sugarcane, cotton, rice, vines, olives, citrus, bananas and tobacco. In the Andes, potatoes, beans, cereals and fruit are grown at varying altitudes. The farming potential of the eastern sector is undeveloped apart from some coffee, cocoa and subsistence crops. Sheep, llamas and alpacas are grazed on highland pastures. Agricultural exports include sugar, cotton, wool and coffee.

Mining

Minerals, accounting for 40% of exports, have a vital place in the Peruvian economy. Most mining activity is located in the mountains at altitudes of over 3,000 m; the main centre is Cerro de Pasco (4,300 m), about 170 km northeast of Lima. Mines in this zone, worked since the seventeenth century, yield silver, copper, lead, zinc, bismuth and vanadium. One of the world's largest stores of copper is found near Toquepala in the south, and large amounts of iron ore are exploited at Marcona on the coast. Other valuable deposits include tungsten, platinum, manganese, mercury, phosphate and potash. Peru is a major world producer of silver.

Industry

The manufacturing sector is expanding steadily and now includes food-processing, cotton and woolen textiles, petro-chemicals, steel, cement, oil-refining, metallurgy and vehicle-assembly. Peru's fishmeal industry, with over a hundred plants, is the largest in the world. Except for smelters and refineries in mining zones, industrial development is mainly situated along the coast and the Lima-Callao region in particular.

Energy

Peru's considerable energy resources include coal at Cerro de Pasco, vast hydro-power potential in the Andes and oil on the northwest coast near Talara, in the Ucayali valley and near Lake Titicaca.

People & towns

About 41% of Peruvians are Amerindians, 39% are mestizos and a further 19% are whites. Two-thirds of the population, including many scattered Indian groups, live in the mountains; the chief Andean city is Arequipa (236,000) in its magnificent setting below El Misti. The coastal zone, although containing only a quarter of the population, dominates the country economically; in addition to Lima, industrial centres include Callao (420,000), Trujillo (197,000), Chiclayo (180,000) and Chimbote (137,000).

Transport

Surface systems are poor because of the difficult terrain and so air services from Lima to all parts of the country are important. There are two main railways: the spectacular Central Railway runs from Callao up into the Andes, climbing 4,800 m in 170 km while the other connects the southern port of Mollendo with the world's highest steamship service across Lake Titicaca to Bolivia. The main features of the road network are the 3,400 km section of the Pan American Highway which follows the coast and the 800 km Trans-Andean Highway from Lima to Pucallpa. Llama trains are used in the high Andes where no roads exist. In the remote eastern lowlands the Amazon is the main artery, but distances are formidable: the chief river port, Iquitos, is 3,700 km from the Atlantic. Callao, near Lima, is the country's leading seaport.

Bolivia

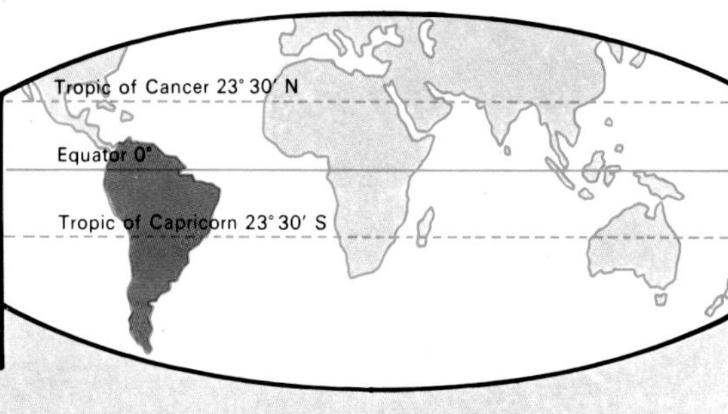

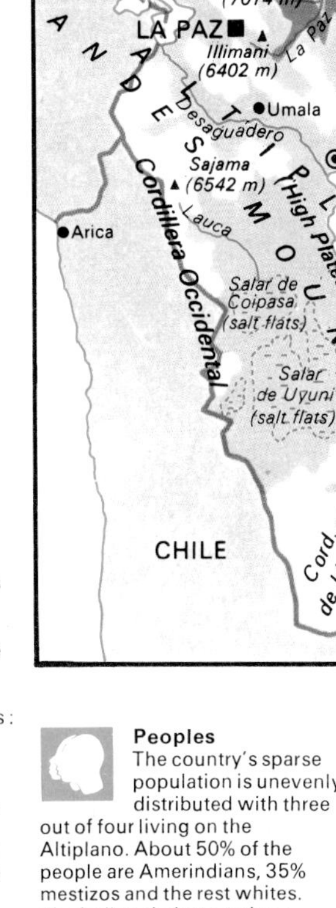

Area
1,098,587 km²/424,165 sq miles
Location
9°40′—22°40′ S
57°30′—69°40′ W
Population
4,688,000 (1976)
Population density
4 per km²/11 per sq mile
Administrative capital
La Paz: 654,500 (1976)
Legal capital
Sucre: 63,000 (1976)
Language
Spanish
Major imports
machinery, foodstuffs, vehicles, iron and steel goods
Major exports
tin, silver, crude petroleum, other minerals, wool, nuts, skins
Currency
peso (1 peso = 100 centavos)
Gross National Product
2,120 million US dollars (1975)
Status
republic

Physical features

Land-locked Bolivia has two sharply contrasting regions: the mighty Andean system in the west and the low eastern plains. The Andes are at their widest in Bolivia (640 km) and comprise two chains: the western branch, along the Chilean border, features volcanic peaks over 6,000 m; the snow-capped eastern ranges include the lofty summits of Ancohuma (7,014 m), Illampu (6,485 m) and Illimani (6,402 m). Between these two chains lies the Altiplano (high plateau) at 4,000 m. At the plateau's northern end is Lake Titicaca, the world's highest navigable lake, drained southwards by the Desaguadero into shallow Lake Poopó. From here, the water disperses into vast and barren salt flats in the south of the Altiplano. Beyond the eastern ranges, the land falls in a tangle of ridges and gorges to the great plains that cover 70% of the country.

Climate

Bolivia is one of South America's driest regions: apart from the north-east, which shares the high rainfall of the Amazon basin, annual rainfall ranges from 60cm near Lake Titicaca and in the eastern foothills to 10 cm on the desert-like southern Altiplano. Temperatures are high on the lowlands but decrease with altitude in the mountains: Cochabamba at 2,500 m averages 18°C while La Paz at 3,665 m averages 9°C.

Peoples

The country's sparse population is unevenly distributed with three out of four living on the Altiplano. About 50% of the people are Amerindians, 35% mestizos and the rest whites. The Indians belong to three ethnic groups: Quechua, Aymara and Guarani. The largest group, the Quechuas (1 million) are mostly found in the southeast of the plateau; the Aymaras (750,000) inhabit the northern Altiplano; the Guaranis live near the Paraguayan border.

Flora & fauna

On the treeless Altiplano, natural vegetation is sparse; coarse grass predominates giving way to cacti and other drought-resistant plants in the south. The banks of Lake Titicaca are thick with totora reeds, used by Indians for making boats and thatching. The eastern Andean valleys are forested in the north and scrub-covered further south. Dense tropical jungle flourishes on the northeast lowlands while savanna and swamp characterize the southeast. Wildlife includes vicunas and condors in the Andes and, at lower levels, jaguars, pumas and alligators.

Agriculture

Although 70% of the population is engaged in agriculture (mostly at subsistence level), Bolivia is not self-sufficient in food. Arable farming is centred on the valleys of the Andean foothills and the Santa Cruz area. Sugar, coffee and cotton are exported while rice, bananas, cassava and maize are the main food crops. Conditions on the Altiplano are unsuitable, but some potatoes, barley and native crops are grown, especially near Lake Titicaca. Livestock farming includes cattle in the Andean valleys and the Santa Cruz region and llamas, alpacas and sheep on the Altiplano. There is some export of wool and skins.

Forestry & fishing

Forests, covering 40% of the territory, occur mostly in the Andean foothills and the northeast lowlands. Although they contain valuable hardwoods such as walnut and mahogany, timber output is low because of transport difficulties. Rubber, from wild trees, and brazil nuts are the main forest exports. Commercial fishing is centred on Lake Titicaca and the Pilcomayo river in the south.

Mining

Mining has played a fundamental part in the economy since 1534 when the Spaniards discovered vast silver reserves at Cerro Rico, making Bolivia the world's leading silver producer. By the 1900s, silver output had declined and tin was the major export; Bolivia is now the world's second largest supplier of tin. Other minerals produced in significant amounts and exported are copper, antimony, tungsten, silver, zinc, lead, bismuth and gold. Further deposits are so far unworked because of inadequate transport. Most minerals occur in a belt about 800 km long and 100 km wide, running along the eastern Andean chain. Minerals make up 95% of exports, tin accounting for 60%. Oil and natural gas are exploited in the southeast and are exported, via pipeline, to Argentina and Chile.

Industry

There is little manufacturing and most consumer goods have to be imported, but the development of oil and gas resources is expected to stimulate industrialization. Factories are mostly located in La Paz, Cochabamba and Santa Cruz.

Transport

Bolivia's poor transport systems are a major obstacle to economic progress. The 25,000 km road network is mostly unsurfaced and even the Pan-American highway is partly impassable during the December-March rainy season. The most important and busiest road is the La Paz-Cochabamba-Santa Cruz highway. On the Altiplano, llamas are widely used as pack animals. The skeletal rail network, totalling only 3,500 km, links the main urban centres and connects with neighbouring systems. As Bolivia has no coastline, trade passes through the Pacific ports of Antofagasta and Arica in Chile and Matarani in Peru (via Lake Titicaca). In addition to Lake Titicaca, the Beni, Pilcomayo, Desaguadero and Mamoré river systems provide 19,000 km of navigable waterway. The national airline, Lloyd Aereo Boliviano, flies to Peru, Brazil, Argentina, Chile and operates internal services.

Cities

In 1898, attempts to move the capital from isolated Sucre to the more vigorous and accessible La Paz resulted in civil war; since then, Sucre, a commercial and agricultural centre, remains the legal capital while La Paz is the seat of government. La Paz, lying in a river valley of the same name at an altitude of 3,665m, ranks as the world's highest capital. Next in importance are the cities of Santa Cruz (255,000), Cochabamba (204,000) and Potosi (77,000). Santa Cruz and Cochabamba both have some industrial development, including oil refineries; Potosi is a major mining centre.

Paraguay

Uruguay

Paraguay and Uruguay

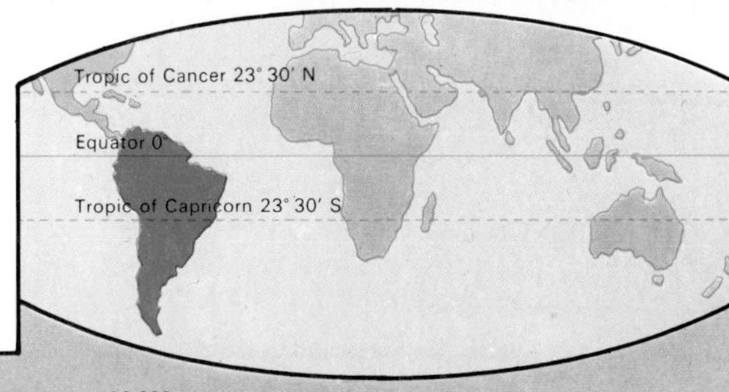

Paraguay
Area
406,752 km²/157,047 sq miles
Location
19°20′—27°40′ S
54°15′—62°40′ W
Population
2,572,000 (1974)
Population density
6 per km²/16 per sq mile
Capital and largest city
Asunción: 417,000 (1973)
Language
Spanish, Guarani
Major imports
fuels, machinery, vehicles, iron and steel, foodstuffs
Major exports
meat products, timber, tannin, cotton, tobacco
Currency
guarani (1 guarani = 100 centimos)
Gross National Product
1,300 million US dollars (1974)
Status
republic

Physical features

The river Paraguay, flowing from north to south, divides the country into two distinct regions. To the west stretches the Gran Chaco, a vast, monotonous lowland of alluvial silts, shifting streams and brackish swamps. East of the Paraguay lies an undulating upland zone, 300 to 600 m high. Apart from the Paraguay, the main rivers are the Paraná (which flows through a deep canyon) and the Picomayo. Vegetation includes deciduous and evergreen forests on the eastern plateau, marsh and palm savanna on the Paraguay plain and grass, and thorn scrub and quebracho thicket on the Chaco.

Climate

The climate is sub-tropical with relatively high temperatures throughout the year. Asunción averages 28°C in January and 17°C in July. Rainfall, heaviest in summer, decreases from 150 cm in the uplands to under 80 cm on the Chaco.

Transport

For landlocked Paraguay, river transport provides a vital trade outlet to the Atlantic ports of Buenos Aires and Montevideo. Large vessels can reach Concepción on the Paraguay and Puerto Stroessner on the Paraná; smaller boats navigate the tributaries. Asunción, 1,520 km from the sea, is the chief port. The road network is being improved; two major highways link Asunción with Paranagua port in Brazil via Puerto Stroessner and with Encarnación. The main railway also runs from the capital to Encarnación where it connects with the Argentinian system. Domestic air services are expanding.

People & towns

The population is 98% mestizo (mixed Spanish and Guarani Indian); minority groups include 40,000 Indians, 14,000 Mennonites (of German and Canadian origin) and 8,000 Japanese colonists. Most people live east of the Paraguay and, except for Mennonite and Indian settlements, the Chaco is virtually uninhabited. The country's only large town is Asunción; other important urban centres are Encarnación, Concepción and Villarrica.

Farming & forestry

Agriculture, concentrated in the east, is the basic economic activity and employs 50% of the population. Cattle-raising is the leading sector with livestock products accounting for 30% of all exports. Arable farming, mostly at subsistence level, covers only 2% of the land. Crops grown for local use are maize, cassava, rice, sugarcane, wheat, yerba maté (tea), coffee and a variety of fruits. Some tobacco, cotton and oilseeds are cultivated for export. Although forest resources are underexploited, they provide 25% of exports, mainly quebracho timber and tannin from the eastern Chaco.

Industry

Paraguay ranks as one of South America's poorest states. Industry is basically limited to processing farm and forest products and includes meat-canning, oilseed-crushing, cotton-ginning, sawmilling and tannin extraction. Nearly all manufacturing is located in Asunción. Small deposits of iron, copper and manganese exist but are so far unworked. Eastern Paraguay has vast hydro-power potential and there are plants on the Acaray and Monday rivers.

Uruguay
Area
186,925 km²/72,172 sq miles
Location
30°—35° S
53°—58°25′ W
Population
2,764,000 (1975)
Population density
15 per km²/38 per sq mile
Capital and largest city
Montevideo: 1,230,000 (1975)
Language
Spanish
Major imports
crude oil, machinery, chemicals, vehicles
Major exports
wool, meat, hides
Currency
peso (1 peso = 100 centesimos)
Gross National Product
3,100 million US dollars (1975)
Status
republic

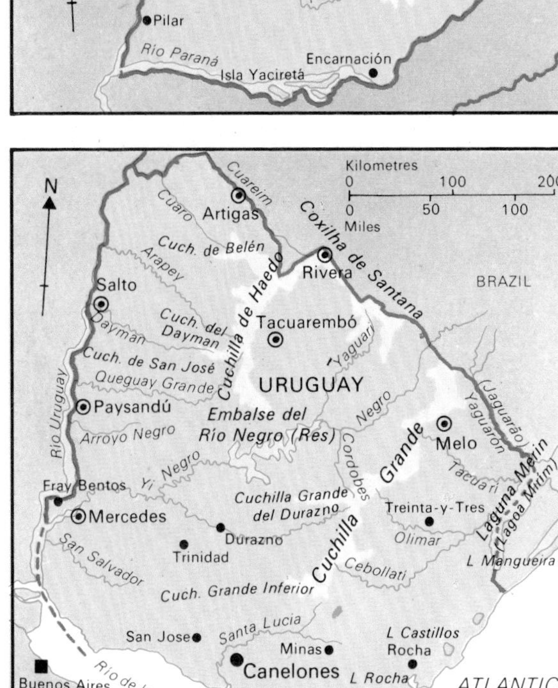

Physical features

Uruguay is the continent's third smallest state and the only one lying wholly outside the tropics. Gently rolling hill country, rising to 500 m in the north, covers most of the territory. Lowland areas comprise the flood plain bordering the Uruguay and Plata and the sandy coastal belt, fringed by lagoons. The Plata system, which includes the Uruguay and Negro, dominates the country's drainage.

People & towns

As most Uruguayans are of European descent, the mestizo element accounts for under 10% of the population. Four out of five people live in urban centres. Montevideo, with 45% of the entire population, is one of South America's largest cities. The country's other main towns—Salto, Paysandú, Mercedes and Fray Bentos—are all on or near the Uruguay; Canelones, Durazno and Rivera are important regional centres.

Climate

The climate, modified by the sea's proximity, is uniform throughout the country. Average temperatures range from 11°C in winter to 23°C in summer. Rainfall, about 120 cm, occurs mostly in autumn and winter but there is no marked dry season.

Agriculture

Uruguay is primarily a pastoral country with 80% of its land used for livestock. The 11 million cattle and 15 million sheep are mostly bred north of the Negro then fattened further south; animals and animal products make up about 50% of all exports. Arable farming is less important and is concentrated in the south on the Uruguay and Plata plains. Crops include wheat, maize, rice, potatoes, oilseeds, sugarcane and beet. Some fruit and vegetables are exported.

Mining & industry

Mining activity is limited to some quarrying of marble and granite. The lack of minerals and other raw materials hampers industrial growth, consequently, most manufacturing remains linked to agriculture: canned meat, sugar, woollen fabrics, vegetable oils and wine are some of the leading products. Other expanding sectors include light-engineering, chemicals, cement and paper. About 75% of industry is concentrated in Montevideo. Major hydro-power schemes are under construction on the Negro and Uruguay and are expected to stimulate industrial development.

Transport

The country's size and topography have resulted in good road and rail networks, both converging on Montevideo. The Uruguay is bridged at Fray Bentos and Paysandú and there are ferries across the Plata; both rivers are busy waterways. Montevideo is the chief port followed by Fray Bentos, Paysandú and Salto. The national airline operates local services and flies to other South American countries.

Chile

Area
756,946 km²/292,257 sq miles
Location
17°30′—56° S
67°—75°40′ W
Population
10,400,000 (1974)
Population density
14 per km²/36 per sq mile
Capital and largest city
Santiago: 3,700,000 (1972)
Language
Spanish
Major imports
foodstuffs, machinery, electrical goods, transport equipment
Major exports
copper, iron ore, chemical products, paper and pulp, fruit and vegetables
Currency
peso (1 peso = 100 centavos)
Gross National Product
7,100 million US dollars (1975)
Status
republic

Physical features

Chile, only 200 to 300 km wide, extends along the Pacific coast for almost 5,000 km. This long, narrow land is overshadowed by the Andes which run north-south along its entire length and occupy half the area. The mountains are highest in the north and centre where they rise to 6,880 m in Ojos del Salado, Chile's highest peak. In the south, the chain is lower and fragmented with lakes, deep valleys, glaciers, fjords and thousands of offshore islands. West of the Andes is Chile's main lowland area, the Central Trough, which features salt lakes and flats in the north but gives way further south to an alluvial zone; below Puerto Montt the trough has been drowned. A low coastal range separates the trough from the ocean; in the far south, the range is submerged and appears as a maze of islands. Rivers, short and fast-flowing, all drain into the Pacific. Chile lies in an unstable zone and is subject to earthquakes and tidal waves.

Climate

Because of its length, Chile spans various climatic zones. The north is very arid—years can pass without rain—but the Andes and the cold Humboldt current modify temperature. Between latitudes 31° and 37°, Mediterranean conditions prevail: temperatures average 10°C in July, 27°C in January and rainfall (occurring in winter) totals 75 cm. Southern Chile is cool and wet with summer temperatures of 20°C and all-year rain (120 cm). The extreme south, including the islands and western Tierra del Fuego, is stormy with high winds, lashing rain (500 cm) and heavy snow; temperatures range from —4°C to 15°C.

Flora & fauna

The desert north is barren except for small valley oases and stunted scrub on the Andean foothills. Grassland and deciduous forest characterize 'Mediterranean' Chile while the south is densely forested with Chile pine (monkey-puzzle), evergreen beech, larch, cypress and thick undergrowth. Wildlife includes pumas, mountain goats, guanacos, condors and parrots.

Mining

Chile's wealth lies in its minerals which are mostly located in the north. Copper, providing 80% of exports, dominates the economy. Reserves represent 40% of the world total and Chile ranks as the third largest copper producer and second exporter. The main mines are at Chuquicamata, El Teniente and El Salvador. High grade iron ore, occurring in Atacama and Coquimbo provinces, is next in importance followed by nitrates from the northern desert; iodine and potassium salts are major by-products. In addition to these leading minerals, many others exist; those worked include gold, silver, manganese, lead, zinc, sulphur and molybdenum. There is some coal-mining near Concepción and oil (from fields in Tierra del Fuego and the Strait of Magellan's north shore) provides 30% of domestic requirements.

Agriculture

Chile's agricultural potential is under-exploited, resulting in large imports of basic foods. The main farming region is the Mediterranean zone, particularly the irrigated, fertile central valley. Here the chief crops are maize, barley, rice, peaches, apples, grapes and vegetables; there are also extensive pastures. About 60% of Chile's cattle, however, are kept further south on small farms in the forest zone; these farms also grow most of the country's wheat, oats and potatoes. In the extreme south, on the Patagonian steppe and in Tierra del Fuego, large flocks of sheep are grazed. Agricultural exports (only 5% of all exports) include wine, fresh and dried fruit, wool and meat.

Forestry & fishing

Southern Chile, between Concepción and Puerto Montt, is extensively forested but, so far, commercial exploitation of timber is limited. The quick-growing pine is the basis of paper and cellulose manufacture, while oak, beech and elm are supplied to the construction industries. Traditionally, Chileans eat few fish, but efforts are being made to boost fish consumption and expand the fishing industry; some shellfish and fishmeal are exported.

Energy

As domestic supplies of oil, natural gas and coal are inadequate, Chile's vast hydro-power potential is being developed to meet the country's expanding energy needs. Most hydro plants are located in the Andes, but the resources of the coastal range are also being harnessed. At present, about half of Chile's electricity is water-generated.

Industry

In recent years, manufacturing has grown significantly and now employs a quarter of the total workforce. Many plants process domestic raw materials to produce steel, woollen textiles, cement, wine, dried fruit, paper, cellulose, furniture, leather goods, petrochemicals and so on, but other sectors have to rely on costly imported materials. Industry is concentrated in the three main urban centres: Santiago, Valparaíso and Concepción.

Transport

Chile's extraordinary shape has a major impact on transport systems. Coastal shipping has always been significant, especially in the south where there are no surface routes beyond Puerto Montt; the road to Punta Arenas, the world's southernmost city, passes through Argentina. The Santiago-Valparaíso road and the Pan-American Highway, from Arica to Puerto Montt, are the two most important roads. Railways consist of a main line between Pisagua and Puerto Montt with branches. Most imports pass through Valparaíso, the chief port; mineral exports are shipped from Antofagasta, San Antonio, Huasco and Chanaral. There are five international airports.

People and towns

Widespread intermarriage between the Spanish and Indian communities has resulted in a predominantly mestizo population. About 70% of Chileans live in the 'Mediterranean' zone which contains the country's three largest cities: Santiago, Valparaíso (300,000) and Concepción (200,000). Santiago, in its beautiful setting below the Andes, is the country's economic hub and houses over a third of the population. The second city and chief port is Valparaíso. Concepción, near the mouth of the Bío Bío, is a modern city which has been rebuilt many times after earthquakes; its port is Talcahuano.

Argentina

Area
2,791,810 km²/1,077,919 sq miles
Location
22° — 55° S
53°40' — 73°30' W
Population
25,400,000 (1976)
Population density
9 per km²/24 per sq mile
Capital and largest city
Buenos Aires: 2,972,453 (1970)
Language
Spanish
Major imports
machinery, metals, chemicals, vehicles, paper
Major exports
cereals, meat, linseed, wool, hides, textiles
Currency
peso (1 peso = 100 centavos)
Gross National Product
38,500 million US dollars (1973)
Status
federal republic

Physical features

Argentina, South America's second largest state, occupies most of the continent below the Tropic of Capricorn and east of the Andes. For nearly 4,000 km, the country's western boundary runs along the high Andean crestline. Towards the north, the mountain zone widens to include a bleak, desert plateau some 4,000 m high. South of this lies Cerro Aconcagua (7,163 m), highest peak in the Western Hemisphere. East of the northern highlands lies the Chaco, an extensive lowland made up of alluvia swept down from the Andes and crossed by the rivers Salado, Bermejo and Pilcomayo. Mesopotamia, the region between the Paraná and Uruguay rivers, is low lying except for a spur of the Brazilian plateau in the northeast. Fanning out from Buenos Aires is Argentina's heartland, the *Pampas*: vast and monotonous grasslands that cover 20% of the country. Southwards, towards the Colorado river, the land rises slowly; beyond the river extends the Patagonian plateau, a rugged, desolate lakeland.

Climate

Argentina's climate, spanning 33° of latitude, ranges from subtropical heat to sub-antarctic cold. The north has hot, wet summers (25°C) and long, dry, mild winters (13°C); rainfall increases from 50 cm in the west to 120 cm in the east. Buenos Aires averages 23°C in summer and 10°C in winter with both temperature and rainfall decreasing towards the southwest. Patagonia is arid and windy and although winters are not severe (2°C), summers are short and cool (16°C).

Population

The indigenous Indians, decimated by the Spaniards, now number under 30,000 and are concentrated in the northwest. As there has been little intermarriage, 97% of Argentinians are white and only 2% (found in the Andean zone) are mestizos. Two-thirds of the people live on the pampas which contain, in addition to the capital, such major cities as Rosario (810,000), Córdoba (801,000), La Plata (500,000) and Sante Fé (252,000). Greater Buenos Aires, with over 9 million inhabitants, is South America's largest urban centre.

Agriculture

Agriculture, centred on the pampas, forms the base of the economy: it supplies most of the country's food and provides 90% of all exports. Stockraising is the principal sector, making Argentina the world's largest raw-meat exporter and fourth largest producer of both beef and wool. Pasture covers almost half the territory: 50 million cattle are grazed on the pampas and 45 million sheep are kept, mostly in Patagonia. Arable farming, occupying 11% of the land, is also concentrated on the pampas. Wheat is the leading crop followed by maize, linseed, alfalfa (for fodder) and sunflower seed. Crops grown beyond the pampas include rice, tea and maté in Mesopotamia; cotton in the Chaco; sugar-cane and citrus in the northwest. Vines are cultivated in the Andean foothills, especially near Mendoza; Argentina ranks as the fourth largest wine producer in the world.

Mining

Apart from oil and natural gas, Argentina lacks mineral wealth and has to import supplies for industry. There are small, scattered deposits of iron ore, lead, zinc, tin, silver, gold, copper, sulphur, tungsten, mica, manganese, cobalt, vanadium and uranium, but only a few of these are worked. Some coal is mined in southern Patagonia but it is low-quality and located too far from urban areas to be important. Argentina is, however, self-sufficient in oil: the main fields are in Patagonia, centred on Comodoro Rivadavia and in the western provinces. Natural gas occurs in the same areas and a network of oil and gas pipelines crosses the country.

Industry

Not surprisingly, much of Argentinian industry is based on agriculture; products include wool and cotton textiles, canned meat, cigarettes, wine, vegetable oils, flour, sugar and leather goods. Other major sectors are steel, petro-chemicals, engineering, cement, electronics and motor cars. Buenos Aires is the main manufacturing centre, but San Nicolas (on the Paraná) has the country's leading steel plant and San Lorenzo (further upstream) is the site of a giant refining and petrochemical complex.

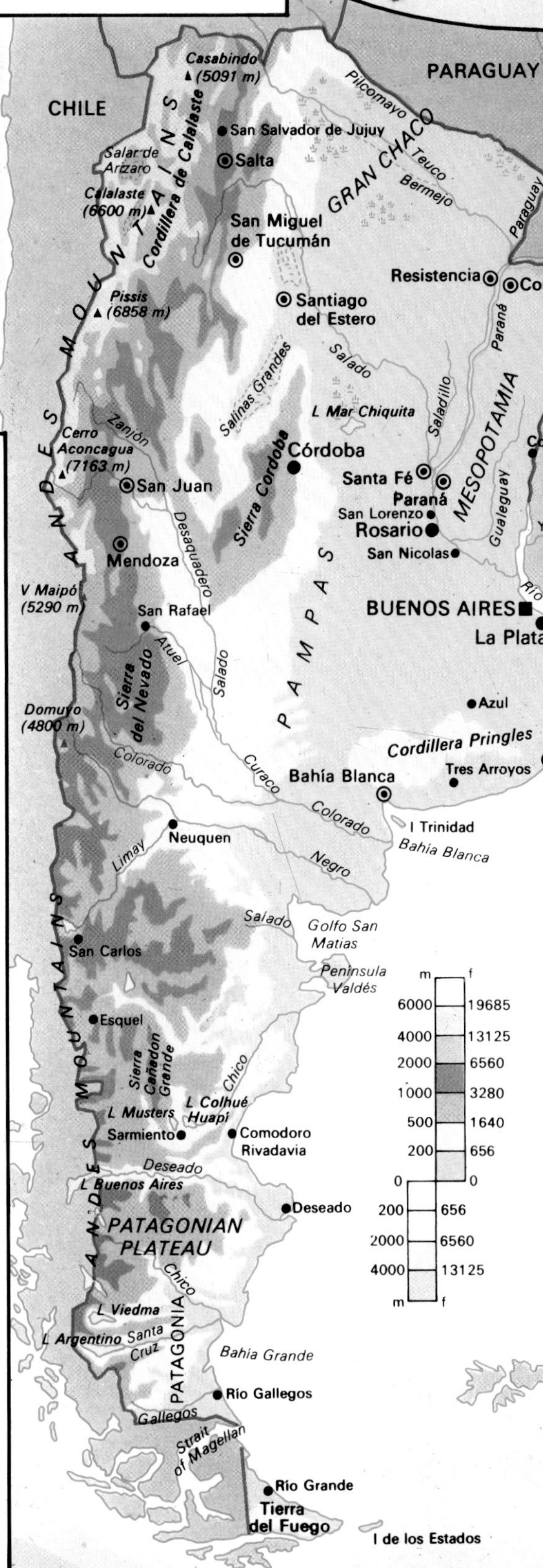

Transport

Argentina's transport services, among the best in South America, are mostly concentrated on the pampas. However, the 40,000 km rail network, spreading out from Buenos Aires, serves all areas except Patagonia; international routes include a spectacular trans-Andean line to Santiago (Chile). The road system, totalling 944,000 km, is being improved for although major highways are good, minor roads are generally unsurfaced and many become impassable in rain. There are steamer services on the Rio Plata, Paraguay, Paraná and Uruguay. The main port, handling 75% of trade, is Buenos Aires followed by Bahía Blanca, Rosario and La Plata. Internal air services, vitally important in remote Patagonia, are well-developed; three international airports link Argentina to all parts of the world.

Flora & fauna

The cold Andean plateau is barren apart from scattered tussocky grasses and stunted drought-resistant shrubs; forests of beech and pine characterize the foothill zone except in the arid south. Deciduous woodland, spiny thorn scrub, savanna and swamp cover the Chaco; Mesopotamia has rolling grassy plains and dense forests. The wide, treeless grasslands of the pampas are richest in the wetter east. In Patagonia, vegetation is reduced to low bushes and coarse grasses. Wildlife includes jaguars, pumas, alligators and parrots in the forests; condors and vultures in the Andes; and the guanaco (wild llama) and rhea (ostrich-like bird) on the pampas.

Forestry

Argentina's extensive hardwood forests, mainly in the Chaco and northern Mesopotamia, are under exploited. A significant product is tannin dye, extracted from the quebracho tree. Softwoods have to be imported.

Fishing

Off-shore fish resources have recently been developed. The fishing industry, centred on Mar del Plata, supplies fish (principally hake and anchovy) for human consumption and for processing into animal feeds.

Atlantic Ocean Islands

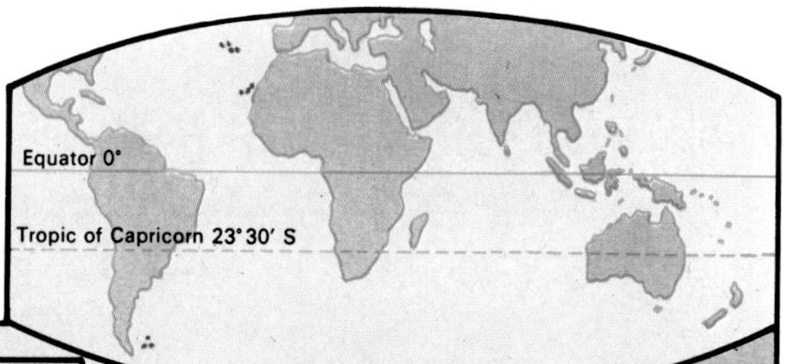

Falkland

St Helena

Azores
The Azores, politically part of mainland Portugal, have a total area of 2,335 km^2 and comprise nine main islands in three widely separated groups: São Miguel and Santa Maria in the east; Graciosa, Terceira, São Jorge, Pico and Faial in the centre; Flores and Corvo to the northwest. The archipelago, 1,300 km west of Portugal, is volcanic in origin. Mountain masses rise steeply from rocky coastal belts and reach 2,351 m on Pico. The climate is mild and damp: the temperature averages 16 C and rain, falling throughout the year, 100 cm. Most of the 291,000 islanders live along the coast and are engaged in farming and fishing. Cereals, fruits, sugar cane, vegetables and tobacco are grown while the fish catch mainly consists of tunny and mullet. Exports include oranges, pineapples, bananas, canned fish and sperm whale oil. The chief towns are the capital on Ponta Delgada, Angra and Horta—all major ports.

Madeira
Madeira, administered as part of Portugal, lies 700 km southeast of the Azores. The volcanic archipelago, 796 km^2 in area, comprises two inhabited islands, Madeira and Porto Santo, plus uninhabited islets and rocks. Madeira, the largest island, consists of central mountains rising to 1,861 m in Pico Ruivo, forested spurs and deep valleys; Porto Santo is hilly. The climate is warm and humid with average temperatures of 17 to 21 C and 50 cm of rain a year. Agriculture dominates the economy: coastal areas and terraced lower slopes are used for growing vines, sugar cane, cereals and a wide range of fruits and vegetables. Wine, bananas and sugar are the main exports. There is some fishing for tunny and swordfish. Tourism is important and traditional handicrafts, notably embroidery and wickerwork, are commercially significant. Funchal the capital, is the major port and leading tourist centre; Vila is the chief town on Porto Santo. The total population of the archipelago is about 253,000.

Canary Islands
The Canary Islands, part of Spain, have an area of 7,273 km^2 and a population of 1,170,000. Situated 100 km off the African coast, the archipelago consists of two groups: to the west, the mountainous islands of Tenerife, Gran Canaria, La Palma, Gomera and Hierro are all peaks rising directly from the ocean floor; Pico de Teide (3,718 m) on Tenerife is Spain's highest point. In the east, Lanzarote, Fuerteventura and adjacent islets are of volcanic origin. The climate is warm but uncertain rainfall often causes drought and irrigation is necessary. Agriculture is the main economic activity. Bananas, citrus, sugar cane, vegetables, coffee, dates, and tobacco are grown below 400 m and cereals, grapes and potatoes up to 700 m. Bananas, tomatoes and sugar are the chief exports. There is some local fishing for sardines and tunny. Tourism is important. The leading towns are Las Palmas and Santa Cruz de Tenerife and these are also the major ports.

Cape Verde Islands
The Cape Verde archipelago, in the central Atlantic 480 km west of Africa, is a Portuguese overseas territory comprising 10 islands and 5 islets. The islands, with a total area of 4,033 km^2, are divided into two groups: Barlavento (windward) and Sotavento (leeward)—the prevailing winds being northeast. Of volcanic origin, the islands are mountainous and rugged and Fogo has an active volcano. The climate is hot (25 C) and humid but there is little rain and droughts are common. About 10% of the territory is used for agriculture with maize and beans as the main food crops while coffee, bananas and peanuts are grown for export. Other exports are canned tuna, salt (produced on Sal, Maio and Boa Vista), pozzolana (a volcanic rock) and corals. Industry includes food-processing and textiles. The capital is Praia on São Tiago but Mindelo on São Vincente is the chief commercial centre, main port and a major refuelling station for transatlantic shipping. Sal has an international airport. The islands have a total population of 280,000.

São Tome e Príncipe
The Portuguese overseas province of São Tome e Príncipe in the Gulf of Guinea is 270 km off the African coast and has a total area of 964 km^2. The two main islands, São Tome (854 km^2) and Príncipe, are of volcanic origin and consist of rugged, jungle-covered highlands with Pico de Tome reaching 2 024 m. Situated just north of the equator, the islands have a hot and humid climate. A third of the land has been cleared for agriculture and the economy is based on cocoa (accounting for 60% of exports) and coffee—both grown on plantations. Other products exported include coconuts, palm oil, copra and cinchona. The main food crops are cassava, sweet potatoes and yams—there is also some fishing. Nearly all the 80,000 inhabitants live on São Tome and work on the plantations. Most of them are contract labourers from the Cape Verde islands.

Falkland Islands
The Falkland Islands are a British colony lying in the south Atlantic some 500 km off the Argentine coast. The group, with a total area of 12,200 km^2, comprises two main islands—East Falkland (6,495 km^2) and West Falkland (5,880 km^2)—plus 200 smaller islets. The desolate landscape consists of mountains and moorlands while the coast is broken by deep fjords. Strong winds and low temperatures characterize the climate. Almost the entire territory is used for sheep-farming. There are some 600,000 sheep with wool the main product but some hides are also exported. Postage stamps are another source of income. Small quantities of oats, potatoes and vegetables are grown, but nearly all the islands' food is imported. About 2,000 people live in the colony, half of them in Stanley—the only town. There is a monthly shipping service from Stanley to Montevideo and direct sailings to the United Kingdom several times a year. Inter-island transport is by seaplane.

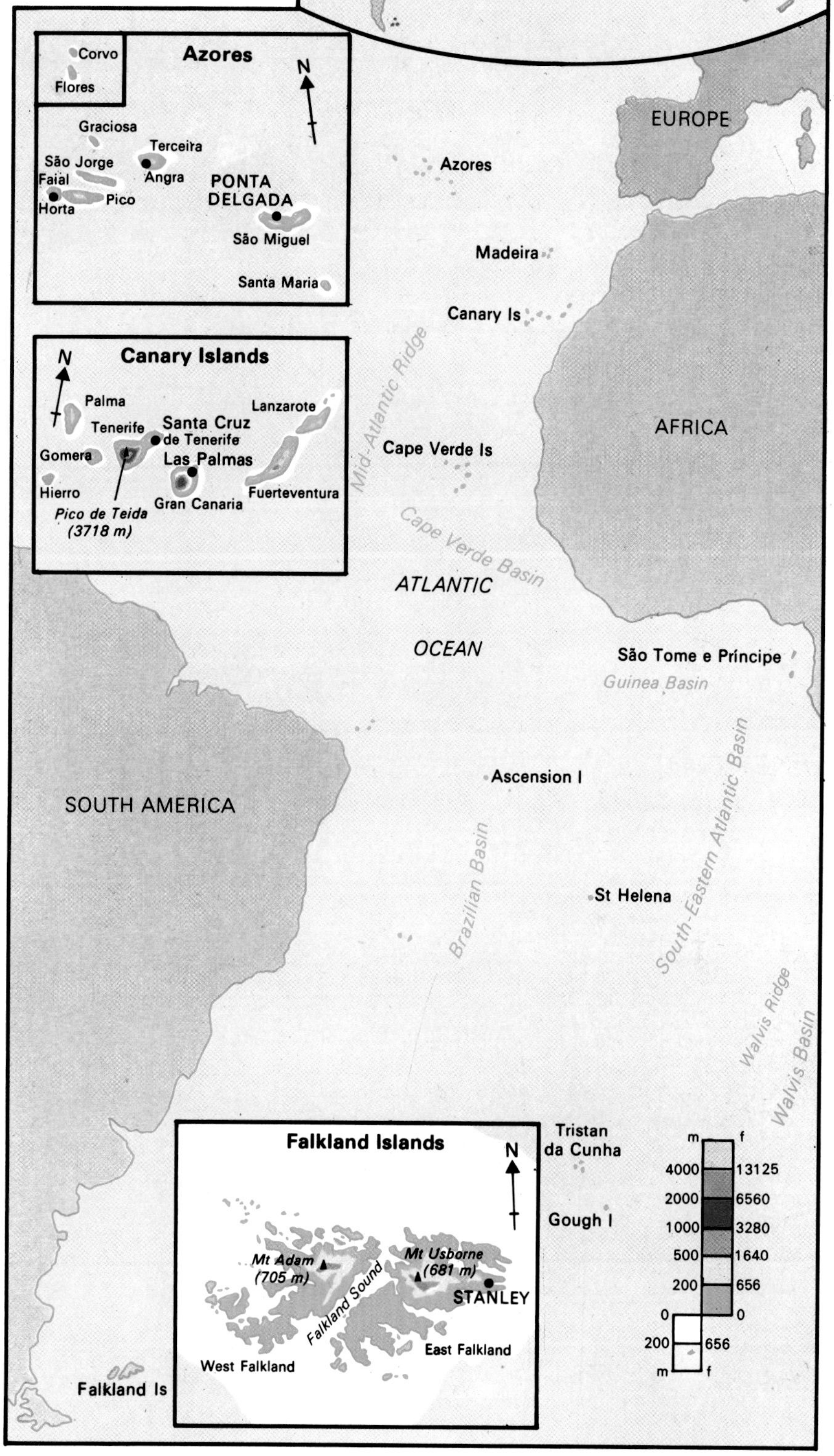

St Helena
The British colony of St Helena, a volcanic island 1,900 km off west Africa, has an area of 122 km^2 and a population of 5,000. Edged with steep cliffs, it has a mountainous interior rising to 823 m in Diana's Peak. The climate, influenced by the southeast trade winds, is temperate. Farmland covers a quarter of the island: potatoes and other vegetables are the main crops and there are some cattle. Fish provides the main source of protein. Jamestown (population 1,600) is the capital and chief port.

Ascension Island
Situated 1,120 km northwest of St Helena, Ascension (88 km^2) is of volcanic origin and is barren except on Green Mountain (875 m). The climate is tropical but dry. Only 4 ha are cultivated, producing vegetables and fruit. The 1,230 inhabitants are mostly employed in the telecommunications and satellite tracking stations situated there. Georgetown is the main settlement. The island, a dependency of St Helena, is famous for its wild life—particularly sea turtles (which lay their eggs on the beaches) and sooty terns.

Tristan da Cunha
The Tristan da Cunha group, halfway between the Cape and South America, is a dependency of St Helena. Tristan (98 km^2) is the largest island and consists of a volcanic cone 2,000 m high. The 290 inhabitants live by farming (potatoes, sheep, cattle) and fishing. There is a crayfish-freezing plant. 50 km south are the small islands of Inaccessible and Nightingale. Rugged Gough Island (90 km^2) lies 400 km to the southeast. All 3 islands are uninhabited and are noted for their rare plants and birds.

Mauritania, Morocco and Western Sahara

Morocco Mauritania

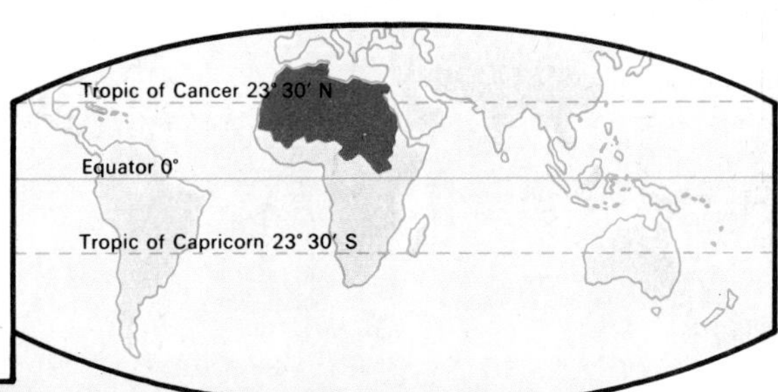

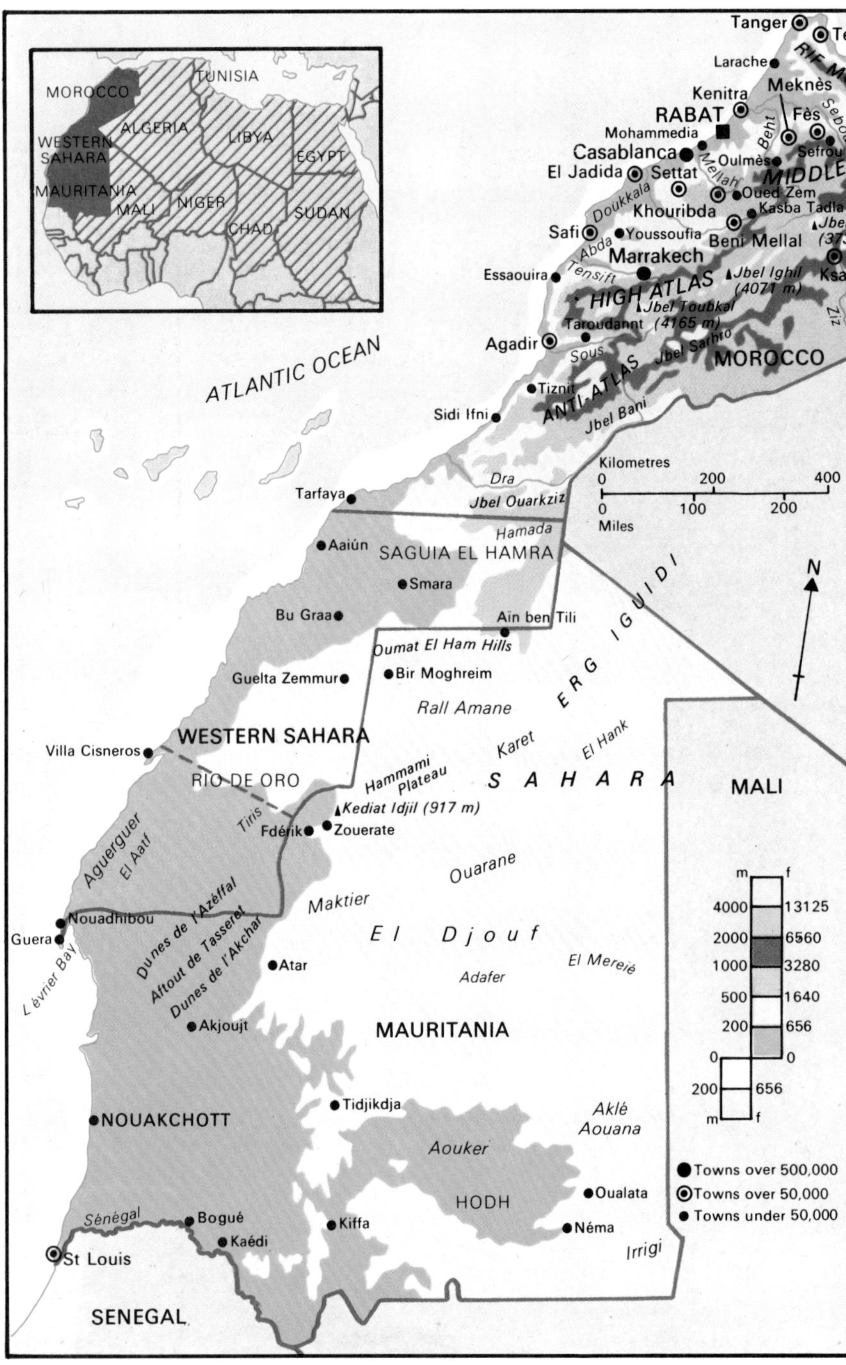

Mauritania
Area
1,030,700 km²/397,950 sq miles
Location
14° 49'–27° 23'N; 4° 50'–17° W
Population
1,180,000 (1972)
Population density
1 per km²/3 per sq mile
Capital and largest city
Nouakchott: 55,000 (1973)
Languages
Arabic and French
Major imports
machinery, transport equipment, foodstuffs, fuels
Major exports
iron ore, fish, cattle, copper
Currency
ougiya (1 ougiya = 5 khoums)
Gross National Product
275 million US dollars (1973)
Status
republic

The land

Mauritania consists of a vast plateau sloping down from 220 m in the northeast to 45 m in the southwest. The monotonous landscape is broken by a series of west-facing scarps, including the Adrar range (490 m), and by isolated peaks such as the Kediat Idjil (917 m). Half the plateau consists of gravel desert; the remainder is dune-covered. Southwest Mauritania is drained by tributaries of the Sénégal; elsewhere, the plateau is dissected by wadis (dry riverbeds) that are very occasionally filled with floodwater. A hot, arid climate with summer temperatures of 30°C and under 10 cm of rain annually prevails over most of the country. The coast is cooler, the south wetter.

The economy

Agriculture, mostly stock-raising, supports 85% of the population. Cattle are bred in the south, sheep and goats along the desert fringe and camels in the north. Arable farming is confined to the alluvial Sénégal region and the oases. Millet and dates are the main crops; maize, beans, yams and cotton are also grown. The waters of Lévrier Bay are rich in fish and the fishing industry, based at Nouadhibou, is important. There are extensive deposits of iron ore at Zouerate and copper at Akjoujt. Iron ore, accounting for 80% of exports, is shipped from Nouadhibou; copper from Nouakchott. There is little industry apart from food-processing and packaging.

Morocco
Area
458,730 km²/177,117 sq miles
Location
27°40'–35°50'N; 1°–13°10'W
Population
16,800,000 (1974)
Population density
37 per km²/95 per sq mile
Capital
Rabat: 724,000 (1974)
Largest city
Casablanca: 1,950,000 (1974)
Language
Arabic
Major imports
food, fuels, textiles, vehicles, machinery, iron and steel
Major exports
phosphates, citrus fruits, fish, tomatoes, lead ore, wine
Currency
dirham (1 dirham = 100 centimes)
Gross National Product
3,222 million US dollars (1972)
Status
constitutional monarchy

The land

Morocco is a rugged country dominated by the Atlas mountains. These mountains sweep across the centre from northeast to southwest and rising from 2,750 m in the Middle Atlas to over 4,000 m in the High Atlas; Jbel Toubkal (4,165 m) is the highest peak. To the south the Anti-Atlas (the uplifted edge of the Saharan platform) reaches 2,000 m. The coastline is extensive: in the north, the Rif mountains rise steeply from the Mediterranean while the Atlantic seaboard is flanked by lowland areas such as the Sebou, Oumer Rbia, Tensift, Sous and Dra river basins. The longest river, the Moulouya, flows into the Mediterranean. Northern Morocco has a Mediterranean climate with hot, dry summers and warm, wet winters; the Atlas zone is dryer and colder while the southeast, verging the Sahara, is very hot and arid.

Transport

The mountainous interior is largely uninhabited except for nomadic tribesmen and, consequently, the 25,000 km road network is mainly concentrated in the populated coastal areas. Railways (40% electrified) cover 1,770 km. Main lines link Casablanca to Tanger, Marrakech and Algeria (via Oujda); branch lines connect with the mining areas. Casablanca, handling 75% of Moroccan trade, and Safi are the chief freight ports; Tanger is important for passengers. Other major ports are Mohammedia, Kenitra and Agadir. Royal Air Maroc is the national airline.

Agriculture

Farming and fishing employs 70% of Moroccans, supplies 85% of the country's food needs and provides 40% of total exports. Arable land is concentrated along the coast where the main crops are wheat, barley, sugarbeet, oilseed, cotton, olives, citrus, almonds and vegetables. Berber tribesmen graze sheep and goats in the mountain valleys and camels in the arid south; some cattle are raised on the lowlands. Forests cover many highland areas and products include cork, cedar timber and tannin. The Atlantic coastal waters abound in tunny, sardines, mackerel and anchovies. Agadir, Safi, Casablanca and Essaouira are the chief fishing ports. The leading agricultural exports are citrus, tomatoes, processed fish and olive oil. Morocco ranks as the world's second largest citrus exporter.

Mining & industry

Morocco is a major world producer of phosphates, mined at Khouribga and Youssoufia and exported via Casablanca and Safi. Cobalt, lead, zinc and manganese are also worked in significant quantities. Supplies of energy minerals (coal, oil and gas) are inadequate and fuel is imported; 80% of electricity used comes from hydro-electric power plants. Industry mainly consists of preparing goods for export (olive processing, fish-canning, fruit-packing, wine-making and phosphate processing). Flour-milling and sugar-refining serve the domestic market. Textiles, leatherwear, vehicles, cement, paper and chemicals are also important. Casablanca is the leading industrial centre.

Cities

Casablanca, extending 20 km along the Atlantic coast, ranks as Morocco's largest and most important city and port. The country's second city, Marrakech (464,000), is the chief town in the south. Known as the 'red city' because of its red clay buildings, it is a trading centre for the Atlas and Sahara regions. Fès (448,000), the former northern capital, is a major religious centre. The present capital of Rabat is mainly administrative.

Western Sahara

Formerly Spanish Sahara, Western Sahara (266,000 km²) is part administered by Morocco and part by Mauritania. It is a desert country with a dune covered coastal plain rising inland to a plateau 300 m high; in the northeast, mountains reach 600 m. The main towns are Aaiún (24,000) and Villa Cisneros (5,400). The 75,000 inhabitants are mostly nomads who live by herding sheep, goats and camels; some barley and maize are grown. The fishing industry, based at Guera, is important. The territory's principal resource is the Bu Graa phosphate deposits. These are among the richest in the world but are not yet exploited. Fish, phosphates and skins are exported.

Tunisia Algeria

Tunisia and Algeria

Tropic of Cancer 23° 30′ N
Equator 0°
Tropic of Capricorn 23° 30′ S

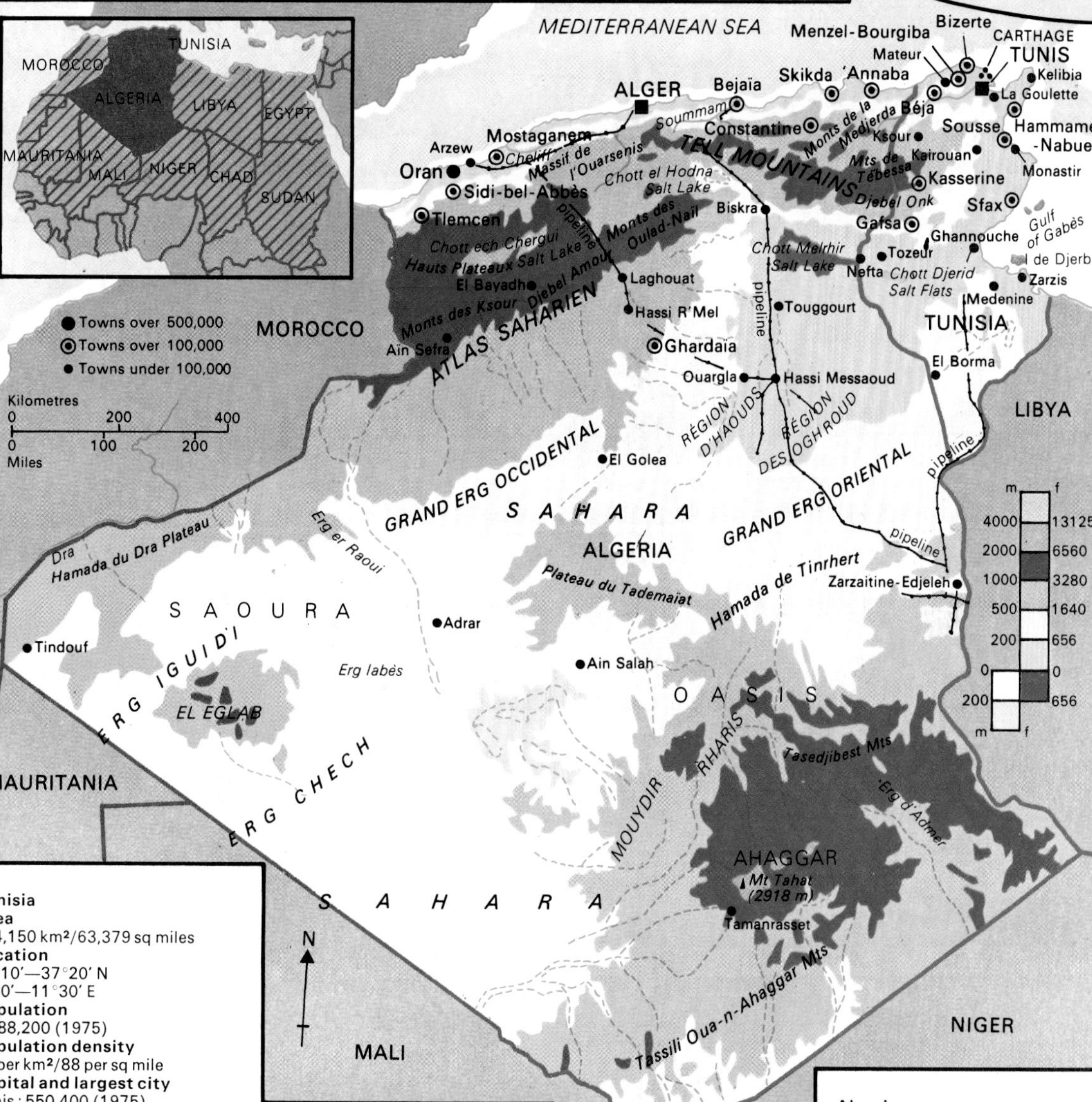

Tunisia
Area
164,150 km²/63,379 sq miles
Location
30°10′—37°20′ N
7°30′—11°30′ E
Population
5,588,200 (1975)
Population density
34 per km²/88 per sq mile
Capital and largest city
Tunis: 550,400 (1975)
Language
Arabic
Major imports
machinery, metal goods, transport equipment, foodstuffs
Major exports
oil, olive oil, phosphates, wine, citrus, iron and steel
Currency
dinar (1 dinar = 1,000 millimes)
Gross National Product
3,150 million US dollars (1974)
Status
republic

The land

Northern Tunisia consists of a plateau some 500 m high. This plateau, an extension of the Atlas mountains, is drained by the Medjerda—the only permanent river. Steppe lands and salt flats, such as the Chott Djerid, characterize central Tunisia which merges southwards with the Sahara. The coast has warm dry summers and mild winters: Tunis averages 12°C in January and 25°C in August. Inland conditions are more extreme: winter temperatures in the plateau drop to 0°C while the desert records over 50°C in summer. Rainfall is low, decreasing from 80 cm in the north to 10 cm in the south.

Agriculture

Tunisia is an agricultural country and 60% of the population lives off the land. The main cereals are wheat and barley grown in the Medjerda valley. Wine-grapes and citrus predominate in the northeast, olives along the coast between the Gulfs of Hammamet and Gabès, and dates in the desert oases. Other crops include sugarbeet, potatoes, tomatoes, figs, apricots and almonds. There is little irrigation and crop yields fluctuate because of the variable rainfall. Animals, mostly sheep, are grazed on the southern steppes. Other products include cork and esparto grass.

Mining

Tunisia is a leading world producer of phosphates. Production is centred on the Gafsa region and phosphates, phosphoric acid and fertilizers are major exports. Iron ore, lead and zinc are also mined and exported. Oil, supplying domestic needs and accounting for 40% of total exports, comes from El Borma and the Gulf of Gabès; natural gas from Ras el Tib and near Sfax.

Industry

Food processing is the main industry: products include olive oil, wine, sugar (at Béja), flour, canned fish and preserved fruit and vegetables. Paper is made from esparto grass at Kasserine, and wool and leather are also processed. Among newer projects are an oil refinery at Bizerte, a steel complex at Menzel-Bourgiba and a phosphoric acid plant at Ghannouche. Other industries include cement, vehicle assembly, fertilizers and electronics. Tourism is based on east coast resorts such as Hammamet-Nabeul and Djerba.

Tunisian transport

Except for the coastal highways to Libya, road and rail networks are concentrated in northern Tunisia. The main seaports are Tunis-La Goulette, Bizerte, Sousse and Sfax. Tunis-Air, the national airline, operates internal and overseas flights; international airports are situated at Tunis, Djerba and Monastir.

Algeria
Area
2,466,833 km²/952,445 sq miles
Location
19°—37°10′ N
8°30′W—12°E
Population
16,275,000 (1974)
Population density
7 per km²/17 per sq mile
Capital and largest city
Alger: 1,700,000 (1974)
Language
Arabic
Major imports
machinery, iron, steel, transport equipment, foodstuffs, textiles
Major exports
oil, wine, gas, fruit and vegetables, iron ore
Currency
dinar (1 dinar = 100 centimes)
Gross National Product
4,400 million US dollars (1971)
Status
republic

Algerian transport

About 90% of surfaced roads (27,000 km) are in the north. The 4,000 km rail network connects with Morocco and Tunisia and serves the main ports: Alger, Oran, 'Annaba, Bejaïa, Skikda and Arzew. Air Algérie is the national airline with airports at Alger, Oran and 'Annaba.

The land

The Tell mountains separate the rocky coast from a belt of high plateaux (1,200 m) and interior basins containing salt lakes such as the Chott el Hodna and the Chott ech Chergui. The southern rim of this semi-arid zone is formed by the Atlas Saharien. Beyond this mountain wall lies the Sahara, occupying 80% of the country and consisting of bare rock, gravel deserts and *ergs* (vast sand seas). In the southeast the desert rises to Algeria's highest peak, Mt Tahat (2,918 m). The coast has a Mediterranean climate—12°C in January, 27°C in August; the desert has frosts in winter but high summer temperatures. Rain varies from 100 cm in the eastern Tell to zero in the Sahara.

Agriculture

Agriculture, employing half the people, is confined to the coastal zone and adjacent valleys. Grapes are the main cash crop and wine accounts for 65% of agricultural exports. Other leading crops are wheat, barley, olives, citrus, vegetables and tobacco. The Tell and plateau are used for grazing, mostly sheep and goats; the plateau also yields esparto grass. Forests cover parts of the Tell and Atlas ranges; products include timber, cork and dye barks. The oases have date palms and Algeria is a major producer of dates. Sardine, anchovy and tunny fishing is important. Algeria is not self-sufficient in food and large imports are necessary.

Mining

Oil and gas make up 75% of Algerian exports. The two main oilfields, accounting for 60% of total output, are Hassi Messaoud and Zarzaitine-Edjeleh; there are refineries at Hassi Messaoud, Arzew, Skikda and Bejaïa. By 1980, gas is expected to be more important than oil. Production is centred on Hassi R'Mel. In the mid-1970s, gas was liquefied before export but direct pipelines to Spain and Italy were planned. Oil and gas are used to generate 75% of the country's electricity; hydro-electric power supplies the remainder. There are deposits of iron ore (Ouenza), lead-zinc (El Abed) and phosphates (Djebel Onk). Copper, mercury, antimony, marble and salt also exist.

Industry

Excluding oil, 40% of industrial output consists of foodstuffs such as wine, olive oil, dried fruit and flour. Other manufactures based on domestic agriculture are cigarettes, leather goods, textiles and paper. Large scale industrial development, with the emphasis on heavy industry, dates from independence in 1962. Modern concerns include oil refineries, gas liquefaction plants, an iron and steel complex at 'Annaba, fertilizer plants at Arzew and Annaba, a chemical factory, engineering works and cement plants. Algerian industry is 70% state-controlled.

Libya

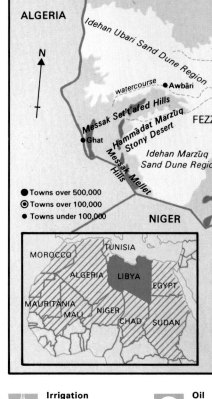

Area
1,759,540 km²/679,358 sq miles
Location
19°—33°10′ N
9°10′—25° E
Population
2,259,500 (1973)
Population density
1.3 per km²/3 per sq mile
Capital and largest city
Tripoli: 551,477 (1973)
Language
Arabic
Major imports
machinery, foodstuffs, transport equipment, textiles, chemicals, building materials
Major exports
petroleum and petroleum products
Currency
dinar (1 dinar = 1,000 dirhams)
Gross National Product
6,280 million US dollars (1973)
Status
republic

Physical features
Libya, roughly square-shaped, is a vast, arid land. Except for the Mediterranean coastal belt, the country consists of barren rock deserts, undulating sand seas, salt-marsh depressions and mountains that rise to 1,200 m in the southwest and to 1,800 m in the southeast. In the north, the coast is flanked by the Jabal al Akhdar hills in the northeast and by the Jabal Nafusah range in the northwest. Between the Jabal Nafusah and the sea, the coastal strip widens and forms the Gefara plain—Libya's most fertile zone—which extends westwards into Tunisia. There are no permanent rivers.

Climate
Climatically, Libya is influenced by both the Mediterranean and the Sahara. The coastal region has a Mediterranean climate: winters are mild with 25 to 40 cm of rain and summers hot and dry. Tripoli averages 13°C in January, 28°C in July. Conditions in the desert interior are extremely hot and arid: annual rainfall ranges from 0 to 12 cm and summer daytime temperatures rise to 45°C but fall at night to under 30°C. An unpleasant feature of the summer months (April to September) is the *ghibli*, a burning southerly wind that brings dust and sand storms and temperatures of over 50°C.

Crops
Arable land covers less than 2% of the total area and is confined to the Gefara plain, the lower slopes of the Jabal Nafusah and Jabal al Akhdar, the Cyrenaica peninsula coast (especially near Al Marj) and inland oases such as Al Kufrah, Brach and Al Jufrah. Farming is most intensive in the northwest: dates, olives, citrus, groundnuts, potatoes, melons and tomatoes are grown along the Gefara coast while further inland the plain supports wheat and barley (the main cereals), olives, vines, citrus and almonds. Olives, vines, figs, apricots, apples and tobacco thrive on the Jabal Nafusah. Vines, olives and dates are important in Cyrenaica and dates predominate in the oases. Libya is not self-sufficient in agriculture and food accounts for 30% of imports. Some olives, tomatoes, groundnuts and almonds are exported.

Irrigation
Since rainfall is negligible, irrigation is vital for Libyan agriculture. The Gefara plain is the most intensively irrigated area but there are other major irrigation and reclamation schemes in the Al Kufrah oasis, the Jabal al Akhdar, the Tāwurghā region, at Awbāri, Sarir and in the Brach/Sabhah district. There is also some irrigated land at oases in the south where wells penetrate underground water. Libya's groundwater resources are, however, limited and supplies for irrigation are reducing the water table.

Livestock
Before the discovery of oil, agriculture (in particular, livestock farming) was the basis of the economy: hides, skins and wool were leading exports. Animals are still important as three-quarters of Libya's productive land is suitable only for grazing. Nomads, accounting for 22% of the population, herd sheep and goats along the desert margins and products include meat, milk, wool and skins. Camels and donkeys are kept for draught purposes. Dairying is being developed on the northeast and northwest coastal belts.

Oil
Oil, discovered in 1957 has transformed Libya from a poor agricultural state into one of Africa's richest nations. Petroleum now dominates the Libyan economy and accounts for 97% of total exports. The most important fields are in the Sirte basin and include Zelten, Hofra, Gialo and Sarir. These are linked by pipeline to terminals at Tubruq, Ras Lanuf, As Sidar, Az Zuwaytīnah and Marsa el Brega. Libya is the leading oil producer in Africa and the fourth largest producer in the Middle East.

Mining
Libya's mineral resources are largely unsurveyed and unexploited. Marine salt is produced near Tripoli, natron (a sodium carbonate compound) is mined in the southwest and chalk, limestone and marble are quarried. Important iron ore reserves have been discovered in the southwest but other mineral deposits are less significant. These include potash and sulphur in the Sirte basin and potassium and magnesium salt in the Marādah region. Mining activity is hampered, however, by inadequate transport systems.

Fishing
Although Libya has a 1,900 km coastline, fishing is of limited importance. The industry is most developed in the northwest and is based at Misrātah, Zuwārah and Al Khums. The catch consists of tunny, mullet and sardine.

Industry
Ambitious programmes of industrialization financed by oil revenues are being checked by a lack of skilled labour, poor communications and a small domestic market. Traditionally, Libyan industry consists of processing local raw materials: manufactures include olive oil, cigarettes, matting, carpets, leather goods, flour, embroidered fabrics and paper (made from esparto grass which grows wild). Recently established industries produce cement, soft drinks, soap, detergents, textiles, petroleum and petrochemicals. Large-scale projects planned for the future cover foodstuffs (canned fruit and vegetables, date processing, dairy products), building materials (iron and steel, aluminium fittings, glass, bricks, cement), clothing, footwear and animal feedstuffs. Tripoli and Benghāzī are the chief industrial centres.

Transport
Libya's transport system is poor but is currently being developed. The 6,000 km road network includes two major highways: a coastal road links Tripoli and Benghāzī (and extends east to Alexandria and west to Tunis) and a route from Tripoli to Sabhah. Minor roads serve the Tripoli and Benghāzī regions and link the oil fields to the Gulf of Sirte ports. A highway to Al Kufrah is under construction and road links with Niger and Chad are planned. The railways have not been in operation since 1964. Tripoli is the main port followed by Benghāzī, Darnah and Tubruq. Libyan Arab Airlines operate international flights from Tripoli and Benghāzī.

Cities
Most Libyans live on the coastal plains in the northwest and northeast and 25% of the population is concentrated in the two main cities: Tripoli and Benghāzī. Tripoli, founded by the Phoenicians, is the administrative, commercial and industrial capital and a major tourist centre. Benghāzī (282,200) is also industrialized. The third largest town is Misrātah (103,300).

Mali, Niger and Chad

Mali (top left)
Niger (top)
Chad (left)

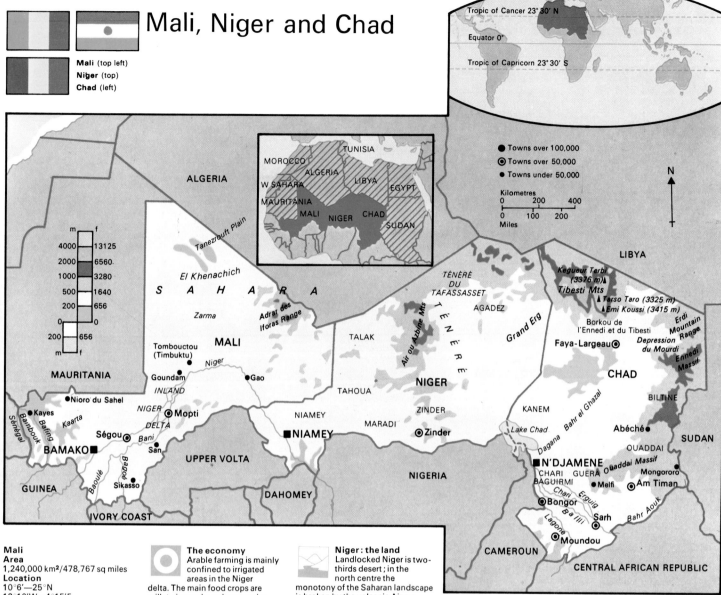

Mali
Area
1,240,000 km²/478,767 sq miles
Location
10°6′—25°N
12°10′W—4°15′E
Population
5,376,000 (1973)
Population density
4 per km²/11 per sq mile
Capital and largest city
Bamako: 350,000 (1973)
Language
French
Major imports
foodstuffs, machinery, vehicles, fuels, chemicals
Major exports
cotton, livestock, groundnuts, vegetable oils, dried fish
Currency
franc (1 franc = 100 centimes)
Gross National Product
352 million US dollars (1970)
Status
republic

Mali: the land

Mali is a vast landlocked state. The northern half of the country is part of the Sahara and consists of gravel-covered plateaux and great sand seas. The Adrar des Iforas range, rising to over 1,000 m, dominates the northeastern corner. Southern Mali is crossed by the Niger—in its middle section, between Ségou and Tombouctou, the river splits into numerous channels and flows through a swampy shallow basin, called the Inland Niger Delta, which floods annually. The mountainous southwest is drained by the Sénégal. Mali has a hot, arid climate. In the desert, temperatures reach 60°C and rainfall is negligible; the south is cooler and wetter with temperatures of 30°C and 75 cm of rain falling June to October.

The economy

Arable farming is mainly confined to irrigated areas in the Niger delta. The main food crops are millet, rice and sorghum; maize, yams and cassava are also grown. Cotton and groundnuts are the chief cash crops and sugar-cane and tobacco are being developed. Livestock (cattle, sheep and goats) is important, particularly in central Mali. There is extensive fishing on the Niger and 20% of the catch is exported. Limestone and marble are quarried but known deposits of other minerals, such as iron, bauxite, manganese, phosphates and gold, have yet to be exploited. Industry, based on local produce, is small-scale and includes rice-milling, sugar-refining, groundnut oil extraction, cotton-ginning and cement manufacture.

Niger
Area
1,267,000 km²/489,190 sq miles
Location
11°40′—23°28′N
0°20′—16°E
Population
4,304,000 (1973)
Population density
3 per km²/9 per sq mile
Capital and largest city
Niamey: 102,000 (1972)
Language
French
Major imports
vehicles, textiles, fuels, food, machinery, iron and steel
Major exports
uranium, live animals, groundnuts and groundnut oil, cotton
Currency
franc (1 franc = 100 centimes)
Gross National Product
424 million US dollars (1972)
Status
republic

Niger: the land

Landlocked Niger is two-thirds desert; in the north centre the monotony of the Saharan landscape is broken by the volcanic Air ou Azbine mountains rising to nearly 2,000 m. The country is lowest around Lake Chad in the southeast and along the river Niger valley in the southwest. Niger is hot (Niamey averages 35°C) and dry: annual rainfall decreases from 56 cm along the Nigerian border to 18 cm in the centre.

Agriculture

Arable land, covering only 3% of the country, is located in the south on the sandy soils of the Nigerian border and along the Niger valley (irrigated by seasonal flooding). Food crops include millet, sorghum and, to a lesser extent, maize, cassava, onions and rice. The main cash crops are groundnuts and cotton. Cattle are grazed on the pastures in the Niger valley with sheep and goats kept on the desert margins. Half the fish catch, from the Niger and Lake Chad, is exported.

Mining & industry

Uranium, mined at Arlit, is Niger's leading export. Some salt and tin are also produced in the Air ou Azbine. Other mineral resources, including iron ore from Say and gypsum and phosphates at Tahoua, are still unexploited. Rice mills, flour mills, cotton ginneries, slaughter houses, tanneries and groundnut oil extraction plants all rely on domestic agricultural produce. Newer projects include a textile factory, a cement works and some light industries.

Chad
Area
1,284,000 km²/495,750 sq miles
Location
7°25′—23°28′N
15°—24°E
Population
3,869,000 (1973)
Population density
3 per km²/9 per sq mile
Capital and largest city
N'Djamene: 193,000 (1973)
Language
French
Major imports
fuels, foodstuffs, vehicles, minerals, textiles, machinery
Major exports
cotton, meat, livestock, hides and skins
Currency
franc (1 franc = 100 centimes)
Gross National Product
333 million US dollars (1971)
Status
republic

Chad: the land

Chad is named after the lake on its western border. Lake Chad (16,000 km²) is marshy with an average depth of only 4 m. It is fed by the Chari and Logone—the only rivers to be used for irrigation and navigation. From the lake, at an altitude of 250 m, the country fans out forming a great basin rimmed by the Tibesti mountains (3,400 m) in the north and by the Ennedi and Ouaddai massifs in the northeast and east. Temperatures average 28°C; rainfall ranges from 120 cm in the extreme south to 2 cm at Faya.

Agriculture

Agriculture forms the basis of the Chad economy and most people live by farming and stock-raising. Arable land is limited to the southern part of the country. Sorghum, millet and rice are produced for food, while cotton and groundnuts are the leading cash crops. Wheat, maize, cassava, sugar-cane and tobacco are also grown; dates predominate in the northern oases. Cattle graze on the open grasslands of central Chad and sheep, goats and camels are herded in the more northerly, arid zone. The rivers Chari and Logone and Lake Chad are rich in fish which is dried and either sold locally or exported.

Mining & industry

Chad's mineral resources are mostly unsurveyed. Natron, produced in the Lake Chad region, is the only mineral of commercial significance. It is used as salt for human consumption, for preserving meat and skins and in soap production. There is little manufacturing. Cotton-ginning is the main industrial activity. Other concerns include a sugar refinery, textile mill, abattoirs, flour and rice mills, groundnut oil extraction plants and a bicycle-assembly works. In Chad, as in Mali and Niger, transport is a major problem—roads are few and railways non-existent. All three countries are land-locked and far from any port. This hinders foreign trade.

Egypt

Area
1,002,000 km²/386,873 sq miles
Location
22°—31°35′ N
25°—35°40′ E
Population
36,420,000 (1974)
Population density
36 per km²/92 per sq mile
Capital and largest city
Cairo: 6,588,000 (1974)
Language
Arabic
Major imports
foodstuffs, machinery, chemicals, transport equipment
Major exports
cotton, rice, cement, phosphates, petroleum and products, onions
Currency
pound (1 pound = 100 piastres)
Gross National Product
9,287 million US dollars (1974)
Status
republic

Information given includes that part of Sinai which in 1976 was under Israeli military administration.

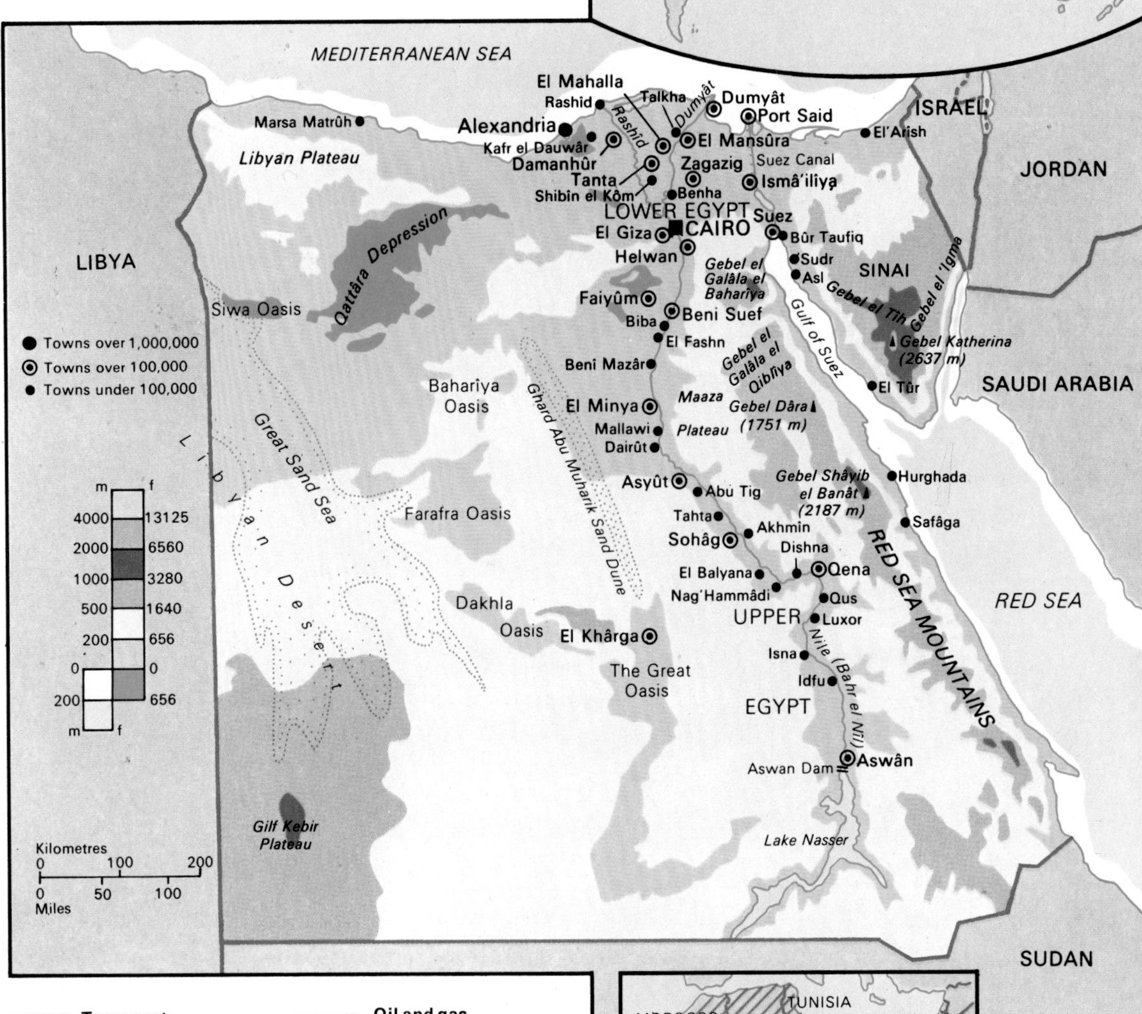

Physical features
About 96% of Egypt is desert. The area west of the Nile is an arid plateau some 200 m high, crossed by belts of sand dunes in the centre and west. There are also several depressions with accessible underground water which are cultivated and settled such as the Qattâra Depression and the oases of Bahariya, Siwa, Farafra, Dakhla and Khârga. The desert extends east of the Nile to the Red Sea mountains, a coastal range 1,500 to 2,000 m high. To the northwest, these highlands give way to a barren limestone plateau which stretches east into Sinai; southern Sinai is mountainous, rising to 2,637 m in Gebel Katherina. The Nile is Egypt's most important feature. For 300 km from the Sudanese border, the narrow valley is flooded by Lake Nasser formed by the giant Aswan dam. Below Aswân, the valley widens—this is a densely populated region. The Nile divides 25 km north of Cairo into the Rashîd and Dumyât—the two main channels of the 22,000 km² delta. The alluvial deltaic plain is fringed with lagoons and swamps along the coast.

Climate
Egypt is very hot and dry. In summer (May to October) temperatures rise to 37°C in Cairo and 43°C in the desert during the day, but at night can drop by as much as 20°C. Winter is slightly cooler with midday averages of 21°C in the north and 27°C in the south. Rainfall is minimal: Cairo receives only 6 cm annually, while the desert often has no rain at all. The prevailing wind is northerly, but in March and April hot winds from the Sahara bring scorching sandstorms. The Mediterranean coast is milder and wetter with 25 cm of rain a year.

Irrigation
Irrigation is vital to Egyptian agriculture. The Nile is the basic source of water and, with the aid of dams and barrages, supplies an extensive network of distributary canals. The most important scheme is the Aswan dam which holds back valuable flood water. In desert oases, wells reach the underlying water table.

Transport
Transport systems, centred on Cairo, are well developed in the Nile delta and valley. The 25,000 km road network includes major highways from the capital to Alexandria, Port Said, Ismâ'iliya, Suez and Aswan. Railways, totalling 4,300 km, serve the delta and run south to Aswân; there is also a line linking the Bahariya iron ore mines to Helwan. There is considerable inland shipping on the delta waterways and the Nile. The Suez canal, closed from 1967 to 1975, is being deepened and widened. About 80% of Egypt's imports and exports pass through Alexandria, the chief seaport. Port Said is the other main Mediterranean port, while Suez handles trade with the Far East. The national airline, Egyptair, operates domestic and overseas services; there are international airports at Cairo, Alexandria, Luxor, Aswân and Marsa Matrûh.

Mining
Phosphates, iron ore, manganese, salt and asbestos are the chief minerals exploited in Egypt. The main phosphate reserves are in the eastern desert and on the Red Sea coast, particularly near Isna and Safâga. Iron ore is mined east of Aswân and in the Bahariya oasis area. There are manganese deposits east of Luxor and in southwestern Sinai. Other minerals worked in small quantities include gypsum, talc, lead-zinc and tungsten; there are adequate supplies of building stones.

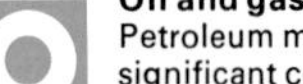

Oil and gas
Petroleum makes a significant contribution to the economy: Egypt is now self-sufficient in oil and has moved into the export market. The total annual output is 18 million tonnes: 60% of this comes from off-shore fields in the Gulf of Suez; the bulk of the remainder is produced along the western shore of the Gulf of Suez. There are also oilfields in Sinai. Refineries are situated in Suez, Mostorod, Tanta and Alexandria and a pipeline is under construction from Suez to Alexandria. Natural gas, from fields in the delta and the western desert, is used to power industries in Helwan and Talkha. Oil, however, is the country's principal source of energy followed by hydro-electric power.

Cities
Cairo, the 'city of victory', was built in 968 at the head of the Nile delta. The largest city in Africa and the Middle East, it contains some of Islam's finest architecture and also has a priceless collection of Pharaonic treasures in the Egyptian Museum. There is some manufacturing in the city, but heavy industry is concentrated at Helwan. Alexandria (2,590,000), at the western edge of the delta, was founded by Alexander the Great in 332 BC. The ruins of its famous lighthouse (one of the Seven Wonders of the World) can still be seen. It is Egypt's main industrial centre and leading port with a canal link to the Nile.

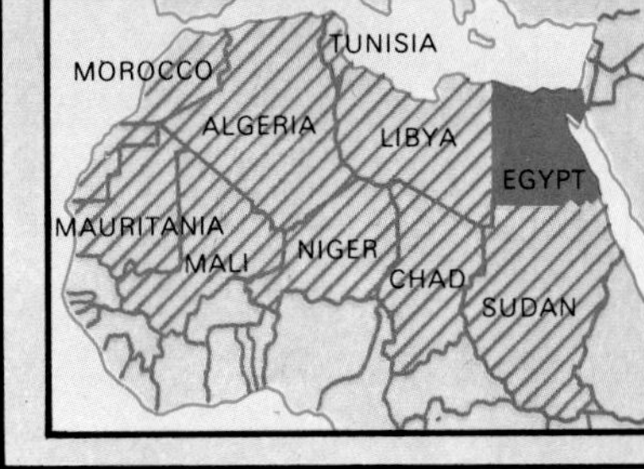

Agriculture
Agriculture is the main sector of the economy: it employs over half the workforce and provides 50% of exports. Although farmland, confined to the Nile valley, delta and oases, covers only 5% of the total area, most of it yields two or three crops a year. The main crop is cotton, grown on 14% of the cultivated area; Egypt leads the world in the production of long-staple cotton. Egypt also ranks as the world's third largest rice exporter. Ricefields, accounting for 10% of farmland, are mainly in the delta region. The leading food crops are wheat and maize and the country is self-sufficient in cereals. Other crops include sugarcane, millet, barley, beans, onions, potatoes, citrus and dates. Livestock farming is being developed in order to supply domestic meat and milk requirements. Cattle and buffaloes are also kept as draught animals and nomads herd sheep and goats in the desert. There is local fishing along the Nile and coast.

Industry
Manufacturing is steadily developing and now accounts for 14% of employment and 35% of exports. Industry is largely located in the delta region—the main centres being Helwan, Shubrâ el Kheima (a Cairo suburb), Mahalla el Kubra, Kafr el Dauwâr and Alexandria. There is also some development in the Suez canal zone. Textile manufacture, using cotton, wool, silk and artificial fibres, is the leading sector and supplies 30% of the total industrial output. It is based on Mahalla el Kubra, Kafr el Dauwâr and Shubrâ el Kheima. Food-processing is next in importance: this includes flour-milling, sugar-refining and fruit and vegetable-canning. Other major industrial products include cement (Cairo, Alexandria), iron and steel (Helwan), petro-chemicals (Suez), engineering (Helwan), fertilizers (Talkha) and aluminium (Nag'Hammâdi). Tourism is growing and new resorts are planned for Marsa Matrûh and the Pyramids (Gîza).

Sudan

Flora and fauna

In the north, the only extensive vegetation consists of cultivated fruit trees (mostly date palms) along the Nile and in oases. The desert gives way to a broad belt of savanna which in turn gives way to stretches of equatorial rain forest and vast expanses of elephant grass. Papyrus, in the Sudd swamp, grows up to 5 m high. Except for antelope, addax and ostrich, there is little life in the desert, but the savanna and southern forests are the home of many animals including elephants, giraffes, buffaloes, hippopotami, crocodiles, leopards, lions, hyenas and white and black rhinoceros.

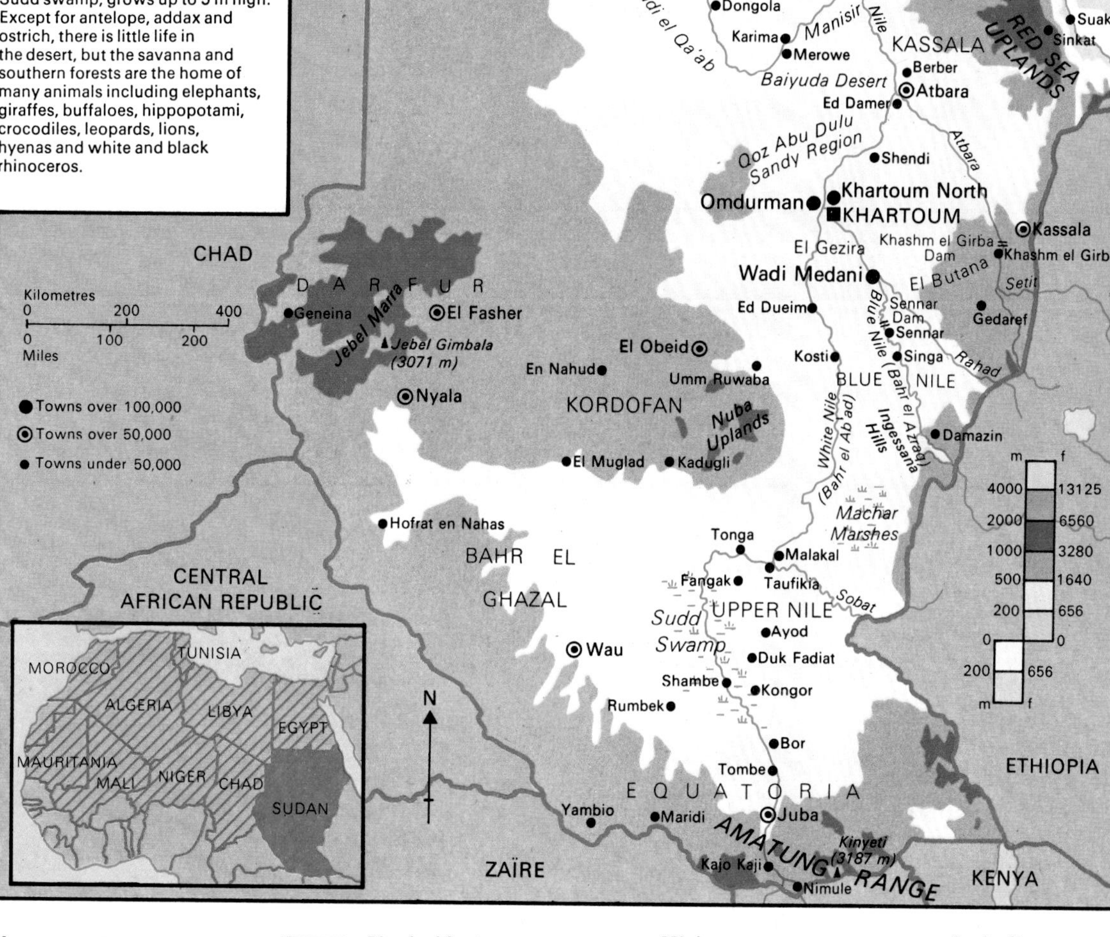

Climate

As Sudan lies wholly in the Tropics and is almost completely land-locked, it has a tropical, continental climate. Maritime influences from the Red Sea are confined to the coastal plain and the eastern slopes of the Red Sea hills. Temperatures are always high: in Khartoum they range from 32°C in winter (November—March) to 41°C in summer (April—June). Rainfall increases from under 5 cm in the north to 150 cm in the south. The rainy season corresponds to July—October in the centre, but lengthens to March—October in the south. In the Nubian desert, dry northerly winds prevail and sandstorms are common.

Industry

Sudan is primarily an agricultural country and manufacturing is underdeveloped. Sudanese industry is mainly concerned with processing agricultural raw materials for the domestic market. There are flour-mills, canning plants, textile mills, tarneries and soap factories. The principal industries centred on the overseas market are cotton-ginning, groundnut-shelling and date-processing. By 1980, Sudan aims to export sugar and textiles: the most important sugar factory is at Khashm el Girba, while new textile plants are being built with foreign aid. Industrial growth is hampered by inadequate power supplies although some industries (cotton-ginning, suga and oil processing) generate their own electricity from by-products. Although all major towns are supplied, many parts of Sudan are without electricity.

Transport

Sudan has an inadequate transport system. Most of the roads are cleared tracks which become impassable after rain. There are only 330 km of surfaced roads and 60% of these are in the Khartoum area. The 4,750 km rail network connects the major centres and is used for nearly all freight movements. There is all-year shipping on the Nile between Kosti and Juba and between Dongola and Karima; other routes are seasonal. Port Sudan, the only seaport, is to be developed following the re-opening of the Suez canal. Sudan Airways operates international and domestic services. A petroleum pipeline links Khartoum to Port Sudan.

Area
2,505,824 km²/967,500 sq miles
Location
3°40′—22°N
21°50′—38°30′ E
Population
16,900,000 (1973)
Population density
7 per km²/17 per sq mile
Capital
Khartoum: 334,000 (1973)
Language
Arabic
Major imports
machinery, vehicles, textiles, metals, chemicals, petroleum
Major exports
cotton, gum arabic, sesame, groundnuts, animal feeds, hides and skins
Currency
pound (1 pound = 100 piastres)
Gross National Product
2,100 million US dollars (1973)
Status
republic

Tourism

A growing number of tourists visit Sudan each year. Attractions include big game hunting and photo safaris, archeological remains in the Nile valley (some dating from 4,000 BC), fishing and skin-diving in the Red Sea.

Physical features

Sudan, the largest state in Africa, has only 640 km of coast-line and that is situated along the Red Sea. Most of the country consists of a vast plateau which is crossed by the Nile and edged by mountains on the east, south and west. The foothills of the Ethiopian plateau extend along the eastern border and the Red Sea coast; the southern Amatung range contains the country's highest peak, Kinyeti (3,187 m), and in the extreme west the Jebel Marra massif rises to 3,071 m. The Nubian desert is an extension of the Sahara which occupies a third of the territory in the north. A huge papyrus swamp, the Sudd, created by the seasonal flooding of the White Nile and its tributaries covers southern Sudan. The Sudd, one of the largest swamps in the world, acts as a reservoir and the flow of the White Nile is consequently relatively even throughout the year. In contrast, rivers draining the Ethiopian highlands (the Sobat, Blue Nile and Atbara) are torrential during the rainy season but otherwise almost dry. The White and Blue Niles meet at Khartoum to form the Nile.

Mining

The mineral resources of Sudan are largely unexploited. There is limited production of iron ore in the Red Sea uplands, chromite in the Ingessana hills, copper at Hofrat en Nahas and gold near Wadi Halfa and in Kassala province. Deposits of mica, manganese and quartz are also worked and marble is quarried in the Red Sea hills. Output from the salt pans at Port Sudan meets domestic requirements and provides a surplus for export. Other minerals known to exist include lead, asbestos, barites, zinc, graphite, sulphur, talc, gypsum and oil (discovered in the Red Sea). Minerals account for less than 1% of total exports: salt is most important, but some copper, iron, mica, manganese and chromite are also exported.

Forestry

The central savanna is largely composed of acacia trees which provide Sudan with its second most important export: gum arabic. Sudan supplies over 90% of the world's gum arabic, used in the manufacture of perfume, confectionery and adhesives.

Agriculture

Agriculture dominates the Sudanese economy. Although less than 5% of the land is farmed, the country is self-sufficient in basic foods and Sudan's chief exports are agricultural products. About 15% of arable land is irrigated. The main irrigation scheme, using water from the Sennar Dam on the Blue Nile, is in El Gezira while another major project based on the new Khashm el Girba dam on the Atbara, serves the El Butana region which now specializes in sugarcane. Cotton is the principal cash crop: long-staple varieties are grown under irrigation, especially in El Gezira; short-staple cotton, cultivated in the extreme south and the Nuba uplands, is rainfed. Other crops include wheat, maize, sesame, groundnuts, millet, oilseeds, sorghum, dates, citrus and mangoes. Tea, coffee, rice and tobacco are being developed in the south. Livestock is important: nomads rear camels, sheep and goats in the north, cattle in the south. Cotton accounts for 60% of total exports; groundnuts, sesame, hides and skins are also exported. There is fishing along the Red Sea coast.

Cities

The population is unevenly distributed: half the country is uninhabited and most Sudanese live in the Nile valley, Khartoum and the provincial capitals. Khartoum is three cities in one. The old town, Khartoum (meaning 'elephant trunk' after the shape of its site), was a centre of the slave and ivory trade in the last century. On its northeast side is Omdurman (290,000), a commercial centre famous for its livestock market. Across the river to the north of the old city is the industrial town of Khartoum North (150,000).

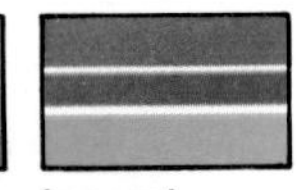
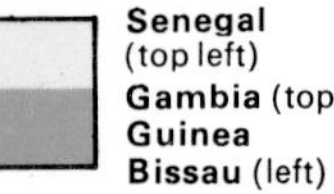

Senegal (top left) **Gambia** (top) **Guinea Bissau** (left)

Senegal, Gambia and Guinea Bissau

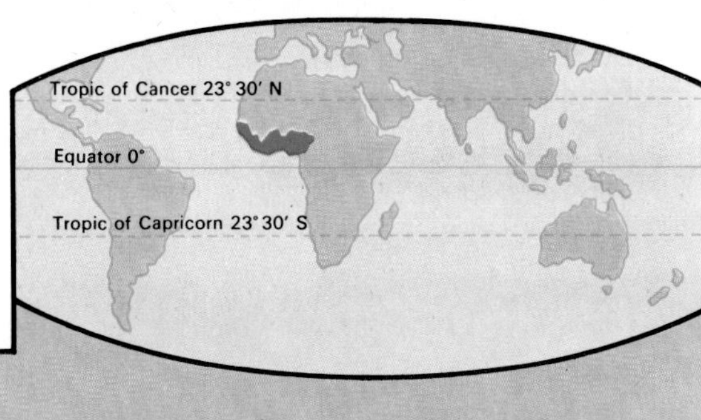

Senegal
Area
196,192 km²/75,750 sq miles
Location
12°20′—16°30′ N
11°20′—17°33′ W
Population
4,230,000 (1973)
Population density
22 per km²/56 per sq mile
Capital and largest city
Dakar: 581,000 (1973)
Language
French
Major imports
foodstuffs, machinery, petroleum products, vehicles
Major exports
groundnut oil, oilseed cake, phosphates, fish, cotton textiles
Currency
franc (1 franc = 100 centimes)
Gross National Product
864 million US dollars (1970)
Status
republic

The land
Except for uplands along the east and south-east borders, Senegal consists of monotonous, low-lying plains crossed by the wide valleys of the Casamance, Gambia, Saloum and Sénégal rivers. Sand dunes and swamps fringe the Atlantic while Cape Verde (Africa's most westerly point) is of volcanic origin. Inland, Senegal is hot (29°C) and, in the south, has up to 160 cm of rain (wet season: June to October). The coast is much cooler (22°C) and drier (average annual rainfall is 50 cm).

Industry & mining
Rich deposits of lime and aluminium phosphates near Thiès provide Senegal with a valuable export. Small quantities of ilmenite, zircon, rutile and sea salt are also produced and some limestone is quarried. Processing domestic raw materials accounts for 90% of manufacturing. Groundnut oil extraction, employing 25% of the industrial workforce, is the main industry but others produce flour, sugar, canned fish, cement, cotton textiles and shoes. Chemical, metallurgical and engineering industries are being developed. Dakar is the chief industrial area.

Transport
Senegal's 13,300 km road network includes major routes to neighbouring countries and the trans-Gambian highway from Ziguinchor to Kaolack. There are five main railway lines totalling 1,200 km. River traffic is important on the Sénégal, Saloum and Casamance. Dakar is the main seaport and has an international airport; Air Afrique (jointly owned by eleven African countries) flies overseas while Air Senegal operates internally.

Agriculture
Groundnuts dominate the economy: they are grown on 50% of the cultivated area and provide 75% of export earnings. Cotton is being developed as a second cash crop. The main food crops are millet, sorghum and rice with cassava, maize, sugar-cane, fruit and vegetables also grown. Cattle, sheep and goats are raised in the drier northern region. Fish, from rivers and sea, supplement the national diet and are also processed for export. Some gum arabic is produced.

Gambia
Area
11,371 km²/4,265 sq miles
Location
13°10′—13°50′ N
13°50′—16°50′ W
Population
494,300 (1973)
Population density
43 per km²/116 per sq mile
Capital and largest city
Banjul: 39,500 (1973)
Language
English
Major imports
foodstuffs, textiles, machinery, transport equipment, fuels
Major exports
groundnuts, groundnut oil, oilseed cake, palm kernels, fish
Currency
dalasi (1 dalasi = 100 butut)
Gross National Product
45 million US dollars
Status
republic

The land
Africa's smallest state is a narrow strip bordering the navigable section of the Gambia river. The country extends east for 320 km and has an average width of 35 km, broadening at the estuary to 48 km. The river banks are edged with mangrove swamps, backed by seasonally flooded grasslands called *banto faros*; behind these lie low sandy plateaux. The coast, with its palm-fringed beaches, is the centre of an expanding tourist industry. The climate is hot and dry with a short, intense wet season in summer. Banjul averages 25°C and has 125 cm of rain. Inland temperatures reach 28°C.

The economy
Gambia is economically dependent on groundnuts. This one cash crop, grown on the sandy uplands, accounts for 70% of the cultivated area and provides 95% of total exports. Food crop production (sorghum, millet and maize) is also centred on the higher, flood-free zone and rice cultivation is being developed in the banto faros. There is some fishing for shad, shrimp and prawns. Apart from groundnut shelling and oil extraction, other concerns (mostly in Banjul) are small-scale—these include fish processing and cotton-spinning and weaving. The river, navigable to Fatoto, is the main highway; ocean-going vessels reach Georgetown. Transport is otherwise poor: there are no railways or internal air services and few all-weather roads. Banjul is the main seaport and the country's international airport is at Yundum.

Guinea-Bissau
Area
36,125 km²/13,948 sq miles
Location
11°—12°40′ N
13°40′—16°45′ W
Population
510,000 (1973)
Population density
14 per km²/37 per sq mile
Capital
Madina do Boé
Largest city
Bissau: 71,170 (1970)
Language
Portuguese
Major imports
rice, textiles, fuels
Major exports
palm kernels, groundnuts, timber
Currency
escudo (1 escudo = 100 centavos)
Gross National Product
122 million US dollars (1971)
Status
republic

The land
The coast with its shallow, drowned estuaries, mangrove swamps and palm trees, is backed by a plain rising to a low, savanna-covered plateau. Near the Guinea border, uplands reach 300 m. Islands, including the Bijagos archipelago, lie offshore. The main rivers (Cacheu, Geba and Corubal) are also major routeways. Guinea-Bissau is hot and wet: temperatures average 26°C and rainfall, occuring May to October, is over 200 cm.

The economy
Guinea-Bissau is an agricultural country. The staple crop is rice, grown in the coastal swamps and along flooded river valleys. Other food crops are maize, beans, cassava and coconuts. The main agricultural exports are groundnuts (grown in the interior) and oil-palm products (from the coast and islands). Livestock is kept on the plateau. Oil and bauxite have been discovered but remain unexploited. Except for some food processing, there is little industry. Waterway transport is important as there are no railways and few roads. Bissau is the main port and has an international airport.

Guinea & Sierra Leone

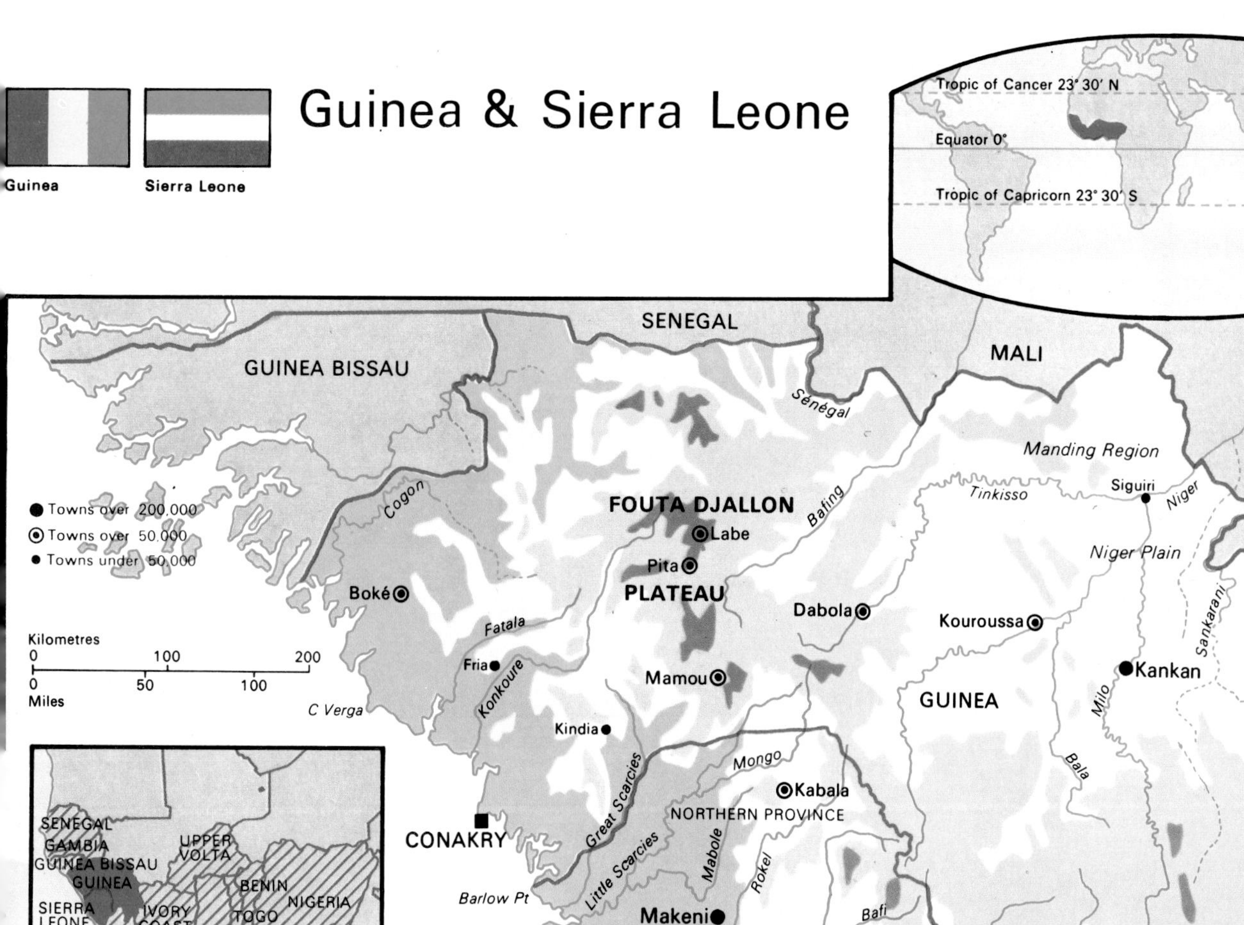

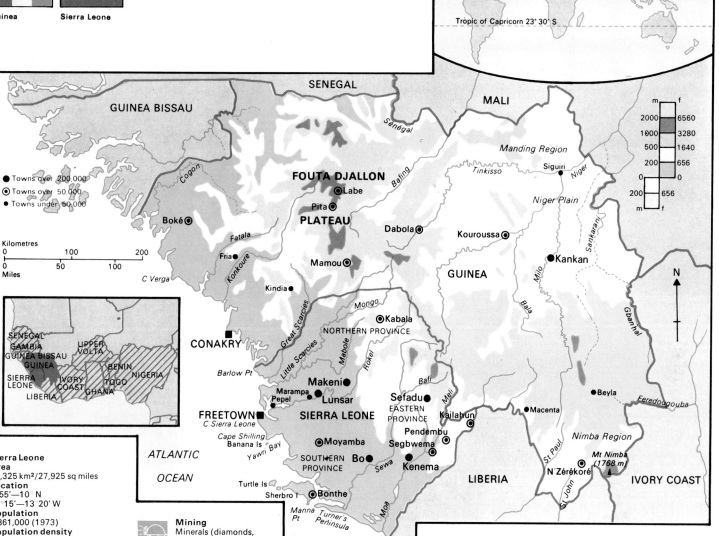

Sierra Leone
Area
72,325 km²/27,925 sq miles
Location
6°55′—10° N
10°15′—13°20′ W
Population
2,861,000 (1973)
Population density
40 per km²/102 per sq mile
Capital and largest city
Freetown: 300,000 (1975)
Language
English
Major imports
textiles, machinery, foodstuffs, vehicles, chemicals, fuels
Major exports
diamonds, iron ore, coffee, cocoa beans, palm kernels, bauxite
Currency
leone (1 leone = 100 cents)
Gross National Product
575 million US dollars (1973)
Status
republic

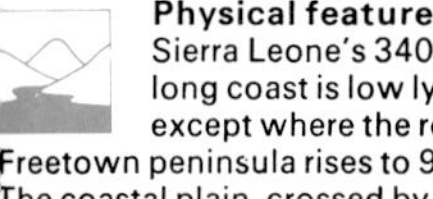

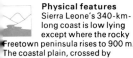

Physical features
Sierra Leone's 340-km-long coast is low lying except where the rocky Freetown peninsula rises to 900 m. The coastal plain, crossed by the rivers Moa, Sewa, Jong, Rokel, Great and Little Scarcies, is characterized by mangrove swamps, grasslands and rain forests; the plain stretches inland for 100 km then climbs to a plateau 450 m high with savanna and woodlands. Near the eastern border, mountains reach heights of over 1,750 m.

Climate
The climate is tropical with an average temperature of 26°C and marked wet and dry seasons. During the wet season (May to October) over 300 cm is recorded. From December to February (in the middle of the dry season) the northeasterly *harmattan wind* lowers temperatures and brings a haze of very fine dust across from the Sahara.

Mining
Minerals (diamonds, iron ore, bauxite and rutile) account for 85% of total exports. Diamonds are found mostly in river gravels in the southeast and east. Iron ore, mined near Marampa, is exported via Pepel. Sierra Leone's reserves of bauxite and rutile are among the largest in the world; exports are shipped from Bonthe. Chromium, gold, platinum and molybdenum have also been discovered.

Industry
There is little industry. Freetown has a few factories producing goods such as cigarettes, soap, textiles, shoes, biscuits, sweets, beverages, plastics and paper for the domestic market. In the rest of the country, industry is concerned with processing agricultural and forest products including palm oil extraction, rice milling, fish canning and furniture construction. Among traditional village activities are fish curing and smoking, hand weaving and leatherwork.

Transport
Rivers are a vital element in Sierra Leone's transport system and are used extensively for carrying freight. The 8,000 km road network is only 10% hard-surfaced. Railways have been closed with the exception of a line from the Marampa mine to Pepel port. Freetown is the leading port, handling all imports and agricultural exports. Sierra Leone Airways flies internally and overseas from Freetown international airport.

Agriculture
Agriculture employs 75% of Sierra Leoneans. Rice is the chief food crop, followed by sorghum, millet, groundnuts, cassava and maize. Export crops are coffee, cocoa beans, palm kernels, kola nuts, ginger and piassava (a fibre obtained from the leaf stalks of certain palms). Cattle raising is important in the north, while poultry, eggs and pork are produced on the Freetown peninsula. The forests yield lumber—mainly mahogany. Canoe-based fishing for bonga and sardines is significant.

Guinea
Area
245,857 km²/95,000 sq miles
Location
7°20′—12°40′ N
7°40′—15° W
Population
4,210,000 (1973)
Population density
17 per km²/44 per sq mile
Capital and largest city
Conakry: 525,700 (1972)
Language
French
Major imports
textiles, fuels, rice, machinery and metals
Major exports
alumina (Al_2O_3), pineapples, palm kernels, coffee, bananas
Currency
sily (1 sily = 100 corilles)
Gross National Product
481 million US dollars (1971)
Status
republic

Guinea: the land
The coast, with its swamps and shallow estuaries, is backed by a plain some 60 km wide. Beyond the plain, the Fouta Djallon rises to over 1,000 m comprising a level plateau dissected by deep valleys. This great sandstone block gives birth to West Africa's three main rivers: the Niger, Gambia and Sénégal. Smaller rivers, such as the Fatala and Konkoure, flow west into the Atlantic Ocean. Grasslands, drained by the Niger, lie to the east; in the extreme southeast, the isolated Guinea Highlands reach 1,768 m at Mt Nimba. The climate is hot and wet. Conakry averages 27°C and has 430 cm of rain between April and October. The Fouta Djallon is drier (180 cm) and slightly cooler (25°C), but on the Niger plain temperatures rise to 40°C.

Agriculture
Agriculture is mainly concentrated along the coast and in the fertile valleys of the Fouta Djallon. The leading cash crops are pineapples, coffee, palm kernels, bananas and citrus. Rice, grown in the coastal swamps and in the flooded valleys of the Niger plain, is the staple crop; millet, maize, cassava and groundnuts are also produced for domestic consumption. The Fouta Djallon is the chief livestock region and cattle, sheep and goats are grazed on its pastures. There is some production of hardwoods from the rain forests on the coastal plain. Fishing is of local significance only.

Mining
Mining plays a dominant role in the economy. Guinea has the world's third largest bauxite deposits and ranks as the sixth bauxite producer; the chief mines are at Fria, Boké and Dabola. The bauxite is converted to pure alumina (aluminium oxide) on site; alumina accounts for 60 % of exports. Iron ore is worked in the Nimba region. Diamonds are found near Macenta; limestone and gold are mined to a lesser extent.

Industry
Manufacturing is mainly based on local raw materials and includes rice milling, groundnut oil extraction, fruit and meat canning, orange juice pressing and cement production. There is a textile mill and a vehicle assembly plant. A plant under construction in 1976 will convert alumina to aluminium using hydro-electricity.

Transport
Communications in Guinea are poor. The principle road runs from Conakry to Kankan (the chief city in the interior) with secondary roads branching off to provincial towns and neighbouring countries. Less than 5% of the road network is hard-surfaced. The only main railway also connects Conakry to Kankan but local lines run from the Fria and Boké bauxite mines to the coast. A new line is being built to serve the Mt Nimba iron ore deposits. Conakry, the leading port, has an international airport.

Liberia and Ivory Coast

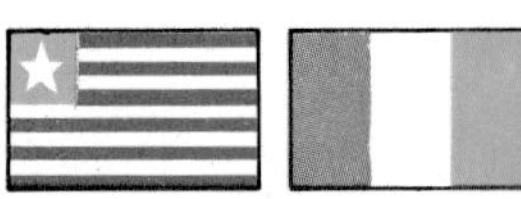

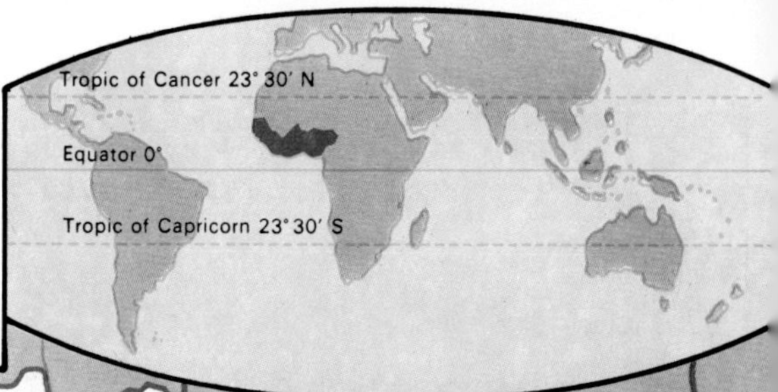

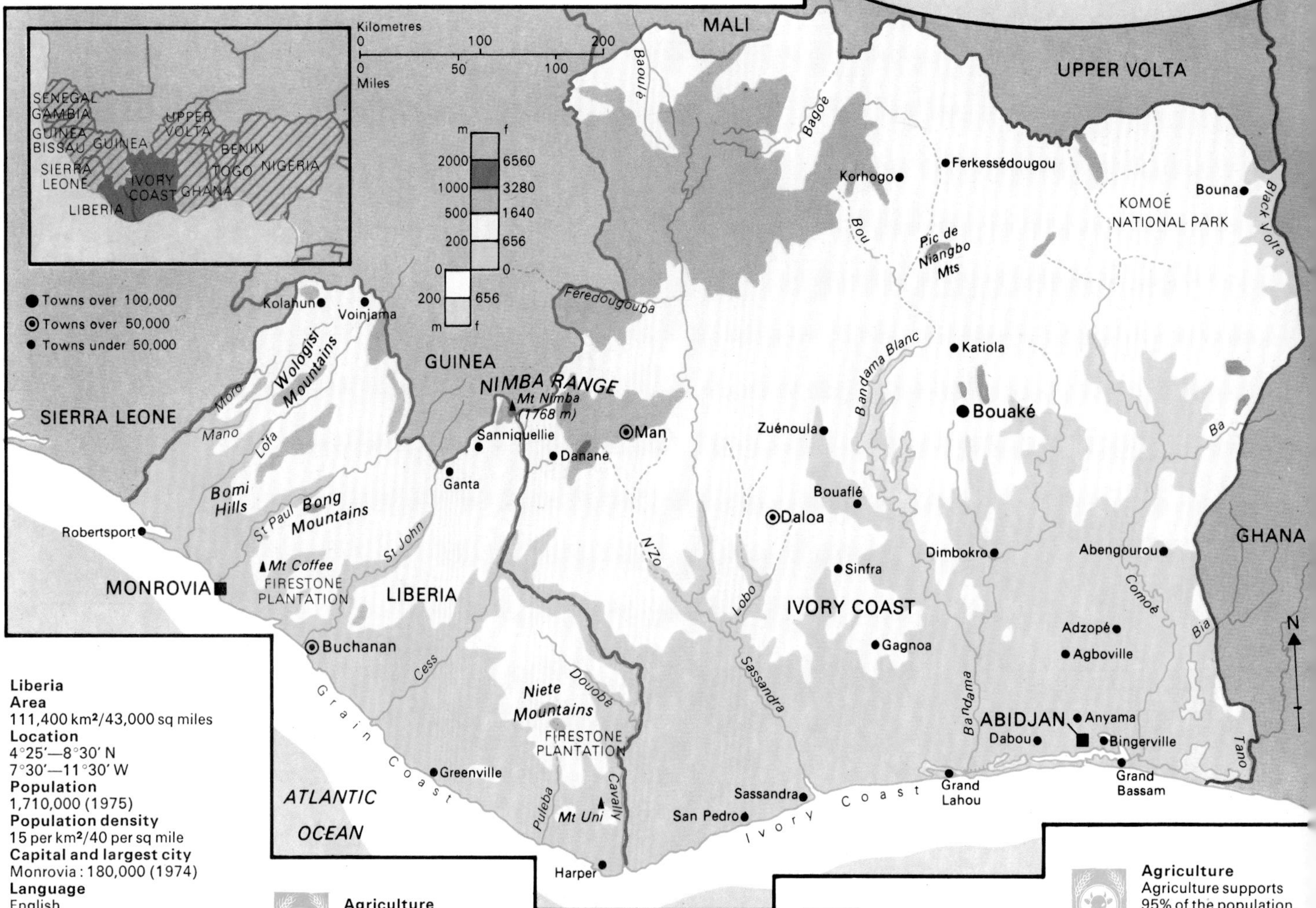

Liberia Ivory Coast

Liberia
Area
111,400 km²/43,000 sq miles
Location
4°25'—8°30' N
7°30'—11°30' W
Population
1,710,000 (1975)
Population density
15 per km²/40 per sq mile
Capital and largest city
Monrovia: 180,000 (1974)
Language
English
Major imports
machinery, transport equipment, manufactured goods, food, fuels, chemicals
Major exports
iron ore, rubber, diamonds, palm kernels, timber, cocoa, coffee
Currency
dollar (1 dollar = 100 cents)
Gross National Product
357 million US dollars (1971)
Status
republic

The land

Liberia, founded by freed American slaves in 1847, is Africa's oldest republic. Behind the swampy shoreline and low coastal plain, the land rises to a forested, undulating plateau some 500 m high. There are several small mountain ranges up to 1,800 m in height. The main rivers flow along parallel northwest-southeast courses. The climate is equatorial with high temperatures (27°C), high humidity (80%) and high rainfall: between May and October, 375 cm of rain falls along the coast and 250 cm in inland areas.

Industry

Manufacturing, centred on Monrovia, is limited. Products include canned fish, tyres, cement, beer, explosives and chemicals. Monrovia consumes 95% of the country's electricity (75% of which comes from the Mt Coffee hydro-electric plant). The iron and rubber industries have their own supply.

Agriculture

Three Liberians out of four live off the land. Rice is the staple crop, grown on 33% of farmland, but low yields make imports necessary. The other basic food is cassava. Rubber is Liberia's second main export and chief cash crop accounting for 24% of the area under cultivation. Over half the output comes from plantations held by the Firestone Tyre Co. who ship the rubber, as latex concentrate and crepe, to the US. Coffee and cocoa are also major commercial crops. Tropical forests cover 25% of the country and products include timber and palm kernels. A few cattle and goats are raised in the interior.

Mining

Liberia's fortunes largely depend on minerals, particularly on iron ore which accounts for 70% of total exports. Mines are located in the Bomi Hills, the Nimba range, the Bong mountains and at Mano river; further reserves have been discovered. There are rail links from the Bomi, Bong and Mano river mines to Monrovia and from Nimba to Buchanan. Iron ore accounts for 90% of cargo handled by Monrovia port. Liberia ranks as Africa's leading producer and the world's fourth largest exporter of iron ore. Diamond production, from the Lofa river area, is significant and gold deposits are worked on a small scale. Bauxite, manganese, kyanite, lead-zinc, copper and rutile also occur.

Transport

The main road runs from Monrovia via Ganta into Guinea with branches serving east and west Liberia. There are no railways apart from the lines carrying iron ore to the coast. Monrovia, with its free zone, is the chief port followed by Buchanan, Greenville and Harper. The registration of foreign ships under a Liberian flag of convenience contributes to the national income and gives Liberia the world's largest merchant navy. East of Monrovia there is an international airport.

Ivory Coast
Area
322,463 km²/124,504 sq miles
Location
4°25'—10°30' N
2°30'—8°30' W
Population
6,055,000 (1975)
Population density
14 per km²/37 per sq mile
Capital and largest city
Abidjan: 900,000 (1975)
Language
French
Major imports
machinery, vehicles, metals, petroleum
Major exports
coffee, timber, cocoa, palm oil
Currency
CFA franc (1 franc = 100 centimes)
Gross National Product
1,600 million US dollars (1971)
Status
republic

The land

Inland, the Ivory Coast consists of a savanna-covered plateau about 300 m in altitude but rising to over 1,000 m in the northwest. A fertile, forested plain separates the plateau from the coast which is fringed by lagoons and sand-bars. The climate is equatorial: in the south, temperatures are high (27°C) and rainfall is heavy (200 cm); the north is slightly cooler and drier.

Transport

The country's transport system is centred on Abidjan. The road network radiates from the capital and includes highways to all five neighbouring states. The only railway runs north from the capital to Upper Volta. Abidjan is also the main port; situated on a lagoon, the city has access to the sea via the Vridi canal. Other ports are Sassandra, Tabou and San Pedro. Air Ivoire operates internally and Air Afrique internationally from Abidjan.

Forestry

Dense forests cover 40% of the country, mainly in the south, and contain over 30 commercially valuable species including teak, mahogany, ebony and cedar. Timber accounts for 25% of total exports and the Ivory Coast ranks as Africa's leading exporter of tropical woods. There are many sawmills and plywood plants. Kola nuts are also important.

Agriculture

Agriculture supports 95% of the population. The staple crops are maize and millet in the northern savanna, rice in the southwest, and yams, plantains and cassava in the southeast. The leading cash crop is coffee, grown in cleared zones in the south and accounting for 35% of total exports. The other major tree crop is cocoa, cultivated mainly in the southeast and providing 25% of total exports. Bananas and pineapples are also important. The Ivory Coast is the world's third largest producer of coffee and cocoa, fourth producer of pineapples and sixth of bananas. Other commercial crops include oil palms (4th largest supplier), rubber in the southwest, copra along the coast and cotton and sugarcane in the centre and north.

Mining & industry

Mining activity is limited to alluvial diamonds in the river Bou and manganese near Grand Lahou. Iron ore is known to exist in the northwest. Since the 1960s there has been considerable industrial development. Food-processing is the most important sector and products range from powdered coffee, cocoa butter and beer, to flour (using imported wheat), canned pineapples and frozen fish. New concerns include a vehicle assembly plant, textile mill, cigarette factory, plastics works and paper factory. Most power stations are oil-fired, but hydro-electric plants are in operation on the river Bia, Bandama and Kossou.

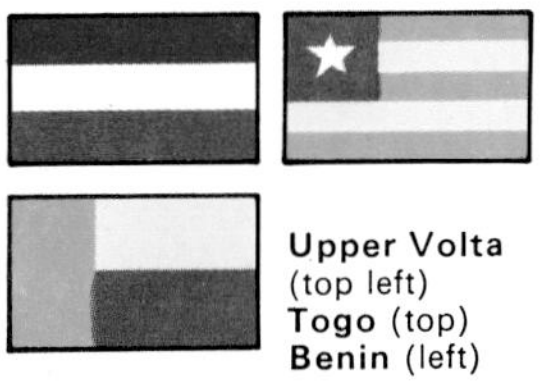

Upper Volta, Togo and Benin

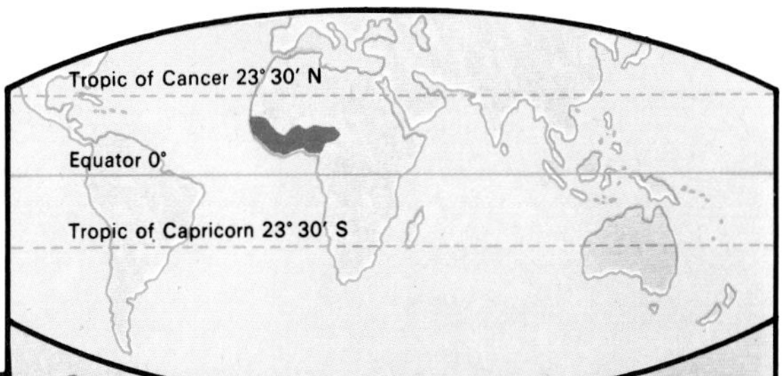

Upper Volta (top left)
Togo (top)
Benin (left)

Tropic of Cancer 23° 30′ N
Equator 0°
Tropic of Capricorn 23° 30′ S

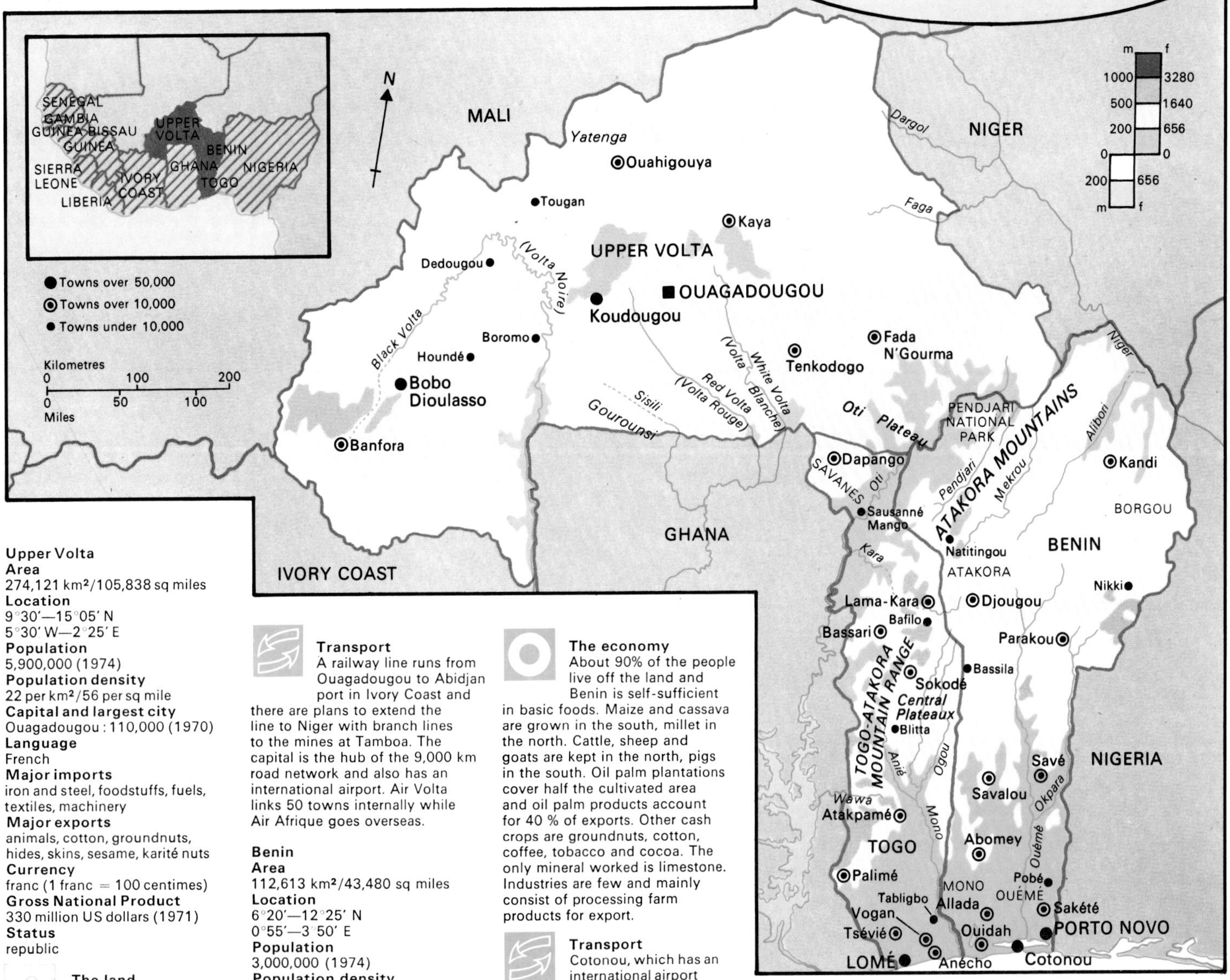

● Towns over 50,000
◉ Towns over 10,000
• Towns under 10,000

Kilometres 0 100 200
0 50 100 Miles

m f
1000 3280
500 1640
200 656
0 0
200 656

Upper Volta
Area
274,121 km²/105,838 sq miles
Location
9°30′—15°05′ N
5°30′ W—2°25′ E
Population
5,900,000 (1974)
Population density
22 per km²/56 per sq mile
Capital and largest city
Ouagadougou : 110,000 (1970)
Language
French
Major imports
iron and steel, foodstuffs, fuels, textiles, machinery
Major exports
animals, cotton, groundnuts, hides, skins, sesame, karité nuts
Currency
franc (1 franc = 100 centimes)
Gross National Product
330 million US dollars (1971)
Status
republic

The land
Upper Volta is landlocked and consists of a plateau some 300 m high and tilted slightly southwards. This granite block, covered with poor, infertile soils and savanna-type vegetation, is crossed by the deep valleys of the Black Volta, Red Volta and White Volta which meet in Ghana to form the Volta. The climate is hot and dry with temperatures of up to 40°C and 90 cm of rain a year which falls between June and September.

The economy
Agriculture is the basis of the economy and employs 95% of the population. Subsistence farming predominates and exports (of sesame, groundnuts, karité nuts and cotton) largely consist of surplus production. The main food crops are sorghum in the south and millet in the north; others are maize, rice and yams. Cocoa and sugar have been introduced. Cattle, sheep and goats are raised in the north and east; live animals, meat, hides and skins account for 40% of total exports. Large manganese deposits at Tamboa are being developed but other mineral assets are, so far, unexploited. Industrial development is limited.

Transport
A railway line runs from Ouagadougou to Abidjan port in Ivory Coast and there are plans to extend the line to Niger with branch lines to the mines at Tamboa. The capital is the hub of the 9,000 km road network and also has an international airport. Air Volta links 50 towns internally while Air Afrique goes overseas.

Benin
Area
112,613 km²/43,480 sq miles
Location
6°20′—12°25′ N
0°55′—3°50′ E
Population
3,000,000 (1974)
Population density
27 per km²/69 per sq mile
Capital
Porto Novo : 100,000 (1972)
Largest city
Cotonou : 175,000 (1972)
Language
French
Major imports
textiles, food, chemicals, machinery, vehicles
Major exports
palm kernels, nuts and oil, cotton, coffee, tobacco, groundnuts
Currency
franc (1 franc = 100 centimes)
Gross National Product
247 million US dollars (1971)
Status
republic

The land
Benin is about 96 km wide and extends 656 km north from the Gulf of Guinea to the Niger. The coast, with sand-bars and lagoons, is backed by a belt of fertile clay. Beyond this lies a seasonally-flooded swamp. The rest of the country consists of forested and savanna-covered plateaux 150 m high. In the northwest, the Atakora mountains reach 650 m, but in the northeast the land slopes down to the Niger. The average temperature is 27°C with 130 cm of rain (less inland).

The economy
About 90% of the people live off the land and Benin is self-sufficient in basic foods. Maize and cassava are grown in the south, millet in the north. Cattle, sheep and goats are kept in the north, pigs in the south. Oil palm plantations cover half the cultivated area and oil palm products account for 40 % of exports. Other cash crops are groundnuts, cotton, coffee, tobacco and cocoa. The only mineral worked is limestone. Industries are few and mainly consist of processing farm products for export.

Transport
Cotonou, which has an international airport and a new harbour, is the hub of Benin's transport system. Railways link this major city to Lomé (Togo), Parakou and Pobé. The two main highways are also centred on Cotonou : one runs east-west to Nigeria and Togo, the other goes north to Niger. The lagoons and the Ouémé, Mono and Couffo rivers are navigable.

Togo
Area
56,000 km²/21,621 sq miles
Location
6°10′—11°10′ N
0°10′ W—1°51′ E
Population
2,170,000 (1974)
Population density
39 per km²/100 per sq mile
Capital and largest city
Lomé : 200,000 (1971)
Language
French
Major imports
machinery, vehicles, chemicals, oil, food, cement, iron, steel
Major exports
phosphates, cocoa, coffee, palm kernels, cotton, tapioca
Currency
franc (1 franc = 100 centimes)
Gross National Product
330 million US dollars
Status
republic

Transport
Togo's transport systems are centred on Lomé. Three railway lines connect Lomé with Anécho, Palimé and Blitta. The 7,000 km road network is 10% hard-surfaced; the two main routes are from Lomé to Upper Volta and along the coast between Ghana and Benin. Lomé has a deepwater port and an international airport; Air Togo operates domestic flights while Air Afrique (6% owned by Togo) flies overseas.

The land
Togo is Africa's second smallest state. Behind the sandy, lagoon-fringed coast, a low plateau, composed of fertile red clay soils, stretches inland for 30 km. The land then rises to a 450 m high tableland drained by the Mono. This central upland is bordered in the north and north-west by the forested Togo-Atakora chain which has peaks up to 900 m. Beyond this lies the savanna-covered Oti plateau. The climate is hot and humid; temperatures average 27°C and about 75 cm of rain falls on the coast increasing to 180 cm inland.

Agriculture
Agriculture supports 90% of the population and provides over 50% of exports. Cash crops include cocoa, coffee and palm kernels, grown in the south, and coffee and groundnuts in the north. Food production includes yams, cassava, millet, sorghum and maize. Rice, sugarcane, fruit and vegetables are grown under irrigation. Livestock (kept in the north) and fish supplement the national diet.

Mining & Industry
Phosphates, mined northeast of Lomé, account for almost half of total exports. There is also some production of limestone and marble, but iron ore, bauxite, uranium and chromite deposits are not yet exploited. Electricity comes from a thermal station at Lomé and a hydro-electric power station at Palimé, with some imported from Ghana. Industry, based on agricultural produce, is small-scale and includes coffee roasting, cassava flour-milling, cotton-ginning and palm-oil extraction. A few consumer goods are manufactured.

Ghana

Area
238,540 km²/92 100 sq miles
Location
4°45′—11°10′ N
3°15′ W—1°20′ E
Population
9,360,000 (1973)
Population density
39 per km²/102 per sq mile
Capital and largest city
Accra: 852,000 (1973)
Language
English
Major imports
food, machinery, manufactured goods, chemicals, fuels
Major exports
cocoa beans and products, timber, gold, diamonds, manganese, bauxite
Currency
cedi (1 cedi = 100 pesewas)
Gross National Product
2,120 million US dollars (1972)
Status
republic

Physical features

Two-thirds of the country consists of the low-lying basin of the Volta river and its tributaries, the Black Volta, White Volta and Oti. To the north, west and southwest, this savanna-covered plain is rimmed by great sandstone escarpments. These scarps overlook a 300 m high plateau in the northwest and the dissected Ashanti plateau in the southwest. In the east, an upland range rises to 600m along the Togo border. Near the end of its course, 70 km from the sea, the Volta flows through a narrow gorge; at this point the Akosombo dam holds back the river to form Lake Volta, one of the world's largest man-made lakes.

Climate

Southern Ghana, exposed to the monsoonal southwest wind, has two wet seasons (May-June and October-November) with an average annual rainfall of 180 cm; the southeast corner, however, is sheltered and relatively dry with Accra having under 80 cm of rain a year. In the north there is only one wet season (June to October) with annual totals of between 100 and 130 cm of rain. During the rest of the year, the arid dusty harmattan wind from the Sahara blows across the interior. Temperatures are high with annual averages ranging from 26°C on the coast to 30°C inland.

Agriculture

Agriculture is the most important sector of the economy. It employs about 60% of the population but accounts for less than 25% of Ghana's surface area. Around 30% of farmland is used for the main cash crop, cocoa, which provides 65% of all exports. Ghana ranks as the world's leading cocoa producer the annual output from the Ashanti plateau area being about 400,000 tonnes. Other cash crops, also grown in the southern half of the country, are coffee, copra, bananas, kola nuts, oil palms, tobacco and rubber. The chief food crops are plantain, maize, cassava, yams and cocoyams in the south and guinea corn, millet, groundnuts and sheanuts in the drier north. Cattle-raising is limited to the tsetse-free northern savanna and the Accra plain by the coast.

Forestry

Tropical rain forests cover much of the Ashanti plateau and commercially valuable species include wawa (African whitewood) sapele and African mahogany. The industry is centred in the southwest and logs are floated down such rivers as the Ankobra and Ofin to the coast for processing or export. Timber accounts for 15% of total exports; half is shipped as logs, the remainder as sawn timber, plywood and veneer. The timber processing industry is being expanded.

Fishing

The fishing industry is well developed and supplies about 90% of domestic requirements. Just over a third of the catch comes from Lake Volta. Traditional canoes, often equipped with outboard motors, predominate and these operate from open beaches along the coast; there are also some motorized vessels working from harbours. The principal fishing centres are Takoradi, Winneba and Apam; Tema, with its modern facilities, is the base of the deep-sea fishing fleet.

Cities

Accra, which is a corruption of *nkran* (the name of the black ants found locally), grew up round three villages and now extends 25 km along the coast. Also on the coast is Sekondo-Takoradi (160,900); in 1963 the old town of Sekondi merged with the modern port of Takoradi to form a single city. Sekondi harbour is now used by fishing boats and pleasure craft. Kumasi (345,100), at the heart of the cocoa region, is a major industrial town and route centre.

Mining

Mining, centred on the Ashanti plateau, is a leading source of income and provides almost 20% of total exports. Gold, as the country's previous name of *Gold Coast* suggests, is important and accounts for 50% of mineral exports. Some gold is extracted from river deposits, the rest is mined; Obuasi has one of the world's largest gold mines. Diamonds are next in importance and provide a further 30% of mineral exports, with production based on Oda and Kade in the Birim valley northwest of Accra. The other minerals exploited are manganese at Nsuta and bauxite at Awaso; bauxite deposits at Kibi are to be developed. Salt is obtained from the sea and lagoons. Oil exists offshore.

Lake Volta

Completed in 1965, the Akosombo dam on the Volta has created a giant lake. Lake Volta is 320 km long and covers 8,482 km² or 3.5% of Ghana's total surface area. The lake has several functions. Primarily, it is a source of hydro-electricity: the Volta dam supplies over 90% of the country's electricity and provides power for export to Togo and Benin. As a reservoir, the lake stores water for domestic and industrial consumption and for irrigation; sugar and rice are to be grown under irrigation along the 7,200 km shoreline. Freshwater fisheries have been established and provide the surrounding area with a valuable source of protein. Lake Volta is navigable and serves as a major route from the north to the coast.

Industry

About 70% of the hydro-electricity generated is consumed by the country's largest concern, the aluminium smelter at Tema. The two other main industries process timber and cocoa; about 12% of cocoa exports are in the form of cocoa butter and paste. Small-scale manufacturing, aimed at the local market, includes flour-milling, sugar-refining, brewing, meat-processing, vehicle assembly, textiles, chemicals and some oil refining. Industrial development is centred on Accra-Tema, Sekondi-Takoradi and Kumasi.

Transport

Road and rail networks are most dense in southern Ghana. Roads total 32,000 km but many are impassable during the wet season; main routes radiate from Accra and Kumasi. The rail network serves the mining and cocoa regions and forms a triangle linking Takoradi, Kumasi and Accra with several branch lines. Exports of manganese, bauxite, logs and cocoa account for 80% of freight carried. The two main ports, Takoradi and Tema (replacing Accra port) are both artificial; a third deep-water port was under construction in 1976. Ghana Airways operates domestic and international services from Accra airport, the largest in the country.

Nigeria

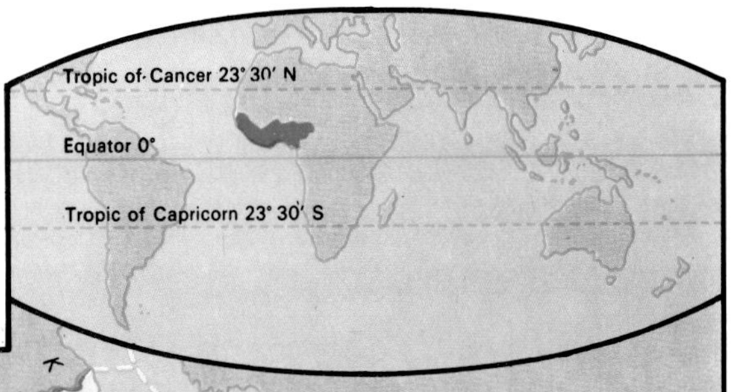

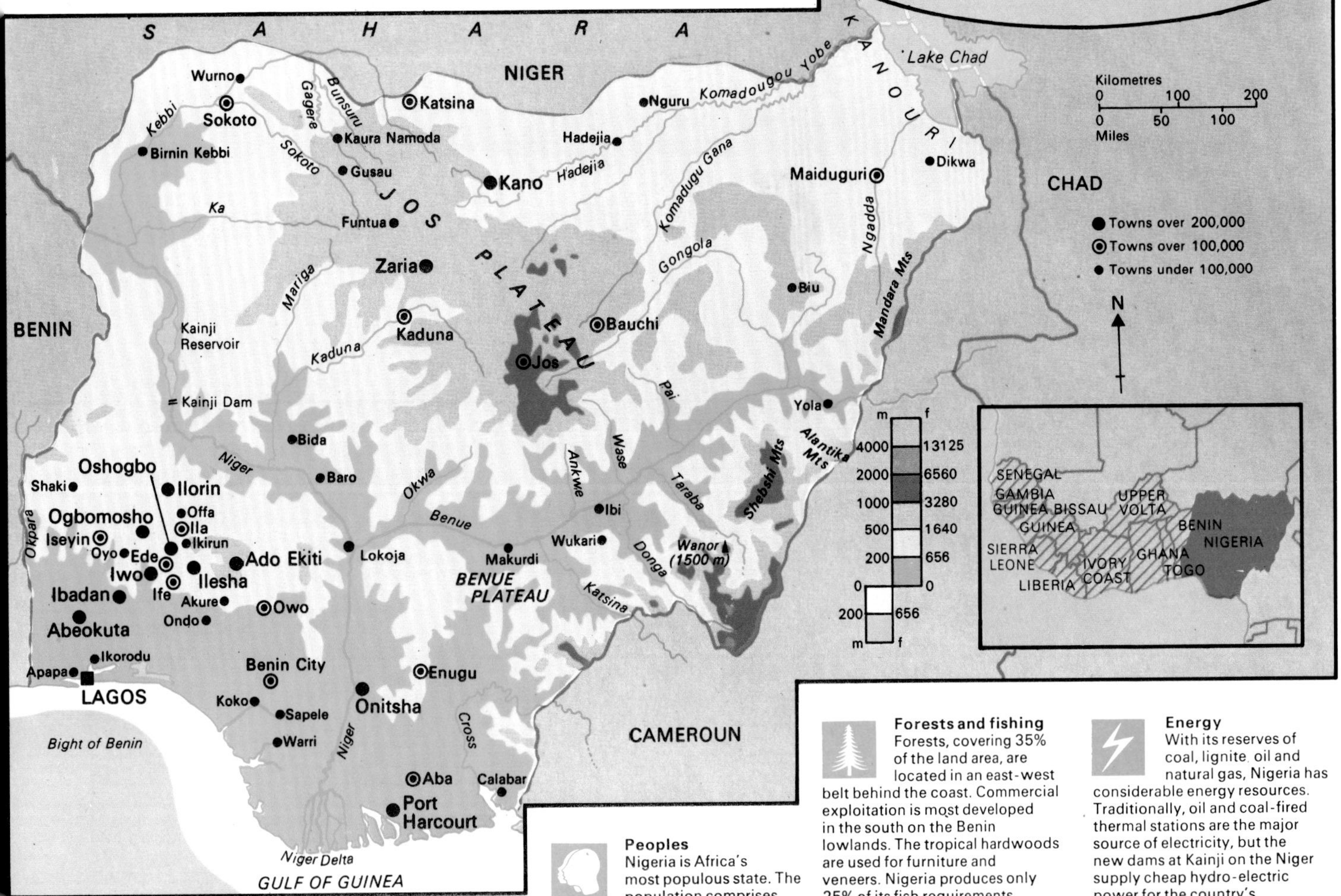

Area
923,773 km²/356,669 sq miles
Location
4°20′—13°15′ N
3°—14°40′ E
Population
79,759,000 (1973)
Population density
86 per km²/224 per sq mile
Capital and largest city
Lagos: 900,970 (1971)
Language
English
Major imports
machinery, iron and steel, textiles, vehicles, food
Major exports
petroleum, cocoa, groundnuts, rubber, palm kernels, tin, timber, hides and skins, cotton
Currency
Naira (1 Naira = 100 kobo)
Gross National Product
9,900 million US dollars (1971)
Status
federal republic

Flora and fauna

Mangrove swamps line the coast; behind lies a belt of tropical rain forest containing hardwood trees and oil palm. Savanna predominates on the plateau with tall grasses and some trees such as baobab and tamarind. Short grass and thorny trees characterize the far north. Nigeria's wildlife is plentiful. Camels, lions, cheetahs, hyenas and a few giraffes roam the savanna; elephants and chimpanzees are found in the forests; crocodiles and hippopotamuses live in the rivers. Leopards are plentiful but gorillas almost extinct.

Physical features

Nigeria's main feature is the Niger—the third longest river in Africa. It flows south-eastwards across west Nigeria to Lokoja where it is joined by its main tributary, the Benue. The river then continues due south and enters the Gulf of Guinea through a broad delta. Behind the lagoons and swamps of the coastal belt lies a thickly-forested hilly region which gives way to the wide Niger and Benue valleys. The northern half of the country consists of the undulating Jos plateau which rises to over 1,500 m in the centre. This tableland is a major watershed with streams flowing both north and south. In the extreme north, the land drops to a sandy plain some 600 m high which merges into the Sahara. Another range runs along the Cameroun border.

Climate

Nigeria's climate is influenced by two winds: the dessicating Harmattan from the Sahara and the moisture-laden south-west wind. The Harmattan, with its dust haze, blows during the dry season (November-April) and causes daily variations of temperature, particularly in the north: at Kano, temperatures range from 8°C to 43°C. The wet south-west wind prevails from May to October bringing rain which decreases inland. Over 400 cm falls on the coast, but only 50 cm near Lake Chad. Coastal humidity is high.

Peoples

Nigeria is Africa's most populous state. The population comprises over 250 ethnic groups each with its own language or dialect. The four largest groups are the Yoruba (13 million) in the southwest, the Ibo (8 million) in the southeast, the Hausa (7 million) and the Fulani (5 million) in the north. Other prominent groups are the Edo in the Benin area, the Tiv, Nupe and Kanuri on the plateau and the Ibidio in the southeast. Although English is the offical language, 35% of the population (mainly in the north) speak Hausa; the Yoruba language predominates in the west and Ibo in the east. The south, in particular the southeast, is the most densely populated region with densities of up to 400 per km². The north-centre and northwest, with cities such as Sokoto and Kano, are also well populated, but the middle zone and the Lake Chad area are largely uninhabited.

Agriculture

Two-thirds of the population work in agriculture, which provides 60% of total exports. The various cash crops are grown in distinct zones: cocoa in the west, rubber in the mid-west, oil-palm in the east, groundnuts and cotton in the north, soybeans in the Benue basin and tobacco in the north and west. Nigeria ranks as the world's second largest cocoa exporter. The country is almost self-sufficient in basic foods: yams and cassava are grown in the south; millet, maize and rice in the north. Cattle are grazed on the northern savanna.

Forests and fishing

Forests, covering 35% of the land area, are located in an east-west belt behind the coast. Commercial exploitation is most developed in the south on the Benin lowlands. The tropical hardwoods are used for furniture and veneers. Nigeria produces only 25% of its fish requirements (mainly from Lake Chad) and has to rely heavily on imports.

Mining

Mining makes a significant contribution to Nigeria's economy. Petroleum, occurring in the southern part of the country, accounts for a third of all exports; production is centred on the Niger delta. Columbite and tin, both mined on the Jos plateau, are next in importance; Nigeria holds first place for world production of columbite. Coal is worked near Enugu. Marble, limestone, lignite and gold are mined in small quantities.

Industry

Nigeria's industry is expanding rapidly. The principal sector is food-processing and products include palm oil, groundnut oil, beer, sugar, margarine, fruit juices and canned foods. The textile and leather industry, located mainly in the north, supplies two-thirds of the country's needs. Cement manufacture is important with plants at Lagos, Sokoto and Enugu. New industries include vehicle-assembly and chemicals and there is an oil refinery at Port Harcourt. Two more refineries, an iron and steel complex, gas liquefaction plants and more cement works were being planned in 1976. Main industrial centres are Lagos and Ibadan in the west, Port Harcourt, Enugu, Aba and Calabar in the east and Kano, Zaria, Kaduna and Jos in the north.

Energy

With its reserves of coal, lignite oil and natural gas, Nigeria has considerable energy resources. Traditionally, oil and coal-fired thermal stations are the major source of electricity, but the new dams at Kainji on the Niger supply cheap hydro-electric power for the country's developing industries.

Transport

The rail network, totalling 3,500 km, comprises two main lines: Port Harcourt to Maiduguri and Lagos to Kano, with branches to Kaura Namoda, Nguru and Baro. There are 38,000 km of roads, 17% hard-surfaced. The principal highways run north-south with east-west branches. On the 6,500 km of inland waterways, shipping is mostly seasonal: the Niger, Benue and Cross are the most important rivers with the Benue used for Cameroun transit freight. Boats also ply the coastal lagoons between Lagos and the Cross estuary. Lagos and Port Harcourt are the chief ports, followed by Warri, Calabar, Koko and Sapele. Nigerian Airways operate domestic and overseas services from Kano and Lagos.

Cities

Lagos stands on a series of lagoon islands. As well as being the administrative capital, it is also the country's commercial and industrial centre accounting for 30% of total manufactures. Apapa, the port of Lagos, handles 50% of Nigeria's foreign trade. The other main towns—Ibadan (758,300), Ogbomosho (386,700), Oshogbo (252,500) and Ilorin (252,000)—are all in the south. The one exception is Kano (357,100) which is in the north. Built of mud and enclosed by a 17 km long wall, Kano originated as a trans-Sahara trading centre.

Somalia; Afars & Issas (FTAI)

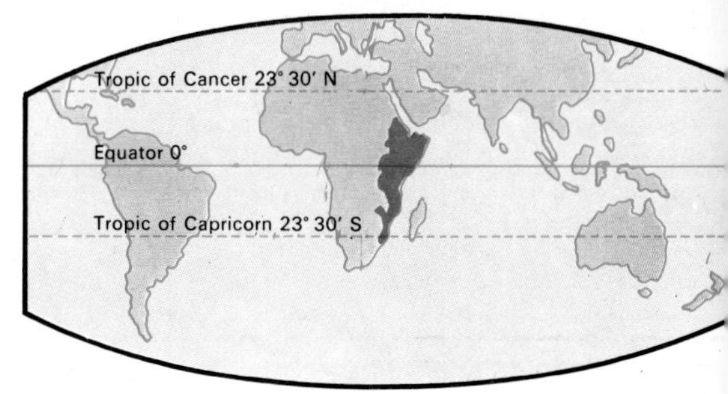

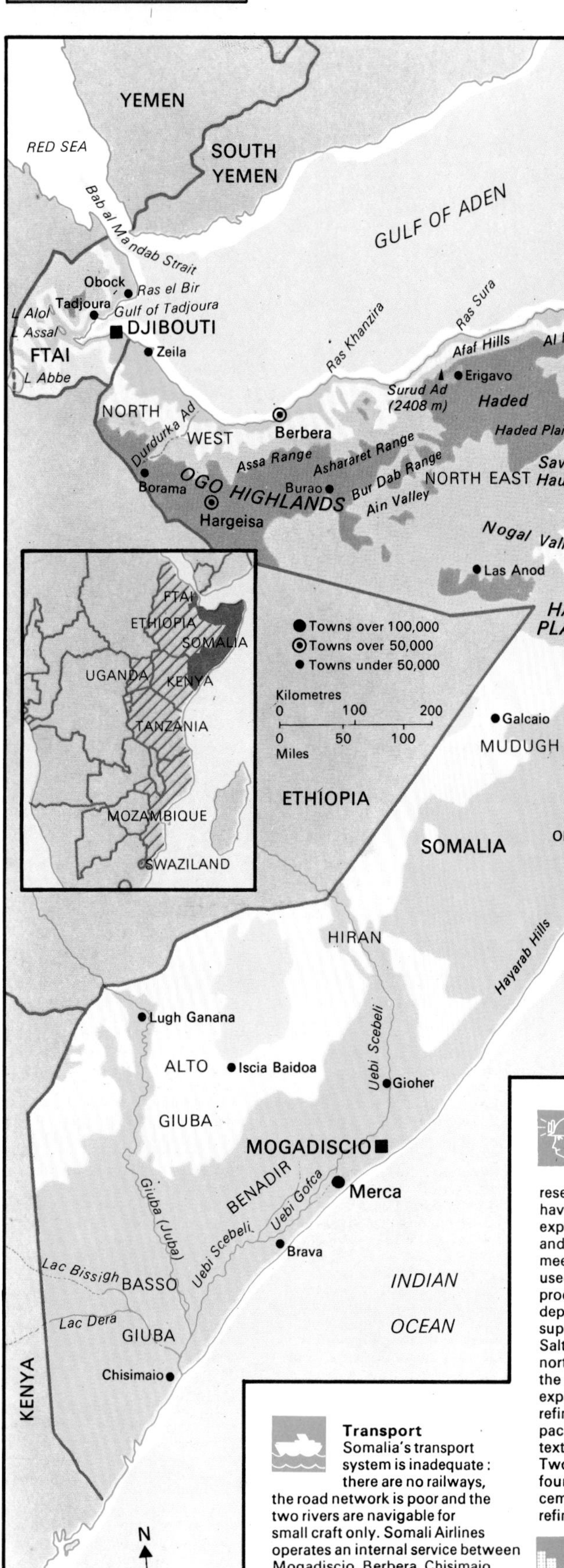

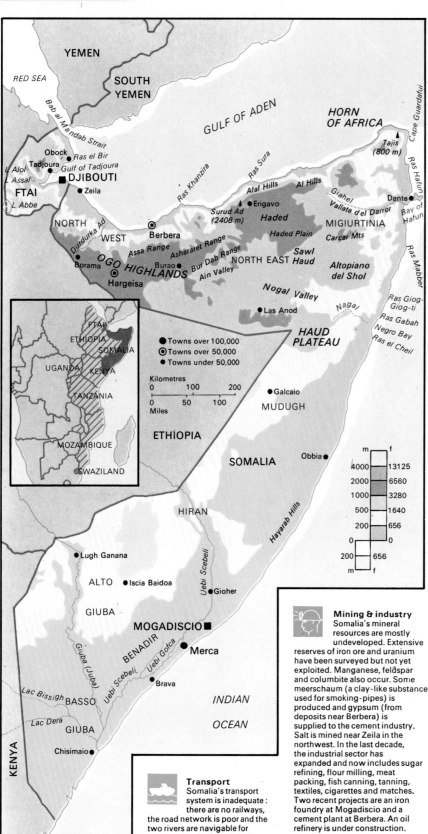

Somalia
Area
637,661 km²/246,201 sq miles
Location
12°N—1°45′ S
41°—51°20′ E
Population
5,000,000 (1975)
Population density
8 per km²/20 per sq mile
Capital and largest city
Mogadiscio : 260,000 (1975)
Languages
Somali, Arabic
Major imports
machinery, transport equipment, cereals, chemicals, fuels
Major exports
live animals, bananas, hides and skins, meat
Currency
shilling (1 shilling = 100 cents)
Gross National Product
175 million US dollars
Status
republic

Physical features
The Somali Republic lies along the coast of the African Horn, the continent's northeastern corner. Most of the country consists of a low plateau under 500 m which extends to the coast in the north and east. The tip of the Horn, Cape Guardafui, is a sheer 300 m high precipice. Ras Hafun promontory, Africa's most easterly point, is 160 km south of the cape. Parallel to the Gulf of Aden coast, a mountain belt rises above the plateau to altitudes of 2,000 m. The south-eastern coast, bordering the Indian Ocean, is flanked by a wide, sandy plain. This arid lowland is crossed by the country's only two rivers: the Giuba (which enters the sea near Chisimaio) and the Uebi Scebeli which usually disappears into marshes near the coast.

Climate
Inland Somalia is hot and dry; coastal areas are hot and humid. The Gulf of Aden shore is one of the world's hottest regions: average temperatures at Berbera are 24°C in January (the coldest month) and 54°C in July (the hottest); the annual average for Mogadiscio is 27°C. Precipitation is light: the winter monsoon brings 5 cm of rain to the north coast; the summer monsoon brings 50 cm to the central plateau.

Agriculture
Somalia is a pastoral country: 80% of the population, mostly nomads, depend on livestock-raising and about 20 million animals (sheep, goats, cattle and camels) are grazed on the interior plateau. Arable farming is confined to irrigated zones bordering the Giuba and Uebi Scebeli rivers where maize, sorghum, sugarcane and bananas are the main crops; production of cotton, rice, groundnuts, sesame and citrus fruit is increasing. Live animals, hides and skins, meat and meat products provide over 60% of total exports and bananas account for a further 30%. Some frankincense and myrrh, from aromatic shrubs on the plateau, are also exported. Fishing is being developed.

Mining & industry
Somalia's mineral resources are mostly undeveloped. Extensive reserves of iron ore and uranium have been surveyed but not yet exploited. Manganese, feldspar and columbite also occur. Some meerschaum (a clay-like substance used for smoking-pipes) is produced and gypsum (from deposits near Berbera) is supplied to the cement industry. Salt is mined near Zeila in the northwest. In the last decade, the industrial sector has expanded and now includes sugar refining, flour milling, meat packing, fish canning, tanning, textiles, cigarettes and matches. Two recent projects are an iron foundry at Mogadiscio and a cement plant at Berbera. An oil refinery is under construction.

People & towns
The Somalis, a well defined ethnic group, are basically nomadic and only 10% live in towns. Four of the five main centres are ports: Mogadiscio, Merca (100,000), Berbera (50,000) and Chisimaio (30,000); Hargeisa (60,000) has a pleasant site in the uplands.

Transport
Somalia's transport system is inadequate: there are no railways, the road network is poor and the two rivers are navigable for small craft only. Somali Airlines operates an internal service between Mogadiscio, Berbera, Chisimaio and Hargeisa: Mogadiscio and Hargeisa have international airports. The two chief ports are Mogadiscio and Berbera, but Merca and Chisimaio handle the banana trade. The merchant fleet, which is jointly owned with Libya, is being expanded.

Afars & Issas (FTAI)
Area
21,783 km²/8,410 sq miles
Location
10°55′—12°45′ N
41°40′—43°25′ E
Population
200,000 (1973)
Population density
9 per km²/24 per sq mile
Capital and largest city
Djibouti : 100,000 (1973)
Language
French
Major imports
excluding transit trade: textiles, machinery, food
Major exports
excluding transit trade: skins, leather, shoes
Currency
franc (1 franc = 100 centimes)
Gross National Product
65 million US dollars (1971)
Status
French overseas territory

Physical features
The French territory of Afars and Issas, formerly French Somaliland, is arid and barren. It consists of stony desert with extensive lava sheets and volcanic hills, some rising to over 1,500 m. A depression, parallel to the Red Sea, contains the salt lakes Alol and Assal; there are no permanent rivers. The Gulf of Tadjoura thrusts inland for some 50 km. Apart from mangroves along the coast, palms in the dry watercourses an sparse stretches of forest in upland areas, vegetation consists of stunted acacia and scrub.

Climate
FTAI has a hot, humid climate. Along the coast, temperatures average 28°C but rise to 45°C in July, the hottest month. Inland, conditions are slightly cooler. Rainfall, occurring in winter (October to February) is very low: under 10 cm a year.

People
The territory's name incorporates its two main ethnic groups: th Afars (82,000) and the Issas (62,000). Both groups are Mosle nomadic pastoralists. The Afars live mostly in the north and the Issas, a Somali tribe, in the south. The only important centre is Djibouti, the capital and port.

The economy
The shortage of water severely restricts arable farming but dat and vegetables are grown on a small scale under irrigation at oases. The rural population is largely nomadic and lives by herding camels, sheep, goats and a few cattle; there is some fishing in the Gulf of Aden. Mineral production is limited to salt, obtained by evaporation from the sea and Lake Assal, but deposits of gypsum, sulphur, mica and amethyst are thought to exist. Most of the FTAI's income, however, is derived from transit trade. Djibouti, as an important port and the coastal terminus of the Addis Ababa railway, handle a major share of Ethiopian exports—in particular, coffee, hides and skin, and oil seeds.

Ethiopia

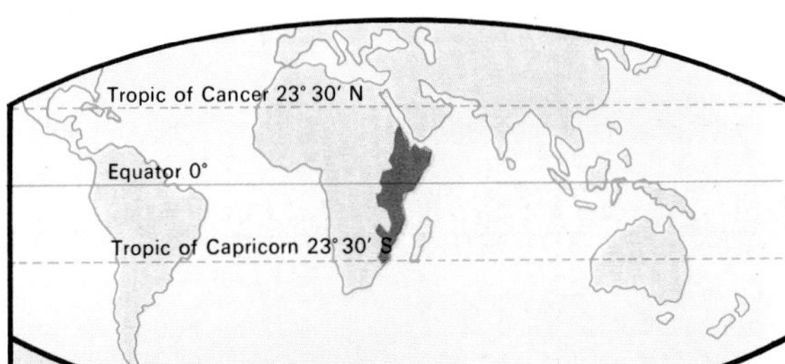

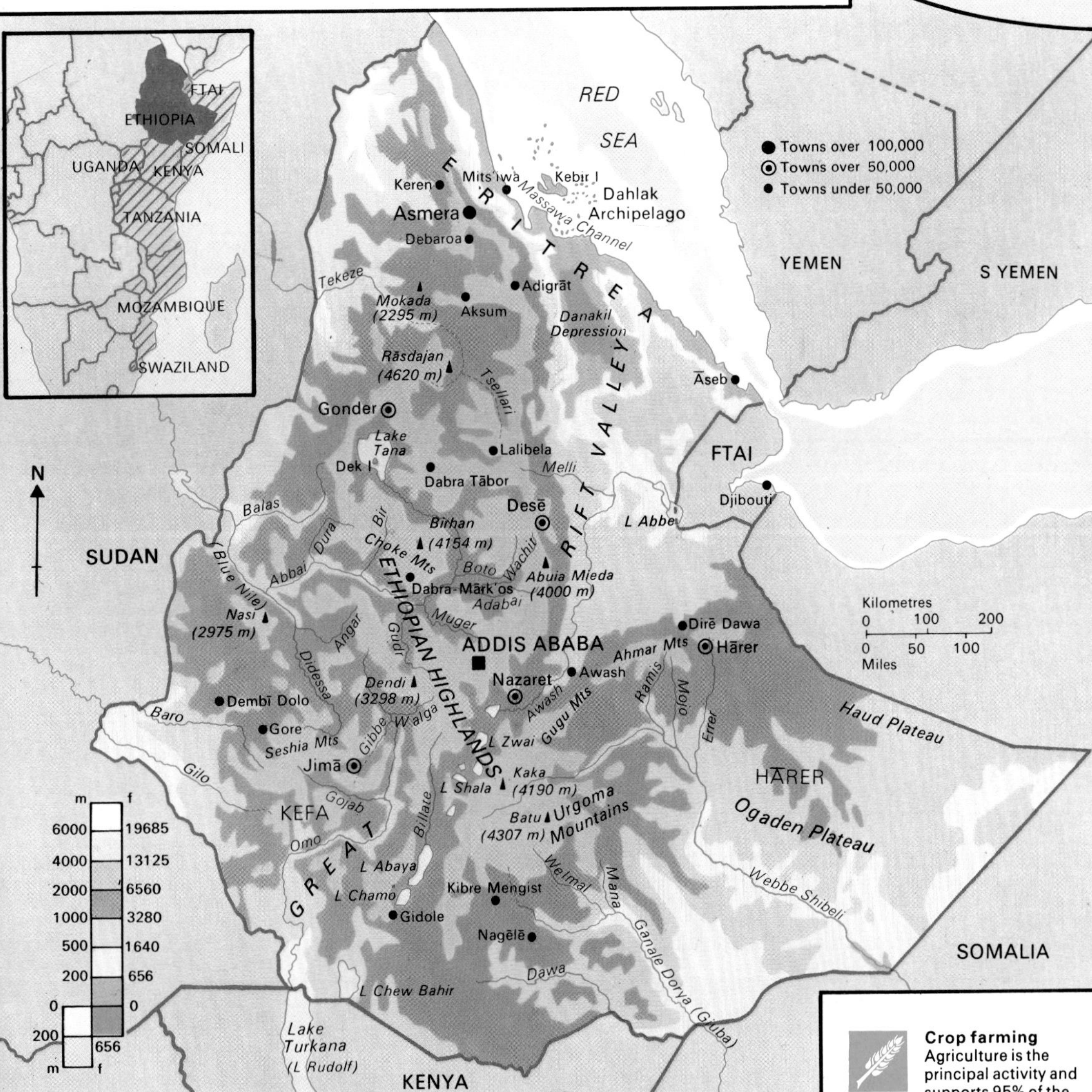

rea
,221,905 km^2/471,778 sq miles
ocation
°30′—18° N
3°—48° E
opulation
7,400,000 (1974)
opulation density
2 per km^2/58 per sq mile
apital and largest city
ddis Ababa: 912,100 (1972)
anguages
mharic, English
Major imports
machinery, vehicles, textiles,
ood, fuels, chemicals
Major exports
offee, fruit, vegetables and
ulses, hides and skins,
esame seeds, meat
urrency
ollar (1 dollar = 100 cents)
ross National Product
,680 million US dollars (1974)
tatus
epublic

Flora & fauna

Arid grasslands predominate below 1,800 m while the plateau orests have mostly been cleared or firewood and agriculture. Wildlife includes elephants, ons, rhinoceros, hyenas, striches, flamingos and eagles.

Physical features

Ethiopia's main feature is a high plateau (mean altitude 2,400 m) of volcanic origin. This plateau is split by the Great Rift Valley along a northeast-southwest line between the town of Awash and Lake Turkana. The Rift Valley, a long, narrow trench dotted with lakes, broadens in the north to form the parched Danakil depression which is mostly below sea level. North and west of the valley, the Ethiopian Highlands rise above the plateau to over 4,000 m and include Africa's third highest peak, Rāsdajan (4,620 m). This mountain zone is broken by steep gorges, some 1,500 m deep, cut by rivers such as the Abbai (Blue Nile) and Omo. The Abbai rises in the country's largest lake, Tana, and carves its way towards the Sudan in an enormous arc. The Urgoma mountains, to the east of the Rift Valley, are less rugged. In the northeast, the plateau drops sharply to a narrow plain fringing the Red Sea; the 800 km coastline lies wholly within Eritrea, a former Italian colony that now forms part of Ethiopia. In the southwest lies the arid Ogaden plateau.

Climate

Climate is influenced by altitude. On the plateau conditions are pleasant: Addis Ababa (2,400 m) averages 14°C in July, the coolest month, and 18°C in March, the hottest. In contrast, areas below 1,800 m (the coastlands and southern plains) are very hot; the Danakil depression is one of the world's hottest places with day temperatures of over 55°C. Humidity is high by the Red Sea. Rainfall ranges from 10 cm in the northeast to over 200 cm in the southwest: 80% of the annual total falls between June and September with smaller amounts between February and April.

People

Ethiopia contains about 40 ethnic groups with 70 languages and 200 dialects. The main peoples are the Christian Amhara and the predominantly Muslim Galla. The Amharas, from the central plateau, are the traditional ruling class although outnumbered by the pastoral Galla who account for 50% of the population and live in the south and east. In the far south and west, there are Negro and Nilotic tribes.

Crop farming

Agriculture is the principal activity and supports 95% of the population. Cultivated land, covering only 10% of the country, is concentrated on the plateau. The leading food crops are teff (a type of millet), wheat, barley and oats. Sugar and cotton are grown under irrigation in the Awash valley. Coffee, taking its name from the southwest province of Kefa where it originated and still grows wild, is the chief cash crop and accounts for over 50% of exports. The main plantations are in the southwest and on the eastern plateau in Hārer province. Other commercial crops are pulses (peas, beans, lentils), oilseeds (in particular, sesame), vegetables, and fruits such as citrus, apricots, figs and grapes. Gum arabic, beeswax, frankincense and myrrh are collected from the bush but have little economic value.

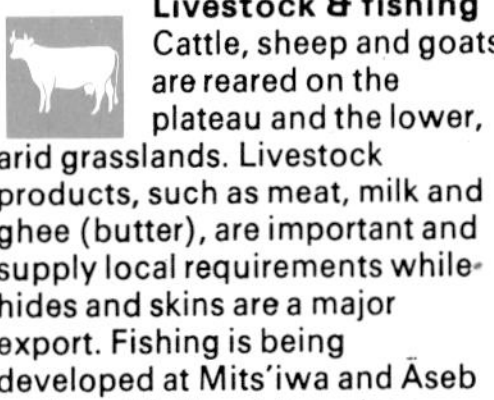

Livestock & fishing

Cattle, sheep and goats are reared on the plateau and the lower, arid grasslands. Livestock products, such as meat, milk and ghee (butter), are important and supply local requirements while hides and skins are a major export. Fishing is being developed at Mits'iwa and Āseb and pearl fishing takes place off the Dahlak archipelago.

Mining

Mineral production is limited. Some gold is mined at Kibre Mengist in the south and near Asmera and small amounts are exported. Potash and salt are obtained from the Danakil depression, copper is exploited at Debaroa in Eritrea and limestone is quarried on a small scale. Natural gas has been located in the Ogaden plateau and zinc, manganese and platinum also occur. The Red Sea coast is being prospected for oil.

Industry

Industrial development is in its early stages and the manufacturing sector employs less than 5% of the total workforce. Food processing is the most important branch and includes sugar refining, vegetable oil extraction, coffee cleaning, fruit, meat and vegetable canning and the manufacture of dairy produce. Other industrial products are textiles, cement, cigarettes, leather goods, pharmaceuticals and furniture. Addis Ababa and Asmera are the principal manufacturing centres. Ethiopia lacks adequate power supplies but output has been increased by recent hydro-electric power installations on the Awash.

Transport

Ethiopia's rugged mountains, escarpments and gorges make communications difficult. Animals are still widely used: horses and mules on the plateau and camels on the plains. A network of main roads radiate from Addis Ababa to Asmera, Dirē Dawa, Hārer and Jimā with two new highways connecting the capital to the Red Sea port of Āseb and with Nairobi (Kenya). Altogether, roads (mostly unsurfaced) cover 8,000 km. The main railway (780 km) links Addis Ababa to Djibouti and carries a major share of imports and exports. External trade also passes through the Eritrean ports of Mits'iwa and Āseb and via the Giuba river in the south to the Somali port of Chisimaio. Ethiopian Airlines provide a domestic service to over 40 towns and fly overseas from the international airports at Addis Ababa, Asmera and Dirē Dawa.

Towns

Addis Ababa has a pleasant site in the Ethiopian highlands. Its modern, cosmopolitan centre with tall buildings and wide, tree-lined avenues contrasts sharply with the sprawling mass of tin-roofed, mud huts that house most of the capital's million people. The second largest city is the Eritrean capital, Asmera (300,000) which is linked to Mits'iwa port.

Tourism

The spectacular scenery and long, rich history of Ethiopia give it considerable tourist potential. Attractions include the Blue Nile Falls (Bahir Dar), Awash Game Park, 800-year-old rock-hewn churches at Lalibela, island monasteries on Lake Tana and medieval castles at Gonder.

Uganda

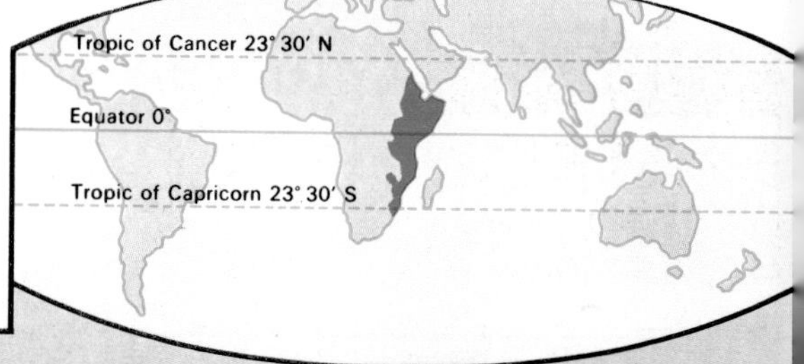

Area
236,860 km²/91,451 sq miles
Location
4°16′ N—1°30′ S
29°36′—35° E
Population
11,172,000 (1974)
Population density
47 per km²/122 per sq mile
Capital and largest city
Kampala: 330,700 (1969)
Language
English
Major imports
machinery, transport equipment, chemicals, food, fuels
Major exports
coffee, cotton, tea, copper, hides and skins, oilseeds
Currency
shilling (1 shilling = 100 cents)
Gross National Product
1,300 million US dollars (1971)
Status
republic

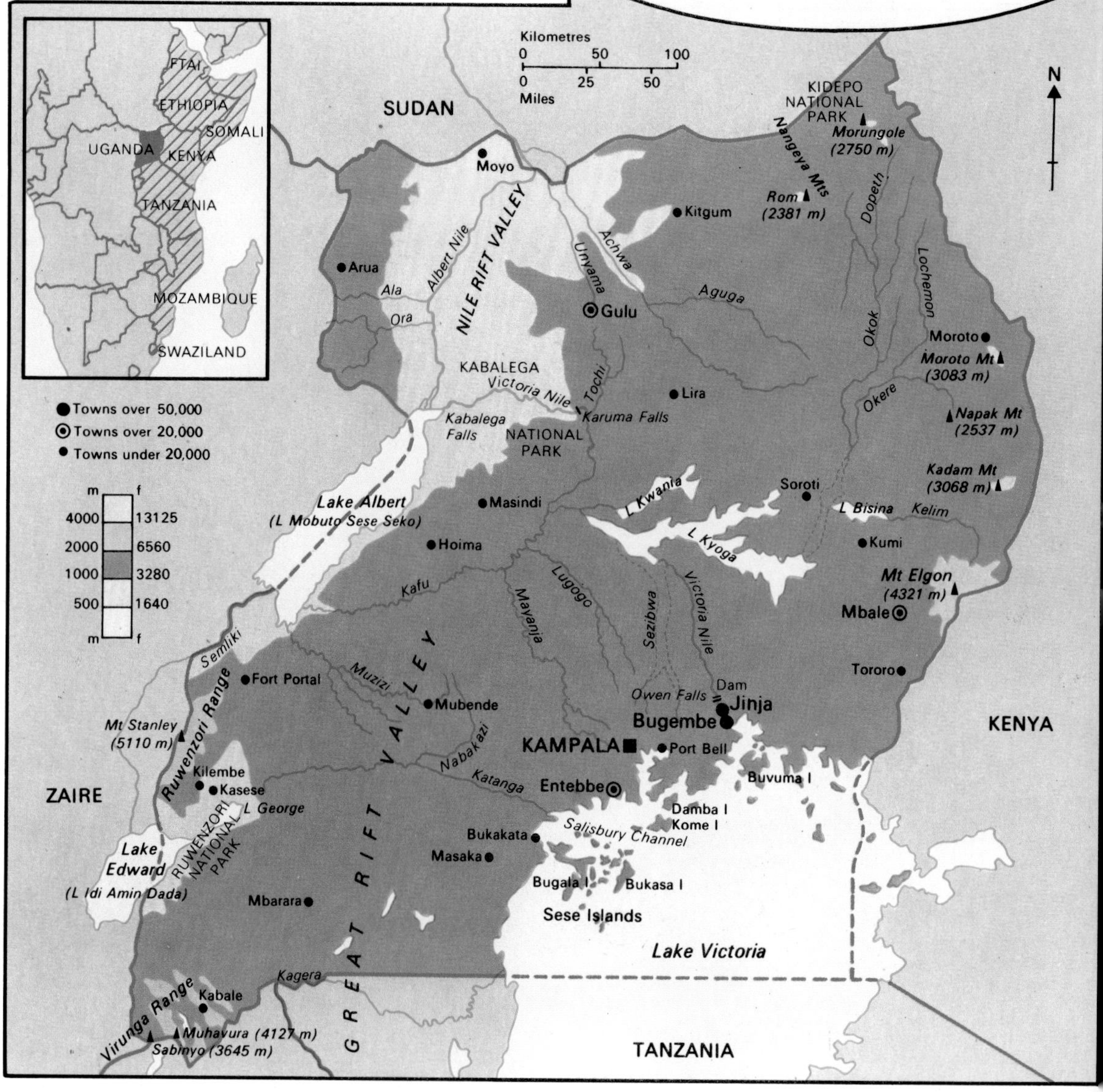

Tropic of Cancer 23° 30′ N
Equator 0°
Tropic of Capricorn 23° 30′ S

FTAI
ETHIOPIA
SOMALI
UGANDA
KENYA
TANZANIA
MOZAMBIQUE
SWAZILAND

● Towns over 50,000
◉ Towns over 20,000
• Towns under 20,000

m		f
4000		13125
2000		6560
1000		3280
500		1640

Kilometres 0 50 100
Miles 0 25 50

SUDAN, KENYA, ZAIRE, TANZANIA, KAMPALA, Jinja, Bugembe, Entebbe, Gulu, Mbale, Lake Victoria, Lake Albert (L Mobuto Sese Seko), Lake Edward (L Idi Amin Dada), NILE RIFT VALLEY, GREAT RIFT VALLEY, KABALEGA NATIONAL PARK, KIDEPO NATIONAL PARK, RUWENZORI NATIONAL PARK, Mt Elgon (4321 m), Mt Stanley (5110 m), Sese Islands

Physical features

Uganda is situated on a plateau more than 900 m above sea level which forms the floor of the Great Rift Valley. There are highlands to the east and west. In the east lies Mt Elgon (4,321 m), an extinct volcano, while in the west, between Lakes Edward and Albert, is the Ruwenzori range which rises to 5,110 m in snow-capped Mt Stanley. This range falls sharply to the Semliki river valley which broadens into the Nile Rift Valley. The plateau is characterized by undulating plains, low hills and swampy tracts. Over 15% of Uganda is covered by lakes, including parts of Victoria, Edward and Albert; Lake George and, in the central swampy area, Lakes Kyoga, Kwania and Bisina. The main rivers are the Semliki, Albert Nile and the fast-flowing Victoria Nile with its rapids and waterfalls and the spectacular Kabalega Falls.

Agriculture

In the north, where there is a marked dry season, food crops include maize, millet and pulses; in the wetter south, plantains, sweet potatoes, cassava and bananas are the staples. Coffee is the main cash crop; two main types are grown: *robusta* and *arabica*. Robusta predominates, partly because of its suitability for instant coffee, and is grown around Lake Victoria; arabica is grown on higher ground, particularly on the slopes of Mt Elgon. Cotton is next in importance and is produced in central parts of the plateau. Coffee and cotton make up 85% of all exports. Other commercial crops are tea (from the Ruwenzori region and the southwest), tobacco (from the northwest), sugarcane (grown on estates near Lake Victoria) and groundnuts. In areas with less then 75 cm of rain a year, in the east especially, cattle, sheep and goats are kept.

Energy

Uganda lacks energy minerals and the country's power comes from the hydro-electric plant at the Owen Falls dam near Jinja. Construction began in 1948 and the last turbine, the tenth, was installed twenty years later. The Owen Falls scheme supplies electricity to all Uganda and sends some to Kenya via a direct power line to Nairobi.

Climate

Although Uganda lies on the Equator, its climate is modified by altitude. Temperatures are fairly uniform throughout the year averaging 23°C on the plateau and 27°C in the Nile Rift Valley. In the equatorial south, rain occurs every month—often as violent thunderstorms—with two wetter periods (March-May, October-November). In the north, there is a dry season from December to February. Amounts vary from under 75 cm in the northeast to over 150 cm on the shores of Lake Victoria and up to 400 cm in the Ruwenzori mountains. Most parts of the plateau receive about 100 cm of rain a year.

Flora & fauna

Tall elephant grass occurs in the wetter areas, merging into rain forest in the south and southwest. Bush savanna covers drier regions, changing to semi-desert vegetation in the north-east. Uganda's wildlife, which is partly protected in three national parks, includes antelopes, elephants, lions, leopards, giraffes, gorillas and the rare white rhinoceros.

Forestry & fishing

Forests, covering only 7% of Uganda, are mostly found in the southwest. Hardwoods predominate: cedar is used for building and camphor and podocarp (yellow-wood) for furniture. Softwood plantations are being developed. With over 35,000 km² of lakes and rivers, Uganda has one of the world's largest fresh-water fisheries. Production averages 11 kilos per inhabitant and comes mainly from lakes Victoria, Kyoga, Edward and George. Carp and tilapia are the main species caught; some frozen fish is exported.

Industry

Most industries are based on the country's agriculture and include cotton ginning, textile weaving, coffee processing, tea packing, cigarette manufacture, sugar refining, flour milling, vegetable oil extraction and leather curing. Other industries process minerals and wood and include copper smelting, cement manufacture, fertilizers, plywood and paper production. Some consumer goods are produced. Kampala, Jinja-Bugembe and Tororo are the chief industrial centres.

Mining

Copper, accounting for 6% of total exports, is Uganda's chief mineral resource. It is mined at Kilembe in the Ruwenzori and railed to Jinja for smelting. All copper exports are sent to Japan. Limestone (used for cement) and phosphate (for fertilizer) are mined near Tororo and there is some production of tin, tungsten and beryl in the southwest. Other minerals existing include gold, nickel, cobalt (in the Kilembe copper ore), bismuth and mica.

People & towns

Uganda is one of Africa's most densely populated countries. The Nile roughly divides the country ethnically: to the north and east are the Nilotics and Nilo-Hamitics (related to Sudanese peoples); to the south and west are the Bantu or Africans who account for 70% of the population. Three main towns are situated by Lake Victoria: Kampala (the capital) and the industrial hub formed by Jinja (100,000) and Bugembe (50,000). The fourth largest town is Mbale (25,000) at the foot of Mt Elgon. Less than 10% of the population live in towns.

Tourism

Uganda has great tourist potential. Its scenery ranges from verdant lake shores to snowy mountain peaks and its abundant wildlife includes a wide variety of birds by the lakes and swamps. There are three national parks (Kidepo, Ruwenzori and Kabalega) and 14 game reserves.

Transport

Because of Uganda's inland position, good external communication are vital to trade. There is a direct rail link, via Tororo, to the Kenyan port of Mombasa which handles the bulk of Ugandar imports and exports. Substantial amounts of coffee, cotton and sugar are also shipped across Lake Victoria from Bukakata, Port Bell (Kampala) and Entebbe to Kisumu (Kenya) and then sent by rail to Mombasa. Internally, the railway serves only a small part of the country (Tororo-Arua, Tororo-Kasese) and road transport is growing in importance. The 46,000 km road network (25% all-weather) includes a major highway into Kenya. Uganda's international airport is at Entebbe, 40 km from Kampala.

Kenya

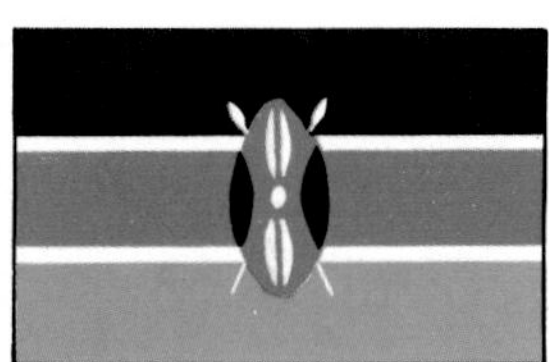

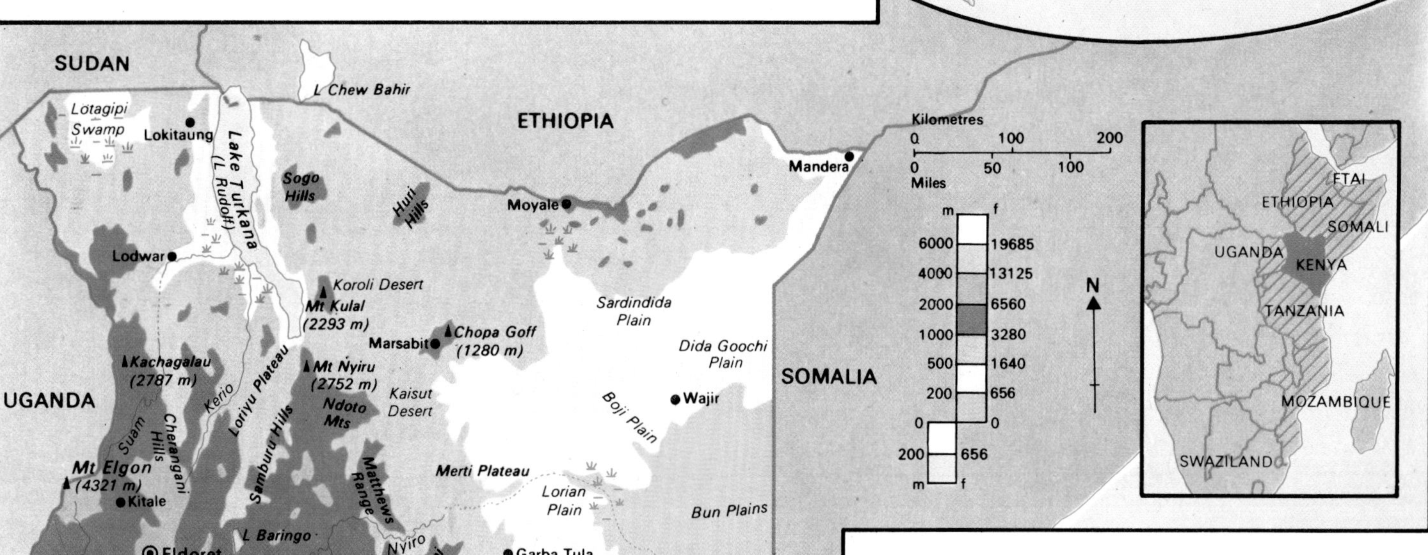

Area
582,647 km²/224,960 sq miles
Location
4°35′ N — 4°40′ S
33°58′ — 41°45′ E
Population
12,912,000 (1974)
Population density
22 per km²/57 per sq mile
Capital and largest city
Nairobi: 723,000 (1974)
Languages
Swahili, English
Major imports
machinery, oil, vehicles, fertilizers, food
Major exports
coffee, petroleum products, tea, sisal, fruit and vegetables, meat, pyrethrum
Currency
shilling (1 shilling = 100 cents)
Gross National Product
2,500 million US dollars (1974)
Status
republic

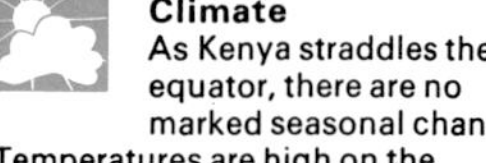

Climate
As Kenya straddles the equator, there are no marked seasonal changes. Temperatures are high on the humid coast but modified inland by altitude: Mombasa averages 26°C, Nairobi 20°C and Eldoret 17°C. Although no month is really dry, there are two wetter seasons: the long rains (March to June) and the short rains (November to December). Amounts vary from over 100 cm in the highlands, the Lake Victoria region and along the coast to under 50 cm on the Nyika and only 10 cm in the northeast where semi-desert conditions prevail.

Physical features
The narrow coastal belt, fringed with rain forest and mangrove swamps, is backed by a vast, arid, scrub-covered plain, the Nyika, which makes up 60% of the territory. The rest of the country, mostly at altitudes of between 1,500 m and 2,500 m, consists of rugged plateaux with grass savanna and forested mountains and includes the 150 km long Aberdare Range (3,994 m) and two mighty peaks: Mt Elgon (4,321 m) on the Ugandan border and Mt Kenya (5,200 m), Africa's second highest summit. This highland zone is cut by the Great Rift Valley which forms a north-south trench, 600 to 900 m deep and contains several lakes including Lake Turkana (Rudolf), 2,473 km². From the western rim of the Rift Valley, the plateau slopes down to the shores of Lake Victoria. The main river, the Tana, drains off Mt Kenya and the Aberdare range and enters the Indian Ocean at Kipini. Many small rivers flow into Lakes Turkana and Victoria.

Agriculture
Agriculture dominates the economy, employing 75% of the population and supplying 80% of all exports. Cultivated land, only 15% of the total area, is concentrated along the coast, in the Tana valley and in the highlands. Maize, found on almost every farm, is the staple food followed by yams, nuts, cassava, wheat and rice. Commercial farming is centred on the highlands. Coffee, grown south of Mt Kenya, is the chief cash crop and provides 30% of total exports. Tea, from the Kericho and Limuru districts, is next in importance and Kenya ranks as Africa's largest tea producer. Other major cash crops are sisal (grown in the coastal belt and along the Nairobi railway), pyrethrum (Kenya produces 80% of the world's supply of this non-toxic insecticide obtained from a white daisy), fruit and vegetables. Copra and coir are produced along the coast. The plateau grasslands support an expanding livestock industry.

Forestry & fishing
Although forests cover only 3% of the country they are commercially important. The coastal mangrove swamps yield tanning bark and poles for building (highly suitable as the wood is resistant to rot and white ants). Above 1,700 m, the highland forests include cedar (for construction and making pencils), camphor and podocarp (for furniture) and bamboo and eucalyptus (for pulp and paper). There are several plywood mills and a fibre-board factory. The Eldoret and Kitale districts have extensive wattle plantations; wattle bark, used in tanning, is a major export. Fishing is primarily based on the lakes.

Mining & energy
Kenya is steadily developing its mineral resources. The most important product is sodium carbonate dredged from Lake Magadi and railed, via a special branch line, to Mombasa. Fluorspar output, from the Kerio valley, is increasing rapidly and is mostly exported. Other minerals exploited are lead-silver-zinc at Kinangoni, limestone at Koru and Kajiado, rubies, green garnets and magnetite. Electricity is generated partly by thermal stations using imported fuels and partly by hydro-electric schemes in the highlands; some power is imported from the Owen Falls hydro station in Uganda.

Industry
Over half of the manufacturing sector is based on processing primary agricultural products and includes coffee milling, meat packing, fruit canning, flour milling, sugar refining, fish freezing, cotton ginning, tanning, rope and sacking manufacture, coir matting and pyrethrum extraction. Other industries produce textiles, clothing, wood, furniture, paper, chemicals, cement and light engineering goods. Vehicle assembly plants have been built in the 1970s. Nairobi is the chief manufacturing centre followed by Mombasa which has a wide range of industries including a ship repair yard and an oil refinery (a major export earner). Other industrial centres are Nakuru, Kisumu, Eldoret, Thika.

Transport
The main road and rail route runs from Mombasa through Nairobi and across the highlands into Uganda. There are branch lines off this railway to Tanzania (via Voi), Nanyuki and Kisumu (the chief port on Lake Victoria). Only 10% of the 47,500 km road network is paved. Mombasa is the main port which also serves Uganda, parts of northern Tanzania and eastern Zaire. There is an international airport at Nairobi and internal air services link the capital with Mombasa, Malindi and Kisumu.

Towns & people
About 95% of the population is African and includes around 40 different tribes. The Kikuyu (nearly 2 million—the largest ethnic group) are from the highlands south of Mt Kenya, followed by the Luo (1,200,000) and the Luhya and Kamba (one million each). Most of the people are cultivators or pastoralists and less than 10% live in towns. Nairobi, in the highlands (1,700 m) mid-way between the Indian Ocean and Lake Victoria, is East Africa's leading industrial and commercial centre. Kenya's second city is the busy port and tourist resort of Mombasa (338,600). Kisumu (146,700), the third largest town, is a lake port and the commercial centre of a major grain-producing area.

Tourism
Kenya is the land of the safari and tourism has overtaken coffee as the leading foreign exchange earner. The country's three main attractions are its coasts, its scenery and its wildlife. The coast has some of the world's finest beaches where the blue ocean contrasts with white sand and green palms. The interior is visually magnificent, ranging from desert to snow-covered Mt Kenya, from vast savannas to the dramatic Rift Valley. Large areas have been set aside as national parks for the conservation of wildlife and contain lions, elephants, giraffes, antelopes, zebras, jackals, baboons, hyenas, buffaloes and many other animals. Lake Nakuru is famous for its flamingos. Almost half a million tourists visit Kenya annually.

Tanzania

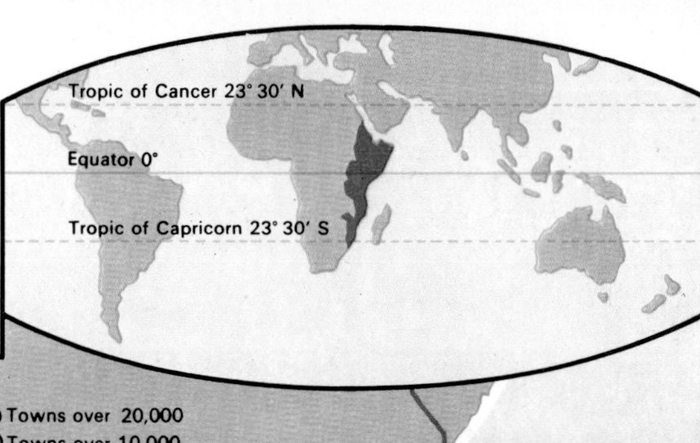

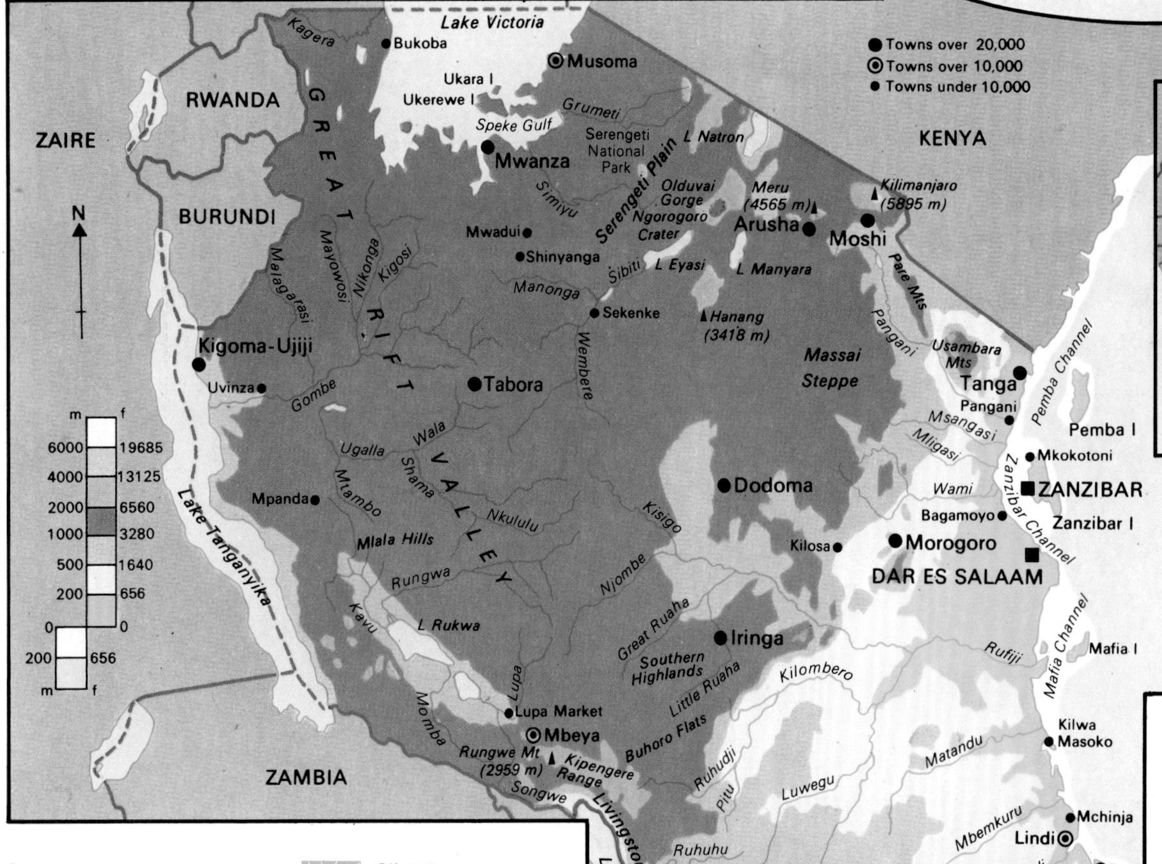

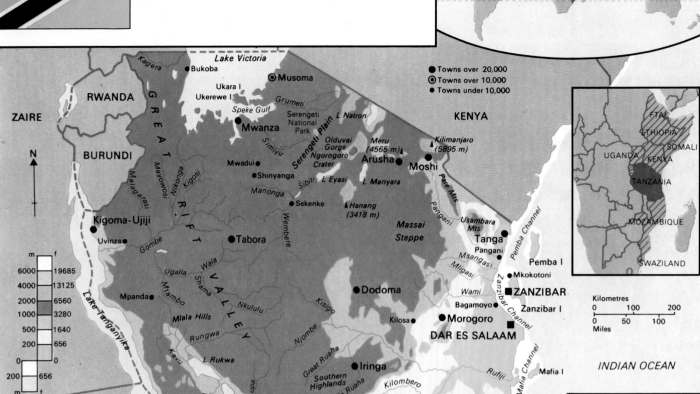

Area
939,704 km²/362,820 sq miles
Location
1°—11°45′ S
29°20′—40°30′ E
Population
14,760,000 (1974)
Population density
16 per km²/41 per sq mile
Capital and largest city
Dar es Salaam: 517,000 (1975)
Language
Swahili
Major imports
machinery, vehicles, fuels, food, textiles, iron and steel
Major exports
coffee, cotton, cloves, sisal, diamonds, cashew nuts
Currency
shilling (1 shilling = 100 cents)
Gross National Product
2,200 million US dollars (1974)
Status
republic

Physical features

Tanzania, East Africa's largest state, was formed in 1964 by the union of Tanganyika and Zanzibar. Tanganyika, the mainland, consists of a great plateau, 1,000 m high, with flat, grassy plains, woodlands and isolated hills. The plateau is broken by mountains in the southwest and northeast, including Africa's highest peak, Kilimanjaro (5,895 m). The territory contains 53,500 km² of water including part of Lake Victoria in the north and sections of Lakes Tanganyika and Nyasa on the western border of the Great Rift Valley. The coastal plain, flanking sandy beaches and mangrove swamps, is narrow except along the lower course of the Rufiji, the country's longest river. Zanzibar (1,658 km²) and Pemba (984 km²) are low-lying coral islands fringed with reefs.

Climate

The mainland coast and islands have an equatorial climate with high temperatures (26°C) and high humidity. There is no dry season and rainfall varies from 180 cm on Zanzibar to 120 cm at Dar es Salaam. The plateau is hot and dry: temperatures, with extreme daily variations (up to 20°C), average 22°C while rain (falling between November and April) seldom exceeds 70 cm.

Mainland agriculture

The severe handicaps imposed by the tsetse fly and low rainfall mean that less than 10% of the country is cultivated. Crop-growing is confined to the coastal plain, the northeastern highlands and to the areas bordering Lakes Victoria and Nyasa where rainfall is slightly higher. Subsistence farming predominates. Maize and millet are the basic foods, followed by groundnuts, rice, cassava and bananas. Coffee, cotton, sisal and cashew nuts make up 50% of total exports; Tanzania is the world's leading sisal producer. Coffee is grown on the slopes of Kilimanjaro and in the Bukoba district; cotton comes from the Mwanza region; sisal is produced in the Dar es Salaam and Tanga regions; cashew nuts are cultivated along the coast between the Rufiji and the Mozambique border. Other cash crops include tea, coconuts (copra and oil), pyrethrum and tobacco. Irrigation has been developed for the Kilimanjaro coffee plantations and for sugar plantations near Arusha and in the Kilombero valley. Cattle-raising is important but is limited to tsetse-free zones.

Island agriculture

In contrast to the mainland, Zanzibar and Pemba are largely self-sufficient in food. As their east coasts have dry, infertile soil, arable farming is based on the central and western zones. Rice, maize, millet, cassava and bananas are the staple foods. The main cash crop, cloves, accounts for 90% of the islands' exports. Two-thirds of output comes from Pemba and together the islands supply 80% of the world's cloves. Coconut palms are widespread and coconut products (copra, oil, rope and matting) are the other leading exports. In an attempt to diversify commercial farming, cocoa, citrus fruits and tobacco are being developed.

Forestry & fishing

Tanzania's few forests have been substantially reduced by shifting cultivation, but re-afforestation programmes are now making good this loss. Highland areas yield hardwoods such as camphor and mahogany, while the mangrove swamps along the coast provide building timber and tanning bark. In Zanzibar, fish are a major source of protein; sardines and tuna are also exported. On the mainland, almost 90% of the catch comes from inland waters, notably Lake Victoria.

Mining

Mining is centred on the country's diamond deposits at Mwadui in the north and diamonds provide 7% of total exports. Some gold is produced in the Musoma, Sekenke and Lupa districts and salt is obtained from seawater along the coast. The new Tanzam railway, linking Tanzania and Zambia, opens up the mineral potential of the southwest and extensive reserves of coal and iron ore are being surveyed near the Livingstone mountains

Industry

Industrial development is in its early stages and is mostly based on agricultural produce. It includes cotton ginning, coconut-oil extraction, textile manufacture, coffee processing, rice milling and cement manufacture (from coral limestone). There are also factories producing soap, paint, plastics, shoes, beer and light engineering goods. An oil refinery has been built at Dar es Salaam and a fertilizer plant at Tanga. Dar es Salaam, Tanga and Mwanza are the main industrial centres. Tanga benefits from the country's principal hydro-electric installation which is on the Pangani river. There is considerable hydro-power potential in the southwest.

Transport

Although the 3,000 km rail network is inadequate, it does connect the major producing areas to the coast. The central line (1,246 km) runs inland from Dar es Salaam via Dodoma and Tabora to Kigoma on Lake Tanganyika; branch lines go to Mwanza and Mpanda. In the north, a line links Tanga to Arusha while the southwest is now served by the new Tanzam line from Dar es Salaam to Zambia. The main ports are Dar es Salaam, Tanga and Mtwara on the coast and Mwanza on Lake Victoria. East African Airways (Tanzanian Region) operates internally and there are international airports at Dar es Salaam, Arusha, Lindi and Tabora.

Tourism

Tanzania has the finest game parks in Africa: the most famous, the Serengeti National Park, covers 13,000 km² and contains a million animals including elephants, lions, antelopes, giraffes, leopards, zebras, buffaloes, rhinoceros and hippopotami. Tanzania also offers tourists scenic landscapes and some of the continent's principal historic sites; the oldest human fossil on record (1.5 million years) was found at Olduvai Gorge in the north.

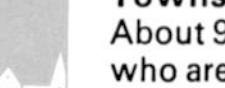

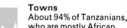

Towns

About 94% of Tanzanians, who are mostly African, live in rural areas and there are few large towns. Dar es Salaam, the 'haven of peace', is the main industrial centre and chief port, but the title of capital is to be transferred to Dodoma (25,000), an old, centrally-located trading settlement. Tanzania's second largest town, the port of Zanzibar, dates back to the 8th century when the Arabs colonized the island. The other main centres, Tanga (61,000), Mwanza (35,000) and Arusha (34,000), are being developed.

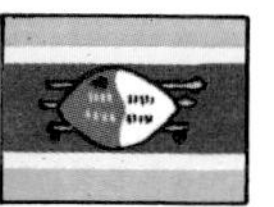

Swaziland

Mozambique

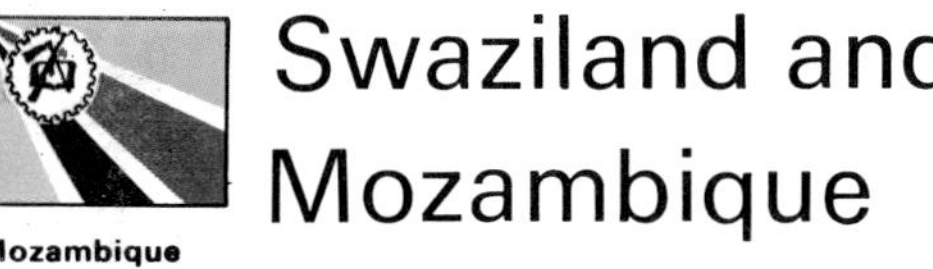

Swaziland and Mozambique

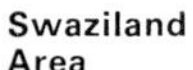

Swaziland
Area
17,366 km²/6,705 sq miles
Location
25°30′—27°20′ S
31°—32°20′ E
Population
477,000 (1975)
Population density
27 per km²/71 per sq mile
Capital and largest city
Mbabane: 24,000 (1975)
Languages
Siswati, English
Major imports
machinery, vehicles, manufactured goods, fuels, chemicals
Major exports
sugar, woodpulp, iron ore, asbestos, citrus, canned fruit, meat and meat products
Currency
lilangeni (1 lilangeni = 100 cents)
Gross National Product
77 million US dollars (1971)
Status
absolute monarchy

Physical features
Swaziland, smaller than Wales, is wedged between Mozambique and South Africa. There are three main regions: the rugged High Veld (averaging 1,200 m) in the west, the undulating Middle Veld (600 m) in the centre and, in the east, the malarial Low Veld (300 m). The low Lebombo mountains run along the Mozambique border. The main rivers, such as the Imbuluzi, Usutu and Ngwavuma, flow east from the High Veld across the country and cut through the Lebombo in deep gorges while the Komati swings north into South Africa finally to join the Sabie.

Climate
The climate varies with altitude. The High Veld is cool and wet with annual averages of 16°C in temperature and 120 cm of rain, while the Low Veld is hot and dry (21°C temperature and 65 cm of rain). Rain occurs mainly as heavy summer storms and causes extensive soil erosion.

Agriculture
Farming, mostly at subsistence level, supports 70% of Swazis; maize is the staple food. Commercial agriculture, under non-Swazi control, includes sugar (accounting for 25% of total exports), citrus, cotton, rice, pineapples and tobacco. Apart from cotton, these export crops are grown under irrigation. About 15% of the country is cultivated. Cattle are widespread and over-grazing contributes to soil erosion; live animals and meat are exported. Forests have been planted to conserve the soil and now provide 20% of exports. Woodpulp is the chief product.

Mining & industry
Iron ore and asbestos make up a third of total exports. Iron ore, mined northwest of Mbabane, is taken by rail directly to Maputo (Mozambique) and shipped to Japan. Asbestos comes from the Havelock mine near Pigg's Peak. Coal is produced in the southeast and 50% of output is exported. Industrial development, centred around a hydro-electric power scheme on the Usutu, mainly consists of sugar refineries, pulp mills and fruit-canning plants.

Transport
The 2,400 km road network is 70% surfaced and includes, in the east, a major highway from South Africa to Mozambique. The 220 km railway, built for carrying iron ore, links with the Mozambique system. Manzini (10,000), the country's commercial centre, has the principal airport and there are connecting flights by Swazi Air to Johannesburg and Maputo.

Mozambique
Area
784,961 km²/303,073 sq miles
Location
10°30′—26°50′ S
30°15′—40°45′ E
Population
9,000,000 (1975)
Population density
11 per km²/30 per sq mile
Capital and largest city
Maputo: 440,000 (1972)
Language
Portuguese
Major imports
machinery, transport equipment, base metals, oil, wheat
Major exports
cashew nuts, cotton and textiles, sugar, wood, tea, sisal
Currency
escudo (1 escudo = 100 centavos)
Gross National Product
1,915 million US dollars (1971)
Status
republic

Physical features
Mozambique is a straggling country extending 2,700 km from north to south and varying in width from 80 km in the south to 800 km in the centre along the Zambeze. A broad coastal lowland, including the Zambeze and Limpopo deltas, occupies about 40% of the territory. Infertile, sandy soils predominate except for alluvial zones bordering rivers such as the Limpopo, Save, Buzi, Pungue and Zambeze. In the south, the coastal plain stretches inland almost to the western border, but in the centre and north the interior is undulating, rising to 900 m on the north-western plateau; the plateau surface is broken by the Namuli massif (2,419 m).

Climate
The coastal belt is hot, humid and unhealthy with temperatures averaging 22°C in winter and 29°C in summer. The interior uplands are only slightly cooler. Rain, falling during the summer months between November and May, is heaviest along the coast (150 cm at Beira) with inland areas, excluding the plateau, drier.

Agriculture
About 90% of the workforce is engaged in agriculture. Subsistence farming predominates: maize, yams, cassava, groundnuts and bananas are the basic crops. Commercial farming, supplying 80% of total exports, is mostly located near the major ports. The main cash crops are cashew nuts (Mozambique is the world's chief producer), cotton, sisal and coconuts (for copra) with tea grown on the plateau and sugar from irrigated areas in the Zambeze and Limpopo valleys. Some cattle are kept in the south. Rain forests along the rivers provide hardwoods for export.

Mining & energy
When developed, Mozambique's mineral resources could transform the economy. They include coal, iron ore, copper, fluorite, gold, bauxite, diamonds and the world's largest deposits of tantalite and second largest of beryl. There are also big reserves of natural gas. So far, only the coal at Tete is exploited in significant quantities. Electricity is generated by coal-fired thermal stations and hydro-electric power plants on the Revue and Zambeze (the Cabora Bassa project).

Industry
The country's few industries, based on local produce, include sugar refineries, cotton mills, tea factories and copra and cashew processing plants.

Transport
Over 75% of trade passing through the main ports (Maputo, Beira, Mozambique, Nacala) is handled on behalf of other states: Zaire, Zambia, Malawi, S Africa and, before 1976, Rhodesia. The rail network reflects this transit trade—there are east-west lines linking the interior to the coast, but no north-south routes. There are also good road connections to neighbouring states. Maputo and Beira have international airports.

Towns
The chief towns are on the coast. Maputo, formerly Lourenço Marques, is not well situated for a capital city as it is remote from most of the country, but it is the leading port and manufacturing centre and has become a tourist centre. Beira, the second largest city, is one of Africa's busiest ports. The two main towns in the north are the new ports of Nacala and Mozambique. Quelimane and Inhambane are regional centres.

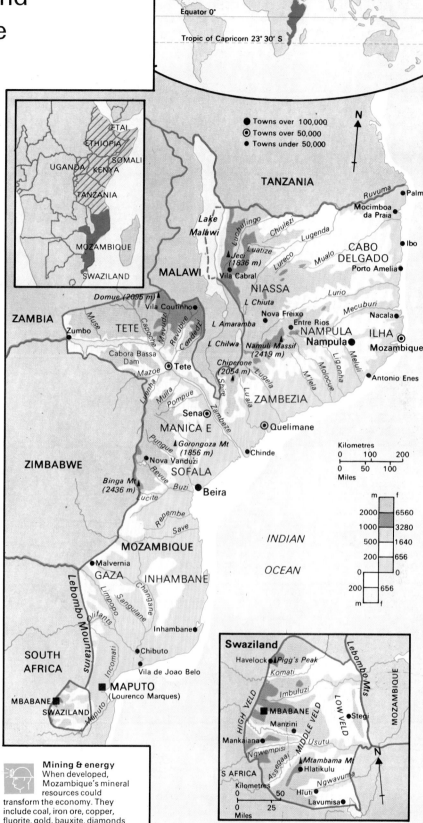

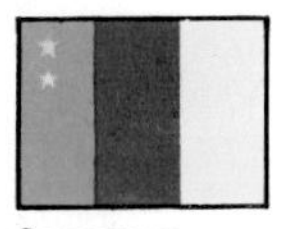
Cameroun

Central African Empire

Cameroun, Central African Empire

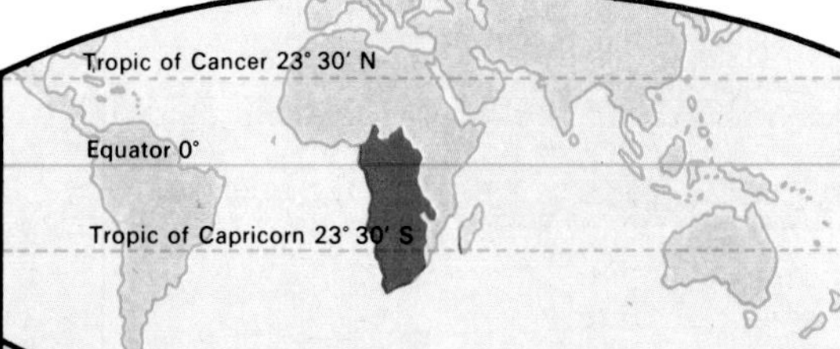

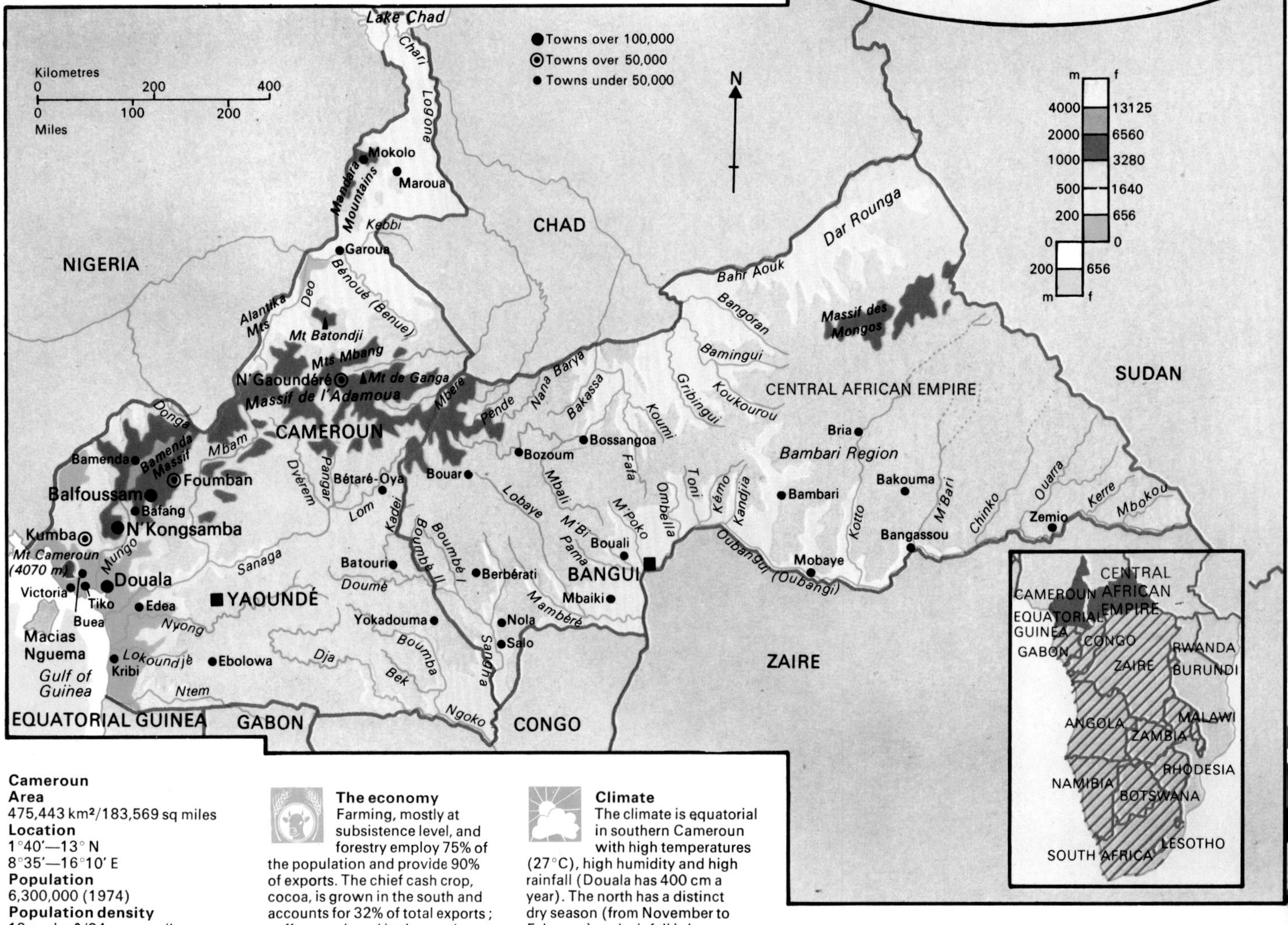

Cameroun
Area
475,443 km²/183,569 sq miles
Location
1°40'—13° N
8°35'—16°10' E
Population
6,300,000 (1974)
Population density
13 per km²/34 per sq mile
Capital
Yaoundé: 230,000 (1973)
Largest city
Douala: 340,000 (1973)
Languages
English, French
Major imports
manufactured goods, transport equipment, machinery, food, fuels
Major exports
cocoa, coffee, timber, aluminium, cotton, bananas
Currency
franc (1 franc = 100 centimes)
Gross National Product
1,050 million US dollars (1970)
Status
republic

Physical features
Behind the narrow swampy coastal plain lies an upland belt covered with dense rain forest. This zone merges northwards into the central plateau where high grasslands rise to over 1,000 m. In the northern part of the country, savanna slopes down to the shores of Lake Chad. Mountains extend along the western border reaching their highest point in volcanic Mt Cameroun (4070 m) which dominates the coastline. The central plateau acts as a watershed: to the north, streams flow either into the Benue (and then into the Niger) or into Lake Chad via the Logone; southwards, streams drain into the Sanaga and Sangha (a tributary of the Congo).

The economy
Farming, mostly at subsistence level, and forestry employ 75% of the population and provide 90% of exports. The chief cash crop, cocoa, is grown in the south and accounts for 32% of total exports; coffee, produced in the southwest highlands, represents a further 25%. Other export crops are cotton and groundnuts from the north, timber, bananas, palm kernels, rubber and tobacco from the south. Yams and rice are grown for food in the south, millet and sorghum in the north. Livestock is raised on the central grasslands and northern savanna. About 60% of the country's fish is taken from inland waters, notably the lower Lagone and Lake Chad. Because of poor communications, bauxite deposits in the central plateau are not fully exploited and the Edea aluminium smelter, the main industry, uses imported ore. Other industries, concentrated in the Douala-Yaoundé region, are small-scale and consist of processing local produce. The hydro-electric power station at Edea on the Sanaga provides 95% of the country's electricity.

Transport
Inadequate transport is retarding industrial development. The main railway runs from Douala to N'Gaoundéré and will, eventually, extend to Chad. At the moment, goods from the north go to Garoua and are exported through Nigeria via the Benue. Douala handles 90% of sea trade and is the main port followed by Tiko, Kribi and Victoria. The 40,000 km road network is being improved. Douala and Yaoundé have airports.

Climate
The climate is equatorial in southern Cameroun with high temperatures (27°C), high humidity and high rainfall (Douala has 400 cm a year). The north has a distinct dry season (from November to February) and rainfall is less with only 60 cm near Lake Chad.

Central African Empire
Area
622,985 km²/240,535 sq miles
Location
2°10'—11° N
14°25'—27°20' E
Population
1,637,000 (1971)
Population density
3 per km²/7 per sq mile
Capital and largest city
Bangui: 301,793 (1968)
Language
French, Sangho
Major imports
machinery, vehicles, textiles
Major exports
diamonds, coffee, cotton, timber, tobacco
Currency
franc (1 franc = 100 centimes)
Gross National Product
229 million US dollars (1971)
Status
empire

Physical features
The Central African Empire lies landlocked in the heart of Africa and consists of a savanna-covered plateau some 760 m high. This upland block acts as a watershed: to the north, streams drain into the Chari, Logone and their tributaries; southwards, most streams flow into the Oubangui and so into the Congo. Dense rain forest covers the southwest.

Climate
In the south, there is a short dry season from December to January and a long wet season from June to October; annual rainfall averages 200 cm. The north has a longer dry season, from November to April, with less rain—about 80 cm a year. Temperatures are high and average 27°C.

Transport
The empire's transport systems are poorly developed. Only a third of the roads in the 21,000 km network are all-weather and there are no railways. Inland waterways play a significant role in carrying freight and there is considerable seasonal traffic on the Oubangui and Sangha. The Oubangui is navigable below Bangui and barges ply between the capital and Brazzaville (Congo). From Brazzaville goods are taken by rail to the coast. Salo is the chief port on the Sangha but, upstream, Nola is being developed as a timber port. The empire's products are also exported via Cameroun: a main road connects Bangui to Douala and there are plans to link the two countries by rail. Such a railway would cross the south-western region and help develop the area's agricultural, forest and mineral resources. Bangui is the centre for domestic and international air services.

Agriculture
In the Central African Empire, 90% of the population live off the land, yet only 2% of the land area is under cultivation. Subsistence farming predominates and the principal food crops are millet, maize, sorghum, beans, cassava, groundnuts and rice. The leading cash crops, mainly from the southwest, are cotton and coffee which together account for over 40% of total exports. Tobacco, rubber, sisal and palm kernels are also exported. Timber production from the southwestern forests is hampered by poor transport facilities; at present, logs are floated down the Oubangui and Congo rivers for export. Stock-rearing is hindered by the tsetse fly and is largely confined to herds kept by nomads in the west and in the Bambari region.

Mining & industry
Alluvial diamonds, from the west of the country, make up half the empire's exports. Important reserves of uranium, located near Bakouma, are so far unexploited. Industry is limited to a few concerns processing primary materials, especially cotton: there are several cotton ginneries and a spinning, weaving and dyeing complex. The hydro-electric power station at Bouali is the chief source of electricity.

Equatorial Guinea and Gabon

Equatorial Guinea **Gabon**

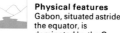

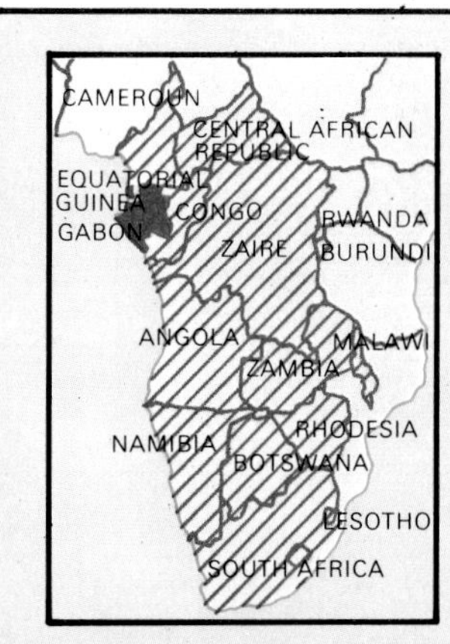

Equatorial Guinea
Area
28,051 km²/10,831 sq miles
Location
3°45′N—1°25′S
5°35′—11°20′E
Population
298,000 (1973)
Population density
11 per km²/28 per sq mile
Capital and largest city
Malaba: 37,237 (1960)
Language
Spanish
Major imports
vehicles, fuels, tobacco, cement, machinery
Major exports
cocoa, coffee, timber, palm oil, copra, bananas
Currency
peseta (1 peseta = 100 centimos)
Gross National Product
61 million US dollars (1971)
Status
republic

The land

Equatorial Guinea consists of the mainland territory of Río Muni (26,017 km²) and five islands: Macías Nguema, formerly Fernando Poo (2,034 km²), Pigalu (17km²), Corisco (15 km²) and Elobey Grande and Elobey Chico (together covering 2.5 km²). Río Muni comprises a plateau which rises in a series of steep steps from the densely forested coastal plain; mountains, reaching 1,200 m, rim the plateau. The principal river, the Benito, divides the country in two. Macías Nguema, the main island, is formed from several extinct volcanoes; thick forests cover the coastal lowlands while savanna and grass-lands characterize the interior mountains. Santa Isabel, the highest peak, reaches 3,007 m. An unhealthy equatorial climate prevails with high temperatures, humidity and rainfall. Malaba averages 26°C and has 200 cm of rain a year; Río Muni is slightly drier than the islands.

Towns

The capital, Malaba, is on the north coast of Macías Nguema and stands on cliffs overlooking a natural harbour formed from a submerged volcano crater. Bata (27,000) is the mainland's chief town and leading port with Niefang, Mikomeseng, Ebebiyin and Evinayong serving as market centres in the interior. Pigalu island is over-populated and many people leave to work in Río Muni or Macías Nguema.

The economy

Equatorial Guinea's economy, based on agriculture and forestry, is undeveloped. Cocoa is the main cash crop, accounting for over half of total exports; 90% of output comes from the fertile Macías Nguema where it is mostly grown on plantations. Coffee, providing 25% of exports, comes from the Cameroun border region of Río Muni. Other commercial crops are palm oil from the mainland, bananas from Macías Nguema and copra from Pigalu. Cassava and sweet potatoes are the staple foods and there is some livestock on the uplands of Macías Nguema. Fishing is well established off the islands. Timber accounts for 16% of exports and production is centred on the forests of Rio Muni; okoumé, a softwood used in making plywood, and mahogany are the principal species exploited. Industry is very limited and is confined to small-scale processing of primary products such as cocoa, coffee and timber. Macias Nguema is more developed than Rio Muni.

Transport

There are no railways and only 1,200 km of roads, mostly unsurfaced. The main tarred routes run from Bata to Rio Benito and Ebebiyin and from Malaba to Luba and Ri-Aba. Malaba, handling general cargo and cocoa, is the chief port followed by Luba (bananas), Bata (general cargo), Rio Benito (wood) and Puerto Iradier (wood). Malaba and Bata have international airports.

Gabon
Area
267,000 km²/103,088 sq miles
Location
2°15′N—3°55′S
8°45′—14°30′E
Population
520,000 (1973)
Population density
2 per km²/5 per sq mile
Capital and largest city
Libreville: 251,400 (1975)
Language
French
Major imports
machinery, metals, transport equipment, chemicals, textiles, foodstuffs
Major exports
crude oil, timber and wood products, manganese, uranium
Currency
franc (1 franc = 100 centimes)
Gross National Product
180 million US dollars (1970)
Status
republic

Climate

Gabon's hot, wet climate is typically equatorial. High humidity and high temperatures (26 to 28°C) prevail throughout the year and there is no dry seaon except in the south. Rainfall, averaging 250 cm, is heaviest in the northwest: Cocobeach, near Equatorial Guinea has up to 400 cm of rain a year.

Physical features

Gabon, situated astride the equator, is dominated by the Ogooué river system. Except for the extreme northwest and southwest, the Ogooué and its tributaries drain the entire territory and have cut their way through the broad forested plateau, some 600 m high, occupying the interior. Mountains, up to 1,800 m in altitude, edge the plateau. The sandy coastal plain, fringed with mangrove swamps, is narrow in the north and south but widens in the Ogooué region.

Mining & industry

Minerals dominate the economy and account for over 60% of exports. Petroleum, from fields at Gamba and off Port Gentil, is the most important followed by manganese from Moanda in the southeast (this ore is exported by rail via the Congo). Gabon ranks as the world's leading exporter of manganese. Uranium is mined at Mounana, also in the southeast. Large reserves of iron ore at Mekambo, in the northeast, are to be exploited; zinc, gold and phosphate also occur. The industrial sector, based on local raw materials, is poorly developed; it includes plywood and veneer factories, an oil-refinery at Port Gentil, coffee and oil-palm processing plants and flour mills.

Agriculture

In Gabon, subsistence farming predominates. The staple crops grown are cassava, maize, yams, rice and bananas but output is not sufficient and food imports are necessary. Cash crop production is very limited with coffee, cocoa, palm oil and kernels accounting for less than 1% of total exports. Coffee and cocoa are grown in the fertile north-west, oil palms and coffee in the Lambaréné region. Few animals are kept because of the tsetse fly. After minerals, timber is Gabon's principal resource providing 35% of exports. Forests cover 75% of the country and include valuable hardwoods as well as okoumé. The okoumé tree grows only in Gabon, Río Muni and Congo; Gabon is the world's largest producer of okoumé wood, used for plywood and veneers. Other timbers exported are mahogany, ebony and walnut.

Transport

Economic development is hampered by inadequate communications. Roads are poor and often impassable during rain. The only railway links the Moanda mine with the Congo network, but a trans-Gabon line is planned and work has begun on the first stage, Owendo to Booué. The Ogoové is navigable up to Ndjolé. There is a new deep-water port at Owendo. As well as an international airport at Libreville, there are over 80 airfields, many of them owned by timber and mining concerns.

Congo and Zaire

Congo, Zaire

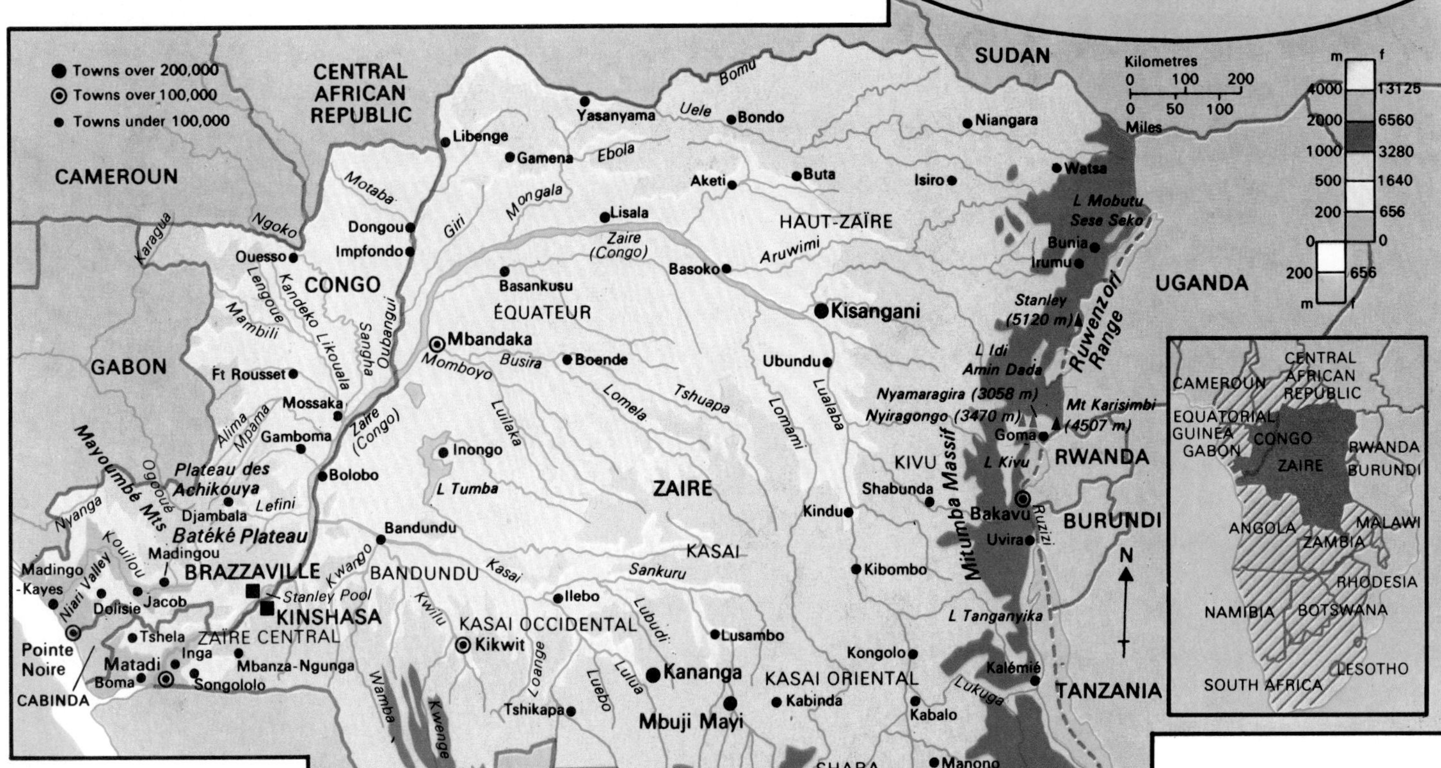

Congo
Area
342,000 km²/132,000 sq miles
Location
3°40′ N—5° S
11°—18°40′ E
Population
1,300,000 (1974)
Population density
4 per km²/10 per sq mile
Capital and largest city
Brazzaville: 289,700 (1974)
Language
French
Major imports
machinery, iron and steel, vehicles, chemicals
Major exports
timber, veneers, plywood, sugar, potash
Currency
franc (1 franc = 100 centimes)
Gross National Product
327 million US dollars (1970)
Status
republic

The land
The Congo's short coastline, backed by lagoons, is sandy in the north but more swampy in the south. From the narrow coastal plain, the Mayoumbé mountains rise steeply to almost 800 m. Beyond this forested ridge lies the broad Niari valley, edged to the north by the Chaillu massif which acts as a divide between drainage into the Kouilou and the Zaïre. Further inland, the country consists of the savanna-covered Batéké plateau which is dissected by the forested valleys of tributaries of the Zaïre. For 1,000 km, the eastern border is formed by the Zaïre and a major tributary, the Oubangui. The climate is typically equatorial with high temperatures ranging from 21 to 27°C and a high annual rainfall of between 200 and 260 cm. There is no dry season except during winter in the extreme north (between December and January) and south (between June and July).

Forestry & farming
Forests, covering half the country, provide the Congo with its leading export: timber. Production is centred on the Mayoumbé and Chaillu highlands, especially along the Congo-Océan railway and the Sangha in the north. Okoumé and mahogany are the main commercial species. Agriculture employs 70% of the population. The chief export crops—sugar, tobacco and groundnuts—are grown in the Niari valley; this fertile depression is also used for food crops such as cassava, maize, bananas and rice and dairy farming. Other cash crops are coffee and cocoa from the forested zones and palm oil from northern river valleys.

Mining & industry
The country's chief mineral resource is potash, mined near Pointe Noire. Petroleum (offshore), lead, zinc, tin, coppper, gold and diamonds are also produced. Iron ore, phosphate and bauxite have been discovered. Industries, located in Brazzaville, Pointe Noire and the Niari valley, process local raw materials. They include sawmills, plywood plants, flour mills, sugar refineries and cigarette factories.

Transport
The 515 km Congo-Océan railway, from Pointe Noire to Brazzaville, plus navigable stretches of the rivers Zaïre, Oubangui and Sangha form the country's principal highways. A main road links Pointe Noire, the chief seaport, with Brazzaville and Ouesso and with Gabon. There are international airports at Brazzaville and Pointe Noire.

Zaire
Area
2,344,885 km²/905,361 sq miles
Location
5°30′ N—13°25′ S
12°14′—31°25′ E
Population
24,165,770 (1974)
Population density
10 per km²—27 per sq mile
Capital and largest city
Kinshasa: 1,990,700 (1974)
Language
French
Major imports
machinery, vehicles, petroleum products, cereals, textiles, chemicals, iron and steel
Major exports
copper, cobalt, diamonds, coffee, palm oil and kernels, zinc, rubber, tin
Currency
zaire (1 zaire = 100 makuta)
Gross National Product
2,400 million US dollars (1972)
Status
republic

Cities
Kinshasa, the capital, stands on the shore of Stanley Pool at the lower limit of inland navigation on the Zaïre. Kananga (600,000), in the heart of the country, is the chief town of the Kasai province. Zaïre's third largest city, Lubumbashi (400,000), is the capital of Shaba in the extreme northeast.

Physical features
After the Sudan, Zaire is the largest state in Africa. Its major feature is the world's sixth longest river, the Congo or Zaïre (4,800 km). The Zaïre rises in the Shaba plateau and curves across the country from the south-east to the southwest; below Kinshasa it breaks through mountains in a series of falls before widening into a 150 km long estuary. The Zaïre basin, forming the major part of the republic, is a vast shallow depression 300 to 600 m above sea level. It contains swamps and lakes, such as Tumba and Mai Ndombe, and an intricate network of tributaries, among them the Lomami, Kasai and Kwango. The basin is almost entirely surrounded by uplands. To the east, the edge of the Great Rift Valley features lakes Mobutu, Idi Amin, Kivu, and Tanganyika and high ranges including the Mitumba and Ruwenzori massifs.

Climate
Zaire has an equatorial climate averaging 27°C and 160 cm of rain. Rain occurs throughout the year near the equator but is more seasonal towards the tropics.

Agriculture
Subsistence farming is widespread. Basic foods are cassava, maize, yams, rice, groundnuts and bananas. Cash crops play a minor role in th economy; the main products are coffee, palm oil and kernels, cotton, rubber and sugar. Livestock is limited and provides only 6% of meat requirements. Forestry is underdeveloped.

Mining & industry
Minerals dominate Zaire's economy and account for 70% of exports. Large deposits of copper, cobalt, manganese, zinc, tin and uranium occur in Shaba making it the republic's most productive area. Zaire holds first place for world production of cobalt and sixth for copper. Half the world's supply of industrial diamonds comes from alluvial deposits in the Kasai river. Gold is mined northwest of Lake Mobutu. There are few industries.

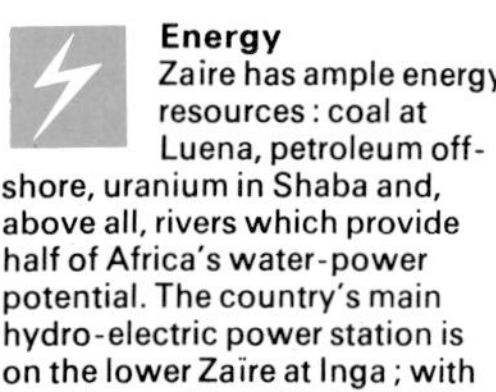
Energy
Zaire has ample energy resources: coal at Luena, petroleum offshore, uranium in Shaba and, above all, rivers which provide half of Africa's water-power potential. The country's main hydro-electric power station is on the lower Zaïre at Inga; with a total capacity of 30,000 MW, it is one of the world's largest.

Transport
The country's size plus the fact that its major producing areas lie far inland make transport a vital issue. The main network, which is 16,400 km long, is formed by the Zaïre and its tributaries; Kinshasa is the chief river port. The leading sea ports are Matadi, linked by rail to Kinshasa, and Boma on the northern bank of the Zaïre estuary. Kinshasa, Lubumbashi and Kamina have international airports.

Rwanda

Burundi

Rwanda and Burundi

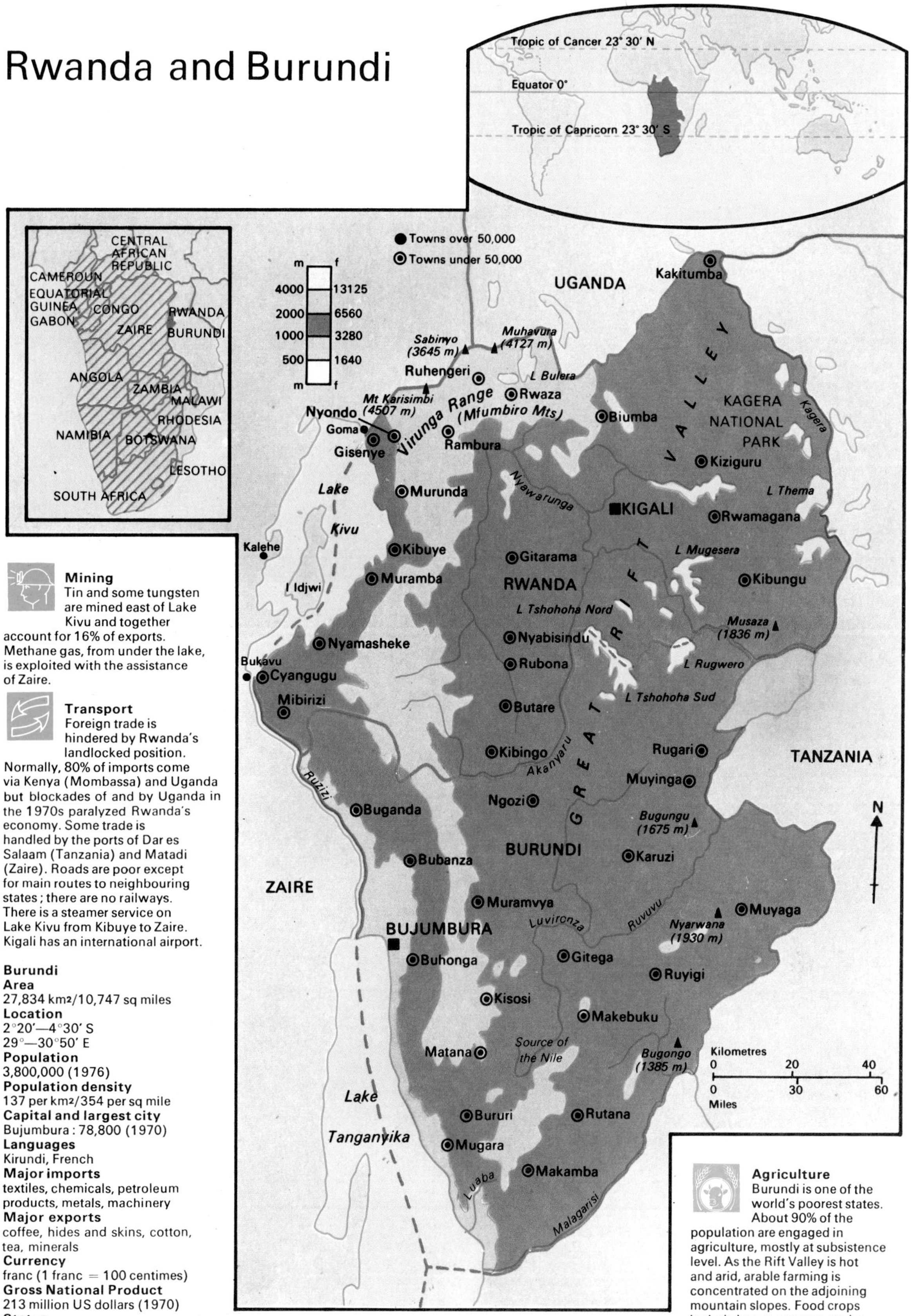

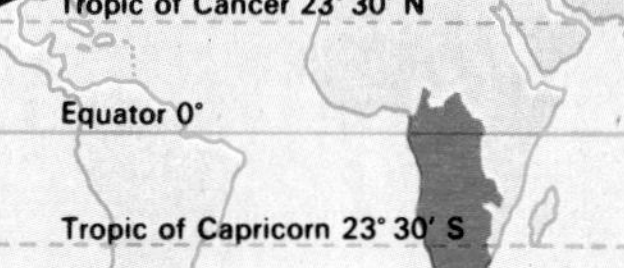

Rwanda
Area
26,338 km²/10,169 sq miles
Location
1°—2°50′ S
28°50′—30°55′ E
Population
4,160,440 (1974)
Population density
158 per km²/409 per sq mile
Capital and largest city
Kigali: 54,400 (1970)
Languages
Kinyarwanda, French
Major imports
vehicles, petroleum products, chemicals, cereals, machinery, textiles
Major exports
coffee, tin, tea, tungsten, pyrethrum
Currency
franc (1 franc = 100 centimes)
Gross National Product
224 million US dollars (1970)
Status
republic

Physical features

Landlocked Rwanda is one of Africa's smallest and most densely populated states. The western part of the country, containing Lake Kivu, occupies a section of the Great Rift Valley. In the northwest, the volcanic Virunga range includes the country's highest peak, Mt Karisimbi (4,507 m). The land slopes down from these mountains to a hilly central plateau 2,000 m high then, further east, gives way to a region of swamps and lakes which border the upper Kagera river.

Climate

The climate is warm with relatively low rainfall occurring in two wet seasons (January-May, October-December); Kigali averages 19°C and 100 cm of rain a year. Altitude modifies temperature: mountain areas are cooler, while the Great Rift Valley is slightly hotter (23°C).

Agriculture

Subsistence farming is the main economic activity. The chief food crops are maize, sorghum, sweet potatoes, cassava, beans, peas and rice; bananas are grown for food and for beer-making. Cash crops are developing slowly and account for less than 10% of total agricultural production. Coffee provides 69% of exports; others are tea, cotton and pyrethrum (from which an insecticide is made). Livestock is being increased. Rwanda's forests have largely been destroyed for fuel; conservation measures include reafforestation and limits on charcoal-burning.

Industry

Industry is poorly developed and is concerned with processing farm products such as coffee, tea, sugar and bananas (beer). There are also some small-scale textile, chemical and engineering plants.

Energy

Rwanda's relief is ideal for power production. In addition to a big hydro-electric plant on the Ruzizi, there are three other stations. Further projects are planned, especially in the Kagera basin.

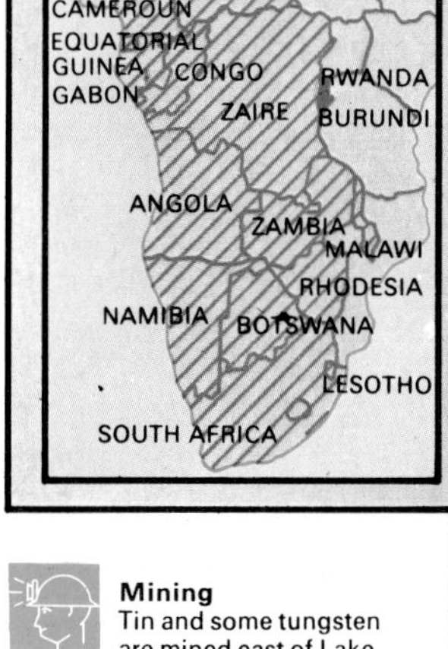

Mining

Tin and some tungsten are mined east of Lake Kivu and together account for 16% of exports. Methane gas, from under the lake, is exploited with the assistance of Zaire.

Transport

Foreign trade is hindered by Rwanda's landlocked position. Normally, 80% of imports come via Kenya (Mombassa) and Uganda but blockades of and by Uganda in the 1970s paralyzed Rwanda's economy. Some trade is handled by the ports of Dar es Salaam (Tanzania) and Matadi (Zaire). Roads are poor except for main routes to neighbouring states; there are no railways. There is a steamer service on Lake Kivu from Kibuye to Zaire. Kigali has an international airport.

Burundi
Area
27,834 km²/10,747 sq miles
Location
2°20′—4°30′ S
29°—30°50′ E
Population
3,800,000 (1976)
Population density
137 per km²/354 per sq mile
Capital and largest city
Bujumbura: 78,800 (1970)
Languages
Kirundi, French
Major imports
textiles, chemicals, petroleum products, metals, machinery
Major exports
coffee, hides and skins, cotton, tea, minerals
Currency
franc (1 franc = 100 centimes)
Gross National Product
213 million US dollars (1970)
Status
republic

The land

To the west, Burundi is bordered by the Ruzizi river and Lake Tanganyika, both lying on the floor of the Great Rift Valley. The steep eastern edge of this valley consists of a narrow mountain range averaging 1,800 m in altitude. The remainder of the country comprises broken plateaux (between 1,300 and 1,700 m) sloping down to the Malagarasi river in the southeast. The Rift Valley is dry for its latitude and hot: Bujumbura averages 23°C and 75 cm of rain (falling between February and May). The plateau is cooler (averaging 20°C) and wetter (125 cm).

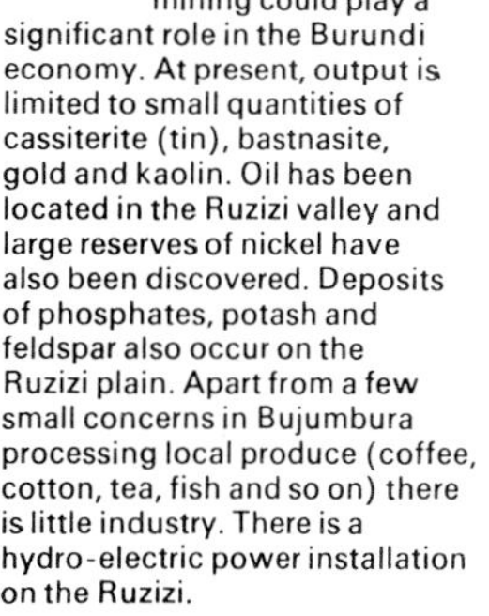

Mining & industry

When mineral resources are fully developed, mining could play a significant role in the Burundi economy. At present, output is limited to small quantities of cassiterite (tin), bastnasite, gold and kaolin. Oil has been located in the Ruzizi valley and large reserves of nickel have also been discovered. Deposits of phosphates, potash and feldspar also occur on the Ruzizi plain. Apart from a few small concerns in Bujumbura processing local produce (coffee, cotton, tea, fish and so on) there is little industry. There is a hydro-electric power installation on the Ruzizi.

Transport

The road network is extensive but in very poor condition: out of a total of 6,000 km, only 130 km are hard-surfaced. The two main routes connect Bujumbura to Zaire and Rwanda. There are no railways. Lake Tanganyika plays a vital role in Burundi's overseas trade. The two main routes to the exterior are by steamer from Bujumbura either to Kalémié in Zaire and so, via river and rail, to Matadi (2,000 km), or to Kigoma in Tanzania and then by train to Dar es Salaam (1,400 km). Bujumbura has an international airport with the national airline, STAB, operating services to Rwanda and Zaire.

Agriculture

Burundi is one of the world's poorest states. About 90% of the population are engaged in agriculture, mostly at subsistence level. As the Rift Valley is hot and arid, arable farming is concentrated on the adjoining mountain slopes. Food crops include beans, cassava, maize, sweet potatoes, yams and bananas; millet, wheat and barley are grown in the higher zones. There is some rice production in the Ruzizi valley. The main cash crop, providing 80% of total exports, is coffee; other commercial crops are cotton and tea. Cattle, grazed on the plateau, are important for their hides. There is a small fishing industry on Lake Tanganyika.

People

Burundi's economic development has been hindered by friction between the two main ethnic groups: the aristocratic and former ruling group, the Tutsi (15% of the population), and the Hutu farmers (84%).

Angola and Namibia

Angola
Area
1,246,700 km²/481,351 sq miles
Location
4°20′—18° S
11°50′—24°10′ E
Population
6,211,000 (1974)
Population density
5 per km²/13 per sq mile
Capital and largest city
Luanda: 480,600 (1972)
Language
Portuguese
Major imports
vehicles, iron and steel, machinery, pharmaceuticals, textiles, cereals
Major exports
crude petroleum, coffee, iron ore, diamonds, fishmeal, sisal, cotton
Currency
escudo (1 escudo = 100 centavos)
Gross National Product
1,700 million US dollars (1970)
Status
republic

Physical features
Angola, which includes Cabinda (a coastal enclave separated from the main territory by Zaire) is an immense country. The 1,600 km Atlantic coast is bordered by a narrow plain that rises in giant steps to the central plateau. This great tableland, ranging in altitude from 1,000 to 2,000 m, covers 60% of the country. Its northeast slopes are drained by the Kwango and Kasai (both tributaries of the Zaire) while the headwaters of the Zambezi rise in the east. The Cuanza, flowing west, is Angola's longest river (960 km) and is navigable up to Dondo. Other rivers which run into the Atlantic, such as the Dande, Catumbela and Cunene, have steep courses suitable for hydro-electric schemes.

Climate
Angola has a tropical climate, but temperatures are modified inland by altitude and along the coast by the cool Benguela current: Luanda averages 23°C. The wet season, from October to March, brings about 130 cm of rain in Cabinda, decreasing to under 30 cm of rain in the south.

Industry
Industry is developing steadily. The leading sector is food-processing, followed by textiles using local cotton. The main industrial centres are the city-ports of Luanda, Lobito, Benguela and Moçâmedes, but new factories are being built inland. Power is mostly of hydro-electric origin: there are important dams on the Cuanza and Catumbela and on the Cunene where a second major plant is planned.

Transport
In recent years, communications have greatly improved and Angola now has an extensive network of all-weather roads. Railways extend inland from the main ports but do not interconnect. The main line runs from Lobito via Benguela into Zaire and carries a considerable volume of transit trade. The leading ports are Moçâmedes, Luanda, Lobito, Cabinda and Benguela. Luanda has an international airport and the Angolan airline, TAAG, also operates internally.

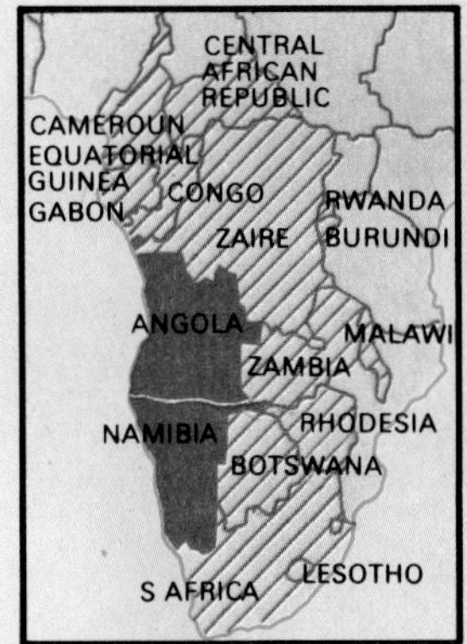

Mining
Angola is rich in minerals. Oil is the principal resource and provides 50% of total exports; the main field lies off Cabinda but vast reserves have been discovered off Santo Antonio do Zaire. Diamonds from the northeast are another 10% of exports. Significant quantities of iron ore, copper and manganese are also produced. Other minerals occurring include bauxite, gypsum, phosphate, uranium, iron and gold.

Agriculture
The basic food crops are cassava, yams and maize in the north and millet in the south. Coffee, the main cash crop, is chiefly grown on plantations north of the Cuanza river—it accounts for 25% of total exports, making Angola Africa's second most important coffee producer. The other major export crops are sisal (grown along the coast), cotton (from the plateau) and bananas (produced in the northwest). Some oil palm products, coconuts and tobacco are also exported. Livestock is limited, largely because of the tsetse fly and inadequate pasture. Fishing, based on Porto Alexandre, Moçâmedes and Benguela, is important and there are several processing and canning plants; fresh fish, fishmeal and oil are exported. Forests in Cabinda yield valuable hardwoods and there are softwood plantations, used for pulp and paper, near Benguela.

Namibia
Area
823,172 km²/317,827 sq miles
Location
17°—29° S
11°45′—25°05′ E
Population
852,000 (1974)
Population density
1 per km²/3 per sq mile
Capital and largest city
Windhoek: 76,000 (1974)
Languages
English, Afrikaans
Major imports
machinery and transport equipment, foodstuffs
Major exports
diamonds, copper, lead, zinc, fish products, livestock, karakul pelts
Currency
rand (1 rand = 100 cents)
Status
international territory. (South Africa continues to administer Namibia in spite of a ruling by the International Court of Justice in 1971 that its administration is illegal.)

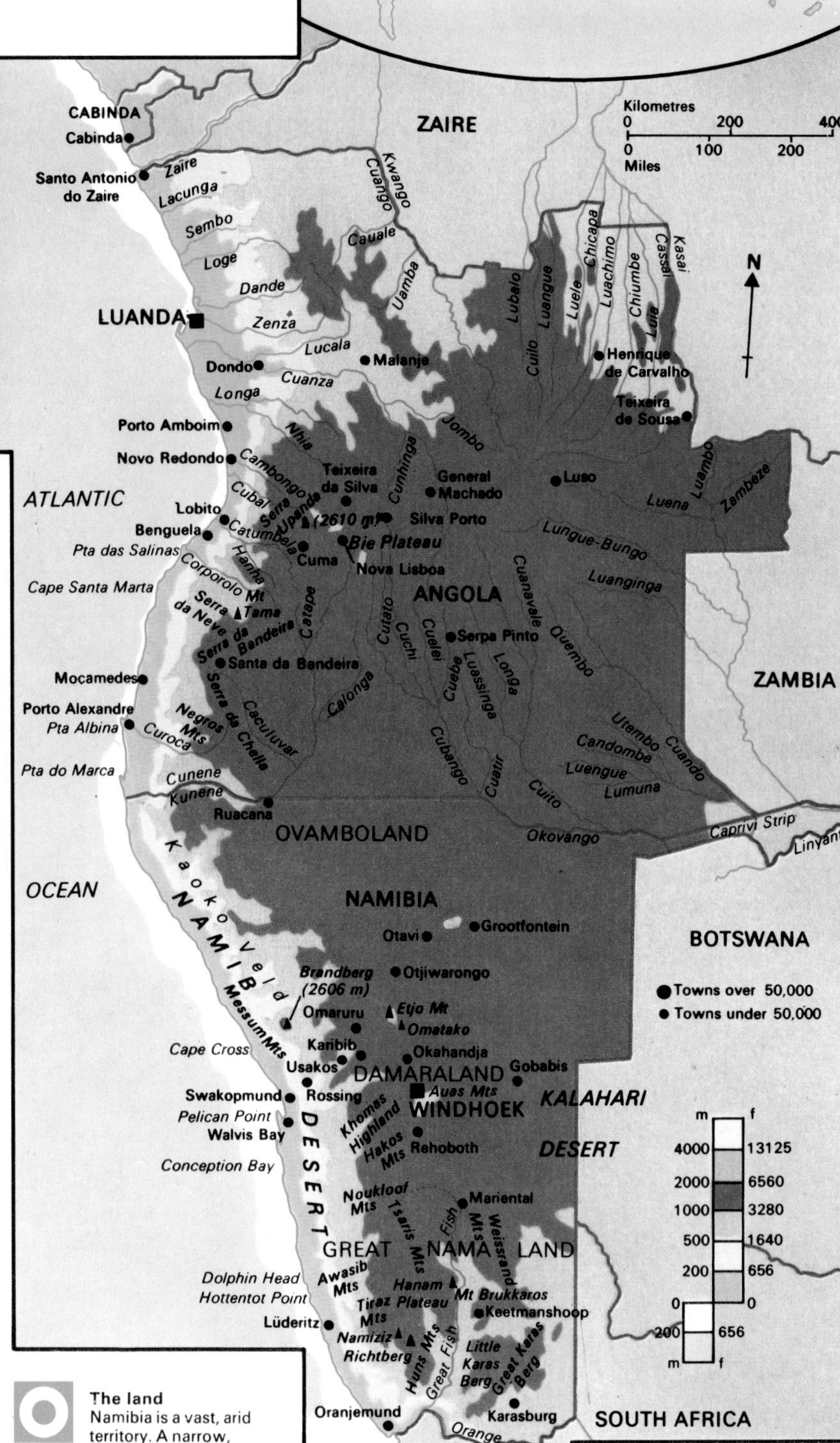

The land
Namibia is a vast, arid territory. A narrow, dune-covered desert belt, the Namib, runs 1,600 km along the entire Atlantic seaboard. The rest of the country consists of a plateau with an average height of 1,100 m but which rises to over 2,000 m in the centre. Semi-desert scrub gives way northeastwards to grasslands and tree savanna. There are no permanent rivers apart from those flowing along the borders, such as the Cunene, Okovango, Orange and Zambezi. The main climatic feature is low rainfall, especially along the coast where less than 2 cm falls annually; on the plateau, amounts range from 5 cm in the south to 60 cm in the north. Temperatures are modified in the Namib by the cool Benguela current: Walvis Bay averages 17°C, Windhoek (at 1,700 m) averages 19°C.

Mining
Namibia's wealth lies underground. Diamonds, accounting for 60% of minerals exported, are produced between Oranjemund (which has the world's richest gem diamond mine) and Lüderitz. Copper, worked at Otavi, is next in importance; the ore also contains large amounts of lead and zinc. Uranium is obtained from a huge opencast mine at Rossing. Smaller quantities of tin, vanadium, manganese and rock salt are extracted elsewhere. A new hydro-electric plant at Ruacana will greatly increase power supplies.

Agriculture
After mining, the main economic activities are fishing and subsistence farming. Fishing, for pilchards and snoek, is important and there are canning and processing plants at Walvis Bay and Lüderitz. The population is concentrated on the plateau, particularly in the better-watered north where some maize, potatoes, beans and groundnuts are grown, partly under irrigation. However, Namibia is primarily a pastoral country and livestock accounts for 90% of farming activity. Cattle are raised on most parts of the plateau and karakul sheep are kept in the centre and south; the tightly-curled pelts of the new-born lambs are a valuable export.

Botswana and Lesotho

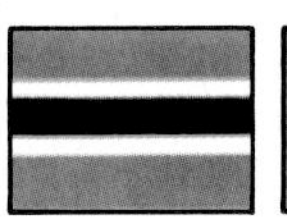
Botswana

Lesotho

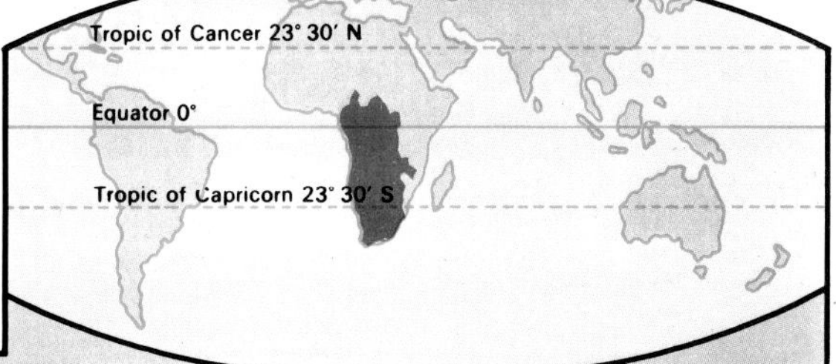

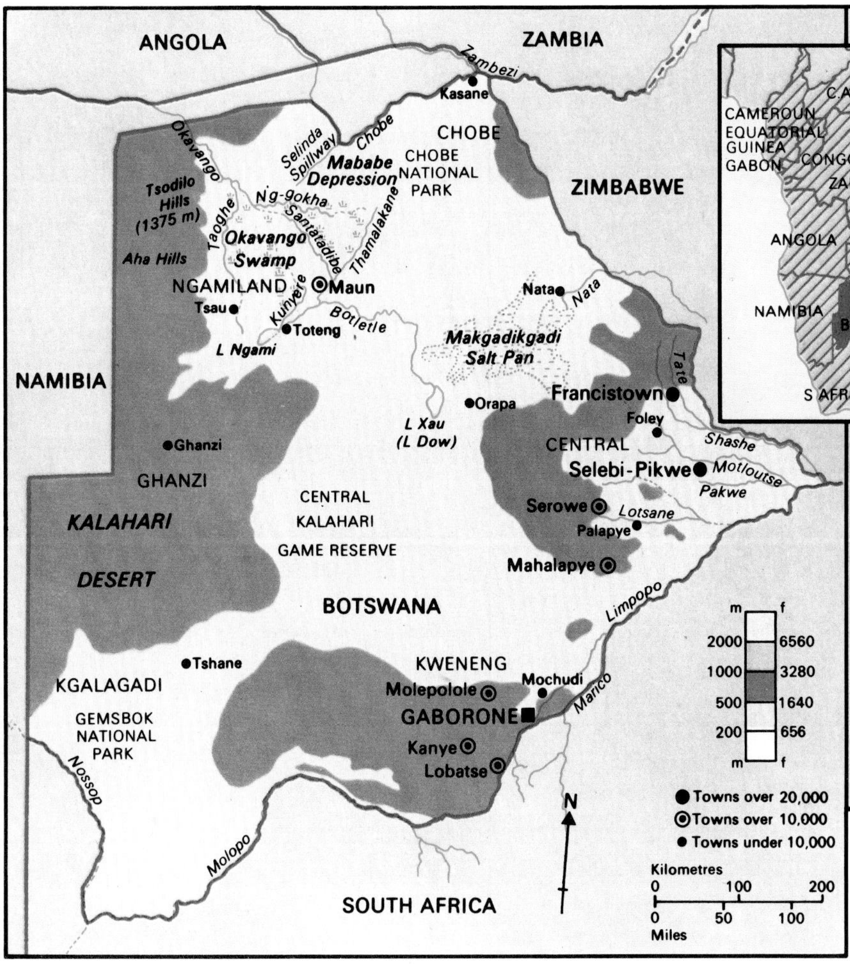

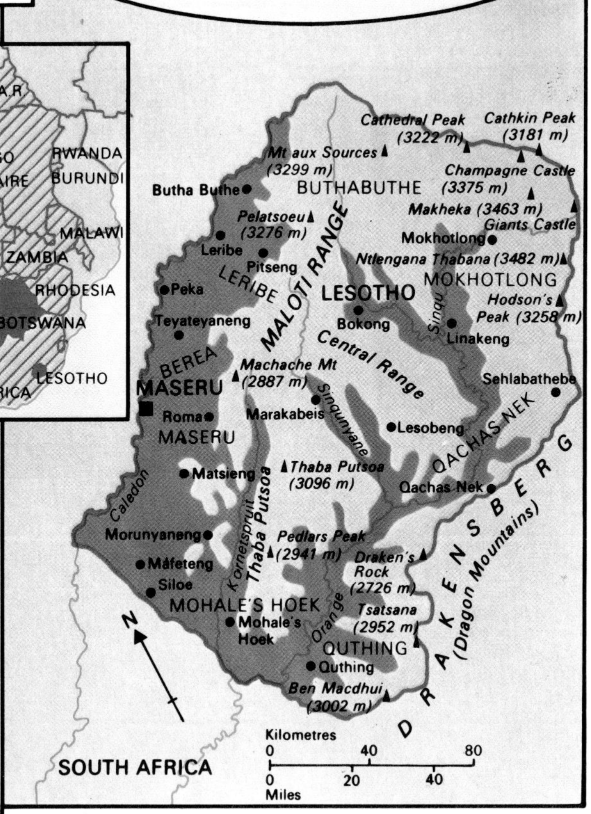

Botswana
Area
575,000 km²/222,000 sq miles
Location
17°50′—26°50′ S
20°—29°20′ E
Population
661,000 (1974)
Population density
1 per km²/3 per sq mile
Capital and largest city
Gaborone: 38,000 (1975)
Second largest city
Selebi-Pikwe: 23,000 (1975)
Languages
Tswana, English
Major imports
machinery, manufactured goods, vehicles, foodstuffs, petroleum products, chemicals
Major exports
meat and meat products, diamonds, copper, nickel, hides
Currency
pula (1 pula = 100 thebe)
Gross National Product
67 million US dollars (1971)
Status
republic

People
About 80% of Batswana (people of Botswana) live in the eastern part of the country which contains the capital and other major towns: Selebi-Pikwe, Serowe (16,000), Kanye (11,000) and Molepolole (10,000). The population, almost totally African, comprises eight main tribes; the largest is the Bamangwato. Botswana is also the home of one of Africa's oldest races, the Kalahari Bushmen.

The land
Botswana is a dry, bush-covered plateau some 900 m high. Around 85% of the territory consists of the Kalahari—a semi-desert country with scrub, grasslands, sand dunes and sandstone ridges. Apart from border rivers (Chobe, Zambezi, Limpopo and Molopo) drainage is internal and the only permanent watercourse is the Okavango. This river loses itself in a vast inland delta (10,000 km²), the Okavango swamp, from which there is a seasonal flow through Lake Ngami and the Botletle river to the extensive Makgadikgadi Salt Pan. The climate is hot and dry: temperatures average 21°C and rainfall decreases from 60 cm in the north and east to a scant 10 cm in the south and west.

Transport & tourism
Communications are poor and many areas in the west and south are not easily accessible. All-weather roads connect the main centres in the east; most of these towns are also linked by the Rhodesia-South Africa railway which crosses the country. Air Botswana flies to neighbouring states and also operates internally between Gaborone, Francistown, Selebi-Pikwe and Maun. Tourism is being developed with wildlife as the chief attraction; several national parks and game reserves have been created with facilities for visitors such as lodges and safari camps.

Agriculture
Although mining is becoming more important, Botswana is primarily a pastoral country. An extensive programme of sinking boreholes and damming small rivers has increased the area available for agriculture and almost 70% of the territory is now used for grazing. There are an estimated two million cattle, one million goats and half a million sheep; animal products form a major share of exports. Arable farming, limited to the wetter, eastern area, is at subsistence level. Half the area under cultivation is used for sorghum; other foods grown are maize, millet and beans. Cash crops are being introduced and include cotton, groundnuts and sunflower seeds. The Okavango Swamp, with its irrigation potential, may be developed for agriculture.

Mining & industry
Botswana's underground wealth is transforming the economy. The diamond mine at Orapa, fully operational since 1972, is the world's second largest and another mine is being developed nearby. In the northeast, there are vast deposits of copper and nickel and the Selebi-Pikwe mining complex began production in 1974. Some coal is exploited at Mahalapye, while manganese and asbestos, also occurring in the eastern sector, are produced in smaller amounts. Meat processing is the main industry.

Lesotho
Area
30,344 km²/11,716 sq miles
Location
28°30′—30°40′ S
27°—29°25′ E
Population
1,200,000 (1976)
Population density
40 per km²/102 per sq mile
Capital and largest city
Maseru: 20,000 (1975)
Languages
Sesotho, English
Major imports
foodstuffs, machinery, transport equipment, manufactured goods, petroleum products
Major exports
wool and mohair, live animals, diamonds, labour
Currency
rand (1 rand = 100 cents)
Gross National Product
90 million US dollars (1971)
Status
constitutional monarchy

The land
Lesotho, entirely surrounded by South Africa, is a rugged highland state. In the north and east, the Maloti range and Drakensberg (Dragon mountains) lie above 2,300 m, rising to 3,482 m in the country's highest peak, Thabana Ntlenyana. This mountain zone, southern Africa's main watershed, is drained by the Orange and its tributary, the Caledon. Rugged foothills (over 2,000 m) cover the rest of the territory except in the west where the land drops to an undulating plain 1,500 m above sea level. Because of altitude, Lesotho has a mild, moist climate. Although summer temperatures reach 33°C, the annual average at Maseru is 15°C. Rainfall ranges from 70 cm in the west to 100 cm in the Drakensberg.

People
Lesotho is a purely African territory. Its people, the Basotho, live mostly on the western lowlands but some have settled in mountain valleys. Over-population plus lack of resources and industry have caused many people to seek work in South Africa: 40% of the adult male workforce is continually absent.

The economy
In spite of poor soils, steeply sloping land and serious soil erosion, subsistence agriculture supports 80% of Basotho. Arable farming predominates in the west with maize, sorghum and wheat as the main crops, but production falls short of demand and cereal imports are high. The more fertile basalt uplands in the east are used for grazing cattle, sheep and goats; livestock products, in particular wool and mohair, form the chief exports. Alluvial diamonds are also exported. Manufacturing, except for some handicrafts, is almost nonexistent, but tourism is emerging as a growth industry. Attractions include spectacular mountain scenery, prehistoric caves and rock paintings.

Transport
Transport systems are inadequate. There are 900 km of gravel roads and a further 3,000 km of dirt roads and tracks; on the lowlands, many of these are impassable during the summer rains. Apart from the 1.6 km line connecting Maseru to the South African network, there are no railways. Lesotho National Airways flies from Maseru to Johannesburg; there are also over 30 airstrips for local flights.

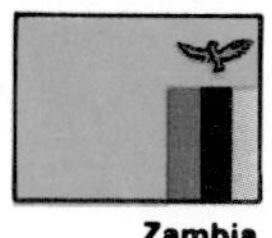
Zambia

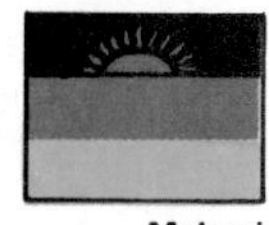
Malawi

Zambia and Malawi

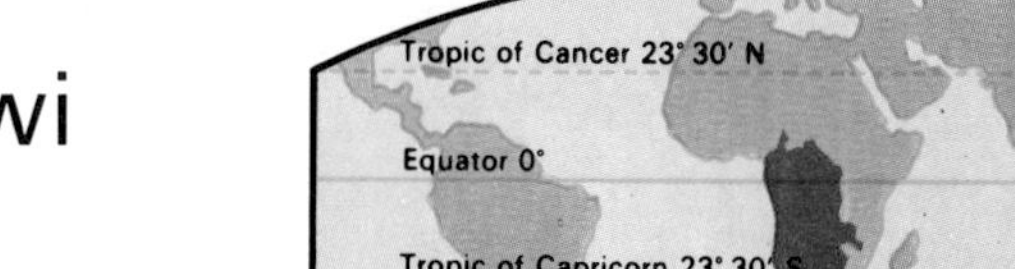

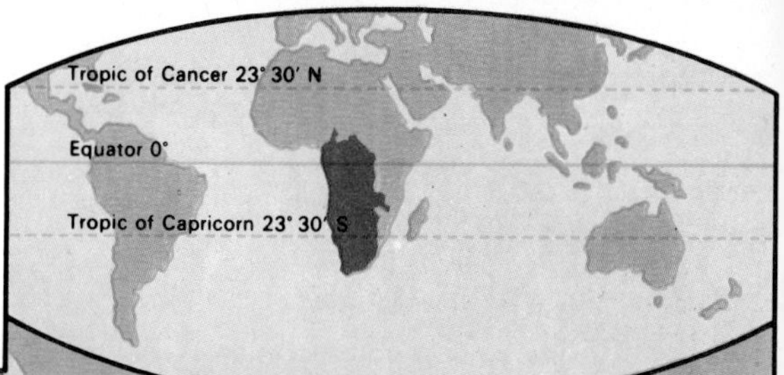

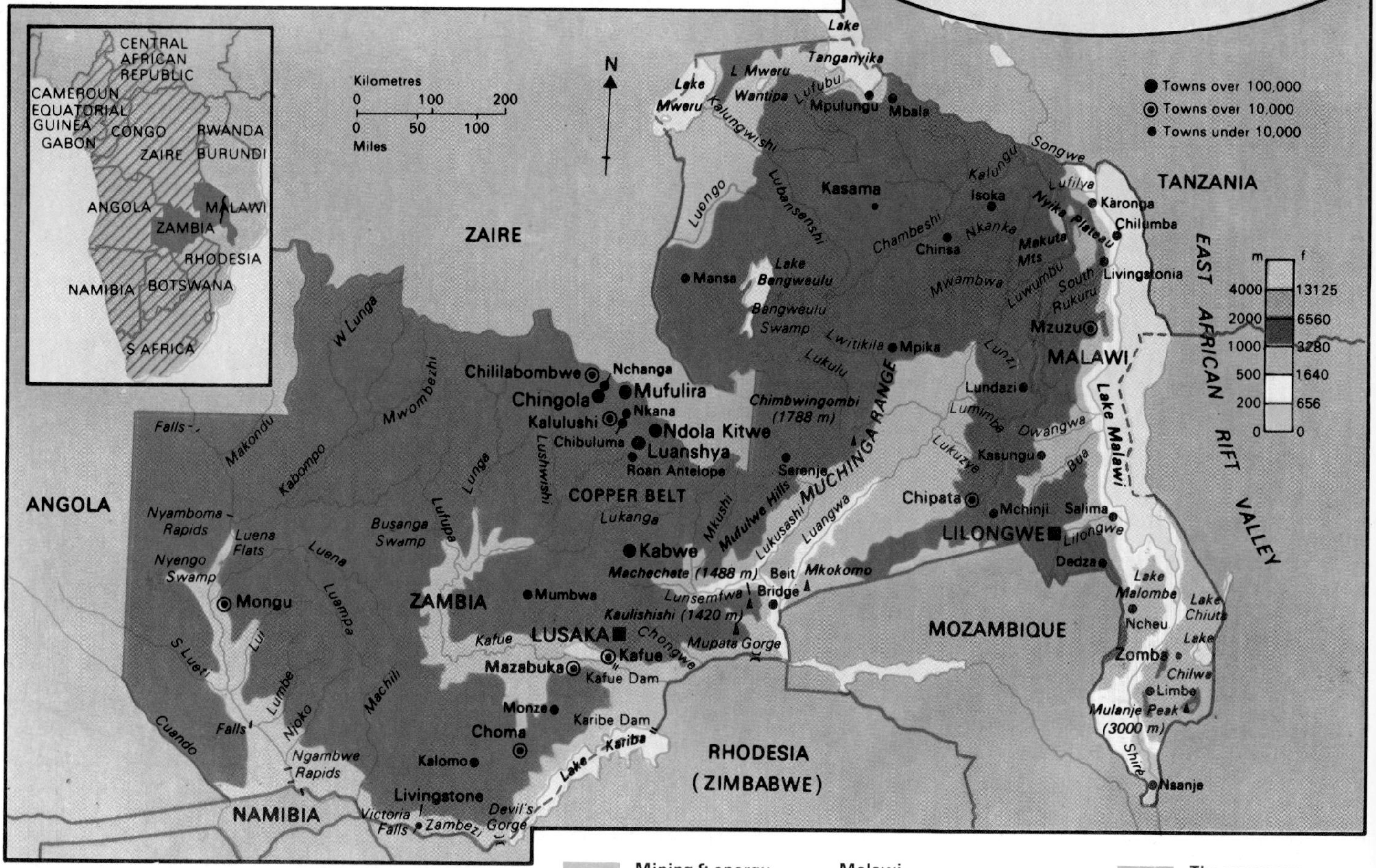

Kilometres 0 100 200
Miles 0 50 100

● Towns over 100,000
◉ Towns over 10,000
• Towns under 10,000

m 4000 2000 1000 500 200 0
f 13125 6560 3280 1640 656 0

Zambia
Area
752,618 km²/290,586 sq miles
Location
8°15′—18°10′ S
22°—33°40′ E
Population
4,750,000 (1974)
Population density
6 per km²/16 per sq mile
Capital and largest city
Lusaka: 415,000 (1974)
Language
English
Major imports
machinery and transport equipment, oil, chemicals, food
Major exports
copper, other metals
Currency
Kwacha (1 Kwacha = 100 ngwee)
Gross National Product
2,700 million US dollars (1974)
Status
republic

Physical features
Landlocked Zambia lies on a plateau 1,000 m high, rising to 1,500 m in the central Muchinga range and to over 2,000 m along the mountainous northeastern border. The upland is dissected by rivers flowing through broad, deep valleys: in the west, the Zambezi and Kafue, in the centre, the Luangwa. The Zambezi's course includes the spectacular Victoria Falls and Lake Kariba (5,180 km²) one of the biggest man-made lakes in Africa. The plateau is so flat that drainage is poor and there are extensive waterlogged areas such as the Nyengo swamp, Luena flats, Busanga swamp, Bangweulu swamp and the Chambeshi valley in the north.

Climate
Zambia's tropical climate is modified by altitude. On the plateau conditions are pleasant but in the valleys it is torrid and unhealthy: Lusaka (1,277 m) averages 17°C in the cool season (May-August) and 24°C in the hot season (September-October); the corresponding figures for Beit Bridge (400 m) on the Luangwa river are 21°C and 31°C. Rain, falling from November to April, ranges from 150 cm in the north to 75 cm in the south. Humidity is high in the valleys.

Agriculture
In most parts, subsistence agriculture predominates; the basic foods are millet, groundnuts, beans and cassava. Large-scale farming has developed along the Livingstone-Lusaka-Copper Belt railway line: beef and dairy cattle are raised between Livingstone and Lusaka, while the area north of the Kafue river is used for maize, cotton, tobacco, sugar and potatoes. Tobacco is also cultivated near Chipata and there are coffee plantations in the Mbala district in the extreme north. Some tobacco, cotton and coffee are exported.

Industry
The industrial sector is under-developed. Food, textiles and cement are the main products. Newer projects include a vehicle-assembly plant at Livingstone and a chemical plant at Kafue.

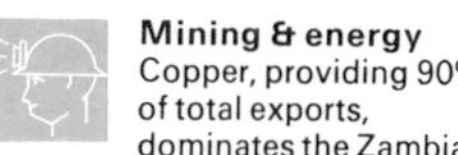

Mining & energy
Copper, providing 90% of total exports, dominates the Zambian economy. Production is concentrated in the Copper Belt where the chief mines are at Nchanga, Mufulira, Roan Antelope Chililabombwe and Chibuluma; further deposits have been discovered in the northwest. Zambia ranks as the world's third-largest copper producer. Other minerals exported are cobalt, from the Nkana and Chibuluma mines, and lead and zinc from Kabwe. Zambia is rapidly increasing its power supplies: coal is mined 200 km northeast of Livingstone and a major hydro-electric power (HEP) station has been built at the Kariba dam. There is a new HEP scheme on the lower Kafue and oil is piped from Dar es Salaam (Tanzania) to a refinery at Ndola.

Transport
Zambia is handicapped by its landlocked position. Political events of the mid-1970s have stopped goods, mainly copper, from being exported via Rhodesia and Angola. Copper is now sent by road or the new Tanzam railway to Dar es Salaam, and by road to the Mozambique ports of Beira and Nacala via Malawi. There are plans for a direct road link with Mozambique. Some trade is handled by Mpulungu port on Lake Tanganyika. Zambia has an adequate network of roads but many are impassable during rain. The rivers, punctuated by falls and rapids, are unsuitable for navigation but small craft ply Lake Bangweulu. The national airline is Air Zambia.

Malawi
Area
118,485 km²/45,747 sq miles
Location
9°30′—17°10′ S
32°45′—35°50′ E
Population
4,929,000 (1974)
Population density
42 per km²/108 per sq mile
Capital
Lilongwe: 102,000 (1974)
Largest city
Blantyre: 193,000 (1974)
Languages
ChiChewa, English
Major imports
vehicles, petroleum products, chemicals, machinery
Major exports
tobacco, tea, groundnuts, cotton, maize
Currency
Kwacha (1 Kwacha = 100 tambala)
Gross National Product
800 million US dollars (1975)
Status
republic

The land
Malawi is a long, narrow mountainous country bordering the southern-most part of the East African Rift Valley. The lakes occupying the valley—Malawi (570 km long), Chilwa and Chiuta—make up 20% of the total surface area. The rest of the country consists of highlands, 1,000 to 1,500 m in altitude, but rising to 2,400 m on the Nyika plateau and to 3,000 m in Mulanje Peak. In the south, the uplands are cut by the deep Shiré valley. Temperatures vary with altitude but are generally high: Zomba averages 20°C, Nsanje, 24°C. During the November-March wet season, most parts receive between 75 and 100 cm of rain.

The economy
Malawi is an agricultural country and farm products account for 75% of exports. Tobacco, grown on the Shiré highlands and in the Lilongwe area, is the chief cash crop. Other commercial crops are tea (from plantations on the slopes of Mulanje Mountain), groundnuts (from the central highlands) and cotton (from the lake shore and Shiré valley lowlands). About 75% of all cultivated land is used for maize, the staple food; any surplus is exported. Other food crops are cassava and millet. Livestock is limited by the tsetse fly. About 25% of Malawi is forested and production of woods such as mahogany, cedar and eucalyptus is increasing. There is some fishing in Lake Malawi. Industry, based on farm produce, includes tea and tobacco processing; fish, fruit and vegetable canning; cigarette and cotton textile manufacture. Hydro-electric power stations are being developed.

Towns & transport
Lilongwe, in the central highlands, replaced Zomba (24,000) as the capital in 1975. The chief industrial and commercial centre, however, is Blantyre in the south. The railway, from Nsanje to Salima, is linked directly to the Mozambique ports of Beira and Nacala; a spur is to be built from Salima to Lilongwe. The road network (10,670 km long) is centred on Blantyre and Lilongwe and is 60% all-weather. There are cargo and passenger services on Lake Malawi. Air Malawi flies overseas, from Blantyre airport, and internally.

Rhodesia (Zimbabwe)

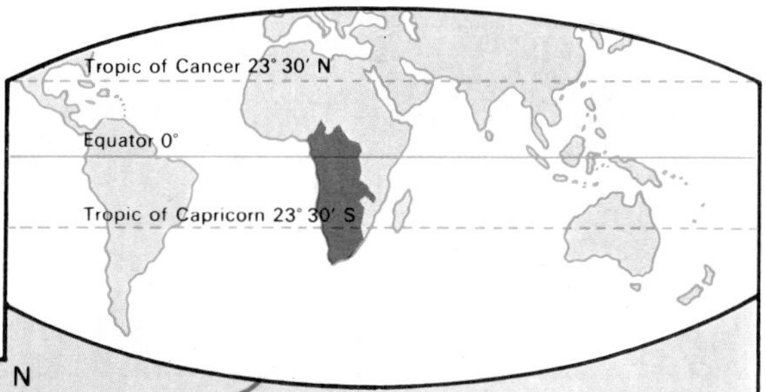

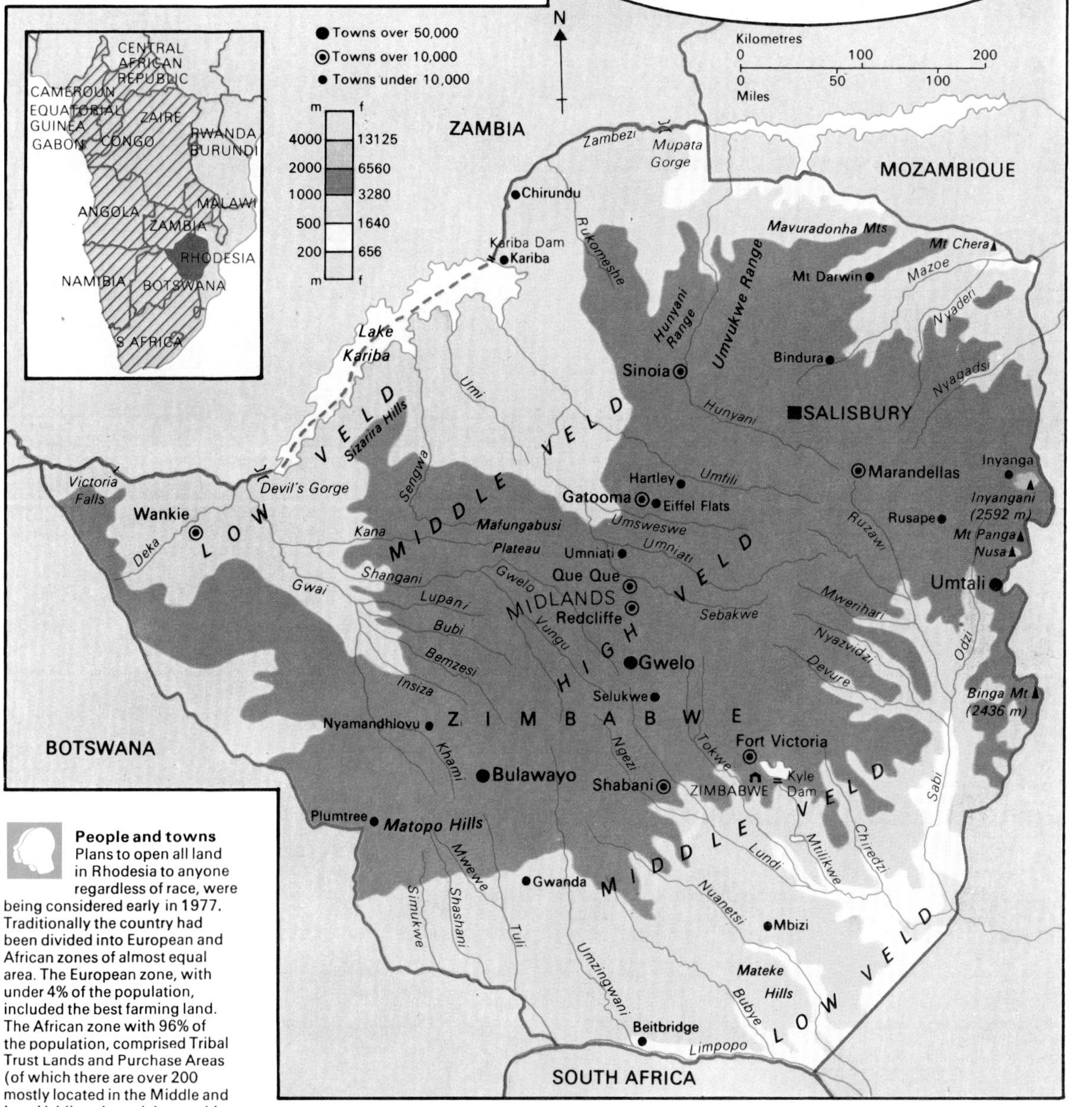

Area
390,623 km²/150,820 sq miles
Location
15°40′ — 22°25′ S
25°20′ — 33° E
Population
6,200,000 (1974)
Population density
16 per km²/41 per sq mile
Capital and largest city
Salisbury: 501,930 (1973)
Language
English
Major imports
machinery, transport equipment, petroleum products
Major exports
asbestos, chrome, tobacco, maize, copper, meat, sugar
Currency
dollar (1 dollar = 100 cents)
Gross National Product
1,540 million US dollars (1970)
Status
Rhodesia was a self-governing colony under the British Crown but in 1965 its government, led by Ian Smith, issued a unilateral declaration of independence (UDI) and, in 1970, proclaimed a republic.

Physical features

Landlocked Rhodesia is a rugged plateau country lying between two great rivers: the Zambezi in the north and the Limpopo in the south. The central region consists of the High Veld, a wide upland belt over 1,200 m high which runs from the northeast (where it is most extensive) to the southwest. This is flanked by the Middle Veld, 900—1,200 m, which gives way to the Low Veld, land under 900 m comprising the Zambezi, Limpopo and Sabi basins. Tree savanna, densest in the north, covers highland areas while hardwood forests fringe the river valleys.

Climate

Although Rhodesia lies wholly within the tropics, its climate, because of altitude, is more temperate than tropical. On the High Veld and Middle Veld, summers are warm and winters cool, often with night frosts. Salisbury averages 21°C in November (the hottest month) and 13°C in July (the coolest month). In contrast, the deep river valleys are hot and humid with temperatures of up to 50°C in November. Rain, usually with thunderstorms, occurs in summer (November to March) and decreases from 250 cm in the northeast to 50 cm per year in the southwest.

UDI

At official talks in 1964-5, Britain refused to grant Rhodesia independence until its white leaders accepted (black) majority rule. In order to preserve white supremacy, the Rhodesian government unilaterally declared independence (1965) and, five years later, set up a republic. Britain proclaimed both these moves illegal and, since UDI, officially ceased trading with the colony. The UN also imposed economic sanctions. In 1976, as a result of growing economic and political pressures, including guerilla attacks in border areas the Smith régime finally agreed to the principle of majority rule. By the end of 1976, the reality of a legally independent state ruled by its majority seemed, however, still a long way off.

People and towns

Plans to open all land in Rhodesia to anyone regardless of race, were being considered early in 1977. Traditionally the country had been divided into European and African zones of almost equal area. The European zone, with under 4% of the population, included the best farming land. The African zone with 96% of the population, comprised Tribal Trust Lands and Purchase Areas (of which there are over 200 mostly located in the Middle and Low Veld) and special townships attached to cities (in which about one third of Africans live). About 40% of Europeans live in Salisbury, central Africa's largest city. Founded in 1890, the capital is an important commercial centre, particularly for tobacco. Bulawayo (339,000) is the country's main industrial city and hub of the rail network. The third largest town, Gwelo (62,000), is the manufacturing centre of the Midlands.

Industry

As a result of sanctions there has been an increase in the production of previously imported consumer goods such as textiles, food, beverages and furniture. Heavy industry is also expanding since Rhodesia has adequate supplies of coal, iron ore, limestone and power and is therefore not dependent on imports; there are iron and steel plants at Bulawayo, Redcliffe and Gwelo. Salisbury and Bulawayo together account for 80% of Rhodesian industry; the remainder is located in Umtali and the Midlands (Gwelo, Que Que, Hartley, Redcliffe, Gatooma).

Agriculture

Sanctions have made Rhodesia diversify its agriculture and aim at self-sufficiency in food production. Maize, grown on 75% of all cultivated land, is the staple crop and a surplus is exported. Tobacco, largely from the northeastern parts of the High Veld, is the main cash crop. Other major crops, for both domestic and export markets, are: citrus (produced near Inyanga and Salisbury and on irrigated estates in the south-east), cotton (from the Hartley-Gatooma region), sugar (grown under irrigation in the Low Veld) and tea (from the Umtali region). Except in the north and northwest, Rhodesia is free of the tsetse fly and livestock is important. Beef cattle predominate in the dry southwest, while the chief dairying region is along the Bulawayo-Salisbury railway. The country is self-sufficient in meat and dairy products and meat is a significant export. Fishing is centred on L Kariba. In spite of sanctions, Rhodesia manages to export its main commodities.

Mining

Mining makes a major contribution to the economy and provides Rhodesia with its chief exports. High-quality asbestos is the country's most valuable mineral resource: it is mined in the Shabani area and also about 100 km northwest of Salisbury. Next in importance are: chrome (obtained near Sinoia and Selukwe), copper (also mainly produced in the Sinoia region), nickel (occurring near Bulawayo, Gwelo, Gatooma and Bindura), gold from scattered deposits near Gwanda, Bulawayo, Gwelo, Fort Victoria, Que Que, Gatooma and Salisbury, and tin from Wankie. More than twenty other minerals are worked in Rhodesia, among them several which form the basis of local industries. These include iron ore (Que Que), iron pyrites (Bindura) and limestone (Que Que and south of Bulawayo near the Botswana border). Also of vital importance to industry are Rhodesia's coal fields; these are mainly located in the southeast and west and are unexploited except for the Wankie field.

Transport

The main railway runs from Bulawayo, via Salisbury to Umtali with branch lines serving mining and industrial centres. As part of sanctions, road and rail links with neighbouring countries have been severed (except for South Africa). Losing access to the Mozambique ports of Beira and Maputo was particularly harmful to Rhodesian trade as all imports and exports now have to be shipped via South Africa which is a longer and more costly route.

Energy

Except for oil, Rhodesia is self-sufficient in energy resources. Over 90% of the country's electricity is generated by hydro-power. The principal hydro-electric plant, at Kariba, supplies power to Salisbury, Bulawayo and the Midlands. Wankie coal is also used to produce electricity; the main thermal stations are at Salisbury, Bulawayo, Umtali, Umniati, Shabani and Wankie. Following sanctions, the oil pipeline from Beira was closed.

South Africa

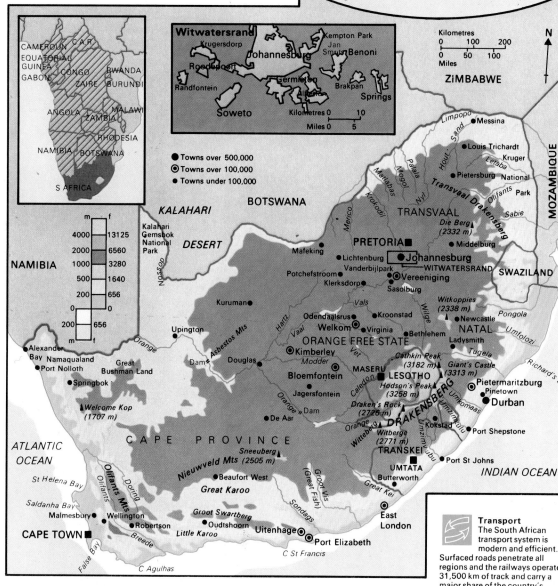

Area
1,221,042 km²/471,445 sq miles
Location
22°10'—34°55' S
16°30'—32°55' E
Population
25,470,000 (1975)
Population density
21 per km²/54 per sq mile
Administrative capital
Pretoria : 563,400 (1970)
Legislative capital
Cape Town : 1,108,000 (1970)
Largest city
Johannesburg : 1,441,400 (1970)
Languages
Afrikaans, English
Major imports
machinery and transport equipment, manufactured goods, chemicals, metals, foodstuffs, oil
Major exports
gold, diamonds, copper, other minerals, fruit, iron and steel, maize, wool, sugar, hides and skins
Currency
rand (1 rand = 100 cents)
Gross National Product
33,700 million US dollars (1975)
Status
republic

Physical features

South Africa's dominant feature is its height : most of the country is over 1,000 m and only the narrow coastal plain lies under 300 m. From the coast, the land rises steeply to the great escarpment encircling the interior plateau ; this mountain rim is highest in the east where the Drakensberg reach 3,300 m. In the south, minor ranges enclose the arid basins of the Little and Great Karoo ('Karoo' comes from a Hottentot word meaning dry or bare). The plateau, over 1,200 m high, is like a huge saucer : from the escarpment rim the land slopes inwards down to the Kalahari desert in the north. Vast featureless plains with scattered low ridges and shallow river valleys characterize the landscape. The country's main river, the Orange, fed by the Caledon and Vaal, flows 2,250 km westwards to the Atlantic.

Climate

South Africa has a relatively temperate climate because of latitude, altitude and proximity to the sea (nowhere more than 800 km away). Mean annual temperatures in the north and south are remarkably uniform : 17°C for both Cape Town and Pretoria. The west coast, subject to the cold Benguela current is cooler (Port Nolloth : 13°C) ; the east coast, with the warm Mozambique current, is hotter (Durban : 20°C). Over most of the country, rain occurs as summer thunderstorms ; amounts decrease from east to west : Durban has 100 cm annually, Bloemfontein has 55 cm and Port Nolloth only 6 cm.

Towns

Johannesburg, founded in 1886 as a gold-mining camp, is now South Africa's largest city and leading industrial and commercial centre. The republic's second largest city, Cape Town, dates from 1652 when Jan van Riebeeck built a fort at Table Bay for the Dutch East India Company ; as the legislative capital it contains the Houses of Parliament. Durban (851,000) is the third largest city.

Agriculture

As much of South Africa is arid or mountainous, only 10% of the land is cultivated. The main food crops are maize, sorghum, groundnuts, potatoes and wheat. A wide variety of deciduous, citrus and tropical fruit is grown in the western Cape Province and fresh and canned fruit is the top agricultural export—it is also a major wine-producing area. Other exports are sugar, tobacco and flowers. About 70% of the country is used for grazing. With 40 million sheep, South Africa is the world's fifth wool producer : 60% of the wool comes from Cape Province ; karakul sheep, prized for their pelts, are found in the dry northwest. Angora goats are kept in the extreme south and the republic ranks as the world's third producer of mohair. Beef and dairy cattle predominate in the east and north. Fishing is important with 90% of the catch (anchovy, pilchard, crayfish, mackerel and hake) coming from the cold waters off the west coast. Cape Town is the main fishing port. Forests cover less than 1% of the total area.

Mining

South Africa has immense mineral wealth. It supplies 70% of the world's gold, 65% of its diamonds, 45% of vanadium and is a leading producer of platinum, uranium, manganese, chrome, iron ore, asbestos, antimony and vermiculite. About 40 other minerals are also exploited. The republic's seven goldfields form a 500 km arc across the centre, extending from Evander in the east through Johannesburg and Klerksdorp to Welkom and Virginia. The main diamond mines are at Kimberley, Jagersfontein, Finsch and Pretoria ; alluvial diamonds are found in the Vaal and Orange and on the west coast at Namaqualand. Large coal deposits occur in Transvaal and Natal.

Tourism

In the last decade, the number of tourists visiting South Africa has doubled and is expected to reach one million by 1980. The country's main attractions are its unspoilt beaches, magnificent scenery, game reserves and its sun : Cape Town has twice as much sunshine as London or Paris.

Energy

Of the electricity generated on the African continent, 57% is produced in South Africa, mostly by coal-fired thermal stations in Transvaal, Natal and the Orange Free State. Hydro-power is being developed : the giant Orange River Project, to be completed by the year 2000, includes 20 hydro-electrical plants. The country's first nuclear station, using Transvaal uranium, will operate from 1978.

Industry

The chief industries are : food-processing (canned fruit and vegetables, refined sugar, meat and fish products) ; wool and cotton textiles ; chemicals (oil from coal at Sasolburg, fertilizers, pharmaceuticals) ; iron and steel (Pretoria, Vanderbijlpark, Newcastle) and engineering. Manufacturing is concentrated in four main areas : southern Transvaal (47% of total industrial output), Durban/Pinetown (14%), western Cape (11%) and Port Elizabeth/Uitenhage (8%). The republic is Africa's most industrialized state.

Transport

The South African transport system is modern and efficient. Surfaced roads penetrate all regions and the railways operate 31,500 km of track and carry a major share of the country's freight. There are 4 main ports : Durban (handling 60% of all cargo), Cape Town, Port Elizabeth and East London (the only river port). SAA (South African Airways) flies overseas and internally and Johannesburg is the chief airport.

Apartheid

South Africans are divided into four groups : Whites (17% of the population), Coloured (10%), Asian (3%) and Bantu or Blacks (70%). Of the nine homelands for the Bantu (covering 13% of the land) Transkei has been made independent. About 50% of the Bantu live in townships attached to the industrial cities.

Transkei

The Transkei republic, home of 3 million Xhosa, is an enclave of 38,557 km² on the southeast coast. Farming is the main activity and irrigation projects, using streams from the Drakensberg, are increasing the cultivable area. Maize is grown for food, while cash crops include flax and tea ; cattle grazing and forestry are also important. Industry is centred on Umtata, the capital, and Butterworth.

Seychelles

Mauritius

Indian Ocean Islands 1

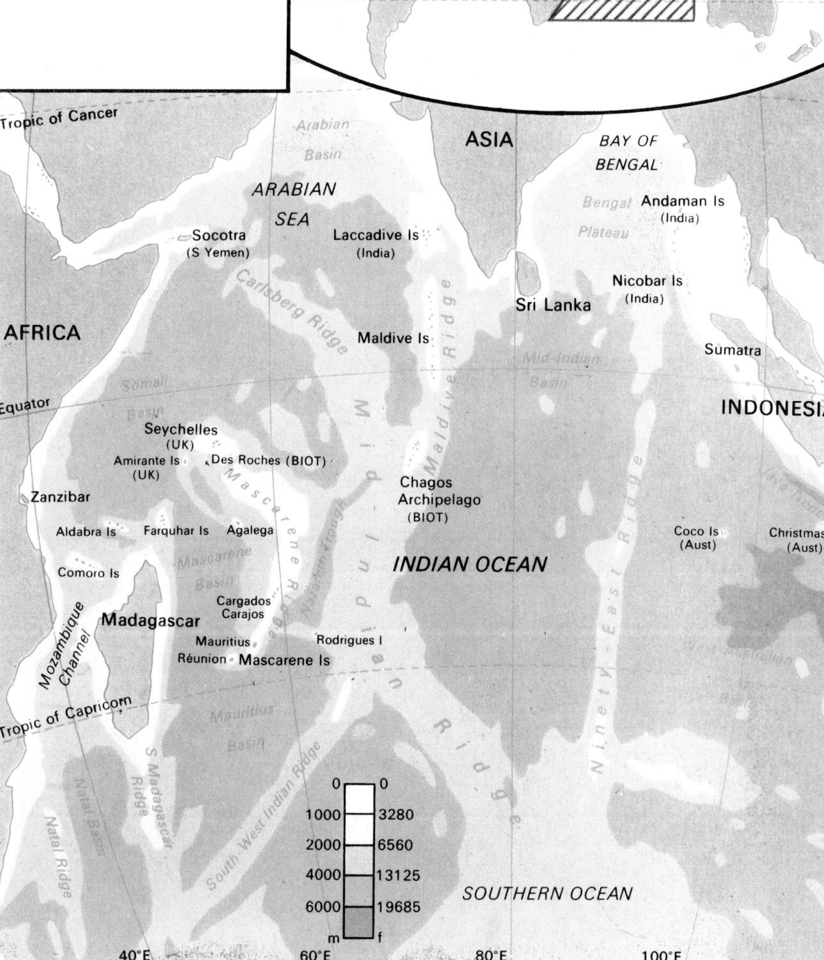

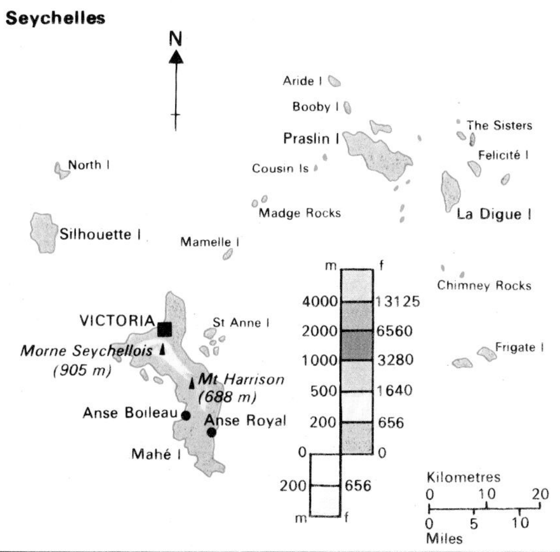

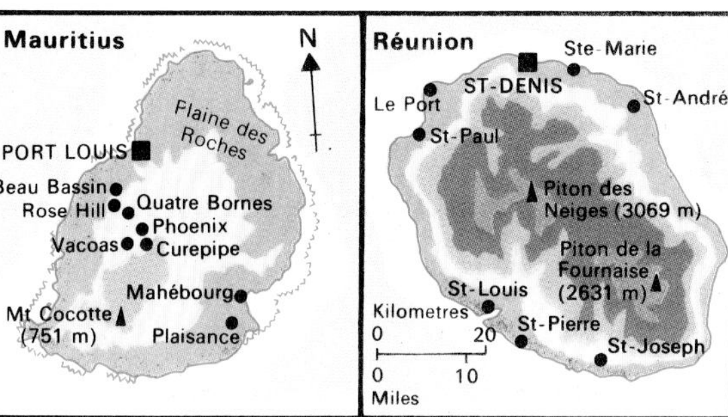

Seychelles
Area
277 km²/107 sq miles
Location
4°30′ S; 55°40′ E
Population
58,000 (1975)
Population density
209 per km²/542 per sq mile
Capital and largest city
Victoria: 14,500 (1972)
Language
English
Major imports
foodstuffs, petroleum products, vehicles
Major exports
copra, cinnamon bark and oil, guano, fish
Currency
rupee (1 rupee = 100 cents)
Gross National Product
21 million US dollars (1975)
Status
republic

Seychelles: the land
The Seychelles, lying 1,000 km northeast of Madagascar, consist of some 85 granitic and coralline islands. The granitic islands, with mountainous interiors up to 900 m, are all situated within 60 km of the principal island, Mahé (148 km²), and include Praslin (41 km²), Silhouette (15 km²) and La Digue (10 km²). The scattered coral islands are low-lying atolls and reefs. The wet season, from December to April, is hot (29°C) and humid with up to 250 cm of rain. The rest of the year is slightly cooler (24°C). Most of the islanders are either African or Afro-French (the Seychelles were first colonized by France): 80% of the population lives on Mahé.

Seychelles: economy
The Seychelles have an unbalanced economy and exports (mainly copra and cinnamon bark) pay for only a quarter of the massive import bill. As well as copra, the palms growing on the fertile volcanic soils of the granitic islands provide coconuts, coconut oil and coir. Other export products are vanilla, patchouli, tortoiseshell, fish and guano (phosphate-rich topsoil formed from bird droppings and used for fertilizer). Tea cultivation has been introduced. The islanders' staple diet consists of rice (mostly imported), lentils and fish. In the last few years, tourism has been developed and visitors to the islands increased from 500 in 1970 to 80,000 in 1976. Inter-island links are by boat and plane; there is an international airport on Mahé.

BIOT
The British Indian Ocean Territory (BIOT) was formed in 1965 to link, politically, some small, widely scattered coral islands and atolls. The Territory, with a total land area of 453 km², consists of the Chagos Archipelago and the islands of Aldabra, Farquhar and Des Roches. Copra and guano are the main products. Except for imported labour on the Chagos Archipelago copra plantations, the islands are uninhabited. The largest island in the Chagos Archipelago, Diego Garcia (28 km²), is a US defence base. Aldabra island, northwest of Madagascar, is famous for its giant tortoises and rare birds and is leased to the Royal Society for research.

Mauritius
Area
1,865 km²/720 sq miles
Location
20°15′ S; 57°30′ E
Population
856,000 (1975)
Population density
459 per km²/1189 per sq mile
Capital and largest city
Port Louis: 136,800 (1974)
Languages
English, French
Major imports
rice, petroleum products, machinery
Major exports
sugar, molasses, tea
Currency
rupee (1 rupee = 100 cents)
Gross National Product
548 million US dollars (1974)
Status
independent Commonwealth nation

Mauritius: the land
Mauritius, 880 km east of Madagascar, is a hilly, volcanic island fringed by coral reefs. The central plateau, 600 m high consists of craters from which lava flowed down to form a fertile coastal plain. Basalt mountain blocks rise to over 800 m in the southwestern part of the plateau. The climate is hot and humid: average temperatures range from 24°C in August (the coolest month) to 30°C in February (the hottest). During the wet season (December to June), the southeast trade winds bring 500 cm to upland areas, but under 100 cm to some coastal districts. The heavy rains have cut deep gorges on the plateau. Cyclones occur frequently during the wet season damaging crops and houses

Mauritius: economy
Sugar dominates the economy, accounting for 90% of exports, 90% of cultivated land and 28% of the workforce. The chief secondary crops are tea, grown in the Curepipe area, tobacco and aloe (used in fibre manufacture). Subsistence farming is small-scale, so food makes up 25% of imports. Industry is based on agriculture: products include refined sugar, molasses, rum and aloe fibre. Power comes from hydro-electric plants and from the re-cycling of sugar by-products. Tourism is being developed.

Mauritius: transport
There is a good network of surfaced roads and regular bus services cover all areas. There are no railways. Port Louis has a modernized harbour and, 22 km away at Plaisance, there is an international airport.

Dependencies
Rodrigues, Agalega and Cargados Carajos are all dependencies of Mauritius. Rodrigues (104 km²) lies 585 km east of Mauritius and comprises a central volcanic ridge, a coastal plain and an encircling coral reef. The 26,000 islanders live by fishing and livestock farming: live animals and salted fish are sent to Mauritius. The coral islands of Agalega and the Cargados Carajos group have a combined area of 71 km² and a total population of 400. The main products are copra (from Agalega), salted fish and guano (from Cargados Carajos); all trade is with Mauritius.

Réunion
Area
2,512 km²/970 sq miles
Location
21°10′ S; 55°30′ E
Population
467,700 (1974)
Population density
186 per km²/482 per sq mile
Capital and largest city
St-Denis: 103,500 (1974)
Language
French
Major imports
rice, pharmaceuticals, machinery vehicles
Major exports
sugar, rum, essences, vanilla
Currency
franc (1 franc = 100 centimes)
Status
French overseas department

Réunion: the land
Réunion, situated 780 km east of Madagascar, is a mountainous island of volcanic origin—its highest peak is Piton des Neiges (3,069 m). The climate is tropical with heavy rainfall between December and March and high temperatures (from 23°C to 27°C).

Réunion: economy
The island's economy depends on sugar cane. Grown on plantations covering 20% of the territory, the cane is processed at St-Denis, St-Pierre and St-Paul; the chief products are sugar, rum and molasses. Other cash crops include vanilla, tobacco, tea and perfume plants for essences. Maize and manioc are the staple foods. There is one major road and a railway which follow the coast and link all main towns.

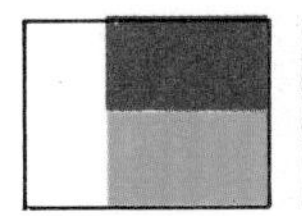

Malagasy Republic

Comoro Republic

Indian Ocean Islands 2

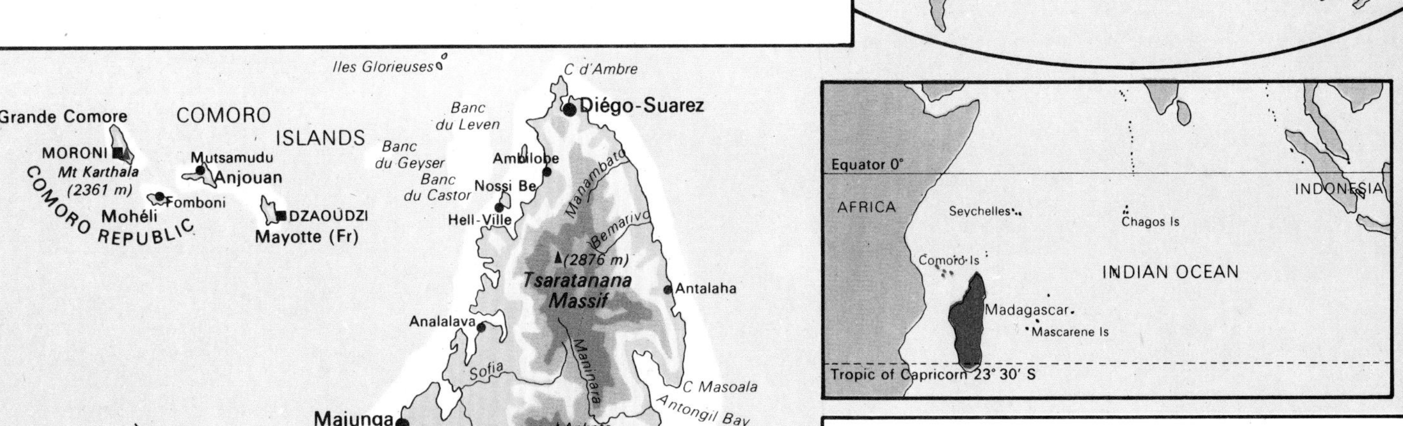

Malagasy Republic
Area
587,041 km²/226,657 sq miles
Location
11°58′—25°34′ S
43°20′—50°30′ E
Population
7,930,000 (1973)
Population density
14 per km²/35 per sq mile
Capital and largest city
Tananarive: 390,000 (1973)
Languages
Malagasy, French
Major imports
machinery, vehicles, metal products, chemicals, textiles
Major exports
coffee, cloves, vanilla, sugar, petroleum products, rice, tobacco, raffia
Currency
franc (1 franc = 100 centimes)
Gross National Product
1,360 million US dollars (1975)
Status
republic

Physical features
Madagascar, the world's fifth largest island, is about 1,600 km long and 580 km across at its widest point. The island's main feature is the central plateau (between 900 and 1,200 m high). Two ranges rise above the plateau: in the north, the Tsaratanana massif climbs to 2,876 m and in the middle, the Ankaratra range reaches 2,643 m. To the east, the uplands fall abruptly in steep steps to a narrow coastal plain fringed by lagoons and reefs; westwards, the land descends in terraces to a 150 km wide alluvial plain. The west coast is characterized by mangrove swamps and offshore islands. The central highlands act as a watershed: the short, swift rivers in the east cut deep gorges while the longer, western rivers flow through broad fertile valleys. Tropical rain forest occurs along the wet east coast, savanna covers the plateau while elsewhere scrub and grasslands predominate. Animal life includes crocodiles in the west and most of the world's lemurs, which are indigenous.

Climate
Coastal temperatures range from 23°C in the south and east to 27°C in the north and west. The plateau is cooler (18°C). Rainfall is heavy on the east coast (over 250 cm) but decreases westwards to 140 cm on the plateau and to under 50 cm in the west and south. During the summer (from January until April), cyclones are common in the north and east.

Agriculture
About 30% of the island is cultivated and half this area is used for rice, the staple food. The western coastal swamps and river valleys are the main rice-producing regions. Other subsistence crops are cassava, maize, millet and potatoes. Coffee, grown near the east coast, is the chief cash crop and accounts for 30% of exports. Vanilla, cloves, tobacco, sugar and pepper are also important commercial crops (Madagascar ranks as the world's leading vanilla producer). Livestock is important and cattle outnumber people 2 to 1. Cattle are raised on the plateau and western plain while sheep are grazed in the south.

Mining & industry
Madagascar's minerals are only partially developed. Sizeable amounts of graphite and chromite and smaller quantities of mica and beryl are exported. There is also some production of iron ore and alluvial gold. Deposits of coal, bauxite and nickel have yet to be exploited. The island's isolated position has encouraged industrial development. As well as traditional activities based on agriculture (such as rice milling, meat packing, oil-seed crushing and brewing) the industrial sector now includes vehicle assembly, oil refining, textiles, chemicals and cement.

Transport
The steep gradients from the coast to the plateau make communications difficult, particularly in the east. The main railway runs from Tamatave to Tananarive. The 38,000 km road network is mostly dryweather and travel is arduous during the wet season (November-April). In the west, the rivers are navigable for up to 160 km while in the east, the 640 km Pangalanes canal runs parallel to the coast between Farafangana and Foulpointe. The chief ports are Tamatave, Majunga and Diego-Suarez. There is an international airport near Tananarive and Air Madagascar flies overseas and internally.

Towns
Tananarive, 'city of a thousand warriors', stands high on the plateau. It is linked by rail to Tamatave (60,000), the chief port. The second city and second port, Majunga (67,000) serves the northwest—especially the Betsiboka valley.

Comoro Islands
Area
2,274 km²/878 sq miles
Location
11°20′—13° S
43°15′—45°20′ E
Population
294,800 (1973)
Population density
130 per km²/336 per sq mile
Capital and largest city
Moroni: 15,900 (1973)
Language
French
Major imports
rice, consumer goods, petroleum products, vehicles
Major exports
ylang-ylang, copra, vanilla, essences, cloves
Currency
franc (1 franc = 100 centimes)
Gross National Product
40 million US dollars (1970)
Status
the islands were French colonies; now, Grande Comore, Mohéli and Anjouan form the Comoro Republic but Mayotte remains, by choice, under French rule.

The land
The Comoro archipelago, lying 300 km off the Mozambique coast, comprises the volcanic islands of Grande Comore (1,147 km²), Anjouan (424 km²), Mayotte (400 km²) and Mohéli (290 km²), plus numerous coral islets and reefs. The four main islands are mountainous and thickly forested; Grande Comore is dominated by Mt Karthala (2,361 m), an active volcano. The climate is tropical: summers (November to April) are wet and hot (27°C), while winters are dry and cooler (23°C).

Transport
Settlement is concentrated along the coasts and boats are widely used. Roads, totalling 750 km, also follow the coast. Inter-island links are maintained by boat (between Moroni, Fomboni, Mutsamudu and Dzaoudzi) and by air. The republic's airline, Air Comores, also flies to Kenya, Tanzania and Madagascar.

The economy
There is no mining or industrial activity and the archipelago's undeveloped economy depends solely on agriculture. Most islanders are engaged in subsistence farming, using primitive methods on over-exploited land. Output of basic crops (rice, cassava, sweet potatoes and maize) is insufficient and food accounts for 50% of imports. There is some livestock; lobster and shrimp fishing is being developed off Mayotte. Plantations, occupying a third of land area, produce commercial crops: the chief products are copra, vanilla, essential oils for perfumes (from ylang-ylang, lemon grass, jasmine, orange flower and tuberose), sisal, cocoa, coffee, cloves and cinnamon. Together, ylang-ylang (the base of 90% of French perfumes), copra, vanilla and cloves provide over 90% of all exports. Small quantities of timber, from the forested interior of Grande Comore, are also exported.

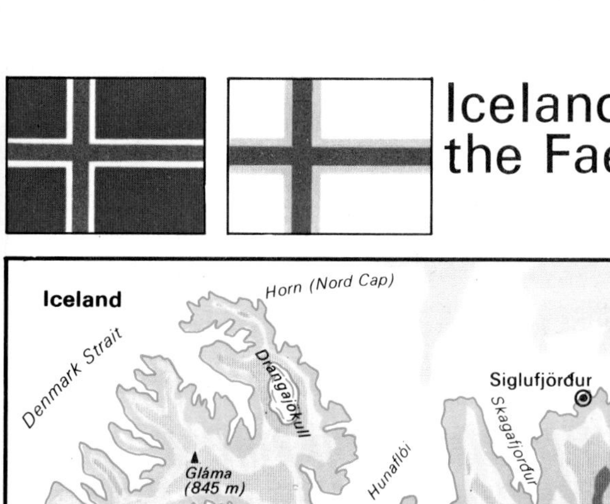

Iceland and the Faeroes

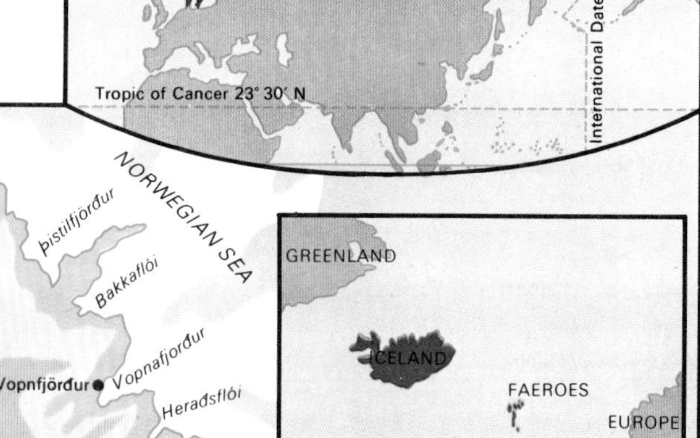

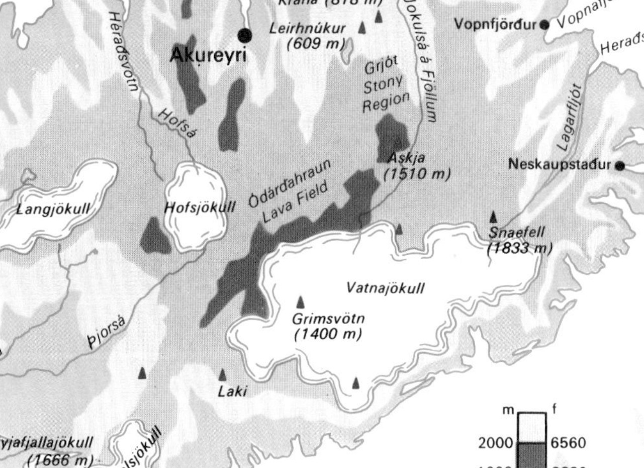

Iceland
Area
103,000 km²/39,770 sq miles
Location
63°25'—66°32'N
13°30'—24°30'W.
Population
213,070 (1973)
Population density
2 per km²/5 per sq mile
Capital and largest city
Reykjavik: 84,300 (1973)
Language
Icelandic
Major imports
transport equipment, fuel oil, foodstuffs, aluminium ore
Major exports
fish, fish products, aluminium
Currency
krona (1 krona — 100 aurar)
Gross National Product
1,025 million US dollars (1973)
Status
independent republic

Physical features
In spite of its name, Iceland is one of the world's major geological hot-spots. Nearly all of the island—a bare plateau over 600 m high—has been built by volcanic activity and one third of the country is still actively volcanic with an average of one eruption every five years. The active zone lies north-south along the Mid-Atlantic Ridge and contains many types of volcanoes from snow-capped Hekla (a lava volcano) to Askja (a complex volcano with an 11 km wide crater). Some of these volcanoes are perpetually under ice as 12% of Iceland is covered by glaciers, the largest being Vatnajökull (8,400 km²). Volcanic activity also produces the many hot springs, steam vents and mudpots.

Climate
The climate of Iceland is influenced by wind and sea. Arctic waters bring fog and ice to the north coast, but the Gulf Stream gives mild winters and cool summers. South-west winds bring heavy rain and snow in the south: as much as 380 cm a year. In contrast, the north has only 33 cm.

Fishing
Iceland is a one industry state and that industry is fishing. It accounts for over 80% of exports and so pays for most imports. As Iceland has no coal, valuable minerals or timber and very little agriculture, all necessities have to be imported and hence its dependence on fishing. The country has about 900 fishing vessels which catch mainly cod and herring on the continental shelf surrounding the island. The total catch landed by Icelanders represents only half the fish taken from the Icelandic shelf: foreign fishermen carry home the rest. Intensive fishing by foreign fleets has reduced stocks alarmingly: catches have decreased, younger fish are being caught and spawning has decreased through the reduction in mature fish. Faced with the destruction of its fishing banks (and consequently its economy) Iceland extended its fishing limit to 320 km in 1975.

Energy
With thousands of hot springs and steam fields, it was natural that Iceland should pioneer the use of geothermal energy for heating. Today, half the population lives in houses heated by hot water. Geothermal power is also used to heat greenhouses and to power a small electricity plant. The other electricity plants are hydro-electric—harnessing the energy from Icelands waterfalls, especially on the rivers Thjórsá and Ölfusa. A cement plant at Akranes, a fertilizer factory at Reykjavik and an aluminium reduction plant at Straumsvik are powered by electricity.

Agriculture
Mountains, glaciers, lava flows, lakes and bogs (which are all unproductive) make up 80% of Iceland. Only 1% of the surface is cultivated: hay, potatoes and turnips are grown along the coast and in the valleys. The rest is rough grazing land, mainly for sheep which outnumber cattle 12 to 1. Agricultural produce, including hothouse grown fruit, vegetables and flowers, is processed and marketed co-operatively: dairies, meat-packing stations and slaughter-houses are also joint concerns.

Transport
When, about a thousand years ago, the Vikings settled in Iceland they brought their horses with them. Until recently, these unique, sturdy animals only 13 hands high were the Icelanders' sole means of transport. The internal combustion engine has since eased the horse's load and Iceland's roads were improved by British and American troops during the Second World War. There are no railways but domestic air services are well developed.

Reykjavik
Reykjavik (or 'smoking bay') was the name given by Iceland's first settler, a Norseman called Arnarson, who was fascinated by the smoke coming from hot-springs near his home on the edge of Faxaflói bay. That was in 874. Today, Reykjavik is Iceland's main port and commercial centre with shipbuilding, textile and fish-processing industries. The second largest town is Akureyri.

Faeroe Islands
Area
1,400 km²/540 sq miles
Location
61°26'—62°24' N
6°15'—7°41' W
Population
39,160 (1972)
Population density
28 per km²/73 per sq mile
Capital and largest city
Thorshavn: 11,200 (1974)
Language
Faeroese and Danish
Major imports
food, machinery, fuels, textiles
Major exports
fish and fish products
Currency
krona (1 krona = 1 Danish krone)
Gross National Product
105 million US dollars (1972)
Status
self-governing community within the kingdom of Denmark

Agriculture
In the Faeroes, three days out of five are wet (annual rainfall is over 150 cm), fogs are frequent and temperatures are low (3°C in January, 10°C in July). Climate, together with infertile soil, restricts vegetation and produces conditions which do not favour agriculture. Less than 4% of the surface is cultivated—the main crop being potatoes. Much of the uncultivated land, especially the heaths, is used for grazing sheep. Sheep rearing is a traditional Faeroese activity with early records showing that the islands were originally called *Faereyiar* which means 'sheep islands'.

Physical features
The Faeroe Islands, situated mid-way between the Shetlands and Iceland, are of volcanic origin. Formed by Tertiary eruptions, they consist of layers of basaltic lava and volcanic ash with a thin covering of glacial deposits. Glaciation left a rugged landscape with steep cliffs, ravines and mountains—the highest of which is Slættaratindur (881 m) on the island of Østerø.

Economy
As agricultural conditions are poor, the Faeroese, who inhabit 17 of the islands, are forced to earn their living from the sea. The islanders fish off Newfoundland, Greenland and in their own coastal waters and the catch, which is principally herring and cod, is the basis of the Faeroese economy. There is a hydro-electric power station at Vestmanhavn on the island of Strømø which, as well as satisfying domestic requirements, powers the local industries. These include fish-processing (frozen, salted, canned and dried) and fish products (such as fish meal and cod liver oil). Industry is also concerned with the fishermen's needs such as ropes, nets and reels as well as ships. There are eight shipyards on the island. Fish and fish products account for 95% of exports. The main port is the capital of Thorshavn on Strømø. The one airport is on Vågø.

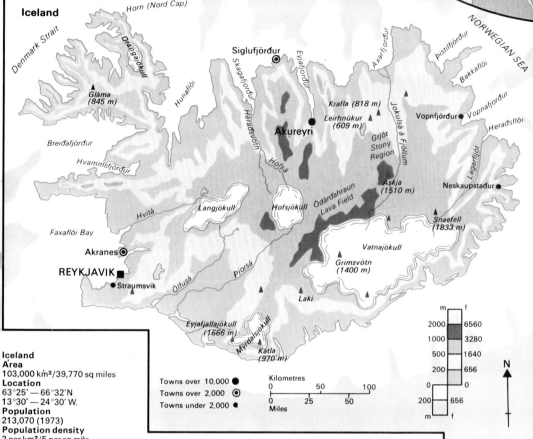

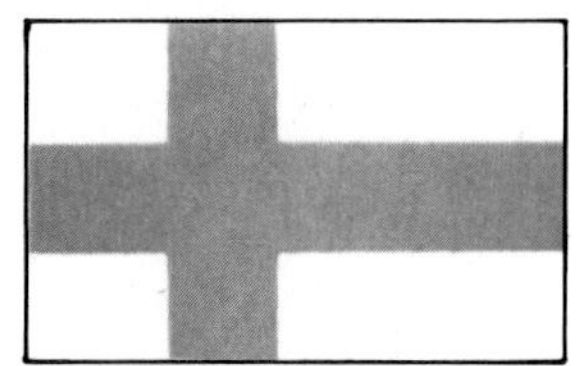

Finland

Area
337,032 km²/130,128 sq miles
Location
59°30′—70°05′ N
19°07′—31°35′ E
Population
4,665,000 (1974)
Population density
14 per km²/36 per sq mile
Capital and largest city
Helsinki: 505,300 (1974)
Languages
Finnish and Swedish
Major imports
machinery, transport equipment, fuels, chemicals, food
Major exports
forest products, engineering products, textiles
Currency
markka (1 markka = 100 penniä)
Gross National Product
21,800 million US dollars (1974)
Status
independent republic

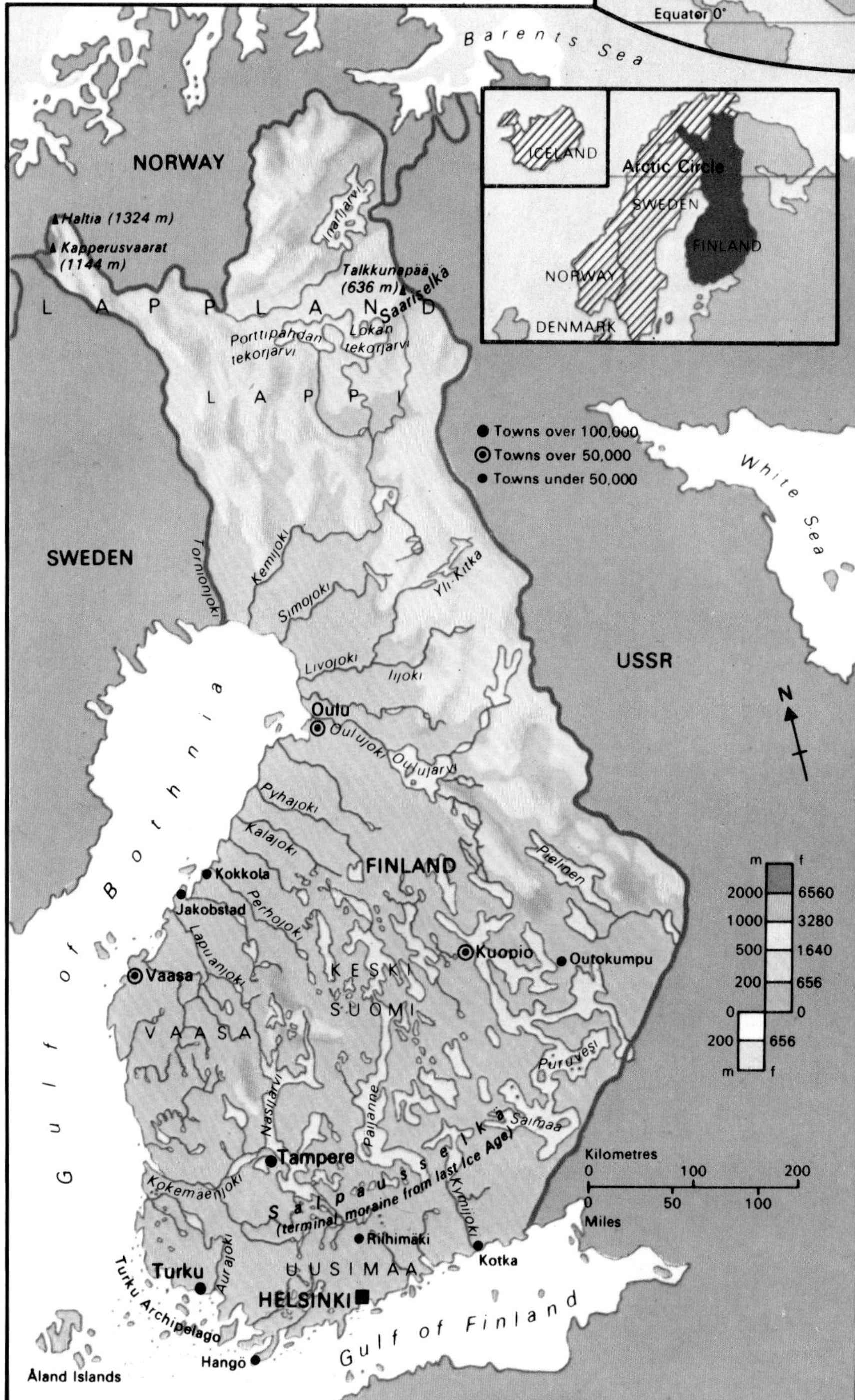

Physical features

Finland is a low-lying country covered with forests and lakes (its Finnish name, *Suomi*, means 'lakeland'). There are about 60,000 lakes which cover 10% of the country's total area. These are Ice Age souvenirs: severe glaciation left the land stripped of soil, scattered with rock ridges (like the Salpausselkä) and pitted with hollows. These water-filled hollows are concentrated in the densely forested central plain 100 m above sea-level known as the Lakes Plateau. They include the Saimaa, Päijänne and Näsijärvi. To the north of this plateau is a harsh region of swamp, fells and forest stretching far into the Arctic Circle. To the south lies the coastal plain with contrastingly fertile clay soil and, off-shore, some 30,000 islands: the two most important groups are the Turku archipelago and the Åland islands.

Climate

In Finland, the winter snow lasts for seven months in the north and for three months in the south with lakes, waterways and ports frozen over. Winter is also cold: minimum temperatures are as low as —30°C. In contrast, the short summer (two months long in the north and four in the south) is warm, partly because of the Gulf Stream. Maximum temperatures reach 30°C. As in all countries with an Arctic (or Antarctic) zone, northern Finland experiences the midnight sun: on the 70th parallel there are 73 days of uninterrupted light in summer and 51 days of darkness in winter.

Agriculture

Farming in Finland is a fight against terrain and weather. Except in the south, land for cultivation has to be carved out of forest or reclaimed from swamps. The result is isolated smallholdings covering only 9% of the country. In northern Finland climate limits crop production but farmers do grow potatoes, oats and barley and keep cattle up to 250 km north of the Arctic Circle. On the central plateau, most smallholders also own some woodland which provides both winter work and extra income. Finland's main farming area is the fertile coastal plain where wheat, rye and cattle predominate. Butter and cheese are exported.

Industry

Many of the rivers plunging over the 180 m high Salpausselkä have been harnessed for hydro-electricity, as have rapids in the north. Thermal stations, using imported oil, also help supply Finland with energy. Much of this power is consumed by the country's main industrial sector—the metal and engineering industries—concentrated at Tampere, Helsinki and Turku and accounting for 27% of total exports. In the engineering field, which includes shipbuilding at Helsinki and Turku, Finland has drawn on its own experiences to produce such items as paper-making machines, forest tractors, ice-breakers, oil rigs, car ferries and other special ships.

Mining

Copper is Finland's most abundant metal and is used, for example, on roofs and in kitchen utensils. Mined at Outojumpu, copper is essential to the expanding electrical industry where it is used in wires and cables. Other metals mined include zinc, cobalt, nickel, lead and, most important, vanadium (used in special steels). Finland is the world's fourth largest producer of vanadium. Also of commercial importance are clay and sand. Clay is essential to the brick, tile and porcelain industries (the Arabia factory at Helsinki is Europe's largest china works). Sand is the basis of the glass industry centred on Riihimäki and Lahti. Finland has no fuels except peat.

Shipping

With 4,600 km of coast and 6,600 km of navigable lakes, rivers and canals, water transport is important—especially for trade with other countries (including neighbouring Sweden which has a different railway gauge to Finland). Almost 90% of Finland's trade is done by sea and over half of this is in Finnish vessels. Because the Gulfs of Bothnia and Finland are both low in salinity and nearly tideless, ice once blocked most ports during the winter months, but now these harbours are, kept open by ice-breakers. Helsinki is the largest port, but others of importance are Kotka (timber), Hangö (dairy produce) and Turku which is Finland's main link with Sweden.

Forestry

For centuries Finland has lived off its forests. Although the metal and engineering industries have recently assumed equal importance at home, wood and wood products are still Finland's leading export—providing 57% of total export income. The forest, mostly privately owned, covers 70% of the land giving Finland the third largest area in Europe after the USSR and Sweden. The main trees grown are pine and spruce (which are used principally for pulp) and birch (used in plywood manufacture). To increase production, improvements such as swamp drainage, the use of fertilizers, and the replacement of slow-growing species are being made. Road construction, especially in the north-east, has opened up new areas. Much of Finland's timber is still floated—the 41,600 km of floatable waterways carry timber (placed on the ice before the spring thaw) to lakeside sawmills and processing plants. Each plant is usually a complex of factories that process a variety of products including pulp, paper, board, plywood and veneers of which approximately 80% is exported.

Nordic co-operation

Finland works closely with the other Scandinavian (Nordic) countries (consisting of Denmark, Iceland, Norway and Sweden) through a co-ordinating body called the Nordic Council. The results of this co-operation are numerous. For example, laws have been harmonized, citizens of member states can travel within the Nordic area without passports, it costs no more to send a letter from one country to another than within one of the countries, and the power grids of Denmark, Finland, Norway and Sweden are inter-connected. Many radio and television programmes are jointly produced and Nordic citizens may work in any member country without restrictions—like the 200,000 Finns at present working in Sweden.

Helsinki

Helsinki is, after Reykjavik in Iceland, the world's most northerly capital at a latitude of 60°10′ N. One Finn in five lives there, either in the city proper or in the suburbs which lie to the north (the sea surrounds Helsinki in all other directions as it is built on a peninsula). Its coastal position has made Helsinki Finland's leading port—its five harbours handle more than half the country's imports, but only 10% of exports (some of which are manufactured in the capital itself). As the centre of Finnish industry, Helsinki specializes in food processing, printing, textiles and metal goods. Because many of the main official buildings are painted in very light colours, Helsinki is known as the 'white city of the north'. It is a relatively modern city which has developed rapidly since it was made the capital in 1812.

Norway

Area
323,797 km²/125,018 sq miles
This does not include the Arctic territories of Spitsbergen and Jan Mayen Island, nor Peter I Island, Bouvet Island and Queen Maud Land in the Antarctic.
Location
57°57′—71°11′ N
4°30′—31°10′ E
Population
4,000,000 (1975)
Population density
12 per km²/32 per sq mile
Capital and largest city
Oslo: 465,000 (1975)
Languages
bokmal ('book language') and nynorsk (Neo Norwegian)
Major imports
machinery, transport equipment, metals, fuels, textiles, food and chemicals
Major exports
fish, forest products, ores, ships, electro-chemical and electro-metallurgical products
Currency
kroner (1 kroner = 100 øre)
Gross National Product
22,897 million US dollars
Status
constitutional monarchy

Physical features

Stretching down the western edge of the Scandinavian peninsula, Norway is the fifth largest country in Europe and, after Iceland, the least populated. Its peaks and high plateaux are generally uninhabitable and settlement is confined to the deep valleys cut by glaciers in the Ice Age and to the sides of fjords. Fjords are a characteristic of Norway's coastline. They are narrow valleys carved by glaciers and subsequently flooded by the rising sea level. The longest fjord is Sognefjorden with a length of 203 km. Islands are another characteristic of Norway's coastline: some 50,000 of them lie offshore, the most famous being the archipelagos of Lofoten and Vesteralen. The mountains of the Scandinavian peninsula rise sharply in the west and slope down gently towards the Gulf of Bothnia in the east. They are highest in the vicinity of the Swedish-Norwegian border and especially in the southwest where the Dovrefjellen, Jotunheimen and Hardangervidda ranges form a central mass. Norway's highest peak is Glittertind (2,470 m) in the Jotunheimen range.

Climate

Norway's climate is influenced by latitude, topography (high mountains, deep valleys) and its proximity to the sea. Winter temperatures range from 1°C at Bergen to —14°C at Hammerfest. Summer temperatures at the same places average 15°C and 9°C. The amount of rain and snow is even more varied. The prevailing onshore winds are the main cause of the heavy rainfall typical of western Norway, but inland areas are drier: Bergen has over 300 cm of rain a year, but Oslo only 100 cm. The coast is also subject to severe storms and in winter force 9 gales are quite common.

Communications

Fjords, mountains and inclement weather make railways and roads difficult to build and costly to maintain. Railways corkscrew up and down mountains, or tunnel through them; roads are a sequence of hairpin bends that follow the chasm's edge and only 15% of them are hardsurfaced. Travelling by public transport often means using two, if not three, forms of transport: buses pick up where trains stop and ferries link one road to another. Water transport is the most used with almost 700 vessels operating across fjords and between coastal and island towns. Norway shares an airline with Sweden and Denmark (SAS) and has seven international airports.

Forestry

About 76% of Norway is unproductive consisting of bog and mountain. The remainder is mostly forest, making forestry a major Norwegian activity. Two-thirds of the forest (mainly spruce) belongs to farmers with the rest owned either by the government or by industry, but all forest areas are under government supervision. The industry is being increasingly mechanized. Cutting is done with power saws and the lumber is transported by truck, funicular or winch to road and rail heads. Woodpulp and paper are the main exports while timber is now aimed more at the home market.

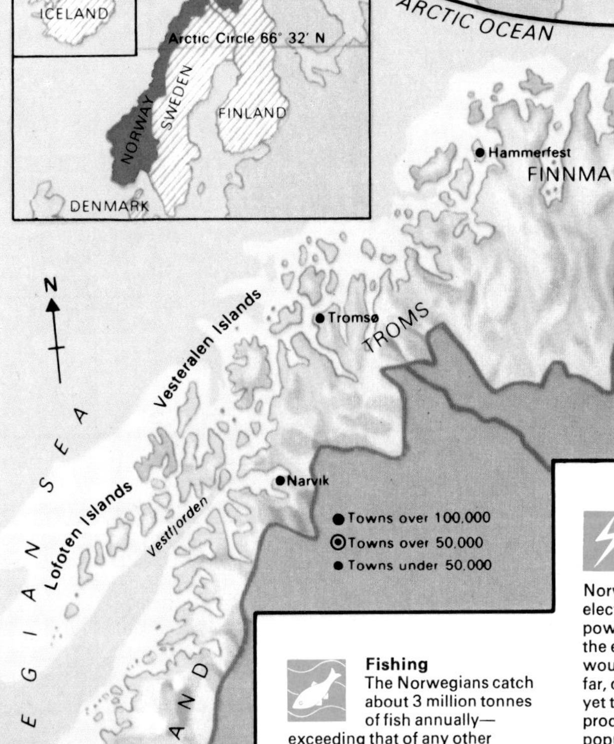

Fishing

The Norwegians catch about 3 million tonnes of fish annually—exceeding that of any other European nation. Cod, capelin, herring and mackeral are the major varieties. Until recently, Norwegian fishing was predominantly coastal with fish-farmers going out in their own motorboats. Now, the emphasis is placed on ocean fishing with modern steel vessels. Herring are caught off More og Romsdal, cod off the Lofoten islands and, further afield, both cod and herring off Greenland and Iceland. Norway only uses between 10 and 15% of the catch. The rest is exported in one form or another (fresh, frozen, canned, salted, smoked, as fish-meal or oil). Of the various processing industries, freezing is now the most important with 235 plants and a fleet of factory freezer trawlers. Alesund (40,000) is the largest fishing port and a sealing base for operations off Newfoundland and Greenland.

Farming

Barren, mountainous Norway is not easily farmed and, of the total area, only 3% is under cultivation. This cultivated land is largely concentrated into two areas: one in the Oslo region, the other centred on Trondheim. The farms, cramped in valleys or alongside fjords, are small; so small that 65,000 farmers (just over half) get their main income from elsewhere. By the coast farmers are often fishermen; inland, lumbermen. But they invariably own their own farms and do all the work themselves—Norwegian farms are highly mechanized. About 65% of the agricultural area is given over to hay and pasture where cattle, sheep, pigs and poultry are the main livestock groups. The corresponding products of cheese, milk, beef, pork, eggs, poultry and wool are marketed through cooperatives. The rest of the land is used for crops—mainly barley, oats and potatoes. Often, extra income is earned through fur farming.

Energy

Heavy rain and snow plus high, steep mountains form the basis of one of Norway's main assets: hydro-electricity. If all the water-power resources were developed, the estimated annual production would be 135,000 million kWh. So far, only 50% has been exploited, yet the amount of electricity produced is, per head of population, greater than in any other country. The largest output is in the Rjukan area where there are six plants. Cheap and plentiful power was the beginning of the electro-chemical and metallurgical industries and now both are major exporters—using 45% of the country's electricity. The remaining 55% meets other demands at home and abroad. Norway supplies Sweden with about 5,000 million kWh annually. In turn, when water levels are low, power is imported from Sweden.

Merchant shipping

Norway's merchant fleet is the world's fourth largest (after Liberia, Japan and the UK). As 97% of the fleet operates between foreign ports, earnings from freight are a major source of national income. This foreign-going traffic consists mostly of tankers, bulk carriers and liners. The other 3% (by weight) of the fleet includes cargo and passenger vessels working along Norway's coasts as well as fishing boats. Norwegian shipping is in the hands of some 300 private companies, each owning or managing anything from one to 50 ships. These ships are generally modern—older ones are exported before becoming obsolete. New vessels are imported, mainly from Sweden and Japan, but about a quarter of the fleet is built in Norway itself. The most important shipyards are at Stavanger (85,000) which is also the centre of the fish-canning industry.

Oslo

Oslo is situated at the head of Oslofjord. It is surrounded by forested hills which are maintained as recreational areas. Much of the city's economic importance comes from its position: Oslo harbour is the largest and busiest in Norway and handles much of the country's trade.

Sweden

Area
449,800 km²/173,665 sq miles
Location
55°20′—69°05′ N
11°—24°10′ E
Population
8,160,000 (1974)
Population density
18 per km²/47 per sq mile
Capital and largest city
Stockholm: 1,500,000 (1974)
Language
Swedish
Major imports
machinery, fuels, food, textiles, chemicals
Major exports
engineering products, forest products, transport equipment, iron and steel
Currency
krona (1 krona = 100 øre)
Gross National Product
55,630 million US dollars (1974)
Status
constitutional monarchy

Physical features

Sweden occupies the eastern part of the Scandinavian peninsula and is almost 1,600 km long. It divides into two main regions: Norrland and the southern-central region. From the mountains of Norway, the broad Norrland plateau slopes eastwards to the Gulf of Bothnia. This plateau, forested and unpopulated, is crossed by many rivers which, in their upper reaches, spread into lakes. In all, Sweden has 96,000 lakes covering 9% of the country. The largest of them, Vänern, Vättern, Malaren and Hjälmaren, are in central Sweden. Central Sweden, like the south, is mainly lowland. The Baltic and Bothnian coasts are edged with archipelagos resulting from land uplift—as great as 1 cm a year in the north.

Climate

The Gulf Stream of the north Atlantic makes Sweden's climate mild for its latitude. In July, the average temperature for most of the country is 15 to 17°C; in January it varies from —1°C in the south to —14°C in the north. Rain is heaviest in the mountains: the Sarek mountains in the north receive over 200 cm a year. Continental influences on the eastern side cause hotter summers and colder winters and at the head of the Gulf of Bothnia coastal ice lasts for nine months.

Agriculture

Agriculture involves only 8% of Sweden's land area. In the north, where winters last at least six months, farms are generally small concentrating on fodder plants and pasture for cattle and pigs. The west and south, however, influenced by the warm Gulf Stream, are more suited to cultivation. Farms are bigger and major crops include cereals, sugar beet and potatoes. Fishing also presents a varied pattern. The 7,600 km long shoreline plus over 38,000 km² of lake water provide ample fishing space, but other factors are missing. For example, moraine lakes in forests give poor nutriment and the Baltic's low salinity means small fish and few varieties. Also, 200 days of ice a year in the Arctic Circle restricts fishing methods. Off the west coast, however, conditions are better and herring fishing is particularly important.

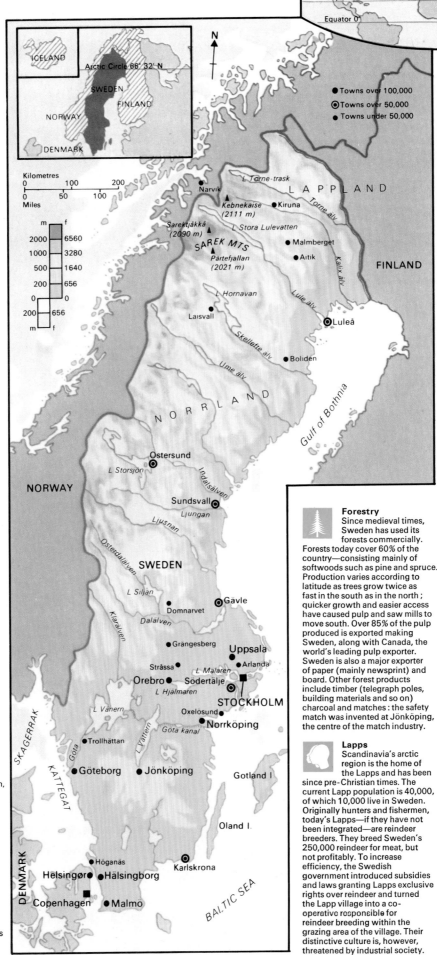

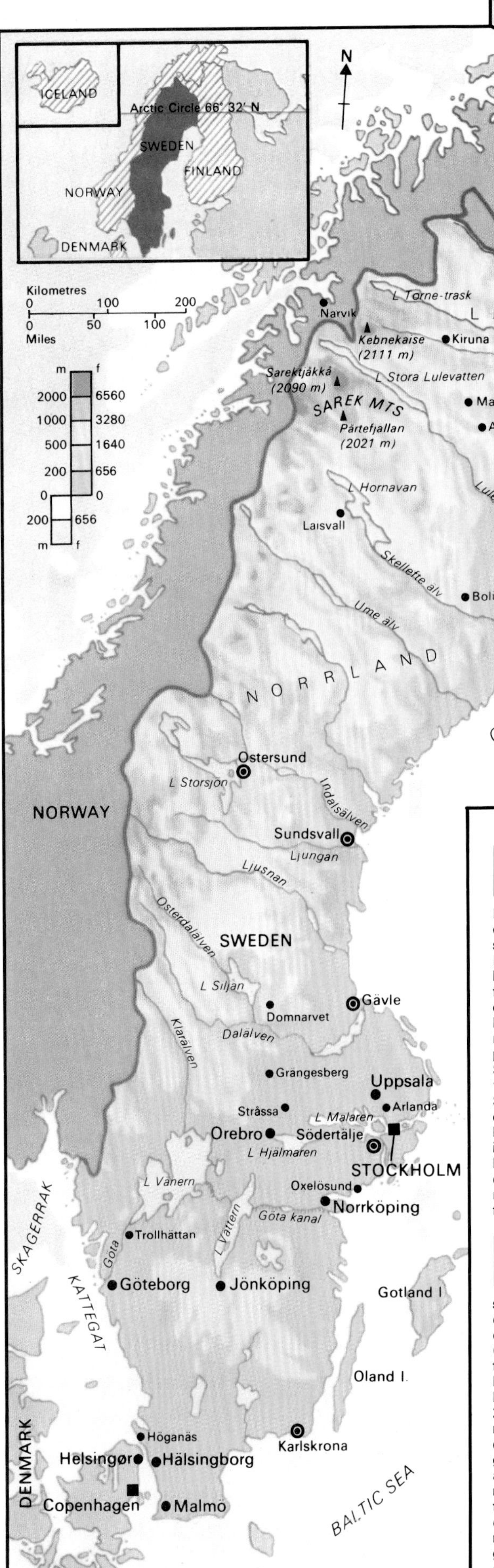

Mining

The growth of steel industries in Europe has created a demand for ores: in meeting this demand Sweden has become the world's fifth largest iron-ore exporter. About 90% of Swedish iron-ore comes from Kiruna and Malmberget. This area, which also has Sweden's biggest copper mine, Aitik, is linked to two ports: Luleå (ice-bound in winter) and Narvik (in Norway). Sweden's two other mining districts are between Boliden and Laisvall (sulphide ores) and Grängesberg and Stråssa in central Sweden, where iron and sulphide ores are shipped via Oxelösund. Mining also includes limestone quarrying (for use in the cement industry) and coal extraction near Höganäs.

Industry

One factor leading to the industrialization of Sweden was water-power. Hydro-electricity compensates for the scarcity of coal and oil deposits, providing about 75% of Sweden's electrical energy. Industry is concentrated mainly in the centre and south: the steel industry, noted for high quality steel, is based at Domnarvet and heavy engineering is concentrated around Stockholm, Göteborg and Malmö. Allied to these basic industries is the manufacture of telephones, ball-bearings, sewing machines, cutlery and so on. The chemical industry is also important, producing fertilizers, explosives paints and pharmaceuticals.

Forestry

Since medieval times, Sweden has used its forests commercially. Forests today cover 60% of the country—consisting mainly of softwoods such as pine and spruce. Production varies according to latitude as trees grow twice as fast in the south as in the north; quicker growth and easier access have caused pulp and saw mills to move south. Over 85% of the pulp produced is exported making Sweden, along with Canada, the world's leading pulp exporter. Sweden is also a major exporter of paper (mainly newsprint) and board. Other forest products include timber (telegraph poles, building materials and so on) charcoal and matches: the safety match was invented at Jönköping, the centre of the match industry.

Lapps

Scandinavia's arctic region is the home of the Lapps and has been since pre-Christian times. The current Lapp population is 40,000, of which 10,000 live in Sweden. Originally hunters and fishermen, today's Lapps—if they have not been integrated—are reindeer breeders. They breed Sweden's 250,000 reindeer for meat, but not profitably. To increase efficiency, the Swedish government introduced subsidies and laws granting Lapps exclusive rights over reindeer and turned the Lapp village into a co-operative responsible for reindeer breeding within the grazing area of the village. Their distinctive culture is, however, threatened by industrial society.

Transport

For every car on the road 20 years ago there are now ten and Sweden has the most cars per head in Europe. In the same period, rail passenger traffic fell but freight transport increased. The busiest line from Narvik in Norway to Luleå carries iron ore from the Kiruna-Malmberget region Other materials, such as stone, pyrites and petroleum, are often moved by ship. There are 186 coastal ports and some canals (such as the Trollhättan and the Södertälje) take sea-going vessels. During the winter, ice-breakers hold open Baltic and lake ports. To meet the demand of growing air traffic, a new airport has been built at Malmö and facilities extended at Göteborg and Arlanda (Stockholm) Future projects include a bridge-tunnel between Malmö and Copenhagen and a Hälsingborg-Helsingør tunnel.

Shipbuilding

Sweden comes second after Japan in shipbuilding. Of the tonnage launched by Swedish yards (concentrated between Göteborg and Malmö) 75% is exported, and half of this to Norway. Many of the ships are tankers, but ore and paper carriers are also produced to meet the needs of Swedish industry. Over 80% of Sweden's merchant fleet trades between foreign ports. The leading port and second largest city in Sweden is Göteborg (442,000). With its deep, ice-free harbour, shipbuilding and shipping are the main activities.

Denmark

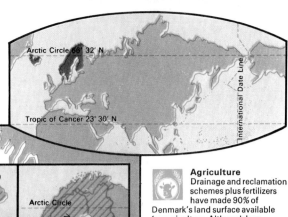

Area
43,070 km²/16,630 sq miles
Location
54°34′—57°45′ N
8°05′—15°12′ E
Population
5,060,000 (1975)
Population density
117 per km²/303 per sq mile
Capital and largest city
Copenhagen: 802,400 (1975)
Language
Danish
Major imports
machinery, metals, fuels, transport equipment, textiles
Major exports
machinery, meat, live animals, dairy produce, eggs, fish and fish products
Currency
krone (1 krone = 100 øre)
Gross National Product
27,300 million US dollars (1973)
Status
constitutional monarchy

Climate

Generally Denmark's climate is moderate: the average temperature of the coldest month, February, is just below freezing, and that of the warmest, July, 17°C. Winter is tempered by the surrounding seas: to the west, the North Sea and the warming current of the Gulf Stream; to the east, the Baltic which, separating Denmark from the continental land mass, acts as a heat reservoir. But, on the rare occasions when ice closes the Baltic, cold air from the east spreads over Denmark causing very harsh weather. On one such occasion in 1940, the temperature fell to a record —31°C. Conversely, in summer the same easterly air-stream may hold off the westerly sea winds and cause a heat wave: the highest temperature recorded was 36°C. Rainfall varies from 80 cm a year in south-west Jylland to about 40 cm in the Store Bælt area.

Fishing

With sea on all sides (except for its 67 km frontier with Germany) Denmark enjoys excellent fishing conditions. The 10,000 vessels of the Danish fishing fleet are mostly privately owned. A third of them are rowing boats, but increasingly, steel vessels over 200 tonnes are replacing the smaller types. The catch consists of herring, cod, plaice and mackerel from the North Sea and the Skagerrak, and eel and shrimp from the Baltic. Esbjerg (79,000), with canning and processing factories, is the main fishing port followed by Skagen, Hirtshals and the new port of Hanstholm.

Porcelain

One of Denmark's traditional manufactures is porcelain using kaolin from Bornholm and also the UK. The most famous centre is the Royal Copenhagen Porcelain Manufactory. It was founded in 1775 as a private company with royal support—the Queen herself supposedly suggested the factory's trade mark, three blue wavy lines symbolizing the Lille Bælt (Little Belt), Store Bælt (Great Belt) and the Oresund (Sound). Four years later, the factory was taken over by the King and for nearly 100 years remained a royal possession before reverting to private ownership. Its products are exported all over the world.

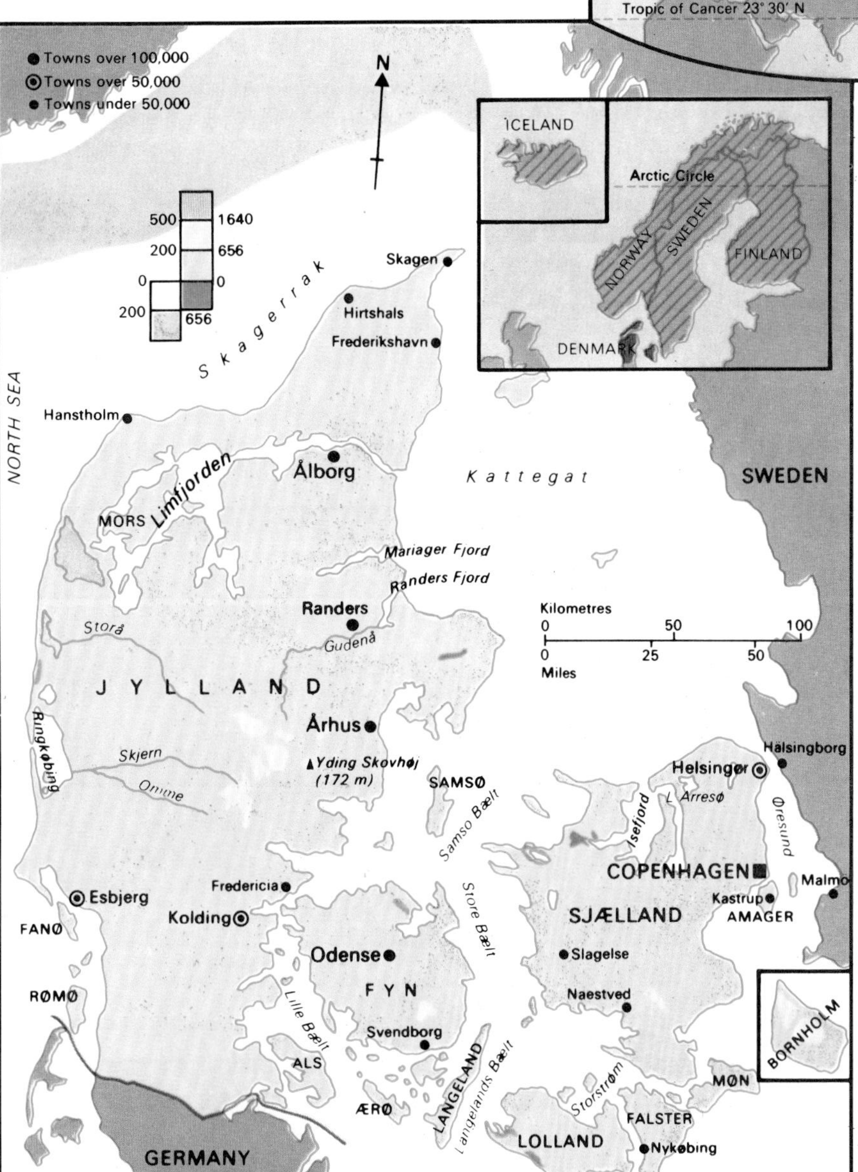

Physical features

Denmark almost forms a land bridge between the continent of Europe and the Scandinavian peninsula and separates the North and Baltic Seas. Its land area is divided between Jylland (Jutland: 29,650 km²) and 406 islands (of which 97 are inhabited) which are mostly concentrated at the Baltic entrance. The largest of these islands are Sjælland (Zealand), Fyn (Funen), Lolland, Falster and, in the south Baltic, the granite island of Bornholm. The country is low-lying with Denmark's highest point, Yding Skovhøj in east Jylland, only 172 m above sea level. Glacial moraine deposits cover the surface to form undulating plains alternating with low hills and lakes. The biggest lake is Arresø (41 km²). Jylland's west coast is characterized by dunes, the north is swampy while the east coast is broken up by inlets leading back into valleys. Denmark's longest river, the Gudenå (157 km), follows a series of such valleys, formed by glacial melt water.

Cities

Copenhagen, or Merchants' Harbour, was founded in 1167 and became Denmark's capital in 1417. The city centre is the medieval Raadhuspladsen (Town Hall Square) with Strøget, the main shopping street now open to pedestrians only, leading off it. Built opposite Malmö on the east of Sjælland and the north of Amager, Copenhagen lies at the entrance to the Baltic. Its position led to its commercial, and later industrial, importance: for centuries Copenhagen controlled trade in the Baltic and today is its leading port. More than 35,000 ships visit Copenhagen annually, handling 60% of Danish imports, but only about 30% of exports (since trade in dairy produce and bacon with the UK is dealt with by Esbjerg on the west coast of Jylland). The second largest city is Århus (245,000) in east Jylland, followed by Odense (168,000) on Fyn. Although three out of four Danes live in urbanized areas, there are few major towns apart from these.

Industry

There is no coal, iron, oil or water power in Denmark, but there is an enormous output of agricultural produce. One of Denmark's main industries is food processing which ranges from meat packing to pharmaceuticals (Denmark is the world's principal supplier of insulin). Another major industry using a domestic raw material, chalk, is cement. Ålborg in Jylland has the world's largest rotary cement kiln. The second biggest industrial sector, employing 36% of the total labour force and using imported materials, is engineering and electronics. Products range from ships and their engines (one diesel-powered vessel in three is fitted with an engine built either in Denmark or under Danish licence) to car components (but not cars) and hearing aids. The other main sector, employing imported materials, is textiles. About 80% of Danish firms employ less than 50 people and many of these small units specialize in high quality craft goods.

Agriculture

Drainage and reclamation schemes plus fertilizers have made 90% of Denmark's land surface available for agriculture. Although less than one tenth of this is for permanent grazing (barley, oats, sugar-beet and green forage are grown on most of the remaining land) farming is mainly concerned with cows and pigs and the major part of the harvest (about 90%) is used for feeding animals. There are over a million dairy cattle in the country; the most popular breed is the Red Danish which can produce 5,000 litres (8,750 pints) of milk a year. Milk is collected from farms in tankers and taken to co-operative dairies where it is processed into butter, cream and cheese. The by-products, such as skimmed milk, butter milk and whey, are sold back to the farmers as pig feed. The pigs are all of the Danish Landrace breed which is well suited for bacon. Increasing demand for meat and meat products had led to concentrated and efficient pig raising systems without the use of battery farming techniques. Each year, about 12 million animals are slaughtered and 80% of the resulting meat is exported. Denmark is the world's biggest exporter of pigmeat, second biggest exporter of butter and the third largest exporter of cheese. Although only 8% of Danes work in agriculture, they produce enough animal-based foodstuffs to feed over 15 million people. This is about three times the total population of Denmark and the reason why Denmark is able to export two-thirds of its farm produce. (It is exported to over 140 countries.) Another major animal-based export is mink skin. Danish breeders produce about 3.5 million mink pelts annually of which about 95% are exported. This makes Denmark the world's third biggest mink producing nation. Mink auctions are held five times a year in Copenhagen. Market gardening is also important and one of the main production areas which supplies Copenhagen is Amager.

Transport

Apart from the Jylland peninsular, Denmark consists of a number of small islands which require a combination of land and sea communications. Ferry and steamer services between islands co-ordinate with rail and bus networks overland. For example, trains from Jylland to Copenhagen cross the Store Bælt (between Fyn and Sjælland) by ferry. A feature of the road and rail networks is the number of bridges involved: the largest is Storstrøm bridge, a 3 km link between Sjælland and Falster. Denmark has a large merchant fleet, mainly serving overseas trade and earning about 2,000 million kroner (about 350 million US dollars) in foreign currency. International air transport is handled by SAS and Copenhagen airport (Kastrup) is the fourth busiest in Europe. From Copenhagen there are domestic flights to nine provincial airports.

West Germany

Area
248,600 km²/95,980 sq miles
Location
47°12′—54°55′ N
6°—12° E
Population
62,000,000 (1974)
Population density
248 per km²/643 per sq mile
Capital
Bonn : 283,350 (1974)
Largest city
Berlin (West) : 2,120,000 (1974)
Language
German
Major imports
foodstuffs, metals, chemicals, fuels, textiles
Major exports
engineering products, electrical goods, chemicals, road vehicles
Currency
Deutsche Mark (= 100 Pfennige)
Gross National Product
383,800 million US dollars (1974)
Status
independent republic

Physical features

The Federal Republic, consisting of 10 *Länder* (states), divides into three physical zones : the Alpine region, the Central Uplands and the north German plain. The Alpine region in the extreme south comprises the Bavarian Alps—a continuation of the main Alpine system which contains Germany's highest peak, the Zugspitze (2,962 m). The undulating foreland, which extends to the Danube, has numerous lakes and peat bogs. The Central Uplands is a region of ancient plateaux and ranges. The main highland masses are the Harz, Fichtelgebirge and Bohemian Forest in the east, the Schwäbische and Fränkische Alb in the south, the Hohe-Rhön and Vogelsberg in the centre and, bordering the Rhine, the Schwarzwald (Black Forest), Odenwald, Taunus, Westerwald, Sauerland, Eifel and Hunsrück. Between these highlands and the coast lies the north German plain. In the south this is covered by fertile loess but, further north, infertile sand, clay and moorlands predominate. The low-lying marshy coast is fringed by the East Friesian Islands. With the exception of the Danube, the main rivers flow into the North Sea.

Climate

In the coastal regions of Germany, the climate is affected by the North and Baltic Seas with cold (but not severe) winters and warm summers. At Emden, winter and summer temperatures are 1°C and 17°C respectively. In the southern interior the climate is more continental with hotter summers and colder winters : January and July averages for Munich are —2°C and 18°C. Rain is heaviest in highland areas : the Alps receive over 200 cm a year, the Central Uplands have 75 cm and the lowlands only 50 cm.

Energy

Thermal stations generate 90% of Germany's electricity. Half of these are fired by coal, the rest by lignite (brown coal), oil and natural gas. Hydro-electric plants, mostly situated in the south, produce 8% and nuclear power stations only 2%. About 90% of Germany's oil requirement has to be imported as well as 40% of natural gas.

Agriculture

Although 54% of the country is farmed, agriculture accounts for only 4% of the GNP and employs under 9% of the workforce. It does, however, provide 75% of the nation's food. Almost half the cultivated land is used for wheat, barley, rye, oats, potatoes and sugarbeet. The main arable regions are the northern plain (the loess belt is West Germany's best farmland and sandy regions are heavily fertilized), the 'Cologne bay' (a fertile lowland area at the northern end of the Rhine gorge) and valleys in the Central Uplands. Between Basel and Mainz, the Rhine flows through a broad rift valley. Here, summers are warmer and maize, tobacco, fruit and vines are grown. Federal Germany is Europe's fourth largest wine-producing country. Hops are cultivated near Munich. Livestock is mainly located on the reclaimed marshlands in the north, but there are also pastures in upland areas. Forests, covering 29% of the country and largely coniferous, are concentrated in the south. About 50% of Germany's fish requirement is covered by domestic production mainly caught in distant Atlantic waters. Bremerhaven is the main fishing port.

Mining

About 90% of German coal comes from the Ruhr with the remainder from Saarland and the Aachen district. Lignite is worked west of Cologne and in Hessen and Bavaria. Oil production, centred on the northern plain, meets 7% of Germany's needs. Natural gas is also obtained from the oil-fields. Mines in Lower Saxony, Hessen and Baden-Württemberg yield 60% of the world's potash of which half is exported. Other mineral resources are limited. Iron ore, mined mainly at Salzgitter, is of low quality and meets only 7% of domestic requirements. Some lead and zinc are mined in the Harz mountains.

Transport

Transport in Federal Germany is highly developed. The Autobahn (motorway) network is the longest in Europe with secondary roads and the rail network coming second. Germany also has Europe's busiest waterway, the Rhine, which, with its tributaries, serves the east, centre and south. The North Sea is connected to the Baltic by the Kiel canal and will be linked to the Black Sea by the Main-Danube canal now under construction. Hamburg is the main seaport, followed by Bremen, Bremerhaven, Emden, Wilhelmshaven and Lübeck. The airline, Lufthansa, operates domestic and overseas flights.

Industry

Since the Second World War, German industry has made a dramatic recovery and Germany is now a leading industrial nation. Of the world's top ten companies, five are West German. The Ruhr, the most concentrated industrial zone in Europe, produces 70% of West Germany's steel. The main steel and engineering centres are Dortmund, Bochum, Essen, Duisburg and Düsseldorf. Other industries established in the Ruhr are textiles at Wuppertal, Krefeld, Mönchengladbach and Rheydt, and chemicals at Cologne, Leverkusen and Rheinport. Steel is also produced at Neunkirchen and Saarbrücken in Saarland and at Salzgitter and Bremen. Frankfurt is the hub of another manufacturing region with engineering, textile, chemical and food-processing industries. Other major industrial zones include Aachen, Munich (München), Nürnberg, Stuttgart and the Braunschweig-Wolfsburg-Hannover-Salzgitter area. Important Rhine towns are Mainz, Mannheim and Karlsruhe. Federal Germany is the world's third largest producer of automobiles and ships. Shipyards are located in Hamburg, Bremen, Bremerhaven, Emden and Kiel.

Cities

The federal capital, Bonn—a university town on the Rhine and Beethoven's birthplace—is an administrative centre. The largest city and leading industrial centre is West Berlin isolated 150 km inside East Germany. The second largest city as regards size and industry is Hamburg (1,817,000) on the Elbe. The third largest city is Munich (München : 1,341,000) in Bavaria where brewing is a traditional industry. Cologne (Köln : 1,100,000) is an industrial and communications centre. Essen (689,200) is the leading Ruhr town and Frankfurt am Main is the country's financial capital.

The Netherlands

Area
36,946 km²/14,265 sq miles
Location
50°45′—53°30′ N
3°20′—7° E
Population
13,540,000 (1974)
Population density
364 per km²/943 per sq mile
Capital and largest city
Amsterdam: 791,770 (1975)
Language
Dutch
Major imports
petroleum, chemicals, textiles, iron and steel, metal products and machinery
Major exports
machinery, transport equipment, chemicals, petroleum products, agricultural produce, textiles
Currency
guilder (1 guilder = 100 cents)
Gross National Product
69,600 million US dollars (1974)
Status
constitutional monarchy

Physical features

The world's most densely populated country, the Netherlands is situated on the North Sea at the estuaries of three rivers: the Rhine, Maas and Schelde. Popularly known as Holland, this small state, which has a maximum length and breadth of 312 km and 120 km respectively, is very flat: most land lies below 30 m and half the total area is below sea level. Sand dunes fringe the coast; the dune barrier has broken to form the Friesian Islands in the north and, in the south, the Maas-Rhine delta islands. Behind the dunes are the polders—reclaimed tracts of land surrounded by dykes. Eastern Holland, lying above sea level, consists of a sandy plain with stretches of pine forest and peat bog. The country's highest point, Vaalseberg (322 m), is in the Limburg district near Maastricht. Apart from the Maas, the main rivers draining the country are the IJssel, Lek and Waal.

Climate

The Netherlands has a marine-type climate with cool summers and mild winters. The average temperature in July is 17°C and in January —1°C. In winter, snow is common and frosts are sufficiently severe to freeze canals, lakes and small rivers; skating is a traditional pastime. Rainfall is moderate (between 60 and 80 cm a year) and occurs throughout the year, but summer is the wettest season. The prevailing westerly and south-westerly winds are strongest along the coast where they sometimes reach storm force.

Mining

The Netherlands has no metal ores and few minerals. Salt is mined at Hengelo and Delfzijl in the east and 60% of output is exported. Coal used to be worked in south Limburg, but production ceased as oil and natural gas became increasingly important. The Schoonebeek and Rijswijk oilfields yield two million tonnes annually, enough to supply 10% of domestic needs. Gas from Slochteren, the world's largest natural gas field, is piped throughout Holland and exported to W Germany, France and Belgium.

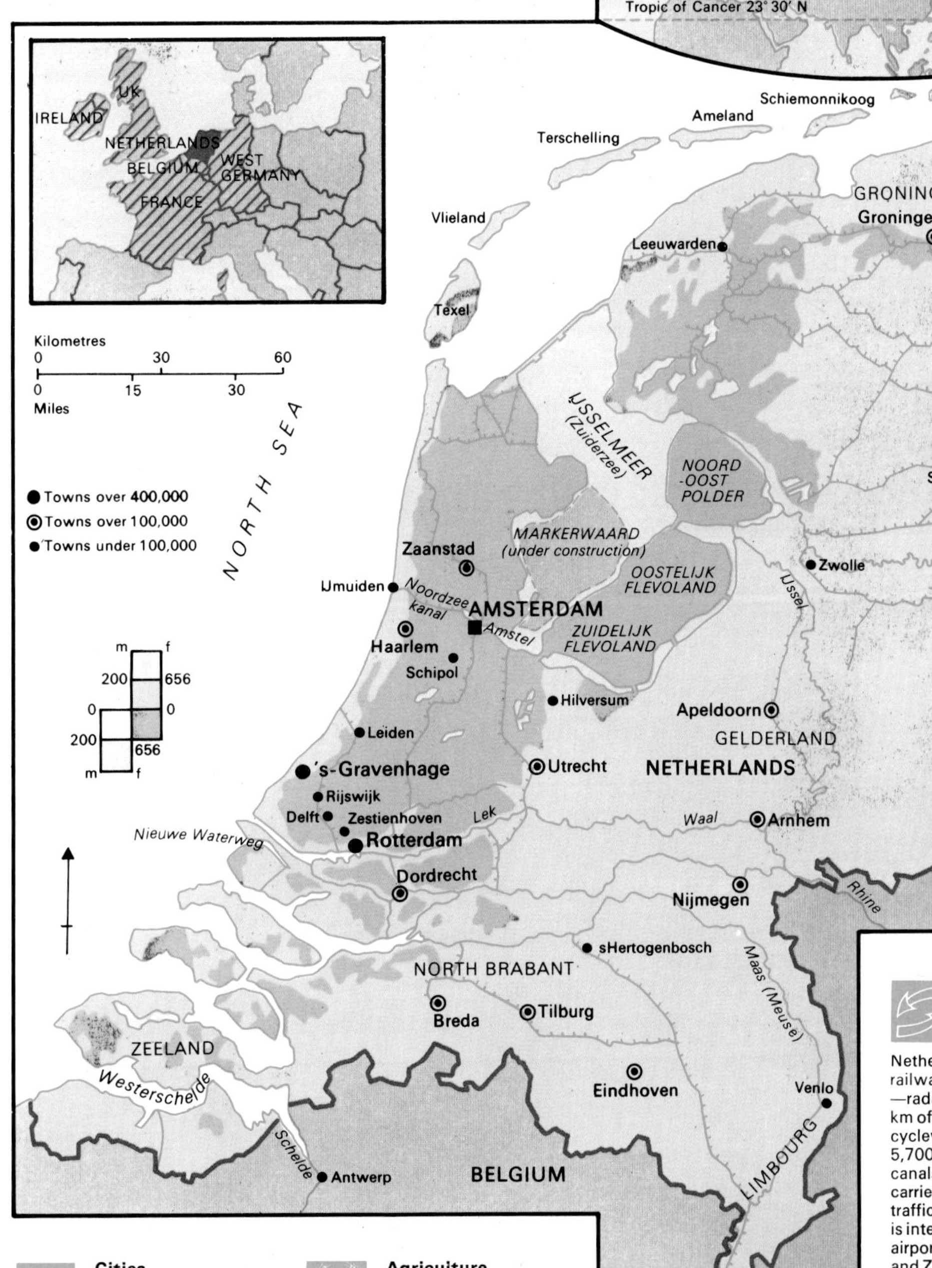

Cities

Amsterdam originated in the 13th century as a port at the mouth of the Amstel river on the old Zuiderzee. Over the centuries, it spread on to adjacent swamp land: hence its many canals, its 800 bridges and its houses built on piles. Today, despite the closure of the Zuiderzee, it ranks as the world's 15th largest port having canal links to both the North Sea and Rhine. Industrial suburbs extend along the Noordzeekanaal to IJmuiden. Although Amsterdam is the capital, it is not the seat of government: parliament, ministries and foreign embassies are located in the third largest city, 's-Gravenhage (the Hague: 510,360). The Netherlands' second city, Rotterdam (654,020) has the world's largest port. 75% of cargo handled is transit trade. Access to the North Sea is by a deep ship canal, the Nieuwe Waterweg. Near its mouth is the new Europoort, built to take large ships. The conurbation formed by Amsterdam, Rotterdam, the Hague and Holland's fourth city, Utrecht (464,050)—accounts for 46% of the population.

Agriculture

About 75% of the country is used for agriculture but, as farming is highly intensive and mechanized, it only employs 6% of the labour force. Livestock is kept on 63% of agricultural land, especially on the rich polder pastures. Dairy farming is important and the main products exported are butter, cheese (Edam and Gouda) and condensed milk. The Netherlands is the world's leading cheese exporter. Other exports include meat, bacon and eggs. Arable farming, covering 31% of agricultural land, predominates in Zeeland and Groningen. The main crops are wheat, barley, sugarbeet and potatoes. Horticulture occupies the remaining 6% of farmland. The leading sector is bulb growing, which is concentrated between Leyden and Haarlem, and millions of bulbs (tulips, hyacinths and daffodils) are exported annually. Most vegetables, especially tomatoes, cucumbers and lettuces, are grown in glasshouses just south of the Hague and there are orchards in Gelderland, North Brabant and Limburg.

Land from water

The first polders were created in the 13th century. Since then, the Dutch have gradually won more and more land from rivers, lakes and the sea. Two major schemes are currently in progress. In the Delta project, all the Rhine-Maas-Scheldt delta estuaries are being closed except the Waterweg and the Westerschelde to allow access to Rotterdam and Antwerp. This scheme, designed to protect the area from flooding, will reclaim 150 km² of land and create a 520 km² fresh-water lake. The Zuiderzee project involves a 30 km dam. The Zuiderzee is being turned into five polders, totalling 2,260 km², and a 1,200 km² reservoir, the IJsselmeer.

Transport

The flatness of the country facilitates all forms of transport. The Netherlands has 3,150 km of railways (with 50% electrified) —radiating from Utrecht; 70,000 km of roads; 7,000 km of cycleways and, most important, 5,700 km of navigable rivers and canals. About 60% of freight is carried by water and half the traffic on Holland's waterways is international. The two main airports, Schipol (Amsterdam) and Zestienhoven (Rotterdam) are the only airports in the world below sea level. Schipol is the base of KLM, the world's oldest civil aviation company.

Industry

Industry employs 42% of the workforce and accounts for 70% of all exports. The leading sector—metallurgy and engineering—uses imported raw materials and is therefore mainly located near the coast: there are works at Amsterdam, Rotterdam, IJmuiden and Dordrecht; at Arnhem and Nijmegen (both river ports) and in Limburg, near the old coalfield. The food and tobacco industry ranks second. Activities such as cheese manufacture, gin distilling, sugar refining and vegetable canning are based on Dutch produce; other manufactures, like chocolate and cigars, process imported materials. The electro-technical industry is dominated by Holland's biggest firm, Philips, based at Eindhoven. Other major industries include chemicals, textiles, tourism and, in Amsterdam, diamond cutting.

Belgium

Area
30,514 km²/11,780 sq miles
Location
49°30′—51°30′ N
2°35′—6°25′ E
Population
9,800,000 (1974)
Population density
319 per km²/826 per sq mile
Capital and largest city
Bruxelles: 1,055,000 (1974)
Languages
French, Flemish (Dutch), German
Major imports
fuels, metals, iron and steel, chemicals
Major exports
engineering goods, steel products, textiles, chemicals, foodstuffs
Currency
franc (1 franc = 100 centimes)
Gross National Product
53,077 million US dollars (1974)
Status
constitutional monarchy

Physical features

Although Belgium is small, it offers a varied landscape. The 66 km long coast is marked by a line of broad dunes backed by polders. This belt of reclaimed land (about 10 km wide) runs into the Flanders plain—a sandy lowland drained by the Schelde and its tributary, the Lys. Kempenland in the north is similar with an undulating sandy plain, but with stretches of heath, bog and pine forest. Central Belgium, lying between the Sambre-Meuse and the Schelde, is a low fertile plateau from 40 to 200 m in height and drained by the Demer, Dijle, Senne and Dender (all tributaries of the Schelde). In the south-east lie the Ardennes. The foothills consist of limestone valleys and forested sandstone ridges with an average altitude of 300 m. Behind these lies the Ardenne plateau, formed over 250 million years ago. It is a region of forests and moorlands between 300 and 600 m high. In the north-east is Belgium's highest point, Botrange (694 m). The winding rivers of the Ardennes—the Meuse and its tributaries, the Semois, Ourthe and Vesdre—flow through deep valleys.

Climate

Belgium has a temperate climate with damp mild winters and cool summers. Bruxelles averages 2°C in January and 17°C in July. Atlantic air masses cause variable weather and the prevailing westerly winds brings frequent rain: most of the country has between 80 and 100 cm a year. Regional differences in climate are determined by altitude and distance from the coast. In the Ardennes, for instance, temperatures are lower (January, —4°C), rainfall is heavier (140 cm) and snow lies for between 35 and 50 days (less than 10 days on the coast).

Energy

Belgian coal is now in competition with oil and natural gas. Oil is mostly imported, but there is some exploitation of the North Sea reserves. Natural gas is piped from Holland. Blast-furnace gas, a by-product of steel manufacture, is used in industrial areas. Many of the power stations are coal-fired and located in the Kempenland region. There are a few small hydro-electric power stations in the Ardennes.

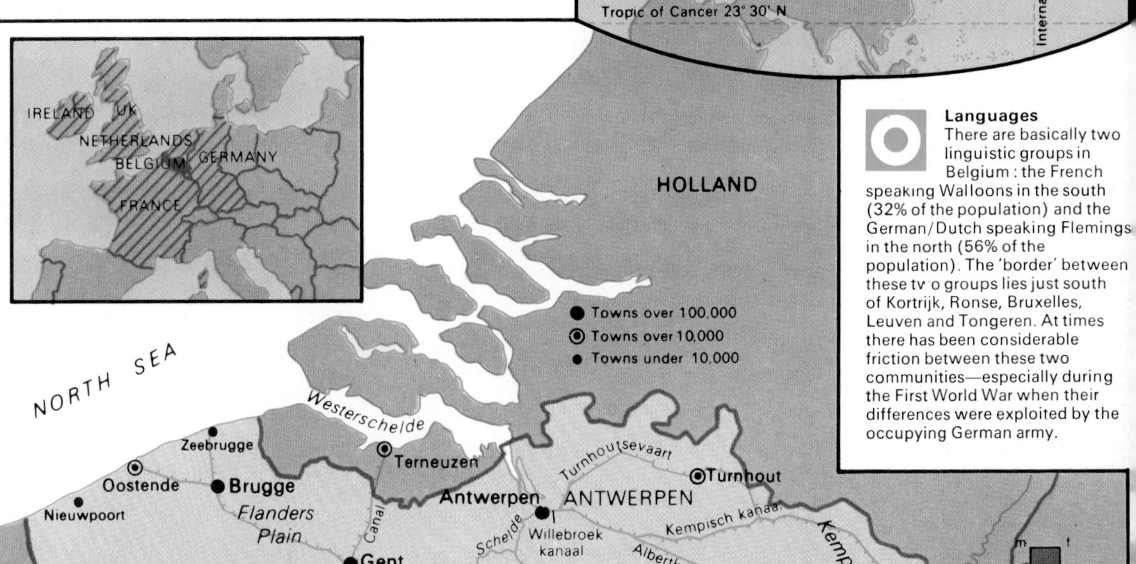

Languages

There are basically two linguistic groups in Belgium: the French speaking Walloons in the south (32% of the population) and the German/Dutch speaking Flemings in the north (56% of the population). The 'border' between these two groups lies just south of Kortrijk, Ronse, Bruxelles, Leuven and Tongeren. At times there has been considerable friction between these two communities—especially during the First World War when their differences were exploited by the occupying German army.

Mining

Belgium's mineral resources are limited to coal, sand, limestone and clay. Coal, located in the Sambre-Meuse valley and in the Kempenland region, is the most significant. The Sambre-Meuse deposits, which led to the industrialization of Mons, La Louvière, Charleroi, Namur and Liège, are now nearly exhausted and yield only 20% of total production. The remaining 80% comes from Kempenland, centred on Genk, Beringen and Zolder. Sand, worked near Charleroi and in Kempenland, is the basis of an important glass industry.

Industry

Belgium is highly industrialized with mechanical engineering the most important industry accounting for 20% of total industrial output. Products range from ships and bridges to bolts and screws. Other major industries include steel manufacture (Belgium produces over 10% of the EEC output), chemicals, glass (products range from large plate glass to Val St-Lambert crystal), textiles (including traditional linen, tapestries and lace) and non-ferrous metals (Belgium is the world's leading processor of cobalt and radium). Oil refining, food processing, cement, paper manufacture and sugar refining are also important industries. Belgium's chief port, Antwerpen, is a major diamond-cutting centre. Approximately 40% of Belgium's industrial output is exported.

Agriculture

Although only 52% of the total area is farmed, Belgian agriculture meets 80% of the country's food requirements. Wheat, barley and sugarbeet are grown on the fertile loess and loam soils of central Belgium; barley, potatoes, flax and hops predominate on the Flanders plain while some fodder crops are grown on the polders and in the lower Ardennes. The high Ardennes, Kempenland and most of the polders are used for dairy farming. Market gardening and glasshouse cultivation are located on the polders and near major cities: horticultural products, such as asparagus, endives, roses and orchids are exported. About 80% of Belgian farms are less than one hectare (2.5 acres) in area and much of the work is done by women and children as the men are often employed in industry. Fishing, in the North Sea and Atlantic, meets 30% of domestic demand. Eight out of 10 Belgian trawlers are based at Oostende; the two other fishing ports are Zeebrugge and Nieuwpoort. Forests, mainly situated in the Ardennes, cover 19% of the country, but timber imports are still necessary.

Transport

The 4,165 km Belgian rail network, radiating from Bruxelles, is one of the densest in the world. And for every 1 km of railway, there are 3 km of main roads, including sections of European expressways. There are over 1,500 km of navigable inland waterways and these are used for bulk freight transport. The major arteries are the Albertkanaal, linking Liège and Kempenland with Antwerpen; the Willebroek kanaal, joining the Schelde and Sambre via Bruxelles; and the two ship canals linking the ports of Brugge and Gent with the sea at Zeebrugge and Terneuzen (Holland) respectively. Antwerpen is Belgium's first (and the world's third largest) port. Other main ports are Brugge/Zeebrugge, Oostende, Gent and Bruxelles. The national airline is Sabena.

Cities

Bruxelles, by the river Senne, is Belgium's leading industrial, commercial and cultural city. It is also a major European centre—housing the headquarters of the EEC. Antwerpen (666,000), on the Schelde estuary, is the heart of an urban area containing half a million people. The port serves Flanders via the Schelde and the east via the Albertkanaal. Gent (220,300) is Belgium's third largest city and port. Traditionally a textile centre, it has developed new industries—many of them located along the ship canal. Both Gent and Brugge (120,000) have many ancient buildings and are popular with tourists. Around 25% of the population lives in the Sambre-Meuse region where the largest towns are Liège (436,000) and Mons (61,000).

Luxembourg

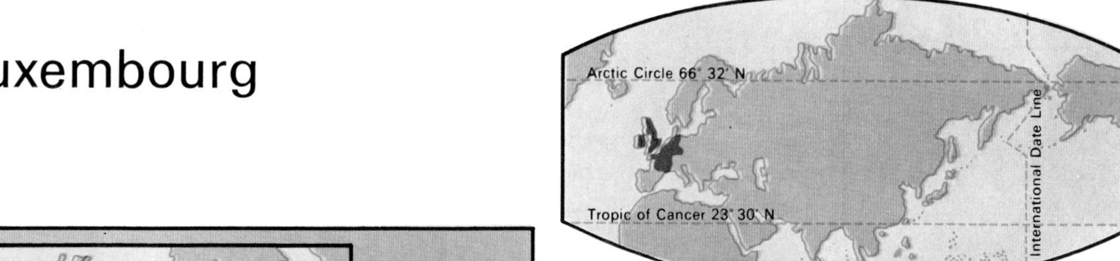

Area
2,586 km²/998 sq miles
Location
49°26'—50°10' N
5°44'—6°31' E
Population
352,700 (1973)
Population density
136 per km²/353 per sq mile
Capital and largest city
Luxembourg : 78,000 (1972)
Languages
French, German, Letzeburgesch
Major imports
mineral products, consumer goods, foodstuffs
Major exports
steel, chemical products (including plastic and rubber), textiles, machinery, wine
Currency
franc (1 franc = 100 centimes)
Gross National Product
1,810 million US dollars (1973)
Status
constitutional monarchy

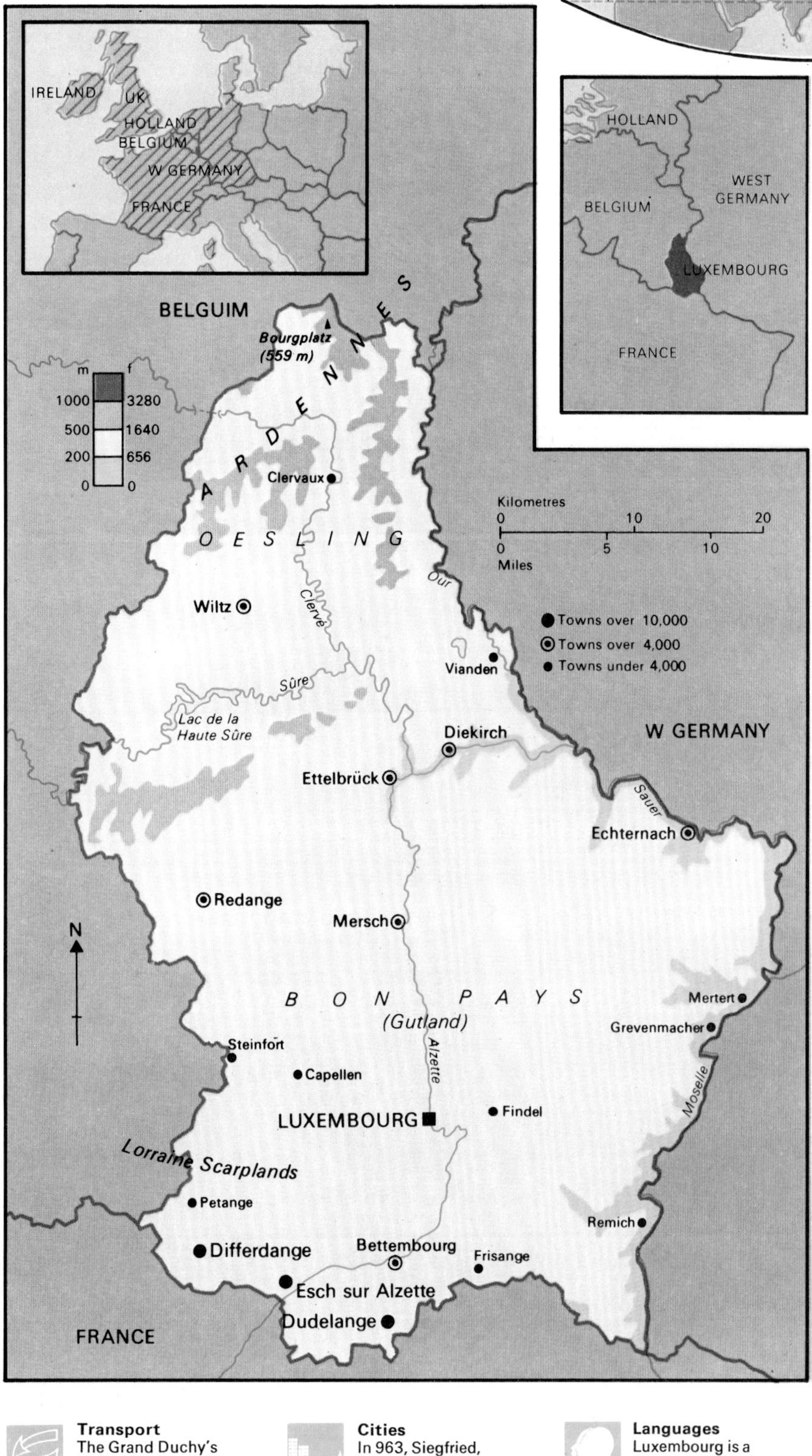

Physical features
The Grand Duchy of Luxembourg, lying between Belgium, Germany and France, is the EEC's smallest member state: its maximum length is 82 km, and width, 57 km. The Grand Duchy divides into two regions. In the north is the Oesling, an extension of the Ardennes, covering about a third of the total area. These forested uplands contain the country's highest point: Bourgplatz, 559 m. The remaining 68% of the territory corresponds to the Bon Pays or Gutland (Good Land). This region, a continuation of the Lorraine scarplands, is less hilly than the north and has an average height of 228 m. The two main rivers are the Alzette and Sûre which, together with their tributaries, flow through deep, picturesque valleys. The Alzette and Sûre drain into the Sauer, a tributary of the Moselle. The Moselle, Sauer and Our flow along the 135 km border with Germany.

Climate
Prevailing south-westerly and north-westerly winds have a moderating influence. As a consequence, Luxembourg has warm summers and cool winters: in the capital, July averages 19°C, January, 2°C. Mean temperatures in the Oesling are about two degrees lower. Rainfall occurs throughout the year, but is heaviest in winter when it often falls as snow. Amounts vary from 70 cm in the Moselle valley to 100 cm in the northern hills.

Mining and Energy
Industry in Luxembourg is based on the country's iron ore deposits. These deposits, which correspond to the northern tip of the Lorraine iron ore field, are worked in opencast mines near Dudelange, Esch and between Rodange and Differdange. Annual production amounts to some 3 million tonnes; a further 12 million tonnes has to be imported. There is some stone and slate quarrying. The main sources of energy are imported coal and oil, electricity and, since 1972, natural gas from the Netherlands. 60% of electricity is generated thermally, using blast furnace gas—a by-product of the steel industry. The remainder is produced by hydro-electric plants on the Sûre, Moselle and Our.

Transport
The Grand Duchy's 5,000 km of roads radiate from the capital; the main international routes are to Germany (via Echternach), to France (via Frisange), and to Belgium (via Steinfort). The rail network totals only 271 km. Luxembourg is a transit country for Belgian and Dutch railways to Switzerland and Italy. Over 50% of cargo handled by the river port of Mertert, on the Moselle, is connected with the steel industry. Luxembourg airlines, Luxair and Cargolux, operate from the international airport, Findel, located 6 km east of the capital.

Cities
In 963, Siegfried, Count of the Ardennes, built a castle high above the Alzette. In the course of time, the castle grew into a powerful fortress known as 'the Gibraltar of the North'. The development of the modern city began in 1867 when the fortress was dismantled. Today's city, an urban agglomeration of nearly 80,000 people, houses several European institutions including the Court of Justice and the Monetary Fund. The Grand Duchy's other leading towns are in the south-western industrial zone: Esch (27,600), Differdange (17,500) and Dudelange (14,900).

Languages
Luxembourg is a linguistic puzzle: French, German and Letzeburgesch are all official national languages. Letzeburgesch, a Germanic dialect, is used in conversation, German is popularly used for written communication, while French is the language of government. In this way, a parliamentary debate is conducted in Letzeburgesch; the report of that debate, for general circulation, is printed in German; the law resulting from that debate is drawn up in French. To cope with this situation, children are taught all three languages at school.

Agriculture
Around 50% of the country is under cultivation and this area divides almost equally into arable land and pasture land. Livestock farming predominates in the Oesling where the soils are thin and infertile. In contrast, the Bon Pays, with its limestone, sandstone and clay, supports mixed farming. The main crops are barley, potatoes, oats and wheat; both dairy and beef cattle are kept as well as poultry and some pigs. In the south, there are also orchards, market gardens and, along the Moselle valley, vineyards. White wines are produced and about 50% of output is exported, mainly to Belgium and the Netherlands. Most farms are small: one in three is under 10 hectares. Every year the total number of farms and that of agricultural workers decreases by about 4%. This is due to the amalgamation of small units and to mechanization. Agriculture contributes less than 5% to the national income and employs only 9% of the workforce.

Industry
The steel industry dominates the Luxembourg economy employing 45% of the industrial workforce and accounting for 69% of all exports. Steel manufacture, centered on Dudelange, Esch, Differdange and Rodange, is dependent on imported materials: 65% of iron ore comes from Lorraine, while West Germany supplies nearly all the industry's coke requirements. The annual steel output is about 5.5 million tonnes and nine-tenths of this is exported as rolled steel, mostly to EEC countries. 90% of steel production is in the hands of Luxembourg's largest firm, Arbed. Three other leading firms are all connected with chemicals—the country's second industrial sector—and are all American subsidiaries: Goodyear make tyres; Du Pont make polyester foils and Monsanto, synthetic fibres. Traditional chemical manufactures include fertilizers, dyes and explosives.

Tourism
Tourism is playing an increasingly important role in the Luxembourg economy. The Grand Duchy's assets as a tourist country include varied landscape, relatively sparse population, industry concentrated in the south-western corner and scope for outdoor activities such as sailing, climbing and riding. The main problem encountered by the developing tourist industry is the short duration of the season, July-August. Most visitors come from Belgium and the Netherlands.

Benelux
1944 saw the creation of Benelux, an economic union of Belgium, the Netherlands and Luxembourg. As a result of the union, goods, people and capital now circulate freely within the three member states. The Benelux countries also have agreements on postal and transport rates, on welfare systems and on overseas trade policies.

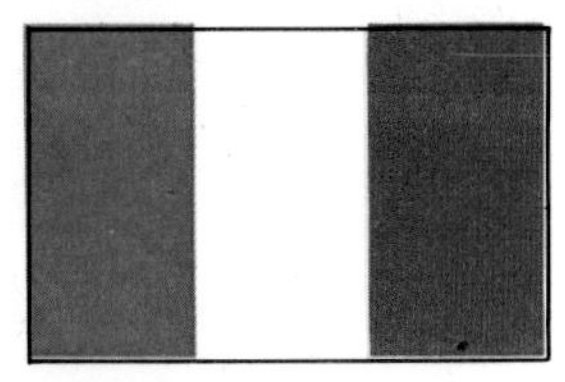

France

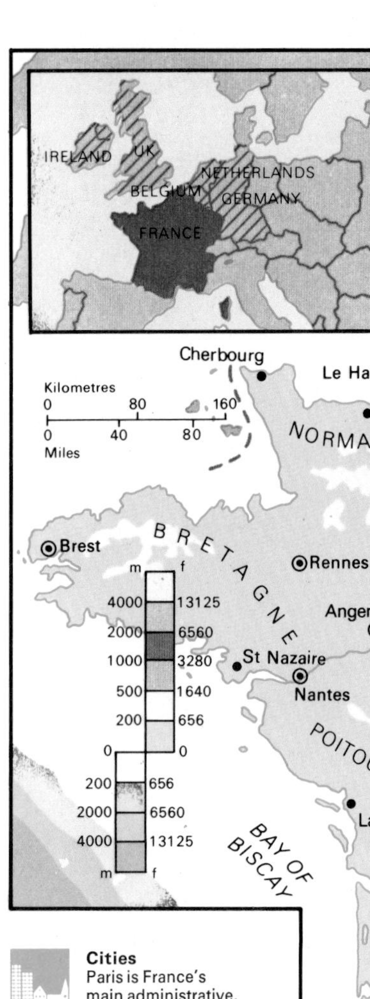

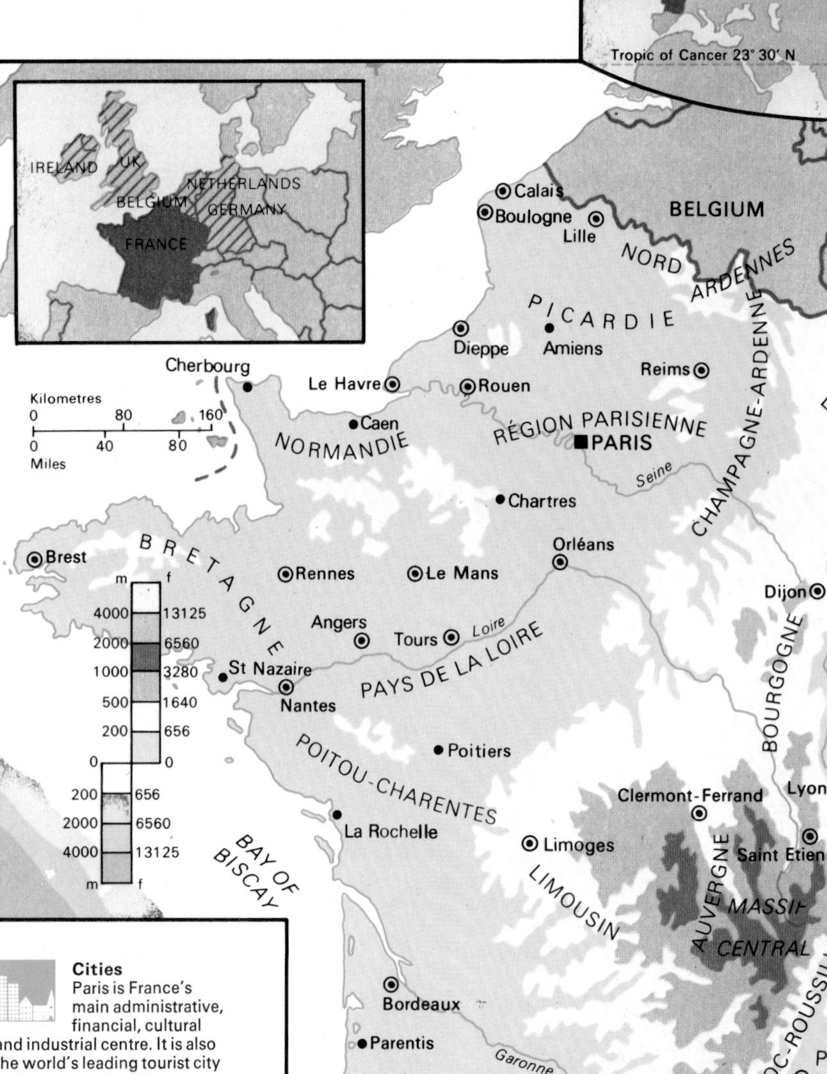

Area
551,000 km²/212,750 sq miles
Location
42°20'—51°5' N
5°55'—8°10' E
Population
53,186,000 (1978)
Population density
94 per km²/244 per sq mile
Capital and largest city
Paris: 8,196,746 (1968)
Language
French
Major imports
fuels, metals, chemicals, machinery, foodstuffs
Major exports
machinery, transport, iron and steel, cereals, dairy produce, wine, textiles, soap
Currency
franc (1 franc = 100 centimes)
Gross National Product
276,000 million US dollars (1974)
Status
independent republic

Physical features

The USSR apart, France is Europe's biggest state. Although it contains the highest point in western Europe—Mont Blanc, 4,807m—60% of the country lies below 250m. There are three main lowland areas, each drained by a major river. The largest is the Paris basin. In the south-west is Aquitaine, drained by the Garonne, while the third area corresponds to the Rhône-Saône valley. These lowlands are bordered by mountains and plateaux. In the south and west, high ranges—the Pyrénées, Alps and Jura—separate France from her neighbours: Spain, Italy and Switzerland. The less rugged plateaux comprise the Vosges, the Ardennes, Armorica and the Massif Central, which covers 15% of the total area and has an average height of 1,000 m. With the exception of the Rhône and its tributaries, the main rivers—including the longest, the Loire—drain into the Atlantic.

Climate

Because of the Atlantic and the Gulf Stream, most of France has a temperate, oceanic cimate which is mildest in the west. January averages 7°C in Brest and 2°C in Strasbourg; respective July temperatures are 17°C and 20°C. Although the rain-bearing winds are westerly, many eastern areas are wetter than the west because of altitude: average annual rainfall in Besançon is 110 cm, but only 66 cm in Rennes.

Mining and energy

Coal, iron and bauxite constitute the major part of France's mineral wealth. Coal, from the north and east, meets 70% of domestic needs. France is the world's third largest producer of iron ore—main deposits are in Lorraine and Normandy—and is also a leading producer of bauxite (named after the village of Lex Baux, in Provence, where it was first mined in 1882). Other minerals worked include uranium, gold and potash. Most oil has to be imported, as domestic output, chiefly from Parentis, is low. In contrast, natural gas, from Lacq and other smaller fields, supplies 32% of demand. 59% of electricity is of thermal origin, 40% hydroelectric and 1% nuclear.

Cities

Paris is France's main administrative, financial, cultural and industrial centre. It is also the world's leading tourist city and has some 3 million visitors a year. Principal attractions include the Eiffel Tower, Notre-Dame cathedral, the Louvre palace with its art collection and Montmartre. France's second city, Lyon (1,083,000), stands at the confluence of the Rhône and Saône. Founded by the Romans, it later became famous for its silk, which is still an important manufacture. Marseille (965,000), first settled by the Greeks in 600 BC, is the country's oldest and third largest city as well as being its chief port. Lille (881,271), at the heart of the industrial north, is a major textile centre.

Transport

Paris is the centre of France's transport system: it has three airports, is a major river port and serves as the hub of the country's dense road and rail networks. Trains—the fastest in Europe—and lorries carry the bulk of freight. A further 25% is transported on the 8,600 km of inland waterways. The Seine, Rhine and Rhône are particularly important; chief river ports are Strasbourg, Rouen and Paris. Marseille is France's first, and Europe's third, seaport, followed by Le Havre, Dunkerque, Nantes and Bordeaux. The national carrier, Air France, is the world's third, and Europe's second largest airline. It has various subsidiaries, including Air-Inter which operates internally.

Industry

France is a major industrial nation. The iron and steel industry, formerly concentrated in the north and east near coal and iron reserves, has gravitated to the coast—at Dunkerque and Fos-sur-Mer—in order to take in imported fuel and ore. Of the various sectors using steel, the automobile industry, centred on Paris, is the most important. Throughout the world, one car in ten is French. The chemical industry is located in Paris and Lyon and on the coalfields; petro-chemicals are associated with the oil-refineries at Dunkerque and on the lower Seine in the north, and at Etang de Berre in the south. Textiles, including synthetic fibres, are important in Lyon, Paris and the Lille-Roubaix-Tourcoing conurbation. The tourist season is year-long: the most popular holiday areas are the Alps in winter, and the coasts in summer.

Agriculture

After the USSR, France is Europe's leading agricultural nation and is largely self-sufficient; agricultural products account for 20% of total exports. Wheat, grown extensively in the Paris basin, is the chief cereal followed by barley and maize. Two other leading crops are potatoes and sugar-beet, cultivated in Brittany and the north. Fruit and vegetables are grown in Brittany, the Rhone and Loire valleys, and near Paris. France is the world's leading wine-producer; major production areas are Languedoc, Burgundy, Bordeaux, Champagne, the Loire and Alsace. Livestock is important: cattle predominate in the north-west and north; sheep in the Massif Central and southern Alps. With over 300 varieties, France is the world's second largest cheese manufacturer. The fishing industry is concentrated in Brittany and the north-west; Boulogne is the main fishing port.

Corsica

Corsica (8,722 km²), situated in the Mediterranean 170 km south-east of Nice, is part of France. Except for the low-lying east coast, the island is mountainous, rising to 2,710 m in Monte Cinto. Tourists—about half a million a year—and sheep are basic to the economy. Cheese from sheep's milk accounts for 75% of exports. Fruit and vegetables are grown on the coastal plain and olive oil, citrus, almonds and wine are exported. 33% of the total population of 269,800 lives in Bastia—the largest town and chief port and in Ajaccio, the capital and Napoleon's birth-place. Industry is small-scale.

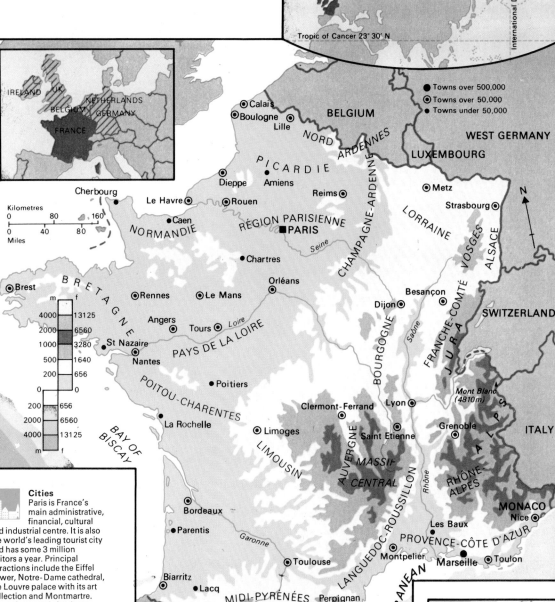

Great Britain

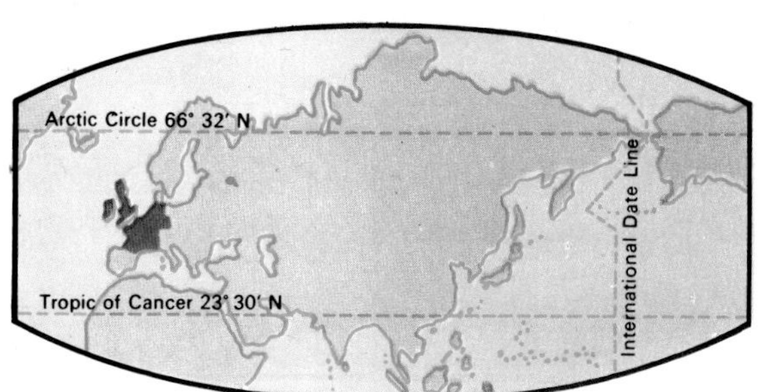

The United Kingdom

Area
(including Northern Ireland)
244,021 km²/94,217 sq miles
Location
49°10'—60°50' N;
1°45'E—8°10' W
Population
55,965,000 (1974)
Population density
229 per km²/594 per sq mile
Capital and largest city
London: 7,300,000 (1974)
Languages
English. Welsh and Gaelic used by minorities in Wales and Scotland respectively.
Major imports
fuels, machinery and transport equipment, foodstuffs, metals and ores, chemicals
Major exports
engineering products, chemicals, metals, foodstuffs, textiles
Currency
pound (£1 = 100 pence)
Gross National Product
176,400 million US dollars (1973)
Status
constitutional monarchy
Statistics refer to whole of UK. Text excludes N. Ireland.

Physical features

Great Britain, largest of the British Isles—a group of islands lying off northwest Europe—divides into highland and lowland areas. Lowland Britain, situated south and east of a line from the mouth of the river Tees to the mouth of the river Exe, consists of a series of chalk and limestone hills—such as the Cotswolds, Chilterns, North and South Downs—separated by broad clay valleys. Highland Britain, over 300m and lying to the north and west, comprises Scotland, the Lake District, Wales, the central upland known as the Pennines and the south-western peninsula of England. The highest point in the British Isles—Ben Nevis, 1,342 m—is in the Grampians in Scotland. Britain's longest river, the Severn, 354 km, rises in central Wales and flows in a wide arc to the Bristol Channel.

Climate

Britain has a mild, temperate climate. The changeable weather is largely determined by a series of depressions brought in from the Atlantic by the prevailing south-westerly winds. The average temperature in the coldest months, January and February, is 4°C, and in the warmest, July and August, 16°C. Rain, occurring throughout the year, averages 70 cm in the lowlands and 250 cm in highland areas; annual rainfall on Snowdon (1,085 m) and Ben Nevis is between 400 and 500 cm.

Islands

Most of the smaller islands round the British coast—such as the Isle of Wight, Scilly Isles, Orkneys and Shetlands—are part of the UK. There are two exceptions: the Isle of Man (588 km²; pop: 56,000) and the Channel Isles (194 km²; pop: 125,000) which are Crown dependencies. Manx is spoken in addition to English in the Isle of Man, while French is still the official language of Jersey, the biggest of the Channel Isles.

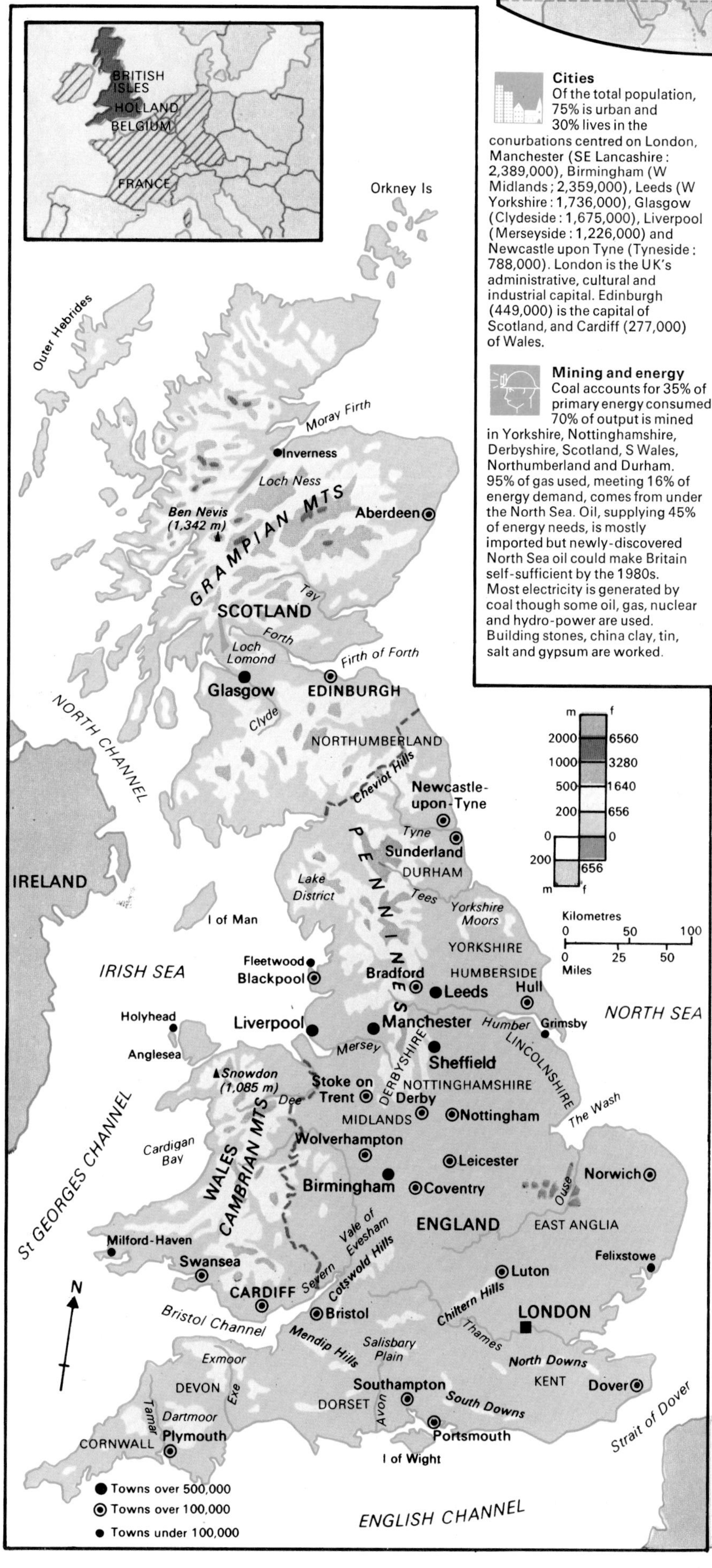

Cities

Of the total population, 75% is urban and 30% lives in the conurbations centred on London, Manchester (SE Lancashire: 2,389,000), Birmingham (W Midlands; 2,359,000), Leeds (W Yorkshire: 1,736,000), Glasgow (Clydeside: 1,675,000), Liverpool (Merseyside: 1,226,000) and Newcastle upon Tyne (Tyneside: 788,000). London is the UK's administrative, cultural and industrial capital. Edinburgh (449,000) is the capital of Scotland, and Cardiff (277,000) of Wales.

Mining and energy

Coal accounts for 35% of primary energy consumed; 70% of output is mined in Yorkshire, Nottinghamshire, Derbyshire, Scotland, S Wales, Northumberland and Durham. 95% of gas used, meeting 16% of energy demand, comes from under the North Sea. Oil, supplying 45% of energy needs, is mostly imported but newly-discovered North Sea oil could make Britain self-sufficient by the 1980s. Most electricity is generated by coal though some oil, gas, nuclear and hydro-power are used. Building stones, china clay, tin, salt and gypsum are worked.

Agriculture

British agriculture, employing 3% of the workforce, produces over half of domestic food requirements. 79% of land is used for agriculture and crops are grown on 38% of this area. Arable farming predominates in East Anglia, Kent, Lincolnshire, Humberside and the coastal lowlands of east Scotland. Main crops are wheat, barley, oats, potatoes and sugarbeet. Dairying is widespread but is most concentrated in southwest Scotland, western England and southwest Wales. Beef-cattle and sheep are kept in upland regions, while pigs are important in lowland areas. The chief fruit-growing regions are Kent and East Anglia. Apples make up 65% of the harvest.

Fishing and forests

Britain is almost self-sufficient in fish. 82% of the catch is white-fish—notably cod, haddock and plaice—taken in distant waters such as the W Atlantic and the Barents Sea, and in coastal areas. Herring, from Scottish waters, and shellfish are also important. 45% of fishing vessels come from Scotland. The main fishing ports are Grimsby, Hull, Aberdeen and Fleetwood. Forests cover less than 8% of Great Britain and production meets only 8% of demand.

Industry

Britain is highly industrialized: over 80% of exports are manufactured goods, 55% of the workforce is employed in industry and it ranks as the world's fifth steel-producing nation. Metallurgy and engineering employ 50% of the industrial workforce and account for over half total exports. The chemical industry supplies 13% of exports; expanding sectors include plastics, petrochemicals and pharmaceuticals. The textile industry provides 6% of exports; high-quality woollens and synthetic fibres are important. The food industry also accounts for 6% of exports: major items are whisky, confectionery and biscuits. Other leading industries include cement, rubber, glass, paper, leather and footwear. The chief manufacturing regions are London, the Midlands, Yorkshire, Humberside, NW and NE England Wales and central Scotland.

Transport

In Great Britain, 90% of passengers and 64% of freight travels by road. The 345,400 km road network includes some 2,000 km of motorways; a further 1,000 km are being built. There are 18,170 km of railways. Only 17% of the 4,000 km of navigable waterways are used commercially; Manchester is the chief inland port. The British merchant fleet is the world's third largest. London is the leading port followed by Southampton. Other major ports include Liverpool (exports), Dover (passengers), Milford-Haven (oil) and Felixstowe (containers). There are some 150 airports; Heathrow (London) is the world's busiest.

Ireland

Republic of Ireland (Eire)
Area
70,282 km²/27,136 sq miles
Location
51°27'—55°25' N
6°—10°30' W
Population
2,978,248 (1971)
Population density
42 per km²/110 per sq mile
Capital and largest city
Dublin: 680,000 (1972)
Languages
Irish and English
Major imports
machinery, foodstuffs, transport equipment, metals, chemicals, petroleum
Major exports
meat, live animals, dairy products, textiles and clothing, engineering goods, pharmaceuticals
Currency
pound (1 pound = 100 pence)
Gross National Product
6,740 million US dollars (1974)
Status
independent republic

The following text includes Northern Ireland (14,139 km²; pop: 1,547,000).

Physical features
Ireland, the second largest island in the British Isles, consists of a broad limestone plain ringed by coastal highlands. The central lowland, mostly under 100 m, is covered with glacial deposits of clay and sand, extensive bogs and numerous lakes. The most spectacular scenery lies in the southwest where a series of east-west sandstone ranges are separated by drowned valleys. The island's highest point, Carrantuohill, 1,040 m, towers over the lovely Killarney lakes. In the southeast, the rounded Wicklow mountains, rising to 926 m in Lugnaquilla, form the largest granite mass in the British Isles. Granite also predominates in the Mourne Mountains—which include N. Ireland's highest point: Slieve Donard, 852 m—and in the desolate western uplands. Of the many lakes, the biggest are Lough Neagh, 396 km², Lough Corrib, 168 km² and Lough Erne, 137 km².

Climate
Ireland, lying in the path of moisture-laden southwesterly winds and the warm waters of the Gulf Stream, has a mild wet climate. As the island is small, with no part more than 112 km from the sea, temperatures are uniform throughout the country. Average temperatures in January and February are between 4°C and 7°C, and in July and August, between 14°C and 16°C. Annual rainfall ranges from 150 cm in the western hills to 75 cm on the east coast.

Tourism
In the Republic, tourism is a leading industry. The eight million visitors who come to Ireland annually are attracted by the varied scenery—particularly in the southwest—the unspoilt countryside, the traffic-free roads and the relaxed way of life. In the 1960s and 70s tourism in Northern Ireland has been adversely affected by the political unrest.

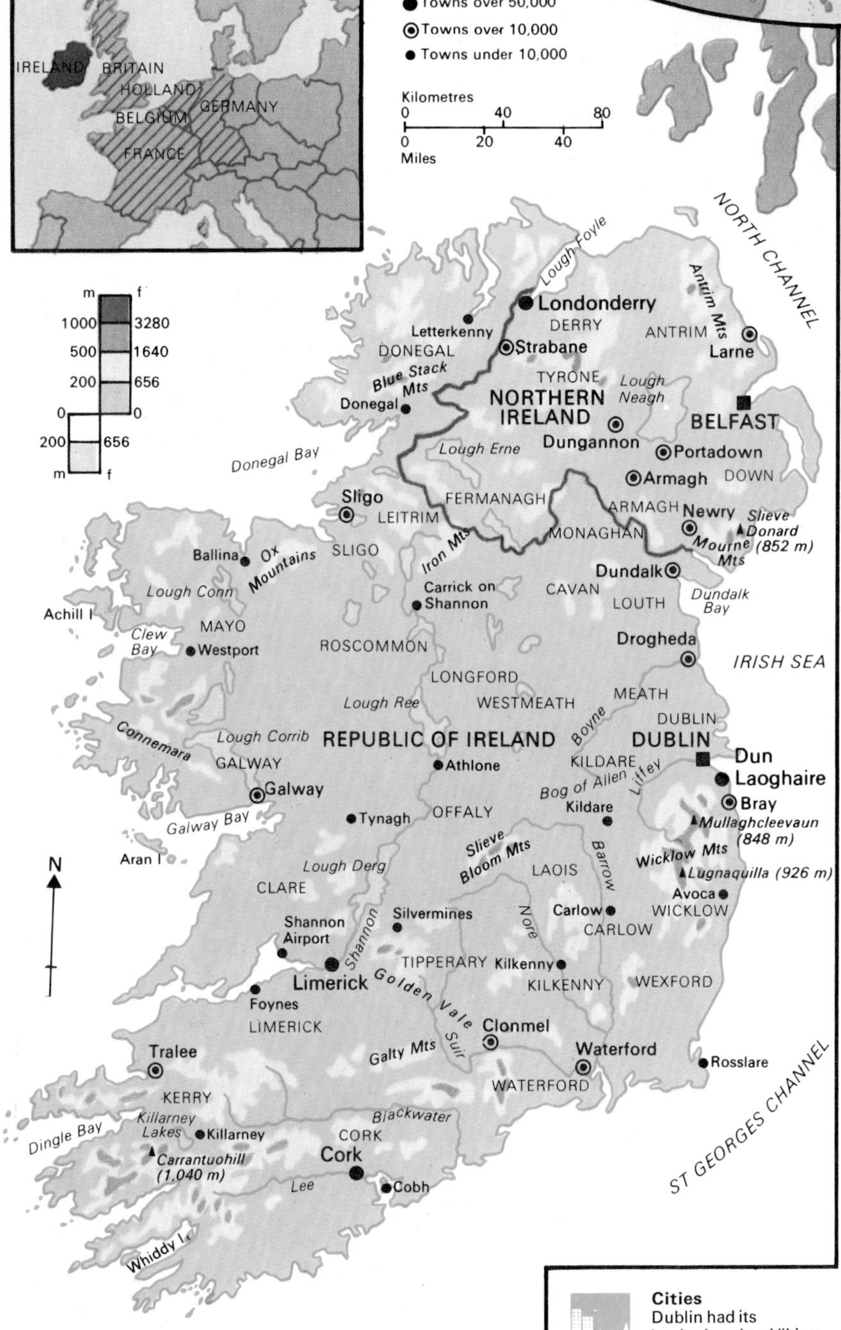

Transport
Throughout Ireland, people and goods travel mainly by road and most areas are served by buses and freight services. Road transport has developed at the expense of rail. The main line in the North runs from Londonderry via Belfast to the border and then to Dublin. In the South, there are rail links from Dublin to Sligo, Galway, Limerick, Tralee, Cork, Waterford and Rosslare. Major ports are Belfast Larne, Dublin, Cork, Dun Laoghaire, Rosslare, Waterford, Limerick, Foynes and Whiddy Island (oil). The Republic's airline, Aer Lingus, operates from international airports at Shannon, Dublin and Cork. Flights from Belfast also go to the UK.

Agriculture: arable
In Northern Ireland, crops like hay, barley, oats and potatoes are of minor importance and are mainly for the farmer's own use. In the Republic, only 7% of the land is used for crops, compared with 63% for livestock. Arable farming is concentrated in the southeast, particularly in County Wexford where oats, barley and wheat are grown. Some fodder crops, such as turnips, potatoes oats and barley, are produced in Counties Carlow, Kilkenny and Waterford: market gardening is important on the coastal plain near Bray. Sugar-beet is grown in the southwest and some fodder crops in the midlands. Productivity is hampered by the small size of farms.

Cities
Dublin had its beginnings in a Viking fortress built on high ground at the mouth of the River Liffey. The modern city owes its development to the growth of the port and trading activities in the 17th century. Today, the port and its outport of Dun Laoghaire are vital to Dublin's role as the country's leading commercial and industrial centre. Industries include food-processing, brewing, engineering, clothing and electrical goods. Cork, on the River Lee, originated as a seventh-century monastery. Now the Republic's second-largest city (134,000) and second port, its industries range from oil refining and chemicals to steel manufacture and flour-milling; trans-Atlantic trade is handled at the outport of Cobh. A third of N. Ireland's people live in the capital, Belfast (392,000), in the east.

Agriculture: livestock
Agriculture, employing 27% of the workforce and accounting for 45% of total exports, is vital to the Republic's economy. 80% of agricultural output consists of livestock and livestock products. Beef cattle are reared on the wet pastures in the midlands and along the fertile Nore, Barrow and Suir valleys in the southeast. Dairy farming predominates in the south and southwest, especially in the Golden Vale of Limerick and Tipperary. The milk is sent to co-operatives for cream, butter and cheese manufacture. Skimmed milk is returned to farms and fed to pigs. The main pig-farming areas are the southwest and southeast; there are bacon and ham-curing factories at Limerick and Cork. Sheep are grazed on the Wicklow mountains and in the west. In Northern Ireland livestock farming also dominates agriculture and accounts for 20% of total exports. Beef cattle are concentrated in Armagh and Co. Down; dairy farming is important in Fermanagh and parts of Antrim and Co. Down; sheep are grazed on the Mourne Mountains, the Antrim Hills and the highlands of Donegal.

Mining and energy
Ireland lacks mineral resources. In N. Ireland, some limestone, sand, gravel, basalt, chalk and clay are worked but the fuels and minerals needed for industry have to be imported. Electricity generating stations use coal and oil. The Republic has valuable deposits of lead, silver and zinc at Tynagh and Silvermines; copper, silver and mercury at Gortdrum; copper and pyrites at Avoca. Other minerals exploited include barytes, gypsum, marble, building stone and some low-quality coal. Peat, from the central plain and the western coast, is used as a domestic fuel and to fire seven generating plants producing 33% of the country's electricity. A further 33% is generated by coal, the remainder is hydro-electric.

Industry
In the Republic, food and drink manufacture is a leading industry. Creameries, flour-mills, beet-sugar refineries, distilleries, breweries and bacon factories all process local produce. Textile and light engineering are also important. With the aim of promoting industrial development, the Government provides financial incentives to help Irish industrialists expand and to attract overseas firms to Ireland. Many of the foreign factories—largely British, American and German—are on industrial estates in Galway, Waterford and at Shannon airport. N. Ireland's industry, concentrated in Belfast, is based on imported raw materials. The main industry is engineering, especially shipbuilding and aircraft manufacture. The chief shipbuilding firm, Harland and Wolff, has the world's largest shipbuilding berth. N. Ireland is also a major textile centre—traditionally famous for its linen produced since the 13th century.

Switzerland

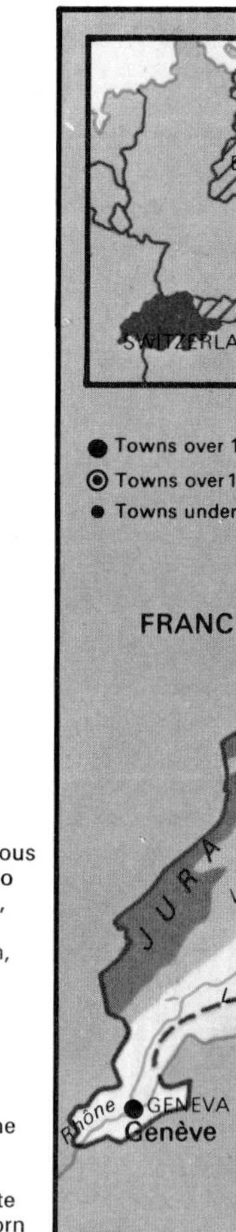

Area
41,287 km²/15,941 sq miles
Location
45°50′—47°54′ N ; 6°—10°30′ E
Population
6,462,500 (1974)
Population density
157 per km²/405 per sq mile
Capital
Bern : 284,737 (1974)
Largest city
Zürich : 719,324 (1974)
Languages
German, French, Italian, Romansch
Major imports
industrial raw materials, fuel, foodstuffs
Major exports
machinery, chemicals, watches, textiles, cheese, chocolate
Currency
franc (= 100 centimes/Rappen)
Gross National Product
46,970 million US dollars (1974)
Status
independent republic

Physical features

Landlocked, mountainous Switzerland divides into three regions : the Jura, the Alps and the plateau. The Jura mountains, rising to 1,800 m, stretch along the French border and consist of limestone ridges and deep forested valleys. The frontiers with Italy, Austria and Liechtenstein are formed by the Alps, comprising two northeast-southwest ranges separated by the Rhine and Rhone valleys. The southern mass contains Switzerland's highest peak, Monte Rosa (4,634 m) and the Matterhorn (4,476 m) ; the northern chain, the Bernese Oberland, includes the Finsteraarhorn (4,274 m), the Jungfrau (4,158 m) and the Eiger (3,970 m). The Alps act as a giant watershed : the Rhine flows to the North Sea, the Rhone to the Mediterranean ; the Ticino runs via the Po to the Adriatic while the Inn meanders eastward to the Danube and the Black Sea. Between the Jura and the Alps lies the Swiss plateau, a region of rolling hills stretching from Lake Geneva to Lake Constance. There are 1,484 lakes in Switzerland ; the biggest are Lakes Geneva and Constance.

Climate

Switzerland has a central European climate modified by altitude. Winter is cold with widespread and heavy snowfall ; January averages 0°C in Zürich, —6°C in Davos and 2°C in Lugano. Summer is wet and warm ; the average July temperature is 17°C in Zürich, 11°C in Davos and 21°C in Lugano. About one-seventh of the country is permanently under snow and ice.

Languages

The Swiss Confederation is a union of 22 cantons —miniature states, each with its own history, culture and dialects. These dialects are used locally ; nationally, there are four official languages. 65% of the population speaks German ; 18%, French ; 12%, Italian and less than 1%, Romansch. The remainder, mostly immigrant workers, belong to other language groups. French predominates in the west, Italian in Ticino, while the Romansch-speaking minority is located in Graubünder.

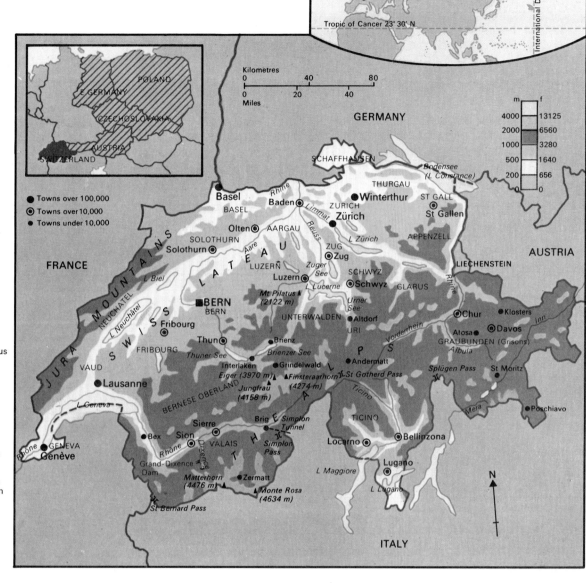

Mining and energy

Switzerland lacks minerals. Mining activity is limited to salt—from the Rhine valley above Basel and the Rhone valley near Bex—and to iron ore, worked in Gonzen and the Fricktal. Some peat, cut on the moors and former lake bottoms, is used locally for fuel. However, Switzerland does have one great natural asset : water. Several thousand hydro-power plants transform the energy of alpine torrents and rivers into electricity. There are 44 artificial lakes and the Grande-Dixence dam in Valais is the world's second highest (284 m). Water-power generates 90% of the country's electricity ; the rest is of thermal or nuclear origin. Yet electricity meets only 20% of Swiss energy requirements ; imported oil supplies the remainder.

Tourism

Switzerland is one of Europe's major tourist centres. Its attractions include the beautiful mountain and lake scenery, facilities for sports—especially mountaineering, walking and sailing, and thermal springs. It is equally popular with visitors in winter : as well as skiing, provision is made for skating, curling and ice-hockey.

Agriculture : livestock

A quarter of Switzerland consists of unproductive rocks, glaciers, rivers and lakes. A further 25% is forested, leaving just half the country for agriculture. 87% of this area is used for livestock. Dairy farming is important and is the basis of 3 major exports : cheese (Gruyère and Emmenthal), condensed milk and milk chocolate. In the Jura and Alps, cattle are still-fed in winter and grazed on mountain pastures in summer. There are also some sheep in mountain areas. Both cattle and pigs are kept on the plateau ; the pigs are fed on skimmed milk, a dairy by-product.

Agriculture : arable

Mixed farming predominates on the plateau—the main agricultural region. Crops include wheat, rye, barley, potatoes, sugar-beet and vegetables. Some fodder crops—hay and lucerne—are also grown in mountain valleys. Orchards on south-facing slopes in the valleys and the midlands yield apples, pears, cherries and plums. Fruit and fruit products, such as jam and pectin, are exported. There are vineyards on the south-facing slopes above Lake Geneva, Neuchatel, Biel and Zürich and in Graubünden and Ticino.

Forestry

Swiss forests, covering a quarter of the country, are located in the Jura and on the lower slopes of the Alps. The timber is used for fuel, chalet construction, furniture manufacture and for wood-carving. In the Alps, the forests also protect settlements from avalanches.

Industry

Almost all raw materials have to be imported, yet Swiss industry—specializing in quality goods for export—is highly developed and employs 50% of the workforce, compared with 7% engaged in agriculture. The 5 major industries are engineering, watches, textiles, chemicals and food-processing. 70% of Swiss engineering products, ranging from marine diesel engines to sewing machines, are exported. Watchmaking, dating from the 16th century, is traditionally located in the Jura. Textile manufacture is centred on the cantons of St Gall and Zürich. The chemical industry, based at Basel, accounts for 20% of total exports, chiefly drugs and dyes. With the exception of the building trade, the food industry has the largest labour force. Swiss cheese, chocolate, condensed milk and preserved foods are world-famous.

Transport

In spite of the many mountains, railways reach all parts. The 3,417 km-long network incorporates over 5,000 bridges and 612 tunnels—including Europe's longest, the Simplon : 19.8 km. In the mountains there are also some 400 cog railways, funiculars and aerial cableways. The 18,511 km road network is supplemented by 3,680 km of mountain post roads served by postal buses. Of the 25 major Alpine passes, the St Bernard, St Gotthard and Simplon are the most important. Apart from traffic on the Rhine, water transport is limited to lake steamers. There are 43 airfields and 4 international airports.

Cities

The 5 main cities—Zürich, Basel, Genève, Bern and Lausanne—house 1 in 4 of the population. Zürich, the home of Swiss banking, has textile and engineering industries. Basel (381,500) handles 50% of Swiss foreign trade through its port. Genève (321,100), famous for international meetings, is the seat of the International Red Cross and various UN agencies. The capital, Bern, is noted for engineering and watchmaking. Lausanne (226,700) is the centre of French-speaking Switzerland.

Austria

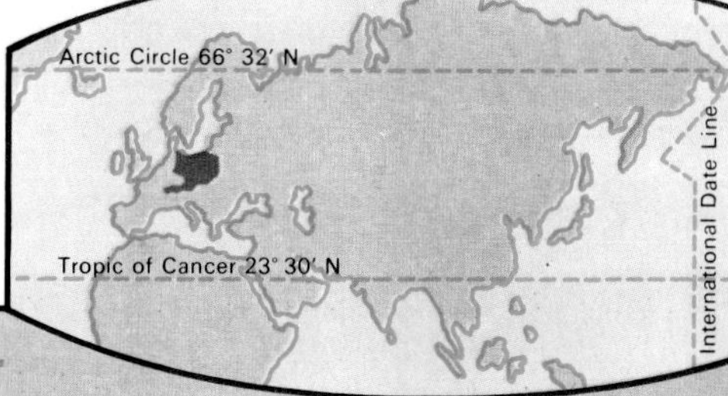

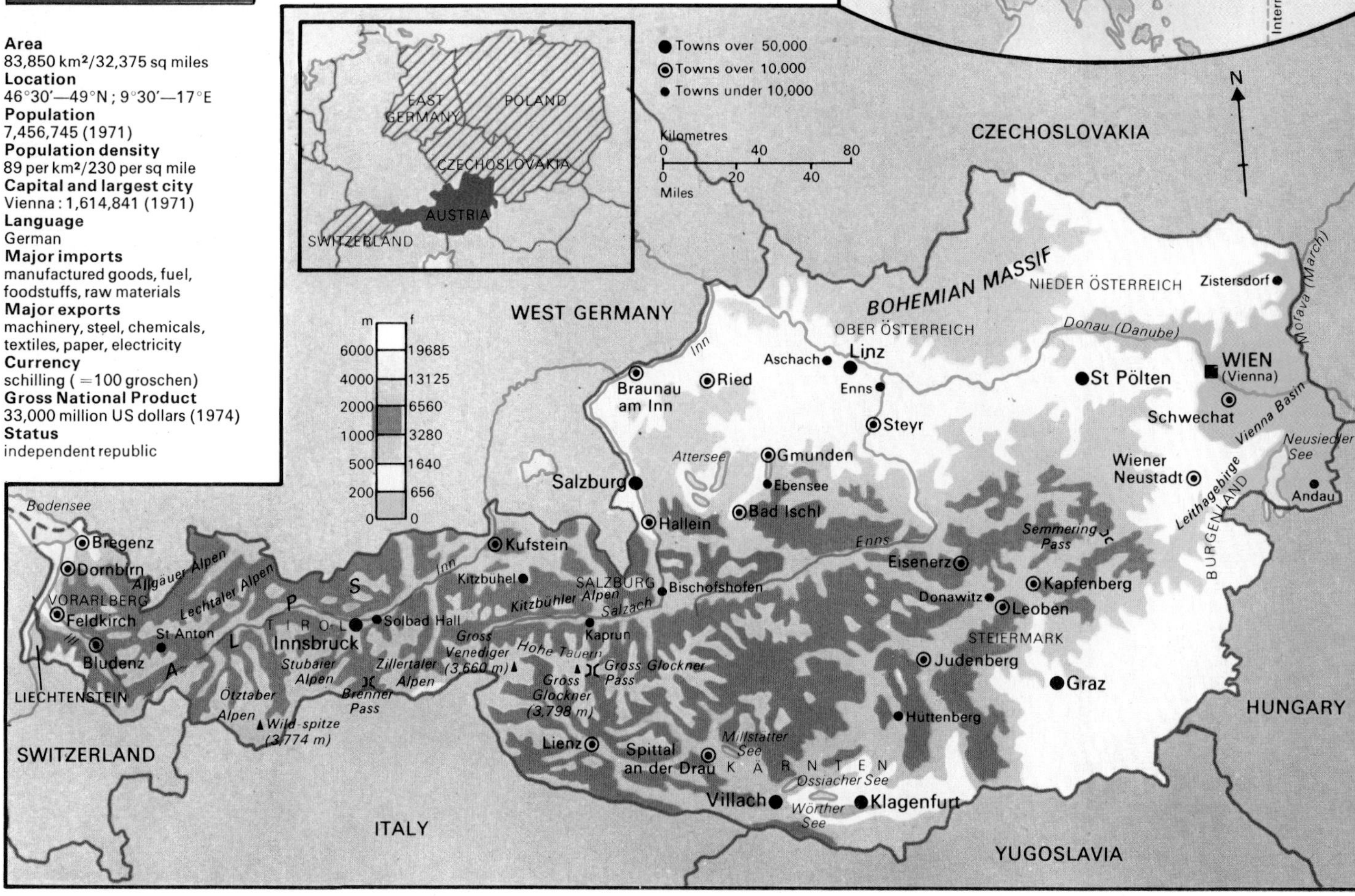

Area
83,850 km²/32,375 sq miles
Location
46°30′—49°N ; 9°30′—17°E
Population
7,456,745 (1971)
Population density
89 per km²/230 per sq mile
Capital and largest city
Vienna : 1,614,841 (1971)
Language
German
Major imports
manufactured goods, fuel, foodstuffs, raw materials
Major exports
machinery, steel, chemicals, textiles, paper, electricity
Currency
schilling (= 100 groschen)
Gross National Product
33,000 million US dollars (1974)
Status
independent republic

Physical features

Austria, one of Europe's most mountainous states, falls into three main regions. The largest, covering 70% of the country, consists of the Alps—two parallel ranges divided by the east-west sections of the Inn, Salzach and Enns river valleys. The more southerly range is the highest and contains Austria's tallest peak, Gross Glockner (3,798 m). North of the Alps are the Danube lands. The Danube or Donau, flows for 352 km across northern Austria, and its tributaries drain most of the country. From the German border to Linz, the river rushes through a narrow gorge, flanked by the rolling hills of the Alpine foreland to the south and by the forested Bohemian massif to the north. Below Linz, the valley broadens and enters the third region, the Vienna basin. The Leithagebirge mountains separate the Vienna basin from Burgenland, a steppe-like plain.

Climate

Austria has a central European climate with cold winters and hot summers moderated by altitude in many areas. In winter, snowfall is heavy and temperatures often remain below freezing, with a January average of —2°C in Salzburg and —1°C in Andau. The Vienna basin and Burgenland are the warmest parts in summer, Wien (Vienna) and Andau averaging 20°C in July and Salzburg 18°C. Rainfall, heaviest in summer, increases from east to west and coincides with rising heights—Andau receives 57 cm of rain a year, Salzburg 137 cm.

Agriculture

Although only 20% of the total land surface is used for arable farming and 20% for livestock, Austrian agriculture supplies 84% of the country's food needs. Cattle predominate in the Alps and Alpine foreland and dairy produce exported includes dried milk, butter and cheese. Arable farming is most important in the Vienna basin and Burgenland where the main crops are potatoes, sugarbeet, wheat, barley and maize. Stock-raising, dairying and pig-farming are also practised in these areas and beef and pork are exported. Orchards and vineyards are sited on south-facing terraces in the Leitha-gebirge and in the lower Donau valley. North of Wien, the Weinviertel (wine district) is famous for its vineyards. Arable farming extends up to 2,000 m above sea-level and in Alpine valleys some wheat, maize, fruit, vines and tobacco are grown.

Forestry

Forested areas, covering 38% of the country, largely correspond to the Alpine provinces, where conifers predominate, and to the Bohemian massif. The industry is most developed in the provinces of Steiermark and Karnten. Forest products include fuel, construction timber, pulp, matches resin and turpentine. Paper mills are located in the valleys and much of their output is exported. An important timber fair is held annually in Klagenfurt, capital of Karnten.

Mining

Austria's chief mineral resources are iron ore, graphite and oil. Opencast mines near Erzberg in Steiermark produce 75% of the iron ore output. The remainder is mined at Huttenberg in Karnten. Austria is a leading world producer of graphite and magnesite and is one of Europe's major oil-producing countries. Oilfields are located in Zistersdorf and between the rivers Inn and Enns in Ober Osterreich province. The refinery at Schwechat near Wien handles domestic output as well as imported oil pumped by pipeline from the Adriatic port of Trieste. Natural gas from the same fields is piped direct to factories and power stations. There is also some production of copper, lead, zinc, salt, bauxite and lignite.

Energy

One of Austria's greatest natural resources is water. Hydro-power plants, sited on the Donau and on fast-flowing Alpine rivers such as the Ill, Inn, Salzach and Enns, generate 80% of the country's electricity. The highest station, 2,036 m above sea-level, is at Kaprun in Salzburg province, while the 1,700,000 kW Aschach installation on the Donau, producing 10% of Austrian hydro-electricity, is the largest in Europe outside the USSR. Thermal stations are fired by coal, oil or natural gas. Electricity is exported via international power lines to neighbouring countries, particularly West Germany and Czechoslovakia.

Industry

The iron and steel and engineering industries account for 35% of industrial production. Steel manufacture, using Erzberg ore, is based on Donawitz, Judenburg and Kapfenberg and on Linz where ore is imported via the Donau. Steel is the basis of the construction industry, and of the engineering industry whose products range from turbines to bicycles. The second main industry, food-processing, includes dairy products, sugar, canned fruit, beer and confectionery. The chemical industry, centred on Lenzing (synthetic fibres), Linz (fertilizers) and Schwechat (petro-chemicals) is expanding. Textile manufacture is next in importance. Vorarlberg specializes in lace and cotton ; Wien and the Inn valley in wool. The traditional glass industry has developed to include optical instruments. Industrial goods make up 70% of total exports.

Tourism

In Austria, tourism contributes more to the gross national product than in any other European country. Tirol is the main holiday province both in summer and winter, St Anton, St Christoph and Kitzbuhel all being major skiing resorts. Salzburg, another Alpine province, ranks second in popularity, followed by Karnten which is noted for lakes such as the Worther See, the Ossiacher See and the Millstatter See. Wien is also a leading tourist centre.

Transport

Centrally situated, Austria has become a bridge for traffic between eastern and western Europe. Wien, in particular, is the focus of several major routes—to Germany via the upper Donau, to eastern Europe and the Black Sea via the lower Donau, to Poland and the Baltic via the Morava valley, and to Italy and the Adriatic via the Semmering Pass. The railways, stretching 5,891 km, are almost 50% electrified. The extensive road network covers 32,000 km, including some 600 km of motorways. The Donau provides a means of water transport, coal, coke and oil making up 65% of freight carried. Six airports—Wien, Salzburg, Innsbruck, Linz, Graz and Klagenfurt—serve the national airline, Austrian Airlines.

Cities

One Austrian in four lives in Wien, the country's economic centre. Main industries include engineering, food-processing, printing and clothing manufacture. Wien's magnificent past and its active tradition of music and theatre attract many foreign visitors. Austria's second largest city is the old cathedral and university town of Graz (248,500) where industry has been developed using Alpine hydro-power. Linz (202,874), dating from Roman times, is a leading industrial centre and major river port. Salzburg (128,845), Mozart's birthplace, and Innsbruck (115,197) are both tourist centres.

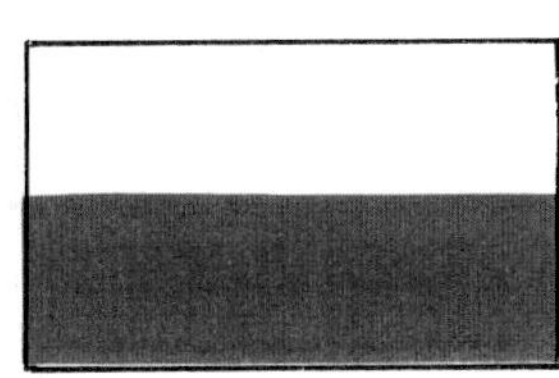

Poland

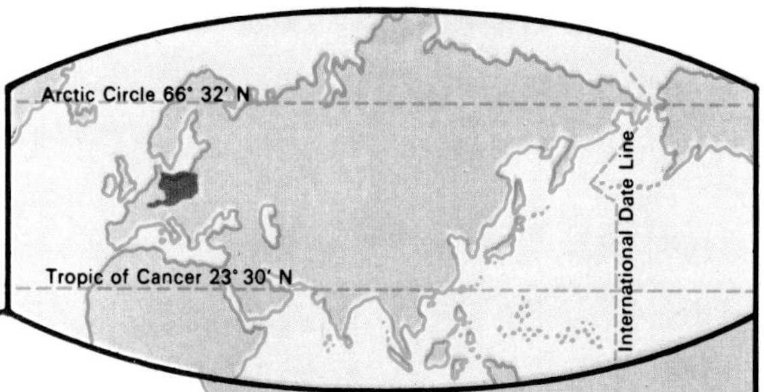

Arctic Circle 66° 32′ N
Tropic of Cancer 23° 30′ N
International Date Line

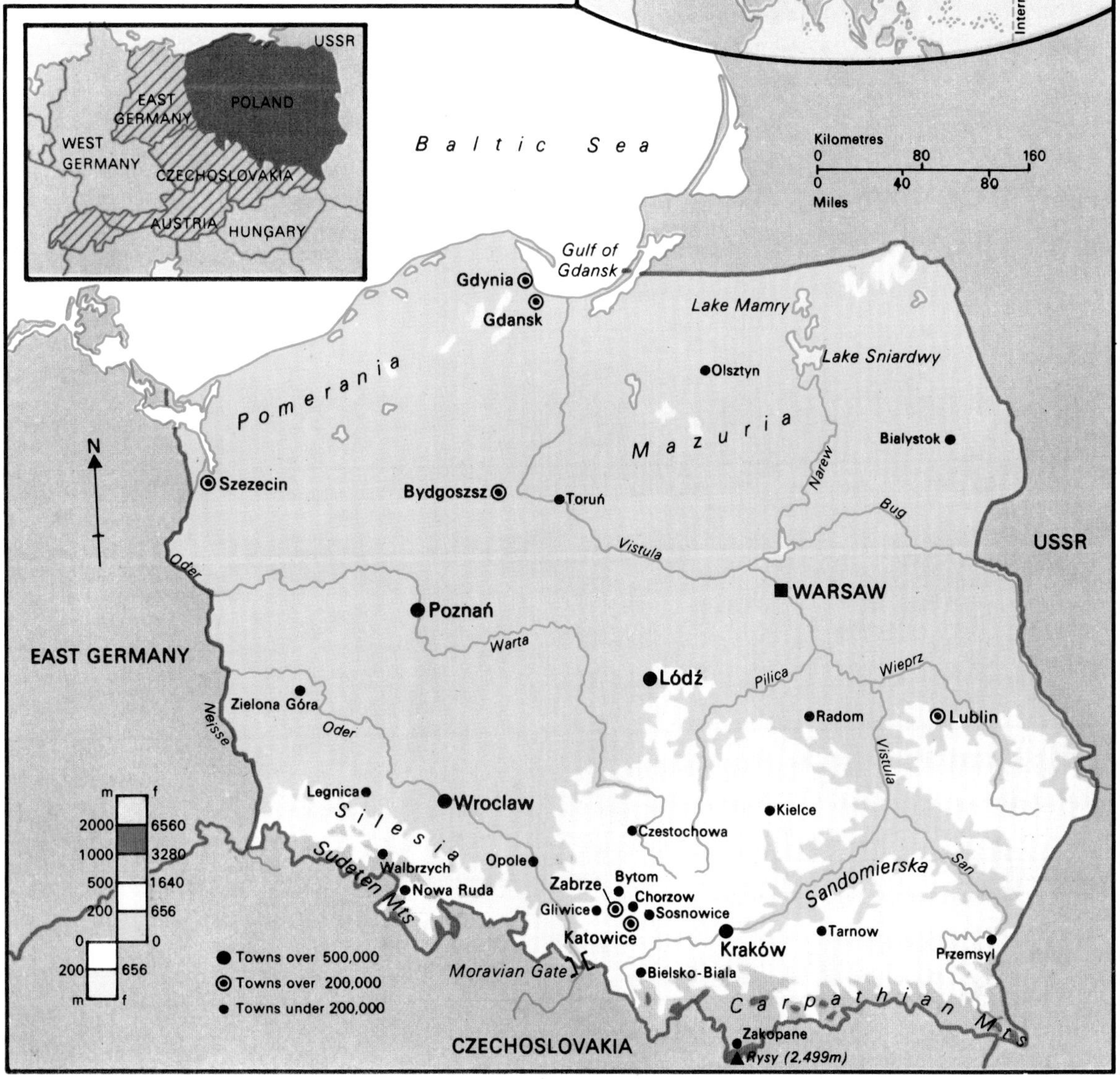

USSR
POLAND
EAST GERMANY
WEST GERMANY
CZECHOSLOVAKIA
AUSTRIA
HUNGARY

Baltic Sea
Kilometres 0 80 160
0 40 80 Miles
Gulf of Gdansk
Gdynia
Gdansk
Lake Mamry
Lake Sniardwy
Olsztyn
Pomerania
Mazuria
Bialystok
N
Szezecin
Bydgoszsz
Toruń
Narew
Bug
USSR
Vistula
Oder
WARSAW
Poznań
Warta
EAST GERMANY
Łódź
Pilica
Wieprz
Zielona Góra
Neisse
Oder
Radom
Lublin
Vistula
Legnica
Wroclaw
Silesia
Kielce
Czestochowa
Walbrzych
Opole
Sudeten Mts
Nowa Ruda
Zabrze
Bytom
Chorzow
Gliwice
Sosnowice
Katowice
Sandomierska
San
Tarnow
Kraków
Przemysl
Moravian Gate
Bielsko-Biala
Carpathian Mts
Zakopane
Rysy (2,499m)
CZECHOSLOVAKIA

m	f
2000	6560
1000	3280
500	1640
200	656
0	0
200	656

● Towns over 500,000
◉ Towns over 200,000
• Towns under 200,000

Area
312,677 km²/120,725 sq miles
Location
49°—54° N; 14°07′—26°08′ E
Population
33,846,000 (1974)
Population density
108 per km²/280 per sq mile
Capital and largest city
Warsaw: 1,410,000 (1974)
Language
Polish
Major imports
machinery, ores, petroleum, cereals, chemicals
Major exports
engineering products, coal, foodstuffs, textiles, sulphur
Currency
zloty (1 zloty = 100 groszy)
Gross National Product
50,800 million US dollars
Status
independent republic

Physical features

Poland is predominantly low-lying; 90% of the country is under 300 m. In the north, the Baltic coast areas consist of shallow, sandy beaches backed by dunes, marshes and lagoons. Further inland lies a belt of morainic hills, rising to over 300 m in places and containing thousands of lakes: the two largest are Sniardwy (114 km²) and Mamry (104 km²). Southwards, the lake zone gives way to the central plain. This gently undulating lowland has large areas of infertile glacial sands and, in the east, bogs. The plain is separated from the mountainous southern rim by uplands enclosing the loess-covered basins of Silesia and Sandomierska. Two major ranges, divided by the Moravian gate, line the Czech border: in the west the Sudetens, in the east the Carpathians, which include the Tatra mountains and Poland's highest peak, Rysy (2,499 m). The country is drained by the Vistula (961 km) and Oder (512 km) and their tributaries notably the Narew, Bug, San and Warta.

Climate

Poland's climate varies from oceanic to continental. The west and Baltic coast, affected by the proximity of the Atlantic and the warm Gulf Stream, are relatively mild. In contrast the east, subject to continental air masses, is more extreme, with colder winters and hotter summers. Temperatures in the south are modified by altitude. January averages 0°C in Gdansk and —5°C in Zakopane; respective July temperatures are 17°C and 15°C. Rain, falling mostly in summer, is heaviest in the mountains: Szczecin (Stettin) has 56 cm per year; Zakopane 112 cm. In the mountains, winter precipitation falls as snow.

Forestry

Forests, covering 27% of Poland, are located in the Sudetens. 82% of these are coniferous, with pine trees in the lowlands, spruce in the mountains. Forestry production consists of timber plus by-products such as resin, dye barks, Christmas trees, fruit (bilberries in particular), mushrooms, herbs and game. Both mushrooms (dried, salted or pickled) and bilberries are significant export items.

Mining

Poland is a major producer of coal, copper and sulphur. 90% of all Polish coal comes from Upper Silesia near the Moravian Gate; there is also some production at Walbrzych and Nowa Ruda. Half the total annual output of 150 million tonnes is exported. Lignite, mined in the Turoszow and Konin regions, is less important. Copper production is centred on Glowgow and Boleslawiec, while sulphur deposits, among the world's largest, are worked near Tarnobrzeg. Lead and zinc, from Bytom, Chrzanow and Olkusz, are also exported. Low quality iron ore, worked near Czestochowa and Kielce, meets only 10% of Polish industry's needs. Other minerals exploited include nickel, salt, kaolin and building stone. Oil production from fields east of Krakow is small, but natural gas reserves, mainly in the Lubaczow region, are extensive.

Energy

Thermal stations, using coal and lignite, generate over 90% of all Poland's electricity. A further 3% comes from hydro-electric plants in the Sudetens and Carpathians. Other stations are fired by oil or gas imported by pipeline from the USSR.

Agriculture

Agriculture, employing 25% of the workforce, covers two-thirds of Poland. Only 20% of farm-land is state-owned; the remainder is worked privately by peasants. In the lake belt and central plain, dairying and pig-farming are important and, despite infertile soils, some oats, rye, potatoes and sugar-beet are grown. In contrast, the loess-soils of Silesia and areas further east give high yields of wheat, barley, sugar-beet and potatoes: the potato crop is the world's second largest. Cattle and sheep graze on the lower slopes of the Sudetens and Carpathians. Fruit and vegetables, mainly cabbages, onions, apples, pears and plums, are grown near Warsaw. Farm exports include bacon, butter, eggs and sugar.

Fishing

The fishing industry, conducted by the state, by co-operatives and by private individuals, is based at Gydnia, Swinoujscie and Szczecin. Poland has developed a fleet of deep-sea trawlers and factory ships and 70% of fish landed—mainly cod, herring, sprat and haddock—comes from distant Atlantic waters. About 14% of the catch is exported.

Industry

Engineering, including electrical engineering, is Poland's leading industry, accounting for 30% of total industrial production. Products range from combine harvesters and computers to rolling-stock and radios. Ship-building is important, in particular fishing vessels such as factory trawlers. Steel production is centred on Upper Silesia but there are also plants at Szczecin, Warsaw and Czestochowa. Total steel output will almost double when the new mill at Katowice comes into operation. Food-processing is the second most important sector, providing 17% of industrial production. The chemical industry, based on domestic reserves of coal, salt, sulphur and natural gas, is expanding rapidly. Leading products are sulphuric acid, fertilizers and synthetic fibres, but plastic production is insufficient for domestic needs. Other major industries include textiles (cotton and woollen manufactures and clothing) wood and paper. The traditional home of Polish industry is the Upper Silesian coalfield, near Gliwice, Zabrze, Bytom, Sosnowiec, Katowice and neighbouring towns towns of Krakow and Opole.

Transport

Railways, with a total length of 26,717 km, carry 25% of Poland's freight traffic, mostly coal, coke, ores, metals and stone. Road transport, operating over 140,576 km, has recently been developed and is now more important than rail, accounting for two-thirds of both freight and passenger traffic. Navigable waterways, totalling 6,907 km, transport only 6% of freight, in particular sand, gravel and fertilizer. 60% of waterway traffic is on the Oder between Silesia and the Baltic. Szczecin is the leading sea-port, followed by Gdansk and Gydnia. The national airline, LOT, provides both overseas and domestic services.

Cities

Warsaw, originally a 13th-century trading centre on the Vistula, was totally devastated during the Second World War but has since been rebuilt in its former style. Lodz (787,000), the second largest city is the centre of Polish textile manufacture. The country's third town and former capital, Krakow (668,300) was founded in the 9th century, on a hill by the Vistula. Its proximity to the Silesian coalfield led to industrialization.

Czechoslovakia

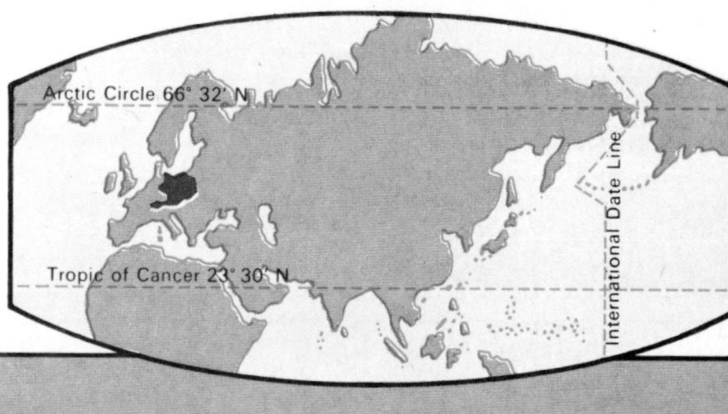

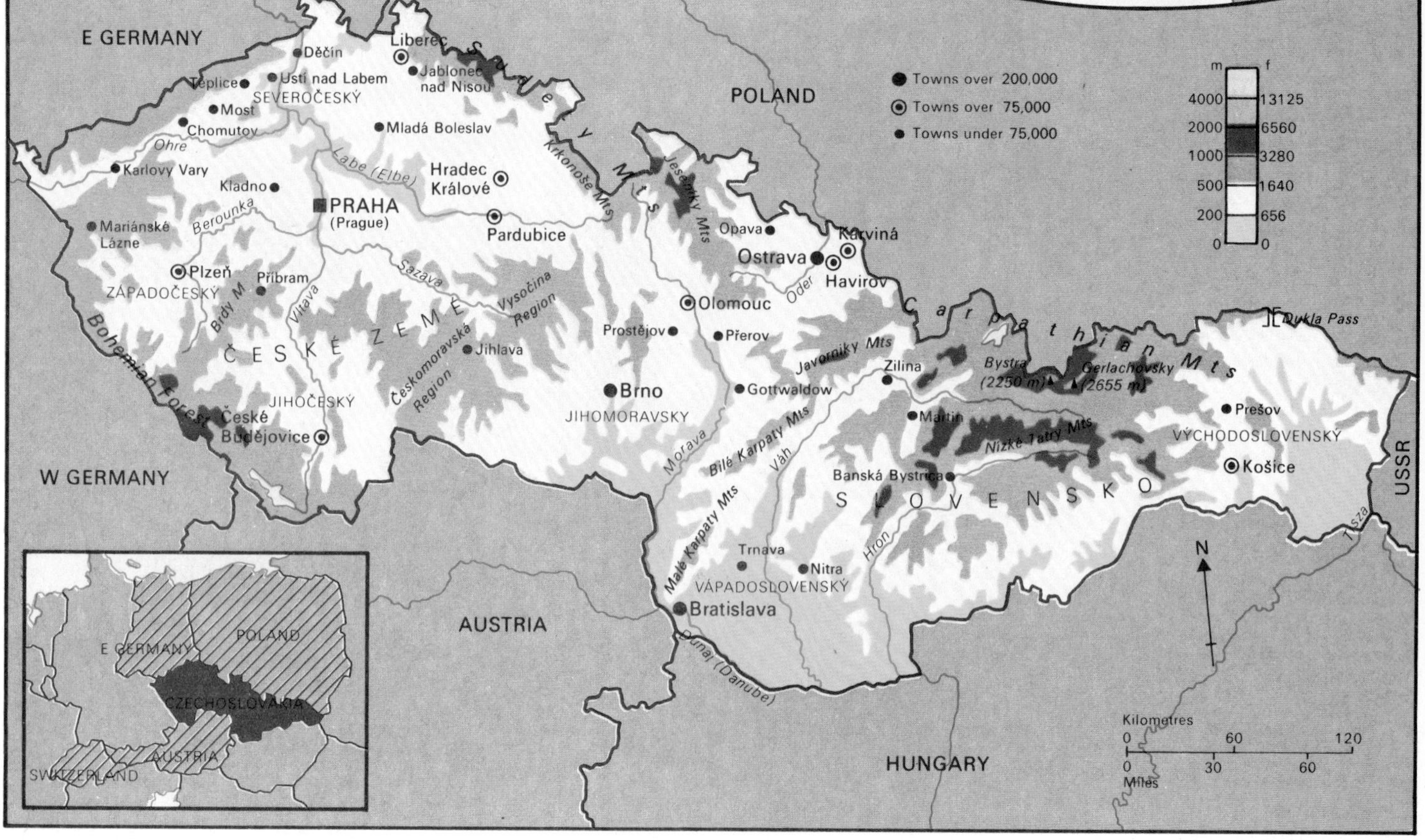

Area
127,877 km²/49,373 sq miles
Location
47°43'—51°03' N
12°05'—22°34' E
Population
14,634,747 (1974)
Population density
114 per km²/296 per sq mile
Capital and largest city
Prague: 1,091,449 (1974)
Languages
Czech, Slovak
Major imports
fuels, ores, metals, machinery, chemicals, cereals and livestock products
Major exports
machinery, sugar, transport equipment, forest products, textiles, shoes, glass
Currency
koruna (1 koruna = 100 hellers)
Gross National Product
38,665 million US dollars
Status
federal republic

Cities

Czechoslovakia is a federal republic made up of two nations: the Czech and the Slovak Socialist Republics. The federal capital, Prague, is also the Czech capital. Situated on the Vltava, Prague is the only city in Czechoslovakia with over a million inhabitants and is a leading industrial and commercial centre. Brno (353,866), also in the Czech Republic, is the country's second largest city with important engineering works and textile factories. The third largest town, Bratislava (325,035), a major river port on the Danube, is the Slovak capital. Karlovy Vary is world famous for its mineral waters.

Physical features

Czechoslovakia stretches 758 km along the highlands of central Europe. Bohemia, in the west, consists of a central basin ringed by mountains: Sudetens, Moravian Heights, Bohemian Forest, Ore Mountains and Giant Mountains. This mountainous rim is broken in the north-west by the Labe (Elbe) gorge with its sheer sandstone cliffs. Central Bohemia comprises rugged uplands in the south and, in the north, the Polabi plain, covered with fertile loess and alluvium. The region is drained by the Labe (396 km) and its tributaries: the Ohre and Vltava. Moravia corresponds to the undulating lowlands of the Morava (352 km) and Oder river valleys. Slovakia, in the east, is dominated by the Carpathians, which include the High Tatras and Czechoslovakia's highest peak: Gerlachovasky (2,655 m). Southwards, lower ranges give way to the Dunaj (Danube) plain. Slovakia is drained by tributaries of the Dunaj, notably the Vah (433 km).

Climate

Czechoslovakia has a central European climate. Summers are hot (20°C in July) and stormy; winters are cold and dry, but milder in the west due to moderating Atlantic winds. January averages 0°C in Prague, —3°C in Kosice. Rainfall, with a July maximum, varies according to altitude: lowlands receive 40-60 cm a year; highlands, up to 200 cm, including heavy snow in winter. Relief also modifies temperature: in the High Tatras, January temperatures fall to —40°C.

Forests

Woodland, mostly state-owned, accounts for 35% of the country. Spruce predominates in the Bohemian highlands and in the Carpathians; beech, pine and some oak cover central Slovakia and low hills in Bohemia and Moravia. As forests are in mountainous regions, the timber industry and associated manufacture benefit from local hydro-electric power. Products include lumber, cellulose, pulp, paper, matches, furniture and toys. Timber, paper, cellulose and matches are exported.

Agriculture

Farmland covers two-thirds of the country and 75% of this agricultural area is arable. In the most fertile regions—the alluvial Polabi plain, the Moravian lowland and the Danube plain—the main crops are wheat, barley, sugar-beet and potatoes with some maize, flax, hops, tobacco and hemp in southern Slovakia and in Moravia. Highland areas are less fertile and rye, oats and potatoes are the principal crops grown along mountain valleys and on lower slopes. In central Slovakia, south-facing slopes support orchards and vineyards. Dairy farming is important in lowland Moravia and Slovakia; beef cattle are reared in the Bohemian foothills while sheep-grazing predominates on the mountain pastures of Slovakia; pigs are kept in most lowland zones. Czechoslovak agriculture is almost totally socialized and state farms and co-operatives account for 86% of farmland and 70% of agricultural production.

Mining

Coal is Czechoslovakia's most important mineral asset. 85% of hard coal output comes from Ostrava-Karvina; smaller fields are sited at Kladno, Plzen, Trutnov and Rosice. Most brown coal and lignite is mined in north-west Bohemia at Chomutov and Sokolov. Reserves of other minerals are less significant. Iron ore is worked in central Slovakia and the Berounka valley; copper and manganese in central Slovakia; kaolin at Plzen and Karlovy Vary; glass sand at Jablonec. There is also some production of uranium, tin, antimony and building stone. Oil and natural gas is largely imported from the USSR but small amounts are obtained from the Hodonin field.

Transport

The 13,293 km rail network, centred on Prague and Bratislava, is vital to Czechoslovakia's transport system and carries most long-distance heavy freight such as coal, ores, building materials, cereals and sugar beet. So far, only 16% of lines are electrified. Since 1947, the road network has been substantially improved and now totals 73,400 km. Public bus services are important: some 6,000 routes over 234,000 km. There are 473 km of navigable rivers but winter ice and spring floods limit their use. The Labe (giving access to the North Sea), the Vltava and the Dunaj (leading to the Black Sea) account for most waterway traffic. CSA (Czechoslovak Airlines) operate international flights from Prague, while Brno, Bratislava, Olomouc and Kosice also have airports.

Energy

Over 95% of electricity is generated in thermal stations. Two-thirds of these are fired by brown coal and lignite. The remainder use oil and, to a lesser extent, natural gas; both fuels are imported via pipeline from the USSR: oil comes from the Vloga area, gas from Siberia. Hydro-electric installations on the Vltava and Vah produce under 5% of the country's electricity.

Industry

Czechoslovak industry is highly developed and is based on natural resources supplemented by imports of fuel and ores from the USSR and other Comecon countries. Engineering accounts for 25% of total industrial output and 50% of exports. Major steel plants and engineering works are located in Prague, Plzen, Ostrava and Kosice; Brno, Kladno and Chomutov are also engineering centres. Leading products range from rolling mills and locomotives to machine tools and looms. Food-processing comes next in importance and includes flour-milling, meat-canning, cheese and butter manufacture, sugar-refining and brewing; main products exported are ham, sausages, sugar and beer—Plzen (Pilsen) is the traditional brewing town. The expanding chemical industry, based on coal from the Chomutov and Ostrava fields, and on imported oil at Bratislava, produces fertilizers, sulphuric acid, synthetic fibres and plastics. Footwear production is important and the Bata shoe factories at Gottwaldov are the world's largest.

Hungary

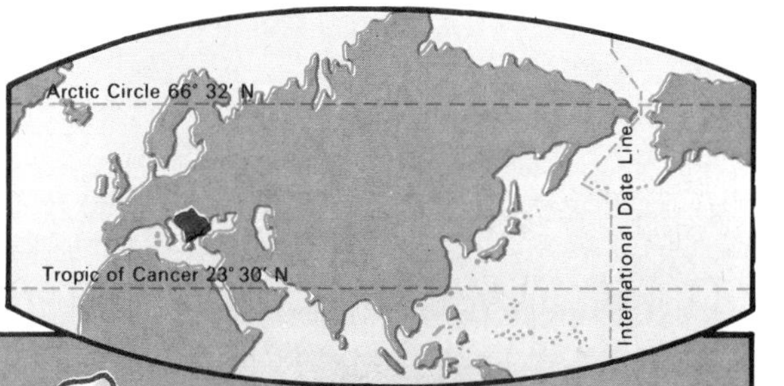

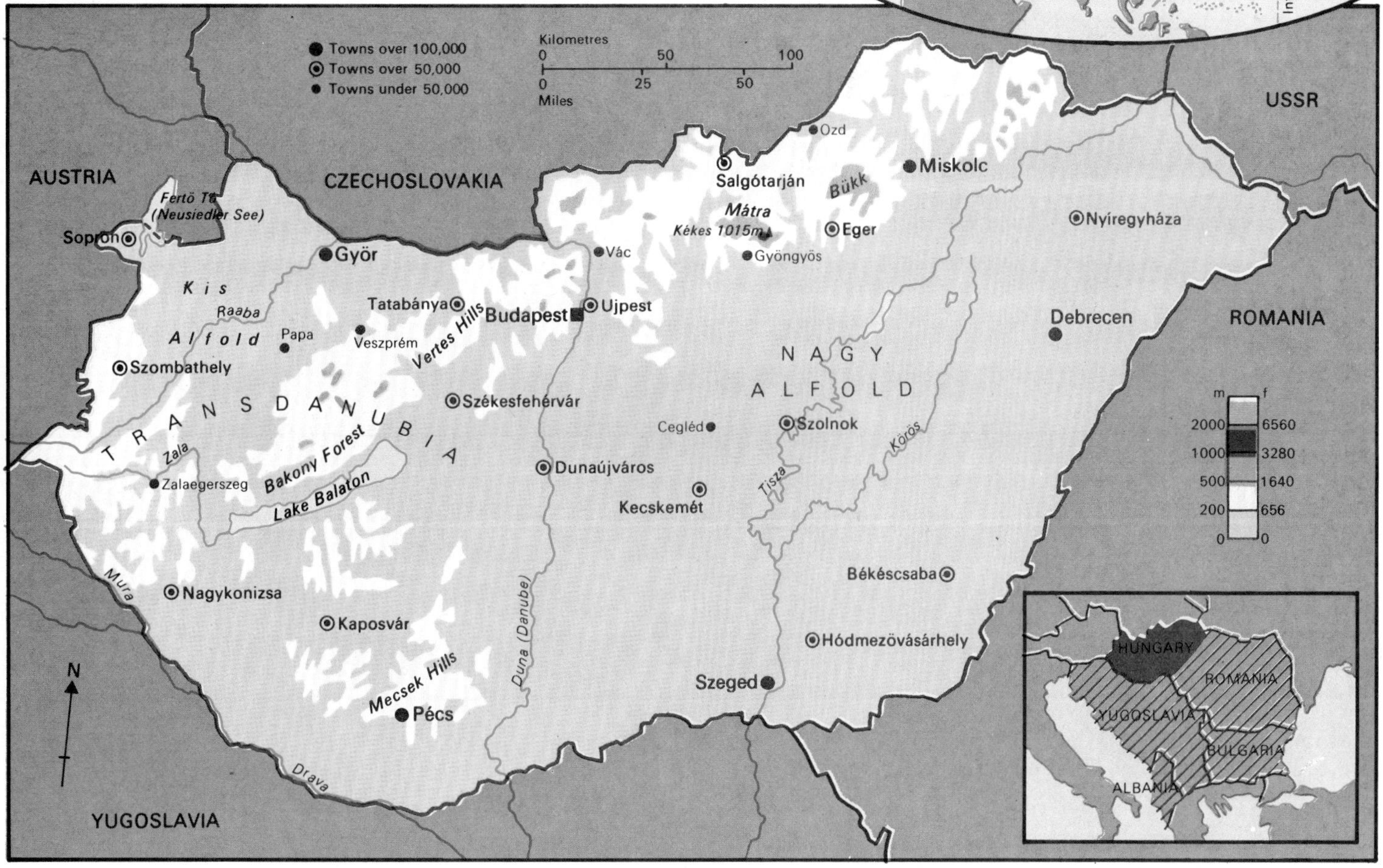

Area
93,032 km²/35,911 sq miles
Location
45°48′—48°40′ N
16°05′—22°55′ E
Population
10,510,000 (1975)
Population density
113 per km²/293 per sq mile
Capital and largest city
Budapest: 2,058,000 (1975)
Language
Hungarian
Major imports
fuels, iron ore, machinery, foodstuffs, cotton, timber
Major exports
vehicles, pharmaceuticals, bauxite, alumina, steel
Currency
forint (= 100 fillers)
Gross National Product
18,402 million US dollars
Status
independent republic

Mining

Hungary's underground resources are limited. Bauxite, mined in the Bakony Forest and Vertes Hills, is the most important mineral and the only one to be exported in significant quantities—mostly to the USSR and Poland. Iron ore output, centred on Miskolc, meets only 15% of requirements; imports come primarily from the USSR. Coal deposits consist mainly of low quality brown coal at Ozd, Miskolc, Salgotarjan, Tatabanya and Ajka. Supplies of hard coal, mined at Pecs, are supplemented by imports from other Comecon countries. Small amounts of oil are drilled near Zalaegerszeg, and some natural gas is produced east of the Tisza near Hortobagy and Bekescsaba.

Climate

Hungary's continental climate is moderated by Atlantic and Mediterranean influences: although summers are hot and winters cold, temperatures are seldom extreme. In Budapest, January averages −1°C and July 22°C. As the country is sheltered by the Carpathians and the Alps, rainfall is slight: Transdanubia and the northern hills receive only 30 cm of rain a year, while the Nagy Alfold has even less. The summer months are particularly arid. The Danube, frozen in winter, often floods in spring.

Physical features

The Danube, flowing 417 km from north to south across Hungary, divides the country roughly in half. East of the river lies the Nagy Alfold, the Great Plain, a flat, monotonous lowland less than 200 m above sea level. Loess covers most of the plain, but there are stretches of infertile sand and, in the river basins, of marsh-land. The Nagy Alfold is drained by the Tisza (579 km) and its tributaries. To the north, the Great Plain is bordered by the Carpathian foothills which contain Hungary's highest point, Kekes (1,015 m). The landscape west of the Danube (Transdanubia) is more varied. In the north-west is the flat, and sometimes, swampy Kis (Little) Alfold. Central and southern Transdanubia consist of rolling upland broken by the Bakony and Mecsek highlands, both rising to over 700 m. These two ranges are separated by Europe's largest natural lake, Balaton (596 km²).

Agriculture

Three-quarters of Hungary is agricultural land and 65% of this area is used for arable farming. Maize is the chief crop and is grown extensively in the Nagy Alfold. Other crops on the Great Plain include wheat, sugar-beet, sunflowers, rye (on sandy stretches) and rice in the irrigated valleys of the Tisza and Koros. Rye, oats, potatoes and sugar-beet predominate in lowland Transdanubia. Sandy soils between the Danube and Tisza and in the north-east favour fruit-growing. Vineyards near Pecs, Lake Balaton, Eger and Tokaj produce world-famous wines. There are some 8 million pigs, mostly swill-fed, and over 40 million hens. The 2 million cattle are largely stall-fed but there is some grazing for both sheep and cattle on infertile grasslands in the Nagy Alfold and on upland pastures in Transdanubia. State and collective farms account for 95% of agricultural land.

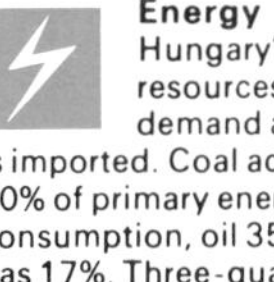

Energy

Hungary's energy resources do not meet demand and 42% of fuel is imported. Coal accounts for 40% of primary energy consumption, oil 35% and natural gas 17%. Three-quarters of the country's oil needs are imported via pipeline from the USSR; another pipeline brings gas from Romania. Electricity is largely generated in thermal stations but there is a major hydro-power plant near Vac. Production does not meet internal needs so 30% of electricity used is imported, mainly from the USSR.

Forestry

Much of Hungary's woodland has been cleared but 17% of the country is still tree-covered. The forests, located on the upper slopes of the Transdanubian and northern hills, consist mainly of oak and beech. Timber production does not meet the requirements of the construction, furniture and paper industries and substantial imports, especially of softwoods, are necessary.

Industry

Industry, employing 36% of the work-force, accounts for 87% of exports. Iron and steel production relies on ore and coke imports from the USSR; major plants are located at Miskolc, Ozd and Dunaujvaros. Hungary's metallurgical industry also includes aluminium: bauxite is exported to the USSR and Poland for smelting and aluminium ingots are then imported; Szekesfehervar is the main aluminium centre. The Ikarus bus factory in Budapest—Europe's largest—makes 10,000 buses a year, 80% of them for export. Other engineering products include diesel engines, TV sets and machine tools. In the last 15 years Hungary's chemical industry has grown rapidly and produces fertilizers, pesticides, plastic, pharmaceuticals, and synthetic fibres. Textile manufacture is also expanding; cotton, wool and silk fabrics, clothing and, in particular, shoes, are exported. The food industry processes domestic produce and exports salami, canned fruit and vegetables, wine and jam.

Transport

Budapest is the focal point of Hungary's transport system and both road (29,700 km) and rail (8,600 km) networks radiate from the capital to all parts of the country. Lorries and buses are gaining ground at the expense of trains: 55% of goods and passengers travel by road compared with 40% by rail. Although the country has two major rivers, the Danube and Tisza, water transport is insignificant. The national airline, Malev, operates international flights from Ferihegy (Budapest) airport; domestic services were discontinued in 1969.

Cities

Just over a hundred years ago the capital was still two separate towns—Buda, lying among the hills on the west bank of the Danube, and Pest, built on the east bank lowland. Today, eight bridges link the two parts of the city. Budapest is Hungary's cultural, commercial and industrial centre, having 70% of the country's factories and accounting for 40% of industrial output. Other Hungarian cities are all much smaller than the capital. Miskolc (190,800), the second largest town, is heavily industrialized; Debrecen (180,000), in the Nagy Alfold, is a cultural centre with some manufacturing; in spite of its rapid industrialization Pecs (159,000) has retained its historic character; Szeged (165,000), a cultural and commercial centre on the Tisza, is noted for its paprika.

Yugoslavia

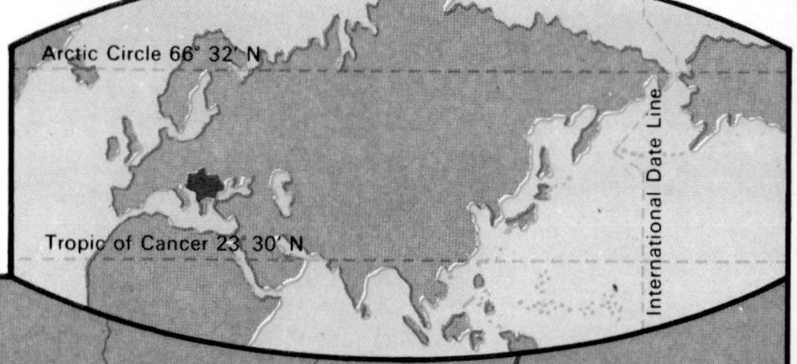

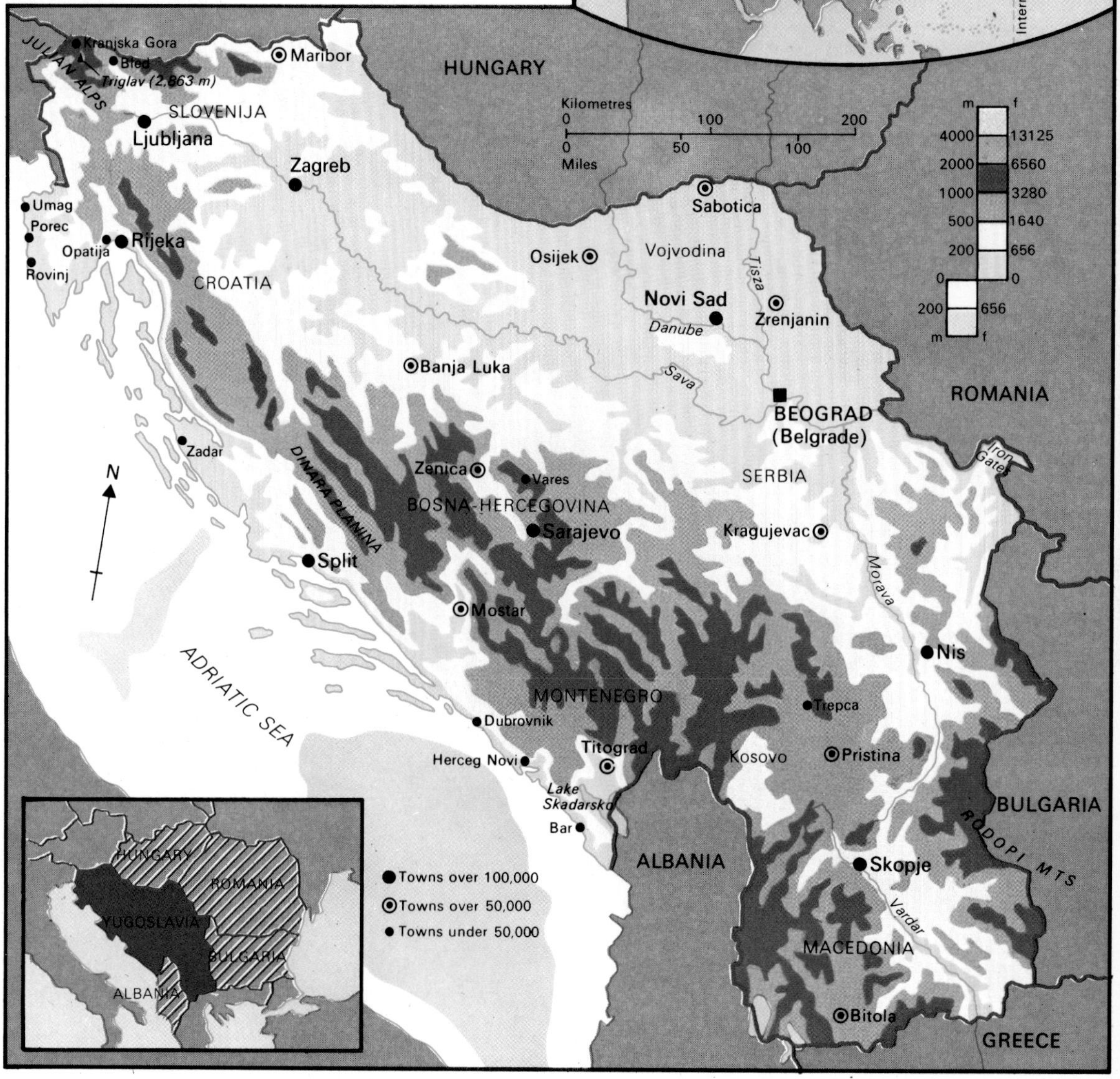

Area
255,804 km²/98,725 sq miles
Location
40 51′—46 53′ N
13 23′—23 02′ E
Population
21,322,000 (1975 estimate)
Population density
83 per km²/216 per sq mile
Capital and largest city
Belgrade: 764,000 (1971)
Languages
Serbo-Croatian, Macedonian
Slovenian
Major imports
petroleum, coal, fertilizers, iron and steel
Major exports
machinery, vehicles, electrical goods, ships, minerals, metal products, timber, food
Currency
dinar (1 dinar = 100 paras)
Gross National Product
13,400 million US dollars (1974)
Status
federal republic

Peoples
Yugoslavia is composed of 6 republics: Bosna-Hercegovina, Montenegro (Crna Gora), Croatia (Hrvatska), Macedonia (Makedonija), Slovenija and Serbia (Srbija: containing the 2 autonomous provinces of Vojvodina and Kosovo). It has the most diverse population in Europe outside the USSR. There are 5 major nationalities, all Slavs: Serbs, Croats, Slovenes, Madeconians and Montenegrins. In addition, there are important Albanian and Hungarian communities and some 15 other minority groups. Serbo-Croat is the most widely used language, but has equal status with Macedonian and Slovenian, which together involve 2 alphabets: Latin and Cyrillic.

Physical features
Mountains, covering 75% of Yugoslavia, stretch from the extreme north-west to the southeast of the country. The Julian Alps, with steep ridges and deep valleys, occupy the northern area; they rise to 2,863 m in Triglav, Yugoslavia's highest peak. A series of parallel ridges, the Dinaric range (Dinara Planina), extends south-eastwards to Lake Skadarsko. Forest covers the northern Dinarics, but further south barren limestone plateaus, drained by underground rivers, predominate. A narrow lowland strip separates these highlands from the island-fringed Adriatic coast. In the southeast, the Rodopi massif extends from Bulgaria into Makedonija and Serbija. A depression, drained by the Morava and Vardar, lies between the Rodopi and Dinarics. North-eastwards, the Dinarics give way to the plains of eastern Slovenija, Croatia and Vojvodina.

Climate
Yugoslavia has 3 climatic regions. The coast has a typical Mediterranean climate with hot drysummers (24°C) and warm, wet winters (7°C); annual rainfall averages 75cm. In the mountains, summers are cool and short, winters, long and cold with heavy snow; precipitation ranges from 200-500 cm. A continental climate prevails in the northeast with January and July averages of —1°C and 27°C and 80 cm of rain.

Agriculture
Agriculture, employing 49% of the population, accounts for 20% of overall exports. Farmland covers half the total area and is largely concentrated on the low-lands of the Danube (Dunav) and its tributaries. Maize and wheat are the main cereals and Yugoslavia is self-sufficient in grains. Industrial crops include hemp, sugar-beet, potatoes and sunflowers; tobacco is important in Makedonija. Orchards and vineyards are located on the foothills and along the coast; tree crops include apples, plums, olives, figs and walnuts. Livestock is kept in highland areas and Kosovo. Meat, fruit, wine and tobacco are exported. Only 20% of cultivated land is socialized; the remainder (in units of 10 ha or less) is held by peasant farmers.

Forestry
A third of Yugoslavia is wooded. 85% of the forests are deciduous with beech and oak predominating. Conifers, mainly fir, grow on the higher slopes. The timber-processing industry is most developed in Slovenija, Bosna, Croatia and Makedonija. Sawn timber, fuel, veneer, pulp and cellulose are all exported.

Mining
Yugoslavia has extensive mineral resources and is a leading world exporter of lead, bauxite and copper. Antimony, chrome, mercury and zinc are also exported in significant quantities. Trepca (Kosovo) is the main lead-zinc centre; copper is mined chiefly at Bar (Srbija); bauxite is exploited in the southern Dinarics. The Dinarics also have deposits of salt, lead, zinc, barite, asbestos, copper, nickel and chrome. The principal iron ore mines are in western Makedonija and at Vares and Ljubija in Bosna. Coal comes from Bosna and Srbija; oil and natural gas from Vojvodina.

Cities
Beograd stands at the confluence of the Danube and Sava. It is a major route centre and handles 50% of Yugoslav foreign trade; the rivers Danube, Sava and Morava provide access to the Black Sea, Adriatic and Aegean. With engineering, chemical and textile works, Beograd accounts for 10% of the country's industrial output. Yugoslavia's main industrial centre and second largest city is Zagreb (566,000). Zagreb is the capital of Croatia.

Energy
Many rivers in the Julian Alps, the Dinarics and the Rodopi have been harnessed and hydro-power supplies 60% of Yugoslav electricity. There is also a major installation, part Romanian, at the Iron Gates gorge on the Danube. Thermal stations are sited near lignite deposits in Slovenija, Bosna and Srbija. The country's first nuclear plant is under construction in Slovenija.

Industry
Yugoslavia is one of Europe's least industrialised states and development is based on domestic resources: minerals, agricultural produce and timber. Industry is invariably located near the materials used: there are sugar refineries, breweries and canneries in Vojvodina, copper works at Bor, cigarette factories in Makedonija, iron and steel mills at Skopje and near Sarajevo, lead and zinc foundries in Kosovo and aluminium plants at Mostar and Titograd. Textile wood-working, engineering (industrial and agricultural machinery, motor vehicles, machine tools), electrical and chemical industries are also important.

Transport
The road and rail networks are most developed in the north-west, but measures have been taken to improve facilities in the south and south-west. These improvements include the Beograd-Bar railway and the Adriatic highway from Rijeka to Skopje. There are almost 2,000 km of navigable waterways; the most important are the Danube, Sava and Tisza. The main seaports are Dubrovnik, Split, Rijeka, Zadar and Bar; ferries link the mainland to the Adriatic islands. There are 13 international airports; the JAT national airline operates both domestic and overseas services.

Tourism
60% of the 6 million foreign tourists who visit Yugoslavia each year stay in Croatia which contains the main Adriatic resort such as Herceg Novi, Dubrovnik, Opatija, Porec, Rovinj and Umag. Tourism is also being developed in inland Yugoslavia. Many mineral spring spas have been established in the mountains of Slovenija and northern Croatia. Mountain zones also offer winter sports; ski centres include Bled, Kranjska Gora and Jahorina.

Romania

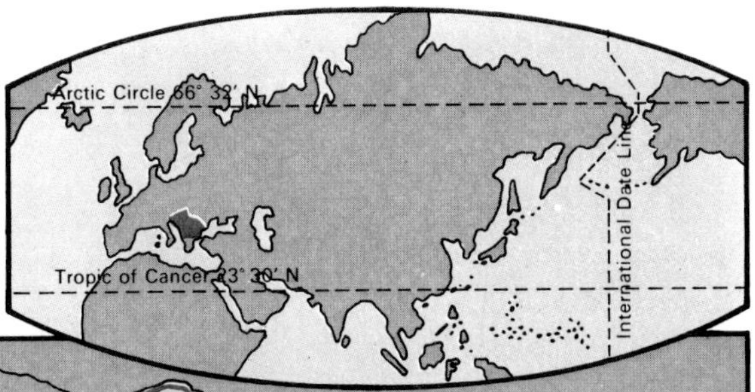

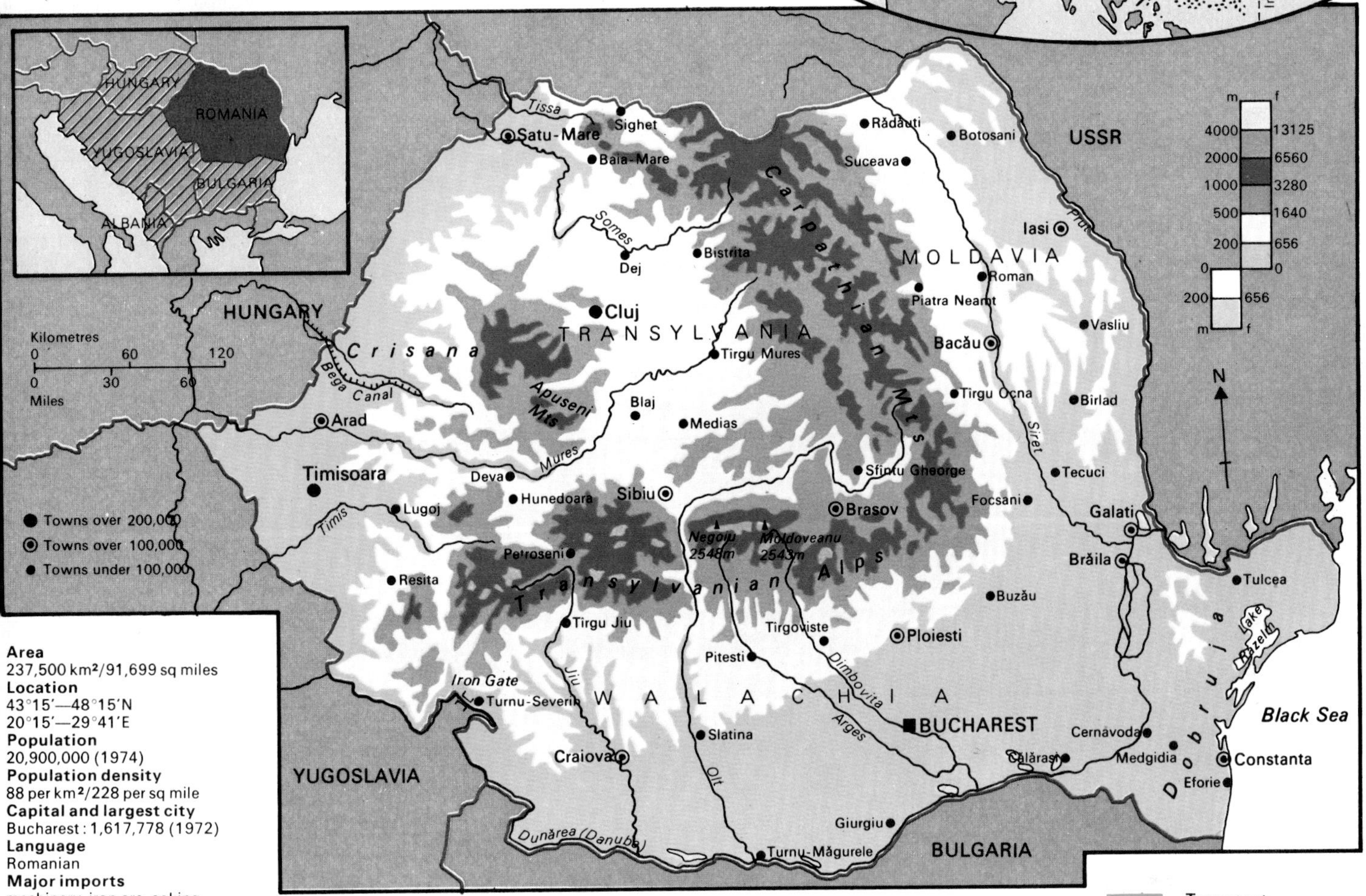

Area
237,500 km²/91,699 sq miles
Location
43°15'—48°15'N
20°15'—29°41'E
Population
20,900,000 (1974)
Population density
88 per km²/228 per sq mile
Capital and largest city
Bucharest: 1,617,778 (1972)
Language
Romanian
Major imports
machinery, iron ore, coking coal, metals, vehicles
Major exports
engineering products, oil, foodstuffs, chemicals
Currency
leu (1 leu = 100 bani)
Gross National Product
16,720 million US dollars
Status
independent republic

Mining and Energy

Romania's leading mineral resource is oil: the annual output of 14 million tonnes is the highest in Europe outside the USSR. The chief oilfields are Ploiesti, Bacau, Pitesti, Craiova and Tirgu-Jiu. Romania also ranks as the world's fifth producer of natural gas, with production mainly centred on the Cluj-Tirgu-Mures area. Although there is a lack of high-grade coal, there are major deposits of lignite near Rovinari, Motru and Oradea and low-grade coal at Petroseni. Output of iron ore, mined in the western Carpathians, does not meet industrial requirements. However, there are adequate reserves of other minerals: the western Carpathians, notably the Apuseni mountains, are rich in copper, lead, zinc, chromium, gold, silver, bauxite and mercury. Salt is worked near Ploiesti and Turda. Thermal stations, fired by lignite, oil and gas, account for 80% of electricity. Hydro-power is being developed: the most important installation, half-owned by Yugoslavia, is at the Iron Gates gorge. A nuclear station under construction uses uranium from the Apuseni range.

Physical features

At the heart of Romania lies the Transylvanian Basin, a hilly tableland some 400 to 500 m high. This is enclosed by the Carpathians which are greatest in the south, where the Transylvanian Alps rise to over 2,000 m and include Romania's highest peak: Negoiu (2,548 m). The country's major lowland is in Walachia and corresponds to the broad, loess-covered Danube valley. The lowlands in the extreme west are also loess-covered; in contrast Moldavia in the east and Dobruja in the south-east are both rock plateaus. Romania's rivers—such as the Somes, Mures, Jiu, Olt, Arges, Dimbovita, Siret and Prut—rise in the Carpathians and drain directly or indirectly into the Danube. The Danube enters the Black Sea via three channels which enclose Europe's largest delta, a marshy area covering over 3,750 km².

Climate

Romania has a central European climate with a mean annual temperature of 11°C in the south and 8°C in the north. In the highlands, snow lasts for up to 3 months. The eastern plain, exposed to north-easterly winds from Russia, is subject to severe cold in winter and burning heat in summer: Bucharest averages —5°C in January and 24°C in July. Rainfall decreases from west to east and is heaviest in the mountains: the Transylvanian Alps have about 130 cm annually but Dobruja has less than 40 cm.

Agriculture

70% of Romania is used for agriculture and a third of this area is arable land. Wheat and maize are the chief cereals and are grown in the Transylvanian Basin, Walachia, the western lowlands and Moldavia. Other crops include sunflowers and sugar-beet in Walachia and the west; barley, oats and potatoes in the Transylvanian Basin, hemp near Oradea and tobacco in Walachia. Terraces in the Carpathian foothills support orchards and vineyards. Moldavia is also a major wine-producing area. There is intensive market gardening near large cities such as Bucharest and Timisoara. Livestock is reared in the Carpathians and Dobruja and on the Danube marshlands. Crop production has been increased by drainage in the Danube lands and by irrigation in the south-east. Agriculture is 90% collectivized.

Forestry and fishing

Forests, covering 27% of the country, consist mainly of beech, spruce and fir. Commercial exploitation is centred on the Carpathians and major processing plants (producing timber, plywood and furniture) are sited at Blaj, Pitesti, Dej, Tirgu-Jiu, Oradea, Caransebes and at the ports of Braila and Constanta. Fish is an important food source: trout predominate in mountain streams, carp in larger rivers. Sturgeon are caught in the Danube delta and caviar (from the roe or eggs) forms a valuable export.

Industry

Romania is the most industrialized country in South-East Europe. The iron and steel industry is well established: some plants, like those at Resita and Hunedoara, use domestic ore and coal, while others, on the lower Danube, rely on Russian imports. 60% of steel produced comes from Romania's biggest iron and steel combine at Galati. Steel is the basis of an engineering industry which accounts for 30% of industrial output and 25% of total exports. Products range from oil refinery equipment and ships to tractors and lathes. The chemical industry, using local oil, gas, coal and salt, has expanded dramatically and now provides 8% of exports; reeds from the Danube delta supply the Braila cellulose plant. Since the 1960s consumer industry has developed and some goods—shoes and clothing—are exported.

Tourism

Some four million foreigners visit Romania annually, making tourism an important sector of the economy. The principal tourist regions are the Black Sea coast with modern resorts such as Mamaia and Eforie; the Carpathians, equally popular in summer and winter; Poiana Brasnov, the main ski resort; northern Moldavia, famous for 15th-century monasteries with exterior frescoes; and the Danube delta, the home of over 300 bird species and the only place in Europe where pelicans breed.

Transport

In the Carpathians, numerous valleys and depressions facilitate communication between the Transylvanian Basin and the lowlands, and 12 railway lines and over 30 trunk roads cross the mountains. Although the roads, totalling 76,304 km are being modernized, the 10,370 km rail network (used for long-distance freight) is still the most important feature of Romania's transport system. The Danube is a major highway but winter shipping is hampered by ice. Galati, Braila, Giurgiu and Turnu-Severin are the main river ports. Cross-Danube ferry services are important as there are only three bridges: at Giurgiu Giurgeni and Cernavoda (rail). The state airline, TAROM, links 17 cities and operates international flights from Bucharest and Constanta.

Cities

Bucharest, on the Dimbovita, was founded in 1459 and became the national capital four centuries later. Romania's urban population doubled between the 1950s and mid-1970s and besides Bucharest there are 13 other towns with over 100,000 inhabitants. Among these are Cluj (208,125), a 2,000-year-old cultural and manufacturing centre; Timisoara (199,987), a commercial town on the Bega canal; Iasi (193,998) in Moldavia and industrial Brasov (188,828). Galati (187,010), located at the confluence of the Danube, Siret and Prut, is noted for its steel and shipbuilding industries.

Bulgaria

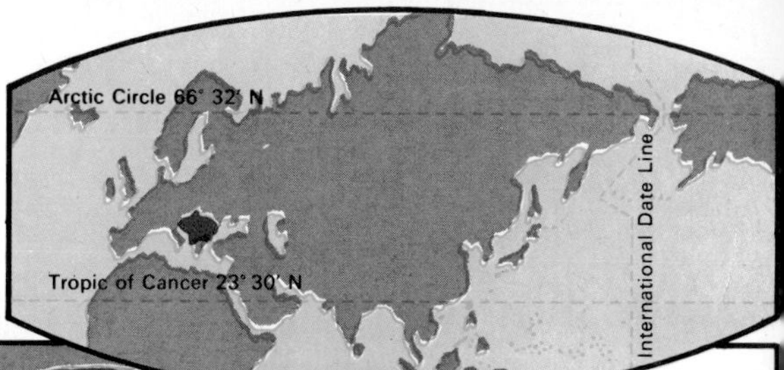

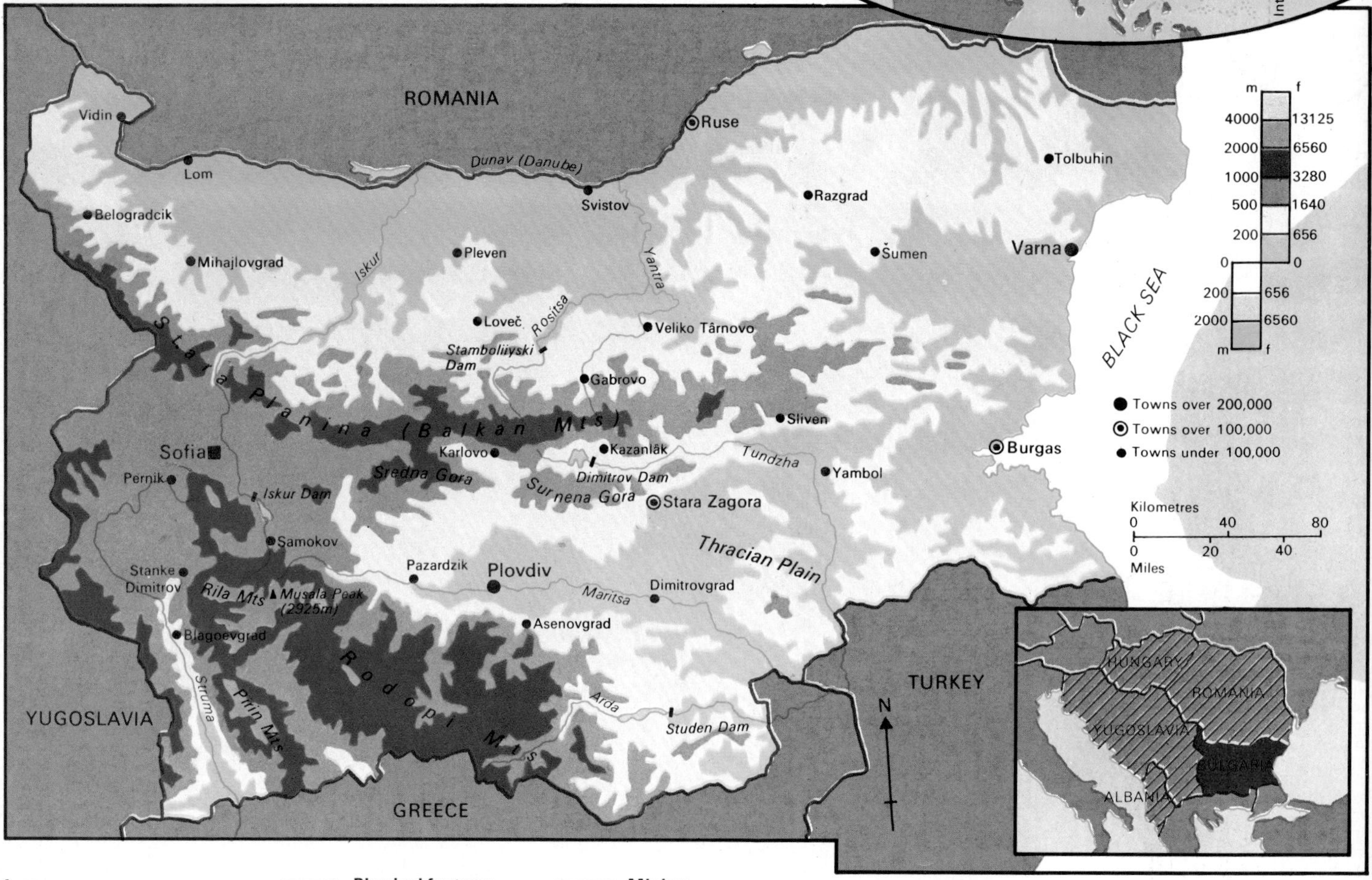

Area
110,912 km²/42,823 sq miles
Location
41°15′—44°10′N
22°20′—28°25′E
Population
8,594,493 (1972)
Population density
77 per km²/201 per sq mile
Capital and largest city
Sofia: 927,833 (1972)
Language
Bulgarian
Major imports
fuel, machinery and transport equipment, chemicals
Major exports
food products, tobacco, metals textiles, rolling stock
Currency
lev (1 lev = 100 stotinki)
6,500 million US dollars
Status
independent republic

Cities

Sofia, on the banks of the Iskur at the foot of the Rodopi mountains, is Bulgaria's cultural, commercial and industrial centre. Plovdiv (261,732), the second largest town, is on the Maritsa. Its food-processing and textile industries are based on the rich agriculture of the Thracian plain. The port and resort of Varna (251,888) has become industrialized, with shipbuilding, oil-refining and petro-chemicals. Ruse (163,012) the leading Danube port, has a bridge link with the Romanian town of Giurgiu. Bulgaria's main port, Burgas (142,137), is also a leading tourist centre. Stara Zagora (117,543), of Roman origin, is famous for its archaeological and architectural treasures.

Physical features

Mountainous Bulgaria divides into a series of east-west zones. In the north lies a platform some 100 m high which ends in a steep cliff fall to the Danube. Southwards, the Danubian platform rises gently to the Balkan Mountains (Stara Planina), which have an average height of 870 m. This massif is separated from a parallel and more southerly range—the Sredna Gora—by a series of depressions extending from Sofia in the east to Sliven in the west. South of the Sredna Gora is the Thracian plain—a broad alluvial lowland drained by the Maritsa. South-west Bulgaria is dominated by the majestic Rodopi mountains which rise to 2,925 m in Musala Peak, the highest point in the Balkan Peninsula. The main rivers are the Danube, Maritsa, Iskur, Struma, Arda, Tundzha and Yantra.

Climate

Bulgaria has a temperate continental climate with hot summers and cold winters, Pleven averaging —4°C in January, 23°C in July. There are distinct regional differences. The Danubian platform, with summer rainfall, is subject to seasonal extremes of heat and cold brought about by north-easterly winds from Russia. The southern border has a Mediterranean climate with winter rain and summer drought. The central region is transitional between these two climatic types, while the Black Sea coast has mild winters but cooler summers.

Mining

Bulgaria has few energy minerals and is largely dependent on Russian imports for supplies of high-grade coal, oil and gas. Small quantities of oil and natural gas are produced at Dolni Dabnik Tjulenovo and off-shore near Varna. There are, however, major lignite deposits at Pernik and Stara Zagora. Lead and zinc are mined in the eastern Rodopi range and in the western Balkan mountains; copper comes from the western Balkans and near Burgas; manganese is worked in the Varna area and north of Sofia; iron ore is extracted near Sofia, in the Maritsa basin and at Belogradcik.

Transport

With the growth of industry the Bulgarian transport system has been modernized. Roads, covering a total of 30,800 km, have developed at the expense of rail and now account for 80% of freight and passengers carried. The 6,000 km rail network is centred on Sofia. Although the increase in road traffic has caused inland shipping to decline, the Danube is still important. Ruse is the leading river port, followed by Lom, Vidin and Svistov. Burgas, the main seaport, handles a large share of Bulgarian exports; it also has an oil refinery. Varna, the second Black Sea port, is equipped with modern shipyards. The state airline, Balkan, links 14 cities and operates international flights from Sofia, Varna and Burgas.

Agriculture

With almost 50% of the land used for arable farming, Bulgaria ranks as South-East Europe's leading agricultural state. The main cereals, grown on the Danube platform and in the Sofia basin, are wheat, maize and barley. Farming is most intensive on the fertile, alluvial soils of the Thracian plain, where the emphasis is on fruit and industrial crops such as cotton, tobacco, sunflowers and sugar-beet. The Black Sea coast, the lower slopes of the Stara Planina and river valleys in the south-west are also fruit-growing areas; plums are a Bulgarian speciality. Market gardening is important in the Maritsa and Sofia basins and on the coastal lowlands. Petals from the world's largest rose gardens near Kazanluk are used to make the famous Bulgarian attar of roses, a perfume base. Livestock—cattle, sheep, pigs and poultry—is widespread. 90% of farmland is collectivized.

Forestry and fishing

Forests cover a third of Bulgaria and are largely concentrated in highland regions. Deciduous trees predominate on the plains and lower slopes: chestnut and walnut on the Thracian plain and oak and beech in the Balkan mountains. The higher slopes of the Rodopi range are forested with conifers. Fishing is mainly in the Black Sea, but some boats go out to the Mediterranean.

Energy

Thermal stations, predominantly fired by lignite, produce 90% of Bulgaria's electricity. The remaining 10% is provided by about 100 hydro-electric installations. A new 800,000 kw nuclear power station will generate a quarter of the country's requirements. Other nuclear and hydro plants are under construction.

Industry

Since the Communist take-over of 1947, the Bulgarian economy has been transformed. Industry has has been developed round local raw materials: iron ore (steel), lignite and oil (chemicals), ores (metallurgy), cotton (textiles), timber (wood and paper), agricultural produce (food-processing). Food-processing is the main industry, accounting for 25% of industrial output; products exported include jam, canned fruit and sugar. Engineering is next in importance, followed by chemicals and metallurgy. The country's two steelworks at Pernik and Kremikovci form part of the major industrial zone centred on Sofia-Pernik. The region—producing 25% of industrial output—also contains important engineering, chemical and textile plants. Other leading industrial centres are Plovdiv, Dimitrovgrad, Stara Zagora, Varna and Burgas. The tourist industry based on the Black Sea coast, is also expanding at several modern resorts.

Albania

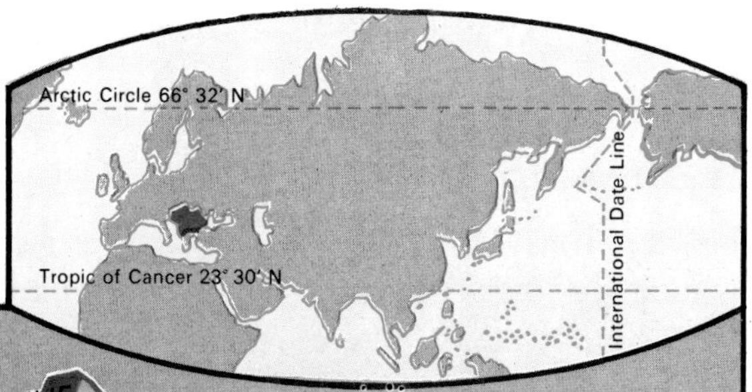

Area
28,748 km²/11,100 sq miles
Location;
39°40'—42°40' N
19°15'—21°5' E
Population
2,230,000 (1971)
Population density
78 per km²/202 per sq mile
Capital and largest city
Tiranë (Tirana): 171,000 (1971)
Language
Albanian
Major imports
iron and steel, fuels, machinery, transport equipment, chemicals
Major exports
fruit and vegetables, wine, tobacco, copper products, wood, crude oil, bitumen, chrome ore
Currency
lek (1 lek = 100 quintars)
Gross National Product
1,300 million US dollars (1970)
Status
independent republic

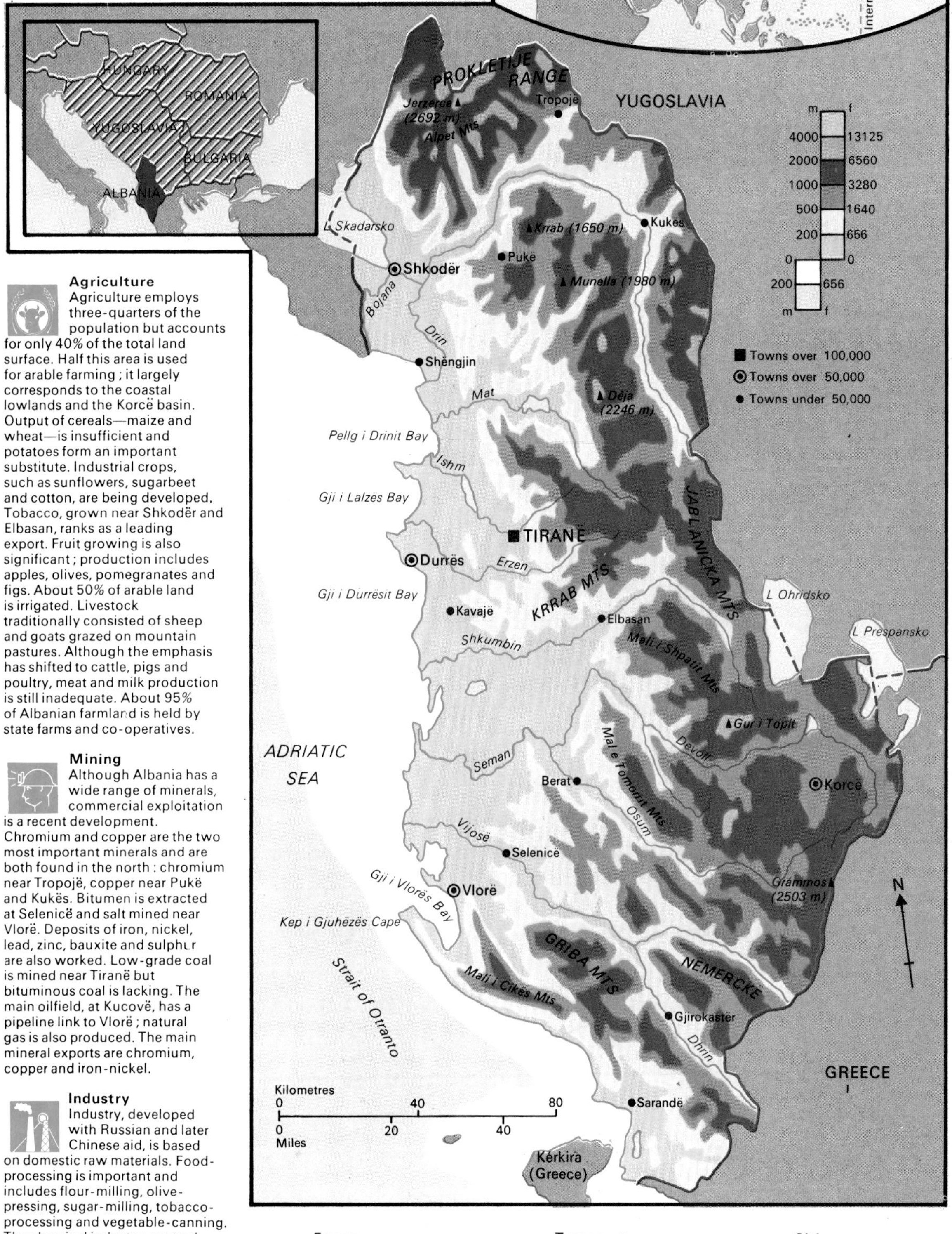

Physical features

Albania, on the west coast of the Balkan peninsula, is eastern Europe's smallest country, in both area and population. Highlands, covering the interior and extending to the coast in the south, account for 70% of the territory. In the northeast, the limestone Prokletije rise to over 2,500 m; the mountains, dissected by steep gorges and often impenetrable, continue southwards and include the Korab, Jablanica, Griba and Nëmerckë ranges. Lowland Albania is confined to the north and central coast. In the north, the coastal strip is narrow, but further south it widens into a triangular plain between Durrës, Elbasan and Vlorë. This plain is largely composed of fertile alluvium interspersed with swampy tracts and low scrub-covered hills. The main rivers, notably the Drin, Mat, Shkumbin, Seman and Vijosë, are swollen in winter and spring with rain and meltwater, but almost dry in summer. In its upper course, the Drin flows from south to north, draining Lake Ohridsko; to the south-east is another lake, Prespansko.

Climate

Coastal Albania has a Mediterranean climate with hot dry summers and mild, wet winters; in January, the average temperature is 8°C and in July, 25°C. Inland, altitude causes a decrease in temperature and an increase in rainfall; in the northeast, January averages —1°C and July, 21°C. Precipitation, occurring mostly in winter, ranges from 109 cm a year at Vlorë to over 260 cm in the Prokletije.

Flora and fauna

Characteristic Mediterranean scrub, or maquis, predominates on the coastal lowlands. The mountainous interior is forested: oak grows on the lower slopes and is succeeded by mixed forest, mainly composed of elm and beech; pine is the principal species in higher zones. In all, woodland covers 47% of Albania. Wild animals—mainly wolves, boars and deer—are found in remote forest and mountain areas.

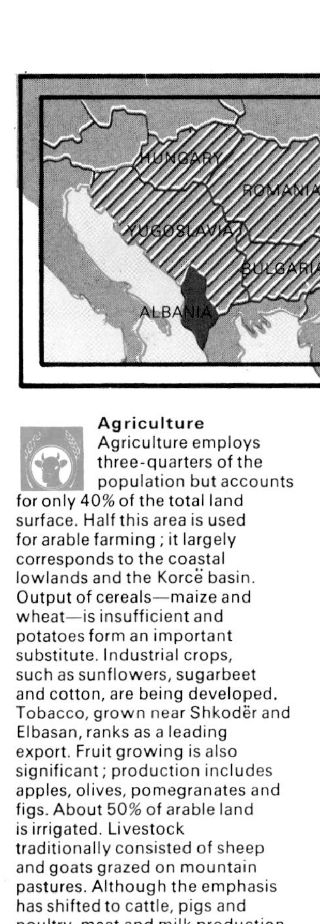

Agriculture

Agriculture employs three-quarters of the population but accounts for only 40% of the total land surface. Half this area is used for arable farming; it largely corresponds to the coastal lowlands and the Korcë basin. Output of cereals—maize and wheat—is insufficient and potatoes form an important substitute. Industrial crops, such as sunflowers, sugarbeet and cotton, are being developed. Tobacco, grown near Shkodër and Elbasan, ranks as a leading export. Fruit growing is also significant; production includes apples, olives, pomegranates and figs. About 50% of arable land is irrigated. Livestock traditionally consisted of sheep and goats grazed on mountain pastures. Although the emphasis has shifted to cattle, pigs and poultry, meat and milk production is still inadequate. About 95% of Albanian farmland is held by state farms and co-operatives.

Mining

Although Albania has a wide range of minerals, commercial exploitation is a recent development. Chromium and copper are the two most important minerals and are both found in the north: chromium near Tropojë, copper near Pukë and Kukës. Bitumen is extracted at Selenicë and salt mined near Vlorë. Deposits of iron, nickel, lead, zinc, bauxite and sulphur are also worked. Low-grade coal is mined near Tiranë but bituminous coal is lacking. The main oilfield, at Kucovë, has a pipeline link to Vlorë; natural gas is also produced. The main mineral exports are chromium, copper and iron-nickel.

Industry

Industry, developed with Russian and later Chinese aid, is based on domestic raw materials. Food-processing is important and includes flour-milling, olive-pressing, sugar-milling, tobacco-processing and vegetable-canning. The chemical industry, centred on oil and gas, and metallurgy, using chromium, copper, iron and nickel, are expanding. The steelworks at Elbasan is supplied by Albanian iron ore but for coal is dependent on imports. Timber-processing is also important and wood is exported. Engineering works have been established but, as yet, the range of products is limited. Heavy industry has developed at the expense of light manufacturing, but textile, clothing and shoe production is increasing. Albanian industry, which is totally nationalized, is concentrated on the Adriatic coastal plain; Tiranë is the chief manufacturing centre.

Energy

Power production has been a major priority of the Communist government and by 1971 every Albanian village had been supplied with electricity. The fast-flowing streams, characteristic of the mountainous interior (particularly in the north and south), are suitable for generating power and several hydro-electric installations have been built; others are under construction. Thermal stations are fired by coal and natural gas. A plant with a capacity of 400 MW, under construction in 1976, was to be the largest in the country.

Transport

The Communist government has developed transport, since the previously inadequate system hindered economic expansion. Roads now serve agricultural regions, industrial centres, mining zones and forested areas. The network is 3,100 km long, but many northern mountain districts remain inaccessible to motor traffic. Railways, totalling 150 km and centred on Durrës and Vlorë, have been established since 1947. Durrës is the main port, followed by Vlorë, Sarandë and Shëngjin. The country's only airport is near Tiran.

Cities

Tiranë, originally a sixth-century fortress, became the capital in 1920. About 32 km inland, on the Ishm river, the city is at the heart of an agricultural region where maize, olives and vines are grown. Under the Communists, who came to power in 1945, Tiranë has become increasingly industrialized. It is linked by rail to Durrës, the principal port. The country's other main industrial towns are also former agricultural centres. They include Shkodër (55,000), Durrës (53,000), Vlorë (50,000), Korcë (47,000) and Elbasan (42,000).

Greece

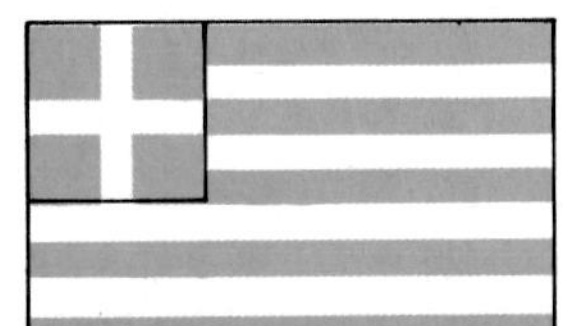

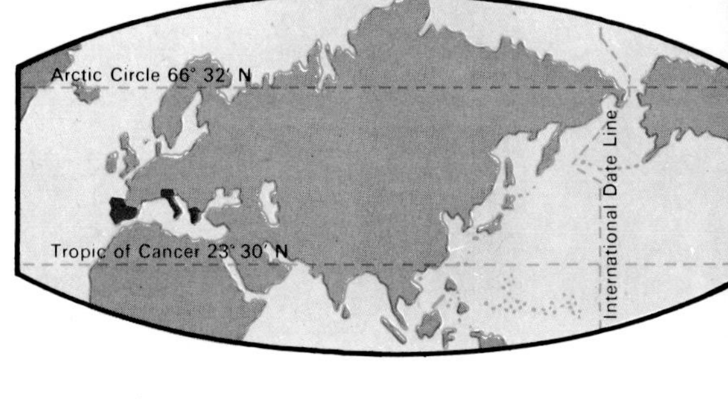

Area
131,944 km²/50,943 sq miles
Location
34 50′—41 45′ N
19 20′—28 15′ E
Population
8,960,000 (1974)
Population density
68 per km²/176 per sq mile
Capital and largest city
Athens: 2,540,240 (1971)
Language
Greek
Major imports
machinery, transport equipment, iron, steel, petroleum, meat, dairy products, pharmaceuticals and textiles
Major exports
tobacco, fresh and processed fruit and vegetables, olive oil, aluminium, cotton, minerals and handicrafts
Currency
drachma (1 drachma = 100 lepta)
Gross National Product
19,860 million US dollars (1974)
Status
republic

Climate

Most of Greece has a Mediterranean climate with warm wet winters and hot dry summers—especially the Pelopónnisos and the islands. In Athens (Athínai), January temperatures average 14°C, in July 27°C. Continental extremes in temperatures prevail in Thrace (Thraki) and Mecodonia (Makedhonia). Thessaloníki averages 6°C in January, 29°C in July. Throughout the country, rainfall occurs in winter and is heaviest west of the Pindhos mountains: Corfu (Kérkira) receives 130 cm of rain a year while Athínai receives only 30 cm per year.

Fishing

Greece, with its long coastline and numerous islands, has a well-established fishing industry and fish is an important item in the national diet. The eastern Mediterranean, however, has limited fish stocks (except for mullet, squid, sardines and tunny) and, as a result, Atlantic fishing is increasing in significance.

Mining and energy

The mountains contain a wide range of minerals including bauxite, iron ore, magnesite, copper, chromite, lead-zinc, sulphur and barite, but in most cases reserves are limited. Bauxite is the most notable exception: some 2 million tonnes are mined yearly, mostly near Elevsis, making Greece one of Europe's main bauxite producers. The island of Náxos is the world's chief supplier of emery and Greek marble is world-famous. With lignite the only energy mineral found in significant quantities, Greece is largely dependent on imported fuels; 75% is used for electricity production. Hydro-electric power currently generating 30% of electricity, is being developed in the Pindhos mountains.

Cities

Athínai, encircled by mountains, is situated 8 km inland. The heart of the city is the Acropolis with world-famous monuments suc as the Parthenon—the shrine of the goddess Athena. On becoming the capital of modern Greece in 1833, Athínai expanded rapidly. It has now merged with the port of Piraievs and forms the country's main industrial region inhabited by a third of the Greek population. The second largest city, Thessaloníki (345,800), is the only major industrial centre outside Athínai.

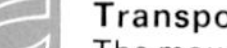

Transport

The mountainous interior has hindered development of land transport and both road and rail networks are poor although they are being modernized. Roads, totalling 36,000 km, are 50% unpaved. New highways link Athínai to Thessaloníki and to Igoumenítsa via Patrai. Greece is a seafaring nation; shipping is the main foreign-currency earner and the merchant fleet is one of the world's largest. Piraeus (Piraievs), near Athínai, is the chief port, followed by Thessaloníki and Pátrai. There are regular steamer services to the islands. The privately owned Olympic Airways operates domestic and international flights.

Tourism

The expanding tourist industry, catering for over 3 million visitors a year, is a major source of income. The country's main assets are its climate, its archeological wealth and its many beaches (no point is more than 130 km from the sea). Popular historical sites include Mycenae, Olympia and the Acropolis (which means 'city at the top') in Athínai.

Agriculture

Agriculture is still basic to the Greek economy: it employs half of the population and provides over 50% of exports. Rough pastures cover 40% of the country and arable land (mostly in Thessalía and Makedhonia) less than 30%. Wheat is the chief cereal and sufficient is grown for some to be exported. Greece is a leading exporter of tobacco, cultivated mainly in Makedhonia, Thraki and Thessalia. Cotton is also a valuable lowland crop; others include sugarbeet and rice. Vines are particularly important in the Pelopónnisos and on the islands and the chief products are currants, raisins and sultanas—Greece is a major supplier of dried fruits. The principal tree fruit is the olive and Greece is the world's third largest producer of olive oil. Citrus production is also significant with oranges, lemons and mandarines exported. Apples, peaches, apricots and vegetables are also cultivated. Farm output is being increased by reclamation and irrigation schemes and by the use of fertilizers. Livestock consists largely of sheep and goats.

Industry

Traditionally, Greek industry is concerned with processing agricultural produce (wheat, tobacco, grapes, olives, tomatoes and so on) but in the last decade there has been considerable growth in the chemical, textile and metallurgical sectors. Industrial development is still in its early stages but recently completed projects include a giant refinery and petro-chemical complex at Diavata, iron and steelworks at Elevsis, an aluminium smelter near Delphi., shipyards at Elevsis and an automobile plant at Pátrai. Most industry is concentrated in the Athínai-Piraievs and Thessaloníki conurbations, but manufacturing is being established in other centres such as Iráklion (Kríti), Lárimna, Vólos, Ptolemaïs and Kavalla. With the growing tourist industry, handicrafts have increased in significance and typical products range from lace, carved knives and icons to alabaster ware, hand-woven carpets and pottery.

Physical features

Greece occupies the southern extremity of the mountainous Balkan peninsula. The barren limestone Pindhos chain, running northwest-southeast and rising to 2,500 m, constitutes the principal mountain axis. Other ranges run from this highland spine to the coast where they project as rocky promontories, then continue as islands. Lowlands consist of mountain-enclosed areas such as the plain of Thessaloníki and the Thessalía basin. The range separating these two major lowlands contains Greece's highest peak, Olympus (Ólimbos: 2,917 m). In the south lies the Pelopónnisos, a rugged peninsula joined to the mainland by the isthmus of Corinth. Kriti (8,331 km²) is the largest of the Greek islands and an extension of the Pelopónnisos ranges. Greece has almost 500 islands accounting for 20% of its area. There are relatively few rivers as the limestone causes water to flow underground. The longest river is the Aliákmon (256 km).

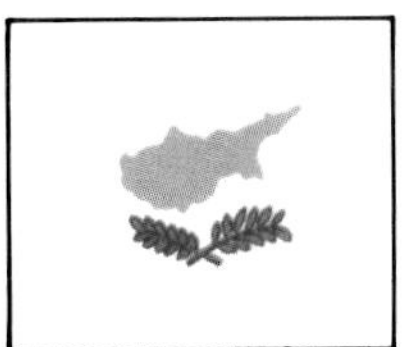

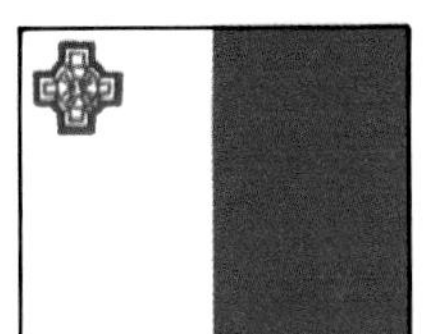

Cyprus and Malta

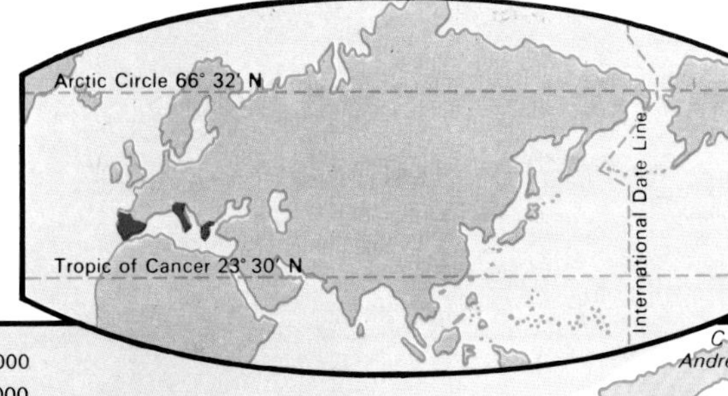

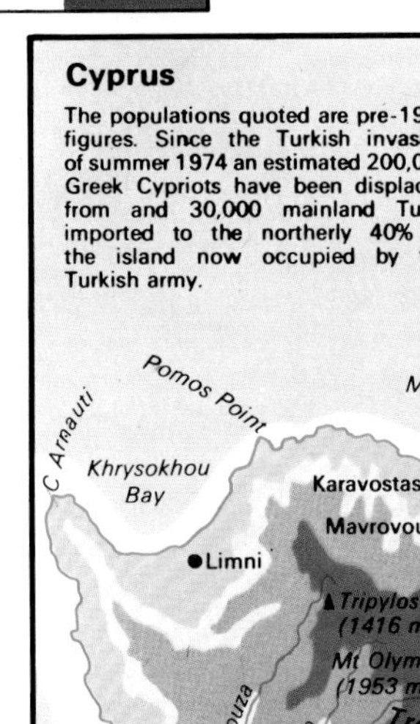

Area
9,251 km²/3,572 sq miles
Location
34°33′—35°41′ N
32°17′—34°35′ E
Population
660,000 (1973)
Population density
71 per km²/184 per sq mile
Capital and largest city
Nicosia: 118,300 (1972)
Languages
Greek and Turkish
Major imports
food, textiles fuels, machinery, transport equipment
Major exports
citrus, potatoes. copper products, wine, asbestos, iron pyrites
Currency
pound (1 pound = 1,000 mils)
Gross National Product
960 million US dollars (1974)
Status
independent republic

Cyprus: the land
Cyprus, the third largest island in the Mediterranean, has a maximum length of 240 km and a maximum width of 96 km. The island consists of two mountain systems separated by a central plain, the Mesaöria. The Kyrenia range, rising to 1,000 m, runs along the north coast and the Troödos massif covers the south-west and includes the island's highest peak, Mt Olympus (1,953 m). The wide Mesaöria lowland has fertile soils. Summers are hot and dry and winters wet and mild. Nicosia averages 29°C in July, 9°C in January. Annual rainfall ranges from 40 cm on the plain to over 100 cm in the mountainous districts.

Cyprus: agriculture
Agriculture, employing 35% of the total workforce, is the basis of the Cypriot economy and provides almost 80% of total exports. About half the island is farmed and most arable land lies in the Mesaöria plain. Here, the chief crops are wheat, barley, potatoes, carrots, vegetables, melons, tobacco, almonds, carobs and olives. The major cash crop is citrus, grown in coastal areas often under irrigation. About 80% of citrus production (oranges, mandarins, lemons, grapefruit) is exported, accounting for 40% of exports. In the southern mountains, orchards and vineyards cover the terraced hillsides; Paphos and Limassol are both noted for their wines. Livestock consists mainly of sheep and goats grazed on upland pastures. Forests of pine and cypress cover the higher mountain slopes and supply 30% of the island's timber needs.

Cyprus: industry
Cypriot industry is traditionally based on agricultural produce: flour-milling, brewing, fruit and vegetable canning wine-making, distilling, biscuit manufacture, tobacco processing and so on. Since independence, other light industries have been developed including clothing, shoes, carpets, cement, bricks, furniture, animal feeds and pharmaceuticals. Tourism is growing in importance with over half a million people visiting Cyprus annually.

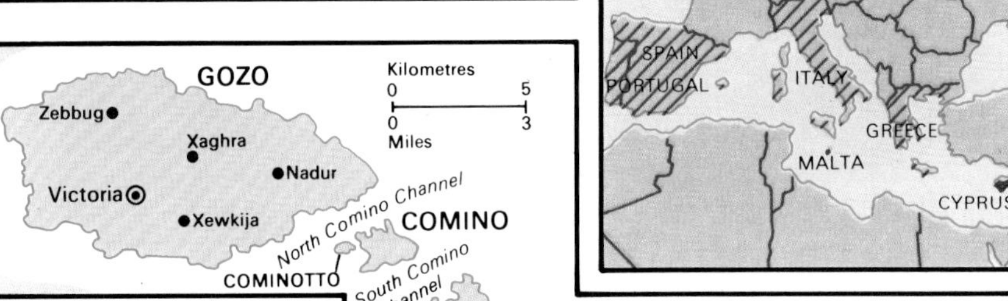

Cyprus: mining
In antiquity, Cyprus was famous for its copper (which derives its name from the island) and this is still the principal metal exploited. Two of the mines, at Mavrovouni and Skouriotissa, have been in use for thousands of years. There are also important deposits of asbestos, iron pyrites and chromite, mostly in the Troödos range. Minerals, handled by the ports of Limassol, Vasilikos, Limni, Xeros and Karavostasi, account for 20% of total exports.

Cyprus: Nicosia
Nicosia, some 5,000 years old, is situated on the Pedieas river in the Mesaöria plain. The city's light industry includes food-processing, cigarette manufacture, clothing and footwear. The capital has good road links with the port of Famagusta.

Cyprus: transport
The island's 9,200 km road network is 50% unsurfaced and there are no railways. Up to 1974, Nicosia was the only civil airport but this has since been closed. Larnaca is now being developed for international flights. The main port of Famagusta (43,000) is also closed. Other ports include Limassol (54,000), Larnaca (21,000), Paphos (10,000) and Kyrenia (4,000). Oil is discharged at Larnaca and, in smaller quantities, at Akrotiri, Moni and Vasilikos.

Malta

Mellieha Bay
St Paul's Bay
Salina Bay
San Pawl il Bahar (St Paul's Bay)
Gharghur
Sliema
Marsamxett Harbour
Naxxar
St Julian's
VALLETTA
Mosta
Balzan
Birkirkara
Grand Harbour
Lija
Hamrun
Zabbar
Attard
Marsa
Siggiewi
Rabat
Zebbug
Qormi
Paola
Luqa
Zetjun
Luqa International Airport
Mdina
Gudja
Ghaxaq
Marsaxlokk
Mqabba
Safi
Qrendi
Zurrieq
Birzebbuga
Marsaxlokk Bay
Towns over 10,000
Towns over 5,000
Towns under 5,000
MALTA
FILFLA

Malta: agriculture
Agriculture employs 16% of the workforce but two thirds of these also have part-time jobs in industry. Farmland, accounting for 30% of the country, is located on the plain and in the valleys which are intensively terraced. The chief crops are wheat, vegetables and fruit, including grapes and wine. Production is mostly consumed locally but potatoes, onions, tomatoes and flowers are exported. Livestock consists mainly of sheep, goats and pigs; meat and dairy products are imported. The Maltese fishing fleet operates off the coast with the bulk of the catch landed between May and November.

Malta: industry
The shipyard, formerly the British naval base, is a vital source of income. The yard, employing 5% of the workforce, undertakes repairs, new building and tanker cleaning. Processing agricultural produce ranks next in importance: products include bacon, margarine, tomato purée, potato crisps, frozen peas, wine and cigars. Other established manufactures are textiles, clothing and footwear. New industries include light engineering (machine tools and electrical), car assembly and chemicals. With the development of tourism, traditional crafts such as jewellery, lace and filigree work have been encouraged.

Malta
Area
316 km²/122 sq miles
Location
35°48′—36° N
14°10′—14°35′ E
Population
300,280 (1975)
Population density
950 per km²/2,461 per sq mile
Capital and largest city
Valletta: 15 400 (1971)
Languages
Maltese and English
Major imports
machinery, transport equipment, foodstuffs, fuels, metals, metal products, textiles
Major exports
clothing, fabrics, rubber and plastic goods, electrical apparatus, potatoes
Currency
pound (= 100 cents = 1,000 mils)
Gross National Product
360 million US dollars (1974)
Status
independent republic

Malta: the land
Situated in the middle of the Mediterranean, the Maltese archipelago comprises Malta (246 km²), Gozo (67 km²), Comino (2 km²) and two uninhabited islets, Cominotto and Filfla. The main island, Malta, is a maximum 27 km long and 14 km wide and consists of a limestone block which has been tilted eastwards resulting in 250 m high cliffs on the west coast and drowned valleys in the east. The northern part of the island is characterized by east-west ridges and alluvial valleys; a clay-covered plain lies to the south. There are no rivers or mountains. The climate is Mediterranean with mild winters (14°C) and hot summers (23°C) tempered by sea breezes. Some 50 cm of rain falls annually, mostly between September and April.

Malta: Valletta
In the 16th century, Malta was ceded to the Knights of St John who subsequently built a new capital and named it after the Grand Master of the Order, Jean de la Valette. Valletta stands on a rocky promontory between two harbours: Marsamxett and Grand Harbour. Grand Harbour is the country's main port and handles nearly all domestic and transit trade. The capital has bus links to all parts of the island; there are no railways. The international airport is Luqa (6 km southwest).

Spain

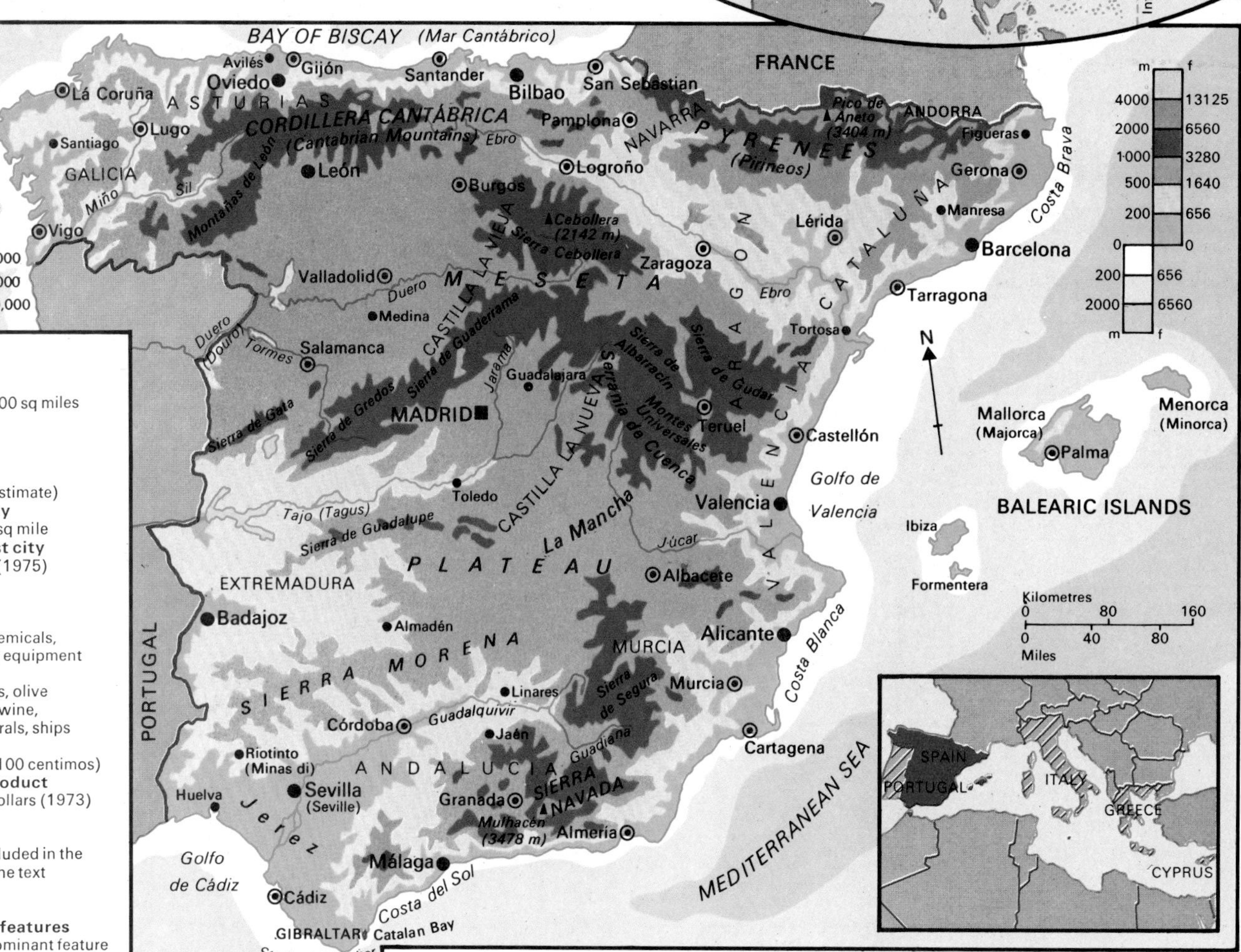

Area
510,000 km²/197,000 sq miles
Location
36°—43°47′ N
9°20′ W—4°20′ E
Population
36,161,000 (1976 estimate)
Population density
71 per km²/184 per sq mile
Capital and largest city
Madrid: 3,792,000 (1975)
Language
Spanish
Major imports
machinery, fuels, chemicals, foodstuffs, transport equipment
Major exports
citrus and other fruits, olive oil, vegetables, fish, wine, cotton textiles, minerals, ships
Currency
peseta (1 peseta = 100 centimos)
Gross National Product
60,800 million US dollars (1973)
Status
Monarchy
The Canaries are included in the statistics but not in the text

Physical features

Spain's dominant feature is the central Meseta, a vast plateau some 600 m high, which is crossed by a series of east-west ranges (the Gata, Gredos and Guaderrama mountains). The Meseta is bounded by the Cantabrian mountains in the north, the Serrania de Cuenca in the east and by the Sierra Morena in the south. West of the Cantabrian chain is Galicia, a region of green hills and *rias* (drowned river valleys). The Cuenca ranges are separated from the Pyrenees by the broad basin of the river Ebro, while in the south another great depression (drained by the Guadalquivir) lies between the Sierra Morena and the Sierra Navada which contains the country's highest peak, Mulhacén (3,478 m). The Meseta tilts slightly towards Portugal so that its main rivers, the Duero, Tajo (Tagus) and Guadiana, drain westwards. Spain's 4,000 km coastline is mostly cliffed and rocky with long sandy beaches. The Balearic islands (5,014 km²) lie off the east coast.

Climate

The northwest coast is mild and wet: in Lá Coruña, January averages 9°C, July 18°C. Rainfall, in all seasons, is over 100 cm. The mediterranean coast is warmer and drier: Valencia has 10°C in January, 24°C in July and 25 cm of rain, mostly in winter. The interior has a continental climate: Madrid records 4°C in January, 26°C in July with 40 cm of rain falling mostly in spring and autumn.

Mining and energy

There are two main mining areas. In the north, the Cantabrians contain coal and high-quality iron ore. In the south, the Sierras Morena and Nevada yield mercury (Almadén), copper pyrites (Riotinto), lead, zinc, sulphur and manganese. Spain is the world's leading producer of mercury and third producer of pyrites. Other deposits include tungsten and tin in the extreme northwest, potash and bauxite in the northeast and uranium in the northeast and near Jaén. Minerals are exported via Bilbao and Huelva. In contrast, Spain has to import fuels (coal and petroleum) as domestic supplies are inadequate. About 50% of electricity is generated by hydro-electric plants, mostly in the northeast. Nuclear power is being developed.

Transport

Madrid is the hub of both road (150,000 km) and rail (18,000 km) networks. Roads are 50% unsurfaced and still used by mules and donkeys in many rural areas. Buses cover the country and carry more passengers than trains. Spain has some 200 ports of which the main ones are Bilbao, Barcelona, Cartagena and Cádiz. There are 33 cities with airports, mostly in tourist areas. Iberia is the national airline.

Cities

Madrid, at the heart of Spain, is primarily administrative and it is Barcelona (1,745,000) which acts as the country's industrial and commercial capital. Although industrialized, Valencia (654,000), Sevilla (548,000) and Zaragoza (480,000) are all centred on important agricultural regions.

Agriculture

Low rainfall and poor soils predominate, but Spain is primarily agricultural. The Meseta is the main cereal region: wheat is in the lead, followed by barley, oats and rye. Maize is grown in the northwest and rice, under irrigation, in the Ebro delta and Valencia. Potatoes, sugarbeet and vegetables are also important. The most fertile zone is the irrigated Mediterranean coast. Citrus, a major export, is the chief fruit in the Valencia area. Other tree crops include apples and pears in the northwest; dates figs and almonds in the south and Balearics; peaches and apricots in the southeast; olives in Andalucia. Spain is the world's leading producer of olives and olive oil and also ranks as the third wine-producing country. Vines are cultivated in the upper Ebro valley, La Mancha, the Mediterranean coastlands and Jerez (sherry). Livestock consists of cattle in the northwest and sheep and goats on the Meseta plateau and the Balearic islands.

Forests and fishing

Most of Spain was once forested but now only mountain areas are wooded and timber imports are necessary. There are, however, extensive cork oak forests in the southwest and Spain is second only to Portugal in cork production. Fishing is widespread but is most important on the Atlantic coasts where the chief centres are Vigo and Lá Coruña. The catch, consisting mainly of sardine and anchovy, is Europe's second largest (after Norway). Galician boats fish cod in the Atlantic waters off Newfoundland.

Industry

Although still not as advanced as other European countries, Spain is rapidly becoming industrialized. Most industry is concentrated in the north and northeast. The north accounts for 80% of steel production: major centres include Avilés (60% of the country's steel output), Gijón, Santander and Bilbao. Engineering (in particular, ship-building) is also important in the north. Barcelona and surrounding Cataluña is noted for textiles (supplying 80% of total production), chemicals and vehicle assembly. A third industrial zone with metallurgical, chemical and ceramic works is growing round Madrid. The food-processing industry includes flour-milling on the Meseta, olive-oil refining in Andalucia and fish-canning in Galicia.

Tourism

Tourism accounts for 75% of foreign currency earnings and ranks as Spain's leading export industry. The tourist boom is also benefitting other industries such as building, handicrafts and transport. Most of the 35 million foreigners who visit Spain each year are attracted to the Mediterranean coasts, in particular the Costa del Sol, the Costa Brava and the Balearic islands of Mallorca and Ibiza.

Gibraltar

Gibraltar, 6 km² in area, is a narrow peninsula jutting out from the southernmost tip of Spain into the Mediterranean. The peninsula consists of a limestone block north-south for almost 5 km; in the north it is over 400 m high but slopes down to 30 m at Europa Point. The climate is mild with average temperatures of 15°C in January and 27°C in August. Rain (80 cm a year) falls in winter. Most of the 29,000 inhabitants live in Gibraltar City, situated on the wet side; Catalan Bay, a village on the east side, is the only other settlement. Rocky, infertile Gibraltar has no agriculture, little livestock and no mineral resources. In addition to a small ship-repair yard there is some light industry such as clothing manufacture, beer bottling and watch assembly, but the economy is largely dependent on the British naval base and tourism.

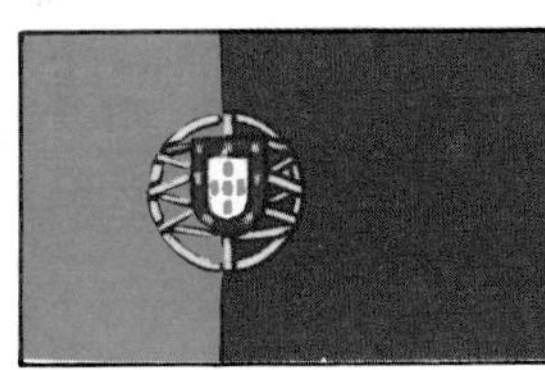

Portugal

Area
88,500 km²/34,170 sq miles
Location
37°—42°15′ N
6°20′—9°30′ W
Population
8,870,000 (1971)
Population density
100 per km²/260 per sq mile
Capital and largest city
Lisbon: 770,000 (1970)
Language
Portuguese
Major imports
vehicles, foodstuffs, fuels, iron and steel, textile fibres
Major exports
wine, cork, wood and wood products, sardines, cotton textiles, minerals, fruit ·
Currency
escudo (1 escudo = 100 centavos)
Gross National Product
11,600 million US dollars (1973)
Status
independent republic
This information does not include Madeira and the Azores, both part of Portugal.

Physical features
Portugal, a rectangular country about 560 km long and 220 km wide, consists of the western margin of the Spanish Meseta and an extensive coastal plain. Highland Portugal lies north of the river Tejo (Tagus) and is characterized by mountains, plateaux and the deep narrow valleys of the Douro and its tributaries. In the centre, the Serra da Estrêla rises to 1,993 m, the country's highest point. Southern Portugal consists of the flat Alentejo plain, the wide alluvial valleys of the rivers Tejo and Sado, and, in the extreme south, the Serra do Caldeirão. The coast, 830 km long, is low and sandy and along the Algarve is fringed by dunes and lagoons. Portugal's main rivers, the Minho, Douro, Tejo and Guadiana, rise in Spain.

Forests
Woodlands, covering 28% of the country, are vital to the Portuguese economy. Cork oak accounts for a quarter of the forested area and predominates in the Tejo valley and in western Alentejo. Portugal is the world's leading producer and exporter of cork (most of the cork is exported crude, but processing plants are being developed). A third of the woodland consists of pine, particularly in the north and pine lumber, pulp, resin and turpentine are all exported. The other main species grown in Portugal's forests are holm oak, chestnut and eucalyptus.

Fishing
Fishing is one of Portugal's chief industries. The main sector is sardine fishing, based at Matozinhos, Setúbal, Portimão and Olhão. Most of the catch is tinned in home-produced olive oil and exported. The tunny fisheries, centred on Vila Real, are also important. The fish are caught in the early summer as they enter the lagoons to spawn. Anchovy is the other main species taken in coastal waters. Every spring the cod fleet leaves for Newfoundland and Greenland and returns in the autumn, but the catch does not meet demand and dried cod has to be imported.

Climate
Southern Portugal has hot dry summers and mild winters: January averages 10°C in Lisboa (Lisbon), 12°C in Faro; corresponding August temperatures are 22°C and 24°C. Lisbon has 75 cm of rain a year, Faro 45 cm. The wettest period is October to March. The mountainous north is wetter and cooler with temperatures of 4°C in winter rising to 20°C in summer. On the Serra da Estrêla, annual rainfall reaches 250 cm and snow lasts from November to April. Winter fogs are common along the north coast.

Agriculture
Portugal is largely agricultural. Farmland covers over half the country—the main areas being the coastal lowlands, the Douro, Tejo, Sorraia and Sado valleys, the Alentejo and the Algarve. The north is characterized by very small farms and polyculture (beans, potatoes, maize and rye) while the Alentejo has vast estates and monoculture of wheat. Rice is grown in the Sorraia and Sado basins. But cereal production is inadequate and imports are necessary. Tree crops, such as olives, figs, almonds and citrus predominate in the Algarve. There is market gardening north of Lisboa. Vines are the leading crop in value and the chief vineyards, producing port wine for export, are on the terraced slopes of the Douro valley. Olives, grown in the south and the Douro valley, are also important; olive oil is both exported and used in fish canning. Irrigation is being developed in the south. Livestock consists of cattle in the north, sheep and goats in the south and pigs (reared on acorns) in the widespread oak forests.

Industry
Traditional industries (cork manufacture, wine, olive oil processing and fish canning) are based on domestic raw materials. The long established textile industry, centred on Porto and Braga, uses imported cotton. New industries are being developed, mostly in the Lisboa and Porto areas, and include steel production (Seixal), shipbuilding (Lisboa and Leixões), engineering (Porto, Setúbal and Lisboa), chemicals (Barreiro, Setúbal, Estarreja and Porto) and motor-vehicle assembly (Lisboa, and Azambuja). a major factor contributing to industrial expansion is increased power production. About 80% of electricity is generated by hydro-electric plants and there are major installations on the Tejo, Cavado, Douro and Zezere.

Cities
Lisboa, on the north side of the Tejo estuary 14 km from the Atlantic is dominated by the medieval castle of São Jorge. Most of the other old buildings were destroyed by one of the world's worst earthquakes which wrecked the city in 1755. The industrial zone lies south of the Tejo and is expanding towards Setúbal (44,500). The world-famous port wine takes its name from Porto (310,000), on the north bank of the Douro. The wine trade is based in nearby Vila Nova de Gaia (45,700). Other leading towns are Coimbra and Braga.

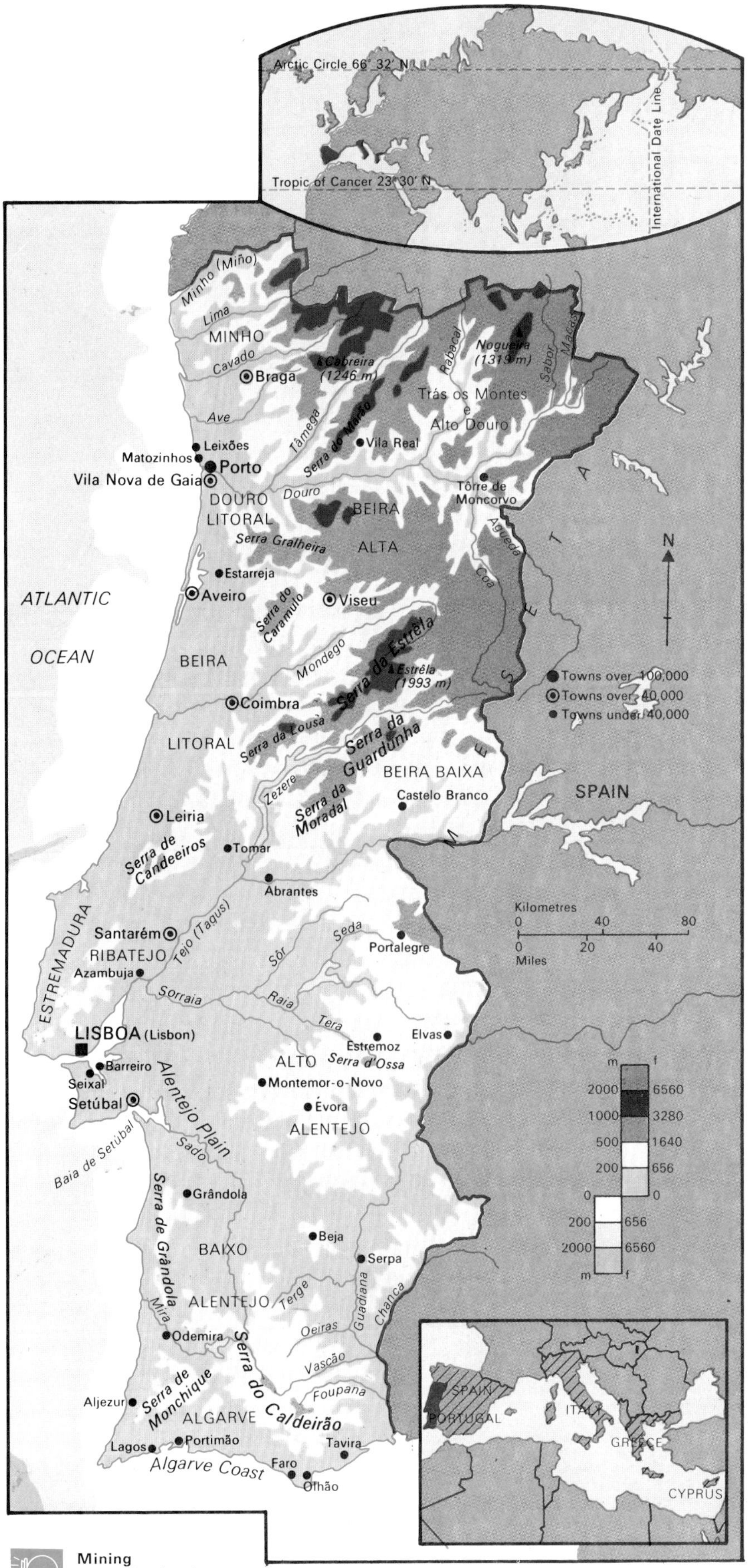

Mining
Portugal's mineral resources are limited and, in many cases, not fully developed. The most significant commercially is tungsten, mined in the north; Portugal ranks as the world's third largest exporter of tungsten. Copper pyrite, mostly from Beja, is also exported. There are iron ore deposits at Torre de Moncorvo, Montemor-o-Novo and in the Guadiana valley. Small amounts of manganese and tin are also produced. Fuels are lacking except for a little coal near Porto.

Transport
Lisboa-Coimbra-Porto is the principal axis of the road and rail networks. There are also several main road links with Spain and major rail routes via the Douro and Tejo valleys. Shipping is vital to the economy: the two leading ports, Lisboa and Leixões handle 80% of Portuguese trade. The national airline, Tap, operates overseas flights from Lisboa, Porto and Faro.

Tourism
Portugal's thriving tourist industry was badly hit by the overthrow in 1974 of the Caetano dictatorship and the ensuing political unrest. As tourism played a major part in the economy, the Government is now trying to re-establish the industry. Previously, four million people visited Portugal annually; the most famous resorts lying on the Algarve coast.

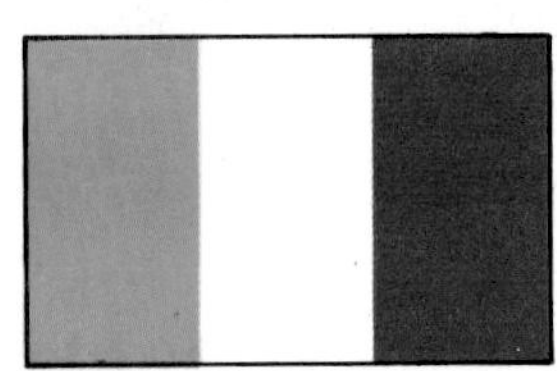

Italy

Area
301,054 km²/116,237 sq miles
Location
36°40′—47°05′ N
6°33′—18°30′ E
Population
55,360,000 (1974)
Population density
184 per km²/476 per sq mile
Capital and largest city
Rome: 2,800,450 (1971)
Language
Italian
Major imports
metal ores, fuels, cereals, meat, iron, steel, machinery, timber and paper
Major exports
fruit, vegetables, metal goods, machinery, fabrics, footwear, vehicles, chemicals
Currency
lira
Gross National Product
149,000 million US dollars (1974)
Status
independent republic

Physical features
The main mountain systems are the Alps and the Apennines. The Alps sweep across northern Italy and are highest in the north-west where Monte Rosa rises to 4,638 m. Alpine lakes, such as Garda (370 km²), Maggiore and Como, are of glacial origin. The Apennine chain extends from the western Alps to the southern tip of the mainland; Monte Corno (2,914 m) is its highest peak. The principal lowland is the fertile northern plain formed by Italy's longest river, the Po (652 km) and its tributaries. In the peninsula there are smaller lowlands such as Campania, Campagna, Maremma, Tavoliere della Puglia and Salentina. Peninsula rivers like the Tiber (Tevere), Arno and Volturno, have a seasonal flow. The two main islands are Sicily (Sicilia: 25,707 km²) and Sardinia (Sardegna: 24,089 km²). Mountainous Sicilia (an extension of the Apennines) is dominated by Etna (3,322 m)—Europe's largest active volcano. Sardegna consists of a desolate plateau broken, in the south, by the Campidano plain.

Climate
Italy divides into two climatic zones. The northern plain has a modified central European climate with long warm summers and short cold winters. Milano averages 25°C in July, 1°C in January. In contrast, a Mediterranean climate prevails in peninsula Italy and the islands with hot summers and mild winters. Palermo averages 27°C in July, 12°C in January. In the north, rain falls throughout the year but is heaviest in autumn; the plain receives about 80 cm a year, the Alps over 125 cm. The south has less than 60 cm of rain a year.

Energy
Hydro-electric power stations in the Alps, central Apennines and Calabria supply 35% of electricity; geothermal power (in Larderello, using steam of volcanic origin), 6%; nuclear plants, 5%; the remainder is generated thermally. As domestic oil production meets only 4% of Italy's energy needs, natural gas 10% and coal only 13%, fuel imports are high.

Agriculture
In spite of industrial growth, agriculture is still important and provides 25% of total exports. Farmland covers 67% of the country. The most fertile area is the Po plain, but other regions with a high turnover from agriculture are Piemonte, Lazio, Campania and Puglia. Wheat, the main cereal, is grown throughout lowland Italy; other cereals include rice (Piemonte, Lombardia) and maize. Italy produces 25% of the world's wines with Piemonte, Veneto, Toscana, Lazio and Sicilia the main vine growing areas. Olives are important, especially in Puglia, Calabria, Sicilia and Toscana. Other tree crops are apples, peaches and pears from the north and citrus fruits from Calabria and Sicilia. The main industrial crops are sugar beet, tobacco and hemp. Dairying is concentrated in Lombardia and Emilia; products include Gorgonzola and Parmesan cheese. Emilia is the chief pig-breeding zone; sheep and goats predominate in the south.

Forests and fishing
Forests, covering 20% of the country, are mostly in the Alps, Abruzzi and Gargano. Deciduous woods grow to 1,000 m then give way to conifers. The timber industry is particularly important in Alto Adige. Thousands of small boats operate off the 8,500 km long coast. Of the seas around Italy, the Adriatic is richest in fish; consequently the chief fishing ports (Chioggia, Fano, San Benedetto, Pescara and Molfetta) are along its coast. The catch includes sardines, anchovies, mullet, octopus, tunny.

Tourism
With 40 million foreign visitors a year, Italy ranks as Europe's leading tourist nation and second in the world after the US. Some of the most popular centres are Roma, Venezia, Florence (Firenze), the Italian Riviera (Liguria) and Campania. Tourism is being developed in Calabria, Sardegna and Sicilia.

Mining
Although Italy has a variety of minerals, deposits are usually small and often unworkable. The principal mining regions are Sicilia (sulphur, potash), Toscana (mercury, salt, pyrites), Sardegna (lead-zinc), Piemonte (asbestos, manganese) and Lombardia (asbestos). Some iron is mined in Valle d'Aosta and on Elba and there is bauxite in Abruzzi. Low quality coal comes from Sardegna and the Alps and lignite from Toscana. Natural gas is produced in the Po basin and oil at Gela in Sicilia. Marble quarrying is important: the Toscana centres of Versilia (Massa, Carrara and Garfagnana) form the world's largest source.

Transport
Railways total 20,000 km and consist of 4 main lines: Ventimiglia-Reggio Calabria, Padova-Lecce, Milano-Roma and Torino-Trieste. The 300,000 km road network includes Europe's second longest motorway system—the most famous being the 1,250 km Autostrada del Sol from Milano to Reggio Calabria. Inland shipping is mainly concentrated on Lakes Garda, Maggiore, Como and Iseo. The main sea ports are Genova, Venezia, Trieste, Palermo, Napoli, Savona, Livorno and Ancona and Italy has the world's eighth largest merchant fleet. There are 30 major airports in Italy served by the national airline, Alitalia.

Cities
Roma was founded on the Palatine hill in 753 BC and within 400 years had spread to 6 other hills on the south bank of the Tiber (Tevere). As one of the greatest historical and relgious cities in the world, Roma's main source of income is tourism. Milano (1,725,700), a major route centre, is Italy's industrial, commercial and financial capital. Napoli (1,234,230) is the only major industrial city in the south and is backed by Vesuvius, the mainland's one active volcano. The fourth largest city, Torino (1,178,400), is dominated by Europe's leading car producer, Fiat, which has some 20 plants in or near the city.

Industry
Italy's recent industrial growth has been most marked in steel and engineering (aircraft, rolling stock, vehicles, machine tools). This heavy industry is concentrated in the Milano-Torino-Genova triangle, but there are also steel plants and engineering works at Piombino, Napoli and Taranto. Genova and Trieste are major ship-building centres. The chemical industry is located in the ports, the Alps (using hydro-electricity) and Torino, Milano, Mantua, Ferrara and Ravenna. Textile manufacture in cotton, silk, wool and artificial fibres is also concentrated in the north (Lombardia and Veneto) but with some production in Napoli and Salerno. Food processing is the only industry evenly distributed throughout the country: exports include cheese, wine, pasta and canned vegetables. Tourism has increased the demand for traditional craft products such as glass (Venezia) and onyx (Siena).

Small European States

Andorra

Monaco

Liechtenstein

San Marino

Vatican City

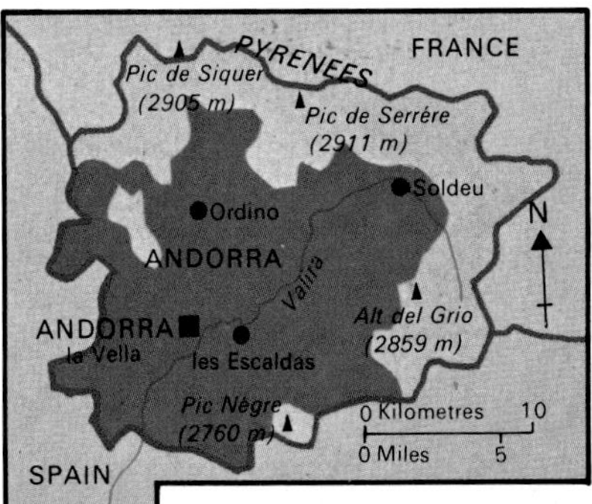

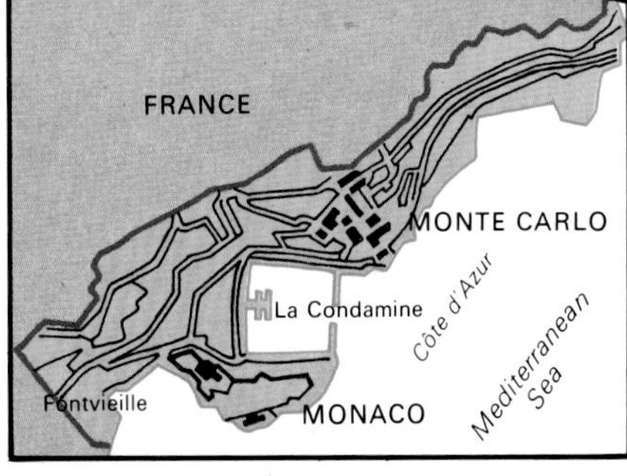

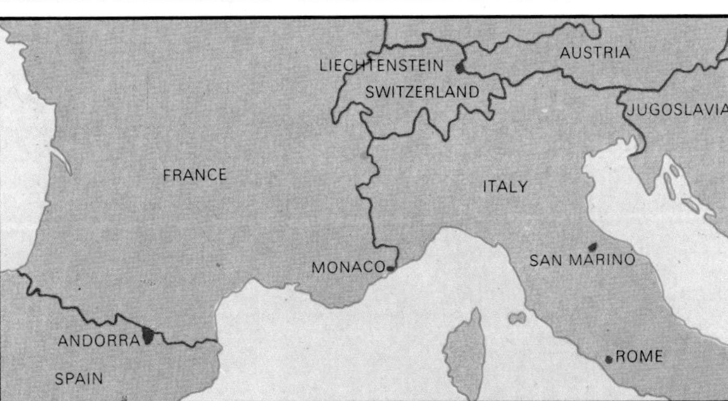

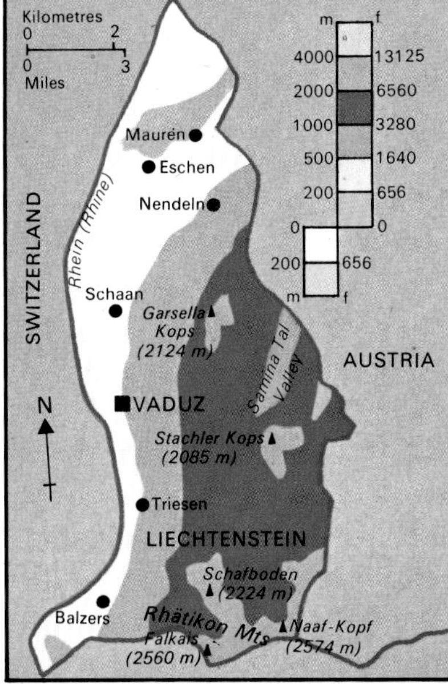

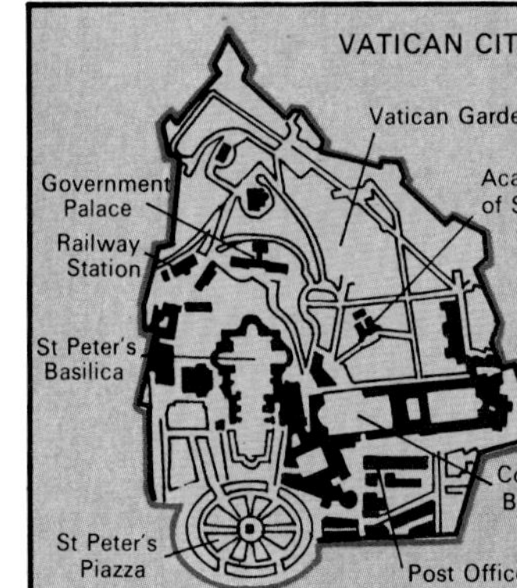

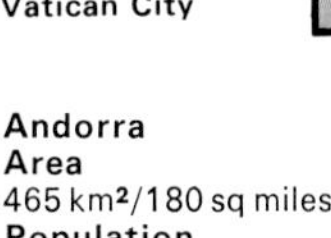

Andorra
Area
465 km²/180 sq miles
Population
23,000 (1973)
Capital
Andorra la Vella : 7,000 (1973)
Language
Catalan
Exports
dairy products, timber, stamps and furniture
Currency
Spanish peseta, French franc
Status
co-principality

Monaco
Area
1.9 km²/0.7 sq miles
Population
23,500 (1971)
Capital
Monte Carlo : 10,000 (1971)
Language
French
Currency
French franc
Status
principality

Liechtenstein
Area
160 km²/62 sq miles
Population
22,300 (1972)
Capital
Vaduz : 4,000 (1972)
Language
German
Exports
manufactured goods, dairy products, wine and stamps
Currency
Swiss franc
Status
principality

San Marino
Area
61 km²/24 sq miles
Population
19,000 (1972)
Capital
San Marino : 4,500 (1972)
Language
Italian
Exports
wine, manufactured goods, stamps
Currency
Italian lira
Status
republic

Vatican City
Area
0.4 km²/0.15 sq miles
Population
1,000
Languages
Italian, Latin
Currency
lira
Status
ecclesiastical state

Vatican City
Vatican City, the headquarters of the Roman Catholic Church, is the smallest independent state in the world. Situated in north-west Rome near the west bank of the Tevere (Tiber) it is dominated by St Peter's basilica, the world's largest Christian church. The adjacent palace, containing over 1,000 rooms, includes the Sistine chapel with Michelangelo's ceiling, museums, libraries and catacombs. The Pope is the head of state and most citizens are Vatican employees, many of them priests and nuns. The city has its own flag, radio station (broadcasting in 30 languages), bank, army, telephone exchange, railway station, daily newspaper (*L'Osservatore Romano*), and a rarely-used prison. It also issues its own coins (accepted throughout Italy), postage stamps and car licences.

Monaco
Monaco lies at the foot of the Alps on the Mediterranean coast about 10 km on the French side of the border between France and Italy. Sheltered from cold winds by the Alps, Monaco has a mild climate : winter averages about 12°C. summer 23°C. The whole territory is built up and consists of four districts : Monaco-Ville (the old city standing on a rocky promontory), the sophisticated capital of Monte Carlo, La Condamine (the port area) and Fontvieille (an industrial zone partly constructed on land reclaimed from the sea). The economy is based on tourism : some of Monaco's major attractions are its luxury yacht harbour, the Casino, international events such as the Monte Carlo Rally and the oceanographic museum. Other sources of income are taxes on gambling and the sale of postage stamps. The industrial sector is growing rapidly with products such as fish preserves, textiles, electronic apparatus, plastics and pharmaceuticals.

San Marino
San Marino, the world's smallest republic, is entirely surrounded by Italy. It is located in the northeast Apennines and, for the most part, consists of Monte Titano (739 m). The capital, San Marino town, perches high on the mountain's west side ; its main suburb, Borgo Maggiore, stands below. Serravalle, an agricultural and industrial centre, is the only other town. Because of its height, a modified Mediterranean climate prevails : temperatures rise to 26°C in summer, but fall to —7°C in winter. Three roads connect San Marino with Italy and there is a helicopter link with Rimini in summer. A funicular runs from Borgo Maggiore to San Marino town. The republic's economy is based on manufacturing, tourism, agriculture and the sale of postage stamps. Industrial development is recent and includes woollen textiles, ceramics, tiles, paints, varnishes and furniture. Tourism is important : some 3 million tourists visit San Marino annually, mostly on day-trips. The volcanic soil of Monte Titano is very fertile : vineyards cover the lower slopes and red wine is a leading export. Wheat, maize and barley are grown on the encircling lowlands and there is also a limited amount of dairy farming.

Liechtenstein
Liechtenstein occupies a small section of the Rhine valley between Austria and Switzerland. In the east, the Rhätikon foot-hills rise to over 2,500 m while the western part of the country (the most densely populated) consists of an alluvial lowland along the right bank of the Rhine. Because of its sheltered position, Liechtenstein has a relatively mild climate. There are bus links with Switzerland and Austria and the Paris-Vienna railway crosses the north of the country. In the last 30 years, Liechtenstein has developed a wide range of light industries such as pharmaceuticals, textiles, precision instruments, ceramics and food-processing. Agriculture also makes a contribution to the economy. Stock raising and dairying, based on the rich alpine pastures, are important. Arable farming is concentrated on the Rhine plain where wheat, maize, potatoes and fruit (plums, apples, pears and cherries) are produced. Vineyards grow on the terraced hill sides. The tourist industry, centred on Vaduz, is expanding. Frequent issues of postage stamps are another source of income. There are several hydro-electric power stations and some of the electricity generated by these power plants is exported to Switzerland.

Andorra
Andorra, situated high in the eastern Pyrenees between France and Spain, consists of mountain peaks rising to between 2,000 and 3,000 m and steep valleys. No point is below 900 m. Winters are severe, but summers are hot and dry. Most settlements, including the capital Andorra la Vella, lie in the valley of the river Valira. There are bus services to France and Spain, but in winter the main road is often snow-bound near the French border. Traditionally, Andorra is a pastoral country : in summer, livestock is grazed on the mountain slopes ; in winter, cattle are stall-fed while sheep are taken to lower pastures in France. Arable farming is confined to the terraced sides of the valleys where potatoes, maize, oats, rye and the main cash crop, tobacco, are grown. Forests, notably pine, still cover much of the country. Industry, based on local raw materials, consists of cigar and cigarette manufacture, food-processing and furniture-making. The mainstay of the economy is, however, tourism. Apart from scenic beauty, Andorra offers its 3 million visitors a year ideal conditions for fishing, riding, walking and, in winter, skiing. Other attractions include tax free shops, thermal springs and colourful stamps.

German Democratic Republic

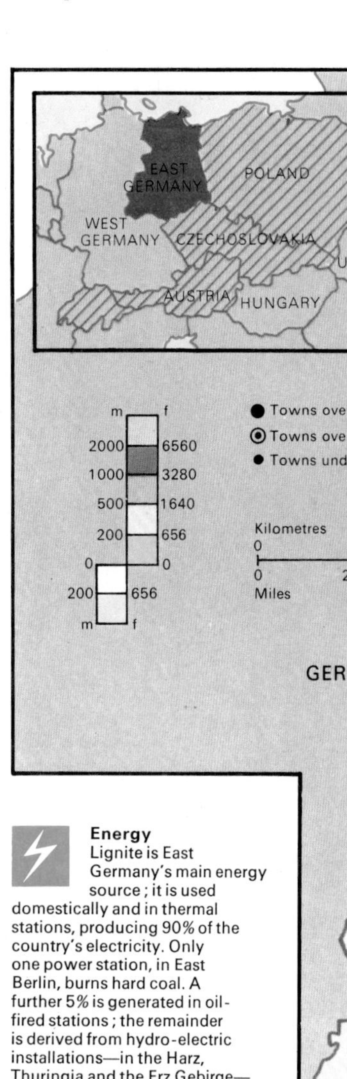
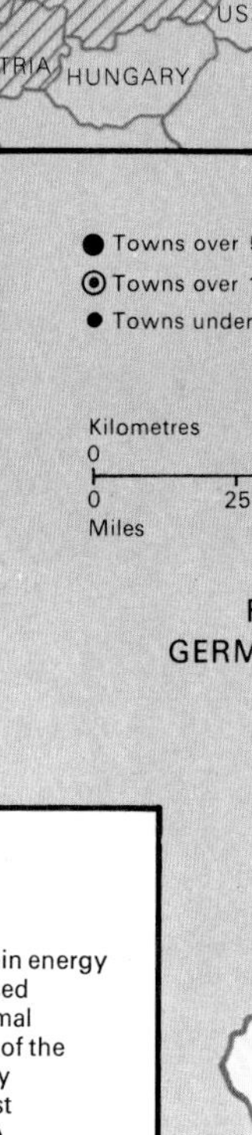

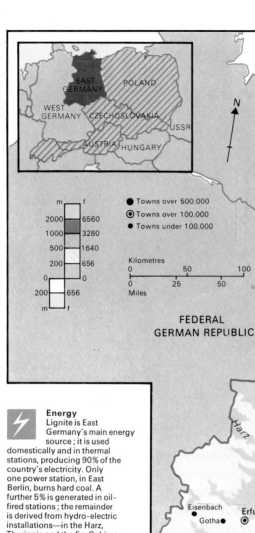

Area
108,178 km²/41,768 sq miles
Location
50°10'—54°41'N; 9°54'—15°2' E
Population
16,924,700 (1974)
Population density
156 per km²/405 per sq mile
Capital and largest city
East Berlin: 1,089,962 (1974)
Language
German
Major imports
fuels, metal products, foodstuffs, textiles
Major exports
machinery, chemicals, transport equipment, minerals
Currency
Mark (1 Mark — 100 pfennige)
Gross National Product
43,000 million US dollars
Status
independent republic

Physical features
Most of the German Democratic Republic (GDR) forms part of the north European plain. The largely infertile central area consists of morainic ridges separated by broad, shallow marshland valleys. In the north, low undulating clay hills with numerous lakes back the Baltic coast, which is characterized by swamps and sandbars. The southern margin of the plain is marked by a wide belt of loess. Beyond this fertile zone lies a plateau over 1,000 m high. These highlands include the granite Harz mountains, the thickly-wooded Thuringian Forest and the Erz Gebirge, with the country's highest point, Klinovec: 1,244 m. Steep, gorge-like valleys cut into the mountain blocks. East Germany is drained by the Elbe and its tributaries; the Oder and Neisse form the eastern border with Poland.

Climate
East Germany's climate is transitional between oceanic and continental. Winters are relatively mild and damp, but increase in severity towards the east—the Oder is frozen for almost three months—while summers are warm and stormy. January averages—1°C in both Greifswald and Dresden; corresponding July temperatures are 17°C and 19°C. In the lowlands, rainfall is fairly evenly distributed: Schwerin has 51 cm of rain a year, Berlin 57 cm. The southern highlands are considerably wetter: on west-facing slopes, annual precipitation ranges between 150 and 200 cm, although sheltered basins can be arid.

Mining
East Germany has vast reserves of lignite and potash: the 250 million tonnes of lignite mined annually account for 35% of world output. Most of it comes from the Lusatian field, north-east of Dresden, and the Halle-Leipzig field lying west of the Elbe. Vast potash beds are worked open-cast on the eastern edge of the Harz near Halle, giving an annual output of 2.5 million tonnes. Small quantities of hard coal are mined in the Karl-Marx-Stadt-Zwickau area. There is some iron ore production in the Harz and in Thuringia, copper at Mansfeld and uranium in the Erz Gebirge.

Energy
Lignite is East Germany's main energy source; it is used domestically and in thermal stations, producing 90% of the country's electricity. Only one power station, in East Berlin, burns hard coal. A further 5% is generated in oil-fired stations; the remainder is derived from hydro-electric installations—in the Harz, Thuringia and the Erz Gebirge—and from the GDR's one atomic power station. Electricity output is insufficient for the country's needs and oil is piped from the USSR to be refined at Schwedt.

Cities
Following war destruction, East Berlin was rebuilt and industry reconstructed; the capital is now the GDR's leading industrial city with electrical and mechanical engineering, textiles, chemicals and food-processing. Leipzig (572,976), at the confluence of the Weisse Elster, Pleisse and Parthe, is a major industrial and commercial town. Dresden (506,752), on the Elbe, was devastated in the war but has been restored and is an industrial, cultural and tourist centre. The famous Dresden china is made nearby at Meissen.

Forestry and fishing
Forests, mostly coniferous, cover 27% of the country. Spruce predominates in the Harz, Thuringer Wald and the Erz Gebirge, while fir, Scotch pine and larch grow on sandy areas in the central plain and coastal region. The production of lumber, pulp and paper is most important in the southern highlands. Demand exceeds output, however, and timber has to be imported. Fish must also be imported as catches, often from distant Atlantic waters, do not meet domestic needs. The deep-sea fleet is based at Rostock.

Agriculture
Agriculture, organized collectively and consisting of state farms and co-operatives, accounts for 58% of the land surface, and almost three-quarters of this area is used for arable farming. The most fertile region corresponds to the southern loess belt which gives high yields of wheat, barley and sugar-beet. Rye and potatoes are grown throughout the rest of the northern plain, with some sugar-beet and fodder crops on the semi-fertile clays near the coast. Livestock is less widespread: beef and dairy cattle and pigs are kept in the Baltic region; dairy farming is important on drained pastures south and west of Berlin; cattle are stall-fed in the loess belt and both cattle and sheep are grazed in the southern highlands. Market gardening is important near most major towns, particularly in the industrial south. Although crop yields are fairly high, the GDR still has to import much of its food.

Transport
The 14,384 km rail network basically serves the industrial south, where it links the principal cities and connects the region with Berlin and the Baltic ports of Rostock and Stralsund. 70% of freight is carried by rail and only 25% by road. Like the railways, the 45,570 km road network is dense in the south, but less developed in the north; it includes the incomplete motorway (autobahn) system which radiates from Berlin. As the inland waterways, totalling 2,546 km, do not connect with the south, they transport less than 5% of freight; tourist traffic, however, is expanding. The main navigable routes are the Elbe, Saale, Havel and Oder plus east-west linking canals. Rostock has been enlarged to include a deep-water harbour, modern shipyards and oil terminal and is now the GDR's leading port; it also serves the Czechoslovak hinterland. The national airline, Interflug, operates overseas and internally.

Industry
The GDR is Eastern Europe's leading industrial country. Natural resources are the basis of the main industrial regions: Halle-Leipzig (lignite, potash); Zwickau-Karl-Marx-Stadt (coal); Lusatia (lignite). Engineering leads in importance and accounts for 40% of total exports, which include machine tools, vehicles, electrical goods and precision instruments. The major centres are Leipzig, Halle, Magdeburg, Karl-Marx-Stadt, Zwickau and Dresden. The chemical industry, ranking second, is located in the Halle-Leipzig area and is based on lignite, potash and oil. Chemical products, making up 17% of exports, range from fertilizers, plastics and artificial fibres to drugs, paints and explosives. Food-processing is third in importance, followed by textile manufacture; imported wool and cotton are being replaced by home-produced synthetic fibres. The expanding metallurgical industry includes several steelworks and an aluminium smelter.

USSR 1

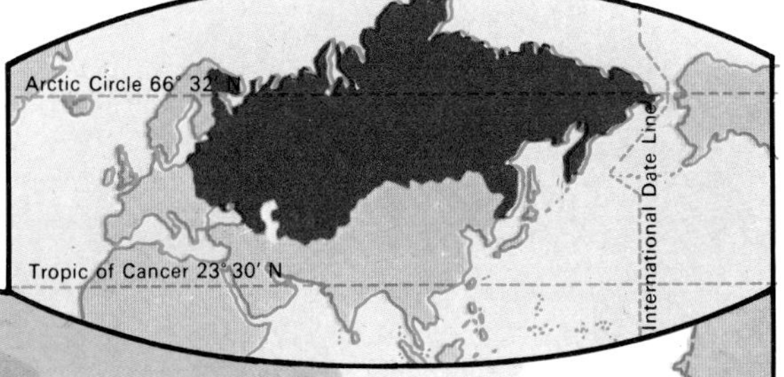

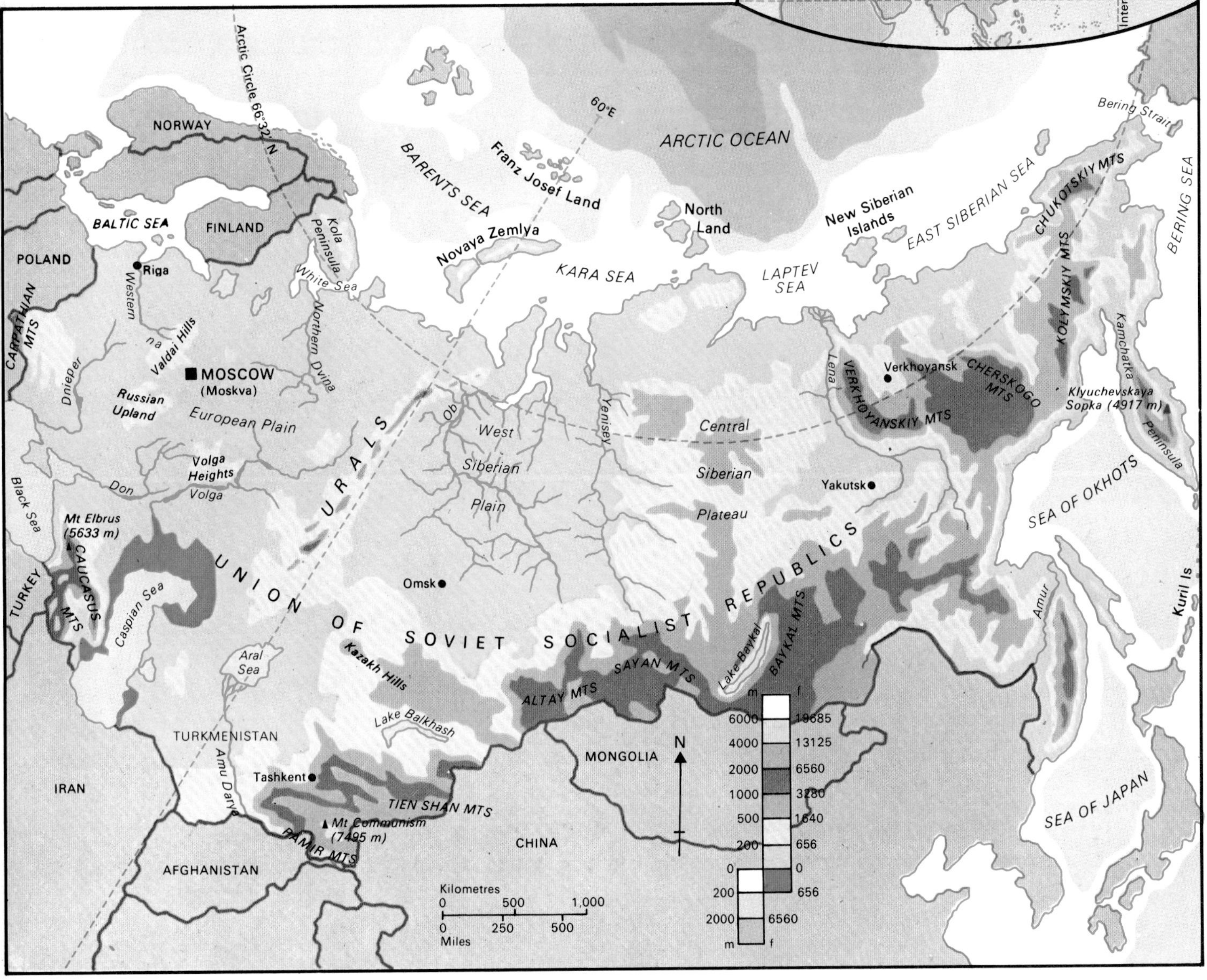

Area
22,402,200 km²/8,649,500 sq miles
Location
35°10'—77°45' N
19°40' E—169°40' W
Population
253,259,000 (1975)
Population density
11 per km²/29 per sq mile
Capital and largest city
Moscow: 7,635,000 (1975)
Language
Russian
Major imports
machinery, fuel and raw materials, foodstuffs, consumer goods
Major exports
crude oil, coal, iron ore, paper, lumber, cotton, vegetable oil, motor vehicles, clocks, watches
Currency
rouble (1 rouble = 100 kopeks)
Gross National Product
540,000 million US dollars (1972)
Status
federal union of republics

Each of the 15 republics comprising the USSR is the home of a major ethnic group. The largest and most important republic, which contains 75% of the total area and over 50% of the total population, is the Russian Soviet Federated Socialist Republic.

Physical features
The USSR is the largest country in the world: twice the size of China, three times as big as Australia, it stretches across Europe and Asia and covers 17% of the world's land surface. There are two main divisions: lowlands, largely corresponding to the plains west of the Yenisey river, and highlands which are concentrated in peripheral zones. The European plain, west of the Urals, is bordered by the Baltic, White and Barents Seas in the north, the Carpathian mountains to the west and the Black and Caspian Seas in the south. The Caucasus has Europe's highest peak, Mt Elbrus (5,633 m). The lowland is broken by the Valdai hills, the Central Russian Upland, the Volga Heights and the Kola Peninsula mountains. The region is drained by the Northern Dvina, flowing to the Arctic, the Western Dvina to the Baltic, the Dnieper and Don to the Black Sea and by the Volga (Europe's longest river, 3,690 km) which flows into the Caspian. The Urals, with an average height of between 500 and 800 m, form the traditional barrier between Europe and Asia.

The West Siberian Plain extends 3,200 km eastwards from the Urals to the Yenisey river and is one of the largest lowlands in the world. This region is mainly drained by the Ob. East of the Yenisey lies the Central Siberian Plateau which stretches to the Lena. The plateau has an average height of 600 m, but is rimmed by the Baykal and Sayan ranges (2,000 to 3,000 m) in the south. Two principal Asian rivers, the Amu Darya and Syr Darya, flow to the Aral Sea through the semi-arid depression separating the Urals from the Kazakh hills. These hills, up to 1,000 m high, stretch southwards to Lake Balkhash and the high mountain mass: the Pamir, Tien Shan and Altay ranges. The Pamir range includes the USSR's highest peak: Mt Communism, 7,495 m. The area between the Lena and the Pacific is mountainous, containing the Verkhoyanskiy, Cherskogo, Kolymskiy and Chukotskiy ranges. The Kuril islands are an extension of the volcanic Kamchatka peninsula which contains Asia's highest active volcano, Klyuchevskaya Sopka (4,917 m). Lake Baykal (33,000 km² and 1,940 m deep) is the world's biggest freshwater lake.

Climate
The USSR has a continental climate. Winters are long and harsh: January temperatures in most parts are below freezing. Conditions are most severe in the north-east where rivers are frozen for eight months and the land is snow-covered for six. In the west, the Baltic, Black and Caspian Seas have a moderating influence. Average January temperatures are: Riga —5°C, Tashkent —5°C, Moscow —10°C, Omsk —19°C and Yakutsk —40°C. At Verkhoyansk, —72°C has been recorded. In contrast, summers are warm: the hottest area is Turkmenistan where 32°C is not uncommon; the coolest zone is the Arctic coast, but here prolonged sunshine raises the temperature to 10°C. July averages are: Riga 17°C, Moscow 18°C, Tashkent 26°C, Omsk 19°C and Yakutsk 18°C. Rainfall, occurring in spring and summer, is generally moderate and light and most of the country receives less than 60 cm a year. The wettest areas are the Black Sea coast (250 cm) and the south Pacific coast (75 cm). Central Siberia has under 25 cm, Turkmenistan under 10 cm.

Flora and fauna
Distinct vegetation zones, related to latitude, extend from east to west in great broad belts. In the extreme north is the tundra. Only mosses and lichens grow on the waterlogged soils of this treeless plain where the subsoil is permanently frozen. Tundra wildlife is limited to reindeer, lemmings, Arctic foxes and migrating birds. Southwards, the tundra merges into the taiga, a belt of coniferous forest some 1,000 km wide. This is the world's most extensive forest zone with spruce, pine, fir and larch. Wolves, brown bears, squirrels, foxes and rabbits inhabit this area. The mixed forest belt of oak, ash, birch and fir is widest in European Russia where animal life has been depleted through clearance. In the east, however, leopards, tigers and black bears are found. The forest gives way to the steppes—treeless grasslands with rich, black soil. Cultivation has driven away much of the wildlife, but wolves and foxes remain. South of the steppes are desert areas. Peripheral mountains are largely forested and inhabited by goats, snow leopards and ibexes.

USSR 2

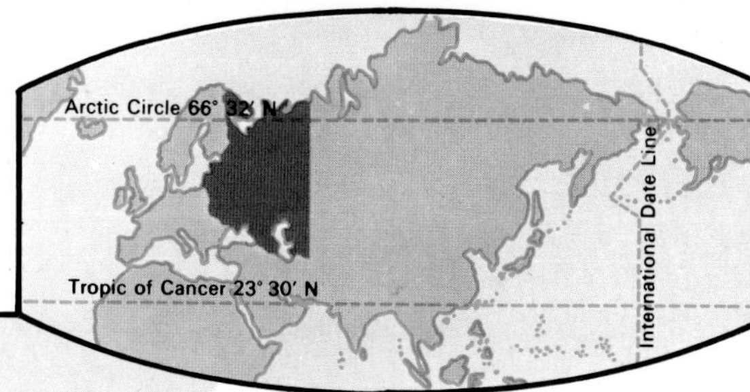

Agriculture

In the last 50 years, the USSR has evolved from an agricultural to an industrial nation. About 46% of the population, however, is still rural and a third of the total labour force is employed in farming. Only 25% of the country is used for agriculture, including grazing. Less than half this area is under cultivation and roughly corresponds to the triangle between Leningrad, the Black Sea and Lake Baykal: this takes in the mixed forest zone and the steppes with their rich black earth. Almost 70% of farmed land lies in European USSR.

Farm organization

The USSR has two types of farm: the collective farm, *kolkhoz*, and the state farm, *sovkhoz*. A collective farm, covering an average of 30 km^2 and grouping some 440 families, is worked as a co-operative. Most of the output is sold to the state and the proceeds are used to buy equipment, fertilizer etc., or to improve cultural amenities. Each household has a private plot and the fruit and vegetables grown on this land may be consumed or sold by the owner as he wishes. There are about 33,000 collectives, mainly situated in traditional farming areas, and together they produce 92% of the country's sugar beet, 76% of its cotton and 54% of its grain. The 15,500 state farms, each with an average of 60 km^2 and 600 workers, are mostly located in newly developed agricultural regions. These farms are highly mechanized, state owned establishments and the workforce consists of state employees. They provide 75% of the USSR's meat.

Crops

Over 30% of the land under cultivation is used for wheat and another 30% for rye, oats, barley, rice and maize. The main wheat zones are the black earth belt, western Siberia and Kazakhstan. Rye, oats and barley predominate in the northwest, maize in the steppes and the Caucasus and rice in Soviet Central Asia and Kazakhstan. Other major crops are sugar beet, grown in the black earth belt, Soviet Central Asia and western Siberia; flax, potatoes and vegetables in the western steppes and northwest; sunflower (the most important oil plant) in the southeast steppes, the Caucasus and western Siberia; and cotton, grown under irrigation in Soviet Central Asia and in Transcaucasia. The sub-tropical conditions in western Transcaucasia also favour tea, citrus fruits and tobacco. Deciduous fruits and grapes are grown in eastern Transcaucasia, Moldavia and Central Asia.

Irrigation

Approximately 120,000 km^2 of land is irrigated and further schemes are under construction. Wheat, rice, cotton and fruit are the main crops grown in these irrigated areas. They are largely concentrated in Kazakhstan and Soviet Central Asia where water is available in summer from snow melting in Pamir, Tien Shan and Altay ranges.

European USSR

Towns over 1,000,000; Towns over 100,000; Towns under 100,000

m	f
6000	19685
4000	13125
2000	6560
1000	3280
500	1640
200	656
0	0
200	656

Kilometres 0 250 500; Miles 0 100 200

Fishing

The USSR has the world's largest fishing fleet yet, in terms of production, it holds third place after Japan and Peru. Much of the Soviet catch comes from distant waters in the Atlantic and Pacific. Coastal fishing is most important in the northwest and eastern seas. The two leading ports in the northwest are Archangel and ice-free Murmansk; principal varieties caught are cod, haddock and flatfish. Vladivostok is the main eastern fishing port and base of the Soviet whaling fleet. Salmon and crab are important and, in arctic areas, whales, walruses and seals. The Baltic catch, largely landed at Riga, includes cod, salmon, lamprey and sprat. Sturgeon from the Caspian and Black Seas are the source of caviar.

Forestry

The USSR has more forested area than any other country in the world. Forests cover 40% of the total land surface—mainly in the east and north-west. The eastern forests yield 17% of the country's timber. Saw and pulp mills are sited on the Trans-Siberian railway, on the Pacific coast and on the Yenisey. A further 13%, mostly spruce and pine, comes from the northwest. Archangel, with over 150 sawmills, has become the country's main lumber port—logs are floated down the Northern Dvina. Riga is a leading Baltic lumber port.

Iron ore

The USSR claims 41% of the world's iron ore reserves. Half of this comes from Krivoy Rog in the Ukraine. Other high grade deposits are worked at Bakal, Magnitogorsk and Nizhniy Tagil in the Urals, at Kerch in the Crimea, Atasu and Gornaya Shoriya in Kazakhstan, and at Orlenegorsk in the Kola peninsula. Low grade reserves are situated in the northern Urals and Kazakhstan. The USSR is also the world's leading iron ore producer.

Livestock

In spite of measures to develop livestock, such as importing new stock and expanding fodder sources, meat and dairy production is still below national requirements. Cattle, pig and poultry farming, based on fodder crops, are practised extensively in the mixed forest and steppes zones, particularly west of the Volga. Dairy herds predominate in the north, beef cattle in the south. Sheep and goats are grazed in the Caucasus, the mountains of Soviet Central Asia and southern Siberia and in the desert zone south of the Urals. There are some 140 million sheep and their wool is the basis of the world's largest woollen textile industry. Reindeer herding takes place in the tundra. Natural pasture is used in the steppes east of the Volga and the Lena valley.

Coal

With an annual output of 700 million tonnes, the USSR is the world's leading coal producer. About 33% of production comes from the Donbass field in the Ukraine, 16% from the Kuzbass in western Siberia, 5% from Karaganda in Kazakhstan, and 3% from Pechora in the north. These four fields are important as output exceeds local demand and the surplus is sent to other parts of the country. The Moscow and Ural fields consist largely of lignite suitable only for generating electricity. At present, scattered mines in eastern Siberia and the Far East yield only 12% of total production, but vast reserves are known to exist, particularly in the Tunguska and Lena basins. Peat is used in European USSR.

Oil and gas

An annual production of 500 million tonnes makes the USSR the world's second largest oil producer. About 70% of the country's petroleum comes from the Ural-Volga area which has been developed since 1940. Before that, 80% of oil came from the Baku and North Caucasus fields; today, these yield only 15% of the total output. The remainder mainly comes from recently discovered fields in western Siberia and Kazakhstan. The USSR exports 20% of its oil. Natural gas production is also expanding rapidly with 50% of output linked to oil-fields in the Ural-Volga, Baku and North Caucasus. There are new gas fields east of the Urals: one of the largest is at Gizli in Uzbekistan.

Other minerals

In terms of world production, the USSR holds first place for manganese and phosphate and second place for potash, copper and zinc. Manganese production, accounting for 50% of the world's supply, is centred on Nikopol, Ukraine, and on Chiatura, Georgia. The Urals and Kazakhstan are major mineral-producing areas. The Urals have deposits of gold, copper, bauxite, platinum and potash. Chrome, copper, lead, zinc, bauxite, sulphur and phosphate are worked at Kazakhstan. Eastern Siberia is noted for gold and diamonds.

USSR 3

Population

The bulk of the Soviet population lives in the European USSR where the average density is 30 per km², but cities and major industrial zones have higher levels: the Ukraine, with only 3% of the total area and 19% of the population, has a density of 81 per km². In contrast, Siberia and the Far East, covering 50% of the area, has only 10% of the population—a density of 2 per km². Due to the mechanization of agriculture and the creation of new urban-industrial complexes, the urban population is increasing. At the moment, however, approximately 50% of the total population lives in an urban environment.

Water transport

The USSR has over 144,000 km of inland waterways. The network is most extensive on the European plain where rivers and canals link the White, Baltic, Black and Caspian Seas. The Volga alone carries 50% of water freight, serving the industrial areas of Moscow, the Urals and Donbass. Coastal shipping is hampered in winter when the major ports of Riga, Vladivostok, Archangel and Leningrad are frozen. Murmansk, however, remains ice-free and Odessa and other Black Sea ports are also free during the year.

Other transport

In a country as vast as the USSR, transport is vital. The 140,000 km rail network carries 70% of freight and 45% of passenger traffic. It is most extensive in the European USSR where Moscow is the heart of the network. In the Asiatic sector, the famous Trans-Siberian route (Moscow to Vladivostok) is now supplemented by other lines to serve new industrial areas. Less than 33% of the 1,500,000 km road network is surfaced and only 7% of freight travels by road—usually to the nearest railhead. In remote regions, air transport is important. The Soviet airline, Aeroflot, operates domestic and international flights.

Energy

The role of traditional fuels (coal, lignite and peat) is decreasing. These now supply only 36% of the USSR's energy, as against 59% supplied by oil and gas. Gas directly supplies 40% of domestic needs; it is also piped to industry and, along with coal and oil, is used in thermal power stations. About 80% of Soviet electricity is still generated thermally in spite of vast hydro-electric projects. Initially, hydroelectric stations were centred in European USSR, on the Don, Dnieper and Volga, but recently plants have been built east of the Urals, notably on the Ob, Yenisey and Angara. The world's largest station is at Krasnoyarsk on the Yenisey. It has a kilometre-long dam and produces 6,000 MW. There are nuclear power stations at Obninsk, Novovoronezh and Byeloyarskaya. It is hoped to establish a national power grid by 1980. It has been estimated that approximately 70% of the electricity generated in the USSR is used by industry.

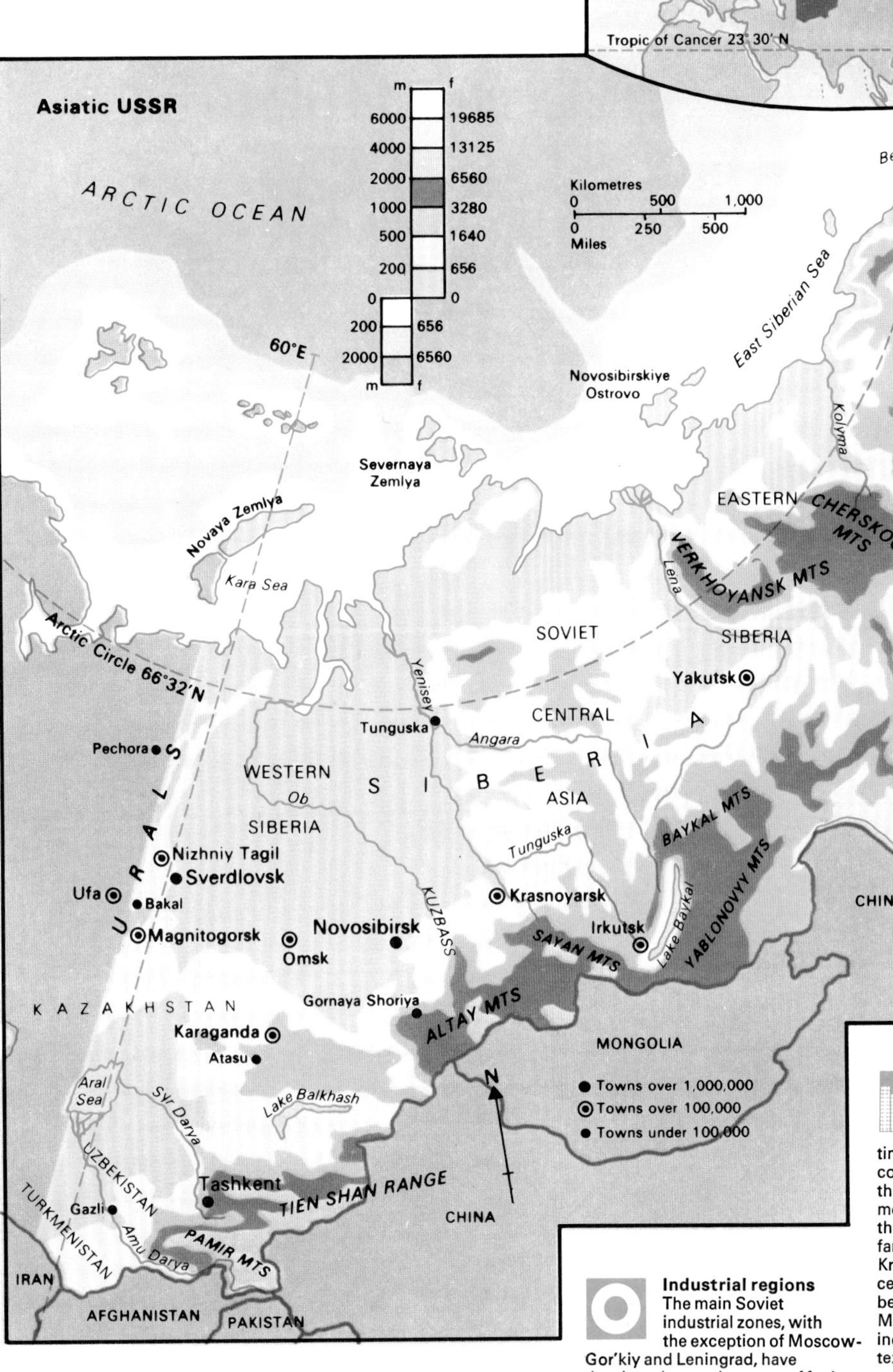

Heavy industry

Fifty years ago, the USSR was industrially backward, but today it is a major industrial power and, in many sectors, rivals the USA. The USSR is the world's leading producer of steel and pig-iron. About 40% of steel and 50% of pig-iron are produced in the Ukraine. A further 30% of both comes from the Urals. Other branches of the metallurgical industry are similarly developed, especially aluminium and copper. Engineering, which employs 30% of the Soviet industrial work-force, is centred in the Ukraine, Urals, Leningrad and the Moscow-Gor'kiy region. The USSR leads the world in the production of diesel locomotives and tractors. Engineering products are exported to East European countries. The chemical industry, traditionally based on minerals such as salt, phosphate and sulphur, now includes major installations using oil and natural gas.

Consumer industry

During the initial stages of Soviet industrialization, development was uneven with the emphasis being placed on heavy industry at the expense of consumer goods industry. In recent years, however, a stimulus has been given to these lighter manufactures and the Soviet people are consequently enjoying a higher standard of living. The USSR's traditional textile centre is Moscow, and the Moscow-Gor'kiy region still accounts for 80% of cotton textiles. The textile industry is also being developed in cotton-growing and sheep-grazing areas. Food-processing is based on urban centres such as Moscow, Leningrad and Kuybyshev as well as growing areas: for instance, fruit canning factories in Transcaucasia, flour mills and sunflower oil extraction in the Ukraine and fish-processing plants in Vladivostok. Cameras, clocks and watches are exported.

Industrial regions

The main Soviet industrial zones, with the exception of Moscow-Gor'kiy and Leningrad, have developed around sources of fuel and raw materials. The leading industrial region is the Ukraine based on Donbass coal, iron ore from Krivoy Rog and Kerch, Nikopol manganese and hydro-electric power from the Dnieper and Don. The Urals owe their industrial importance to extensive mineral wealth and to natural gas at Ufa and Berezovo. Oil is brought in from the Volga fields, while Karaganda and the Kuzbass supply coal. Industry in the Volga lands developed with the discovery of petroleum and the construction of hydro-electric power stations on the river; local phosphate, sulphur and salt are significant. Caucasian industry is also based on oil at Baku and on manganese deposits at Chiatura. The industrial growth of the Moscow-Gor'kiy and Leningrad regions stems from these major urban centres where fuel and raw materials have to be imported. Kazakhstan is the main manufacturing zone in Asiatic USSR with coal and iron ore.

Cities

Moscow was founded as a fortress on the river Moskva in 1147. At that time, the entire settlement was contained within the walls of the citadel, or Kremlin. The modern city (inhabited by 3% of the Soviet population) has spread far beyond the old walls, but the Kremlin remains and is now the centre of government. As well as being the leading cultural city, Moscow has developed as a major industrial centre specializing in textiles, engineering, food-processing and chemicals. The former capital, St Petersburg, is now known as Leningrad (4,311,000), and is the second largest city. Built by Peter the Great in 1713 at the mouth of the Neva, St Petersburg was the principal outlet of Russia to Western Europe. Its industry relies on raw materials supplied by the rest of the USSR and on hydro-electricity from plants on the Volkhov and Svir. The city builds 75% of Soviet ships, particularly ice-breakers. The USSR's third city (and the Ukraine's first) is Kiyev (1,947,000), a major engineering centre on the Dnieper. Completely rebuilt since the Second World War, Kiyev is noted for its parks which cover 33% of its area. The following Soviet cities also have over a million inhabitants: Tashkent (1,595,000), Baku (1,383,000), Kharkov (1,357,000), Gor'kiy (1,283,000), Novosibirsk (1,265,000), Sverdlovsk (1,147,000), Minsk (1,147,000), Tbilisi (1,006,000) and Odessa (1,002,000).

Mongolia

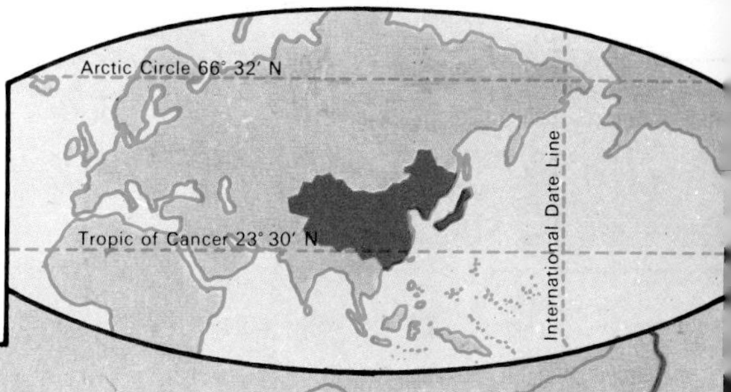

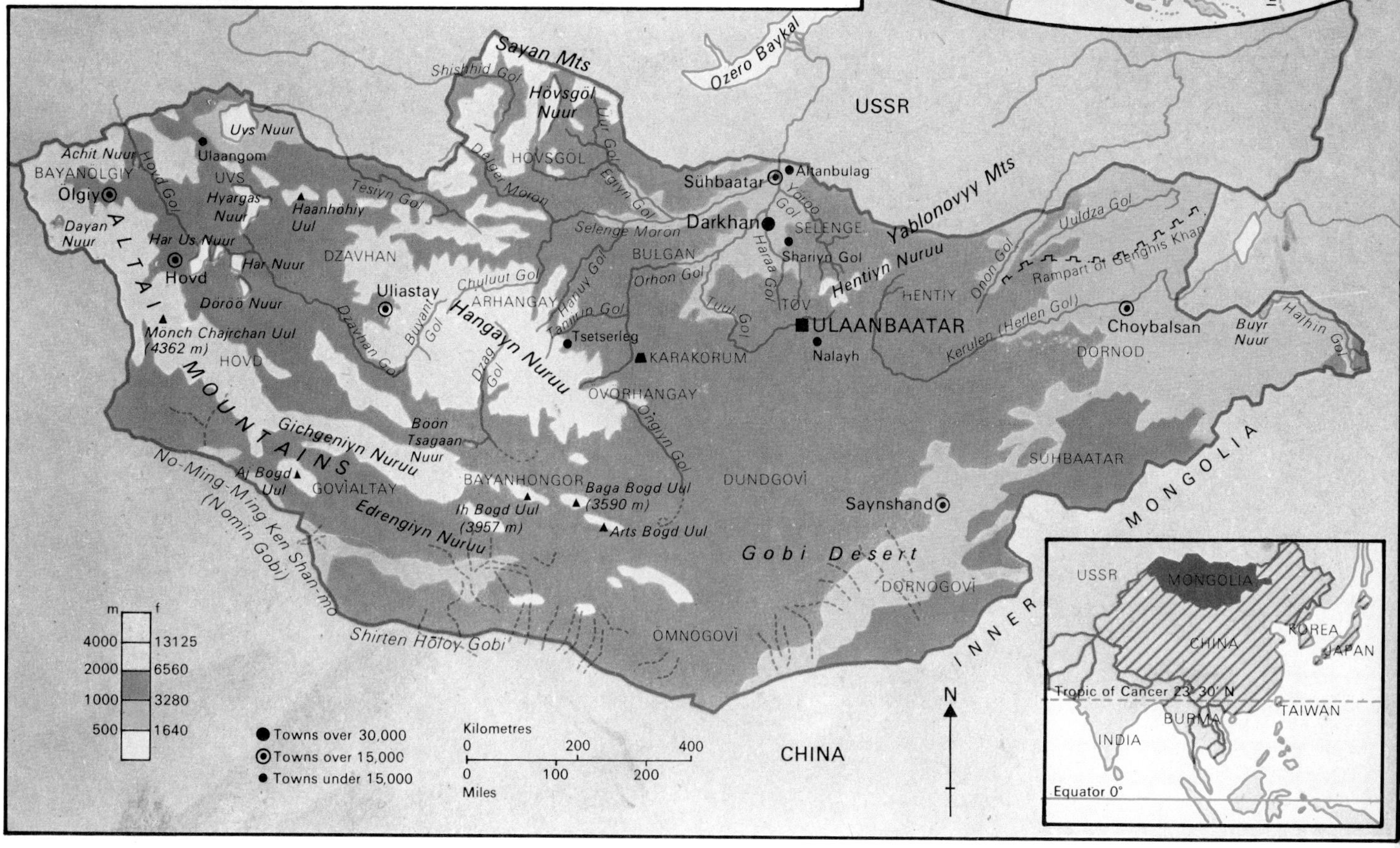

Area
1,565,000 km²/604,247 sq miles
Location
41°30′—52°10′ N
88°10′—119°40′ E
Population
1,468,600 (1976)
Population density
1 per km²/2 per sq mile
Capital and largest city
Ulaanbaatar: 334,000 (1976)
Language
Mongolian
Major imports
machinery, petroleum, transport, equipment, consumer goods
Major exports
livestock and animal products (meat, wool, hair, hides), fluorspar, tungsten
Currency
tugrik (1 tugrik = 100 möngö)
Gross National Product
590 million US dollars (1970)
Status
people's republic

Population

Mongolia is one of the world's most sparsely populated countries. Formerly, most Mongols were nomadic herdsmen but, under the present system, they have been encouraged to settle so that 48% of the people now dwell in towns and the remainder are mostly grouped in villages; only a few still live in the traditional round, felt-covered tents (*yurts*). Half the urban population is concentrated in the capital. Founded in 1649 as a monastery town, Ulaanbaatar is now the republic's industrial, commercial and cultural centre. Darkhan (30,000), which is on the main road and railway to the USSR, is the site of a major industrial complex.

Physical features

The Mongolian People's Republic, the world's largest landlocked state, lies on a high plateau between 1,500 and 1,800 m above sea level. Mountains dominate the north and west: snow-capped peaks of the Altai rise to over 4,300 m and the parallel Hangayn range are almost as high. The Hangayn chain is separated from the northerly Hentiyn mountains by the fertile basin of the rivers Selenge, Orhon and Tuul. The Selenge-Orhon-Tuul system drains northwards into Lake Baykal (USSR); Mongolia's other major river, the Kerulen, flows east into China. Between the mountain blocks there are many large, deep lakes; among them is Hövsgöl with an area of 2,620 km² and a depth of 240 m. In the southeast, the plateau drops down to the Gobi desert which extends into China; the desert landscape features undulating sand seas as well as barren sheets of rock and stone.

Climate

Mongolia has a harsh, dry continental climate with short hot summers and bitterly cold winters; in Ulaanbaatar temperatures average 18°C in July and drop to —26°C in January. During the severe winter, lakes and rivers are frozen but there is little snow. Precipitation, varying from 30 cm in the northwest mountains to under 5 cm in the southeast desert, occurs mostly as heavy summer showers and often causes flooding. The country is exposed to frequent strong winds and dust storms and is also liable to earthquakes.

Flora & fauna

The southern fringe of the Siberian *taiga* (the great coniferous forest belt) covers the border lands of northern Mongolia. Except for this forested zone, the plateau is largely grassland steppe; towards the southeast, vegetation becomes sparser and is reduced to patches of tufted grass and scrub along the desert margins. The Gobi is the home of the wild camel, wild horse, wild ass, gazelle and dzeren (antelope); wildlife in the north includes bear, snow leopard, wolf, sable, beaver and ermine. Furs are a valuable export.

Agriculture

Traditionally, Mongols are herdsmen and, although crop growing is expanding, stockraising is still basic to the Mongolian economy and provides the bulk of exports (live cattle and horses, meat, wool, hair, hides, skins, butter). In all, there are 24 million animals: sheep account for 55% of the total and goats 20%; horses, cattle and camels make up the remainder. Some nomadic herding still occurs in the Gobi but stock-breeding has generally been collectivized and, like arable farming, is organized into co-operatives and state farms. In the last twenty years the arable sector has been substantially developed. The ploughing of virgin lands in the wetter north greatly increased the area under cultivation and Mongolia is now self-sufficient in flour; in addition to cereals, fodder, potatoes and vegetables are grown. Some fruit is cultivated under irrigation.

Mining & energy

Mining activity is being expanded with technical aid from the USSR and other Comecon countries. Fluorspar and tungsten are mined and exported and there is also some production of gold. Major deposits of copper and molybdenum are being developed and reserves of tin, lead, phosphates, silver, fluorite and uranium have been discovered. There are important coal fields at Nalayh and Shariyn Gol; the coal is supplied to industry in Ulaanbaatar and Darkhan and to a new thermal electricity plant at Darkhan which also serves the capital. There are some smaller thermal stations but in most provincial centres electricity is provided by diesel generators. Wood and dried dung are the main domestic fuels in rural areas.

Industry

Industrialization, based on Soviet assistance, is making some progress but is hampered by the lack of skilled labour, inadequate power supplies and limited domestic market. Manufacturing is still primarily concerned with processing agricultural products including woollen textiles, leather footwear, flour, butter and vodka. Light engineering is also important. About 50% of Mongolian industry is located in Ulaanbaatar; the other centres are Darkhan and Choybalsan. Economic plans emphasize the need for export-orientated industries to help reduce the country's chronic trade deficit. About 80% of trade is with the USSR and a further 15% with other Comecon states.

Transport

Modern transportation systems have been introduced as part of the country's economic development programme. Railways are particularly important, accounting for 70% of all freight and 30% of passenger traffic. The main route is the Trans-Mongolian line linking the capital with Moscow and Peking; there are spurs to the Nalayh and Shariyn Gol mines. Another line connects Choybalsan with the Trans-Siberian railway. The 9,000 km road network is surfaced in the Ulaanbaatar and Darkhan regions and at points along the Soviet border. In rural areas, oxen, horses and camels are still widely used. There are boat services on Lake Hövsgöl and the rivers Selenge and Orhon. The state airline, MIAT, flies to the USSR and operates internally.

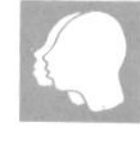

People

The people belong to the Mongoloid race with such typical features as round face, straight black hair, small nose and 'almond eyes'. The Mongolian people are mostly *Khalkhas* (Mongols from the north) but about 5%, concentrated in the west, are Turkish-speaking *Kazakhs* and *Uighurs*. In the 13th century, under Genghis Khan, the Mongols adopted a form of lamaist Buddhism; 70 years ago, lamas and novices accounted for 15% of the population but, with the growth of Soviet influence, most people have abandoned their Buddhist traditions. The Mongolian language, quite unlike Russian or Chinese, is now written in a modified Cyrillic script.

China

Peoples Republic of China

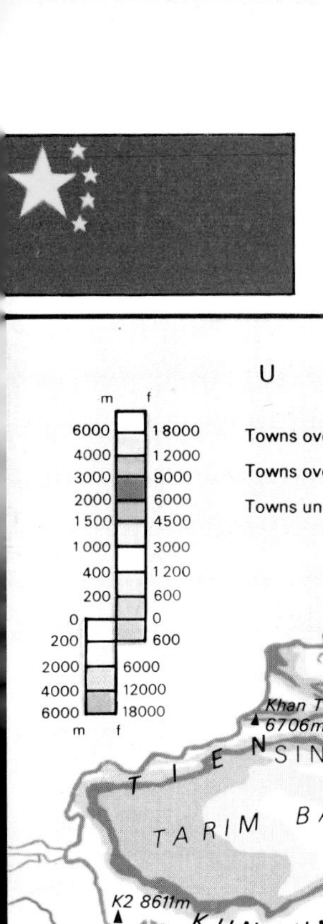

Area
9,561,000 km²/3,691,500 sq miles
Location
18°30'—55°N
70°—113°E
Population
800,000,000 (1974 est.)
Population density
84 per km²/217 per sq mile
Capital
Peking: 8,000,000 (1974 est.)
Largest city
Shanghai: 11,000,000 (1974 est.)
Language
Mandarin, Cantonese and Hakka dialects
Gross National Product
223,000,000,000 U.S. dollars
Major imports
machinery, cereals, metals, chemicals, raw cotton
Major exports
agricultural products, textiles, minerals, manufactured goods, tea
Currency
100 fen = 10 Chiao = 1 yuan
Status
Independent republic

Forestry

Over the centuries, a shortage of fuel led to the widespread destruction of China's forests; today, only 10% of the land is forested. More than half this timber is located in the north-east uplands where there are extensive coniferous and deciduous forests. Other wooded areas, producing tung oil and teak, are situated along the south-east coast and in Yunnan and Szechuan.

Climate

China's climate is dominated by two air masses. From November to March, polar air moves south from Siberia, giving harsh winters in the north and west. Winter temperature differences between the north and south, which remains mild, range from 30°-50°C: in January, the coldest month, the average in Canton is 13°C and in Harbin, —19°C. From May to October tropical air from the Pacific brings warm, damp winds and 80% of the country's annual rainfall. Summer temperatures are more uniform: in July, the hottest month, the average in Canton is 27°C and in Harbin, 23°C. Rainfall is heaviest in the monsoonal south-east, where some areas receive over 250 cm a year, whereas the Mongolian plateau receives less than 10 cm.

Livestock

In a country where nearly all fertile land is used for crop production, there is little pasture. Farmers in the east limit their livestock to work animals, such as oxen and water buffalo, and to ducks, hens and pigs. Conversely, stock-raising predominates in the arid interior. In Inner Mongolia, where milk is basic to the economy, sheep, cows, camels and goats are all kept for their milk. Similar herds are grazed in Sinkiang while Tibet's animal, the yak, is kept for its milk, meat, skin and hair.

Physical features

China, stretching 5,000 km from north to south and from east to west, is one of the world's largest countries, second only to the USSR. More than half the surface area is made up of plateaux and mountains; these are highest in the west and descend gradually to the eastern plains. The highest region is the 4,800 m Tibet tableland in the far west which is enclosed to the south by the Himalayas and, to the north, by the Kun Lun range. North of Kun Lun lies the desert basin of Tarim which has as its northern edge another range of mountains the Tien Shan. South-east of the Tibet plateau is the slightly lower Yunnan plateau. A range of mountains north of Yunnan separate it from the fertile Szechuan basin—where the Yangtse river is joined by three major tributaries—known as the red basin because of its coloured sandstone. Continuing north, the Tsinling Shan range runs between Szechuan and loessland—an area covered with a 100 m layer of yellow silt and bounded to the north by the Mongolian plateau. China's two main rivers, the Yangtse (5,800 km) and the Huang Ho (4,845 km) both rise in Tibet. The Huang Ho flows through loessland; hence its name, the Yellow River.

Minerals

China is relatively rich in minerals and is the world's leading producer of tungsten, from Kiangsi, and of antimony, from Hunan. Two other minerals exported are tin, mined at Kochin (Yunnan), and molybdenum, in Liaoning. Main centres of iron ore production are at Anshan (Lianoning), Tayeh (Hupeh) and Bayin Obo (Inner Mongolia).

Energy

Coal supplies 90% of China's energy needs. Although almost all provinces have some coal, 80% of reserves are in Shensi and Shansi, but the most important basins are at Kailan, Fushun, Huainan and Tatung. An annual output of some 400 million tonnes makes China the world's third-largest coal-producing country. In the last 15 years oil production has rapidly increased and China now claims to be self-sufficient. Major oiltields are in Kansu (Yumen) and in Sinkiang (Karamai, Wusu). China has great hydro-electric power potential, but so far only 1% has been exploited—mostly in the north-east. The greatest potential, in the centre and south, is largely untapped because of inaccessibility.

Autonomous regions

China is composed of 22 provinces and five autonomous regions. Originally, these five regions—Inner Mongolia, Sinkang-Uighur, Tibet, Ninghsia-Hui, Kwangsi-Chuang—were inhabited by national minorities but today the indigenous population has often been outnumbered by immigrant Han Chinese. Three of these regions—Tibet, Inner Mongolia and Sinkiang—are great interior lands on China's perimeter; the other two are in China proper. Kwangsi, in the Canton hinterland, is the home of eight million Chuangs—the largest of China's minorities. Ninghsia lies on the edge of loessland.

Inner Mongolia, part of the former Mongol empire created by Genghis Khan, is a 1000 m high plateau with an area of 1,177,500 km². The climate is dry with extreme differences in temperature between summer (21°C) and winter (—30°C). Agriculture predominates: cereals and sugar beet are grown in some areas; elsewhere the nomadic Mongols graze their animals. Industrial development, except for iron and steel at Paotow, is linked to agriculture: flour mills, sugar refineries and dairy plants. Huhehot is the capital.

Sinkiang, to the north of Tibet, has an area of 1,646,800 km². The region consists of two desert basins, the Tarim and the Dzungaria, separated by the Tien Shan mountains. In both basins oasis agriculture has been developed and crops include wheat, maize, rice, cotton and fruit. Livestock is kept on the less arid mountain slopes. Local oil, coal and iron has led to industrialization, centered on the capital, Urumchi.

Tibet consists of a high, bleak tableland, covering 1,177,500 km². Most of the two million Tibetans live in the south where they can grow maize, wheat, barley and potatoes in the Indus, Sutlej and Brahmaputra valleys. Livestock is also important. So far, there has been little industrial development, but some manufactures based on agriculture, such as leather factories, have been set up in Lhasa, the capital.

Eastern China

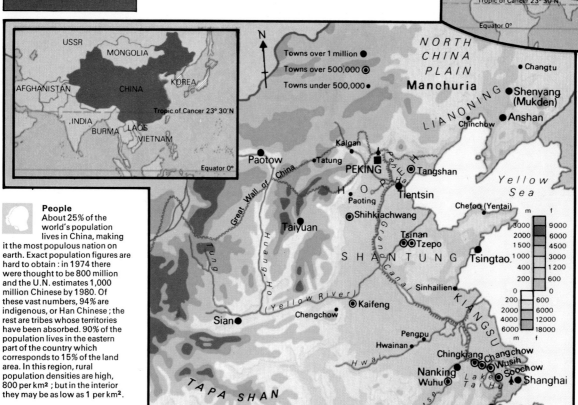

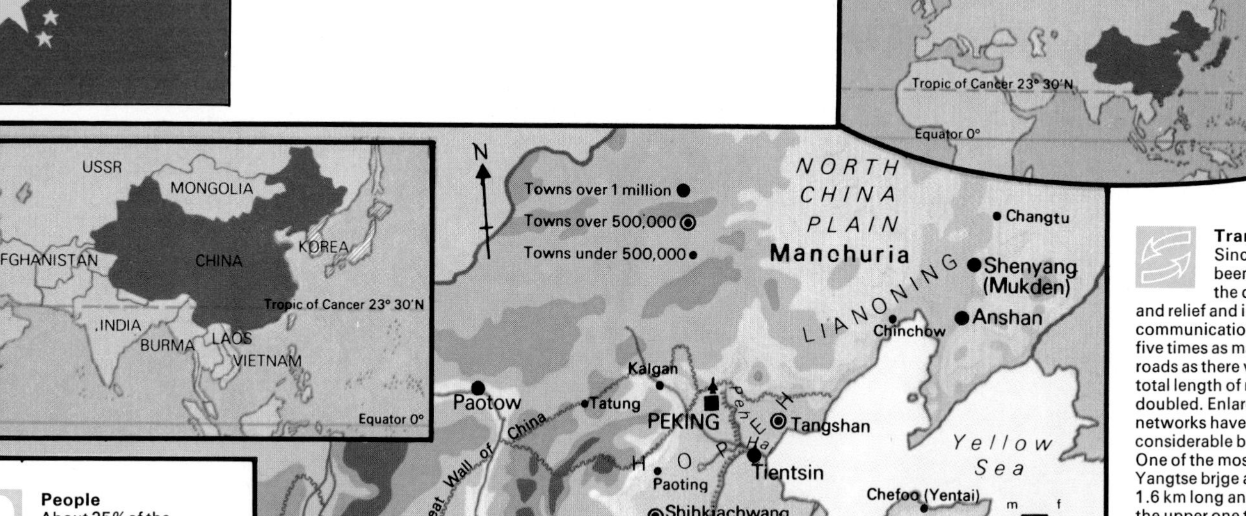

People

About 25% of the world's population lives in China, making it the most populous nation on earth. Exact population figures are hard to obtain: in 1974 there were thought to be 800 million and the U.N. estimates 1,000 million Chinese by 1980. Of these vast numbers, 94% are indigenous, or Han Chinese; the rest are tribes whose territories have been absorbed. 90% of the population lives in the eastern part of the country which corresponds to 15% of the land area. In this region, rural population densities are high, 800 per km²; but in the interior they may be as low as 1 per km².

Communes

When the Communists came to power in 1949, radical land reforms were introduced. Initially, large private estates belonging to the rich were broken up and redistributed to the peasants who were encouraged to form mutual-aid teams. The second stage of communisation began in 1953 with the introduction of a larger unit, the producers' co-operatives. In 1958 a third stage saw the grouping of co-operatives into People's Communes. A commune, with an average of 4,600 families, is not just concerned with farming; it is also an industrial and social welfare unit and runs small factories, schools, etc. Although the commune has proved too large for some activities, it is ideal for major projects such as irrigation and afforestation.

Industry

After 1949, one of the Communists' first objectives was industrialisation. Today, there are major iron and steel plants at Anshan, Wuhan, Paotow, Chungking, Peking, Shanghai and Taiyuan. Steel is the basis of other developing manufactures, particularly agricultural machinery and transport equipment; main engineering works are sited at Shanghai, Shenyang and Tienstin. Another expanding sector is the chemical industry—plastics, synthetic fibres and fertilizers—based in Shanghai, Nanking, Tienstin and Lushun. As most light industry is concerned with processing agricultural produce such as cotton, tobacco and sugar, factories are located in the producing regions; 70% of industrial capacity, however, is concentrated in the north and north-east. Shanghai is the chief industrial city with iron and steel, textiles, engineering, chemicals and food processing.

Cities

According to current estimates, China has about 20 cities with over one million inhabitants. The biggest is Shanghai: its population of around 11 million makes it the world's largest city. Situated on the south bank of the Yangtse, Shanghai is the country's leading port and industrial city. Three other major cities are on the Yangtse; the former capital, Nanking (pop 1.75 m), 240 km from the sea, is an important textile centre; Wuhan (pop 2.75 m), the hub of the middle Yangtse basin, has iron and steel works; Chungking (pop 3 m), the largest settlement in the Szechuan basin, is a commercial and industrial city built on steep cliffs overlooking the river. Peking (pop 8 m), is the Republic's capital.

Silk

Silk production in China dates from 2700 BC and, over the centuries, Chinese silk became much coveted, especially in Imperial Rome. This trade gave rise to the Silk Road, the major land route out of China at that time. Silk is still being produced in China today, mainly as a cottage industry. Over 50% of the country's silk comes from the Tai Hu area in Kiangsu; the other two main silk regions are the Szechuan basin and the Canton delta.

Physical features

Eastern China is the country's lowest and most fertile area. The gently undulating Manchurian plain, hemmed in by mountains, is in the north-east. The basins of the Huang Ho and Yangtse rivers, separated by mountains in central China, merge nearer the coast to form an alluvial lowland 1,120 km long. The Nan Ling mountain system covers most of the area south of the Yangtse, except for the Canton hinterland where the rivers Tung, Peh and Si join to form the Pearl delta. Lying off the Luichow peninsula is the tropical island of Hainan. Although eastern China is mountainous in the centre, tropical produce such as coconuts and pineapples are grown in coastal areas. The coast is flat and smooth north of Shanghai, but to the south it is hilly, indented and island-fringed.

Water Transport

Some 170,000 km of navigable rivers and canals form a major transport system. The most important is the Yangtse which, together with its tributaries, accounts for 40% of China's waterways. This river, the world's fourth largest, is open to shipping as far as Ipin, in Szechuan, while ocean-going vessels can reach Wuhan. Other major networks are provided by the Pearl River, the Huang Ho and the Sungari. The Republic's main canal—and the world's longest artificial waterway—is the Grand Canal running 1,768 km from Peking to Hangchow. Coastal shipping is limited and tends to be divided into two zones, centered on Shanghai and on Canton. There are about 200 ships in China's ocean-going fleet and these are largely second-hand vessels from Europe and Japan.

Transport

Since 1949, steps have been taken to overcome the dual problem of size and relief and improve China's communications. There are now five times as many kilometers of roads as there were, while the total length of railways has been doubled. Enlarged road and rail networks have entailed considerable bridge-building. One of the most famous is the Yangtse brjge at Wuhan which is 1.6 km long and has two tiers: the upper one takes cars and pedestrians, the lower one carries trains. Railways are particularly important and handle 80% of all freight and passenger traffic. Fifteen main lines cover the country, even going as far West as Urumchi, in Sinkiang; the only region not accessible by rail is Tibet. Domestic air services are being developed and over 70 towns have airports; international flights operate from Peking, Shanghai and Canton.

Fishing

After Japan and Peru, China is estimated to be the world's third fishing nation. Fish is one of the main sources of protein and over one million Chinese exploit the seas off the coast, which are generally less than 200 m deep. These shallow waters make ideal fishing grounds for more than a thousand varieties of fish. In the north, where cod is the main catch, there are major fishing ports with processing plants at Chefoo and Tsingtao, both in Shantung, and at Luta, in Lianoning. Shanghai and Canton are the country's other two main fishing centres. One predominantly fishing region is the south-eastern coast where mountains and infertile soils have turned the population towards the sea. The traditional junk is still widely used and, recently, thousands have been motorised. Inland, many farming communities supplement their income by fresh-water fishing in rivers, ponds and rice fields.

Agriculture

In spite of growing industrialisation, China remains essentially an agricultural country and at least 70% of its people are engaged in farming. Only 13% of the land is under cultivation, mostly in the east. China is the world's leading rice-producer; the main growing area, yielding two or three crops a year, is south of the Yangtse. North of the Yangtse, wheat and millet are grown but, as consumption exceeds production, China has to import wheat from the West. Other crops include cotton, maize, millet and sugar beet in the north; sweet potatoes, potatoes, maize and fruit in the south; and, in the far south, citrus, sisal, rubber, tea and sugar cane. Primitive farming methods, like hand-sowing, are still widely used, but most communes now have a bulldozer, mini-tractors and water-pumps. Drainage, irrigation and afforestation schemes are being implemented to fight the Chinese farmer's traditional enemies: flood, drought and soil erosion.

North

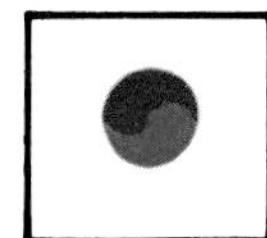

South

North and South Korea

North Korea
(Democratic Peoples Republic)

Area
121,247 km²/46,814 sq miles
Location
37°59′—43°1′ N
124°3′—130°57′ E
Population
15,501,000
Population density
129 per kms/333 per sq mile
Capital and largest City
Pyongyang: 1,500,000 (1974 est)
Language
Korean (Hangul script)
Major imports
Chemicals, machinery, transport equipment, wheat, fuel
Major exports
Fresh fish, graphite, tungsten iron ore, copper, zinc and lead
Currency
Won (1 won = 100 chon (jun))
Gross National Product
4,500 million US dollars (1974)
Status
Independent Republic

Industry
During the Japanese occupation of 1910-45, the north became established as the industrial centre of Korea. After the establishment of the People's Democratic Republic in North Korea, all industry was nationalized and land was distributed among the peasants. The north is rich in minerals, with large deposits of coal, iron, lead, copper, zinc, tin, silver and gold. Most gold comes from two mines at Unson and Suan. The richest anthracite coal mine in East Asia is near Pyongyang. Development has concentrated on heavy industry particularly iron and steel, electricity, heavy machinery, cement and chemicals. The Hwanghai iron works is the centre of iron and steel production and reached 4 million tonnes in 1973. Large scale automation in light industry increased production in the textile industry, centred around Pyongyang and Sinuiju, which produced over 600 million metres of natural and synthetic fibres. Industry relies mainly on hydro-electric power for which North Korea has great potential. Despite such advances, North Korea is turning increasingly towards the West for sophisticated machinery and technology.

Agriculture
Most arable land is concentrated in the relatively flat western provinces of Pyongyang and Hwanghai, with another area in the Hamyong province on the east coast, where the mountains extend almost to the sea. Paddy (rice) is the main crop, covering 27% of cultivated land, followed by maize, potatoes, pulses, millet, wheat and barley. Meat production, especially pigs and cattle, is generally more predominant than in China and Japan. Serious shortages of Agricultural labour made farm mechanization a high priority and a factory for agricultural machinery in South Hwangchai stared production in 1959. Successful programmes for farm mechanization plus recent irrigation schemes, including the construction of 40,000 km of canal, have meant that North Korea now produces a surplus for export.

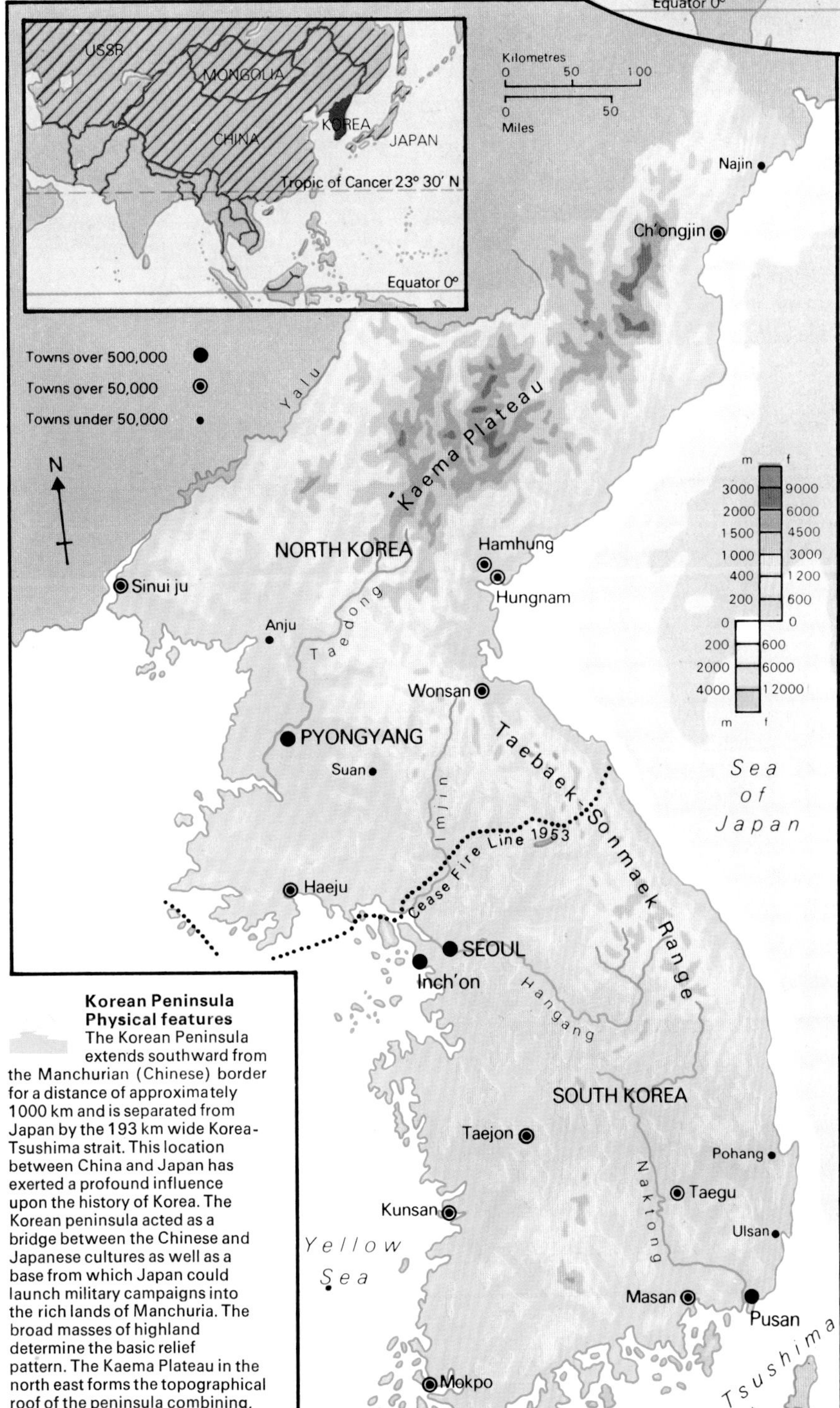

Korean Peninsula Physical features
The Korean Peninsula extends southward from the Manchurian (Chinese) border for a distance of approximately 1000 km and is separated from Japan by the 193 km wide Korea-Tsushima strait. This location between China and Japan has exerted a profound influence upon the history of Korea. The Korean peninsula acted as a bridge between the Chinese and Japanese cultures as well as a base from which Japan could launch military campaigns into the rich lands of Manchuria. The broad masses of highland determine the basic relief pattern. The Kaema Plateau in the north east forms the topographical roof of the peninsula combining, with other mountain ranges, to form a chain across the north from the south-west to the north-east which rises to over 1,829 m. A second major mountain range, called Taebaek-Sonmaek, runs the entire length of the peninsula parallel to the east coast. Thus the main lowland areas, which are also the areas of maximum cultivation and population density, are found in the south and west. Flowing away from the eastern highlands, the rivers of Korea drain mainly westward into the Yellow Sea. The valley plains of these rivers are major agricultural regions because of their relatively rich alluvial soils. The longest river is the Yalu, flowing south-west for 806 km. The south and west coasts are fringed with many islands and natural harbours.

Climate
The Korean Peninsula has a monsoon climate which is cold and dry in winter and hot and wet in the summer months when up to 70% of the annual rainfall falls. Mean temperatures in January range from —22°C in the northern interior to 2°C in Pusan on the south coast, and in August, from 20°C to 25°C respectively. The wider range in northern temperatures is produced by the continental influence. Rainfall also increases towards the south with 61 cm on the northern plateau and 140 cm on the south coast. Typhoons sometimes occur.

Vegetation
The natural vegetation of the Korean peninsula is temperate forest of mixed deciduous and coniferous trees. It resembles that of Japan, with pines, oaks and walnuts in the south and conifers and birch in the north. Forests once covered about 70% of the surface but the mountains of central and southern Korea have been severely deforested, resulting in flooding and soil erosion. There has been a considerable amount of afforestation but, nevertheless, the green valleys provide a marked contrast to the bare, eroded hills.

South Korea
(Republic of Korea)

Area
98,484 km²/38,025 sq miles
Location
33°0′—38°30′ N
125°—130° E
Population
33,459,000 (1974)
Population density
345 per km²/893 per sq mile
Capital
Seoul: 6,289,600 (1973)
Language
Korean (Hanguk script)
Major imports
wood, wheat, petroleum, textiles, fabrics, machinery, raw cotton
Major exports
Textiles and clothing, plywood electrical machinery, fish
Currency
Won (1 won = 100 chun (jeon))
Gross National Product
17,164 million US dollars (1974)
Status
Independent Republic

Industry
Next to Japan and China, South Korea has the highest economic growth rate in Asia. In 1973 it reached the record level of 16.5%. All parts of the country are rich in mineral resources. The largest tungsten mine in the world is located near Songdong while the steel mill at Pohang is the centre of the iron and steel industry and capable of satisfying home demand entirely from domestic resources. Coal, gold, graphite, anthracite and fluorspar are also plentiful. New manufacturing industries such as electronics, cotton and silk textiles, machine building, food processing, plywood, plastic goods and chemicals are increasingly the source of South Korea's economic strength. A petrochemical plant at Ulsan was completed in 1973—as was the largest shipyard in the world, which quadruples the annual ship-building capacity to 1.1 million gross tones. South Korea's exports totalled US $4,600 million in 1974, her major trading partners being the USA and Japan. Most of the exports pass through Pusan (population 1.5 million) in the south, the oldest and largest port of Korea, followed by Inch'on (550,000) near Seoul and Masan free export zone in the south. The silk industry has increased considerably in South Korea where climate and farm labour conditions are ideal for the production of high-quality raw silk at low cost. Ulsan, with its deep-sea fishing base and processing plants, is the centre of the fishing and sea culture industry which produces over US $100 million a year in exports.

Agriculture
In 1974, 50.4% of the working population was still involved in agriculture and fisheries. Rice accounts for two-thirds of all food-grain production, followed by wheat, barley, sweet potatoes and tobacco. The widespread use of chemical fertilizers, pesticides and improved, high-yield seed, together with the practices of double cropping, deep ploughing and intensified irrigation, have greatly increased agricultural production.

Japan

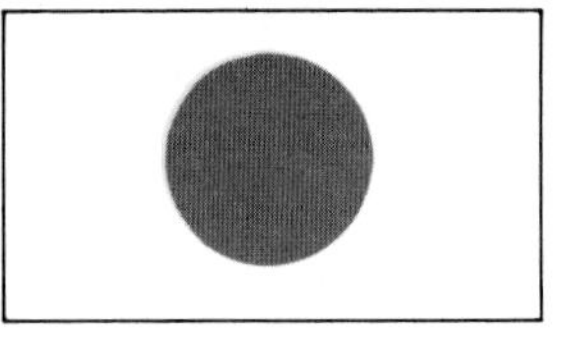

Area
377,484 km2/145,747 sq miles
Location
26°59′—45°31′ N
128°6′—145°49′ E
Population
110,049,000 (1974)
Population density
295 per km2/764 per sq mile
Capital and largest city
Tokyo : 11,519,000
Language
Japanese
Major imports
Oil, raw wool, iron ore, timber (raw materials, fuel, foodstuffs)
Major exports
Ships, motor vehicles, iron and steel, radios, synthetics
Currency
Yen (1 yen = 100 sen)
Gross National Product
430,332 million US dollars
Status
Constitutional Monarchy

Physical features
The four main islands of Japan—Hokkaido, Honshu, Shikoku and Kyushu—and its many smaller islands, lie off the east coast of Asia. The northernmost, Hokkaido, is about 1,300 km from Vladivostok in the USSR. Of the total area of Japan, 85% is mountainous and 580 of its peaks, many of which are volcanic, are more than 2,000 m high. Mount Fuji, now dormant, is the highest cone at 3,776 m. There are many active volcanoes today, including Mount Aso in Kyushu, and one of their by-products is numerous hot springs. Many fast-flowing streams cut through the mountains and provide good sources of hydro-electric power; the most important of these are the Teshio and Ishikari on Hokkaido, the Kitakami, Shinano and Tenryu in Honshu, and the Chikugo in Kyushu. The largest lake, Biwa-Ko in southern Honshu, covers 674 km². There is an acute shortage of cultivable lowland in Japan : the only lowland areas are formed by river deltas and flood plains. The largest is the Kanto plain (east central Honshu).

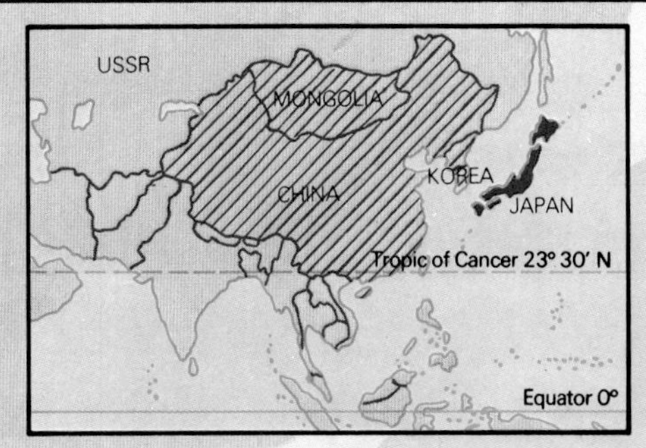

Climate
The winter monsoon (late September to early March) brings heavy rain and snow to the western parts of the islands, but the central mountains shield the east producing drier, windy weather. The summer monsoon, lasting from mid-April to early September, however, comes from the east and south and produces warm rainy weather throughout. The warm Kuroshio Current contributes to the warm temperatures on the east coast up to latitude 35° N, but causes dense sea fog when it meets the cold Oyashio Current off east Hokkaido and north-east Honshu. Minimum and maximum temperatures in Kagoshima in southern Kyushu are 7°and 27°C respectively, compared with —9° and 21°C in Asahikawa in north Hokkaido. Annual average temperatures for Tokyo are 15°C. The average annual rainfall varies from 94 to 400 cm but in most areas it is over 100 cm. Snow covers the whole of Hokkaido, and the interior of Honshu from November to April.

Agriculture
Only 15.6% of the land is arable, of which about 58% is paddy. Japan has therefore to import much of her foodstuffs, especially wheat, soyabeans, sugar and fodder grains. Agriculture accounts for less than 8% of the net national income (and its share in decreasing) and yet it involves more than 17% of the working population. The average size of a farm is still little more than three acres and much of the land consists of terraced hillsides which severely limits the use of machinery. The national output of rice in 1973 was over 12,000 million tonnes, but many farmers are responding to the increasing domestic demand for livestock, sugar and vegetables.

Industry
After an unprecedented rate of growth, Japan is now one of the top three industrial nations in the world. The iron and steel industry, centred in northern Kyushu, produced over 220 million tonnes of steel in 1973 and made US $ 5,000 million in exports. Osaka is the centre of the largest shipbuilding industry in the world which, in all, comprises over 1,000 shipyards of which 28 produce over 90% of total output. Exports in 1973 amounted to US $ 3,819 million. In car production, Japan has an output of over 4.5 million vehicles per year—an export commodity worth over US $ 3,500 million. The petro-chemical industry is of growing importance with eleven major installations linked to refineries around the coast. Despite the recent shift in emphasis from light to heavy industry, Japan still exports US $ 1,600 million worth of textiles and clothing. Factories are to be found in Nagoya, Kyoto and many other industrial towns.

Energy
Japan has few indigenous energy resources and has, therefore, to rely heavily on imported oil. The demand is over 1.5 thousand million barrels per year which represents 70% of Japan's total energy consumption. This is met by importing US $ 6,000 million worth of crude oil —mostly from the Middle East. Attempts to diversify power sources include off-shore oil exploration and several nuclear power stations. Japan already ranks third after the USA and USSR in nuclear energy capacity. Small amounts of liquified natural gas have also recently been imported from Alaska. Japan is also developing her own oil refineries in the Middle East and Africa : 10% of oil supplies are already 'Yen Oil'. A joint project with the USSR is currently planned to develop resources in Siberia.

Fisheries
Japan is the chief fishing nation in the world after Peru, producing over 10 million tonnes of fish per year. This industry has, however, tended to slow down in recent years. About 250,000 individual households still produce about 40% of the catch, particularly in coastal fishing and shallow-sea culture (fish farming), which only require small boats or nets. Species raised include pearls and oysters, yellow-tail prawn and octopus. Offshore fishing is undertaken by slightly larger enterprises requiring boats from 10 to 100 tonnes while the really large companies are involved in long-distance deep-sea fishing, with large fleets and a mother ship handling the processing and packing on-the-spot. Their activities range from trawling off the African coast to whaling in the Arctic Ocean and salmon fishing in the North Atlantic. Ocean currents around Japan provide many varieties of fish.

Transport
Japan has one of the most highly developed transport systems in the world. The Tokaido railway, linking Tokyo and Osaka, is capable of speeds up to 250 km per hour and is part of a total railway network of over 24,000 km. Japan's three major industrial cities, Tokyo, Nagoya and Kobe, are linked by modern expressways, part of a planned highway system of 7,600 km by 1985. Japan's three major ports ; Kobe, Nagasaki and Yokohama, harbour a merchant fleet of over 30 million tonnes. Ships are an important means of transport between Japanese ports. There are two international airports, at Tokyo and Osaka, and a third is being built near Narita City about 40 km from Tokyo.

Forestry
About two-thirds of the Japanese archipelago is forested, providing an important source of building materials, paper-pulp and fuel. The most valuable timber forests are mixed conifer and deciduous and the most valuable trees are the Sugi (Japanese Cedar), Hinoki (Japanese Cypress) and Akamatsu (Red Pine). Japan now imports up to 56% of her timber requirements.

Cities
Japan's capital, Tokyo, on the main island of Honshu, is the centre of heavy industry as well as the seat of government. The thriving port of Yokohama is 34 km south of the capital. Another major industrial area is situated further south and contains Kyoto and the ports of Osaka and Kobe.

● Towns over 1,000,000
◉ Towns over 500,000
• Towns under 500,000

Hong Kong, Macao and Taiwan

left **TAIWAN** (Formosa)

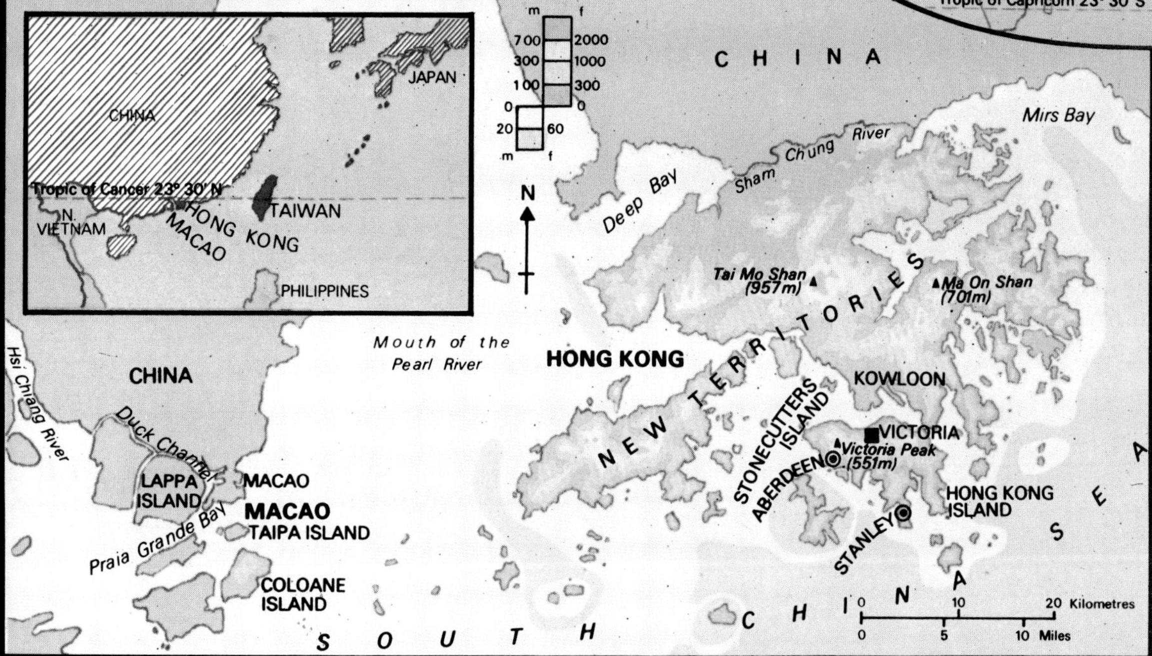

Hong Kong
Area
1046 km²/404 sq miles
Location
22°9'—22°37' N
113°52'—114°30' E
Population
4,345,000 (1974)
Population density
3,924 per km²/10,164 per sq mile
Capital
Victoria: 671,000
Language
English, Cantonese and Mandarin
Gross Domestic Product
5,921 million US dollars (1973)
Major imports
Food, raw materials
Major exports
Clothing, textiles, manufactured goods
Currency
Hong Kong dollar
Status
British Crown Colony

Physical features

Hong Kong is situated on the south east coast of China on the east side of the Pearl River estuary. The crown colony consists of Hong Kong island and islets (75 km²), the Kowloon Peninsula and Stonecutters Island (9.7 km²) and the New Territories (945 km²). The colony's main asset, the 44 km² Victoria Harbour, lies between Hong Kong and the mainland. Most of the land is volcanic rock with hills rising directly from the sea. The highest peak, Tai Mo Shan on the mainland, rises to a height of 957 m. The main agricultural area is north of the Kowloon ridge on the mainland, particularly around Deep Bay where the Sham Chun River, which forms the natural border with China, flows out to sea. The rest of Hong Kong is urban.

Climate

The subtropical climate brings hot, humid summers (28°C in July) and cool, dry winters (16°C in January). Over half the normal annual rainfall of 216 cm falls in the summer monsoon months of June to August. This is usually a period of bad weather with high winds and typhoons.

Population

The population of Hong Kong has grown from 600,000 to 4 million in 25 years, owing largely to the influx of Chinese from Communist China and South-East Asia. The Chinese form 98% of the population and of the remainder about 29,000 are of British origin. Recently, the government has undertaken huge housing projects, of which the largest, Tuen Wan houses 400,000 of the population.

Agriculture

Only 13% of the total area is cultivated and this employs 4.5% of the work force. The traditional main crop is 'paddy' (or rice), but there is a shift towards land-intensive farming of vegetables (74% of total production value), fruit and flowers—also poultry and fish farming. The remaining land is either marsh, coarse grassland or eroded highland. Marine fishing, which employs 50,000 men, is a major industry and source of exports valued at about HK$ 137 million.

Industry

Hong Kong's exports of manufactured goods now account for 25% of total world industrial exports from developing countries. Its post-war economic expansion is based mainly on a large immigrant labour force, the import of cheap foodstuffs from China, a laissez-faire economy and, until recently the free trading advantages of a colony. The major industry and the source of 45% of exports is textiles and clothing manufacture. Total exports are worth nearly HK$ 23 billion (1974). Other light industrial products include plastics, optical and electronic equipment and watches. Heavy industries include shipbreaking and repairing. All the colony's raw materials are imported, as is much of its food. Invisible earnings come from tourism, shipping and new foreign investments. Nearly half of Hong Kong's goods go to the United States and Britain.

Macao
Area
16 km²/6.2 sq miles
Population
321,000
Population density
17,500 per km²/45,300 per sq mile
Language
Portuguese, Cantonese
Major imports
Fabrics, yarn, food
Major exports
Clothing
Currency
1 pataca = 100 avos
Status
Portuguese Overseas Province

Macao is situated 64 km west of Hong Kong on the mouth of the Pearl River. It consists of the Macao peninsula, and the islands of Taipa and Coloane. The capital of the province is Macao which is situated on the mainland peninsular. 98% of the population is Chinese and only 8,000 are Portuguese. Over 2 million tourists visit Macao annually from Hong Kong and about 60% of annual revenue derives from hotels, restaurants and gambling. The textile industry provides 60% of Macao's exports while much of her imports, (cheap food and clothing) come from China.

Taiwan/Formosa/ Nationalist China
Area
35,962 km²/13,885 sq miles
Location
21°45'—25°38' N
120°—122° E
Population
15,772,800 (1974)
Population density
438 per km²/1134 per sq mile
Capital and largest city
Taipei: 1,998,620 (1974)
Language
Mandarin (official), also Fukien, Hakka (mainland Chinese) and aboriginal dialects
Major imports
Timber, wheat, maize and cotton
Major exports
clothing, televisions, plastics
Currency
New Taiwan dollar
Gross National Product
10,226 million US dollars
Status
National republic

Land and climate

The Chungyang Shanmo mountains run from north to south and cover almost three-quarters of the island. In the east, they rise steeply from the coast, but in the west they slope gently down towards alluvial plains, the island's only arable land. The range includes many peaks over 3,000 m, the highest being Yushan (3,996 m). The main rivers are the Tan-Shui Ch'i flowing north and the Cho-Shui Ch'i flowing west. The climate is subtropical in the north and tropical in the south but is strongly affected by ocean currents such as the warm Kuroshio current from Japan. Summer temperatures average 20° to 30°C and winter temperatures about 15°C. The summer monsoons bring floods.

People and places

Apart from 150,000 aborigines, the 15.7 million Taiwanese are all descended from Chinese settlers from the Fukien and Kuomintang provinces. About 45% of the people live in rural areas and are engaged in agriculture. Settlements around paddy fields are highly concentrated, particularly in the south where water is scarce. In the north and in the hills, villages are smaller and more scattered. The only ports are Kee-Lung, serving Taipei the capital, Kao-Hsiung in the south-west and Hua-Lien in the east. Most of the industrial development is based around these towns.

Industry

Traditionally an agricultural community, Taiwan is gradually becoming industrialized, although only 12% of the population is engaged in manufacturing industries. Natural resources are limited, so manufacturing industries based on imported raw materials have grown up around Kee-Lung and Kao-Hsiung—the main ports. The textile industry is very important, accounting for 10% of Taiwan's exports. Other exports include chemical products, electrical appliances, cement, paper, sugar and machinery.

The Philippines

(Republika ng Pilipinas)

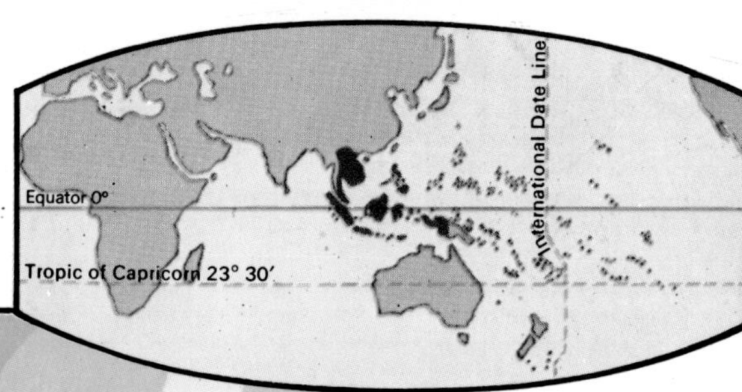

Statistics

Area
300,000km²/115,830 sq miles

Location
4°25′-21°20′N;
116°55′-126°40′E

Climate
tropical monsoon

Population
39,500,000 (1972)
41,170,000 (1973)

Population density
132 per km²/341 per sq mile

Capital
Quezon City: 745,452 (1974)

Largest city
Manila: 1,966,622 (1974)

Languages
Filipino, English, Spanish

Gross National Product
5,355 million US dollars

Major imports
machinery, fuel, transport equipment, metals, foodstuffs, textiles

Major exports
timber, coconuts and coconut products, sugar, abaca (manila hemp) copper

Currency
peso (100 centavos = 1 peso)

Status
Independent republic.
The Filipino people are basically Malay, but there has been extensive inter-marriage with Chinese and Spanish settlers.

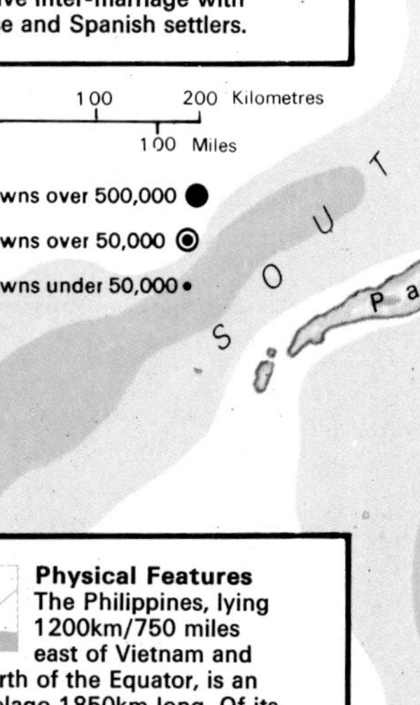

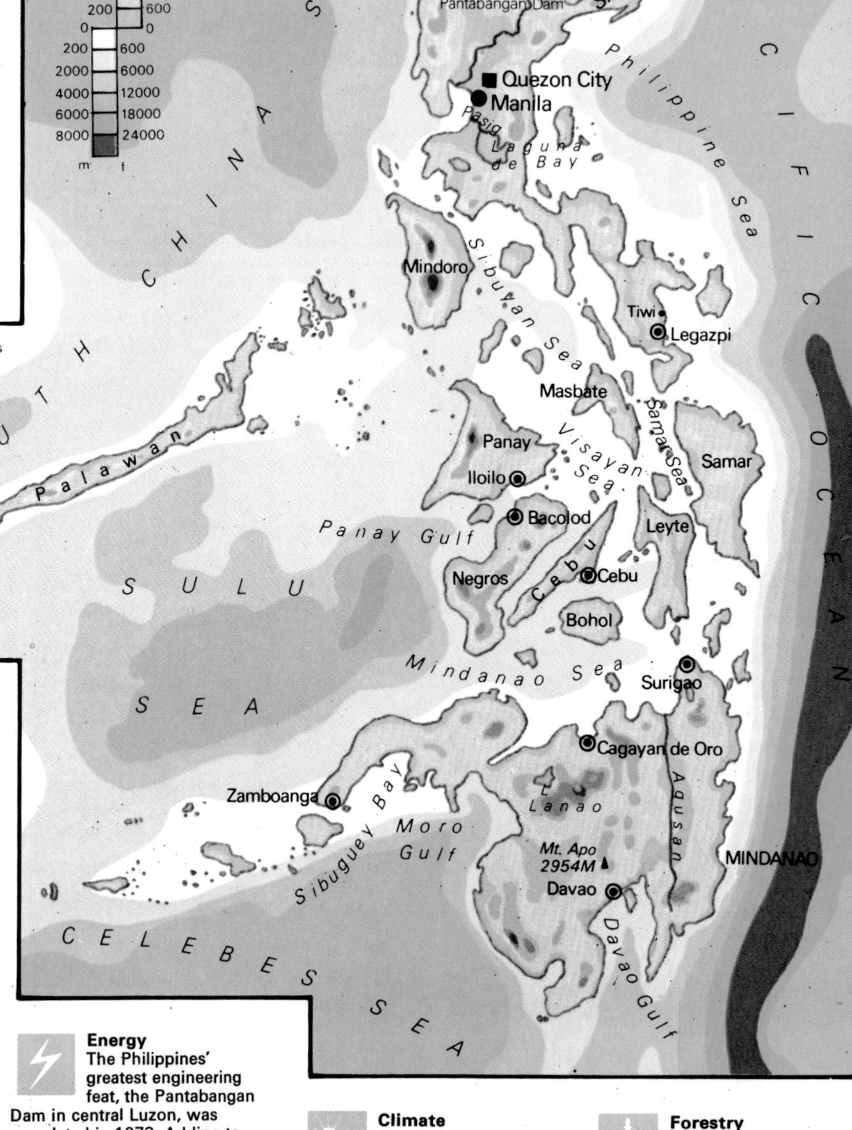

Physical Features

The Philippines, lying 1200km/750 miles east of Vietnam and 15° north of the Equator, is an archipelago 1850km long. Of its 7,107 islands only 2,773 have names and 6,377 are uninhabited. Some 94% of the total land is accounted for by the 11 major islands, each of which has an area exceeding 259 km². Luzon (108,380km²) and Mindanao (94,630km²) are the two largest; the others are Samar, Negros, Palawan, Panay, Mindoro, Leyte, Bohol and Masbate and Cebu—the most densely populated. A north-south mountain range of volcanic origin runs the length of the archipelago; its densely-forested slopes leave only narrow coastal plains. The rivers are fast-flowing and most drain north; the three longest, each over 320km, are the Cagayan, on Luzon, and the Agusan and Rio Grande on Mindanao. These two islands also have the most extensive lowland areas in the archipelago, and there are other large plains on Panay and Western Negros. Mt. Apo, a dormant volcano on Mindanao, is the country's highest peak: 2,954m. The coast is fringed with coral reefs. East of Surigao, on Mindanao, is the Philippine Deep, 10,973m, thought to be one of the world's deepest ocean troughs.

Energy

The Philippines' greatest engineering feat, the Pantabangan Dam in central Luzon, was completed in 1973. Adding to the country's hydro-electric output, it is also used for irrigation and flood control. A new project is geothermal power using underground steam. The first geothermal plant was set up at Tiwi, Luzon, and more geothermal wells are being dug. By 1990, Tiwi's estimated potential of 600 megawatts—enough to supply all Luzon, including Manila—should be realized. By that time, the total geothermal production is expected to cut the country's oil imports by 60%.

Climate

The Philippines are humid and warm. The average temperature at sea level is 27°C, but about 9°C lower in the mountains. Rainfall, varying from 102cm to 508cm, is heavy in the east particularly during the October-March north-east monsoon. At the same time it is dry in the west. From June to November, typhoons are a constant hazard, especially in Luzon and Samar, where high winds cause widespread damage and torrential rain leads to flooding and soil erosion.

Forestry

Nearly half of the total land area is covered with rain forests with over 3,000 tree species. About 60% of this forest, which is government-owned, is of commercial value—many of the hardwoods are especially suited to the furniture and construction industries—but is not yet fully exploited. Timber and wood veneers are the country's leading export making it the world's sixth largest lumber producer. Other forest products include gums, tan and dye barks, bamboo, rattan and vegetable oils.

Agriculture

Agriculture, employing 60% of the work force, dominates the economy. One half of all cultivated land is used for rice, Other domestic crops include maize, sweet potatoes and bananas. The main cash crops are coconuts, sugar and abaca (the fibre of this plant, Manila Hemp, is used in rope making). With 310 million coconut trees giving almost 10 billion nuts a year, the Philippines accounts for 44% of the world's coconut output and is its leading coconut producer. Some 12 million Filipinos are engaged in coconut growing or processing; coconuts and coconut products are the country's second largest export after timber The third major export is sugar, from Luzon, Negros and Panay, followed by abaca, grown on Luzon, Samar and Leyte. Other export crops are tobacco, coffee and pineapples.

Mining and industry

The Philippines is rich in minerals and ranks as a major world producer of gold, which is found on Luzon. Other important deposits being exploited on Luzon are copper, chromite, lead, zinc and iron; silver and manganese are also mined. Industrialization is slow and most of the country's factories process agricultural crops such as coconuts, sugar, rice and tobacco. Coconut-based manufactures, for example, inlcude margarine, soap, cosmetics, cattle-food and pesticides. Textile factories and cement works have been established recently.

Cities

The largest city and former capital is Manila, situated at the mouth of the Pasig river on the west coast of Luzon. Heavy industry is centred south of the river, while light industry lies to the north. The great urban concentration around Manila is known as Metro Manila and has a population of 7,000,000. Metro Manila comprises four cities and 17 municipalities; the largest of these, after Manila itself, is Quezon City, the capital. Lying to the north-east, Quezon is the seat of government offices and the University of the Philippines.

Communications

The road network is one of the best in Asia and is 60% hard-surfaced. Although trains run on Luzon and Panay, these are in competition with buses and planes. Altogether, four domestic airlines operate inter-island services between some 80 airports. Shipping is vitally important. Manila, handling 80% of all shipping, is the main port: its north harbour takes domestic traffic, the south harbour handles international trade. Other international ports are Cebu—more important than Manila for inter-island shipping—Iloilo, Davao, Zamboanga and Bacolod.

VIETNAM

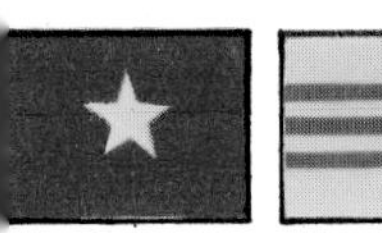
North

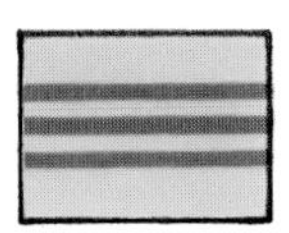
South

Climate

Although both regions have a tropical monsoonal climate, the North has more pronounced seasons because of higher latitude. Average temperatures in Hanoi range from 16°C in January to 29°C in July, but in Saigon there is little variation: 27°C in January, 30°C in July. Most rain comes in summer with the SW monsoon: Hanoi receives an average of 177 cm, Saigon 203 cm, while parts of the Tonkin mountains and Annamese Chain receive over 406 cm. A feature of winter in the North is the 'crachin' or drizzle which permits the cultivation of an extra rice crop. Coastal areas in the South which are exposed to the NE monsoon, may receive up to 25 cm of rain in January.

Physical features

Vietnam is a mountainous country. The Annamese chain stretches almost the entire length of the country, with several peaks more than 2,000 m high. This range spreads eastwards to the sea, leaving only a narrow coastal plain. In the South, the mountains give way to the vast alluvial delta of the Mekong river, covering 37,814 km². Vietnam's other great lowland region is in the North: the Red River delta extending over 14,502 km². This area, liable to severe flooding, is bordered to the west by the rugged Tonkin mountains which rise to over 3,000 m in places. Some 80% of Vietnamese live on the deltas where population densities reach 1,525 per km². The Mekong delta has extensive swamps.

Agriculture

Vietnam is an agricultural or, more specifically, rice-growing country. In the North, 90% of cultivated land—mostly in the Tonkin lowlands—is devoted to rice, producing two or three crops a year. The remaining farmland is used chiefly for groundnuts, cotton, sugar and maize. South Vietnam's arable land, concentrated in the Mekong delta, yields only one crop of rice a year. Other major crops include rubber, sugar, tobacco, tea and cinnamon. Fish is the main source of protein: 250,000 South Vietnamese and twice as many North Vietnamese work as fishermen in the Gulf of Tonkin and the South China Sea. About two-thirds of Vietnam is forested. The tropical forests on the interior highlands mainly consist of valuable hardwoods such as teak, but the lumber industry is still underdeveloped.

The recent Vietnamese conflict seriously affected agriculture, industry, transport, trade, etc. As the immediate post-war period is one of confusion and change, the facts here relate to normal conditions. The political status of North and South Vietnam remain undetermined.

North Vietnam
(Democratic Republic of Vietnam)
Area
158,750 km²/61,294 sq miles
Location
17°—23°15′ N
102°20′—108°E
Population
23,787,000 (1974)
Population density
150 per km²/388 per sq mile
Capital and largest city
Hanoi: 950,000 (1974 est.)
Language
Vietnamese
Gross National Product
2,180 million US dollars
Major imports
machinery, transport equipment, petroleum, foodstuffs
Major exports
coal, minerals, handicrafts, cement, teak and forest products
Currency
dong (100 xu = 10 hao = 1 dong)

South Vietnam
(Republic of Vietnam)
Area
173,809 km²/67,108 sq miles
Location
8°40′—17°N
104°40′—109°30′E
Population
19,367,000 (1973)
Population density
111 per km²/289 per sq mile
Capital and largest city
Saigon: 1,845,400 (1973 est.)
Language
Vietnamese
Gross National Product
3,700 million US dollars
Major imports
foodstuffs, petroleum, machinery, transport equipment, textiles
Major exports
rubber, tea, groundnuts, copra
Currency
piastre (= 100 centimes)

Cities

Saigon, sometimes called Ho Chi Minh City, has a greater urban' population of over three million. Its wide avenues, reflecting its French heritage, contrast sharply with the shanty towns developing round the perimeter. Built on the Saigon river, the city is a major port with 5 km of quays and an industrial centre. Hanoi, at the confluence of three rivers, is protected against floods by dikes 15 m high. A feature of the old city are its eleventh-century pagodas, while the modern sectors were built by the French in the nineteenth century. Hanoi is the North's industrial and commercial centre.

Mining

At Quang Yen, north of the Red River, North Vietnam has S.E. Asia's richest coal field; the 3 million tonnes mined annually meet domestic needs and provide 1 million tonnes for export. Iron ore is mined at Thai Nguyen—also the site of a major steel works, and of phosphate mines. The phosphate is used to manufacture fertilizer at Lao Cai. Other deposits include zinc, tin, antimony, bauxite and chromite. In contrast, South Vietnam has few minerals apart from phosphate deposits on the Paracel islands, a small coal field near Da Nang, and silica (used for glass-making), in coastal sands. There are also salt-beds along the coast in both North and South Vietnam.

Industry

North Vietnam is more industrialized than the South, largely because of its mineral wealth and investment from Russia and China. Hanoi is the main centre, with engineering and food processing plants, and a range of light industries. Haiphong, with shipyards, cement plants, engineering works and textile mills, comes second. Other developments include the steel complex at Thai Nguyen, a textile combine at Nam Dinh and chemical plants at Viet Tri. In South Vietnam, industry—food processing and textiles—is concentrated in the Saigon area. Other manufactures are glass, forest products, cement and cigarettes. In both countries handicrafts are important.

Transport

Inland waterways are vital in both North and South Vietnam. The South is served by the great Mekong River and its branches, while in the North the Red River, the Black River and the Song Lo are important. Hanoi stands at the confluence of these three rivers and is also the hub of the country's railways which link it with China, Dong Hoi and the sea port of Haiphong, the only port for ocean-going ships. The South has an equally sparse rail network—the main line runs from Saigon to Hue—but twice as many roads as the North. Internal air services are being developed and both Hanoi and Saigon have international airports.

Cambodia

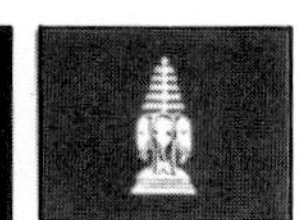

Laos

Cambodia and Laos

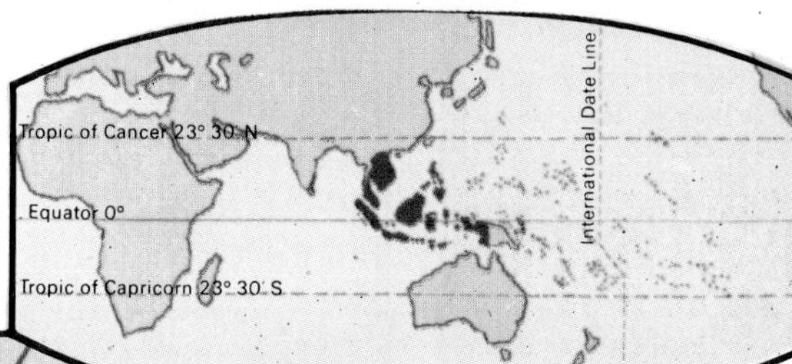

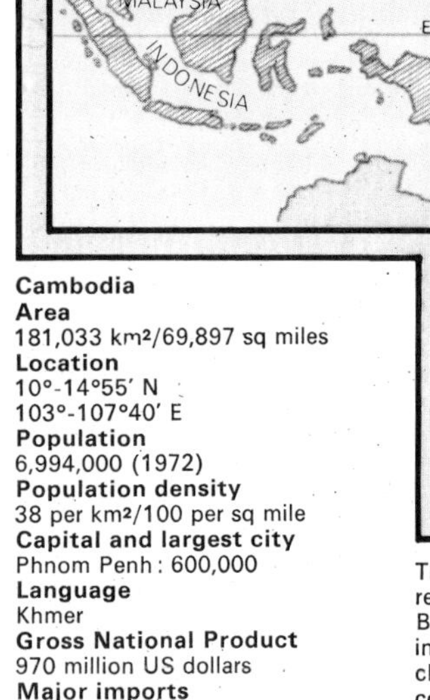

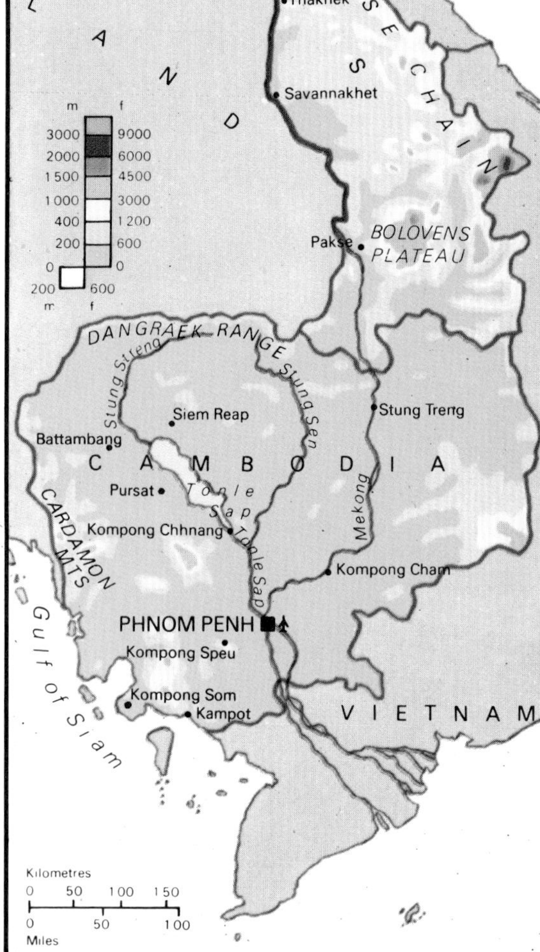

Cambodia

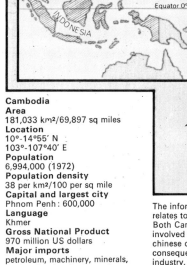

Area
181,033 km²/69,897 sq miles

Location
10°-14°55' N
103°-107°40' E

Population
6,994,000 (1972)

Population density
38 per km²/100 per sq mile

Capital and largest city
Phnom Penh: 600,000

Language
Khmer

Gross National Product
970 million US dollars

Major imports
petroleum, machinery, minerals, foodstuffs, chemicals, textiles

Major exports
rubber, rice, maize, forest products, pepper

Currency
riel (100 sen = 1 riel)

Status
independent republic

Laos

Area
236,800 km²/91,400 sq miles

Location
14°-22°40' N;
100°10'-107°50' E

Population
3,257,000 (1974)

Population Density
13.7 per km²/35.6 per sq mile

Capital and largest city
Vientiane: 176,637 (1973)

Language
Lao

Gross National Product
350 million US dollars

Major imports
petroleum, foodstuffs, machinery, transport equipment, textiles, chemicals

Major exports
tin, timber (teak), green coffee

Currency
kip (100 at = 10 bi = 1 kip)

Status
constitutional monarchy

Climate
The climate in both Laos and Cambodia is tropical monsoonal with three seasons: a hot, wet season during the S-W monsoon, which lasts from June to October; a cool, dry season (November-February); and a hot, dry season (March-May). Some 80% of rain falls during the S-W monsoon period. In Cambodia, rainfall on the central plain is relatively low—127 cm a year—because of its sheltered position, but rises to over 508 cm in the Cardamon mountains. In Laos, most areas receive 178 cm of rain, with more than twice as much on high ground like the Bolovens Plateau. Temperatures in Cambodia range from 27°C in January, the coldest month, to 35°C in April. Corresponding temperatures in Laos are lower.

The information given here relates to normal conditions. Both Cambodia and Laos were involved in the recent Indo-chinese conflict with devastating consequences for agriculture, industry, communications, energy supplies, trade and population distribution.

Physical features
Laos and Cambodia have one major feature in common: the mighty Mekong River that rises in Tibet and flows 4,160 km to the South China Sea. In Laos, the Mekong forms the western boundary with Thailand. With its tributaries, it is bordered by lowlands hemmed in by the Annamese Chain along the Vietnam frontier, and by the north-eastern mountains which are over 2,500 m high. Cambodia is like a great saucer. The mountains of the Phanom Dang Raek range and the Cardamons, which rise to 914 m, edge the central lowland which has the Tonle Sap Lake and the Mekong river as its focal points. During the S-W monsoon, flood waters from the Mekong surge into the Tonle Sap: while in the dry season the lake covers 2,590 km² and is 1.5 m deep, in the rainy season its area increases to 10,360 km² and its depth to 15 m. This flooding is vital for rice growing.

Transport
Cambodia has some 19,312 km of navigable rivers and canals and Phnom Penh is an international port, able to take ships of up to 4,000 tonnes. These waterways are an indispensable means of transport, especially in the north and west, as roads mainly serve the south-east. The rail network consists of two lines linking Phnom Penh to Thailand and to the country's only ocean port, Kompong Som. In Laos, where there are no railways and few roads, the Mekong is the main highway. Away from the river and its tributaries, oxen are used. Elephants are also important as work animals—the country was once called Lanxang 'the land of a million elephants'. Both countries are developing domestic air services and Phnom Penh and Vientiane have international airports.

Fishing
In both countries, fish is the most important source of protein. Cambodia has the greatest fresh-water fish resources in South-East Asia and 70% of the Cambodian catch comes from the Tonle Sap. Most fishermen are also farmers, except in the Tonle Sap. Nearly all the catch is used locally, half of it as dried fish. Marine fishing in the Gulf of Siam is of lesser importance. In Laos, the fish resources of the Mekong are not yet fully exploited.

Mining
Tin, from Phong Tiou, is Laos' leading export. Major reserves of iron ore in Xieng Khouang province have not yet been exploited; neither have smaller deposits of coal, lead and gold in the north, and copper in the south. In Cambodia, known mineral resources are few. Phosphate is mined near Kampot and a small quantity of gold and precious stones mined in the north-west. There is iron ore in the north but it remains unexploited.

Industry
Industry is primarily based on processing raw materials. In Cambodia most provincial capitals have rice mills, sugar refineries and textile mills. Other industries which have been established in major centres, notably Phnom Penh and Kompong Som, include vehicle-assembly plants, cement works and distilleries. In Laos, where large-scale operations are limited to rice-milling and saw-milling, cottage industries are important: hand-weaving, pottery, silver-engraving, leather-curing and wood-carving. Some light industries have also been introduced, producing cigarettes, soft drinks and shoes. In both countries, ambitious hydro-electric schemes are planned along the Mekong which should contribute to industrialization.

Agriculture
Both countries are agricultural with 80% of the population engaged in farming. The main areas under cultivation, where 9 out of 10 farmers grow rice, are the Mekong lowlands in Laos and the Cambodian central plain. Poor irrigation facilities mean that rice yields in both countries are among the lowest in monsoon Asia: Laos has to import rice although, in good years, Cambodia has a small surplus available for export. In Cambodia maize and rubber are grown in the south, and there are small pepper, tea and coffee plantations in the south-west. Other cash-crops include tobacco, cotton and kapok. Commercial crops grown in Laos are maize, tobacco, cotton, coffee and, in the north, opium. As most people in both countries are Buddhists and therefore vegetarians, animals such as water buffalo are mainly raised for work. The timber industry is more developed in Laos, where forests cover 70% of the area, than in Cambodia which is 50% forested.

People
In Cambodia, the majority of the people are Khmer. There are a number of urban minorities like the Chinese and Vietnamese, and other groups like the Cham, and highland peoples like the Jarai. In Laos, most of the population is Lao, but there are large minorities of other peoples like the Miao.

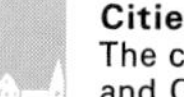

Cities
The capitals of Laos and Cambodia are both on the Mekong River. Vientiane, like Laos' other towns, is small: a famous sight is the That Luang, a 16th-century temple. Some 800 km further south, where the Mekong meets the Tonle Sap River, is Phnom Penh, the Cambodian capital. Although there are another 290 km/180 miles to the sea, Phnom Penh is a busy port. It is also the Republic's main industrial centre with food processing plants, rice mills, distilleries and textile factories. The other major towns in Cambodia are Battambang, Kompong Cham and Kampot. The ancient city of Angkor Wat was the capital of the Khmer empire (*c.*800-1430 AD).

Thailand

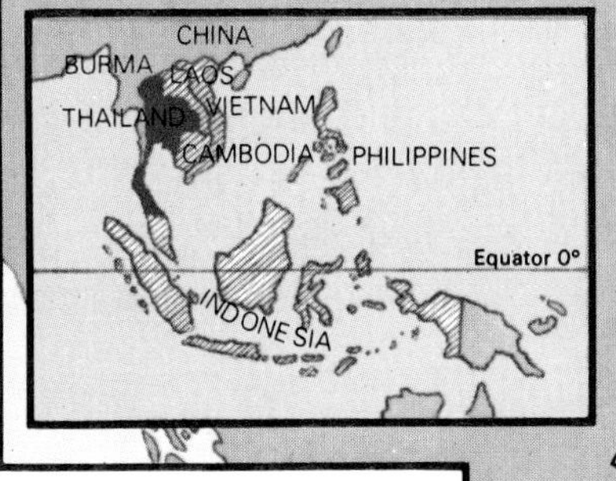

Physical features

The northern mountains which include Thailand's highest, Doi Inthanon, 2,595 metres high, give way to a central plain drained by tributaries of the Chao Phraya. The lower part of this plain corresponds to the Chao Phraya delta which has rich alluvial soil and is subject to seasonal flooding. This area is used almost entirely for rice and is the most densely settled. The Korat plateau, in the north-east, has an average height of 150 metres to the east, the low Phu Phan hills separate the lakes and swamps of the Mekong basin from the Chi-Mun rivers, while the mountains extend along the Burmese border and into the peninsula. The Chao Phraya is Thailand's principal river. One of its tributaries, the Nan, which flows 1,000 km before joining the Chao Phraya is the longest. The coasts are largely fringed with mangrove swamps and there are numerous offshore islands. The forests and river valleys of Thailand are alive with many kinds of wild animal such as the tiger, leopard and monkey, as well as exotic species of birds.

Forests

About 60% of Thailand is forested. Deciduous trees predominate in the north with tropical evergreen forests further south. The northern forests include teak which provides Thailand with its fifth most important export. Elephants and other animals are used for hauling the cut timber to extraction points—veneer quality logs are then transported by rail, but the majority go by water. The logs are drifted singly to the rafting stations at Tak and Sawankhalok where they are tied together in batches of 150 -350 before floating on to Bangkok. Rafting is confined to the early and late flood seasons: July-August, November-December. Other forest products are yangwood, firewood, charcoal, rattan, oil and bamboo. Extensive mangrove forests along the southern shores of the Gulf of Siam are now being exploited to produce timber and charcoal.

Industry

Industrial activity is basically related to processing raw materials such as sugar, tin, timber, tobacco and rice: there are, for instance, over 6,000 rice mills. In recent years, however, the government has established other industries. These include cement works, textile factories, paper mills, chemical plants, steel rolling mills and oil refineries. Energy requirements are partly met by hydro-electricity, but mostly by electricity generated in thermal plants using gas or solid fuel such as lignite. A nuclear power station is being built at Chon Buri. While major industries are concentrated in Bangkok, many world-famous Thai products are handmade in villages. These cottage industries include silk spinning and weaving, lacquer work, nielloware, silver and gold engraving, esparto grass weaving, wood carving, ceramics, jewelry and basketry.

Area
514,000 km²/198,455 sq miles
Location
5°40'—20°30' N
97°20'—105°40'E
Population
39,950,306 (1974)
Population density
70 per km²/182 per sq mile
Capital and largest city
Bangkok: 3,967,081
Language
Thai
GNP
9,369 million US dollars
Major imports
transport equipment, iron and steel, machinery, petroleum
Major exports
rice, maize, timber, tin, rubber
Currency
baht (100 satangs = 1 baht)
Status
constitutional monarchy

Climate

Thailand, with a tropical monsoon climate, has three main seasons: dry, rainy and cool. The hottest and driest month is April, when Bangkok has temperatures of 33°C and in the north, Chiang Mai has 31°C. The cooler period lasts from November to February when temperatures in Bangkok fall to 24°C and in Chiang Mai to 19°C. The rainy season, caused by the southwest monsoon, extends from May to September and most areas receive three-quarters of their rainfall during these months. Amounts vary according to distance from the sea and exposure to the prevailing monsoon: Chiang Mai has 135 cm and Bangkok 88 cm of rain a year. The peninsular has less temperature variation and is generally wetter. Here, rainfall is recorded at Phuket as 228 cm a year.

Bangkok

In 1971, Bangkok and neighbouring Thon Buri were merged and became Bangkok metropolis. About half of Thailand's urban population lives in this metropolitan area which is the country's chief port and leading industrial city. Situated on the Chao Phraya river some 30 km inland, the city is known as the Venice of the East because of its many *khlongs* or canals. The administrative area is centred on the Grand Palace, while the commercial sector largely corresponds to the Chinese quarter, Sam Peng. Heavy industry is located near the port which handles nearly all Thailand's imports. Less than a third of these pass through the interior: most are either consumed or processed in the capital.

Transport

Thailand has 3,765 km of railways and some 17,000 km of roads, half of them surfaced. Further roads are planned, some to link railheads and important inland waterways with agricultural areas. There are 9,180 km of canals and rivers and over 10 million people live along waterways using boats for transport. Over 80% of rice produced is carried to mills by water and every year some 200,000 logs are floated down the rivers. Bulk cargoes, such as petroleum and building materials also move by water, both inland and along the coast. Bangkok is the main port, handling 85% of the country's foreign trade. There are several domestic air routes and Bangkok has an international airport.

Mining

Thailand, producing over 31,000 tonnes of tin a year, is the world's third largest supplier of this mineral. There are about 650 tin mines, mostly on the peninsula and Phuket island, and the ore goes to an oil-fired tin smelter on Phuket. Tin ranks as Thailand's fourth most important export. There are also extensive deposits of wolfram. Other mineral resources include small amounts of lead, antimony, iron ore, manganese, gypsum and fluorite. Lignite, a brown coal, is processed into solid fuel.

Agriculture

Thailand is a predominantly agricultural country. The main crop, covering three-quarters of all cultivated land, is rice. Most of the rice farms, which employ 72% of the population, are situated in the central lowland area. Annual production exceeds 13 million tonnes. Some two million tonnes are exported—mainly to Indonesia, Japan, Malaysia and India—and account for 36% of Thailand's export earnings. Other major export crops are maize and jute, grown in the northern uplands, and rubber, which comes from the southern region: Thailand is the world's third largest rubber producer. Coconuts, grown along the sandy coasts, are also important. Livestock farming—cattle and water-buffalo—is being developed in the north-east; poultry and eggs already form a significant export item. An annual fishing catch of 1.5 million tonnes exceeds domestic requirements so some, particularly shell-fish, is exported. The country's marine fishing grounds cover three-quarters of the shores on the Gulf of Thailand and the eastern shore between Burma and Malaysia.

Malaysia, Singapore and Brunei

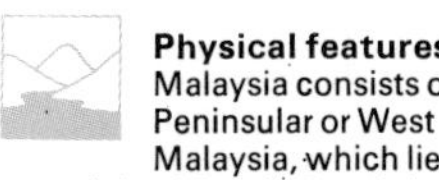

(top left)
Malaysia
(top)
Singapore
Brunei (left)

Physical features
Malaysia consists of Peninsular or West Malaysia, which lies on mainland South-East Asia between Thailand and Singapore, and East Malaysia comprising Sabah and Sarawak on the north-west coast of Borneo (some 600 km lie between East and West Malaysia.) The peninsular has a series of central mountain ridges bordered by narrow coastal plains. More than 58% of West Malaysia is over 152m above sea level and the highest point is Gunong Tahan 2,189m. South of the Pahang, the largest river, are the Johore lowlands. Sabah and Sarawak are both mountainous (Mt Kinabalu is Malaysia's highest peak, 4,101m) with very narrow coastal belts. The two main rivers are the Rajang and the Kinabatangan. Brunei, which is divided into two by Sarawak, consists of a fertile coastal plain rising to a hilly interior. Singapore, made up of the main island and 54 islets, is low-lying and swampy (although many areas have been drained) with a central hill region. The island is criss-crossed by streams, yet the main river, Sungei Seletar, is only 14.5 km long.

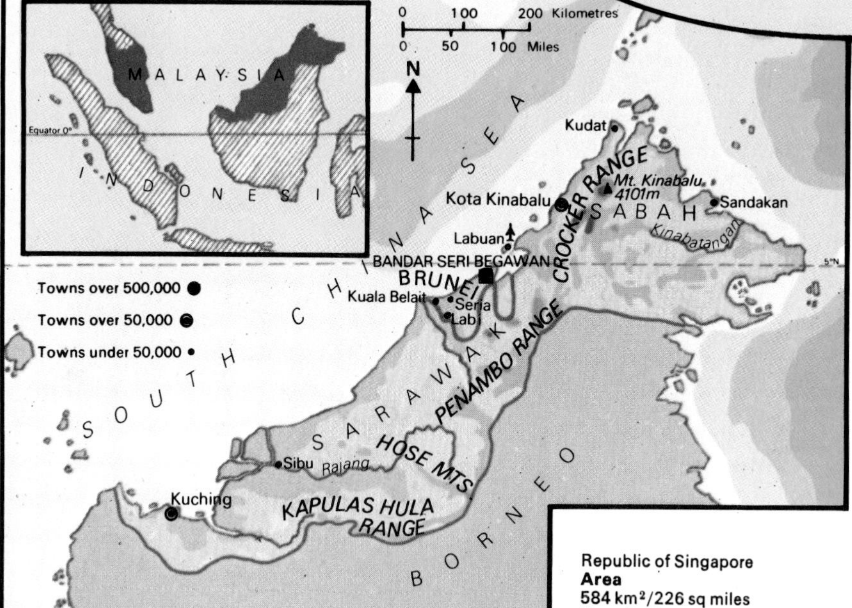

Malaysia
Area
333,403 km²/127,316 sq miles
Location
1° – 7° N ; 100° – 119° E
Climate
equatorial
Population
11,700,000 (1974)
Population density
35 per km²/92 per sq mile
Capital and largest city
Kuala Lumpur : 500,000 (1974)
Language
Bahasa Malaysia
Gross National Product
8,150 million US dollars
Major imports
machinery and transport equipment, manufactured goods, foodstuffs
Major exports
rubber, timber, tin, palm oil, iron ore
Currency
Malaysian dollar (100 cents = 1 dollar)
Status
independent constitutional monarchy

Republic of Singapore
Area
584 km²/226 sq miles
Population
2,219,100 (1974)
Population density
3,784 per km²/9,750 per sq mile
Capital and largest city
City of Singapore : 1,247,000 (1970)
Languages
Malay, Mandarin, Tamil, English
Gross National Product
4,145 million US dollars
Major imports
foodstuffs, machinery, petroleum
Major exports
petroleum products, rubber, ships
Currency
Singapore dollar (100 cents = 1 dollar)
Status
ndependent republic

Brunei Darus Salam
Area
5,765 km²/2,226 sq miles
Population
145,170 (1973)
Population density
25 per km²/65 per sq mile
Capital and largest city
Bandar Seri Begawan : 37,000 (1971)
Language
Malay
Gross National Product
110 million US dollars
Major imports
machinery, transport equipment, manufactured goods, foodstuffs, chemicals
Major exports
crude oil, natural gas, petroleum products
Currency
Brunei dollar (100 cents = 1 dollar)
Status
self-governing sultanate under British protection

Climate
The climate is humid and hot. East Malaysia and Brunei are slightly hotter than the peninsular and Singapore. Rainfall is affected by the monsoons and is heaviest from November to March during the north-east monsoon ; the period from June to October is relatively dry except along the south-west coast of Sabah. But rainfall everywhere varies with altitude. In Brunei, for example, the coast receives 250 cm/100" a year, while parts of the interior receive 500 cm/200".

Forests
A quarter of the forest, which covers 70% of West Malaysia and 80% of East Malaysia, is commercially exploited, making timber the country's second largest export. In Brunei, three-quarters of which is forested, timber exports are restricted and the emphasis is on wood products : a new veneer and plywood factory at Muara will use timber from the Temburong district and forests in the Kuala Belait and Labi areas will eventually supply a pulp mill at Kuala Belait.

Industry
Of the three countries, Singapore is the most industrialized. There are engineering works, shipyards, oil refineries, petrochemical plants, saw mills and textile, electrical and food-processing factories. In Malaysia, traditional industries are concerned with agricultural and mineral products : rubber-processing, saw milling, tin-smelting, copra-milling and, recently, oil-refining. New industries include steel, vehicle assembly, chemicals and the manufacture of consumer goods. Brunei is undergoing industrialization : there are plans for a glass factory using local silica, a petrochemical plant, a pulp mill, a plywood factory and a sago-processing plant.

Agriculture
Malaysia's economy is largely based on agriculture and this employs more than half the work force. The country is the world's largest producer of rubber—which accounts for 32% of export earnings—palm oil and pepper. Other cash crops are coconuts and, of lesser importance, sago and tea. After rubber the second main crop is rice, supplying 90% of domestic requirements. Rubber and pepper are also grown in Brunei but here, agricultural products make up less than 1% of exports. In an effort to reduce food imports, Brunei is trying to increase rice production and to develop livestock farming. Singapore also has a high level of food imports, but is self-sufficient in pork, poultry and eggs, while intensive market gardening meets half the state's vegetable needs. There are also rubber and coconut plantations. Fishing is growing in importance and both Brunei and Malaysia export prawns—some to Singapore which is not self-sufficient in fish.

Cities
In Singapore, 9 out of 10 people live in the capital. To combat overcrowding (in some areas there are over 40,000 people per km²/100,000 per sq mile) the government sponsors rehousing programmes. The city, which includes an industrial sector, is a free port and much of the cargo handled is in transit. The capital of Malaysia, Kuala Lumpur, is near the west coast of the peninsular on the Kelang and Gombak rivers. It is the country's major industrial city and is served by the port of Kelang. Brunei's capital, Bandar Seri Begawan, is an agricultural market town and river port.

Transport
A causeway links Singapore to Malaysia where there are good road and rail networks, especially in the rubber and tin belt. East Malaysia and Brunei have few roads ; the only railway is in Sabah, so river transport predominates. The main shipping ports are Singapore (the fourth largest in the world) ; Penang and Kelang in West Malaysia ; Kota Kinabalu, Sandakan and Kuching in East Malaysia ; Muara and Kuala Belait in Brunei. There are international airports at Kuala Lumpur, Kota Kinabalu, Penang, Singapore and Bandar Seri Begawan.

Mining
Over a third of the world's tin supply comes from Malaysia, making it the world's largest tin producer. Deposits are concentrated in Peninsular Malaysia and the most important are found in the western belt running from Perak to Negri Sembilan. Tin accounts for 13% of exports. Iron ore and bauxite are also exported. The petroleum industry is expanding : oil strikes have been made off eastern Peninsular Malaysia and off Sabah and Sarawak ; petroleum and petroleum products already make up 5% of total exports. In Brunei, a leading petroleum producer, oil and natural gas are essential to the economy and account for 99% of export earnings. Most of the output, coming from the onshore field at Seria and the offshore fields of Ampa, Fairley and Champion, goes by pipeline to refineries in Sarawak. Brunei also has the world's biggest liquefied natural gas plant.

Indonesia

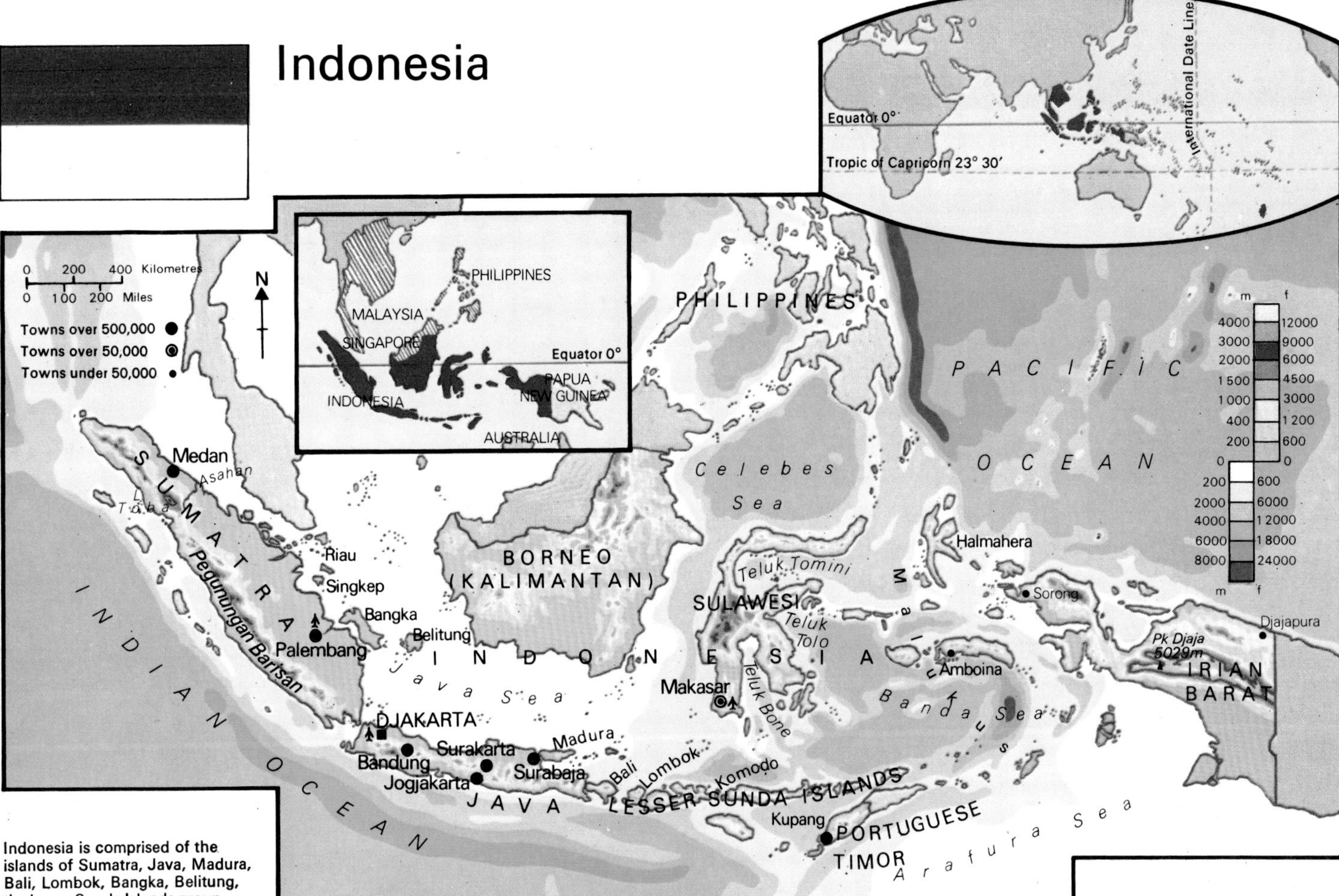

Indonesia is comprised of the islands of Sumatra, Java, Madura, Bali, Lombok, Bangka, Belitung, the lesser Sunda Islands group, Sulawesi, the Riau-Lingga Archipelago, the Maluku Islands, part of the islands of Borneo and Timor and the western half of the island of New Guinea (Irian Barat).

Land Area
1,904,344 km²/735,268 sq miles
Location
5°55'N-11°S; 95°-141°E
Population
124,030,000 (1972)
Population density
65 per km²/168.6 per sq mile
Capital and largest city
Djakarta: 4,700,000 (1972)
Language
Bahasa Indonesia
Major Imports
cotton, wheat flour, rice, machinery, fertilizers
Major Exports
oil, timber, rubber and latex products, tin, coffee
Currency
rupiah (100 sen=1 rupiah)
GNP
10.63 billion US dollars
Status
independent republic

Climate

Indonesia's position, straddling the equator, gives it a tropical climate. Temperatures range from 19°C to 36°C, with an average at sea level of 26°C. Humidity is high and rain is heavy throughout the year. In the very wet, mountainous zones, annual rainfall averages 609cm and Djakarta receives 203cm. In most areas rain is heaviest from November to March, the west monsoon season. In contrast, the east monsoon, coming from the dry interior of Australia from June to October, is not a major rainbearer and, in the extreme south-east, is even arid. Kupang, on Timor, for example, has only 3.7cm of rain during this five-month period and a few islands, like Komodo, are so parched that vegetation is very sparse.

Physical features

Indonesia, the largest country in South-East Asia, lies between the Indian and Pacific Oceans and occupies most of the Malay archipelago or East Indies. It consists of over 13,600 islands; the three largest—Kalimantan, Sumatra and Irian Barat—make up to 70% of the total land area. Nearly all the islands are mountainous. On some, like Sulawesi, the Malukus and the eastern Lesser Sundas, the land rises steeply straight from the sea; on others, there are lowland areas. Sumatra and Kalimantan have coastal swamps, while wide river valleys and alluvial plains characterize Java, Lombok and Bali. Indonesia's central mountain range reaches its highest point in Irian Barat at Mt Djaja (5029 m). The range includes over 400 volcanoes, 100 of which are active: on Bali, Gunung Agung, sacred as the home of the gods, last erupted in 1963.

Forests

About 60% of Indonesia is covered with dense forests. In coastal areas these forests are largely mangrove and nipa palm, while tropical rain forests grow in the interior. Timber production, which increases as new roads are built, is mainly carried out by men with the help of work animals, such as oxen and water buffaloes, rather than machines. Teak is the major timber export, followed by ebony, sandalwood and ironwood. Other important forest products are seeds used for drugs and dyes; mangrove bark for tannin; bamboo, rattan, resin; and cajuput oil, used in treating skin diseases. Tidal forests on Sumatra and Kalimantan are major sources of charcoal and fuel wood.

Agriculture

Indonesia is primarily agricultural; its rich lowlands and abundant rainfall create ideal conditions for farming, in which 80% of the population is engaged. The country is not, however, self-sufficient in the production of its staple food, rice, which is cultivated on both dry fields and terraced, wet fields. The latter, known as 'giant staircases to the heavens', are best because they yield two harvests a year. Other crops grown for domestic use include cassava, coconuts, peanuts, soya beans and sweet potatoes. The main cash crop is rubber. Other important exports are palm oil; coffee, which is grown on Java, Kalimantan, Bali and Sumatra; tea and tobacco, both produced on Java and Sumatra; sugar, mostly from Java; copra and spices. Recent projects affecting agriculture have included irrigation schemes—essential for rice—and transmigration, whereby Indonesians from overpopulated Java are moved to areas in need of workers

Crafts

Indonesia has many traditional crafts, but the most famous is batik, a method of hand-printing textiles. Starting with plain cloth, the batikmaker applies hot liquid wax to the areas he does not wish to dye, then dips the cloth into a vat of dye. The waxing and dyeing process is repeated for each colour, until the cloth is intricately patterned. Two other popular crafts are silver-work (practised in Jogjakarta on Java, Bali, South Sulawesi and Sumatra) and wood-carving. The best wood-carvers, who use modern themes influenced by the country's Hindu and Islamic heritage, are found on Bali and at Djapara.

Energy and industry

Indonesia has enough resources to provide for all her energy needs; wood, coal (which is mined in both Sumatra and Kalimantan) and oil are the major sources, but hydro-electricity is also important: three large plants are being built on the Asahan river in Sumatra and on the Djatiluhur and Brantas rivers in Java. Although Indonesia has industrial potential the economy is still basically agricultural, and less than 10% of the work force is engaged in manufacturing. Most major industries are connected with agriculture and mining: rubber-processing plants, rice and sugar mills, oil refineries, a fertilizer plant near the Palembang oil fields and a chemical works at Surabaja based on salt from Madura; the important textile industry uses yarns imported from overseas.

Mining

Indonesia's mineral wealth is vast. Petroleum and tin, mined on Bangka, Belitung and Singkep, are the most important. The republic is the largest oil producer in the Far East, production coming from Sumatra, Kalimantan and Java. Many of the oil fields are in dense jungle which makes drilling and transport difficult; helicopters are often used to bring men and equipment to the sites. About 15% of the crude oil produced is sufficient to supply domestic needs; the rest is exported. There is an important production of bauxite on the Riau islands, and nickel on Sulawesi and Halmahera. Other mineral deposits—not yet fully exploited, partly because of poor communications—include iron ore, manganese, copper, gold, silver, platinum and diamonds.

Cities

Although Java only comprises one-seventh of Indonesia's total land area, it is the most important island and the home of two out of three Indonesians. Djakarta (4,700,000), the country's capital, is on the island's north-west coast, built on swampy ground at the mouth of the Tji Liwung. The city, which has traditional bamboo-mat houses alongside concrete office blocks, is the republic's commercial and financial centre. Its port, Tandjung Priok, is the most important in Indonesia and handles nearly all imports which are then often re-shipped to other domestic ports. The republic's second and third largest cities are also on Java: Surabaja (1,600,000) is a major port and industrial centre; Bandung (1,300,000), on a volcanic plateau 610m/2,000 ft high, has many light industries. Other major cities are Medan (which has Indonesia's largest mosque) and Palembang, both on Sumatra, and Makasar.

Communications

Transport facilities vary from island to island. Java and Sumatra have adequate road networks, but in many other areas there may be no links between major settlements, and the local roads are unpaved. Rail transport is particularly important on Java, where the high population density makes it difficult to build new roads; Madura and Sumatra also have railways. Inter-island freight traffic moves by sea, while passenger traffic goes by air. The inter-island shipping fleet includes vessels from small barges to 500 tonne ships and serves some 300 ports; the three most important are Tandjung Priok, Surabaja and Belawan (Medan). A domestic air service, linking almost 40 towns, is provided.

Burma

Area
676,580 km²/261,228 sq miles
Location
9°30'—28°35' N
92°10'—101°10' E
Population
28,890,000 (1973)
Population density
43 per km²/111 per sq mile
Capital and largest city
Rangoon: 2,056,118 (1973)
Language
Burmese
Major imports
machinery, transport equipment, textiles, metals
Major exports
rice, timber, rubber, minerals
Currency
kyat (1 kyat = 100 pyas)
Gross Domestic Product
2,129 million US dollars
Status
Independent republic

Physical features

Burma falls into three major regions: the western ranges, the central basin and the eastern plateaux. In the far north, mountains rise to 6,000 m: Hkakabo Ravi is the country's highest peak at 6,289 m. Running southwards are the western ranges. These stretch from the northern border with India to the Rangoon delta and include the Naga hills, the Letha Range, the Chin hills (Rongklang Range) and the Arakan Yoma. To the east is the 920 m high Shan plateau which becomes lower as it continues southwards into the Tenasserim peninsula. Between these two mountain systems is the central basin formed by the valleys of the Irrawaddy, Chindwin and Sittang rivers. The Irrawaddy and Sittang, divided in their middle courses by the Pegu Yoma, have adjoining deltas with a total area of 15,000 km². Although the 2,090 km long Irrawaddy is Burma's major river, the Salween is the longest. Rising in Tibet, it flows 2,815 km to the sea at Moulmein. Burma extends down the Tenasserim peninsula for over 300 km to Victoria Point—this is the narrowest region of the peninsula, only 50 km wide. The peninsula is a hilly region with peaks between 1,000 and 1,500 m while the west coast is studded with many islands.

Agriculture

Rice dominates the Burmese economy. Rice-fields, covering 70% of land under cultivation, are concentrated in the Irrawaddy delta. Although double-cropping is rare, Burma produces a surplus and is one of the world's leading exporters of rice. In drier areas—the middle Irrawaddy basin and the lower Cindwin valley—various crops are grown: maize, millet, sesame, tobacco, peanuts, cotton and pulses. There are sugar plantations in the Sittang valley and rubber is important on the Tenasserim peninsula. The government is developing jute cultivation in the delta so as to abolish the import of bags for rice. Other government schemes include irrigation projects and the increased use of fertilizers. Apart from rice, which accounts for 60% of total exports, rubber, pulses and oil-cake are exported. As Buddhists do not eat meat, cattle and buffalo are raised only for work. After rice, fish is the main food, coming mostly from rivers. Marine fishing is being developed.

Cities

About 80% of Burmese people live in the country and, of the remaining 20%, more than half live in the capital, Rangoon. Built beside the Rangoon river, 40 km from the sea, the city has grown round the great gold-coated pagoda of Shwe Dagon. Rangoon is the country's leading port and main industrial city with rice- and saw-milling, food processing, chemicals, textiles, soap, rubber, oil refining and steel. Burma's second largest town, Mandalay (pop. 417,266), is 619 km north of Rangoon. Mandalay is an important Buddhist centre noted for its monasteries and pagodas, especially the Maha Mya Muni pagoda which has a very old brass Buddha, 4 m high. Built beside the Irrawaddy, it is the hub of road, rail, water and air networks in the interior. Its traditional industries include silk-weaving and jade-cutting. Other major towns include Moulmein and Mergui.

Climate

The climate is monsoonal: most areas receive 80% of rain during the south-west monsoon (May-October). This warm, wet wind cuts across the NW-SE alignment of the mountains giving a varied rainfall pattern: coastal zones are wet (Moulmein, 494 cm), while the central basin is dry (Mandalay, 76 cm). This monsoon is followed by the NE monsoon which lasts until February. January is the coldest month with averages of 22°C in Mandalay, 25°C in Rangoon. April, in the transitional hot dry period, is the warmest month: 32°C in Mandalay, 30°C in Rangoon.

Forestry

Over 60% of Burma is tree-covered and, after agriculture, forestry is the main occupation. Commercially, the most important forests grow in areas where rainfall is between 100 cm and 200 cm, especially on the Arakan Yoma, the Pegu Yoma and the Shan plateau. These monsoon forests produce teak, used for ships and furniture, also ironwood, used for railway sleepers. About 4,000 elephants are employed to haul logs to the river banks. The wood is then piled on bamboo rafts and floated downstream to the sawmills. Timber, mostly teak, accounts for 15% of exports. Swamps and mangroves cover the Irrawaddy delta.

Industry

Industrialization is still in its early stages. Traditional industries, rice-and saw-milling are based on the country's leading raw materials. New developments include textile factories at Rangoon, Myingyan and Paleik; fertilizer plants at Sale and Kynchaung; a steel works and a chemical plant at Rangoon and a cement works at Thayetmyo, fired by natural gas. Further industrialization partly depends on energy supplies. Current sources of power are a thermal plant at Rangoon and three hydro-electric stations. Larger supplies can undoubtedly be provided by an increased petroleum production and by harnessing the vast hydro-electric potential of Burma's rivers. About 1.5 million people are employed in the power, construction and manufacturing sectors. In rural areas, the state encourages the development of cottage industries such as ivory-carving, silver-work and weaving.

Mining

Burma's mineral wealth is largely under-exploited. The most important are petroleum, tin, tungsten and silver-lead. Oil-fields are situated along the valleys of the middle Irrawaddy and Chindwin with production centered on Chauk, Yenangyaung and Myingyan. The petroleum is refined at Chauk and Syriam, near Rangoon. Deposits of tin and tungsten occur in a belt running from the Shan plateau to the Tenasserim coast. The Bawdwin mines, also on the Shan plateau, yield lead, silver and zinc and, in smaller quantities, copper and nickel. Future mining developments could include coal found at Kalewa in the Chindwin valley and iron, at Taunggyi. More famous, though of less commercial value, are Burma's precious stones. Rubies, amethysts and sapphires, come from the mines at Mogok, in the Shan uplands; jade comes from Myitkyina in the extreme north, and gold from the banks of the Chindwin and Irrawaddy.

Transport

The Irrawaddy is the backbone of Burma's transport system. The river is navigable up to Myitkyina, 1,600 km from the sea, and its tributary, the Chindwin, is navigable for a further 650 km. The delta streams provide a 3,200 km network open to vessels and a canal, 96 km long, links the Sittang to the Irrawaddy. These inland waterways are essential to the rice trade: almost every ricefield is accessible by water and boats take the unhusked rice to the mills. Burma has four ports open to international shipping: Bassein, Moulmein, Sittwe and Rangoon—the country's main port, handling over 80% of exports. The waterway network is supplemented by rail. Branch lines spread out from the main line which runs from Rangoon to Myitkyina, via Mandalay. Roads are less important. Internal air services link 50 towns and both Rangoon and Mandalay have international airports.

People's Republic of Bangladesh

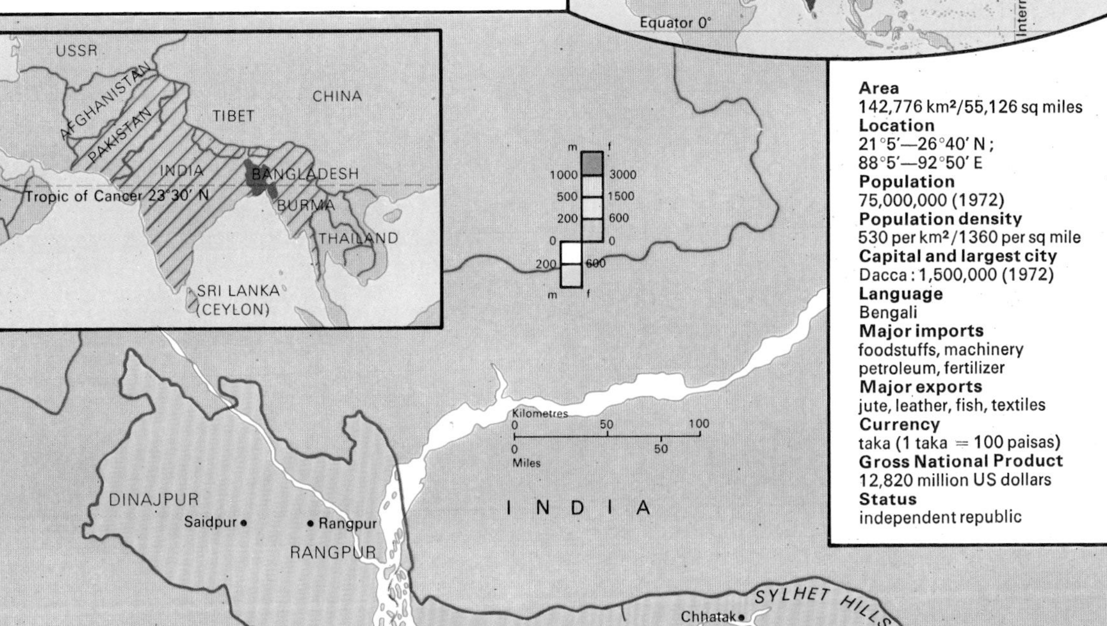

Area
142,776 km²/55,126 sq miles
Location
21°5′—26°40′ N;
88°5′—92°50′ E
Population
75,000,000 (1972)
Population density
530 per km²/1360 per sq mile
Capital and largest city
Dacca: 1,500,000 (1972)
Language
Bengali
Major imports
foodstuffs, machinery
petroleum, fertilizer
Major exports
jute, leather, fish, textiles
Currency
taka (1 taka = 100 paisas)
Gross National Product
12,820 million US dollars
Status
independent republic

Forestry

Forests cover 15% of the country. Commercially, the most important areas are the Chittagong Hills and the delta mouth, the Sundarbans, home of the Bengal tiger. Covering an area of 5,960 km², the tidal Sundarbans forest is largely mangrove, but also contains gewa, a softwood used for newsprint, matches and boxes, and sundari, which gives the forest its name and is used for boat-building. The tropical rain forest on the Chittagong Hills yields teak, used for furniture, and bamboo, which is the basis of the country's paper industry. An associated forest product is honey with an annual yield of over 240,000 kg.

Physical features

Bangladesh is situated in the world's largest delta formed by the rivers Ganges, Brahmaputra and Meghna at the head of the Bay of Bengal. This vast alluvial plain, now extensively cleared for cultivation, was once completely covered with tropical rain forest. In places, it is less than 10 m above sea level and extremely vulnerable to flooding. Swampy islands, covered with mangrove forests known as the Sundarbans, fringe the coast. The delta is ever changing with the three main rivers and, more importantly, their many tributaries frequently altering course. Furthermore, the delta region is continually growing through the accretion of silt. The only major upland area in Bangladesh is in the southeast: the Chittagong Hills. These are a series of jungle-covered parallel ranges with an average height of 600 m. This densely forested region covers an area of over 3,000 km². There are also low hills, with a maximum height of 250 m, in the north-east near Sylhet. On the plain itself there are stretches of old alluvium which rise above the general level.

Industry

Bangladesh is still an agricultural country. The country has enormous resources such as peat, coal, oil and natural gas but these are, as yet, undeveloped. Although coal has been discovered, it is not yet mined and the country has to rely on imports. Petroleum also has to be imported as the production of oil from the Bay of Bengal is in its early stages. An oil refinery has, however, been built to exploit these oil reserves. On the other hand, natural gas, found in the Sylhet and Comilla districts, is fully exploited. In 1966, the first hydro-electric power station was installed. Situated by the Kaptai dam on the Karnafuli reservoir near Chittagong, this provides 80,000 kW of electricity. A nuclear power station is presently being built at Ruppur near the town of Pabna. Industry is concerned with the processing of raw materials. There are jute mills at Dacca, Narayanganj, Chittagong, and Khulna and a cement works at Chhatak which utilizes the country's limestone resources. Bamboo and softwoods supply paper mills at Chandraghana near Chittagong, Khulna and Pabna.

Agriculture

In Bangladesh, 60% of the land is used for agriculture and this employs 80% of the population. Of this cultivated area, 75% is used for growing rice—the chief food crop. Although double-cropping is common, the annual production of 200 kg per person is insufficient for food and seed requirements and most people live at subsistence level. The chief cash crop is jute and Bangladesh produces 50% of the world's supply. Like rice, jute requires standing water and high temperatures for ripening: the regularly flooded delta plain is therefore ideal for both crops. The country's second cash crop, tea, also requires heat and humidity but, as it does not grow in water, plantations are located on the Chittagong and Sylhet hills. Other products include sugar-cane, also grown in the Sylhet region, tobacco, cotton, wheat and oilseeds. The country's many rivers and streams are rich in fish, the main food after rice. The annual catch from inland waters is 50,000 tonnes and from the Bay of Bengal, 60,000 tonnes. More efficient farming is dependent on flood control and a number of drainage and storage schemes are being implemented.

Climate

The climate of Bangladesh is monsoonal. During the summer monsoon (May to October) the country receives 80% of its rainfall. The annual average on the plain is about 180 cm; high ground has up to twice this amount. Winter, which is warm and dry, lasts from November to March. The average temperature in Dacca for January the coldest month, is 21°C and for April, the hottest month, it is 27°C. The maritime influence causes high humidity which is over 90% during the wet season. There are frequent storms in May and October and winds of up to 150 km per hour rage over the Bay of Bengal, whipping up waves to as high as 7 m. These cause extensive flooding and often disastrous loss of life.

Cities

Only 5% of the population are urban-dwellers, and 80% of these live in either Dacca, Chittagong or Khulna. Dacca, the capital, is the country's largest and main industrial city. Traditionally, the city is famous for its muslin, embroidery and gold and silver-work. Current industrialization is based on jute-processing, rice-milling and cotton manufacture; the jute industry is centered on Narayanganj, a river port 16 km south of the capital and included in Greater Dacca. The second largest city, Chittagong (pop. 680,000), is also the country's leading port and handles nearly all jute, tea and leather exports. Khulna (500,000) is a commercial and industrial centre in the south-west.

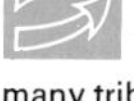

Communications

The three main rivers, the Ganges, Brahmaputra and Meghna, and their many tributaries provide a comprehensive transport system. Nevertheless, these same rivers and the many other inland waterways that dissect the country, together with the persistent floods, have prevented the development of an extensive road and rail network. These are limited to some 2,800 km of railways and 5,800 km of roads. A domestic air service operates between major towns and there is an international airport north of the capital of Dacca.

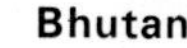

Nepal Bhutan

The Himalayan States

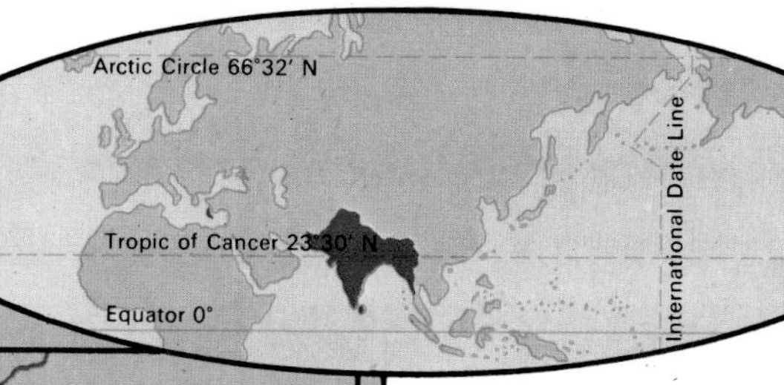

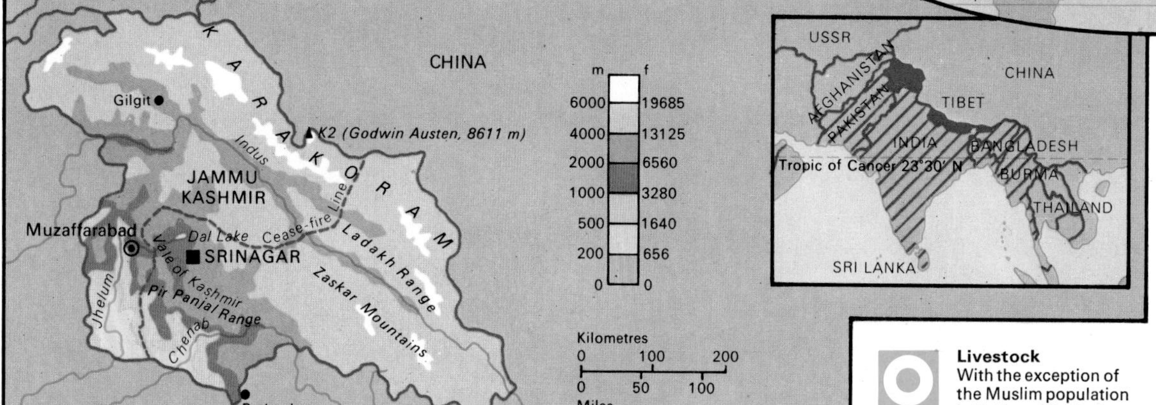

Nepal
Area
140,798 km²/54,362 sq miles
Location
26°20′—30°10′ N
80°15′—88°15′ E
Population
11,700,000 (1973)
Population density
83 per km²/215 per sq mile
Capital and largest city
Katmandu: 353,756 (1971)
Language
Nepali, but English, Hindi, Lepcha and Bhutanese also spoken
Major imports
manufactured goods, foodstuffs, minerals, fuels, machinery and chemicals
Major exports
food and live animals, jute, timber, medicinal herbs, hides
Currency
Nepalese rupee (rupee = 100 paise)
Gross National Product
920 million US dollars
Status
constitutional monarchy

Bhutan
Area
46,600 km²/17,992 sq miles
Location
26°45′—28° N 89°—92° E
Population
1,100,000 (1971)
Population density
24 per km²/61 per sq mile
Capital and largest city
Thimphu: 60,000 (1971)
Language
Dzongkha
Major imports
textiles, machinery
Major exports
fruit, timber, jam, distillery products
Currency
Indian rupee (rupee = 100 paise)
Gross National Product
47 million US dollars
Status
democratic monarchy

Jammu and Kashmir
Area
222,770 km²/86,012 sq miles
Location
32°15′—37°20′ N
72°40′—80°30′ E
Population
5,900,000 (1971)
Population density
26 per km²/69 per sq mile
Capital and largest city
Srinagar: 403,612 (1971)
Status
officially, Jammu and Kashmir is part of India but Pakistan has disputed this since 1947. The current cease-fire line gives about 30% of the state to Pakistan

Sikkim
Area
7,298 km²/2,818 sq miles
Location
27°—28° N
88°10′—89°5′ E
Population
208,600 (1971)
Population density
29 per km²/74 per sq mile
Capital and largest city
Gangtok: 15,000 (1971)
Status
formerly an Indian protectorate with internal autonomy, Sikkim became part of the Indian republic in 1975

Cities

The capital of the Indian sector of Jammu and Kashmir is Srinagar, standing 1,600 m above sea level on the banks of the Jhelum river in the Vale of Kashmir. Canals, crossed by wooden bridges, flow through the picturesque city which has both Hindu temples and Moslem mosques. Srinagar is a major tourist centre and a leading attraction is the Dal Lake with its floating gardens. Bazaars display a wide range of Kashmiri crafts: carpets, embroidered silk, silverware, papier mâché and wood-carvings. Jammu, some 200 km south of Srinagar and over 1,000 m lower, is the winter capital and well-known for its traditional paintings. The chief town in the Pakistani sector is Muzaffarabad. Katmandu, the Nepalese capital, is situated at an altitude of 1,325 m near the confluence of the Baghmati and Vishnumati rivers. A city of palaces and temples, it is an important commercial centre at the heart of a densely populated farming region. Gangtok is the capital of Sikkim and an agricultural market town. With the royal palace as its focal point, Thimphu, the capital of Bhutan, is also a market town.

Minerals

The mineral wealth of the Himalayan states remains largely unexploited. In Kashmir, coal and bauxite deposits have yet to be developed but some lignite is mined in the Vale. Lignite is also worked locally in eastern Nepal; elsewhere in the country there is limited mining of copper, iron, dolomite and cobalt. Exploitation is more developed in Sikkim where lead, copper and zinc are mined at Rhotang. Graphite and gypsum have also been located. Bhutan is currently planning to develop its resources of coal, dolomite, graphite and gypsum.

Industry

Industry is generally limited to processing local produce and to traditional crafts. In Kashmir, the main industry after tourism is silkworm breeding which employs 8% of the population. Important crafts are wood-carving, carpet weaving, leather work and papier mâché. In Bhutan, sawmills, jam factories, distilleries and a furniture plant use local materials, and there are several craft industries including hand-weaving, embroidery, wood-carving and metalwork. As well as traditional manufactures and distilleries, Sikkim has a few small factories producing items such as nails and candles. In Nepal, factories process domestically produced jute, sugar, tobacco, timber and leather; new projects include a chemical works and an iron and steel complex. Hydroelectric plants are being constructed in all four states.

Livestock

With the exception of the Muslim population in Pakistani Kashmir, most of the Himalayan peoples are either Buddhists, and therefore vegetarians, or Hindus, who do not eat beef. Consequently, meat production is limited and animals are raised mainly for their hair, skin and milk. In the Nepalese valleys, cattle and buffaloes are often stall-fed as all available ground is cultivated. Goats and sheep graze in the mountains. In Kashmir and Sikkim, yaks and sheep provide hair and wool for woven goods.

Physical features

Nepal, Sikkim and Bhutan lie between the Ganges Plain and the High Himalayas. Nepal has three zones. In the south is the Terai, a narrow, swampy malarial plain. North of this are the mid-Himalayas, a series of parallel ranges broken by transverse valleys. Beyond these ranges rise the snow-covered peaks of the High Himalayas, including Mount Everest (8,882 m) the world's highest mountain. Sikkim, drained by the Tista river, is very mountainous. Bhutan also has three zones: peaks of over 7,000 m in the north descend to a belt of low ranges crossed by valleys with the hot and steamy Duars plain in the extreme south. Kashmir is composed of a series of steps rising from 600 m to the great Karakoram range with the world's fourth highest peak, K2, at 8,951 m. The major flat area is the Vale of Kashmir, an alluvial basin drained by the Jhelum.

Climate

The average temperature for July in Srinagar is 23°C, in Katmandu it is 25°C. January figures are 0° and 10°C respectively. Altitude is an obvious influence and in the High Himalayas temperatures are always below freezing. In Bhutan, Nepal and Sikkim, most rain falls during June-September and is heaviest in the east: 760 cm a year in the Duars, 100 cm in western Nepal. In Kashmir, rain occurs mostly in the winter, averaging 66 cm per year.

Agriculture

Agriculture dominates the economy of all four states. In Bhutan, cultivation is concentrated in the central valleys. Rice and maize are grown on the valley floors while wheat and barley cover adjacent slopes. State orchards produce a variety of fruit, mostly for export. Sikkim is the world's leading producer of cardamom. Other cash crops include potatoes, apples, mandarin oranges, ginger and tea; principle food crops are rice and maize. In Nepal, 15% of land is under cultivation. Of this, 75% is in the Terai and the remainder is in the mid-Himalayan valleys. Half the arable land is used for rice; maize, millet and wheat are the other food crops. The two leading cash crops, jute and sugar, are grown in the Terai; fruit, tea and tobacco are being developed in the mid-Himalayas. In Kashmir, rice, maize and wheat are the main cereals. Fruit is the major cash crop and apples, apricots, peaches and plums are exported. Mulberry leaf production for silkworm breeding is important.

Forestry

Forests, ranging from tropical hardwood to coniferous, cover 35% of Bhutan, Sikkim and Nepal, but only about 12% of Kashmir. Exploitation is very limited in Sikkim, but in Bhutan and Kashmir there is some production of timber, gums and resins. The industry is most developed in Nepal where hardwoods from the Terai and sal from the slopes are exported to India, and Terai softwoods are used for the manufacture of matches. In all four states, forests yield medicinal herbs.

Transport

Communications are poor and most people travel on foot or use animals, such as buffaloes. Nepal has the most developed transport system; there are about 3,000 km of roads mainly in the Terai and the Katmandu valley; railways link Raxaul (India) to Amlekhganj (48 km), and Jaynagar (India) to Bijalpura (53 km) while the Royal Nepal Airlines operate flights to some 35 Nepalese towns as well as to India, Bangladesh, Burma and Thailand. Sikkim has few roads and no railways or airports. Bhutan is also without railways but has an air service between Paro and Calcutta and 1,500 km of roads built with Indian aid. Kashmir is linked to the rest of India by road and rail from Jammu to Pathankot and by air from Srinagar and Jammu to Delhi. Internally, there are 5,600 km of roads.

Pakistan

Area
801,408 km²/309,424 sq miles
Location
23°41′—36°50′ N
60°55′—75°30′ E
Population
64,892,000 (1972)
Population density
81 per km²/210 per sq mile
Capital
Islamabad: 250,000 (1972)
Largest city
Karachi: 3,500,000 (1972)
Language
Urdu
Major imports
transport equipment and machinery, iron and steel, chemicals and fertilizer
Major exports
raw cotton and cotton manufactures, rice, leather, fish
Currency
rupee (1 rupee = 100 paisa)
Gross National Product
3,575 million US dollars
Status
independent republic

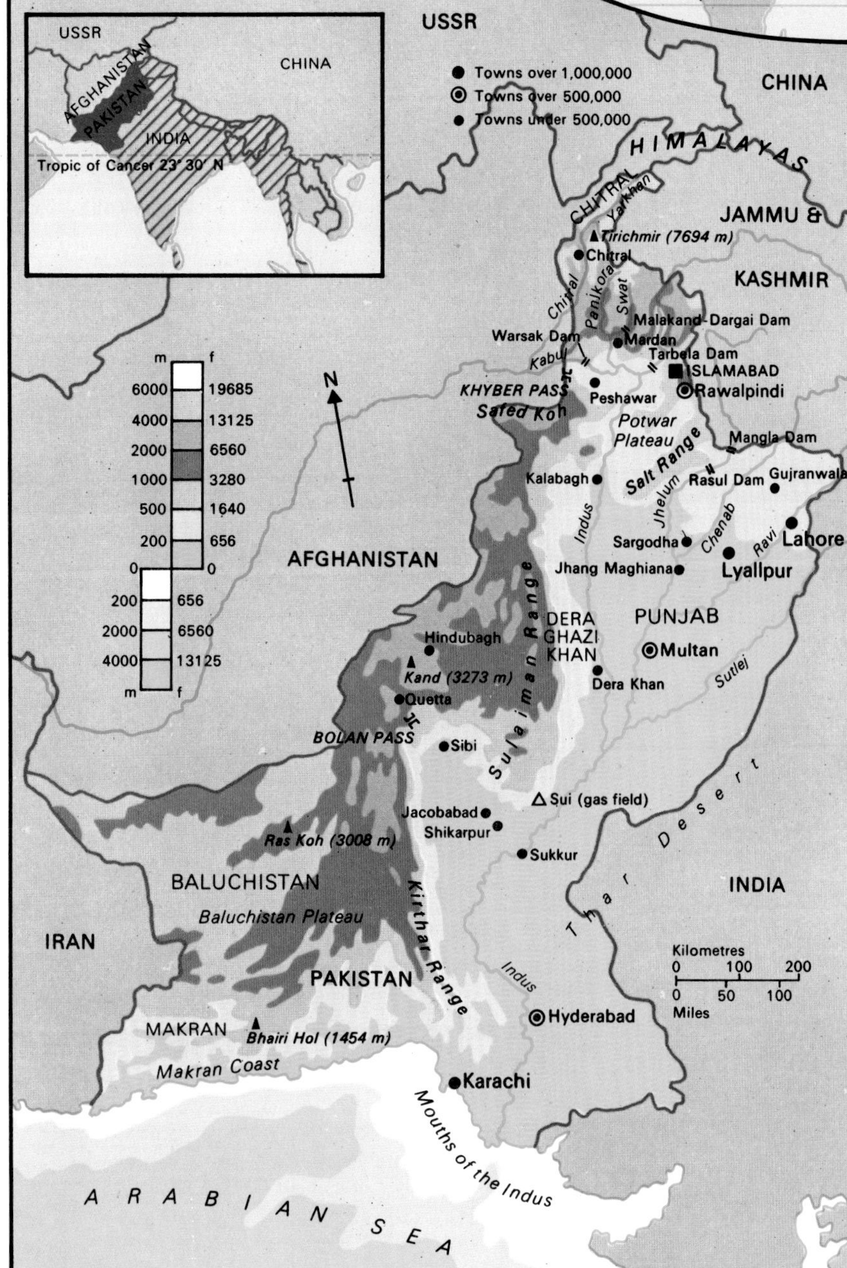

Physical features

Pakistan divides into three geographical regions. Mountains dominate the north and north-west. These are highest in the north and situated there is Pakistan's highest peak, Tirichmir (7,694 m). In this area, the rivers Yarkhan, Swat, Chitral and Panjkora flow through deep gorges. Along the north-west frontier lie a series of lower ranges: Safed Koh, Sulaiman and Kirthar. The most famous pass across this mountain wall is the Khyber, linking Pakistan with Afghanistan. A second zone corresponds to the 900 m high desert plateau of Baluchistan, situated west of the Kirthat range. Finally, stretching from the Himalayan foothills and the Salt Range to the Arabian Sea is the alluvial plain formed by the Indus and its Punjab tributaries: Jhelum, Chenab, Ravi, Beas and Sutlej. The arid Thar desert lies east of the lower Indus.

Climate

Although classified as tropical monsoonal, the climate has continental characteristics. Winter (October to March) is dry and cold; in the mountains, temperatures are low (Lahore, 10°C) but increase southwards (Karachi, 16°C). Summer begins with a hot, dry season. Temperatures are highest inland: the May average is 33°C, (in Karachi, 28°C). Jacobabad has the highest temperatures—up to 50°C. Light rain, brought by the south-west monsoon, falls from June to September. The annual average is 50 cm in Lahore, 20 cm in Karachi and less than 10 cm in Baluchistan.

Communications

The 8,530 km rail network was once the key element of Pakistan's transport system, but roads (with a total length of over 40,000 km) are increasing in importance. Both road and rail link Karachi with Peshawar—the frontier town guarding the Khyber Pass. Karachi is the leading port and its natural harbour is visited by over 2,000 ships a year. There are international airports at Karachi and Lahore with domestic flights also operating from Peshawar and Rawalpindi.

Cities

Only one Pakistani in five lives in a city and 25% of this urban population is concentrated in Karachi, the former capital and largest city. Situated west of the Indus delta, it is a leading industrial and commercial centre. It is also Pakistan's main port, handling 75% of foreign trade as well as serving landlocked Afghanistan. The new capital, Islamabad, is situated 14 km north-east of Rawalpindi at an altitude of 600 m. A blend of traditional Islamic and modern architecture, the city became operational on completion in 1965. The second largest city, Lahore (1,985,800) is situated on the left bank of the Ravi and is a major textile-manufacturing centre. Pakistan's third city is Lyallpur (1,016,400) which is an industrial centre and an agricultural market. Three other major towns are Hyderabad (785,700), Rawalpindi (615,000) and Multan.

Mining

Pakistan has limited mineral resources and those that do exist are not fully exploited. Low quality coal, mined in north-east Baluchistan and the Salt Range, meets half the country's requirements. Iron ore, worked at Kalabagh, is also low-grade; small higher-grade deposits are known to exist in the Chitral area but exploitation is hindered by inaccessibility. Chromite, extracted near Hindubagh, is largely exported to the US. Other minerals being exploited include limestone, quarried in the Salt Range; gypsum, mined at Sibi; rock salt from the Salt Range and uranium from the Dera Ghazi Khan region. Small oil fields on the Potwar plateau near Rawalpindi supply 10% of Pakistan's needs. The search for oil led to an important discovery: enormous reserves of natural gas. Gas is currently produced from Sui which is one of the world's largest fields, and at Mari.

Energy

Until recently, most of Pakistan's energy needs were supplied by coal-fired thermal plants. The situation, however, is changing with the development of hydro-electric power and natural gas. In the last 20 years, great progress has been made in harnessing the country's hydro-electric potential—the biggest project being the Tarbela Dam on the Indus with a capacity of two million kilowatts. Other major plants include the Mangla Dam on the Jhelum, Warsak on the Kabul, Malakand-Dargai on the Swat canal and Rasul on the Jhelum canal. Since the late 1950s, natural gas has radically increased Pakistan's power output. Pipelines from the Sui field supply gas to homes and industry in Karachi, Multan, Lahore, Lyallpur, Rawalpindi and Islamabad. A nuclear power plant at Karachi which is currently using imported uranium will shortly switch to uranium from Dera Ghazi Khan.

Industry

Pakistan's first steps towards industrialization centred on the processing of its agricultural products. Cotton is the leading industry and employs 40% of industrial workers: cotton yarn and manufactures together make up 60% of exports. Hides and skins are the basis of the important leather industry: tanneries are widespread and there are several large shoe factories. Food-processing plants, found in most towns, include sugar, rice and oilseed mills; local tobacco is made into cigarettes. More recently, non-agricultural industries have been developed: the cement industry uses lime-stone; fertilizer manufacture and petro-chemical products are based on natural gas. Engineering industries, such as vehicle assembly and irrigation machinery, use imported materials. Apart from Karachi, Hyderabad and Sukkur, industry is concentrated in the zone between Multan, Lahore and Peshawar. Manufacturing employs less than 20% of the population; in rural areas a further 10% is engaged in handicrafts such as hand-woven fabrics, pottery, metalware and leather goods.

Irrigation

As rainfall is low, agriculture in Pakistan is dependent on irrigation and 70% of cultivated land is watered in this way. Most irrigation water flows through perennial canals: dams have been built across the Indus, Jhelum and Chenab and the water stored behind these dams is supplied to the plains by the largest network of irrigation canals in the world. Other more traditional systems include wells, underground water tunnels and flood irrigation. This last method is seasonal as canals, built above low-water level, only fill when rivers are in flood.

Agriculture

Agriculture is basic to the economy and employs about 80% of the population. The cultivated area, covering 25% of the country, largely corresponds to the irrigated Indus basin. The main cereals are wheat, grown as a winter crop, and rice and maize, both grown as summer crops. Rice surpluses are exported. The leading cash crop is cotton, valued not only for its fibre but also for its seed which is used for fodder and vegetable oil production. Other major cash crops include sugar cane, oilseeds and tobacco. Apricot, peach and apple orchards are sited on irrigated areas in Baluchistan, while dates are grown along the Makran coast. Livestock farming is important: oxen, mules and camels are used as work animals, sheep provide wool used for textiles and carpets in addition to meat and dairy produce. Cattle hides are the basis of leather manufacture. The fishing industry, located on the coast and lakes in the lower Indus basin, is expanding and part of the catch, principally tuna and shellfish, is exported. Many fish farms have been established around the lakes of Sind.

India 1

Area
3,046,283 km²/1,176,171 sq miles (excluding Jammu and Kashmir, Sikkim)
Location
8°—33°15′ N
68°5′—97°25′ E
Population
546,750,000 (1971—excluding Jammu, Kashmir and Sikkim)
Population density
179 per km²/465 per sq mile
Capital
New Delhi: 3,629,842 (1971)
Largest city
Calcutta: 7,040,362 (1971)
Languages
Hindi, English, regional and tribal languages
Major imports
Machinery, steel, petroleum, raw cotton, fertilizers, chemicals
Major exports
jute products, leather, tea, cotton textiles, iron ore
Currency
rupee (1 rupee = 100 paise)
Gross National Product
57,300 million US dollars
Status
federal republic

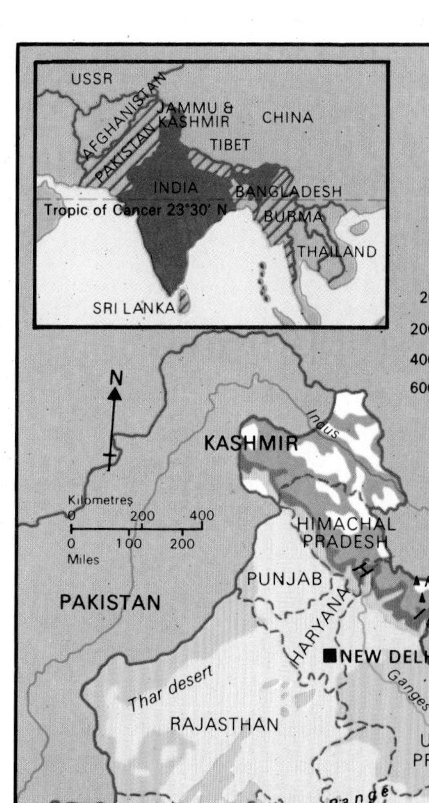

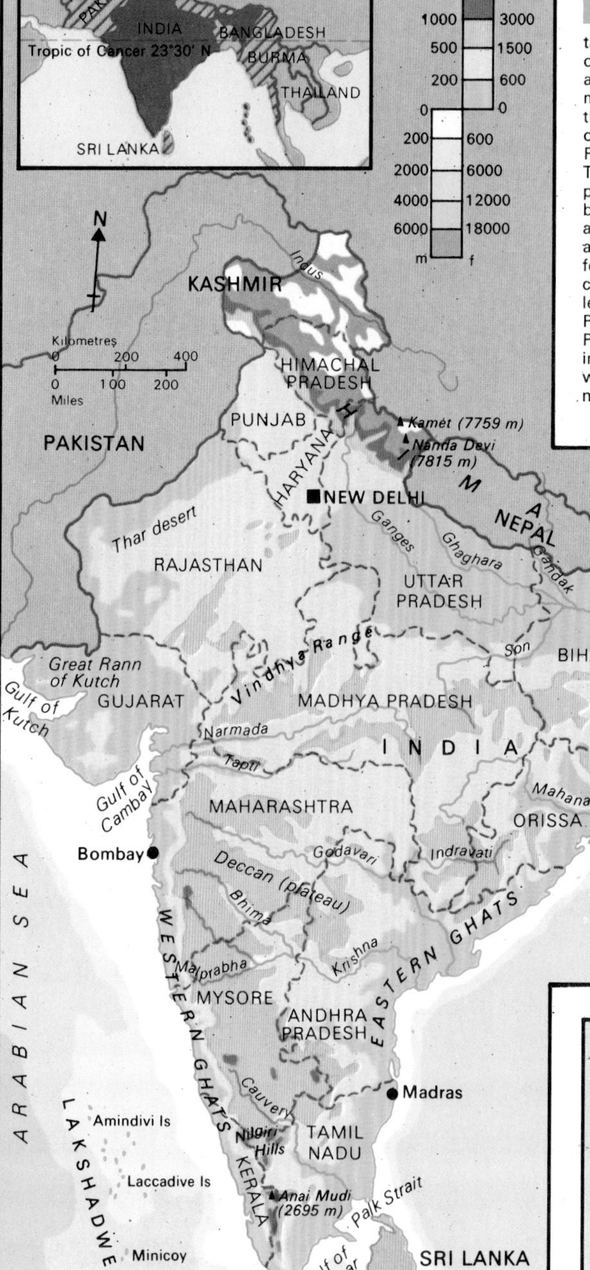

Physical features

India divides naturally into three regions: the Himalayas, the northern plain and the peninsula. The highest mountains in the world, the Himalayas, form a barrier across the north and although Mount Everest is actually in Nepal great peaks such as Nanda Devi (7,815 m) and Kamet (7,759 m) do lie in India itself. The Himalayas give way to the northern plain. This vast alluvial lowland, 350 km wide and stretching 4,000 km from east to west, is formed by the river basins of the Indus, Ganges and Brahmaputra. The peninsula plateau, the Deccan, lies south of the lowland and is separated from it by the Vindhya mountains. The Deccan is highest in the west where it rises to the Western Ghats with an average height of 1,200 m. Eastwards, it slopes down to the Eastern Ghats, 600 m. The Arabian Sea coastal strip is narrow, but between the Eastern Ghats and the Bay of Bengal there is a broad coastal plain crossed by the peninsula's main rivers: the Cauvery, Krishna, Godavari and Mahanadi.

Climate

India has four seasons: the cool season (December to February), the hot season (March-May), the S-W monsoon (June-October) and the retreating monsoon (November). The cool season is dry and sunny except in Madras where rainfall is heavy. In the coldest month, January, temperatures are 24°C in Madras and Bombay, 19°C in Calcutta and 14°C in Delhi. The hot season is dry and temperatures in May, the hottest month, are 33°C in Madras, 29°C in Bombay, 30°C in Calcutta and 32°C in Delhi. The southwest monsoon brings India 90% of its rain. One arm comes in over the Malabar coast depositing 500 cm on the Western Ghats. The other arms goes up the Bay of Bengal bringing rain to the north and east with the Khasi Hills, northeast of Bangladesh, receiving up to 2,000 cm. In contrast, the Thar desert on the borderland region with Pakistan receives as little as 12 cm.

Population

India is the world's second most populous country. The population is made up of many different peoples with distinct cultures. Communications are hampered by language problems: there are 15 major languages and 250 dialects. The official language, Hindi, is spoken by only 40% of the people, mostly in the north. India also has many religions: the main one, Hinduism, claims 85% of the population and has a profound influence on life in India. About 80% of the people live in rural areas where rainfall is sufficient for agriculture: the northern plain and the coasts of Kerala and Tamil Nadu.

Famine and food

In India, hunger is an everyday word. In the last 15 years, medical advances have caused a dramatic increase in population; the government responded by introducing a national birth-control campaign. Even if a lower birth-rate is achieved, food production must rise by at least 2% a year. Indian agriculture, however, is backward with small farms, primitive methods and only 20% of the land irrigated. Droughts and floods are common. Government projects to increase food production include fertilizer factories, irrigation and flood control schemes and improved seeds.

Agriculture: food crops

Agriculture employs 70% of the population and takes up 55% of the land. Most of this area is under cultivation and 30% of it is used for rice, the main food crop. Rice is grown in the Ganges basin (Bihar and parts of Uttar Pradesh and Madhya Pradesh) and along the east coast. These ricelands are densely populated, especially the Ganges basin where rich alluvial soil and adequate water for irrigation favour agriculture. The second staple food is wheat, grown as a winter crop in areas where rainfall is less than 100 cm such as the Punjab, Uttar Pradesh and Madhya Pradesh. Millets are grown mainly in regions with poor soil and where the rainfall is uncertain, notably on the Deccan.

Agriculture: cash crops

India is the world's leading tea producer and this crop accounts for 20% of exports. Tea plantations are situated on hillsides in Assam, West Bengal, Kerala and Tamil Nadu. India is also the world's leading producer of sugar (grown on the Deccan and the northern plain), of pepper (from Kerala) and of groundnuts (mainly from Tamil Nadu, Maharashtra and Gujarat). Groundnuts, as well as sesame, linseed and others produce oil for domestic and industrial use. Two other major crops are cotton and jute. Cotton is produced in the NW Deccan while jute is concentrated in West Bengal. Other important cash crops include coffee and rubber, both grown in the south.

Livestock

India has 20% of the world's cattle, yet livestock is under-exploited. Only 5% of the land—usually arid scrub—is used for grazing so the country's 176 million cattle and 51 million buffaloes are kept for work and not for milk. As Hindus consider the cow sacred, it is not slaughtered and beef production is negligible. There are also 40 million sheep but the wool yield is low. Its coarse quality is best suited for carpets. Dung is dried and used as fuel rather than fertilizer.

Forestry and fishing

Originally, most of India was forested, but the land and fuel needs of the growing population led to deforestation. Today, forests cover only 21% of the country and play a minor role in the economy. Products include teak, from Madhya Pradesh and Mysore, sal from the north-east and softwoods from the Himalayas. Fishing also contributes little to the economy despite enormous potential. Kerala and Orisa are important for marine fishing, West Bengal for freshwater fish.

Island territories

Three island groups belong to India: the Andaman and Nicobar Islands and Lakshadweep. The Andaman and Nicobar Islands, administered jointly, are situated in the Bay of Bengal, 1,200 km east of Madras. They have a total area of 8,200 km² and a population of 115,000. The Andaman group consists of 204 islands, many of them forested. The main exports are Andaman redwood, gurjan (used for plywood) and softwoods which are used for matches. The Ten Degree Channel separates the Andaman Islands from the Nicobar group which consists of 19 islands. Coconuts are a staple food and also the chief export item. The capital of the joint territory is Port Blair on South Andaman Island. Lakshadweep lies 300 km west of Kerala in the Arabian Sea. Its 27 islands have an area of 32 km² comprising the Laccadives, Minicoy and Amindivis. They have a population of 32,000.

India 2

Minerals

With an annual production of 100 million tonnes, India is the world's sixth largest coal-producing country. Of this, 95% comes from West Bengal and Bihar. India is also rich in iron-ore and has about 20% of the world's reserves. The main deposits occur in the north-east Deccan and 75% of the output is exported. In contrast, the country is short of other metallic minerals and has to import copper, zinc and nickel. Manganese and bauxite are both found in the north-east Deccan and India is the world's third largest producer of manganese. Some gold is mined at Kolar in Karnataka. The chief non-metallic mineral is mica and 80% of the world's supply comes from India, mostly from mines in Bihar and Rajasthan. Also important is monazite, found in the Kerala beach sands. Salt is obtained by the evaporation process along the west and south-east coasts. India produces about 30% of its oil needs from fields in Gujarat and Assam. Drilling for more oil is in progress in the Gulf of Cambay.

Energy

More than half of India's electricity is generated by thermal plants, mostly coal-fired. Hydro-electricity is being developed but faces the problem of seasonal variations in river flow. So far, only 10% of the hydro-power potential has been harnessed, mainly in the Western Ghats, the Nilgiri Hills, the Damodar valley and the Himalayas. Nuclear power is also being developed, especially to serve industrial zones away from coalfields such as Madras, Bombay and Ahmadabad, and plants have been built in Tamil Nadu, Maharashtra and Rajasthan. Electricity production is increasing yearly and it is now estimated that 14% of villages are electrified. As yet, there is no national grid which means that there are power surpluses in some regions and shortages in others.

Industry

The introduction of heavy machinery dates from between 1907 and 1911 when the Jamshedpur steel-works, based on locally produced coal, iron, limestone and manganese, were established. Two other iron and steel complexes have been built west of Jamshedpur at Rourkela and Bhilai and two more in the Damodar valley at Durgapur and Bokaro. The Damodar valley, rich in coal and hydro-electricity, is a major industrial region. As well as steel, there are cement, chemical, aluminium, fertilizer and engineering works. Another great manufacturing zone is based around Calcutta, home of India's jute industry. Cotton textiles dominate the two industrial conurbations of Bombay and Ahmadabad and are important in the fifth industrial zone formed by Madras, Bangalore, Coimbatore and Madurai which is better known for its light- and electrical-engineering. Apart from these five major zones, most towns have factories which process local products such as cotton, leather, sugar, rice, wheat and salt.

Cottage industry

Although not as profitable as factory production, cottage industries are encouraged by the government as they provide employment in rural areas. These are often organized on a co-operative basis. Of the 25 million people working in village industries, a quarter are handloom operators engaged in making khadi (a hand-spun and hand-woven cotton cloth). Other home industries include hand-woven silk, particularly in Karnataka and Assam, filigree work in Orissa and Andhra Pradesh, brass and copper ware, carved ivory and leather goods, and bicycle assembly.

Irrigation

In a country where rainfall is seasonal, unreliable and, in places, almost non-existent, irrigation is essential to agriculture. Traditional methods are wells, tanks and canals. Wells are most common in the northern plain; water is brought to the surface in a variety of ways, often by animals hauling up skin buckets or turning a wheel composed of scoops. Tanks, formed by low earth walls, predominate in the south. The government has included irrigation schemes in all of its five-year plans and most of the projects involve multi-purpose storage dams providing power as well.

Land transport:

Roads are a minor element in India's transport system: they total only 1,300,000 km and less than a third are surfaced. Road building is therefore a government priority and it is hoped that by 1981 no village will be more than 6 km from a surfaced road. There are 13 national highways, with a total length of 24,000 km, linking state capitals and major ports. In contrast to the inadequate roads, India's railways are important. The 60,130 km long network, which carries over 10,000 trains a day, is one of the world's longest. Although trains are slow, they are not expensive and 6 million people travel on them every day. Rail freight consists mainly of coal, ores and cereals.

Other transport:

Traffic on India's 14,400 km of navigable waterways is declining, except in West Bengal and Kerala. Marine shipping is, however, increasing. The country's leading ports are Calcutta, Bombay, Madras, Cochin, Marmagao, Kandla, Vishakhapatnam and Paradip. The two main ship-yards, equipped to build ocean-going vessels are at Vishakhapatnam and Cochin. Air transport is developing rapidly. There are two corporations: Indian Airlines, which flies to over 80 towns within India and to adjacent countries such as Sri Lanka, Burma and Nepal; and Air India, which operates overseas flights from international airports at Delhi (Palam), Bombay (Santa Cruz), Calcutta (Dum Dum) and Madras.

Cities

Four Indian cities have a population of over two million. The largest is Calcutta (7,040,400). Situated 140 km upstream from the River Hooghly estuary, Calcutta is a major port and handles 40% of the country's exports, notably jute and tea. The city has a wide range of manufactures; the most important is jute-processing. Overcrowding is a serious problem and there are innumerable slum and street dwellers. The second largest city is Bombay (5,969,500), the main port on the Arabian Sea and the country's financial centre. Cotton dominates the city's industry with raw cotton and cotton textiles as major export items. Delhi (3,630,800) is the third largest city and includes the nation's capital, New Delhi, which lies 5 km to the south. Old Delhi, on the Jumna river, is noted for its traditional metalwork, embroidery and ivory carvings. New Delhi's modern government buildings (built in 1912) contrast with the old city's monuments such as the 17th century Red Fort and Jami Masjid mosque. The fourth largest city is Madras (2,470,300), which is the cultural and commercial centre on the east coast of southern India.

Trade

Traditionally, India is a major exporter of jute products, cotton textiles and tea; these are still the main exports together with hides and iron ore. In spite of the increasing production of other commodities such as sugar and steel, the value of exports is well below that of imports. This is partly explained by a series of poor harvests which have made large imports of food necessary. Raw materials, such as chemicals and petroleum, for India's expanding industry are another major import item. India's main trading partners are the USSR, USA, UK and Japan.

Caste system

One feature of Hinduism which has greatly influenced the structure of Indian society is the caste system. This divides Hindus into several thousand classes, or castes. A Hindu is born into a certain caste and can never leave it. His caste invariably determines his social status, his occupation (some jobs are traditionally associated with specific castes) and his choice of wife (it is rare to marry outside one's caste). This rigid social order has often checked economic progress: high-caste individuals consider it their right to own land but not to work it; low-caste persons are condemned to menial jobs. Recent laws, however, have been introduced against caste discrimination and the barriers between castes are slowly being broken down, especially in cities.

Sri Lanka (Ceylon) and the Maldive Islands

Sri Lanka Maldives

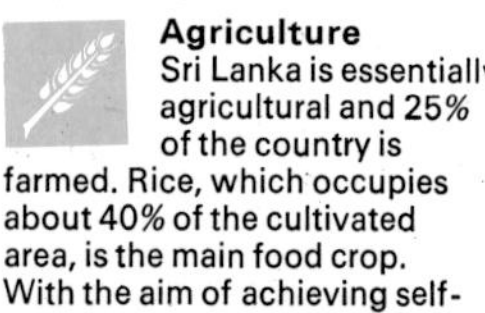

Agriculture

Sri Lanka is essentially agricultural and 25% of the country is farmed. Rice, which occupies about 40% of the cultivated area, is the main food crop. With the aim of achieving self-sufficiency in rice, more land is being made available through irrigation schemes such as those on the Gal Oya, Mahaweli and Walawe. The three leading cash crops—tea, rubber and coconut—make up 90% of exports; tea alone accounts for 55%. They are mostly grown in the wet zone: tea plantations are located mostly in the hills up to heights of 1,800 m; rubber covers the lower slopes and coconuts grow on the plains. In world production, Sri Lanka holds second place for tea and fourth for rubber. Coconut products include timber, palms, arak, coir, copra and oil. Other cash crops are cocoa and citronella. The main crop grown in the Maldives, both for domestic consumption and export, is coconut.

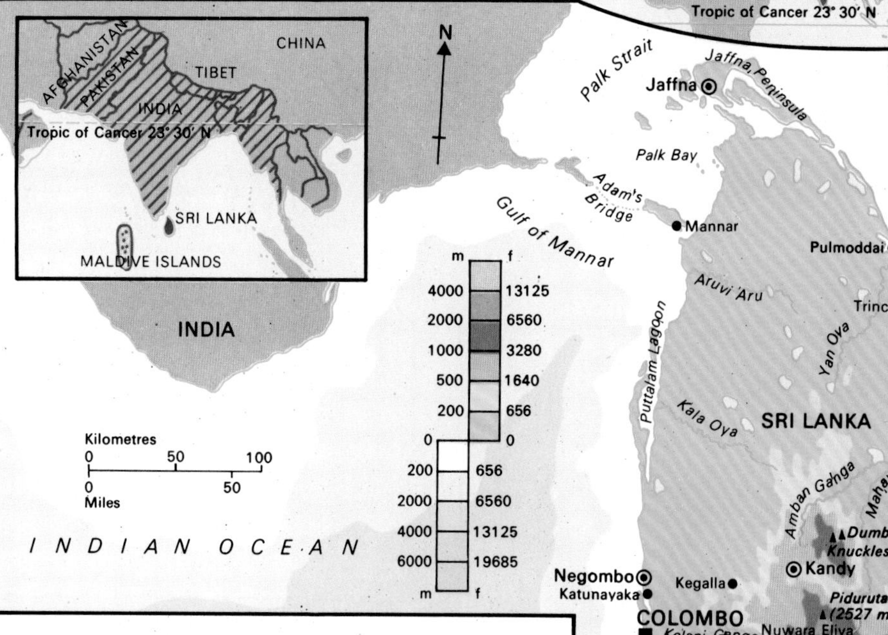

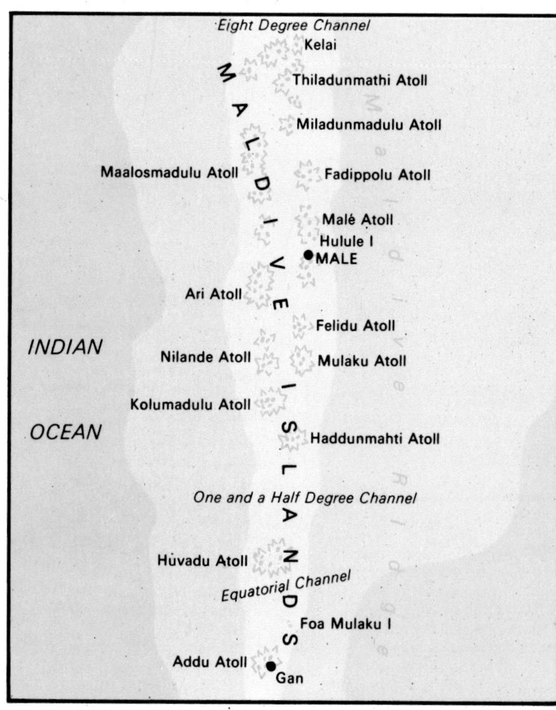

Physical features

Sri Lanka is linked to India by a line of sandy islands known as Adam's Bridge. The island is 432 km long and 224 km at its widest point. There is a mountainous zone in the south with peaks rising to over 2,000 m: the highest point being Pidurutalagala (2,527 m). These mountains are flanked by hilly uplands which give way to an alluvial coastal plain, broadest in the north and narrowest in the west and south. In the far north is the limestone Jaffna peninsular. The coast is fringed with sand dunes and lagoons. Sri Lanka's rivers radiate from the hilly interior: the longest is the Mahaweli Ganga (332 km). The Maldives, located 640 km south-west of Sri Lanka, consist of some 2,000 coral islands covered with grass, scrub and coconut palms—only 215 are inhabited.

Climate

Both countries are affected by the south-west and north-east monsoons. These bring an average rainfall of 150 cm to the Maldives. In Sri Lanka, the south-west (the wet zone) has up to 500 cm of rain a year but the rest of the island has less than 120 cm a year. Sri Lanka's high temperatures are modified by sea breezes and altitude. At Colombo the January temperature is 25°C, at Nuwara Eliya (1,890 m) 14°C; in May it is 28°C and 16°C respectively. The Maldives are hot and humid (av. temp: 27°C).

Transport

Sri Lanka's roads (about 19,000 km total length) cover the island adequately and are supplemented by 1,450 km of railways. Colombo is the principal port and handles nearly all exports, except tea which is shipped mainly from Trincomalee—one of the world's finest natural harbours. Galle and Jaffna are also major ports. There are several airports including Ratmalana (domestic) and Katunayaka (international) near Colombo. Steamers link Sri Lanka with the Maldives. Under construction is an airport on Hulule, an island 2 km from Male.

Fishing

The Maldivian economy is dominated by fishing which employs over 50% of the population. Every day several thousand sailing boats made of coconut wood make for the fishing grounds—up to 30 km away. The catch, mainly bonito and tuna, is cooked, cured and dried then exported to Sri Lanka. While the men are fishing the women are collecting shells, entirely for export. Some of the rarest shells come from the Maldives. In Sri Lanka, both island and sea-water fishing are being developed. Pearl fishing, once important in the shallow waters of the Gulf of Mannar, is in decline because of poor yields.

Minerals & energy

Sri Lanka has a limited range of minerals. High-grade graphite is the most important and 80% of production is exported. Other commercially valuable minerals include ilmenite (extracted at Pulmoddai and mainly exported to Japan) and monazite, rutile and zircon (all found in beach sands). High-quality iron ore occurs in the centre and south of the island. There are also deposits of phosphates, china clay, quartz (used in glass) and, in the north, limestone. Sri Lanka is famous for its gemstones found in the Ratnapura region. These include ruby, sapphire, aquamarine garnet, moonstone, topaz and chrysoberyl. Salt production, by evaporation, is centred on the islands' lagoons. There is no coal or oil and power is supplied either by thermal stations using imported fuels or by hydroelectric plants, often linked to irrigation and flood-control schemes.

Industry

Partly because of Sri Lanka's limited mineral and power resources, industrialization is still in its early stages. The processing of tea, rubber and coconuts is important and industries using domestic raw materials include cement (limestone), bricks and ceramics (clay), paper (rice straw), tyres (rubber) and leather goods. Imported materials are the basis of industries such as oil and sugar production, textile manufacture and steel-rolling. Handicraft production is considerable: wood and ivory carving, basketry, handloom weaving, lace, jewellry and tortoise-shell ware. Maldivian industry deals with processing fish and coconuts; copra is an important export. Coconuts are also the basis of two cottage manufactures produced almost exclusively by women: coir (fibre) and cadjan (palm) weaving. Two other traditional island crafts are reedware and lacquer work. Tourism is being developed in both countries.

Towns

Sri Lanka's capital, Colombo, is on the west coast near the mouth of the Kelani river. The port has one of the world's largest artificial harbours and, with its central position in the Indian Ocean, is an important supply and refuelling base. Industries in Colombo are concerned with processing imports. The second largest town is Jaffna (107,800), a leading port in the north, followed by Kandy (93,600), a former capital and a tea and rubber centre. The Maldivian capital, Male, handles most of the islands' trade.

Sri Lanka
Area
65,610 km²/25,332 sq miles
Location
5°55′—9°50′ N
79°42′—81°52′ E
Population
12,711,143 (1971)
Population density
194 per km²/502 per sq mile
Capital and largest city
Colombo: 563,000 (1971)
Language
Sinhala, Tamil and English
Major imports
foodstuffs, fuels, machinery and textiles
Major exports
tea, rubber, coconut products, cocoa and cinnamon, gems
Currency
Sri Lanka rupee (1 Sri Lanka rupee = 100 cents)
Gross National Product
1,680 million US dollars
Status
independent republic

Maldive Islands
Area
298 km²/115 sq miles
Location
3°15′—8° N
73°—74°20′ E
Population
118,818 (1971)
Population density
399 per km²/1033 per sq mile
Capital and largest city
Male: 13,610 (1970)
Language
Divehi (a dialect of Sinhala), Arabic is widely read
Major imports
rice, textiles, chemicals
Major exports
fish (especially dried bonito), copra, shells, millet, coconut products such as coir (a coconut fibre)
Currency
Maldivian rupee (1 Maldivian rupee = 100 larees)
Status
independent republic

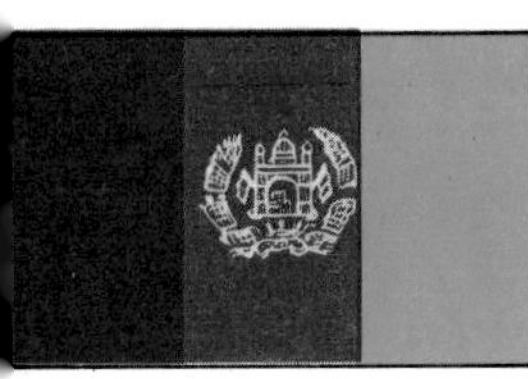

Afghanistan

Area
647,500 km²/250,000 sq miles
Location
29°30'—38°35' N
60°50'—75° E
Population
17,882,000 (1972)
Population density
28 per km²/72 per sq mile
Capital and largest city
Kabul: 500,000 (1971)
Languages
Pushtu (or Pashto), Dari
Major imports
foodstuffs, machinery, petroleum products, chemicals
Major exports
hides and skins, fruit (fresh, preserved and dried), nuts, cotton, carpets, natural gas
Currency
afghani (1 afghani = 100 puls)
Gross National Product
1,700 million US dollars
Status
independent republic

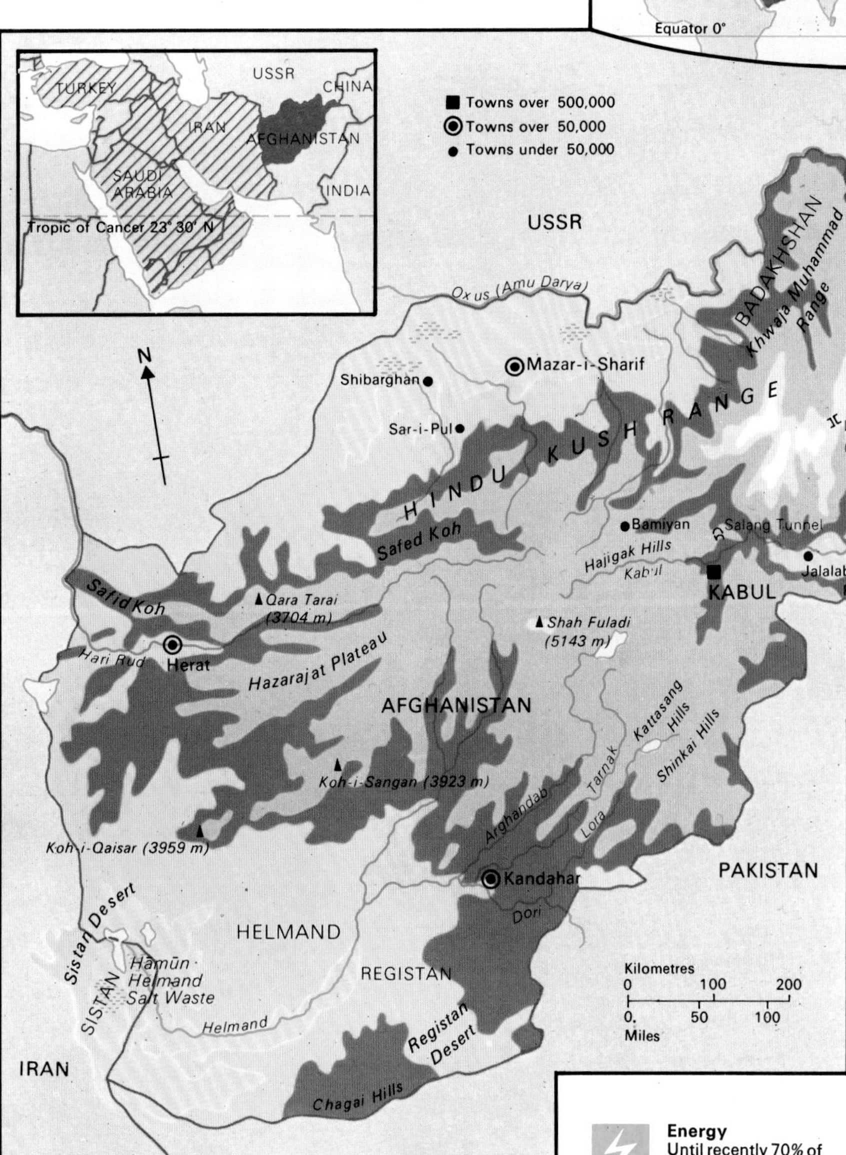

Physical features

The mountainous, land-locked country of Afghanistan has a minimum height of 1,200 m and is dominated by the Hindu Kush mountains. This great range which has an average altitude of 4,000 m is highest in the north-east: some of the peaks in the Wakhan district rise to over 6,500 m. Lowland areas include the region between the Hindu Kush and the river Oxus (Amu Darya), the south-western deserts of Sistan and Registan and the fertile valleys around Kabul, Bamiyan and Jalalabad. Four major rivers flow out of the Hindu Kush water-shed: the Oxus (which forms the northern border with the USSR) the Hari Rud (ending in a closed salt basin on the Iranian frontier), the Helmand (which drains the south-west—ending in the Hamun Helmand salt waste in Iran) and the Kabul in the east, eventually joining the Indus.

Climate

The climate of Afghanistan is characterized by extreme temperatures, dryness and strong winds. Summer is hot and arid: in Jalalabad, July temperatures rise to over 45°C; the highland areas are cooler—Kabul (at 1,800 m), 38°C. Between June and September the strong north-west 'wind of 120 days' blows across the Iranian plateau at speeds of up to 160 km per hour. Winter is cold. January temperatures on the central Hazarajat plateau fall to —26°C, at Jalalabad to —4°C. A little rain falls between November and May with up to 15 cm in the north and west and about 30 cm in the east. Perpetual snow lies on mountains over 4,000 m.

Forestry and fishing

Following widespread deforestation (mostly for fuel) forests now cover less than 3% of the country. Mainly located in the east and on the northern slopes of the Hindu Kush, they include both coniferous and deciduous trees. They provide timber for construction and furniture-making nuts such as pine kernels and pistachios, resins, tan and dye barks. Replanting has begun in some places. To combat protein deficiency in the national diet, fishing is being developed in the country's rivers and lakes.

Agriculture

Farming is the main economic activity in Afghanistan. About 20% of the land (corresponding to fertile valleys and plains) is cultivable although only half of this is currently in use. Inadequate rainfall makes irrigation vital. This ranges from wells to major schemes such as the Helmand valley project. In this way, 70% of the cultivated land is watered. Wheat is the staple food crop followed by barley, maize and rice. Sugar-beet and cane, and oilseeds are also important, but production is low and imports are necessary. The two major cash crops are cotton (grown near Mazar-i-Sharif, Herat and in the Helmand valley) and fruit. Grapes account for 50% of fruit production and raisins are exported to Europe, USSR and China. Afghanistan is essentially a pastoral country. Its 10 million sheep provide meat, grease (used as a butter substitute) and wool. Around 70% of the wool is exported, the rest is woven into carpets. In the northern provinces there are also 4 million Karakul sheep; their valuable skins, made into fur coats, are a leading export.

Mining

Afghanistan's mineral resources are, for the most part, unexploited. At present, the most important asset is natural gas found in the north near Shibarghan and Sar-i-Pul. Over half the output is piped direct to the USSR, accounting for 15% of exports. Coal has been located in the northern slopes of the Hindu Kush but, so far, extraction is confined to mines at Dara-i-Suf, Karkar and Ishpushta. Mines are, however, being prepared for production near Herat. Afghanistan is the world's leading producer of lapis lazuli; this semi-precious stone has been mined in Badakhshan province for thousands of years. Gypsum, limestone, salt, talc and chromite are also currently worked. Deposits not yet exploited include copper, lead, zinc, beryl, mica, manganese, baryte, gold, silver, asbestos and sulphur; petroleum exists in the north. There are also important high-grade iron-ore reserves in the Hajigak hills, 100 km north-west of Kabul. The use of natural gas as an energy source for the reduction of this ore is being studied.

Energy

Until recently 70% of Afghanistan's energy needs were supplied by imported petroleum. This was supplemented by domestically produced coal and wood. With the development of natural gas and hydro-electric power, however, the pattern is changing. Although much natural gas is exported, some is retained for domestic consumption and the first gas-fired thermal station is in operation at Mazar-i-Sharif. With its major rivers rushing down through the mountains, the country has great hydro-electric potential yet to be harnessed.

Cities

The capital, Kabul, which is situated by the Kabul river at an altitude of 1,800 m, is over 3,000 years old. A former trading centre between East and West, the city is still the country's major market place. Industrial developments include food-processing plants and textile mills. Kandahar (134,000), the second largest town, was built 200 years ago by Ahmad Shah Durrani—the founder of the state of Afghanistan. It is a commercial and industrial centre in the agricultural south-west. Other towns include Herat (104,000) in the west and Mazar-i-Sharif (47,000) in Karakul sheep country near the gas reserves.

Transport

In the last 10 years Afghanistan, with Soviet and American aid, has built a network of trunk roads linking Kabul to all leading towns. An outstanding feature of this network is the high-altitude Salang tunnel in the Hindu Kush. There are no railways but a regular internal air-service is operated by Bakhtar Afghan Airlines to 14 provincial centres. The international Ariana Afghan Airlines flies from Kabul airport. A few waterways are navigable. There is some barge traffic on the Oxus (Amu Darya) and, in the east, rivers are used for floating logs. As the country is landlocked, Afghanistan has transit rights with its neighbours: Iran, the USSR and Pakistan. The bulk of foreign trade is taken by truck over the Khyber Pass to Peshawar, then by train to Karachi.

Industry

Industry employs less than 1% of the working population and is primarily concerned with processing domestic raw materials. Afghanistan's first established industry was cotton textile manufacture and today there are six major spinning and weaving plants. Cloth production, however, still accounts for only 75% of national requirements. There are also factories manufacturing woolen and rayon textiles. Other industries based on agricultural produce include sugar-refining, leather-tanning, fruit-preservation, raisin-cleaning and oilseed crushing. Other industries include cement (from limestone) and nitrogen fertilizers (from natural gas). A copper-smelting plant is planned. Industry still contributes less to the national income than traditional handicrafts which include metalware, leather work, jewellry, tiles and especially carpets and rugs. These carpets and rugs, hand-woven in rural areas, are a major export item and are particularly popular in West Germany and the UK.

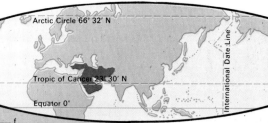

Iran

Area
1,648,000 km²/636,290 sq miles
Location
25°—39°45′ N
44°—63°30′ E
Population
31,000,000 (1973)
Population density
19 per km²/49 per sq mile
Capital and largest city
Tehran: 3,700,000 (1973)
Language
Farsi
Major imports
machinery and transport equipment, iron and steel, foodstuffs, chemicals, textiles
Major exports
petroleum and petroleum products carpets, fruit (fresh and dried) hides, leather, mineral ores
Currency
Rial (1 Rial = 100 dinars)
Gross National Product
11,000 million US dollars
Status
constitutional monarchy

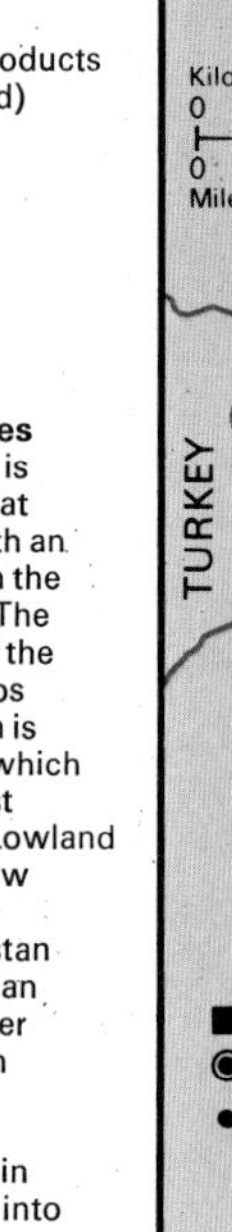

Forestry and fishing
Forests cover 11% of Iran and are concentrated on the northern slopes of the Elburz, along the Caspian coast and in the Zagros. Before 1963, destructive exploitation badly depleted timber resources, then forests were nationalized and a programme of afforestation initiated. The annual yield of timber is mainly used for construction purposes. Fishing is increasing in importance in both the Caspian and the Persian Gulf. The Caspian fisheries are famous for caviar: of the 200 tonnes produced annually, 195 are exported of which the USSR takes half. With the introduction of sturgeon breeding stations, caviar production is expected to double by 1983. The Persian Gulf catch, containing over 100 varieties of fish, is consumed locally.

Physical features
The centre of Iran is occupied by a great desert plateau with an average height of 1,500 m in the west and 900 m in the east. The southern and western rim of the plateau consists of the Zagros mountains. The northern rim is formed by the Elburz range which rises to 5,780 m at its highest point—Mount Damavand. Lowland areas are limited to the narrow coastal strip bordering the Caspian Sea and the Khuzestan plain at the head of the Persian Gulf. The most important river is the Karun which is 800 km long. On the plateau, most rivers flow inland from the mountain rim and terminate in closed basins which dry out into salt marshes in summer. Westwards, near the Turkish border, many rivers drain into Lake Urmia, a salt lake.

Climate
The central plateau has a climate of extremes. Summer is characterized by high temperatures (rising to 50°C), dryness and the scorching 'wind of 120 days'. Winter is cold with temperatures below —20°C and snow on high ground. Most of the plateau receives less than 25 cm of rain a year, coming mainly in winter. Tehran has temperatures of 37°C in July and —3°C in January. The Caspian lowlands are warm and humid with 125 cm of rain a year, mostly in summer. The Khuzestan plain is also humid with milder winters: in Abadan, temperatures are 45°C in August and 7°C in January.

Transport
The basis of Iran's transport system is a 40,000 km network of roads. Railways are less extensive. There is a 1,400 km long main line which goes from Bandar-e Shahpur via Tehran to Bandar-e Shah. Principal branches from this serve Tabriz, Mashhad and the steelworks at Esfahan. Iran National Airlines fly to 15 Iranian cities, to neighbouring countries and to Europe. Tehran and Abadan have international airports. The main port is Khorramshahr, handling 50% of Iran's non-oil cargo, followed by Bandar-e Shahpur, Bandar Abbas, Bushehr, Lengeh and Chah Bahar. Bandar-e Pahlavi and Bandar-e Shah trade with the USSR.

Oil
Iran has an oil-based economy. Petroleum and petroleum products account for 89% of exports. It is the world's fourth largest oil-producer and 90% of the production comes from fields lying between the Iraqi border and Shiraz. Crude oil is exported via Kharg Island, the world's largest oil terminal. The world's biggest oil refinery at Abadan has an output of 500,000 barrels a day. There is another refinery at Shiraz and two more are under construction at Tabriz and Neka. The oil industry which, in spite of its importance, employs under 1% of the population is nationalized.

Mining
The steel plant at Esfahan uses iron ore from Bafq near Yazd and coal from Kerman. Coal is also mined in the Elburz mountains. Lead and zinc are mined at Bafq and near Qom. Chrome and turquoise are produced for export and other important deposits include sulphur, salt, limestone, ochre and kaolin. In the last 10 years, substantial copper deposits have been located, especially near Kerman and Iran could soon be a leading producer of copper. Iran also has the world's second largest reserves of natural gas, found in the south and in the Elburz mountains. Some of the gas is piped direct to the USSR. Iran's mineral wealth is rapidly being developed.

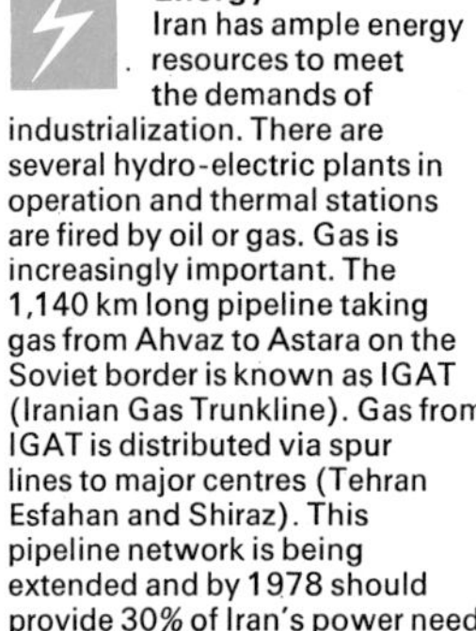

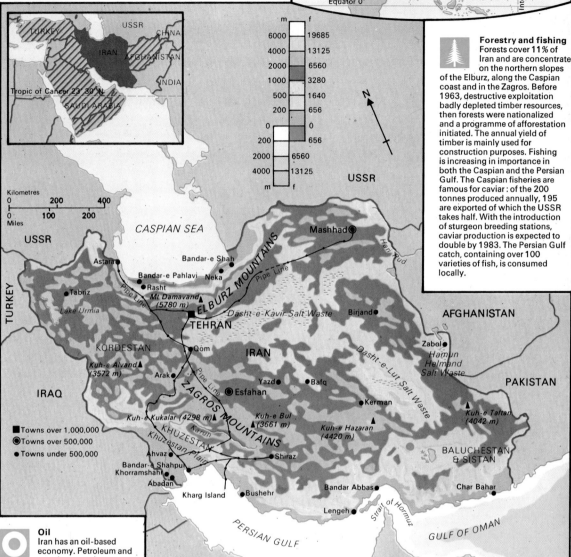

Energy
Iran has ample energy resources to meet the demands of industrialization. There are several hydro-electric plants in operation and thermal stations are fired by oil or gas. Gas is increasingly important. The 1,140 km long pipeline taking gas from Ahvaz to Astara on the Soviet border is known as IGAT (Iranian Gas Trunkline). Gas from IGAT is distributed via spur lines to major centres (Tehran Esfahan and Shiraz). This pipeline network is being extended and by 1978 should provide 30% of Iran's power needs.

Cities
Tehran is situated on the southern slopes of the Elburz at an altitude of 1,200 m. The bazaars and narrow streets of the old city contrast with the modern sector lying to the north. Over 50% of Iran's manufactured goods, ranging from cigarettes and shoes to textiles and china, are produced in Tehran. Esfahan (700,000) is the second largest city and the country's textile centre. This town now has Iran's first steel mill. Mashhad (600,000) is a commercial centre for the north-east.

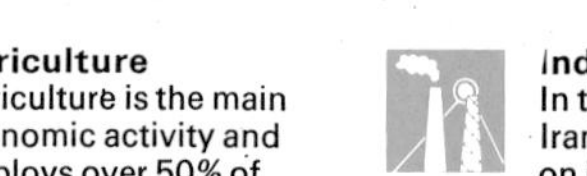

Agriculture
Agriculture is the main economic activity and employs over 50% of Iranians. About 25% of the country is cultivable but less than half of this is under cultivation. The main cereal crops are wheat and barley, grown on the Gulf coastlands and the southern Elburz slopes. Rice is cultivated in the Caspian lowlands. Two of the main cash crops, cotton and sugarbeet, are extensively grown; a third, tobacco, is limited to the Caspian area. Other crops produced commercially include tea, olives, nuts, fruit (grapes, citrus, melons, apricots) and, in the extreme south, dates. About 25% of the cultivated area is irrigated, mainly from traditional underground water ducts; modern water storage projects are being developed. Along the Turkish and Iraqi borders, agriculture is rain-fed. Output is being increased by mechanization, fertilizers and the establishment of farming co-operatives in most villages. Livestock is important: the wool provided by some 30 million sheep, principally grazed in the Zagros mountains, is the basis of the carpet industry. Many of the herds belong to nomadic tribesmen who bring them to the coastlands in winter.

Industry
In the last 10 years Iran has concentrated on industrialization in an effort to reduce its dependence on oil and agriculture. Traditional industries have been expanded; for example, the processing of local raw materials such as cotton at Esfahan, silk in the Caspian area, sugar refining, rice milling, fruit canning, flour milling, tanning, cement and construction materials and cigarette manufacture. New industries have been introduced. In exchange for Iranian natural gas, the Russians helped build a steelmill at Esfahan, a machine plant at Arak and a machine tool factory at Tabriz. Foreign capital has also contributed to an aluminium smelter at Arak and a petrochemical complex at Bandar-e Shahpur. Many European vehicle manufacturers have production plants in Iran. The main industrial centres are Tehran, Esfahan, Tabriz, Arak, Mashhad, Shiraz and Rasht. Handicrafts are widespread and include pottery, metalware, jewellery, leatherwork and, most important, carpet-weaving. Hand-woven carpets are Iran's chief non-oil export which is expected to earn 500 million US dollars by 1978.

Iraq and Kuwait

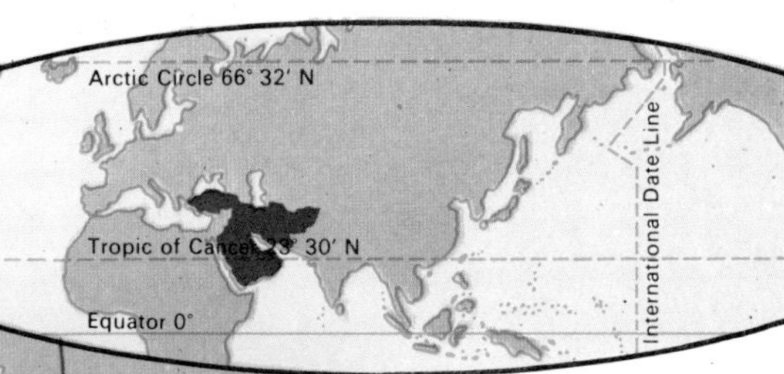

Iraq
Area
438,446 km²/169,284 sq miles
Location
29°—37°20′ N
38°45′—48°30′ E
Population
11,124,253 (1975 estimate)
Population density
25 per km²/66 per sq mile
Capital and largest city
Baghdad: 2,200,000 (1970)
Language
Arabic
Major imports
machinery and transport equipment, iron and steel, sugar, textiles
Major exports
crude oil, dates, wool, skins and hides, cement
Currency
dinar (1 dinar = 1,000 fils)
Gross National Product
3,200 million US dollars
Status
independent republic

Kuwait
Area
17,818 km²/6,880 sq miles
Location
28°30′—30° N
46°30′—48°40′ E
Population
990,380 (1975)
Population density
56 per km²/144 per sq mile
Capital
Kuwait: 80,400 (1970)
Largest city
Hawalli: 106,500 (1970)
Language
Arabic
Major imports
machinery, transport equipment, manufactured goods, foodstuffs
Major exports
petroleum and petroleum products, fertilizers, fish
Currency
dinar (1 dinar = 1,000 fils)
Gross National Product
3,000 million US dollars
Status
constitutional emirate

TURKEY
SYRIA
IRAN
IRAQ
SAUDI ARABIA
KUWAIT
NEUTRAL TERRITORY
PERSIAN GULF
USSR
CHINA
AFGHANISTAN
INDIA
Tropic of Cancer 23° 30′ N
Zakho
Tel Kotchek
Oil Field
Ayn Zalah
Mosul
Arbil
Lesser Zab
Greater Zab
Oil Field
Kirkuk
KURDISTAN
Jabal Hamrin Mountains
Kuhe Haji Ebrahim (3600 m)
Pipe Line
Ad Dawr
Kifri
Nahr al Uzaym
Diyala
Samarra
Khanaqin
Zagros Foot Hills
Mandali
Al Falluja
BAGHDAD
Badiet esh Sham Plateau
Tigris
An Najaf
Euphrates
Sahra Hijarah Desert
Al Haniyah Ridge
Ad Dibdibah Plain
Shatt al Arab
Basra
Shuaiba
Rumaila
Az Zubayr
Oil Field
Al Faw
Umm Qasr
Oil Terminal
Bubiyan I.
Kuwait Bay
Shuwaykh
Hawalli
Faylakah I.
Mina al Ahmadi
Al Ahmadi
Shu'aybah

m	f
4000	13125
2000	6560
1000	3280
500	1640
200	656
0	0
200	656

Kilometres 0 50 100
Miles 0 100

■ Towns over 1,000,000
◉ Towns over 100,000
● Towns under 100,000

Physical features
Iraq is dominated by the Tigris and Euphrates. These two rivers flow south-eastwards across the country then into the Gulf via a combined estuary, the Shatt al Arab. South of Baghdad the Tigris-Euphrates plain is low, alluvial and prone to flooding. North of Al Fallujah and Samarra the land is high and barren. A low limestone plateau, forming part of the Syrian desert, lies to the west and south of the Euphrates. East of the Tigris the land rises to the Zagros foothills. North of Khanaqin the mountains of Kurdistan penetrate Iraq with peaks over 3,000 m. Four main tributaries of the Tigris flow down from these ranges: Greater and Lesser Zab, Nahr al Uzaym and Diyala. The Euphrates has no tributary within Iraq. Kuwait consists of undulating desert with occasional low ridges rising to 150 m, particularly in the south. As rainfall is extremely low, there are no rivers in Kuwait. The principal coastal features of Kuwait are the large bay on which the capital is built and the sandy offshore islands which include Bubiyan and Faylakah—these are being developed as beach resorts.

Cities
The capital of Iraq, Baghdad, is situated on the Tigris 560 km from the Persian Gulf. Flooding was once common but the city is now protected by the Samarra barrage. The greater part of Iraqi industry, ranging from steel and bricks to leather and cigarettes, is located in the capital. Iraq's second city, Basra (371,000), is 112 km inland on the west bank of the Shatt al Arab and is the country's leading port. The Kuwaiti capital, situated on the south side of Kuwait Bay, developed as a trading centre and today is a major Gulf port. One of its suburbs, Hawalli, has become the state's largest city.

Climate
Both countries have hot, arid summers. In July and August day temperatures, normally 50°C, rise to 70°C. Sandstorms are common in June and July. Winter is cold and damp. In January the average temperature in the capital of Kuwait is 20°C, in Mosul in the north of Iraq it is 8°C. Rain occurs between November and April and is heaviest in north-east Iraq. Kuwait has about 10 cm a year, Basra 15 cm, Mosul 40 cm and in the north-east mountains up to 100 cm—falling mainly as snow. In April and May, melting snow causes the Tigris and Euphrates to flood.

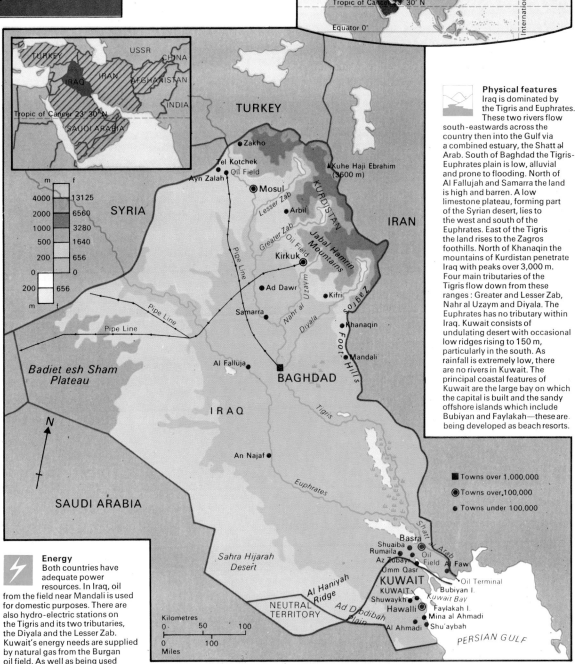

Energy
Both countries have adequate power resources. In Iraq, oil from the field near Mandali is used for domestic purposes. There are also hydro-electric stations on the Tigris and its two tributaries, the Diyala and the Lesser Zab. Kuwait's energy needs are supplied by natural gas from the Burgan oil field. As well as being used for domestic consumption, the gas also powers the state's electricity generating stations.

Transport
In Iraq, a main road runs from the Jordanian frontier through Baghdad to Basra. Other major routes link Baghdad to Zakho, Khanaqin and An Najaf. The main railway goes from Basra via Baghdad and Kirkuk to Arbil. A line from Baghdad to Tel Kotchek connects with the Syrian network and provides a through service from the Gulf to Europe. Inland waterways are important locally. Basra is the leading port but Umm Qasr is being developed. The state airline, Iraqi Airways, operates international services from Baghdad and Basra. Kuwait has no railway, but an efficient 1,600 km road system links the capital to Al Ahmadi, other oil-producing zones, and the Iraqi and Saudi borders. Kuwait is the chief port followed by Shuwaykh and Shu'aybah. Some 20 airlines, including Kuwait Airlines, serve the one international airport.

Agriculture
Just ove 25% of Iraq is cultivable and half that area is now under cultivation. In the north-east, where agriculture is rain-fed, wheat, barley, tobacco and fruit are the main crops. On the plains, the growing of wheat, barley, maize, millet, sesame and cotton relies on irrigation. About half of the land under cultivation is irrigated. In the Hawr al Hammar lake area, rice and dates are grown. Iraq produces over 300,000 tonnes of dates a year and, together with Egypt, ranks as the world's leading date exporter. Livestock, in particular sheep, are reared and wool is exported. Forests in the north-east yield timber for construction as well as licorice, dye-barks and gum tragacanth. In Kuwait, less than 0.1% of the total area is cultivated. Of this, two-thirds is used for vegetables such as tomatoes, radishes, melons and cucumbers. Fishing is a traditional Kuwaiti activity; prawns and shrimps are exported.

Mining
The major mineral resource in both countries is oil. Crude oil accounts for over 90% of Iraq's exports. The three main production areas are at Kirkuk, at Ayn Zalah (north-west of Mosul) and at Rumaila and Az Zubayr, south of Basra. Oil from the northern fields is taken by pipelines to Mediterranean ports in Lebanon and Syria. Output from the south is exported via Al Faw. The main refinery is at Ad Dawr. Kuwait is the world's seventh largest oil producer. The Burgan oilfields are the most important. These are situated on the Ahmadi ridge and gravity takes the oil down to the two coastal terminals and offshore-tanker terminal. The world's first all-hydrogen refinery at Shuaiba supplies petroleum products for domestic consumption and export. No other mineral resources have been located in Kuwait but, in Iraq, deposits of iron, chrome, copper, lead and zinc have been found.

Industry
In Iraq, all leading industries are nationalized. These include cement, asbestos, bricks, steel, textiles, flour, sugar, leather-tanning, cigarettes and paper. A smaller but equally important activity is date-packing. The current five-year plan aims at developing the petrochemical electrical and food-processing industries. Baghdad, Basra and Mosul are the principal manufacturing centres. With a view to diversifying its economy, Kuwait has embarked on a major industrialization programme. The three main development areas, in addition to petrochemicals, are chemical fertilizers (accounting for 62% of Kuwait's non-oil exports), building materials (such as cement and bricks) and flour production (including biscuits and pasta). Two industries connected with traditional activities are boat-building and fish-freezing. At Shuwaykh, Kuwait has the world's largest desalination plant.

Turkey

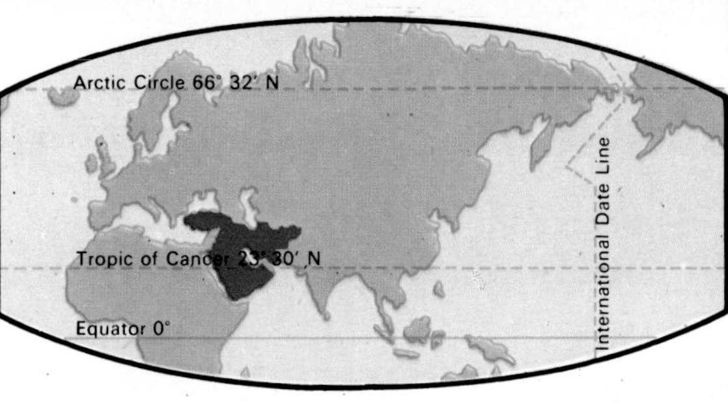

Climate

The west and south coasts of Turkey have a Mediterranean climate with hot summers and mild, rainy winters. The average temperature in July is 28°C, in January it is 11°C and annual rainfall, occurring between September and May, is about 75 cm. The Black Sea coast and Istanbul have slightly lower temperatures: 23°C in July, 7°C in January and rain in all seasons. The central plateau has hot summers with temperatures up to 33°C and severe winters with temperatures dropping to —12°C (snow is common). South-eastern Turkey has a semi-arid desert climate: hot summers, cool, damp winters.

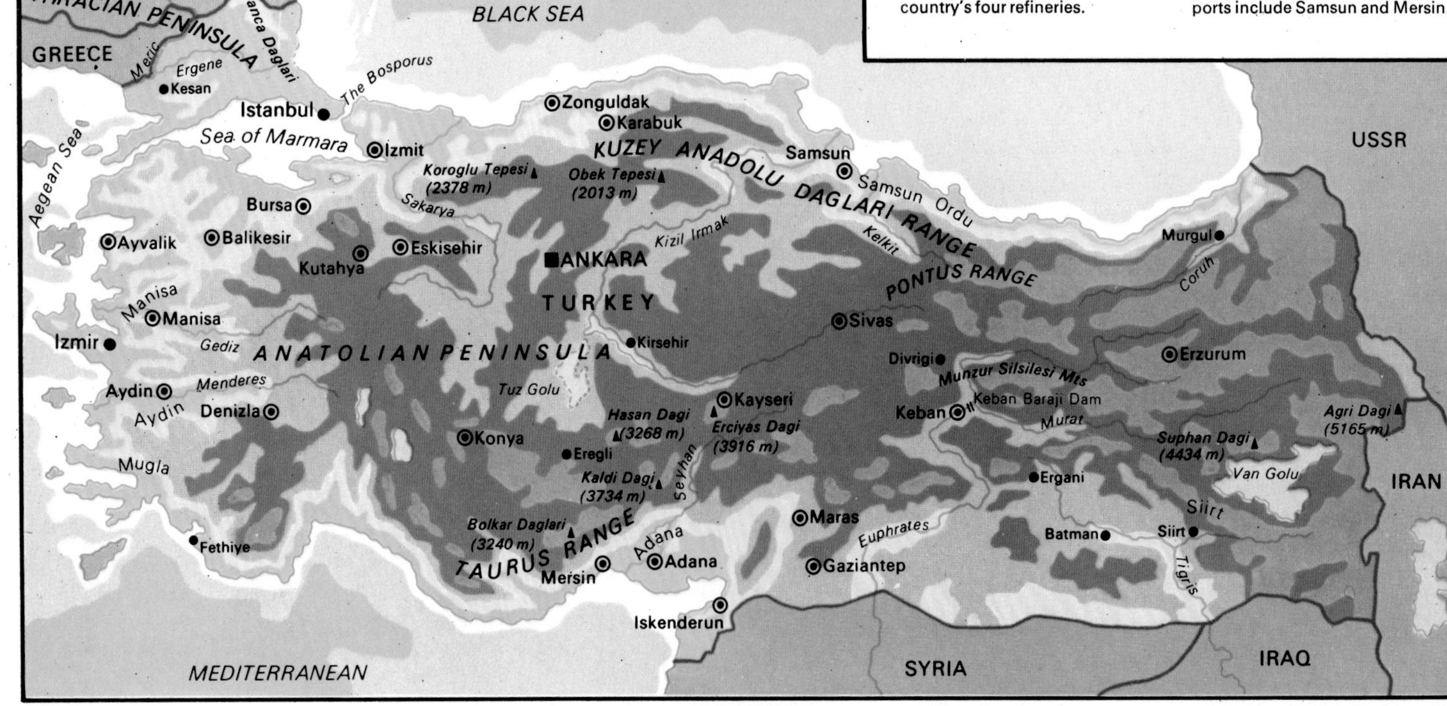

Mining

There are important chrome deposits near Maras and Fethiye and Turkey is one of the world's four leading chrome producers. Other mineral exports include copper (from Murgul and Ergani) and, in smaller quantities, zinc, manganese, mercury, borax and antimony. At Konya there is an aluminium plant using local bauxite. The output of iron ore, mined at Divrigi, does not meet the increasing domestic demand. Lignite and coal are mined in small quantities and the main coalfields are at Eregli and Zonguldak. Oil, coming mostly from the Siirt region, provides 30% of the throughput of the country's four refineries.

Transport

The government is taking steps to improve Turkey's road and rail system. There are 35,000 km of state highways (50% of which is hard-surfaced) and a further 186,500 km of minor roads. In 1973 the world's fourth longest bridge, linking Europe and Asia, was opened at Istanbul. Work has begun on a highway running from Greece, via Istanbul and Ankara, to Syria. New stock is being built for the 8,200 km rail network. Of the country's 18 airports, two (Ankara and Istanbul) are international. The two main ports are Istanbul, which handles over 50% of Turkish imports, and Izmir. Other leading ports include Samsun and Mersin.

Area
779,452 km²/300,950 sq miles
Location
35°50′—42°5′ N
25°40′—44°50′ E
Population
40,000,000 (1974)
Population density
49 per km²/127 per sq mile
Capital
Ankara: 1,461,346 (1973)
Largest city
Istanbul: 2,376,296 (1973)
Language
Turkish
Major imports
machinery, iron and steel, oil, transport equipment
Major exports
cotton, fruit and nuts, tobacco, cereals, minerals, livestock
Currency
lira (1 lira = 100 kurus)
Gross National Product
20,840 million US dollars (1973)
Status
independent republic

Tourism

Tourism is a major growth industry. In the last five years the number of visitors to Turkey has trebled and the income from tourism has increased six-fold.

Physical features

Turkey links Europe and Asia. European Turkey, the Thracian peninsular, has an area of only 23,764 km². Thrace is a land of wide, undulating plains, with highlands in the north-east and south-west. Asian Turkey, the Anatolian peninsular, is much bigger. Central Anatolia consists of a vast plateau with an average height of 1,200 m, broken by ridges and volcanic outcrops. In the extreme east is Turkey's highest peak, Agri Dagi (Mt Ararat), 5,165 m. This central plateau is bordered to the north by the Kuzey Anadolu Daglar Range which extends eastwards into the Pontus range. In the south, the plateau is bordered by the Taurus range which extends north-eastwards to the Munzur Silsilesi mountains and the higher mountains in the east. The main rivers draining off the plateau are the Tigris, Euphrates, Seyhan, Menderes, Gediz and Kizil Irmak. There are about 65 lakes: the largest is Van Golu, 3,738 km² in area and 1,800 m deep, followed by Tuz Golu which has an area of 1,642 km² and is over 800 m deep.

Agriculture

Agriculture employs 60% of the population and accounts for 65% of exports. About 60% of the land is under cultivation. On the Anatolian plateau the cultivated area is used for cereals: wheat and barley are the main crops. Cash crops are concentrated on the fertile coastal plains. These include sugarbeet, cotton (grown in the Adana, Manisa and Mugla regions) and tobacco (from the Ordu, Samsun, Manisa and Aydin districts). Citrus fruits, grapes, figs and hazelnuts are extensively grown and dried fruit is exported through Izmir. Olives, used mainly to produce oil, are cultivated in the west. Silk production is centred at Bursa. Animals, principally sheep and goats, are important and livestock is exported. Forests cover 25% of the country. Half of this is of low commercial value but Turkey is self-sufficient in timber, firewood, resin and turpentine. Fishing is being developed, but at present only 20% of the potential catch is landed. Recent measures to assist agriculture include irrigation and machinery.

Industry

Although Turkish industry is expanding, it is still primarily concerned with supplying the domestic market and few manufactures are exported. The textile industry, centred at Istanbul, Aydin, Denizli, Adana, Gaziantep and Kayseri, is the most important: output is 80% cotton, 20% woollen. Iron and steel production was formerly confined to the Black Sea coalfield with works at Eregli and Karabuk but, with Soviet aid, a third steel mill has been built at Iskenderun. Another major industrial activity is petroleum refining: crude oil is imported from Iran and Iraq and refined at Izmit, Mersin, Batman and Izmir. Other industries include paper manufacture, flour-milling, sugar-refining, cement production, vehicle assembly and fertilizers; a petro-chemical plant was opened at Izmir in 1971. Traditional crafts are important and some products, such as woven carpets from Siirt, Kirsehir and Sivas, are exported. Turkish ceramics are also known internationally; the two main centres are Istanbul and Kutahya.

Energy

Although the output of power has quadrupled in the last ten years, 60% of the population is still without electricity and wood and dried dung are widely used for domestic purposes. Thermal stations generate 80% of the energy supply and these use oil and lignite. The remainder is from hydro-electric stations: there is a major dam at Keban and another hydro-electric station is under construction at Ayvalik.

Cities

Ankara, which lies 200 km south of the Black Sea on the edge of the Anatolian plateau, has been the capital since 1923. About 350 km to the west is Istanbul, the country's largest city. This was the former capital of the Byzantine Empire, then of the Ottoman Empire and, finally, of Turkey. It is built on a peninsular surrounded on three sides by water: the Sea of Marmara, the Bosphorus and the Golden Horn. Istanbul's historic monuments, which include many mosques, have made it an important tourist centre.

Saudi Arabia

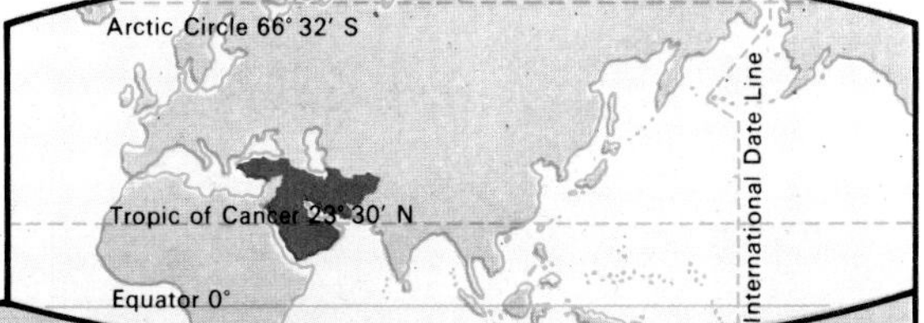

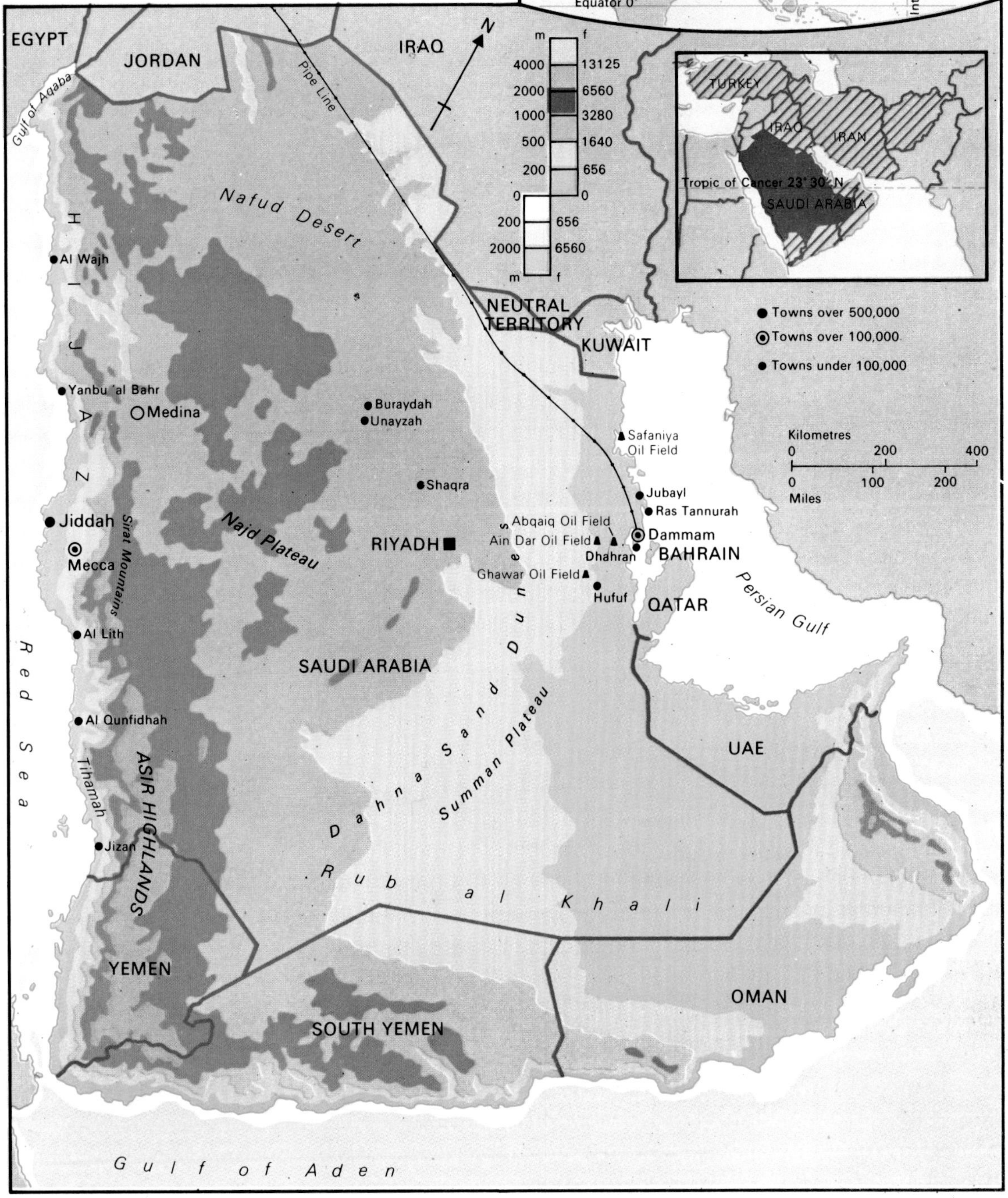

Area
2,300,000 km²/888,000 sq miles
Location
16°—32°10′ N
34°30′—56° E
Population
8,200,000 (1973 estimate)
Population density
3.6 per km²/9 per sq mile
Capital and largest city
Riyadh: 600,000 (1975 estimate)
Language
Arabic
Major imports
foodstuffs, machinery, transport equipment, building materials, textiles
Major exports
petroleum and petroleum products
Currency
rial (1 rial = 20 qurush)
Gross National Product
5,000 million US dollars (1972)
Status
absolute monarchy

Physical features

Saudi Arabia is situated between the Red Sea and the Persian Gulf and occupies 80% of the Arabian peninsular. It consists of a block of old, hard rock, highest along the Red Sea and tilted downwards towards the north-east. A narrow coastal plain, the Tihamah, borders the Red Sea. This is paralleled by steep ranges varying in height from 1,500 m in Hijaz to 2,500 m in the Asir highlands. East of these mountains lies the arid Najd plateau. A sandy strip 1,300 km long links the Nafud desert in the northwest to the uninhabited 'empty quarter', the Rub 'al Khali desert in the south. The barren Summan plateau separates the Dahna sand dunes from the low plains adjoining the Persian Gulf. Surface water is rare and there are no permanent rivers—seasonal streams evaporate into wadis (dry valleys). There is, however, abundant underground water which provides numerous oases and wells.

Climate

Saudi Arabia has one of the hottest summer climates in the world. Inland, July and August temperatures often rise to 50°C. The coasts are slightly cooler—Jiddah 32°C, Dammam 35°C—but the humidity, which can be as high as 90%, is intolerable. Winter temperatures are 23°C in Jiddah, 17°C in Dammam and 14°C in Riyadh. It is coldest in the Asir highlands where frost and snow occasionally occur. Rainfall is slight: Dammam and Riyadh have about 10 cm a year, Jiddah 6 cm while the Rub 'al Khali frequently has none. In contrast, the Asir mountains receive over 35 cm.

Transport

Roads are a government priority in Saudi Arabia. These now total over 16,000 km and a further 1,000 km are being built annually. A major achievement is the coast-to-coast route which runs from Jiddah via Riyadh to Dammam. There is only one railway, the 575 km line between Dammam and Riyadh. The state-owned Saudi Arabian Airlines operates scheduled internal and overseas services as well as special flights for pilgrims. There are international airports at Jiddah, Dhahran and Riyadh. The main ports are Jiddah and Dammam.

Cities

Although Riyadh is the administrative capital, Jiddah (500,000), with the Saudi Ministry of Foreign Affairs and embassies, is the diplomatic centre. Jiddah, which originated as a meeting place for pilgrims on their way to Mecca, is now Saudi Arabia's leading industrial city and chief Red Sea port. The country's third largest town is Mecca (300,000), the birthplace of Mohammed. Built around an oasis on a caravan route in the Sirat mountains, Islam's holy city is visited by a million pilgrims each year. Non-Muslims are not allowed inside the city; they are also barred from Medina (100,000), 523 km north of Mecca. Medina, where Mohammed governed and died, is Islam's second most sacred city and also a place of pilgrimage.

Agriculture

About 25% of the population is employed in arable farming. The cultivated areas, representing 0.2% of the total land surface, are concentrated in the Asir (where agriculture is rain-fed) and in the east (which is irrigated). The main cereals are wheat, millet and maize; other crops include fruit, melons, coffee and dates. Although output has increased, particularly of fruit and vegetables, food is still imported. A further 50% of the population is engaged in herding. Camels, sheep and goats are raised for their milk, meat, wool, hair and skins. Half of these pastoralists are nomadic Bedou who roam the deserts with their camels. Desalination plants, irrigation and desert reclamation schemes are being developed to improve agriculture.

Industry

Industrialization is still in its early stages and production is aimed at the domestic market. Major projects currently in operation are petrol refineries at Ras Tannurah and Jiddah, cement plants at Jiddah, Riyadh and Hufuf, a steel-rolling mill at Jiddah, a fertilizer factory at Dammam and three desalination plants. Industrial estates have been set up at Jiddah, Riyadh and Dammam and a fourth is planned for Jubayl. A refinery at Riyadh, flour and sugar mills, vehicle assembly works as well as additional fertilizer factories and cement plants are all under construction. There are plans for the further diversification of industry including aluminium manufacture, iron and steel production, mining and the liquefaction of gas.

Mining

Saudi Arabia, with almost 20% of the world's oil, has the largest reserves in the world. It is also the world's leading oil exporter and, after the USA and the USSR, holds third place for production. The oil industry is centred at Dhahran; the main fields are Ghawar, Abqaiq, Ain Dar and Dammam, all in the east, and offshore, Safaniya. About 75% of the crude oil is shipped from the Ras Tannurah terminal, mainly to Europe and Japan; 15% goes through Tapline (the Trans-Arabian Pipeline) to the Mediterranean port of Saida in the Lebanon; the rest is piped to refineries on Bahrain Island and at Ras Tannurah and Jiddah. Deposits of copper, zinc, iron, phosphates and uranium have been located but are not exploited commercially.

Oman and Yemen

People's Republic of Yemen (PRY)
Yemen Arab Republic (YAR)

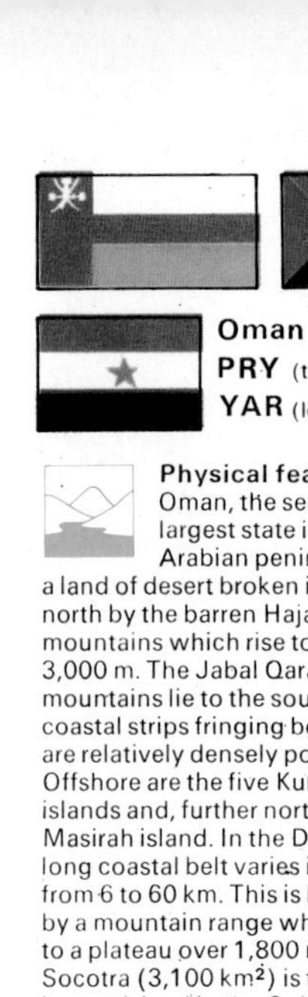

Oman (top left)
PRY (top)
YAR (left)

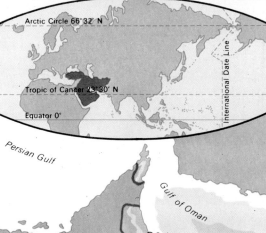

Physical features
Oman, the second largest state in the Arabian peninsula, is a land of desert broken in the north by the barren Hajar mountains which rise to over 3,000 m. The Jabal Qara mountains lie to the south. The coastal strips fringing both ranges are relatively densely populated. Offshore are the five Kuria Muria islands and, further north, Masirah island. In the DRY, the long coastal belt varies in width from 6 to 60 km. This is backed by a mountain range which rises to a plateau over 1,800 m high. Socotra (3,100 km²) is the largest island in the Gulf of Aden. The YAR's coastal plain, the Tihamah, is an arid strip of sand dunes. About 50 km inland, the plain rises to the Upper Tihamah, a foothill zone flanked by rugged mountains rising to heights of over 3,000 m—75% of the population is concentrated in this highland region. The Rub al Khali (Empty Quarter) lies further inland.

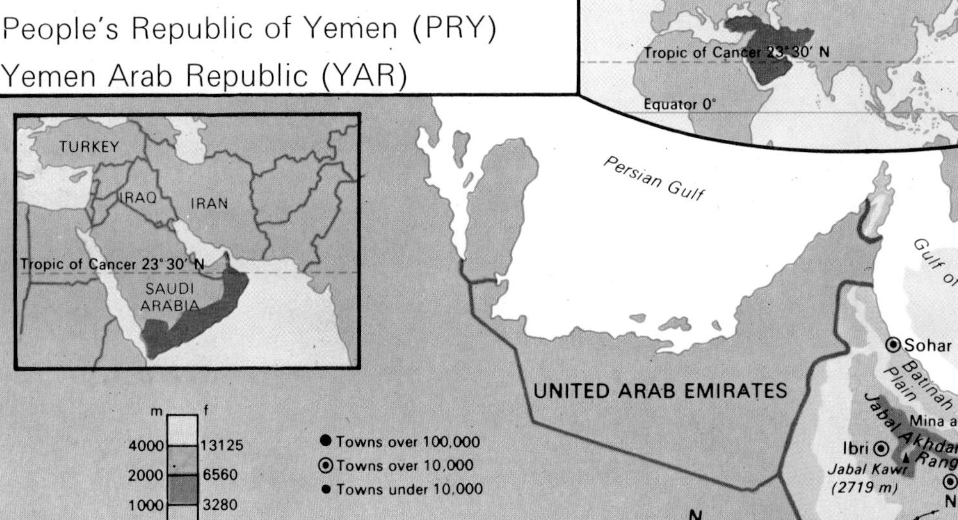

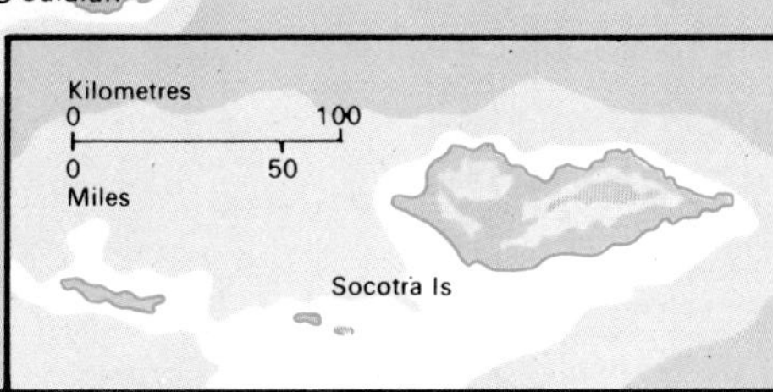

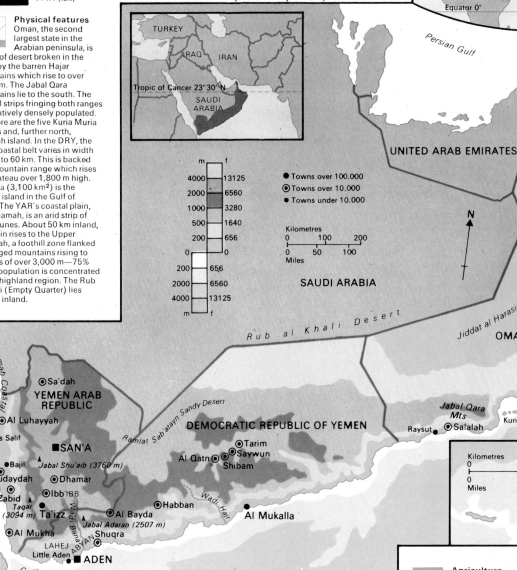

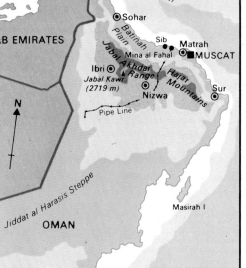

Oman
Area
212,400 km²/82,000 sq miles
Population
750,000 (1970)
Population density
3.5 per km²/9 per sq mile
Capital and largest city
Muscat: 18,000 (1970)
Language
Arabic
Major imports
foodstuffs, machinery and transport equipment, cement
Major exports
crude oil, limes, dates, fish
Currency
Rial (1 rial = 1,000 baiza)

Democratic Republic of Yemen
Area
293,000 km²/113,130 sq miles
Population
1,600,000 (1974)
Population density
5 per km²/13 per sq mile
Capital and largest city
Aden: 250,000 (1974)
Language
Arabic
Major imports
crude oil, foodstuffs, textiles
Major exports
refined petroleum, cotton, dried fish, coffee
Currency
Dinar (1 dinar = 1,000 fils)

Yemen Arab Republic
Area
200,000 km²/77,220 sq miles
Population
7,500,000 (1974)
Population density
30 per km²/78 per sq mile
Capital and largest city
San'a: 150,000 (1974)
Language
Arabic
Major imports
foodstuffs, machinery and transport equipment, chemicals
Major exports
cotton, coffee, hides, skins, salt
Currency
Riyal (1 riyal = 40 bugshas)

Climate
In the three states, coastal areas are humid (over 80%), hot and arid. In January, Aden has an average temperature of 25°C, in June it is 33°C—annual rainfall, which occurs in winter, is under 10 cm. In Oman and the DRY rainfall increases in the mountains to 25 cm. It is even heavier in the YAR highlands: the Upper Tihamah receives up to 50 cm and the main ranges about 100 cm—falling mostly in summer. The YAR highlands are cooler—average annual temperature is 18°C.

Mining
Oil dominates the Omani economy. Production began in 1967 and has increased as new fields, all in the interior, have been developed. The oil is piped to the terminal at Mina al Fahal, near Matrah. Important copper deposits have been discovered in the north, but so far remain unexploited. In the DRY, salt is mined in the north-east. About a million tonnes a year are also mined at As Salif in the YAR. Other minerals known to exist include coal, iron, sulphur, uranium, gold and silver.

Transport
In Oman, new roads, an international airport at Sib and a deep-water port at Matrah have all been financed by oil revenues. Two other major ports are at Raysut and Sur. In the DRY, most roads are unsurfaced except near Aden. The port of Aden handles nearly all the DRY's trade and is a re-fuelling stop for international shipping. In the YAR, main roads connect San'a, Ta'izz and Al Hudaydah, the chief port. As Salif port is used for the salt trade. None of the states has a railway.

Agriculture
In all three states, agriculture employs over 70% of the population. In Oman, the main cultivated areas are the Batinah plain, the Jabal Akhdar and parts of the Hajar range. About 50% of the land under cultivation is used for dates; other crops include limes, coconuts and bananas. The staple food, rice, has to be imported. There are beef and dairy herds in the Qara mountains. In the DRY, the main cash crop is cotton, grown intensively in Abyan and Lahej, followed by coffee and tobacco. The main food crops, sorghum, millet and sesame, have to be supplemented by imports. Agriculture is the basis of the YAR's economy. The main export crops are cotton (grown on the humid Tihamah) and coffee: this is grown in the highlands and known as mocha as it was formerly exported via the port of Mocha (Al Mukha). Qat (a narcotic), dates and tobacco are also cash crops. Cereals, fruit and vegetables are grown in the highlands where sheep, goats and cattle are also raised. Fishing is important in Oman and the DRY. In the DRY, the industry is centred on Aden and Al Mukalla; anchovy, tuna and sardine are dried and exported. Some Omani ports have cold store facilities.

Industry
Industry is undeveloped in the three states and handicrafts, such as weaving, pottery and leatherwork, are still important. In Oman, the income from oil has stimulated industrialization: a cement plant is under construction near Muscat and future projects include a flour mill, a fertilizer complex using natural gas and a desalination plant. The oil refinery at Little Aden accounts for 80% of the DRY's industrial output. Other activities include fish-processing, ship-building and repair and cotton textiles. In the YAR, industry is based on local raw materials. There are cotton mills at San'a and Bajil, a rock salt factory at Salif and a fish-canning plant at Al Hudaydah.

Cities
Matrah (15,000), a suburb of Muscat, is Oman's chief port and a departure point for caravans taking goods to the interior. About 2,000 km south-west is Aden, the biggest port between Suez and India. Its role as a trading centre has been seriously affected by the closure of the Suez canal. The YAR capital, San'a, situated in the mountains about 130 km inland, is a noted Moslem centre with over 40 mosques.

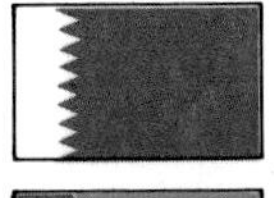
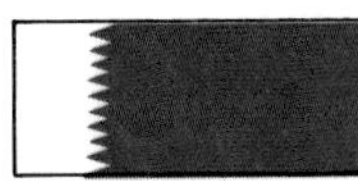

Bahrain, Qatar, United Arab Emirates (UAE)

Bahrain (top left)
Qatar (top)
UAE (left)

Bahrain
Area
662 km²/256 sq miles
Location
25°45′—26°27′ N
50°25′—50°54′ E
Population
224,000 (1972)
Population density
338 per km²/876 per sq mile
Capital and largest city
Al Manamah : 90,000 (1971)
Language
Arabic
Major imports
Machinery and transport equipment, textiles, foodstuffs
Major exports
refined petroleum, aluminium, fish
Currency
Dinar (1 dinar = 1,000 fils)
Status
independent emirate

Qatar
Area
11,400 km²/4,400 sq miles
Location
24°35′—26°30′ N
50°45′—51°30′ E
Population
180,000 (1971)
Population density
16 per km²/41 per sq mile
Capital and largest city
Doha : 120,000 (1971)
Language
Arabic
Major imports
machinery and transport equipment, foodstuffs, textiles
Major exports
petroleum and petroleum products
Currency
Riyal (1 riyal = 100 dirhams)
Status
independent sheikdom

United Arab Emirates
Area
83,655 km²/32,300 sq miles
Location
23°—25°52′ N
51°—56°23′ E
Population
342,000 (1974)
Population density
3.5 per km²/9 per sq mile
Capital
Abu Dhabi : 80,000 (1974)
Largest city
Dubai : 90,000 (1974)
Language
Arabic
Major imports
foodstuffs, transport equipment, manufactured goods
Major exports
petroleum
Currency
Dirham (1 dirham = 100 fils)
Status
independent federation

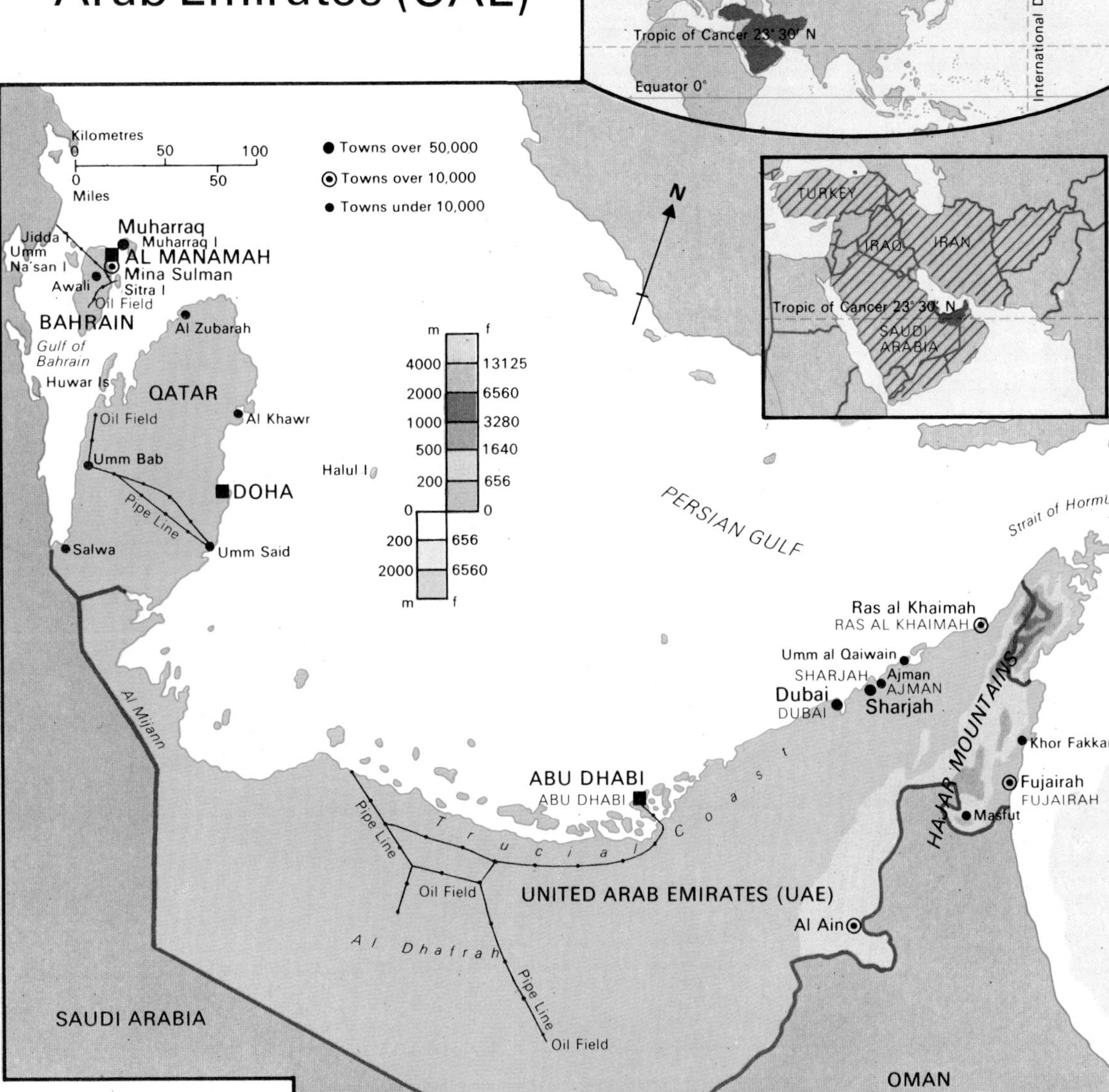

Transport

Of the three territories, Bahrain has the best road network. The international airport on Muharraq (a stopping-point for long distance flights to the Far East and Australia) was the first in the world to be purpose built for Jumbos. There are steamer services from the main port, Mina Sulman, to destinations in the Gulf, India and Pakistan. In Qatar, the interior network is poor; the state is linked to other countries by an airport at Doha, ports at Doha and Umm Said and a road to Saudi Arabia. In the UAE, the main road runs along the coast. The chief ports are Dubai, Abu Dhabi and Khor Fakkan and there are international airports at Abu Dhabi, Dubai and Sharjah.

Climate

Most of the region has a hot, dry, desert climate. Summer temperatures range from 30° to 50°C, but drop in winter to 20°C. Rainfall occurs between December and March and is very light. The annual average is under 10 cm except in the Hajar mountains which may have up to 45 cm. In Bahrain, humidity is high.

Physical features

Bahrain consists of 33 islands in the Persian Gulf. The biggest island, Bahrain, is 48 km long and 16 km wide and fringed with coral reefs. The other main islands are Muharraq, Sitrah (both linked to Bahrain by causeway), Umm Na'san and Jidda. Nearer Qatar are the Huwar islands which are inhabited only by a few fishermen. All the islands are low-lying—the highest point being Jabal ad Dukhan (135 m) on Bahrain. The Qatar peninsula is also low-lying, rising to a maximum height of 75 m. The country is largely arid with sand dunes predominating in the south. The shallow coastal waters are dotted with islets and coral reefs. Five of the seven states comprising the UAE have similar features: desert, salt flats and populations centred on coastal towns. The exceptions are Ras al Khaimah and Fujairah, which both have fertile zones situated in the northern fringes of the Hajar mountains.

Agriculture

In Bahrain, agriculture is limited to the north of the main island where springs and artesian wells make irrigation possible. Dates are grown on two-thirds of the cultivated area with the rest used for vegetables, fruit (mango, banana, citrus, pomegranate) and dairy farming (which is being developed). Prawn fishing is important with production exported to Japan, Europe and the USA. As a result of poor soils and lack of water, Qatar has little agriculture. It is, however, self-sufficient in vegetables and even exports melons, tomatoes, marrows, aubergines and cucumbers. Orchards have been planted. Fishing is important and 7 tonnes of shrimps are caught each day—mostly for export. Agriculture is also restricted in the UAE. The main cultivated areas are found in Ras al Khaimah, Fujairah and at Al Ain, an oasis. Dates, wheat, barley, millet and fruit are grown and Al Ain is famous for its mangoes. Fishing for mackerel and tuna is traditional, particularly at Sharjah, Ajman and Umm al Qaiwain and at Fujairah on the Gulf of Oman.

Industry

All three countries are using their oil revenues to develop industry. Bahrain's first major project was an aluminium smelter. Other industries include ship repair and prawn processing. Mina Sulman is a free port with a thriving entrepôt trade. Traditional activities such as building dhows (sailboats), weaving and pearl fishing are in decline. In the last five years there has been considerable industrial expansion in Qatar with a fertilizer factory, flour mill, cement works and a shrimp processing plant already in operation. An iron and steel mill, a petrochemical complex and an aluminium smelter are being planned. A similar industrialization programme is being implemented in the UAE, particularly at Abu Dhabi and Dubai. Dubai is a free port and has become the federation's commercial centre. In all three countries, water for industry is supplied by desalination plants.

Mining

Oil was discovered in Bahrain in 1932, making it the first oil-producing state in the Gulf. Production from the field at Jabal ad Dukhan is relatively low—about 3 million tonnes a year. This crude oil, plus a further 9 million tonnes piped from the Dammam field in Saudi Arabia, is refined at Sitrah where there is also a 5 km long tanker terminal. Natural gas reserves have recently been exploited and are used to power the refinery, aluminium smelter and a thermal power station. About 11 million tonnes of oil (50% of Qatar's production) comes from the Dukhan field on the west coast; the other half coming from offshore fields. A pipeline runs from Dukhan to the tanker terminal at Umm Said. Natural gas powers thermal stations and desalination plants. The leading UAE oil producer is Abu Dhabi with onshore and off-shore fields: oil revenues make Abu Dhabi, per capita, the world's richest state. Oil is also produced from offshore fields in Dubai and Sharjah. In the federation, mineral surveys are being made. It is thought that asbestos exists in Ras al Khaimah, and chrome and copper in Ajman. Marble is quarried at Masfut.

Syria

Area
185,180 km²/71,500 sq miles
Location
32°20′—37°15′ N
35°35′—42°20′ E
Population
7,300,000 (1975 estimate)
Population density
39 per km²/102 per sq mile
Capital and largest city
Damascus: 836,000 (1970)
Language
Arabic
Major imports
machines, metals, foodstuffs, chemicals, transport equipment
Major exports
cotton and cotton textiles, crude oil, wool, livestock, wheat
Currency
pound (1 pound = 100 piastres)
Gross National Product
2,000 million US dollars (1972)
Status
independent republic

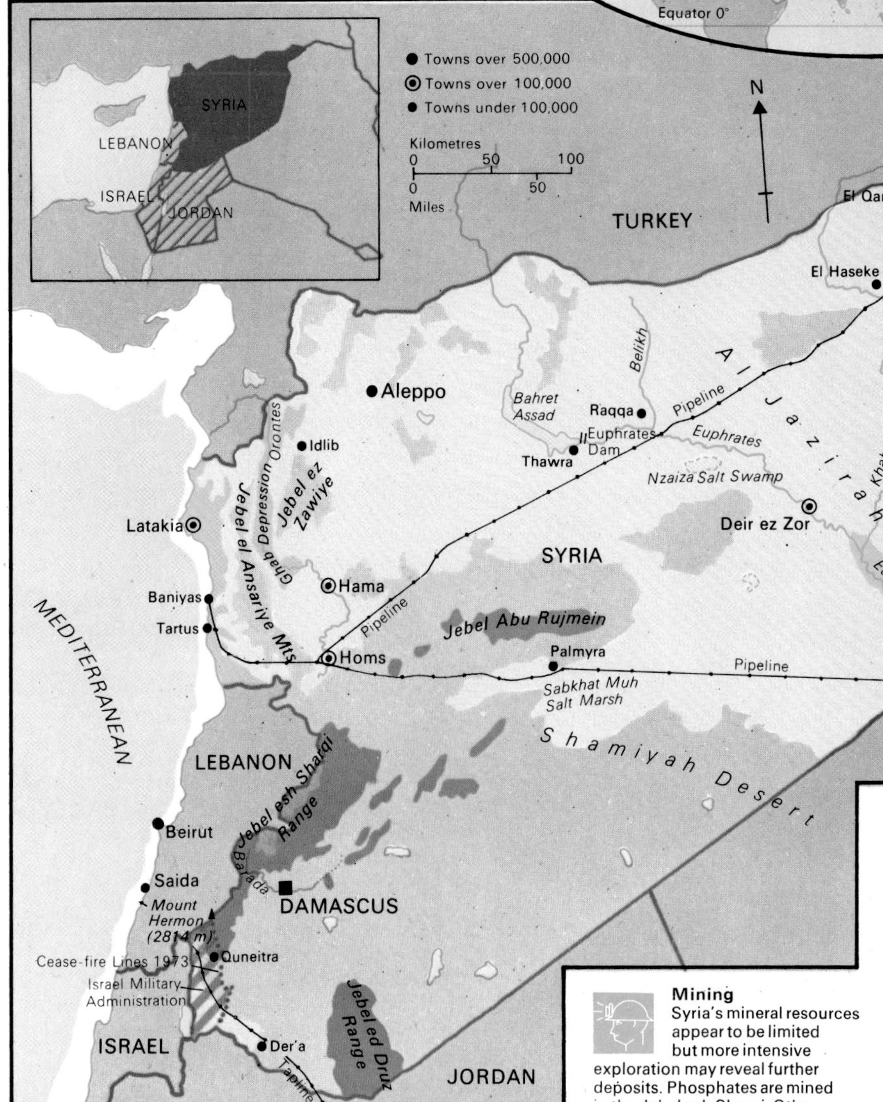

Physical features
A narrow coastal plain separates the Mediterranean from the Jebel el Ansariye mountains. This range stretches from the Turkish border in the north to the Lebanon mountains in the south. East of the Jebel el Ansariye is the swampy Ghab depression—part of the Great Rift Valley that continues through the Red Sea and into East Africa. The Orontes river, which rises in Lebanon, flows 325 km northwards to Turkey through the Ghab. South of Homs, the Lebanese border follows the Jebel esh Sharqi and Mount Hermon ranges. Mount Hermon itself is Syria's highest peak at 2,814 m. The remainder of the country is largely desert steppe extending eastwards to the Euphrates. The most important features of the steppe are low ridges near Palmyra, the volcanic Jebel ed Druz range in the south and the plateau's western rim, the Jebel ez Zawiye. The region north-east of the Euphrates, the Al Jazirah, is drained by the Belikh and the Khabur. The Euphrates, which flows across Syria for 600 km, is the longest river. The source of the Euphrates is in Turkey and its total length is 2,330 km.

Climate
Inland Syria has a more extreme climate than on the coast and in the western mountains. In the desert, summer temperatures rise to over 40°C, but can fall to 0°C in winter. Rainfall, occurring in winter, is very low: less than 12 cm a year. Along the coast, summer temperatures range from 25°C to 32°C. Winters are mild (about 10°C) and wet. The coastal belt and mountains receive over 75 cm of rain between October and May. On the mountain peaks this often falls as snow: Mount Hermon is snow-covered until June or July.

Flora and fauna
The desert plateau is barren except for patches of sparse grazing. In spring, however, the fringes of the plateau are bright with colourful wild flowers. The western mountains were once thickly forested, but are now mostly scrub-covered. Thin forests (mainly oak and pine) remain in the Jebel el Ansariye. Gazelles and foxes are found in the desert, while wolves, wild boar and bears live in the mountains.

Agriculture
Agriculture plays a major role in the Syrian economy and agricultural products account for over 60% of exports. Rain-fed farming is practised on the western margins of the steppe (where precipitation reaches 50 cm a year), along the coast and on the mountain slopes. Other areas under cultivation are irrigated: the Euphrates and Khabur valleys, the Damascus oasis and parts of the Ghab where swamp land has been reclaimed. Wheat, barley, millet and maize are mainly grown in the unirrigated steppe regions. In good years, Syria exports up to one million tonnes of cereals. Cotton, providing 30% of total exports, is the chief cash crop. Other crops include rice (in the Euphrates valley), tobacco (from the Latakia district), citrus fruits (grown along the coast) and, at higher altitudes, olives, grapes and deciduous fruits. Modernization schemes include mechanization, co-operatives, fertilizer production and irrigation projects. Sheep, goats and cattle are important and the region north of the Euphrates is a major stock-raising area. Forests cover only 5% of Syria. Fishing is also under-developed and catches are consumed locally.

Euphrates dam
The key to Syria's economic future is the Euphrates dam situated at Thawra. This giant project is now nearing completion. The dam will revolutionize Syrian agriculture by doubling the area under irrigation. A further 360,000 hectares will be reclaimed when a subsidiary scheme, harnessing the river Khabour, is completed. The dam will also promote industrial growth: its hydro-electric power station, with a capacity of 1,200 MW, is scheduled to meet the future energy needs of Syrian industry.

Oil
Crude oil accounts for 35% of Syrian exports. Production comes from the fields at Qarachuk, Rumailan and Suwaydiyah in the north-east. The oil is piped to the port of Tartus for export and to Homs for refining. A second refinery at Baniyas on the Mediterranean coast is near completion. The Syrian oil industry is nationalized. Three oil pipelines cross Syria. Two Iraqi pipelines cut through from Kirkuk to Baniyas and Tartus and, in the extreme south-west, the Tapline from Saudi Arabia crosses Jordan and Syria to Saida in Lebanon.

Mining
Syria's mineral resources appear to be limited but more intensive exploration may reveal further deposits. Phosphates are mined in the Jebel esh Sharqi. Other minerals worked include sandstone (found near Palmyra and used in glass manufacture), asphalt (used in road construction), limestone (quarried near Aleppo) and marl (used in cement production). Rock salt is exploited in the Deir ez Zor and salt is also produced from the salt lakes. Iron ore deposits have been discovered near Palmyra, Aleppo, Homs and Damascus. Lignite, manganese, chromite and asbestos exist and natural gas has been located in Al Jazirah.

Transport
Damascus and Aleppo are the focal points of Syria's transport system. The 17,000 km of roads radiate from these two centres. New highways are being built linking Damascus with Aleppo, Beirut (Lebanon) and Amman (Jordan). Three railways of varying gauges serve the main towns in the west and there are also rail links with Iraq, Lebanon, and Turkey. Two new links under construction are El Qamishliye to Latakia and Damascus to Aleppo. Latakia is the main port but there are oil-tanker terminals at Tartus and Baniyas. El Qamishliye, Aleppo, Latakia and Damascus have airports. The communications network was badly damaged by the war in October 1973.

Industry
The textile industry is the most developed. The production of cotton, wool, silk and artificial fabrics is centred on Damascus, Aleppo, Homs and Hama. Cement production is next in importance: there are currently seven plants in operation and a further four are planned for 1977. Other leading industries include flour, sugar, vegetable oils, soap, shoes, glass and refrigerator assembly. Two major projects have recently been completed: a nitrous fertilizer plant near Homs with an annual capacity of 250,000 tonnes and a metallic bar factory near Hama. The latter is to be part of a giant metallurgical complex which will manufacture sheet-iron, iron-wire, steel and which will be powered by electricity from the Euphrates dam. At present, the metallic bar factory uses imported materials, but it is hoped that the needs of the new complex will, in part, be supplied by the iron-ore discovered in Syria.

Cities
Damascus, situated on the Barada River at the desert's edge, is one of the world's oldest cities and has been inhabited for over 4,000 years. Biblical Damascus stands side by side with the modern city which was planned in 1929. It is a centre of light industry—particularly textiles and leathergoods—and is an important link in trade between Baghdad, Beirut and Amman. The capital is also noted for its handicrafts which include ceramics, glassware and mother-of-pearl work. Aleppo (639,000) is Syria's second city. It is an industrial centre manufacturing textiles (especially silk) and processing food. Homs (215,000) is the next largest city and is also a manufacturing and trading centre.

Lebanon

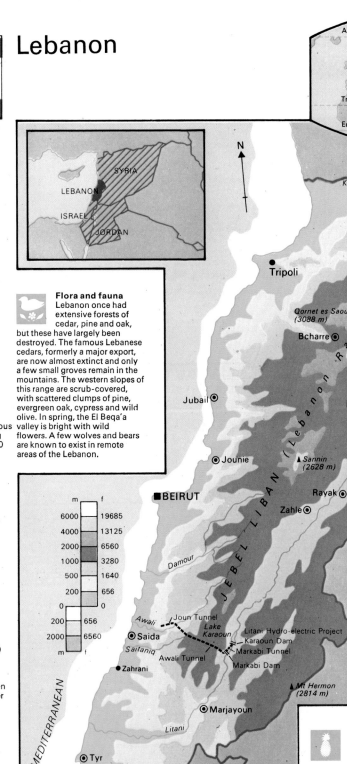

Area
10,400 km²/4,000 sq miles
Location
33°04'—34°40' N
35°05'—36°40' E
Population
2,855,000 (1972)
Population density
274 per km²/711 per sq mile
Capital and largest city
Beirut: 800,000 (1972)
Language
Arabic
Major imports
machinery, textiles, foodstuffs, transport equipment, chemicals, precious stones and metals, base metals
Major exports (& re-exports)
fruit and vegetable products, machinery, textiles, precious stones and metals
Currency
pound (1 pound = 100 piastres)
Gross National Product
2,120 million US dollars (1972)
Status
independent republic

Physical features

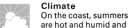

Lebanon is a mountainous land about 220 km long and varying between 30 and 60 km wide. The fertile coastal belt is very narrow and rises abruptly to the Lebanon mountains. This range, which is highest in the north, runs parallel to the coast: its main peaks are Qornet es Saouda (3,088 m) and Sannin (2,628 m). The country's eastern border is formed by the Anti-Lebanon (Jebel esh Sharqi) and Hermon ranges rising to 2,814 m (Mt Hermon). Between the Lebanon and Anti-Lebanon ranges lies the El Beqa'a valley, a flat alluvial plain some 150 km long and 16 km wide. This depression is part of the Great Rift Valley. Lebanon's two main rivers rise in the El Beqa'a near Ba'albek: the Orontes flows north into Syria but the Litani (145 km long) remains in Lebanon, entering the Mediterranean north of Tyr. A third river, the Kebir, flows along the northern border between Lebanon and Syria. The remainder of the country's drainage is seasonal with winter torrents rushing down mountain slopes.

Climate

On the coast, summers are hot and humid and winters mild. The average temperature is 32°C in July and 16°C in January. In the El Beqa'a valley, away from the sea, temperatures are slightly more extreme: 35°C in July and 10°C in January. The mountains are cooler and at an altitude of 1,500 m temperatures are 8°C cooler than on the coast. Rain occurs between October and May—ranging between 30 cm in the El Beqa'a and 150 cm in the mountains with 80 cm on the coast. The mountains are snow-covered from December to May, hence the origin of the country's name from laban which is Aramaic for 'white'.

Tourism

Each year some two million people visit Lebanon attracted by its scenery, climate, biblical sites, history (which goes back beyond the Phoenicians) and its beach and ski resorts. In recent years, however, the Arab-Israeli conflict and internal disturbances have adversely affected the industry.

Flora and fauna

Lebanon once had extensive forests of cedar, pine and oak, but these have largely been destroyed. The famous Lebanese cedars, formerly a major export, are now almost extinct and only a few small groves remain in the mountains. The western slopes of this range are scrub-covered, with scattered clumps of pine, evergreen oak, cypress and wild olive. In spring, the El Beqa'a valley is bright with wild flowers. A few wolves and bears are known to exist in remote areas of the Lebanon.

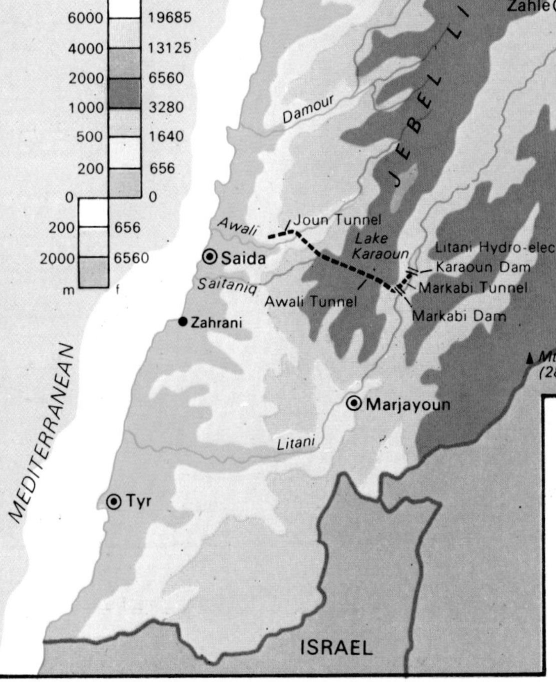

Mining and energy

Lebanon has limited mineral resources. Small deposits of iron-ore, lignite and phosphates are worked but these have no commercial significance. On the other hand, large quantities of building stone are quarried and salt is extracted from sea-water. Other deposits include copper, oil-shale, asphalt, glass-sand and clay (suitable for ceramic manufactures). The output of fuel from the Saida and Tripoli refineries is sufficient for domestic needs. There is a surplus of electricity (augmented by the Litani hydro-electric project) which is exported to Syria.

Transport

Beirut international airport, one of the busiest in the Middle East, is used by over 30 airlines, including the two national carriers: Middle East Airlines and Trans Mediterranean Airways. The leading port, Beirut, handles over 3,000 vessels a year. There are oil terminals at Tripoli and Zahrani, while Jubail, Saida and Tyr are used by local steamers and fishing boats. The road network is good and 75% of roads are paved. Bus and long distance taxi services cover the country. There are three railway lines: Saida-Tripoli, Beirut-Rayak-Damascus, Tripoli-Homs.

Agriculture

Although over 50% of the country is uncultivated, Lebanon is essentially agricultural. The area under cultivation comprises the coastal strip, terraced mountain slopes and the El Beqa'a valley but only half of this is under full irrigation. Wheat and barley are the chief cereal crops and these are grown mainly in the El Beqa'a but, as only 20% of total farmland is used for cereals, flour imports are necessary. The leading cash crops, forming Lebanon's main export, are fruit and vegetables. Citrus fruits (oranges, lemons and limes) are the most important, followed by apples. Other export crops include grapes, bananas, olives, figs, onions, tomatoes, potatoes and cucumbers. Cotton and tobacco are also grown, mainly for local consumption. Livestock is limited as grazing is scarce, but about 600,000 goats, sheep and cattle are raised, primarily for dairy purposes. Poultry is being developed and about 60% of the total 600 million eggs which are produced annually is exported.

Industry

Lebanon is crossed by two oil pipelines: one from Iraq to Tripoli, the other from Saudi Arabia to Zahrani, near Saida. There is a refinery at the terminal of each pipeline and the combined annual input of crude oil is 2.5 million tonnes. By Middle East standards, manufacturing in Lebanon is relatively well-developed. The most important sector is food-processing, which includes sugar refining, flour-milling, biscuit factories and milk pasteurization. The other main industries, mostly organized on a small scale, are textiles, cement, wood and furniture, pharmaceuticals, chemicals and aluminium. There are two steel mills. In spite of industrial growth, commerce (especially transit trade) remains the basic source of national income. Craft products, such as copper goods, hand-woven kaftans, olive-oil soap and glassware, are a major tourist attraction.

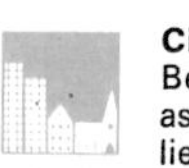

Cities

Beirut, which originated as a Phoenician city, lies at the crossroads of Asia, Europe and Africa. It is Lebanon's leading commercial city with a stock exchange, free port facilities and a free money market. The capital is also the major industrial centre and 80% of Lebanese industry is located in the Beirut region. The cosmopolitan city, which houses 40% of the country's urban population, is divided into distinct communities—for example, there are separate Christian and Moslem sectors. Lebanon's second largest city, Tripoli (150,000), is also a major port and industrial centre. It has Byzantine remains but many buildings are medieval.

Jordan

Area
96,188 km²/37,140 sq miles
East Bank : 89,555 km²
West Bank : 6,633 km²
Location
29°20′—33°25′ N
34°55′—39° E
Population
2,570,000 (1973)
East Bank : 1,850,000
West Bank : 720,000
Population density
27 per km²/69 per sq mile
East Bank : 21 per km²
West Bank : 109 per km²
Capital and largest city
Amman : 521,000 (1973)
Language
Arabic
Major imports
machinery, foodstuffs, textiles, minerals, chemicals
Major exports
phosphates, fruit and vegetables, cement, cigarettes
Currency
dinar (1 dinar = 1,000 fils)
Gross National Product
1,125 million US dollars (1974)
Status
constitutional monarchy

As a result of the Arab-Israeli war in 1967, the territory lying west of the River Jordan—known as the West Bank and representing 6% of the total area—came under the control of Israel. The information here refers mainly to the East Bank.

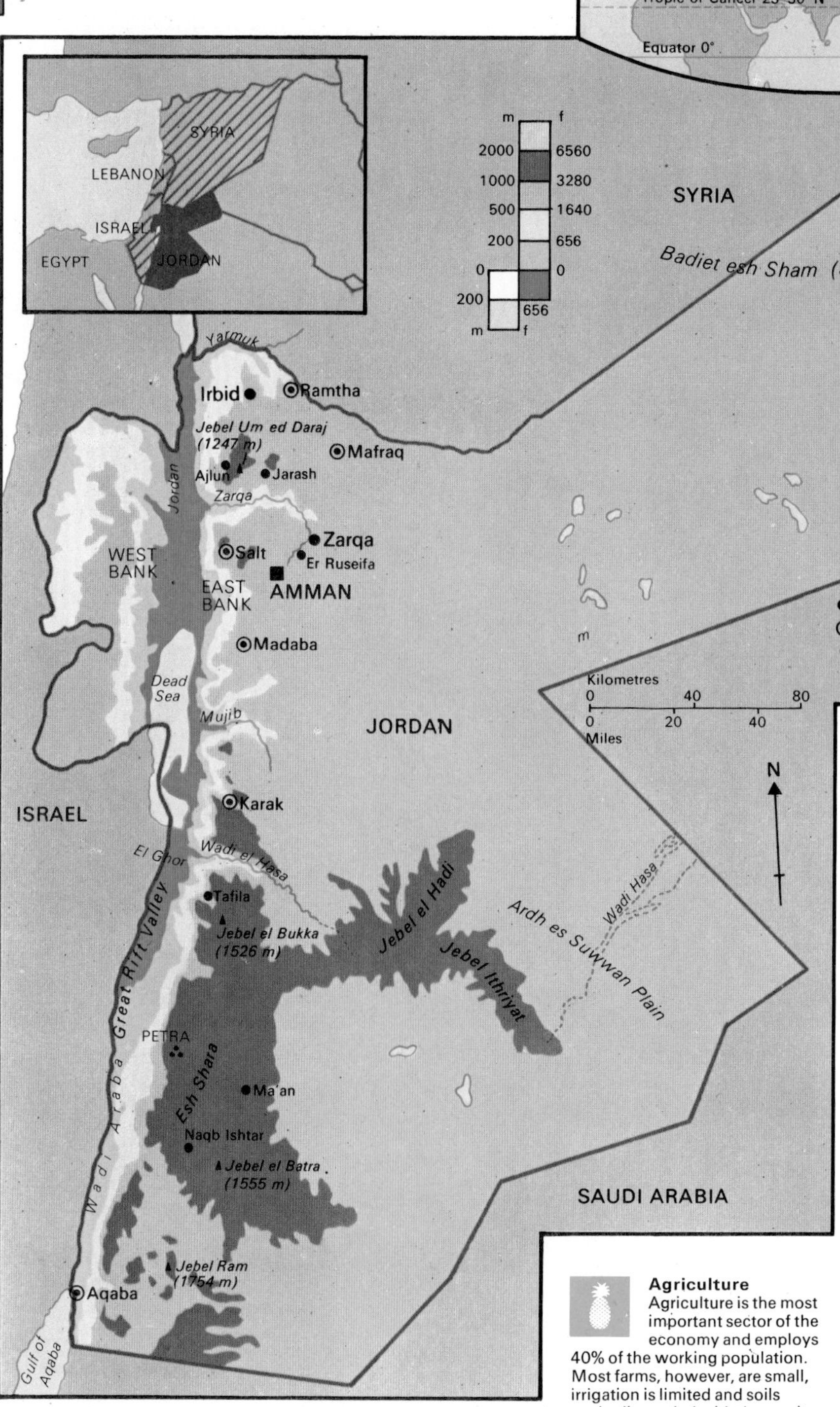

Physical features
About 80% of Jordan is desert. The fertile area is located in the west—mainly in the Jordan river valley. In the Israeli-occupied zone west of the river, limestone hills rise to over 900 m. In the north-west, the border with Syria and the Israeli-held Golan Heights is formed by the River Yarmuk, a tributary of the Jordan. The 250 km-long Jordan valley, part of the Great Rift Valley, lies below sea level. The river flows into the Dead Sea which has no outlet; the rift valley, however, continues to the Gulf of Aqaba where Jordan has 20 km of coastline. To the east, the mountains rise steeply from the narrow fertile belt. Beyond these mountains, which are highest in the south (Jebel Ram: 1,754 m), the land descends gradually to the arid, stony desert.

Climate
In Amman, 720 m above sea level, the average temperature in summer is 28°C, in winter, 10°C. The climate is more extreme in the desert and the Jordan valley where August temperatures frequently reach 40°C. Rainfall occurs during winter: the hills on the West Bank receive 80 cm a year, the Aqaba region, 10 cm and the desert has less than 4 cm.

Cities
The ancient Graeco-Roman city of Amman has recently expanded to become the country's main industrial centre. Leading manufactures include food-processing, tobacco, textiles, plastics, cement, electrical goods and paper products. Amman is also the hub of Jordan's transport system. Other East Bank towns which have developed rapidly are Zarqa (214,000) and Irbid (113,000), both in the north.

Transport
As economic development in Jordan is hindered by poor communications, transport is a current government priority. The 9,000 km road network (75% surfaced) links Amman to all main towns. Major highways connect the capital with Aqaba, Syria (via Jarash) and Iraq (via Mafraq). There is only one railway: a single line track running from Der'a (Syria) via Amman to Naqb Ishtar. This is now being extended to Aqaba. Aqaba is the only port and phosphate exports account for over 50% of the trade handled there. Alia (Royal Jordanian Airlines) operates a domestic service between Amman, Aqaba and Ma'an and overseas flights from Amman. A new international airport is being built near the capital.

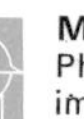

Mining
Phosphates are the most important of Jordan's mineral resources and make up 25% of total exports. Over one million tonnes a year are produced from rich deposits at Er Ruseifa and near the Wadi el Hasa. Two other minerals exploited commercially are marble (near Amman) and potash (from the Dead Sea). Clay and feldspar deposits are also worked and a ceramics industry is based on local materials. Copper has been discovered in Wadi Araba and excavation is due to begin in 1976. Other minerals known to exist include iron ore, nickel, manganese, quartzite and barite. The country's one oil refinery at Zarqa is supplied by Tapline (the Trans-Arabian Pipeline) which crosses Jordan.

Agriculture
Agriculture is the most important sector of the economy and employs 40% of the working population. Most farms, however, are small, irrigation is limited and soils are badly eroded with the result that farming is often at subsistence level. The main cereals are wheat and barley, grown in unirrigated areas. Production therefore varies according to rainfall, but even in good years the bulk of Jordan's grain requirements has to be imported. Tomatoes are the leading export crop; other exports include citrus, grapes, melons, aubergines, cucumbers and cauliflowers. Tobacco is also a major industrial crop. The output of fruit and vegetables was severely affected by the loss of the West Bank: 80% of the fruit growing area and 45% of the vegetable growing area are under Israeli administration. The Bedou graze sheep, goats and camels on the sparse desert pasture. There is some fishing in the rivers Jordan and Yarmuk and in the Gulf of Aqaba.

Industry
The three principal industries are phosphate extraction, cement manufacture and oil-refining. Cement production is increasing and now accounts for 15% of total exports. Output from the oil refinery at Zarqa meets domestic requirements; the two main electricity generating plants, fired by oil, are at Amman and Zarqa. In recent years, a range of small industries, based on local raw materials, has been established including cigarette manufacture, fruit and vegetable canning, olive oil refining and soap manufacture. With the loss of the West Bank, Jordan's growing tourist industry suffered a major setback: nearly all the Holy Places, including Jerusalem and Bethlehem, are under Israeli control. However, Jordan still has some outstanding tourist attractions, such as the ancient rose-red rock city of Petra, 40 km west of Ma'an. The tourist trade stimulates handicrafts such as mother-of-pearl work, wool and goat-hair rugs, tapestries and ceramics.

Flora and fauna
Much of the country has no vegetation other than desert scrub. The main forested regions are in the highlands near Ajlun, Jarash and Ma'an where evergreen oak and Aleppo pine predominate. Junipers and wild olives are found in areas with less rainfall. Ibex, panther, wolf, gazelle and wild boar still exist in remote areas, particularly the southern uplands.

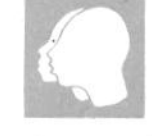

Peoples
The Arab-Israeli conflict has created population problems for Jordan. In 1948, and again in 1967, Palestinian refugees, fled to Jordan from Israeli-occupied territory. There are some 750,000 refugees, accounting for 33% of the total population. The economic difficulties of absorbing the Palestinians into Jordan are heightened by racial, cultural and religious differences.

Israel

Area
89,359 km²/34,500 sq miles
Location
27°45′—33°20′ N
32°06′—35°50′ E
Population
4,241,400 (1973)
Population density
47 per km²/123 per sq mile
Capital
Jerusalem: 304,500 (1973)
Largest city
Tel Aviv-Yafo: 362,900 (1973)
Language
Hebrew, Arabic
Major imports
rough diamonds, machinery, iron and steel, ships, aircraft, foodstuffs
Major exports
polished diamonds, citrus fruits, textiles, minerals
Currency
pound (1 pound = 100 agorot)
Gross National Product
8,900 million US dollars (1973)
Status
independent republic

As a result of the 6-day war in June 1967, the following areas came under Israeli administration: Gaza Strip, Sinai peninsula, West Jordan and the Golan Heights. These administered areas are included in the information given here.

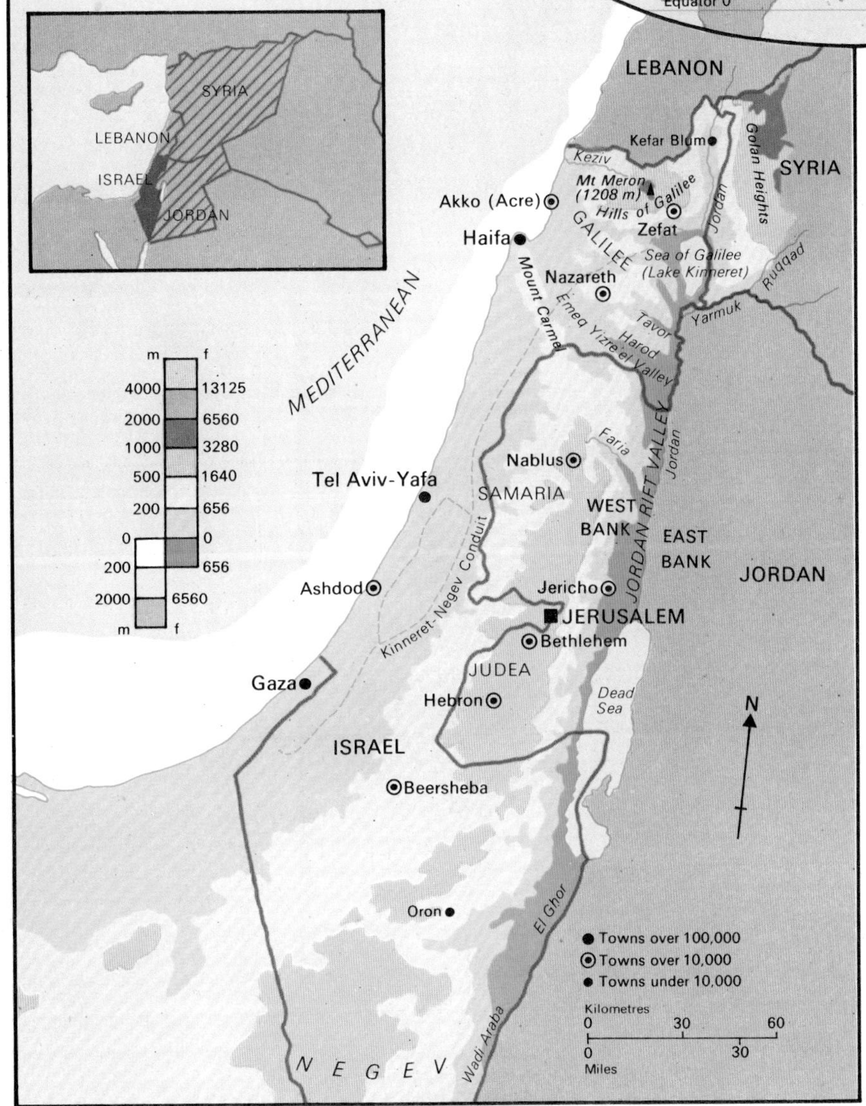

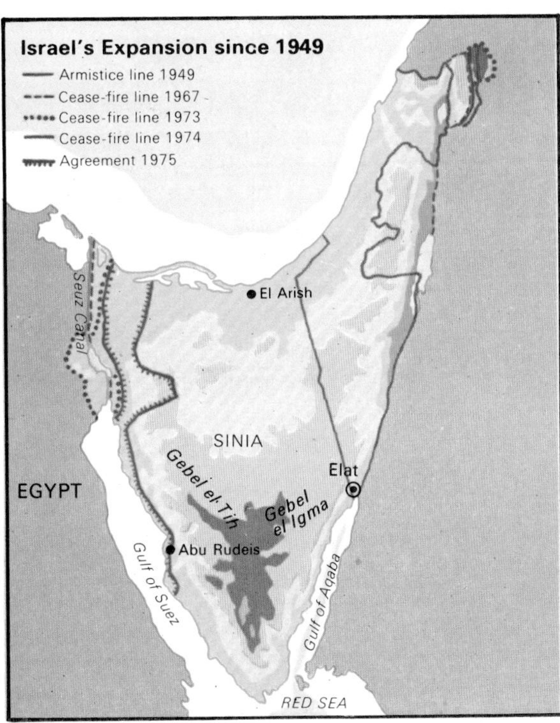

Physical features
Israel divides into four regions. The Mediterranean coastal plain, fringed with sand dunes, has an average width of 4 km and is split into two by Mt Carmel, a limestone ridge of 546 m high. This alluvial lowland is flanked by the central mountain zone—the hills of Galilee, Samaria and Judea—which has its highest point in Galilee: Mt Meron (1,208 m). Galilee is separated from Samaria by the Emeq Yizre'el valley, a traditional route from the Mediterranean to Jordan. South of this valley, the Samarian and Judean hills (with an average height of 600 m) slope eastwards to the deep Jordan Rift Valley—the third region. The Jordan river links two internal seas: the Sea of Galilee (Lake Kinneret) and the Dead Sea (the lowest point in the world at 392 m below sea level). The Dead Sea has no outlet and evaporation balances inflow, but the Rift Valley continues to the Red Sea and is known as the Araba. The fourth zone corresponds to the Negev and Sinai deserts. Much of Sinai is an arid limestone plateau which has a mountainous southern rim over 2,000 m high.

Climate
On the coast, winters are mild, summers hot. In Tel Aviv, the average temperature in January is 20°C, in August 30°C. The mountains are cooler: in Jerusalem, the January temperature is 15°C and in August, 28°C. The hottest parts of the country are the Rift Valley and the desert. The January and June temperatures for Kefar Blum are 21 and 34°C and for Elat, 23 and 33°C. Rainfall, occurring mainly in winter, is heaviest in the northern mountains (where it sometimes falls as snow) and lowest in the desert. Tel Aviv receives about 72 cm a year, Beersheba has about 53 cm a year, while Elat has only 2 cm.

Agriculture
Agriculture in Israel is highly efficient. Farming is capital intensive and employs only about 10% of the working population in the three main areas of agriculture, forestry and fishing. The country is self-sufficient in fruit, vegetables, cotton, poultry, eggs, milk and dairy produce. Half the land under cultivation is irrigated. The coastal plain and the Emeq Yizre'el valley are the main agricultural areas for mixed farming, citrus fruits, vine-yards and poultry. In the hills, tobacco and olive plantations predominate. About 20% of the cultivated area is devoted to citrus fruits, of which 95% of the output is exported (fresh, dried or processed into fruit juices). Poultry and dairy cattle are important in the lowlands, while sheep and goats are mainly grazed in the Galilee hills and the Negev. On the West Bank, vegetables are the main export crop. In Sinai, approximately half of the land under cultiv-ation is used for growing citrus fruits, but melons are also important. With Israel's modern fleets, most marine fishing takes place in the Atlantic and Indian Oceans.

Irrigation
As Israel lives on the edge of a desert the supply of water is vital. The principal sources of water—Lake Kinneret and the Jordan—are in the north, while the areas most in need of irrigation are in the south. To overcome this problem the National Water Carrier was devised. The NWC pumps water via canal and tunnel, mainly by gravitation, to the Negev. There are also desalination plants at Elat and Ashdod.

Mining
A major part of Israel's mineral resources is found in the Dead Sea: potash and bromine are extracted from its waters. The only other deposits of commercial significance are copper, mined near Elat, and phosphate, at Oron in the Negev. Natural gas and oil are produced in the northern Negev. (Control of the Abu Rudeis oilfield in the Gulf of Suez was relinquished by Israel after the 1975 agreement with Egypt.)

Industry
Although most raw materials have to be imported, industry has developed rapidly and industrial products (excluding diamonds) now make up 35% of all exports. The main industries produce electrical and electronic goods, textiles, processed food, chemicals and vehicles. Israel is also one of the world's major diamond-polishing centres: the worked diamonds are almost all marketed abroad and account for 40% of total exports. Heavy industry, such as steel, engineering, cement and oil-refining is largely concentrated at Haifa, the main port. The other leading industrial area is Tel Aviv-Yafo.

Transport
An extensive road network is the principal feature of the Israeli transport system and buses are the main form of public transport; railways are less important. A domestic air service links major towns; overseas flights are operated by El Al from Lod airport, 14 km from Tel Aviv. In the last 20 years, the Israeli merchant fleet has quadrupled. Haifa is the largest port, handling over 50% of total cargo; Ashdod, the second port, came into operation in 1965 and replaced facilities at Tel Aviv and Jaffa. Israel's third port, Elat, is on the gulf of Aqaba which runs into the Red Sea and is used to offload oil for trans-shipment to Ashdod, via pipeline.

Cities
Jerusalem, situated in the Judean hills, 27 km west of the Dead Sea, first became the capital of the Jewish nation 3,000 years ago under King David. Known as the Holy City, it is a place of pilgrimage for Jews, Moslems and Christians. Between 1949 and 1967 the city was divided between Israel and Jordan. The largest city was formed in 1950 when the old port of Jaffa merged with its modern suburb of Tel Aviv. Tel Aviv-Yafo is Israel's cultural, commercial and industrial centre.

Nauru (top left)
Tonga (top)
Samoa

Micronesia and Polynesia

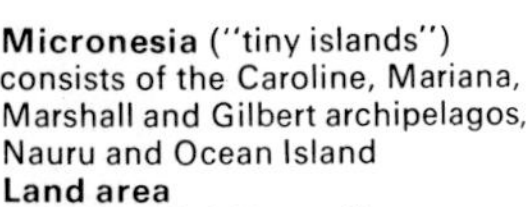

Micronesia ("tiny islands") consists of the Caroline, Mariana, Marshall and Gilbert archipelagos, Nauru and Ocean Island
Land area
2,800 km²/1,100 sq miles
Largest islands
Guam (Marianas) : 541 km²/209 sq miles ; Babelthuap and Ponape (Carolines) : each 339 km²/130 sq miles
Population
260,398 (1970)
Population density
93 per km²/236 per sq mile
Major imports
foodstuffs, fuels, machinery, textiles
Major exports
copra, phosphate, handicrafts
Status
Trust Territory of the Pacific Islands (Carolines, Marshalls, Marianas except Guam) : UN trust territory administered by USA ; Guam : US territory ; Gilberts and Ocean Island : UK colony ; Nauru : independent republic

Polynesia ("many islands") includes Samoa ; Ellice, Line and Phoenix Islands ; Tokelau Islands ; Wallis and Futuna Islands ; Tonga ; Cook Islands and Nieu ; French Polynesia ; Pitcairn and Easter Island
Land area
9,507 km²/3,741 sq miles
Largest islands
Savai'i (W. Samoa) : 1,657 km²/703 sq miles ; Upolu (W. Samoa) : 1,191 km²/430 sq miles ; Tahiti : 1,042 km²/400 sq miles
Population
415,794 (1970)
Population density
44 per km²/111 per sq mile
Major imports
foodstuffs, fuels, machinery, textiles
Major exports
copra, bananas, handicrafts
Status
Tonga : independent state ; W. Samoa ; independent state ; American Samoa : US territory ; Cook, Tokelau and Nieu Islands : NZ territories ; Ellice, Line, Phoenix and Pitcairn Islands : UK colonies ; French Polynesia, Wallis and Futuna : French territories ; Easter Island : Chilean dependency.

Physical features
The islands are generally classified as high or low. The high islands are the summits of ocean-floor volcanic mountain ranges. Mount Silisili on Savai'i rises to 1,858 m. These volcanic islands have a jagged landscape : cliffs, canyons, peaks and ridges. As the mountains are high enough to trap rain, the surface is often forested like the wooded Wallis and Futuna Islands. The low islands are coral atolls : a chain of islands enclosing a lagoon. In the Carolines, for example, many of the atolls are only 2.5 m above sea-level, while some of the Tongan islands have been uplifted to 18 m The Kwajalein atoll in the Marshalls is the world's largest : 38 islands surround a lagoon of 2,202 km² Many archipelagos include both high and low, such as the Cook Islands : in the south these are high volcanic, further north they are low atolls.

Scattered across the Pacific Ocean, between 130°E and 130°W—a distance of 11,265 km —are thousands of islands with a total land area of 260,000 km², excluding New Zealand and New Guinea. These islands fall into three great divisions : Melanesia, Micronesia and Polynesia.

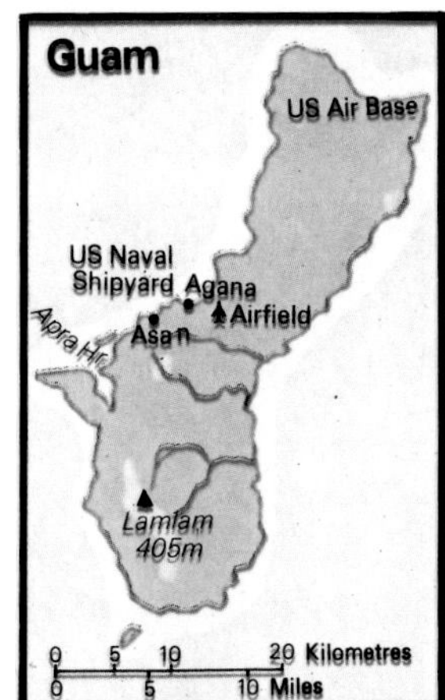

Climate
The climate, influenced by latitude and sea, is both tropical and oceanic. Humidity is high : on average 80%. Temperatures are also high and mostly uniform throughout the year. On Guam, the average annual temperature is 27°C with a mean annual range of less than 2 degrees. Even on remote Easter Island, temperatures only range from 16°C to 23°C and, although the nights are cold, humidity remains high. Rainfall is less uniform. Across the east and central Pacific the N.E. and S.E. tradewinds bring rain to windward coasts, while western Micronesia is subject to year-round monsoons and, from July to November, typhoons. Relief greatly affects rainfall : the high islands of the Carolines receive as much as 1,016 cm a year, but the neighbouring low atolls of the northern Marshalls receive only 50 cm. In some places rainfall is very uncertain. Nauru, for example, has to import 165 million litres of water a year.

Agriculture
On all the islands subsistance agriculture provides the islanders' food. Main root crops include taro, yam and sweet potato ; principal tree crops are coconut, bananas and breadfruit. The volcanic islands have a greater range of crops than the coral atolls, but on both farming methods are traditional and production is in the hands of individual families. In many places the islanders' farming and fishing rights are carefully guaranteed. In Tonga, for instance, where all land belongs to the Crown, each male over the age of 16 is granted an allotment amounting to 3.3 hectares. On the island of Nauru, the Baudu lagoon is divided between families, each family having exclusive fishing rights in its area. The one product grown for export in nearly every territory is copra. Bananas are also important, and cacao, pepper and coffee are being introduced as prospective cash crops.

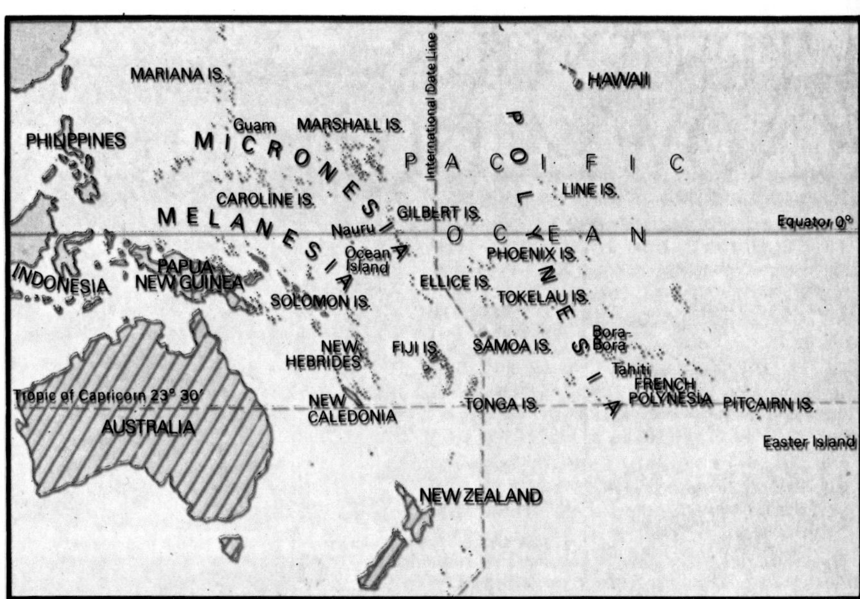

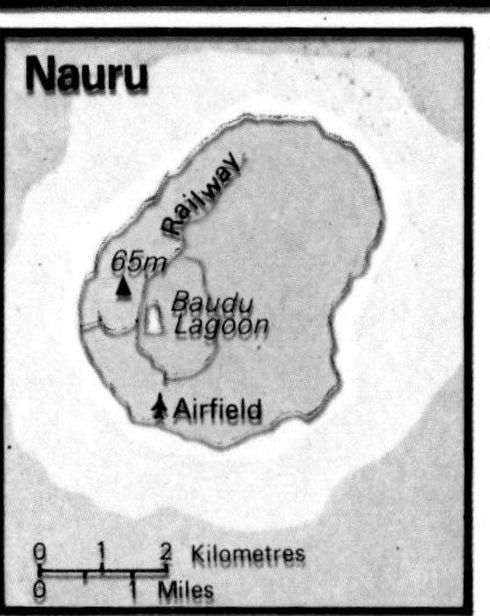

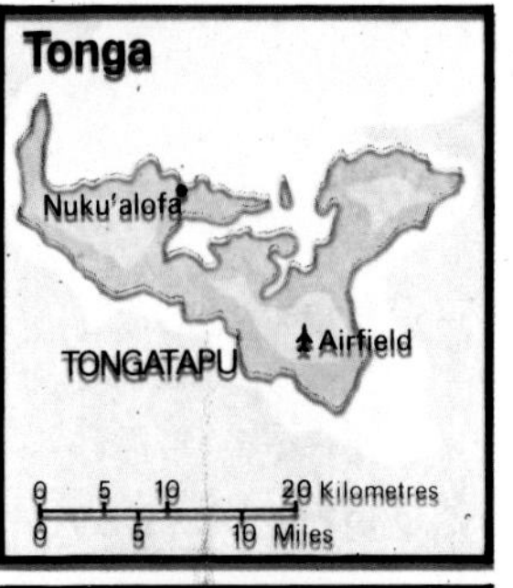

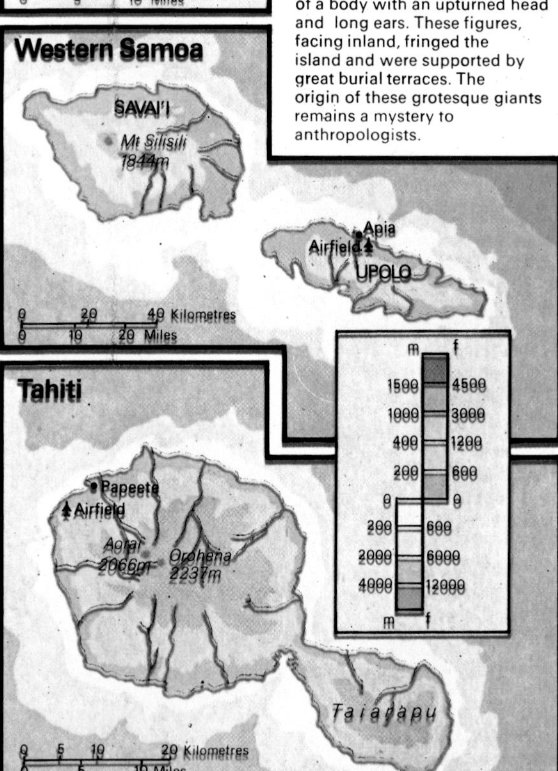

Communications
In most territories, the traditional forms of inter-island transport —canoes and schooners—have been supplemented by air services. There are internal flights within French Polynesia for instance, and remote islands, such as Nieu near the Cook Islands, have air links with important centres like Tonga. Regular air and shipping services operate between the major island groups and New Zealand, Australia and Japan. The transpacific flights of international lines use Easter Island, Tahiti and Guam as stopovers. Transport on larger islands is usually by bus or taxi.

Easter Island
The most isolated Polynesian island is the most famous : Easter Island. The island is known for its colossal statues of the 'big-eared' men. These statues, from 3.6 m to 10 m high and weighing up to 100 tonnes, are carved out of volcanic rock from the Rano-raraku crater in the north-east of the island. Each statue represents the upper half of a body with an upturned head and long ears. These figures, facing inland, fringed the island and were supported by great burial terraces. The origin of these grotesque giants remains a mystery to anthropologists.

Industry
Industry is very sparsely developed and is invariably connected with processing local produce. In many places, the islanders are engaged in handicrafts. On Pitcairn, for instance, they sell woodcarvings and baskets woven from pandanus palm leaves to passing ships. Visitors to Tonga may buy tapa cloth, grass skirts and tortoise-shell ornaments. In addition to handicrafts, Tonga has a dried coconut works, a tobacco factory and a rope works. Western Samoa also has several factories : wood veneer, soap and soft drinks. American Samoa and the Carolines both have tuna-canneries, while fruit and fruit juices are tinned in the Cook Islands. In Guam, a factory assembles watches from Swiss-made components but most activity is centred on the US naval shipyard and air base. Several islands are developing a tourist industry. Nearly all islands issue exotic postage stamps, prized by philatelists all over the world.

Mining
The economies of Ocean Island and Nauru are both based entirely on phosphate industry. On Ocean Island, the land is leased by the British Phosphate Commission and the phosphate—about 600,000 tonnes a year—is shipped overseas for processing. It is estimated that the phosphate deposits will be exhausted by 1980 and, as nearly all the 2,192 inhabitants are employed by the BPC, alternative industries such as fishing and tourism are being explored. The phosphate deposits on Nauru, producing some 2 million tonnes a year, are expected to last another 25 years. 50% of the production—used for fertilizer—is exported to Australia and 25% each to New Zealand and Japan. 75% of the revenue from exports is being invested to provide an income for the Nauruans when the phosphate is exhausted. Extra labour is hired from the Gilbert and Ellice Islands and Hong Kong.

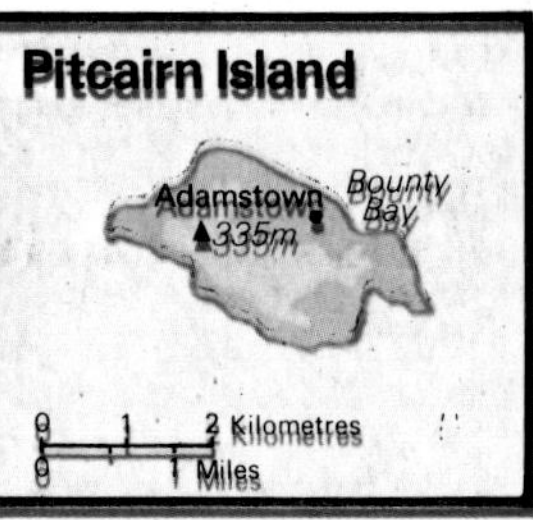

Papua New Guinea **Fiji**

Land Area
552,675 km²/213,389 sq miles
Largest Islands
Papua New Guinea: 461,700 km²/178,260 sq miles (the whole of New Guinea covers 876,100 km²/338, 260 sq miles); New Caledonia: 19,100 km²/7,374 sq miles; Bouganville (Solomons): 10,620 km²/4,100 sq miles; Viti Levu (Fiji): 10,390 km²/4,011 sq miles
Population
3,310,000 (1971)
Population density
6 per km²/15·5 per sq mile
Major imports
machinery, foodstuffs, fuels
Major exports
copra, timber, cocoa, coffee, minerals, bananas, sugar
Status
Papua New Guinea is composed of Papua: Australian territory; independent state from 16 September 1975 and New Guinea: UN trust territory administered by Australia (includes Bismarks, and Bougainville and Buka in the Solomons); independent with Papua; Solomon Islands: UK protectorate; independence scheduled for 1977; New Hebrides: Anglo-French condominium; New Caledonia: French territory; Fiji: independent state

Papua New Guinea and Melanesia

Melanesia ('black islands') is the most westerly Pacific island group. Lying between the equator and the Tropic of Capricorn, it includes New Guinea—divided politically into Irian Barat and Papua New Guinea—the Bismarks, Solomons, New Hebrides, New Caledonia and Fiji.

Physical features

Many Melanesian islands are continental: they are associated with the submerged margins of Asia and Australia and are generally mountainous. The highest peak in the New Guinea Trust Territory is Mt. Wilhelm 4,508 m and, in Papua, Mt. Victoria 4073 m in the Owen Stanley Range. These are occasionally snow-covered. Two of the island's main rivers are in the eastern half: the Sepik drains north, and the Fly, south. Both have swampy lowland plains, huge deltas and are liable to flood. Off the north-east coast, especially near the Huon peninsula, there are coral reefs rising more than 610 m above sea level. The remaining territories comprise mountainous volcanic islands such as Espiritu Santo (New Hebrides), Choiseul (Solomons), New Britain and Vanua Levu, and low-lying coral atolls, like the Fijian Lau group and the Loyalty Islands (New Caledonia). Several islands in the New Hebrides, including Ambrym, Lopevi and Tanna, have active volcanoes; New Caledonia has the world's second longest coral reef.

Communications

A traditional form of transport, the canoe, is still widely used, especially along reef-bound coasts and on narrow rivers. As roads are generally scarce waterways are necessary. In Fiji, for example, bananas are floated on rafts downstream to the coast. Fiji has Melanesia's only railway, built to meet the needs of the sugar-refining industry. Links between the islands and beyond are by sea and air. Nandi airport on Viti Levu is a recognized stopover for transpacific flights. Air Melanesia and Air Pacific operate regional services and, for internal flights, many islands have their own airline, like Air Niuguini on Papua New Guinea, Solomon Islands Airways and Fiji Air Services.

Mining

The island richest in minerals is New Caledonia where ores and semi-processed metals account for over 90% of exports. Nickel, chrome and iron are the most important, but cobalt and manganese are also mined. Other manganese deposits being exploited are on Efate and on Fiji. Fiji also has small amounts of silver and copper, but its main mineral resource, and third largest export, is gold mined at Vatukoula on Viti Levu. Gold is also mined in the Marobe district of Papua and on Guadalcanal. Bougainville's main mineral wealth lies in the copper at Panguna: a special town, Arawa, is being built to service the mine and deposits are expected to last 30 years. A smaller output of copper comes from the Star Mountains in Papua.

Climate

The climate is basically hot and humid with a wet season from November to April and a slightly drier, less humid period from May to October when the cooler south-east trade winds prevail. In New Guinea and the Solomons, rainfall is heavy: high ground in New Guinea receives 750 cm of rain a year. Both the New Hebrides and New Caledonia are subject to violent storms and rainfall is unevenly spread: in the New Hebrides, annual rainfall averages well over 200 cm; in New Caledonia, it ranges from 200 cm in the east to 100 cm in the west. In Fiji rainfall also varies from 300 cm in the east to 175 cm in the west, and average temperatures range from 20°C in July to 30°C in February.

Agriculture

With the exception of New Caledonia, the Melanesian economy is dependent on agriculture. The most important cash crop is copra, followed by coffee and cocoa. In Papua these three products make up 50% of exports and in the Solomons, copra alone brings in half the overseas earnings. In Fiji, sugar dominates. Other crops grown in smaller quantities throughout the region are rubber, tea, oil-palm and spices. Subsistence farming includes yams (on dry ground), taro (in heavy rainfall areas) and bananas, maize, cassava, breadfruit and pineapples. The staple food grown by the Solomon islanders is rice. Livestock farming is limited to cattle in Papua, New Caledonia and Fiji, and pigs in the New Hebrides, but there are also goats. A further 45% of Papua's exports consists of forest products. Timber, mostly mahogany and kauri pine, is also grown commercially in New Caledonia, the Solomons and the New Hebrides. Fishing is also important: shellfish, octopus and tuna are caught offshore, while lagoons yield mullet, bream and turtles.

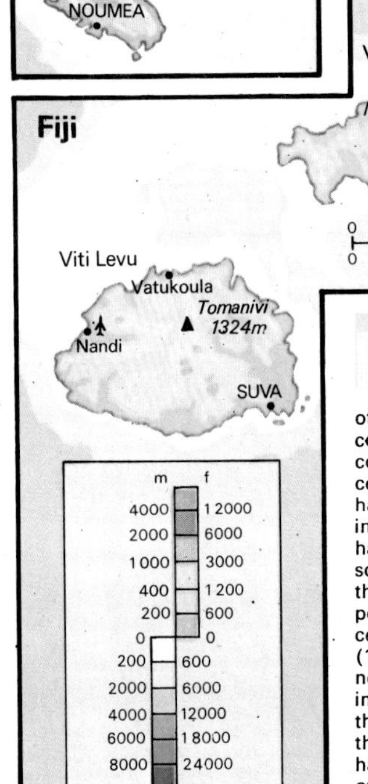

Industry

Although secondary manufactures, such as packaging materials, fibreglass products and footwear are being developed, industry is essentially based on primary products. New Caledonia, for instance, has nickel-processing plants, sawmills, meat-preserving factories and coffee-barking mills while Fiji's main industries are centred on cane-crushing, gold-refining, processing copra into coconut oil and meal, pineapple-canning and timber-processing. Other leading Fijian manufactures are cement and biscuits. Biscuits, as well as twist tobacco and baskets, are made in the Solomons—among the least developed of the Pacific islands. Baskets, and other traditional crafts are also characteristic of the New Hebrides where industrial activity is based on meat-canneries, a fish-freezing plant, soft-drink factories, a cement works and a shipyard. Tourism, currently being developed in the New Hebrides and New Caledonia, is of major importance in New Guinea as well as in Fiji where it has surpassed sugar as the major foreign exchange earner.

Cities

The largest city in Melanesia is Suva (63,000), the capital of Fiji. On the south-east coast of Viti Levu, Suva is the country's light industrial centre and leading port, handling over 800 ships a year in its natural deep-water harbour. Noumea (50,490) in the south-west of New Caledonia is the territory's capital and only port. The capital and commercial centre of the New Hebrides, Vila (12,000) is also a port with a new deep-water quay completed in 1972. Honiara (11,191) on the north coast of Guadalcanal is the capital of the Solomons and handles most of the territory's overseas trade. Papua New Guinea is administered from Port Moresby (42,000).

Australia-West

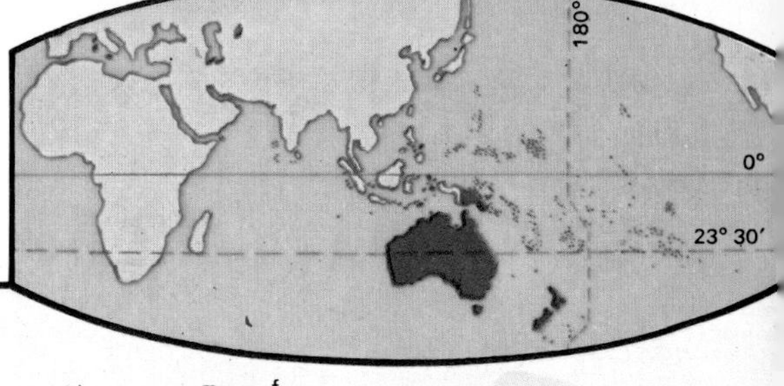

Area
7,686,884 km²/2,967,909 sq miles
Location
10°40′ – 43°40′S.
113°10′ – 153° 40′ E
Population
13,268,300 (1973)
Population density
1·7 per km²/4·4 per sq mile
Capital
Canberra: 184,000 (1974)
Largest city
Sydney: 2,874,380 (1973)
Language
English
Gross National Product
21,350 million US dollars (1974)
Major imports
machinery, transport equipment, textiles, petroleum, chemicals
Major exports
wool, meat, ores, cereals, sugar, coal, dairy products
Currency
Australian dollar (100 cents = 1 dollar)
Status
The Commonwealth of Australia is a federal state and constituent member of the Commonwealth of Nations.

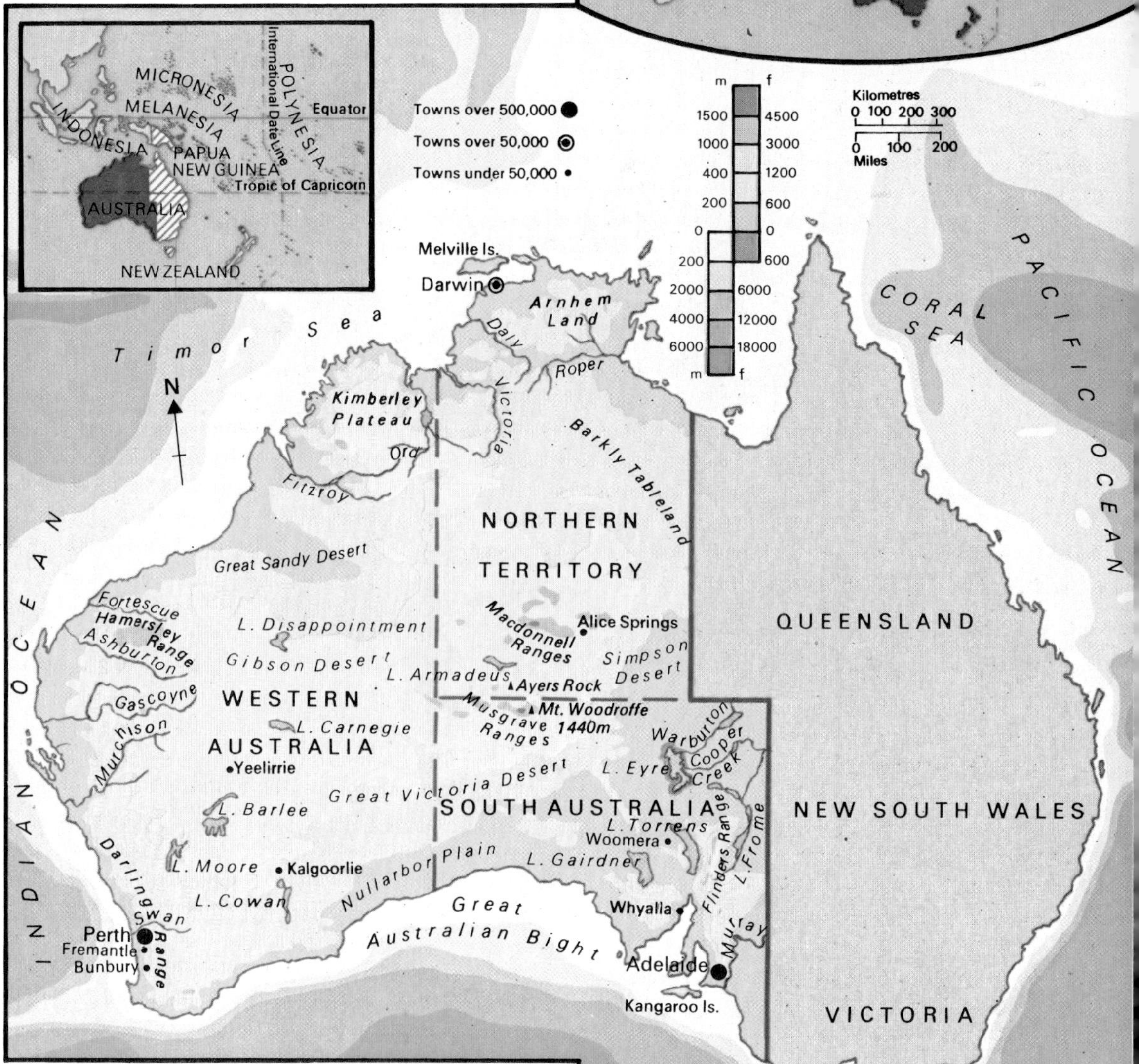

Physical features

Australia, the only continent occupied by a single nation, is the world's sixth largest country. It is also the world's lowest and flattest land mass. Almost 75% of the continent is a vast, ancient plateau, formed more than 3,000 million years ago, with an average height of 300 m. To the east of this is lowland of less than 150 m, followed by a highland belt stretching along the coast. The dominating structure, the Great Western Plateau, emerges from the Indian Ocean coastal plain to cover almost the whole of Western Australia (the largest state, occupying one third of the continent), much of the Northern Territory, South Australia and a part of Queensland. The monotony of the plateau, largely desert, is broken by the Kimberley, Hamersley, Macdonnell and Musgrave ranges and by isolated outcrops such as Ayers Rock, a giant red rock 335 m tall.

Climate

As Australia covers more than 30° of latitude—the distance from Switzerland to Ghana—the climate is varied, but it is modified by the oceans and the absence of high mountains. The north lies within the tropics and has high temperatures, heavy rain and cyclones. In Darwin, annual temperature range is from 23°C to 32°C and the average annual rainfall, coming in the January–March wet season, is 154 cm. 60% of the country is in the temperate zone with warm summers and mild winters. January and July temperatures in Sydney are 26°C and 16°C, and in Perth, 29°C and 17°C. Winter, however, does bring snow to the Alps in the south-east. Rainfall is uneven. S.E. trade winds carry rain to the east coast: for example, 120 cm a year in Sydney. Westerly winds bring light rain to the south, but the interior around Lake Eyre receives less than 15 cm a year.

Islands

Among the territories administered by Australia are three island groups. Norfolk I., 1,676 km north-east of Sydney, has an area of 35 km² and 1,700 inhabitants. Once a penal colony, its economy is now firmly based on tourism. Christmas I., in the Indian Ocean, 1,400 km from Australia, is 135 km² in area. Its sole economic activity, employing nearly all the 2,741 residents, is the recovery of phosphate. The Cocos (Keeling) Is., 27 coral islands in the Indian Ocean, are 2,767 km north-west of Perth and 14 km² in total area. The population of 640 is engaged in copra production.

Communications

Transport in Australia faces the problem of distance—4,000 km separate east from west, and 3,500 km north from south. Distance is made worse by the distribution of population—6 out of 10 Australians live in a city, mostly in one of the state capitals which are all on the coast and at least 640 km apart. A transport system has evolved which includes 880,000 km of roads, 50% unpaved; 40,000 km of government railways; and 120,000 km of air routes travelled by 8 million passengers a year.

Iron and steel

Iron and coal deposits are the basis of the world's tenth largest steel industry. The nation's entire output of steel is in the hands of the Broken Hill Proprietary Company and its subsidiaries. BHP's major steelworks are at Port Kembla near Sydney, Newcastle, Whyalla and Kwinana near Fremantle. Dependent on steel is the car industry operated by subsidiaries of foreign companies such as Ford, Leyland and Renault. Also associated with steel is a shipbuilding industry.

Sheep

64% of the continent is farmland but, because of low rainfall, 90% of this is only rough grazing for sheep. The country's 148 million sheep, mostly merinos, constitute 15% of the world's sheep and produce 33% of the world's wool, making Australia the world's leading wool producer and exporter. Sheep are found in all states. In arid areas, where drought can halve sheep numbers, merinos are grazed exclusively. In high rainfall zones, like Tasmania, different breeds are raised to give super-fine wools. The main markets for Australian wool—its leading export—are Japan, the USSR and EEC countries.

Minerals

Australia is rich in minerals. Iron, mainly from the Hamersley Range, is the most important and is Australia's biggest mineral export. Australia is the world's largest bauxite producer. Other major deposits exploited are nickel at Kalgoorlie, manganese, found in Western Australia and in the Northern Territory, and copper, occuring throughout the continent. Australia is fourth in the world production of lead and zinc, mined at Broken Hill, Mount Isa and Read-Roseberry, and sixth in gold production. Recently, uranium has been discovered in the Northern Territory and at Yeelirrie. Mines at Lightning Ridge are the world's major source of opals. Australia now produces 70% of its crude oil requirements, mostly from fields in the Bass Strait which also have natural gas.

Cities

Adelaide is the capital of South Australia and the continent's fourth largest city (868,000). Ringed by fertile plains, the city was originally a market for agricultural produce, but has now become industrialized and specializes in engineering, textiles and chemicals. Australia's fifth largest city, Perth (740,000), on the Swan River 19 km from the sea, is the capital of Western Australia. Half the state's population lives there. Heavy industry is concentrated in the suburbs of Perth and Fremantle which, situated at the mouth of the Swan River, is Australia's third largest port. The capital of the Northern Territory, Darwin, is smaller (43,000) and is closely associated with the Territory's two main economic activities: mining and beef cattle.

Australia-East

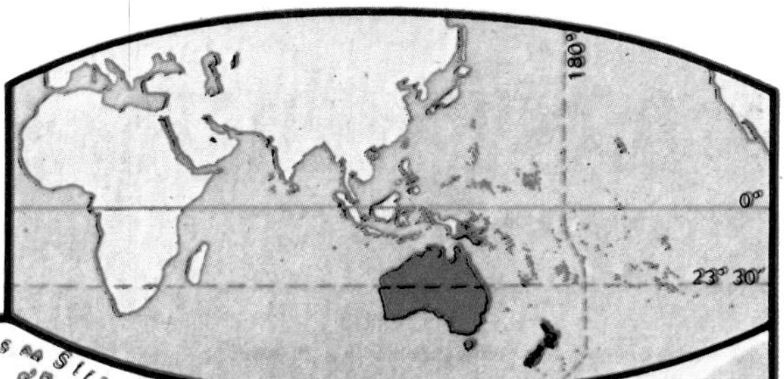

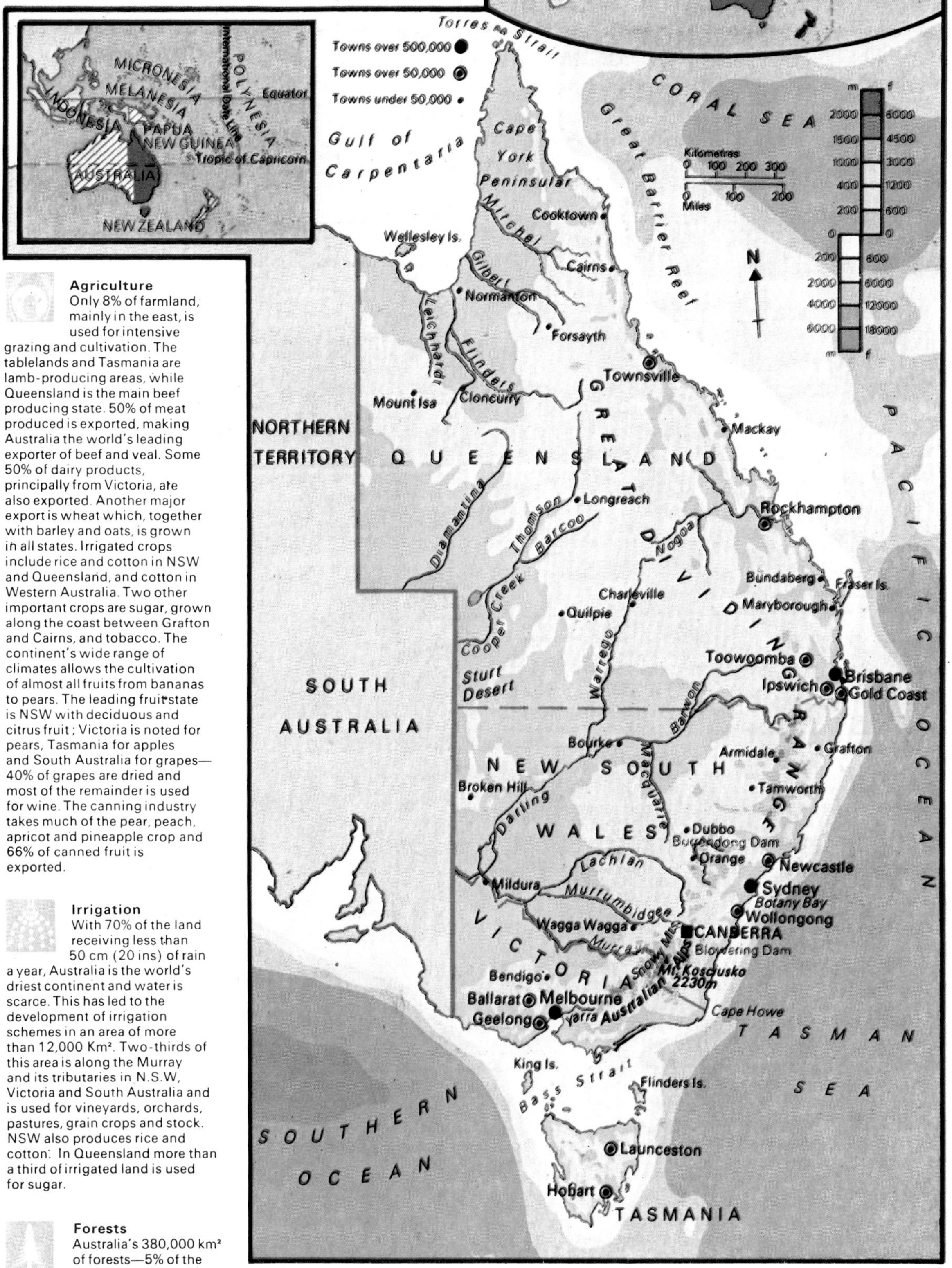

Physical features

East of the western plateau, and stretching from the Gulf of Carpentaria to South Australia, are lowlands. On average, these are less than 150 m high and Lake Eyre is nearly 12 m below sea level. Following the coast from Cape York to south Tasmania is a 3,200 km long chain of highlands, the Great Dividing Range. Most Australians live east of this on the coastal plain, which ranges from 50 to 400 km wide. The Great Divide mountains are faily low except for the Australian Alps in the south-east, which include the continent's highest peak, Mount Kosciusko, 2,228 m (7,300 ft). The seaboard from Tasmania to Brisbane is a succession of rocky headlands and sandy beaches. North of Brisbane, the coast is in the lee of the Great Barrier Reef, a belt of coral reefs and islands extending 2,000 km up to New Guinea. Australia lacks the big river systems of mountainous continents and many of its rivers only flow after heavy rain. Its largest system is the Murray and its tributaries, Darling, Murrumbidgee, Lachlan, which drain 1,057,000 km². But even the Murray takes a year to empty into the sea what the Amazon River in South America discharges in 36 hours.

Industry

Since the Second World War, Australian industry has greatly expanded. In addition to steel, engineering and paper, main industries include foodstuffs, chemicals and textiles. Australia produces a lot of surplus food, and exports of raw and processed food bring in a third of the nation's export income. The chemical industry, from local resources such as coal, molasses, salt and sulphur, produces basic chemicals used for explosives, plastics, fertilizers, cosmetics, etc. The rapid growth of oil refining has given an impetus to petro-chemicals and the textile industry is able to rely on local resources.

Cities

The national capital, Canberra, situated in the Australian Capital Territory 310 km from Sydney, is mainly administrative but has some light industry. Australia's oldest and largest city, Sydney, is built on low hills by the south Pacific. Capital of New South Wales (NSW), Sydney is Australia's financial centre and major port. Its most famous structure is the single span steel harbour bridge, the second longest in the world : 503 m (1,650 ft). The nation's second largest city and former capital is Melbourne (2,585,000). Capital of Victoria, the city houses 75% of the state's industry—metals, textiles, foodstuffs, paper. Brisbane (911,000), Queensland's capital and Australia's third city, has shipyards, engineering works, oil refineries, food-processing factories and sawmills. The most southerly city is Hobart (158,000), capital of Tasmania, and mainly concerned with fruit. Its port is most active during the apple season and fruit-processing is a major industry.

Agriculture

Only 8% of farmland, mainly in the east, is used for intensive grazing and cultivation. The tablelands and Tasmania are lamb-producing areas, while Queensland is the main beef producing state. 50% of meat produced is exported, making Australia the world's leading exporter of beef and veal. Some 50% of dairy products, principally from Victoria, are also exported. Another major export is wheat which, together with barley and oats, is grown in all states. Irrigated crops include rice and cotton in NSW and Queensland, and cotton in Western Australia. Two other important crops are sugar, grown along the coast between Grafton and Cairns, and tobacco. The continent's wide range of climates allows the cultivation of almost all fruits from bananas to pears. The leading fruit state is NSW with deciduous and citrus fruit ; Victoria is noted for pears, Tasmania for apples and South Australia for grapes—40% of grapes are dried and most of the remainder is used for wine. The canning industry takes much of the pear, peach, apricot and pineapple crop and 66% of canned fruit is exported.

Irrigation

With 70% of the land receiving less than 50 cm (20 ins) of rain a year, Australia is the world's driest continent and water is scarce. This has led to the development of irrigation schemes in an area of more than 12,000 Km². Two-thirds of this area is along the Murray and its tributaries in N.S.W, Victoria and South Australia and is used for vineyards, orchards, pastures, grain crops and stock. NSW also produces rice and cotton. In Queensland more than a third of irrigated land is used for sugar.

Forests

Australia's 380,000 km² of forests—5% of the land area—are mainly found in the wetter zones near the east and south-east coasts and in Tasmania. Most of this is eucalyptus forest which fills all the country's hardwood requirements and most of its paper needs. The nation's 16 pulp and paper mills are concentrated mainly in Victoria, Tasmania and NSW. Australia exports veneers, sleepers and woodchips but, because conifers are deficient, has to import softwoods. To tackle this deficiency, softwood has been planted over 4,000 Km².

Flora and fauna

About 50 million years ago, links with other land masses disappeared, cutting off Australia and its plant and animal life from the rest of the world. Species evolved that are unknown elsewhere, such as the emu—a flightless bird—and the kangaroo, which can bound at 40 kph (25 mph). Like the koala, it is a marsupial : it rears its young in a pouch. Best known native trees are the acacia and eucalyptus, in which the koala lives.

Energy

Australia's greatest engineering project is the Snowy Mountains Hydro-Electric Scheme in NSW. The scheme provides about 2,344 million m³ of irrigation water a year and its total generating capacity is almost 4,000 megawatts. Another major hydro-electric scheme in Tasmania supplies nearly all that state's electricity. Taking the continent as a whole, however, over 70% of electricity comes from thermal plants fuelled by coal.

Aboriginals

The Aboriginals are thought to have arrived in Australia some 30,000 years ago. In a difficult environment they lived as semi-nomadic hunters and food-gatherers. When European settlement began almost 200 years ago, conflict and disease reduced their numbers drastically. Today the Aboriginal population is about 140,000. Many still live a traditional life in the 350 Aboriginal reserves, but others are moving to cities.

New Zealand

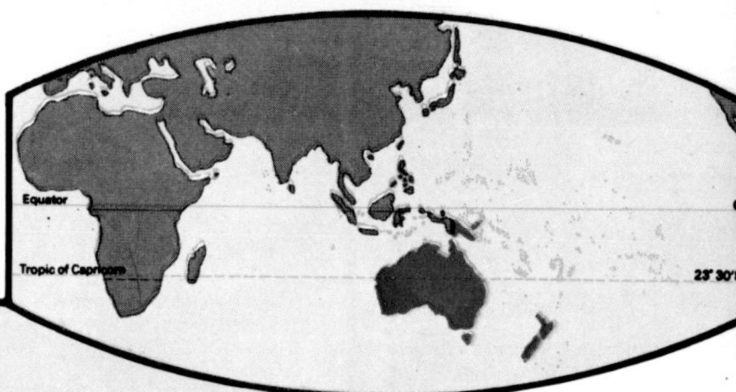

Maoris
The first Polynesians probably arrived in New Zealand in 800AD. They were the Maoris—hunters of the now extinct moa bird. More arrived in the great migration of 1350 and these original settlers, fishermen and farmers, were undisturbed until European colonization in the 1800s caused bitter conflict in some areas. Today, however, the Maoris—about 8% of the population—are an integral part of New Zealand society, proud of their culture and active in politics. Many now live and work in cities. Auckland is the world's largest Polynesian city.

Cities
The country's capital, Wellington, is on the southern tip of the North Island and is partly built on reclaimed land. It is New Zealand's political and commercial hub, but the biggest city is Auckland. On an isthmus between the Waitemata and Manukau harbours, Auckland is also the largest port. It handles 33% of exports and 50% of imports, and is the main industrial complex, producing one third of the country's manufactured goods. These include machinery, timber products, chemicals, processed food, textiles, plastics and cement. The second largest industrial centre is Christchurch.

Climate
Although New Zealand's climate ranges from subtropical in the north to almost continental in the central South Island, conditions are not extreme: winters are mild, summers warm. In the coldest month (July) minimum temperatures are 3°C in Dunedin and 8°C in Auckland. In January, summer maximums range from 19°C to 23°C. Prevailing westerly winds bring rain to the west coast all year, but the areas east of the ranges are drier, especially in summer and autumn, when hot, arid north-westerlies blow. In winter, snow covers the mountains and, in bad years, settles on the lowlands south of Christchurch.

Area
268,675 km²/103,736 sq miles (excluding the Pacific island territories of Tokelau and Niue)
Location
34°05' – 47°20' S
166°10' – 178°20' E
Population
3,094,900 (1975)
Population density
11 per km²/29 per sq mile
Capital
Wellington: 346,900 (1974)
Largest city
Auckland: 775,469 (1974)
Language
English
Gross National Product
9,130 million US dollars
Major imports
machinery, transport equipment, metals, textiles, fuels, foodstuffs, fertilizers
Major exports
dairy produce, meat, wool
Currency
NZ dollar (100 cents = 1 dollar)
Status
independent monarchical state and constituent member of the Commonwealth of Nations
National bird
kiwi

Transport
The road and rail networks on both islands are linked by ferries from Wellington to Lyttelton (the port of Christchurch) and across Cook Strait to Picton. An internal airline, the National Airways Corporation, operates services from 24 airports. Three of these airports—Auckland, Wellington, Christchurch—are also used by Air New Zealand for international flights. The country's seaports handle more than 13 million tonnes of foreign trade cargo a year. The chief ports are Auckland, Wellington, Lyttelton and Tauranga, with oil imports coming in at Whangarei.

Industry
In the last 20 years, New Zealand's industry has grown dramatically. Apart from the expansion of industries based on agricultural and forest products—timber, pulp and newsprint are now major exports—other domestic raw materials are being exploited. These include clay for bricks, limestone for cement, and ironsands, found along the west coast of the North Island and used in the Glenbrook steel plant near Auckland. Wax is also extracted from peat for use in paints and explosives. Essential to New Zealand's industrialization is cheap hydro-electricity. This led to the siting of a giant aluminium smelter at Bluff which uses imported Australian bauxite.

Agriculture
Although only 12% of the population works in farming, New Zealand's foreign trade depends on agricultural products which make up 80% of exports. It is the world's largest exporter of dairy products and lamb, and second largest exporter of wool. 22,000 dairy farms produce 6,000 million litres of milk a year. The milk is taken to co-operatives where it is processed into more than 100 products including butter and cheese. Between them, the country's 40,000 sheep farmers own 60 million sheep producing 315,000 tonnes of wool a year. Britain takes 19% and other major customers are the USA, Belgium, France, Japan and the USSR. Sheep rearing gives rise to New Zealand's other major export, lamb, which is sent to more than 100 countries. Beef is also produced and other associated exports are sausage casings, tallow, hides and skins. The country's success in livestock farming lies in its ability to grow good grass and clovers (seeds are exported world-wide) thanks to even rainfall, plentiful sunshine and fertilizers. The other factor is mechanization: aircraft, for instance, are used for top-dressing, spraying and sowing. Arable farming is equally successful and New Zealand is self-sufficient in wheat and in hops. Fruit growing has also become important and apples and pears and exotic local fruits are air-freighted abroad.

Physical features
The three islands of New Zealand lie 2,000 km south-east of Australia and 10,000 km west of Chile. The two larger islands, North (114,453 km²) and South (150,718 km²), are long and narrow: no point is further than 110 km from the sea. The third, Stewart Island, is smaller (1746 km²). The mountains in the South Island, the Southern Alps, include the country's highest peak, Mount Cook (3,764 m), and a network of lakes and glaciers. In places, glaciers spread down to 300 m above sea level. In the centre of the North Island is a volcanic plateau, dominated by the volcanic peaks of Ruapehu, Ngauruhoe and Tongariro, by geysers and hot springs and by New Zealand's largest lake, Lake Taupo (606 km²). Although 75% of New Zealand is more than 200 m above sea level, there are lowland areas. The most extensive are on the Canterbury Plains, crossed by rivers, which cover 12,500 km² of the South Island's east coast. The North Island has rich grasslands round the Waikato.

Energy
New Zealand's energy needs are largely supplied by hydro-electricity. In the North Island, stations are concentrated on the Waikato river. The newest stations are in the South Island, where the major Clutha and Waitaki river schemes offer great potential. Electricity also comes from thermal plants using coal, oil, natural gas and geothermal steam. The Kapuni field near New Plymouth produces natural gas and a larger field, off the Taranaki coast, is being developed. Of lesser importance is coal, mined in Westland and Waikato valley.

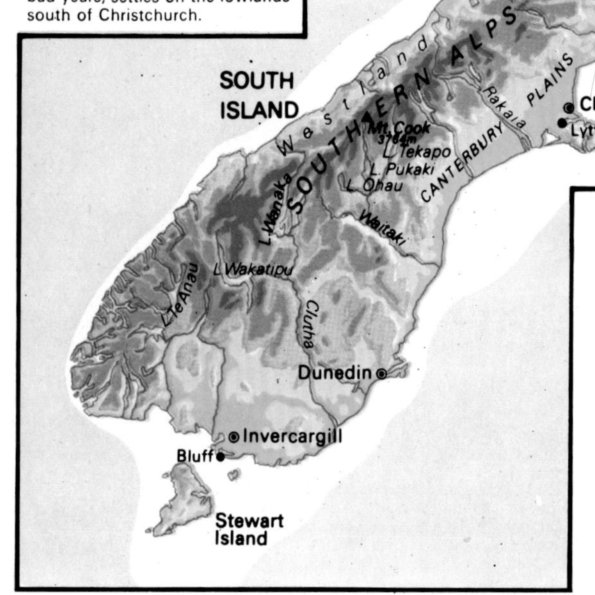

The Antarctic

The Antarctic

The Antarctic comprises the continent of Antarctica and its surrounding seas and numerous islands; these include the South Shetlands, the South Sandwich Islands, the South Orkneys, South Georgia, Bouvet Island, Heard Island, the Balleny Islands, Scott Island and Peter I Island. Various boundaries are used to define the region: the Antarctic Circle at 66°32′S; the political limit corresponding to latitude 60°S; and the Antarctic convergence—the border generally accepted for geographical and scientific purposes. This oceanographic boundary, a belt of water 30 to 50 km wide, lies between latitudes 50° and 62°S—the zone where cold northward-moving antarctic surface water sinks below warmer subantarctic water.

Antarctica

Antarctica, centred on the South Pole, is the world's coldest and most desolate continent. It is also unique in its isolation, situated 960 km from South America, 2,700 km from Australia and 4,000 km from South Africa. Except for the deep indentations of the Ross and Weddell seas and the projecting Antarctic peninsula, the continent is roughly circular in shape and lies almost wholly within the Antarctic Circle. With a total area of 13.8 million km² it is the world's fifth largest continent, nearly equal in size to the US and Europe combined. Antarctica is surrounded by the Southern or Antarctic Ocean, formed from the southern waters of the Pacific, Indian and Atlantic oceans and extending northwards to the tips of the neighbouring continents.

Climate

Antarctica has a far harsher climate than the Arctic, largely because of its average altitude but also because the ocean, frozen in winter, insulates the continent from the warming influence of open water. Inland temperatures often drop to –56°C and the world's lowest recorded temperature of –88°C was at the Soviet station, Vostok. The coast is milder but even in summer no point has a monthly mean above freezing. Bitter winds, rushing seawards, are a constant feature of Antarctic weather; speeds average 80 kph but gusts exceed 300 kph. Loose snow, driven by these winds, causes dense blizzards. Precipitation, in the form of snow, is very low (equal to 5 cm of rain) making Antarctica one of the Earth's great deserts.

Vegetation

The continent's severe temperatures and extreme aridity are hostile to plant life except for algae, mosses, lichens and, in the northern part of the Antarctic Peninsula, some small flowering plants.

The land

Ice covers 95% of Antarctica; exposed areas comprise sections of mountain ranges, projecting peaks and, along the coast, dry valleys known as 'oases'. Most ice-free zones occur in Victoria Land and the Antarctic Peninsula. The principal mountain chain is the Transantarctic range which rises to over 4,500 m and extends from Victoria Land to Coats Land. Other ranges fringe the coast: the Ellsworth mountains contain Antarctica's highest peak, the Vinson Massif (5,140 m). The Transantarctic chain divides the continent into two parts. The larger part, East Antarctica, is a continental shield composed of old, hard rocks. The smaller section, West Antarctica, is more recent in origin and consists of folded ranges and plateaux; Mt Erebus, on Ross Island, is an active volcano. The Antarctic Peninsula, with its magnificent ice-capped plateau and fjord-indented coast, is probably an extension of the Andes; it is linked to Tierra del Fuego by the submarine Scotia Ridge of which the South Shetlands, the South Orkneys and the South Sandwich Islands are outcrops.

Land ice

Antarctica is a vast dome of ice formed by the snows of past millennia. At the dome's summit, near the Pole of Inaccessibility (800 km from the South Pole), the ice is about 4,000 m thick; its average thickness of 2,000 m makes Antarctica the highest continent. This enormous ice-sheet, representing 90% of the world's ice, is in constant motion: under its own pressure the ice flows slowly outwards and downwards to the sea. Surface features include giant terraced steps, wave-like dunes and crevasses up to 40 m deep and 20 m wide. Most of the glacier sheet terminates at the coast but some of the ice spills out over the sea as floating ice-shelves; the largest is the Ross Ice Shelf, covering 806,000 km².

Sea ice

Antarctica is surrounded by pack-ice that ranges from huge flat-topped icebergs (160 km long and 50 m high) to small fragments only a few centimetres across. Wind and currents keep the ice moving and, in summer, create a maze of lanes through which ships can pass. Access is easiest via the Ross Sea which is almost ice-free in February and March; in contrast, navigation on the Weddell Sea is difficult as the ice jams against the peninsula. In winter, the pack-ice extends northwards for hundred of kilometres and effectively doubles the area of the continent.

Wildlife

Except for a few wingless insects, Antarctica has no land animals, but marine and bird life are more plentiful. The ocean floor abounds with molluscs and small creatures such as sponges, sea-urchins and starfish while seals and whales swim in the Antarctic waters; the various species include the blue whale weighing up to 150 tonnes. Gulls, petrels and penguins are the most common birds; the emperor penguin is the only one that winters on shore; the others migrate to the edge of the pack-ice.

Man in Antarctica

The rigorous climate is inhospitable and dangerous to man. As a result, Antarctica is the only continent with no permanent human inhabitants. The current population (about 1,000) consists mostly of scientists engaged in research. Various countries maintain research stations in Antarctica and seven of them (Norway, Australia, France, New Zealand, Chile, the United Kingdom and Argentina) claim territory. The claimed sectors are segments running from the coast to the South Pole; only one zone, Marie Byrd Land, remains unclaimed. In 1959 an international treaty was signed suspending all territorial claims for 30 years and guaranteeing the free use of the continent for peaceful purposes only.

Usefulness

Primarily, Antarctica is a great scientific laboratory. In addition, there are valuable minerals in Greater Antarctica but the high costs involved make exploitation uneconomic: some whaling and sealing occur in the Southern Ocean.

Index

Entries and numerals in italics refer to illustrations.

The index is in two sections. Part I refers to information contained in the articles. Part II indexes the Gazetteer, showing where to find major cities, rivers, mountain ranges etc. Numerals in italics refer to illustrations.

A

B

C

D

E

F

G

H

I

J

K

L

M

T

U

V

W

XYZ

The Gazetteer

A

B

C

D

E

F

G

H

I

J

K

L

M

N

O

P

R

S

T

U

V

W

X

Y

Z